HISTORIC SPOTS IN CALIFORNIA

FOURTH EDITION

Historic Spots in
CALIFORNIA

by
Mildred Brooke Hoover
Hero Eugene Rensch
Ethel Grace Rensch
William N. Abeloe

Revised by Douglas E. Kyle

STANFORD UNIVERSITY PRESS · STANFORD, CALIFORNIA

Historic Spots in California was originally published in three volumes: *The Southern Counties* (1932), by H. E. and E. G. Rensch; *Valley and Sierra Counties* (1933), by H. E. and E. G. Rensch and Mildred Brooke Hoover; and *Counties of the Coast Range* (1937), by Mildred Brooke Hoover. A revised edition, in one volume, was published in 1948. A third edition, revised and expanded by William N. Abeloe, was published in 1968. The present edition has been extensively revised and updated by Douglas E. Kyle and was first published in 1990.

Stanford University Press, Stanford, California

Photographs on pp. 210, 211 courtesy of the State of California
Department of Parks and Recreation
All other photographs by Douglas E. Kyle

Published with the assistance of the L. J. Skaggs and Mary C. Skaggs Foundation

Printed in the United States of America

CIP data appear at the end of the book

Original printing 1990
Last figure below indicates year of this printing:
04   03   02   01   00   99   98   97   96   95

Preface

Historic Spots in California is now in its fourth edition and has an interesting history of its own. The work began as a project of the California State Conference of the National Society, Daughters of the American Revolution. It was published, then as now, by Stanford University Press. The first edition appeared in three volumes, the first being *The Southern Counties* (1932), written by Hero Eugene Rensch and his wife, Ethel Grace Rensch. In the following year, *Valley and Sierra Counties* appeared, with Mildred Brooke Hoover as coauthor with Mr. and Mrs. Rensch, her sister and brother-in-law. The third volume, *Counties of the Coast Range*, completed the project in 1937 and was entirely written by Mrs. Hoover.

In the 1930's Californians could see many efforts being made to preserve and to commemorate the history of their state. Anthropologists were publishing extensively on the world of the California Indians. Many crumbling buildings of the missions, perhaps the most famous Spanish enterprise in California, were being restored. In old cities like Los Angeles and Santa Barbara, historic buildings were being identified and refurbished. The gold rush period seems to have produced one book or journal article every month in that decade. Historically important State Registered Landmarks were beginning to be identified and labeled. *Historic Spots in California*, therefore, appeared when there was a considerable interest in California's past, and it found a receptive audience.

The second edition of the work was published in 1948. The three original volumes were brought together into a single volume, which kept the previous geographical divisions and was updated and revised by Ruth Teiser. This book included the Introduction from the first edition by Robert Glass Cleland, an established California historian. A select bibliography followed each county's history in this edition, as it did in the volumes of the first edition.

World War II wrought a massive transformation of California. The state's population rapidly increased, in part due to many new government operations. When the war ended, many of the newcomers decided to stay, and they were joined by many more. In 1963, California became the most populous of the United States. This growth was in some part made at the expense of California's historical spots. It was obvious that many historic buildings in the vicinity of the burgeoning urban complexes might soon be destroyed.

In 1962, Stanford University Press engaged Reverend William N. Abeloe to make a third edition of *Historic Spots in California*. Father Abeloe was an enthusiastic student of California history and was teaching this, among other subjects, at Bishop O'Dowd High School in Oakland. He quoted with evident approval from the first edition that one of the purposes of this book was "to arouse a state-wide interest in the preservation of those vanishing historic landmarks which still survive." He made some substantial changes in the book, the first of which was to put county chapters in alphabetical order. He added photographs taken on his trips throughout the state and maps for each county. The cities of Los Angeles and San Francisco and the Pomona–Ontario–San Bernardino region had inset maps indicating historic sites. The text was updated to note those buildings or landscapes that no longer existed. This third edition, which was in several places thoroughly rewritten by Father Abeloe, was published in 1966. It became a popular book and went through several reprintings; in 1978, Father Abeloe added an update preface to acknowledge those State Registered Landmarks which had been made since 1966.

California, geologists and historians agree, is always on the move. Twenty years after the third edition appeared, it was decided to take a fresh look at these spots, and this edition is the result of that decision.

Historic Spots in California has never claimed to be a history of California; rather it is a book about the historical landmarks of the state. To provide historic background, I have written a short introductory essay. As was done in earlier editions, there is a rough chronology followed in each county's chapter, beginning with pertinent facts on geography, continuing with Indian life, following with the coming of the Spanish and other Europeans, and then the American conquest and, in those areas where it had a major impact, the gold rush. The text then continues into the period of industrialization, railroads, intensive agricultural development, the growth of cities, and on into the twentieth century. An effort has been made to give the address and general interest of the museums in the state, but it is important to remind the reader that visitors should make local inquiries as to days and hours when a museum or other historic spot is open.

For the fourth edition the text has been extensively rewritten to reflect the recent developments in California historical preservation. We include all of the State

Registered Landmarks and many, but not all, of the places on the National Register of Historic Places. While the latter identify only currently existing buildings and sites, State Registered Landmarks (SRL followed by a number in the text) include many places that no longer exist and in some cases have not even been marked with a sign or monument. A number of private organizations have also placed markers about the state; among them we can note the Native Sons of the Golden West, the Native Daughters of the Golden West, the Daughters of the American Revolution, and E Clampus Vitus (the last is a twentieth-century revival of a social group originating in the Mother Lode in the 1850's).

The photographs in this edition, mostly the work of the author, are designed to show prominent landmarks and some not so well known. It was decided to omit maps from this edition. Good up-to-date maps can be obtained through automobile organizations, book shops, and service stations, and these will reflect the current status of roads. The text has been written with the idea that the reader might use the book while traveling around the state, and thus mileage and specific locations have been given where it was thought necessary to do so. Numbered roads are identified as follows: interstates as, for example, I-5; U.S. highways as U.S. 101; and state routes as SR 1.

The bibliography has been updated to the end of 1988 and includes some of the established classics in California history as well as more recent material.

When Father Abeloe and I, as members of the board of directors of the Alameda County Historical Society, were among those working with Leonard Verbarg on his book *Celebrities at Your Doorstep*, Verbarg looked around the table after a long session and noted: "It takes teamwork when you deal with history." Certainly this book owes a great deal to the efforts and suggestions of many people, and the following people are herewith thanked for their input.

At Stanford University Press, the editorial and design work of Colleen Forbes, Stella Hackell, Norris Pope, and Ellen F. Smith brought readability and order to the manuscript and illustrations. I am much in their debt. Sandra Elder and Maryln Bourne Lortie of the State Office of Historic Preservation, Department of Parks and Recreation, gave me the information I needed on updates of State Registered Landmarks.

From many counties in the state came information, often from a corresponding secretary of a historical society, and all of this was personally corroborated by the author in a visit at one time or another. Alameda County received information from Arthur H. Breed, Jr.,

Frances Buxton, David and Heidi Casebolt, Peter T. Conmy, Ann Doss, Frederick J. Monteagle, Janet Newton, Lois Over, and Bernadine Swadley. For Alpine County, Ilean Price Long and Nancy Thornburg provided information. Amador County benefited from the input of Frank Aliberti, Evelyn Angier, Clyde Berriman, Larry Cenotto, Jock and Muriel Thibaut, and Frank Tortorich.

Butte County's material came in part from James Lenhoff, Lois McDonald, Lillian Pinker, and Charles Randolph. Calaveras County had contributions from Judith Cunningham and W. P. Fuller, Jr. Contra Costa County contributors include Beverly Clemson, Duane Norgren, Donna Roselius, and Justine Sellick. In Del Norte County, Paul Hamby and Mary Lu Miller were helpful; in El Dorado County, material came from Nan Hauser Cotton, Betty Harvey, and Jack Schlappi. Fresno County had information provided by Steve Emanuels, Donald C. Fillmore, and William B. Secrest, Jr. Glenn County's Richard A. Jacobson and Gene H. Russell were helpful, as was Humboldt County's Arlene Hartin.

Kern County benefited from the contributions of Harland Boyd and of Glen and Doreen Settle; Lake County, from Orville Magoon and Norma Wright. Lassen County's Tim I. Purdy gave useful update information.

Los Angeles County contributors included Flora Twyman Baker, Helen Beiner, Mary Borgerding, Louis C. Bourdet, Barbara Brink, Joe Da Rold, Maria A. Edwards, Michael E. Engh, Zona Gale Forbes, Betty Forsyth, Joyce Lawrence, Bruce R. Lively, Elizabeth L. Marsh, Elva Meline, Hollis Page, Donald H. Pflueger, Gerald C. Reynolds, Teena Stern, and Dorothy B. Welles.

Madera County's material in part came from Mildred Eaves and Doris Seabury; the Marin County chapter owes much to Laurie Huffman, Roger Rehm, and May Ungemach. Merced County had contributions from Catherine Julien and Albert Shumate, and Modoc County from Claude Singleton. Monterey County received material from Amelie Elkinton, Michael Jay Nicolette, and Edward T. Planer. Napa County material was supplied by Jess Doud. In Nevada County, information came from Bruce C. Bolinger, Steven D. Moore, and Edwin L. Tyson. Orange County had input from Clifford Bodamer and Diann Marsh.

Placer County was commented on by Doris Parker-Coons; Plumas County information came from Robert Cooke and Marilyn Morris. Riverside County had material supplied by Michael Rounds, and Sacramento County benefited from the advice of Alan Wilson. San Benito County has information from Janet Brians. San Bernardino County owes much to the contributions of

Fred Holladay. For San Diego County, material came from Eugene Chamberlin, Karna Webster, and Thomas Whayne.

San Francisco County contributors include Douglas S. Brookes, Milton B. Halsey, Jr., Daniel Rosen, Jean Sherrell, and Albert Shumate. Material on San Joaquin County was supplied by Glenn A. Kennedy, R. S. Minnick, and Horace A. Spencer. In San Luis Obispo County, information was provided by Eleanor Garrissere and Russell C. Goodrich. San Mateo County had input from George Miller, Katie Murdock, Irene Neasham, Donald R. Newmark, Hadley Osborn, Earl Schmidt, Albert Shumate, and Mary Vallejo. Santa Barbara County contributors Dennis and Carolyn Naiman, Michael Redman, and Karen L. Schultz were most helpful.

In Santa Clara County, a large group of people participated in the up-dating of information, including James M. Arbuckle, Peggy Coats, Frances Fox, Leon Kimura, Bea Lichtenstein, Kenneth Malovos, Laurella O'Brien, James O'Connor, Melita Oden, Mary A. Prien, Dorothy Regnery, Roger Rehm, Bartolome Sepulveda, James H. Stone, and William A. Wulf. In Santa Cruz County, contributors included Evelyn Baird, Margaret Koch, Alzora Snyder, and Stanley D. Stevens.

Shasta County benefited from the information of Richard B. Eaton, Mary Hendricks, Lindsay Jewett, Daniel Rosen, and Marjorie M. Weidert. For Solano County, acknowledgment is made of information from Mary Higham and Jack Nunnerly. The Sonoma County chapter was helped by material provided by James B. Alexander and Roger Rehm. Stanislaus County benefited from the input of Claude Delphia, and Sutter County

from information given by Dewey Gruening. Tehama County historians Lester Bodine, Patricia Felthouse, Ruth Hitchcock, and Rosemary Tingley gave useful information.

From Trinity County came material courtesy of Alice G. Jones. I benefited from Tulare County information from Annie R. Mitchell and Richard and Josephine Pratt. Tuolumne County material came from Madeline Iverson, Dolores Nicolini, and Mary Paquette. Ventura County was helped by material from Alberta Word. In Yolo County, Joanne Larkey, Roger Rehm, and Shipley Walters were very helpful, and in Yuba County W. H. Hutchinson supplied useful information.

In acknowledging all these contributions from others, I alone remain responsible for the final writing. If there are errors of fact or of interpretation, I would greatly appreciate having corrections, in hopes of incorporating them in future editions.

Finally, I want to acknowledge the help and support given to me by my family. My late parents, Oliver and Helen Kyle, began my interest in history when I learned that I was the great-grandson of Dr. Willard Pratt, the founder of Prattville in Plumas County. My children Charles, Lucile, and William and his wife Lynn, were full of very helpful advice throughout, and sometimes accompanied us on our travels. And Judith Butts Kyle, my wife, companion, and dearest friend, was with me all the way, through thousands of miles on the highways and back roads of California and untold hours of preparing this book. It is altogether fitting and appropriate that I dedicate this work to her.

Douglas E. Kyle

Contents

Historical Introduction

This overview is intended as a brief and very basic introduction to California history in order to provide some background for readers not already acquainted with it and also to avoid the need to repeat information throughout the chapters. Readers seeking more detailed information should consult the first section of the Bibliography, which lists works on the general history of California.

California's earliest verified historic date is September 28, 1542, when two small ships flying Spanish colors sailed into a harbor on the Pacific coast of North America. Juan Rodríguez Cabrillo, commander of the expedition, called his anchorage the Bay of San Miguel. Sebastián Vizcaíno, whose expedition entered the port 60 years later, called it the Bay of San Diego, and that name is the one which has survived. Changes of names would often happen in the history of California.

Spain was, by the middle of the sixteenth century, the foremost military and naval power of western Europe, with growing colonies in the Caribbean and on the continents of North and South America, and trade interests that spanned the Pacific to the Philippine Islands and Japan. Voyages by Cabrillo and his contemporary Hernando de Alarcón (who may have been the first European to set foot on California soil, in what is now Imperial County, around 1540) were part of the Spanish program of expansion, financed in part by the incredible wealth that the Spaniards found in Mexico and Peru and driven both by imperial needs and by dreams of gold and magical lands.

The name California was taken from a popular romantic narrative written in 1501, *Las Sergas de Esplandían* (*The Exploits of Esplandían*), which referred to a fabulous island ruled by an Amazon, Queen Calafia. The name was later given to the land lying west of Mexico, thought at that time to be an island, but actually the peninsula now known as Baja (Lower) California. Also somewhere to the West—which has, in Western civilization, always represented the future, unknown but potentially golden—the land of El Dorado was supposed to lie. The legend of El Dorado told of a kingdom so rich that its ruler was daily anointed with gold dust, thus becoming "El Dorado," the Gilded Man.

Meanwhile, in 1579, Spain's hegemony in the Pacific was briefly challenged by the Englishman Francis Drake. After raiding Spanish ports on the Pacific coast of South and Central America, Drake anchored his ship for three weeks, probably in California's Marin County. On his departure he claimed the land for Queen Elizabeth, a loyal but basically empty gesture. No other English voyager is known to have called on the California coast for more than two centuries.

After Cabrillo's voyage, the next official Spanish voyage of discovery was that of Sebastián Vizcaíno in 1602, seeking a possible anchorage on the North American coast for the great cargo ships that sailed from Manila to Acapulco. Vizcaíno discovered Monterey Bay, which he named for the Conde de Monterey, Viceroy in Mexico. However, Vizcaíno's glowing reports of what he saw in traveling perhaps as far north as Cape Mendocino did not stimulate further expeditions. Spain claimed the Pacific coast of North America as being within her empire, and no other European power challenged that claim. This remained a stable situation until the middle of the eighteenth century.

The area claimed by Spain as Alta (Upper) California was, in fact, already home to some 300,000 indigenous people, whose ancestors had been living there for at least 12,000 years. California's generally dry climate and abundance of plant and animal life made it possible for the Indians to harvest and store a generous supply of food without the need for farming or a nomadic life style. By the time Europeans began to explore the coast of California, the Indians had evolved into a complex of cultures, encompassing 104 language groups and living, usually in permanent settlements (later called *rancherias* by the Spanish), in every region of the present-day state except the high Sierra. Generally peaceable, their societies were further enriched by cooperative labor and extensive patterns of trade. They were, however, completely unprepared to withstand the Europeans, who showed no understanding or appreciation of the Indian way of life and whose attitude of superiority was to have tragic consequences.

By the 1760's Spain was forced to review her situation in the New World; Britain, France, and Russia were claiming more and more territory in North America. The northwestern frontier of the empire was unfortified and vulnerable to foreign penetration.

The Spanish occupation of Alta California was thus a deliberate act of colonization. Spanish subjects would be induced to move into these northern territories, assured of military protection and remission of taxes in the first five years of settlement. The Church would be provided with a fresh field in which missionary work could be done among the Indians—it was remembered that they were subjects of the King and could be introduced to the benefits of Spanish culture. The military would fortify strategic locations and deal with possible Indian or foreign resistance.

In 1769 a two-part expedition set out for Alta California and arrived at San Diego in the summer of that year. Three ships carried colonists and soldiers from Mexico, and an overland party traveled from Sonora with Gaspar de Portolá, governor of Baja California, as military commander and Father Junipero Serra as spiritual leader. Portolá had been instructed to find the Bay of Monterey of the Vizcaíno reports. Serra was to begin the establishment of the missions to the Indians of Alta California.

After the two groups came together at San Diego, Father Serra and his Franciscan brethren established the first mission. Portolá, ordering the foundations for a presidio, took a party northward to find Monterey Bay. The settlers took possession of the land. Not unexpectedly, this act was challenged by the local Indians; every activity of the Spanish was protected by a small military force.

Ultimately, four presidios, or fortified places, were established by the Spaniards in Alta California, all before the end of the eighteenth century, at San Diego, Santa Barbara, Monterey, and San Francisco. In addition, 21 missions were founded by the Franciscans along the coast, from San Diego de Alcalá in 1769 to San Francisco Solano in Sonoma in 1821. Many became extensive operations, containing churches, a padre's residence, workshops and storehouses, and quarters for both Indian neophytes and the king's soldiers. Using Indian labor, the missions developed gardens, orchards, vineyards, and pastures and began an extensive trade in hides and tallow. Between the missions, normally a day's ride apart, a rough pathway developed—El Camino Real, "The King's Highway." The name has been retained in several communities and is closely followed by today's U.S. Highway 101 between Petaluma and Los Angeles, and Interstate Highway 5 between Los Angeles and San Diego.

A third type of Spanish settlement, the pueblo or town, was also begun in Alta California, to be home for Spanish colonists. Many inducements were made to bring settlers into the province. Two pueblos, Los Angeles and San Jose, survived to become major California cities; a third, Branciforte, languished; its site is now part of the city of Santa Cruz.

Alta California was thought of as a northern extension of New Spain, as Mexico was known in Spanish days. For a dozen years, overland expeditions brought in settlers, livestock, seeds, and tools, culminating in the founding of the Pueblo of Los Angeles in 1781. In that year, a massacre of Spaniards along the Colorado River by Mojave Indians abruptly brought the overland route to a halt. Henceforth, the connection between Alta California and the governors in Mexico was made by sea, and a sense of distance obtruded between the two areas, which was never overcome, in either the Spanish or the Mexican years.

Spain's rule over Alta California has come under vigorous criticism by many historians in the last hundred years. The attack centers on the impact of Spanish Christian culture and domination upon the native California population. Clearly Europeans of the eighteenth and early nineteenth century believed their ways to be highly superior to those of the rest of the world, and this was evident in Alta California. Every European who left memoirs of a visit during the Spanish period wrote disparagingly of the Indians, who were described as ugly, naked, lethargic, and behaving much like animals. Rounded up into communities under Spanish rule, the Indians were cut off from their traditional ways; they were also exposed to European diseases, which worked with terrible force. Zealous and devout missionary priests, among them the recently beatified Serra, would doubtless be horrified to learn that a later age would charge them with genocide, but one fact stands above the waves of historical interpretation: the Indian population of California had declined to less than 50,000 by the middle of the nineteenth century. Once in a while rebellion occurred, always to be crushed. That Indian culture survived at all is almost miraculous.

The Europeans who visited California and wrote their accounts were many. Among them was the Englishman Captain George Vancouver, who twice visited the province in the 1790's and commented on what he considered to be the weak defenses of the area. There was no significant improvement of the defenses of the California coast, and in 1806 a Russian ship easily entered San Francisco Bay to begin negotiations with the local authorities for supplies to the destitute colony of Sitka in Russian America, now Alaska. Although Spain's mercantile economic policy sought to keep foreigners out of her imperial trade, the authorities in remote Alta California agreed to permit a limited amount of trade between the province and the Russians. When a Russian settlement was made north of San Francisco at Fort Ross (Sonoma County) in 1819 the Spaniards were unable to oust these traders and indeed were grateful for the services of the colony's artisans.

Spain's empire was feeling pressure from a new area, that of the United States of America. An occasional American ship had already been seen along the California coast in these early years of the nineteenth century, as the whaling industry and the China trade began to bring Yankee ships into Pacific waters, hitherto a Spanish monopoly. In 1819, the Adams-Onís Treaty between Spain and the United States drew a boundary line between Spanish and American claims in North America, and followed the 42nd parallel of latitude westward from the Rocky Mountains to the Pacific Ocean, the boundary line between California and Oregon today. The Oregon Country became an American outpost on the Pacific, from which many Americans would emigrate into California in the gold rush days.

In 1822 New Spain threw off Spanish rule and became the Republic of Mexico. Alta California had little choice but to accept this political change, although many of her leaders were Spanish by birth or by loyalty, particularly among the padres of the Church. Thus a level of hostility was added to the sense of distance that already existed between Mexico and Alta California. Spain had been an imperial power of global scope; Mexico was an impoverished country with no tradition of political self-government and no system of efficient internal communications.

Mexican rule did bring significant changes from that of Spain. A governor appointed from Mexico was to rule the province. The seat of government often moved from one administration to another, usually between Monterey in the north and Los Angeles in the south. (Briefly, in 1832–33, the quarrel between the north and the south resulted in two governors and two capitals! North-south conflict in California is an old story.) A provincial legislature, the *diputación*, was created; its authority was limited, and its deeds were few. Municipal government appeared, and the *alcalde*, the town's chief official, became the most important person in the region.

By Mexican revolutionary standards, the Church was hopelessly reactionary. As owner of extensive lands, it was also a major economic force in a poor country. Philosophy and fiscal needs combined to bring on the secularization of the missions beginning in 1834. The property of the missions was taken over by the state and sold to eager buyers. Those Indians who lived in the vicinity of the missions were supposed to get land of their own in this process, but in fact few did so.

Land was the one permanent element in this period of change. In the Spanish days, each of the missions received a grant of land for its sustenance. A few private individuals had also been given the right to occupy specific tracts of land, and most of these two dozen awards were confirmed under Mexican law in the 1820's. Mexico began the policy of making outright grants of land to trustworthy citizens. The land was allocated by leagues; a linear league would be 2.63 miles in today's measurements, and a square league would be about 4,439 acres. These parcels of land were known as *ranchos* and often mark the first attempts made in the history of California to make specific identification of land. Thus many of the historic spots in California have their first mention as ranchos. (The chapters in this book that deal with the coastal counties often contain subheadings based on ranchos, followed by the names of the towns that now sit on that land.) About 500 grants of land were made in the quarter-century of Mexican rule.

The economic backwardness of Mexican California invited outsiders. After 1822, more and more of these were young bachelors, American or British, seeking their fortune; many of them married the daughters of established California families and were baptized into the Catholic faith, which accounts for such a name as Juan Bautista Rogers Cooper of Monterey. Jedediah Strong Smith headed the first party of Americans to arrive in Alta California overland from the United States, in 1826; other mountain men and fur traders, some from the Hudson's Bay Company in the Oregon Country, were active in California in the late 1820's and the decade of the 1830's. Unable to keep them out, Mexico permitted foreigners who were willing to acknowledge Mexican law to become citizens of the republic, and as citizens these newcomers could become landowners. Men such as Robert Livermore and George C. Yount were now peers of established families like the Carrillos, the Lugos, and the Yorbas. These Hispanic grandees were chiefly concerned with cattle raising on their extensive lands. The newcomers tended to dominate the commercial and business life of Alta California.

Overland migration of American settlers into California began in 1841, when the Bidwell-Bartleson Party arrived from the Mississippi Valley. The traverse of the West was formidable: trails were random, water was scarce, and livestock perished. The people making this crossing endured great hardship in their migration, of which the Donner Party (whose story is told in the Nevada County chapter) was a frightful example. Despite adversities, the newcomers made a considerable addition to the American presence in California by 1846.

Between 1835 and 1846, relations between Mexico and the United States gradually deteriorated. In part, this was due to Mexican suspicion that the United States was seeking territorial expansion at Mexico's expense. In 1835, Mexico turned down an American offer to purchase San Francisco Bay. In the following year, Americans in Texas staged a successful revolution that drove Mexico out and created an independent Lone Star Republic, officially annexed to the United States in 1845. In 1842, Thomas ap Catesby Jones, U.S.N., commodore of the U.S. Pacific squadron, having heard a rumor that war had broken out, brought his four ships into Monterey Bay and demanded the surrender of the province. In the early 1840's, expansion toward the Pacific Coast became the announced goal of the majority Democratic Party, which in the election of 1844 put its candidate James K. Polk into the presidency and controlled both houses of Congress. The American annexation of Texas early in 1845 caused Mexico to sever diplomatic relations with the United States, and by May 1846 the two countries were at war. Although the major events of the war took place along the Texas border and on into Mexico, the opportunity to gain control of California was not wasted.

John Charles Frémont, an Army officer and son-in-law of Senator Thomas Hart Benton of Missouri, had begun his career with expeditions exploring the passes of the Rocky Mountains. He reached the Oregon Country in 1843 and entered Alta California the following year, where he too noted the weak defenses of the region. His *Report of the Exploring Expedition to Oregon and North California*, written with his wife Jessie in 1845, was very well-received and brought California more than ever to the attention of American officials. By the end of 1845, Frémont was back in California, where he and his men openly defied the Mexican authorities, going so far as to erect a fortification atop Gabilan Peak in San Benito County, overlooking the Salinas Valley. He abandoned the fort before any formal hostilities ensued. In May 1846, while Congress was receiving President Polk's war message, Frémont returned to California from a short sojourn in Oregon, captured Sutter's Fort at Sacramento, took Captain Sutter as prisoner, and encouraged Americans to rise against Mexican rule.

On June 14, 1846, a party of Americans took possession of the town of Sonoma and raised the Bear Flag of the California Republic over the plaza. Within three weeks, an American naval force appeared on the coast and formally proclaimed American rule over the presidios and coastal towns. Throughout the remainder of 1846, several incidents of Californian resistance to the American conquest took place, the most serious being the Battle of San Pasqual in San Diego County, where 21 American soldiers were ambushed and killed in December. On January 13, 1847, Frémont accepted the surrender of Governor Pío Pico and commander José María Flores. The captured province was officially annexed to the United States by the Treaty of Guadalupe Hidalgo early in 1848, ending the Mexican War.

Just a few days before the treaty was signed, James Marshall, an employee of Captain John Sutter, discovered abundant gold in the bed of the South Fork of the American River, at Coloma in El Dorado County. Nothing could keep this news from spreading, and throughout 1848 there were many other discoveries. President Polk's message to Congress in December acknowledged the bonanza. By 1849 the great gold rush was on. From as far away as Australia, Chile, China, and Europe, gold-seekers came to California by sea. A greater number of Americans ventured overland, on the trails already established by earlier pioneers. The excitement continued even after the easily discovered streambed nuggets were gathered and men realized that they had to mine the Sierra foothills in search of more gold.

In this Mother Lode region, new camps and towns set up almost overnight, many lasting no more than a few months. "Dame Shirley," the pen name of one of the few women in a mining camp, left memorable descriptions of Rich Bar, Plumas County, in 1852, which are a classic of reporting. The ruins of these short-lived mining centers are still to be seen throughout the state, from Tumco and Havilah in the south up to Hawkinsville and Orleans in the north. A number of other towns, such as Nevada City and Sonora, have survived and remain important regional centers.

Extensive hydraulic mining was practiced throughout the gold region until halted by a court order in 1884, largely because of environmental damage. Rivers had filled with debris, necessitating levees along the Feather and Sacramento rivers to hold back the spring floods, an annual problem that has persisted into the twentieth century. Malakoff Diggins State Historic Park in Nevada County and the enormous tailings east of Folsom in Sacramento County were the result of this kind of mining.

California, newcomers realized, presented many other opportunities beyond the haphazard search for gold. The mild climate and good soil invited developments in agriculture, ultimately the state's most valuable economic activity. The new cities of the gold rush—San Francisco, Sacramento, and Stockton in particular—needed skilled workmen and entrepreneurs. California's isolation encouraged the development of domestic industry, which by the federal census of 1860 boasted more than 3,500 manufacturing establishments.

The migration into California was so large that a movement toward statehood was underway even before civil territorial government began. In September 1849 a state constitutional convention met in Monterey. Of the 48 delegates, only seven were native Californians. The new state government included a popularly elected governor holding office for two years, a bicameral legislature, and a hierarchy of courts. A bill of rights contained a ban on slavery. As it happened, fifteen states in 1849 were free-soil and fifteen were slaveholding, a balance deliberately maintained since the Missouri Compromise in 1820. No slave territory was available to match free-soil California, whose admission to the Union was feared by the slave-holding South as placing that region at a disadvantage when sectional issues were voted on by Congress. Nonetheless, California entered the Union as a free state by the Compromise of 1850, which also included a more stringent fugitive slave law.

When the Civil War came, the need to link loyal California to the Union became urgent. As early as 1853, plans for a federally underwritten transcontinental railroad had been discussed, but nothing came of them for nearly a decade. In 1862, Congress enacted the Pacific Railroad Bill, just at the time when the forces of the Union seemed to be losing ground. (Travel by sea from New York to California, even using the short-cut over the Isthmus of Panama, was still a matter of many weeks under the best of conditions.) Before the completion of the railroad in 1869, however, telegraph lines connected California with the Mississippi Valley, and so on to the Eastern states. San Franciscans learned of President Lincoln's death the morning after his assassination in April 1865.

Lincoln's Republican party, which received California's electoral votes both in 1860 and 1864, advocated federal support for internal development; this included the encouragement of railroad lines in the West by extensive land grants. With Republicans dominating both the federal and the state political scene for many years after the end of the Civil War in 1865, the railroads had friends in high places. The Central Pacific Railroad, the western half of the transcontinental project of 1862–69, became the Southern Pacific Railroad system by the end of the century and exerted much influence on California politics. Its landholdings created towns such as Barstow, Roseville, and Tulare, and its power brought on such events as the Mussel Slough Tragedy in 1880, a story told in the Kings County chapter.

In these years (1850–80), a major development in California history resulted from policies adopted concerning Mexican land grants. These grants had been made in the days when a registered *diseño* (a sketch map and description of the land) was sufficient evidence of a valid land claim. Few Mexican ranchos had fences or any clear boundaries. Although Article IX of the Treaty of Guadalupe Hidalgo declared that Mexican land titles would be honored under the new American regime, ambitious newcomers into California laid claim to attractive areas of old land grants or simply "squatted" on these lands and defied the owners to drive them out. The early histories of both Oakland and Sacramento give ample evidence of how effective squatter settlement could be.

A federal statute in 1851 attempted to regulate the process whereby land claims in California could be approved (or "patented") by a commission appointed to that end. Holders of Mexican land grants had two years to prove before the courts that theirs was a valid title; the burden of proof was upon the Mexican owners, not the new squatters. The Land Commission met from 1852 to 1856 and, at great length and at the disadvantage of claimants (none of the commissioners knew the Spanish language, for example), determined the status of each claim. On the average, it took seventeen years for a claim to be patented. Often, the original litigants had died; even more often, the costs of litigation compelled the rancho owners to sell off their land piecemeal. Between 1865 and 1880, to cite one example, the Sepulveda family had to contend with 80 separate lawsuits in their efforts to keep Rancho Los Palos Verdes in Los Angeles County. The result of all this litigation was that about three-quarters of the Mexican claims were accepted or patented by Federal officials, but in fact most of the litigants had already sold most of their holdings. Albany, Berkeley, Emeryville, and northern Oakland now stand on the lands of José Domingo Peralta, who was so impoverished by legal fees that, at his death in 1865, his family required financial aid for his burial. Thus the old ranchos became divided into many new holdings.

With railroad transportation out of California a reality after 1869, the pace of California life stepped up dramatically. Migration from East to West increased, particularly into the area of Los Angeles. The 27 original counties of California were gradually subdivided and increased to reflect these changes in population until there were 58 by 1907. Many new towns were incorporated, chiefly in the Los Angeles basin and in the Great Central Valley. New faces were seen in the land. Chinese laborers, some early gold miners and others imported to build the railroads, stayed on, and San Francisco's Chinatown had 47,000 inhabitants by an 1875 estimate. Settlers from France, Italy, the Austro-Hungarian and the German empires, all established colonies for their countrymen. One could see Chinese joss houses and Jewish synagogues in the towns. The one population group that was languishing was the California Indian. A last hard-fought resistance against overwhelming odds, the Modoc War of 1873, was to little avail in the decline of the indigenous Californians.

In the late nineteenth century California was discovered by artists and writers, attracted to the magnificent landscapes and natural beauty of the state and to the fascinating spectacle of rapid social and economic change. Some great works of this period, such as the paintings of Albert Bierstadt or the essays of John Muir, were done by men born in Europe but raised in America, who came in their maturity to California. Health seekers flocked to the balmy climate: many tuberculosis sanitaria were established between 1880 and 1920, for example. A new kind of "El Dorado" myth began, composed of oranges, sunshine, outdoor life, and a wholesomeness that was contrasted with the squalor of Eastern industrial cities.

In these years of great change, some believed that California's past was being obliterated. In 1871 the California Historical Society was organized at the University of Santa Clara. In 1875 the Native Sons of the Golden West was begun, followed in 1886 by the Native Daughters of the Golden West. These groups were all concerned with the commemoration and recording of California history. They encouraged the keeping of local history, and they erected monuments throughout the state, reflecting all sorts of California's historic activities. Many of these are today State Registered Landmarks (SRL) and are so identified in the text that follows.

California politics between 1875 and 1924 frequently involved anti-Oriental movements, whose leaders declared that Chinese labor was undercutting white labor and that Japanese entrepreneurs were acquiring excessive amounts of land. Under pressure from the California Congressional delegation, the United States in 1882 stopped any further immigration from China, the first time that a nationality had been so excluded. Japanese immigration was halted by an Executive Agreement in 1908 and banned in 1924. In 1913 California's Webb Act prohibited Japanese not born in the United States from acquiring California land. In the years after 1924, official relations between the United States and the Empire of Japan grew more and more estranged: the Pearl Harbor attack on December 7, 1941, brought into the open a long-standing hostility, to which California politics had made some contribution. Although all Japanese on the West Coast were forced into "relocation centers" in the early days of World War II, most Japanese living in the United States were loyal to this country. The Manzanar site in Inyo County remains as a reminder of this period of wartime tension.

Political issues in these years were a chief subject of the press, always important as a means of communication in a state as large and diversified as California. Many leading newspapers had joined the concerted effort in the 1910 election to drive the Southern Pacific Railroad from its dominant position in the state; this campaign was successful with the election of Progressive Republican reformer Hiram Johnson as governor and a sympathetic legislature.

The major publishing names of the twentieth century, among them Chandler, De Young, Knowland, McClatchy, and Storke, were also concerned with historic preservation. William Randolph Hearst, the most influential publisher in California's history, supported several historical restorations. His San Simeon estate, in San Luis Obispo County, is a kind of treasure house of collections, and is a major tourist attraction today.

Water is an issue that repeatedly makes the headlines, for the simple reason that southern California has the larger population while northern California has 70 percent of the water in the state. Agriculture depends on irrigation to get through the long dry summers. Dams and reservoirs, aqueducts, and pumping systems have been installed throughout the state, often after considerable acrimony and debate. The city of Los Angeles acquired water rights in the Owens River Valley around the turn of the century, a measure still hotly debated. Great aqueducts brought the water to Los Angeles, leaving the Owens River basin in a dessicated condition. More aqueducts brought water from the Colorado River; the Salton Sea is the result of an overflow of water from the Colorado in 1905. The federal Central Valley Project, begun in 1935, dammed the Sacramento and San Joaquin rivers to provide irrigation for the Great Central Valley. The larger state project, the California Water Plan, involves moving millions of acre-feet of water every year from the northern to the southern part of the state; Butte County's Oroville Dam and Lake Oroville are the biggest elements in this project, without which California might not have grown as it has.

Petroleum became important in California as early as 1880, as numerous oil strikes were made in Kern and Los Angeles counties. By the first years of the twentieth century, the state was the largest oil producer in the United States. Over all, the value of petroleum far exceeds that of gold produced in the state, although California prefers to be known as the golden state.

Economic struggles came to the fore in California as the twentieth century began, and workers began to organize, particularly in the industrial city of San Francisco. Although often at odds with management, such groups as the International Longshoremen's Association wielded considerable power in the city; in 1934 they led a successful general strike in San Francisco, the only such occurrence in California history. Meanwhile, though the ports continued to be important for the shipment of goods, more and more commerce was being carried by trucks on the expanding highway system. All too often these highways were built through and over old areas of historic interest.

One industry closely connected with California since the early 1900's is that of motion pictures (and more recently, television), centered around the Hollywood district of Los Angeles. "Hollywood" became synonymous with glamor and opulence, not only on the screen but in the homes of Bel Air and Beverly Hills. The area has been a tourist attraction for decades. Movies were also shot on location throughout California, creating a new category of historic spots. When the Hooker Oak (SRL 313) in Bidwell Park, Chico, fell in 1977, newspapers identified it chiefly as part of the setting of the 1938 film *Robin Hood*.

World War II brought great changes to California, among them many new or expanded military bases. California lay within the Pacific theater of operations; in the early months of the war there was actually an enemy attack on the Santa Barbara County coast. Hundreds of thousands of military personnel were moved through California ports. There had been an influx of migrants from the Dust Bowl states into California in the 1930's, but the new wave was ten times that of the previous decade. The defense industry, which became one of California's most important, sought workers from all over the country. One group who responded in large numbers were black Americans from the South. The 1940 census reported 124,000 blacks in California; by the 1950 census, their number had risen to 462,000. Established California cities became larger, and new ones arose seemingly overnight, particularly in the San Francisco Bay Area and in the Los Angeles basin.

As California approached the end of the twentieth century, new population movements were occurring, many a result of war in Southeast Asia. People from Cambodia, Laos, and Vietnam now made their homes in America: Fresno became not only a city of many Armenians; it had now the world's largest Hmong population. The assimilation which some Californians have feared and others have championed will doubtless continue to add color and new dimensions to the history of California in the future. One encouraging sign is the return of native Americans. From near-extinction in 1900, the Indian population of California is today more than 200,000, the largest of any state, in part because of migration of Indians into California from other parts of the United States.

The account of California's historic spots which follows will inevitably require updating as time, fire, flood, and freeways take their toll. New events will produce new landmarks or new meanings for old ones (many will always think of the San Francisco City Hall for the 1978 assassinations there). So this must be regarded as a chapter in a history still unfolding, still fascinating, and worth visiting.

HISTORIC SPOTS IN CALIFORNIA

Alameda County

Alameda County was created in 1853 from portions of Contra Costa and Santa Clara counties. The county seat was originally at Alvarado. It was moved to San Leandro in 1856, and from there in 1873 to Oakland, where it has remained.

The primary meaning of *alameda* is "a place where poplar trees grow." It is derived from the Spanish word *alamo*, meaning "poplar" or "cottonwood." The county doubtless received its name from El Arroyo de la Alameda (Alameda Creek), which, when first discovered, was lined as it is now with willow and silver-barked sycamore trees, giving it the appearance of an *alameda* or road lined with trees.

The Emeryville Shell Mound

From the 1850's the shell mounds found along the shores of San Francisco Bay excited the curiosity of the incoming white settlers. These mounds were first studied scientifically in the spring of 1902 by Drs. John C. Merriam and Max Uhle of the University of California. They made careful excavations on the site of the prominent Emeryville mound and published methodical considerations of the evidence obtained. N. C. Nelson in 1908 completed a survey of the entire San Francisco Bay region, in which he located, numbered, and mapped nearly 425 shell heaps, analyzing them in detail and publishing a summary of his observations and conclusions.

The Emeryville mound, designated no. 329 in the Nelson survey, was situated on the eastern shore of San Francisco Bay almost due east of the Golden Gate. It lay on the western side of the old Peralta grant, or that part of Rancho San Antonio apportioned to Vicente Peralta by his father, Don Luís María Peralta. This section became known later as Emeryville, now an incorporated town lying between the cities of Oakland and Berkeley. The shell mound (SRL 335) was located between the Bay and the Southern Pacific Railroad tracks. Shellmound Street identifies the site; no official marker has been placed there.

"The first people who came to this site," writes W. Egbert Schenck, "camped just above the shoreline, possibly on little hummocks at the edge of the marsh. As shell-fish were obtained, the shells were thrown aside, and these with the by-products of daily life increased the camp ground and gradually crept out into the marsh. . . . As the shell area increased, subsequent people utilized it because it was drier, placing camps, perhaps, over what had previously been marsh. . . . This shell area grew until it covered some hundreds of thousands of square feet."

Virtually every trace of the shell mounds has vanished today; fortunately, one mound can still be seen in Coyote Hills Regional Park in Fremont. Encroaching tidal waters, bulldozers leveling grounds for factory sites, city streets and modern residences, the farmer's plow or the search for fertilizer, all these and other factors have entered into the gradual demolition of the fascinating monuments of a vanished race.

The Emeryville mound was located at a point that was favorable for use as a camping ground by prehistoric peoples. Lying on the narrow alluvial plain that stretches from north to south along the Contra Costa ("opposite coast") between the foothills and the Bay, it was bordered on the north by open, almost treeless plains, and on the south by a willow thicket some twenty acres in extent. Further south the thicket merged into a marsh extending about one and one-half miles along the shore and gradually increasing in width until at its southern end it was three-quarters of a mile wide. Beyond the marshes stretched a mile of rolling, oak-studded fields, the Encinal de Temescal.

Temescal Creek held an important relation to the mound in prehistoric times. The creek itself supplied fresh water to the nomadic people who visited its banks, and the abundant shellfish beds at its mouth supplied food, while the quiet reaches of the Bay were full of sea otter, hunted perhaps from tule rafts. Waterfowl filled the marshes, and deer were plentiful in the willow thicket and the oak grove to the south; acorns, seeds, and other vegetable foods were abundant, as the numerous mortars found in the vicinity indicate. The willow thickets too supplied ample firewood.

To this favored spot groups of Indian peoples came yearly from the surrounding country, perhaps from long distances. They may have spent six months out of each year at this site, fishing and hunting, drying and pounding the shellfish for future food supplies, and taking the otter skins for clothing.

Although there may be older mounds in the Bay region and although no certainty can be attached to any estimate of when human beings first camped at the spot, scientists compute that the maximum age of the Emeryville mound is about 1,000 years. Likewise, there is no certain evidence on when the place was last used as a rendezvous for nomadic tribes. Schenck says that it was apparently unoccupied when Fages passed that way in 1772, for no mention is made of it in the chronicles of that expedition. Anza, in 1776, and Gabriel Moraga, in the early 1800's, also failed to mention having seen Indians in the Oakland-Berkeley neighborhood, although they did note their presence both to the south and to the north. Yet even if these early explorers did not see Indians there, and even though there were no fogs concealing their whereabouts, it is very possible that the oak groves of which Father Crespí wrote, together with the willow thickets near the mouth of Temescal Creek, may have formed an effectual screen behind which the Indians at the Emeryville mound were encamped—or perhaps took refuge—when the first white travelers passed that way.

Vicente Peralta erected his adobe dwelling not far from Temescal Creek and about one and one-half miles east of the Emeryville mound about 1836. At the mouth of the creek was the Temescal embarcadero, and the ancient mound was a landmark familiar to travelers along the old creek road during those early days.

In 1857 the Peralta grant was surveyed and mapped by Julius Kellersberger, and in 1859 Edward Wiard purchased that portion of it on which the mound stood. Maps of that date show buildings on both the eastern and the western parts; in 1871 Wiard leveled a section of the eastern side and laid out the mile race track that became known as the Oakland Trotting Park. On the western side in 1876 he opened the Shellmound Park, a holiday resort and picnic grounds long popular among pleasure seekers of the entire Bay Area until the destruction of the mound in 1924. The Emeryville shell mound, in the amusement park days, was a picturesque landmark. On its low, truncated summit were a circle of trees, some windmills, and the round dance pavilion surrounded by a high cypress hedge. A historical atlas dated 1878 shows this mound with the residence of J. S. Emery in the foreground.

The Emeryville mound was leveled in 1924 in order to convert the area into a factory site. John Hubert Mee, president of the Mee Estate, which owned the property, made known his intentions and permitted the University of California to explore the site, while Captain Ludwig Siebe, proprietor of Shellmound Park, rendered every assistance possible in the work of excavation. The mound was razed by steam shovel; careful observations were made and collections were taken during the process. After the leveling operations were completed, controlled excavations of its lower levels were made by hand. Many skeletal and artifact materials were collected. The pile was found to be composed principally of shells—mostly clams, mussels, and oysters, with a plentiful mixture of cockleshells. Certain other kinds, found only in rare quantities, had been treated in the manner of possessions. Besides human burials, the accumulation disclosed the skeletal remains of birds, quadrupeds, sea mammals, and fish. Many of these bone remains were placed in the Museum of Vertebrate Zoology at the University of California.

The Lincoln Park Shell Mound

One shell mound of the 425 mapped by Nelson in 1906–8 has been memorialized. The site of this mound, located in the city of Alameda and now covered by modern streets and residences, extended over three acres of ground bounded roughly by what are now Central, Johnson, and Santa Clara avenues and Court Street. The mound was removed by the city authorities in the summer of 1908, and the earth, combined with tons of shells, was used for the making of roads on Bay Farm Island.

The lower levels of this ground were examined by Captain W. A. Clark, who, working the ground carefully with a hand trowel, was able to save a number of fine relics. These were placed in the Alameda Public Library, where they are still on display.

A stone monument bearing a bronze tablet was placed in Lincoln Park near the site of the old Indian mound. The inscription reads: "One thousand feet due west was a prehistoric mound, 400 feet long, 150 feet wide, 14 feet high. The remains of 450 Indians, with stone implements and shell ornaments, were found when the mound was opened in 1908. Erected by Copa de Oro Chapter, D.A.R., 1914."

Other Indian Sites

From Albany in the north to Mowry's Landing in the south, there were at least twenty shell mounds scattered along the bayshore in Alameda County when they were catalogued and mapped by Nelson in 1906–8. Nelson in his report states that the 425 mounds found in the greater Bay Area probably did not include all of them, and that some doubtless had been obliterated in past years.

At the curve of Indian Rock Avenue where it meets the south end of San Diego Road in north Berkeley, a huge, irregular rock mass looms above the drive. From its level summit there is a commanding view of the valley and of the Bay beyond. At the base of the main boulder are a number of smaller rocks in which are deeply worn holes or mortars where the Indians once ground acorns for meal. Gnarled buckeyes and green bays encircle this spot, and at the foot the city of Berkeley has planted a garden in Mortar Rock Park. A few hundred feet lower down on Indian Rock Avenue at the head of San Mateo Road is Indian Rock Park, another prehistoric landmark set among small live oak and tall eucalyptus trees.

In the Trestle Glen neighborhood of Oakland there is a level spot where an Indian village once stood. It was originally called Indian Gulch because Indians still lived there when the first white people came to that region. Nothing remains today as a reminder of the Indians, and Trestle Glen Road winds through a narrow canyon still shaded by immense live oaks and other trees.

Temescal

Temescal, a name of Aztec origin meaning "sweat house," was brought to California by the Franciscan Fathers. A. L. Kroeber describes the *temescal* thus: "From the outside its appearance is that of a small mound. The ground has been excavated to the depth of a foot or a foot and a half, over a space of about twelve by seven or eight feet. In the center of this area two heavy posts are set up three or four feet apart. These are connected at the top by a log laid in their forks. Upon this log, and in the two forks, are laid some fifty or more logs and sticks of various dimensions, their ends sloping down to the edge of the excavation. It is probable that brush covers these timbers. The whole is thoroughly covered with earth. There is no smoke hole. The entrance is on one of the long sides, directly facing the space between the two center posts, and only a few feet from them. The fireplace is between the entrance and the posts. It is just possible to stand upright in the center of the house. In Northern California, the so-called sweathouse is of larger dimensions, and was preeminently a ceremonial or assembly chamber."

Dr. L. H. Bunnell, in his history published in 1880 of his discovery of the Yosemite Valley, notes some interesting details of the use of the sweat house. "It . . . was used as a curative for disease, and as a convenience for cleansing the skin, when necessity demanded it. . . . I have seen a half-dozen or more enter one of these rudely constructed sweathouses through the small aperture left for the purpose. Hot stones are taken in, the aperture is closed until suffocation would seem impending, when they would crawl out, reeking with perspiration, and with a shout, spring like acrobats into the cold waters of the stream. As a remedial agent for disease, the same course is pursued."

Through what is now a busy part of Oakland, Temescal Creek wandered down from the Piedmont hills to San Francisco Bay. When white men first came to this section of the country, it is said that they found an old Indian sweat house on the arroyo and that because of this circumstance they named it Temescal Creek. W. E. Schenck, however, believes that the name may have arisen, not from the presence of a native Indian village and sweat house, but because the Indian retainers on the Peralta rancho doubtless set up a *temescal* on the bank of the creek near their cabins. The Vicente Peralta adobe was built about two blocks north of the point where the present Telegraph Avenue crosses the creek, near 51st Street. Around this nucleus the settlement of Temescal grew up. The name first appears on the Kellersberger survey map of 1857 as "Temesconta," which, Schenck says, "may or may not be Temescal."

Temescal Creek flowed about 450 feet southeast of the center of the Emeryville shell mound and discharged into the Bay some 800 feet southwest of the center of the mound. The creek seems to have been the determining physiographical feature of the region in prehistoric as well as in pioneer times, tending to focus population by its supply of fresh water and food; until about the 1880's, for instance, it had salmon runs. With the coming of the Spaniards to the eastern side of the Bay, Mission San José was settled, and later the great ranchos of San Antonio, San Leandro, San Pablo, San Lorenzo, and others were granted. Gradually embarcaderos sprang up along the eastern shore of the Bay. Among others the Temescal landing at the mouth of Temescal Creek near the old Emeryville shell mound became a landing place for occasional parties from San Francisco. The path of the old Temescal Creek road doubtless followed the general course of the creek as far east as Telegraph Avenue and beyond.

The owners of the great ranchos of Alta California between 1833 and 1846 lived in a time when the missions were breaking up, the presidios were practically deserted, and land could be had almost for the asking. Theirs was a simple, carefree life, or so it seems in contrast to the terrific challenges that came to them after 1848.

During this period, visitors landing in boats at the mouth of Temescal Creek continued to the ranchos or to the mission by way of the Vicente Peralta adobe one and one-half miles inland. All who came were sure to be hospitably entertained. From there they would proceed close to the foothills to Antonio Peralta's adobe near what is now Fruitvale Avenue, and thence to Ignacio Peralta's on the bank of San Leandro Creek. The next stop was the Estudillo rancho on the south side of the creek, and from there they went to Guillermo Castro's adobe at the site of the present city of Hayward. Here roads led east to Amador's and Livermore's ranchos and south to Mission San José.

The old Temescal Creek Road no longer exists (though

a portion of SR 24 follows the creek bed in some places), and the free flow of the stream was stopped in 1866 when it was dammed up in the hills to form the reservoir still known as Lake Temescal. At that time it furnished the principal water supply for several thousand inhabitants. The course of the arroyo itself is still plainly indicated in some places by a winding lane of native oak, willow, bay, elder, buckeye, and cottonwood trees. The creek itself runs through culverts underground and in places runs freely; it forms part of the boundary between Emeryville and Oakland.

Ortega First to See the "Contra Costa"

In the fall of 1769, while he was encamped on San Francisquito Creek (on the San Mateo–Santa Clara county line), after his historic discovery of the great Bay of San Francisco, Gaspar de Portolá sent out a reconnoitering party. Commanded by José Francisco de Ortega, the expedition's purpose was to find a land route up the eastern shore of the newly discovered bay to Point Reyes in Marin County and Cermeño's harbor. It seems to have been anticipated that a settlement to be named San Francisco would be established on that harbor and there would be founded the mission dedicated to St. Francis.

Passing around the southern end of San Francisco Bay, Ortega and his men forded the Guadalupe River (in Santa Clara County). From there, wrote Father Juan Crespí, chronicler and chaplain to Portolá, "they went forward on the other side of the estuary eight or ten leagues, but there was still a long distance for them to go. At this distance of ten leagues, they came upon another very large stream with a very strong current, and its bed was also wooded and its course was through a great plain which was also quite well wooded." They must have gone as far north as Niles or farther, says Bolton, and the second "very large stream" with wooded arroyo was doubtless Alameda Creek, from which the county takes its name.

On the evening of November 10, 1769, "the explorers returned, very sad. . . . They said that all the territory which they had examined to the northeast and north was impassable because of the scarcity of pasture and especially because of the ferocity and ill-temper of the heathen, who received them angrily and tried to stop their passage. They said also that they had seen another estuary [San Pablo Bay] of equal magnitude and extent with the one we had in sight and with which it communicated, but that in order to go round it one would have to travel many leagues . . . and that the mountains were rough and difficult."

The austere aspect of what the Spaniards came to call the Contra Costa ("coast opposite" San Francisco) on that November day two centuries ago put dismay into the hearts of Portolá's weary, half-starved soldiers. They had gone far enough north to sight San Pablo Bay, but the view had only made further passage seem an impossible undertaking. Already disheartened because the long-sought port of Monterey had not been found, they voted unanimously to return to the Point of Pines in Monterey County.

Fages, Trail Blazer of the Contra Costa

Alameda County was again penetrated by white men in the autumn of 1770, when Pedro Fages, one of Portolá's men left by him in command at Monterey, decided on his own initiative to make another attempt to reach Point Reyes by land. It was on this trip that Fages opened the first inland route from Monterey to the future site of San Jose. From there he continued over the trail opened the year before as far as Niles and on to a point "seven leagues beyond the point reached by Ortega."

During this time the party had, Bolton writes, "skirted the Contra Costa for two days. . . . From the Berkeley hills they looked west through the Golden Gate and to the north they beheld San Pablo Bay cutting across their route to Point Reyes."

Fages made a second attempt in the spring of 1772 to reach Cermeño's bay. Accompanied by Father Juan Crespí, "six Catalonian volunteers, six leather-jackets, a muleteer, and an Indian servant," he followed the trail that he had opened more than a year before. Northwest to the region of Hayward the party retraced the ground already twice covered by Ortega and Fages.

Crespí's chronicle for Wednesday, March 25, reads: "On this day of the Incarnation, after Mass had been said, we set out . . . in the direction of the north-north-west. At the start we travelled about a league from the estuary at the foot of a bare mountain range, and after travelling a short distance we were three leagues from the estuary. All the land is level, black, and very well covered with good grass, mallows, and other herbs. . . . We passed five villages of heathen, which are all on the banks of the arroyos with running water. . . . We halted on the bank of a large arroyo close to the mountains skirting the broad plain. The bed of the arroyo is very full of alders, cottonwoods, and willows."

Their route, like that of the long line of travelers who were to follow in their steps, lay close to the hills, and camp was made at San Lorenzo Creek, called San Salvador de Horta by Crespí.

Advancing as far as the site of Fruitvale on March 26, they pitched camp about where Mills College is today.

During the day they had their first view of elk, which Crespí thought were buffalo but which the soldiers called mule deer. Five arroyos of running water had been crossed, their banks green with alder, cottonwood, live oak, and bay trees. At the end of five leagues, Fages and his men saw the Alameda peninsula, now an island, and the intervening *encinal* or live-oak groves. "The site," wrote Crespí, "is very suitable for a good settlement . . . on account of the proximity of the forest. . . . This place was called Arroyo del Bosque"— probably Fruitvale Creek.

From here the march, as described by Bolton, crossed country now thoroughly urbanized, but then only a pleasant wilderness: "On the 27th they turned inland to round the estuary and the adjacent marshes, and emerged from the hills near the site of Lake Merritt. Near the [Oakland] Technical High School Father Crespí made his observations of the Golden Gate. The islands which he describes in the gate are Alcatraz Island, Goat (Yerba Buena) Island, and Angel Island. The arroyo where they camped, a league north of the point of observation, was probably Strawberry Creek, and the campsite near the western side of the campus of the University of California. On the 28th they continued past the sites of Berkeley and Albany to eastern Richmond" in Contra Costa County.

In 1977, the Alameda County Historical Society placed a plaque on the campus of the California College of Arts and Crafts at 5200 Broadway in Oakland at what is believed to be the actual vantage point from which the 1770 Fages expedition first looked at the Golden Gate.

On the return trip in 1772, the first stop made in Alameda County was made on April 1 at what is now the grounds of the Castlewood Country Club near Pleasanton. On April 2 "they descended Arroyo de la Laguna, crossing it near Suñol. Leaving Suñol Valley they crossed Alameda Creek, ascended Mission Pass, re-entered the valley of San Francisco Bay, and continued past the head of the bay at a point near Milpitas" (in Santa Clara County).

The second Fages expedition seems to have been decisive in determining the location of San Francisco. Clearly Point Reyes was less attractive a site than the newly discovered bay. A settlement south of the Golden Gate would be accessible from Monterey both over land and by sea.

Anza Follows the Contra Costa Trail

After he had explored the sites for the presidio and the mission to be established at the port of San Francisco, Captain Juan Bautista de Anza, accompanied by Lieutenant José Moraga, his second in command, and by Father Pedro Font, master chronicler and chaplain of the second overland expedition from Sonora to California, passed around the southern extremity of San Francisco Bay into Alameda County. With eleven soldiers, six muleteers, and servants, Anza and his companions were on their way to explore the "Rio Grande de San Francisco"—Carquinez Strait and the waters above it.

On the frosty Sunday morning of March 31, 1776, after Father Font had said Mass, the travelers left their camp on the Guadalupe River and, meeting with a network of sloughs and marshes along Coyote Creek, where it runs west, were forced to twist their way about for three leagues until they emerged on higher ground at the foot of the hills. From this point forward, the line of march followed "far away from the water . . . through very level country, green and flower-covered all the way to the estuary, but with no other timber or firewood than that afforded by the trees in the arroyos which we encountered."

Font's map showed that the line of march was now close to the hills all the way, and Bolton identifies it as the route passing by way of the Arroyo de la Encarnación, probably Scott Creek, and from there into what is now Fremont. The arroyo "about half way on the road" was apparently Alameda Creek, with its "very deep pools, many sycamores, cottonwoods, and some live oaks and other trees." It was here that a band of about 30 armed but peaceful Indians ran out to greet them with shouts of "Au, au, au, au," which seemed to Father Font "like something infernal."

Passing three arroyos and two deserted Indian villages, Anza and his men crossed the fifth stream, San Lorenzo Creek, near which they pitched their tents. Here they met a lone Indian, who appeared to be much frightened by their sudden appearance. This is the last mention of Indians until Wildcat and San Pablo creeks were reached in Contra Costa County.

Mass was said in a thick and "very damp" fog on Monday, April 1, and a small army of mosquitoes pursued the travelers. Continuing along the foothills, the route was much the same as that followed by Foothill Boulevard today. Professor Bolton has identified and sketched the way for us: "The arroyo where they saw the bears was San Leandro Creek. Two leagues beyond they crossed the creek at Mills College. Just beyond they climbed the hill and from there Font drew the sketch of the Oakland Estuary and oak-covered Alameda Peninsula, now Alameda Island. . . . Descending the hill they crossed Arroyo del Bosque, a stream in eastern Fruitvale. Continuing northwest they crossed the site of Oakland. It was from Berkeley that Font sighted through

Lime Point and Point Bonita to determine the trend of the north shore of the Golden Gate. It was in Berkeley, too, that the elk were chased, 'at the Arroyo de la Bocana' of Crespí, a place of 'very little water' and 'a small growth of trees.' Farther down this arroyo there was 'a grove or growth of not very large timber.'" This was what is now known as Strawberry Creek.

Leaving the stream and its brushy coverts behind them, the explorers passed over a level plain and low hills into Contra Costa County. Following Suisun Bay as far as Antioch, they turned south on April 4. After a tiring struggle with impassable tulares and the blinding, wind-driven ash of burned tules, they proceeded some six leagues "along the general course of the Old River." At a point just south of Bethany, Anza decided to give up his attempt to approach the Sierra Nevada, on account of the seemingly limitless and impassable tulares that intervened, and to return to Monterey.

Continuing south, the party entered the Lomas de las Tuzas, evidently by Midway Valley. Ascending Patterson Grade to the vicinity of the pass, they looked down into Livermore Valley and "descried in the distance the range of redwoods on San Francisco Peninsula. . . . Continuing southeast along the northeastern edge of Crane Ridge for seven or eight miles, about to the San Joaquin County line, they climbed to the top of Crane Ridge, perhaps up Sulphur Springs Canyon, reaching the summit west of Eagle Mountain. Continuing south they descended to Arroyo Mocho, striking it about at Callahan Gulch, some two miles north of the Santa Clara County line."

The Founding of Mission San José

"In 1794," Bancroft writes, "the eastern shores of San Francisco Bay were almost a tierra incognita to the Spaniards." For nearly twenty years after the coming of Anza in 1776, there is no record of any exploring expedition until 1795, when Sergeant Pedro Amador visited the southern part of Alameda County some time before June. In his report, acknowledged by Governor Diego de Borica on June 2, 1795, Amador used the name of Alameda, the first known official use of that designation. The Alameda was again visited in November 1795, when, in accordance with the governor's orders, Hermenegildo Sal and Father Antonio Danti set out from Monterey to search for suitable mission sites.

"Having arrived at Santa Clara on the 21st," says Bancroft, "they were joined by Alférez Raimundo Carrillo, and started the next day to examine the Alameda previously explored by Amador, whose diary they had." The party journeyed northward nearly to the site of modern Oakland, then returned to the Alameda and continued to the south. At the base of what is now called Mission Peak, a suitable site was found. The place was twelve miles north of Mission Santa Clara, in an area which proved to have fertile soil and a healthy climate.

It took some time before official permission was forthcoming to establish Mission San José. In June 1797 Padre Presidente Fermín Francisco de Lasuén and a few soldiers set out for the new site, called Oroysom by the natives. An *enramada*, or temporary chapel, was erected, and on June 11, Trinity Sunday, Father Lasuén celebrated the first Mass at the site.

Five days after the founding, temporary buildings constructed of native timbers and thatched with grass were begun, and on June 28 Fathers Isidoro Barcenilla and Agustín Merino arrived to take charge of the new mission. Barcenilla served until 1802, when Father Luís Gil y Taboada succeeded him, and Merino was replaced in 1799 by Father José Antonio Uría. Luís María Peralta succeeded Miranda in command of the mission guard in 1798.

Of the various fathers who served Mission San José, Narciso Durán, a native of Catalonia, who came to California from Mexico in 1806, was the most prominent. He went at once to Mission San José and, with Father Buenaventura Fortuni, began his long ministry, which continued until 1833, when he moved to Santa Barbara. Father Fortuni left the mission in 1825, and from then on Father Durán served alone, being also Padre Presidente of the missions during the years 1825–27, 1831–38, and 1844–46. He was especially noted for his earnest and successful missionary work. Throughout the troubled years of secularization, he managed the affairs of the mission with marked ability, attaining something close to what would today be called popularity with most people with whom he came in contact. An accomplished musician, he taught the Indians to read music and trained an orchestra of 30 Indians, with flutes, violins, trumpets, and drums.

The German explorer Georg Heinrich von Langsdorff, who came to California on the Russian ship *Nadeshda* in 1806, visited Mission San José early in May. He was the first non-Spanish foreigner to tread the southeastern bay shores. He received a warm reception from Father Pedro de la Cueva, then in charge of the mission, and a great Indian dance was given for his benefit. Since he was particularly interested in the manners and customs of the natives, he devoted much space to them in his narrative of the expedition. Langsdorff also wrote enthusiastically of the orchards and gardens of Mission San José: "The quantity of corn in the granaries far exceeded my expectations . . . and a proportionate quantity of maize, barley, pease, beans, and other grain. The kitchen garden is extremely well laid out, and kept in very good order; the soil is everywhere rich and fertile, and yields ample returns. . . . A small rivulet runs through the garden, which preserves a constant moisture. . . . The situation of the establishment is admirably chosen, and according to the universal opinion the mission will in a few years be the richest and best in New California."

Langsdorff's prophecy was fulfilled to a large degree, for Mission San José grew and prospered throughout the years of its service, before the inevitable decline following secularization at last set in about 1841. Bancroft pictures this growth with the following statistics: "By the end of 1797 there were 33 converts, and in 1800 the number had increased to 286, the baptisms having been 364. . . . Meanwhile the large stock came to number 367, and there were 1,600 sheep and goats. Crops in 1800 were about 1,500 bushels, chiefly wheat."

Ten years later the number of neophytes had increased to 545. There were 1,806 people at the mission in 1824, when it was second only to Mission San Luís Rey in population, and in the number of baptisms San José greatly exceeded any other mission. It was fourth in the number of cattle and sheep raised, as well as in the average production of grain crops.

The highest population attained at Mission San José was 1,877 in 1831; the number fell to 1,400 in 1834, and to 580 in 1840. However, this mission for the entire decade of the 1830's maintained a remarkable record and was probably the most prosperous of all the California missions both before and after secularization, which was effected in Alta California between 1834 and 1837. Crops were good, and the livestock increased steadily. Engelhardt gives the last available official report (1832) as 12,000 cattle, 13,000 sheep, and 13,000 horses.

San José was the last mission but one to be secularized. In November 1836 the property was turned over to José de Jesús Vallejo, *comisionado*, and the transfer was completed in December. Vallejo remained in charge until April 1840, when he was succeeded by José María Amador. Temporal management of twelve missions, including San José, was restored to the padres in March 1843, but in May 1846 Mission San José was finally sold by Governor Pío Pico to Andrés Pico and J. B. Alvarado for $12,000.

Most of the mission lands finally fell into the hands of strangers. The greater part of the estate of Mission San José was secured by E. L. Beard, who was described in 1876 as still residing at the mission and who possessed one of the loveliest places in the state. The Beard homestead at Mission San José is now a Dominican convent.

Mission San José was a center for the social life of the ranchos on the east side of San Francisco Bay during the 1830's and 1840's. It was also a stopping place for expeditions sent against the Indians in the years when Spanish and Indian peoples were often at odds with each other. During 1849 and 1850 it provided a wayside station for those gold seekers who used the land route from San Francisco to the mines by way of Mission Pass and Livermore. At this time Henry C. Smith, a member of Frémont's California Battalion in 1846, had a trading post in the old adobe mission building.

Of the original buildings at Mission San José (SRL 334), only a part of the padres' living quarters remains today. It has been incorporated into the museum at the mission. To the north is the reconstructed church, completed in 1982, one of the most ambitious historical reconstructions in California. While the project was under way, archeologists found the grave marker of Robert Livermore underneath the old church site. A leader in this restoration project was the late Father William N. Abeloe, who revised and edited the third edition of *Historic Spots in California*. Nearby is the Dominican Convent cemetery, with its background of cypress and olive trees. Ohlone College lies at the southern edge of the mission. A mile west on Washington Boulevard is the Ohlone Indian burial ground.

Although it is located nowhere near the Guadalupe River, Mission San José is often referred to as "San José de Guadalupe." Guadalupe was not a part of its original title, and was probably acquired somehow through association with the Pueblo de San José de Guadalupe, now the city of San Jose, some fifteen miles away.

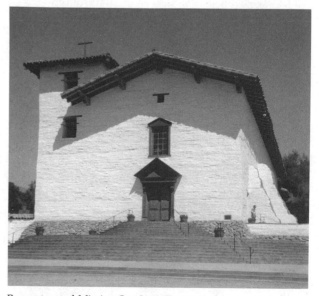

Reconstructed Mission San José, Fremont

In 1956, the old community of Mission San José became part of the city of Fremont, at almost 100 square miles one of the largest municipalities in the state in area. The other four unincorporated towns that joined with the old mission town to form the new city were Centerville, Irvington, Niles, and Warm Springs.

Mission Pass, an Old Spanish Trail

Mission Pass, the starting point of an old Spanish and pioneer American trail, cuts through the Mount Hamilton Range just northeast of Mission San José. The winding SR 21 long followed the route approximately, but now it has been straightened and widened into a freeway and taken into the interstate highway system as part of I-680.

Crossing over the lower hills, the old trail dropped down into Sunol Valley, where it went in two directions. One branch skirted the western edge of Livermore Valley along the Arroyo de la Laguna and proceeded up the Amador and San Ramon valleys to the site of Concord, and from there on to the San Joaquin Valley. The other branch, the more traveled route, went straight across Livermore Valley through the hills into the San Joaquin Valley.

In 1772 Pedro Fages and Father Juan Crespí came over the first of these trails by way of Concord on their return from the north, after having discovered the mouth of the San Joaquin River. Many later expeditions went through the same pass, among them the one led by Gabriel Moraga that opened up the Sacramento Valley region. Various expeditions against the Indians, made by Moraga, Vallejo, and others, started from the mission through this pass, as did later gold-seekers.

Jedediah Strong Smith, a Prisoner at Mission San José

In May 1827, while Father Narciso Durán was in charge of Mission San José, Jedediah Strong Smith, the great American pathfinder, wrote a letter to the padre. Durán was suspicious of the strangers. Four hundred of the neophytes had run away from the mission on May 15 and 16, and the fur hunters were unjustly suspected of having been the instigators of the desertion.

Unsuccessful in his attempts to cross the Sierra Nevada, far from home, and low on all supplies, Smith addressed to Durán a letter dated May 19 in which he made a frank statement of his purpose and condition and concluded with the words: "I am, Reverend Father, your strange, but real friend and Christian brother, J. S. Smith." Father Durán did not read the letter but forwarded it to Monterey for translation.

After his historic passage of the Sierra Nevada late in October, Smith, with three of his men and some Indian guides, proceeded from his camp on the Stanislaus River to Mission San José, where he hoped to procure the supplies needed for his journey out of California. Father Durán, however, was still on the defensive, and the unwelcome strangers were put in the guardhouse.

A visit from Captain J. B. R. Cooper, an influential citizen of Monterey, greatly relieved the uncertainty of the situation, since he offered to aid Smith in every way within his power. However, the pathfinder was detained at the mission for twelve or fourteen days before receiving a letter from the governor and a guard to escort him to the capital. At Monterey, on November 12, Cooper signed a bond in favor of Smith.

Smith returned to Mission San José on November 24, and for two weeks he and his men were busy preparing for the journey out of California—rounding up their horses, drying meat, repairing their guns, and baling the goods allowed them by Governor Echeandía's orders. On Sundays and holy days they attended services at the mission and there listened to the father address his people in Latin or in Spanish. Smith makes special note in his journal of the music, which, he says, "consisted of 12 or 15 violins, 5 base vials and one flute."

Having obtained permission from Father Durán, Smith removed his company on December 24 "to a sheep farm belonging to the mission called St. Lorenzo, where there was plenty of grass and a pen in which I could shut up my horses and mules."

Impatient at continued delays and fearing further obstacles to an immediate departure, Smith finally "settled off with the father under pretence of moving to better grass," and on December 30, in rain and mud, the band began its march northward, not by way of Bodega and Fort Ross, as officially planned, but through Mission Pass across the Livermore Valley to the Old River branch of the San Joaquin (sometimes called the Pescadero by the Spanish), and from there up the Sacramento Valley as far as Tehama, where Smith blazed a new trail out of California through Trinity, Humboldt, and Del Norte counties.

Rancho San Antonio

The present cities of Alameda, Albany, Berkeley, Emeryville, Oakland, Piedmont, and a part of San Leandro are located on what was once Rancho San Antonio (SRL 246). This vast estate extended five leagues along the eastern shore of San Francisco Bay, from San Leandro Creek on the south to El Cerrito Creek, now the boundary between Alameda and Contra Costa counties, on the north. It comprised all of the land lying between the Bay on the west and the crest of the Contra Costa hills on the east, a total of about ten square leagues.

In August 1820, Pablo Vicente de Solá, the last Spanish governor of Alta California, ordered the grant of Rancho San Antonio to be made to Luís María Peralta. Peralta was thereby rewarded for his loyalty, dedication, and service beyond the call of duty in almost 40 years in the Army, and for the valuable assistance he rendered in the establishment of the missions of Santa Cruz and San José. A native of Tubac, Sonora (now in Arizona), Peralta was baptized in 1759. He came to California with the Anza expedition in 1775–76, and enlisted in military service about five years later. He was in command of the guard at Mission San José from 1798 to 1800, and from 1807 to 1822 he was *comisionado* of the Pueblo de San José. In 1784 he married María Loreto Alviso, with whom he had seventeen children, of which four sons and five daughters lived to adulthood. Don Luís never made his home on Rancho San Antonio but maintained his residence in San Jose, where part of his adobe dwelling still stands at 184 West St. John Street.

Rancho San Antonio was occupied by the four living sons of Don Luís—Hermenegildo Ignacio, José Domingo, Antonio María, and José Vicente—and the original adobe home was located in what is now the Fruitvale district of Oakland. There in the 1820's the first permanent settlement, after Mission San José, on the east side of San Francisco Bay was erected, and there for a number of years the four brothers stayed whenever they visited the rancho.

The site of this adobe is at 2511 34th Avenue at the northwest corner of Paxton Avenue, one block east of Coolidge Avenue, near the north bank of Peralta Creek (SRL 925). The adobe was torn down in 1897. Some of the adobe bricks were used to construct a small house in Dimond Park. This building, overshadowed by the gigantic gnarled branches of an evergreen oak (*Quercus agrifolia*), was used for years by the Boy Scouts, but was finally destroyed by fire. Part of the adobe construction was saved, however, and incorporated into the present building under the old oak. A few of the bricks from the original Peralta adobe were also used in a home built by a descendant of Ignacio Peralta at 384 West Estudillo Avenue in San Leandro, where they may be seen today near the front entrance.

Soon each of the Peralta brothers began to build his own adobe on the section of the rancho later apportioned to him. To these homes they brought their wives, and there they reared their children. Their surroundings and mode of life were patriarchal. Thousands of horned cattle grazed among the oak trees. Sometimes

Don Luís Peralta's former companions in arms from the Presidio de San Francisco would cross in small boats to participate in rodeos and to enjoy the festivities of the Contra Costa. To the north (in Contra Costa County) the Castros held Rancho San Pablo, while to the south there were the Estudillos, the Higueras, the José de Jesús Vallejos, and the Guillermo Castros, all living on vast estates of their own before 1842.

The legal division of the lands of Rancho San Antonio took place in 1842. At this time, Don Luís Peralta came up from San José to divide the estate among his four sons. As they rode over the land together, the father parceled it out among them, marking out the boundaries by natural objects. It was divided, as nearly as possible, into four equal parts, each running from the hills to the shore of the bay. The total area was over 43,000 acres.

Ignacio, the oldest, was given the southern end of the grant, bordering on the north bank of San Leandro Creek. Domingo was given the northern end, where the cities of Albany and Berkeley now stand. Antonio received what is now East Oakland (where the original house stood) and the Encinal de San Antonio (now the city of Alameda). And to Vicente fell the Encinal de Temescal, the portion that is now occupied by Emeryville, Piedmont, and central and north Oakland.

To the south of the original adobe on the present 34th Avenue, Antonio Peralta built a second adobe in 1840, and also an eight-foot wall enclosing an area of about three acres. Two additional structures were erected that year on the same plat, one of which was a guest house. These later buildings were all leveled in 1870, the year in which Antonio built a frame structure on Paxton Avenue. In 1897 this was moved to the southwest corner of Paxton and 34th avenues, where it still stands.

Ignacio erected his first house on the north bank of San Leandro Creek about 1835, after his term as *alcalde* of San José. The site is at the end of 105th Avenue, near the Nimitz Freeway; the house, as well as a second adobe built nearby in 1842, disappeared in the 1870's.

About 1860 William Toler built a brick house (SRL 285), said to be the first in Alameda County, for Ignacio Peralta, his father-in-law. It is now the Alta Mira Club House and stands at 561 Lafayette Avenue in San Leandro, one block west of East Fourteenth Street. The furnishings are all from the twentieth century, but the old walls and exterior remain as they were.

The adobe of Domingo Peralta was built in 1841 on the site of what is now 1304 Albina Avenue in Berkeley, just off Hopkins Street and on the south bank of Codornices ("quail") Creek. Neither this home nor a frame

Peralta House, Oakland

dwelling later built on Hopkins Street is still standing.

The first adobe house of Vicente Peralta was erected in 1836 in that part of Oakland known as Temescal at 5527 Vicente Street. A second adobe was later built at 486 55th Street; both are long vanished. A frame structure on Vicente Street, later moved to Claremont Avenue, is also gone.

A section of the old *camino* of Rancho San Antonio (SRL 299, an unmarked site) that led from Temescal south to San Leandro is closely followed by Santa Clara Avenue, and the MacArthur Freeway (I-580) parallels this road.

The pleasant years of the 1830's and early 1840's on the old ranchos of the Contra Costa were but a brief episode in the history of California. Americans began to visit the region as early as 1846, and the Peraltas soon found that their fertile lands were the envy of these shrewd newcomers, who saw that they could be made valuable for other than pastoral purposes. In 1850, when the greater portion of the territorial patrimony of Domingo and Vicente Peralta was sold, the first encroachment upon Rancho San Antonio was made. Don Luís Peralta, the grantee of the original princely estate, died on August 25, 1851, on or about his 92nd birthday, having lived to realize that what he had given to his sons was one of the most valuable tracts of land in California and that it was gradually melting away before their eyes.

A series of bitterly contested lawsuits helped destroy the Peralta patrimony. Daughters of the family and their husbands claimed a share of the lands, it was alleged that the father was mentally incompetent when he made his will, and American squatters brought continual legal problems before the courts.

The rancho and the four Peralta brothers are jointly commemorated by a bronze tablet set in a boulder and placed in Lakeside Park in Oakland by 11 Bay Area chapters of the Daughters of the American Revolution. The spot is just above the boathouse on the northern shore of Lake Merritt.

Rancho San Ramón (Dublin and Contra Costa County)

José María Amador, the first white settler of Murray Township, arrived there before 1830, according to local tradition. He brought with him a rich heritage of ingenuity and industry from his father, Pedro Amador, the Mexican soldier who had come to California with Portolá in 1769. Don José, himself a soldier, had been born in San Francisco in 1794, and had served as a private in the San Francisco Company from 1810 to 1827, being stationed in the Escolta or military guard at Sonoma from 1824 to 1827. He took part in the expedition of Luís Arguello to the Sacramento Valley in 1821 and went with Gabriel Moraga to Fort Ross and Bodega that same year. After his discharge in 1827 he was mayordomo at Mission San José, and in 1834 and 1835 he was granted more than four square leagues of the rancho later known as San Ramón, the greater part of which lay in Contra Costa County.

The economy of Alta California did not rely entirely upon the sale of hides and tallow. Some domestic manufacturing was begun in the nineteenth century. Amador was one of the first manufacturers and farmers in Alameda County, herding vast numbers of cattle over his broad, unfenced acres and making leather, soap, saddles, harness, blankets, shoes, and even wagons in the adobe workshops on his rancho with the aid of Mexican labor. At one time 300 to 400 horses, 13,000 to 14,000 head of cattle, and 3,000 to 4,000 sheep grazed on his lands. In 1848 the lure of gold drew Amador, along with thousands of others, to the Mother Lode country. According to Theodore H. Hittell, he mined in the county that was later named for him, assisted by a number of Indian laborers.

The site of Amador's two-story adobe is on the northwest corner of Dublin Boulevard and San Ramon Road in Dublin. Alamillo Spring still flows nearby. Robert Livermore helped Amador to build another adobe, and Amador reciprocated by assisting Livermore at his Rancho Las Positas, located to the east.

Natural landmarks usually designated the boundary lines between the early Spanish and Mexican land grants, although later surveys often varied from the original, less precise ones; the first surveys that marked out the confines of Rancho San Ramón may still be identified. To the west, the Pita Navaja ("knife point"), a sharp knob above the summit of Bulmer Hill Grade, indicated the division between Rancho San Ramón and Rancho San Lorenzo. It is mentioned frequently in early deeds. The southern boundary was a large oak tree in the small gulch running up the hillside opposite the site of the old Fallon House at 6035 Foothill Road. This tree once bore the marks of early surveyors, who used it as a landmark from which the boundary line between Ranchos San Ramón and Santa Rita was drawn.

Becoming financially involved, Amador gradually sold portions of his estate to various newcomers. Michael Murray and Jeremiah Fallon, natives of Ireland, who had come west together in 1846 and who had settled temporarily at Mission San José, bought sections of the Amador holdings south of the present Dublin Boulevard before 1852. Murray Township, organized in 1853, was named for Michael Murray, the first county supervisor from the district. The old homes of Fallon and Murray survived into the 1960's but have since been pulled down.

John Green, another native of Ireland, was an active pioneer in the area. He was not only storekeeper, postmaster, and supervisor for Murray Township, but also a large-scale rancher who owned lands both at Dublin and in the Livermore mountains to the east. The settlement of Greenville, four miles east of Livermore at the entrance to Altamont Pass, was named for him, since he started the first store there. In spite of his busy days, Green spent his evenings studying law, especially the land-tenure laws pertaining to the Spanish and Mexican land grants. He had learned Spanish during his apprenticeship to a New York drug firm that had trade relations with South America. Thus it was natural that Green became a friend and adviser to the native Californians of the Amador and Livermore valleys, and the old ranchers often drove to Dublin to discuss their increasingly complex land problems with their Irish neighbor.

About the Amador adobes a town gradually grew up, generally known until 1860 as Amador's or Amador Valley. The portion of the settlement south of the Stockton Road, however, was called Dublin. It was said that Mississippi-born settler James Witt Dougherty first called it that when a traveler asked him the name of the community. Dougherty replied that the post office was called Dougherty's Station but that, since there were so many Irish living south of the road, they might as well call that part Dublin. The name stuck, although no post office bore that name until 1963.

The first business house in Dublin was the two-story Amador adobe, which served as a wayside station until its destruction in the 1860's. The oldest business house still standing in Dublin is the old John Green store, now a restaurant, at Donlon Way and Dublin Boulevard; it was built in 1864. Stucco covers the old resawed siding, and the building is much altered from its original appearance.

St. Raymond's Church is a long-standing Dublin landmark. Built in 1859, it was the first church in the township. Land for the church and the adjoining Catholic cemetery was donated by Michael Murray and Jeremiah Fallon, both of whom are buried there. The first interment, in 1859, was of Tom Donlon, who was killed in an accident during construction of the church. The street on which the church stands is called Donlon Way. The nonsectarian portion of the cemetery was given by James W. Dougherty.

The old church gradually fell out of use and was nearly demolished, but in 1966 it was acquired by the Amador–Livermore Valley Historical Society for restoration, which was largely accomplished by 1980. The nearby Murray School is the museum of the Dublin Historic Preservation Association and is open at regular hours.

Rancho Agua Caliente (Fremont)

Warm Springs, a small settlement that is now part of the city of Fremont, is located on what was once Rancho Agua Caliente. This rancho was granted to Fulgencio Higuera in 1839, having been released by its earlier grantee, Antonio Suñol. About two miles south of Mission San José on Mission Boulevard is the area in which the homes of the Higuera family stood.

The hot springs at this point were first frequented by the Indians. To these springs later came the señores and señoras of the 1840's, bringing their linens for their Indian servants to wash and holding their annual rodeos in the vicinity.

The portion of the rancho that includes the springs was purchased by Clemente Columbet in 1850, and buildings for a resort were erected. From this time to the earthquake of 1868 (which did considerable damage to the buildings at Mission San José), Warm Springs was one of the most fashionable watering places in the state. Persons of wealth and leisure as well as invalids from many places came to enjoy the benefits of the hot sulfur water.

Columbet moved a house all the way from San Jose to serve as a hotel at the springs. In 1858 he leased the place to Alexander Beaty, who maintained its reputation for grand festivities. Another hotel was built in 1869 by A. A. Cohen, but it was never used as such. Governor Leland Stanford purchased the estate about the same time and had it planted with orchards and vineyards. His brother Josiah, and later Josiah's son,

Weibel Vineyards and Leland Stanford Winery Marker, Fremont

Josiah W. Stanford, resided in Cohen's hotel. It was owned for a time by the Sisters of the Holy Names and used as a summer villa, but now it is privately owned. The Stanford winery (SRL 642) is now operated by Weibel Vineyards, which uses some of the original brick buildings. It is located east of Mission Boulevard at 1250 Stanford Avenue.

Rancho Las Positas (Livermore)

A young English sailor named Robert Livermore entered California in 1821 on the trading ship *Colonel Young*. Deciding to stay, he worked at various places, apparently gaining the good will of most people wherever he went. In partnership with José Noriega, he applied for the easternmost rancho in the valley that would later bear his name, Rancho Las Positas ("little watering holes"). It was on the frontier between the coastal settlements and the Indian territory of the hills and great central valley and was therefore a place of some danger. By 1835, he was living in a house on the property. In 1838 he married the widow Josefa Higuera Molina, whose father owned Rancho Tularcitos in Santa Clara County, and began to raise a family. In 1839 Governor Juan B. Alvarado granted the land to Livermore and Noriega; Livermore later bought out Noriega's interest.

Robert Livermore became a naturalized citizen of Alta California in 1844. About 1846 he purchased Rancho Cañada de los Vaqueros, most of which lay in Contra Costa County but which skirted the northern portion of Livermore Valley. Under American rule, the two ranchos were confirmed to him, and Livermore became a wealthy man. The rancho was soon well stocked with cattle, but Livermore was more interested in horticulture and viticulture than he was in cows or sheep. After the fathers of Mission San José, he was the first man to plant a vineyard and an orchard of pears and olives in this section of California. He died in 1858, before the birth of the town that was named for him.

One of the first dwellings on Rancho Las Positas was an adobe erected by Livermore, assisted by José María Amador, his nearest white neighbor in the valley. Amador did not forget that Livermore had volunteered aid to him in a like situation several years before. At times, too, Livermore's troubles with the Indians became so heated that he and his family took refuge with Amador for a while.

This friendly house, with its honest, hospitable host, became a popular stopping place for travelers on the Stockton road. In March 1850, when Nathaniel Greene Patterson (a member of the California Battalion in 1846–47 and a gold seeker of 1848) hired the adobe for a hotel, it became the first place of public entertainment in the valley. This house, which stood near the source of Las Positas Creek at a point about one and one-half miles north of the center of Livermore, was partly in ruins by 1876 and was later torn down.

Livermore built a large frame dwelling near the adobe in 1849, the first wooden building in Livermore Valley. A part of the original structure, the timbers of which had been shipped around the Horn, stood until the 1950's. On Junction Avenue, the western approach to the city of Livermore from the freeway, is a monument in honor of Robert Livermore (SRL 241). An arrow on top of the monument points to Livermore's homesite, perhaps one-third of a mile to the north.

The first house to be erected within the present city limits of Livermore was built by Alphonso Ladd, who came to California from New Orleans in 1850. The following year he settled with his wife near the Suñol adobe, then the only white habitation in Suñol Valley. A few years later he took up 160 acres of government land in what was called the Livermore Extension, and in 1855 he built a hotel on the Stockton road at the site of what was to become known as Laddsville, a forerunner of Livermore. The Ladd Hotel, a frame structure built of lumber hauled across the hills from Mowry's Landing, was very prosperous for many years, but after it burned in 1876 the settlement of Laddsville never recovered.

The tracks of the Central Pacific Railroad were laid through the Livermore Valley in 1869. William Mendenhall, who had traveled overland to California from Pennsylvania in 1845, laid out a town that he named in memory of Robert Livermore; this was on what had been part of the gigantic Rancho El Valle de San José. The fire at Laddsville brought an end to the rivalry between the two neighboring towns. Livermore was incorporated in 1876.

The Livermore Collegiate Institute was founded by Dr. and Mrs. W. B. Kingsbury in 1870. For several years it was used as a sanatorium by J. W. Robertson, who sold it to John McGlinchey for use as a private residence. The building has been destroyed by fire; the site is at 1615 College Avenue. Other health facilities still in use include the Arroyo del Valle Sanitarium and the large federal tuberculosis hospital for veterans, both on Arroyo Road. North of the federal hospital at 2647 Arroyo Road is Ravenswood, once the country home of Christopher A. Buckley, one-time boss of San Francisco political life. The Livermore Park and Recreation District has restored the Cottage House, Buckley's Queen Anne home.

The Livermore Heritage Guild has restored the old Highway Garage on Portola Avenue. This was on the Lincoln Highway, the first transcontinental paved highway in the United States, begun in the early 1920's. The restored garage is now a museum of the Lincoln Highway. The Duarte family, builders and longtime operators of the garage, lived next door, and their home has also been preserved. The Livermore History Center is in the old Carnegie Library in the center of town and is open on a regular basis as a charming museum of Livermore history.

The University of California established the huge Lawrence Livermore Laboratory east of the city in 1952 for nuclear weapons research. It has also become an important center for electrical engineering and electronics research.

The Livermore Valley is one of California's famous wine-producing areas. Charles Wetmore's Cresta Blanca wine won the grand prize in the Paris Exposition of 1889, creating international recognition for California's wine-producing capacity. The Cresta Blanca Winery (SRL 586), founded in 1882, is now an operation of Wente Brothers, concentrating on sparkling wine; it is located at 5050 Arroyo Road. The original Wente winery (SRL 957) at 5565 Tesla Road goes back to 1883. The Wentes are proud to be the oldest family-owned, continuously operating winery in California. Also established in 1883 was the Concannon Winery (SRL 641) at 4590 Tesla Road, still managed by Concannon family members although the winery has been sold.

Rancho San Leandro

José Joaquín Estudillo, the first white settler in Eden Township, petitioned for a grant of the land known as the Arroyo de San Leandro in 1837 "with the object of securing subsistence for and supporting a large family, consisting of his wife and ten children, after having been in the military service for a period of seventeen years, four months, and seven days." The title was given in 1839 but the document was lost, and Estudillo lived on his land for "the long term of five years, five months, and several days" before he again secured his grant in 1842. It was well that he did so, for Guillermo Castro, his neighbor on Rancho San Lorenzo, also desired the lands of San Leandro, but Estudillo's long period of actual tenure won the battle for possession.

José Joaquín, son of José María Estudillo and brother of José Antonio Estudillo of San Diego, was born at the Presidio of Monterey in 1800. A member of one of the old Californian families, he held several positions of honor in the military service and in the government in his own right. William Heath Davis, a son-in-law, said that José Joaquín moved to San Leandro early in 1836, after he had first obtained a written permit from Governor Alvarado to occupy the land. He brought with him 300 heifers, by which he increased his herd until, on his death in 1852, he left to his heirs about 3,000 head of cattle. His specialty and pride was "white cattle," because he said their color enabled him "to see his stock at a great distance."

Squatters first encroached upon Rancho San Leandro in 1851, when Americans began to settle there against the wishes of the legal owner. The intruders first made their appearance on the banks of San Lorenzo Creek, at a place subsequently known as Squattersville, now San Lorenzo. They soon overran the rancho, but Estudillo, "an educated, intelligent, and up-right man," with the aid of his sons and sons-in-law consistently "opposed the evildoers in seizing the land. At times . . . there was a tendency . . . towards a bloody affray. But among [the squatters] there were conservative counsellors and prudent squatters, who invariably prevailed on the rougher class to avoid bloodshed." A malicious element among them, however, did much damage, shooting and wounding horses and cattle under cover of darkness, and fencing Estudillo's stock away from the creek. During "all these turbulent times [1851–54] the members of the family were in constant fear of their personal safety."

Through the instrumentality of John B. Ward and William Heath Davis, the squatters were finally brought to terms. Some of the property was deeded to an alien, Clement Boyreau, in order to bring the case into the federal courts. Judges Ogden Hoffman and Matthew Hall McAllister rendered a decision in favor of the Estudillo family. As a result, the squatters took leases from the family pending the final decision of the United States Supreme Court, and eventually they purchased the land from the original owners.

The town of San Leandro was founded for the sole specific purpose of housing the seat of Alameda County. In 1854 Estudillo's two sons-in-law, Ward and Davis, submitted a plan to José Joaquín's widow, Juana Martínez de Estudillo, and her children for laying out a town. The family gave land for county buildings and reserved 200 acres for the town, which was surveyed early in 1855. A popular election in December 1854 brought the county seat to San Leandro from Alvarado. "The family mansion," wrote Davis, "was surrendered to the county for a temporary court house." It was damaged in 1855 by fire, probably set by an incendiary who wished the county seat to be returned to Alvarado. The election of 1854 was declared invalid, since it had not been authorized by the state legislature, and the center of justice went back to Alvarado. By action of the legislature, however, it was again in San Leandro in 1856, where it remained until 1873, when it was moved to Brooklyn, now a part of East Oakland and by that time annexed to the city of Oakland.

The first adobe dwelling built by José Joaquín Estudillo, about 1836–37, was located near the south bank of San Leandro Creek, roughly opposite the home of Ignacio Peralta. Some ten years later he moved to what is now the block bounded by Estudillo Avenue, San Leandro Boulevard, and Davis and Carpentier streets. There he erected a second home, possibly occupied by the spring of 1850. A wooden house, thought to be substantially the same as this second home, stood on that block until about 1947–48, when it was razed for construction of the priests' residence of St. Leander's Church. The site of this house (SRL 279) was marked on the West Estudillo Avenue side on June 7, 1964, coincidentally the 112th anniversary of the death of José Joaquín Estudillo. The dedication was part of the festivities celebrating the centennial of St. Leander's Parish; the present church (1957) and rectory (1948) stand on the site of the old home. The Estudillo family gave the land for the original St. Leander's Church, built in 1864 directly opposite the present church, where the primary school now stands. The venerable Gothic structure was razed in 1957.

A permanent brick courthouse of two stories was erected in 1856–57 in the central part of the block bounded by West Estudillo Avenue and Carpentier, Davis, and Clarke streets, the main entrance being on the latter. It collapsed in the 1868 earthquake but was repaired and used until the county seat was transferred in 1873. In 1881 it became the first convent and school of St. Leander's Parish. Later a three-story wooden building was built around it, and it stood until 1926, when it was replaced by the present convent and school, constructed on either side of it.

María de Jesús Estudillo married William Heath Davis at Mission Dolores in 1847. After her father's death in 1852, she inherited the portion of Rancho San Leandro near the original homesite. The street that now runs west from San Leandro to the Bay and crosses what was once the Davis ranch is called Davis Street.

Casa Peralta at 384 West Estudillo Avenue was built in 1897 for N. G. Sturtevant and bought and remodeled by Mrs. Herminia Dargie of the Peralta family in 1924. Adobe bricks from the first Peralta home are built into the house, now owned by the city of San Leandro and open to the public on a regular basis.

The oyster industry at what is now the San Leandro Marina prospered during the 1890's, becoming the single most important fishery in California. Moses Wicks is credited with having been the first person to bring seed oysters around the Horn and implant them in the San Leandro oyster beds (SRL 824). The industry diminished after 1911 because of pollution in San Francisco Bay.

At the San Lorenzo end of the rancho lands, one finds today the old pioneer cemetery, which has been restored, at Hesperian Boulevard near the Nimitz Freeway. Nearby at 18701 Hesperian Boulevard is the restored McConaghy Estate (1886), once a prosperous farm dwelling; the outbuildings have interesting collections of farm equipment from the late nineteenth century.

Rancho El Valle de San José (Pleasanton and Sunol)

The mission fathers early recognized the advantages of the fertile Arroyo Valle and pastured their herds among the great sycamores there. For many years after Mission San José was secularized, mission Indians still lived around Pleasanton. The original name of the locality was Alisal, from *aliso*, meaning either "alder tree" or "sycamore grove."

Rancho El Valle de San José was granted to four relatives, Antonio María Pico, his brothers-in-law Agustín Bernal and Juan Pablo Bernal, and his sister-in-law María Dolores Bernal de Suñol, in 1839. It was patented to the Bernals and to Antonio María Suñol in 1865.

Antonio María Pico, son of José Dolores Pico, was born in Monterey in 1808. He held various public and military offices throughout his career. He was stationed at San José from 1833 to 1839 and took part in the revolt against Micheltorena in 1845. After having been a member of the Constitutional Convention, he was appointed by President Lincoln as registrar of the United States land office at Los Angeles in 1861. He was a grantee of Rancho Pescadero (San Joaquin County) in 1843 and co-purchaser of the San Rafael Mission estate in 1846. Don Antonio married Pilar Bernal and sold his fourth of Rancho El Valle de San José to Juan P. Bernal.

Antonio María Suñol, a native of Spain who had come to California as a sailor on the French ship *Bordelais*, which he left in 1818, married María Dolores Bernal. He lived at the Pueblo de San José and never took up residence on the Rancho El Valle de San José. A man "of excellent reputation," he held a few public offices but was mainly a stock raiser and trader. He was owner of the Rancho Los Coches in Santa Clara County after 1847 and purchaser of San Rafael Mission in 1846 with Pico.

His son of the same name, Antonio Suñol, had an adobe on the rancho in the pleasant valley of the sycamores and alder trees, where he lived in the late 1840's and early 1850's. The site of this adobe is near the Water Temple of the San Francisco water system, which stands near the intersection of three old valley roads, one from Sunol, one from Pleasanton, and a third through Mission Pass.

Agustín and Juan P. Bernal, sons of Joaquín Bernal, were presidio soldiers who had served at San Francisco and San José. Agustín was in 1853 a claimant for Rancho Santa Teresa in Santa Clara County, of which his father had been grantee in 1834. In April 1850 he moved to his section of Rancho El Valle de San José and erected an adobe home near the foothills at the western rim of the broad Livermore Valley. The picturesque adobe still stands in excellent condition in a beautiful ranch setting west of Pleasanton on the west side of Foothill Road, about a mile south of the Alviso adobe of Rancho Santa Rita. In 1852 Juan P. Bernal, settling near Alisal, constructed an adobe dwelling, no longer standing, on the north bank of Arroyo Valle.

The Bernals were good business managers. Consequently, they were able to secure their large holdings from the aggressive encroachments of foreigners and to maintain possession of the original grant better than most of the native families.

The next settler in the vicinity of Pleasanton was John W. Kottinger, a native of Austria who came to California in 1849 and who married a daughter of Juan P. Bernal in 1850. Late in 1852 Kottinger went to live at Rancho El Valle de San José, and in that year he built at Alisal, later Pleasanton, an adobe and frame dwelling on the south bank of Arroyo Valle opposite Bernal's residence. Kottinger was one of the founders of the town of Pleasanton and the first man to start a store there. His plat lay just south of Arroyo Valle and was surveyed in 1867 and 1869. Kottinger's house was torn down in 1930, but the old barn, also of adobe, still stands at the rear of the residence at 218 Ray Street.

The Castlewood Country Club stands on part of the Rancho El Valle de San José about three miles southwest of Pleasanton. Here Phoebe Apperson Hearst, wife of Senator George Hearst and mother of the publisher William Randolph Hearst, lived in her beautiful Hacienda del Pozo de Verona from 1891 until her death in 1919. The building, later the clubhouse, burned in 1969, but it is still fondly recalled by many visitors to the region.

Rancho Potrero de los Cerritos

The Alvarado district of Union City is on what was once a part of the Rancho Potrero de los Cerritos, granted to Agustín Alviso and Tomás Pacheco in 1844. Agustín Alviso, son of Ygnacio Alviso, was mayordomo of Mission San José in 1840–41. He was a prosperous ranchero, locally well known, who married María Antonia Pacheco in 1830. Tomás Pacheco was a soldier of the San Francisco Company from 1826 to 1832 and later held various offices at the Pueblo de San José from 1834 to 1843.

The old Alviso adobe was so badly damaged in the 1868 earthquake that the family could no longer live in it; soon it was pulled down and a frame house, no longer standing, was built on the spot. The site is just south of Newark Boulevard two-tenths of a mile east of its junction with Jarvis Avenue. The site of Tomás Pacheco's adobe is south of the Decoto district on the south bank of Alameda Creek and on the west side of Decoto Road, which is the northern continuation of Jarvis Avenue.

In 1850 John M. Horner purchased from Alviso 110 acres in the tract that had been the mission grazing lands. He plotted a townsite covering the whole of his purchase, and the first lots were sold on September 9, 1850, the day California became a state (although no one in California knew until later of the official act performed in Washington, D.C.). The town of Union City was a success; it drew the trade of Mission San José from the more southerly sloughs and also provided a more direct outlet for the area east of the hills.

Henry C. Smith bought 465 acres from Alviso and Pacheco late in 1850 and had the town of New Haven laid out at the upper embarcadero adjoining Union City. "These communities," wrote J. N. Bowman, "became rivals of San Francisco. In this neighborhood, grain, vegetable and fruit ranching were proven feasible in California for Americans; flour and sugar factories were later erected, and people and investors were even attracted from San Francisco."

The success of these two towns, Bowman notes, encouraged the development of a third adjacent to them, named for the former Mexican governor Juan Bautista

Alvarado. In March 1853 Henry C. Smith introduced a bill in the state legislature, then meeting in Benicia, creating the new county of Alameda from parts of Contra Costa and Santa Clara counties and designating New Haven as the county seat and Alvarado as the seat of justice. By the time the new county was organized in April New Haven had discarded its old name and was also known as Alvarado.

The site of the New Haven embarcadero and of the building used as a county courthouse (SRL 503) is at Union City Boulevard near Smith Street in the Alvarado District. Some old wooden buildings still stand in the vicinity. Northeast on Dyer Street is the site of the nation's first successful beet sugar factory (SRL 768), established in 1870 by E. H. Dyer. The property is now occupied by the Holly Sugar Company.

The pioneer name of Union City was restored to the area in 1958 when Alvarado and Decoto combined to incorporate as a city.

Rancho San Lorenzo (Castro Valley, Hayward)

There were two divisions of Rancho San Lorenzo. That portion on which the cities of Castro Valley and Hayward are located was granted to Guillermo Castro in 1841 by Governor Juan B. Alvarado and in 1843 by Governor Manuel Micheltorena. The portion west of Hayward and south of San Lorenzo Creek was granted to Francisco Soto in 1842 and 1844.

Guillermo Castro's adobe house was located on Mission Boulevard between C and D streets, on the site of the present Hayward City Hall. The adobe was one of the buildings in the area badly damaged by the 1868 earthquake. Soto's adobe stood on what is now the southwest side of Mission Boulevard opposite the tennis courts of the Hayward Memorial Park.

One of the first Americans to come to Rancho San Lorenzo was William Hayward from Massachusetts. In the fall of 1851 he pitched his tent in Palomares Canyon under the impression that it was government land and that he would obtain there a homestead of 160 acres. Before long, however, he was visited by Guillermo Castro, who informed him that he was a trespasser. However, an agreement was made between Castro and Hayward so that the latter remained, and the relations between the two men continued to be most friendly. Hayward soon removed his tent to the location of the hotel that would later become famous as a resort, on the hill north of A Street and east of Mission Boulevard; the hotel was destroyed by fire in 1923. In 1854 Castro laid out the plat of the town that he called San Lorenzo but instead took the name Haywards, later Hayward. A bust of the pioneer is on display in the Hayward Area

Historical Society Museum at 22701 Main Street, where other artifacts from the region's past can be seen.

The relations of Castro with another American, Faxon D. Atherton, illustrate how shrewd Yankees often bested native Californians. Atherton loaned money to Castro from time to time so that he might gamble. When the latter was unable to repay, Atherton took possession of a piece of land. Finally, Castro and all of his family except a daughter and one son, Luís, later surveyor of Alameda County, moved to South America.

Several large old ranch houses still stand in the Hayward area. Outstanding among these is the beautiful Victorian mansion of William Meek at 240 Hampton Road in San Lorenzo. Meek was one of California's pioneer orchardists. He came West prior to the gold rush, bringing to Oregon, on one trip, a wagonload of grafted trees. There, with Henderson and John Lewelling, he entered the nursery business, which they later moved to Alameda County. By 1866 he had clear title to 2,010 acres, most of which had originally belonged to the Soto portion of Rancho San Lorenzo. Much of this he planted with almond, cherry, and plum orchards. Meek was generous with his time and talent in public service. He was a member of the first board of trustees of Mills College and served four terms as an Alameda County supervisor. His home, surrounded by magnificent trees and gardens, was built in the late 1860's. Destruction of the estate was threatened in 1963, when it was sold to a subdivider for an apartment project. The efforts of citizens and groups, including the Hayward Area Historical Society, however, led to its purchase by the Hayward Area Recreational District for preservation and development of the grounds.

The McConaghy Estate at 18701 Hesperian Boulevard is another project maintained by the Society. This twelve-room farmhouse built in 1886 has been restored to its early appearance; the property also contains a tank house and a carriage house with many displays.

Another old home built about the same time is the former residence of Cornelius Mohr, still owned by the family, at 24985 Hesperian Boulevard in Mount Eden. Here, as at the Meek home, the old carriage house also stands. Most of the Mohr ranch is now the campus of Chabot College. California State University at Hayward, east of Mission Boulevard, is built on what was once the ranch of Timm Hauschildt. Beyond lived Ahapius Honcharenko, Ukrainian patriot and Orthodox priest, from the 1870's to his death in 1916. He published the *Alaska Herald-Svoboda*, a bilingual newspaper, and translated the Constitution of the United States for the Russian-speaking people of Alaska. "Ukraina," the Honcharenko estate, is still a privately owned ranch.

In 1866 Josiah Grover Brickell gave the land for the

first public school in Castro Valley (SRL 776). The site is now Redwood School, on Redwood Road between James and Alma avenues. A landmark still standing in downtown Hayward is the Odd Fellows Hall on B Street, built in 1868.

Rancho Arroyo de la Alameda (Southwestern County)

Rancho Arroyo de la Alameda, taking its name from the stream that flows for many miles through the open plains that drain to the Bay, was granted to José de Jesús Vallejo in 1842. It consisted of 17,705 acres of fertile valley land. Don José, one of thirteen children of Ignacio Vallejo, a Spanish soldier of Alta California, was an elder brother of General Mariano G. Vallejo. He himself was active in military and governmental affairs from 1818 to 1847; among other offices he was *comisionado* and administrator at Mission San José from 1836 to 1840 and military commander at the Pueblo de San José from 1841 to 1842. In 1850 he was appointed postmaster at Mission San José, where his home stood just west of the highway and opposite the mission. Affairs on the rancho were left primarily in the hands of overseers, and an expensive flour mill, erected about 1850, became the most famous asset of the estate.

Where tree-lined Alameda Creek issues from Niles Canyon and passes into the flatland that slopes away to the Bay, the old settlement of Vallejo Mills, now known as Niles, grew up in the 1850's. Historic landmarks may still be found in the neighborhood. Stone foundations of a second flour mill (SRL 46), erected here by Vallejo in 1856, remain in a Fremont city park at the northeast corner of Mission Boulevard and Niles Canyon Road. A mile up the canyon the stone aqueduct, which he built to conduct water to the mill, still parallels the road for some distance. The site of one of the several adobes built by Vallejo for his overseers is located at the entrance of the canyon.

Perhaps the most picturesque reminder of adobe days in this vicinity is the little building in the gardens of the California Nursery Company northwest of Niles off Niles Boulevard. The California Nursery, founded in 1865, has played an important part in the development of the fruit industry and home beautification in California. This adobe, the first of the Vallejo adobes built in the vicinity, has been restored as a guest house.

The town of Niles, now part of the city of Fremont, was named in 1869 for Judge Addison C. Niles, an executive of the Central Pacific Railroad. Here, for several years ending in 1916, was located one of the first motion picture studios in the West. The Essanay Company ("S" for Spoor, "A" for Anderson) had been founded in Chicago by George K. Spoor and Gilbert M. "Broncho

Billy" Anderson. The latter decided to move his base of operations to California and selected Niles as a suitable location. He made the first pictures at Niles in a barn, at the rear of 37467 Second Street, but soon built a block-long, story-and-a-half studio at Niles Boulevard and G Street (it has been razed, but the site is marked). Anderson starred himself in Westerns, frequently using photogenic Niles Canyon as a setting. Other actors who pioneered at Niles included Charles Chaplin, Ben Turpin, and Wallace Beery. Here Chaplin made his great film *The Tramp*. Some of the cottages built by the company along Second Street behind the main studio are still standing and occupied.

The site of the old Washington College, founded in 1871, is on the hill at the northeast corner of Washington Boulevard and Driscoll Road in the Irvington (formerly Washington Corners) district of Fremont. It was established as a nonsectarian institution by certain pioneers interested in education, including E. L. Beard, Henry Curtner, and the Rev. W. F. B. Lynch, who intended to make it a school of science and industrial arts. The Rev. S. S. Harmon, a pioneer missionary, was principal of the school until 1880, when he established a school of his own in Berkeley. In 1883 Washington College was taken over by the Christian Church, and after 1894 it ceased to exist as a college, although a private school was located there for a number of years, last known as the Anderson Military Academy. A 22-room house, built about 1889, remains on the property, surrounded by many of the old trees; it now serves as a private residence.

George Washington Patterson arrived in California to mine gold, but instead found wealth in the marshy lands near the Bay south of Alameda Creek. He arrived here around 1854 with his family, and set out to drain and clear the land. His white frame farmhouse, built in 1856, was the center of what was eventually a 3,000-

Farmhouse, Ardenwood Historic Farm, Fremont

acre farm named Ardenwood, apparently a reference to the Forest of Arden in Shakespeare's *As You Like It*. The house was enlarged around 1880. Some 205 acres of the old property were acquired in the 1970's by the East Bay Regional Park District; they were formally opened to the public in 1985 as Ardenwood Historic Farm. The farm has producing fields that can be harvested in season and a replica of a short-line horse-drawn railroad that operated nearby in the late nineteenth century. Two old farmhouses slated to be demolished to make way for a new subdivision have been added to the property, along with a working blacksmith's shed.

Nearby is Coyote Hills, another East Bay Regional Park, part of which lies on the old Patterson Ranch, at 8000 Patterson Ranch Road in Fremont. Although primarily a natural preserve, the park contains four of the rare intact Indian shell mounds in the Bay Area (only one, however, is open to viewing). The park includes the lower estuary of Alameda Creek down to the shores of the Bay.

Rancho Santa Rita

Rancho Santa Rita once skirted the western edge of the broad Livermore Valley and adjoined Rancho El Valle de San José to the east. It was granted to José Dolores Pacheco in 1839, and included more than 8,800 acres of excellent grazing land. Pacheco was often mentioned in the local annals of San José, where he held a number of public offices off and on between 1838 and 1846. He died in 1852.

Samuel and J. West Martin purchased about 5,000 acres of Rancho Santa Rita in 1854; there were enough cattle included in the sale to provide the purchase money. The little adobe (SRL 510) that still stands beneath a giant oak tree on Foothill Road about three-tenths of a mile south of Dublin was built about 1845, probably by Francisco Solano Alviso, who came to Rancho Santa Rita as mayordomo in 1844.

Oakland

Until the American invasion following the discovery of gold, the coastal portions of Rancho San Antonio were largely untended. Three men who separately had sailed around the Horn were responsible for the beginnings of Oakland: Edson Adams, Andrew Moon, and Horace W. Carpentier, a skillful attorney, who after service in the California militia was known as General Carpentier.

After a short time in the gold fields, the three determined to settle and lay out a town on the Contra Costa, the eastern shore of San Francisco Bay. In May 1850 they landed at what is now the foot of Broadway (Jack London Square) in Oakland and built a cabin on Vicente Peralta's property. Challenged by Peralta, they asserted that the land was public domain. Lawrence Kinnaird continues the tale: "Other squatters quickly followed their lead and the rightful owner found his property overrun by squatters who killed or stole his cattle and cut his timber. All the East Bay rancheros had troubles with squatters but Vicente Peralta suffered most. He finally got a writ of ejectment against Carpentier, Adams, and Moon from the county court at Martinez and Deputy Sheriff Kelly with about twelve men was sent to enforce the order. They found Moon alone at his cabin in a grove of liveoaks. He pretended to be much astonished at the action taken against him and explained that he and his associates had no intention of damaging Peralta, for whom they had the highest regard. Taken in by Moon's smooth talk, Peralta finally agreed to lease the land. Moon and his partners had no intention to comply with the terms of the lease. Instead they took over the land as if they owned it and laid out the town of Oakland." Julius Kellersberger was employed to lay out the area now bounded by First, Fourteenth, Market, and Fallon streets. Streets 80 feet wide were planned, and even wider, at 110 feet, was Main Street, later Broadway. In 1852 a bill sponsored by Carpentier, who had become enrolling clerk of the state senate, was approved by the legislature incorporating the town of Oakland; this came as a great surprise to the 150-odd inhabitants of the settlement, who learned of the bill only after the legislation had been enacted. Two years later the legislature recognized Oakland's status as a city.

The trustees of the town granted to Carpentier the rights to all the waterfront. In a series of intricate financial transactions, the General (who soon would become the first mayor of the city of Oakland) passed control to other members of his family, ultimately selling to the Central Pacific Railroad. Not until 1911 was the city of Oakland able to assert jurisdiction over its entire waterfront, which was subsequently developed into one of the most prosperous on the Pacific Coast.

The original city of Oakland lay on the west side of San Antonio Slough. Several men had settled there before the arrival of Adams, Moon, and Carpentier in May 1850. The first, in the winter of 1849, was Moses Chase. He was followed by the Patten brothers, Robert, William, and Edward, in February 1850. These four men turned their attention to the east side of the slough and leased land there from Antonio Peralta. They laid out the town of Clinton on a tract of 480 acres in 1853, and in the same year a bridge was built across the slough to connect Clinton with Oakland. The area included in

Clinton lay, approximately, between East Eighth and East 24th streets and Lake Merritt and Fourteenth Avenue, which was then a small creek. On the other side of this creek the town of San Antonio was surveyed on a tract of 200 acres in 1854. A flurry of excitement over a small gold discovery passed through the San Antonio region in 1856; hundreds of claims were staked out, but not enough gold was found to warrant continued enthusiasm. Small traces of gold were found at the site of Merritt College, in the hills between Redwood Road and Skyline Boulevard, but not enough to support further activity.

By 1856 Clinton and San Antonio constituted a single town called Brooklyn. In 1870 Brooklyn was incorporated, and two years later it was annexed to the city of Oakland. For some time it had been under consideration as a possible county seat to replace San Leandro, where the courthouse had been devastated by earthquake in 1868. In 1873 the people of Alameda County voted to move the seat of government to Oakland, and the site chosen was in what had been Brooklyn. The old wooden courthouse stood into the 1960's at 1952 East Fourteenth Street, and behind it, at 1417 Twentieth Avenue, was the building that housed the hall of records and the jail. Clinton Square, San Antonio Park, and Brooklyn Avenue in East Oakland commemorate these early towns.

In 1874 it was decided to move the county offices to a downtown location. When Julius Kellersberger mapped the town in 1853, he had set aside two squares, Washington and Franklin, for a civic center. They were used instead as parks until the city of Oakland gave them to the county of Alameda for the new county buildings. The courthouse was opened in 1875 on Washington Square (bounded by Fourth, Fifth, and Washington streets and Broadway), and the hall of records about a year later on Franklin Square (bounded by Fourth, Fifth, and Franklin streets and Broadway). The old courthouse stood until 1950 and the hall of records until 1964. The Oakland City Hall was erected in 1911.

On November 8, 1869, the first train to arrive in Oakland over the newly completed transcontinental railroad pulled up to the station on Seventh Street. A salute of 37 guns was fired and a grand celebration was held at which notables addressed the enthusiastic citizens. Actually, Oakland had been preceded by Alameda as the western terminal about two months earlier. While construction of the line continued, a temporary connection had been made with the San Francisco, Alameda, San Leandro and Haywards Railroad (opened in 1865), and the first transcontinental train arrived in Alameda on September 6, 1869. The terminal (SRL 440) where festivities took place that day was located at the wharf

at the foot of Pacific Avenue in Alameda, now on the grounds of the Alameda Naval Air Station.

Lake Merritt, covering 160 acres, is unique in that it is a wildfowl sanctuary in the middle of a large city. It was named in honor of Samuel B. Merritt, a graduate of the medical department of Bowdoin College, who came to California in 1850 and practiced medicine for a while before becoming engaged in business activities in Oakland. He served as mayor in 1868–69 and furthered many projects favorable to the development of the young city. Merritt Hospital was founded by his bequest, and Merritt College bears his name.

San Antonio Slough once spread over a large region at the head of the San Antonio Estuary. Into it flowed salt tides from San Francisco Bay as well as several creeks carrying the freshwater drainage from the outlying foothills of the Coast Range. Dr. Merritt was instrumental in having a dam built to impound these waters—the first step in the formation of Lake Merritt as it is today, a saltwater lake with a broad causeway and a moveable floodgate. Lake Merritt was set aside by the state in 1869 as a wildfowl refuge and is the oldest one in the United States. In 1909 the City of Oakland completed acquisition of the entire lake frontage and began to develop Lakeside Park. Organized feeding of birds began in 1915, and in 1926 banding of ducks was inaugurated.

The lake is a major attraction of the city, and in the 1930's was further embellished by a "necklace of lights" that lined the 3.18 miles of its shore. Terminated as a wartime economy measure in 1942, the long string of lights was restored as a civic project in 1987.

St. Mary's Catholic Church, at Eighth and Jefferson streets, was established as a mission in 1853 and a parish in 1858. The foundations of the present building were laid in 1868 and it was dedicated in 1872. The wooden structure has undergone much remodeling through the years, including a partial brick facing. St. James' Episcopal Church (SRL 694), at Twelfth Avenue and Foothill Boulevard, was founded in 1858; the structure built the following year still stands next to the present church and is now used as a social hall. The First Unitarian Church (SRL 896) at Castro and Fourteenth Streets dates from 1890; its Romanesque design is embellished with remarkable stained glass windows.

A number of interesting old houses are still to be seen in Oakland. The gabled house of J. Mora Moss, built in 1864, stands in Mosswood Park at MacArthur Boulevard and Broadway. The 24-room home of James DeFremery, a native of Holland, was erected in 1868 and is preserved in DeFremery Park at Eighteenth and Adeline streets. The home of John and James Treadwell, owners of the Tesla coal mine in eastern Alameda

County, stands on the campus of the California College of Arts and Crafts at 5212 Broadway. The Camron-Stanford House, at 1426 Lakeside Drive, was built in 1876 as the home of William Camron, who married Alice Marsh, the daughter of Dr. John Marsh, famed pioneer of Contra Costa County. Four rooms have been restored to their appearance in 1880 when President and Mrs. Rutherford B. Hayes came to have tea with the David Hewes family, who then owned the home. Josiah Stanford, brother of Governor Leland Stanford, was the third owner.

The residence of George C. Pardee is located at 672 Eleventh Street. Pardee was a physician, mayor of Oakland (like his father before him) from 1893 to 1897, and governor of California from 1903 to 1907. The house is owned by a private foundation and will eventually be opened to the public. Preservation Park is in the vicinity of the Pardee home. The Dunsmuir House, a handsome Colonial Revival mansion at 2960 Peralta Oaks Court, was built in 1899. Acquired by the City of Oakland in 1961, it stands on 40 acres of hill and gardens and has been used as background for a number of films.

Oakland's historic preservation districts include the Bret Harte Boardwalk on Fifth Street between Jefferson and Clay, honoring the writer who lived here (in a house no longer standing) with his sister Margaret and his stepfather, Colonel Andrew Williams, in 1854. Williams became Oakland's fourth mayor three years later. Victorian Row on Ninth Street is a street of old buildings, mostly commercial.

Along Broadway and Seventeenth Street are perhaps California's most extensive grouping of Art Deco buildings from the 1920's and the early 1930's. The Paramount Theater (SRL 884) at 2025 Broadway opened in 1931 and was a movie palace until 1970. Its opulent style has made it famous; it was the home of the Oakland Symphony for many years.

The Oakland Free Library was established in 1878 with Ina Coolbrith, later California's first poet laureate, as the first librarian. She encouraged the literary career of young Jack London, who was born in San Francisco but raised in Oakland. In 1893, upon his return from his first ocean voyage, Jack London entered a prize-winning manuscript, "The Story of a Typhoon off the Coast of Japan," in a contest managed by the *San Francisco Morning Call*. He lived with his first wife, whom he married in 1900, at 1130 East Fifteenth Street, and the following year they moved to a house of the Italian-villa type, the former home of sculptor Felix Peano, at First Avenue and East Twelfth Street near the shore of Lake Merritt. Scenes from the windows of this house, which looked toward the bridge at Eighth Street, are described in London's *Martin Eden*. While he wrote *The Call of the*

Wild, he was living with his family in a bungalow in Piedmont on Blair Avenue. The most familiar Oakland landmark associated with Jack London is Heinold's First and Last Chance Saloon at 50 Webster Street, where he spent many hours. The tavern was near the Webster Street bridge to Alameda, then a dry town, and travelers would get their first or last drink there, depending on whether they were going to or coming from Alameda. Nearby is a wooden one-room cabin brought here from the Klondike region, where London lived in 1898 during the gold rush there. Jack London Square, at the foot of Broadway, is now an area of fine restaurants and shops.

The Hights, situated on the wooded hills overlooking San Francisco Bay and the Golden Gate, is on Joaquin Miller Road. This was the estate of Cincinnatus Heine ("Joaquin") Miller, "Poet of the Sierra," who lived his last years here from 1870 to 1914. It is now an Oakland park. The Abbey, his small home (SRL 107), is not open to the public. On the extensive grounds are stone monuments erected by his hands: the "Sanctuary to Memory," the "Funeral Pyre," the "Tower to Robert Browning," and the "Tower to General John C. Frémont." The latter was placed on the spot where Frémont, who named the Golden Gate, is said to have stood when he first saw the San Francisco Bay opening out into the Pacific.

Redwood Regional Park, a part of the East Bay Regional Park District, contains two historic landmarks. A short distance above The Abbey in the Roberts Recreational Area, is SRL 962. Here stood the tall redwoods called the Blossom Rock Navigational Trees. Mariners entering San Francisco Bay, upon sighting these trees, were able to plot a course that would avoid the submerged menace called Blossom Rock. The Army Corps of Engineers destroyed the rock in 1870.

At the Fishway by the Redwood Regional Park office a plaque (SRL 970) commemorates the identification of the rainbow trout, *salmo irideus*. At nearby San Leandro Creek (now known as Redwood Creek and Upper San Leandro Creek), three specimens were taken in 1855. Dr. W. P. Gibbons, the founder of the California Academy of Natural Sciences, identified these as a new species, but closely related to the steelhead, *salmo giardinerii*, previously classified. The rainbow trout was successfully introduced into rivers and streams throughout the world.

Robert Louis Stevenson lived off and on in Oakland before leaving in 1888 for his last voyage to the South Seas. The poet Edwin Markham called Oakland home from 1892 to 1899. After his famous "The Man with the Hoe" was published in 1899, he and his family moved to New York.

Gertrude Stein grew up in East Oakland, where her

playmates included Isadora and Raymond Duncan; all three found their careers in Europe. Of her childhood home, she wrote: "It was wonderful there in the summer with the dry heat and the sun burning and the hot earth for sleeping; and then in the winter with the rain and the north wind blowing that would bend the trees." On a visit to California in 1934, Gertrude Stein was disappointed to see that her childhood home was gone and the neighborhood had changed; in her cryptic style, she lamented that "there was no there there."

Dr. Cyrus Mills and his wife conducted the Benicia Seminary in Benicia from 1865 to 1871. Then they moved to what is now East Oakland, where they hoped to make their school the Mount Holyoke of the Pacific. Mills College, originally Mills Seminary, has been a prominent institution of higher education ever since; after many years as a women's college, it is now coeducational. Mills Hall (SRL 849), one of the original buildings from 1871, is still in use. The long, four-story wooden structure was once considered to be the most beautiful educational building in California.

Julia Morgan's architectural work is much in evidence on the Mills College campus. Miss Morgan was the first woman to graduate from the École des Beaux-Arts in Paris and is perhaps best remembered for her work on William Randolph Hearst's San Simeon estate. At Mills, the campanile she designed and whose installation she supervised was her first independent commission (1904), and it triumphantly survived the earthquake two years later that laid waste so many Bay Area structures. The library is largely her work. In 1923 she designed the charming Quong Ming orphanage for Oakland's Chinese community. The building was then far from downtown Oakland, and in 1936 it was sold by its patrons to Mills College, which acquired title to the grounds on which it stands. Renamed Alderwood Hall (but still containing its Oriental decorative embellishments), it is the official guest house for the college and a frequent meeting center.

A tiny cemetery of the Mills family called Sunnyside is at the eastern side of the campus, and it is said that it was responsible for preserving much of the Mills College grounds in the 1950's when the freeway (now I-580) was pushing through the district. The state might override the claims of a college, but a cemetery could not be moved.

St. Mary's College, founded in San Francisco in 1863, moved to Oakland in 1889. The site of the old building (SRL 676) at Broadway and Hawthorne has been marked by a tablet on the structure at 3093 Broadway. In 1928 the college moved from Oakland to its present campus at Moraga in Contra Costa County.

The Oakland Museum at 1000 Oak Street includes a history gallery within its complex, superbly capped by

Alderwood Hall, Mills College, Oakland

a garden area. It offers a range of exhibits about California history, one of which is the old Assay Office from Nevada City. The East Bay Negro Historical Society has a museum in the library building at 5605 San Pablo Avenue, reflecting the contributions to Oakland's history made by black Americans. The Judah L. Magnes Memorial Museum at 2911 Russell Street in Berkeley is the home of the Western Jewish History Center. All of these museums are open to the public.

The College of California began as the Contra Costa Academy in Oakland in 1853. It was founded by the Rev. Henry Durant, a Yale graduate, and the Rev. Samuel H. Willey, one of the four commissioned Protestant missionaries sent to California by the American Home Missionary Society. The college was first located on Broadway and Fifth Street, but eventually settled at what is now the corner of Thirteenth and Franklin streets (SRL 45), adjacent to the *Oakland Tribune* building. The site was abandoned in 1873 when the college, by then the University of California, moved to Berkeley.

Berkeley

Ocean View was the name of the community north of Oakland, originally Jacobs' Landing on the bay shore. Two miles inland, the first telegraph line to the rest of the Union was put up in 1861, along what are now Telegraph and Claremont avenues. As the Telegraph Road branched out northward from downtown Oakland, development began along its path. The State Asylum for the Deaf, Dumb, and Blind attracted many newcomers. By 1865 Samuel Willey built the first house in the area at what is now 2709 Dwight Way. He was among those who thought that the emerging community ought to have an inspirational name. The name of Berkeley was first discussed as being appropriate for the new college town. Bishop George Berkeley, the renowned English philosopher and seer of what he believed to be the westward march of civilization, wrote the line

"Westward the course of Empire takes its way" in his poem "On the Prospect of Planting Arts and Learning in America," written in 1752. Berkeley's name, although not his pronunciation, was thus given to the city that began around the University of California at Berkeley (SRL 946). Ocean View was annexed in 1878.

Chartered in Oakland in 1868, the University of California moved to Berkeley in 1873. The one original building still standing is South Hall, just west of the Campanile. At the site of the old North Hall is the Bancroft Library, one of the most valuable collections of books and materials on the history of California, located in the library annex. The nucleus of this collection is the personal library of the great bibliophile and historical patron Hubert Howe Bancroft. Phoebe Apperson Hearst was the great benefactress of the university; the Hearst Memorial Mining Museum, built in 1907 in memory of her husband, and the Greek Theater are among the structures she endowed.

The University of California has been the scene of some of the most notable discoveries in the field of atomic physics and chemistry. Here Ernest O. Lawrence invented the cyclotron. In Room 307 of Gilman Hall, on the night of February 23–24, 1941, the man-made element plutonium was first identified by Professors Joseph W. Kennedy, Glenn T. Seaborg, and Arthur C. Wahl. Number 94 on the periodic table, plutonium is used in nuclear reactors and in atomic explosives. The small laboratory where this history-making discovery took place has been registered as a National Historic Landmark by the Department of the Interior.

The First Church of Christ, Scientist, at 2619 Dwight Way, built in 1910, is considered a masterpiece of Bernard Maybeck, the renowned California architect of the early twentieth century. Its style includes elements of the Japanese, Byzantine, Gothic, and Romanesque. The church has been registered as a National Historic Landmark.

Across Bowditch Street from the Church is an open area owned by the university but since the 1960's occupied by a motley crowd of people and unofficially known as "People's Park." This is one visible reminder that the area near the university was the scene of great protest in that decade of the Free Speech Movement and anti-war demonstrations. The future of the property is uncertain.

The Berkeley City Club (SRL 908) at 2315 Durant Avenue represents one of the finest works of Julia Morgan; it was constructed in 1929–30.

The view from the Berkeley Hills across San Francisco Bay to Marin County, the islands of the Bay, the Golden Gate, and the San Francisco skyline is among the most famous in California. Over the years the hills have been covered by homes in a remarkable variety of styles, with those of Maybeck, Morgan, and John Galen Howard among the most numerous from the days before the outbreak of World War II. Guides to historic buildings are easily available in bookstores and make Berkeley a living architectural treasury to walk through.

Alameda

Alameda is locally famous for the preservation and restoration of its old homes and public buildings. The red brick City Hall, at Santa Clara Avenue and Oak Street, was built in 1896 in the fashionable Romanesque style. The nearby area bounded by Oak and Park streets and Lincoln and Encinal avenues is the Park Street Historic Commercial District. The Croll Building (SRL 954), at 1400 Webster Street, was first put up as a hotel in 1883. It has since been converted into offices and stores. The "Gold Coast" area, centered on St. Charles Avenue, has dozens of well-preserved Victorian houses in an area that is also a favorite for walking tours.

The China Clipper made the first transpacific air flight. On November 22, 1935, the first plane of this route took off from Alameda Naval Air Station. It put down at Pearl Harbor in the Hawaiian Islands, touched at the islands of Wake, Midway, and Guam, and finally, six days after it left Alameda, put down in Manila in the Philippine Islands. There is an excellent display on the China Clipper in the Treasure Island Museum, and a marker (SRL 968) at the main gate of the Alameda Naval Air Station commemorates its first flight.

Piedmont

The springs in Piedmont Park first attracted visitors to this area in the hills above Oakland, where a resort hotel was built in 1870. The spectacular view from here across San Francisco Bay to the city and the Golden Gate beyond was an early inducement for settlers. They put up small houses, such as the Wetmore House at 342 Bonita Avenue, built in 1879 in the distinctive Galveston style once popular on the Texas coast; this is now on the National Register of Historic Places and a privately owned dwelling. Jack London and his friends were part of a Bohemian colony in the Piedmont hills for a short time early in the twentieth century, living in scattered "bungalows."

After the 1906 earthquake, a rush was made from San Francisco to the East Bay, where many new and very large houses were built on the splendid avenues that today make Piedmont one of the most impressive residential communities in the Bay Area. Piedmont Community Church began its ministry in the charming

Romanesque structure it now occupies at 400 Highland Avenue in 1918, having been organized nine years before. Piedmont Park is now a city-owned area in one of the many canyons running from the hills down to the flatlands adjacent to San Francisco Bay. Incorporated as a city in 1907, Piedmont is entirely surrounded by Oakland.

Altamont

At the southeastern corner of Alameda County where it touches Contra Costa and San Joaquin counties, Altamont Pass (elevation 1,009 feet) is a low declivity in the hills that separate the San Joaquin Valley from the San Francisco Bay Area. This area is subject to very high winds at certain times of the year, and on the slopes of Altamont Pass nearly four thousand wind turbines have been erected to derive electrical energy from winds that have been clocked at more than 80 miles per hour. The first of these modern windmills was installed in 1982, and today the group constitutes about half of those in operation in the state of California. They may be as important in the future of the state as the oil fields were in California's past.

Though no marker is posted there, the Altamont Speedway, just off I-580 near Altamont Pass, has a special and tragic historical significance. Here, on December 6, 1969, a Rolling Stones concert attracted thousands of enthusiasts. The presence of Hells Angels gang members acting as guards may have contributed to the highly charged atmosphere: a riot broke out, and a spectator was stabbed to death. An active and revolutionary decade in California's cultural life thus ended on a disturbing note of violence.

Alpine County

Alpine County (named for its similarity to the alpine country of Europe) was created March 16, 1864, from parts of El Dorado, Calaveras, Tuolumne, Mono, and Amador counties. The county seat was at first located at Silver Mountain but was transferred to Markleeville in 1875. Until 1863 the region was thought to be a part of Nevada, to which it is more closely united geographically; even today, most of its social and economic ties are with Nevada.

Frémont's Crossing of the Sierra

Among the few government explorers who came to the Pacific Coast before the Mexican War was John C. Frémont. In his company were French trappers familiar with the Western trails. Kit Carson, almost as famous as his noted leader, was the chief guide.

Fired by a desire to see Klamath Lake, Mary's Lake, and the fabled Buenaventura River, Frémont left Oregon for St. Louis in November 1843. Following a circuitous route through Oregon and western Nevada, he finally reached the Carson River. By this time supplies had become greatly depleted, and the horses and mules were in no condition to negotiate the rough Rocky Mountains. Frémont therefore made the bold decision to find a pass through the Sierra into California.

Perhaps no part of the entire journey was more difficult than that through the rugged region that is now Alpine County. The trail necessarily followed along the ridges, where the wind had cleared away a little of the snow and sometimes exposed grass and brush on which the half-starved animals could feed. Because of the difficulty of beating a path through the deep snows, the party had to make camp every few miles. On February 2 or 3, 1844, a halt was made at a spot one and one-half miles northeast of Markleeville, near the confluence of Markleeville Creek and the East Fork of the Carson River. On the following night, camp was made near Grover's Hot Springs, five miles farther west.

On February 6, Frémont had his first view of the great Sacramento Valley lying in the dim distance far below him. From the top of a high peak Kit Carson, who had gone to California with Ewing Young fifteen years before, recognized the low mountains of the Coast Range 100 miles to the west.

On February 14, in company with Charles Preuss, Frémont climbed to the summit of another peak, for many years assumed to have been Stevens Peak, although Red Lake Peak was probably the one in question. From this height Frémont beheld a great sheet of crystal-clear water, which his first map designated merely as the Mountain Lake, but which he later named Lake Bonpland, after Aimé Jacques Alexandre Bonpland (1773–1859), the noted French botanist and companion of Baron von Humboldt. Maps of the 1850's designated it Lake Bigler, but today it is known as Lake Tahoe.

At last, on February 20, they reached the summit at the granite ridge immediately north of Elephant's Back, about three-quarters of a mile south of what was later known as Kit Carson Pass, at an elevation of about 8,600 feet. Here on the 21st Frémont and his companions looked out across the magnificent panorama of snowy ridges and towering peaks interspersed with deep canyons. Far in the distance they saw the Sutter Buttes, the Sacramento Valley, and the Coast Range. They proceeded to the American River along a ridge that runs from Red Lake Peak to the river in the vicinity of Strawberry.

At the summit of Carson Pass a bronze memorial plate (SRL 315) commemorates this heroic passage of the Sierra, giving special honor to the man for whom the pass was named. A portion of the tree that once stood here, on which Carson carved his name in 1844, was removed when the tree was felled in 1888 and is now in the museum at Sutter's Fort in Sacramento.

The Overland Emigrant Trail

Each year after 1844 saw more and more pioneers setting out for California from their homes east of the Mississippi River. The "California" or "Overland Emigrant Trail" was really several routes across the Sierra Nevada, and in recent years efforts have been made to mark these various passages. The Nevada Emigrant Trail Marking Committee, under the auspices of the Nevada Historical Society, has marked that portion of the Overland Emigrant Trail passing through Alpine County with seven distinctive yellow-painted iron markers and plaques, the easternmost of which is at SR 88 and the emigrant trail about one mile north of Woodfords. Others are in or near Snowshoe Springs Campground, Hope Valley, Red Lake, Kit Carson Pass, Caples Lake, and Emigrant Pass.

Three miles west of Carson Pass on SR 88, a monument (SRL 661) has been erected at the point where the old emigrant road of 1848 swung down across a meadow now covered by Caples Lake. A quarter of a mile east of the summit of Carson Pass are some large rocks on which a party of pioneers in 1849 inscribed their names and the emblem of the Independent Order of Odd Fellows. Some of the names are still legible. In 1941 the Grand Lodge of California, I.O.O.F., placed a plaque nearby and dedicated the spot as a memorial to the pioneer Odd Fellows (SRL 378). And at the crest of Carson Pass is a striking obelisk dedicated to the memory of "Snow-Shoe" Thompson, the top portion of which is broken off and embedded in the base, symbolizing a life cut off in its prime.

"Show-Shoe" Thompson

From 1856 to 1876, John A. "Snow-Shoe" Thompson braved the winter storms of the High Sierra to deliver the United States mail to early pioneers in the days before railways. Many stories are told of his courage, stamina, and reliability; no matter how wild the mountain storms, he never failed to come through, usually on time.

Early in January 1856, while on his ranch at Putah Creek, Thompson read in the papers of the difficulties experienced in getting the mails across the summit of the Sierra Nevada in winter. He made himself a pair of "snow skates," or skis, such as he had used in Norway when he was young Jon Tostensen, and began the arduous and heroic work that he carried on for two decades. His first trip was made in January 1856, from Placerville to Carson Valley, Nevada, a distance of 90 miles over the old emigrant road on which Placerville was the principal town. Not only was Thompson "the father of all the race of snowshoers in the Sierra Ne-

Monument to "Snow-Shoe" Thompson, Carson Pass

vada," but he was also the forerunner of the stagecoach and the locomotive over the High Sierra.

Thompson made his home until 1876 on a ranch in Diamond Valley, at the head of Carson Valley, close to the Nevada boundary line. This was near Woodfords, and Thompson was taken from that point to the deep snow line by sleigh or saddle horse. He had two general routes. One went from Woodfords to Placerville, following approximately the course of the present state highway along the West Fork of the Carson River to a point near the mouth of Horse Thief Canyon, four and one-half miles from Woodfords. There, he bore directly west in the direction of Thompson Peak. The other route was from Woodfords to Murphys, by way of Indian Valley and sometimes by way of the Border Ruffian Pass and Blue Lakes. On a few occasions he took the trail through Ebbetts Pass, stopping at Silver Mountain. These three routes to Murphys converged in Hermit Valley.

"Snow-Shoe" Thompson died at his ranch on May 15, 1876, not yet 50 years of age. He is buried at Genoa, Nevada; a pair of skis are incised on his marble tombstone. A monument was placed near the site of his home in Diamond Valley by the social and historical society E Clampus Vitus in 1956. A pair of his "snow-shoes" are on display in the visitor center of the Plumas-Eureka State Park at Johnsville in Plumas County.

Alpine Highways

The surface of Alpine County is elevated and rugged and on every side the view is grandly picturesque. The summit of the Sierra Nevada bisects the county. All but a small portion of the county lies within three National Forests: El Dorado, Stanislaus, and Toiyabe. A road, said to have been the first surveyed route over the High Sierra, was constructed as early as 1857, from Hermit Valley to Hope Valley by way of Twin Lakes Pass. Hope Valley was named by members of the Mormon Battalion on their return to Salt Lake City in the summer of 1848. The emigrant trail through Ebbetts Pass (SRL 318) to Angels Camp was opened up in the early 1850's, but no road went that way until 1864, when, as a result of the opening up of the Comstock Lode in Nevada, a toll road was completed under the name of the Carson Valley and Big Tree Road. It was over this trail, in September 1861, that a little group of Bactrian camels from the Gobi Desert in Mongolia was driven from San Francisco to Nevada, where they were used for transportation in the mines. The experiment was not a success, it seems, for the Nevada state legislature in 1875 passed "an act to prohibit camels and dromedaries from running at large on or about the public highways."

Alpine Ghost Towns

Silver Mountain, founded as Kongsberg (Königsberg) in 1858 by Scandinavian miners, existed until 1886. The county seat was located there from 1864 to 1875. A ghost of Alpine's once thriving silver camps, it is marked today only by the crumbling walls of the old stone jail, the first in the county, near the site of the old courthouse. Silver Mountain is located on SR 4 a few miles southwest of its junction with SR 89, a junction that was once the location of the town of Mt. Bullion or Bulliona. En route to the jail ruins at Silver Mountain a tall brick chimney is passed on the right. This was part of the reduction plant of "Lord" Chalmers, an Englishman who came to Alpine County in 1867. Here, next to the chimney and by Silver Creek, is his home, called the Chalmers Mansion, and still containing some of the furnishings of the past.

Of Silver King, located on the headwaters of the East Fork of the Carson River west of US 395, only a little wreckage of old buildings remains to mark the site. Monitor, flourishing from 1858 to 1886 and entirely deserted by 1893, showed some return to activity (under the name of Loope) from 1898 to 1911, when it was again deserted until 1930, at which time there was a brief revival of mining for a few years.

Although silver predominates in the Alpine region, in large low-grade ledges gold is encountered in nearly every mineralized district. "Uncle Billy Rogers'" Copper Mine, situated in Hope Valley in the northwest angle of the county, is said to have been the first deposit (1855) of this ore ever opened in California or anywhere on the Pacific Coast, antedating the Comstock discovery by several years.

Chalmers Mansion, Silver Mountain

Woodfords

In 1847 Sam Brannan, on his way to Salt Lake City, stopped at the present site of Woodfords and left two men to establish an outpost—the first white settlement in this area. The project was abandoned, but other settlers arrived at what had come to be called Brannan Springs. Daniel Woodford, who came in 1849, erected a hotel, the first building of any permanence. About 1851 a man named Cary, whose first name seems to have been lost to history, built a sawmill, and the growing town became known as Cary's Mills, yielding in 1869 to Woodfords. Cary built a house, still standing but now generally called the Wade house, in 1852–53, from lumber milled at his own establishment. During the initial five weeks of its operation in 1860, the Pony Express was routed through Woodfords and maintained a re-mount station (SRL 805) at Cary's barn, the site of which is across the road from the present Woodfords store.

Markleeville

The town of Markleeville is California's smallest county seat and the seat of its least populous county, which has neither high school nor hospital within its borders. The picturesque settlement had its beginning in the cabin of Jacob J. Marklee, who settled there in 1861, only to be shot and killed during a quarrel two years later. On the site of his dwelling (SRL 240) stands Alpine County's beautiful little courthouse, built of native stone in 1928.

By 1864 Markleeville had a population of over 2,500, but in 1875, when it succeeded Silver Mountain as the county seat, the entire county could boast only a few more than 1,200; such was the effect of the decline of silver mining. Although a fire about 1886 destroyed much of Markleeville, a few interesting old buildings still stand. The tall Alpine Hotel was originally built in

Webster School, Alpine County Historical Complex, Markleeville

Silver Mountain as the Fisk Hotel and was moved to its present location in 1885.

On the hill above the town is the Alpine County Historical Complex, an interesting group of buildings. The old wooden jail is open to visitors. Nearby the Webster School, in use from 1882 to 1929, was completely restored in 1968 by the Historical Society of Alpine County. Two years later a new museum building was completed, housing a collection of mining and domestic artifacts.

Three miles west of town is Grover Hot Springs State Park. The springs here boasted a hotel for many years, operated by the Grover family; the state acquired the property in 1959. The water that emerges from the earth at a temperature of 140 degrees is channeled into a pool where it cools somewhat and refreshes bikers, hikers, skiers, and other visitors to the area.

Amador County

Amador County was created in 1854 when the legislature allowed the voters of Calaveras County to decide whether to divide the county at the Mokelumne River. Although the actual results were contested and never certified by Calaveras officials, organizers formed the new county nevertheless. Jackson was chosen as its

county seat and remains so today. Amador's Creek, later Amador City, which gave its name to the county, was itself named for miner and settler José Maria Amador, a trader at the creek in 1848–49 and formerly a mayordomo of Mission San José. The county's first northern boundary was Dry Creek, but it was later extended to the Cosumnes River. In 1864, Amador lost its easternmost territory when Alpine County was formed.

The Moraga Expedition

Gabriel Moraga's expedition of 1806 through the Sierra foothills in all probability passed through part of Amador County. The evidence lies not in documents or in diaries but in the fact that about 50 years later, miners near Mokelumne Hill found a bullet or slug embedded in a pine tree with some 50 growth rings around it. No gun-toting people are known to have been there at the appropriate time except Moraga and his followers. There may have been solitary trappers in the foothills in later years, but no documentary evidence proves this.

Sutter's Pine Woods

More certain is the fact that in the fall of 1844 or the spring of 1845 John A. Sutter sent employees out from New Helvetia (now Sutter's Fort), his estate in what is now Sacramento, to search the mountain lowlands for a good supply of cedar and pine trees for lumber. A logging project was established at Pine Woods, of which no trace remains today, although it is thought that it lay on the ridge five miles east of the later town of Sutter Creek, between Amador and Sutter creeks. The distance from Pine Woods to New Helvetia (from where Sutter planned to sell his Sierra lumber) was estimated in 1845 by John Bidwell, then in Sutter's employ, to be some 40 miles. A reliable sawmill was needed at a site closer to Sutter's Fort, and so James Marshall, another of Sutter's men, was sent in the fall of 1847 to look for a better location. It was at the new site, at what is now Coloma in El Dorado County on the South Fork of the American River, that Marshall discovered gold in the stream bed in January 1848. If Sutter had decided to build his sawmill on one of the two creeks below the ridge at Pine Woods, gold might have been discovered earlier, and Amador County would be hailed as the discovery site.

The Emigrant Trail

One branch of the old emigrant trail went through Jackson. A later stage road to Virginia City, Nevada, and the present SR 88 have followed its general direction. On this trail, near the El Dorado–Amador county line, the Tragedy Springs massacre occurred on June 27, 1848. While members of the Mormon Battalion were returning to Utah, three scouts of the party were killed by Indians. An account of the event and the names of the scouts were carved on a tree at the spot; the carved section of the tree is preserved in the museum at Sutter's Fort.

Near Tragedy Springs, a monument (SRL 662) indicates where the emigrant road crosses SR 88. Less than two miles west of this point, beside the highway, is the "Maiden's Grave" (SRL 28), the last resting place of one of the many emigrants who did not have the stamina to complete the long trek.

Kirkwood's stage station and inn (SRL 40), built in 1863 by Zack Kirkwood, still stands on SR 88, eight miles northeast of Tragedy Springs. Looking as sturdy as the day it was built, the place serves as a bar and restaurant. Kirkwood's log cabin, built around 1858, has been incorporated into the main building. When Alpine County was created in 1864, the division left the barn and milk house belonging to the Kirkwoods in Alpine, while the county line went directly through the barroom of the inn.

The Volcano Cutoff brought overland traffic into the central part of what is now Amador County in 1852, when Stockton and Volcano merchants paid a contractor to construct a wagon road from Volcano to the Emigrant Trail near Corral Flat. About this time, the name of Kit Carson was attached to the Emigrant Trail, although he had never been on it. The Volcano Cutoff is now followed by the Fiddletown–Silver Lake Road, which joins SR 88 at Dewdrop Station.

Plasse's Resort

Raymond Peter Plasse followed the Volcano Cutoff to the Emigrant Trail in 1852. Born in France, he had arrived in San Francisco in 1850 and had headed for the mines to try his luck. At the south end of Silver Lake he established a trading post near the roadway and placed a claim for 160 acres in the neighborhood. The log cabin he built in 1852 is now used as a generator house, and it is believed to be the oldest building still standing in the length of the Sierra Nevada. The Plasse family ultimately lived on a ranch south of Jackson but retained the mountain property as a summer place and pasturage, and in time other buildings joined the first log cabin on the property. Around 1900 the family opened a summer resort that is still in operation. Historian Larry Cenotto observes that this property has been in the hands of the same family for over 130 years, something of a record for the gold country of California.

Gold Bars of the Mokelumne

Possibly the first gold found in Amador County was discovered somewhere along the Mokelumne River, in the spring of 1848, by Captain Charles M. Weber, the founder of the city of Stockton. During the summer of the same year, within two months' time, a company of eight men headed by James P. Martin took out several thousand dollars' worth of gold each. In the autumn a mining expedition of one hundred men recently mustered out of the army came to the river; they had seen service in the war with Mexico under Colonel J. D. Stevenson.

Thousands of eager miners from all over the world flocked to the gulches and rivers of the Sierra in 1849, and during the first years of the 1850's they continued to swarm up and down the rivers, building small towns overnight at all of the rich river bars. Within the two decades that followed, an almost unbelievable change took place. Historian J. D. Mason, writing in 1881, described the transformation even then evident to one walking along the banks of the Mokelumne River. Hardly could one realize, he said, "that the stillness, broken only by the murmur of the river, was ever otherwise." Today, scarcely a fragment remains of the numerous cabins where "the miner fried his flapjacks or dried his wet clothing after a day's toil under a broiling sun in the ice-cold water."

Big Bar (SRL 41) was one of the prominent camps along the Mokelumne. One of the old inns, Gardella's, still stands at the Amador end of the bridge where SR 49 crosses the river. After the placers on the bars had been depleted, the center of trade moved across the river to Mokelumne Hill, in Calaveras County. The rushing river and the rugged canyon remain at Big Bar.

Middle Bar (SRL 36), two miles below Big Bar, was a larger community than its neighbor, and in the 1920's it had a brief lode mining revival. The old homesteads, however, were soon purchased by the East Bay Municipal Utility District, which built the Pardee Dam across the Mokelumne River six miles below Middle Bar. This district was formed when eleven San Francisco Bay Area cities joined forces to secure water and power, and selected the Mokelumne River as the source of the purest water. Former governor George Pardee was president of the company when the dam was completed in 1930. This region, where hundreds of busy miners with pans or cradles once washed the gold from the river, is now covered with water. The old lode mines included the Big Tunnel or Mammoth, the Hardenburg, the Marlette, and the St. Julian or Caminetti, successors of the earlier placers and all big producers in the past.

Lancha Plana

Farther down the Mokelumne River, in the southwestern part of the county, many mining camps centered about Lancha Plana, among them Poverty Bar (in Calaveras County), Winter's Bar, Oregon Bar, and Put's Bar. This area is now inundated by the Camanche Reservoir of the East Bay Municipal Utility District. Lancha Plana ("flatboat"), just across the river from the exceedingly rich gravels of Poverty Bar, came into existence as the mooring place for the flatboat ferry, which carried miners from the north side of the river across to Poverty Bar and the mines of Calaveras County. Lancha Plana (SRL 30) reached the height of its prosperity after 1856, when hill and bluff mining were bringing greater returns than mining in the river had ever brought.

Buena Vista ("beautiful view") was the name applied to a settlement about six miles north of Lancha Plana, as well as to a mountain and a valley in the vicinity. Buena Vista, over the years, was a more important settlement than Lancha Plana. The old store at the intersection of the Pardee-Ione Road and the Jackson Valley Road still serves the public well in its "new" location. It was originally built in Lancha Plana by William Cook in 1859. When the miners moved away to other fields, all business languished in Lancha Plana. Cook decided to set up in the more promising town and had the sandstone blocks of the Lancha Plana store taken down and rebuilt at Buena Vista in 1877.

Butte City

The Ginocchio Store (SRL 39), on SR 49 about one and one-half miles south of Jackson, is all that remains of what was once Butte City, a thriving mining camp in the Mother Lode country in the 1850's. As early as 1856 Xavier Benoist had a store and bakery in this building. For a time Butte City, located at the south side of Butte Basin, a section rich in auriferous deposits, rivaled Jackson. Today the spot is typical of the many ghost towns that are reminiscent of California's early mining activity: a roofless stone structure stands by the highway in the midst of open fields where for a short time a thousand miners' cabins stood, and on the hill lies a lonely graveyard of the forgotten miners. The damaged store is now fenced off and, unless it can be repaired in some way, will soon become another ruin of the Mother Lode.

Drytown

At Drytown (SRL 31), a mining camp on Dry Creek nine miles north of Jackson, mining for gold was first begun in the spring of 1848. It was not unusual, in 1849, to wash as much as $100 in gold from a single pan in the surrounding canyons. These canyons had a grisly collection of names—Blood Gulch, Murderer's Gulch, and Rattlesnake Gulch among them. Although there were doubtless plenty of steady, industrious miners at Drytown, there were also desperate characters who left their mark. The town prospered until 1857, when fire swept the place. It never recovered from this disaster, for gold was already becoming worked out there. But some charming old buildings still stand at Drytown, including an old brick house (1857) that has been owned by members of the same family since it was built, the old brick store where George Hearst, then neither a millionaire nor a United States senator, kept his mining records for a while in the late 1850's, and the old Town Hall, which was used by a popular little-theater group until its destruction by fire in 1987.

Rancheria

Mining at Rancheria, two miles east of Drytown, began in 1848. A mixed population, in which Mexicans and Chileans predominated, gathered there to the number of five or six hundred. From that year, the new American rulers of California became increasingly antagonistic to the Mexicans and Chileans moving into the state seeking wealth; the state legislature imposed the Foreign Miners Tax (1851) in a blatant attempt to drive these people out of the state. Law enforcement officials reflected this anti-Hispanic bias, the Chileans and Mexicans said, and violence against the "greasers" (an ugly term often used by the Americans of that time for all Spanish-speakers) resulted in a kind of ethnic civil war in some parts of California. One result of this conflict was a Mexican backlash. On the night of August 6, 1855, Rancheria was assaulted by a gang of Mexican horsemen, who sacked the town and killed nine people, five in one family. The retaliation was as brutal as the offense, and to this day it is not certain how many Mexicans were lynched or otherwise killed by vigilantes. It is certain that the Spanish-speaking population of most of the Mother Lode nearly disappeared after 1855. A monument on the mass grave of the slain Dinan family stands near the road from Amador City to Rancheria Creek.

Volcano

Volcano (SRL 29) is located at the bottom of a deep cup in the mountains, hence its name. It was a prospective mining town like many others, with the accident of geography thrown in: it lay between the Emigrant Road at the northern border of the county and the more populated region around Jackson and Sutter Creek. In 1852, the Volcano Cutoff (also called the Pennsylvania Cutoff in early accounts) was made by the merchants of Stockton and Amador County to bring wagons down from the trans-Sierra route into the settled region of the

county. Volcano was thus on the highway of its day. It never became a ghost town, although the authors of the previous (1966) edition of *Historic Spots in California* described it in romantic, eerie words: "Volcano's population has dwindled considerably since the 1850's, and its isolation, together with the weirdness of the gray rocks washed out by the miners of long ago, make it a veritable 'Sleepy Hollow' of the West. Almost one looks for goblins among the ghost rocks, or for a headless horseman to come galloping down the steep wooded mountain road."

This was a very rich hydraulic mining district in early days, a million dollars in gold having been taken out of one mine alone, which was worked for over 30 years. Some gold is still found in the region, but activity of other sorts is more evident; Volcano, nearby Daffodil Hill, and Indian Grinding Rocks (Chaw-Se) State Historic Park are major tourist attractions, and retirement communities, vacation homes, and the commercial activities necessary for their support have certainly changed the region, like many other places in the Sierra foothills.

Volcano today is a curious combination of modern-day activities and old surroundings. Several old stores on Main Street have only their stone facades left. Other buildings are very much occupied. The Kaiser General Store is claimed to have been serving the public continuously since it was built in 1852. The Odd Fellows and Masonic Hall, still in use, dates from 1856, as does the old Bavarian Brewery, now a private residence. The most grandiose structure in Volcano, and something of a Mother Lode highlight, is the St. George Hotel, three stories high. Built in 1863, the St. George is the fourth hotel built on the site since the early 1850's, and still accommodates guests. An E Clampus Vitus plaque on the hotel celebrates its history. Another "Clamper" plaque in the center of town notes that in 1934 plans were afoot to build a dam and to flood Volcano, but, in the words of the plaque, "Geology and water rights negated plan so Volcano didn't drown. Not by a dam site."

An interesting relic is "Old Abe," the six-pound bronze cannon on display next to the old Sing Kee Store. The cannon was cast in Massachusetts in 1837 and brought to California some time after the end of the Mexican War. In 1861, as the Civil War broke out, it was brought to its present site by the Volcano Blues, a pro-Northern militia unit, and local tradition says that although it never fired a shot in anger, the presence of the Union cannon was enough to discourage Confederate sympathizers in the region. Since virtually all the six-pound bronze cannons in the United States were melted down in the early months of the war to make twelve-pound pieces, "Old Abe," far off in the West,

Chaw-ses, Indian Grinding Rocks State Historic Park

Ceremonial Roundhouse, Indian Grinding Rocks State Historic Park

may be the only remaining six-pound bronze cannon in the nation.

Another relic from Civil War days is the bell presented to the town by Reverend Thomas Starr King, whose eloquent speech here on behalf of the Union in 1861 elicited generous contributions from the community. The bell was given by Union sympathizers in Boston to replace the one lost when Volcano's Methodist Church burned. California had relatively few men in arms during the Civil War, but her contribution in gold was crucial to the ultimate victory of the Union. The bell is now displayed in the center of town.

Volcano is three miles from SR 88 at Pine Grove. Between the two towns is Indian Grinding Rocks (Chaw-Se) State Historic Park, where the remarkable grinding rock, 173 feet by 82 feet, contains 1,185 *chaw-ses*, or mortar cups, and some 363 rock carvings. A Northern

Miwok center, the park also contains replicas of native buildings, including a ceremonial roundhouse. The visitors' center has good displays of local artifacts and natural history. Four miles north of Volcano, on Shake Ridge Road, is the site of the earliest known amateur astronomical observatory in California (SRL 715), built in 1860.

Pine Grove

Pine Grove has the appearance of a fairly new town, and indeed it has attracted many residents in the past quarter-century. The place began as an inn, the Pine Grove House, built in 1855 by Albert Leonard on the road between Volcano and Jackson. The Pine Grove Hotel that one sees today replaced the former hostelry in 1881. Older by two years is the Town Hall, originally the Dance and Temperance Hall, which has been the community center for over a century. The public school built in 1869 is now a small museum and open to the public. All of these are located on SR 88 at Pine Grove.

Plymouth

In the northern part of Amador County numerous mining camps were once located on the Cosumnes River and its branches. Some of these camps have long since vanished, only scarred hills and an occasional chimney marking the spots where miners once toiled or where their crude cabins stood. Other camps remain today as mountain hamlets, while a few are marked only by an aging building.

The richest location in the district was situated on the river bar at the main forks of the Cosumnes, and was called by the Indian name Yeomet. Several stores and a somewhat pretentious hotel were standing there in 1853, but the miners gradually took over the town, one building after another giving way to the diggings, until nothing was left except the old toll bridge.

On the stage road to Sacramento, four or five miles south of Yeomet, was Plymouth, whose history is largely bound up with the quartz lodes of the region. The town was kept busy into the 1940's by the Plymouth Consolidated Gold Mine. On the south side of Plymouth's main street, next to the old Roos Building, is a brick structure (SRL 470) built in 1857 and at one time used as the office and commissary of the consolidated mining company. At the southwest end of the flat on which Plymouth is located was the hamlet of Pokerville, or Puckerville, at the site of which a unique building remains. The Old China Store, built around 1880, has side walls of local fieldstone, but the front and back are of brick, which is also used around the corners in a series of zig-zag steps; a brick front was often thought to be a status symbol in the late nineteenth century. The original proprietor was a Mr. Ming, whose nationality probably led to the present-day name of the building.

Fiddletown

A few miles east of Plymouth is the picturesque settlement of Fiddletown (SRL 35), immortalized in Bret Harte's story "An Episode of Fiddletown." It was first settled in 1849 by a party of Missourians. "They are always fiddling," said a Missouri patriarch; "call it Fiddletown." And Fiddletown it was until 1878, when the name was changed to Oleta. The change was made by the state legislature at the insistence, it was said, of Judge Purinton, a prominent citizen who on frequent business trips to Sacramento and San Francisco had been embarrassed at being known as "the man from Fiddletown." Through the efforts of the Committee on Historic Landmarks of the California Historical Society, the old name of Fiddletown was restored in 1932. Some buildings dating from the 1850's can be seen on the main street; the rammed-earth adobe built for a Chinese doctor and his family later was a general store and home until its owner, Chow Fong You, died in 1965. Chow's store and home was preserved and opened to the public by the Fiddletown Preservation Society and Amador County in 1988.

Across the street from Chow's store is another building from the 1850's, known locally as the Chinese Gambling House. The forge next door is also from the 1850's, as is the general store a few doors east; this is one of the oldest such places in California still doing business in its original location. The tall Schallhorne building was a smithy and wagon shop when it was built in 1870; it serves now as a garage. Fiddletown is an exceptionally charming town for a stroll on a summer's afternoon.

In the 1850's and 1860's Fiddletown was the trading center for a number of rich mining camps, American Flat and American Hill, French Flat, Loafer Flat, and Lone Hill among them. The entire region, including the ridge between Bridgeport (once Suckertown) and Slate Creek, is within an area of extensive old river deposits.

Central House, a popular stage station that stood on the road between Plymouth and Drytown where SRs 16 and 49 now join, was built of timbers brought around the Horn. Another much-frequented hostelry on this route was at Willow Springs, a few miles west of Drytown on the way to Sacramento. Forest Home, Arkansas Creek, and Yankee Hill were neighboring camps farther west.

Adobe Store, Fiddletown

The region around Fiddletown and Plymouth is now a prosperous dry-farming community, growing grapes, walnuts, pears, and various farm products. Shenandoah Valley, north of Plymouth, has been a rich farming section since the early 1850's, and descendants of pioneer settlers still occupy many of the old homesteads. The D'Agostini Winery (SRL 762), eight miles northeast of Plymouth, was founded in 1856. Its original stone cellar is still in use, and is open to the public on a regular basis. More than a dozen newer wineries can now be visited in the Shenandoah Valley, one of the important wine-making districts of California.

Sutter Creek

Sutter Creek (SRL 322) was named after John A. Sutter, the first white man to come to that region in 1846, and the first to mine the locality in 1848. There was little activity at Sutter Creek until 1851, when quartz gold was discovered. Quartz mining was a very hazardous occupation in the early days. The art of timbering the shafts and tunnels was not understood and many cave-ins resulted. The capital outlay, too, was so great and the profits were so uncertain that many men were ruined financially by the venture. Alvinza Hayward stands preeminent as the man who emerged victorious. Buying out several mines, ultimately, in the face of great odds, he made them produce millions. The Central Eureka, discovered in 1869, and at one time part of the Hayward holdings, continued production even after most of the mines were closed down by World War II. The shaft reached almost the 5,000-foot level and the mine produced about $17 million in gold. The Old Eureka Mine was first opened in 1852. It was located at the foot of the great sweeping curve of the highway (SR 49) going north into Sutter Creek.

In the late 1850's Leland Stanford, later governor of California and founder of Stanford University, financed the Lincoln Mine, between Sutter Creek and Amador City, for Robert Downs, maintaining a controlling interest in it during the years from 1859 to 1872. The returns proved so rich that Stanford, then a Sacramento businessman and merchant, had a considerable fund with which to begin construction of the Central Pacific Railroad.

Sutter Creek is still a thriving town, with several deep, though inactive, quartz mines nearby. The first foundry and furniture manufacturing establishment in the gold country was built here, and the Knight Foundry, started in 1877, still operates on Eureka Street; it is believed to be the only water-powered foundry in the United States. Educational and religious activities also thrived here from the beginning, making Sutter Creek a cultural center distinct from the wilder mining camps of the region. The Methodist Church at the south end of town was built in several portions, the earliest in 1862; the spire was added to the church tower in 1976. The Sutter Creek Grammar School was first used in 1870 and is now being refurbished by the Sutter Creek Woman's Club. Sutter Creek was hit by a number of fires, and few buildings from before 1888 exist. Among the old dwellings is an inn, the oldest part of which goes back to 1859. An interesting house on Spanish Street at the end of Hayden was ordered from a catalogue in 1930 and assembled on the spot. As in many California cities of historical interest, walking guides may be obtained in the town that describe these old buildings.

Amador City

Amador City, located on Amador Creek three miles north of Sutter Creek where it intercepts the Mother Lode ledge, had its beginnings as a mining center in 1848. But the placers were never very rich and, like Sutter Creek, the history of Amador City has been connected chiefly with quartz mining. The first quartz discovery in Amador County was made there in February 1851 by S. A. Davidson, a Tennessee Baptist preacher. Since three other ministers were associated with him, the mine was called the "Ministers' Claim." Soon thereafter the vein was discovered on the north side of the creek, and became known as the "Original Amador Mine."

Amador Hotel, Amador City

The Keystone Mine at Amador was the result of the consolidation of the Original Amador with the Spring Hill, Granite State, and Walnut Hill mines in 1857. But the enterprise was not a success until the discovery of the Bonanza in 1869, when the first month's crushing paid $40,000. This high production continued for over a decade. The Keystone has been closed since early in this century, but there are people who believe that millions of dollars in gold still lie hidden within the earth thereabouts and that Amador City may yet renew its old-time activity.

Amador City is now chiefly a cluster of old buildings along SR 49, most of which are still in use. A beautiful brick building, the office and residence of former Keystone Mine superintendents, still stands in good repair. Built in 1881, it is now a motel with period furnishings. The Amador and Imperial Hotels both go back more than a century. Most of the buildings still standing are of brick, since the 1878 fire destroyed most of the older wooden structures. A building that escaped the fire is the old schoolhouse on the hill behind the cemetery, with its old bell in place in the belfry. Although it has never been a very populous place, Amador City has been an incorporated city since 1915, the smallest incorporated city in California both in population and in area.

Jackson

Jackson, county seat of Amador County, is rich in old buildings reminiscent of the mining days of the 1850's. Built largely of brick, with massive doors, iron-shuttered windows, and balconied upper stories, they speak eloquently of the days before our own. The presence of these old iron-barred stores gives the town an Old World atmosphere, which is reflected in the diversity of its townsfolk. The people of Jackson come from Italian, Serbian, Slavonian, and Mexican backgrounds, as well as from pioneer American families.

Most of the stone and brick buildings on Main and Court streets were constructed immediately after a disastrous fire destroyed the town in 1862. The Independent Order of Odd Fellows Hall, of red brick, is one of the tallest three-story buildings ever erected. Like the nearby National Hotel, it was built after the 1862 fire. An earlier structure is the drug store (1855) on Main Street, which in Civil War days housed the *Amador Dispatch*. The authorities came to believe that this newspaper was pro-Confederate and unpatriotic. When the news of President Lincoln's assassination arrived in California in April 1865, U.S. cavalrymen arrested the publisher and editor of the paper, put them in Alcatraz Prison (then a military station) in San Francisco Bay, and closed down the paper.

At 113–115 Main Street is the Pioneer Hall (SRL 34), where the Native Daughters of the Golden West were organized in 1886. At the corner of Water Street and Broadway is the Masonic Building (1854), one of the oldest in town. Jackson's most picturesque building is the little white Serbian Orthodox Church of St. Sava, which stands at the northern edge of the town on Jackson Gate Road. This is the mother church for the denomination in North America, and it was built in 1894.

Commemorative plaques have been placed at several places in Jackson. One along Main Street identifies the site of Jackson's "Hanging Tree," where ten men were executed between 1851 and 1855. In front of handsome St. Patrick's Catholic Church (1868), another marker, placed by the Knights of Columbus, honors Jackson-born Angelo Noce (1848–1922), "Father of Columbus Day," who "devoted his life to the memory of Christopher Columbus . . . [and] through whose efforts were founded the national holiday which now bears his name." In the schoolyard at the corner of Church and North streets another marker (SRL 865) commemorates the first Jewish synagogue in the Mother Lode, begun on the spot in 1857 but no longer in existence.

The Amador County Museum is housed in the A. C. Brown House, at 225 Church Street, which was built of brick in 1859. The entire block, including wrought-iron fences, a Victorian carriage house, and the two-story residence itself, is maintained in excellent condition. Models of some of the mine structures from various parts of the county are among the many displays in the museum.

Jackson was named by early miners (1849) in honor of Alden M. Jackson, a capable New England-born lawyer and prominent early citizen, who was often given the honorific "Colonel," although the rank was never actually awarded him. The location had formerly been known as Bottileas (Bottles), apparently because of the debris scattered about by transients on their way to the mountains.

The diggings in the immediate vicinity of the town were not rich, but, being the logical center for a large mining area and a convenient stopping place on the road from Sacramento to the southern mines, Jackson grew and prospered in the early 1850's. The richest location in the neighborhood was below the forks of Jackson Creek, where a few prospectors took out as much as $500 in a day.

The flats and gulches in the vicinity of Tunnel Hill, a mile and one-half south of Jackson, at Scottsville, were also good producers, as was the hill itself. A number of tunnels sunk into its sides gave rise to the name. This very rich deposit was worked to bedrock; the scarred hills are now grass-grown and serve as pasturelands.

Another rich gravel digging was at Jackson Gate (SRL 118), a mile north of town. A deep, narrow fissure in the rocks through which the creek flows gave the place its name. Here is Chichizola's Store, built in the early 1850's. Ohio Hill and Squaw Gulch nearby were also very rich producers. During a winter's work at the former place, the operators of one mine took out from forty to fifty thousand dollars, while "Madame Pantaloons," a woman dressed as a man and working like the men, accumulated a hundred thousand dollars and then sold her claim for twenty thousand more.

Quartz mining continued to bring prosperity to Jackson after other forms of mining had ceased to be remunerative. Several deep quartz veins in the hills above the town were worked until World War II. The famous Argonaut and Kennedy mines (SRL 786), among the deepest in the world, are located here. The Argonaut, discovered in the early 1850's, experienced many failures as well as successes, but it operated continuously from 1893 to 1942 and reached a vertical depth of 5,570 feet. Here, in August 1922, 47 miners lost their lives when they were trapped by fire in the lower levels, the greatest loss of life in a mine accident in California history. The total production of this mine has been estimated at over $25 million. The Argonaut can be located many miles away by its lofty water tower.

Across SR 49 from the Argonaut is the Kennedy, opened prior to 1870. It, too, had its ups and downs, vast sums being expended with little returns. Later, however, it became a record producer, yielding a total estimated $45 million in gold. In this century modern equipment was installed, including a second hoist at the 4,600-foot level of its vertical shaft, which reached an

Tailing Wheel, Kennedy Tailing Wheels Park, Jackson

place became prosperous and many brick and stone structures were put up, none of which survive.

Irishtown (SRL 38), seven miles northeast of Jackson at the junction of SR 88 and the Clinton Road, has also vanished, and the story of its lively citizens is almost forgotten. The first white settlers on this spot found it a "city of wigwams," and hundreds of mortars in the rocks testify that this was an established Indian encampment. Pine Grove lies two miles beyond.

Ione Valley

Ione was variously known in the gold rush days as "Bed Bug" and "Freeze Out." But the place grew, and the more euphonious name of Ione replaced the older ones. Ione is a heroine in the Bulwer Lytton novel *The Last Days of Pompeii*, and some believe this is the source of the town's name; others cite Ione in Illinois, perhaps the home of an early pioneer. One also hears of William Hicks, who came to California with the Chiles-Walker party in 1843, and for a while settled in the area. He was the first to prospect the valley, which he left in 1850. When asked by a visitor who owned all the land, Hicks is said to have replied, "I own it," giving rise to another Amador County tall tale.

Ione was a supply center, not a gold town, and as agriculture gradually made headway throughout the state, the town prospered. The town's first school and its Methodist Episcopal church were both started here in 1852. When a larger church structure was needed, Bishop Matthew Simpson laid the cornerstone in 1862 for a striking brick building of Gothic design (SRL 506), which was completed in 1866. Among the old business buildings lining the streets of Ione, the Daniel Stewart Store (SRL 788) from 1856 is the oldest; it was operated by the Stewart family until they sold the business in 1973. A double structure across Main Street houses the Masonic Lodge Hall on the second-floor west and the Native Sons of the Golden West Hall on the second-floor east. The Scully home on West Marlette Street dates from the 1850's and has been lived in by the Scully family since 1882. Charles Howard Park has been the scene of Ione's homecoming picnic since 1876; held on the first weekend in May, this is one of California's longest-established community events.

The Preston School of Industry was built between 1890 and 1894 as a school for juveniles referred by the courts; it is now a facility of the California Youth Authority. The principal building (SRL 867), known locally as "The Castle," is the major example of Romanesque Revival architecture in the Mother Lode. The old building no longer houses inmates, although it is still part of the large institution. The California Division of Forestry

ultimate depth of 5,912 feet before mining was stopped. A half-mile east of the Kennedy Mine are four huge tailing wheels, used to raise the tailings, or mill waste, to the summit of a small hill, beyond which lay the disposal dump. Built in 1902, these wheels are among the most photographed landmarks in the Mother Lode Country; they are located in Kennedy Tailing Wheels Park, operated by the city of Jackson on North Main Street.

North and east of Jackson, remnants of several smaller mining camps may still be found among the hills. Clinton (SRL 37), eight miles east of Jackson, with its Catholic church built in 1877, is now surrounded by small ranches. Many miners were attracted to the region after water had been brought in through canals in the 1850's, but the diggings were never rich; this was a center for quartz mining as late as the 1880's.

On the Clinton Road, five miles east of Jackson, Slabtown exists only as a site. Formerly a rich mining area, it is now a prosperous agricultural community known as Milligan District. The first citizens of Slabtown were too poor to afford anything better than shacks of rough slabs of wood with the bark left on; later the

Fire Academy was established in Ione in 1967 and is another major state facility in the town.

Muletown, about two miles north of Ione, was a lively camp in the 1850's, and many stories are told of the strikes in its rich foothill ravines: an Argentinian washed out $100 a day there; a Chinese miner, picking up a piece of gold weighing 36 ounces, was so elated that he immediately left for his homeland. After the ravines had been worked out, the surrounding hills were attacked by hydraulic power and outdid the ravines in treasure produced. Some claims paid as high as $1,000 per week per man. During its palmy days Muletown claimed several hundred inhabitants, a large proportion of them Irish. There is nothing left of the place today.

Nor does anything remain of the Q Ranch, Irish Hill, or Quincy, all of which were important for a while and then vanished; their sites are to the north and west of Ione in the vicinity of SR 104. A new state prison is under construction in the area that will include some of this territory within its grounds and there are plans for the land to be annexed to the city of Ione.

Butte County

Butte County (named for the Sutter Buttes, the high hills to the south, in Sutter County) is one of the original 27 counties of the state, at first encompassing an area much larger than it does today. The first county seat was at Hamilton, but in 1853 it was moved to Bidwell's Bar, and again in 1856 to Oroville.

U-I-No, the Cliff of the Giant

U-I-No, familiarly known today as Bald Rock, in the Grand Gorge of the Middle Fork of the Feather River near where Fall River empties into the larger stream, was believed by ancient Indian tribes to be the home of a giant evil spirit. Towering sheer above the seething river for 3,600 feet, utterly devoid of vegetation, its white granite majesty resembles that of El Capitan in Yosemite Valley.

The entire region is one of spectacular beauty and is so wild and rugged that Indians, early white explorers, and prospecting miners either avoided or failed to penetrate it. In 1889 Emery Oliver, later a great railroad engineer, ran a survey through the entire Middle Fork Canyon, including that portion now known as Bald Rock Canyon. In 1908, two Geological Survey men also passed through it. There are immense granite boulders, deep caverns, and, above all, the superb beauty of Feather Falls, one of the most imposing of Sierra waterfalls. The falls drop sheer 500 feet, with an additional 200 feet of cascades, and fill the canyon with heavy mist and iridescent lights for half a mile. The area is now Feather Falls Scenic Area within Plumas National Forest; Bald Rock Canyon on the Middle Fork of the Feather River has been designated a Wild River. Feather Falls can be reached by trail from the village of Feather Falls, about three miles to the east; another way to see the falls is by boat from the surface of Lake Oroville.

Rancho Chico

John Bidwell came to California in 1841 as one of the leaders of the first overland company of Americans to come to California with the intention of making it their home.

On his arrival, Bidwell was employed for a time by John A. Sutter at Sutter's Fort, but in the late 1840's he bought Rancho Chico from William Dickey and Edward A. Farwell, the original grantees of Rancho Arroyo Chico and of the Farwell Grant, both made in 1844. On Rancho Chico Bidwell built a brick mansion that is now a State Historic Park. On his ranch he founded the town of Chico in 1860, later donating land for public schools, set-

Bidwell Mansion, Bidwell Mansion State Historic Park, Chico

ting aside a plot of ground for each church organization, and designating a large section for the Northern Branch State Normal School, started in 1887, which is today California State University at Chico.

John Bidwell was one of the foremost builders of the commonwealth of California. He was a member of the senate and served in the state militia during the Civil War, where he attained the rank of general, by which title he was often known in later years. He was a pioneer agriculturist and horticulturist, and a man interested in humanitarian, educational, and reform movements. He was three times nominated for governor and in 1892 won the nomination for President of the United States on the Prohibition ticket, receiving the largest number of votes of any one ever nominated by that party. But after serving a single term in Congress from 1865 to 1867, he was never again elected to public office. During his term in Washington, he met Annie E. Kennedy, of an old Washington family. They were married in a wedding attended by President Andrew Johnson and many prominent persons of the day before going to California, where they spent the remainder of their long lives.

General Bidwell had a reputation for being friendly to the Indians, treating them fairly, providing rancheria lands, hiring them to work on his estate, settling disputes, and providing both cultural and material advantages. He and his wife maintained a school and a church for the use of the Indians.

On the site of the Mechoopda adobe, built for Bidwell on Rancho Chico (SRL 329), a marker has been placed by the Pioneer Historical Society and the Native Sons of the Golden West, assisted by the Chico Chapter of the D.A.R., in honor of General Bidwell. The marker also commemorates the fact that the Oregon Emigrant Trail passed the place.

Treaty G, one of the eighteen unratified treaties of the United States government with the California Indians, was drawn up and signed at Rancho Chico on August 1, 1851. These treaties, made in 1851–52 by duly authorized agents of the federal government in the administration of President Millard Fillmore, were pigeonholed in the archives of Congress during the California gold rush and were not brought to light until 1905. They covered scattered areas throughout California.

Beginning as early as 1847 and continuing until his death, General Bidwell maintained an experimental orchard near his house. It contained at least one specimen of over 400 varieties of fruit and at the time of his death in 1900 included 1,800 acres of every species and variety adapted to the locality. He was the father of the raisin industry in that region as well as a pioneer in the manufacture of olive oil. He began wine making in 1864

or 1865, but after his marriage to the ardently prohibitionist Annie Kennedy, the vineyard was dug up and no wine grape was ever again planted on his land. In 1886 Bidwell presented some 30 acres of land to the state as a forestry experiment station. The gift was neglected by the State Forestry Commission and in time came to be owned by the city of Chico. The site has been marked by a plaque (SRL 840.2) at Cedar Grove and East Eighth streets in Bidwell Park.

The entire estate of Rancho Chico was remarkable for its splendid trees, both native and exotic. On July 10, 1905, five years after the General's death, a tract of the most desirable land along Big Chico Creek comprising more than 1,900 acres and including Oak Forest, Iron Canyon, and other spots of great beauty was donated to the city of Chico by Mrs. Bidwell and was named Bidwell Park. In 1911 Mrs. Bidwell added another 301 acres to the gift, making Bidwell Park the second-largest city park within California, after Los Angeles's Griffith Park. She also donated an area along Lindo Channel to the state of California; this is now held by Butte County as an undeveloped park area. Two miles southeast of the city are 240 acres owned by the United States Department of Agriculture and used as an experimental station.

Four miles northeast of downtown Chico, off Manzanita Avenue near Hooker Oak Avenue, is the site of the mammoth Hooker Oak (SRL 313), perhaps the most famous of California's valley oaks (*Quercus lobata*, the largest of all the American oaks). The tree was named in honor of the great English botanist Sir Joseph Hooker, who visited Rancho Chico in 1877. Just one hundred years later, the tree, badly damaged by a storm in 1962, finally toppled. The valley oaks were discovered in 1792 by Spanish naval officers and were often mentioned in the narratives of Vancouver, Frémont, and other early explorers. In its prime, the Hooker Oak was calculated to be over 100 feet tall and 28 feet around its base.

Chico

Chico, named for the rancho and the creek (Chico being Spanish for "little"), is today a bustling city centered on the university and surrounded by prosperous farmlands. The older district of the city, shaded by fine trees, contains some interesting old buildings. The Gage house at 410 Normal Avenue, built in 1861, is the oldest standing in town. Nearby is the Stansbury House at 307 West Fifth Street, built in 1883 for Dr. Oscar Stansbury of Mississippi. Dr. Stansbury practiced medicine for many years in Chico; his daughter Angelina, on her death in 1974, bequeathed the home to the city of Chico. It is open to the public and maintained by a preservation association. The Masonic Hall at 131 West First Street is the oldest (1871) public building still standing, although a portion of the Bidwell Building, ten years older, is still extant within the structure at 100 Broadway. The City Plaza bounded by Broadway, Main, Third, and Fourth streets was General Bidwell's gift to the new city at the time of its incorporation in 1872, although the plans for a county courthouse on the square never materialized since Oroville held on to its position as the seat of government. Local tradition has it that the elms shading the plaza today were planted by Bidwell himself. The handsome Main Post Office (1915) on the plaza is now on the National Register of Historic Places.

Of particular interest are two old cemeteries. The Mechoopda Indian Tribal Cemetery on West Sacramento Avenue at Mechoopda Street is close to the site of the old Mechoopda Indian village. Annie Bidwell established a church near the site in the early 1870's, and the cemetery was begun about that time. The Mechoopda Tribal Association still maintains and uses the old cemetery. Unfortunately, many of the older graves are no longer marked. At 700 Camellia Way is the Chico Cemetery, dating from 1860. It was begun as a Bidwell family plot (both the General and Mrs. Bidwell are buried there); relatives and family servants were also interred there, and in time it became the city burial ground, some 35 acres in extent.

The Chico Museum at Salem and Second streets has, among other displays, parts of a Chinese temple reconstructed from the days when a large Chinese community ("Chinatown") was part of many northern California towns. The state university campus is a particularly attractive one to visit. The administration building (1929) is the oldest part of the campus; it replaced the Normal School building of 1887, which was destroyed by fire in 1927.

Chico Landing, first known as Bidwell's Landing, where steamers plying the Sacramento River unloaded, was an important place in the 1850's. It was located on nearby Rancho de Farwell, about five miles west of the present city of Chico.

Rancho Esquón

The headquarters of Rancho Esquón, granted to Samuel Neal and John A. Sutter in 1844, were located on Butte Creek seven miles south of Chico. Neal, a native of Pennsylvania, had come to California with Frémont earlier in 1844, and with the latter's permission had remained at Sutter's Fort as a blacksmith. Two years later, in April 1846, Neal entertained Frémont on Rancho Esquón, while the Captain was on his way to Oregon.

The next month Neal helped guide Gillespie up the Sacramento Valley in an attempt to overtake Frémont and to deliver to him certain instructions from the government in Washington.

Hamilton

Hamilton was a mining town situated on a bend in the Feather River above Marysville. Its story is characteristic of many ghost towns on the Feather River and in other old mining regions. The first mining was done at this point in the early spring of 1848 by John Bidwell and others. By 1849, mining for gold in the river became active and a town grew up.

Hamilton won over Bidwell's Bar in the contest for county seat in 1850, but, as the latter town (25 miles farther up the river) became richer and more prosperous, people left Hamilton, and Bidwell's Bar became the county seat in 1853. Within the old cemetery, largely of the Moore family, is a monument erected in 1917 to mark the first county seat of Butte County. There is nothing else left of Hamilton today. Part of its site disappeared as the river changed its course. Just above the site was a settlement of Chinese miners, who worked in the same red hills that over a century later were the source of clay for the impervious layer in the construction of Oroville Dam.

Bidwell's Bar, the Oroville Dam, and Lake Oroville

Bidwell's Bar (SRL 330) was one of the many flourishing mining camps along the Feather River in the Sierra Nevada in the 1850's. Gold was discovered there by John Bidwell in July 1848. The camp was located on the Middle Fork of the Feather River, 39 miles above the town of Marysville. In 1853 three daily stages ran to Bidwell's Bar directly from Marysville. As the mines at Bidwell's Bar became more or less exhausted, the inhabitants moved down the river to Ophir City, later called Oroville, where rich deposits were found. Oroville became the county seat in 1856, succeeding Bidwell's Bar, where the seat of government had been located since 1853.

The Oroville Dam is called the Keystone of the California Water Project, authorized by legislative action in the 1950's. The purpose of the project is threefold: to impound and distribute water, to create sources of electrical energy, and to make new recreational facilities. The Oroville Dam was completed in 1968. At 770 feet, it is the highest earthfill dam in the world and the highest dam of any kind in the United States. The waters of Lake Oroville, which the dam has created, cover an area of 24 square miles with over 160 miles of shore line.

The "Mother Orange Tree," Lake Oroville Recreation Area

Bidwell Bar Suspension Bridge and Toll House, Bidwell Canyon Marina

Three relics of Bidwell's Bar, which now lies beneath the waters of the lake, have been preserved. The "Mother Orange Tree," planted at Bidwell's Bar in 1856 by Judge Joseph Lewis, is probably the oldest living orange tree in California. It still bears fruit. It was carefully moved and successfully replanted at the State Division of Water Resources headquarters on Glen Drive off Oroville Dam Boulevard, about a mile east of Oroville proper. The suspension bridge (SRL 314) and brick toll house that once were at Bidwell's Bar have been relocated at the Bidwell Canyon Marina on Lake Oroville. The bridge, the first of its kind in California, was shipped around the Horn from New York in 1853 and installed in 1856.

Mining Camps of the South Fork of the Feather River

On the South Fork of the Feather River above Bidwell's Bar were other mining camps. Stringtown, about four miles east, was so called because its buildings were strung out in a narrow, rambling line along the canyon. Its history is brief and phenomenal. Dating from 1849, it had become very populous by 1850. In July 1856 the *Butte Record* published its obituary in the following words: "The string of Stringtown has been pulled out."

About seven miles east of Stringtown on the river was Forbestown, founded in September 1850 by B. F. Forbes. It was a center of mining activities for 30 to 40 years. It was a town of some cultural importance also, with a private academy and a general assembly hall, where lectures were given during the week and where large congregations gathered for services on Sunday. This once bustling camp could be described about 1930 as "a derelict town lost in a mountain cove where a second growth of timber is fast replacing a one-time virgin forest. Heaps of debris and old foundations mark the sites of large buildings that have collapsed or been torn down. Other structures with crumbling roofs and gaping doors are verging on dissolution." Today the only noteworthy landmark remaining is the restored Masonic Hall, built in 1855. Old Forbestown is now reached by a side road, a mile or so north of the present post office and stores that perpetuate the name Forbestown. Near Forbestown is Clipper Mills, an early lumber camp, on the La Porte Road.

Oroville, the City of Gold

The first miners came to the site of Oroville on the Feather River in 1849, and in 1850 a mining camp was formed there that was named Ophir City. By 1856 the town had been renamed Oroville, and its importance had increased so considerably that it was ambitious to be chosen as the county seat. Since Bidwell's Bar, then the county seat, was waning as a mining center, Oroville received the honor by popular election. The new county seat soon became a trading center for the mining towns in the surrounding hills, along Table Mountain, and up the Feather River.

Immediately east of Oroville were important river mining operations in the 1850's and some years after. The river was diverted from its course in order that the gravel of the bed might be mined. From Oroville to the junction of the North and Middle forks of the Feather River the most extensive activities of this kind in California were carried on, but all evidence of this is under Lake Oroville now.

Several miles above Oroville was Long's Bar, founded in 1849 with the establishment of a store by the Long brothers. The first pan of gold washed out at Long's Bar netted $400. The place became one of the principal settlements of the region during the 1850's. A marker was placed at Long's Bar in 1982 by the Butte County Historical Society, the Masons, and E Clampus Vitus. At the Cape Claim, in 1855, the fluming of the river is said to have netted $1,000,000 in 60 days. Lynchburg, another thriving camp with rich surface diggings, was located in this vicinity. It was a rival of Oroville in the contest for county seat, putting forth the claim of a superior climate. Centerville, or Middletown, was a camp near the site of the Southern Pacific depot in the present city of Oroville. Thompson's Flat, first called Rich Gulch and mined as early as 1848, had so increased in population by 1854 that the town, then called New Philadelphia, was moved to the top of the hill, which still bears the name of Thompson. Morris Ravine, near Thompson's Flat, also saw some of the earliest mining in the county.

Because of all this activity up and down the river, Oroville had become a stage center of some importance by 1856, as is indicated by an article in the *North Californian* for November of that year: "Coaches are rattling through our streets at all hours of the day and night. We have ten, semi-daily, connecting this place with different parts of the world. There are six daily stages to Marysville, three for Spanishtown, one for Shasta, one for Bidwell, one for Forbestown, one for Bangor." Numerous pack animals also traveled up and down the highways and along the narrow trails into the higher mountains where no wagon roads yet led.

In February 1857, the *Gazelle* arrived at Oroville, the first of the river steamers to penetrate that far. The last steamboats arrived there during the flood of 1862.

Beginning in the late 1850's and continuing through the 1880's, hydraulic mining was the chief activity at Oroville and Cherokee and in the surrounding country. Evidence of extensive hydraulic operations may still be seen in the form of canals, ditches, old flumes, and deeply scarred hills.

The decline of hydraulic mining was followed by the development of the gold-dredging industry, which originated at Oroville and from there spread around the world. The great gravel fields about the city give some idea of the extent of the industry, which gleaned many millions in gold from the land. One dredging company offered to move the entire town of Oroville and rebuild it at the company's expense if it might be allowed to dredge beneath the town and remove the great treasure trove over which the city had been built. Oroville today

is nurtured by the rich agricultural region nearby and by tourism and vacation activities generated by the Lake Oroville State Recreational Area, but some mining is still carried on in neighboring towns in the hills. When the Oroville Dam was built, much material for its construction came from the tailings left by the gold dredges.

Oroville's Chinatown, said to have housed 10,000 souls, was one of California's largest, second only to San Francisco at one time. The Chinese Temple (SRL 770), dedicated in the spring of 1863, is now open as a museum, having been restored by Oroville women's clubs; it is located at 1500 Broderick Street. A few blocks away is the Lott House in Sank Park, 1067 Montgomery Street, owned and maintained by the city of Oroville. The restored Victorian Gothic house, built in 1856, was lived in by the same family until 1961 and is open to the public on a regular basis. The gardens are maintained in a formal Victorian style. The Ehmann Home, built in 1911 at 1480 Lincoln Street, is now the headquarters of the Butte County Historical Society. The Butte County Pioneer Memorial Museum at 2300 Montgomery Street contains much material relating to early days in a building fashioned like a miner's cabin.

About two miles east of Oroville, on the Oroville-Quincy Highway just north of its junction with SR 162 (Olive Highway), is the site (SRL 809) of the discovery of Ishi, last of the Yahi tribe and the last known Indian of California to have lived without contact with white settlers. On August 29, 1911, the emaciated survivor of years of wandering and persecution stumbled into the corral of a slaughterhouse at this location. He was at first lodged in jail but fortunately came into the hands of two University of California anthropologists, Thomas T. Waterman and Alfred L. Kroeber, who provided a home for him until his death in 1916. Ishi made an extremely valuable contribution to our knowledge of California Indian languages, history, and customs.

Cherokee

The old town of Cherokee is ten miles north of Oroville and one mile west of that stretch of Lake Oroville that was formerly the West Branch of the Feather River. The Spring Valley Gold Mine here was the largest hydraulic gold mine in California at one time. Diamonds were found in the diggings around Cherokee as early as 1853. Over 300 diamonds, mostly of industrial quality, have been discovered there; at no other place in North America has an equal number been found. Stone walls and a vault still mark the site of the Spring Valley Mine and Assay Office, a picturesque remnant of for-

Spring Valley Mine and Assay Office, Cherokee

mer days. The well-kept Pioneer Cemetery at Cherokee is overlooked by the massive bulk of Table Mountain, a remarkable picture in the spring when wildflowers cover its flanks. The Cherokee Museum is situated in what was once a boarding house for miners, and is one of the many small, charming, and informative museums one encounters throughout California.

Oregon City and Yankee Hill

Scores of mining camps were once located in the hill region north of Oroville. The early locations on the river bars were followed by those on the flats somewhat back from the streams, and finally the ridges and hills were worked. In some instances, the names of these camps remain to mark their location, but often even the name has been forgotten. Throughout the Feather River district the remains of crudely constructed fireplaces, sometimes found in lonely and forgotten places, are almost the only evidence of pioneer habitation.

As early as the autumn of 1848 gold-seekers from Oregon began to arrive, the first from outside California. Their presence in the mining regions is evidenced by the names of Oregon City and Oregon Gulch, halfway between Oroville and Cherokee on Derrick Road. Oregon City (SRL 807) no longer has many inhabitants, but there are impressive restorations there. The 1877 schoolhouse was in service until 1922, when it became a community hall. In 1981 it was acquired by E Clampus Vitus and the Butte County Historical Society, and it has been restored as a historical museum. The covered bridge one crosses to reach the school grounds is not a cherished relic from the past, as is everywhere else the case in California, but a new (1982) structure, a replica of a previous structure.

Perhaps the liveliest of these North Feather River

camps was Spanishtown, so named because the rich diggings in the vicinity had been discovered in 1855 by Spanish-speaking Chileans and Mexicans. By 1856 a town had sprung up, twenty miles north of Oroville and one mile from Frenchtown, that in turn became the chief town of the region, Yankee Hill. Old Yankee Hill lies to the east of SR 70 and newer Yankee Hill to the west a mile north, where modern retirement homes are to be seen under the old oaks.

Magalia, Paradise, and Inskip

Twenty-five miles north of Oroville on the West Branch of the Feather River was Dogtown, now the thriving community of Magalia. An old French woman, so one story goes, lived in the area with a kennel of hounds, poodles, and mastiffs that were known all over the countryside. (The E Clampus Vitus plaque at the center of town says she was Mrs. Basset, with no reference to her nationality.) The name Dogtown was applied not only to the town but to the entire ridge as well. Two miles east of the town a gold nugget was discovered in 1859 that is said to have been the largest ever found in Butte County. This "Dogtown Nugget" weighed 54 pounds in the rough and was valued at $10,690. On the Skyway near Magalia a monument points to the site of the discovery of the Dogtown Nugget (SRL 771). The old brown-shingled church at Magalia, also a community center, is on the National Register of Historic Places.

About five miles southwest of Dogtown is Paradise, the only one of the old communities in the region that is a major town today. It began to grow rapidly after the completion of the Butte County Railroad from Chico to Stirling City in 1902. Then it was a center of the apple industry; today its population has swelled primarily because of the great influx of retired people who have discovered that its clear air and wooded hills make it truly a "paradise" for their golden years. A few miles west of Paradise on Honey Run Road from Chico, the Honey Run covered bridge crosses Butte Creek. Built in 1894, the bridge is a local landmark, well restored today and in a county park.

Exceptionally rich diggings were found in the late 1850's at Lovelock, nine miles north of Dogtown, and at Inskip, twelve miles north of Lovelock. These communities are all linked today by the Skyway, a good modern highway leading from SR 99 south of Chico to Inskip. Inskip is today a very small community, but its hotel is still in operation and is listed on the National Register of Historic Places. The E Clampus Vitus plaque on the hotel notes that this structure, built in 1869, is the only one remaining of the five hotels that once served the district.

Two other "Clamper" plaques on the Skyway south of Inskip commemorate Stirling City and DeSabla. The former was established by the Diamond Match Company, which in 1902 built the railroad to the town, named for the Stirling boilers used to heat the first workers' quarters. Eugene J. DeSabla, Jr., was the engineer who is sometimes called the "Father of the Pacific Gas and Electric Company." The DeSabla Reservoir nearby is part of the huge power project that DeSabla began around 1900 and that ultimately became absorbed into the present-day corporation.

Dogtown was only one of a number of mining camps and stage stations on the road from Oroville to Susanville. Twelve miles north of Oroville, Manoah Pence and several partners located the Lyon ranch in 1850, opening a store and an eating place in a tent. The place grew and by 1864 a post office, under the name of Pentz, had been established there, with Pence as post-master. Butte Community College, founded in 1968, is on SR 191 three miles west of Pentz; its present campus opened in 1974.

Bangor and Wyandotte

Bangor, ten miles southeast of Oroville, was settled in 1855 by the Lambert brothers from Bangor, Maine. With the discovery of the Blue Lead Mine it became quite important, consisting of 50 buildings. An 1880's one-room frame church there has been acquired by the Butte County Historical Society and is now a local history museum. Northwest of Bangor was Wyandotte, named after a company of Wyandotte Indians who mined there in 1850. It reached its greatest prosperity around 1853; in 1857 its "magnificent brick fireproof hotel" was cited as the only of its kind in the county. Bangor and Wyandotte are today centers of the orange and olive industries, and the old mining ditches are used for irrigation.

Calaveras County

Calaveras County took its name from the river named by Gabriel Moraga on his expedition of 1808. Moraga had noticed exposed skulls (in Spanish, *calaveras*) along the banks of the river. Calaveras was one of the original 27 counties. Pleasant Valley, later known as Double Springs, was designated by the legislature as the first county seat on February 18, 1850, and was followed successively by Jackson, Mokelumne Hill, and finally San Andreas in 1866.

Wayside Inns

Along the old Mokelumne Hill road from Stockton by way of Linden (now SR 26), many a wayside inn refreshed the traveler of early gold days. Just one-third of a mile east of the San Joaquin–Calaveras county line was the famous Red House, a two-story hostelry, no longer standing. Its stone corral (SRL 263), however, is intact today. Beyond Stone Corral, on the old river road to Jenny Lind, was the Pleasant Valley House, a two-story building since destroyed by fire. Halfway between Jenny Lind and Valley Springs on the north side of the road and across from the headquarters of present-day Rancho Calaveras was the North America House, where the stage horses were changed; a mile and a half below the North America was the Tremont House, built of lumber brought around the Horn. The Spring Valley House, between Valley Springs and San Andreas, about one-half mile above Mountain Gate, was a two-story structure with barns and corrals. None of these old hostelries still exists.

The Kentucky House, about two miles south of San Andreas and the center of mining activities on the South Fork of the Calaveras River, was a stage stop between Sonora and Sacramento. The Calaveras Cement Company now has a plant there. The original Kentucky House was destroyed by fire, but a later building was erected on the same site and has been remodeled by the cement company as a clubhouse.

Double Springs

Double Springs (SRL 264), one of the ghost towns of the Mother Lode mining region, became a thriving center after it was named county seat in 1850. Neighboring towns, however, were also growing and soon wished to hold this coveted position. One of these was Jackson (then in Calaveras County), north of the Mokelumne

River. The story of the contest for the position of county seat is typical of what took place in various parts of the state during the pioneer period. In July 1851, a few ambitious young men at Jackson drove over to Double Springs, where some of their number treated the county clerk quite liberally at the tavern bar. Meanwhile the others went to the building used as a courthouse, loaded the archives into their wagon, and hurried back across the river to Jackson. Although this high-handed action was illegal, Jackson retained its position until April 16, 1852, when by popular election Mokelumne Hill took first place. It is said that the votes cast were "out of all proportion to the number of voters."

In 1854 Amador County was separated from Calaveras County, and Jackson became the county seat of the new county. In 1866 San Andreas was given that honor in Calaveras County, in place of Mokelumne Hill, and it remains the county seat today.

Double Springs lies at the junction of SR 12 and SR 26, about four miles east of Valley Springs. The two springs for which the town was named still keep green the meadow that lies between the low hills. Here, surrounded by oleanders, orange trees, and aged locusts, stands the lovely old mansion of squared sandstone built in 1860 by Alexander R. Wheat. On the hill across the road, under the shadow of a great live oak, is the family cemetery where he lies. The building that was the county courthouse when Double Springs was the county seat is behind the Wheat house and is no longer open to the public.

Angels Camp

Angels Camp (SRL 287), named for its founder, Henry Angel, retains several iron-shuttered stone buildings reminiscent of the early gold days. Some of the

St. Vasilije Serbian Orthodox Church, Angels Camp

Main Street, Angels Camp

most noteworthy landmarks are Angels Hotel, the Stickels Store (1856), and the famous Utica Mine, which was originally sold for a song and which later produced millions during its great period from 1893 to 1916. Utica Park stands over the site of the mine; the Utica Mansion nearby, built in 1882, is on the National Register of Historic Places. At the north edge of town stands St. Vasilije Serbian Orthodox Church (1910), one of the first of that denomination to be built in California.

In January 1865 Mark Twain, stopping at Angels Hotel (SRL 734), obtained the nucleus for his famous story "The Celebrated Jumping Frog of Calaveras County." The story was told him by Ben Coon, a bartender at the hotel. The present hotel was built in 1855, its predecessor (known as the Lake Hotel) having been destroyed by the disastrous fire of that year. A bronze frog surmounts the marker in front of the hotel. Since 1928, a Jumping Frog Contest has been held annually at Angels Camp; in recent years it has been combined with the

Calaveras County Fair, held on the third weekend in May in nearby Frogtown.

Bret Harte

Francis Brett Harte (1836–1902) made a sizable reputation for himself as a storyteller of the Mother Lode. His actual connection with the area was rather tenuous, limited to about two months late in 1855, but from this visit he gathered impressions that he reworked for many years to come, both in California and in England, where he spent his last years. His popularity was greater in places such as London, where few people had any knowledge of actual conditions in the West, than in California, where critics agreed that his stories showed little intimate knowledge of mines or miners. Among the locations in Calaveras County that are believed to have influenced him are Angels Camp, McLean's Bar (a now-vanished spot on the Stanislaus River), and Fourth Crossing.

Carson Hill

Carson Hill (SRL 274), about four miles south of Angels Camp, has been called "the classic mining ground of California," for it was considered to be the richest camp in all the Mother Lode. There in November 1854 a mass of gold was found at Morgan Mine weighing 195 pounds and valued at $43,534, said to be the largest nugget in the United States. (It was really a pocket weathered out of a quartz vein, and not a nugget at all.)

Between Carson Hill and Hanselman's Hill at Albany Flat, about two miles south of Angels Camp on SR 49, is the elaborate James Romaggi stone house, built before 1856. It was located on the old road to Los Muertos, that wild camp on Arroyo de los Muertos ("creek of the dead") where the Battle of Six Mile Creek was waged between American and Mexican miners in the autumn of 1852. Los Muertos, with its predominant Mexican and Chilean population, is one of the many spots in California said to be a haunt of the bandit Joaquín Murieta.

The Morgan Mine on the north slope of Carson Hill produced some $26 million in gold, yielding a million dollars in a year as late as 1925. There are plans to revive mining in this region, which was unusually productive even by Mother Lode standards. James H. Carson, for whom Carson Hill and nearby Carson Flat on Carson Creek were all named, discovered gold on the flat as early as August 1848 and, according to his own report, panned 180 ounces of gold in a period of ten days.

On a two-ton mine car at Carson Hill a plaque has been mounted in honor of Archie Stevenot (SRL 769), member of a pioneer Carson Hill family, who was born half a mile to the west in 1882. One-time manager of the Carson Hill Mining Company, Stevenot in his retirement helped publicize the attractions of California's gold country and became affectionately known as "Mr. Mother Lode."

On the south slope of Carson Hill on the Stanislaus River is Melones (Spanish for "melons"). It was originally called Robinson's Ferry (SRL 276), the name Melones (from the shape of the gold found in the vicinity by Mexican miners) having been borrowed in 1902 from a former camp midway between Carson Hill and the present town of that name. In the summer of 1849, within six weeks' time, $10,000 in tolls was collected at Robinson's Ferry. The settlement of Melones today is on the shores of New Melones Lake, the Stanislaus River being impounded by the New Melones Dam a few miles to the south.

Altaville

Altaville (SRL 288) dates from 1852 and was formerly known as Cherokee Flat. It is located only one mile north of Angels Camp, and the two communities have grown to meet each other. D. D. Demarest established a foundry at Altaville in 1854, producing most of the stamp mills and a large part of the mining machinery erected in Calaveras and Tuolumne counties. After many years, the foundry closed and its buildings were pulled down in 1985 to make room for a shopping center. The outstanding landmark at Altaville is the Prince and Garibardi Store (SRL 735), built in 1857 and still a strikingly handsome stone building. The old red brick grammar school (SRL 499), erected in 1858 and used until 1950, is being restored by the Calaveras County Historical Society.

North of Murphys Grade Road about half a mile east of Altaville is Bald Hill, on the slope of which is the virtually hidden shaft of the old Mattison Mine. Here, at a depth of 150 feet, the famous Calaveras Skull was alleged to have been found by Mr. James Mattison, of Angels Camp, in February 1866. It was pronounced a genuine relic of prehistoric man by Professor J. D. Whitney, then state geologist of California, at a public meeting later that year. Many were unconvinced of the skull's real antiquity (Bret Harte's mocking poem "To the Pliocene Skull" expressed this sentiment), and modern research has placed the skull's origin in a less ancient cave burial.

Five miles northwest of Altaville and just west of SR 49 is Fourth Crossing (SRL 258). The old stone bridge, built in 1857, may be the oldest bridge still standing in California. Between Altaville and Fourth Crossing is the site of Hawkeye.

The Mokelumne Hill Region

Mokelumne Hill (SRL 269), perched on the top of a mountain above the Mokelumne River, is one of the most picturesque towns in the mining region. It was the county seat from 1852 to 1866 and was the leading town in the central Mother Lode at that period.

Several interesting old buildings remain from mining days, as well as some ruins. Outstanding among the buildings is the International Order of Odd Fellows Hall (SRL 256), formerly housing the Wells Fargo Office; its two lower floors were built in 1854 and the third story was added in 1861. The Leger Hotel includes the building that served as the courthouse of Calaveras County (SRL 663) from 1852 to 1866. When the county seat was moved to San Andreas, George W. Leger acquired the building and made it a part of his adjoining hotel, which had also been built in 1854, with a second story added in 1874. The Congregational Church (SRL 261) was erected in 1856, and is believed to be the oldest church building of that denomination in the state.

Overlooking the town of Mokelumne Hill is French Hill, the scene of one of the skirmishes in the so-called "French War" of 1851. The envy of Americans had been aroused by the good fortune of French miners throughout the region. On the pretext that they had hoisted the French flag and defied the American government, the French were attacked by a band of Americans. The defenders erected a temporary fort at French Hill, but the Yankee power prevailed and the French were expelled.

A mile and a half east of Mokelumne Hill a deteriorating stone building can be seen on the south side of SR 26; this was the winery of the Louis Baudin family, who lived across the road in a settlement, now gone, called Happy Valley. Just one-tenth of a mile east of this building a road branches to the right and leads 3.5 miles to the settlement of Jesus Maria (SRL 284) on the creek of the same name. Nearby a road sign indicates the junction of Jesus Maria Road with Whiskey Slide Road, this writer's favorite California intersection. Whiskey Slide, later called Clear View, and McDonald or Poverty Flat were now-vanished settlements in the region, which is still only sparsely populated.

A road going southwest from Mokelumne Hill leads to Campo Seco (SRL 257), a rich placer camp in early days. After the 1860's it was the site of the rich Penn Copper Mine. Although its heyday was the first two decades of the twentieth century, the Penn Mine was still producing copper after World War II. One of the state's oldest and largest cork oaks (*Quercus suber*) grows at Campo Seco. Stone ruins and the pioneer cemetery are reminders of the past. The road from Mokelumne Hill to Campo Seco passes through Paloma, an old mining town formerly called Fostoria (SRL 295). Beyond Campo Seco was Camanche (SRL 254), a picturesque community with several old stone buildings. It was leveled in 1964 for the construction of Camanche Reservoir of the East Bay Municipal Utility District. The graves from the cemetery of nearby Poverty Bar, now like Camanche under the water of the reservoir, were moved to the old Pioneer Cemetery near San Andreas and the People's Cemetery in San Andreas.

At Chili Gulch (SRL 265), two miles south of Mokelumne Hill on SR 49, a little group of Americans were driven from their claim by a superior force of Chileans in December 1849. Later American retaliation drove the Chileans out, but not before considerable diplomatic protests had been made by both the United States and the Chilean governments.

There are several places named "Rich Gulch" in Calaveras County. On the Lower Rich Gulch, which leads from Paloma to the Mokelumne River, is the famous Gwin mine, once owned by State Senator William Gwin, Jr., whose father and John C. Frémont were the first two United States senators from California. The mine was an excellent producer for many decades.

To the east of Mokelumne Hill is another Rich Gulch, a once populous camp of which little remains; six miles beyond that is Railroad Flat (SRL 286), once a placer and quartz-mining center, where a store, a post office, and a few of the old homes can be seen. A near neighbor was Independence Point (SRL 268), where numerous small but rich quartz ledges were once worked by Mexicans and other miners. It is now a quiet mountain community with many homes of retired people. A few old buildings in the business district are to be seen among newer ones. Two and one-half miles southeast of West Point on SR 26 is Sandy Gulch (SRL 253), where little more than an old cemetery remains. About nine miles northwest of Mokelumne Hill, where the road forks to West Point and Railroad Flat, is Glencoe (SRL 280), once called Mosquito Gulch. Near West Point (formerly Bummerville), the Blazing Star Mine is in operation once more, producing both gold and tungsten.

Murphys

The country around Murphys (SRL 275) was first mined in July 1848 by two brothers, Daniel and John Murphy, who came in the same company with Henry Angel and James Carson. Like others of the group, the Murphys struck out for themselves on reaching the diggings and set up camp at a site on Angel's Creek, which was soon known as Murphy's Diggings, later Murphy's Camp, and ultimately Murphys.

The town is one of the most photographed and painted in all the gold country; tree-shadowed Main Street is lined with historic old buildings, most of which are very much in operation today. The Peter L. Traver Building (SRL 466) was constructed in 1856; this, the oldest stone building in town, was the sole survivor of a disastrous fire in 1859. Today it houses the Old-Timers Museum, filled with artifacts from the town's past. The original portion of the Traver house on Jones Street was built before 1862. What is now the Murphys Hotel was originally Sperry and Perry's Hotel when it was built in 1856; damaged in the 1859 fire, it was restored and still serves as a hostelry. On Main Street may also be seen the Compere Trading Post (1860), now a private home, the Jones Apothecary Shop (1860), and the Thompson Building (1862). On the western exterior wall of the Thompson Building is the Wall of Comparative Ovations of E Clampus Vitus, which bears more than 70 plaques commemorating men, women, and events of California's history—certainly one of the most colorful and amusing historical commemorations in the state.

At 350 Main Street stands the Chase House (1862), where Albert A. Michelson lived as a child; he went on to become the first American scientist to be awarded the Nobel Prize (1907) for his pioneering work on the velocity of light. An E Clampus Vitus plaque commemorates him.

Two blocks north of Main Street, where it was missed by the great fire of 1859, stands St. Patrick's Catholic Church, built in 1858 with gold, contributions, and labor from the miners of Murphys. The present Congregational Church stands in a building completed in 1895 next to the original (now gone) church building of 1853, in use until 1896. The restored Masonic Temple on the next block of Church Street, on the site of an earlier temple (1862), dates from 1902. Near the eastern edge of town, by SR 4, the old Murphys School stands. Built in 1860, it was used for many years as an elementary school and now serves as an adult educational center. Murphys makes good use of its historical buildings.

West of Murphys is the site of French Gulch. One mile east of Murphys on Pennsylvanian Gulch Road was Brownsville (SRL 465), a thriving mining camp in the 1850's and 1860's. About one mile northwest of Murphys are Mercer's Caverns, notable limestone formations in several successive "rooms"; discovered by Walter Mercer of Murphys in 1885, the caverns are open as a commercial attraction.

From Murphys, SR 4 climbs northeast up the Sierra Nevada about twenty miles to the famous Calaveras Big Trees State Park, a beautiful stand of the *Sequoia gigantea*, the larger of the two species of California sequoias. While on a scouting expedition in 1841, John Bidwell came upon one of the fallen giants of the Calaveras, the first white man known to have seen this grove. This reserve actually contains both a North and a South Grove, acquired by the state in 1931 and 1954, respectively. The park now contains 5,437 acres of forest and meadow.

San Andreas

In most of the present-day Mother Lode towns one finds old and new structures within a neighborhood, and townspeople daily pass in the shadow of historic buildings. San Andreas (SRL 252) is an exception; the older area remains a small enclave. The Calaveras County Museum and Archives Building, at 30 North Main Street, was once the County Hall of Records. It stands next to the old two-story brick County Courthouse; both of these buildings are now part of the county historic center. The Odd Fellows Building dates from 1856, and the Cassinelli adobe (now disguised as a white wood-framed apartment house) is nearly as old.

About eight miles east of San Andreas is El Dorado (SRL 282) or Mountain Ranch, where some of the old adobe buildings from mining days are still standing. The Domenghini family has operated a general store here since 1901, in the building that was the Domenghini Saloon, erected in the 1850's. This was the loca-

Old Courthouse and Hall of Records, Calaveras County Museum, San Andreas

tion of an early sawmill. The original Mountain Ranch post office was located about a mile west of here but was moved to the town of El Dorado in 1868. Southeast of here was Cave City (SRL 956), the first cave in California to be operated as a commercial attraction. When the mines there gave out, its school was moved to El Dorado, but the district retained the name of Cave City. Between Mountain Ranch and Murphys is Sheep Ranch, one of several profitable investments made by Senator George Hearst. By the time the mine closed in 1942, it had produced more than $8 million in gold and reached 3,100 feet in depth. A plaque placed by E Clampus Vitus commemorates the Sheep Ranch Mine.

Six miles southeast of San Andreas are Old Gulch and Calaveritas (SRL 255), where one old adobe building stands and the ruins of others are to be seen. The region is one of great tranquillity, showing no trace of the twentieth century beyond the rather worn road.

Three miles northwest of San Andreas is Cottage Spring, and three miles west are North Branch and Central Hill, noted for their once productive gravel mines. Farther west is Valley Springs (SRL 251), founded in 1884 when the railroad was constructed in this area. The large stone Late Ranch House was built in 1862 by the Scottish stonemason William Watt, who built several other homes in the vicinity including the Wheat home in Double Springs. The town of Valley Springs was laid out on property formerly belonging to the Late Ranch.

On the main road about two miles west of San Andreas on the south bank of the North Fork of the Calaveras River is the old Pioneer Cemetery (SRL 271), the oldest in the county and, sadly, much vandalized.

Vallecito

Vallecito ("Little Valley," SRL 273) is about five miles east of Angels Camp. A few landmarks from mining days remain, among them the Dinkelspiel Store (originally Cohen and Levy's Store), still in operation after more than a century. There is also an old church bell, which was brought up from San Francisco by an itinerant preacher in the early days. The bell was mounted on a large oak tree, and every Sunday morning scores of miners answered its summons. The bell is now mounted on top of a stone monument (SRL 370).

To the north, between Vallecito and Murphys, is Douglas Flat (SRL 272), on the so-called Central Hill Channel, an ancient river deposit extending through the middle of the county from which vast quantities of gold have been taken. The old Gagliardo Building (1862), once a store and bank, is a roadside landmark here; the identifying sign is misspelled "Gilleado."

Jenny Lind and Copperopolis

Jenny Lind (SRL 266), on the north bank of the Calaveras River, was once the center of most of the mining operations on the lower Calaveras; today it is a pleasant community of new and old homes. A few stone and adobe ruins remain from earlier days. Six miles south of Jenny Lind is Milton (SRL 262), the first town in Calaveras County to be connected to the railroad. The Southern Pacific arrived in 1871, and Milton was born. From here freight and passengers were conveyed by wagon and stage to other parts of the county.

Prior to the discovery of the large copper deposits in the northern part of the state, Copperopolis (SRL 296), in the southwestern part of Calaveras County, was the principal copper-producing center in California. In 1867 it boasted a population of nearly 2,000 and had three schools, two churches, four hotels, and stores and workshops of all kinds. A fire in September 1867 destroyed much of the town, and it was never rebuilt, the mines having closed in the same discouraging year. The town of today retains memories of its one-time importance in the disintegrating smelters, chutes, and shafts of the old mines, in the handful of brick stores flanking the highway, and in the pioneer Congregational Church, which has been the community center since the 1950's. The neighboring Copperopolis Armory, an imposing brick structure, was built in 1861 to train troops in the days of the Civil War; it is now part of the community center. Near Copperopolis, at Funk Hill, Black Bart, the "gentleman bandit," committed his last stage robbery in 1883.

On the road from Copperopolis to Mountain Pass was O'Byrne's (or Byrne's) Ferry (SRL 281). The ferry of pioneer days was supplanted by a covered bridge, which spanned the Stanislaus for almost a century. The structure, 210 feet in length, was removed in 1957 when Tulloch Dam was constructed. The little triangular valley, shared with neighboring Tuolumne County, hemmed in by steep and rugged mountain slopes covered with chaparral, is now filled with the waters of Tulloch Reservoir. Above it, "like the ruins of a Rhineland castle," as one writer described it, tower the lava-topped crags of Table Mountain.

Colusa County

Colusa County was one of the 27 original counties. The name comes from the Ko-ru-si Indians, and the county was originally known as Colusi, the present usage being adopted in 1854. Monroeville, now in Glenn County, was the first county seat, but it was superseded by Colusa in 1854. A portion of Tehama County and all of Glenn County to the north were included in the original area of the county.

Ko-ru-si Indian Villages

Colusa was built on the site of the old Indian village Ko-ru, tribal capital of the Ko-ru-si. In 1850, there were a thousand or more of these Indians living in villages scattered up and down the Sacramento River within the present boundary of the county. As early as 1846 Americans began to settle along this part of the river, and by the close of the nineteenth century only two of the Indian villages remained, Tat-no, four miles above the town of Colusa, on what was at that time the Colonel Hagar Ranch, and Wy-terre, on the upper end of the Rancho Jimeno.

There were at least thirteen of these villages. Loch-loch, at the head of Sycamore Slough, was where the town of Sycamore now stands. To the north was Coo-coo, then Doc-doc; Colusa lies on the site of Ko-ru, the head village of the tribe. Across the river from Ko-ru was Cow-peck; Tat-no was north of Ko-ru on the same side of the river. This is today the Colusa Indian Reservation, where the remnants of the tribe now live, about five miles north of the town of Colusa. Si-cope occupied the bend of the river east of the site of the old Five Mile House, while at the Seven Mile House was Cah-cheal. At the bend of the river, on the upper end of what became the Judge Hastings Ranch, was Si-ee ("view"), where there were no trees. On the Rancho Jimeno was Wy-terre ("turn to the north"). Cha was at the Senator Boggs Ranch and Ket-tee was where the present town of Princeton now stands; north of Princeton, at what is now the Colusa-Glenn county line, was Tu-tu.

The Larkin Grant

John Bidwell was the first recorded white explorer of Colusa County, in the years 1843–44, while in the employ of John A. Sutter. In July 1844, Bidwell mapped out a grant of land that extended along the west bank of the Sacramento River north of what is now the town of Colusa and into the present Glenn County. This was the first land grant made in Colusa County and was known as the Larkin Grant, having been secured for the children of Thomas O. Larkin, American consul at Monterey. John S. Williams, brother of Isaac Williams, owner of Rancho Chino in southern California, was the first white settler in Colusa County. In 1847 he was employed to look after the Larkin Grant, and on it he built the first house in the county. Senator John Boggs later bought that part of the Larkin Grant on which Williams lived, just below the present town of Princeton. The town of Williams, incidentally, is named not for John S. Williams but for W. H. Williams, who laid out the townsite on the route of the Southern Pacific Railroad.

The Sacramento Valley Museum has displays of shops and activities from the pioneer days of Colusa County and the Sacramento Valley as well as an interesting exhibit of farm machinery. It is at 1491 E Street in Williams.

Colusa

On the spot where Ko-ru, chief settlement of the Ko-ru-si, had been located only a few years before, Colusa was founded in 1850. The land on which the new town was laid out and land beyond it were included in the grant made to John Bidwell in 1845. When Dr. Robert Semple, founder of Benicia, visited the country in 1847, he was so impressed with its beauty and fertility and its nearness to the great river that he saw possibilities of a future city there.

Colonel Charles D. Semple, a brother of Dr. Semple, came to California in 1849. The Doctor immediately told him of this fine country to the north, and Charles was most favorably impressed. He purchased the land from Bidwell the same year, and in a small homemade launch started up the river the following spring to found a new city. Mistaking the site originally chosen by his brother, the Colonel landed seven miles to the north, at a place afterward known as the Seven Mile House, but a visit by the doctor soon rectified the error. Barges came up the river from Sacramento, and trade from the northern mines was good; Semple's hopes seemed justified, and the new town prospered.

In 1853 Dr. Robert Semple and his nephew, Will S.

County Courthouse, Colusa

Green, purchased Rancho Alamo on Freshwater Creek, six miles from Williams. Dr. Semple died there the following year and was buried on the ranch; later his body was removed to the Williams Cemetery, where a bronze tablet and monument stand at his grave. Another marker has been placed at the Semple ranch west of Williams on SR 20. Green became known as the crusading editor of the Colusa *Sun*.

Although Colusa did not become a great city, it prospered and in 1854 was made the county seat. Today it is the center of a thriving agricultural region. The courthouse (SRL 890) was built in 1861. Its neoclassical architecture reflects the taste of early settlers who came from the South; during the Civil War Colusa County

Oddfellows Building, Colusa

was notorious for its pro-Confederate sympathies. The I.O.O.F. Building nearby dates from 1892, its top story faithful to the time of its construction, the ground floor modernized into stores and offices. Whereas old Carnegie Library buildings throughout California are being abandoned and turned into museums and the like, Colusa has taken its 1906 library, in use until 1964, and made it the headquarters for the police department.

The Grand Island Shrine

The brick shrine a mile and a half south of Sycamore on SR 45 commemorates the first Roman Catholic service in Colusa County, a Mass celebrated on May 1, 1856, by Father Peter Magagnotto, C.P., of Marysville. According to Father Henry Walsh, the service was held in the home of Jacob Meyers on the Sacramento River, an area known as Grand Island. In September 1864 a mission was preached to the people of Grand Island by Father P. G. Laufhuber, S.J., and a piece of land was donated for a church. On September 14, at the close of the mission, a 27-foot wooden cross was erected on this property. No church was ever built, but in 1883 Father Michael Walrath put up the shrine, a tiny structure that will hold no more than four persons at one time. Mass is occasionally celebrated there, and the little house of worship is a constant attraction for tourists. The cross was later replaced by one of concrete.

The River Road

The old River Road, following the west bank of the Sacramento River from Colusa to Shasta City, was the only road in Colusa County in the early 1850's. Its popularity rivaled that of the river steamers, which plied as far north as Red Bluff. The volume of traffic over the road to the northern mines resulted in the building of many inns or stage stations along its course. From Wilkins' Slough in southern Colusa County to the mouth of Stony Creek in what is now Glenn County, a fringe of farms bordered the river, many with facilities to refresh travelers and their pack animals on the long trip to the gold fields.

Colusa was the most important center on the route, from which as many as 50 freight wagons often started for the north in one day. Distances and names were often calculated from Colusa. Among the several stations on the River Road were the Five Mile House, where the Maxwell road branches off to the west; the Seven Mile House, where Colonel Semple made his first Colusa settlement; the Ten Mile House, built by L. H. Helphenstine and owned by the family for over

Grand Island Shrine, near Sycamore

ward carried away many of the stones. The Old Stone Corral (SRL 238), as it was long known, has been restored by the Colusa Parlor, Native Sons of the Golden West. It is located on the ranch at the south side of the Maxwell-Sites Road, where it crosses Stone Corral Creek.

Letts Valley

Jack and David Lett settled in a small valley near the northwest corner of Colusa County in 1855. Letts Valley (SRL 736) is now the site of a lake and a campground, completed in 1959, within the Mendocino National Forest. The spillway is built on the site of a tunnel constructed by the brothers to facilitate drainage. The campground is located where the brothers met their death in 1877 while trying to prevent squatters from settling on their land. The area is southwest of Stonyford via Fouts Springs.

College City

Pierce Christian College at College City was named after Andrew Pierce, who at his death in 1874 left a large amount of land to the Christian Church for religious and educational advancement. In 1876 a board of trustees established a college on the land and laid out a town about it. For years, this was the only school of higher rank in that part of California, and at one time most of the teachers of Colusa County had been educated there.

In 1896 the Pierce College grounds and buildings were given to the Union High School District of College City. This happened in many districts in northern California during the last decade of the nineteenth century, when denominational and other private schools gave their lands and buildings for the use of the newly established high schools. The college had been discontinued because the Christian Church had decided to consolidate its various colleges scattered throughout the state into one adequately endowed institution, finally established at Los Angeles. In March 1937 Pierce Union High School was moved to its new campus in Arbuckle, and in the three years following, the college buildings at College City were razed.

70 years; the Sterling Ranch, or Fourteen Mile House, where John S. Williams built the first house (an adobe) in Colusa County in 1847, and where Charles B. Sterling, the second settler, succeeded him in 1849; the Sixteen Mile House, two miles above the Sterling Ranch, where Princeton now is; and the Seventeen Mile House, owned by Hiram Willits, later founder of Willits in Mendocino County.

The small town of Princeton had a special celebrity for many years, since the only remaining ferry on the Sacramento River crossed from here to Glenn County, a journey usually lasting two minutes. Despite valiant efforts to save it, the Princeton Ferry closed down in June 1986. Recently, however, service has been resumed on a limited basis.

Stone Corral

Six miles west of Maxwell is a hollow hemmed in on three sides by high hills, forming a natural site for a corral. The place may have been used by vaqueros as early as 1848, but the construction of the stone fence is generally attributed to Granville P. Swift, whose cattle operations covered a vast area of the Sacramento Valley in the early 1850's. After 1855 it was used by John Steele, who made further improvements. Settlers after-

Contra Costa County

Contra Costa County was one of the original 27 counties of California. It was first seen by the Spanish from San Francisco, and thus was given the name "opposite coast." The significance of the name Contra Costa was lost when that portion directly across the Bay from San Francisco became part of Alameda County, created in 1853. Martinez has always been the county seat.

Mount Diablo

Perhaps no other place name in California has gathered about itself so many legends as that of Mount Diablo, in Spanish *Monte del Diablo* or "Mountain of the Devil." Standing out above the plain and the lesser mountains almost in the exact center of Contra Costa County, its isolation makes it one of the most conspicuous landmarks in the state. There are actually two peaks on this eminence, Mount Diablo proper at 3,849 feet and North Peak about a mile to the north at 3,563 feet. A ridge declining about 800 feet connects the two summits. On a clear, windy day, it is still possible from the higher point to see over 60 percent of California's area; Professor Josiah D. Whitney estimated in 1862 that from this vantage point one could see an area of land equal to that of the six states of New England. Increasing air pollution and the haziness brought on in part by intensive irrigation in the Central Valley have lessened the number of such viewing days. The beacon erected at the summit in 1928 by the U.S. Commerce Department and the Standard Oil Company of California is now lit only on December 7, a memorial to the men killed at Pearl Harbor when that base was attacked by enemy forces in 1941.

General Mariano G. Vallejo, in his report to the legislature in April 1850, gave the following story of the derivation of the name in its Spanish form: "In 1806 a military expedition from San Francisco marched against the tribe 'Bolgones,' who were encamped at the foot of the mount; the Indians were prepared to receive the expedition, and a hot engagement ensued in the large hollow fronting the western side of the mount. As the victory was about to be decided in favor of the Indians, an unknown personage, decorated with the most extraordinary plumage and making divers movements, suddenly appeared near the combatants. The Indians were victorious and the incognito, *Puy*, departed toward the mount. The defeated soldiers, on ascertaining that the spirit went through the same ceremony daily and at all hours, named the mount 'Diablo,' in allusion to its mysterious inhabitant, who continued to make his appearance until the tribe was subdued by the troops in command of Lieutenant Gabriel Moraga, in a second campaign of the same year. In the aboriginal tongue *Puy* signifies 'Evil Spirit'; in Spanish it means 'Diablo,' and doubtless it signifies 'Devil' in the Anglo-American language."

Erwin G. Gudde, on the other hand, wrote that "Monte Diablo" referred originally to an Indian village at the present site of Concord, with *monte* used in the sense of "thicket" or "woods" rather than "mountain"; apparently early American settlers misunderstood the term and applied the name to the mountain.

An unsuccessful attempt was made by the state legislature in 1865–66 to change the name of Mount Diablo. Although the legislature might say "Coal Hill," the people continued to say "Mount Diablo," and Diablo it has remained.

The mountain was a landmark for explorers and pioneers from the earliest days. In the spring of 1772 Pedro Fages and his trailblazers skirted the western side of the mountain. During the spring of 1776, Juan Bautista de Anza also passed that way, after retracing Fages's steps as far as the junction of the Sacramento and San Joaquin rivers. Dr. John Marsh established his rancho at the base of the great mountain in 1836. The Bidwell-Bartleson company, the first overland emigrant train to enter California by way of the Sierra Nevada, was guided by the peak in 1841 to Dr. Marsh's estate.

A government cabin and telescope were placed on the summit of Mount Diablo in 1851, when it was chosen as the base point for United States surveys in California. With the exception of southern California and the Humboldt district, the locations of all lands in the state are determined by their situation with reference to the Mount Diablo "base and meridian" lines. The summit is at 37°52′54″ north latitude and 121°54′49″ west longitude.

Between 1860 and 1864 much of California was surveyed by an official geological survey party headed by Professor Josiah D. Whitney. William H. Brewer, principal assistant to Whitney, made a series of notes and observations on the work of the party, from which some of his observations on the Mount Diablo region are taken. They noted the magnificent white oaks (*Quercus hindsu hindsii*) that studded the fields, "their great spreading branches often forming a head a hundred feet in diameter." Camp was pitched on May 6, 1862, "in one of the loveliest localities, a pure rippling stream for water, plenty of wood, fine oaks around"; and behind it Mount Diablo rose grandly, its summit "burning with the Tyrian fire of evening." The town of Clayton, with its store, tavern, and other buildings, stood a short distance from the campsite. The discovery of coal in the region had caused the settlement to spring up only a few months before.

Early on the morning of May 7, five of the Whitney party, with their guests who had arrived the previous evening from San Francisco, climbed the mountain. The day was one of those rare, crystal-clear days when the view from the summit stretched for hundreds of miles. "Probably but few views in North America are more extensive—certainly nothing in Europe." The Whitney party remained in the region until May 28, making investigations and measurements of the natural phenomena.

The superb beauty of Mount Diablo, the loveliness of its wildflowers, and the profuse scattering of juniper, piñon, oak, sycamore, and other trees very early attracted nature lovers as well as scientific explorers to its craggy summits. Two good wagon roads were laid out in 1874, one from Concord on the northwest and the other from Danville on the south side of the mountain, and two stages ran daily to the Mountain House. This hostelry was built some distance below the summit because the last part of the trail was too steep for vehicles. The Mountain House enjoyed some years of popularity in the 1870's and 1880's, but it was abandoned in the following decade when the government cabin burned and local ranchers shut off access to the summit.

Mount Diablo was again made accessible to the public when Mount Diablo State Park was created in 1931. In 1939, work was begun on an observatory and museum at the crest of Mount Diablo, which was completed in 1941. Except in very dry weather, when fire is a constant threat, and during severe storms, when roads become difficult of access, the park and the top of the mountain are open on a regular basis, and campers and hikers make year-round use of the slopes.

Indian Shell Mounds

One of the largest of the more than 400 shell mounds or kitchen middens that existed in the San Francisco Bay region when the first white men came to its shores was located within the present city limits of Richmond at what is now the foot of Eleventh Street. Twelfth Street intersects the site of the old mound as it extended across the marsh.

A large part of the Ellis Landing shell mound, as it was long called, was removed for grading purposes in 1907, and the final leveling took place in 1924. Like the one at Emeryville in Alameda County, this mound was of particular significance because of its unusual size and because of the extensive scientific explorations by the Department of Archaeology of the University of California. During the years 1906–8, a detailed study and report of this and other mounds was made by N. C. Nelson, and for two weeks in 1907 extensive scientific excavations were made. At that time about 67,500 cubic feet of material was removed, while 265 artifacts and 126 human skeletons were uncovered.

Before the ancient pile was torn down, it measured 460 feet in length, 250 feet in width, and about 30 feet in height, and its volume approximated 1,260,000 cubic feet. Scientists estimate that the process of accumulation extended over a period of from 3,000 to 4,000 years. It consisted largely of broken shells, principally from common clams and mussels mixed sparingly with oyster, cockle, and abalone shells. Many broken rocks, pebbles, and ashes were also found, as well as fifteen house pits.

The Ellis Landing campsite seems to have afforded few of the advantages usually sought by the mound dwellers. In summer there was no fresh water for drinking, and except for drift there was no firewood, while at all times the location was exposed to strong winds. Since it lay on the shore edge directly north of Brooks Island with 600 yards of marshland at its back, access to it was difficult, and at high tide on stormy winter days it became an island completely surrounded by water.

The natural barriers about the shell heap long served to protect it from the plow, which has ruined many of these deposits. A Mr. Ellis, who lived at the landing for about 40 years, stated that as late as 1890 the mound was still intact. His father ran a small canal from one of the marsh creeks up close to the mound on the landward side and began hauling away its rich soil.

Before humans began its destruction, however, nature had already made inroads upon the mound. Because the base of the pile was from eleven to eighteen feet below sea level before the leveling, the encroaching tides were yearly undermining the steep sea wall and were fast destroying the deposit itself. Since it rested upon solid gravel but was more than half buried in fine silt, Nelson estimated that "the region has sunk at least eighteen feet since the ancient inhabitants began to accumulate the refuse deposit."

The Great Discovery

The Pedro Fages expedition continued in the latter part of March 1772 up the Contra Costa in search of a land route to Point Reyes. Leaving their camp on Strawberry Creek in Alameda County and continuing past the sites of Berkeley and Albany on March 28, the little band turned into the Contra Costa County hills and descended past them into the arroyo later known as Wildcat Creek. At the Indian village on its banks, the strangers were met in a most friendly manner by the natives, who presented them with generous gifts of native foods and "two dead geese, dried and stuffed with grass to use as decoys." The white men reciprocated by offering colored beads, which were eagerly received by the Indians.

Four more arroyos "with running water" were passed before Fages at length halted his men on the bank of a fifth stream "at the foot of some hills." Before them "lay a large, round bay, which resembles a great lake," wrote Father Juan Crespí. This was San Pablo Bay, and in it they saw Mare Island close to the opposite shore. Camp was made at or near the present town of Pinole.

On the following day the explorers climbed the hills that come down close to the shore of San Pablo Bay, still confident that they could reach Point Reyes from this place. To their disappointment they found the passage completely shut off by Carquinez Strait. All day they roamed over the hills and gullies of the rough regions above the strait, passing "five large villages of very mild heathen . . . [where they] were well received . . . and presented with some of their wild food." Many other villages could be made out on the opposite shore.

"According to scientists," writes Mrs. Sanchez, "the name Carquinez is derived from Karkin, the name of an Indian village in that region. . . . Fray José Viader, diarist of the Moraga expedition of 1810 . . . [and] other diarists speak of this Indian village and tribe under the name of the Carquines, making it fairly certain that the origin of the name is Indian." Crespí called the strait the Río de San Francisco.

Breaking camp near Martinez on March 30, the party crossed a deep arroyo "well grown with oaks, cottonwoods, alders, and laurels," which, says Professor Bolton, was probably Pacheco Creek. The expedition then entered the broad, oak-studded Concord Valley, which Crespí called Santa Angela de Fulgino and thought would be an excellent place for a settlement. Two native villages were seen in this neighborhood.

Leaving the valley behind them, the little cavalcade pressed forward over the western spur of Mount Diablo. From one of the high hills of the range they gazed out across a vast new territory never before looked upon by any white man. Before them lay the great central valley of California and the Sacramento and San Joaquin rivers, which converge at the head of Suisun Bay, and, far away to the southeast, "some high mountains," which probably were the Sierra Nevada.

Thus the trail had been blazed through the Contra Costa, and although the specific goal of the expedition was never attained, a discovery of far-reaching magnitude had been made. The vast inland empire of Alta California with its great intersecting watercourses had been opened to future exploration and ultimate settlement.

Camp on this eventful evening was probably pitched between Pittsburg and Antioch. "From this place," wrote Crespí, "we decided to return to . . . Monterey, in view of the fact that our passage to Point Reyes . . . was cut off by these rivers." Before turning back, however, the expedition "went ten leagues from Pacheco Creek, reaching an Indian village near Antioch," writes Bolton.

Camp near the San Joaquin River was broken early the next morning. The range was crossed north of Mount Diablo, and Concord Valley was reentered north of Clayton. Continuing west to Walnut Creek, the party turned southeast and proceeded past the site of Danville through the San Ramon Valley. Camp was set just south of Danville. The trail of Pedro Fages through this area has been commemorated by a plaque (SRL 853) at 856 Danville Boulevard.

Early on the first day of April Fages and his men traveled south through the San Ramon Valley and on into Livermore Valley, passing "many and good arroyos, and with numerous villages of very gentle and peaceful heathen. . . . It is a very suitable place," Crespí's diary records, "for a good mission, having good lands, much water, firewood and many heathen."

In the Footsteps of Pedro Fages

On April 1, 1776, Father Pedro Font mapped, from his position east of Richmond, the Richmond Peninsula, which he took to be an island. Juan Bautista de Anza was the leader of that epoch-making march up the Contra Costa. On the banks of Wildcat Creek, the "rather deep arroyo with a growth of trees and little water," the party came upon an abandoned Indian village. Crossing the creek near San Pablo, they came to a second arroyo with a "very deep" bed and a "heavy growth of live oaks, sycamores, and other trees." Here they found a native village where they were greeted by some 23 men and 7 women, who presented the travelers with a feast of roasted cacomites (a species of iris) in exchange for the glass beads that Anza gave them.

More hills and two or three small arroyos were passed, and another village of friendly Indians greeted them. At nightfall the travelers came to a "high hill" from which they could see a wide expanse of the Bay and hear the waves on the shore. This, says Bolton, was evidently one of the hills at the edge of Rodeo. Camp was made at Rodeo Creek.

At sunrise on the morning of April 2 the camp was visited very early by a delegation of some ten Indians from a village nearby. They came singing and dancing and bearing gifts of cacomites and chuchupate roots. After Mass had been said, Anza accepted the invitation of his visitors to go to their village. Still singing and dancing, they led the way, the padre now and then interrupting their demonstration by chanting the Alabado, the morning hymn.

The village, which they soon reached, stood in a valley on the bank of a small arroyo at about the site of Tormey. The Indians welcomed the strangers "with an indescribable hullabaloo," and, with banners made of feathers and the skins of rabbits, they led the white men to a level spot in the center of the village, where the singers resumed the dance of welcome accompanied by "much clatter and yelling." After an exchange of gifts, Anza and his men continued their journey, apparently to the sorrow of the villagers.

The next halt was made just east of Selby and west of Carquinez Bridge. Here at the edge of the water longitudinal measurements were taken, and Father Font devoted himself to a diligent refutation of previous reports made by Fages and Crespí "that Carquinez Strait and Suisun Bay constituted a Rio Grande." At this point, too, they found Indians fishing with nets from "launches" or rafts, in which the fishermen afterward crossed to the opposite shore.

The next lap of the journey followed the line of the present road from Selby to Martinez. Professor Bolton outlines the route as follows: "Two leagues along the top of the hills took them nearly to Port Costa, where the road forks half a mile from town. From here the highway follows a canyon for two and one-half miles and comes out at the coast opposite Benicia." They were looking upon the great interior rivers and valleys of the Sacramento and the San Joaquin, beyond which lie the Sierra Nevada.

Dropping down to the Martinez Valley, where the Indians from across the strait joined them, the little band continued southeast along the present route of the highway that goes to Walnut Creek. Camp was made at about Pacheco on the edge of the Concord Valley and somewhat more than a league from the Puerto Dulce. Father Crespí had thought that this pretty wooded spot would be an attractive place for a mission but the arroyo did not prove to have enough permanent water.

April 3 "dawned very fair and warm but with a pleasant northwest wind blowing." After Mass, the cavalcade moved forward ten leagues to where Antioch Bridge now is. "Leaving camp, they passed the site of Concord, ascended a canyon (Willow Pass) to the top of the ridge [from which they again saw the Sierra Nevada], descending on the east side, and continued to an Indian village on the site of Antioch, swung southeast about a league to or beyond Oak Grove Cemetery, and then northeast a league to the bank of the San Joaquin River near Antioch Bridge where camp was made." Here the tule marsh, some of which still covers the river bank at this point, caused the party to turn west about a quarter of a league to the site of an abandoned Indian village. Font's observations here further convinced him that what he saw (the San Joaquin River) was a "fresh water sea," rather than a river, as Fages and Crespí believed.

Nevertheless, the commander of the expedition determined to follow the watercourse, to cross the plain, and to explore in the direction of the Sierra Nevada. With this purpose he set out on April 4 in the general direction but "to the left of the highway that runs from Antioch through Knightsen to Tracy. Just east of the starting point," Bolton continues, "was the large marsh east of Antioch Bridge. Leaving the river, therefore, Anza swung southeastwardly past Oakley, keeping on the right the live oaks which continue to Knightsen, then suddenly disappear. At a point not far from Knightsen, Anza swung northeast for a league but encountered the tulares, perhaps at Rock Slough."

Escaping not without difficulty from the mire of the treacherous tules, the weary soldiers trudged through the blinding, wind-blown dust of the dry swamps east of Byron Hot Springs. They followed the general course of the Old River some six leagues to a point just south of Bethany, where Anza finally abandoned his plan to approach the Sierra Nevada and decided to return to Monterey instead.

Rancho San Pablo

Rancho San Pablo, at first called Rancho Cochiyumes, consisted of four leagues of land bordered on the west and north by the bays of San Francisco and San Pablo, and on the east by low verdant hills. There were no fences on all its vast acres and no roads; only divergent trails twisted through the grasses that stretched like a vast sea on all sides. Here and there the tract was dotted by islands of huge oak trees. It was home to numerous wild creatures: bears, coyotes, and herds of deer and elk.

Into this wilderness Don Francisco Castro drove the first herd of cattle north of Rancho San Antonio. Like the herds of the Peraltas, it soon multiplied into roving bands of untamed animals that supplied the rancho with food and the Yankee traders with hides and tallow. Here, too, the first fruit trees in the county and grape cuttings from the mission were set out.

Francisco María Castro, a native of Mexico, was a settler at San Francisco in 1800. For thirteen years he served as a soldier, and in 1822 he was a member of the Governor's Council, the *diputación*. In June 1823 he acted as *diputado*, or official representative, of the exploring expedition led by Father José Altamira north of San Francisco Bay, and in that year also he obtained, provisionally, the grant of Rancho San Pablo on the Contra Costa.

As early as 1826, Francisco Castro took up residence on this land, and there he lived until his death in 1831, three years before the official confirmation of the grant in 1834. The estate was left half to his widow and half to his eleven children. Through years of litigation, during which, says Bancroft, the whole Castro family was "kept in a state of landed poverty," the vast grant gradually dwindled to a few acres about the adobes at El Cerrito and San Pablo.

The venerable Castro adobe (SRL 356) stood until it was destroyed by fire in 1956 on the site of what is now El Cerrito Plaza shopping center. This is on the north bank of El Cerrito Creek, which here forms the boundary between Contra Costa and Alameda counties. To the west rises El Cerrito ("the little hill"), long a landmark for early travelers and settlers along the northwest shore of the Contra Costa. This hill, round and smooth and high, cast a bold silhouette against the sky in the old days before it was planted with eucalyptus, and it constituted one of the more substantial and permanent designations of the boundary line between Rancho San Pablo and its neighbor to the south, Rancho San Antonio.

About 1842, Jesús María Castro, one of the sons of Don Francisco, built an adobe building on what is now the west corner of San Pablo Avenue and Church Lane in the city of San Pablo. Martina, daughter of Francisco Castro, married Governor Juan Bautista Alvarado in 1839, and the governor thus came into possession of the portion of the estate that Martina inherited on her mother's death in 1851. This included the adobe at San Pablo, to which the governor had retired in 1848, remaining there until his death in 1882. Gradually, the vast acreage had been relinquished until, at the time of his death, only about 50 acres of the princely estate that once surrounded the adobe remained.

The Alvarado adobe (SRL 512) stood for many years behind a grocery store at the corner, and, covered with a wooden superstructure, was used as a storeroom. In September 1954, despite the efforts of local citizens and organizations to preserve it, the old adobe was razed for the construction of a motel. A bronze plaque has

Blume House Museum, San Pablo

been placed on an apartment house that was built later on the front portion of the lot.

In 1976, a replica of the Alvarado adobe was built on Alvarado Square nearby; this is now a museum of the San Pablo Museum and Historical Society. Across from the Alvarado Square complex, which also houses the city offices of San Pablo, is the Blume House Museum. The ranch house and the bunkhouse of the Blume family, built elsewhere in 1905, were moved to this site in 1971 when the original site was purchased by Chevron Land and Development Corporation. The buildings are open to the public.

The Gutiérrez adobe, built about 1850 and one of the finest mansions of its day, stood on the south bank of San Pablo Creek, northwest of San Pablo within the city limits of Richmond. Located west of Garden Tract Road and south of Parr Boulevard, it was razed in 1946. The home of Candido Gutiérrez and his wife, Jovita Castro Gutiérrez, was pleasantly situated on the bank of the arroyo, where schooners came up the creek to the back door, bringing supplies and taking away products from the rancho.

The pastoral lands once occupied by the great Rancho San Pablo are now covered by miles of residences and paved highways; the cities of Richmond, El Cerrito, and San Pablo have grown up around the pioneer settlements, and with the passing of the old adobes, nothing remains to remind us of other days.

Rancho San Ramón

The vast acreage of Rancho San Ramón lay mostly within Contra Costa County after Alameda County was created in 1853. Two square leagues of this rancho were granted to Bartolomé Pacheco and Mariano Castro by Governor José Figueroa in 1833. Four leagues were granted by the same governor to José María Amador in

1834 and 1835. Leo Norris, a native of Kentucky who had come across the plains to California from Missouri in 1846, filed claim for one square league, which he purchased from Amador, and this was confirmed and later patented to him.

Pacheco and Castro divided their grant, Pacheco taking the southern half and Castro the northern. Neither lived on the rancho. Castro lived at Rancho Pastoria de las Borregas (in Santa Clara County) and sold his share of the San Ramón to his brother-in-law, Domingo Peralta of Rancho San Antonio (in Alameda County), in 1852. Pacheco died in 1839, and his land came into the hands of his son Lorenzo, who himself died in 1846. Lorenzo's widow, Rafaela Soto de Pacheco, eventually deeded part of this southern league to Horace W. Carpentier, who had also acquired much of Domingo Peralta's land. Early American settlers on the rancho, including John M. Jones, Daniel Inman, Albert W. Stone, and James Tice, had to pay Carpentier in order to get clear title to their land.

When Leo Norris came to the rancho in the autumn of 1850, he found, according to J. P. Munro-Fraser, a branch of the Soto family residing in an adobe house then standing about 150 yards from the site of his residence. Apparently these were brothers of Rafaela Soto de Pacheco who planned to settle there, but they moved elsewhere when all their horses were stolen by Indians.

Leo Norris lived at Mission San José from June 1847 until the early autumn of 1850, when he and his son William migrated to the San Ramon Valley. With them went their relative, William Lynch, a native of New York, who had landed in San Francisco in June 1849 from the pilot boat *W. A. Hackstaff*. Lynch was a journeyman carpenter and practiced his trade in San Francisco before going out to the fertile valley of San Ramon, where he aided Norris in erecting his house, the first frame dwelling in the valley, from lumber hauled from the San Antonio redwoods. The old Norris dwelling, which stood on Norris Canyon Road at the mouth of the canyon, about half a mile west of San Ramon Valley Boulevard, was destroyed by fire about 1950.

Other American pioneers purchased portions of Rancho San Ramón. Joel Harlan, a native of Indiana, came to California with his parents in the spring of 1846. After a trip to the mines, followed by his marriage in April 1849, Harlan lived at different times in Napa City, San Francisco, Sacramento, San Jose, and San Lorenzo (in Alameda County), where he was one of the first settlers at Squattersville.

Finally, in 1852, Harlan purchased a tract of land on Rancho San Ramón in Contra Costa County. There he erected a dwelling, which, when Alameda County was created, was one of the points defining the boundary line. Notwithstanding the unique, if somewhat indefinite, position of his house, Harlan always maintained that it stood on the Contra Costa side of the line. A huge oak tree in the corner of the original Harlan yard long served as a landmark. The spot is just west of the junction of Alcosta and San Ramon Valley boulevards north of Dublin. The iron milepost erected in 1895 on the county line by Elisha Harlan and his mother, Minerva (Mrs. Joel) Harlan, has been moved to the southeast corner of this intersection.

Approximately 2,000 acres purchased from the Norris tract were added to the Harlan estate in 1856. The following year the house at the county boundary line was moved north to a site three miles south of the town of San Ramon, and there in 1858 Harlan built the fine old country mansion now known as El Nido ("the Nest"). The original dwelling was incorporated into a wing of the two-story building, which is set back from the road at 19521 San Ramon Valley Boulevard.

Another early settler who purchased a portion of Rancho San Ramón was David Glass, a native of Pennsylvania, who had arrived with his family in California from Iowa in August 1850. After a short stay in Placerville, he settled in November of that year in the vicinity of Walnut Creek. It was not until some nine years later that he purchased the ranch of 718 acres located three and one-half miles south of San Ramon. The original Glass house no longer stands, but a two-story residence built in the 1880's, now known as the Hillside Ranch Sanitarium, remains at 19801 San Ramon Valley Boulevard.

Christian Wiedemann, who came to San Francisco from Germany in 1852, settled on Rancho San Ramón in 1855. He built his home, still owned by his descendants, in 1858 on a 400-acre tract. It is located about one-half mile south of Norris Canyon Road at a point two and one-half miles west of San Ramon Valley Boulevard.

Alamo

The towns of Alamo, Danville, and San Ramon are located on the northern (Castro-Pacheco) portion of Rancho San Ramón. The name Alamo (Spanish for "poplar") was given to the town because poplar or cottonwood trees once grew abundantly in the valley and along the streams. The old buildings of the place have all been leveled to make way for newer structures. The Union Academy was built here in 1859, with the Reverend David McClure as master; he had conducted the first services of the Presbyterian Church in the San Ramon Valley in 1857. When the building (about where El Portal Road meets Danville Boulevard, on the western side) burned in 1868, it was not rebuilt.

Danville

It has been said that Danville was named for Daniel Inman, the pioneer who formerly owned the land on which the town now stands. In a story told in the *Danville Sentinel* of 1898, Inman noted that settlers wanted to name the new post office Inmanville, "but my brother Andrew and I objected to that. Finally, 'Grandma' Young, my brother's mother-in-law, said: 'Call it Danville,' and as much or more out of respect to her, as she was born and raised near Danville, Kentucky, it took that name."

In 1858, S. Wolf, M. Cohen, and Henry Hoffman dissolved the firm of Wolf and Company at Alamo and opened a store in Danville. About the same year H. W. Davis opened a hotel at the junction of the Tassajara road and the highway through Danville. It burned in 1873, but a newer Danville Hotel (first known as the Railroad Hotel) was built on the same spot in 1891 and still serves as a popular bar and restaurant.

San Ramon (Limerick)

The northern boundary of the Norris division of Rancho San Ramón is just south of the town of San Ramon. Originally known as Lynchville, this town, like Dublin to the south, long retained the sobriquet of Limerick because the settlers of the vicinity were primarily Irish. When the population in the neighborhood justified the creation of a post office in 1873, it was given the name San Ramon, although the settlement continued to be known popularly as Limerick for some time. An earlier post office named San Ramon had existed in the vicinity from 1852 to 1859. The Catholic church dedicated to St. Raymond was built in 1859 at Dublin, where it still stands.

Rancho El Sobrante de San Ramón (Tice and Stone Valleys)

In 1844 Inocencio Romero and his brother José claimed Rancho El Sobrante de San Ramón of five leagues. This was the *sobrante* ("leftover" or "excess") of land lying between the ranchos of "Moraga, Pacheco, and Welch." Some six or seven years before the Romeros petitioned for the grant, the tract had been claimed by Francisco Soto but had never been used or cultivated by him.

The large adobe residence of the Romeros, in Tice Valley southwest of Walnut Creek, was razed in 1900, but a small stone and mud house remained for some years afterward. El Sobrante de San Ramón was never confirmed to the brothers because of certain legal complications and vagaries, and James Tice, for whom the valley was named, later came into ownership of the property. Joseph Napthaly began to acquire land in the valley in 1874. He built a winery where Del Valle High School now stands. The former station of Saranap on the Sacramento Northern Railroad was a contraction of Sara Napthaly. In 1930 the Napthaly Ranch was sold to Stanley Dollar, the steamship magnate, and in 1960 it became Rossmoor Leisure World, a retirement community. About 1965 some children from Tice Valley School discovered in the hills a large sandstone rock with the chiseled inscription "J. W. Tice 1855."

The portion of San Ramón Sobrante that lies immediately east of Alamo was long known as the Stone Ranch and is still called Stone Valley. Albert W. Stone, a native of Pennsylvania and a blacksmith by trade, had come to California from Iowa in 1852. After returning to Iowa the following year, he again crossed the plains to California, this time with his family. For a while he lived in Colusa County on land later occupied by Dr. Hugh J. Glenn, but in 1858 he moved to Contra Costa County, where he purchased the farm of 800 acres adjoining Alamo. The family built a frame house that long stood at 2144 Stone Valley Road. Later a two-story house was built nearby, where Francisco García had erected a small adobe house around 1850. None of these are standing today.

Rancho Acalanes (Lafayette)

Rancho Acalanes, lying among the fertile little valleys west of Lafayette, was granted in 1834 to Candelario Valencia, a soldier of the San Francisco Company. The name, says Kroeber, was probably derived from Akalan (or a similar name), a Costanoan Indian village in the vicinity, which was called by the Spaniards the Acalanes "tribe." Like many another Californian of the old Spanish and Mexican regime, Valencia eventually became indebted to a foreigner and, being unable to clear himself of entanglements, was forced to sell his land. Thus it was that Rancho Acalanes fell into the hands of William A. Leidesdorff of Yerba Buena, who put it up for sale.

Meanwhile, Elam Brown, a native of New York, had arrived in California in October 1846 as captain of a company of fourteen families and sixteen wagons that apparently had crossed the mountains in company with the Boggs and Cooper parties. Brown spent his first summer in California whipsawing lumber in the San Antonio redwoods and hauling it to the San Antonio Landing, where it was shipped across the Bay to San Francisco. Learning that Rancho Acalanes was for sale,

Brown purchased it from Leidesdorff, together with 300 cows the latter had obtained from Vásquez at Half Moon Bay.

Brown took his family through the Moraga Valley to their new home, where they arrived in February 1848. They were the second American family to settle in Contra Costa County. The Browns' first two settlements had to be abandoned for lack of adequate water. They finally settled in a redwood house on the site of the present La Fiesta shopping center in Lafayette, at the southwest corner of Hough Avenue and Lafayette Creek.

At first Brown had to make long, tedious trips on horseback or by ox team via the San Ramon Valley in order to carry his wheat and barley to Sansevain's mill in San Jose, where it was turned into flour. To eliminate the necessity for this trip, Brown purchased a horse-power mill at Benicia in 1853 and set it up near his house. The millstone was placed in the Lafayette plaza in 1955 as a memorial to Elam Brown. The gristmill was located beside the creek south of this monument, next to the Park Theater. Brown, who died in 1889, was for many years a respected and prosperous citizen of Contra Costa County. He was a member of the convention that framed the state constitution in 1849 and also of the first two legislatures after its adoption.

Conveyance of one-tenth of Rancho Acalanes was made to Nathaniel Jones in the autumn of 1847, soon after Brown had acquired the property. Jones, a native of Tennessee, had started for Oregon from Missouri in April 1846 in company with 15 or 20 other families. Circumstances diverted the immigrants to California, and Joseph Chiles induced Jones at Fort Sutter to go to Rancho Catacula in Napa County. With three or four other families the Joneses arrived in Chiles Valley in November 1846. After volunteering and participating in the Battle of Santa Clara, Nathaniel Jones returned to Rancho Catacula.

Jones took his wife and small son to the San Antonio redwoods in Alameda County, and with the proceeds of the work that he did that summer he purchased a part of Rancho Acalanes from Elam Brown for $100.

Nathaniel Jones and Elam Brown moved to their new homes about the same time, and early in 1848 Jones built his house. In the spring of the following year he began to set out black locust trees, which gave the name of Locust Farm to his ranch. The seed of these trees had been brought to California by Major Stephen Cooper in 1846 and subsequently presented to Jones. A few of the trees may still be seen on Lower Happy Valley Road, north of Lafayette.

The settlement was named in 1853 in honor of the French hero of the War of American Independence; it is one of several Lafayettes in the United States. A traveler passing by the Brown residence in 1852 was induced to remain. This was Benjamin Shreve, who taught school there during the winter of 1852–53 and later opened a store and built a home. The store building (1855) still stands at 3535 Plaza Way. Shreve is credited with naming the town, and he was the first postmaster when the post office was established in his store in 1857. Lafayette's first school was located near the plaza; it no longer stands, but the second school is now used as a tavern at 3535 Mount Diablo Boulevard, and the third has been incorporated into the Lafayette Methodist Church at 955 Moraga Road.

Among the first industries in Lafayette was a blacksmith shop established by Jack Elston and purchased by Peter Thomson in 1859. This shop was situated at what is now 3530 Mount Diablo Boulevard. Milo Hough operated a hotel here from 1853 to 1855. Very early a church was built and a cemetery laid out. Thus, about Elam Brown's hospitable home, the town of Lafayette grew up.

Rancho Sobrante (El Sobrante, Orinda)

The *sobrante* granted to Juan José and Victor Castro in 1841 was entirely surrounded by other grants, in a day when boundaries were everywhere uncertain. Governor Alvarado in making the grant stipulated that its boundaries should be determined by the boundaries of the surrounding grants—Ranchos San Antonio, San Pablo, El Pinole, La Boca de la Cañada del Pinole, Acalanes, and La Laguna de los Palos Colorados. The effect of this proviso was to throw the boundaries of the new *sobrante* into legal conflicts that lasted for 40 years. When a grant of over 20,000 acres was confirmed to the Castro brothers in 1883, thousands of acres had already gone to pay attorneys' fees. A survey map of 1893 showed Victor Castro, who survived his brother, as the owner of 549 acres. The family still resides in the area on Castro Ranch Road.

In 1980 the Orinda Historical Society placed a marker at the spot where the boundaries of Ranchos Sobrante, Acalanes, and Boca de la Cañada del Pinole converged, at the end of Dalewood Drive in Orinda.

Rancho La Boca de la Cañada del Pinole (Bear Creek Valley)

In about 1824, Ignacio Martínez occupied the area that he called Rancho El Pinole. Five years later he invited Felipe Briones, who had been a *regidor* or pueblo councilman in San Jose, to live on the ranch in exchange for various services rendered. In 1839, while Martínez's petition for Rancho El Pinole was still pending, Briones filed for a grant of land that apparently included El Pinole. When it was pointed out that Martínez had long been a resident there and that Briones's house was really at El Corral de Galindo, Briones changed his petition to request the area called La Boca de la Cañada de Pinole, which bordered on but did not include El Pinole.

In 1840 Briones was killed while trying to recover horses stolen by Indians. His widow continued the petition and received the grant in 1842, about the same time that Martínez, who had supported her claim, received his grant at El Pinole.

Rancho El Pinole (Pinole, Martinez)

Ignacio Martínez was born in Mexico City in 1774 and, coming to California, entered military service as a cadet at Santa Barbara in 1799. He was promoted to be *alférez* of the San Diego Company in 1806 and in 1817 was again recommended for promotion, this time to go back to Santa Barbara. To his chagrin, an error in the making out of his papers sent him to San Francisco instead. He was retired in 1831, after having been *comandante* at San Francisco during the last four years of his military service. He was a *regidor* at San Jose in 1834–35, but then settled on his claim in Contra Costa, granted to him in 1842. One of his daughters married the pioneer William A. Richardson.

The town of Pinole (a Mexican word meaning "cereal meal") carries the name of his rancho, and the town of Martinez at the edge of his land is named for his family. The site of the Ignacio Martínez adobe is where Pinole Valley Road jogs while crossing the creek twice in a short distance. Two of the old El Pinole rancho houses may still be seen in the vicinity of Martinez. One is on the John Muir Ranch in Franklin Canyon about two miles south of town, and the other is farther south on the John Swett Ranch in the Alhambra Valley.

The home of John Muir (SRL 312), explorer, scientist, and author, is located at Alhambra Avenue and Franklin Canyon Road. The large old-fashioned house where Muir lived from 1890 until his death in 1914 stands on a knoll overlooking the orchards and homes below and the hills that hem them in on all sides. The house was built by Dr. John Strentzel, Muir's father-in-law.

John Muir was born in Dunbar, Scotland, on April 21, 1838. He came to the United States in 1849 and went on to California while still a young man. Most of his life was spent exploring, studying, and writing about the great mountains of California and Alaska, their valleys,

Home of John Muir, John Muir National Historic Site, Martinez

glaciers, and wildlife. Many of the mountain peaks and glaciers up and down the Pacific Coast were discovered and named by him. He was one of the foremost advocates of national parks, and his books, which have literary as well as scientific value, have done much to cause people to know and love the natural wonders of the Pacific Coast states. Perhaps the best-known and most beautiful of his writings is *The Mountains of California*, published in 1894.

The property is now the John Muir National Historic Site, operated by the National Park Service. The site also includes the Vicente Martínez adobe (SRL 511), which was the home of ranch employees during Muir's time. Vicente, a son of Ignacio Martínez, built the adobe in 1849. Four years later he sold it to Edward Franklin, who resided there a short time and for whom Franklin Canyon is named.

John Swett has been called the "father of the California public schools" because of his untiring efforts on their behalf while he was superintendent of public instruction from 1863 to 1867. He was born in New Hampshire and came to San Francisco in 1853, where he was at once employed as a teacher. Throughout his long career as a teacher and administrator he did more than any other man to build up the public school system of California.

The John Swett Ranch, at the end of Millthwait

Drive off Alhambra Valley Road, lies in the heart of the Alhambra Valley in the midst of orchards and residential developments. The big old house itself is hidden among the trees along a stream. Beside it is a little white adobe built by Abilino Altamirano about 1849 and carefully preserved by Swett and his descendants.

Bernando Fernandez settled near the mouth of Pinole Creek in the 1850's; he became a merchant and grain factor and an early developer of Pinole. The two-story mansion he built on Tennent Avenue in 1894 is now owned and maintained as a public facility by the city of Pinole and is on the National Register of Historic Places.

Rancho Los Medanos (Marsh Creek and Eastward)

Father Narciso Durán, accompanied by Father Ramón Abella and Captain Luís Antonio Arguello, made a boat voyage up the Sacramento River in May 1817. It was on this expedition, according to Chapman, that the sand banks or dunes that lie along the Carquinez Strait between Pittsburg and Antioch were mentioned as *Los Medanos*, "the sand banks." During the late 1830's two adjoining ranchos were granted, both of which, according to Bancroft, received the name of Los Medanos, apparently because of the sand dunes lying along the left bank of the San Joaquin River in their vicinity. Later writers, however, have tried somewhat ambiguously to distinguish the two by calling the rancho originally granted to José Noriega and later purchased by Dr. John Marsh "Los Meganos" and the New York Ranch (where Pittsburg now stands) "Los Medanos."

José Noriega, who was aboard the *Natalia*, wrecked at Monterey in 1834, became *depositario*, or receiver, at Mission San José the following year. In October 1835 he also became grantee of Rancho Los Medanos in Contra Costa County, where he built some corrals and a few outbuildings. In 1837 Noriega sold his rancho to John Marsh, who settled upon it the same year and occupied it until his death in 1856.

Marsh, a native of Massachusetts, graduated from Harvard University with the degree of Bachelor of Arts. After spending some time in Wisconsin, he left the United States for New Mexico in 1835. He traveled through a portion of Old Mexico and entered southern California early in 1836. He displayed his Harvard diploma to the *ayuntamiento* of Los Angeles, who received it as a medical diploma; Marsh was given a license to practice medicine. In his sympathetic biography, John W. Winkley points out that Marsh had in fact completed his medical education and had practiced for some years; although he lacked a formal medical degree, he was well qualified as a physician and surgeon.

By December 1837 Marsh had come north and acquired the rancho in the shadow of Mount Diablo. The Indians of this region became the doctor's friends and helpers, and he called his estate the Farm of Pulpones (evidently a corruption of Bolbones or Bolgones), from the name of an Indian tribe or village in the vicinity of Mount Diablo. Marsh maintained good relations with his Indian neighbors—healing their sick, purchasing their pelts, and leaving their ancient rancheria undisturbed. In return, the Indians helped the "Señor Doctor" to build a four-room adobe with attic on the bank of the stream opposite their village. They brought grape cuttings from Mission San José to this first house and his grander mansion and helped him to plant a vineyard and an orchard of pears, figs, and olives. They plowed his field for him and helped him to sow it with wheat. When he died, it was said that the Indians watched beside his bier and mourned his passing.

Disappointment and tragedy experienced during his sojourn among the Indians in Wisconsin before he came to California had left their stamp upon the life and character of John Marsh. To all but his Indian neighbors he was notoriously parsimonious and often unkind. When the Bidwell-Bartleson party reached his rancho in 1841, the first party to cross the Sierra Nevada into California, he received them, but he made them pay well for his services. Even the Yankee traders complained about his sharp methods when he tried to beat them at their own game. His treatment of the 1841 party is understandable in that several of the members had killed some of Marsh's trained work animals.

But there were those who admired the seemingly hard and tightfisted doctor, and several Californians, including General Vallejo, spoke of him in terms of warm praise. Dr. Marsh was the first and for several years the only man to practice medicine in the San Joaquin Valley. He often traveled many leagues to minister to the sick, his services usually being paid in cattle. "The greater the distance," George Lyman notes, "the more cows he expected, but it was generally agreed that he brought comfort and relief to the households he visited. His reputation spread. Cows or no cows, his services were in demand."

Although naturalized as a Mexican citizen in 1844, Dr. Marsh joined Sutter's forces against the Californians in 1844–45 but took little part in the troubles of 1846–47. Nevertheless, he increasingly wanted to see California come into the possession of the United States, and almost every wagon train to the East carried letters to his friends praising the glories and possibilities of the land. Most of these communications were to Missourians and were published in Missouri newspapers.

These letters, written from direct observation, exerted a far-reaching influence on immigration to California, especially from Missouri. Their influence, coupled with the practical efforts of Antoine Robidoux, probably helped the movement that resulted in the first emigrant party to California via the Rocky Mountains and the Sierra Nevada, led by Bidwell and Bartleson in 1841. The Marsh letters are still a valuable source of information on the life and times of pioneer California.

In June 1851 Dr. Marsh married Abbie Tuck, the daughter of a minister in Chelmsford, Massachusetts, and a beautiful and accomplished young lady who had come to California in 1850 for her health. John Marsh dreamed of something better than his crude adobe for his wife and planned a stone mansion with a library, marble fireplaces, a tower, and a suite of rooms for Abbie and himself. She selected the site almost directly opposite the old adobe but never lived in the mansion. About three years after the birth of their daughter, Alice, Abbie sickened and died. The peak of John Marsh's happiness and prosperity passed quickly. His Mexican neighbors were becoming increasingly irritated and vengeful over the doctor's parsimonious acts and unkind attitude toward the rights of others. On September 23, 1856, he was murdered by three of these desperate young Californians on the lonely road between his rancho and Martinez. Ten years later one of the murderers was apprehended and sent to prison for life. After 25 years he was pardoned. The site of the murder (SRL 722) is marked on Pacheco Boulevard two miles north of Pacheco.

Set in wide, open fields about four miles southwest of Brentwood via Walnut Boulevard and Marsh Creek Road, Marsh's stone house is one of the most striking landmarks of Contra Costa County. Its steep English gables, its solid masonry of native stone, and its three stories give it an appearance that was already being praised before the house was completed.

Here Alice Marsh, orphaned at an early age, was to experience poverty and hardship before she finally came into her inheritance. The Marsh estate was divided between Alice and Charles, the doctor's son by his common-law wife in Wisconsin, at whose death John began his travels to California. It was largely through the efforts of Charles that justice was finally obtained for the two children and the property was freed from the hands of unscrupulous persons.

The state of California acquired the Marsh home and the few acres around it from Contra Costa County in 1979, and extensive restoration has been undertaken. The house will be open to the public when restoration has been completed.

Salvio Pacheco Adobe, Concord

Rancho Monte del Diablo (Concord)

Salvio Pacheco, having held high offices in the government of Mexican California, was granted the Rancho Monte del Diablo, of 18,000 acres, in 1834. About ten years later he moved to it and soon built the adobe house (SRL 515) still standing in the present town of Concord, originally called by him Todos Santos, which was surveyed in 1868. The adobe is located at 2050 Adobe Street between Salvio and Central streets, and is now modernized as an office building.

The adobe home of Salvio's son Fernando Pacheco (SRL 455) stands at 3119 Grant Street. It was built in the 1840's on a 1,500-acre tract given him by his father. Long neglected, it was restored by the Contra Costa County Horsemen's Association in 1941 and serves as their headquarters.

Rancho Laguna de los Palos Colorados (Canyon, Moraga, Orinda)

This rancho was granted to Joaquín Moraga and Juan Bernal in 1835. Moraga was the grandson of José Joaquín Moraga, founder and first *comandante* of the Presidio of San Francisco, and Bernal was the younger Moraga's cousin. The redwoods for which the rancho was named were in the canyons between Moraga's home and Rancho San Antonio of the Peraltas. The small community of Canyon lies in a deep redwood canyon between Moraga and Oakland. The laguna, or lake, was located at the present site of Campolindo High School on Moraga Road in Moraga.

The adobe built by Joaquín Moraga (SRL 509) and completed in 1841 was acquired and restored a century later by Katheryn Brown White Irvine. A private home, it stands at 24 Adobe Lane in Orinda.

Orinda and the East Bay Connection

William Camron, a cousin of Elam Brown of Lafayette, came to California in 1849 with his family and was orphaned five years later when he was eleven years of age. Raised by his uncle, Judge Thomas A. Brown, he came to be a speculator in East Bay real estate. In 1871 he married Alice Marsh, daughter and heiress of John Marsh. "After the marriage," Muir Sorrick writes, "William managed her estate, eventually with disastrous results." He also acquired property on the eastern slope of the Berkeley hills, which he named Orinda Park in 1876. "Orinda" was the pen name of Katherine Philips, an English poet of the seventeenth century, and it is thought that Alice Marsh Camron derived the name from the copy of Dr. Samuel Johnson's *Lives of the Poets* that she had inherited from her father. It probably was a name more euphonious and pleasing to the ear than anything else, and in time would become (without the "Park") associated with a community naturally endowed with a beautiful landscape and climate. Orinda, with some reluctance, became an organized city in 1985.

Orinda has historically been the connection between Contra Costa County and Oakland via various thoroughfares across the steep range of hills. William Camron was highly interested in building a toll road from Berkeley to Orinda, but he was financially strapped and unable to undertake the project. Theodore Wagner, who had a ranch in the lower Bear Creek Valley (part of which is a nature preserve today), undertook to build a road in 1889; it was ultimately paid for by official stipends and private contributions. Its course is today approximately followed by Wildcat Canyon Road, which runs from the San Pablo Dam Road in Orinda west through the Berkeley hills into Tilden Regional Park.

A more direct but more difficult route between the shoreline communities and those of the interior was the Telegraph Road, which was built in 1861 along the new telegraph line extending from Oakland to Nevada. The route followed what is today Telegraph Avenue in Oakland, then Claremont Avenue in Oakland passing into Berkeley, and from there over the summit (of 1,315 feet) and down what is now Fish Ranch Road to Orinda. The distance was short but the climb and descent were formidable. Most traffic between San Francisco or Oakland to Contra Costa came slowly by roads and later by railways along the shores of the Bay. Without better access, Contra Costa entrepreneurs feared their region would become a backwater.

After considerable prodding of their boards of supervisors, Contra Costa and Alameda County boosters rejoiced in the opening of a tunnel under the summit in 1903. It was narrow and dark and had a deceptive bend in the middle where the counties met but their road crews had not. Vehicles passed through it only with difficulty, and it was subject to occasional earthslides. Around 1915 the tunnel had to be closed for a year for repairs and cleaning.

In 1928, after considerable pressure had been put on the state legislature, a special highway district was formed for the purpose of creating a new "low-level" tunnel (that is, at a lower elevation). Ground was broken in June 1934, with President Franklin D. Roosevelt and Governor Frank F. Merriam in attendance on the Oakland side. The two-bore tunnel was opened to traffic in 1937. It was named for Thomas E. Caldecott, an Alameda County supervisor and president of the Highway District. Since then a third bore has been added, with a fourth planned within the next few years.

Under the highway tunnel, a 3.5-mile-long train tunnel, one of the longest in California, connects the Rockridge and Orinda stations of the Bay Area Rapid Transit (BART) System, an extensive rail line that connects San Francisco and Oakland with communities as far away as Concord, Daly City, Fremont, and Richmond. The system went into operation in 1972 after extensive planning and developments, and was one of the technological innovations of its day. Both BART and the Caldecott Tunnel have greatly increased movement between Contra Costa County and the Bay Area, so that Orinda, once an idyllic country retreat, is today only a short journey from the city scene.

Rancho Arroyo de las Nueces y Bolbones (Walnut Creek)

In the central part of the county is Rancho Arroyo de las Nueces y Bolbones, whose 17,782 acres were granted to Juana Sánchez de Pacheco in 1834. This rancho, located on the western flank of Mount Diablo, was patented to her heirs in 1866. Arroyo de las Nueces is now called Walnut Creek and has given its name to a thriving city. Bolbones was the name of a tribe of Indians in the vicinity of Mount Diablo.

One of the early American settlers on this rancho was James T. Walker, who acquired some 1,400 acres in the 1850's, and in 1868 built a home that is still standing at 1200 North Gate Road between Walnut Creek and Mount Diablo State Park. In 1867 Walker's uncle came to live with him. This was Joseph Reddeford Walker, trapper, trailmaker, guide, and stock buyer of the 1830's and 1840's, for whom Walker Pass is named. The elder Walker moved into the new house with his nephew and lived there until his death in 1876 at the age of 77.

He is buried in Alhambra Cemetery in Martinez, where his headstone recounts the highlights of his career.

Almost directly across the road from the Walker home is the Borges Ranch, which was placed on the National Register of Historic Places in 1981. It has been acquired along with 2,300 acres of meadow and woodland by Contra Costa County and designated an Open Space Area. Built around the turn of the century, the ranch home is still the center of a working farm. The county is planning to expand the farm and to develop museum and display facilities.

The Shadelands Museum at 2660 Ygnacio Valley Road is lodged in the 1902 farmhouse of Hiram Penniman. This modest two-story building is filled with some of his family's possessions and is maintained as a Walnut Creek museum of history. It too is on the National Register of Historic Places.

Martinez

Contra Costa's county seat was incorporated in 1876, although county government had been in operation there since 1850. A center for wheat shipping until the railroad came through in 1879, Martinez was also the southern terminus for the busy ferries that crossed Carquinez Strait from Benicia until the Benicia-Martinez bridge was opened in 1960. Two disastrous fires in 1894 and 1904 all but destroyed the downtown area, which centered on Main and Ferry streets, today the heart of the Martinez Historical District. Two buildings from 1904 serve as restaurants today. At 825 Main Street a marker commemorates the site of the *Contra Costa Gazette*, a paper founded there in 1858; it moved to Pacheco in 1863 and returned to Martinez in 1873, where it is now the *Martinez News Gazette*.

The north-south streets in downtown Martinez are named for the old California families into which the daughters of Don Ignacio Martínez married: Castro, Richardson, Estudillo, and Berrellessa. At 1005 Escobar Street is the cottage built in 1890 by Dr. J. S. Moore as his residence and dental office. It is now the home of the Martinez Historical Society and houses a vast collection of city memorabilia. Martinez has proven to its satisfaction over the years that the martini cocktail originated in this city and that the present name is a corruption.

Pittsburg, "The New York of the Pacific"

Colonel Jonathan D. Stevenson brought the First Regiment of New York Volunteers to California by sea, arriving in three transports in March 1847 to take part in the American occupation. In 1849 he purchased Rancho Los Medanos from the original grantees, José Antonio Mesa and José Miguel García.

On this ranch, Stevenson laid out the site for a city about where Pittsburg now stands. He called it New York of the Pacific, after his home city, and the rancho was called the New York Ranch. The colonel hoped that his new city would become a large and prosperous seaport, and to that end he attempted to locate the state capital there in 1850, but the city of Vallejo won the honor by popular election.

When the Mount Diablo coal mines began operation in the 1860's, Pittsburg Landing was the coal shipping point. The industry was short-lived, however, because of the poor quality of the coal, and the town was not of real importance until the twentieth century, when it became a manufacturing center of considerable extent. The name was officially changed to Pittsburg in 1911, although New York had long ceased to be used. Los Medanos College recalls the name of the old rancho.

Contra Costa's Mining Towns

South of Antioch and Pittsburg, the lingering ghosts of coal-mining days remind one of the brief excitements that took place there from the middle 1850's to the middle 1880's. Nortonville and Somersville, Stewartsville and Empire, West Hartley and Judsonville, with their shipping counterparts at New York and Pittsburg landings, dominated the affairs of the county for a period of 30 years; in the case of Somersville, limited activities continued as late as 1905. High-quality sand was also mined between 1920 and 1949.

A unique population found its way into the Mount Diablo coal district from the coal fields of Wales and Cornwall. In 1882 about 300 men and boys were employed in the mines at Nortonville, while the entire population of the place registered about 900.

Bancroft states that coal was discovered in Contra Costa County as early as 1848. George W. Hawxhurst settled in 1855 at the place where the town of Somersville later grew up, and after prospecting for coal he discovered the Union vein in March of that year. Four years later, in December 1859, Francis Somers and James T. Cruikshank discovered the famous Black Diamond vein. With his associates, H. S. Hawxhurst and Samuel Adams, Somers located the lands afterward known as the Manhattan and Eureka coal mines, which comprised, with the Union and Independent, the mines forming the basin that held the town of Somersville. In the 1880's the Pittsburg Railroad connected the district with Pittsburg Landing at the mouth of the San Joaquin River.

The Black Diamond, Cumberland, and Mount Hope

mines, located about a mile west of Somersville on the same vein, were opened by Somers and another group of men. Since they were unable to finance the building of necessary roads, they never secured title to these lands. Very soon, however, Noah Norton, from whom Nortonville received its name, came upon the scene and took over the Black Diamond, while Frank Luch and others undertook to develop the Cumberland. Luch soon disposed of his share to a group of men from Martinez, who took hold of the Cumberland diggings and made a success of the enterprise and also assisted Noah Norton in getting the Black Diamond under way. Roads were opened to Clayton and to Pittsburg Landing, and in the 1880's a railroad connected the latter place with the Nortonville mines.

The first slump in coal mining in the Mount Diablo district occurred in 1878, when the Somersville mines were closed temporarily, with the hope that they would soon reopen. Meanwhile, new locations were being made. One of these was the Empire Mine, opened near Judsonville in 1878, five miles south of Antioch and about three and one-half miles east of Somersville. A lavish outlay of capital was made, but competition demanded a cut in production cost, and this, in turn, brought the inevitable dispute between capital and labor over wages. Work was suspended early in 1880, to be continued with new men later that year.

Activities speeded up in 1881, when the railroad was extended from Judsonville to the Central Mine. Fifteen new houses and a large hotel were built, and the town of Stewartsville came into existence one mile east of Somersville. Nevertheless, competition was still strangling the industry. Since the newer mines were able to pay relatively low wages for a short time and the cost of production at Nortonville was increasing, coal mining at that place was doomed by 1883. In 1885 the Black Diamond Mine found that it could no longer stand the heavy expense of keeping the shaft clear of water, and by March the mines were permanently closed. Nortonville was deserted overnight. Lodges, churches, and schools were closed or moved to Martinez. Many of the houses were taken apart by their owners and moved to other places. Nothing remains of any of these little short-lived mining towns today except for the cemetery and a few place names.

Activity in Mount Diablo's sandstone belt has been temporarily resumed at various times. For nearly three decades sand was mined at Somersville. In 1932 the coal mines at Nortonville were briefly reopened and worked again. The coal taken out then was given to the poor and unemployed in the vicinity.

While ranching took over the surface, the uncovered mine shafts were a menace that claimed the lives of sev-

Cemetery, Nortonville

eral youthful and inexperienced explorers in the following years. In 1972 the East Bay Regional Park District acquired 2,763 acres of land in the area, including the Black Diamond Mine, and created Black Diamond Mines Regional Preserve. In the springtime, the mine is opened to the public on a restricted basis. The preserve is a beautiful natural area to wander in. It can be reached from Antioch by way of Somersville Road. A short road connects the parking area with Rose Hill Cemetery, recently restored after decades of senseless vandalism. Five stately cypress trees guard the spot. Among the burial markers are those of Welsh miners with inscriptions in their native language.

Clayton, southwest of Nortonville and southeast of Concord, was an important center in coal-mining days. It had a more diversified economy than the mining towns and survived to become an incorporated town in 1964. Joel Clayton ran a dairy farm when he was not a part-time coal miner. He wanted to name the settlement after the Italian patriot Garibaldi, but residents preferred the name of their neighbor.

Clayton's Main Street has some interesting old buildings, including the much-remodeled Pioneer Saloon from the 1860's, the Christian Endeavour Hall just off Main Street at Oak and Center, built in 1867 and now a community center, and the charming Clayton Museum at 6101 Main Street. The DeMartini or Clayton Winery building on the north side of Main Street at the western edge of town still stands. The Old Mount Diablo Winery on the east side of Marsh Creek Road is having a resurgence as a soft-drink bottling warehouse.

Antioch

The story of Antioch begins with twin brothers, William Wiggin Smith and Joseph Horton Smith, born in New Hampshire in 1811. Both brothers were carpenters and ordained ministers in the Christian Church, and both took their families to California to seek their fortunes in 1849.

Since carpenters were in demand, the Smith brothers agreed to go to work at a place called New York of the Pacific. Arriving there in July 1849, they were welcomed by Dr. John Marsh and were able to obtain the two quarter sections of land where Antioch now stands. Here in December they broke ground and set up tents. Working their lands enough to hold them, the Smiths continued their carpentry work at New York of the Pacific, often going to Smith's Landing, as it was known at first, to cut firewood for the New York House, the hotel and eating establishment the brothers founded.

Joseph Smith died of malaria at New York of the Pacific in February 1850. The following summer, a shipload of settlers arrived in San Francisco aboard the *California Packet* from Maine. This group of New England frontier families had sailed to California to found a colony. Hearing of the new arrivals and of their wish to settle in California, William Smith hastened to San Francisco to meet them. He invited them to come to Smith's Landing; although the gold mines proved too enticing for some of the company, a number accepted the invitation.

A street plan was now laid out, and to each family that wished to settle on the land Smith presented a lot on which to build a home. The first house built was that of George W. Kimball, captain of the *California Packet*, at Third and E streets. Nearby, a plaque at the foot of F (once Kimball) Street commemorates the first settlers.

At what is now the rear of the Campanil Cinema at 600–604 Second Street, a picnic was held on July 4, 1851, at Smith's home. The all-absorbing question of the day was "What shall we name our town?" One proposed "Minton," the name of a river boat, in the hope that it might be induced to stop at the landing; another proposed "Paradise," which was rejected because of the uncertainty of land titles in California, a circumstance that might result in "Paradise Lost" for the holders. At length Smith proposed that, inasmuch as the first settlers on the spot were disciples of Christ and one of them, his brother, had died and was buried on the land, it be given a Biblical name in his honor. He proposed that they adopt the name of Antioch for their town, because "at Antioch, Syria, the followers of Christ were first called Christians." The name was accepted at once.

Although many of Antioch's old buildings have succumbed to fire or the ravages of time, an area known as Old Town can still be seen, bounded by E, I, and Sixth streets and the San Joaquin River. The home of Stephen McKellips, the first engineer on the Empire Railroad that ran to the Empire Mine, was built in 1882 and still stands at 504 Sixth Street. At 302 and 308 I Street are the old McGuire and DeWitt homes; the Hard Home at 815 First Street was built about 1870 by Roswell B. Hard, first mayor of Antioch. Here the first city council met in 1872 when Antioch was incorporated.

Crockett

On the site of an old Indian village, Thomas Edwards, Sr., built a home in 1867, the nucleus of the town of Crockett. He had purchased land the previous year from Judge Joseph B. Crockett, who had acquired 1,800 acres in the area. As other settlers arrived, Edwards opened the first store. "The Old Homestead" (SRL 731), as the Edwards residence is called, stands with its tall palm trees on the south side of Loring Avenue. The timbers, some of which came around the Horn, are well preserved. For years Crockett has been the company town of the California and Hawaiian Sugar Refinery.

Port Chicago and Clyde

Port Chicago, where the Sacramento River meets Suisun Bay, began as Bay Point, built by the C. J. Smith Lumber Company of Minneapolis. The name was changed in 1931 to Chicago and changed again at the request of the U.S. Post Office to Port Chicago. In 1942 the United States Navy took over the riverfront area for an ammunition loading dock. At the docks on the night of July 17–18, 1944, one of the great disasters in California's history occurred when an explosion destroyed the ammunition ships SS *Quinault Victory* and SS *E. A. Bryan*, killing 322 stevedores and servicemen instantly and wounding 390 more. The blast broke windows as far away as the St. Francis Hotel in San Francisco. Miraculously, no one was killed in the town of Port Chicago, but the Navy henceforth was determined to move civilians out of a hazardous area. After many attempts, Congress provided sufficient funds to buy out the residents in 1969. The site is now the United States Naval Magazine, Port Chicago.

The nearby town of Clyde owes its origin to the contract drawn up during World War I by the federal government with the Pacific Coast Shipbuilding Company to build ships at Bay Point. The town of Clyde—named for the River Clyde in Scotland, a center of the British ship-building industry—was to be the residence for the workers. The government did not want flimsy temporary homes and commissioned Bay Area architect Bernard Maybeck to design permanent buildings.

Although the war was soon over, building continued at Clyde until 1922, by which time a large 176-room

1919 Maybeck House, Clyde

hotel and 103 houses had been constructed in the distinctive Maybeck style. The hotel burned in 1969; in the same year the Navy closed down Port Chicago, some of whose houses were moved to Clyde. The town, though its distinctive character is threatened by the burgeoning development in this part of Contra Costa County, remains an interesting period piece.

Byron Hot Springs

Before white settlers came, Miwok and Costanoan Indians had known of the bubbling mud pots and mineral springs in eastern Contra Costa County. In 1868, after an unproductive attempt to produce salt from the region, Orange Risdon, Jr., and his nephew Lewis Risdon Mead saw the possibility of creating a health resort, such as were springing up all over California. In 1888, Mead replaced the early cottages with a hotel. This burned in 1901 and was replaced by a second hotel, which met a like fate in 1912. The third hotel on the spot—by now known as Byron Hot Springs after the town of Byron, three miles to the north, from which the springs were reached—was put up in 1914 along with other structures; one, known as the Mead Memorial, built by Lewis Mead's widow in memory of her husband, was said to be the only building in the world equipped with natural hot and cold springs.

The resort's mineral waters were famous and often prescribed for their therapeutic value, but as the fashion for such watering spots waned during the 1930's, the place declined. World War II saw it taken over by the government for the internment of high-ranking German and Japanese prisoners of war. Since 1945 several owners have had plans for the renovation and reopening of the property, but nothing had been done by 1988.

Other Historic Spots in Contra Costa County

Tao House, in the hills about one and one-half miles west of Danville, was the home of Eugene O'Neill and his wife, Carlotta Monterey, from 1937 to 1944. Here the playwright, winner of the Nobel Prize for literature in 1936, wrote some of his greatest works. The house is a National Historic Landmark and is owned and administered by the National Park Service; after many years of isolation, it is now open to the public on a restricted basis.

Point Richmond, at the eastern end of the Richmond–San Rafael Bridge, overlooks San Francisco Bay. Like Sausalito in Marin County, it is both an artist colony and a residential area. The business district contains a number of buildings from the early 1900's, when the Standard Oil Company and the Santa Fe Railroad developed their facilities nearby. The town is on the National Register of Historic Places. At Point Molate, now a U.S. Naval Fuel Depot, stood a building called Winehaven. It was said to be the largest winery not only in the United States but, from 1911 to 1917, in the world. It was a victim of Prohibition and never reopened.

The Richmond Museum at 400 Nevin Avenue in Richmond has many displays about the maritime and commercial history of the city.

East Brother Lighthouse, established in March 1874 on a tiny island off the Contra Costa shore at Point San Pablo, was one of a series of small lighthouses erected in inland waters in the late nineteenth century. Despite government attempts to shut it down in 1934 and again in 1968, local protests kept the station in operation. The principal building of the station is now a bed-and-breakfast inn, and the lighthouse is still maintained by the Coast Guard.

Del Norte County

Del Norte County was organized from a portion of Klamath County in 1857, and Crescent City was made the county seat. Del Norte is Spanish for "of the north"; the county is in the extreme northwestern corner of California.

Klamath County, which had been established in 1851, extended from the Pacific coast to the summit of the Coast Range and from the Oregon boundary to the mouth of the Mad River. Trinidad was the first county seat; it was moved to Crescent City in 1854 and to Orleans Bar in 1855. A small population and low assessed values made county government burdensome, and in 1874 the legislature was petitioned by referendum to divide the remainder of the county between Siskiyou and Humboldt counties. This was done in 1876. Klamath is the only California county to have been disestablished. Between 1851 and 1857, all of what is now Del Norte County was part of Klamath County.

Trailbreakers

Taking a northwest course across the Coast Range through what are now Trinity and Humboldt counties to the sea, Jedediah Strong Smith, trapper and explorer, in 1828 first opened a line of communication from northern California to the Oregon country—a route the Hudson's Bay Company was quick to take advantage of. Crossing the Klamath River at the site of the present city of Requa in May 1828, the great pathfinder and his party traversed what is now Del Norte County slowly and with difficulty. Trails had to be blazed over steep and rugged mountains, while progress was often impeded by heavy fogs. The scarcity of wild game, which was almost their only food, added to their hardships.

A level, grassy bottom near the mouth of the Klamath River on Hunter's Creek was reached on June 5, and camp was pitched at a spot along the present US 101 near Requa. At this point, the exhausted and half-starved men and animals of the party rested for three days and nights.

Unfruitful attempts to replenish their failing food supply occupied them the first two days in camp. The last dog and a horse had to be killed for meat. On June 7, ten to fifteen Indians visited camp, "bringing with them a few Muscles and Lemprey Eels and some raspberries" (thimbleberries). In a brisk trade the white men exchanged for these delicacies the glass beads brought for such occasions.

From the Hunter's Creek camp, Smith and his men crossed over to Wilson Creek on June 8. "We were weary and very hungry," wrote Smith; again several Indian lodges near the camp supplied them with mussels and small fish in exchange for the prized beads. They also brought "dried sea grass mixed with weeds and a few muscels. They were great speculators and never sold their things without dividing them into several small parcels asking more for each than the whole were worth. They also brought us some Blubber not bad tasted but dear as gold dust. But all these things served but to aggravate our hunger and having been long accustomed to living on meat and eating it in no moderate quantities nothing else could satisfy our appetites."

That afternoon Smith killed three elk, "thanks to the great Benefactor." The camp was changed from "the moody silence of hunger to the busy bustle of preparation for cooking and feasting." At the Wilson Creek camp, the explorers occupied the time making salt and cutting and drying the meat. The unblazed trail that they cut from June 11 to 16 through the wilderness of Del Norte County was rough and difficult. The prairie south and east of Crescent City was reached on June 16. Although there were no mountains on this lap of the journey, the dense redwood forest, the thick brush, and swamps made travel difficult.

They made camp in the vicinity of Crescent City on June 17, and on June 18 Earl Lake was discovered by a reconnoitering party. On June 19 Smith himself discovered the river that in later years bore his name. On the north bank of Smith River, tents were set up on June 20. The next day Smith pushed on northward, and soon he was in Oregon.

Alexander Roderick McLeod, at the head of the trapping expedition of the Hudson's Bay Company, entered California from the north in 1829, trying vainly to follow Smith's trail but finally coming southward via the Umpqua Valley and Klamath Lake.

The Klamath, River of Mystery

A mystery to early explorers and mapmakers was the Klamath River. Its source in the Klamath lakes and its upper course were known almost a quarter of a century before it was determined that its mouth was in the present Del Norte County. In the fall of 1826 a trapper of the Hudson's Bay Company, Peter Skene Ogden, set out from Fort Vancouver on the Columbia River for the region of the "Clamitte." His diary gives the earliest account of the visit of white men into the country north of Mount Shasta. Between 1827 and 1850, British and American trappers continued to trap for beaver on the upper Klamath and its tributaries, but not one expedition followed the river to its mouth. Thus the lower course of the river was unknown, and the spot where it emptied into the sea was long a matter of conjecture. Most maps represented the Klamath as entering the ocean north of the present California-Oregon boundary line, and the lower Klamath was represented as a continuation of the present Trinity River. These two rivers, together with the South Fork of the Trinity, extended from the southeast to the northwest and on early maps were represented as one river named Smith's River.

The Klamath was the river course traveled by Jedediah Strong Smith and his party of trappers in the spring of 1828 when he blazed a northwest trail from the Sacramento Valley into Oregon. The first Indian agent, who arrived on the Klamath in 1851, was familiar with the maps of the region that indicated its chief waterway by the name of Smith's River, and he sought to locate that stream. But by 1851 "Smith's River" had become a lost river. The true course of the Klamath had been determined late in 1850 by a party of miners who traversed its whole length from the mouth to the junction with the Shasta River, prospecting every bar for gold. Later the name "Smith's River" was given to an unnamed stream in Del Norte County also discovered by Smith.

The early miners in northwestern California had never known of a river called Smith's but were familiar with the Trinity River, first named by Major Pierson B. Reading in 1845. Reading had discovered gold in this stream, and as a consequence the upper course of the river with its tributaries was teeming with miners in 1849–50. The approach was from the Sacramento Valley. More direct access to the sea was desirable, and soon vessels left San Francisco to explore the northern coast with the hope of finding the mouth of the Trinity River at Trinidad Bay. No river was found at Trinidad Bay, but farther north a large river was discovered (the Klamath) that many believed to be the Trinity River.

Soon all the streams of the region were being prospected for gold, and the Klamath, crossed and recrossed, was mistaken at first for the Trinity or the Salmon. Gradually, however, the true course of the Klamath was determined, and its tributaries were identified.

Klamath City

Miners came into the region in increasing numbers, and Klamath City, near the mouth of the Klamath River, directly opposite the present Requa, was established in 1851. This short-lived city arose with great expectations of becoming the port of entry for the back country, rich in gold. But, because of the shifting sandbars at the mouth of the river, navigation was uncertain, and the place was deserted soon after 1852.

The Story of the Lost Cabin

It has been said that a great part of northwestern California and of southern Oregon was explored, prospected, and settled as a result of the spread throughout California and the Eastern states of one or another of the "Lost Cabin" stories during the 1850's, when new strikes seemed to be made everywhere. The founding of Crescent City itself, according to one early account, was due to a wandering prospector in search of the "Lost Cabin." The following account comes from A. J. Bledsoe, writing in 1885.

"In the very earliest days of the mining excitement in California, a miner more adventurous than his fellows, armed with his rifle and supplied with necessary mining implements, crossed the Coast Range and prospected the gulches and ravines of the foothills near the sea-shore. One lucky day he 'struck it rich.' The rich earth yielded its yellow treasures in abundance, and the solitary miner erected a cabin in the wilderness, with the sole thought of amassing a fortune and returning to home and friends in the East. And there in the 'forest primeval' with the giant trees towering above him, the lonely gold-hunter toiled as if for life, day by day, for many weary months, adding to his store of gold until it amounted to a fabulous sum. The prowling Indians found his retreat at last, and attacking him in overwhelming numbers left him senseless on the ground, apparently dead. The treasure was too well hidden to be easily found, and failing in their search for it, the savages set fire to the cabin, burning it to ashes. When they had gone, the miner recovered consciousness, but not his reason—the light of his mind had gone out, and left a flickering flame of disconnected thought. Bereft of his reason, he wandered out of the forest and into the home of civilization. How he succeeded in finding his way back to his friends in the East the legend saith not. But (so the story goes) he did succeed in reaching home and there, after a brief period, he died. Before his death his reason returned to him, and calling his friends around him he told them the story of his hidden treasure, describing minutely the locality of the cabin, and from the account he gave, it was evident that the lost cabin was situated somewhere on the northern coast of California."

Tributary Gold Camps of Southern Oregon

Mining areas along the Klamath River, of which Happy Camp (now in Siskiyou County) was the trade center, as well as the gold camps of southern Oregon, were long tributary to Crescent City in Del Norte County. These regions were populated and flourishing one or two years before the city itself was laid out. The Klamath section was mined and settled as early as 1851, in the wake of the party of miners who had prospected their way up the Klamath River from its mouth to its source. Happy Camp, Wingate Bar, Woods Bar, and Indian Creek Diggings were among the prosperous camps established as the result of the discovery of rich gold mines.

In the territory now included in southern Josephine and Jackson counties in Oregon, the first discovery was made at Kirbyville in 1851. Another discovery made by a group of seafaring men led to the founding of Sailor Diggings, later called Waldo after a prominent California politician. Discoveries were made in Jackson Creek in 1852, and Jacksonville became the chief center of activities. Soon a thousand and more miners rushed to the scene of these discoveries and numerous mining companies sprang up.

The first port of entry to this region was Scottsburg, in Oregon, but more direct access to the sea became desirable after the experience of high prices and famine in the winter of 1851–52. Consequently, the trail to Crescent City was opened up in the spring of 1853, and pack trains soon brought in the necessary supplies. Agitation for a wagon road was started in 1854, the surveys being made by T. P. Robinson, who in June 1854 determined the Oregon-California boundary line. Work was finally commenced in 1857 by the "Crescent City and Yreka Plank and Turnpike Company," and in 1860 the wagon road between Waldo (Sailor Diggings) and Crescent City was completed. A monument commemorating this old turnpike (SRL 645) stands on US 101 at Elk Valley Road in Crescent City.

As the surface gold was depleted, most of the population departed. Hydraulic mining was introduced in the 1860's and 1870's, and some localities were producing as late as the 1880's. The bulk of the activity had passed long before, although Waldo was still an important center in the 1880's. The road to Crescent City was closed for many years because of the heavy cost of keeping it in repair. The present US 199 avoids Waldo, so that it is necessary to reach it by a side road from O'Brien, Oregon, but there is virtually nothing there today. On US 199 is the Randolph Collier Tunnel, one-third of a mile long and one of California's longest highway tunnels. It was named for longtime state senator Randolph Collier, the "father of the California freeway system."

During the height of mining activity, southwestern Oregon was always connected more closely with California than with Oregon. Indeed, before the boundary line was determined, the miners considered themselves Californians. Regarding this boundary, Bledsoe says: "The decision caused some excitement . . . as the miners did not like to be so suddenly transported from California to Oregon. They had before voted in both California and Oregon Territory and had refused to pay taxes to either."

Of this period of southern Oregon's history A. G. Walling wrote in 1884: "In every respect it resembles and is identical with the history of the mining counties of California, with which state Jackson County has far closer affiliations than with the exclusively agricultural portion of Oregon. Indeed, it is a rather striking and in some sense regrettable act that it is not a part of the former state. . . . The surface mining industry grew up under the same conditions, attained its maximum at the same time and has declined in the same proportion."

A half-serious movement on the part of some residents of Del Norte, Siskiyou, Modoc, and Lassen counties in California and of Curry County in Oregon made headlines in late November 1941; angered by what was said to be neglect of highway and public works projects in their remote areas, these people proposed to secede from their respective states and form "the sovereign state of Jefferson." The attack on Pearl Harbor the following week diverted attention from the idea, which has not been revived since.

Crescent City

Settlers flocked to the northwest coast of California in 1850 as a result of the discovery of gold on the Trinity. Eureka, Arcata, and Trinidad were established as trade centers, but, although a number of vessels—the *Paragon*, the *Cameo*, and the *Laura Virginia*—had anchored in the crescent-shaped bay as early as 1850, no settlement was made north of the mouth of the Klamath River until after 1852.

The site of Crescent City was first observed from the landward side in the spring of 1851, when searchers looking for the legendary "Lost Cabin," led by Captain McDermott, looked westward from the summit of French Hill toward the ocean and saw in the far distance an indentation like a bay. Reports of this discovery spread to the interior, where miners were eager to make a shorter communication line to the sea. In September 1852 another party set out from Althouse Creek (now in Oregon), and after a perilous and fatiguing journey they cut their way to the coast. Elk Valley, located northeast of Crescent City, was named at this time for large herds of elk seen there by the miners.

Setting up camp on the beach, the party dispatched one of their number to San Francisco to charter a vessel. In due time the schooner *Pomona* arrived with prospective settlers, and in February 1853 the town of Crescent City was laid out. By the summer of 1854, 300 buildings had been erected and the town was the center of an increasing trade from the interior.

Crescent City, despite many ups and downs, continued to hold its own as the chief port of entry and as the supply center for the gold miners of southern Oregon, Siskiyou to the east, and a part of Trinity County, as well as for the camp in the vicinity of Crescent Bay. It was made the county seat of Klamath County in 1854, but in December of 1855 lost this position to Orleans Bar. Incredibly, some civic boosters launched a campaign in that year to have the state capital transferred to Crescent City, but nothing came of this endeavor.

The business activity and social life of that early time in Crescent City were feverish in the extreme. Every day saw some new project for improvement. New hotels and business houses were opening continually. Soon the town was encroaching on the forest and even covered the beach. Fraternal organizations were established and a fire department organized.

By the summer of 1855, trails were completed to the gold camps of southern Oregon and to the large area to the east that drained into the Klamath River. The trail that shortened the way to Yreka was long known as the Kelsey Trail.

Meanwhile, new rich diggings were being uncovered in the hills immediately adjacent to Crescent City. In 1854 and 1855 the miners on Myrtle Creek twelve miles to the northeast were making from five to fifteen dollars a day. New diggings were also found on the South Fork of the Smith River, where individual miners were making from ten to twenty dollars a day.

Diggings were also found closer at hand. In November 1854 discoveries were made six miles from the city, on a creek that emptied into Smith River at the White and Miller Ferry, later known as Peacock's Ferry. Even the beach in front of the city was staked off into mining claims. In the Bald Hills six miles to the east gold mines were found in 1856. Here Villardville, named for a Frenchman, A. Villard, was laid out. Many other mining camps and districts in the neighboring hills about

Crescent Bay lived their brief day and then vanished, Redwood Diggings, Big Flat, Growler Gulch, Hurdy Gurdy Creek, Blacks Ferry, Altaville, and Low Divide among them.

Altaville was a center for copper and chrome mining during the 1860's, and was full of life and activity. By the 1880's its glory had departed, and it lay surrounded by peace and quiet. Black mouths of tunnels appeared on the hillsides, and heaps of bluish rock showed the location of mines.

A landmark at Crescent City is the site of an old Indian village (SRL 649) on Pebble Beach between Pacific Avenue and Freeman Street. For many years Tolowa Indians lived near the beach, and this site was occupied as late as the latter part of the nineteenth century. At this spot were redwood huts, a *temescal* or sweat house, a ceremonial dancing pit, and a burial place. Requa, south of Crescent City at the mouth of the Klamath River, is still an Indian settlement (the name comes from the Yurok *re'kwoi* or "creek mouth"). The old Indian "Family House" was restored there in the 1950's.

Crescent City figures, too, in modern history. A 10,745-ton General Petroleum Corporation tanker, SS *Emidio*, was the first ship torpedoed and shelled by a Japanese submarine off the Pacific Coast during World War II. The attack took place on December 20, 1941, at a point about 200 miles north of San Francisco. Five lives were lost. The disabled vessel drifted north and foundered on the rocks off Crescent City. Some pieces of the hull, salvaged in 1950–51, are preserved on the waterfront at Front and H streets; E Clampus Vitus has marked the site (SRL 497).

Relics from the SS *Emidio*, Crescent City

Battery Point Lighthouse, Crescent City

On March 27, 1964, the town was devastated by a tsunami, a great wave engendered by Alaskan earthquakes. Over 24 blocks of the downtown business district were inundated, and much property was destroyed, although miraculously no lives were lost.

Two other points of historical interest in the vicinity of Crescent City are Whale Island, where in June 1855 a company engaged in the whaling business was located, and Battery Point, where three brass cannons were placed in 1855. They had been salvaged from the steamer *America*, which was burned and wrecked on June 24, 1855.

A lighthouse was established at Battery Point in 1856 (SRL 951). Made of huge stone blocks with a masonry tower, it survived the 1964 tsunami. By that time the station had been automated and was no longer in service; the main floor of the lighthouse had been taken over by the Del Norte County Historical Society as a museum. Later the tower was opened to the public. Since 1982, it has once again been a working lighthouse, a Private Aid to Navigation, with a light shining from dusk to dawn every night. The Battery Point Lighthouse Museum is offshore on an island at the foot of A Street and can be reached at low tide on a rough causeway.

The Del Norte County Historical Society Museum is located in the former County Hall of Records at Sixth and H Streets in Crescent City. The building was first used in 1926 and was acquired for a museum in 1963; it

has been open since 1965. The Indian Room features an exceptionally fine collection of Yurok and Tolowa Indian artifacts and baskets.

A Seacoast Cemetery: The Tragedy of St. George Reef

On the bluff overlooking the sea to the west of Crescent City is an old cemetery, in which many of the headstones recall the terrible tragedy that occurred during the summer of 1865. On July 30 the *Brother Jonathan*, owned and operated by the California Steam Navigation Company, plying off the coast west of Point St. George under the command of Captain Samuel J. De Wolfe, was overtaken by a severe storm. Attempting to seek a port of safety, the vessel struck St. George Reef with such force that her foremast went through the hull. There was very little time to get passengers and crew off the doomed ship. Between 80 and 90 drowned, while only one boatload was saved. The *Brother Jonathan* Cemetery (SRL 541) on Pebble Beach Road has been converted into a park. Some of the old headstones are to be seen in the Del Norte County Historical Society Museum in Crescent City.

Headstone, *Brother Jonathan* Cemetery, Crescent City

The Lighthouse of St. George Reef

The St. George Reef Light has guided scores of vessels away from the treacherous hidden reefs that lie at its base. The lighthouse is on a small, lonely isle seven miles directly off the coast and thirteen miles from Crescent City. The keepers of the lighthouse were virtual prisoners the year round; the men could barely step out of doors, and in stormy periods even this was impossible. During moderate weather, however, they were permitted to take turns visiting ashore.

The St. George Reef Lighthouse is one of the greatest structures of its kind ever erected by the United States government. Costing $750,000, it took four years to build, because work could be carried on only in fair weather. It was completed in 1891. The tower is of rock transported by barge to the lonely island. The base covers 6,000 square feet, described as "the enclosure within which men must work and exist and have all that is necessary to their labor."

This unique outpost was closed by the United States Coast Guard in May 1975, when the beacon light was replaced by a computerized buoy. While the lighthouse stands as it did in the past, the Coast Guard has removed the 18-foot-high Fresnel lens from the tower. In 1982 it presented the 5,000-pound lens to the Del Norte County Historical Society Museum in Crescent City, where it is handsomely displayed today.

Fort Ter-Wer

Six miles from the mouth of the Klamath River, and to the east of the present town of Klamath on SR 169, Fort Ter-Wer (SRL 544) was established by First Lieutenant George Crook, U.S.A., in October 1857 as an outpost to guard the Klamath River Indian Reservation and to encourage peace between the Indians and the whites. The name seems to be a variant of the Yurok name that was first applied to a native village and later given to nearby Terwah Creek. The fort was abandoned in 1862.

Camp Lincoln

Camp Lincoln was temporarily formed northeast of Crescent City in the Smith River area. Following destructive floods throughout this part of the state in 1862, Camp Lincoln was established in September of that year at Elk Valley on what is now Kings Valley Road, about three miles north of US 199 (SRL 545). The original officers' quarters can be seen from the road. All the other buildings of Camp Lincoln, which was abandoned in May 1870, are gone. Some important artifacts from the days of Camp Lincoln are on display at the Del Norte County Historical Society Museum in Crescent City.

The Redwood Region

Del Norte County was for many decades California's most inaccessible county, rivaled only by Alpine County in the High Sierra. These are two of the four counties in California that the railroads could not penetrate; the others are Lake and Mariposa. US 101 is the principal access into the county today. From Humboldt County in the south, one drives north through Redwood National Park, established in 1968 and subsequently expanded. This corridor of coastal forestland extends from Orick in Humboldt County to Crescent City. The preserve surrounds Del Norte Coast Redwoods State Park to the south of Crescent City and Jedediah Smith Redwoods State Park to the east, as well as Prairie Creek Redwoods State Park to the south in Humboldt County.

El Dorado County

El Dorado County was one of the original 27 counties. The first county seat was Coloma, but it was superseded by Placerville in 1857.

The Spanish term *El Dorado* has the connotation of "the gilded man." The general understanding is that the name was given to this county because gold was discovered there. The name arose from legend. Andean Indians, perhaps hoping to persuade their Spanish conquerors to go elsewhere, told of a land ruled by a king. So rich in gold was this land that the king's body was gilded every morning with a fresh coating of gold dust, which was washed away every night. The Land of the Gilded Man ("El Dorado") thus became a term for a fabulously rich region waiting to be discovered by the Spaniards.

Coloma

In the latter part of 1847, John A. Sutter, founder of "New Helvetia," later Sacramento, sent foreman James W. Marshall into the foothills to find a suitable site for a sawmill. Marshall chose a stretch along the South Fork of the American River, about 45 miles northeast of Sutter's Fort, and work soon began on the mill.

On the morning of January 24, 1848, while inspecting the site, Marshall noticed shining particles in the stream bed. These were tested and found to be gold. Marshall reported his discovery to Sutter, who immediately recognized its meaning and attempted to keep the news from leaking to the outside world. But the secret could not be kept, and although work went ahead and the sawmill was completed in March, the gold fever was already at work, and history's greatest rush was on. California would become world-famous within the year.

Coloma, the earliest of California's mining towns, was founded on the site of Marshall's discovery early in 1849. Like most of these towns, its initial prosperity soon peaked, and it settled into a quiet village with a few old houses and sporadic mining activity in the vicinity.

As the site of Marshall's discovery of gold, however, Coloma has been of special interest to Californians. In time, therefore, the state established the Marshall Gold Discovery State Historic Park, which includes the stretch of the river where the discovery was made and about three-quarters of the town of Coloma, nearly 300 acres all told.

The discovery site (SRL 530) on the bank of the river is marked by a stone monument where the original mill stood. Nearby, an electrically operated replica of the mill can be seen and is run by park rangers from time to time. Half a mile up the hill behind Coloma is the huge monument erected by the state to Marshall (SRL 143); it was completed at the cost of $9,000 in 1890, five years after Marshall died in poverty. He lies beneath the granite pile, which is surmounted by a bronze statue of him; the right hand points downward to the site of the gold discovery.

This was not the first discovery of gold in California; that honor belongs to Placerita Canyon, described in the Los Angeles County chapter, where gold was found in 1842. The Coloma discovery, however, was followed by hundreds of other strikes in a short time, touching off a population rush never equaled in American history.

Coloma, briefly El Dorado's county seat, has few old buildings left today. The Wah Hop Store, one of the two nearly identical stone buildings, is a remnant of the days when a large Chinese population lived in the foothills; it is today a state museum. The Emmanuel Episcopal Church, also used by Methodists and Presbyterians over the years, has stood on High Street since 1856. Nearly as old is St. John's Catholic Church, a block further up the hill. The Protestant cemetery on the hill is one of the oldest in the Sierra country. Near it is the reconstructed cabin that Marshall, who grew grapes in his later years, built and lived in until 1868.

The museum of the Marshall Gold Discovery State Historic Park has displays on early mining and on the lives of Marshall and Sutter; it is located on SR 49, which passes through the park, across from the gold discovery site. Coloma, a National Historic Landmark, is seven miles northwest of Placerville, nineteen miles southeast of Auburn, and fourteen miles southwest of Georgetown.

The Coloma Road

The earliest roads in the mining region, in reality mere pack trails, were developed in El Dorado County. The first of these was marked out in 1847–48 by Sutter and his men, Marshall among them, as a way to his new sawmill on the South Fork. Running along the south side of the river from Sacramento to where Folsom now is, this first trail followed approximately the same line as that taken later by the railroad and by US 50. From Folsom it passed into El Dorado County by way of Mormon Island, Green Valley (modern Rescue), Rose Springs, and Uniontown (modern Lotus) to Sutter's Mill, the early name for Coloma—the present route of a country road along which a few old landmarks still stand. The Pleasant Grove House (SRL 703) is at the left of Green Valley Road, nine and a half miles east of Folsom. This was a changing station for the Pony Express when it utilized this route in 1860–61. It contains the

Site of James Marshall's Discovery of Gold, South Fork of the American River

only original horse barn from Pony Express days still standing in California, for which it has received national landmark status. A mile and a half northeast of Rescue, where the Green Valley Road turns toward Placerville, the old Coloma Road continues north to Lotus. On the right, three-quarters of a mile from this point, stands the Gordon House, the material for which was brought around the Horn.

The Coloma Road evolved from a narrow pack trail into a well-beaten, crowded highway soon after Marshall's discovery of gold in 1848. Over it thousands of gold-seekers directed their footsteps toward Coloma. Soon after the arrival of a ship at San Francisco, the Coloma Road became thronged with men on foot or on horseback, making their way to the diggings. Mexicans with long trails of pack mules loaded with freight and miners' supplies joined the procession. Oregonians very early brought in the first wagons. A mail business developed, of such magnitude that wagonloads of letters never reached their destination and had to be sent to the dead-letter office. In 1849 the Coloma Road became the route of California's first stage line, established by James E. Birch.

Soon all available land about Coloma was staked out to claims, and newcomers were forced to seek other locations. Thus the mining area quickly expanded in all directions, with numerous trails opening up fresh diggings and newer El Dorados for the onward-moving Argonauts.

The first, and for a long time the principal, branch of the Coloma Road turned north at New York Ravine three miles east of Mormon Island. Crossing the South Fork at Salmon Falls (at first by ferry and later, in 1853, by toll bridge), this road proceeded, as it still does (although realigned around Folsom Lake), to Centerville (modern Pilot Hill), where it branched again, one fork going through Greenwood to Georgetown. From Georgetown a road led northwest to Spanish Bar on the Middle Fork of the American River, where it crossed over into Placer County. Continuing by way of Paradise and the North Star House, this trail to Todd's Valley and Forest Hill was much traveled during the 1850's and 1860's. Another crossing farther up the Middle Fork at Volcano Bar led to Michigan Bluff, in Placer County.

Another branch road starting at Centerville took a more direct route to Forest Hill by way of Murderer's Bar, located a few miles above the confluence of the Middle and North forks of the American River. The present SR 49 follows this road, but instead of crossing the Middle Fork at Murderer's Bar it now proceeds directly to Auburn via Lyon's Bridge.

Crossing the South Fork at Mormon Island, still another branch of the Coloma Road paralleled the North Fork, connecting the populous river-bar camps. Along the fifteen miles of the North Fork above its confluence with the South Fork, crossings were made at Beal's, Condemned, Whiskey, Rattlesnake, and Oregon bars.

At first crude ferries were used—ships' boats brought up from Sacramento, flimsy rafts, and sometimes even the beds of abandoned emigrant wagons. Soon, regular ferry boats, or scows, large enough to carry a wagon, were constructed, only to be supplanted by rough bridges, which were usually washed away by the succeeding winter's flood. Structures of a more substantial and permanent character ultimately replaced these first primitive ones. All, however, were built by private capital for profit. So great was the traffic to and from the mines that many fortunes were made from tolls collected by the owners of pioneer ferries and bridges.

At Whiskey and Rattlesnake bars, wire-rope bridges were constructed in 1854, and in 1856 W. C. Lyon built the Condemned Bar bridge, later torn down when he moved farther up the river.

The first regular ferry in El Dorado County was operated at Coloma early in 1849. In February 1851 this was superseded by a bridge, also the first in the county. All along the South Fork numerous bridges were erected to take the place of the ferries of an earlier date. The amount of travel was tremendous and the profit reaped from tolls was correspondingly great. At the old Uniontown Bridge it was not uncommon to collect from $600 to $800 monthly during the early 1850's, and the Rock Bridge a few miles farther downstream was almost as well patronized.

Of the maze of roads and branch roads radiating from Coloma to the scores of camps that sprang up, fewer than half a dozen are maintained today: the Georgetown road through Garden Valley (now SR 193), the little-traveled Ridge Road to Kelsey, the Gold Hill Road to Cold Springs and Placerville (now in an area of much recent development), and SR 49, the Mother Lode Highway, from Placerville via Coloma and Pilot Hill to Auburn. These old roads are rich in reminders of the historic past: scars of abandoned diggings; here and there the dark mouth of a tunnel reaching into the hillside; foundations of buildings long since vanished; crumbling walls of brick or stone standing neglected by the roadside; remnants of apple orchards; a few gnarled locust trees beneath whose shade inns or farmhouses welcomed the wayfarer; lonely hilltop cemeteries marking once thriving communities.

Monuments commemorating the importance of the Coloma Road have been erected at Sutter's Fort, Nimbus Dam, Rescue (SRL 747), and Coloma (SRL 748).

The Carson Emigrant Road

The main route to Coloma and the gold diggings in 1849 and the early 1850's was the Carson Emigrant Road by way of the Kit Carson Pass. John C. Frémont and a few picked men, including Kit Carson himself, were the first to cross the Sierra Nevada by a route close to this pass, in 1844, and also the first to cross the length of what is now El Dorado County. Crossing the summit at the granite ridge immediately north of Elephant's Back, they proceeded along a ridge that runs from Red Lake Peak to the South Fork of the American River near Strawberry. They forded the stream and climbed the opposite wall of the canyon to the southern edge of the Georgetown Divide, down which they proceeded to the Sacramento Valley and Sutter's Fort.

In the summer of 1848 members of the Mormon Battalion, on the way to rejoin their group in Salt Lake City, were the first known white men to use Carson Pass. In the spring of 1849, Jefferson Hunt, a captain in the Mormon Battalion and later founder of San Bernardino, brought the first wagon that way, thus opening the Carson Emigrant Road to the host of Argonauts who entered California by this route in 1849 and afterward.

Winding its way over a pass 8,573 feet high, the Carson Emigrant Road was long and difficult, but, according to Bancroft, "the immigrants . . . in order to avoid the sharper hills and deeper gulches of a possibly lower pass, had preferred to climb to an elevation of nine thousand feet to secure a road less broken. As they arrived at the pass late in summer when the snow was off the ground this would do very well."

The course of the old road through El Dorado County may be traced on modern maps by the names of campsites, once important places along the divide between the Cosumnes River and the South Fork of the American River: Tragedy Springs (on the Amador County line), Leek Spring, Camp Springs, Sly Park, Pleasant Valley, Diamond Springs, Mud Springs (now El Dorado), Shingle Springs, Clarksville, and White Rock Springs (in Sacramento County). From White Rock Springs to El Dorado, US 50 follows roughly the same route today, but from El Dorado to Silver Lake in the High Sierra no through travel goes over the old road, the Carson Emigrant Road having been superseded by the Placerville Road, now part of US 50.

Traffic over the Carson Road was enormous during the early 1850's, and a chain of wayside stations was established along its entire length between Mormon Station (later Genoa, Nevada) and Hangtown (Placerville). Every mile had its inn or hotel. Few remnants of these early taverns remain, and even the sites of many would be difficult to determine exactly.

From the main road a number of branches diverged at various points, chiefly at Diamond Springs, where the stream of emigrants turned off to Coloma by way of Hangtown and (as new diggings were discovered) to Salmon Falls, Pilot Hill, Georgetown, Kelsey's Diggings, and numerous other camps. Two main branches led to the southern mines, one by way of Grizzly Flats to Brownsville (Mendon), Indian Diggins, and Fiddletown (in Amador County), and another via Mud Springs to Logtown, Quartzburg (Nashville), Saratoga (Yeomet), and Drytown (in Amador County). At Clarksville still another fork of the Carson Road went to Folsom, and thence to Auburn and the river-bar camps on the North Fork of the American River. Many of these arms of the old Emigrant Road may be traveled today over good county roads, with historic reminders of the past visible on every hand.

Although the Carson Road continued to be used for twenty years or more, increased transportation necessitated the development of easier routes. As an all-year road, the Carson Pass route, subject to deep snows, was impossible, and a road over a lower pass became imperative. This need led to the survey and construction of the Placerville Road over Echo Summit and down the canyon of the South Fork of the American River to Hangtown.

The Placerville Road

Deviations from the Carson Emigrant Road began very early. Gold-seekers, impatient to reach their destination quickly, often took great risks in trying new routes. The most popular of these shorter trails took the so-called Johnson's Cutoff, later the Placerville Road. With the construction of Bartlett's Bridge on the South Fork of the American River near the Pacific House, this route was made passable for wagons before 1854, and a large proportion of the overland emigration was early diverted to it.

The tremendous growth of population in California during the early 1850's and a corresponding increase in overland transportation hastened the demand for improved, all-year highways to take the place of those first long and precipitous trails over the higher passes of the Sierra. After much agitation, the state legislature in 1855 passed a bill authorizing the survey and construction of such a road, the cost of which was not to exceed $105,000. No appropriation was made for the work, however, and the expense of preliminary surveys had to be met by private subscription.

Keeping to the southern exposures of the ridges and canyons, and avoiding, as much as possible, the higher altitudes in order to chart a route that could be kept open throughout the winter, Surveyor General H. S. Marlette and his assistant, Sherman Day, finally recommended that part of the Johnson's Cutoff route that followed the canyon of the South Fork of the American River as far as Echo Summit and from there through Luther's Pass, Hope Valley, and the canyon of the West Carson River to the state line. This path avoided the steep eastern declivity over the western summit of the Sierra negotiated by the Carson and Johnson routes.

The Placerville Road was actually being used by some emigrants and toll companies had been constructing it piece by piece when in 1858 it became the joint project of El Dorado, Sacramento, and Yolo counties, which together appropriated $50,000 for construction. Before the road was graded or leveled, J. B. Crandall's Pioneer Stage Company began to operate between Placerville and Genoa, Nevada, making the trip in 24 hours. Meanwhile, George Chorpenning had obtained a government contract to carry the weekly mails between Placerville and Salt Lake City, with an annual stipend of $136,000, and the first overland mail via this central route arrived in California at 11:00 P.M. on July 19, 1858. With this demonstration it was proved once and for all that "a highway over the 'terrible' Sierra was both possible and practicable."

State and county governments, however, continued to be lethargic. Failing to make appropriations for further improvements or maintenance of the road, the whole enterprise, so nicely started in 1858, would have collapsed, and the Placerville Road would soon have become impassable but for the timely discovery of the rich silver deposits of the Comstock Lode in Nevada. Private companies immediately obtained charters to establish toll roads, and immense sums were expended on the four or five detours routed by these new companies. So great was the traffic over the Placerville turnpikes that the promoters not only cleared all expenses but made vast fortunes from the toll collections.

During the years 1859 to 1866, this "grand artery of travel" witnessed a great era of staging and freighting by horse-drawn vehicles. By day continuous streams of one- to eight-span teams moved in both directions, while at night from four to six Concord coaches rumbled in and out of Placerville loaded with bullion, passengers, and mail. Mule trains, filling the canyons with the music of their bells; cumbersome freight schooners, rumbling over the rough roads; aristocratic Concord coaches, rattling at breakneck speed over the narrow, tortuous thread of road; Pony Express riders filling the night with the clop of galloping hooves—all passed over this great thoroughfare through country once traversed only by Indians.

An actual check made of this overland commerce as it passed by Swan's tollhouse during three months of 1864 revealed that 6,667 foot travelers, 833 travelers on horseback, 3,164 stage passengers, 5,000 pack animals, 2,564 teams, and 4,649 head of cattle had gone that way. During the years 1864 and 1865, 320 tons of freight passed through Placerville daily, while the combined freight charges of 1863 could not have been less than $12,000,000. William H. Brewer, who camped at Slippery Ford in August 1863, says that 5,000 teams were then employed steadily in the Virginia City trade. Mark Twain's humorous version of Horace Greeley's stage ride over the old Placerville Road in the summer of 1859 is one of the choice passages of *Roughing It*.

Landmarks of the Stagecoach Trail

The present Placerville Road, US 50, has been converted to freeway, and thus misses most of the historic sites. The traveler in search of the past is therefore advised to follow, as far as possible, the old highway through Camino, Pollock Pines, and other settlements where there are still some reminders of the old stage road and of the former inns along the way. Many years ago, the Forest Service of the El Dorado National Forest placed a chain of "Pioneer Days" markers designating the sites of the old landmarks, but most of these signs have disappeared at the hands of time and vandals. A number of the old stone mileposts designating the distance from Placerville can still be found. During the centennial of the Pony Express in 1960, markers were placed by the state of California at the sites of the remount stations along the route. These markers indicated that US 50 actually touches and utilizes bits of the still older road from Placerville to Meyers at the southern end of Lake Tahoe and beyond. Other fragments of the earlier road are plainly visible on the sides of the steep canyon walls above or below the highway.

Leaving Placerville, one may take the short bypath through Smith Flat, a former mining town, before swinging again to US 50. The old Smith Flat House, built in 1852, still stands by the roadside, now doing duty as a restaurant. The site of the Three Mile House, later known as the Home Ranch and eventually one of 93 mile-marker houses on this road, marks the beginning of the actual ascent of the high mountains. Beyond Cedar Grove was the junction with the west end of the old Plank Road.

In Cedar Grove is the site of the original Sportsman's Hall (SRL 704), also known as Twelve Mile House. The plaque notes that it was both a stage stop and "a relay station of the Central Overland Pony Express. Here, at 7:40 A.M., April 4, 1860, pony rider William (Sam) Hamilton rode in from Placerville and handed the express mail to Warren Upson, who two minutes later sped on his way eastward." The present building is of a later date. During the mid-1860's stable room for 500 horses was maintained here.

A stone monument, erected by the Native Sons and Native Daughters of the Golden West of Placerville in honor of the brave pioneer officers of the law, stands at Bullion Bend high above the great canyon of the South Fork. This is now on a bypassed and virtually abandoned stretch of road below the highway and about a mile beyond Pollock Pines. At this point two coaches of the Pioneer Stage Line running between Virginia City and Sacramento were held up and robbed by a gang of fourteen men on the night of June 30, 1869. Eight sacks of bullion and a money chest were taken. An attempt was made to capture the bandits, resulting in an encounter at the Somerset House (in the southern part of El Dorado County) in which one deputy sheriff, Joseph Staples, lost his life, and another, George C. Ranney, was badly wounded. Later, one of the bandits, Thomas Poole, was captured and executed at Placerville.

Near here the first glimpse is had of the South Fork of the American River, a narrow silver ribbon gleaming amid the pines more than a thousand feet below, while far to the east snow-patched Pyramid Peak stands silhouetted against the sky. Here the road begins to drop slowly into the canyon, passing Fresh Pond and the Pacific Ranger Station before reaching the Pacific House one mile beyond Fresh Pond. Built in 1859, the original hostelry at this site housed many a famous wanderer in the early days. Here Horace Greeley, Mark Twain, and Thomas Starr King all stopped on their way to Sacramento over the old emigrant trail.

Passing the site of the old Brockliss Grade (used from 1859 to 1864 by stages only), one can see the Esmeralda Falls tumbling down the mountainside above the road. At the junction with Ice House Road a monument indicates the site of Moore's Station (SRL 705), where Baker's fast rig changed horses in toll-road days. This area was later called Riverton, and a resort developed at the very edge of the South Fork. From here the highway follows along the north bank of the river for several miles.

The site of the original White Hall watering place and saloon a few miles up the river is now occupied by the White Hall store and resort. On the right is the site of the old bridge, which once stood at the east end of the Oglesby Grade, one of the four or five detours used between 1861 and 1864 on the Placerville Road. The west end of this grade was at the Fourteen Mile House.

The sites of Sol Perrin's Road House and the Sugar Loaf House (SRL 706) are the next points of historic interest. A mile beyond Sugar Loaf is Kyburz, where a small community forms a center of trade for campers and tourists. Trails to the Silver Lake country lure the modern vacationer into the magnificent scenic highlands of this region.

Narrowing to a rocky gorge, the canyon of the South Fork becomes wilder and more spectacular as the site of the old Riverside House is approached. Mother Weltie's (or the Leon Station), the Champlain House, the Georgetown Junction House, Log Cabin Number Two, and the Watcheer House, once a well-patronized hotel, are sites passed in quick succession as one swings up the canyon.

One of the most interesting points along the entire Placerville Road is reached at Strawberry Flat, to the right of which the perpendicular walls of Lover's Leap rise more than 1,000 feet above the floor of the little valley. To the left the rocky summit of Pyramid Peak towers 4,000 feet above the river, with Horsetail Falls gleaming white against the gray and barren crags far up the mountainside.

In a beautiful Sierra meadow, surrounded by river and canyon and mountain, stands the Strawberry Lodge, formerly a popular teamsters' resort. The present building has supplanted the original Strawberry Valley House (SRL 707), which stood below the present site not far from the river. An annual profusion of wild strawberries appeared here.

Turning up the canyon toward Echo Summit, the highway passes by or near several more historic sites. Toll House Flat, where today may be seen modern summer camps half hidden among the pines and luxuriant meadows of wildflowers, is the site of George Swan's Upper Toll House. Next the traveler comes to the sites of the Snow Slide House of pioneer days and of Phillips Station, where modern facilities are located. The post office for this station is Little Norway, formerly Vade. Audrain Station is next, then the beginning of the old Hawley Grade into Alpine County, over Luther Pass, used from 1859 to 1861. Finally, at 7,382 feet, one reaches Echo Summit, where in pioneer days the Sixty Mile House was located. From this vicinity a magnificent panoramic view may be had of Lake Valley, the Upper Truckee River, the southern end of Lake Tahoe, and the barren mountains of Nevada on the horizon beyond.

From Echo Summit the highway drops quickly to the floor of Lake Valley. Here, near Echo Creek, once stood the Osgood Toll House. The road from Woodfords (in Alpine County) joins US 50 near Meyers, located on the site of Yank's Station (SRL 708). Following around the southern end of Lake Tahoe, the old Placerville Road continued on into Nevada by one of two routes, the Carson Valley route via Daggett Pass, and the later road along the eastern side of the lake by way of the old Glenbrook station in Nevada. Friday's Station, the easternmost remount station of the California Division of the Pony Express (SRL 728), lay about three-quarters of a mile east of the California-Nevada state line, although the landmark site is on the west side of the line on US 50. On October 20, 1861, the Pony Express gave way to the transcontinental telegraph; the extraordinary enterprise acknowledged by the markers on the Placerville Road lasted just eighteen months.

River Bars

In the summer of 1848, after Marshall's gold discovery, other discoveries followed, and soon mining was being carried on along the river bars above and below Coloma. Prospectors also pushed out across the Georgetown Divide to the Middle Fork of the American River, where many stopped to pan. By 1849, thousands of newcomers were working every foot of the Middle and South forks of the American River, as well as the various branches of the Cosumnes River.

Practically nothing remains today to mark the exact sites of these old river camps. Some are inundated by Folsom Lake. The bars themselves have changed location, and all of the buildings have disappeared. In El Dorado County there were scores of such camps, for the Middle Fork of the American River was generally considered to be the richest river mining region in California. At least 10,000 men worked on this fork during the late summer and autumn of 1849, extracting something like ten million dollars' worth of gold dust from the river sands.

Along the junction of the North and South forks on the El Dorado side of the river were the following bars: Condemned, Long, Granite, Whiskey, and Oregon. East of the confluence of the North and Middle forks were numerous other bars: Louisiana, New York, Murderer's, Wild Cat, Willow, Hoosier, Green Mountain, Maine, Poverty, Spanish, Ford's, Volcano, Big, Rocky, Sandy, Grey Eagle, Yankee Slide, Eureka, Boston, and Alabama. Murderer's Bar, two or three miles up the Middle Fork from its junction with the North Fork, was the scene, in the spring of 1849, of the massacre of five white men by Indians in revenge for the murder of some Indians at the place by these very men several days before. Spanish Bar, mined as early as 1848 by men who came from Coloma, was one of several bars that produced more than a million dollars.

Among the hundreds of claims along the South Fork were the following bars: Dutch, Kanaka, Red, Stony, Ledge, Missouri, Michigan, and Chili. Along the Co-

sumnes River and its branches were a dozen or more river camps, among them Big Bar, Michigan Bar, Diving Bell Bar, Wisconsin Bar, Nashville Bar, Yeomet Bar, Pittsburg Bar, and Buck's Bar.

Placerville

Placerville (SRL 475), at first known as Old Dry Diggins, and then as Hangtown, was founded in 1848. James Marshall stated that in the summer of that year he had located the Old Dry Diggins. Usually, however, this discovery has been credited to William Daylor, owner of a ranch on the Cosumnes River not far from New Helvetia (Sacramento). Daylor did pan for gold on Hangtown Creek during that spring, in company with Perry McCoon and Jared Sheldon. With the help of a number of Indians, they took out from one small ravine, "not more than a hundred yards long by four feet wide and two or three feet deep," as much as $17,000 in one week's time. Governor R. B. Mason, who had the spot pointed out to him that July, included it in his report to the federal government, mentioning Daylor and McCoon as the men who had worked it.

The Old Dry Diggins had become quite a camp by the autumn of 1848. At first it was practically free from crime, but the motley society that began pouring in by 1849 brought with it the criminal element of all nations. Robberies and murders became prevalent, and because there was no organized government, the people took matters into their own hands—a phenomenon found elsewhere in the state at this time. By the fall of 1849, three men had been flogged and hanged, thus giving rise to the name of Hangtown. The site of one of the hangman's trees is at 305 Main Street (SRL 141). By 1850, Hangtown had become a well-ordered community, and in May 1854 the town was incorporated under the name of Placerville in preference to Ravine City, also suggested as a substitute for the earlier designation.

The dry diggings on Hangtown Creek fluctuated with the seasons—in winter there was "water and prosperity," in summer "dullness and departures." But with the building of the South Fork Ditch, prosperity became more stabilized, and the place grew to be one of the leading mining centers of the county and one of the most populous of all the early mining camps. Its voting population in 1854 was the third largest in the state, and in 1857 it was made the county seat. As early as 1856, however, a decline had begun, owing to the diminution of activity in the gold fields and the occurrence of two severe fires. A revival followed the discovery of the fabulously rich Comstock Lode in Nevada and the subsequent building of the Placerville Road. From 1859 until the building of the Central Pacific Railroad, Placerville witnessed an even greater period of activity, marked by the construction of permanent church buildings, an academy, hotels, and business houses. Placerville was a relay station of the Central Overland Pony Express from April 4, 1860, to June 30, 1861; on July 1, 1861, it became the western terminus of the route, and remained so until the Pony Express ran its final course on October 26, 1861. A marker (SRL 701) in honor of this brief episode of Western history is located at Main and Sacramento Streets.

Much of the charm of present-day Placerville is due to the fact that its streets conform to the topography. Following the courses of the streams and gulches and the contours of the surrounding hills, the earliest settlers pitched their tents or built their first log cabins along these meandering paths. Later the builders of the permanent town were content to emulate the early example set them. As the traditional cowpaths set the pattern for the streets of Boston, so the pack-mule trails of the miners to the diggings are responsible for the intriguing course of Placerville's Main Street along Hangtown Creek, as well as for the direction of the side streets and alleyways that penetrate the ravines and the steep hillsides, many now covered with old-fashioned homes and shaded gardens.

Placerville's central area was swept by fire in 1856, but the brick and greenstone John Fountain (or Nuss) Building at 524 Main Street, erected four years before, survived the fire and still stands today. The nearby Placerville Hardware Store was constructed after the 1856 fire and is one of the oldest continuously operated hardware businesses in California. The old City Hall at 487 Main Street was originally built in 1860 as the house for Confidence Engine Company No. 1, in the days of volunteer fire companies. It became Placerville's seat of government in 1902. Next door, at 489 Main Street, a plaque placed by the Native Daughters of the Golden West on a two-story balconied structure honors "Emigrant Jane [Shrovers Johnson, who] drove a band of horses across the plains and from the proceeds of that sale erected this building in 1861." A fire tower (1898) at the plaza in the center of Main Street still carries alarms to the community.

At 300 Main Street is the Cary House, built in 1857. It was a stage stop for the Wells Fargo and Pioneer Lines. Mark Twain was one of its early guests, as was Horace Greeley, who stayed there in 1859 on his overland journey to San Francisco in the interest of a transcontinental railway. It is reported that he addressed the citizens of the town from the veranda (no longer in existence). In the Comstock silver bonanza, Wells Fargo passed $90,000,000 in bullion through this office alone. For

Fire Tower, Placerville

many years known as the Raffles Hotel, it has been considerably remodeled and once again is known as the Cary House.

Among other residents of early Placerville were the merchants Mark Hopkins and Collis P. Huntington, two of the "Big Four" entrepreneurs who brought the first railroad to California (the other two being Charles Crocker and Leland Stanford); Philip Armour, a Placerville ditching contractor who became the meat-packing king of Chicago; and the poet and educator Edwin Markham, who also lived briefly in Coloma. John M. Studebaker, a wheelwright and blacksmith, worked from 1853 to 1858 in a shop (SRL 142) at 543 Main Street, where he made wheelbarrows for the miners and amassed the capital for the factory that he later started with his brothers in South Bend, Indiana. There, instead of wheelbarrows, they manufactured wagons and buggies. With the advent of the automobile, the Studebakers became distributors of the car that they later bought out and manufactured under their own name. Early in this century, the elderly J. M. Studebaker revisited Placerville, the scene of his initial success, keeping a promise made on leaving the place that he would return in 50 years. A little group of pioneers banqueted with him on this occasion.

In 1986, the Native Sons of the Golden West marked the Bee-Bennett Mansion at 643 Bee Street as a historic site. Now the Elks Hall, it was built in 1853 by Colonel Frederick A. Bee, who founded the Bee Telegraph Company, one of the first telegraph companies in California and a parent of Western Union. For many years after

1889, Judge Marcus Bennett and his family lived in the remodeled mansion.

The old Hangtown bell, used in the early days to call out the vigilantes as well as for fire alarms, has been removed from the plaza where it stood for many years and is now at the park on Bedford Avenue.

At the intersection of Main Street and Cedar Ravine stands the Druid Monument, erected to commemorate the organization in 1859 of the first Grove of the United Ancient Order of Druids to be established west of the Rocky Mountains.

Placerville's historic churches began with the erection of the Methodist church in 1851, which has been moved to Thompson Way near Cedar Ravine and reconstructed as a pioneer memorial (SRL 767). The Episcopal Church of Our Savior at Coloma and Conrad streets dates from 1865. It is architecturally interesting for its vaulted ceiling, an inverted clipper ship frame with joints and bracing following the shipbuilding practices of the day; Mother Lode churches often employed former shipwrights from San Francisco. It is currently being thoroughly renovated.

The Gold Bug Mine is a unique walk-through museum owned and operated by the city of Placerville. On Bedford Avenue about a mile from the center of town, the mine is part of a park, and visitors can go through its shafts and tunnels and see just how a mine looks. A huge stamping mill stands across from the mine entrance. The Placerville City Museum is housed in the Nuss Building at 524 Main Street, the oldest building still standing in town. The El Dorado County Historical Museum is located on the west side of town at the County Fairgrounds on Placerville Drive.

Placerville's Neighbors

Almost the entire region about Placerville for miles in all directions was very rich in gold, particularly along the ravines and in the depressions of the hills. Yields here averaged an ounce per day per man during the early days of the gold rush. Several ancient auriferous (gold-bearing) river channels run throughout the Mother Lode. These drained the region in prehistoric times and added to the wealth of later streams, creating immense deposits of gold. The oldest and deepest of these channels is the Blue Channel. Above it and intersecting it at many points is the Gray Channel, and the White Channel is uppermost. Placerville was always the supply center for this part of the Mother Lode, and dozens of little camps appeared in its neighborhood.

One of the richest spots in the vicinity was Diamond Springs (SRL 487), three miles south of Placerville. Its name was derived from the presence of crystal-clear springs on the north side of Main Street on what is now mined-out ground. A camp on the old Carson Emigrant Trail and then for a time on the later Placerville Road, Diamond Springs grew rapidly as a mining center. The little town was once noted for its fine sandstone buildings, a few of which have survived the devastating fires that have swept it. Scars of placer diggings and remnants of early quartz mining in the outlying hills indicate the activities of other days.

Weber Creek bears many evidences of early mining operations. It derived its name from Captain Charles M. Weber, founder of Stockton. Weber mined along this stream in the spring of 1848, at about the same time that William Daylor discovered the rich dry diggings on Hangtown Creek. Antonio María Suñol, owner of Rancho El Valle de San José (in Alameda County), was also mining farther downstream at this time. Weber had organized the Stockton Mining Company at Tuleburg (soon to be renamed Stockton) and was working the placers at Weber Creek, assisted by a large number of Indians. A store was established on the creek by Weber and his company in the summer of 1848, chiefly as a place where goods attractive to the Indians could be exchanged for the gold that they dug. The Stockton Company was disbanded in September 1848, Weber having determined to give his attention wholly to the building up of the city of Stockton. The Weber trading post, however, continued to be a center for miners, and other camps soon grew up around it. The site of Weberville, two miles from Placerville, has long since reverted to wilderness.

Coon Hollow, about a mile south of Placerville, was one of the most prosperous of the early camps, no less than $25,000,000 in gold having been mined there from an area five acres in extent, the property of the Excelsior Mine. On the Placerville side of the same ridge, at Spanish Hill and Tennessee Hill, other productive mines were located on the ancient gravel channel. Smith's Flat and nearby White Rock were also profitable early camps in the vicinity; both have since vanished.

Cold Springs, beyond the confluence of Hangtown and Weber creeks about five miles northwest of Placerville, was one of the liveliest of the early mining camps of El Dorado County. During its short heyday it had a population of 3,000 and enjoyed a direct stage connection with Sacramento as well as with Coloma and Placerville. From the fall of 1852 to the spring of 1853 Leland Stanford, with his partner, N. T. Smith, kept a store at Cold Springs, but as business began to decline, they moved to Michigan Bluff in Placer County. As mining activities slackened in the vicinity and no new locations were found, the miners gradually left for richer fields. Stores had to close, the stage took another route, and before long the camp was left isolated and deserted on an unfrequented road. The name persists today in Cold Springs Road, and the grass-grown cemetery on the hill alone bears witness to the life that once animated the now-vanished town.

On the summit of Gold Hill north of the site of Cold Springs and seven miles northwest of Placerville, ruins of the old town of Gold Hill may be seen at the crossroads. The roofless walls of a sandstone building bearing the date 1859 mark the site of this one-time mining camp. The Wakamatsu Tea and Silk Farm was a colony of two dozen or so Japanese, the first to come to America, who settled here in 1869 under the leadership of a Dutchman, John Henry Schnell, who had married a Japanese woman. Japanese agricultural methods and crops had no success, and the colony broke up after the death of its leader two years later. The site (SRL 815) is about where Gold Hill and Cold Springs roads meet. The area today is a flourishing region of orchards and gardens.

El Dorado

Mud Springs, later known as El Dorado (SRL 486), was an important camp on the old Carson Emigrant Trail, subsequently becoming a mining center and crossroads station for freight and stage lines. It was a re-mount station of the Central Overland Pony Express (SRL 700) in 1860–61. The name Mud Springs was bestowed upon the camp because the ground about the springs where the emigrants watered their stock was always muddy—a name applied likewise to a number of other old California campsites. This was changed to El Dorado when the town was incorporated during the height of the gold fever. At that time the population was counted in the thousands, and the place was by all accounts thriving. A traveler in 1930 described El Dorado as "little more than a wide place in the road . . . ruined buildings, roofless, with gaping windows and doors half concealed by rank vegetation." A fire in 1923 had demolished most of what remained of the town; Nathan Rhine's store, built in the mid-nineteenth century, was repaired and still stands.

With El Dorado as its center, a rich placer-mining district spread out in 1849 and 1850 to include new diggings at Loafer's Hollow, Deadman's Hollow, Slate Creek, Empire Ravine, Dry Creek, and Missouri Flat. The last place, about one mile to the north, was a camp of some importance during the 1850's. To the north and south of El Dorado, several rich Mother Lode quartz leads were also uncovered, Logtown being a particularly active area around 1851.

Continuing south from El Dorado two miles on Union Mine Road, one passes the site of King's Store on the North Fork of the Cosumnes River, an important trading station in the early days.

About two miles farther is Nashville, originally called Quartzburg, one of the earliest quartz-mining districts in the state. Here the first stamp mill, brought around the Horn from Cincinnati, was used at the old Tennessee Mine, later called the Nashville. The town of Quartzburg was established on the site of an Indian camping ground, and a large rancheria still existed there when the first miners arrived. Less than a mile south of Nashville and one mile north of the Forks of the Cosumnes River is a flat, east of SR 49 and across the North Fork. Here one of the eighteen unratified Indian treaties with the United States of America was drawn up and signed by O. M. Wozencraft, U.S. Indian agent, and representatives of the Cu-lu, the Yas-si, the Loc-lum-ne, and the Wo-pum-nes tribes, on September 18, 1851.

Shingle Springs and Clarksville

Several refreshing springs on the overland Emigrant Road and a shingle mill built in 1849 gave Shingle Springs (SRL 456) its name. A well-made building of native stone, once the Phelps Store, survives from the 1880's, with deep-set arched doorways in the lower and upper stories. Nearby Clarksville, at first a way point for emigrants and later a mining camp, is marked today by a picturesque stone ruin of a building erected in the 1850's, its roof and doorways gone, and a sturdy locust tree growing up through its foundations. Half a mile west of Clarksville on the old Clarksville–White Rock Emigrant Road was Mormon Tavern (SRL 699), first opened in 1849 and a Pony Express stop in 1860–61.

Old Phelps Store, Shingle Springs

Latrobe

Latrobe, named in honor of the civil engineer who constructed the first railroad in the United States, was laid out in the southwestern part of the county in 1864 as the terminus of the Placerville–Sacramento Valley Railroad. The Odd Fellows Hall is one of the old buildings still standing in this farming community.

Pleasant Valley

Pleasant Valley, ten miles southeast of Placerville, was named by a group of Mormons who camped there en route to Salt Lake City in the summer of 1848. At the northern end of the valley a large corral was built for some of the cattle, and a second one was placed on the South Fork of Weber Creek, one-half mile farther north. Gold was discovered while the pilgrims were at this spot, but even gold could not detain them from the real purpose of their journey, and after a three weeks' rest they resumed their march up the divide and over the Sierra Nevada.

When some of these same Mormons returned to California in 1849, news of their discovery at Pleasant Valley the year before spread quickly, and many miners were soon panning out the yellow dust in the vicinity of the corrals, making an average of eight dollars a day. By July hundreds of Argonauts were pouring into California over what would later be called the Carson Emigrant Trail. Coming by way of Stonebreaker Hill, the golden quest ended for some of these wayfarers at Pleasant Valley. Several camps of rude tents and cabins sprang up: Iowaville, on the low divide between the forks of Weber Creek; Dogtown, at the first of the Mormon corrals; and Newtown, one-half mile southwest of Dogtown. With the building of ditches to carry water to the mines, Newtown grew rapidly. Later on, hydraulic operations were carried on there, but in 1872 the town was destroyed by fire. One old stone store marks the site of this settlement, on the Newtown Road northwest of Pleasant Valley.

With the revival of quartz mining at Grizzly Flats in the 1880's, Pleasant Valley took on new life; Tiger Lily, Hanks Exchange, and Cook's were three wayside stations on the road between Diamond Springs and Pleasant Valley.

Old Camps on the Upper Cosumnes

Grizzly Flats is located 27 miles southeast of Placerville in a wild and rugged region on the ridge between the North and Middle forks of the Cosumnes River. A company of miners who camped here in the fall of 1850 gave the place its name, suggestive of that life of adventure common to the hardy young men of '49 and of the rough country into which the lure of golden treasure had led them. The story is typical: while preparing their evening meal over a glowing campfire, the young men were surprised by the visit of a large grizzly bear, to whom the savory odors of the coffee pot and the frying pan seemed also to have been attractive.

Extensive placers were worked for miles about Grizzly Flats during the spring of 1851, and by 1852 the town had grown to such an extent that it polled 600 votes. Hydraulic mining here was of some importance during the 1870's, and a number of quartz mines were also developed, among them the Eagle, the Steely, and the very rich Mount Pleasant. Lumbering, still an important industry in this neighborhood, had its beginning in 1856, when sawmills were first erected there.

Grizzly Flats today has only a few dozen inhabitants. Several wooden buildings date back to more prosperous days, and indelible scars of old mines mark the surrounding landscape.

Brownsville, Indian Diggins, Fair Play, Henry's Diggings, and Coyoteville, once the locale of many animated scenes in the drama of the Sierra gold regions, were also located in the Cosumnes River region, where hydraulic mining was extensively carried on. Brownsville was renamed Mendon when a post office was established (there being another Brownsville, in Yuba County), but its original name was restored after the post office was discontinued. Brownsville is distinguished as the site of the rich Volcano Claim, discovered by Henry Brown and his companions, which is said to have produced hundreds of thousands of dollars in gold up to the year 1867.

Crossing the South Fork of the Cosumnes River from Fiddletown (in Amador County) in 1849, a party of prospectors located near an old Indian village in Telegraph Gulch. A lively camp, known as Indian Diggins, soon grew up, becoming the center for mines on Indian Creek and in Drummond Gulch as well. A population of over 1,500 had gathered at Indian Diggins by 1855, and three stage lines connected the mines with the outside world. The rich gravel beds of the region were gradually worked out by tunneling and hydraulic processes, fires swept the town in 1857 and 1860, and by 1890 only a hundred people remained in the place. Today it is a ghost town, marked only by an old cemetery and an abandoned farm. The nearest settlement is Omo Ranch, whose school preserves the name of Indian Diggins.

Fair Play, an old camp five miles northwest of Indian Diggins, was described as late as 1890 as "a neat little village prettily situated on a sort of table-land shelving from the slope of a large mountain to the southeast." Provisions were shipped in to Fair Play, and to Slug Gulch to the east, over steep and tortuous mountain roads. The present Fair Play store is about a mile and a half from the original site of the town.

Coyoteville, south of Fair Play on Cedar Creek, received its name from the peculiar type of mining employed there, known as drift mining or coyoteing. Theodore Hittell explains the origins of the word "coyoteing" thus: "Each miner had his separate hole, in which he delved. The men, while at work, were entirely out of sight of a person looking over the bar, flat, or slope in which they were operating, but the approach of night or any alarm or unusual noise would cause them to pop out of their holes; and their supposed resemblance under such circumstances to the Californian animal corresponding with the prairie wolf of the Mississippi states caused these pits, shafts, or tunnels to be called coyote-holes and the character of mining done in them coyote-mining. . . . While it was in vogue, many places were completely honeycombed by so-called coyote-holes."

Folsom Lake's Buried Camps

When Folsom Dam, part of the Central Valley Project, was completed in 1955, the impounded waters of the American River rose and flooded an area extending into El Dorado County. Among the old towns now beneath the water are Negro Hill (SRL 570), a settlement of black miners, Chile Hill, Condemned Bar (SRL 572), Long Bar, and Salmon Falls (SRL 571). State markers are in Folsom Lake State Recreation Area, along with a marker for Mormon Island (SRL 569), on Green Valley Road just east of the El Dorado County line. Across the road is Mormon Island Memorial Cemetery, to which the remains of many pioneers were moved before their original resting places were flooded.

Pilot Hill

Standing up boldly above a wide expanse of hills and forested ravines, the conical promontory of Pilot Hill has served as a landmark for ages. Probaby the first white men to visit the region were John C. Frémont and his men, when, early in March 1844, they followed the well-defined Indian trails leading out of the High Sierra and down over the foothills into the Sacramento Valley.

Mining first began in the vicinity of Pilot Hill in the summer of 1849. During the following winter scores of prospectors from the river bars and higher mountains congregated at this point, and a town bearing the name of Pilot Hill grew up near the northern base of the mountain. Not far away, Centerville and Pittsfield developed

simultaneously, but the three camps soon consolidated under the name of Centerville, a title that clung to the place even after the establishment of a post office officially designated Pilot Hill. The small community of today has been bypassed by a realignment of SR 49, and the few businesses have relocated on the new road. On the old highway, now designated Pedro Hill Road, a decrepit hotel, a relic of 1854, stands among a handful of old cottages and newer homes. The hotel, now cut down to one story, long served as post office, store, and service station. On the slope above the old highway one mile east of Pilot Hill is a small pioneer cemetery, where many graves of the 1850's lie beneath the locust trees.

A quarter of a mile north of the Pilot Hill Hotel stands a grand old relic of the early 1860's, the Bayley House. It was erected by Alcandor A. Bayley, a native of Vermont, who came to California in 1849. From 1851 to 1861 Bayley owned the Oak Valley House at Pilot Hill. After it was destroyed by fire, he built the large three-story brick structure still known by his name. Believing that the overland railroad would pass that way, Bayley expended over $20,000 in the construction of a splendid hostelry. But the dreams he so fondly cherished at the grand opening in 1862 never materialized. Abandoned for many years, the Bayley House is now being restored by El Dorado County. On the Bayley property the first grange in California was organized, Pilot Hill Grange No. 1, in 1870. A monument (SRL 551) stands at the site of the old Grange Hall.

Lotus

Uniontown, one and a half miles down the river from Coloma, has enjoyed a succession of names. In 1849 it was called Marshall, after James W. Marshall; in 1850 the name was changed to Uniontown, in honor of California's admission to the Union; finally, with the establishment of a post office, the town was assigned the exotic and poetic designation of Lotus, its former name having been preempted by Uniontown (now Arcata) in Humboldt County. Lotus it remains today.

In the 1850's, when Uniontown's population was over 2,000, Adam Lohry built a sturdy brick store with iron doors and a fine old brick mansion next to it, now a restaurant. With its pleasant garden, this is a charming gold rush relic.

Kelsey

The mining area rapidly grew outward from Coloma, soon reaching across the river and up into the higher ridges. Among other rich claims was Kelsey's

Diggings, located by Benjamin Kelsey, brother of Andrew Kelsey, for whom Kelseyville in Lake County was named. The two brothers had come overland with the Bidwell-Bartleson party in 1841, and early in 1848 Benjamin had come to this part of El Dorado County, discovering the diggings that took his name. Within a year the place had become a large camp, its prosperity continuing into the 1850's.

Kelsey is best remembered today as the last home of gold discoverer James Marshall, whose declining years were on the whole unhappy and full of disappointment. His blacksmith shop (SRL 319), built in 1872, was restored and carefully preserved inside the walls of a little fireproof building constructed by the state in 1921. A short distance up the road is the site of the Union Hotel, where Marshall died in 1885. On the hill is the cemetery, with many pioneer graves. The first slate quarries in the state, working a large deposit of blue-black slate, of which almost the entire mountain seems to be composed, operated there from the 1890's to 1915.

Greenwood

John Greenwood, an old trapper, established a trading post in Long Valley late in 1848. Soon other stores were built, and in 1850 the new town was christened Lewisville after the first white child born there. When the town attained the dignity of a post office, the name was changed to Greenwood. The town had social advantages not enjoyed by many of its neighbors, notably a well-patronized community theater. In the cemetery a small slab of stone bearing the initials J.A.S. and the date January 24, 1863, marks the grave of John A. Stone, a pioneer songwriter of the 1850's, who lived, sang, and died at Greenwood.

Situated in the midst of an old orchard community, Greenwood is still a trading center for a township of several hundred people. The historical marker in the center of town (SRL 521) is surmounted by a fire bell.

Georgetown

The first mining operations near Georgetown (SRL 484) were carried on along Oregon Creek and Hudson's Gulch by a party of Oregonians in 1849. A company of sailors under the leadership of George Phipps followed, and in 1850 motley camps of tents and shanties grew up on the creek at the foot of what is now Main Street. Known first as Growlersburg, it was destroyed by fire, and the old site was deserted in 1852 for the present situation on the hill. The name, too, was changed to Georgetown in honor of its nautical founder. To keep further fire damage at a minimum, the new town had

Old Wells Fargo Building, Georgetown

unusually wide streets: Main Street is 100 feet across, and side streets 60 feet wide are not uncommon.

Georgetown rivaled Placerville in the number and quality of its early social and cultural institutions. By 1855 it included in its list of attractions a school, a church, a theater, a town hall, a Sons of Temperance Hall, a Masonic Hall, and three hotels, as well as many stores. The cultural advantages of the little town, the beauty of its hill setting among the pines, oaks, and cedars of the Georgetown Divide, and the mild and tonic air of its 2,650-foot elevation won for it the title "Pride of the Mountains."

Along Georgetown's broad Main Street, beneath a double row of giant locusts, stand stores with fronts of brick and stone. The former U.S. Armory, constructed in 1862, is especially attractive. It is now a commercial office. The Wells Fargo office dates from 1852. The imposing Georgetown Hotel is the third structure of that name on that site since 1856; the present building was erected in 1896. The Shannon Knox residence, built in 1864 and marked with an E Clampus Vitus plaque, is now a handsome group of offices. The Odd Fellows Hall stands opposite.

The gardens and orchards of Georgetown were remarkable for the variety of flowers, shrubs, and fruits, all grown from stock obtained from a pioneer nursery established by a Scotsman in the 1860's. Many a beautiful plant, rare today and seldom seen elsewhere, may be found in the old gardens of the town, and the cemetery is full of them. Scotch broom from the same nursery has grown wild all over the hills, glorifying the countryside each spring with golden bloom.

Seam mines, a formation of slate interspersed with quartz seams largely decomposed and varying in thickness from that of a knife blade to several feet, are characteristic of the Georgetown district. The Nagler or French Claim at Greenwood Valley is a seam mine that produced more than $4,000,000 from 1872 to 1885. There are other seam mines at Georgia Slide, two miles northwest of Georgetown. Here an open perpendicular bank of slate rock was found with sheets of gold-bearing quartz coursing through it. Georgia Slide, however, dates back to 1849, when a group of miners from Georgia first worked the spot for its placer gold. The camp was called Georgia Flat at first, but a big mountain slide occasioned the change in name. For years it was a wild, rough place with no outside communication except by pack trail. A few shells of houses mark the former camp at the end of Georgia Slide Road.

The old gravel beds of Kentucky Flat, six miles northeast of Georgetown, and of Volcanoville, three miles northwest of Kentucky Flat, once made production records. Among the many old hill camps dating back to 1851 and 1852 were Mameluke Hill, Bottle Hill, Cement Hill, and Jones Hill.

Johntown, five miles south of Georgetown, was named after a sailor who discovered its gold-bearing deposits. Later, when it became more profitable to raise vegetables there than to mine, the name was changed to Garden Valley. An old store stands there. The Empire and Manhattan creeks join at this point to form Johntown Creek. Below their confluence miners have taken out between two and three million dollars in gold.

Lake Tahoe

One of California's favorite resorts for over a century has been Lake Tahoe, a fuller history of which is recorded in the Placer County chapter. First officially named Lake Bigler, after the governor of the state in 1852, the present name was introduced about the time of the Civil War. In 1859, the first lakefront hotel was erected near what are now Lakeview and Lily avenues in South Lake Tahoe. By all accounts, this was not a luxurious or even a comfortable resort: J. Ross Browne, visiting Lake House in the early 1860's, reported that its eight rooms sometimes held as many as 300 guests a night. When the hotel burned in 1865, it was not rebuilt. In the early twentieth century, as resort hotels began to spread across California, the Al Tahoe Hotel was constructed close to the site of the old Lake House. The hotel closed in 1968, but some of its cottages still stand.

California's first state highway was built in El Dorado County, connecting Placerville with Lake Tahoe in 1896. Paved roads, however, had to wait for several decades.

For many years, well-to-do families maintained summer lodges along the shore of Lake Tahoe, traditionally open between Memorial Day and Labor Day. A mag-

Pope Estate, Tallac Historic Site, Lake Tahoe

nificent example of this rustic splendor is to be seen at the Tallac estate, now maintained by the U.S. Forest Service. The visitor center is on SR 89 about a mile north and west of Camp Richardson. The summer homes of the Pope, McGonagle, and Heller families may be seen in the pine forest by the water, a rare open space on the lakeshore. The Tallac estate was once the site of a beautiful hotel put up by Elias J. Baldwin, better known as "Lucky" Baldwin, a San Francisco-based financier who also had extensive interests in Los Angeles County. After the hotel was razed in 1927, the area became a secluded private compound.

Further north, a distinctive private home stands on the shore of Emerald Bay in the state park of that name. Vikingsholm was built in 1928 for Mrs. Laura Knight in Scandinavian style. A strikingly handsome building that is open to the public during the summer, Vikingsholm can be reached by trail from the highway above or by boat. Still further north on SR 89 is the Hellman-Ehrman Mansion, now part of Sugar Pine Point State Park; this beautifully preserved home was built in the Queen Anne style greatly admired at the turn of the century.

Since World War II, the popularity of winter sports and of the casinos of neighboring Nevada have brought increasing numbers of people to live permanently along the south shore, and in 1965 the town of South Lake Tahoe was incorporated. The Lake Tahoe Historical Society Museum at 3058 Highway 50 is housed in an old log cabin and displays relics from the transportation, lumbering, and resort and entertainment life of Lake Tahoe's past.

Fresno County

Fresno County was organized in 1856 from Mariposa, Merced, and Tulare counties. On eight subsequent occasions its boundaries were altered, the last time being in 1903. Fresno is Spanish for "ash tree" and was first applied to the Fresno River, often spelled "Frezno" in early maps. Millerton was the first county seat; Fresno became the county seat in 1874.

The Old Los Angeles Trail (El Camino Viejo)

The oldest north-and-south trail to traverse the entire length of the San Joaquin Valley was known as the Los Angeles Trail, or El Camino Viejo. It led from San Pedro on the coast to San Antonio, now East Oakland. Following a route identical with that later known as the Stockton–Los Angeles Road as far as the later Chandler Station (Los Angeles County, between Gorman and Lebec), the road descended San Emigdio Canyon to its mouth in the extreme southwestern corner of the San Joaquin Valley. From there the trail skirted the eastern slope of the Coast Range foothills, finally passing out of the valley through Corral Hollow and Patterson Pass southwest of Tracy.

Early in the nineteenth century the Spaniards drove in oxcarts over this route between San Pedro and San Antonio. Some of the old water holes along its course developed into historic places: San Emigdio in the present Kern County; Los Carneros, where there is a spectacular outcropping of Vaqueros sandstone, which composes also Tres Piedras ("Three Rocks"), Joaquín Murieta's stronghold; and Posa de Chiné, six miles east of the present Coalinga.

On the site of an Indian village, Posa ("pool") de Chiné, a small agricultural community made up of a dozen or so Spanish and Mexican families, was long the only Spanish settlement in what is now Fresno County. Later, American pioneers came and established stores and built houses. They also continued the practice begun by the Hispanics of cutting down the neighboring trees for firewood and shelter, gradually rendering the place barren and inhospitable. Today nothing marks the spot where Posa de Chiné stood, the pool itself having been obliterated in the flood of 1862.

Approaching Posa de Chiné from the south, El Camino Viejo crossed El Arroyo de las Polvarduras ("dust clouds"); El Arroyo de las Canoas ("troughs"); El Arroyo de Zapato Chino ("Chinese shoe"); and El Arroyo de Jacelitos, "so named by the Spanish," says F. F. Latta, "because they found there many 'Indian huts' from which the inhabitants had fled in terror." Continuing north from Posa de Chiné, the road passed other campsites on the Arroyo de Cantua, Arroyo de Panoche Grande ("big sugar loaf"), and Arroyo de Panochita ("little sugar loaf").

To the northeast on an eastern branch of El Camino Viejo there was another very early settlement, La Libertad, about five miles east and a half-mile south of the present Burrel. Largely Mexican in population as late as 1870, it was later dominated by English-speakers and was called Liberty; the community was in decline by 1890.

Continuing northward, other settlements were passed either on the main road or on laterals branching from it, among them Pueblo de las Juntas on the west bank of the San Joaquin River at its junction with Fresno Slough north of the present Mendota, and Rancho de los Californios on the south bank of the San Joaquin River several miles east of Fresno Slough, a settlement nearly gone by 1870.

El Río de los Santos Reyes (Kings River)

The Kings River rises in the High Sierra and flows through Fresno, Tulare, and Kings counties, forming the boundary between Fresno and Kings for a short distance. Spanish explorer Gabriel Moraga discovered the river on January 6, 1805, the Feast of the Three Kings or Wise Men, and named the river in their honor. Moraga's was one of several expeditions made by the Spanish into the San Joaquin Valley in the early years of the nineteenth century. Some of these were made to pursue Indian renegades or deserters from the missions, some to explore for purposes that included extending mission activity into the Great Valley. Nothing permanent came of these expeditions, although the discovery in 1852 of a huge pile of adobe bricks near Laton on the banks of the Kings River has been taken by some historians to mean that they were intended for some kind of mission structure.

Caleb Strong Merrill, a stonemason who had come to San Diego in 1831 aboard a Boston hide drogher, worked at Mission San Diego and then at Monterey. Accompanying an expedition into the valley near Laton in the 1830's, he described the region, in the paraphrase made by Latta, "as a vast jungle and swamp. The party was never able to approach Tulare Lake. After climbing the highest trees, all they could see in all directions was more trees and a sea of tules."

Pueblo de las Juntas

Pueblo de las Juntas, a rendezvous for adventurers, refugees, and a few pioneers from the Spanish settlements to the west, was one of the first places in the San Joaquin Valley to be settled by Spaniards and Mexicans, although exactly when this happened is unclear. Much of the history of the San Joaquin Valley in these years was never written down and was only recalled by elderly people who were questioned a long time after events had taken place.

Las Juntas ("junction" or "meeting place") was located at the confluence of the San Joaquin River and Fresno Slough, but the name may have referred to the fact that it was a meeting place for fugitives. In the 1850's and 1860's it had a bad reputation of long standing. Horse stealing, gambling, and drinking went unchecked, and murder was not uncommon. It was said that bandits Joaquín Murieta and Tiburcio Vásquez and their gangs obtained supplies here, where they were safe from the pursuit of American officers. A number of Spanish and Mexican families lived at Las Juntas despite its tough reputation, and in the 1870's the population numbered about 250. The Butterfield Overland Stage passed this way and often stopped at the old pueblo.

Ash trees, abundant along the banks of the slough, gave the name Fresno to the locality. Two large specimens of this tree grew on the banks of the San Joaquin River at Las Juntas, so it too was sometimes called Fresno. When a settlement (near the present Tranquillity) grew up about eighteen miles farther south at the head of Fresno Slough, it too was frequently called Fresno City. However, Las Juntas was the first Fresno.

In 1879, when a canal company bought the townsite, most of the inhabitants of Las Juntas moved to Firebaugh. Soon after, the Miller and Lux ranching empire acquired the land, and the remaining settlers were forced to leave. The tule-thatched houses of brush and mud-brick at Las Juntas have long since disappeared, and today the Delta-Mendota Canal runs through the site.

American Explorers in Fresno County

Jedediah Strong Smith was the first American to arrive in California overland, in 1826. He was detained by suspicious Mexican officials at Mission San Gabriel but eventually was permitted to leave the province by a northern route. En route he came to the stream that Moraga, two decades before, had named the San Joaquin, having come upon it on March 20, the feast day of Saint Joachim. In his journal, first published in 1977 shortly after its discovery, Smith wrote that the Indians called the river Peticutry. Smith soon departed for the Rockies, whence he had come to California, but the men of his party, enthusiastically trapping in the streams leading down from the Sierra Nevada, made a fortune in beaver and otter furs, which were sold to officials of the Hudson's Bay Company at their "factory" or trading post at Vancouver, now in the state of Washington. The British-owned Company in turn sent trappers into California from 1827 to 1846, when Britain and the United States jointly occupied the Oregon Country.

The Hudson's Bay trappers, led by Peter Skene Ogden, soon encountered American adventurers such as Kit Carson, as the outside world became aware of the riches of California. Fresno County was in the line of march of several American expeditions, from that led by Ewing Young in 1829 (Kit Carson's first visit to California) to that led by John C. Frémont in 1845. The accounts of these expeditions, particularly that led by Joseph Reddeford Walker in 1833–34, contain interesting descriptions of the San Joaquin Valley and the Sierra foothills on the eve of the American conquest. They also note that the Indian population seemed to be in a decline, an ominous foreshadowing of the wholesale destruction of the valley's Indian population in the mid-nineteenth century, a destruction due in part to the Indians' susceptibility to the diseases of the white people.

Old Stage Roads

In early pioneer days the Stockton–Los Angeles Road followed along the base of the Sierra Nevada, with many laterals branching off to the mines in the foothills. The route through Fresno County passed by the sites of the present towns of Reedley, Sanger, and Friant. Today only fragments remain of the old road where pack trains traced the first dim course and where the lumbering prairie schooner later beat out a well-worn trail.

The principal streams along this road were crossed by privately owned bridges or ferries. Two detours, Lower and Upper, ran parallel a few miles apart. The Lower Detour crossed the Kings River at Pool's Ferry, settled as early as 1851, and designated one of the two voting precincts when Tulare County was organized in 1852. John Pool was running the ferry there as late as 1857, after which the records are silent. Its location was north of Reedley and eight-tenths of a mile southeast of the intersection of Adams and LacJac avenues; the

Site of Smith's Ferry on the Kings River, near Reedley

site was marked on private property in 1959 by the Jim Savage Chapter of E Clampus Vitus.

Smith's Ferry, established by James Smith in 1855, superseded Pool's and for nineteen years was the most important crossing on the Kings River. Because a crossing could be made at no other point along the river during high water, Smith's Ferry remained open to the public after all the others had ceased to operate. Only after the railroad was completed twelve miles to the west did business slacken, and in 1874 Smith's Ferry was likewise abandoned. This once prosperous place was located approximately one-quarter mile south of the intersection of Dinuba and Reed avenues, less than one-tenth of a mile north of the Reedley Cemetery and of the automobile bridge that crosses the river at this point. The site may be identified by a large grove of eucalyptus trees on the west side of Reed Avenue.

Scottsburg was established at the ferry on the Upper Detour in 1854. It stood on a knoll in the bottom lands of the Kings River east of the present town of Sanger. Following the devastating flood of the winter of 1861–62, when the whole town was washed away, a new site was chosen at the foot of the bluff to the northeast. Here again, in the winter of 1867, floods engulfed the settlement. Soon after, however, the town was established on the bluff and rechristened Centerville, the name it still bears.

The old Stockton–Los Angeles Road also made two crossings of the San Joaquin River, one at Brackman's on the Lower Detour, and the other at Jones's Ferry on the Upper Detour.

The route usually followed by the Butterfield stages during the years 1858–61 turned off from the Stockton–Los Angeles Road east of Visalia in Tulare County and, passing through Visalia, crossed the country to Kingston, located on the south bank of the Kings River in what is now Kings County. From there, the route ran through Fresno County to Firebaugh's Ferry, operated by Andrew Firebaugh from 1853 to 1856, and the site of the modern town of Firebaugh. Hawthorn's Station, established by the Butterfield Company, and Elkhorn Station were stopovers between Firebaugh on the San Joaquin and Kingston on the Kings.

During very wet weather, when the river was too high to cross at Kingston, the Butterfield stages followed the old Stockton–Los Angeles Road along the base of the hills to Smith's Ferry; from there they took the road marked out by James Smith especially for the Butterfield stages, crossing the valley 50 miles to Fresno City.

Fresno City

At certain times of the year, and particularly in years of heavy rain and flooding, many of which followed the declaration of statehood in 1850, the San Joaquin River could be navigated well into the valley by vessels of very shallow draft.

Fresno City was established about 1858 at the head of navigation on Fresno Slough, sometimes called the South or Fresno Branch of the San Joaquin River. A pier was built for unloading freight from flatboats and barges. There were a few warehouses, several homes, and a hotel, the Casa Blanca, something of a landmark on the west side until it was destroyed by fire.

Fresno City was expected to become an important town because of its steamboat commerce, its station on the Butterfield line, and its location on the transcontinental telegraph line being built through the San Joaquin Valley. The expectation was not fulfilled, and by the end of the Civil War Fresno City had been abandoned. The name Fresno was given to another settlement, one that had much less promise but, as it turned out, a far greater future. The site of Fresno City is marked (SRL 488) near the present town of Tranquillity, at SR 180 and James Road.

Millerton

A mining town begun under the name of Rootville in 1851, Millerton became the county seat when Fresno County was organized in 1856. It was located on the south bank of the San Joaquin River in the Sierra Nevada foothills, near the southernmost part of the Mother Lode gold region. The Stockton–Los Angeles Road crossed the river at this point.

The rainy winter of 1861–62 caused flooding on the river that washed away nearly half the town. An even more destructive flood late in 1867 was so catastrophic that few inhabitants stayed to rebuild. In 1870 fire swept the community, which by now was shabby, disheartened, and an embarrassment as the county seat.

Relocated Millerton Courthouse, Millerton Lake State Recreation Area

The new vigor in the county lay in the valley, where the Central Pacific Railroad was being constructed through the developing agricultural regions and where the station of Fresno had been created. In 1874 the burgeoning town replaced Millerton as the county seat, and all the officials of the county hastened to the new location.

Millerton remained a sleeping ghost town until the twentieth century. Friant Dam, part of the great Central Valley Project, impounded the waters of the San Joaquin River and the town now lies at the bottom of Millerton Lake. The old two-story brick courthouse was carefully taken apart and preserved in 1941, thanks to the Native Sons and Native Daughters of the Golden West, and the remains were kept until reconstruction became possible in a project completed in 1970; the result is one of the most impressive anywhere in California. The old courthouse now stands on Mariner Point, overlooking Millerton Lake and Friant Dam, about two miles from its original site. The brick and granite structure stands out against the landscape like a monument. Inside are a small museum, replicas of early county offices, and some modern commercial offices.

Fort Miller

In 1850 the discovery of gold in the Millerton region of the Sierra Nevada foothills attracted a large number of miners. The Indian population in the surrounding hills vigorously opposed the invasion of their lands, and the United States government decided to place a detachment of soldiers there in order to hold the Indians in check. The first post established was known as Camp Barbour, after a Federal Indian Commissioner, George Barbour. It was here on April 29, 1851, that one of the eighteen unratified treaties with the Indians was concluded by Barbour and his fellow commissioners Redick McKee and Oliver M. Wozencraft.

The following month, a more permanent fortification was erected at Camp Barbour and named Camp Miller (in 1852 changed to Fort Miller), after Major Albert S. Miller, commander of the Army station at Benicia. A marker (SRL 584) at Millerton Lake State Recreation Area commemorates the fort, the site of which is now beneath the waters of the lake. About this time, the settlement of Rootville changed its name to Millerton in honor of the fort. The fort was partly evacuated in 1856, and the last troops departed in 1864.

The first school in Fresno County was conducted in the hospital building at Fort Miller early in 1860. This building, along with all of the other buildings of the fort except the blockhouse, eventually fell into decay. Judge Chester A. Hart purchased the fort after the military left it for good, and the property remained in the hands of his family until it was inundated by Millerton Lake, created by the building of Friant Dam.

In 1944, as soon as it was known that the water would cover the site, the blockhouse was carefully moved, piece by piece, and reerected in Roeding Park, in the city of Fresno. In 1954 this century-old building was formally dedicated as the Fort Miller Blockhouse Museum, and it is now open to the public. A tank from World War II is prominently displayed in front of the museum.

The Murieta Rocks

So much fiction has been written concerning the young bandit Joaquín Murieta, and so little has been published of an authoritative nature, that it is difficult to state the facts of his career. A native of Sonora in Mexico, Murieta came to California about 1849, trying his luck at mining near Murphys in Calaveras County. Here he encountered the vicious racism that often developed as the Americans swarmed into the gold country. Murieta's claim was jumped, he was beaten, and his wife was raped. In a second incident, also in Calaveras County, his brother was lynched and Joaquín was horsewhipped. After this, Murieta took up a career of violence against the American invaders.

Murieta tracked down his assailants and put a dozen or more of them to death by dragging them behind his horse. In 1851, Murieta's name (or at least that of a bandit named Joaquín) began to resound throughout much of California. Some historians believe that as many as five different gangs, each calling itself the followers of "Joaquín," made raids on highways, farms, and mining towns alike. Joaquín Murieta himself could not have frequented all of the numerous places in California traditionally associated with his name.

Murieta's chief stronghold was in the Arroyo de Cantua, a place of numerous rocks and caves, some sixteen miles north of the present town of Coalinga. Massive buttes known as Tres Piedras ("Three Rocks"), visible from the valley, protected the hiding place, and from this point the lookout could see for miles in all directions across the surrounding treeless plains. The Murieta Rocks, as they are popularly known, are on private property four miles by foot from the end of Monterey Avenue (locally called Repeater Station Road). There is a monument (SRL 344) with a bronze plaque nine miles north of Coalinga on SR 198, just west of I-5. Fourteen miles further north, another marker indicates a view of the rocks.

By the spring of 1853, Joaquín's depredations had caused the state to offer a reward of $1,000 for his capture. In addition, a special company of rangers was raised to bring Murieta and his gang to justice. Random killings all over the central part of California had stirred up a popular frenzy over the whereabouts of the outlaws. On July 25, 1853, the rangers surprised a group of Mexicans in the Arroyo de Cantua; a gun battle broke out, and six men were either killed or captured. The head of one was cut off and exhibited throughout the state for many years as the head of Joaquín himself; a severed hand that purportedly belonged to Three-Fingered Jack, one of Murieta's henchmen, was also displayed.

There is some reason to believe that the grisly relics came from innocent men whom the overeager rangers murdered deliberately. Murieta, it was said, lived on, eventually succumbing to wounds received at the Cantua. But when the site in Niles Canyon, in Alameda County, locally believed to be Murieta's grave was excavated in 1986, no trace of a burial could be found. State officials were satisfied that their quest had been fulfilled when they paid Captain Harry Love and the rangers the promised reward for destroying the Murieta band. Although other bandits appeared in later years, Joaquín and his men seem to have vanished after the battle at the Cantua.

The Arroyo de Cantua was also a haven for the notorious Tiburcio Vásquez, who in the early 1870's had much of the San Joaquin Valley and the adjacent Coast Range in an uproar. Firebaugh's Ferry and Kingston in Kings County were among the sites of Vásquez's raids, which were usually profitable and marked by senseless killings. Once more the state offered a bounty, and Vásquez was captured in 1874 and executed the following year.

Fresno

Fresno is today the largest city in the San Joaquin Valley. It pioneered the development of gravity irrigation, which changed arid land into fertile farms, and it has used its location in the geographical center of the valley to become one of the largest wholesale trade centers in California. Fresno County is one of the nation's leading producers of grapes, raisins, figs, and cotton.

During the last decades of the nineteenth century, when Fresno was beginning its rise to agricultural prominence, one of the wealthiest landowners in the county was Martin Theo Kearney, whose estate, called "Fruit Vale," lay west of Fresno. Kearney's origins are unclear; some accounts describe him as English, while others maintain that he was an Irishman. While he subdivided and leased much of his land, he retained a part for his own use and built a beautiful tree-lined avenue of three lanes from Fresno to the entrance of his home grounds, seven miles from town, and continuing eight miles beyond to Kerman. To avoid the monotony of an arrow-straight drive through the level valley land, he planned the road to include two graceful curves. On both sides of the wide center lane he alternated plantings of fan palms, eucalyptus, and oleanders. Other picturesque roads he lined with orange, olive, Monterey cypress, and many other trees. Huge and impressive, Kearney's trees still line Kearney Avenue, one of the most striking drives in all California.

Kearney, who was president of the first California Raisin Growers Association from 1898 to 1904, planted sufficient acreage with fruit trees and crops to make the entire estate more than self-sustaining. In 1892 he constructed a two-story residence, largely of adobe, where he lived while he was in the area. This was to be superseded by a grandiose "Chateau Fresno," modeled after the Château de Chenonceaux in France; the two-story building was to become the home of his superintendent. Chateau Fresno was never built; in 1906, just as he was about to commence the project, Kearney died of a heart attack in midocean while sailing to Europe.

By the terms of his will his entire estate was given to the University of California, which gradually divested itself of the property until by 1949 all of the land except the grounds around the house had been sold. The beautifully planted acreage surrounding the residence is now Kearney Park, a recreation area operated by the county of Fresno. The building itself, now called the Kearney Mansion, is open at stated times for a nominal fee as a museum of the Fresno County Historical Society. Many of Kearney's original furnishings have been preserved.

Dr. Thomas Richard Meux practiced medicine in Fresno from his arrival from Tennessee in 1887 to his retirement about 30 years later. The home he built at Tulare and R streets, described by a local paper, on its completion in 1889, as "probably the most elaborate residence in Fresno," was lived in by him and his family until the death of his daughter Anne Prenetta Meux

Kearney Mansion, Kearney Park, Fresno

in 1970. The two-story Victorian structure is noteworthy for its unusual combination of architectural forms, which include an octagonal master bedroom with a turreted roof, a sweeping veranda, many windows with bat-wing shutters, and highly ornamental gingerbread scrollwork on the porches. Now on the National Register of Historical Places, the Meux home was acquired by the city of Fresno in 1973 and has been beautifully restored and maintained as a museum.

The Fresno Metropolitan Museum at 1555 Van Ness Avenue has displays of decorative arts as well as materials relating to local history. The attractive building in which it is housed was formerly the home of the prominent newspaper, the *Fresno Bee*. The Discovery Center at 1944 North Winery Avenue is primarily designed for young visitors but contains Indian baskets and artifacts of interest to all ages.

Fresno is the site of the first fight for free speech in California and the first attempt to organize the unskilled workers of the San Joaquin Valley. The Industrial Workers of the World demonstrated at the corner of Mariposa and I streets from October 1910 to March 1911; the historic event is commemorated by a plaque (SRL 873) at the Fulton Mall Clock Tower nearby at Van Ness Avenue and Fresno Street.

The First Junior College

Fresno can claim an important place in the educational history of California, since it was the home of the first junior college in the state. Institutions of this rank, in which California leads the nation, had their beginning as postgraduate extensions of high school. Fresno Junior College, the oldest two-year college in California, opened in 1910 in the 15-year-old Fresno High School building, with three teachers and an enrollment of 28 students. The first dean was George W. Huntting. The

college was first maintained at local expense, but within several years junior colleges were made an integral part of the state school system. The original site of the junior college (SRL 803) is the block bounded by Stanislaus, O, Tuolumne, and P streets. A fountain and plaque at the corner of O and Tuolumne streets memorialize this pioneer educational endeavor.

The Underground Gardens

About six miles north of downtown Fresno, at 5021 West Shaw Avenue near SR 99, is one of California's most unusual landmarks. An underground home of some 65 rooms, gardens, and grottos, it is the creation of one man, Baldasare Forestiere, who tunneled and burrowed there with only the simplest of tools from 1908 until his death in 1946. Born in Sicily in 1879, he relied on the experience gained as a "sandhog" in the eastern United States, which also taught him a way of escaping the high temperatures of the Fresno area. One of the most interesting features is a tree growing more than twenty feet below the surface of the earth and grafted to bear seven different kinds of citrus fruit. The catacombs, nearly a mile in length and covering an underground area of about seven acres, display the marvelous architectural, horticultural, and engineering skills of a man with virtually no formal education. The place was opened as a commercial enterprise in 1954. In recent years it has for long periods of time been closed to the public.

Water Development and Agricultural Colonies

Intensive agriculture would not be possible in the San Joaquin Valley's long, hot, arid summers without a regular supply of water. It is believed that Indians at Posa de Chiné were the first people of what is now Fresno County to use irrigation canals. After California became a state in 1850, cattle ranching was the dominant activity in the valley. With the coming of the railroad in 1872 and new state laws requiring ranchers to fence in their livestock, cultivation of crops became the principal economic interest in the region, and schemes to build irrigation systems were manifest throughout the San Joaquin Valley. The Miller and Lux interests, for example, helped begin a San Joaquin and Kings River Canal that would extend from Kern County to the Sacramento River delta; the project eventually materialized as the San Joaquin Canal, which extended north from the San Joaquin River just west of its junction with Fresno Slough into Stanislaus County. The Kings River was repeatedly tapped by these new canals, which made possible, among other things, the settlement of the west side of Fresno County. According to Clough and Secrest's *Fresno County: The Pioneer Years*, by 1887 the county had canals that irrigated 610,000 acres of land and carried 3,500 cubic feet of water per second.

Also contributing to the growth of population in Fresno County after 1872 were agricultural colonies, communities of settlers initially dedicated to fruit growing. The first of these seems to have been the Central California Colony, begun in 1875 southwest of Fresno. Today's Cherry and Fig avenues were some of the early roads of the community. Vineyards were also planted, and when the scorching summer of 1875 dried the grapes on the vine at the Central California Colony, the Fresno raisin industry began. The raisins were well received in San Francisco, and a major Fresno County endeavor was launched. The Sun-Maid raisin cooperative was founded in 1913, one of the most successful in American agricultural history.

The prominent Armenian community of Fresno was begun in 1881 when Hagop and Garabed Saropian purchased some orchard land. Their prosperity induced other Armenians to join them in a new and freer environment.

Alternating periods of drought and flood ravaged rural California well into the twentieth century. A federal project to build great dams for water storage, flood control, and hydroelectric power, like the projects in such places as the Tennessee and Missouri river valleys, was begun in California in 1935. The great Central Valley Project had nearly been completed twenty years later. The Friant Dam created Millerton Lake and made possible the Friant-Kern and the Madera canals, which irrigate the eastern side of the San Joaquin Valley to the southeast and to the northwest, respectively.

The Valley Towns: Fowler, Kingsburg, Reedley, Selma

The Central Pacific Railroad created a switch from its main line south of Fresno to the ranches of state senator Thomas Fowler, cattle baron, in 1872; Fowler's Switch was the name given to the site, commemorated by an E Clampus Vitus plaque at Seventh and Merced streets in downtown Fowler. By 1882, the town of Fowler had been established at the spot, then as now a processing and shipping center for valley crops.

Northeast of Kingston on the Kings River, the Central Pacific also established a switch initially called King's River in 1873. In the next three years, the location was renamed Wheatbury, then Kingsbury, then Kingsburgh; the terminal *h* was dropped in 1894. The town received a population boost with the arrival in 1886 of some 50 Swedish families from Michigan. Some disastrous fires late in the 1890's damaged but did not destroy the well-

established town, and Kingsburg continues to serve as an agricultural and transportation center, with an annual Swedish festival.

Reedley was begun as another railroad waystation. The 76 Land and Water Company, an important enterprise in northeastern Fresno County, needed a shipping place for its products, and the site selected was on the Kings River close to old Smith's Ferry. Thomas Law ("T. L.") Reed, a prosperous local wheat farmer, encouraged the railroad to build into the area by granting it a half-interest in a townsite, which was named for him. It was a successful settlement once the railroad arrived. Soon it had several substantial commercial enterprises, as well as a number of churches and schools. Reedley is still proud of its churches and schools, one of which is Reedley College. The Reedley Museum, housed in the former city hall building (1913) at 1752 Tenth Street, contains local Indian artifacts and memorabilia from the turn of the century.

Selma, lying on the railroad line between Fowler and Kingsburg, dates from 1880. There is uncertainty about the source of the name. Selma's history is much like that of neighboring towns. It began as a shipping center for crops; the establishment of local businesses, schools, and churches, several destructive fires, and eventual restoration followed. In 1895, a strong Prohibitionist movement in the community resulted in the first city ordinance in California forbidding the sale or consumption of alcoholic beverages. Opponents were able to get the decree rescinded within a couple of months. On the whole, California has not been receptive to Prohibitionist measures. A plaque commemorating the founding of Selma was placed by E Clampus Vitus in front of Fire Station No. 1, on West Front Street. North of Selma, adjacent to SR 99, is the Pioneer Village Museum, opened in 1980. Among the buildings that were moved to the site are the Apple House (built in 1904), the Lincoln School, St. Ansgar's Lutheran Church, the Unger Opera House, and the Southern Pacific Depot from downtown Selma (built in 1887). All are well maintained and worth a visit.

Coalinga

It is reported that peddlers in Millerton were selling gallon cans of crude oil as early as 1865. The oil was collected from seepages in the hills on the west side of the San Joaquin Valley. Some commercial efforts at oil drilling were made in the area over the next 25 years, none successful enough to warrant further development.

In 1890, the Coast Range Company of Los Angeles sunk a well 135 feet deep in the Oil City field, northeast of present-day Coalinga. Although this well had but a small yield, it foreshadowed a larger strike that was made in 1896 in the same location. Within a year, a significant oil boom was on.

Meanwhile, a coal mine had been opened on the west side of Pleasant Valley. In 1887 the Southern Pacific Railroad opened a line from its station at Huron westward to Alcalde; the three loading sites on the route were called Coaling Stations A, B, and C. Coaling Station A—soon shortened to Coalinga—became a center for the oil boom, and as the coal business died out, petroleum took over. The boom town became renowned for nothing but "hell and jackrabbits" around the turn of the century; the barren fields nearby gave little encouragement to agriculture on any extensive scale.

Coalinga is still a community based on oil. The visitor driving in from the east on SR 198 notices an array of fancifully painted oil booms, some decorated as cartoon characters or whimsical animals, others with futuristic designs; locally known as the "Iron Zoo," most are still working vigorously. The R. C. Baker Memorial Museum at 297 West Elm Avenue offers a superb display of local history, including a great deal of equipment used in the petroleum industry. Baker was a pioneer developer in the field, and the building now housing the museum was once his office. History of another sort was made at Coalinga by the destructive earthquake of May 2, 1983, the worst in a series that hit the community over a period of months.

Exploration of Fresno County's Sierra Nevada

Although the expeditions of Joseph Reddeford Walker and John C. Frémont passed through Fresno County, the first expedition to make an extensive survey of the mountains that constitute the eastern third of the county was that led by William H. Brewer in 1864. Four years earlier, the California legislature had established a geological survey of the state, and in the summer of 1864 Brewer's group turned its attention to this region of the Sierra Nevada. Some of this expedition's discoveries are discussed in other chapters of this book. The principal discovery in Fresno County was of the great canyon of the South Fork of the Kings River. Brewer wrote: "Next to Yosemite this is the grandest canyon I have ever seen. It much resembles Yosemite and almost rivals it. A pretty valley or flat half a mile wide lies along the river, in places rough and strewn with bowlders, and in others level and covered with trees. . . . The river swarmed with trout; I never saw them thicker. . . . On both sides rise tremendous granite precipices, of every shape, often nearly perpendicular, rising from 2,500 feet to above 4,000 feet. . . . The whole scene was sublime—the valley below, the swift river roaring by,

the stupendous cliffs standing against a sky of intensest blue, the forests through which we rode."

Today this canyon is enclosed within Kings Canyon National Park, established in 1940. Also within the park is the Tehipite Valley along the Middle Fork of the Kings River, discovered by Frank Dusy in 1869. On a later expedition, Dusy took his bulky camera equipment into the high mountains; he seems to have been the first to photograph Tehipite Dome, in 1879.

Lumber and Big Trees

The mountains attracted miners, sheepherders, and lumbermen. The first sawmills in the timber country began operation in 1852. Almost at once they faced the problem of getting the finished lumber to market in the emerging valley towns. Early roads were difficult to build and to maintain, and flumes whereby water was

General Grant Tree, Kings Canyon National Park

brought through wood or metal conduits, carrying lumber down to the valley, proved equally difficult to keep in operation. In 1867 the Tollhouse Road was built up the steep incline to the mills in the vicinity of Shaver Lake. The road was named for the building erected, at the place still called Tollhouse, to collect a toll from all vehicles being driven up or down the ten-mile road. The steep grade was sometimes called "Beast Killer." The modern Tollhouse Road largely follows its course. The small town of Academy on the road is named for a private secondary school established there in 1872. Pine Ridge and Swanson Meadow were important early lumber centers.

Fresno is one of seven counties in the state in which the *Sequoia gigantea* is found. A small stand of magnificent trees is contained in the General Grant Grove section of Kings Canyon National Park on the southern boundary of the county in the High Sierra. The southern portion of this park is in northern Tulare County.

The General Grant, 264 feet in height and more than 40 feet in diameter at its base, for which the grove is named, is one of the most noted of its trees. General Grant National Park was created in 1890 to preserve the grove and was absorbed by Kings Canyon National Park when that was created in 1940. There are seven smaller groves in Fresno County, besides the Evans Grove, east of Hume Lake, which contains 500 trees.

What may have saved these redwoods is the fact that, unlike their cousins on the Pacific Coast, they are almost useless for commercial purposes. Before this was known, massive logging operations cleared out thousands of sequoias in the Converse Basin, said by some to have been finer than those of the Giant Forest in Sequoia National Park (in Tulare County). In the Converse Mountain Grove, one monarch survives. This is the Boole Tree, a close competitor of the General Sherman as the largest of all the Big Trees. It was saved by Frank Boole, foreman, for whom it is named.

Glenn County

Glenn County, named after Dr. Hugh James Glenn, was organized in 1891, when it was separated from Colusa County. Willows is the county seat.

The Swift Adobe

The adobe home built by Granville P. Swift stood for many years on Hambright Creek, about a mile north of Orland. This pioneer settler crossed the plains in 1843 and entered California from Oregon with the Kelsey party. He served in Sutter's campaign in 1845, participated in the Bear Flag Revolt, and in 1846–47 served as captain in Frémont's California Battalion. Subsequently he settled near the confluence of Hambright and Stony creeks and made his adobe the headquarters for cattle operations extending as far south as the present Woodland. In 1849, in partnership with his brother-in-law, Frank Sears, he purchased from John S. Williams the cattle and brand of the Larkin Children's Grant. Swift soon had vast droves of cattle, herded annually by Indian vaqueros, and extensive rodeos were held at the adobe on Hambright Creek and at a corral (no longer existing) on what later became the Murdock Ranch west of Willows. Swift also is credited with planting the first barley in the North Sacramento Valley.

When John Bidwell discovered gold at Bidwell Bar, Swift amassed a fortune, it is claimed, by working large numbers of Stony Creek Indians on the Feather River. Legend has it that he buried his gold dust about his adobe; many have dug in the area over the years, but no one has announced success in finding this putative fortune.

Swift moved to Sonoma County in 1854, but his name is perpetuated in Glenn County in Swift's Point, near Hamilton City, a place on the Sacramento River once fordable at low water. The river road from Red Bluff and Shasta City crossed here to points east of the Sacramento.

The site of Swift's long-vanished adobe (SRL 345) is on the south bank of Hambright Creek about 100 yards east of the Southern Pacific right-of-way, north of Orland; the marker is on SR 99-W one mile north of Orland.

Monroeville

Monroeville, at the mouth of Stony Creek (formerly called Capay River) in what is now northeastern Glenn County, was the county seat of Colusa County from 1851 to 1853, before Glenn was separated from Colusa.

It was situated on the Capay Rancho, a grant made to María Josefa Soto, later the wife of Dr. James Stokes of Monterey. Out of this estate a portion at the mouth of Stony Creek was given by Mrs. Stokes to a man named McGee in return for his aid in making the grant official. The first settler on the land, in 1846, was a man known to history only as Mr. Bryant, who also built the first house there.

After the discovery of gold in 1848, other settlers located there, among them U. P. Monroe, whose ranch and hotel became a popular stopping place on the road from Colusa to Shasta. The hotel, which was to double as courthouse, was largely built from the remains of the *California*, one of the first steamers to ascend the Sacramento River. It was wrecked at the right-angle turn in the river on Monroeville Island, about a mile above the mouth of Stony Creek.

The Colusa County boundary had scarcely been defined when a quarrel began over the location of the county seat, a phenomenon seen elsewhere in California and the West. Monroe, an ambitious, aggressive man, was determined that the county seat should be established on his land and named for him. Colusa, however, also wanted to be the county seat. Monroe presented a petition to Moses Bean, a judge in Butte County, requesting that the county be organized and that Monroe's Ranch be designated as the only polling place for the election of county officers. Bean complied, though he had no lawful authority to act, and this high-handed procedure seemingly carried the day. Monroeville assumed the role of the first county seat of Colusi County, as it was originally called.

No scramble for offices followed the election, and those chosen could be persuaded only with difficulty to perform their duties. The mines were too attractive and the opportunity to acquire princely farmlands was too great to tempt anyone to give his time to the irksome and unremunerative task of running the government.

There was, fortunately, a notable exception, William B. Ide, primary leader of the Bear Flag Revolt in 1846. For a time, Ide performed the duties of judge, county clerk, auditor, treasurer, coroner, and surveyor. Death cut short his useful life on December 20, 1852; a victim of smallpox, Ide died at Monroeville and was buried in the local cemetery, which is the only remnant of Monroeville today. A stone monument has been erected to Ide's memory on SR 45 two miles south of Hamilton City, only a few hundred yards from the grain field that was once the site of Monroeville.

In 1853 Colusa won the fight to be named county seat, and Monroeville was soon deserted, even by its founder. South of Monroeville, equally ambitious contemporary "paper cities" arose, among them Placer City,

about three-quarters of a mile north of Jacinto, and Butte City, on the east bank of the Sacramento and formerly in Butte County. All traces of Placer City have long been obliterated, but Butte City is now an agricultural center for that portion of Glenn County east of the river.

Willows

Standing out in bold relief from a vast expanse of treeless plains, a clump of willows bordering on a large water hole fed by several springs was the only landmark in early days between the settlements on the river and those in the western foothills. Travelers guided their course by "the Willows." A marker has been placed on SR 162 one mile east of the city of Willows by the Native Daughters of the Golden West at the site of the water hole, which has since been filled in. This place on Willow Creek, the only live watering place between Cache Creek (Yolo County) on the south and Stony Creek on the north, was taken over in the late 1840's by Granville Swift and was utilized by all the cattlemen of the area at a price to the owner.

When the Central Pacific pushed its rail lines northward to Oregon in the late 1870's, the town of Willows was formed, about a mile west of the old landmark. The post office was known as "Willow" from 1876 until the terminal s was officially added in 1916. Willows became the shipping point for many large wheat and barley ranches, and when Glenn County was formed in 1891 from the northern half of Colusa County, Willows became the county seat. The Willows post office, in the majestic turn-of-the-century Federal style, is on the National Register of Historic Places.

Five miles east of Willows the Beehive Bend gas fields were discovered in the 1950's, the largest in the northern part of the state. The fields are scattered over a large area. To the south and extending into Colusa County is the Sacramento National Wildlife Refuge, the

Post Office, Willows

largest of several wildlife refuges in the valley and one of seventeen in California.

Jacinto and Dr. Hugh Glenn

Now little more than a wide space in the River Road (SR 45), which runs from Hamilton City to Colusa, Jacinto was once the busiest river town in the upper Sacramento Valley. This was at the time Dr. Hugh J. Glenn, for whom Glenn County was named, farmed 55,000 acres of wheat land in all directions except eastward from his headquarters at Jacinto.

Dr. Glenn, a Missouri dentist, came to California in 1849 and worked for a time on a gold claim he had taken up at Murderer's Bar on the American River. He made a number of trips across the plains driving herds of cattle, horses, and mules from Missouri, but finally returned to settle permanently in California. After a few years spent in farming in Yolo County, he purchased land in what is now Glenn County in 1867, to which he moved his family in 1869.

Dr. Glenn began the cultivation of wheat on a large scale in the 1870's, purchasing large tracts of land in Rancho Jacinto (so named for the original grantee, Jacinto Rodríguez, who obtained the land from the Mexican government in 1844), Rancho Capay, and the Larkin Children's Grant. The town of Jacinto, 27 miles above Colusa, was the supply center for the huge Glenn operations and the residence of the two to three hundred men he employed. In the 1880's it included a hotel, a large general store, several blacksmith shops, a butcher shop, a post office (1858–1910), and several immense grain warehouses. The first school in the present county was established there. The Glenn home stood for years in a tangle of trees and shrubbery until it was torn down about 1960. The site of Jacinto is twelve miles south of Hamilton City at the junction of SR 45 and Bayliss Road (County Road 39).

Dr. Glenn was nominated for governor of California by the New Constitution and Democratic parties in 1879 but was defeated by George C. Perkins. The man who eventually became known as the world's "Wheat King" did not live to see the county named for him; he was shot to death at his Jacinto home by an employee on February 17, 1883. His great holdings have since been subdivided into small farms, now all under irrigation.

Elk Creek

Located at the base of the steep Coast Range in an open valley bisected by Stony Creek is the mountain town of Elk Creek, established in the late 1860's as a trading center for the valleys drained by Stony Creek

Roundhouse, Grindstone Indian Reservation

and its tributaries. The post office was opened in 1872, and the town was the stopping place for stages from Colusa, 35 miles to the southeast, to Newville, thirteen miles to the north. Elk Creek today is at the entrance to the far-flung Mendocino National Forest.

A conical hill of historical significance lies one mile across Stony Creek from the little town. A large redwood monument has been placed on "Bidwell Hill" by the Willows Chapter of the Daughters of the American Revolution to mark the encampment of John Bidwell on July 4, 1844, while on an exploratory trip in search of a suitable land grant for the children of Thomas O. Larkin. The trip was unsuccessful, but a year later Bidwell located the desired lands bordering on the Sacramento River, south of the mouth of Stony Creek and north of Colusa.

W. C. Moon and Ezekiel Merritt, both of whom were members of the Bear Flag party, and Peter Lassen quarried and manufactured a large number of grindstones in 1845 on Grindstone Creek, a branch of Stony Creek several miles north of the town of Elk Creek, and packed them on mules over twenty miles to the Sacramento River. Here they loaded them into fragile canoes and drifted with them down the river, selling a number at Sutter's Fort and the rest in San Francisco. These grindstones, Bidwell concluded, were doubtless the first civilized manufacture in Colusa County, if not in the entire northern part of the state. On the Grindstone Indian Reservation at the confluence of Grindstone and Stony creeks may be seen an excellent example of an Indian roundhouse.

Orland

A child of the railroad, Orland was founded in the early 1870's and became one of the larger grain shipping points in northern California. Three pioneer settlers met to select a name for the town. One urged Comstock, another Leland, and the third Orland, "after a town in England," according to one version of the story. Unable to agree, they placed the names in a hat, and a child at the meeting drew out the slip marked Orland.

Just east of the city on the Chico highway the Orland College, a private school for students above the ninth grade, was founded in the 1880's. Professor J. B. Patch, who became its first president, solicited funds from wealthy farmers throughout Colusa County for the two-story building. One of the few institutions of higher learning in the North Valley, it closed in the 1890's, following the opening of the Northern Branch State Normal School, now California State University at Chico.

Orland is the center of the Orland Federal Irrigation Project, an area of 20,000 acres watered by East Park Reservoir (in Colusa County) behind East Park Dam on Little Stony Creek. Formed in 1906, it was at the time the only irrigation project in California installed and operated entirely by the newly formed United States Reclamation Bureau. It was a pilot project for federal irrigation in the state and was the forerunner of the statewide Central Valley Project, which was developed in the 1930's and 1940's. Eight miles northwest of Orland on the main channel of Stony Creek is the $13 million Black Butte Dam (in Tehama County), constructed by the U.S. Army Engineers as a flood control project, and completed in 1963. Black Butte Lake (mostly in Glenn County) contains 150,000 acre-feet of water and is a popular recreational area.

Orland today is a major processing center for almonds, olives, and oranges. The ladino clover crop of the Orland area furnishes much of the seed used in the nation; it is processed at a plant in Artois (once called Germantown), nine miles south of Orland on I-5. Haigh

Field, now Orland's airport, was first used as an auxiliary training field in World War II.

St. John and Hamilton City

Hamilton City, Glenn County's newest town, might well be considered the legitimate descendant of the two pioneer towns that have passed into oblivion: Monroeville, about five miles south, and St. John.

St. John, two miles northwest of Monroeville, was founded by Aden C. St. John about 1856 on the banks of Stony Creek, about where it is crossed by the present SR 45. St. John was the home of the first large general merchandise store in Colusa County and boasted also a hotel and large warehouses and barns, built to handle the overnight ox and mule traffic bound up the west side of the river to the mines at Shasta and Weaverville.

As Monroeville was superseded by St. John, so did St. John fade when Hamilton City was founded in 1905 as the site of a large sugar beet factory, now operated by the Holly Sugar Company. The place was named for J. G. Hamilton, president of the original sugar company.

Three and a half miles north of Hamilton City on the west bank of the Sacramento River, a marker (SRL 831) commemorates Will S. Green, guiding spirit of irrigation in the North Valley and for years editor of the Colusa *Sun*. On December 18, 1883, Green posted the first water notice in California on a nearby oak tree. The notice stated that 500,000 inches of river water were being diverted for irrigation of lands on the west side of the Sacramento Valley. The domination of northern California by the exploitative mining interests, with their appalling hydraulic gushers that wasted soil and water alike, was coming to an end. The area's future would be with those who farmed the land.

Humboldt County

Humboldt County was organized in 1853, with Uniontown, now Arcata, as its county seat. Like Humboldt Bay, it was named for the great German scientist and traveler, Baron Alexander von Humboldt. It was formerly a part of Trinity County, and what is now its northern third was included within Klamath County from 1851 to 1875. When Klamath County was dissolved in 1875, its territory was divided among Humboldt, Del Norte, and Siskiyou counties.

Cape Mendocino

Cape Mendocino, the westernmost point of California, has been for centuries a landmark for mariners along the Pacific Coast. It was named in honor of Antonio de Mendoza, the first viceroy of New Spain. The monumental rock may first have been seen in 1542 by Juan Rodríguez Cabrillo, the discoverer of Alta California, but few writers are agreed on the exact route of his voyage, and it is more generally believed that he went only as far as the Northwest Cape in what is now Sonoma County. The real discoverer may have been Alonso de Arellano, a deserter from the expedition commanded by Father Andrés de Urdaneta in 1565. Before taking his vows as a monk, Father Urdaneta had been a noteworthy navigator, and his expertise was such that he was put in charge of this secular expedition.

In 1565 Urdaneta had opened up the route for the Manila galleon from Asia across the Pacific to New Spain, and in 1566 the galleon made its first trading voyage. For 250 years the Spaniards followed this route, sailing across the Pacific with cargoes of rich silks, satins, and spices from the Orient, and often sighting the coast of California as far north as Cape Mendocino.

The name of the point was apparently unknown to Bartolomé Ferrelo, pilot to Cabrillo, in 1543. It was mentioned by Francisco de Gali, commander of the Manila galleon in 1584, in such a casual manner as to lead one to believe that it was a name well known to him, although he himself did not see it.

Some of the explorers of the coast did sight Cape Mendocino and charted their course by it. Among them were Francis Drake in 1579, on his voyage around the world; Sebastián Rodríguez Cermeño, in 1595, while seeking a northern port for the Manila galleon; Sebastián Vizcaíno, during 1602–3, while exploring the coast from Cape San Lucas to Cape Mendocino; and George Vancouver, sent out by England in 1792 to investigate the extent of the Spanish possessions on the Pacific Coast. Each of these men, and perhaps others, passed by Cape Mendocino, or turned back southward from that point.

Cape Mendocino Lighthouse, no longer in service, was one of the tallest along the coast at 422 feet. It was built in 1868 after a shipwreck took 38 lives at this point. The Fresnel lens, made in France at a cost of $79,000, was visible for 28 miles. The lens and the mechanism that operates it have been removed to a replica of the lighthouse on the Humboldt County Fairgrounds at Ferndale.

Indian Wars

After 1848, Americans flocked to California in large numbers, and explored both the easily accessible regions and those more remote, such as the northern Pacific coast. Soon these newcomers began to settle on lands that the Indian people had always regarded as their own; conflict was the predictable result. Trouble between Indians and whites was prevalent throughout California between 1850 and 1865. The Coast Indians of the Humboldt region were generally friendly and peaceful. But the mountain dwellers were less willing to coexist with the white newcomers, and they set fire to grass, drove off livestock, and killed or drove out, one by one, the white settlers along the Mad River and Redwood Creek and in the Bald Hills, until there were none left between Humboldt Bay and Trinity River.

A. J. Bledsoe, in his 1885 history of the Indian Wars, says: "During the year of 1851 the trouble between the Indians and the whites became acute. The packers and miners used little caution in their treatment of the Indians, many regarding the latter as their natural enemies, to be shot down whenever opportunity offered. The Indians were unable to discriminate between these vicious white men and the more peaceful ones, and as a result when an Indian was killed some white man paid the penalty, and unfortunately it was seldom the man who had committed the wrong. Nor were the whites themselves at all times above this practice, for seldom was the effort made to apprehend the real offender among the Indians, but rather a general attack followed on the nearest rancheria."

The need of military protection for the new settlements caused the establishment of a post at Fort Humboldt (SRL 154), on Humboldt Heights in what is today the southwestern part of Eureka. Brevet Lieutenant Colonel Robert C. Buchanan was entrusted with establishing the fort in January 1853, and within a year or so some fourteen buildings stood on the bluff around a 260-foot-square parade ground. Isolated from the rest of the world, fogbound for days at a time, and confronted with perpetual strife between Indians and settlers, the garrison was not a happy one. The four dreary and half-drunken months he spent there in 1854 convinced Captain Ulysses S. Grant to resign from the Army and to return to his family in Illinois.

For ten years after the establishment of Fort Humboldt, the United States Army sought to pacify the Indians of Humboldt County, without success. In 1863 the Mountain Battalion of the state militia, composed of six companies of volunteers, was organized. During the two years that followed this action, almost ceaseless warfare was carried on.

The incessant wars took their toll on the Indians, as did the diseases of the white settlers. In 1864 the Hoopa Valley Indian Reservation was established, and the Indian Wars came to an end in Humboldt County. Fort Humboldt was abandoned in 1870. In 1893 its land and the one remaining building on the property, the hospital, were sold to W. S. Cooper. Upon his death, his wife gave the property to the city of Eureka, which transferred it to the state in 1955. Now it is Fort Humboldt State Historic Park, overlooking US 101 at Highland Avenue in Eureka. In addition to the museum, visitors will see a remarkable display of logging that traces the history of redwood logging from its beginnings in 1850, highlighted by a Washington slack-line steam donkey, which was capable of hauling immense redwood logs as much as half a mile.

The Mattole Valley, Hydesville, Yager Creek, and Van Duzen districts are full of the history of Indian conflicts. Many military posts were scattered throughout the region, among them Fort Baker (1862–63), 28 miles east of Hydesville; Fort Lyons (1862) at Brehmer's Ranch on the Mad River 25 miles southeast of Eureka; Fort Iaqua (1863–66) on Yager Creek, eight miles south of Brehmer's; Martin's Ferry, on the Klamath River about three miles west of Weitchpec; Camp Grant (1863) on the Eel River about three miles east of Dyerville; Fort Seward (1861–63) on the Eel River, where an old log house still stands near the railroad and the county road, twenty miles southeast of Camp Grant; Camp Anderson (1862–66), near Minor's Ranch, where the road to Hoopa crosses Redwood Creek; and Fawn Prairie (1863) on the Hoopa Trail. One and one-half miles north of Arcata was Camp Curtis (SRL 215), the fort of the volunteer Mountain Battalion from 1863 to 1865.

The "Arrow Tree"

One mile east of Korbel there is a redwood tree, now dead, that is the center of an Indian legend. When white men first passed by the ancient tree, they found it stuck full of arrows for 30 or 40 feet above the ground. It was like a mammoth porcupine. The Indians of the region had a tradition about the "Arrow Tree" (SRL 164) that went back to the time when it was young.

The tribes of the coast lands were at war with the tribes that dwelt in the hill country, and the two met in a great conflict. The hill tribes were defeated and peace was made near the great redwood tree, which was afterward looked upon as a boundary mark between the two nations. Both Chilulas and Wiyots passed the old tree from time to time, and, because it was sacred, they never failed to leave an arrow in its soft bark. "At first," says one account, "the arrows may have been real war arrows, but within the memory of living Indians, they have been merely sharpened sticks. Gradually, the original significance of the tree was partially lost sight of, and it became more and more an altar for worship and a place of prayer."

Korbel is about six miles east of Arcata off SR 299.

The Rain Rock

Near the fishing place on Trinity River in Sugar-Bowl Valley and four miles from Hoopa is a boulder, not over four feet in diameter and not at all conspicuous, called by the white people the "Rain Rock" and by the Hoopa the Mi, or Thunder's Rock. By this rock, the Indians believed, dwells a spirit who, when he is displeased, sends killing frosts, or prolongs the rains till flood time, or brings drought and famine.

Many legends are connected with Sugar Loaf Mountain, and many other mountains, as well as rocks, trees, and rivers throughout the region, have similar legends connected with them. At many of these places Indian ceremonial dances are still held, preceded by much fasting and bathing and accompanied by chanting, singing, and wailing. The climax of the festival follows in the making of medicinal preparations. At Weitchpec, where the Trinity River runs into the Klamath, the largest of these festivals is held annually and is attended by visitors from all over the state.

Indian Island

In 1860 a massacre of Indians who had gathered for an annual festival took place on Indian Island in Humboldt Bay. Bret Harte, who was temporarily in charge of the *Northern Californian*, the Uniontown paper, denounced the outrage, and his attack was upheld by the majority of the community. The resentment of a "violent minority," however, was so acute that it finally caused Harte to return to San Francisco. The massacre was only one instance of numerous Indian troubles that occurred throughout California in those years.

The sites of two shell mounds are on this island. It is now registered as a National Historic Landmark by the Department of the Interior.

The Hoopa Valley Indian Reservation

The Hoopa Valley Indian Reservation may be reached by SR 96 from Willow Creek, 56 miles northeast of Eureka. The Trinity River flows through the center of the reservation and joins the Klamath at Weitchpec, and a corridor of the reservation follows on either side of the Klamath into Del Norte County all the way to the coast. At Weitchpec, representatives of thirteen local Indian tribes gathered in 1851 for the purpose of arranging a treaty with the United States government concerning their lands. This document, signed on October 6 of that year, is now included among the eighteen unratified California Indian treaties on file in Washington, D.C. A military post, Fort Gaston, was established in the Hoopa Valley in 1855, and in 1864 Superintendent Austin Wiley selected the valley and surrounding hills for an Indian reservation.

The Hoopa Valley Indian Reservation is California's largest in area, covering some 93,000 acres. The Hoopa Tribal Museum in Hoopa displays an excellent collection of Hoopa, Yurok, and Karuk artifacts, including Indian basketry, ceremonial regalia, tools, and implements.

Humboldt Bay

The first recorded discovery of Humboldt Bay was made in 1806 by Captain Jonathan Winship, an American employed by the Russian-American Fur Company to hunt seals along the coast of California. With over 40 small boats manned by Aleut Indians, Captain Winship in the *O'Cain* anchored 25 miles north of Eureka. While searching along the shore for sea otter, some of his men discovered the bay, and a few days later the *O'Cain* sailed through the long-obscured entrance and anchored opposite the present site of Eureka. Winship named the harbor the Bay of Indians because of the numerous native villages found along its shore. To the entrance he gave the name Rezanov after Count Rezanov.

In 1827, Jedediah Strong Smith, trapper and pathfinder, penetrated into Humboldt County, discovering the Trinity River, but did not see the bay. It remained for Dr. Josiah Gregg to rediscover the bay that Winship had seen and named 43 years earlier. Gregg had been employed by the government to trace the Trinity River from its source to its mouth. With his companions, he started from Rich Bar, in the vicinity of Weaverville, on November 5, 1849, and reached Trinidad Head on December 7. Here the expedition turned south and on December 20 reached the bay that Dr. Gregg named Trinity Bay. In April of the following year, Lieutenant Douglass Ottinger, in command of the *Laura Virginia*, anchored in the bay and named it Humboldt Bay.

Humboldt Bay lies halfway between Cape Trinidad on the north and Cape Mendocino on the south, a distance of 45 miles. It is very capacious, being almost the only good harbor between San Francisco and Puget Sound. As elusive as the entrance to San Francisco Bay, it was passed and repassed for centuries by navigators unaware of its presence.

Trinidad

Trinidad is on US 101 twenty miles north of Eureka. It seems probable that Sebastián Rodríguez Cermeño may have sighted Trinidad's rocky headland on November 4, 1595, when the *San Agustin*, laden with silks and porcelain from the Orient, first sighted the coast of New Spain a little above 41° latitude. The name was given by the Spanish mariners Bodega and Heceta, who entered the bay on Trinity Sunday, June 9, 1775. Trinidad was next visited in 1793 by Captain George Vancouver, who found the roughly hewn cross left by the Spaniards, with the inscription CAROLUS III DEI G HYSPANIARUM

REX. At the Coast Guard station south of town, a monument (SRL 146) in the form of a granite cross was placed by the women's clubs of Humboldt County. The Trinidad Head lighthouse nearby is now automated.

The Indian village of Tsurai, occupied until 1916, dated from prehistoric times. It was visited by captains Bodega and Heceta, the first outsiders, in 1775. A monument (SRL 838) stands at Ocean and Edwards streets in Trinidad, overlooking the village site.

Trinidad (SRL 216), the oldest town along the northern California coast and the first town in Humboldt County to be settled by Americans, was founded in 1850. It was then in Klamath County (later abolished) and was the county seat from 1851 to 1854.

During the 1850's, Trinidad was a port of entry and one of the principal trading posts for the mining camps in the Klamath and Trinity River drainage areas. As the mining activity waned, Trinidad became one of the most important whaling stations on the California coast. As whaling too died away, Trinidad declined. When lumbering became the chief industry of the region, Eureka, on Humboldt Bay, superseded all other towns in importance.

Humboldt City

This settlement was begun in April 1850, immediately opposite the entrance to Humboldt Bay. Soon the rival settlements of Bucksport, Eureka, and Uniontown were also founded to the north. Despite the efforts of promoters to attract settlers, Humboldt City was at a disadvantage, being farther from the Klamath mines, then the center of activity, and eventually it was deserted. A marker (SRL 882) at Harold Larsen Vista Point on Humboldt Hill Road just above US 101 commemorates the Humboldt Harbor Historical District. Bucksport to the north was named for David A. Buck, an early settler. This community was ultimately absorbed into Eureka and now lies within the southwestern corner of modern Eureka.

Eureka

Eureka (SRL 477), destined to be the metropolis of the Humboldt Region, was the last of the towns to be established there. When the Mendocino Exploring Company arrived in May 1850, they found that the Union Company, located at Uniontown, already claimed the land. An agreement was made to share the establishment of the town, and lots were surveyed the same year under the supervision of James Ryan.

Advancement at first was very slow, since the new settlement was farther away from the Klamath mines than Uniontown. When business shifted from the Klamath to the Trinity mining district, a road was cut to the Trinity area from Eureka, and the latter's position was improved.

Gradually mining was superseded by lumbering. Since Eureka was situated at the head of navigation only seven miles from the entrance of the bay, it soon proved to be the natural shipping center and shot ahead in the race for supremacy, while Uniontown, impeded by a vast extent of mud flats, fell behind. In 1856, the final triumph of Eureka was marked by its victory in the contest for the county seat.

Eureka's outstanding landmark is the beautiful Carson mansion near the bay at Second and M streeets. It is probably the best preserved and most photographed Victorian home in California. Built in the 1880's by lumber magnate William Carson, it consists of three stories and an ornamented tower, with some of the most elaborate wooden scrollwork and embellishment to be seen anywhere in the state. The redwood house remained in the Carson family until the late 1940's and is now a private club, not open to the public.

The area west of the Carson mansion by the waterfront, between C and G streets and Third Street and the harbor, has been designated the Eureka Old Town area. Within this area are the old Eureka Public Library, built in 1902 at 636 F Street, and the Clarke Memorial Museum at Third and E streets. The museum is housed in the former Bank of Eureka building, a handsome example of the Roman Renaissance style. Founded with a bequest from Cecile Clarke in 1960, the museum has a special wing, Nealis Hall, that contains the largest collection extant (some 1,200 pieces) of northwestern California Indian basketry. Other parts of the museum display materials from the history of Eureka and of Humboldt County.

The Humboldt Bay Maritime Museum at 1410 Second Street contains artifacts from the nautical activities of the bay, including relics from the wreck of the USS *Brooklyn* in 1930.

The Samoa Cookhouse

At Samoa, on SR 255 across the bay from Eureka, stands the Samoa Cookhouse, which has been serving gigantic meals since 1900. It was built for the workers of the Hammond Lumber Company. Most of the surrounding bunkhouses and other buildings of the lumber company are gone; one survivor is used as a museum. Cookhouses of this kind were once common throughout the lumbering country; the Samoa Cookhouse, now in business as a public eating place, is the last such establishment in the West.

Arcata

Arcata, on Arcata Bay eight miles northeast of Eureka, was founded in 1850 by a party of men from San Francisco under the leadership of L. K. Wood. Wood was one of the Josiah Gregg party, which discovered Arcata Bay and adjoining Humboldt Bay in 1849, at the point where Arcata now stands. On April 19, 1850, Wood and his party founded their town, which they called Uniontown.

When Humboldt County was organized in 1853, Uniontown became the county seat. It was the center of activity in the days of pack trains, when goods were carried to the mines over the mountain trails that began at Uniontown and followed up the Trinity and Klamath rivers. When the lumbering industry superseded mining, the lumber mills centered at Eureka, which was on deep water, making it the natural shipping point of the bay. The county seat was removed to Eureka in 1856. In 1860 Uniontown was renamed Arcata, the original Indian name for the spot, which is beautifully situated by the bay and surrounded by redwood forests.

The Arcata and Mad River Rail Road is the oldest line on the north coast. Established in 1854, it served as a link between Humboldt Bay and the Trinity River mines. A monument (SRL 842) commemorates the pioneer railroad at the depot at Blue Lake, six miles east of Arcata on SR 299.

The Humboldt State Normal School was established at Arcata in 1913. In later years it became the Humboldt State Teachers College and Humboldt State College; to-

Carson Mansion, Eureka

Jacoby Building, Arcata

day it is Humboldt State University. From its campus, many magnificent scenic trails lead through the primeval redwood groves that flank the Redwood Highway (US 101) in Humboldt County.

Bret Harte, California's noted short-story writer, lived in Arcata from 1857 to 1860 while he worked for the *Northern Californian* newspaper, located in a building that is still standing. He also tutored at the Liscom Ranch in the suburbs of Arcata.

At Eighth and H streets is the Jacoby Building (SRL 783), a pioneer business house of Arcata. Augustus Jacoby built the basement and first story in 1857, and during its early years the structure served periodically as a place of refuge in time of Indian troubles. Various firms supplying the Klamath-Trinity mines were located here for many years.

Orleans Bar

Orleans Bar, once a thriving mining center on the Klamath River, along which the rich mines of northern California were located, is on SR 96 about fifteen miles northeast of the junction with SR 169 at Weitchpec. This was the county seat of Klamath County from 1855 to 1875, when the county was disestablished. Today it is a small village simply called Orleans.

Ferndale

The city of Ferndale (SRL 883) began as an agricultural community as early as 1852. Dairying is still the principal industry. Dozens of ornate commercial and residential buildings of the Victorian era still stand,

drawing tourists in increasing numbers and making Ferndale one of the best-preserved rural cities in California. The five blocks along the center of Main Street are a treasury of nineteenth-century architecture, beautifully preserved. A walking-tour map is available from the chamber of commerce or from the charming Ferndale Museum at Third and Shaw streets. The Ferndale Cemetery and the adjacent St. Mary's Cemetery on the brow of a hill to the south of the town are large and well maintained.

On January 6, 1860, the steamer *Northerner*, one day out of San Francisco, struck a hidden rock off Cape Mendocino and drifted to the Centerville beach, seven miles west of Ferndale. Seventeen passengers and 21 members of the crew were lost. A concrete cross (SRL 173) has been erected by the Native Sons of the Golden West to honor the memory of the 38 people who lost their lives in this disaster. One result of this accident was the construction of the Cape Mendocino lighthouse.

Scotia

Scotia is a town entirely owned by the Pacific Lumber Company, whose giant mill can be visited on a self-guided tour. The old Scotia Inn was first opened in 1888 and still takes in guests. The museum, built in 1920, has a display of logging activities. Scotia is a rare example of the company towns that were once found throughout the logging areas of the West.

Mail Ridge

Mail Ridge was once a part of the old mail stage route from San Francisco into the northwestern part of California before the advent of the railroad. It is about 3,500 feet above sea level with extensive views over the whole southern part of Humboldt County.

To reach the ridge, SR 36 leaves the Redwood Highway (US 101) at Fortuna, eighteen miles south of Eureka, and follows up the Van Duzen River to Bridgeville. From Bridgeville, Alderpoint Road runs south through high mountain country to Blocksburg, and on to Alderpoint on the main line of the railway. Crossing the railway, the route leads uphill for eight miles to the town of Harris, then turns north again and follows along Mail Ridge, the old stage road.

Petrolia

Humboldt County claims the honor of California's first drilled oil wells, and a quiet little town in the Mattole Valley remembers the brief boom in its name, Petrolia. Prior to 1865 the area was mapped by A. J. Doolittle as "New Jerusalem," but the shipment of the first crude oil to a San Francisco refinery by the Union Mattole Oil Company in June 1865 was the occasion for the bestowal of a permanent name. A monument in the town commemorates the oil wells (SRL 543), which are located on private property about three miles east on the North Fork of the Mattole River. Today, although there are occasional efforts to revive the oil industry, the main interests of Petrolia and the Mattole Valley are livestock raising, farming, and recreation.

Covered Bridges

Humboldt County contains two of California's eleven remaining covered bridges. Both are located on the Elk River five to six miles south of Eureka, not far from Fields Landing, and both are 52 feet in length. The Berta's Ranch bridge, built in 1936, is the westernmost covered bridge in the United States. The Zane's Ranch

Berta's Ranch Covered Bridge, near Fields Landing

bridge, farther upstream, was completed in 1937. When these bridges were built there were twelve covered bridges in Humboldt County alone.

The Redwood Groves

One of the great attractions of this area is the magnificent stands of *Sequoia sempervirens*, the Coast redwoods. Although this has been an area of intensive lumbering, groups such as the Save-the-Redwoods League have been active in preserving groves and stands of virgin timber. Prairie Creek Redwoods State Park, along the coast at the northern edge of the county, is noteworthy for being a refuge for the Roosevelt elk that were once numerous in the region. Adjacent to it and extending south for many miles is the Humboldt County area of Redwood National Park. Grizzly Creek Redwoods State Park is a small jewel along SR 36 between Carlotta and Bridgeville. Richardson Grove State Park is another small redwood preserve bisected by US 101 at the southern edge of the county. The largest preserve is Humboldt Redwoods State Park, which contains the spectacular Avenue of the Giants, an alternative to US 101 that passes the many groves set aside as memorials to families and organizations.

The title of the world's tallest tree has long remained among the Humboldt County sequoias. Until 1957 the honor belonged to the Founders Tree in Humboldt Redwoods State Park (height 352.6 feet). Then it was discovered that the nearby Rockefeller Tree in the same park was a few feet taller. In 1963, however, Dr. Paul A. Zahl, senior naturalist of the National Geographic Society, found a redwood over eleven feet taller than the Rockefeller. This 367.8-foot giant stands in a privately owned grove on Redwood Creek southeast of Orick. In the same grove two other trees were discovered that also exceed the Rockefeller Tree in height. It is quite likely that an even taller tree remains to be found.

Imperial County

Imperial County was organized in 1907 from that part of San Diego County known as Imperial Valley, and is consequently the newest of California's 58 counties. El Centro is the county seat.

A Prehistoric Wonderland

Imperial Valley is remarkable for the vast range of prehistoric and geologic relics to be found within its borders. Outlining and in a sense explaining these is the ancient beachline extending from north to south and plainly visible at 260 feet above the surface of the Salton Sea. Professor William P. Blake of the Williamson survey first observed the old beachline and examined its shells while engaged in making the first governmental survey of Imperial Valley in 1853.

Extending southward from Indio in Riverside County, past the Travertine Rock at the county line and on through western Imperial County to the Fish Creek Mountains, this ancient shoreline there turns east and south, skirting Superstition Mountain and crossing I-8 about three miles west of Dixieland. Continuing south along the West Side Canal and down into Mexico as far as Black Butte, it again turns northward, reentering Imperial County eight miles east of Calexico. Here the waterline follows the East Highline Canal northward, passing east of Salton Sea into Riverside County, where the circuit is completed at a point slightly north of Indio.

This beachline, approximately 30 feet above sea level, is that of an ancient freshwater lake that covered Imperial and Coachella valleys. Indications are that in past ages it was filled many times by waters from the Colorado River and stood at this elevation for long periods before the river shifted course again and directed its flow into the Gulf of California. Along the entire length of this ancient beach, or within a short distance from its sands, may be found relics of bygone ages: vast coral reefs, millions of fossils and shells, and even pottery wrought by a long-vanished people. The beachline is not always visible south of the international border. Presumably it is buried beneath silt from the Colorado River.

Travertine Rock is a landmark near SR 86 on the western shore of the Salton Sea. It is actually not true travertine but is covered by a calcareous rock called tufa, left there by receding waters at least a thousand years ago. The chalk-like surface is made even more interesting by the Indian rock writings (petroglyphs) of a prehistoric age. Twelve miles to the south lies a petrified forest.

A group of prehistoric animal tracks, reached by a drive over rough roads and a short hike, are to be seen in a small canyon north of the Fish Creek Mountains. Presumably a water hole where great prehistoric animals came to drink, the canyon is covered by hundreds of huge tracks that geologists believe to be the footprints of mastodons, solidified and preserved by succeeding geological epochs.

Painted Gorge, with its rugged walls tinted in a patchwork of colors like the design of an old-fashioned quilt, is seven miles north of I-8 and 30 miles west of El Centro. At the upper end of the gorge are high coral reefs and well-preserved oyster shells.

The best and most extensive coral formations are found in Shell Canyon across the Coyote Mountains from Painted Gorge. These deposits are reached only by a very difficult desert road followed by three miles of hiking. Two magnificent coral canyons may also be reached from Barrett Well with less difficulty: Barrett Canyon in the Fish Creek Mountains to the north and Garnet Canyon in the Coyote Mountains to the south.

South of I-8 stretches the Yuha plain, with its myriad fish fossils, its beds of oyster shells, and what has been called "the most amazing rock concretions ever discovered in the United States." The latter were first mentioned by Juan Bautista de Anza in 1774 and first described over 125 years later by George Wharton James in his *Wonders of the Colorado Desert*. They consist of "detached rocks of various shapes and sizes, chiefly spherical . . . and resembling petrified fruits, vegetables, and flowers."

The Explorations of Alarcón and Diaz

Hernando de Alarcón may have been the first white man to touch California soil. On May 9, 1540, Alarcón sailed north from Acapulco, Mexico, until he reached the mouth of the Colorado River on August 17 or 18. On several occasions during the fall of 1540, he crossed the river, to a point probably a little beyond the site of Yuma. No documentary evidence has established his specific whereabouts, but a spot five and one-half miles west of Winterhaven (SRL 568) has been landmarked as a probable landing point. There is no monument or marker at this site.

The next white man to walk upon California soil was Melchior Díaz, who had left Coronado's expedition near the present site of Ures, Mexico, in October 1540, with instructions to make contact with Alarcón if possible. Díaz proceeded up the Colorado River as far as the Gila, where his party crossed over on rafts, touching California soil at about the same point as Alarcón. He then traveled down the western bank, passing Pilot Knob on Imperial County soil.

First Passage of the Colorado Desert

A trail from Mexico to the junction of the Colorado and Gila rivers had been blazed as early as 1700 by Father Eusebio Kino, a Jesuit priest, whose purpose was to find an overland route from Sonora to the missions of Baja California. Kino was one of the great missionaries of New Spain. He was in Lower California from 1683 to 1685. The remainder of his life was spent in Pimería Alta, now southern Arizona and northern Sonora, where he founded some 50 missions and chapels.

The desire to find a way to connect the missions of Pimería Alta with those of Lower California led to numerous exploring expeditions. In 1700 Kino went as far as the junction of the Colorado and Gila rivers, and the next year he descended the former nearly to its mouth, which he crossed on a raft. Descending the Colorado again in 1702, Kino went as far as the Gulf. These explorations led him to believe that California was a peninsula and not an island, as had previously been supposed. Furthermore, the way had been opened to the great Colorado Desert, a trail followed over 70 years later by Garcés and Anza.

Father Francisco Garcés, famous priest-explorer, was the first white man to enter the Colorado Desert. In 1771, believing that he was crossing the Gila River, he crossed the Colorado instead. During his wanderings he skirted the Cocopah Range to its terminus at Signal Mountain near present-day Calexico. To the northwest he saw two great gaps in the mountain range, which he believed could be followed into New California without great difficulty.

On this journey, Garcés gained information that exercised a profound influence on the decision of the government, which eventually recommended Anza's plan to go overland to California. It was also this journey, more than any other, that helped to determine the path taken by the subsequent expedition.

In 1774, Juan Bautista de Anza, one of the most heroic figures in the history of California, volunteered to find an overland route to the coast missions in order to avoid the perils and uncertainty of communication by sea, and to ensure the settlement of Alta California. Antonio María Bucareli, then viceroy of Mexico, accepted Anza's offer.

Accompanied by Father Francisco Garcés, Father Juan Díaz, and twenty soldiers, Anza reached the junction of the Gila and Colorado rivers on February 7, 1774, and two days later he crossed the Colorado at the ford above the Gila, camping on the California side.

On the following day, the party went four leagues along the river, passing the geological formation known later as Pilot Knob, which Anza named the Cerro de San Pablo, where the river turns south. Proceeding another league, they stopped for the night at the Ranchería de San Pablo, a Yuma Indian village at the place where the Mission San Pedro y San Pablo was established in the autumn of 1780.

This was just above the present international boundary line, and from here the expedition continued southwest until they reached a lake that Anza called Laguna de Santa Olaya, twelve miles south of the boundary line and eight miles west of the Colorado, "the end of the known land." Beyond lay hostile Indians and league upon league of treacherous sand dunes blocking the way into what is now southeastern Imperial County.

Undaunted, Anza set forth to cross this forbidding waste, but the dunes proved impassable, and he was forced to retreat to Santa Olaya, which the party reached again on February 19. Having rested for several days among the friendly Indians at this oasis, the party resumed its journey on March 2, and finally reentered California on March 7, camping three or four miles southwest of the Yuha Well and about two miles north of the international boundary line. The next morning they reached a little group of refreshing wells, "which, on being opened, distilled an abundant supply of most beautiful water." Here Anza rested for a day, refreshing both the footsore men and the starved horses. These life-giving springs were named by Anza the Pozas de Santa Rosa de las Lajas (the Wells of St. Rose of the Flat Rocks), because of the great number of peculiar rock formations. How the less poetic name of Yuha Well later came to be attached to them is not known. They lie in a basin of the same name six miles southwest of Plaster City.

Anza's last important camp on the first journey across the desert was reached on March 10. It was made at the junction or sink of the San Felipe and Carrizo creeks, called by Anza the San Sebastián, in honor of Sebastián Tarabal, his Indian guide, who had previously passed that way under great hardships and danger. This place, now known as Harper's Well, was at the base of the Fish Creek Mountains, where the western wall of the great Colorado Desert had been reached and where the expedition entered San Diego County by way of San Felipe Canyon and San Carlos Pass.

On his return to Mexico in May, Anza again crossed the desert, camping at San Sebastián on May 7, and from there making a shortcut directly across the desert. On December 11, 1775, he again stopped at the Wells of Santa Rosa, this time to rest and refresh the first caravan of emigrants to enter California, the party destined to be also the first settlers of San Francisco. This caravan, which left Tubac on October 23, 1775, was made up of 240 persons, of whom more than 30 were women and 136 were boys and girls. Only one life was lost on the entire journey of 1,000 miles, and three babies were born en route. Over a thousand animals also began the journey, but many perished in the deserts.

On his final return to Mexico in 1776, Anza again

made a direct cut across the desert, paralleling SR 86 past Kane Spring as far as Westmorland, and camping on May 8 east of Imperial.

The Desert Trail

The old desert trail across Imperial Valley, first opened by Anza and followed later by generations of explorers and trappers, traders and Argonauts, and finally by a long line of home-seekers, has been variously known as the Sonora Road, the Colorado Road, the Emigrant Trail, and the Butterfield Stage Route. That part of the route from the San Felipe Sink via San Carlos Pass was closed after 1782 and has never been used since. In July 1781 the two missions established on the Colorado River the previous year were destroyed by Indians, and in 1781 and 1782 Pedro Fages carried dispatches to Mission San Gabriel concerning these Indian troubles. On the first of these trips he followed Anza's trail all the way, but on the second he traversed it only across the desert to the San Felipe watering place, where he turned up the Carrizo Creek into the unexplored territory to the southwest, thus opening the road that now goes by way of Warner's Ranch, a trail followed by the southern emigrant trains of 1849 and the 1850's and known as the old Emigrant Trail.

Because of the hostility of the Yuma Indians, the desert trail was probably not used again until 1826, although Santiago Argüello, while pursuing Indian horse thieves in 1825, rediscovered Fages's route through the mountains. In 1826, on the approval of Romualdo Pacheco, Lieutenant of Engineers, the Mexican government adopted the desert trail as an official mail route. Pacheco tried to establish a small garrison on the Colorado River the same year; it was unsuccessful and had to be abandoned. From then on, the trail was used to a small extent by traders from Sonora.

The David E. Jackson party in 1831 followed Anza's trail across the desert to Carrizo Creek, where they crossed the mountains via Warner's Pass, probably the first Americans to journey that way. In 1834 Rafael Amador, a messenger for President Santa Anna of Mexico, made the trip in 48 days, record time, and in 1846 Stephen W. Kearney conducted the advance guard of the "Army of the West" across the old desert trail and over the mountains through Warner's Pass.

The Butterfield Stage used approximately the same road from 1858 to 1861, probably the first well-defined trail across the Imperial Valley. The ruined adobe walls of the old Pilot Knob station could be seen for many years at Araz on I-8 a few miles west of Yuma. Except for the

Old Plank Road, near Yuma

station at Indian Wells (also known as Sunset Springs and by various other names), the trail through the shifting dunes from Araz westward is uncertain until Carrizo Creek is reached. It led south of the international boundary line by way of the stations at Cook's Well and Alamo Mocho (both of which have disappeared) and then northwest into the present Imperial County by way of the station at Indian Wells, halfway to the Carrizo station (San Diego County). Indian Wells was located approximately eight miles south and a little west of Seeley. The adobe station building stood there until it was washed away by the flood of 1906.

Another stage station in Imperial County, though not on the Butterfield route, was at Mountain Springs (SRL 194), just east of the San Diego County line near I-8. There are some ruins here and the remains of an old road; tradition says that the Army camped at the spring here in 1846.

Seventeen miles west of Yuma in the sand dunes can be seen what is left of the old plank road built in 1916–17, one of the first automobile roads through this part of the desert (SRL 845). It was wide enough for only one car, with turnouts provided for passing. Nearby is a bypassed stretch of US 80 (Gray's Well Road), built in 1927, which seems like a superhighway next to the plank road. Providing the greatest contrast of all, the I-8 freeway carries one through the dunes in a few minutes. Recreational vehicles today swarm over the area, now viewed as a major dune-buggy park instead of a formidable and impassable region.

The Yuma Massacre

Mission La Purísima Concepción and Mission San Pedro y San Pablo once stood twelve miles apart in the southeastern corner of what was destined to become

Imperial County. The two were established in the autumn of 1780 by four Franciscan padres from Mexico, Fathers Díaz, Morena, Barreneche, and Garcés. The purpose of these missions was twofold: to convert the Yuma Indians living at this point along the Colorado River, and to make a way station on the overland emigrant trail from Mexico to the California missions.

The plan followed at Purísima and at San Pedro y San Pablo was different from that followed in other parts of California. The Indians were allowed to remain on their own rancherias, and the padres visited them there, ministering to their spiritual needs alone.

But this plan was not successful. The fathers had not the means to visit the Indians often, nor had they the necessary trinkets to allure them. Moreover, the soldiers, and the few white settlers who came with them, used for themselves the scant patches of ground on which the Indians raised their melons, beans, and corn, and the white settlers' cattle ate up the precious pasturage that the Indians' stock needed.

Naturally, the Indians soon looked upon the white people as invaders, and in July 1781 one of the most tragic occurrences in the history of California took place. Captain Fernando Rivera y Moncada, lieutenant-governor of Lower California, was bringing a party of settlers from Mexico to establish the proposed pueblo of Los Angeles in California. On reaching the Colorado River, the soldiers and settlers, over whom Rivera exercised little discipline, harassed the Yuma Indians. The families in the train were sent ahead with some of the soldiers, while Rivera remained behind to refresh his exhausted animals. From July 17 to 19, an outbreak among the Indians came to a climax. Rivera and his soldiers, Father Garcés and the other priests at the two missions, and all other males were massacred. The women and children were made captive, being subsequently ransomed by Pedro Fages.

The missions and settlements were not established again on the Colorado, and the route that had been opened with such great effort by Juan Bautista de Anza in 1774 and 1775 became more dangerous to travelers than ever before. The colonists of Rivera's expedition did go on to establish the great city of Los Angeles, but the importance of the Yuma Massacre must not be underestimated. With Anza's land route effectively closed, the only means of supply from and contact with Mexico was the highly unreliable sea route. The Californians soon saw the necessity of development from within and began to draw from California's limitless natural resources. At the same time dependence upon Mexico, both economic and political, was lessening, and contact was being established instead with the foreigners who

Chapel at the Site of Mission La Purísima Concepción

came by land and sea, paving the way for an early and easy American occupation. The Yuma Massacre was thus a turning point in California history.

After declaring independence from Spain, Mexico attempted to reopen the overland road from Sonora into California in 1822. In 1825 Lieutenant Romualdo Pacheco and his soldiers built an adobe fort here, the only Mexican fort in Alta California. On April 26, 1826, Kumeyaay Indians attacked the fort, killing three soldiers and wounding three others, and the discouraged Pacheco abandoned it, taking the soldiers to San Diego. The unmarked site of Fort Romualdo Pacheco (SRL 944) is on the west bank of the New River south of Worthington Road, six and one-half miles due west of the town of Imperial.

In the early 1850's, Fort Yuma was established on the spot where Mission Purísima had stood, and American troops were stationed there for several years. It was besieged by Indians in 1851. On the same spot, in later years, an Indian School, where boys and girls were taught trades as well as reading and writing, was conducted by the Sisters of St. Joseph. The school building standing today on a high hill north of the highway on the California side of the Colorado River was built by the United States government for the education of the Indians on the Yuma reservation.

Today a Catholic chapel for the Indians stands on what is thought to be at least the approximate site of

Mission La Purísima Concepción (SRL 350). Next to it is a statue of the martyred Father Garcés. Some of the old buildings of Fort Yuma still stand nearby (SRL 806). These landmarks are on a hill just across the Colorado River from the famous Arizona Territorial Prison in Yuma, and like the prison they are reached from the former routing of the main highway, which crosses the river by an old, narrow bridge. The Yuma Crossing and historic buildings on both sides of the Colorado River, such as the remains of Fort Yuma on the California side and the Territorial Prison on the Arizona side, have been registered as a National Historic Landmark.

The precise site of Mission San Pedro y San Pablo is uncertain. The marker (SRL 921) is just north of the junction of Imperial Road with Levee Road near the banks of the river nine miles northeast of Yuma and about twelve miles from Winterhaven.

Early Colorado River Ferries

Several ferries were established on the Colorado below its junction with the Gila in 1849 and 1850. The first of these was built by General Alexander Anderson, from Tennessee, in order to transport his party to the California side at a point several miles south of the Gila. Anderson afterward presented his boat to the Indians with a certificate of title, the terms of which seem to have been faithfully lived up to by the latter.

Another ferry, started in September 1849 by Lieutenant Cave J. Couts at Camp Calhoun on the California side, aided gold-seekers across the river. In December Couts sold his ferry to Dr. G. W. Lincoln, reputed to have been a distant relative of Abraham Lincoln.

This ferry was destined to come to a tragic end. When John Glanton, a villainous character, purchased a half share in Lincoln's ferry, the enterprise quickly degenerated. Lincoln was secretly done away with and the neighboring Indian ferry was destroyed in order to prevent opposition. The indignant Indians retaliated by surprising and killing Glanton and his men and destroying their boat.

In the summer of 1850 the ferry was reestablished by L. J. F. Jaeger and others, at a point several miles below the present site of Yuma near the Hall Hanlon ranch. Lumber for Jaeger's ferry was transported across the desert from San Diego by pack train. A ferry was operated at this point until the present old highway bridge was erected in 1915. A marker commemorating these pioneer ferries stands at the old landing on the Arizona side near the Territorial Prison.

Picacho, a Ghost of the Desert

On the west or south bank of the Colorado River, 25 miles north of Yuma, is the site of Picacho, an early gold-mining camp, said to have been discovered by an Indian in 1860. It was first located by Mexican prospectors in 1862 and is said to have been one of the richest placers in California. The population was almost entirely Hispanic during the first few years of its existence, a bit of Old Mexico transplanted to American soil. The Americans came in later and found rich lodes in the neighboring hills, erected large stamp mills, and soon had a payroll amounting to $40,000 a month.

Picacho today is being developed as the Picacho State Recreational Area. It is reached only by a dirt road from the south or by the river itself; few buildings are left. The site of the mines (SRL 193) is four miles south of the area on private land.

Tumco

Tumco, known at first as Hedges, was a mining town of some importance until after the turn of the century. Nine miles north of I-8 and five miles north of Ogilby Station on the Southern Pacific Railroad, it lies in a narrow desert valley hemmed in on either side by two barren mountain ranges. It received its name from the initial letters of a company that later purchased the properties, The United Mines Co. Once inhabited by 2,000 people, Tumco is today a desolate wasteland of ruined adobe walls and stone foundations; it has been marked by a plaque placed in 1985 by E Clampus Vitus. The Tumco mines (SRL 182), originally staked as a claim in 1884, operated until about 1914. The most famous of them were the Golden Queen, the Golden Cross, and the Golden Crown. Five miles northeast of Ogilby was

Ruins at Tumco

the American Girl Mine, developed later than Tumco and worked by fewer than 200 men. Ogilby is itself now a ghost town, with an abandoned cemetery by the roadside.

Water from the Colorado

The first diversion of water from the Colorado River to Imperial Valley was made through a temporary wooden gate, known as the Chaffey Gate, located several thousand feet back from the river a short distance above the Mexican border. The gate was too small and the sill too high; consequently, it was replaced in 1905 by a concrete gate, known as Hanlon Heading, which was located at the last place where rock formation is found on the lower Colorado River. This also was connected to the river by an open canal. This canal became filled with silt during flood periods, and therefore, in 1918, it was replaced by another concrete gate, Rockwood Heading, several thousand feet upstream and adjacent to the Colorado River. It was through these structures that every drop of water used by the people of Imperial Valley for irrigation and domestic purposes was diverted from 1901 until 1942, when the All-American Canal was completed.

It is this water from the Colorado River, conveyed through a vast system of canals and ditches to be deposited upon the rich soil of the Salton Sink, that makes Imperial Valley today a prosperous agricultural community of over 90,000 people. It is appropriate that around this spot should cluster the memories of three pioneers of the idea of reclaiming the Colorado Desert: Dr. Oliver Meredith Wozencraft, Charles Robinson Rockwood, and Charles Chaffey.

Dr. Wozencraft is considered the real father of Imperial Valley, "the first man to actually plan the reclamation of the desert sink for agricultural purposes by bringing the waters of the Colorado to the arid area to the west." He came to California in the gold rush of 1849, and immediately after his arrival in San Francisco he set out on an expedition to the little-known Colorado Desert. It was there, in 1849, that he first conceived the idea of reclamation. The project so possessed him that he was led to devote the rest of his life to making his dream a reality.

Obtaining favorable action from the state legislature in 1859, Wozencraft was given all state rights in the Salton Sink. The next step was to get a patent from the federal government, but in spite of repeated attempts he never obtained this, chiefly because the attention of Congress was entirely taken up with the Civil War and subsequent problems of Reconstruction. Dr. Wozencraft died in Washington in 1887 while making a final effort to obtain Congressional action. His repeated attempts to interest capitalists in his enterprise had been of no avail. However, an appeal made to George Chaffey for support in 1882, although not obtaining results at the time, was no doubt a factor leading to the final accomplishment of the reclamation under the latter's direction from April 1900 to February 1902.

Meanwhile, there was no one to continue the work begun by Dr. Wozencraft until Charles Robinson Rockwood, a civil engineer, rediscovered the agricultural possibilities of Imperial Valley in 1892. The name of Rockwood will always be associated with the early history of Imperial Valley as that of one preeminent among those entertaining the idea of turning the waters of the Colorado upon the parched soil of the Salton Sink. He never gave up hope of success during the eight long years of toil, struggle, and disappointment through which he passed before finally locating the necessary man with capital to finance the work. This man was George Chaffey, who was able to take hold of the project and bring the water to the desert.

George Chaffey had begun his career of founding agricultural colonies based on irrigation at Etiwanda (in southwestern San Bernardino County), in 1881, where he originated the idea of a mutual water company and set up the first dynamo for developing hydroelectric power on the Pacific slope. The next year he laid out the Ontario Colony (also in southwestern San Bernardino County). In 1886 he and his brother William began their work of establishing colonies in the arid regions of Australia. There he learned that it was possible for white people to colonize hot and arid regions, provided that sufficient water could be brought to them. With this experience as a background, Chaffey was ready, when approached by Rockwood in 1899, to undertake the very thing he had refused to do in 1882 when Wozencraft made his appeal.

Chaffey now became the chief factor in the reclamation of the desert. Entering into the work under his own terms, he built up the project from its very foundations, planning and directing the construction of vast canals and ditches. It was he who gave the name of Imperial to the valley.

Water from the Colorado was first turned through the intake gate at Pilot Knob on May 14, 1901. This first heading was located about 500 feet south of the present Rockwood Gate. The construction of the canals was completed in February of the following year.

The necessity of bringing water to Imperial Valley by a canal located in Mexico caused considerable difficulty. Moreover, it was necessary in most years to build either brush dams or sand dams across the river in low-flood periods in an endeavor to divert a sufficient supply of water for the valley. It became apparent that a new location for the diversion point would have to be found. A canal located entirely within the United States was also needed.

Bills toward this end were introduced in Congress beginning in 1918. In 1928 Congress adopted the Swing-Johnson Bill providing for the construction of Boulder (now Hoover) Dam and the All-American Canal. Imperial Dam, the diversion point for the canal, is located about twenty miles north of Yuma. The headworks for the All-American Canal are outstanding, with very large gates through which the water is diverted and a system of desilting that is one of the largest in this country. Along the canal are many large concrete structures, and at three of the drops the Imperial Irrigation District has installed power plants. The district has also installed a power plant at Pilot Knob, where surplus water is discharged into the river through the old Rockwood Heading. Where the All-American Canal emerges from the sand dunes, a branch canal, some 120 miles in length, takes off, flowing northward on the east side of Salton Sea and around Coachella Valley to provide supplemental water for that valley.

There are now 3,000 miles of irrigation and drainage canals serving 500,000 acres of cultivated land in Imperial Valley and its cities and towns. A vast desert waste has become one of the world's most fruitful gardens.

The Salton Sea

In 1905–7 unusual rainfalls caused the whole flow of the Colorado River to break through the intake gates, threatening to fill the entire valley, a phenomenon that had happened before in prehistoric times. The flow of the river was finally turned back into its normal course by February 10, 1907, thus saving most of the valley. The almost superhuman efforts of the Southern Pacific Railroad under its president, E. H. Harriman, were chiefly responsible; ultimately the U.S. government reimbursed the company for the millions of dollars it had spent in the damming project.

The runaway river had, however, left its mark in the newly formed Salton Sea, which had previously been dry land. Two streams from the Colorado, the Alamo and the New rivers, flow northward across the Mexican border and empty into the Salton Sea. This body of water is about 35 miles long and from 9 to 15 miles wide. The elevation varies from year to year but averages 230 feet below sea level. The recreational activities of the Salton Sea have been severely impaired by pollution in recent years, and its future is uncertain.

Other Landmarks of Imperial County

At the present site of Calexico, adjacent to and immediately north of the international boundary, Lieutenant Cave J. Couts, escort commander with the International Boundary Commission, established Camp Salvation (SRL 808) on September 23, 1849. Until the first of December the camp served as a refugee center for the distressed emigrants who were attempting to reach the gold fields over the southern emigrant trail.

The Imperial Valley Pioneers Museum is at the Midwinter Fairgrounds on Aten Road in the town of Imperial. It shows ancient Indian artifacts as well as displays related to the agricultural development of Imperial County.

Inyo County

Inyo County was organized in 1866 from territory that had been set aside two years earlier from Mono and Tulare counties and called Coso County. Coso County was never organized, however, and Inyo took its place. Inyo is a Paiute Indian word meaning "dwelling place of a great spirit." Independence has always been the county seat.

Second-largest of California's counties (10,130 square miles), Inyo contains within its borders an extraordinarily varied topography. On its western boundary stands Mount Whitney, the highest peak in the continental United States; to the east is Death Valley, the lowest spot in the Western Hemisphere. Death Valley abounds in scenic as well as historic interest, with places named Marble Canyon, Mosaic Canyon, the Sand Dunes, Grotto Canyon, Stovepipe Wells, Furnace Creek (a veritable oasis in the desert), Golden Canyon, Mushroom Rock, Pluto's Salt Pools, Badwater, and the Devil's Golf Course.

Mount Whitney

Mount Whitney is the highest peak in the United States outside Alaska and one of a group of splendid mountains more than 13,000 feet in elevation situated in the High Sierra at the headwaters of the Kern and Kings rivers. For many years it was thought that Mount Shasta was the highest summit in California, but in 1864 the Whitney Geological Survey discovered that the summit of Mount Whitney was the highest point in the Sierra and higher than Shasta. The latest accurate measurements of their altitudes are 14,495 feet for Mount Whitney and 14,126 feet for Mount Shasta.

The mountain was named in 1864 in honor of Josiah Dwight Whitney, state geologist and leader of the Geological Survey, by the survey party led by William Henry Brewer. Clarence King, a member of the party and a leading geologist of the West, wrote: "For years our Chief, Professor Whitney, has made brave campaigns into the unknown realm of Nature. There stand for him two monuments: one a great report, made by his own hand; another the loftiest peak in the Union, begun . . . in the planet's youth and sculptured of enduring granite by the slow hand of time."

King, attempting to climb the peak in 1871, missed it on account of obscuring storm clouds and climbed Mount Langley by mistake. Learning of his error in 1873, he hastened west to climb the real Mount Whitney on September 19. He was too late, however, for on August 18 John Lucas, A. H. Johnson, and C. D. Begole had made the first ascent of the great mountain.

Since July 1881 Mount Whitney has been the base of operations for many scientific astronomical observations, the expedition under Professor S. P. Langley that year being the first. A frequently used approach to the mountain is from the eastern side, where a good road runs west from Lone Pine into the mountains to Whitney Portal, from which trails lead through the forest and canyons to the summit. The western approach to Mount Whitney is in Tulare County, through Sequoia National Park.

The Bishop Petroglyphs

Indian petroglyphs, or rock markings, may be found throughout much of the arid West. Those of one area are unlike those of others, and so it is thought that they were made by different tribes. All, however, are similar in their crudeness and simplicity of design. They are generaly made in soft tufa by chipping, and are usually found near springs or streams on natural routes of travel, but sometimes are discovered in secluded mountain nooks.

A few miles north of Bishop, in northern Inyo County and southern Mono County, the largest group of markings in this part of the state is found on the courses of stream beds or near ancient springs. Among the petroglyphs found here are crude pictures of what appear to be deer, footprints of humans and of animals, snakes, many-legged insects, and numerous geometrical designs. At Deep Springs Valley, on the Midland Trail, is a great round boulder covered with these carved pictures: sun symbols, snakes, a bird, what is possibly a rabbit, and concentric circles that some think may be representations of sweat houses. At Little Lake, Coso Hot Springs, and Keeler are rocks on which animal figures predominate. Other petroglyphs are found covering the granite base of the Inyo Mountains at a point near Swansea.

Similar carvings have been found from Alaska to South America, and scientists have sought for years to understand their meaning. Their age is still a matter of speculation and their meaning is enigmatic.

Big and Little Petroglyph Canyons, in the southern part of the county on the grounds of the U.S. Naval Weapons Center, have been registered as a National Historic Landmark by the Department of the Interior. The petroglyphs are accessible by a well-maintained road leading north from the China Lake housing area (in Kern County), but permission to visit them must be obtained from the authorities at the Naval Weapons Center in China Lake.

Winnedumah

Directly east of Independence on the extreme crest of the White Mountains stands a remarkable granite monolith commonly known as the Winnedumah Paiute Monument. It is 80 feet high and is visible on the skyline for many miles. A legend connected with it tells of Winnedumah, a medicine man, who was transformed into this great rock while calling for spiritual help in the course of a battle.

The Bristlecone Pines

High in the White Mountains and straddling the border of Inyo and Mono counties is the Ancient Bristlecone Pine Forest, a region of Inyo National Forest. The bristlecone pine (pinus arustata) has a good claim to be the oldest living thing on earth. Thriving at an altitude averaging some 10,000 feet above sea level, these trees are also found in some other parts of the American southwest. Dr. Edmund Schulman of the University of Arizona discovered that some of the group in the Inyo Forest were over 4,000 years old, one or more proving to be at least 4,600 years old. It is likely that many of these were cut down in the heyday of mining activity in the region to provide charcoal for the kilns of the mines.

The bristlecone pine is a survivor, existing in thin, rocky soil at high altitudes with long intervals of freezing winters and waterless summers. It is a botanical curiosity in that a good part of the visible tree is in fact dead; a thin strand of living bark keeps part of the tree alive for long periods of time.

Owens Valley

Although trappers may have penetrated Owens Valley south to what is now Inyo County as early as 1826, the first authentic record we have is that of Joseph Reddeford Walker, who led a party north through Owens Valley in 1834. He entered the valley again in 1843, this time from the north; following his old trail, he led the Chiles emigrant party, the second wagon train to enter California from the east, south through the pass that was later named for him. In 1845 Walker accompanied the main body of John C. Frémont's second expedition into California over the same route. Frémont himself went by way of Donner Pass with Kit Carson, Richard Owens, and twelve others. Frémont considered Owens to be "cool, brave, and of good judgement," and he gave Owens's name to the river, valley, and lake that still bear it, although the man for whom they were named never saw this region.

William H. Brewer, of the Whitney Geological Survey, and his party crossed the Sierra from the west and descended the eastern slope. He gave an appreciative description of the region in his journal in 1864: "Yesterday in the snow and ice—today in this heat! The thermometer [measured] 96 degrees in the shade, 156 degrees in the sun. . . . Owens Valley is over a hundred miles long and from ten to fifteen wide. It lies four to five thousand feet above the sea and is entirely closed in by mountains. On the West the Sierra Nevada rises to over fourteen thousand feet; on the east the Inyo Mountains to twelve or thirteen thousand feet. The Owens River is fed by streams from the Sierra Nevada, runs through a crooked channel through this valley, and empties into Owens Lake, twenty-five miles below our camp. This lake is of the color of coffee, has no outlet, and is a nearly saturated solution of salt and alkali.

"The Sierra Nevada catches all the rains and clouds from the west—to the east are deserts—so, of course, this valley sees but little rain, but where streams come down from the Sierra they spread out and great meadows of green grass occur. Tens of thousands of the starving cattle of the state have been driven in here this year, and there is feed for twice as many more. Yet these meadows comprise not over one-tenth of the valley—the rest is desert."

Early in the twentieth century, the city of Los Angeles began to acquire land and water rights in the Owens Valley and by 1913 was pumping water out of the valley for the use of the city. This action continues to ignite controversy and to beget lawsuits. The drained valley of today bears little resemblance to the great meadows that Brewer saw more than a century ago.

Death Valley National Monument

Death Valley, on the southeastern border of California, is a long, sunken desert basin, surrounded by fairly high mountains. It includes Badwater, the lowest spot in the Western Hemisphere, 282 feet below sea level. Its grim name is believed to have been given after the William Lewis Manly and Jayhawker parties attempted to cross the valley into California in 1849, tragic episodes in California's history. Manly himself writes on the origin of the name: "We took off our hats, and then overlooking the scene of so much trial, suffering and death spoke the thought uppermost in our minds, saying: 'Goodbye, Death Valley!' . . . Many accounts have been given to the world as to the origin of the name, but ours were the first visible footsteps, and we the party which gave it the saddest and most dreadful name that came to us first from our memories."

During Christmas week of 1849 more than a hundred half-starved emigrants, seeking a shortcut to the California gold fields, entered what some called the Valley of Burning Silence at the mouth of what was later known as Furnace Creek. This gateway (SRL 442), on SR 190 at the eastern entrance to Death Valley National Monument, is now commemorated by a stone monument and a bronze plaque. From this point the Manly party proceeded south, while the Jayhawkers and other groups turned to the northwest. Manly's group crossed the salt flats and found a good spring at what was without a doubt Tule Spring. The site is marked (SRL 444) on the West Side Road. They called this place the Last Camp, for their situation was so critical that it was decided that the party should remain in camp while Manly and John Rogers set out over the mountains to seek help. After incredible suffering and almost insurmountable difficulties, these two brave men finally reached their destination and returned to Death Valley after almost a month to rescue their friends. At Last Camp it was found that only the Bennett and Arcane families remained, the others having attempted to go on alone. (A local name for this spot is the Bennett-Arcane Long Camp.) One Captain Culverwell, who had joined the last party out, died not far from camp. He is the only one of the Manly party known to have perished within the limits of Death Valley itself, but the fate of the others is unknown and it is likely that they too died somewhere in the wilderness.

The story of the Jayhawkers, a high-spirited group of young bachelors who set out from Galesburg, Illinois, in the spring of 1849 with other emigrants, is even more tragic. Traveling by themselves for the most part, the Jayhawkers were often closely associated with the Manly-Bennett-Arcane party in their grim march across the desert, being together at some camps and apart at others. Accounts of the journey by participants in these two main parties differ, but the best authority seems to be that nine of the Jayhawkers perished to the east of Death Valley and four died after leaving it but while still in the desert. One of these, a man named Robinson, died within sight of deliverance not far from the foot of the Sierra. Having separated from Manly's party at what is now Furnace Creek, the Jayhawkers and some others proceeded northwest to a place close to what is now Stovepipe Wells. This place has become known as Burned Wagons Point (SRL 441), for here the emigrants abandoned and burned most of their equipment before they continued westward on foot and, after suffering tremendous hardships, reached safety.

Stovepipe Wells (SRL 826) was the only water hole among the sand dunes in the northwest part of Death Valley. It derives its name from the length of stovepipe inserted in the hole to mark it during times when drifting sand might obscure its location. A plaque has been placed on the Sand Dunes Access Road, one-quarter mile north of SR 190. In 1926 H. W. Eichbaum opened a toll road from Darwin Falls to Stovepipe Wells, the first maintained road into Death Valley from the west. A marker (SRL 848) at Stovepipe Wells commemorates Eichbaum's toll road. As a result of this road, tourism gradually replaced mining as the economic base of the area, and by 1933 Death Valley National Monument had been established. A small triangular plot of the Monument extends into Nevada, and a portion of it lies in San Bernardino County to the south; the rest of its nearly 3,000 square miles lies within Inyo County.

Manly's route lay over the mountain barrier to the south, through Red Rock Canyon, into the Mojave Desert, and on to the San Gabriel Mountains. There the party passed through Soledad Canyon and over Newhall Pass into the San Fernando Valley.

Some contingents of escaping Forty-niners, suffering from the thirst of Death Valley, which they had just left, attempted to secure water from Searles Lake. Finding it unpotable, they despaired and turned northward

and westward across the Argus Range and other mountains in their search for civilization. This bitter disappointment is commemorated by a marker (SRL 443) about six miles north of Trona and just north of the Trona Airport.

This trek across Death Valley is the first recorded tragedy to be associated with it, but it is highly probable that lone wanderers before and since have entered the valley, many never to come out. One of the earliest expeditions from the west was a mining company headed by Dr. Darwin French in the spring of 1860. These men discovered and named Furnace Creek, the presence of a crude furnace at the stream being the occasion for the name. While it has been generally believed that this was built by a Mormon party, it is also possible that it was built by a group of Mexican miners.

The first scientific expedition was made by the State Boundary Commission in 1861. In 1871 the Wheeler Survey (Geographical Surveys West of the One Hundredth Meridian), conducted by Lieutenant George M. Wheeler of the U.S. Army Engineers, mapped this area of California east of the Sierra.

The ruins of the Harmony Borax Works (SRL 773) may still be seen in Death Valley just north of Furnace Creek Ranch and west of the highway. There, in 1880, large deposits of borate were discovered by Aaron Winters and his wife, Rosie. A short while before this, Isidore Daunet, a prospector, had discovered white marshes in Death Valley a few miles north of Bennett's Well and twenty miles southwest of Furnace Creek. On hearing of Winters's find, Daunet opened up the Eagle Borax Works, the first borax corporation in the valley. The product, however, proved to be impure and the plant was closed. Its ruins may be seen from the West Side Road between Shorty's Well and Bennett's Well.

The Winters deposits of borate were finally acquired by Francis M. ("Borax") Smith and his partner, W. T. Coleman, who started the old Harmony Borax Works. In 1889, after the marshes had been thoroughly worked out, Coleman assigned his property to the Pacific Coast Borax Company, and work at the old Harmony plant ceased. Smith then entered the picture in earnest, working his way to the head of the company. A deposit at the base of Monte Blanco, a thousand-foot peak southeast of Furnace Creek, proved to be in a purer state than that previously worked and so rich that even today the mountain seems to be composed of almost solid colemanite, as the deposit was called. The miles of tunnels and drifts into the mountain did not begin to exhaust the supply. A picture of the 20-mule team used to haul the borates 200 miles across the desert to Mojave became the trademark of the company and is used to this day, although the teams were replaced by the Tonopah and Tidewater Railroad in 1907. New borax deposits as rich as those of Death Valley, and far more accessible, were found in Nevada and Oregon and at Trona near Searles Lake in adjacent San Bernardino County. Borax is still present in Death Valley in great quantities, but the difficulties of transportation are too great and the mines are no longer worked.

The Borax Museum at Furnace Creek has an outdoor exhibit of some of the wagons used in the borax trade and an indoor display that shows the process whereby borax was extracted from the mined ores. Furnace Creek is a remarkable flow of water in the midst of a desert; from its emergence behind the Furnace Creek Inn, the creek passes the Visitors' Center and waters the oasis of Furnace Creek Ranch, where a delightful grove of date palms provides cool shade.

In the extreme northern part of Death Valley National Monument is the fabulous Scotty's Castle, built in the 1920's by Walter Scott and his partner, Albert M. Johnson, a Chicago financier. Scott was once a cowboy with Buffalo Bill Cody's Wild West show and in later years was known as a "desert rat," a prospector who may have struck it rich. "Death Valley Scotty" was 91 when he died in 1954, and his house, said to have cost $3,000,000, is now a privately owned enterprise and open to the public for guided tours. A few miles to the west is impressive Ubehebe Crater, half a mile wide and 800 feet deep, believed to be the result of a volcanic explosion 3,000 years ago.

Early White Settlements: Laws and Bishop

Prior to 1861, the only white population in Owens Valley was composed of transient prospectors, mountain men, and travelers to the West Coast, who took a shortcut through the valley or who used this route to reach the gold fields without going over the high Sierra Nevada. In August 1861 A. Van Fleet with three other men drove cattle into the northern end of the Owens Valley from Nevada Territory. A cabin of sod and stone was built, the site (SRL 230) of which is at the big bend of the Owens River about four miles northwest of Bishop, not far from the little community of Laws. The same month Charles Putnam built a stone cabin on Little Pine Creek (now Independence Creek) and started a trading post. These were the first white dwellings in Owens Valley.

Laws became an important town because of its position on the narrow-gauge Carson and Colorado Railroad, which ran from Mound House near Carson City, Nevada, to Keeler, California. The Laws railroad station (SRL 953) was erected in 1883. When the line was sold to the Southern Pacific Railroad in 1900, the station was named for superintendent R. J. Laws. The line worked by the Slim Princess, as the narrow-gauge engines were affectionately called, ceased to operate in 1960, and in the following year the Southern Pacific donated the railroad station and surrounding installations, together with Locomotive No. 9 and a string of cars, to the city of Bishop and Inyo County for the establishment of the Laws Railroad Museum. This attraction also features exhibits of domestic and commercial life in Inyo County around the turn of the century.

Samuel A. Bishop, for whom the town of Bishop was named, came to California in 1849. He was associated with General Edward F. Beale at Rancho Tejón before coming to Inyo County and later, in 1866, he became one of Kern County's first supervisors.

Bishop and his wife came to Inyo from Rancho Tejón in 1861, settling on the creek that now bears his name. Here, where the stream leaves the foothills and enters the valley, about three miles southwest of the present town of Bishop, two small cabins of rough pine slabs were erected on August 22, and the new settlement was named the San Francis Ranch (SRL 208). The site is on Red Hill Road, west of Bishop via SR 168. Bishop did not remain long in the area, moving in 1864 to the abandoned fort at Tejón.

Settlers were in and around the area from the time Bishop arrived. The town of Bishop, now the largest in the county, prospered mainly because of the rich farming land surrounding it, but early mining in the White-Inyo Range also contributed to its growth. The Paiute Shoshone Cultural Center at 2300 West Line Street features exhibits of Indian life in the Owens Valley and is maintained by the tribes.

The early history of Indian-white relations in the Owens Valley was one of conflict and war. A large party of Indians threatened San Francis Ranch in the autumn of 1861, greatly alarming the settlers. Knowing that they could not withstand a siege, they agreed to hold a council with the natives. On January 31, 1862, Indian chiefs met with the white settlers at the ranch and concluded a treaty, which was signed by both parties.

The San Francis treaty proved to be only an episode in the Indian wars of Inyo County, for within two months the natives started hostilities in earnest. In March, Warren Wasson, Nevada Indian agent, asked for aid from United States troops in order to prevent a long and bloody war. He made every effort to settle the difficulty by peaceful means, but without success.

On April 6, between 50 and 60 pioneers under John T. Kellogg and a settler named Mayfield engaged in battle with 500 to 1,000 Paiutes lined up from a small black butte in the valley across Bishop Creek to the foothills in the south. Three settlers were killed, and after the moon had set, the pioneers retreated to Big Pine. A marker has been placed at the Bishop Creek battle-ground (SRL 811) on Bishop Creek Road, about five miles southwest of Bishop on SR 168.

Troops had arrived at Owens Lake on April 2, and on April 8 they joined with the settlers in a second engagement with the Indians. Mayfield and Trooper Christopher Gillespie were killed. The site of this battle (SRL 211) is at the mouth of what was later named Mayfield Canyon, about one-half mile north of the former Wells Meadow Ranger Station, northwest of Bishop off Round Valley Road near Rovana. Temporary peace followed, but by May the valley was in almost undisputed possession of the Paiutes and many of the white settlers left the region. On July 4, 1862, Camp Independence was established. By the fall of 1863 settlers in increasing numbers were coming into the valley and new camps were springing up. Not until 1866, however, was the valley pronounced safe from Indian hostilities, and troops were maintained at the post until 1877.

Independence

On July 4, 1862, Lieutenant Colonel George S. Evans with 201 men of the Second Cavalry California Volunteers arrived on Oak Creek, raised the Stars and Stripes, and established a military post, naming it Camp Independence in honor of the day. The purpose of this post was to protect the few white people in Owens Valley and to act as a fortification in case of an invasion by secessionists from the territories of Nevada and Arizona. With the exception of the year 1864, troops were maintained at Camp Independence until July 1877, when the post was abandoned. The site (SRL 349) is about two miles north of the town of Independence, off US 395. The caves occupied by soldiers and the old cemetery are all that remain, and they are difficult to reach.

A relic of the old post may be seen, however, in the town of Independence. The Commander's House was purchased and moved to the corner of Edwards and Main streets in 1883. It was constructed following the great earthquake of 1872, which rendered the earlier adobe buildings unsafe. The two-story, ten-room frame house with its adobe fireplace has been renovated and is open to the public.

The town of Independence was started with the building of the stone trading post by Charles Putnam in August 1861 and was at first called "Putnam's" or Little Pine after the creek so named. Town and creek derived their new name from the nearby army post. The stone

Home of Mary Austin, Independence

cabin was used as a residence, store, hospital, and fort, and stood on a site (SRL 223) southwest of the present courthouse until it was torn down in 1876. In 1862 gold was discovered in the Inyo Mountains to the east, and for some years the town was the center of a rich mining area. The platting of the townsite was completed in 1866, the first to be found in the county records. Upon the organization of Inyo County that year, Independence became the county seat and has remained so.

The home of Mary Austin (SRL 229), said to have been designed and supervised by the author herself, still stands on Market Street in Independence. There she wrote *The Land of Little Rain* and other books that picture the beauty of Owens Valley and Inyo desert regions. The marker bears a quotation from the first chapter of the book: "But if ever you come beyond the borders as far as the town that lies in a hill dimple at the foot of Kearsarge, never leave it until you have knocked at the door of the brown house under the willow-tree at the end of the village street, and there you shall have such news of the land, of its trails and what is astir in them, as one lover of it can give to another."

The Eastern California Museum at Grant and Center streets is also the Inyo County Museum, with a remarkable collection of artifacts from early times down to souvenirs of the World War II internment camp at nearby Manzanar. The museum administers the Commander's House and the 1865 Edwards House, one of the oldest still standing in Inyo County.

Bell's Mill was the oldest flour mill in Owens Valley and served a vast, sparsely settled territory. Its wooden ruins may still be seen on Oak Creek, northwest of Independence, about half a mile west of US 395, by a road that branches from the road leading to the Mount Whitney Fish Hatchery.

About midway between Independence and Big Pine,

Harry Wright's stage station on Taboose Creek, one and one-half miles north of Aberdeen and a mile west of the highway, was a popular gathering place in the 1860's and 1870's. Only a few locusts and black willow trees mark the site, which is now a public campground.

Manzanar

While there are no traces left of the Shepherd ranch house, it was said to be the first two-story frame dwelling in Owens Valley. The house stood one-half mile west of Manzanar crossroads on the north side of the road. It was built in 1873 by John Shepherd from materials brought by horse- or mule-drawn wagons from San Pedro, on the coast 250 miles away.

The settlement of Manzanar grew up in this area after the turn of the century but was abandoned when the city of Los Angeles bought the land. On February 19, 1942, in the early days of World War II, Executive Order 9066 went into effect, calling for the internment of people of Japanese ancestry. The Manzanar site (SRL 850) was one of ten Japanese War Relocation Centers created in the western United States for that purpose. Ten thousand people, the majority of whom were American citizens, were interned here. The inscription on the state marker at the gates contains a passage like that found on the Tulelake relocation center in Modoc County (SRL 850.2): "May the injustices and humiliation suffered here as a result of hysteria, racism and economic exploitation never emerge again."

Not much remains today on the dusty Manzanar plain to show the heartbreaking desolation of the camp. A pair of Japanese-style stone gates and a few concrete foundations can be seen; a striking monument in the cemetery was completed in 1943 by internee R. F. Kado, a landscape architect and stonemason. The Eastern California Museum has a permanent exhibit of Manzanar memorabilia and a project is under way to collect as much material as possible from what is hoped will remain a unique experience in California history.

Lone Pine

The first cabin at Lone Pine was built in the early part of the winter of 1861–62, and a "fine settlement" was reported there two years later. The town was so named because of a large pine tree that stood at the confluence of Lone Pine and Tuttle creeks. Its shade provided a meeting place for the early settlers, and it was said to have been used in the same manner by the Indians long before then. It blew down in a storm in 1876.

On March 26, 1872, a severe earthquake shook Owens Valley, opening a great fault twelve miles long, parallel-ing the present US 395 and running north from Lone Pine. Along this crevice, land dropped from 4 to 21 feet, and at Lone Pine, a town of adobe houses and stores, 27 persons were killed and dozens injured. On the edge of the fault north of Lone Pine, sixteen of the disaster victims were buried in a single large grave (SRL 507). The quake was felt throughout Inyo County and as far as 250 miles away; two deaths occurred in other areas, but the major damage was done between Olancha and Big Pine. Lone Pine is now a thriving town, the seat of the Interagency Visitor Center, where some fourteen public agencies, from the U.S. Bureau of Land Management to the University of California, have displays and materials on their activities in the region. Some 90 percent of the Owens Valley–Mono Basin region is owned by the federal government or the city of Los Angeles.

The Alabama Hills and Kearsarge

The Alabama Hills run generally north and south and are just west of Lone Pine and east of the alluvial apron at the base of the Sierra Nevada. The name comes from Civil War days. Southern sympathizers, mining in a gulch at the north end of this picturesque stretch of hills in 1863, heard of the damage that the Confederate raider *Alabama* was inflicting on Northern shipping. In their elation over the news, they named the hills for the ship. These hills, with their attractive topography and comparative ease of access, have been the location for the making of many Western films. The visitor today may drive on the Alabama Hills Scenic Road and Movie Road, keeping alert for cinematographic stampedes.

Kearsarge Peak, a few miles to the northwest, and the town that followed the strike made in the Sierra Nevada in 1864 were named for the USS *Kearsarge*, which sank the CSS *Alabama* off the coast of France the same year. These miners were Northern sympathizers and jubilant over the sinking. They named their mine the Kearsarge, and soon the peak, a pass, and the town that grew up under the boom took the same name.

The city of Kearsarge was built at the southern base of the mountain's highest crest and had developed into a considerable camp by the end of 1865. Violent storms raged about the peak in February 1867, bringing rain, snow, freezing, and a sudden thaw. An avalanche swept down the side of the mountain and almost wiped out the settlement; a woman was killed and several men injured. Despite such setbacks, the Kearsarge, Silver Sprout, Virginia Consolidated, and other mines on the slopes of the great mountain continued to be worked for a number of years. The town moved to another location, the site of which is three miles east of Independence at the end of Mazourka Canyon Road, but only crumbling foundations remain of a place that once vied with Independence for the county seat.

Camps on the East Side of Owens River

Notwithstanding Indian hostilities, new settlements were made in the Owens Valley in 1862 and 1863. Owensville lay on the banks of the Owens River four miles northeast of Bishop, close to where Van Fleet had built his cabin in 1861. For a few years it held the distinction of being the chief settlement in the northern part of the valley. In its vicinity more than 50 homestead claims of 160 acres each were taken up; in the White Mountains to the northeast were a number of mines, among them the Golden Wedge and the Yellow Jacket. By the end of 1864, Owensville had started to decline. Its buildings were being torn down and rafted down the river to Independence and Lone Pine. By 1871 the last inhabitant had departed.

Bend City (SRL 209), a mining camp established in the early 1860's, was named by the legislature as the seat of Coso County (which, however, was never organized). Nearly all of the 60-odd houses originally built at the camp were adobe. Their ruins can be seen near Kearsarge, east of Independence. The first county bridge across the Owens River was erected at Bend City, but the earthquake of 1872 changed the river's course and left the already deserted townsite on the bank of an empty ravine.

The White Mountain District

From the earliest coming of the white settlers to Inyo, more than one aspiring city was staked out in the White Mountains east of Bishop, only to be forgotten. Just over the summit of the range from Owens Valley, town plots were actually surveyed for two would-be mining centers, which figured in an attempted election fraud in the fall of 1861. The "Big Springs precinct," with its alleged polling place at what is now known as Deep Springs, was created less than two weeks before the election. In spite of the fact that virtually no population existed in the region, election returns showed a total of 521 votes cast. Investigation finally revealed that the names had been copied from the passenger list of a steamer at San Francisco. White Mountain City, neatly laid out on Wyman Creek on the Deep Springs slope, and its rival, Roachville, on Cottonwood Creek, were only paper cities in 1864 and never became anything else.

Settlements were made near Big Pine Creek in 1861, and the rich farming land fed by the creek was an early attraction to those wanting to locate in the new area. The town of Big Pine on US 395 is near the famous Palisade Glacier, the southernmost glacier in the United States. A road leads westward from Big Pine over scenic Westgard Pass, and the south branch of this road, leading to Eureka and Saline valleys, has been extended into Death Valley, making this recreation area accessible from the north end of Inyo County. Big Pine is also the gateway to the Ancient Bristlecone Pine Area.

The Cerro Gordo Mines

Twenty miles northeast of Olancha, on the ridge of the Inyo Mountains, are the famous Cerro Gordo Mines, believed to have been discovered in 1865 by a Mexican prospector, Pablo Flores, and two companions, who later in the same year located the Ygnacio, San Felipe, and San Francisco claims. The Cerro Gordo ("fat mountain") Mines produced silver, lead, and zinc, and were without doubt the most productive mines in Inyo County. During the 1870's the region had a population of several thousand. Some estimate that the mines yielded $28 million. The last mining operations ceased in 1915. The site is on private property, and the buildings are reported to be in good condition. Cerro Gordo is reached only by a tortuous road from Keeler on the east side of Owens Lake.

Landmarks Around Owens Lake

Ore from Cerro Gordo was hauled to the foot of the Inyo Mountains, where a town named Keeler grew up on the eastern shore of Owens Lake, now dry. From here it was taken across the lake by the steamboats *Bessie Brady* and *Molly Stevens* to Cartago on the far shore, and thence to San Pedro. The process cost more than $50 a ton, thus necessitating the building of smelters in the area. One of these was constructed at Cerro Gordo itself and another at what became known as Swansea, a short distance northwest of Keeler. This place derived its name from the smelter town of Swansea in Wales. At California's Swansea, all that remains of the furnace of the Owens Lake Silver-Lead Company is the old firebox (SRL 752). Across the highway stands part of the adobe house of James Brady, a superintendent of the company and the town's founder. The furnace operated from 1869 to 1874 and, together with the one at Cerro Gordo, produced about 150 bars of silver a day, each weighing 83 pounds.

From Keeler to Laws (near Bishop), a distance of 71 miles, the last remnant of the narrow-gauge Carson and Colorado Railroad operated until 1960. Some of the equipment is on exhibition at the Laws Railroad Museum.

On the western shore of Owens Lake, fifteen miles

Cottonwood Charcoal Kilns, near Cartago

south of Lone Pine and east of US 395, stand two of the Cottonwood charcoal kilns (SRL 537). Here wood was turned into charcoal and taken across the lake by steamboat to the Cerro Gordo furnaces. These kilns were vital to the smelting operations, for all the available wood in the Cerro Gordo area had been used. The kilns are similar to those in Wildrose Canyon, Death Valley.

The town of Olancha is near the southern tip of Owens Lake. Near here M. H. Farley, working for the Silver Mountain Mining Company in the Coso Mountains, completed the first mill and furnace in the Owens Valley by December 1862. Two years earlier he had explored and named Olancha Pass and had conceived the idea of his mill. The site (SRL 796) is on Olancha Creek, about a mile west of the historical marker that stands on US 395 at Williams Road. East of Olancha and southeast of Keeler is another interesting old town, Darwin, named for Darwin French, an early explorer of Death Valley.

Relics of the old steamboats are to be seen in the Eastern California Museum at Independence.

Panamint City

The Panamint Valley lies at the western edge of the Panamint Mountains, a desolate region so remote from the rest of the world that outlaws flourished openly and Wells Fargo, it was said, refused to send a stagecoach through it. High in the mountains at the end of Surprise Canyon, Panamint City was a fast-growing mining town with a reputation for lawlessness equalled only by Bodie in Mono County to the north. By 1875, the Panamint Mining Company and the Surprise Valley Mill and Mining Company were in full operation, and the town boasted some 1,500 people. A torrential downpour in 1876 generated a flash flood so devastating that it is said 200 people were drowned and the loss in buildings was very great. The entire episode was over in less than an hour; Panamint City never recovered.

The road to Panamint City is not easy, but it is highly picturesque. Through Randsburg, by the edge of Searles Lake with its vast deposits of potash and borax, up over the Slate Range, and down into the Panamint Valley, the road leads past the adobe ruins of Ballarat, once described as "a wraith of the desert." From here the road leads on to the site of Panamint City, entering the gateway to the mighty chasm four miles from Ballarat.

Where the canyon widens to several hundred feet is the site of Panamint City, now wrecked by cloudbursts, floods, vandals, and the ravages of time. A tall brick chimney rises from a smelter, and nearby are a few skeleton houses of wood among the juniper and mesquite bushes, while the thick stone walls of former saloons and gambling houses cluster along the base of the cliffs. Over all hangs the stillness, the grandeur, and the desolation of the wilderness.

Greenwater and Skidoo

Two later boom camps, Greenwater and Skidoo, had their start in the 1880's. The former, discovered in 1884 on the eastern side of the Funeral Mountains and just over the summit from where the slope into Death Valley begins, has had few parallels in the "sudden rise, great outlays, small returns, and quick decline" that have attended its brief periods of excitement. Gold, silver, and copper finds each had their day, the latter as late as 1906, when the population increased from 70 to 1,000 within a month. Over a 30-mile stretch of mountain range some 2,500 claims were staked within four months' time, and from them the "copper kings" reaped a rich harvest. But the camps were surrounded by hundreds of miles of barren mountain and desert, and their inaccessibility ultimately caused all claims to be abandoned. A cheerful miner from somewhere in the locality described the situation in vivid terms when he wrote in a letter that he was employed on the "graveyard shift in the Coffin Mine, Tombstone Mountains, Funeral Range, overlooking Death Valley."

Skidoo, located on the summit of the mountain on the western edge of Death Valley, was Greenwater's nearest neighbor. It had the luxury of pure mountain water piped many miles from a spring near the top of Telescope Peak. (This aqueduct was some 23 miles long, and the term "twenty-three Skidoo," popular in the early years of this century, may refer to the satisfaction that comes from the completion of a difficult task.) Skidoo continued to produce gold and silver ores years after its sister mine was deserted.

Although it was not a wide-open, brawling town like others in the Eastern Sierra country, Skidoo had its moment of notoriety. On Sunday, April 19, 1908, Joe

Simpson (familiarly known as Joe Hootch) shot and killed Jim Arnold, the manager of the local store. Simpson was immediately jailed. On Wednesday night following the shooting, while most of the town slept or refused to be aroused by stealthy footsteps, Simpson was taken out of jail and hanged, his swaying body found the next morning. The headlines of the next *Skidoo News*, a weekly paper, read in bold letters: "Murder in Camp, Murderer Lynched with General Approval." As if this did not create enough excitement, when reporters from

daily newspapers arrived shortly thereafter, the body of Joe Simpson was dug up and hanged for a second time, with appropriate pictures made of the event.

Apart from this episode, Skidoo was a rather peaceful town until, its mines worked out, it was abandoned. A few buildings still stand in the town, now on the National Register of Historic Places; it lies within the border of Death Valley National Monument at the top of a steep road branching off from Wildrose Road.

Kern County

Kern County was organized in 1866 from parts of Los Angeles and Tulare counties. Edward Meyer Kern, an artist, was the topographer for the expedition led by John C. Frémont in 1845–46. Frémont named the principal stream in the region the Kern River after his Philadelphia-born colleague narrowly escaped drowning during a crossing. Kern died at the age of 40, two years before his name was given to California's third-largest county.

The first county seat was located at Havilah. Bakersfield, with a more central location, replaced it in 1874.

Garlock's Prehistoric Village

On Black Mountain, about five miles northwest of Garlock, at the edge of the Mojave Desert, are the remains of a prehistoric Indian village, discovered in the 1880's. From the nature of these ruins scientists have concluded that no recent tribe of Indians could have erected the village. On the inside of one of the doorways are stone carvings resembling those found on the famous Posten Butte near Florence, Arizona. From this evidence it is believed by some that the village may have been occupied centuries ago by the same race of people that built the extinct and buried cities of Arizona and Mexico. Other authorities hold that the site was not a true village but rather a religious center used during certain periods of the year and not otherwise occupied.

In neighboring mountains and valleys there are many evidences of more recent tribes, among the most notable being the painted rocks (pictographs) on the Kern River near Lake Isabella.

Grizzly Gulch

Grizzly Gulch, in northeastern Kern County, about seven miles south of the old mining town of White River (Tailholt) in Tulare County, was noted in early days for its large number of grizzly bears. Several prospectors were reported killed or crippled by them, and active mining operations could not be carried on until they had been killed.

The prevalence of fossil bones of prehistoric animals and of archaeological remains of the Yokuts Indians adds greatly to the interest of this region. South of Grizzly Gulch, and particularly in Rag Gulch and north of the Kern River, marks of an ancient shoreline are plainly visible, showing that this was the eastern margin of a great body of water in past ages. For miles, the waterline may be traced by the remains of shellfish and other sea life, and at Shark Tooth Mountain, north of the Kern River, the bones and teeth of prehistoric sharks exist in great numbers.

An Indian rancheria once existed in Grizzly Gulch a little less than half a mile east of Blue Mountain Road. Hundreds of Indian mortars, many of them deeply worn into the granite through the grinding of acorns and seeds for generations, may still be seen in the bedrock and outcropping granite surrounding the little valley.

The Southern Passes

Lying between the southern end of the Sierra Nevada to the east and the Coast Ranges to the west at about the 35th parallel are the Tehachapi Mountains. To the north they fall away into the San Joaquin Valley and the basins into which the rivers flow from the Sierra. Six passes, all of historical interest, cut through this mountain barrier: from east to west, they are Walker Pass, Tehachapi Pass, Oak Creek Road, the original Tejón Pass, the present Tejón Pass or Canyon de las Uvas, and San Emidio Pass.

Walker Pass

One of the pioneer trails to California followed down the Owens River Valley through what is now western Inyo County, passing by Owens Lake, and thence through Walker Pass to the South Fork of the Kern River, and down the South Fork to its junction with the North Fork at Isabella.

There the trail divided. One branch went south by way of Bodfish, Havilah, and Walker's Basin, and then west by several routes to the ferry on the Kern River (called Gordon's Ferry for many years) about five miles northeast of Bakersfield. The other branch crossed the Kern River near Isabella, passing over the Greenhorn Mountains either to Poso Flat or to Linn's Valley (near Glennville), and then turning north to the White River and Visalia.

In 1834, Joseph Reddeford Walker, captain of an exploring party, left California by the latter route, via the White River and the Greenhorn Mountains, and in 1843 he followed the same trail in, while leading the Chiles emigrant party, the second wagon train to enter California from the east. In 1845, John C. Frémont, on his second expedition into California, sent his main party, accompanied by Joseph Walker, via this route, while he and a few others crossed the Sierra at Donner Pass. It was on this expedition that Edward Kern mapped the river that Frémont subsequently named for him. Kern's campsite (SRL 742) at the junction of the North and South forks is now inundated by Lake Isabella, but a monument has been placed on SR 178 on the east side of the lake. The summit of Walker Pass on the same highway has been marked (SRL 99), and in 1963 it was designated a National Historic Landmark by the Department of the Interior.

A marker has been erected at Freeman Junction (SRL 766), a meeting place of old Indian trails that was passed by Walker in 1834 after his discovery of the pass to the northwest. At this point the Death Valley Forty-niner parties diverged west and south after their escape from that inferno of suffering. Later the place became a favorite haunt of the bandit Tiburcio Vásquez. It is now the junction of SR 14 and SR 178. A few miles north of this point on SR 14 is Indian Wells (SRL 457), a station

on the Walker Trail and later on the freight line from Los Angeles to the Cerro Gordo Mines in Inyo County. It derives its name from a rock-walled spring, still in existence, the former location of an Indian village.

The Tejón Passes

The pass that is today named Tejón ("badger") was first penetrated by Pedro Fages, then acting governor of Alta California, in 1772 while he was pursuing deserters from the Spanish Army. A manuscript penned by Fages himself, discovered only in modern times and published in 1937, describes his inland expedition from San Diego to San Luis Obispo. Concerning this document, Professor Herbert E. Bolton writes that "it is a surprising story of an entirely unknown California expedition, ahead of Anza, from Imperial Valley over the mountains to San Bernardino Valley, thence through Cajón Pass, along the edge of the Mojave Desert, through Antelope Valley, through a pass into the southern end of San Joaquin Valley, northwest across it to Buena Vista Hills and Lake, and through the mountains to San Luis Obispo, four years before Garcés entered the valley. . . . It gives Captain Pedro Fages a distinctive position, hitherto unrecognized, as far-travelling trail blazer, and as pioneer in the South San Joaquin."

The pass and canyon through which Fages blazed this trail have had various names. Fages himself called the canyon Buena Vista ("beautiful view"). The Spaniards who came later designated it La Cañada de las Uvas ("the canyon of the grapes"), and it is known today as Grapevine Canyon. The route over the summit, however, is designated on modern maps as Tejón Pass. A monument (SRL 283) has been placed at Lebec, near the summit, in memory of Pedro Fages, the first white man to cross the Tehachapi Mountains by this pass and the first to enter the San Joaquin Valley from the south.

Leaving Grapevine Canyon, Fages traveled 30 miles northwest across the southwestern corner of the San Joaquin Valley to the Buena Vista Hills in the Coast Range, perhaps taking a shortcut by way of the low gap at the neck of Wheeler Ridge. A marker on SR 166, about seven miles west of SR 99, indicates the point (SRL 291) at which Fages's trail was crossed in 1806 by the expedition, in search of mission sites, that included Father José Maria Zalvidea. This party traveled from Santa Barbara Mission to San Gabriel Mission, passing the site of present Bakersfield.

Reaching the foot of the hills on the southwestern shore of Buena Vista Lake, Fages found an Indian village, the existence of which is still attested by vast kitchen middens. Across the floor of the valley and about the lake itself Fages found "a labyrinth of lakes and tulares." The name Buena Vista has been given to the nearby hills and the village at their foot, and is the oldest Spanish place name in the San Joaquin Valley.

The site of the principal Tulamniu Indian encampment (SRL 374) is on Tupman Road, south of SR 119, on the west side of Buena Vista Lake. This was the scene of excavation work done in 1933–34 under the auspices of the Smithsonian Institution.

The second Spaniard to enter the San Joaquin Valley from the south was a Franciscan friar, Father Francisco Garcés, in 1776. Garcés left San Gabriel in April of that year and, ascending the San Fernando Valley, crossed over the Newhall grade to the vicinity of the present town of Castaic, in Los Angeles County, where he swung northeast over the mountains by a trail running east of the present I-5. Near Hughes Lake on the edge of Antelope Valley he crossed Fages's trail of 1772 and then proceeded north across the valley to Cottonwood Creek, up which he climbed to the pass above. From there he descended into the San Joaquin Valley by way of Tejón Creek. To this pass, fifteen miles east of the pass over which Fages had entered the great central valley four years before, rightly belongs the name Tejón.

On April 30, 1776, Garcés visited the locality of the present Arvin, a fact commemorated by a statue of him (SRL 371) in front of St. Thomas Church on Bear Mountain Boulevard at the eastern limit of the town. On May 1 he crossed the Kern River, which he named Río de San Felipe, at a point (SRL 278) about one mile north of the marker on SR 178, eight miles east of Bakersfield. Since the priest could not swim, friendly Indians carried him across the river.

The padre traversed the valley as far north as the White River, near which on May 3 he baptized a dying Indian boy. This site of the first baptism in the south San Joaquin Valley (SRL 631) is marked by a cross on private property three miles north of the monument that stands on Garces Highway seven miles east of SR 65 and sixteen miles east of Delano. Outdoor pageants dramatizing the visit of the pioneer Franciscan have been held in a natural amphitheater on the ranch property. On his return trip, Father Garcés visited, on May 7, an Indian rancheria at or near the site of the present city of Bakersfield. This city has commemorated the first white man to have been within its present limits by a statue (SRL 277) in the traffic circle at Chester and Golden State avenues. A Catholic high school in Bakersfield has been named in Garcés's honor. The explorer returned by way of Arvin on May 10 and 11 en route to the Tehachapi region and the Mojave Desert.

Hudson's Bay Company trappers came as far south as the Tejón region in the 1830's, and in the name of the town of Lebec is preserved the memory of Peter Lebeck, possibly one of these trappers, who was killed on October 17, 1837, by a grizzly bear that he had shot and wounded near the site of Fort Tejón. Authentication is doubtful here, but it is believed that Lebeck was buried under a tree standing at the northeast corner of the old Fort Tejón parade grounds, three and one-half miles north of Lebec.

Rancho El Tejón

Rancho El Tejón is one of the most interesting and important historic spots in the San Joaquin Valley. Here are the sites of several Indian villages that date back to prehistoric times. They were occupied until the last quarter of the nineteenth century.

The first historic record of the region was made by Father Francisco Garcés, who, on his expedition in April 1776, visited and named the Indian village of San Pascual, probably the one located at the mouth of Tejón Creek, later the site of the Los Alamos Butterfield Stage station. For many years this village was the center for traditional Indian ceremonies such as that described by Bishop William Kip, who visited the place in 1855: "It was a wild scene as the glare of the fire fell upon the dancers and a thousand Indians gathered in a circle around them."

General Edward Beale, while Superintendent of Indian Affairs, established a government Indian reservation on Rancho Tejón in the early 1850's, erecting stone and adobe buildings as headquarters for the agency on the site later occupied by the headquarters of the rancho on Arroyo del Paso. One of these buildings, erected in 1856 and formerly used as a store, still stands, in part, although it has been extensively modernized. The thickness of its adobe walls is evident, and the old front doors, bearing the symbol of the Tejón brand, are still in use, having been replaced on the building after its original front portion was torn down. Most of the old buildings were razed following serious damage by the Tehachapi earthquake of 1952. At this location there were also later adobe buildings constructed from bricks salvaged from some of the old structures at Fort Tejón after its abandonment, but these too are gone. After the earthquake new ranch headquarters were built on the east side of I-5 three and one-half miles north of Lebec, opposite Fort Tejón State Historical Monument and on a portion of the old fort site. The old rancho headquarters are fifteen miles east of the highway. Entrance to Tejón Ranch Company properties requires a written permit from the headquarters near Fort Tejón.

A marker beside the highway north of Grapevine

(together with the Rose Station marker) commemorates the government reservation, originally called Tejón but later renamed Sebastian Indian Reservation (SRL 133) in honor of William King Sebastian of Arkansas, chairman of the Senate Committee on Indian Affairs in 1853. Although the reservation failed, General Beale, as owner of Rancho Tejón, encouraged the Indians to remain on the land, employing them as vaqueros and laborers. It is said that when the rancho was finally sold, it was stipulated that the Indian residents should be allowed to remain and that they should be well treated. For years many Indians lived in the little adobe houses scattered up and down Arroyo del Tejón for a distance of several miles, but the adobe houses did not survive the 1952 earthquake.

Rancho El Tejón was a grant made in 1843 to José Antonio Aguirre, a Spanish Basque who was a wealthy trader, and to Ignacio del Valle. The largest Mexican grant in the San Joaquin Valley, it included 97,616 acres of land. It lay in the extreme southeastern corner of the valley, a section of rolling hills and mountains. After the failure of the Indian reservation, General Beale purchased the rancho in 1865 from del Valle and Juan Temple (who had acquired Aguirre's share) and retired to it at the end of his term as United States Surveyor General. The irregularity of the boundary lines of the rancho is due to the fact that an attempt was made to include sufficient water facilities to support the land.

Rancho Tejón today is one of the several combined ranchos owned by the Tejón Ranch Company, incorporated in 1936, totaling over a quarter of a million acres of cattle range. Other old Mexican land grants, each with an interesting history, are included in this vast domain: Rancho de los Alamos y Agua Caliente (partly in Los Angeles County), Rancho de Castac, and Rancho de la Liebre (also partly in Los Angeles County).

Rancho de los Alamos y Agua Caliente was purchased by Beale in 1865 from Agustín Olvera, Cristobal Aguilar, and James L. Gibbens. It had been granted in 1843 and 1846 to Francisco López, Luís Jordan, and Vicente Botello.

Rancho de Castac, traversed throughout nearly its entire length by I-5, extends northward from Castac Lake, near Lebec, to a distance of two miles beyond Grapevine Station. It was granted in 1843 to José Maria Covarrubias, a French citizen of Mexico, who came to California as a teacher in 1834 and later took a prominent part in public affairs. He served as secretary to Governor Pío Pico, and in the autumn of 1849 became a member of the first State Constitutional Convention and later of the state legislature.

Rancho de la Liebre was the first of General Beale's acquisitions in the area, in 1855. His old adobe still stands in Los Angeles County on property of the Tejón Ranch Company. The rancho had been granted to José Maria Flores in 1846.

In a description of historic Rancho Tejón one cannot omit mention of the vast wildflower gardens that each spring display their gorgeous colors along the upland canyons and mountain meadows. The broad valley floor, too, was once covered with miles of blooms, but now the huge acreages under cultivation have caused the wildflowers to become restricted largely to the foothills.

Fort Tejón

Old Fort Tejón (SRL 129) stands in a grove of ancient oaks and sycamores in an exceptionally attractive setting beside the winding mountain stream known on modern maps as Grapevine Creek (Arroyo de las Uvas). It was established in 1854 as the headquarters of the United States Army's First Dragoons, to protect the Indians from extermination and to deter cattle and horse stealing. It was important in the early years of American rule in California.

In 1858 the fort became a station on the Butterfield Overland Mail route, when six-horse stages covered the distance between St. Louis and San Francisco in 23 days. Soldiers from the fort went out to meet the stages and escorted them through the pass, where protection from Indians and bandits was needed. At its peak, the fort was one of the largest settlements in Southern California and the principal military, social, and political center between Visalia and Los Angeles. The men at Fort Tejón traveled on duty to the Colorado and Owens river valleys, escorted groups to Salt Lake City, policed the area, and brought some rule and order into a region that was sometimes a battlefield for miners, Indians, and land claimants. It is an interesting fact that fifteen officers who served at Fort Tejón later achieved the rank of general in the Civil War; eight served with the forces of the Union and seven with the Confederacy.

After the Army abandoned the fort in 1864, the land became part of General Beale's Tejón Ranch, and the buildings on the post were used as residences, stables, and sheds. In 1939, five acres around the ruins of the buildings were granted by the Tejón Ranch to the state of California, which purchased an additional 200 acres from the Tejón Ranch corporation in 1954.

Today, Fort Tejón State Historic Park is easily visited from I-5, which passes directly in front of the visitors' center. Principal structures are the orderlies' quarters, which have been preserved for over 130 years, reconstructed officers' quarters, and a barracks building. Nothing remains for the visitor to see of the Army's fa-

Restored Orderlies' Quarters, Fort Tejón State Historic Park

mous experiment with camels, imported in 1857 to transport supplies to isolated posts in the arid Southwest; the animals were removed in 1861.

The park today still conveys a sense of a more tranquil past, and the modern visitor might well agree with the description written in the 1850's by an admiring visitor: "The post of Tejón is on a little plain, entirely surrounded by high mountains, beautifully situated in a grove of old oak . . . most romantic and beautiful. On the plains and mountain sides, Mother Nature has almost excelled herself, carpeting them with flowers of every hue, giving to the eye one of the most beautiful prospects imaginable; and the air is bracing and exhilarating and inspiring. An oasis in the desert where all is freshness and life."

On the old road between Fort Tejón and Lebec is an adobe building known as "The Dairy." It is owned by the Tejón Ranch Company and was erected in 1886 of adobe bricks salvaged from disintegrating buildings at Fort Tejón. Its circular gable windows are said to have been removed from the fort's original guardhouse.

The Tehachapi Passes

From Bakersfield, SR 58 leads across the Sierra Nevada to the Mojave Desert by way of Tehachapi Pass, a comfortable drive on an excellent multilane freeway. Tehachapi is an Indian word, the meaning of which is uncertain, but Stephen Powers, in his *Tribes of California* (1877), asserts that it was named for a now extinct group of Indians who once lived in the pass. Tradition gives the meaning "land of plenty of acorns and good water" to the name, and the abundance of artesian well water and sturdy oaks seems to justify the interpretation.

The summit of the Sierra is reached just east of the town of Tehachapi, and from there the road descends into the Mojave Desert. The first white man to go through the Tehachapi region was Father Garcés, in 1776. On this expedition Garcés crossed the mountains from the south via Cottonwood and Tejón creeks, and penetrated into the San Joaquin Valley as far north as the White River, passing en route the present site of Bakersfield. Retracing his steps, he crossed the Sierra into the Mojave Desert. His route varied considerably from that followed by the present state highway and the railroad. Instead of going up Tehachapi Creek, Garcés reached Tehachapi Valley via Rancho Tejón and Cummings Valley, where he turned south into the desert, probably by way of Oak Creek Pass. A monument has been placed at the summit of this pass (SRL 97), seven miles southeast of Tehachapi on the road to Willow Springs.

Historians have not been able to determine which of the passes through the Tehachapi Mountains Jedediah Strong Smith traversed in finding his way into the San Joaquin Valley in 1827. Kern County has remembered Smith with a monument (SRL 660) erected on SR 58 about twelve miles east of Bakersfield. Smith traveled where water was obtainable for his party; being primarily a trapper, he investigated the possibility of fur animals being on the several watercourses emerging from the mountains, and so kept close to the foothills. Considering the topography of the area, there is little doubt that he passed at or very near the site of the monument.

Other trappers and hunters went this way from time to time. John C. Frémont, on his way out of California in April 1844, went into the Mojave Desert by way of Tehachapi Creek and Oak Creek Pass, called Tehachapi Pass until the building of the railroad in 1876, when the name was transferred to the present Tehachapi Pass. Later the old trail and wagon road used by the early emigrants followed closely along the trail by Frémont through the original Tehachapi Pass. Frémont himself added to the confusion of subsequent historians by calling this Walker's Pass.

When the Kern River mines were centers of activity in the 1860's, this became an important stage road from Havilah to Los Angeles. Its importance continued during the 1870's, since it was the route between San Fernando and Caliente, which was at that time the southern terminus of the railroad under construction down the San Joaquin Valley from Stockton.

The first permanent settlers came to Tehachapi, in Tehachapi Valley, about 1854. Gold in the China Hill placers brought a large number of miners to the region, but it was not until 1869 that a post office was established there. Before this, the settlers had to get their mail from Los Angeles, a hundred miles away, whenever they or their neighbors went there for provisions.

The original town of Tehachapi was about three and one-half miles west of the present town, originally called Greenwich, which supplanted it when the railroad was built in 1876. At the first location, still known as Old Town (SRL 643), no buildings remain, but a monument indicates the site. The entire countryside is made fragrant each spring with the scent of millions of fruit blossoms, for in hidden nooks and upon sunny plateaus, often lying more than 3,000 feet above sea level, orchards of prize-winning apples and pears flourish.

Signs of twentieth-century industry are also to be seen in the area. The Monolith Portland Cement Company quarry and processing plant, at Monolith, four miles east of Tehachapi, was originally developed for the building of the first Owens Valley–Los Angeles aqueduct. The aqueduct, which crossed Antelope Valley, was completed in 1913. The plant is one of the largest in California and is easily seen from the highway. Further east on SR 58, where the air of the Mojave Desert mingles with that of the mountains, a veritable forest of gigantic wind machines generates electrical energy from the strong winds that rush through this pass and Oak Creek Pass to the south. This remarkable sight is much like that at Altamont Pass on the eastern edge of Alameda County, where similar wind conditions prevail. It is likely that in time machines such as these will become part of the story of California's endless quest for additional sources of power.

San Emigdio

Rancho San Emigdio in San Emigdio Canyon was granted to José Antonio Domínguez in the summer of 1842. Within a year or so, José Antonio's death left his son Francisco in possession. Don Francisco did not occupy the property and had the cattle removed to a location where they would be safer from Indian attacks than they were in the remote rancho. John C. Frémont bought a half-interest in the rancho, and later Alexis Godey occupied the ranch and ran cattle. Godey, "noted plainsman and guide," in the words of an old history, had come to California with Frémont on several occasions. The house he erected still stands on the property, now owned by the Kern County Land Company.

El Camino Viejo

The western San Joaquin Valley retains much of the atmosphere of the early Indians and Spaniards. Even today the sites of many rancherias may be identified, and for years there were many old Hispanic settlers still living along the dry creeks and among the oak-covered hills bordering El Camino Viejo who remembered the location of every water hole along its course. The very names of those numerous arroyos and *aguajes* ("water holes") suggest a significant but little-known Spanish-Californian background.

El Camino Viejo of the Spanish period, which followed the prehistoric Indian trails and the still older paths of antelope as they wandered from *aguaje* to *aguaje* over hill and gully, through tule swamps and plains of blistering alkali, was used chiefly by Spanish and Mexican refugees, who passed over it unobserved from San Pedro to San Antonio (now East Oakland).

For eight months of the year El Camino Viejo crossed a desert waste, to be traveled only when unavoidable; but in springtime it wound through one vast wildflower garden, where every arroyo flowed with abundant, crystal-clear water. Beyond El Arroyo de San Emigdio, the old road passed a campsite at the sink of El Arroyo de Amargosa ("bitter water"), located southwest of Buena Vista Lake. Twenty miles along the road to the northwest of Amargosa was La Brea, a site later occupied by one of several oil camps that have borne the name of Asphalto, five miles east of McKittrick. Many bones of prehistoric animals have been taken from the asphalt deposits at this point, as well as from the spot southwest of McKittrick that is now a registered landmark and discussed later in this chapter.

Another three miles to the northwest was Aguaje de Santa Maria, while still farther on was El Arroyo de los Temblores ("earthquakes"), where were found living springs said to have first issued from the canyon floor as a result of a severe earthquake. Beyond the Creek of the Earthquakes, El Camino Viejo crossed El Arroyo de Chico Martínez, near the mouth of which rise glistening white chalklike bluffs and hills that may be seen for miles across the plains. The arroyo was named for Chico Martínez, a Spanish pioneer in this region, who was known as "king of the mustang-runners" because of his skill in herding wild horses into the corrals built for their capture at Aguaje Mesteño ("mustang springs") and elsewhere.

Traversing an elevated and broken country, El Camino Viejo wound along from El Arroyo de Chico Martínez to El Arroyo de los Carneros ("sheep"). Two chimney-like rocks rising 800 feet above the valley pilot travelers to this water hole. Among these rocks are caves covered with Indian pictographs. Passing successively the Aguajes de en Media ("middle water") and del Diablo ("of the Devil"), and Arroyo de Matarano, the road now ran two miles east of the Point of Rocks, known to the Spanish as Las Tinajas ("tanks") de los Indios, evidently the site of an important Indian encampment. Rock formations here acted as natural reservoirs to hold the water that collected during the winter rains. These cisterns bear evidence of having been improved by the Indians, for deeply worn steps cut into the rock lead down to the water. Indian mortars, rock writings, and other evidence that this was a prehistoric encampment have been found about the rocks.

The next water hole to be reached was at a second Aguaje de la Brea ("tar springs") near the present SR 46 three miles southwest of Devils Den. The oil that covered the water of this spring doubtless deceived many a thirsty wayfarer, who passed it by thinking it only a pool of oil.

At Alamo Solo ("lone cottonwood") three and one-half miles north of La Brea, El Camino Viejo forked, a branch going northeast four miles to Alamo Mocho ("trimmed cottonwood") and thence on to several early Spanish settlements on the west banks of Tulare Lake, Fresno Slough, and the San Joaquin River. The main road continued northward to Poso de Chiné and thence to San Antonio. At Alamo Solo, probably the most unfailing water hole on the entire west side of the valley, there was at one time an Indian encampment that covered approximately 100 acres.

Edward F. Beale

In 1852 General Edward Fitzgerald Beale was made Superintendent of Indian Affairs for California and Nevada. He at once initiated a policy of honest and humane dealings with the Indians. He established a government reservation and later employed them on his ranch.

Like Kit Carson, Beale was a Western pathfinder. He won fame for reaching San Diego with Carson after the Battle of San Pasqual, to warn Commodore Stockton of General Kearny's dangerous situation. He was the first to carry California gold to the East after the discovery of 1848. He explored mountain passes, surveyed routes, and built roads over them, and in 1861 he was appointed Surveyor General of California and Nevada. He acquired the extensive Rancho El Tejón, south of Bakersfield, to which he retired after the Civil War.

Beale, who was an enthusiastic advocate of the camel as a means of transportation across the deserts of the Southwest, brought the first caravan to California from Texas (the animals were originally from Tunis), a trying journey of 1,200 miles, taking from June 1857 to the following January. This feat proved to Americans beyond a doubt the great endurance of the animals. After crossing the Colorado River (where Beale proved that camels can swim), the caravan was driven to Fort Tejón, where some of the animals remained for more than a year.

The camel experiment, however, proved to be a failure, although the animals were used to a limited extent for about two years. Dislike of the creatures and lack of understanding in their care and management, the Civil War, and finally the coming of the railroad, all combined to bring about the ultimate abandonment of the project. In 1863 the camels were sold at auction at Benicia Arsenal, and were soon dispersed to different parts of the country. Rumors were long current that descendants of the original camel corps were occasionally encountered in the desert, but the only physical evidence of them today is the skeleton of one of the animals preserved in the Smithsonian Institution in Washington, D.C.

Butterfield Stage Stations

Following along the old Stockton–Los Angeles Road, the Butterfield stages rumbled back and forth through the Cañada de las Uvas and up the southern San Joaquin Valley on their periodic trips between Los Angeles and San Francisco during the years 1858 to 1861. Most of the stations along the way have long since disappeared. Although little remains today to indicate their sites, one may trace the trail through Kern County by the following names: Fort Tejón, Sink (or Sinks) of the Tejón, Kern River Slough, Gordon's Ferry, Posey, and Mountain House.

The Sinks of the Tejón, also called Agua de los Alamos (or Los Alamitos), were located at the mouth of Tejón Creek. Here, where the water of the arroyo sinks into the dry sands, there was a perpetual spring, long a gathering place of the Indians. It was an important station for the Butterfield stages in the busy years 1858–61; several buildings were erected, including a barn, hostlers' quarters, and a combined general store, post office, and drugstore. This site on the property of the Tejón Ranch Company is now under cultivation, but a monument with bronze plaque (SRL 540) stands six miles west at the intersection of David and Wheeler Ridge roads.

The old stage road continued north past the station at Kern River Slough, where horses were changed. This location is now marked (SRL 588) two miles east of Greenfield on Panama Road. The stage road then crossed the Kern River at Gordon's Ferry (the Kern River Station), about four miles northeast of Bakersfield near the China Grade. No remnant of the Kern River Station can be seen today, but there is a marker (SRL 137) at the south end of the bridge. Major Aneas B. Gordon operated a ferry here for several years before the establishment of the Butterfield route.

Going north, the next station was located at Posey

(Poso) Creek, two and a half miles east of the marker (SRL 539) that stands at the junction of Round Mountain Road and the Bakersfield-Glennville highway. To the north was Mountain House, sometimes called Willow Springs (not to be confused with the Willow Springs near Rosamond in southeastern Kern County). Mountain House had a bad reputation because of several murders that had been committed there, and weird tales developed around it, among them the tale of the white ox that came to the spring to drink and then mysteriously disappeared, and that of the possum that hid at the watering trough, disturbing the flow of water in an uncanny manner. The site of the Mountain House Station is on private property about a mile and a half north of the marker (SRL 589) that stands on the Bakersfield-Glennville highway eight miles southwest of Woody.

Other Landmarks of Stagecoach Days

Rose Station, about four miles north of the present Grapevine Station and one mile east of I-5, was an important stopping place for travel between Bakersfield and Los Angeles during the late 1860's and early 1870's. A monument (SRL 300) stands on the highway at a point from which the site, on Tejón Ranch Company property, can be seen in the distance. This plot of land was first known to history as the Kanawha Ranch, operated by James V. Rosemyre and William W. Hudson. The latter was a native of West Virginia, born on the banks of the Kanawha River. When José J. López and William B. Rose bought the property in 1872, they seem to have recorded their purchase as the Canoa Ranch. *Canoa*, Spanish for "trough," is pronounced very much like "Kanawha," thus creating some historical confusion about the original name of the place that, under Rose's ownership, finally became Rose's Station. The adobe structure erected in 1876 was still standing in good condition in 1933 when this section of the first edition of *Historic Spots in California* was published. By 1946, only a portion of one wall remained standing. In the summer of 1963, Father William N. Abeloe could find only the bare spot where the building had stood, and he noted in the third edition of this book: "So pass our California landmarks."

Willow Springs (SRL 130), about eight miles west of Rosamond, was once an important watering place on the trail connecting the southern San Joaquin Valley and the desert. The springs were used by Indians from ancient times and numerous artifacts have been found there. The site was visited by Father Garcés in 1776, John C. Frémont in 1844, and the Death Valley Forty-niners. On the old Tehachapi Pass route (Oak Creek Pass), it was a stage and freight station until the coming of the railroad in 1876. It was the dividing place for the ordinary stage travel to the Kern River mines by way of Oak Creek and the heavier ox-team traffic by way of Red Rock Canyon, Jawbone Canyon, and the South Fork of the Kern River. Ox teams bound for Inyo County also turned northeast at Willow Springs. Ezra T. Hamilton bought the property from the Beale estate in 1894 and established a resort. Little remains there today except some crumbling ruins and a few old houses.

Another Death Valley Forty-niner water hole that later became a freight station is Desert Spring (SRL 476), one and three-quarters miles southeast of Cantil, which is east of SR 14 and a mile and a half south of the Red Rock–Randsburg Road. Valley Road runs east of Cantil for a mile and then intersects Pappas Road, from which a dirt road branches off to the east for a quarter of a mile to Desert Spring; the historical monument stands on the far side of the wooded clump that surrounds the spring.

North of the junction with the Randsburg Road, SR 14 passes through beautiful Red Rock Canyon State Park, an area of highly colored cliffs that have been eroded into what seem to be pillars, temples, and other fantastic formations. Some of the formations have been given names, including The Great Temple and The Phantom City. The coloration appears more vivid in early morning or late afternoon.

Glennville, Granite Station, and Woody

Forty-two miles northeast of Bakersfield is the pioneer community of Glennville, named for the Glenn brothers, who settled there in the early 1850's. Already at the spot when they arrived was Thomas Fitzgerald, who had built an adobe (SRL 495), still standing, the oldest known residence in Kern County. The tamped-earth structure, restored by the Kern County Museum, was originally a trading post at the intersection of two established Indian trails. Fitzgerald traded with the Indians and also with white trappers. The attractive, well-maintained building still has its original ceiling rafters and a hand-hewn oak door hung on hand-forged iron hinges.

One mile from Glennville on the White River Road a marker (SRL 672) indicates the site of Lavers Crossing, community center for the settlers in Linn's Valley. Here miners and emigrants stopped en route across Greenhorn Mountain to the gold strike of 1854 at Keyesville on the Kern River.

Granite Station and Woody lie on parallel routes leading from Bakersfield into the hills at Glennville. The Kern County Historical Society has marked both places. The Granite Station marker, dedicated in 1981, notes that the place (now virtually deserted) was once known as Five Dogs and was established as a stage route stopover by John Elden in 1873. Woody is still a small town with its own post office; its marker, dedicated in 1982, notes that this early mining center and supply town was named for the pioneer rancher Dr. Sparrell W. Woody, who settled in the area in 1862. A hamlet near Dr. Woody's ranch developed about 1889 and was named for the doctor, who by that time was fully engaged in his farming career. In 1891 Joseph Weringer discovered copper nearby and operated the Greenback Copper Mine and the Weringer Hotel. In the same year the town was renamed Weringdale for its new booster, although by the time Dr. Woody died in 1909 the original name had been restored to the town.

Keyesville

The Kern River, with towering granite walls, banks lined with brilliant green, and "deep-throated roar," is the gateway to one of California's most fascinating mountain regions. Here, in this stupendous natural setting, romance, comedy, and tragedy were enacted during one of California's most important gold rushes.

California historian Robert Glass Cleland said of the discovery of gold on the Kern River and of its importance to Los Angeles and southern California: "Perhaps the most serious drawback to the material development of the south was its deplorable lack of money . . . and under such a handicap economic progress was necessarily slow. . . . In 1855 gold was discovered in considerable quantities on the Kern River. This at once attracted miners from the entire State, and led to a rush of no mean proportions. The southern California merchants were naturally jubilant over this event in which they saw an opportunity of reaping some of the rich harvest their San Francisco, Stockton and Sacramento rivals had previously monopolized."

The first town to spring up in this new field was known as Keyesville (SRL 98), after Richard Keyes, who had opened up a mine likewise named for him. The town was situated in a semicircular cove of the Greenhorn Mountains at the edge of a rocky gulch, and its few stores were scattered about the middle of this flat. There were no streets and the dwelling houses went straying up the slope quite informally.

Keyesville was the scene of gambling resorts and gunmen as wild as in any of the larger camps in the north. The surrounding mountains, too, were wild in the extreme. In 1856 the settlers, expecting an attack from Indians who were waging war in neighboring counties, erected a rude fort on the sage-covered hill just outside the town. The Indians, however, never came and the fort was never used, but a vestige of the trenches may be traced there today. The townsite is at the end of Keyesville Road four miles west of Lake Isabella. The passage of time and the depredations of vandals have almost obliterated old Keyesville; few of the old roughly-hewn board houses, with their shake roofs, remain.

Quartzburg and Whiskey Flat—Rivals

In 1860, Lovely Rogers (this was indeed his first name), a miner from Keyesville, was out looking for a lost mule. In a gulch eight miles north of his home, he found his mule and also a magnificent piece of quartz where the famous Big Blue Mine was later located. That was the beginning of Quartzburg and of its rival, Whiskey Flat, later known as Kernville. The rush to the gulches and mountainsides around Rogers's mine soon resulted in the opening of a dozen quartz mills, and the region became the richest in the state during that period.

On a small ledge above the river the town of Quartzburg sprang up. Water from the mine pumps irrigated the trees and gardens and alfalfa patches, and a homey atmosphere clung about the place from the beginning. Moreover, the influential citizens of Quartzburg believed in local option, and when an attempt was made to start a bar in town, that unwelcome feature was forced to move a mile down the river to a place thereafter known as Whiskey Flat.

Kernville (SRL 132) eventually became the most important town in the Kern River mining region, but for several years it had a rival in the little town up the river. If one tired of the quiet, orderly Quartzburg, it was but a short walk along the riverbank to the bars and gambling resorts of Whiskey Flat.

By 1879 the Kern River region had reached the height of its prosperity, and most of the mines around Quartzburg had been acquired by Senator John P. Jones, who consolidated them into the Big Blue. Soon after this, the senator met with reverses and the mine closed down, thus shutting off the water supply for Quartzburg's houses and gardens. The former were gradually torn down and carted away, while the latter were left to run wild or die. Nothing remains at Quartzburg today to remind one of its past.

Kernville remained until the early 1950's a pleasant town of quaint houses and tree-shaded streets. Now it lies beneath the waters of Lake Isabella, created when two dams were completed in 1953. A new Kernville was begun in 1951 on the bank of the Kern River several miles north of the original site. Some of the old houses were moved to the new community.

The old Kernville Cemetery, however, was not inundated by the lake, and may be seen bordering the highway to new Kernville near the site of vanished Quartzburg. A monument that used to stand at old Kernville is now located in front of the cemetery.

Havilah

Havilah (SRL 100) was named for the Biblical land "where there is gold" by Asbury Harpending, a man with a career almost as exotic as his name. The Kentucky-born adventurer joined William Walker's filibustering expedition to Nicaragua in the 1850's; when that collapsed, he came to California, about 1856. A Confederate sympathizer during the Civil War, he hatched all manner of plots against the Union, for which he was briefly jailed. He made a fortune in gold mining and in real estate and in 1864 learned of a rich quartz deposit just south of Clear Creek, a tributary of the Kern River.

Havilah became the chief settlement of the Clear Creek mining district; Harpending laid out its main street and did a land-office business in selling lots, beginning in July 1864. The region was soon thick with prospectors, and miners from all over the state made it a boom town, aided by favorable publicity by the developers. When Kern County was created in 1866, the flourishing town was made its first county seat.

It was soon found that the ore-bearing deposits lay in deeper veins than had been anticipated, and that the cost of bringing the ore to the surface and refining it was almost prohibitive. Gradually, the mines began to shut down and their developers looked elsewhere. By 1879, mining activity in the region had been abandoned altogether.

Meanwhile, the agricultural future of the San Joaquin Valley was attracting settlers to towns like Bakersfield, which soon challenged remote Havilah to be the county seat. After disputed elections, court hearings, and much bad feeling, it was declared in 1874 that a majority of eligible Kern County voters approved the change to Bakersfield.

Today it is difficult to imagine Havilah as a place where more than 500 people lived in the summer of 1866 or where the business of Kern County was transacted for the next eight years. The courthouse, a one-story frame structure, was restored as a bicentennial project in 1976, and a small display area within is a museum of the palmy days of the settlement, which

Old Kern County Courthouse, Havilah

is now almost deserted. The site is on the Caliente-Bodfish Road, about eight miles south of Bodfish.

Other Mountain Mining Camps

Several other almost-vanished mining towns are to be found in the mountains of Kern County. Due east of Havilah in Kelso Valley in the Piute Mountains is Sageland, a brief mining center of the mid-1860's. Loraine in Caliente Canyon was not developed until the early years of the twentieth century; originally named Paris, which the post office said was already being used elsewhere in the state, its name was changed in 1912. Its decline is attributed to the enactment of Prohibition in 1919 more than to the inevitable falling-off of the mines; having the only saloon for miles around, Loraine was a much-needed social center. It and neighboring Twin Pines continue as small settlements today.

Frazier Park, on the border with Ventura County just west of Lebec and I-5, was a center for borax mining from about 1899 to 1908. Here as elsewhere in Kern County the prodigious labor and expense necessary to get the ore out was ultimately too burdensome to make it a profitable undertaking, although some lumbering activity was also done. Frazier Park is enjoying a second life today as a mountain recreational and retirement community.

Bakersfield

Colonel Thomas Baker was born in Muskingum, Ohio, in 1810, the son of a soldier in the War of 1812 and grandson of a Revolutionary War colonel. Baker himself was made a colonel in the Ohio State Militia when he was nineteen and, having completed his legal studies, was admitted to the Ohio bar. He moved westward first to Illinois and then to Iowa, where he was elected to the first Iowa state legislature, in 1846. A widower by then, Baker caught gold fever and journeyed to California; after brief sojourns in Benicia and Stockton, he moved to the San Joaquin Valley in 1852. That year his name was listed among the pioneer settlers in Visalia, Tulare County. He became active in public affairs, serving as assemblyman, Federal Land Office receiver, and state senator. He married a second time, and in 1863 moved to the banks of the Kern River, where disastrous floods in 1862 had swept away the settlement made there in 1860 by Christian Bohna, a German-born settler, and his family.

The swampy, forested area proved to be productive when reclaimed and drained. Its agricultural potential seemed better than that of the mining ventures that hitherto had been the primary attraction in this part of the state. Soon Baker built an adobe house that became a community center for the incoming population, and planted ten acres of his reclamation land with alfalfa. The place that had been called "Kern Island" for its location on the channels and sloughs of the Kern River was now becoming known as "Baker's Field."

One of the first visitors the Bakers had received after their arrival was Captain Elisha Stevens of the Murphy-Townsend-Stevens overland party of 1844, who made his final home in the area and is buried in Bakersfield. He brought the colonel and his family a welcoming gift of some hogs and chickens from the ranch he had established below the China Grade Bluff. Stevens's homesite is just east of the Greater Bakersfield Memorial Hospital on 34th Street; the marker (SRL 732) is north on Union Avenue at Columbus Street, just west of Garces High School.

By 1870 Bakersfield, with a population of 600, was fast becoming the principal town in Kern County. In 1873 it was officially incorporated as a city, an event that Colonel Baker, who had planned and mapped the townsite, did not live to see, for he died in the typhoid epidemic of the previous year. Baker's insistence on wide streets and even wider avenues and a regular grid pattern for the city was sensible and wise; the city has grown around this nucleus with little change in streets since then. By 1874 Bakersfield had replaced the dying town of Havilah as county seat. Railroads, agriculture, cattle ranching, oil, and highway transportation have continued the boom until today; Bakersfield is now one of the major cities of California.

Alexis Godey, explorer with the Frémont expeditions, made his last home in Bakersfield, having acquired about 66 acres there in 1873. He disposed of much of this land but retained a favorite spot of high ground as his home. The site (SRL 690), facing Nineteenth Street, is now occupied partly by Central Park and partly by business and residential property.

Pioneer Village of the Kern County Museum

The outstanding historical attraction of present-day Bakersfield is the Pioneer Village of the Kern County Museum at 3801 Chester Avenue. Begun in 1950 as an outdoor expansion of the museum's work, the Pioneer Village quickly became the principal repository of buildings and artifacts from Kern County's past. A superb collection of Californiana, this park became the model for others in the state. Its theme is early settlement in Kern County, from about 1860 to about 1900. Most of the buildings are authentic structures that have been moved to the site from various parts of Kern County to be preserved from inevitable destruction in the name of progress. Among these are the Thomas Barnes log cabin, built in 1868, the one-room Norris School from 1882, the modest William Pinckney residence from 1900, the elaborate W. A. Howell house from 1891, and the general store established in Woody in 1899. Specialized buildings include a doctor's office, a dentist's office, a barber shop, an undertaker's parlor, a fire station, a newspaper office, a blacksmith shop, and a bank. The ranching, agricultural, railroad, and oil eras of Kern County history are also represented; a landmark of the village is the wood-framed oil drilling rig from 1910, the oldest known to exist in the United States.

The Kern County Museum, housed in a sturdy two-story building, has detailed exhibits of materials from Kern County's past, from Yokuts Indian artifacts to modern machinery. The Harry D. West Vehicle Collection contains sixteen vintage horse-drawn vehicles, from freight wagons to surreys.

Log Cabin of Thomas Barnes, Pioneer Village, Kern County Museum, Bakersfield

Next to the museum stands a replica of the famous Beale Clock Tower, which stood at the intersection of Seventeenth Street and Chester Avenue for almost half a century until it was razed following the earthquakes of 1952. The original had been given to the city in honor of his mother by Truxtun Beale in 1904. The son of pioneer General Beale had served as United States ambassador to Spain, and the tower was based on one he had seen and admired in that country. The replica was installed in December 1964.

Bakersfield boasts a fine set of modern public buildings housing the city and county departments. These were constructed following the earthquake of August 22, 1952, which wrecked the city hall and courthouse beyond repair. This shock followed the earthquake of July 21 that devastated the town of Tehachapi. In front of the Bakersfield City Hall, at Truxtun and Chester avenues, stands a statue of Colonel Thomas Baker (SRL 382).

The Railroad

Construction had started in the spring of 1870 on the San Joaquin Valley branch of the Central Pacific Railroad, now Southern Pacific, but the tracks did not reach Kern County until 1873. The first station, at the northern boundary, was called Delano for Columbus Delano, then Secretary of the Interior. The railroad bypassed Bakersfield, since its citizens had refused to give the customary subsidy, and established a station called Sumner, a mile and a half east of the town. This place, later called Kern, was consolidated with Bakersfield in 1909, and by that time the Santa Fe Railroad had already established itself in Bakersfield.

The Tehachapi Mountains presented a major engineering obstacle to the continuation of the railroad to Los Angeles County. Construction reached Caliente in April 1875, and here the engineers were faced with the task of raising the railroad 2,734 feet in sixteen miles to scale the pass at a height of 4,025 feet. Caliente (SRL 757) thus became the terminal for about sixteen months while a force of up to three thousand men, mostly Chinese, labored in the mountains. A station just beyond Caliente was named Bealeville (SRL 741) for Edward F. Beale, on whose Rancho El Tejón it was located. (A shortcut from SR 58 to Caliente crosses the railroad at this point.)

The Tehachapis were conquered in 28 miles of track laid on gradual curves and through eighteen tunnels. At one point the track is looped over itself in a remarkable manner, an engineering marvel directed by William Hood, who later became chief engineer for the entire Southern Pacific system. A portion of the famous "Tehachapi Loop" (SRL 508) may be glimpsed from the Woodford-Tehachapi Road at a point about two miles south of Woodford (Keene). A monument has been erected on the spot, and with luck one may see the locomotive of a long train at the top of the loop and the caboose just entering the tunnel below.

A station called Greenwich was established near the summit of the pass, but this soon developed into a town and stole the name and the population of nearby Tehachapi (the place now called "Old Town"). At this time also the name "Tehachapi Pass" was transferred from the pioneer Oak Creek route to the new railroad pass. The railroad was opened through the Tehachapis and across the desert to Mojave on August 8, 1876. With the coming of the railroad to Kern County, the modern era began and agriculture and livestock raising immediately replaced mining as the principal industry.

The desert town of Mojave, child of the railroad, was the rail terminus for the 20-mule-team borax wagons that operated from Death Valley in the years 1884–89. The route, over 165 miles of mountains and desert, ran from the Harmony Borax Works in Death Valley, Inyo County, to the railroad loading dock in Mojave. A round trip required twenty days. A monument (SRL 652) has been placed on the west side of the 16200 block on the Sierra Highway (SR 14) in Mojave.

The United States Borax and Chemical Company, formerly the Pacific Coast Borax Company, began to develop sodium borate mining at Boron, just north of modern Edwards Air Force Base and at the eastern edge of the county. As the Death Valley deposits were gradually exhausted, those at Boron were developed, beginning in 1925; in 1957 this became an open-pit operation and today is one of the largest open-pit mining operations in the world.

Mining in the Mojave

A mining boom was inaugurated at the eastern edge of Kern County with the discovery of gold in 1895 in a group of rounded hills rising out of the Mojave Desert. The mine became known as the Rand, after the prosperous mining district of that name in the Transvaal, South Africa, and a town called Randsburg sprang up nearby. Randsburg soon became the center of several camps, including Johannesburg, Red Mountain, and Atolia, the latter two being in San Bernardino County. Tungsten and silver were later discovered in the area, and there is still some mining activity amid the remnants of boom days. The Rand Mining District is commemorated by a monument (SRL 938) on the eastern side of the junction of Randsburg Road with US 395. The Desert Museum at 161 Butte Street in Randsburg is a branch of the Kern County Museum, featuring mining tools and displays on the history of Randsburg, one of the most picturesque old mining towns in California.

On Garlock Road, one mile north of the Red Rock–Randsburg Road and ten miles west of Randsburg, a marker indicates the ghost town of Garlock (SRL 671), one-time location of four stamping mills serving the Rand Mining District. The first of these was set up by Eugene Garlock near a water hole known as Cow Wells. The post office established there in the following year took his name. The Randsburg area was supplied by freight wagons hauling from the railroad town of Mojave, and Garlock became a regular stopping place. The town quickly grew to a population of 300 and promised further growth, but the completion of a railroad to the Rand area and the erection of a stamp mill at the Yellow Aster (formerly the Rand) Mine caused Garlock to dwindle in importance, and its people gradually moved elsewhere.

Rosamond Mining District

Ezra M. Hamilton discovered gold northwest of Rosamond in 1896, after prospecting for two years. His enterprise was successful; it was purchased in 1909 by the Tropico Mining and Milling Company and its name was changed to Tropico Hill. Two years after the mining operations closed in 1956, Tropico Mine reopened as a public attraction, with an interesting collection of old mining buildings rebuilt on the grounds, three miles west of Rosamond.

North of Rosamond, Standard Hill is the site of a gold discovery in 1894 by W. W. Bowers. Subsequent bonanzas were made in both gold and silver, and the Cactus Queen Mine in the nearby Middle Buttes was the most productive silver mine in California until World War II.

Black Gold

The story of oil in Kern County is essential to a complete picture of the modern era. The county today contributes about one-fourth of the oil produced in California. Even before the county was organized in 1866, oil was being refined in the area. The Buena Vista Petroleum Company was organized and incorporated in 1864, and soon thereafter a refinery was built at the foot of the Temblor Range, eight miles west of the marker that stands at the intersection of SR 33 and Lokern Road, about seven miles north of McKittrick (SRL 504). The refinery operated until April 1867, producing 3,000 gallons of refined oil, but work ceased when freight charges were found to be prohibitive.

There were a number of relatively early discoveries in the McKittrick Field. The California Standard Oil Well No. 1 (SRL 376), not completed until 1899, has been incorrectly designated as the discovery well of that field. The McKittrick area is more famous for the refining of asphalt, the original name of the settlement being Asphalto. About one-half mile south of McKittrick on SR 58 a marker (SRL 498) stands near the location of a brea pit of the Pleistocene period (15,000 to 50,000 years ago), from which the bones of many animals and birds, trapped in the sticky asphalt, have been recovered. These relics, first brought to the attention of scientists in 1929, may be seen in the Kern County Museum in Bakersfield. The pit has now been filled in.

The west side of the county, with its thriving communities of Maricopa, Taft, and Ford City (the last deriving its name from the preponderance of Model-T's there in 1921), is generally associated with Kern's oil industry. But it was in the Bakersfield area that the discovery was made in 1899 that zoomed the county to prominence as an oil producer. Several miles northeast of the city on Round Mountain Road (not far from the site of Gordon's Ferry but on the northern bank of the Kern River), a marker (SRL 290) indicates the discovery well of the Kern River oil field, dug by hand in the summer of 1899. The first commercial well of the area was drilled a few hundred feet away several weeks later, and soon the towns of Oil City, Oil Center, and Oildale came into existence, communicating their prosperity to nearby Bakersfield.

Fellows was a railroad terminal in 1908 but experienced its greatest boom when the Midway Gusher, Well 2-6, blew in on November 27, 1909, with a production of 2,000 barrels a day. The marker (SRL 581) is located a quarter of a mile west of Fellows on Broadway Road.

Although the Midway Gusher started the West Side oil rush, it was eclipsed a few months later when Lakeview Gusher Number One blew in on the evening of March 14, 1910. This is the greatest gusher in the history of the world, producing an unprecedented 18,000 barrels in the first 24 hours. This Union Oil Company well flowed for eighteen months, producing nine million barrels. It presented a major control problem and fire danger, forcing residents of the nearby camp to abandon their homes for a time. At its peak production the output reached 68,000 barrels a day. It is said that the tremendous flow of this gusher brought down the price of oil. Its location is marked (SRL 485) one and one-half miles north of Maricopa on Division Road off SR 33.

The town of Buttonwillow, also on the west side

Site of the Midway Gusher, Well 2-6, near Fresno

of the county, antedates the oil boom. It derives its name from a lone buttonwillow tree (SRL 492), still standing and marked one mile north of town on Button-willow Avenue; the tree was a landmark for early cow-boys in the area and the location of their spring rodeos. It had been an ancient Indian campsite. Henry Miller established the headquarters of the Miller and Lux enterprises at this spot and bestowed the name of the tree on the railroad station and the post office, started in 1895.

Tule Elk State Reserve

California's great Central Valley was home to herds of tule elk, so numerous in the fertile floodplains and lowlands of the northern San Joaquin Valley that they were sometimes observed in groups of one or two thou-sand. Although the coming of the Spanish missions and ranchos had little immediate effect on the tule elk, the aggressive European grasses they introduced spread into the valley and overran the grazing lands of the tule elk. The elk almost vanished altogether when hunters began a systematic slaughter of the animals after 1848. The state legislature made elk hunting illegal through-out the state in 1854, but little seems to have been done to enforce the law. A state fish and game warden could find only a single pair of elk in the state around 1875, in the tule marshes near Buena Vista Lake.

Henry Miller, of the Miller and Lux cattle empire, was determined to preserve the elk. He gave stern in-structions to his employees to protect the animals and offered a generous reward for information about any-one disturbing them. Thus he was able to preserve a

herd. Although they did thousands of dollars of dam-age to his crops each year, Miller nonetheless protected the elk. In 1930 Miller and Lux provided 600 acres as a temporary enclosure for the tule elk until a state refuge could be established.

In 1932 the State Park Commission purchased 953 acres near Tupman to be completely fenced and main-tained as a tule elk sanctuary. Those elk that could be rounded up were maintained here, while wild and free-ranging herds of tule elk were established in Colusa County's Cache Creek area and in the Owens Valley, where they still exist today.

The Tule Elk State Reserve is located four miles west of I-5 and 27 miles west of Bakersfield and can be vis-ited year-round. In recent years, changing water condi-tions have rendered this a less desirable retreat than it formerly was, and the state is considering the establish-ment of another reservation for the tule elk.

The Desert Tortoise Natural Area

The California State Reptile is the desert tortoise (*Gopherus agassizi*). Thirty-eight square miles of natural habitat for these animals were set aside on the western edge of the Rand Mountains by the Bureau of Land Management, U.S. Department of the Interior, in 1977. This refuge is fenced off to prevent larger animals from entering and to keep the few, reclusive tortoises as pro-tected as possible. The visitors' center is located on the Randsburg Road five miles from California City Boule-vard. Some of the area bounded by the fence is still privately owned, although plans are in effect to pur-chase all of the enclosed area for the reserve; once this is done, the Desert Tortoise Natural Area will be the largest wildlife preserve in the United States.

Edwards and China Lake

The largest dry lake in the United States is 65-square-mile Muroc Dry Lake, also known by the name of Rodrigues or Rogers, after a gold- and silver-mining company that operated there early in the twentieth cen-tury. The name "Muroc," which was given to a settle-ment of homesteaders there in 1910, is the reversed spelling of the name of Ralph and Clifford Corum, pio-neer settlers. The hard lake bed has been much used in the past for sports car racing. Its first use by the mili-tary was in 1933 as a bombing and gunnery range op-erating out of March Field near Riverside. In 1942, shortly after the outbreak of World War II, the north end of the lake was used for testing the XP-59, the first jet plane developed in the United States. Muroc Army Air Field became Muroc Air Force Base in 1948. It was established to include the dry lake bed, and since then most of the testing of experimental and production aircraft by the Air Force has been done here, and a number of world speed records have been set. Here, on October 14, 1947, Air Force Captain Charles E. Yeager, at the controls of a Bell X-1 Rocket plane, was the first man in history to fly faster than the speed of sound.

The base was renamed three years later in memory of Air Force Captain Glen W. Edwards, who was fatally injured in the crash of his test plane in 1948. Edwards Air Force Base has been the scene of many aviation triumphs since then; one memorable one was in 1981, with the safe landing there of the first manned space shuttle, *Columbia*.

North of Edwards, but also on the eastern border of the county and also extending into San Bernardino County, is China Lake, site of the United States Naval Weapons Center. The dry lake nearby derives its name from the Chinese who searched Indian Wells Valley for borax in the years following their construction work on the Central Pacific Railroad. The station was established in November 1943 for the development and testing of rockets. The Michelson Laboratory there is named for Albert A. Michelson, who in 1907 was the first American to receive the Nobel Prize in physics.

At Shafter Airport, fifteen miles north of Bakersfield, another aviation landmark was achieved on August 23, 1977, when a man-powered aircraft first completed a mile-long figure-eight flight (the "Kremer Circuit"). Dr. Paul B. MacCready, Jr., designed the aircraft, called the Gossamer Condor. It was operated by Bryan Allen, who won a prize of 50,000 pounds offered by the Royal Aeronautical Society of London for the feat. The flight of the Gossamer Condor is memorialized at the airport (SRL 923).

Kings County

Kings County was named for the river called El Río de los Santos Reyes, "River of the Holy Kings," after the Three Wise Men of the Bible, by a Spanish explorer, probably Gabriel Moraga, in 1805. At the time of the American conquest, the English name "Kings River" was given to the stream, and in 1893 Kings County was organized from territory set off from adjoining Tulare County. Two small additions from Fresno County were made in 1909. Hanford has always been the county seat.

Tulare Lake

Tulare Lake was discovered in 1772 by Pedro Fages, who gave the vast marshlands of the San Joaquin Valley the name Los Tulares ("the place of rushes"). Charles E. Chapman says that as early as 1804 Father Juan Martín of Mission San Miguel crossed the Coast Range into the valley, penetrating as far as an Indian village on Lake Tulare. He goes on to say that "in October 1814 a fresh search for a mission site in the tulares was made. The commander of the expedition was a sergeant (Juan Ortega?), whose name does not appear. The account comes from Father Juan Cabot, who was a member of the party. They went from San Miguel to Lake Tulare." The fur-trapping "mountain-men" also visited Tulare Lake as early as 1827.

Tulare Lake comprises the natural drainage area in the valley for the Kings and Tule rivers and other smaller watercourses. According to government surveys, the lowest point in the bed of Tulare Lake is 175 feet above sea level; the highest water on record reached 220 feet above sea level. In 1865, when its waters covered the present site of the town of Corcoran, it was 35 miles wide and 60 miles long. Its maximum depth has never been more than 45 feet. In times past commercial fishing boats as well as pleasure boats operated on the lake. Sloughs fed a swamp area much larger than the actual lake. In the twentieth century, streams that formerly flowed into the lake have gradually been drained for irrigation purposes, and in dry years the entire lake bed has been given over to cultivation. Wet years still make their appearance, however, and periodically Tulare Lake floods to an impressive extent, sometimes for two or more years at a time. The building of Pine Flat Dam has helped to control some of the worst flooding and irrigation problems.

Stage Stations in Kings County

A stage station known as the Head of Cross Creek was established at Cross Creek in 1856. The site is in the extreme northeastern corner of the county, four miles northwest of Goshen (Tulare County), and in stagecoach days it was the halfway point between Visalia and the Kings River Station at Whitmore's Ferry. After the coming of the Butterfield stages in 1858, the station was called Cross Creek Station. Like the other stations of this section, the Cross Creek post, now vanished, consisted of a board-and-batten barn and a cabin of the same construction for the use of the hostlers, generally two in number. During the drought of 1864, Peter Van Valer built a toll bridge over Cross Creek; it was said to have been the only bridge between Visalia and Stockton at the time.

Kingston, on the south bank of the Lower Kings River eight and one-half miles northwest of Hanford, was founded in 1856 at Whitmore's Ferry, which had been put into operation in 1854 by L. A. Whitmore. After 1858 the town became a stopping place for the Butterfield stages, which established a regular route through the San Joaquin Valley by way of Kingston and Whitmore's Ferry after leaving the old Stockton–Los Angeles Road at a point east of Visalia.

A toll bridge superseded the ferry in 1873, and its piers remain near the riverbank, about a quarter of a mile below the Santa Fe railroad bridge at Laton (Fresno County). On the evening of December 26, 1873, before the tollgates of the bridge were in place, Tiburcio Vásquez and his bandit gang made a bold raid on the little town of Kingston. They bound 39 men and robbed three stores before the alarm was spread, when they fled across the new bridge to horses waiting in a corral on the north side of the river and escaped; two of the bandits and a horse were killed in the attack.

Kingston is now gone, but a marker (SRL 270) commemorating the town has been placed in the park on the south bank of the Kings River, one-quarter mile west on Douglas Avenue from its intersection with Avenue 12-3/4.

El Adobe de los Robles Rancho

One of the oldest houses still in use in the central San Joaquin Valley is a long low adobe (SRL 206), with casement windows of Spanish design, that stands beneath the shade of immense oaks and blue gums on SR 41 five miles north of Lemoore. It was built in 1856 by Daniel Rhoads, who arrived in California in 1846, having come over the Oregon Trail with the caravan of pioneers from which the Donner party separated to take the fateful Hastings Cutoff, later becoming snowbound in the High Sierra. In February 1847 Dan Rhoads became a member of the first relief party, which in the face of untold hardships and even death left Johnson's Rancho to go to the rescue of the starving emigrants at Donner Lake. Much of the material used by Bancroft for his account of the Donner tragedy was drawn from an interview with Rhoads.

Carefully preserved, and containing relics of pioneer days, the old adobe is maintained strictly as a home and not as a museum. The site is noteworthy for its great plantations of trees—stately Australian blue gums and tall cypress trees planted by Rhoads himself and a line of old black olive trees along the driveway—and the many native oaks from which the house derived the name of "El Adobe de los Robles."

Historic Spots of the West Side

The town of Avenal takes its name from the Spanish word for wild oats. Much older than the town is the Avenal Ranch, fourteen miles south of Avenal and six miles off SR 41 in the foothills of the Coast Ranges. The ranch headquarters stand on the site of a prehistoric Indian village. The mission padres from San Miguel passed this way in their search for a mission site in the tulares. Here is located an old adobe barn, probably built in the early 1850's by the original owners, Welch and Cahill from Missouri. There is also the old ranch house, most of the original lumber of which is redwood brought by oxen from the Santa Cruz Mountains.

On the west shore of Tulare Lake an adobe trading post was established in 1870 by Cox and Clark. Since it was the only building on that side of the lake at the time, it served as a landing place for lake boats and as a trading center for the Indians. The site of the old post is three miles south of Kettleman City on SR 41. About three miles north of Kettleman City is the site of another adobe known as the Vaca dugout, built in 1863 by Juan Perría and Pablo Vaca; this was a vaquero headquarters, never a boat landing.

Both of these buildings were on the eastern branch of El Camino Viejo, which left the main road at Alamo Solo, a campsite twenty miles to the south of the Cox and Clark adobe. Alamo Mocho ("trimmed cottonwood") was another campsite on this road, located just south of Kettleman Hills within a short distance of SR 41. At the mouth of El Arroyo de las Garzas ("herons") a camp on the western branch of El Camino Viejo was located. It was here that Dave Kettleman, a cattle rancher, first settled. His name is remembered in Kettleman City and Kettleman Hills, as well as Kettleman Oil Fields, which achieved prominence in 1928.

Lemoore

Dr. Lavern Lee Moore proposed that a post office should be established at the small agricultural community of La Tache, which was growing up north of Tulare Lake. The Post Office Department acceded to his request in September 1875, but gave the new office a name coined from that of the petitioner. Two years later the center of population moved a short distance to the branch railroad built through the area and across the Kings River to the Huron Plains and the important sheep-shearing center at Posa Chiné trading post. In 1890 Lemoore was considered to be the largest wool-shipping center in the United States. The older, pre-railroad crossing of the river to the west side was at what is still called Murphy's Bridge, one-quarter mile south of Jackson Avenue (former routing of SR 198). Lemoore is now noteworthy as the site of a large naval air station.

Hanford

The same branch railroad gave birth in 1877 to Hanford, named for James M. Hanford, a Southern Pacific official, and destined to become the county seat when Kings County was formed. The town's wooden buildings were frequently destroyed by fire; in 1887 the town's first brick building was erected. It still stands at 110–112 East Sixth Street, in the historic district of Hanford. The city boasted one of the largest Chinatowns in California for some years, with as many as 600 residents. A street known as China Alley still remains, as does a Taoist temple dating from 1893.

The Kings County Courthouse is a beautiful structure on Courthouse Square, put up in 1897 and expanded in 1914. Until 1979 it was the seat of county

China Alley, Hanford

government; today the brick and granite building houses offices and commercial establishments. The most striking building is the neighboring sheriff's office and jail, built in 1897 and dominated by an octagonal tower and parapet that give it a neo-Gothic appearance. Locally known as "La Bastille," the building has housed a restaurant since its county offices were moved elsewhere in 1974.

On the north side of Court Street across from "La Bastille" is the Veterans' Memorial Building built in 1925 and still much used by the community. It is claimed to be the first veterans' building in California. The museum located in the old Carnegie Library at 109 East Eighth Street has materials on Kings County and on Hanford on exhibit. At 870 West Davis Street at the Roosevelt Elementary School is "Fort Roosevelt," an outdoor museum of natural history and Indian artifacts; the site was formerly the Southern Pacific freight depot, established in 1893.

The Mussel Slough Tragedy

Mussel Slough is a branch of the Kings River north of Hanford. Here on May 11, 1880, a bloody shoot-out took place between settlers and agents of the Southern Pacific Railroad. The railroad's claim to extensive lands in the San Joaquin Valley was in dispute for some years, during which time the railroad invited settlers to farm some of the property. When its title was confirmed by the courts, the company offered land to buyers without consideration for the settlers already established there; the company also won a court order ejecting those settlers. When Southern Pacific agents, accompanied by a U.S. marshal, attempted to settle two new purchasers on the land, the newly formed Settlers League

Old Jail, Hanford

resisted. In a tense atmosphere, aggravated when a horse reared suddenly and struck the marshal, firing broke out. Five settlers and a railroad agent were killed in less than a minute; two others died of their wounds later. Five settlers eventually went to prison and the others either accepted the railroad's terms or abandoned their lands. The novelist Frank Norris used the incident as the basis for *The Octopus* (1901), an attack on the railroad's treatment of California farmers. The historical marker (SRL 245) commemorating the tragedy is at the roadside on Fourteenth Avenue, between Elaine and Everett avenues, four miles north of Grangeville.

Lake County

Lake County—so named because of the presence within its confines of a large body of fresh water known as Clear Lake—was set off from Napa County in May 1861, and Lakeport was made the county seat. In 1867 the courthouse and all its records were burned. Another was built in 1870–71, but in the meantime the county seat was temporarily located at Lower Lake.

Indians and Their Legends

Accessibility to a convenient food supply is the prime requisite for the habitation of a primitive people. Throughout Lake County the abundance of fish, fowl, berries, nuts, and game met this need and supported a large Indian population, possibly the densest in California.

Tule roots grew abundantly along the shores of the lakes, and here the Indians camped in great numbers during the digging season. Also of economic value were the massive bodies of obsidian found in the county. Those found southwest of Mount Konocti were used for making knives and razors, while those found near the east and northeast shores of Lower Lake were used for making spearheads and arrowheads. From the numerous game birds feathers were taken for decoration. George Gibbs, writing in his journal in 1851, says: "At Clear Lake the women generally wear a small round bowl-shaped basket on their heads, and this is frequently interwoven with the red feathers of the woodpecker and edged with the plume tufts of the blue quail."

A legend of the area concerns Mount Konocti, the most prominent feature of the landscape. Lupiyomi, daughter of the proud and powerful Chief Konocti, was sought in marriage by a rival chieftain, Kahbel. Chief Konocti, refusing consent to the union, was challenged to battle. He took up his stand on one side of the Narrows of Clear Lake, while his opponent took a position on the opposite side. The rocks hurled across the water by these warriors during the combat are the immense boulders that now cover the mountainside. The maiden's tears formed a pool—now Little Borax Lake—a lasting memorial of her grief. The lover Kahbel was killed; his blood is seen in the red splashes on the gashed side of Red Hill, rising on the north shore. Chief Konocti also succumbed and, sinking back, became the rugged mountain that now bears his name. The maiden was so distraught that she threw herself into the lake; her unfailing tears bubble up in Omarocharbe, the Big Soda Spring, gushing out of the waters of Clear Lake at Soda Bay.

Clear Lake

Clear Lake was known to the Indians as Hok-has-ha and Ka-ba-tin, names given to it by two different tribes. It is the largest natural body of fresh water lying wholly within the state and is near the geographical center of the county. Thousands of years ago it was a broad valley draining into the Russian River. When landslides blocked this western outlet, the water rose until it found a new outlet, Cache Creek, which drains eastward into the Sacramento River.

Ewing Young and his party of trappers crossed the Coast Range in 1832 by way of this lake on their journey from the Sacramento River to the Pacific Ocean. James Clyman, in his diary for December 1845, wrote that he camped on the outlet of Clear Lake and feasted on bear ribs and liver. Edwin Bryant, a traveler in California in 1846–47, wrote: "A lake not laid down in any map and known as the Laguna among the Californians, is situated about sixty miles north of the Bay of San Francisco. It is between forty and sixty miles in length. The valleys in its vicinity are highly fertile and romantically beautiful. In the vicinity of this lake there is a mountain of pure sulphur. There are also soda springs and a great variety of the mineral waters and minerals."

Lieutenant Joseph Warren Revere, in command of the northern district for some months after the raising of the United States flag at Sonoma, made a tour to Clear Lake and wrote up his experiences for publication. "Few white men have visited this magnificent Laguna." About sunset one evening, he and his men arrived at the narrowest part of Clear Lake, "opposite a pretty islet" upon which was a native village. The Indians, at first fearful because of the many raids made upon them in search of laborers, were finally persuaded to ferry the travelers across on tule balsas. The island village, protected by this natural moat, had between two and three hundred inhabitants.

Clear Lake is now actually nineteen and one-half miles long. It is shaped like a double-tailed polliwog. The fat body part is Clear Lake proper. The two tails are called East Lake and Lower Lake, and are joined to the body by the Narrows. Clear Lake State Park, near Soda Bay, contains an Indian Nature Trail that displays living plants and explains how they were used by the Pomo and Lile'ek Indians.

Anderson Marsh State Historic Park preserves the sites of 40 Indian villages, some of which go back 10,000 years. Established in 1982 and therefore one of the newer state parks, this thousand-acre preserve was once the homestead of John Anderson, who settled there around 1856. His home, still standing but somewhat modernized, is now the park visitors' center. The park is located on SR 53 between the town of Clearlake and Lower Lake. Archaeological work is continually being done at this park, making it a demonstration of a working dig.

Mount Konocti rises to the southwest almost 3,000 feet above the level of the lake, a majestic, solitary guardian of the scene. Settlement near the summit of this mountain was attempted in the 1870's by O. S. Morford, who built the first wagon road and completed it in 1878 with the intention of establishing a public summer resort far up the mountainside. On May 1, 1878, Morford and two companions ascended to the peak and there unfurled the Stars and Stripes. His plans for a summer resort were never carried out. The first permanent settlers near the summit were the Euvelle Howard family early in the twentieth century. Orchards now grace the slopes of the mountain; the shores of the lake are dotted with both permanent and summer homes, and at Lakeport and other locations annual water carnivals are held.

Kelseyville

General Mariano G. Vallejo founded and was placed in command of Sonoma in 1835. In 1836 an expedition led by his brother Salvador and Ramón Carrillo was made into the Clear Lake country, the first military expedition to enter that region. Salvador Vallejo and his brother Antonio, as early as 1839, applied for a grant of land covering what are now known as the Big, Scotts, Upper Lake, and Bachelor valleys. For several years the Vallejo cattle were herded over its fertile ranges, where they multiplied and became exceedingly wild. A log cabin and corral were built in Big Valley near the present site of Kelseyville, with a mayordomo and ten vaqueros to look after the ranch.

In 1847, Vallejo drove some of his cattle out of the valley and sold the remainder to four men: Charles Stone, a man named Shirland, and two brothers, Andrew and Benjamin Kelsey, who had arrived in California with the Bidwell-Bartleson party in 1841. Stone and Andrew Kelsey took possession of the ranch and employed Indians to erect an adobe house for them west across Kelsey Creek from where Kelseyville now stands. Apparently the white men treated the Indian workers cruelly, and after some particularly brutal punishments, the Indians retaliated by killing Kelsey and Stone in the fall of 1849.

In January 1850 a military expedition came to punish the offenders, but it found that the Indians had taken refuge on various islands in Clear Lake and could not be reached. In May Captain Nathaniel Lyon and a detachment were sent from Benicia for the same purpose, bringing with them two whaleboats on the running gears of wagons and two mountain howitzers. The only Indians they found were gathered on an island in Upper Lake. By using the boats, cannon, and bayonets, the soldiers practically annihilated the group. About a hundred Indians were killed, none of whom, in all probability, had taken any part in the Stone and Kelsey incident. There are differing versions of this massacre, although the outcome is in no doubt. Since that time the place has been called "Bloody Island" (SRL 427), although later reclamation projects have eliminated its water boundaries and it appears to be a hill by the shore of the lake today. A monument with bronze plaque marks the site, about one and one-half miles southeast of the town of Upper Lake, just west of SR 20.

The remains of Stone and Kelsey were moved in 1950 to a monument near the site of their adobe home (SRL 426), west of Kelseyville at Main Street and Bell Hill Road. The adobe stood on the bluff one hundred yards west of the monument.

The town of Kelseyville began in 1857 with Denham's store and blacksmith shop. The oldest business building presently standing is a brick structure on Main Street, built in the 1870's.

A Lost Treaty

To adjust land disputes with the Indian tribes, a commission to negotiate treaties was appointed by President Millard Fillmore shortly after the admission of California into the Union in 1850.

Commissioner Redick McKee, representing the United States government, and the chiefs and headmen of eight local Indian tribes signed a Treaty of Peace and Friendship on August 20, 1851, at Camp Lu-Pi-Yu-Mi on the south shore of Clear Lake. This treaty consisted of eight articles setting forth details of the promises on both sides, and a description of the lands to be given, in perpetuity, to these tribes, as well as certain benefits to be derived by them in recompense for their renunciation. Article III of the treaty states: "The said tribes, or bands, hereby jointly and severally relinquish, cede, and forever quitclaim to the United States all their right, title, claim, or interest of any kind, which they, or either of them, hold to the lands or soil in California." One wonders what this language meant to the tribes. At this council a gift was made to the assembled Indians of "ten head of beef cattle, three sacks of bread, and sundry clothing."

This treaty, along with seventeen others, was sent to the Senate by President Fillmore in June 1852 for approval. Never acted on, it is now referred to as one of the "Eighteen Lost Treaties." Attempts have been made to secure compensation for the Indians of California from the United States in lieu of the values granted them in the treaties, and some reimbursement has been given.

Mexican Grants

Three grants of land were made by the Mexican government within the territory now included in Lake County.

Rancho Lupyomi, about which there was much litigation, was originally granted to Salvador and Juan Antonio Vallejo by Governor Micheltorena in 1844. The map accompanying this grant showed the territory of Laguna de Lu-Pi-Yo-Mi extending sixteen leagues and embracing Upper Lake, Bachelor, Scotts, and Big valleys. In 1854 settlers began to arrive, and by 1861 many families had located on the land, although their titles to it could not be made valid until certain claims were decided. After many delays, Judge Ogden Hoffman rendered a decision that gave satisfaction, and the potential owners met for a "jollification" at Lakeport on October 6, 1866. Soon after this, the land was surveyed and each settler secured a home. Kelseyville is on part of this grant.

Rancho Callayomi, consisting of three leagues of land in Loconoma Valley, was given to Robert T. Ridley in 1844 by Governor Micheltorena. Ridley, an English sailor, became captain of the Port of San Francisco in 1846, a position that he held but a short time. He had been naturalized as a Mexican citizen in 1844 and married Presentación Briones. Within a few years, in 1852, the claim of Colonel A. A. Ritchie and Paul S. Forbes was confirmed to this land, and a patent was issued to them in 1863. This grant was divided in 1871 and disposed of to actual settlers.

Rancho Guenoc, containing six leagues in Coyote Valley, was ceded by Governor Pío Pico to George Rock (Roch) in 1845. Coyote Valley extends for several miles along Putah Creek. According to Bancroft, George Rock came into the valley as early as 1837. For a time he was agent there for Jacob P. Leese, who kept cattle both there and in Loconoma Valley. Rock lived in a cabin on the north side of the valley before 1850. The stone house (SRL 450) now standing on the site of Rock's cabin was built in 1853–54 by Captain R. Steele and Robert Sterling, whose wife was the first white woman in the valley. Colonel Ritchie and his partner, Paul S. Forbes, who had acquired Rancho Callayomi, also received the United States patent for the Guenoc grant in 1865. The stone house was torn down and rebuilt of the same stone about 1894 by Charles M. Young. It stands on private property about six miles north of Middletown on SR 29 at its southern junction with Spruce Grove Road, which meets the highway again to the north.

Mineral Springs

A number of medicinal springs are found in Lake County. The Harbin Springs, four miles from Middletown, were visited by A. A. Ritchie in 1852, but were known to the Indians long before that time. They were already famous when the water was examined by Dr. Winslow Anderson in 1889, and a fashionable resort grew up about them as the population of the state increased. Other Lake County vacation spots, Adams and Anderson springs among them, are still in operation. The French-owned Vittel Company has purchased Bartlett Springs, founded in 1868 in the Middle Fork of Cache Creek, and has built a new plant at Bartlett Springs Road and SR 20 to bottle its waters.

The mountains between Middletown and Clear Lake have been the site of summer resorts since the beginning of the twentieth century; Cobb, Hobergs, and Loch Lomond are among those of long standing. A number of other resorts have been purchased by private organizations or have fallen into disuse.

Old Mills

The many streams of Lake County afforded power for two industries of great importance in a pioneer community: the grinding of grain for food, and, in a few instances, the sawing of lumber for houses. Thomas Boyd built the first mill in the county on the south shore of Boggs Lake. It was a steam gristmill and sawmill combined and was put in operation in 1858. In 1866, H. C. Boggs purchased the mill, which from this date was known as the Boggs Mill, although its location was changed several times. A few remnants mark its last location, three miles north of Harbin Springs.

Another mill, originally known as Elliott's Mill, was erected in Upper Lake Township in 1855 by William B. Elliott, who had come overland from North Carolina, arriving in California in 1845 with his wife and children. He and his sons became successful hunters of the grizzly bears then prevalent in the mountain regions. His mill was in operation until 1867. In time it became known by the odd cognomen of "Whittle-Busy," because, since it ground very slowly, its patrons whiled away the time by whittling.

The old Brown Mill (earlier called the Allison Mill) stood on Kelsey Creek about three miles above Kelseyville. Joel Stoddard's Mill, about three and one-half miles west of Middletown, was known in the 1880's as "one of the neatest and best mills in Lake County." A later mill at the same location was operated by the McKinley family until 1935. The site on SR 29 is marked by an old millstone and a plaque placed by the Native Daughters of the Golden West.

Mines

Although a great variety of minerals have been discovered in the county, the quantities usually have been too small for economic development. Mercury, sulfur, and borax have been mined. The Great Western, a cinnabar (mercury) deposit, first produced in 1873. It is four miles south of Middletown.

The old Sulphur Bank Mine (SRL 428) grew out of the works of the California Borax Company. This was the location of the mountain of sulfur referred to in the journal of Edwin Bryant. It was 40 feet high and some 300 feet long, and was completely removed by mining in 1865–69, having produced two million pounds of sulfur. The first mercury was mined here

in 1873, and the place became a steady and important producer. It has been idle since World War II. The Sulphur Bank Mine is on the eastern end of East Lake south and across the lake from the town of Clearlake Oaks. A monument of native obsidian stands on the highway about one and one-half miles from the town at the junction with the road leading to the mine. In the hills, about one mile east of the monument and on the same side of the highway, stands the Saint Anthony (or Sulphur Bank) Church, which was erected in 1909 as a place of worship for workers in the mine. There are several other old mercury mines in the county, including the Abbott, the Mirabel, and the Helen.

The Manhattan was an old mercury mine in the Knoxville District, where Lake, Napa, and Yolo counties meet. In 1978, gold was discovered on the site. The McLaughlin deposit was so promising that a new operation, the Home Stake Gold Mine and extraction facility, was soon created. The site is on the Berryessa-Knoxville Road about eighteen miles southeast of the city of Clearlake.

The first source of borax in California was Borax Lake, discovery of the mineral having been made in 1856 by Dr. John A. Veatch. The California Borax Company began operation there in 1864. In 1868 all work was transferred to Little Borax Lake, where Dr. Veatch had found borax eight years earlier. Operations were carried on successfully until 1873.

The Mayacamas Mountains, which lie along the Lake-Sonoma county line, include an area of considerable geothermal activity, the best-known evidence of which is probably The Geysers in Sonoma County. The California Department of Water and Power has constructed the Bottle Rock Power Plant, which uses geothermal energy, on the Lake County side of the mountains, off Bottle Rock Road just west of Cobb and Pine Grove. This facility went into operation in 1983 and is designed to provide supplementary power for the state water agencies.

Lower Lake

The first house in the town of Lower Lake, two miles southeast of Clear Lake, was built by E. Mitchell in 1858, although there had been settlers in the area as early as 1848. The town became important for its location on crossroads and was the center of business activity for the surrounding agricultural interests, mountain resorts, and mercury mines. It was a station on the stage line running from Calistoga in later years and was the county seat for two years while the Lakeport Courthouse was being rebuilt after the 1867 fire. Still standing in town is a tiny stone jail (SRL 429), built

Stone Jail, Lower Lake

tween Second and Third streets in Lakeport (SRL 897). It is now the home of the Lake County Museum. Of particular interest are the artifacts of the Pomo Indians, remarkable weavers and craftsmen. A two-story frame structure at 102 Clear Lake Avenue was once the home of Clear Lake College, which held classes here from 1876 to 1896. Like most of the private and local colleges in late-nineteenth-century California, it was unable to compete with the University of California and closed its doors. The Sayre House at 690 Forbes Street was built in 1897 for the family of Judge M. S. Sayre; it has been restored by the Catholic church and is open to the public on a limited basis. The first boat landing at Lakeport, in 1873, is commemorated by a marker on the grounds of the grammar school on Main Street.

Middletown

Middletown lies on SR 29, the principal route from Clear Lake into Napa County to the south, at the junction with roads leading to the resort and geothermal areas to the north and west and to the mines in the east. It is near the center of the Callayomi land grant and was first settled in 1868. The oldest building now standing in the town was the O. Armstrong house, built in 1870; it is on the left side of a stretch of road between the high school and the old bridge on the way to Lower Lake, and is still occupied. In the same year, J. H. Berry built a house that was later used as a hotel on what is now SR 29, the main street through town. This was replaced in 1875 by the larger Lake County House, which burned in 1918. The present Herrick Hotel stands on the site, incorporating some of the brick walls from the former hotel.

The last years of the distinguished scholar Dr. James Blake were spent in Middletown. A native of England and a California pioneer in 1849, Dr. Blake was a writer of medical books and one-time president of the California Academy of Sciences. He retired to Lake County in 1876 because of impaired health. He took up his residence near a large spring, where he built a cottage east of Mount St. Helena and just south of the county line in Napa County, about two miles east of SR 29. Feeling his health vastly improved here, he erected simple buildings where others might be helped, and where he carried on his medical research until he finally moved to Middletown, where he died and was buried in 1893. The main building of Blake's sanatorium is still in existence on a private estate, although the cottage no longer stands. Dr. Blake's house in Middletown also remains, at the southeast corner of Barnes and Young streets.

At the edge of Middletown on SR 29 a stone monu-

in 1876 at the height of the quicksilver mining boom. A plaque on the monument in front of the jail states that Stephen Nicolai, one of the first stonemasons in the area, built the jail from local materials with the help of Theodore and John Copsey. "Theodore and John commemorated the completion of the jail by over-celebrating, thereby becoming the jail's first occupants. Rumor has it they were also the jail's first escapees—as they had failed to bolt down the roof."

Lakeport

Lakeport, on the western shore of Clear Lake, was first named Forbestown. William Forbes owned 160 acres here before the formation of the county in 1861 and deeded 40 acres as a site for the county seat in the vicinity of his previously erected house and blacksmith shop. Forbes Street now commemorates his name. The first place of business in the county was a short distance south of Lakeport, at Stony Point, where Dr. E. D. Boynton built a store and put in a stock of goods in 1856.

The Lake County Courthouse, in use from 1871 to 1968, is a solid two-story building on Main Street be-ment with bronze plaque commemorates the old toll road over Mount St. Helena (SRL 467), built in the 1860's by John Lawley, and the earlier and steeper "bull trail" that it replaced. The Lawley road passed out of existence as a toll road in 1924, but a fragment of it remains to the east of SR 29 just north of Calistoga in Napa County.

The Cache Creek Dam

In 1866 a dam was constructed across Cache Creek near the outlet of Clear Lake by the Clear Lake Water Company. The level of the water in the lake was raised to such an extent that the rich farmland, the established orchards, and the houses within a large radius were flooded. Reasonable appeals to the water company had been ignored, and no compensation for damage had been allowed. On Sunday morning, November 15, 1868, after being led in prayer by the Baptist minister, Rev. B. Ogle, a disciplined crowd began the demolition of the dam and the nearby mill, having taken the sheriff and law enforcement officers into custody. By Tuesday morning, the work was completed, and although litigation ensued, the dam was never rebuilt on this spot. Another dam on Cache Creek, below the town of Lower Lake, was completed in 1914 and is still in use.

The Langtry Farm and the Guenoc Winery

Lillie Langtry, the celebrated English actress known as the "Jersey Lily," in 1888 became joint owner of a property in the southern part of the county. "Freddie" Gebhard, a wealthy New York clubman, was the co-partner in the purchase of this 7,500-acre portion of the old Guenoc grant. At the time of the purchase, a winery was in operation and a few dwellings were on the premises.

Extensive improvements were made, and large

Langtry House, Guenoc Winery, near Middletown

sums were invested in fine race horses by the new owners. Dr. Charles Aby, former manager of the Santa Anita ranch of "Lucky" Baldwin, was put in charge, and a one-mile race track was constructed. Mrs. Langtry visited the place only once, for about two weeks in May 1888. For some years all went well; then in 1897 the partnership was dissolved. Barns, race track, and general operations were concentrated on the Gebhard land, and a stout fence was built to define the two holdings.

The Langtry property was sold in 1906 to George H. Mastick; in the next 60 years it had several owners, who used it primarily as a stock farm. In 1963 it became the property of the Magoon family, who became interested in reviving the vineyard and the wine-making activities that once flourished there. In 1982 the Guenoc Winery was launched on the property. The Langtry house, occupied through all the years, has been refurbished in period style, together with outbuildings, and is part of the private estate, although it can be seen by special appointment. The winery is at 21000 Butts Canyon Road, about seven miles southeast of Middletown.

Lassen County

Lassen County, named for the pioneer Peter Lassen, was organized in 1864 from parts of Plumas and Shasta counties. Susanville has been the county seat from the beginning. The eastern portion of Lassen Volcanic National Park is in Lassen County, but the greater part of the park, including Lassen Peak, is in Shasta County.

Peter Lassen

Peter Lassen was born in Denmark in 1800 and came to America in 1829. After working in Boston at his trade of blacksmithing for ten years, he came west to the Willamette Valley of Oregon in 1839. The next year he moved to Alta California. After brief sojourns at Bodega Bay, Fort Ross, and San Jose, he made his way to the Sacramento Valley, where he was befriended by John A. Sutter. In 1844 he received the grant of Rancho Bosquejo in what is now Tehama County and began intensive cultivation of wheat and grapes. Ultimately, however, he lost the land because of poor management and overspeculation in emigrant projects. His name is linked with the Lassen Trail into California of 1848. In the 1850's he pioneered for a few years in Indian Valley in Plumas County, after which he developed an interest in the Honey Lake region of what is now Lassen County. While prospecting in the area, Lassen and a companion were shot and killed by Indians on the morning of April 26, 1859, a third man escaping to tell the story.

Lassen's grave (SRL 565) stands at the edge of a meadow six miles south of Susanville via Richmond and Wingfield roads. It is marked by a monument placed there by the Masons in 1862. Two old graves from the 1880's, with simple surface markers, are nearby. Lassen had a cabin not far from this spot in 1855; it long ago burned down.

Lassen died in relative poverty, but his contemporaries seem to have thought well of him and his name was bestowed on a number of locations in northeastern California. One early account states that Lassen himself climbed the peak that now bears his name, but there seems to be no corroboration for this statement.

The Lassen Trail

In 1848 Peter Lassen returned to California from a trip to Missouri, joining a wagon party headed west. The wagons followed the Applegate Trail, first opened two years before, across the wastes of Nevada and the extreme northeastern corner of California. Near Goose Lake in Modoc County, Lassen persuaded the group to leave the trail and turn in a southerly direction, which he claimed would be easier. (It is thought that he hoped to induce these and subsequent emigrants to settle on his lands along the Sacramento River once they arrived in California.) The journey was a series of blunders, ending up in the canyon of the Pit River and making a long detour around the base of Lassen Peak. A party of Oregon gold-seekers, coming across the tracks of the party, joined them and rescued them, and they all arrived safely at the Lassen Ranch. This "Lassen Trail" was used again in 1849, but as more reliable trails opened, it gradually fell into desuetude.

A volunteer association, Trails West, Inc., has placed markers along the routes of the Applegate, California, Lassen, and Nobles Trails in California and Ne-

vada in recent years. Many of these are inaccessible to any but the most resolute and well-equipped adventurers; a guide with copious directions has been published by the organization from its headquarters in Reno, Nevada. Fairly close to roads are markers in Little Valley on Lassen County Road 404, 2.2 miles west of its junction with Lassen County Road 407; at Round Barn in Little Valley; at Harvey Valley; and in Westwood at the Community Center on Third Street. Two and a half miles west of Westwood on SR 36 a state historical marker (SRL 678) stands near the Lassen Trail where it passed into neighboring Plumas County.

Another state marker (SRL 763) commemorating part of the Lassen Trail stands on the grounds of the Veterans Building in Clara Bieber Memorial Park, two blocks south of US 199 in Bieber. Next door is the Big Valley Museum of Lassen County, begun in 1976 with collections on the development of the cattle and lumber industries of this corner of Lassen County. The museum also contains a useful reference library and some original documentary materials.

The Nobles Trail

The Nobles Trail was one of the northern cutoffs used by emigrants in the early 1850's. In 1851 William H. Nobles, member of a prospecting party, saw the value of an alternative to the Lassen Trail used by his party and enlisted the support of businessmen of the town of Shasta (in Shasta County). In 1852 he succeeded in raising $2,000 for surveying a wagon road over the new route, with its terminus at Shasta.

The Nobles Trail began at the Humboldt River in Nevada, branching off from the Applegate Trail at Rabbit Springs and continuing west into California toward Honey Lake. Trails West has placed a marker just east of Viewland, an old railroad station along US 395, where there is also a state marker (SRL 677) noting the course of the Nobles Trail. The present highway into Susanville is near the old route; Trails West markers can be seen at Honey Lake Valley, Shaffer Station, Litchfield (or Soldier's Bridge), Willow Creek Crossing (on Lassen County Road A-27), and Roop's Fort in Susanville; another state marker (SRL 675) is in the Susanville County Park. Trails West markers further west that are fairly easily reached on paved roads are at Big Springs, on SR 44 about five miles west of its junction with SR 36; Feather Lake, where the Lassen Trail and the Nobles Trail intersected; Poison Lake; and Butte Creek, at the boundary with Lassen Volcanic National Park. The Nobles Trail was faster and less dangerous than the Lassen Trail, which seems to have been bypassed in the next few years. With the opening of the Sierra passes and the coming of the railroad within the next two decades, both roads became deserted and in places are nearly inaccessible today. But they are historically important because they signify the beginning of a new way of life in this underpopulated and isolated part of the West.

"Nataqua" and the Sagebrush War

Isaac Roop, the first white settler in Honey Lake Valley, was the founder of Lassen County and of the county seat, Susanville. Roop came to Honey Lake from Shasta City in 1853 and returned the next year to build a store on the Nobles Trail, which had recently been opened through that region. Early in 1855 Peter Lassen discovered gold in Honey Lake Valley, and news of the find brought in a number of men from the Feather River mining region. Several land claims were staked out at that time.

Honey Lake Valley was so isolated during the pioneer period that a local government was set up on the initiative of the people themselves. About twenty signers, all original settlers in Honey Lake Valley, met at the Roop cabin on April 26, 1856, and formed the "Territory of Nataqua," with Roop as secretary and recorder and Lassen as surveyor. With the eastern boundary of California not definitely determined, the organizers of the new territory included a good deal of land in the present state of Nevada in "Nataqua." "They made a wild shot at their location. They didn't even live in the territory they had created," says one account. "It was nearly thirty-five miles from their place of meeting to the western line of Nataqua, and the settlers furthest down the lake were almost twenty miles west of it." Moreover, the citizens of the Carson, Eagle, and Washoe valleys were not even notified that they were included within the boundaries of the new political division. Actually, "Nataqua" existed for a short time only, and then merely in the minds of a few men.

Finally, in 1857, the citizens of "Nataqua" decided to cast their lot with those who were petitioning Congress for separation from the Utah Territory with its Mormon dominance. While awaiting Congressional action on their petition for the formation of a new territory, the settlers met again in 1858 to set up a local government. As a result, a constitutional convention was held at Genoa, Nevada, on July 18, 1859, and in the following September, Isaac Roop was chosen provisional governor of the proposed territory.

On March 2, 1861, Congress passed the bill creating the Nevada Territory, which, only with California's consent, was to include the eastern slope of the Sierra Nevada from Inyo to Modoc counties. In creating its first

Isaac Roop's Log Cabin (Fort Defiance), Susanville

counties the same year, however, the Nevada Territory extended its new Lake County to include Honey Lake Valley. In 1862 both Plumas County in California and Lake County in the Nevada Territory held elections in the valley. In February 1863, a skirmish called the Sagebrush or Boundary Line War, waged by 40 or 50 of the original settlers of Honey Lake Valley against Plumas County officials, resulted from the attempt of the Plumas County sheriff to uphold the authority of his county in the valley. The confusion was cleared up by the creation of a separate authority, Lassen County, on April 1, 1864.

Susanville

Susanville was named after the only daughter of Isaac Roop. Roop's old log cabin (SRL 76), called Fort Defiance when it was used as a fort during the Sagebrush War, still stands on the east side of Weatherlow Street in the Susanville city park. Next to it is the William H. Pratt Memorial Museum, which contains many exhibits on the history of Lassen County as well as the various economic developments of the life of Susanville, located where the forests, the brushlands, and the grasslands of Lassen Valley meet.

"The Potato War"

The blunders and atrocities of a few white men against the Indians triggered a bloody conflict by the shores of Honey Lake in October 1857. Unable to distinguish between members of different tribes, a white raiding party mistook a Paiute for a Shoshone and in killing him turned the Paiutes and Washoes against the settlers of the valley. The plundering of settlers' vegetables and livestock earned the skirmish the name "The Potato War." The settlers barricaded themselves in a farmhouse close to what is now the state highway rest stop on US 395 about four miles southeast of Buntingville. In the exchange of shots, twelve Indians were killed and one rancher was wounded.

Another Lassen County fort was located three-fourths of a mile from Janesville; Fort Janesville (SRL 758), as it was called, was built by the people of Honey Lake Valley in preparation for an Indian attack that never materialized. There is no state marker at this site.

Other Historic Spots in Lassen County

Jack's Valley, ten miles north of Susanville on SR 139, contains a cement water trough, built in 1913 for the benefit of travelers, and the only one of its kind in northeastern California. The place was named for "Coyote Jack" Wright, who left the spot in 1869. By 1880, as the E Clampus Vitus plaque placed here notes, five wagon roads converged here; a number of varied establishments stood here over the years.

Milford, on US 395 about seventeen miles southeast of Buntingville, was settled in 1856 by R. J. Scott; the name was bestowed by Joseph C. Wemple in 1861. The first flour mill in northeastern California was built here the same year. E Clampus Vitus placed a marker here in 1985. Honey Lake, now almost a dry basin, was named for the substance deposited on the wild grasses by the honey-dew aphis and valued by the Indians as a food.

Los Angeles County

Los Angeles County was one of the original 27 counties. Its boundaries have been changed many times; at its largest, in 1852–55, it covered an area of 31,000 square miles. The city of Los Angeles ("the angels") has always been the county seat, and its archives contain many pre-statehood records in Spanish.

Juan Rodríguez Cabrillo and Santa Catalina

Juan Rodríguez Cabrillo first sighted the coast of Alta California at San Diego on September 28, 1542. In his honor, a memorial plaque was placed in Exposition Park, Los Angeles, by the Daughters of the American Revolution in 1915. A replica of this tablet was placed at Avalon on Santa Catalina Island. It has recently been argued that Cabrillo died and was buried at an unknown site, not on San Miguel, in the Santa Barbara Channel Islands, as tradition holds, but rather at Santa Catalina Island. Cabrillo, sighting the island on October 7, 1542, named it San Salvador. Sebastián Vizcaíno, sighting it on November 20, 1603, St. Catherine's Day, named it Santa Catalina Island.

Portolá's Trail

In 1769, Gaspar de Portolá left San Diego to find a trail up the coast to the port of Monterey, where the second mission was to be established. Traveling through what are now San Diego and Orange counties, he entered Los Angeles County on July 30, making camp near modern La Puente. The following day the party moved west and made camp in an open space in the valley north of the Whittier Narrows, not far from where Mission San Gabriel was later established.

On August 2 the party reached a spot on the Los Angeles River occupied by the Indian village of Yang-Na, at the center of today's Los Angeles. Camp was probably made near what is now North Spring Street, at the juncture of the Los Angeles River and North Broadway. This site (SRL 655) was marked in 1930 in Elysian Park. The hill, around which the Los Angeles River turned to the south at the point where it is bridged by North Broadway, is mentioned in the journal written by Lieutenant Miguel Costansó of Portolá's expedition.

On the same day, Wednesday, August 2, 1769, the diary of Father Crespí tells how he named the campsite by the river Nuestra Señora la Reina de los Angeles de la Porciúncula (Our Lady the Queen of the Angels of the Porciúncula). Porciúncula or "little portion" refers to a small parcel of land adjacent to the once tiny church of Saint Mary of the Angels in the valley below the hill town of Assisi in Italy. There St. Francis received a revelation on August 1, 1206, and subsequently a basilica was erected on the site; the day became a major event in the Franciscan liturgical calendar.

Leaving their camp and crossing to the west side of

the river, Portolá and his party bypassed the La Brea tarpits, which were discovered by their scouts, and camped the night of August 3 at springs surrounded by sycamores. The approximate site has been marked on La Cienega Boulevard, between Olympic Boulevard and Gregory Way, in Beverly Hills (SRL 665). The next day they moved on to two hillside springs where friendly Indians made them welcome. This campsite was apparently on or near the grounds of the Veterans Administration Center in West Los Angeles. From there the scouts went as far as the beach west of Santa Monica. On the campus of University High School at 11800 Texas Avenue in West Los Angeles are springs that may be those at which Portolá camped on August 4. Many Indian artifacts have been uncovered on the grounds. The springs are known as "Serra Springs" (SRL 522) because it is said that Father Serra said Mass nearby in 1770.

On August 5 the Portolá party followed up Sepulveda Canyon (the route of today's San Diego Freeway) to the mountaintop from which they viewed the San Fernando Valley; they descended to camp at the warm springs now included within Los Encinos State Historic Park at Encino. (The large Indian village here was revisited by Portolá's party on January 15 and April 27, 1770, when they established the east-west route along the south side of the valley and through Cahuenga Pass.) On August 7 they camped northwest of the site of Mission San Fernando, and the next day they traveled over San Fernando Pass to Newhall, pitching camp at a large Indian rancheria on the Santa Clara River near Castaic. From there, they proceeded northward by way of Santa Clara Valley, so named by Portolá on the feast day of Saint Clare.

Mission San Gabriel Arcángel

On August 6, 1771, a party set out from San Diego, consisting of two friars, Pedro Benito Cambón and Angel Somera, and ten soldiers, to establish a mission 40 leagues to the north. On September 8, 1771, Mission San Gabriel Arcángel was founded.

The new mission, being on the direct overland route from Mexico to Monterey, was the first stopping place and supply station after the desert and mountains had been crossed. The padres protected this location with special care, and the mission grew rich and prosperous. It survived the years of secularization and withstood the tide of American immigration and has continued its usefulness to the present time as a thriving parish church.

The original site of the mission was five miles south

Mission San Gabriel Arcángel

of its present location, on a bluff overlooking the Rio Hondo (then called the San Gabriel) at North San Gabriel Boulevard and Lincoln Avenue in Montebello, where a granite marker has been placed (SRL 161). Nothing remains of the old buildings of this "Mission Vieja."

Floods from the Rio Hondo eventually forced the fathers to seek another location for their mission, and the first site was abandoned about five years after its founding. The new land chosen was higher and dryer but no less fertile, and luxuriant gardens and orchards soon flourished about the new buildings. An extensive vineyard, olive groves, and orchards of fig, orange, and pear trees covered several hundred acres of ground, and were protected from wild animals and marauders by a high, thick cactus hedge. Remnants of this old hedge, as well as of the mission orchard, may still be seen here and there in the town of San Gabriel. Other vineyards were planted with cuttings taken from the Mother Vineyard ("Viña Madre") at San Gabriel.

The first church building on the second site of California's fourth mission was dedicated in 1776. This turned out to be only a temporary location. The present church (SRL 158), at 537 West Mission Drive in San Gabriel, was started in 1791 and completed in 1803 under the supervision of Father José Maria Zalvidea. It was solidly constructed of stone and cement as far up as the windows, and of brick above that. Its massive walls and buttresses, its outside stairway leading to choir and belfry, and the bell tower with its several arches built to correspond to the different sizes of the bells make it one of the most unusual and interesting of all the missions. In the yard behind the church there are many reconstructed buildings, including a smithy and a kitchen. An earthquake in 1987 caused much damage to the church, which is closed to the public until restorations are made.

About two miles north of Mission San Gabriel near the site of the present Huntington Hotel, Claudio López, under supervision of Father Zalvidea, built between 1810 and 1812 the first water-operated gristmill in California. The old mill, "El Molino Viejo," was constructed of solid masonry and still stands at 1120 Old Mill Road in San Marino (SRL 302). In 1903, H. E. Huntington bought the building and restored it to its former proportions, retaining the picturesqueness of mission days. For a time after 1923 it was used as a real estate office and then for many years as a private residence. It is now the Southern California headquarters of the California Historical Society.

Anza's Route

Juan Bautista de Anza reached the Santa Ana River on March 20, 1774, crossing it by an improvised bridge the following morning. That night he camped in a wooded valley near San Antonio Creek a little west of the present city of Ontario. At sunset on March 22 the party reached Mission San Gabriel (then located at its original site), where they were given a warm welcome.

Anza remained at San Gabriel for nearly three weeks, awaiting necessary supplies for the journey to Monterey. On the morning of April 10 he proceeded to the Los Angeles River and followed it into the San Fernando Valley, from there turning west around the point of the mountain west of Glendale. Camp was made that night in Russell Valley, in what is now Ventura County.

Anza followed much the same route in 1776 with the band of emigrants who settled San Francisco, the first settlers to come overland to California. The caravan reached the San Antonio Creek campsite on January 2, and on January 3 they halted at the San Gabriel Wash, reaching Mission San Gabriel on the next day. There they rested until February 21 when, refreshed by the welcome hospitality of the mission fathers, they set out once more. Swinging westward to the Los Angeles River, they followed it northwest to a campsite west of Glendale. Crossing the southern edge of the San Fernando Valley on February 22, the party entered the Simi Hills at Calabasas and continued to the vicinity of Las Virgenes Creek. There tents were pitched for the

night, and on the following day the travelers continued beyond the Santa Clara River, camping near El Rio in Ventura County.

Hughes Lake and Antelope Valley

Early in 1772 Pedro Fages passed the site of Hughes Lake on his notable inland journey from San Diego to San Luis Obispo, while in pursuit of deserters from the Spanish army.

In April 1776 the intrepid friar Francisco Garcés crossed Fages's path at Hughes Lake. Leaving San Gabriel, he crossed the San Fernando Valley, went over Newhall Grade to the vicinity of Castaic, and swung northeast over the mountains. Just before he entered the plains, on the edge of Antelope Valley, he mentioned a lake, evidently Hughes Lake, "and near thereto a village where, according to the signs, Señor Capitan Faxes has been."

Antelope Valley, geographically a part of the Mojave Desert, was the hunting paradise of Andrés Pico and other Californios, lured there by the immense herds of antelope that roamed through it and from which it derived its name. In the heart of this valley one of California's most glorious poppy fields adds its flame to the spectacular carpet of wildflowers that each spring spreads out across the valley floor at the foot of Portal Ridge from Palmdale to Del Sur.

North of Fairmont there is a splendid forest of tree yuccas (*yucca arborescens*), with their spires of exquisite waxen lily bells. These striking and distinctive inhabitants of the desert, more commonly known as Joshua trees, are said to have been named by early emigrants to California for their resemblance to the praying prophet.

John C. Frémont, coming down from the north by way of Oak Creek Pass on April 15, 1844, crossed Antelope Valley to the base of the Sierra Madre, following Fages's trail as far as Cajón Pass, where he connected with the Spanish Trail near Victorville. It is interesting to note that on this trip Frémont wrote in his diary of the "strange and singular" yucca forests and the fields of California poppies, as well as other shrubs and flowers in Antelope Valley.

"St. Ann" and Cienega

One mile southeast of the junction of Palomares Avenue with San Dimas Canyon Road is the site of an Indian camping place. In early mission days, logs were hauled here from the San Bernardino Mountains for the building of San Gabriel Mission. The Spaniards called this Ciénega ("a wet place") because of the natural springs that were perpetually seeping up out of the earth.

In 1826, Jedediah Strong Smith, the first American pathfinder to blaze an overland trail into California, camped at a spot designated by the expedition's diarist, Harrison Rogers, "St. Ann, an Indian farm house." George W. Beattie assumes that this was really San Antonio Rancho, one of "the seventeen ranchos for cattle and horses possessed by Mission San Gabriel. The Mexican grant of San José on which both Pomona and Claremont are situated was a combination of the San José and the San Antonio ranchos of Mission San Gabriel."

Before 1870 there was a stage station at the springs on the road from San Bernardino to Los Angeles. This station was probably located near the site of the pumping plant on Palomares Avenue. All that remains of the old San Bernardino Road is a short strip of road less than one-half mile east of the springs, where Palomares Avenue turns southeast at Grand Avenue for a short distance. Many years ago, the seeping springs were pumped dry for irrigation purposes.

The Old Adobes of San Gabriel

San Gabriel once had many quaint and picturesque old adobe homes. Among the few that remain, perhaps the oldest is located between West Mission Drive and Orange Street, at the end of a short, curving lane. Part of it is said to have been built as a home for the mission friars three years before the mission church was erected. In the garden there were once many old trees, doubtless a part of the mission orchard, which was walled in by a cactus hedge. It was from this hedge that the ranch derived its name, Las Tunas ("the cactus"). The history of Las Tunas Ranch is uncertain. It was occupied some time before 1852 by Henry Dalton when he was mission administrator. Hugo Reid may have been another owner. Reid, a Scotsman who married an Indian, is noted for his splendid account of the life and customs of California Indians, which has been much quoted by later writers.

The Ortega-Vigare Adobe (SRL 451) at 616 South Ramona Street was erected during mission days, and is the second oldest adobe in the region. Originally L-shaped, it is now only half its original size. In 1859, the adobe became the property of Don Juan Vigare. In the early 1860's, as San Gabriel's first bakery, it was separated from the mission's lime orchard by a high cactus hedge.

La Casa López de Lowther at 330 North Santa Anita Avenue is surely one of the former mission buildings, being of the type of adobe construction used during mission days. It was restored in keeping with its past by Doña Maria López de Lowther, whose family lived there for many years.

El Pueblo de Los Angeles State Historic Park

El Pueblo de Nuestra Señora la Reina de los Angeles, second of the three pueblos to be established in Alta California, was officially founded on September 4, 1781. A few settlers from Mexico had already arrived by this date. A carved wooden cross, placed on the north side of the present plaza at the south entrance to Olvera Street, commemorates the founding. Close by, an idealized bronze statue commemorates Felipe de Neve, governor of Alta California from 1775 to 1782, who ordered the establishment of the settlement; this statue was erected by the Native Daughters of the Golden West on the 150th anniversary of the founding of Los Angeles.

The first site of the settlement was a nearly dry summer stream that turned into a torrent in the winter. A second site was also flooded out, and what remains today is the third and final site of the pueblo of Los Angeles. The plaza (SRL 156), around which the settlement grew, was established between 1825 and 1830. Homes were built around the plaza by such prominent families as the Ávilas, the Carrillos, the Coronels, the Del Valles, and the Lugos. Gradually the settlement grew outward from the plaza, which remained the center of community life even after the coming of the Americans.

The oldest building on the plaza is the Church of Nuestra Señora la Reina de los Angeles (SRL 144), which was begun in 1818 and dedicated in 1822. It stands at 535 North Main Street, on the west side of the plaza, and is the only building in El Pueblo Park still used for its original purpose. From 1822 to 1844 the city's first cemetery, the Campo Santo, was located just south of the church. In 1981, an archaeological excavation unearthed Indian artifacts from the eighteenth century and the foundations of the old house of the padres (1822).

The oldest dwelling house in Los Angeles is the nearby Ávila adobe (SRL 145) at 14 Olvera Street, which probably dates back to 1818. It is much reduced from its size of a century and more ago, when it was in the possession of the Ávila and Rimpau families. In January 1847 Commodore Robert F. Stockton made his California headquarters there for five days.

The renovation of the Ávila adobe and of Olvera Street was the beginning of historical preservation in Los Angeles. In the 1920's, Mrs. Christine Sterling began a campaign to bring to the public's attention the deterioration of the neighborhood, which had gone so far that the Ávila adobe had been condemned by the city as unfit for human habitation. In 1930, restoration began when Olvera Street was opened to the public; it culminated in 1953 with the establishment of El Pueblo de Los Angeles State Historical Monument (now Historic Park).

The Ávila adobe is now a museum on Olvera Street, where many shops and restaurants are built into the old buildings. A diagonal line of brick in the paving of Olvera Street marks the course of the old *zanja madre* ("mother ditch") that brought water from the river to the pueblo. An exhibit of the "History of Water in Los Angeles," mounted by the City of Los Angeles Department of Water and Power and the state park, traces the history of water in the Los Angeles area and has a model of the plaza in 1860.

La Casa Pelanconi, at 33–35 Olvera Street, was built in 1855–57; it was one of Los Angeles' first brick houses and is presently a restaurant. The site of the Lugo House is on the east side of the plaza on Los Angeles Street (SRL 301). The house was a two-story adobe built before 1840 by Vicente Lugo, who later donated the building to St. Vincent's College (now Loyola University), the first college in Southern California, founded in 1865. The college moved shortly after 1867 to another downtown location, and St. Vincent's Place (SRL 567), off Seventh Street between Broadway and Hill Street, commemorates the site. When the original Lugo home was torn down in 1951, it was found to have been rebuilt of brick. A small park here is dedicated to Father Serra.

El Pueblo de Los Angeles State Historic Park is on the National Register of Historic Places. Of the 27 historic buildings in the park, sixteen are individually listed on the register. Most of these come from the American period.

The Pico House was built by Pío Pico, last Mexican governor of California, in 1869; its three stories made it the tallest building in Los Angeles for a time. Located at 430 North Main Street (SRL 159), the old hotel is now being restored. Next door, at 420–22, is the Merced Theatre (SRL 171), the first theater in Los Angeles. The Masonic Hall at 416 North Main Street is the oldest building (1858) on the south side of the plaza; the second floor contains a Masonic museum. The firehouse, built in 1884 on the southern corner of the plaza (SRL 730), was the city's first. It ceased being a firehouse in 1897 and was the first building to be restored (1960) in the park complex. It is open as a museum and houses historic fire-fighting equipment and memorabilia. The Sepulveda House next door at 130 Paseo Del Plaza dates from 1887; it was built by Señora Eloisa Martínez

Union Station, Los Angeles

de Sepúlveda, and the park's Visitors' Center is located on the ground floor. Henry E. Huntington in 1903–4 built the Plaza Substation on a lot between Olvera and Los Angeles streets to convert electricity from alternating to direct current to power his electric street cars. There are plans to create a transportation museum in this building.

El Pueblo de Los Angeles State Historic Park and the area where Union Station is now located (off Alameda Street across from the park) are the site of Los Angeles' first Chinatown. This was the center of activity of the Chinese population of Los Angeles until the 1930's, when there was an exodus to "Old Sonoratown," a few blocks north.

Restoration and development of the park continues; the most recent addition is an Indian garden landscaped with plants indigenous to the area at the time of the Spanish arrival in 1769.

Rancho San Rafael (Glendale, Eagle Rock, La Canada Flintridge, Verdugo City)

One of the first grants made in Alta California was the great Rancho San Rafael granted to José Maria Verdugo in 1784 and 1798. It was one of the largest of all the grants, comprising 36,000 acres of fertile pasturage from the Arroyo Seco to Mission San Fernando. Today's Glendale, Eagle Rock, La Canada Flintridge, and Verdugo City lie within its area.

Don José died in 1831, leaving the estate to his son Julio and his daughter Catalina; 30 years later they divided it, Julio taking the southern portion while his sister took the more rugged and mountainous section in the north.

Doña Catalina, who had been blind from girlhood,

never married, and as she grew old she tired of living here and there with her nephews and wished for a home of her own. Her nephew Teodoro built for her in 1875 what is now the last Verdugo adobe, one of the five that were at various times erected by the Verdugos on Rancho San Rafael. This modest but charming little house (SRL 637) is set back from the street at 2211 Bonita Drive in Glendale, surrounded by beautiful old trees. The massive oak that stood nearby, under which General Andrés Pico made his last camp before surrendering to Frémont at Cahuenga, has since fallen.

Tomás Sánchez, who married María Sepúlveda, built an adobe home for his wife and their nineteen children in 1865. Now known as the Casa Adobe de San Rafael (SRL 235) at 1330 Dorothy Drive, it is owned by the city of Glendale. The house and the well-kept grounds are open to the public.

The Descanso Gardens at 1418 Descanso Drive in La Canada Flintridge is on 165 acres of land that were once part of Rancho San Rafael. A live-oak forest cut by streams, the tract was purchased in 1937 by E. Manchester Boddy, publisher of the *Los Angeles Daily News*, who gave his land the name of Rancho del Descanso ("rest"). His estate included the largest ornamental camellia garden in the world, along with thousands of other plants. Today the gardens are owned and operated by Los Angeles County; the mild climate enables a year-round series of floral and arboreal displays. The Hospitality House on the grounds was the Boddy residence, built in 1939.

Eagle Rock takes its name from a massive rock that resembles an eagle in flight. It was an important landmark in Hispanic days. The rock, located at the northern end of Figueroa Street, has been declared a historic-cultural monument by the city of Los Angeles.

Grants of Southeastern Los Angeles County

Another early grant in California was made to Manuel Nieto in 1784, just three years after the founding of the Pueblo de Los Angeles. At first it included all the land lying between the Santa Ana and San Gabriel rivers from Coyote Hills to the sea, but this vast tract was later divided among Don Manuel's four heirs. The ranchos thus created were Los Alamitos, Los Cerritos, Santa Gertrudes, Los Coyotes, and Los Bolsas. Los Alamitos, Santa Gertrudes, and Los Coyotes lie partly in Orange County, and Los Bolsas is wholly within it. Old adobes still stand on Ranchos Los Alamitos and Los Cerritos.

Rancho Los Alamitos (Long Beach)

Abel Stearns, a native of Massachusetts and one of the first American settlers in California (1829), helped to introduce Yankee business methods into the largely bucolic life of the Pueblo de Los Angeles. He opened a general merchandise store and became prosperous.

Don Abel married Arcadia Bandini, the beautiful daughter of a prominent family in Alta California. Doña Arcadia reigned as social leader at El Palacio ("the palace"), Don Abel's home, built on the site of his general store. In 1858 he built the Arcadia Block at the rear of El Palacio, fronting on Los Angeles Street. It was a commercial center for many years. After Stearns's death, Doña Arcadia married Colonel R. S. Baker. The Baker block was built about 1878 on the site of El Palacio and stood at the southeast corner of what used to be the intersection of Arcadia and Main streets. Most of that area of Los Angeles has been completely razed and rebuilt for the freeway system.

Stearns was active in public affairs after the American conquest. He was a member of the first constitutional convention, a city councilman, state assemblyman, and county supervisor.

In 1842, Abel Stearns bought Rancho Los Alamitos, on a part of which the eastern section of the city of Long Beach now stands. His prosperity began to wane when he abandoned the cattle business after the great drought of 1863–64, in which cattle died by the thousands. Michael Reese, who held a mortgage on the ranch, foreclosed, and in 1878 Reese's heirs sold the Rancho Los Alamitos to the Bixby family, who had leased it for several years. The Los Alamitos ranch house has remained in the Bixby family ever since. Although it has undergone many alterations, and very little of the original adobe remains, the house retains much of its charm as an American farmhouse of the 1870's, with extensive gardens and interesting barns. The house is located at 6400 Bixby Hill Road, five and one-half miles east of downtown Long Beach, and is open to the public on a limited basis.

The oil well "Alamitos 1" (SRL 580), discovery well of the important Signal Hill field, takes its name from the old rancho. Drilled to a depth of 3,114 feet in 1921, it is located at Hill Street and Temple Avenue in Signal Hill.

Rancho Los Cerritos (Western Long Beach)

La Casa del Rancho Los Cerritos, with its broad balcony stretching the full length of the back, its great patio enclosed on three sides by the long wings of the house and on the fourth by a high adobe wall, is a magnificent building. On the balcony side is a beautiful garden dating from early days, and in the patio is another planted in recent times. Below is the river, and beyond lies the valley. The shaded *corredores*, the many and varied rooms, and the hand-finished woodwork are among its sights. The present tile roof replaced one of redwood shakes; the first roof was of brea, or tar.

This splendid adobe mansion was built in 1844 by Don Juan Temple, another energetic young native of Massachusetts, who, finding life in Alta California agreeable and profitable, married Rafaela Cota, a cousin of Guillermo Cota. Temple bought out the shares that the grandchildren of Manuel Nieto held in Rancho Los Cerritos. He built his mansion at what is now 4600 Virginia Road, about four miles north of the center of the present city of Long Beach, the main part of which stands within the confines of the old rancho. The Los Cerritos adobe (SRL 978) is now owned by the city of Long Beach and is open to the public on a regular basis. It is a National Historic Landmark. For years it was owned by the Bixby family and was rebuilt by Llewellyn Bixby, son of the pioneer Llewellyn, in 1930.

Everything Juan Temple did was successful. He opened the first general store in the Pueblo de Los Angeles, and in front of it he planted pepper trees. He and his brother built the Temple Block, Los Angeles' first office building. Juan Temple's establishments were located in what is now the Civic Center. The Federal Building on Los Angeles Street stands on the site of his general store. The market later became the courthouse, and the Temple Block stood just to the north. The sites of these two buildings are now occupied by the Los Angeles City Hall.

Long Beach Harbor

In Long Beach Harbor are two tourist attractions that have an interesting history. The *Queen Mary*, launched in Scotland in 1936, was one of the great passenger liners in the heyday of Atlantic crossings. After World War II, when it served as a troop transport, it returned to luxury travel. Phased out by the Cunard Line, it was acquired in 1967 by the city of Long Beach, and it is now operated as a hotel, restaurant, and museum complex. Although permanently moored in the harbor, it is still the largest passenger liner afloat, and certainly one of the most handsome.

Nearby, in a specially designed hangar, is the Spruce Goose, the largest aircraft ever built. The work of entrepreneur Howard Hughes, the plane was designed to be a troop transport during World War II. It was not com-

pleted until two years after the war ended, however. On November 2, 1947, with Hughes at the controls, the gigantic seaplane flew a little over one mile at an altitude of 70 feet in Long Beach Harbor. It has never flown again, nor has an aircraft so large ever been built since. The body and wings of the plane are of wood, hence its name.

Rancho Santa Gertrudes (Downey, Santa Fe Springs)

Antonio María Nieto received Rancho Santa Gertrudes, and in 1834 the Mexican government confirmed the title to his widow, Doña Josefa Cota de Nieto. Later, the rancho was sold to Lemuel Carpenter, a Kentuckian who married the beautiful María de los Angeles Domínguez. Carpenter and his wife conveyed a portion of Rancho Santa Gertrudes to José M. Ramírez in 1855; this section became known as the Ramírez Tract. The Carpenters had prospered under Mexican rule, but they failed under the more challenging business methods of the Yankees. On November 14, 1859, the rancho was sold by the sheriff. John G. Downey and James P. McFarland were the fortunate bidders. Carpenter took his own life.

John Gateley Downey had the sort of career that made others think of California as a golden land of opportunity. Born in Ireland in 1827, he came to America as a young man and learned the pharmacy business in Washington, D.C.. He then worked as a druggist in Mississippi and Ohio before coming to California in 1849. He became a naturalized United States citizen in 1851; in the following year he married María Jesús Guirado and was elected to the Los Angeles City Council. In 1850 he opened Los Angeles' second drugstore in partnership with Dr. James P. McFarland, and the two purchased Rancho Santa Gertrudes in 1859. Two months before the purchase, Downey had been elected

Oldest Existing McDonald's Drive-In, Downey

lieutenant governor of California on the Democratic ticket, and when Governor Milton Latham resigned early in 1860 to fill an unexpired United States Senate seat, Downey became governor. A strong Union supporter in the Civil War, he raised five regiments of infantry and six companies of cavalry from California for the federal Army, and presided over the laying of the cornerstone for the state capitol in Sacramento. After his term expired in 1862, he was a trustee of Phineas Banning's Pioneer Oil Company, the first oil company in California. He was also a trustee of the Farmer's and Merchant's Bank, one of the patrons contributing land for the University of Southern California, and a founder of the Historical Society of Southern California. The city of Downey was begun in 1873. The oil-rich community of Santa Fe Springs began on its eastern boundary.

Three twentieth-century historic spots of note are to be found in Downey. The James C. Rives Home at Paramount Boulevard and Third Street (1911) is on the National Register of Historic Places; it was the home of Rives, who was Los Angeles County District Attorney and a Superior Court judge, and his family. The Rockwell International Plant at 12214 Lakewood Boulevard (1929) is the site of the design and much of the technology for the Apollo lunar craft and the space shuttle. And the world's oldest existing McDonald's Drive-In Restaurant has stood with its two golden arches at 10207 Lakewood Boulevard since 1953.

Rancho San Pedro (Compton, Gardena, Wilmington)

The rich grazing lands of Rancho San Pedro covered 43,119 acres, extending from the coast near Wilmington up the estuary of the Los Angeles River halfway to Los Angeles. Gardena and Compton are situated on the northern boundary of the grant. San Pedro is one of the earliest grants in California, and has continued in part in the hands of the descendants of the original grantee. First granted to Juan José Domínguez before 1799 and again in 1822 to his heir, Sargento Cristobal Domínguez, Rancho San Pedro came into the charge of Manuel Domínguez in 1826. Don Manuel lived on the estate until his death in 1882, and his vigorous management as well as his integrity and hospitality made the rancho famous.

Only the shaded eastern *corredor* of the Domínguez adobe (SRL 152) and the historic trees in the garden recall the atmosphere of rancho days long past. Arches and stucco have made the west front decidedly modern. In the chapel of Don Manuel's casa there is a stained-glass window bearing the inscription "Domínguez 1826." A descendant of the Domínguez family presented the old place to the Claretian Order to be a memorial seminary for the training of priests. It is operated by the Claretian Fathers today as a retreat.

Rancho San Pedro was the scene of a battle between Californians and Americans on October 9, 1846. After the citizens of Los Angeles had given their allegiance to the United States, Commodore Robert F. Stockton, acting commander of American forces in California, and Colonel John C. Frémont left the city early in September, leaving Captain Archibald Gillespie in charge of 50 men. Leaving so small a garrison proved to be a mistake. A revolt occurred among the Californians of the city, and the garrison, forced to surrender on September 30, retreated to San Pedro. Meanwhile, Commodore Stockton in San Francisco had heard of the revolt and sent Captain William Mervine and 300 men to assist the American forces.

Gillespie arrived in San Pedro on October 7, and was about to embark when Captain Mervine and his reinforcements arrived on the *Savannah*. The two commanders then joined forces and marched toward Los Angeles. They were halted on October 9 at the Domínguez rancho by a force of 120 mounted Californians commanded by José Carrillo. Armed with a four-pound cannon, the Californians held off repeated American charges until Mervine, with six men killed and a number wounded, retreated to San Pedro on the coast. The American dead were buried on a little island near the mouth of San Pedro Bay. Deadman's Island, as it was christened by the burial party of the American forces, long remained a landmark in the bay, but it has now been entirely removed by harbor construction work.

As a result of their victory on the Domínguez rancho, the revolt of the Californians quickly spread all over California, and the Americans were confronted with the semblance of a real war.

At this point, the clever José Carrillo played a trick on the Americans that temporarily kept them out of Los Angeles. Setting his troopers to rounding up all the wild horses of the neighboring ranchos, he herded them back and forth across a gap in the hills where they kicked up such a dust that Stockton, watching from San Pedro harbor three miles away, took them to be a great body of mounted Californians. Knowing their daring and marvelous horsemanship, he weighed anchor and sailed for San Diego.

The official state marker at the Claretian retreat recounts the history of the Domínguez ranch house and the Battle of the Domínguez Rancho.

The first air meet in the United States was held atop Domínguez Hill on the old rancho from January 10 to 20, 1910. The first competitive meeting of pioneer fliers was held at a time when aviation was considered by many to be a passing novelty. Glenn H. Curtiss set a new air speed record of 60 miles per hour. The site (SRL 718) was marked in 1941 by the Compton Parlors of the Native Sons and Native Daughters of the Golden West, but the marker is relatively inaccessible. Another monument has been placed one-half mile to the northwest, on Wilmington Avenue, one mile north of Del Amo Boulevard.

Wilmington, near the southern edge of Rancho San Pedro, was founded in 1858 by General Phineas Banning, "Father of Los Angeles Transportation." He was famous first as an operator of stage lines and later as the builder of the first local railroads, and was a pioneer in the oil industry as well. His 30-room mansion in Banning Park (SRL 147), at 401 East M Street, was built in 1864. It has been owned by the city of Los Angeles since 1927, and is open to the public as a museum. Drum Barracks (SRL 169) at Wilmington was the central supply station for the Union Army in southern California during the years 1861–68. It was named in honor of General Richard Coulter Drum, a general of the Mexican War. The last surviving building of the Drum Barracks is the officers' quarters, now divided into private apartments, at 1053–55 Cary Avenue. In the 1870's it briefly housed a Southern Methodist college, called Wilson College in honor of its donor, Don Benito Wilson.

Heritage House (SRL 664), at 401 South Willowbrook Avenue, is the oldest house in Compton. The original two rooms were built in 1869 by A. R. Loomis. The house, which originally stood at 209 South Acacia Street, was purchased by the city of Compton and moved to its present site in 1957.

Redondo Beach is at the northwest corner of Rancho San Pedro. At this point it adjoins Rancho Sausal Redondo. Between Pacific and Francisca avenues at the north end of Redondo Beach is the site of an old salt lake (SRL 373) from which the Indians of the area obtained salt. A flourishing salt works operated here in the last half of the nineteenth century.

Rancho Los Palos Verdes (San Pedro, Palos Verdes)

The great Rancho Los Palos Verdes grant was given to the Sepúlveda family in 1827, and the grant was confirmed to José Loreto and Juan Sepúlveda in 1846. It contained 31,629 acres, extending from south of Redondo Beach to San Pedro. San Pedro is now a part of the city of Los Angeles, and it is interesting to note that almost the entire district was carved out of Rancho Los Palos Verdes, not out of Rancho San Pedro, as is often thought.

According to Chapman, Cabrillo discovered San Pedro Bay on October 8, 1542, calling it Bahía de los Fumos ("the Bay of Smokes"), because of the dense smoke arising from burning grass during the Indians' periodic rabbit hunts. However, the Bahía de los Fumos (or Fuegos) has also been identified as Santa Monica Bay.

Sixty years later, Vizcaíno entered the bay, and as early as 1793 San Pedro had become the port of entry for the Pueblo of Los Angeles, three missions, and several ranchos. In that year George Vancouver, the English navigator, on his second voyage to California, named the points at the two extremities of the bay Point Fermin and Point Lasuen, in honor of his friend Father Fermín Francisco de Lasuén, successor to Junípero Serra as Padre Presidente of the missions. The names given by Vancouver were retained on modern maps.

The first Yankee ship to anchor at San Pedro was the *Lelia Byrd* in 1805, with Captain William Shaler in command, on his return voyage from the Sandwich (Hawaiian) Islands to Boston. This was the beginning of a brisk trade between California and Yankee ships from New England. After this, Yankee brigs as well as ships from other nations called regularly at San Pedro, in quest first of otter skins and later of hides and tallow. This was officially contraband trade until 1821, when Mexico, having freed herself from Spain, made it legal. From then on the port of San Pedro grew in importance.

The first harbor improvements were made in 1877, and in 1892 steps were taken for the creation of a deepwater port. Scarcely any of the old landmarks remain today. From 1874 to 1945 a lighthouse operated on Point Fermin, now closed to the public. A pleasant park surrounds the structure, at Paseo del Mar and Gaffey Street. Timm's Point (SRL 384), mentioned by Richard Henry Dana in *Two Years Before the Mast* as the place down which the cargoes of hides and tallow were lowered to Yankee trading ships below, has disappeared with harbor improvements. The point and landing were located off the south end of Beacon Street near present Fisherman's Dock.

The Fort MacArthur military reservation, now much reduced in area, once covered much of the area around Point Fermin. The fort was named for General Arthur MacArthur, father of General Douglas MacArthur. Two gun emplacements from the World War I coastal defenses, Batteries Farley and Osgood, can still be seen in Angels Gate Park (that part of Fort MacArthur now released to public ownership). Here also is the Bell of Friendship between the Korean and the American people, erected in an imposing belfry on a bluff in the

Point Fermin Lighthouse, San Pedro

Don José Dolores had trouble getting his land title cleared, so he took a trip to Monterey to get the matter settled in 1824; on his return, he stopped off at Mission La Purísima and was killed in the Indian uprising that year.

Mission San Fernando Rey de España

Mission San Fernando Rey de España was founded on September 8, 1797, by Father Fermín Francisco de Lasuén. The spot chosen had been provisionally granted to Alcalde Francisco Reyes of Los Angeles. The padres took over the adobe house the alcalde had built, and within two months erected the first small chapel. Another church was completed in 1799, and the present church in 1806. Although heavily damaged by the earthquake of 1812, it was subsequently repaired. The mission was secularized in October 1834.

The first European industry in the Los Angeles area was the burning of limestone to produce lime, a necessary component of the construction of the missions and other adobe structures. Lime was needed for foundation cement, for mortaring and plastering walls, and for whitewash to protect the adobe bricks. It is believed that the *calera*, or kiln, near the present Chatsworth Reservoir was used to obtain lime for the construction of Mission San Fernando. A plaque (SRL 911) has been placed at Woolsey Canyon Road and Valley Circle Boulevard in Chatsworth near the site.

The vast lands of Mission San Fernando were leased in 1845 to Andrés Pico, brother of Governor Pío Pico. In order to obtain money to defend California against the Americans, the governor sold Rancho Ex-Mission de San Fernando in June 1846 to Eulogio de Celís for $14,000. Celís recognized Andrés Pico's lease, and in 1854 Pico bought a half-interest in the rancho. He continued to make the old mission his country home and to herd his cattle on its vast ranges. Romulo Pico, the son or adopted son of Andrés, also came to live on the rancho.

In 1874, senators Charles Maclay and George K. Porter purchased the northern half of the rancho; B. F. Porter became associated with them in 1879. The southern half had already been bought by a group headed by Isaac Lankershim and I. N. Van Nuys, and with these two purchases the era of small farms and the building up of the town of San Fernando and the San Fernando Valley began. The old mission days were ended.

For many years the only intact building of Mission San Fernando was the *convento*, often called simply the "long building," 243 feet in length with nineteen arches. At the east end is the chapel room containing several

park as part of the 1976 Bicentennial celebration. The view from the platform over the Pacific Ocean and the entrance to Los Angeles Harbor is beautiful. The International Korean War Memorial was dedicated in Angels Gate Park in 1987.

The Palos Verdes Peninsula, with its beautiful homes and a major tourist attraction, Marineland of the Pacific, occupies much of the old Rancho Los Palos Verdes. At the residential community of Portuguese Bend a whaling station was located from about 1864 to 1885 (SRL 381).

None of the old Sepúlveda adobes stands today. The home of Diego Sepúlveda (SRL 380) was located in the 700 block of Channel Street in San Pedro and faced on Gaffey Street. Built about 1853, it was the first two-story Monterey-type adobe in southern California. An even earlier adobe stood southeast of Walteria at the foot of the Palos Verdes Hills. The home of José Dolores Sepúlveda (SRL 383), father of Diego, is said to have been built in 1818. The exact site is unknown, but the general area is indicated by old pepper trees at the mouth of the canyon into which Madison Street runs.

ancient paintings and relics of mission days; the building also includes the refectory, kitchen, and underground wine vats. In 1938, under the leadership of Mark R. Harrington of the Southwest Museum, restoration of the other buildings began. The mission church had fallen into ruin, and very little remained of the workshops and living quarters. The Sylmar temblor of 1971 further damaged the church, and the building was demolished. Now the church has been fully restored and part of the quadrangle has been rebuilt. The mission is at 15151 San Fernando Road, in Mission Hills. On the northwest side of the mission is the graveyard where 2,000 Indians lie buried.

In what is now Brand Park (SRL 150), across San Fernando Road from the mission complex, are the immense stone soap vats constructed by the mission fathers and also two beautiful fountains. One of the fountains, a replica of one in Cordova, Spain, was moved 300 feet from its original location in the mission courtyard in 1922. Both of them were a part of the old mission water system.

The Andrés Pico adobe was built in two parts. The earliest part dates from 1834 and was built by Indians from the missions. Pico acquired the adobe and added the second story in 1873. It fell into neglect early in the twentieth century but was purchased and saved by Dr. and Mrs. Mark Harrington in 1930, who restored the building to its earlier condition. The beautiful structure (SRL 362) stands a quarter of a mile southwest of the mission at 10940 Sepulveda Boulevard. It is the headquarters of the San Fernando Valley Historical Society, which maintains it and a small museum within for the city of Los Angeles. It is the oldest house in the San Fernando Valley and second in age only to the Ávila adobe in the city of Los Angeles.

The town of San Fernando began to boom about 1874, when Don Gerónimo López, who had erected an adobe home on Rancho San Fernando earlier, decided to move there. In 1883 his son Valentino built the house at 1100 Pico Street that still stands. The López adobe has been somewhat elaborately restored, but it retains its quaint and picturesque upper balcony and outside stairway, and an old-fashioned garden that keeps the spirit of the past. It is owned by the city of San Fernando and operated by the San Fernando Landmarks and Historical Commission.

The oldest nonsectarian cemetery in the San Fernando Valley is the San Fernando Memorial Cemetery, also variously known as the Morningside Cemetery or the Pioneer Cemetery, on Foothill Boulevard and Bledsoe Street in Sylmar (SRL 753). It is presently being restored by a local citizens' group.

On the Workman Ranch, now called the Shadow Ranch Park, at 22633 Vanowen Street in Canoga Park, there is an adobe-and-redwood ranch house built between 1869 and 1872 and now owned by the city of Los Angeles. In the same area is "Rancho Sombra de Robles," the adobe house and estate of W. W. Orcutt, an early oil engineer and one of the founders of the Union Oil Company, at 23555 Justice Street. This is owned as a Los Angeles city facility and designated the Orcutt Ranch Horticultural Center.

At Chatsworth, the Homestead Acre and the Hill-Palmer house are at 10385 Shadow Oak Drive. This 1.3-acre plot is all that remains of the 230 acres homesteaded by James David Hill and his wife, Rhoda Jane, in the late 1880's. Their seventh child, Minnie, was born here in 1886, later married, and returned to the place to care for her mother. Minnie Hill Palmer continued to live on the remaining land until she reached the age of 90, living in pioneer style, raising vegetables, and canning fruit. She bequeathed the home to the Chatsworth Historical Society for restoration as a monument to pioneers who homesteaded the valley. At Oakwood Memorial Park, at 22601 Lassen Street in Chatsworth, the Chatsworth Memorial Church has been moved from its original (1903) site at 10051 Topanga Canyon Boulevard; this nondenominational Protestant church served the community for over 50 years and is now being restored by the Chatsworth Historical Society.

Rancho El Encino (Encino)

Father Juan Crespí, who with Gaspar de Portolá and his band of explorers first marched through the beautiful valley of San Fernando in 1769, gave it the grand name of El Valle de Santa Catalina de Bononia de los Encinos ("the Valley of Saint Catherine of Bologna of the Oaks"). The Shoshone word *zelzah* ("oasis" or "spring") seems to have been used to describe the springs and vegetation marking the beginning of the Los Angeles River; the name has been perpetuated in a local thoroughfare. The presence of the native oaks also inspired the name of Rancho El Encino, which was granted in 1845 to three Indians, Ramón, Francisco, and Roque. It was purchased by Don Vicente de Osa, who erected there in 1849 the long, low adobe house that still stands a few hundred yards north of the present Ventura Boulevard. The house shows evidences of having been extensively repaired and improved during the 1870's or early 1880's.

Rita de la Osa in 1867 conveyed to James Thompson ("Don Santiago" of Rancho La Brea) all of her interest and that of Don Vicente, who had died in 1861, in Rancho El Encino. Two years later it was purchased by Eugene Garnier, a French Basque, who made of El Encino a great sheep ranch. The broad pool or reservoir in front of the old adobe was constructed by Garnier in 1867 or 1868, and just to the north of it in 1872 he built the quaint two-story stone house that still stands. In spite of his thrift and industry, Eugene Garnier was not able to hold Rancho El Encino. It passed into other hands, including those of three French Basques in succession. At one period the place was a stagecoach stop.

The rancho headquarters are now Los Encinos State Historic Park, at 16756 Moorpark Street, Encino. It includes the springs that feed the lake; the Portolá expedition camped here on August 5, 1769.

In 1984, excavations for an Encino building complex on Ventura Boulevard near Balboa Boulevard turned up what is believed to be the Indian village of "Encino" first visited by the Portolá expedition in 1769. Artifacts from this excavation have been placed on display at the park headquarters.

Rancho El Escorpión (Calabasas)

Besides Rancho Ex-Mission de San Fernando and Rancho El Encino, there were other Mexican grants in the San Fernando Valley. One was Rancho El Escorpión, 1,110 acres, granted to three Indians, Urbano, Odon, and Manuel, and to Joaquín Romero. It came into the hands of Miguel Leonis, a Basque who arrived in California about 1858. Leonis enlarged an adobe that was begun in 1844 and completed in 1846 on public land outside the confines of his rancho. It still stands at 23537 Calabasas Road in Calabasas, a well-preserved two-story house of Monterey style.

Rancho San Antonio (South and East of Los Angeles)

It was said by an admirer that there were "no horses so fast, no cattle so fine, no land so fertile, no rancho more famous than the Rancho San Antonio. No family more prominent, no hospitality more welcome or as freely partaken, no hacienda more lovely, happy or prosperous than that of the Lugos." Rancho San Antonio was granted to Antonio María Lugo in 1810, and for 50 years it remained in possession of the family. Its 29,513 acres of land adjoined the original pueblo grant of the city of Los Angeles on the southeast. Don Antonio and his bride lived at first in a tule house on the site of the present-day town of Bell. In 1819 he built an adobe dwelling in Los Angeles on what is now the east side of San Pedro Street between First and Second, and here his four sons were born. Vicente Lugo, a son of Don Antonio, built a two-story house that was long a

center of social life in the pueblo. Neither house still stands, nor does Vicente's country estate in what is now Bell Gardens. Henry T. Gage, who was governor of California from 1899 to 1903, lived in an adobe a few blocks away from the now-vanished Lugo house; the Gage residence still stands at 7000 East Gage Avenue in Bell Gardens.

Ultimately, the pressure of American business closed in on the great Rancho San Antonio until, bit by bit, it was lost to its original owners. Among the communities now on the old rancho grounds are Bell, Bell Gardens, Huntington Park, Lynwood, South Gate, Vernon, and Walnut Park.

Rancho La Brea (Hancock Park District, Los Angeles)

Rancho La Brea, originally a part of the Los Angeles pueblo lands, was granted in 1828 to Antonio José Rocha and Nemicio Domínguez by José Antonio Carrillo, alcalde of Los Angeles and brother-in-law of Pío Pico. Later, the grant was confirmed by Governor Echeandia. The rancho derived its name from La Brea Pits, where brea, or crude tar, oozed out of the ground in great quantities. Early conveyances of this land all provided that the owners were to allow the inhabitants of Los Angeles to take from the pits as much brea as they needed for the roofs of their adobe houses.

Antonio José Rocha was a Portuguese who came to California in 1815 and became one of the most respected citizens of the Pueblo of Los Angeles. He was naturalized in 1831, and in 1836 was a resident of Santa Barbara. In 1860, his son José Jorge Rocha deeded Rancho La Brea to Major Henry Hancock. Parts of the estate were later conveyed to Cornelius Cole, James Thompson, and Arthur Gilmore, but much of it remained in the hands of the Hancocks. For years, the Hancocks extracted immense quantities of oil from the rancho lands, but the oil gradually decreased, until today the derricks of the once wealthy oil fields have been replaced by the beautiful homes of the Wilshire District. The site of the old pits has become Hancock Park (SRL 170), and the pools are now confined within a park-like enclosure.

In the heavy crude oil that has oozed out of the ground at La Brea Pits since time immemorial, animals, once caught, were unable to free themselves. Thousands of skeletons of prehistoric creatures (and one human being) have been recovered, and more still turn up. Many can be seen in the Hancock Room of the Museum of History and Art at Exposition Park. The George C. Page Museum of La Brea Discoveries at 5801 Wilshire Boulevard in Hancock Park is an excellent source of information on these excavations.

Although Major Hancock began to uncover some of these bones during the 1870's, their importance was not confirmed until 1906, when Professor J. C. Merriam of the University of California investigated them. Merriam and other scientists made extensive studies at the rancho. On June 23, 1913, Major Hancock gave the exclusive right to excavate the beds to the city of Los Angeles, and the Hancock Room was set aside as a memorial to his parents, Major Henry Hancock and Ida Hancock Ross.

Rancho La Brea (Hancock Park) has been registered as a National Natural Landmark by the Department of the Interior.

The adobe house that remains standing approximately ten blocks north of the pits was built by Antonio José Rocha about 1828–30. It is one of the original adobes of the rancho and was restored with great care by oil magnate Earl E. Gilmore, who was born in the old house in the 1880's and died there on February 27, 1964. It stands at 6301 West Third Street, on a private drive between the Farmers Market and the CBS television studio.

Rancho Rincón de San Pasqual (Pasadena, South Pasadena, Altadena)

At 1804 Foothill Boulevard in South Pasadena is the Adobe de las Flores, beautifully restored and now used as a private residence. Begun by Manuel Gárfias in 1839, it was the first house built on Rancho San Pasqual, originally that part of the extensive lands of Mission San Gabriel granted first in 1835 to Juan Mariné, husband of Eulalia Pérez de Guillén, reputedly the oldest white woman in California at that time. This land was a gift made in recompense for Doña Eulalia's long services at the mission as nurse, overseer of spinning and tailoring, cashier, and accountant. Today, the cities of Pasadena, South Pasadena, and Altadena cover the former rancho lands.

The rancho was regranted provisionally to José Pérez, who died in 1840, and eventually came to be owned by Manuel Gárfias, who was a son-in-law of Doña Encarnación Ávila.

The casa has come to be known as the Flores adobe because it was there that General José María Flores, provisional governor of California, took refuge in January 1847 after the Battle of La Mesa, while Kearny and Stockton took final possession of Los Angeles and Frémont held the San Fernando Valley. General Flores and his staff held their last council within this house on the night of January 9, while the California horsemen kept watch on the hills outside. Knowing that surrender was inevitable, they made final plans to leave Andrés

Pico in command while Flores and Manuel Gárfias, both commissioned officers in the Mexican army, fled to Mexico under cover of darkness on the night of January 11. On January 13 the Cahuenga Capitulation Treaty was signed by Frémont and Andrés Pico, and hostilities came to an end.

Pasadena

Pasadena is one of the longest-established residential communities in Los Angeles County. The oldest house in the area was built in 1869, five years before the founding of Pasadena, and is a privately owned adobe, "The Hermitage," at 2121 Monte Vista Street. The Clapp house at 549 La Loma Road is the oldest frame building in the city (1874); Pasadena's first school was located in the parlor of the new home where it originally stood, at the corner of California and Orange streets. The city in time became known for its elegant mansions, one of the most imposing of which is the Wrigley Estate at 391 South Orange Grove Boulevard. Mr. and Mrs. William Wrigley, Jr., purchased the new house in 1914 and lived there until 1958. In 1959 the Wrigley heirs donated the estate to the city of Pasadena; it became Tournament House, the permanent headquarters of the Tournament of Roses Association. It is open to the public on a limited basis. The David B. Gamble House (SRL 871), at 4 Westmoreland Place, is the finest surviving example of the work of the architects Charles Sumner Greene and Henry Mather Greene. Built in 1908, it exemplifies the Arts and Crafts movement of the early twentieth century. The beautiful house in California Bungalow style has been registered as a National Historic Landmark and is open to the public.

The Fenyes Estate, completed in 1905, is a large mansion that was once the Finnish Consulate. Since 1970 it has been headquarters for the Pasadena Historical Society, and the Pasadena Historical Museum oc-

David B. Gamble House, Pasadena

cupies the ground floor. The elegant building is located at 470 Walnut Street. The Norton Simon Museum, the newest of Pasadena's great public buildings, is around the corner at 411 West Colorado Boulevard. The quality of its collections makes it a major world treasury.

The Pasadena Playhouse (SRL 887) opened in 1925. It served as the training ground and launching area for many of Hollywood's finest actors, directors, and technicians. Among those who received early training at the Playhouse are Robert Young, Victor Mature, William Holden, Charles Bronson, Lee J. Cobb, Kim Hunter, Sally Struthers, Raymond Burr, and Dustin Hoffman. The building, in Spanish Colonial Revival Style, is considered by many to be the finest work of architect Elmer Grey. It is located at 39 South El Molino Avenue.

The Huntington Hotel at 1401 South Oak Knoll Avenue is one of the showplaces of southern California. It was begun in 1907 by General Marshall C. Wentworth with the idea that every room in the reinforced-concrete structure would receive direct sunlight at some time during the day—an innovation in hotel building at the time. The Wentworth Hotel closed after one unprofitable season but was reopened as the Huntington by the railroad tycoon and art collector Henry E. Huntington in 1914. Late in 1985 the state of California declared the building to be vulnerable to earthquakes; the principal building is now closed to the public, though cabanas and restaurants are open.

The Rose Bowl stadium in Arroyo Seco Park was built in 1922, although the first Rose Bowl football game was played on New Year's Day, 1902. Since 1916 the Rose Bowl game has been played here on the first day of the year, except during World War II, when it was played in Durham, North Carolina. From here, on January 1, 1927, radio stations across the nation were linked together for the first coast-to-coast broadcast. The first west-to-east color telecast on a nationwide hook-up was of the Tournament of Roses parade and Rose Bowl game on January 1, 1954.

The Pasadena Freeway, originally the Arroyo Seco Freeway, is California's first freeway. A six-mile stretch was opened on December 30, 1940, and two days later California suffered its first freeway congestion—traffic to and from the Tournament of Roses parade and the Rose Bowl game.

San Marino

Standing behind San Marino High School on the north side of Huntington Drive is an old story-and-a-half adobe that was once the home of Michael White (Miguel Blanco), an English sailor who came to California in 1829 and married one of the daughters of Doña Eulalia de Guillén. White obtained a grant of 77 acres

directly north of Mission San Gabriel and lived there for many years after 1843.

The estate of Henry E. Huntington is now the location of the Huntington Library and Art Gallery. The library is one of the foremost depositories of historical material in California. The art gallery has an outstanding collection of eighteenth-century English art. The gardens comprise 130 acres of beautifully kept landscapes in a number of themes and styles. The Huntington, as it is known, is at 1151 Oxford Road.

For many years another adobe house stood in San Marino. It was the residence of George Stoneman, governor of California between 1883 and 1887. His 400-acre estate was called "Los Robles." A monument at the site of the house (SRL 669) on Montrobles Place incorporates some of the old adobe bricks.

The home of Edwin Hubble, one of America's greatest twentieth-century astronomers, stands at 1340 Woodstock Road, and has been registered as a National Historic Landmark. Among other accomplishments, Hubble discovered extragalactic nebulae and their recession from one another.

Rancho Paso de Bartolo Viejo (Whittier)

At first a part of the lands belonging to Mission San Gabriel, Rancho Paso de Bartolo was granted to Juan Crispín Pérez in 1835, the year of the secularization. Pérez was *alcalde auxiliar* of Rancho Santa Gertrudes from 1831 to 1836 and was later mayordomo of the mission during its declining years. Following the original grant, Paso de Bartolo Viejo was finally divided among four claimants, Pérez, Bernardino Guirado, Joaquina Sepúlveda, and Pío Pico. Pico and Pérez finally received their patents to 8,891 acres in 1881.

Pío Pico, last Mexican governor of California, did not inherit his wealth but obtained it by his own efforts. The vast ranchos of Las Flores and Santa Margarita were his, as well as several other extensive properties. He called the 8,000-acre rancho of Paso de Bartolo by the title "El Ranchito," both because of its diminutive size in comparison to his vaster estates and because of the affection in which he had always held it. It was his favorite home place, and at the close of the struggle to compete with American business methods that finally reduced Don Pío Pico from the position of the wealthiest man in California to a pauper's grave, El Ranchito was his last possession in Los Angeles County.

It is uncertain just when the adobe house of Pío Pico was built; in the flood of 1867 the nearby San Gabriel River swept away a portion of the building, and in the winter of 1883–84 additional floods destroyed what was left. The second casa was a blend of Mexican and American styles and was built with a capacious series of rooms and courtyards for the entertaining of guests, which Pío Pico loved. Today it is Pío Pico State Historic Park (SRL 127) at 6003 Pioneer Boulevard in Whittier.

What is now the city of Whittier began as a Quaker colony. Aquilla H. Pickering of Chicago founded the Pickering Land and Water Company about 1887 for the purpose of establishing Quakers on neighboring farms. John H. Thomas had established a ranch there in 1880, and Jonathan and Rebecca Bailey moved into his ranch house in 1887. The house still stands at 13421 Camilla Street; owned by the city of Whittier, it is now the Jonathan Bailey House and Park, and the building is on the National Register of Historic Places.

Nearby is the Whittier Museum at 6755 Newlin Avenue, displaying historical artifacts connected with the early days of Whittier. A Whittier landmark is the huge paradox hybrid walnut tree (SRL 681) in the 600–800 block of West Whittier Boulevard, which divides around it. It was planted in 1907 as part of an agricultural experiment by the University of California.

A legislative act of March 11, 1889, provided for a state school for juvenile offenders, and this was established in Whittier two years later as the Whittier State School for Boys and Girls. Since 1970 it has been known simply as the Fred C. Nelles School, after a longtime superintendent. Located at 11850 Whittier Boulevard (SRL 947), the school has been in continuous use since 1891, although its inmates today are all young men, the women's facilities being elsewhere in the state.

Rancho San José (Pomona)

In the beautiful valley of Pomona west of the Arroyo de San Antonio, the boundaries of the great Rancho San José were first laid out by Ygnacio Palomares and Ricardo Vejar on March 19, 1837, the feast of St. Joseph. Father Zalvidea, who accompanied the party from Mission San Gabriel, performed the first Christian religious service ever held in the valley when he pronounced a benediction upon the two families about to establish their homes in the wilderness of San José. The ceremony was held under an oak tree, the stump of which still stands in the city of Pomona at 458 Kenoak Place. A bronze tablet commemorating this event was placed on the historic tree by the Pomona Chapter, DAR, in 1922.

To Ygnacio Palomares was given the upper portion of Rancho San José, or San José de Arriba, while Ricardo Vejar received the lower half, known as San José de Abajo. Four adobes remain on the rancho, in the city of Pomona and in the foothills to the west.

La Casa Primera, built by Don Ygnacio after 1837, still stands among the orange trees at 1569 North Park Avenue, although the older part of it has been torn down. The low roof of the little house projects over a broad *corredor* extending the full length of the side that faces the old-fashioned garden. About 300 yards southwest, at 1459 Old Settlers' Lane, is the Alvarado house, once the home of Ygnacio Alvarado, close friend of Palomares. In those days when neighbors lived many miles apart, the hospitality of Spanish settlers was proverbial, but in few other instances was it expressed in so friendly and intimate a manner as in the case of Ygnacio Palomares and Ygnacio Alvarado. At the urgent invitation of the former, Alvarado came to Rancho San José and built his home within a stone's throw of his friend's, the only stipulation in the arrangement being that Alvarado should build a chapel in his house, an agreement that was accordingly fulfilled. According to the present owners, the altar in the chapel was so arranged that after religious services were held, it could be turned to the wall and the large room used for secular purposes. The Alvarado adobe is on the National Register of Historic Sites. Both adobes are private houses today, cared for and prized by their owners.

In 1854 Ygnacio Palomares built another adobe (SRL 372) at what is now the corner of Arrow Highway and Orange Grove Avenue. Leaving the old home to his son Francisco, Don Ygnacio made his home at the newer place on the road to Chino and San Bernardino. The adobe became a popular stage station and tavern, where a huge fireplace welcomed many a traveler on chill nights. For many years the deserted adobe mouldered among the roses and oranges, but in time it was restored, and since 1940 has been open to the public as a museum of the Historical Society of Pomona Valley.

At 919 Puddingstone Drive above Puddingstone Dam, about two miles southeast of San Dimas, the Carrión adobe (SRL 386) stands on the lower reaches of the hills. Here on the old San Bernardino road, where the padres and caballeros of Spanish and Mexican times were followed by the pioneers of the early American period, Saturnino Carrión built one of the most attractive of the smaller adobes in southern California. This portion of Rancho San José de Arriba was given to Carrión by his uncle and aunt, Don Ygnacio and Doña Concepción López Palomares, in 1843, when he was only a boy of eleven, but it was not until the year of the great drought, 1863, that he finally came to San José to live. The little house was for many years threatened with decay, but fortunately it has been restored and is occupied as a private residence. Substantial additions were made to the house in the 1950's.

The first American settlement in Pomona Valley was at Spadra, located on Rancho San José de Abajo. Spadra was a stage station on the old Colorado Emigrant Road via Chino in the 1850's and 1860's. Here "Uncle Billy"

Rubottom, the first American settler in the valley, built a tavern in the 1860's, and the place was named Spadra after his native home in Arkansas. The Spadra Cemetery on Pomona Boulevard is the only vestige of this settlement. About a mile east of Spadra at 2640 Pomona Boulevard is the two-story mansion built by Louis Phillips in the late 1860's. It was the first brick house in Pomona and is still in good condition. It is now operated as a Victorian museum by the Historical Society of Pomona Valley. Ricardo Vejar, easygoing and trustful, had lost Rancho San José de Abajo by foreclosure in 1864. A year or two later, it was purchased by Phillips, who proved to be an excellent manager, and in his hands and those of his descendants the great rancho prospered.

Pomona College, founded in 1887, held its first class on September 12, 1888, in a small cottage, the site of which is at the southwest corner of Fifth and White avenues in Pomona (SRL 289). Five months later, the college moved to Claremont. Dr. Cyrus Grandison Baldwin, president of Pomona College, organized the San Antonio Light and Power Company, which built in 1892 the first hydroelectric installation in California for long-distance transmission of alternating current at high voltage. A monument to this pioneer power plant (SRL 514) stands on the upper road in San Antonio Canyon northeast of Pomona, while the foundations of the plant can still be found on San Antonio Creek near the lower road. Pomona College is now one of the Associated Colleges of Claremont, the others being Scripps College for women (founded in 1926) and the coeducational Claremont Graduate School (1925), Claremont McKenna College (1946), Harvey Mudd College (1955), and Pitzer College (1963). The Claremont School of Theology and some special institutes are also affiliated with the association.

Rancho La Puente (La Puente, Hacienda Heights, Industry, Walnut)

On November 5, 1841, a group of 25 emigrants, recruited partly in Missouri and partly among the Americans in New Mexico, reached Los Angeles by way of the Gila and Colorado rivers. Like other early companies, this group was known by the names of its leaders, and history records it as the Rowland-Workman party. Upon their arrival in Los Angeles the two partners, William Workman and John Rowland, began almost immediately to look for a permanent home. Both had lived in New Mexico for more than ten years and were married to New Mexican women, and both had become Mexican citizens there. This entitled them to petition for grants of land in California, which they did in the

spring of 1842, receiving the land formally in 1845.

At first the two friends seem to have owned the great ranges of La Puente jointly, their herds sharing the unfenced pastures and their adobe dwelling houses standing less than a mile apart. Later, the land was formally divided, with Workman taking the western half and Rowland the eastern.

The Workman-Temple Home (SRL 874) at 15415 East Don Julian Road in the City of Industry is a striking example of historic preservation and of different periods of California living. In 1843 William Workman had a simple adobe house built for his family on his portion of the ranch. A later remodeling, before 1872, enlarged the house with two parallel arms and a central patio. By the 1870's, the Workman family had acquired considerable wealth and remodeled the adobe into "an English manor house." Unfortunately, the bank that Workman owned with his son-in-law, Francisco P. F. Temple, collapsed, and the family fortune went with it. The rancho became the property of financier Elias Jackson ("Lucky") Baldwin, and only the old homestead, the acreage immediately around the house, stayed with the Workman and Temple families.

New life came in 1917 when Walter P. Temple, Sr., grandson of William Workman, restored the family's fortune through oil and real estate investments. He and his wife, Laura Gonzalez, then set out to restore the homestead's grandeur. They had a Greek Revival mausoleum put up in El Campo Santo, site of an Indian rancheria from the previous century and of an Indian cemetery; the Workmans made it the first private cemetery in Los Angeles County, and brought the bodies of Pío Pico and his wife from a remote burial spot for entombment here. A new house, La Casa Nueva, was put up not far from the old house, this one exceptionally rich in the decorative arts. Fortune turned away from the Temples after the 1929 crash, and they were forced to sell the property on which so much care and money had been lavished. The homestead was used as a convalescent home and for other purposes.

The City of Industry was incorporated in 1957 to provide an ideal environment for manufacturing, distribution, and industrial facilities within its boundaries, and proved remarkably successful. Not wishing to neglect the historic past of the area, the city took steps that in 1974 resulted in the purchase of the Workman-Temple Homestead, La Casa Nueva, and El Campo Santo. The painstaking restoration is not yet complete, but already the site has attracted many visitors and is a much-visited Los Angeles County showplace.

John Rowland's adobe is long gone, but about 100 yards south of its site a two-story brick house built by him in 1855 still stands. It is located behind the buildings of the Hudson School District on Gale Avenue east of Hacienda Boulevard. At the rear of the stucco-covered brick house is its first kitchen, a separate adobe building. John Rowland is buried in the cemetery at the Workman place. Workman himself was laid to rest beside his partner, but his remains have now been placed in the mausoleum. The site of Rowland's original adobe house near the south bank of San Jose Creek is marked by two ash trees and an olive tree, planted by him around 1850.

Rancho La Merced (Montebello)

Rancho La Merced lay west of Rancho La Puente. It was originally granted to Doña Casilda Soto in 1846. In 1850 she sold the ranch and her adobe house to William Workman, who in 1851 gave it to his son-in-law, Francisco P. F. Temple, and Juan Matías Sánchez. The spot where the Temple adobe stood is near the corner of San Gabriel Boulevard and Durfee Avenue; it has vanished, as has the little settlement of Temple's Corners along the Rio Hondo. Upon Temple's death in 1888, the home tract at Temple's Corners became the property of his widow; this part of Rancho La Merced remained in the Temple family for many years, and escaped the grasp of "Lucky" Baldwin, who acquired much land in the area.

One spring day in 1914, nine-year-old Thomas Workman Temple II, a grandson of Francisco Temple, was looking for tall wild oats, which he used to snare lizards on the hillside across the Rio Hondo from his home at Temple's Corners. On the search he discovered an outcropping of natural gas in a pool of water on the property his father, Walter P. Temple, had purchased in 1912. Operations were begun there in 1917 by the Standard Oil Company. Thus was the famous Montebello oil field established.

On Lincoln Avenue near La Merced Avenue, about two miles southwest of the site of the home of Francisco Temple, stands a fine adobe mansion on a pleasant hill above the Rio Hondo. The older wing, facing the river, was erected by Casilda Soto in the late 1840's. The house was enlarged in the early 1850's by Juan Matías Sánchez, who built the wing facing the hills. Although elaborately remodeled within, some of it as recently as the 1970's, the Soto-Sánchez adobe retains some of its original exterior lines and character. Juan Matías Sánchez had owned 2,200 acres of excellent land about Mission Vieja, site of the first San Gabriel Mission, as well as the Potrero Grande and the Potrero de Felipe Lugo. His friendship for William Workman and Francisco Temple, however, caused him to sacrifice all his possessions in a heroic effort to save the honor of his friends. His last years were spent in poverty, while rich oil wells about his adobe made later owners wealthy and preserved the old adobe house.

First Discovery of Gold in California

The first discovery of gold in commercial quantities in California was made in 1842 by Francisco López at Placerita Canyon. The following year he found gold in San Feliciano Canyon. The story of the first discovery is as follows.

One day in March 1842, López rode into Placerita Canyon. While resting in the shade of an oak tree, he began to gather wild onions. He suddenly noticed some shining particles clinging to the roots of the plants. Picking up more of the roots, he found the same kind of pebbles on them. Later, in Los Angeles, he was informed that they were gold nuggets.

This discovery not only caused considerable excitement throughout the south but also brought numbers of prospectors from Sonora, Mexico. In November 1842, Don Abel Stearns sent the first California gold from the mines at Placerita to the U.S. Mint at Philadelphia. For many years thereafter he continued to send gold dust and nuggets from this region to Philadelphia.

Placerita Canyon State Park is located about four miles east of Newhall in the San Fernando Hills, and about 40 miles northwest of Los Angeles. In the vicinity of the old placers on the west side of the canyon proper, a boulder with a bronze plate was placed in 1930 by the Kiwanis Club and the Native Sons of the Golden West to mark the site of the first discovery of gold in California. Near the marker, the old oak tree under which López rested is still to be seen, below the level of the present main park road. It has been styled the "Oak of the Golden Dream" (SRL 168). Also in the park is the Walker Cabin, built by Frank Evans Walker around 1900. This tiny board-and-batt home housed twelve children and is now a small museum of local history.

Rancho Ciénega o Paso de la Tijera (Crenshaw District, Los Angeles)

There were many natural springs and marshlands (ciénegas) below the hills at Rancho Ciénega, and two narrow valleys between the Baldwin Hills formed a pass that to the imaginative Spaniards resembled a pair of open scissors (paso de la tijera). Thus originated the double name of the great Rancho Ciénega o Paso de la Tijera, granted to Vicente Sánchez, alcalde of Los Angeles, in 1843. Rancho Ciénega was a long day's journey into the country in those days, and Don Vicente's official duties caused him to live in Los Angeles. The vast ranges of his country estate were therefore mainly used for cattle grazing.

After Don Vicente's death, about 1850, his landholdings were partitioned among his heirs, and Tomás A. Sánchez, famous as sheriff of Los Angeles for nearly ten years, received Rancho Ciénega, while his sisters took the property on Calle de los Negros in Los Angeles.

Don Tomás married Maria Sepúlveda, who received a portion of Rancho San Rafael after Fernando Sepúlveda's death. Tomás Sánchez sold Rancho Ciénega and made his home on his wife's little estate at the present Glendale, where a handsome adobe, still standing, was built near the site of the original home.

"Lucky" Baldwin finally became the owner of Rancho Ciénega, and when the estate was settled after his death in 1909, this rancho was listed as one of the most valuable of all his extensive holdings. His luck has held, it seems, for this continues to be very valuable land, no matter how often it is subdivided.

When the Sunset Golf Corporation leased the estate from the Baldwin heirs in the 1920's, a few old adobes were still standing. One of these, at 3725 Don Felipe Drive, was used as the clubhouse for a golf course that no longer exists, and now serves as a women's club.

It was in this Crenshaw or Angeles Mesa district that the world's greatest athletes were housed during the Olympic Games in 1932. The Olympic village, including over 600 two-room dwellings, was built in the hills west of Crenshaw Boulevard; Olympiad Drive and Athenian Way are local street names. The Los Angeles Memorial Coliseum (SRL 960), built in Exposition Park in 1923, was enlarged for this international event.

The 1984 Summer Olympic games were also held in Los Angeles. Many events took place in the Coliseum, but there are now so many activities in an Olympic festival that even in so well-provided a city as Los Angeles they had to be dispersed around the metropolis, as far west as Lake Casitas in Ventura County and as far east as Chino in San Bernardino County.

Rancho Aguaje de Centinela (Inglewood)

Ygnacio Antonio Machado first settled on the Rancho Aguaje de Centinela in the mid-1830's, but did not receive a formal title until 1844. The next year, Machado traded his estate to Bruno Ábila (or Ávila) for a small tract of land with a house, corrals, and a vineyard in the Pueblo of Los Angeles. Today most of the pastures of the Centinela Rancho are covered by the thriving city of Inglewood.

The *aguaje* (water hole) of the Centinela was located in what is now Inglewood's Centinela Park. It was the principal water supply for early settlers, as it had been for Indian people before them. A drinking fountain and plaque (SRL 363) commemorate the Centinela Springs in the park below the pool.

Rancho Centinela had a varied history. Bruno Ávila lost the land in 1857 through foreclosure, and the title passed through several owners. In 1860 it was acquired by Sir Robert Burnett of Crathes Castle, Banchory, Scotland, who came to California in the 1850's, presumably to raise and sell sheep. He also acquired the divided lands of the neighboring Rancho Sausal Redondo. In time he accumulated nearly 25,000 acres, which he named the Centinela Ranch, an area today covered by eight cities and Los Angeles International Airport.

In 1864 Burnett married Matilda Josephine Murphy of New York and brought his bride to the refurbished Centinela adobe. While specializing in the raising of premium wool-producing sheep, Burnett also planted extensive orchards in the 1870's. His improvements, and the rising value of land, brought the baronet $140,000 in gold coin when he sold the ranch in 1885 to Canadian barrister Daniel Freeman. During the real estate boom of 1886–88, Freeman sold the heart of the ranch lands for one of the most spectacular new subdivisions of the era, the town of Inglewood. The community was famed as a center for the raising of poultry, and in the 1920's the world's largest chinchilla farm was started here by M. F. Chapman.

With the location of the aircraft industry in southern California during World War II, the agricultural phase of Inglewood's history neared its end. The United States Air Force initiated the Intercontinental Ballistic Missile Program in 1954 at the old St. John's Catholic School; a bronze plaque at the corner of Manchester Boulevard and Locust Street marks the site where the nation's space exploration program began with the development of the Atlas missile. Ygnacio Machado's Centinela ranch house at 7634 Midfield Avenue remains one of the most beautifully preserved of the smaller adobes of Los Angeles County. Its simple lines, early Victorian furnishings, and well-kept gardens reflect the life-style of the later Burnett and Freeman families. Nestled in the trees on the same grounds stand two other buildings, which the Historical Society of Centinela Valley operates.

The 1887 Centinela-Inglewood Land Company office was moved to the site in 1975; in this building Inglewood's first citizens purchased their lots during the great land boom. Complementing the adobe in style is the Centinela Valley Heritage and Research Center, built in 1980. When the 1889 Freeman-Howland mansion in Inglewood was razed in 1972, the Historical Society of Centinela Valley salvaged paneling, doors, stained glass, and other artifacts, which have been incorporated into the structure of the new center. All the buildings are open to the public.

Rancho Los Feliz (Griffith Park)

Rancho Los Feliz was granted to María Ygnacia Verdugo in 1843, but was occupied by her as early as 1841. The United States government issued a patent in her name for 6,647 acres. The rancho passed successively through the hands of Antonio Coronel, pioneer of Los Angeles; James Lick, a San Francisco pioneer and the founder of Lick Observatory; and Colonel Griffith Jenkins Griffith, who in 1898 deeded 3,015 acres of the rancho to the city of Los Angeles. This is now Griffith Park, the largest urban park in California. The Los Feliz adobe still stands at 4730 Crystal Springs Drive, within the park.

Rancho Santa Anita (Arcadia, Monrovia)

Rancho Santa Anita, comprising 13,319 acres, was granted to Hugo Reid in 1845. For a time it was in the hands of William Wolfskill, but in 1872 his son, Lewis Wolfskill, sold it to H. Newmark and Company for $85,000. In 1875 Elias Jackson ("Lucky") Baldwin, San Francisco mining operator and horseman, purchased it for three times the amount paid by Newmark. Baldwin had made millions, it was said, in the Ophir Mines of Nevada. He soon moved from San Francisco into the ranch house at Santa Anita. Here he continued to win fortunes not only by developing a world-famous breed of racing horses but also by acquiring and selling great landed estates.

Baldwin was a lover of trees as well as of horses. All the roads within his rancho were lined with trees, and many of the eucalyptus trees he planted still can be seen along parts of Huntington Drive and Santa Anita Avenue.

The heart of the Baldwin estate is now the Los Angeles State and County Arboretum at Arcadia. Here, surrounded by beautiful trees, flowers, and lakes, stands the original Hugo Reid adobe (SRL 368), built in 1839 and later occupied by Baldwin as his home. It was restored by the state and dedicated in 1961. The "Queen Anne Cottage" (SRL 367) was built by Baldwin in 1881 as a guest house, and has been restored. Still another landmark is Baldwin's old carriage house. The name of the rancho is continued in Santa Anita Race Track, which adjoins the arboretum.

The neo-Mediterranean home of Upton Sinclair has been registered as a National Historic Landmark. The famed social critic and political writer, an unsuccessful candidate for governor of California in 1934, moved into this house in 1942. It stands at 464 North Myrtle Avenue in Monrovia.

Landmarks of the Mexican War

The Battle of San Gabriel occurred on January 8, 1847, ten miles southeast of Los Angeles at a place on the San Gabriel River (now Rio Hondo) in the southern part of the present city of Montebello. There was quicksand at this point and a high bluff opposite the ford, making passage of the stream difficult. Here the Californians, with 500 or 600 men under command of General José Flores, held the bluff, while the Americans under Commodore Robert F. Stockton and General Stephen W. Kearny, with 600 men, had the difficult task of fording the river with their heavy artillery, under enemy fire. Within an hour and a half, however, the feat was accomplished and the Californians were retiring toward Los Angeles. A monument has been erected at the corner of Washington Boulevard and Bluff Road in Montebello (SRL 385).

On January 9 the two forces met again at La Mesa, the site of the present Union Stockyards in the great central manufacturing district of Los Angeles. La Mesa was of slight importance in itself, merely confirming the course of events at San Gabriel. Like all the so-called "battles" of the American occupation, it amounted to little more than a skirmish. The Californians, realizing the hopelessness of resistance, soon withdrew to Rancho San Pasqual, where their final decision to surrender was made. Camping that night on the outskirts of Los Angeles, Stockton and Kearny marched to the plaza on the following day, the city having already surrendered. With this action, control passed forever from the hands of Mexico.

With Kearny and Stockton in control of Los Angeles and Frémont occupying the San Fernando Valley, the Californians offered no further resistance. Frémont at once sent Jesús Pico to persuade the Californians to lay down their arms, which they agreed to do. Ready to make peace if favorable terms were arranged, the two parties met on January 13, 1847, at the Cahuenga adobe, about a mile from the entrance to Cahuenga Pass. Here Andrés Pico and Frémont signed the Cahuenga Capitulation Treaty, which ended hostilities throughout California.

The site of the old treaty adobe (SRL 151) has been preserved by the city of Los Angeles as a memorial park called "Campo de Cahuenga." It is at 3919 Lankershim Boulevard in North Hollywood, directly across from Universal Studios. Not far from the site, below Lookout Mountain, at a place called Los Alamos, a skirmish took place on February 20–21, 1845, between a band of rebel Californians, under José Castro and Juan Bautista Alvarado, and Governor Manuel Micheltorena's *cholo* army. The governor was forced to retreat to Rancho Los Feliz, where he surrendered, and Pío Pico was made governor in his stead.

The site of Frémont's headquarters in Los Angeles in January 1847 was at the southeast corner of Aliso and Los Angeles streets. There he established himself in the Alexander Bell adobe, after Commodore Stockton had appointed him military governor of the territory on January 19, an office he held for 50 days. The old Bell adobe was torn down long ago, and the site is occupied by a modern public building.

When Stockton and Kearny entered Los Angeles on January 10, 1847, after the Battle of La Mesa, their troops, numbering 600 men in all, were stationed on a hill west of the plaza. On January 11, Frémont and his men came down from Monterey, via Cahuenga Pass, and for several weeks 1,000 American soldiers were quartered on the hill. At this time, work was begun on a temporary fort, but it was never completed. Later, in the summer of 1847, Fort Moore (named for Captain B. D. Moore, killed in the Battle of San Pasqual) was erected on the same spot overlooking the pueblo. Nothing of the old fort remains today, and much of Fort Moore Hill was leveled for the construction of the Hollywood Freeway. What remains of the hill is occupied by the Los Angeles City Board of Education headquarters. At the base the Pioneer Memorial from the 1950's honors the troops "who helped win the Southwest."

El Monte

The "Old Spanish Trail" into California, followed by William Wolfskill in 1830–31, has been proved "to be neither old nor strictly Spanish." The trail was first traversed by a New Mexican, Antonio Armijo, in 1829–30, although his route before reaching California varied considerably from that followed by Wolfskill the following year. Later, it came to be known also as the Santa Fe Trail and was used by many early American pioneers who came into California by the southern route. In the late 1840's and early 1850's this trail, as far as Salt Lake, Utah, was also known as the Mormon Trail. For many of the covered-wagon emigrants, El Monte became the end of the trail, and here on the banks of the San Gabriel River, where natural springs made farming easy and where the land remained unappropriated by Spanish or Mexican grants, they made their homes. At first El Monte was only a place to camp, but as early as 1849 Ira Thompson had established a stage station at a place called "Willow Grove." By 1852 the Dodson and Ryan families had arrived by ox team and Dodson had erected the first house in El Monte, a crude adobe of "sticks and mud." Soon other emigrants arrived, and permanent homes were established in this green oasis. SRL 975 in Pioneer Park, 3535 Santa Anita Avenue, commemorates the first southern California settlement by immigrants from the United States.

In 1852 the first schoolhouse was erected on a site now in the bed of the San Gabriel River, the flood of 1909 having washed out a new channel farther east. The building had previously been removed to what is now 3436 Granada Avenue, where it still stands, remodeled and used as a private house. John Prior, a Baptist minister, organized the first Protestant evangelical church in southern California in this old schoolhouse in 1853. The first church building was not erected until the 1860's.

Glendora

The Glendora Bougainvillea (SRL 912) is believed to be the largest growth of the vines in the continental United States. Planting was done by Ruben Hamlin between 1900 and 1903. It originally bordered an orange grove, which has been subdivided. The vines are at the corner of East Bennett Avenue and North Minnesota Avenue.

Angeles National Forest

Angeles National Forest in the San Gabriel Mountains of Los Angeles and San Bernardino counties was the first national forest in California and the second in the United States. President Benjamin Harrison set the area aside on December 20, 1892, and it was first called San Gabriel Timberland Reserve. In 1907 it became San Gabriel National Forest, and the following year it acquired its present name. The most scenic road in the forest is the Angeles Crest Highway from La Canada to Big Pines. A historical monument commemorating the early forest preserve stands on this highway. The state marker (SRL 717) is at Angeles National Forest Headquarters at 1015 North Lake Avenue in Pasadena.

The side road to Mount Wilson and the observatory branches from the Angeles Crest Highway at the Red Box ranger station. Just south of Red Box a dirt road leads east into the canyon of the West Fork of the San Gabriel River. About six miles along this road is "Old Short Cut" (SRL 632), the oldest building in the Angeles National Forest, erected in 1900. The log structure was the original West Fork ranger station and is said to be the first United States Forest Service ranger station in the nation built with government funds. It takes its name from the Short Cut Canyon Trail, on which it is one of the main stopping points.

Tujunga is a community along Foothill Boulevard near the boundary of Angeles National Forest. It was once an incorporated city but is now a part of the city of Los Angeles. Bolton Hall, a unique building of native stone built in 1913 and at one time the Tujunga city hall, now houses the Little Landers Museum, devoted to the history of the region, at 10110 Commerce Avenue. The Little Landers were original settlers who had small holdings of property.

Hollywood and Motion Pictures

Hollywood, a district of Los Angeles, became "the glamor capital of the world" when the motion picture industry located and flourished there. The first feature-length motion picture made in Hollywood was *The Squaw Man*, filmed in 1913–14 by Cecil B. DeMille, Samuel Goldwyn, and Jesse Lasky, Sr. The studio in which the picture was made was a barn at the corner of Selma Avenue and Vine Street. In 1927 the historic barn (SRL 554) was moved to the Paramount Studio lot and in 1983 to the 2100 block of Highland Avenue, across from Hollywood Bowl. The barn is now the Hollywood Studio Museum and preserves some of the artifacts connected with DeMille.

Barnsdall Park, on Olive Hill at 4800 Hollywood Boulevard, is owned by the city of Los Angeles and is a major cultural center. Here stands Hollyhock House, the first California residence designed by Frank Lloyd Wright. It was built for Aline Barnsdall in 1918–20. The Arts and Crafts Building, by the same architect, was constructed about the same time. In 1927 Miss Barnsdall deeded her property to the city, and in 1954 Wright was engaged to design another building, the Municipal Gallery. Hollyhock House, the Arts and Crafts Building, and the park itself have been declared historic-cultural monuments by the Cultural Heritage Board.

The Griffith Ranch (SRL 716), now privately owned, was the home of the pioneer filmmaker David W. Griffith and the locale of many of his pictures. A marker stands one and one-half miles east of San Fernando at Foothill Boulevard and Vaughn Street.

A major Los Angeles tourist attraction for many years has been bus tours through districts such as Beverly Hills and Bel-Air to see the homes of the film stars. Three such homes have now been set aside as public parks.

The Harold Lloyd Estate, "Greenacres," is at 1740 Green Acres Place in Beverly Hills. At the peak of his career in 1928, Lloyd began construction of a lavish 44-room mansion on the estate he named "Greenacres." This and the beautifully landscaped grounds (SRL 961) were left to the city on Lloyd's death in 1971.

The William S. Hart Ranch, at San Fernando Road and Newhall Avenue in Newhall, is now a Los Angeles County Park. Here stand the original ranch house, built about 1910 by an earlier owner, and the mansion completed by the cowboy actor in 1928. Both are open to the public, as are the extensive grounds.

Will Rogers State Historic Park, at 14253 Sunset Boulevard in Pacific Palisades, includes the home built by the famed humorist in the 1920's. The 190-acre park has extensive hiking trails into the Santa Monica Mountains.

In 1978, Congress set aside 153,000 acres of land for the Santa Monica Mountains National Recreational Area, which surrounds the Will Rogers Park.

Landmarks of the Los Angeles County Coast

Point Dume (SRL 965) was named by the English explorer Captain George Vancouver on November 24, 1793, during his second voyage to California. He named it in honor of Father Francisco Dumetz, of Mission San Buenaventura. The marker is located at Point Dume State Beach at the corner of Cliffside Drive and Birdview Avenue in Malibu.

Frederick and May Rindge acquired the Malibu Ranchero in 1881, and on this land their daughter Rhonda Adamson built an exquisite beach home (SRL 966) in 1929; it is located on Malibu Lagoon State Beach at 23200 West Pacific Coast Highway. An adjoining museum traces some of the Malibu coast's history. Both are open to the public on a limited basis.

The J. Paul Getty Museum at 17985 West Pacific Coast Highway in Malibu was opened to the public in 1974. It is a replica of the Villa of the Papyri in Herculaneum, Italy, which was buried by the lava from the eruption of Mount Vesuvius in 79 A.D. The delightful museum contains a great deal of Greek and Roman art and many treasures of post-Renaissance Europe and is a major cultural resource for the state.

From 1872 to 1890 the Southern Pacific Railroad enjoyed a virtual monopoly on all shipping to and from Los Angeles through the port of San Pedro. As rival rail lines were opened, Collis P. Huntington, president of the Southern Pacific, seeing his power and profits dwindling, put into operation in 1892 a plan to make Santa Monica, rather than San Pedro, the main deep-water harbor for Los Angeles. At that time, the Southern Pacific was engaged in an extensive building program to improve the San Pedro facilities. Huntington directed that that program be abandoned and that construction begin immediately on Port Los Angeles, as he called it, at Santa Monica. The Long Wharf there was completed in 1893. Controversy raged for almost a decade over the various advantages and disadvantages of San Pedro and Port Los Angeles. After Huntington's death in 1900, the Southern Pacific lost interest in the new port and ultimately leased the wharf to an electric trolley line. By 1920 the wharf had been completely dismantled. The site of Port Los Angeles (SRL 881) has been marked at 15100 West Pacific Coast Highway in Will Rogers Beach State Park in Pacific Palisades. San Pedro remains the harbor for the city of Los Angeles to this day.

William Wrigley, owner of Santa Catalina island, built the SS *Catalina* to serve the island as a passenger ferry. It was in operation between 1924 and 1976, when it was sold to foreign interests. A marker (SRL 894) commemorates the ship at the Catalina Island museum on the ground floor of the casino at the west end of Avalon Bay, Santa Catalina Island.

Other Landmarks in the City of Los Angeles

The first commercial orange grove in California was planted in 1857 by William Wolfskill on his ranch near the Pueblo of Los Angeles. For a number of years it was the largest citrus grove in the United States and yielded very heavy crops. In 1885 the owners of the Wolfskill Ranch donated to the Southern Pacific Railroad the site for the Arcade depot, no longer in existence, at Fifth Street and Central Avenue. Soon after, the city rapidly expanding, the remainder of the famous orchard was sold and subdivided.

The site of the Coronel ranch house, where Helen Hunt Jackson was hospitably entertained by Antonio Coronel in the winter of 1881–82, and where she worked on her novel *Ramona*, is at Seventh and Alameda Streets.

In April 1950 an official state marker was placed on Temple Street at the Federal Building to commemorate the centennial of the establishment of the Los Angeles post office. Two markers have been placed on the bank building at Main and Commercial streets. One honors southern California's first newspaper, the *Los Angeles Star* (SRL 789), founded on May 17, 1851. The newspaper office stood at Los Angeles Street and the Santa Ana Freeway, and the plaque has been placed nearby on the Commercial Street side of the bank. The other marker indicates the site of the Bella Union Hotel (SRL 656), Los Angeles' pioneer hostelry, where the first Butterfield stage arrived from St. Louis on October 7, 1858. The Butterfield Overland Mail Company soon acquired the property at 145 South Spring Street and built

there its Los Angeles station (SRL 744), one of the best equipped on the route. A plaque marks the site.

The Bunker Hill district, just west of the Civic Center, was once one of the most fashionable parts of Los Angeles. Thoroughgoing razing to make way for freeways has virtually destroyed both the hill and the residential area. One old house, the Samuel C. Foy residence, was moved to new ground; it is now at 631 South Witmer Street, divided into offices.

The Bradbury Building at 304 South Broadway, another historic-cultural monument, is Los Angeles' most interesting old business building. The exterior of the five-story structure, built in 1893, is undistinguished, but the interior is unique, with a covered court, open corridors, ornamental rails, and exposed elevator cages.

The original building of the University of Southern California (SRL 536), opened in 1880, was moved in 1956 to Childs Way between Hoover Boulevard and University Avenue at the south end of the campus; it is now the Alumni House. In the same part of Los Angeles is the former mansion of oil magnate Edward L. Doheny, at 8 Chester Place, now part of the campus of Mount St. Mary's College. It was built in 1899–1900 and acquired by Doheny in 1901. A little-known fact is that Los Angeles was the birthplace of Adlai E. Stevenson, governor of Illinois, twice Democratic candidate for the presidency, and ambassador to the United Nations. He was born on February 5, 1900, at 2639 Monmouth Avenue, while his father was employed by the *Los Angeles Examiner*. The Doheny mansion and the Stevenson birthplace have been declared historic-cultural monuments by the Cultural Heritage Board.

The same board has officially recognized several old buildings at Sawtelle, the Veterans Administration Center in West Los Angeles, originally the Pacific branch of the National Home for Disabled Volunteer Soldiers. Among the oldest structures is the chapel, built about 1888.

The first organized community effort by the pioneer Jewish settlers of Los Angeles was the acquisition of a sacred burial ground from the city council in 1855. The site (SRL 822) is near Lilac Terrace and Lookout Drive in the Chavez Ravine area.

Nearby, at 1700 Stadium Way, is the Naval and Marine Corps Reserve Center (SRL 972), built in 1938–41; it was then the world's largest enclosed structure without walls. It is the largest and second oldest Navy reserve center in the United States and has been used for many movie and television films. The building was carefully restored after a devastating fire in 1984 and is still an important facility.

In 1887 the State Board of Forestry established the

first experimental forestry station in the United States in Rustic Canyon, Los Angeles. The station was operated by the board until 1893 and by the University of California until 1923. The site of the old Santa Monica Forestry Station (SRL 840) is near the intersection of Latimer and Hilltree roads in Los Angeles.

La Casa de Adobe, at 4605 North Figueroa Street, part of the Southwest Museum, is a faithful and charming replica of an early California home. Built of adobe around a patio planted exclusively with shrubs and plants grown in early California gardens, it is furnished with genuine antiques of the period, most of which were provided by Spanish and American pioneer families. It is open to the public.

El Alisal ("the place of the sycamore") was the home of Charles Fletcher Lummis from 1897 to his death in 1928. "Don Carlos" Lummis wrote and lectured vividly on the Southwest, of which he was a lifelong student. From 1895 to 1910 he edited *The Land of Sunshine*, later changed to *Out West*, a magazine extolling the virtues of his adopted home. In 1894 he founded the Landmarks Club, which was largely responsible for the preservation of the old California missions at the turn of the century, and in 1902 he established the Sequoya League, which had as its goal "to make better Indians by treating them better." He and others founded the Southwest Museum in 1907, now located at 234 Museum Drive in the Highland Park section of Los Angeles, to house the collection of the Southwest Society of the Archaeological Institute of America. He was Los Angeles city librarian from 1905 to 1910. He died at El Alisal on November 25, 1928. This tribute was paid to him: "He was Southern California—he was the Great Southwest."

With his own hands, Lummis built his home of reinforced concrete, faced with river stones found on the site. Building took place from 1897 to 1910 around a giant sycamore. The original sycamores of this Sycamore Grove have been replaced with new ones. El Alisal (SRL 531) is located at 200 East Avenue 43, near the Pasadena Freeway, and is open to the public. It is the headquarters of the Historical Society of Southern California.

At 1765 East 107th Street in the Watts district of Los Angeles is one of California's most unusual landmarks, the Watts Towers. The three spires, highest of which is 104 feet, were the work of one man from 1921 to 1954. Simon Rodia, an Italian immigrant, using only basic tools, constructed what has been called "a paramount achievement of twentieth-century folk art" of steel rods, wire mesh, seashells, broken dishes and bottles, and cement. He intended it as a tribute to his adopted land. In 1959 the towers were threatened with demolition,

The Watts Towers, Los Angeles

but a severe stress test proved their solidity and safety, and the city allowed them to remain. Since then, they have been declared a historic-cultural monument by the Cultural Heritage Board and are open to the public. Rodia died in obscurity in Martinez in 1965 at the age of 90.

The predominantly black Watts area was also the site of one of the first major urban riots of the 1960's. On August 11, 1965, an angry crowd gathered as California Highway Patrol officers arrested Marquette Frye, a young black man, on a drunk driving charge. After Frye was taken away, some members of the crowd began throwing rocks and bricks. Violence escalated over the next four days to fire-bombing, looting, and gunfire. By the time the National Guard restored order on August 15, 35 people had been killed, almost 1,000 seriously wounded, and more than 4,000 arrested. Damage in the 50-square-mile area was estimated at some $46 million.

Other museums of California history in the Los Angeles area are the California Afro-American Museum at 600 State Drive in Exposition Park; the California Historical Society Museum at 6300 Wilshire Boulevard; the California State Museum of Science and Industry at 700 State Drive; Heritage Square Museum at 2612 Main Street in Santa Monica; the Los Angeles Maritime Museum at Berth 84, Harbor Boulevard at Sixth Street in San Pedro; and the Wells Fargo History Museum at 444 South Flower Street.

Landmarks of Northern Los Angeles County

Early in the twentieth century the city of Los Angeles acquired the water rights to the Owens Valley in Inyo County some 250 miles to the north. Under the direction of city engineer William Mulholland, an aqueduct was begun in 1905 and completed in 1913. The terminus of the aqueduct is about four miles north of San Fernando beside I-5. It is called The Cascades (SRL 653), and here water from the eastern slope of the Sierra Nevada may be seen coursing into reservoirs for the use of the metropolis. The Western Hotel in Lancaster was one place where crews were housed during the construction of the aqueduct. It was built in 1874 and still stands at 557 West Lancaster Boulevard in the Antelope Valley town (SRL 658). The St. Francis Dam was built in 1926 as part of the same water project. Two years later, on March 12, 1928, the 185-foot-high dam broke, sending a wall of water down San Francisquito Creek and the valley of the Santa Clara River. Hundreds of homes were washed away, and nearly 500 persons were killed in one of California's worst disasters. Many had been asleep, for it was after midnight. The dam was not rebuilt. A heap of rubble marks the site (SRL 919), on the west side of the road at 32300 San Francisquito Canyon Road outside Saugus.

On the east side of the Sierra Highway, about a mile north of its junction with I-5 near Newhall, is a parking area with several historical markers. Unfortunately, they have been vandalized and are nearly illegible. John C. Frémont went this way in January 1847 on his way from Santa Barbara to Los Angeles, and the crossing of the mountains became known as Frémont Pass. In 1859 General Edward F. Beale and his men cut 50 feet of rock and earth from the gap to enable wagons to make the crossing more easily. One may still see Beale's Cut by hiking about a quarter of a mile east and north of the parking area, across a dry wash. Modern engineers consider it a remarkable feat of pioneer engineering. Frémont Pass was replaced by the Newhall Tunnel, directly west, and this, in turn, has been superseded by the present giant cut of the Antelope Valley Freeway (SR 14).

Today I-5 makes a smooth crossing of the high mountains between the Los Angeles basin and the San Joa-

The First Commercial Oil Refinery, Newhall

quin Valley, but historically the Ridge Route has been a difficult one—far too steep for the railroads, and very taxing for motor vehicles. The first Ridge Route in 1915 had 48 miles of twisting, turning pavement between Castaic and the Grapevine in Kern County. SR 99 superseded it in 1933. From time to time the motorist can see parts of the old road in driving over "The Ridge" today.

Several historic places are located in the vicinity of Newhall, in addition to the already-described "Oak of the Golden Dream" and the William S. Hart Ranch. On the Sierra Highway is the site of Lyons Station (SRL 688), an old stage stop. A small community grew up here in the 1860's; the pioneer cemetery has been expanded into Eternal Valley Memorial Park. The discovery well of the Newhall oil field, CSO-4 or Pico 4, is located in Pico Canyon west of Newhall beyond I-5 (SRL 516). It was spudded early in 1876, completed at 300 feet in September of the same year, and deepened to 600 feet still later in 1876, at which time it produced 150 barrels a day. It is the oldest continuously producing oil well in the world. The oldest oil refinery in the world and the first commercial one in California, also built in 1876, is on Pine Street just off the San Fernando Road (SRL 172).

Farther down Pico Canyon is Mentryville (SRL 516.2), a town formed in the 1880's to support men working in the nearby oil fields and the Star Oil Refinery. The home of founder Charles A. Mentry still stands, along with a barn and a schoolhouse from 1885, but they are on private property and not open to the public.

The site of Lang Station is at Lang Station Road adjacent to the Southern Pacific tracks, ten miles east of Saugus and at the Soledad Canyon exit of SR 14 (SRL 590). Here was driven the "last spike" that united the two sections of the railroad, one coming north from Los Angeles and one coming south from San Francisco over Tehachapi Pass. With Crocker, Huntington, Stanford, and other officials in attendance, the last spike was driven on September 5, 1876, ending the period of isolation that had kept Los Angeles a sleepy and unprogressive town and ushering in the new era in which it would become one of the great cities of the world. The old railroad station has been moved to Newhall, where it is adjacent to William S. Hart Park. It is the headquarters and museum for the Santa Clarita Valley Historical Society, and is open to the public on a regular basis.

The Newhall Chamber of Commerce is housed in a charming frame house at Market and Walnut streets that goes back to 1889.

Robbers' Roost, better known as Vasquez Rocks, is an interesting geologic formation on a high ridge between Soledad and Mint canyons, northeast of Land and west of Acton. It is said that this was one of the hiding places of Tiburcio Vásquez, the most feared of all the outlaws of coastal California during the 1860's and early 1870's. He was captured in the Santa Monica foothills and taken to San Jose, where he was tried, convicted, and executed in 1875. The Vasquez Rocks form a part of the great San Andreas Fault, which extends through California from the Mendocino coast to the Imperial Valley. The disaster of 1906 in San Francisco and elsewhere, like many other earthquakes in California, was caused by this fault system.

Rancho San Francisco (SRL 556), comprising 48,612 acres, was granted to Antonio del Valle in 1839. The marker stands near the junction of I-5 and SR 126, half a mile north of the site of the old rancho headquarters in Valencia. William Lewis Manly and John Rogers obtained supplies here in 1850, whereupon they returned to Death Valley to rescue their starving comrades. Rancho Camulos, to the west in Ventura County, is part of Rancho San Francisco, and Del Valle's beautiful adobe home is still there.

Several homes were built by Martín Ruiz and his sons in the Cañon del Buque, erroneously called "Bouquet Canyon" by General Beale and other early topographers, whose mistake persists on modern maps and road signs. It was in this region that Francisco ("Chico") López, nephew of the Francisco López who discovered gold in Placerita Canyon, pastured his cattle during the 1840's. Later, Francisco Chari, one of his herdsmen, took up land here. Chari was a French sailor whom the Californians nicknamed "El Buque" ("the ship") because of his many tales of the sea and of the ships in which he had sailed.

An old adobe stage station stood into the 1960's at 38839 San Francisquito Canyon Road, about two miles west of Green Valley. It has been torn down, but a later two-story adobe stands next to the site and is occupied. The older building is believed to have been in use at the time the Butterfield stage line passed this way from 1858 to 1861.

On SR 138 in Antelope Valley is a small post office called Llano. It preserves the name of an ill-fated socialistic colony, Llano del Rio, which existed in the area from 1914 to 1918. The founder was Job Harriman, unsuccessful candidate for mayor of Los Angeles in 1910. He was associated with Clarence Darrow in the defense of the brothers James B. and John J. McNamara, arrested for the bombing of the *Los Angeles Times* building on October 1, 1910, during a tense period in the organization of labor. Harriman could well have been elected mayor if the McNamaras had been acquitted, but the brothers unexpectedly changed their pleas to guilty, and Harriman's political career was over. The desert colony he founded in 1914 moved to Louisiana four years later because of an insufficient water supply at the Antelope Valley site. A few ruins, notably the stone pillars and chimneys of the colony's hotel, and two large cisterns stand along the highway half a mile west of the Llano post office.

Another utopian colony, this one with a religious basis, was located in Los Angeles County about the same time. Pisgah Grande was founded by Finis E. Yoakum in the mountains northwest of Chatsworth, very close to the Ventura County line. A number of substantial brick buildings were erected, some of which are still standing. Las Llajas Canyon road and its private extension (with locked gate) lead from Santa Susana to the site of the settlement.

La Casa del Rancho La Liebre stands on property of the Tejón Ranch Company in the northwestern corner of Los Angeles County. It is located about one-half mile south of SR 138 at a point about ten miles east of its junction with I-5 near Gorman. It stands on the floor of a small canyon known as the Cañon de las Osas ("canyon of the she-bears"). The adobe, which was built by General Edward Beale after he acquired the property in 1855, was the headquarters for his Rancho La Liebre ("ranch of the jack rabbit"), 48,800 acres, a part of his vast estate composed of several ranchos and extending north well into Kern County. The house is strong and commodious, suggestive of the efficiency and thoroughness of its builder, and is said to have been his home for two or three years while he was Surveyor General. This region was another of the haunts of Tiburcio Vásquez.

Madera County

Madera County was organized from a part of Fresno County in 1893. Madera is Spanish for "wood" or "timber." It was given the same name as its principal town, Madera, which was made the county seat.

Old Trails

It is unlikely that many of the early Spanish expeditions entered the confines of Madera County, and no Spanish settlements were ever made there. This isolation was due, first of all, to the fact that it was practically impossible to penetrate the tulares from the west or to cross the sloughs that covered the whole central portion of the San Joaquin Valley at high water. In addition to this general inaccessibility, the streams throughout the area of the county were little more than dry, sandy washes except during and immediately following a heavy rainfall. Furthermore, the water holes along the foothills of Madera County were few compared with the broad, perennial streams to the north and south. For many years these conditions repelled both exploration and settlement.

This impenetrable barrier is described by F. F. Latta: "Between Martinez on the north and San Emigdio, two hundred and fifty miles to the south, there were only two places where the San Joaquin Valley could be crossed from east to west except at time of low water. Throughout the course of the San Joaquin River and bordering the lakes to the south was an impenetrable sea of tule, sloughs, mud flats, and water, which, until as late as 1880, was passable only at these same places. When Tulare Lake was below the extreme high water mark, the sand ridge which crossed it from east to west formed a bridge over which we know the Spanish crossed. The other point at which they were able to cross during time of high water was at the head of Fresno Slough near the present town of Tranquillity."

There is evidence, however, that the Pico expedition to the San Joaquin and Kings rivers in 1825–26 entered Madera County, crossing the rivers on tule rafts. Monte Redondo, a large grove of cottonwood trees near the Fresno River about seven miles west of Madera, seems to have been known to people on the coast as early as 1825.

Jedediah Strong Smith passed through what is now Madera County in 1827 and again in 1828. He was soon followed by Hudson's Bay Company trappers and later by Ewing Young, Kit Carson, and other Americans, who followed the trail of the beaver along the numerous streams that come down from the High Sierra on the eastern side of the valley.

The first definite record that we have of a trail across Madera County is that left by John C. Frémont on April 4–6, 1844. By means of rafts the party ferried Bear Creek (in Merced County) and then proceeded southward, their progress being greatly impeded by the numerous sloughs of this section. Continuing up the San Joaquin River, they passed "elk . . . running in bands over the prairie, and . . . along the left bank . . . immense droves of wild horses." Camp was made on the San Joaquin River on the 4th and 5th. On the 6th the party crossed the San Joaquin at Gravelly Ford, west of where SR 145 today crosses the river.

The Millerton or Stockton–Los Angeles Road, the only north and south route that passed through Madera County during the 1850's and 1860's, ran along the base of the foothills, crossing the Chowchilla River at the Home Ranch a little west of where the Merced-Mariposa county line intersects the Mariposa-Madera county line. The San Joaquin River was crossed at Millerton by means of the Converse Ferry, which fell into disuse after the building of the railroad.

Most of the miners at Coarsegold and other mining centers in Madera County migrated south from Mariposa County. Others came from Gilroy via Pacheco Pass, crossed the San Joaquin River just south of the mouth of the Fresno River, and from there proceeded to the Sierra Nevada mines. Alexis Godey, famous plainsman and guide to Frémont, operated a ferry at this point for a short time during the early 1850's.

In the late 1870's a stage road from Madera to the Yosemite Valley was constructed, passing through Bates Station, Kelshaw Corners, Coarsegold, Fresno Flats, Fish Camp, and Clark's Station (Wawona).

The Madera and Mammoth Trail is also known as the French Trail after its promoter, John French, who sought a better route to his mining interests in the Mammoth area. Biweekly trips from Fresno Flats (Oakhurst) to Mammoth City were started about 1880; the travelers were met at the stagecoach and continued the trip to Mammoth by saddle train. The French Trail proper began at the ranch of Jesse B. Ross, who settled there about 1858. Between 1910 and 1930 the property was owned by Samuel L. Hogue and has continued to be known locally as the Hogue Ranch, still privately owned. It is located on Mammoth Pool Road (Road 225), about four miles southeast of North Fork. The log house built by Jesse Ross in 1860 still stands. The property is famous for the apple orchards planted by each successive group of owners. A good road from North Fork now follows the course of the French Trail past the Hogue Ranch (elevation 4,500 feet) and for many miles beyond.

About four miles southeast of the Hogue Ranch, on Road 225, a marker indicates the geographical center of the state of California.

Historic Indian Locations in Madera County

About ten miles northeast of Madera on the River Road is the Adobe Ranch, the site of the old Fresno Indian Reservation established in the early 1850's. This was briefly in existence in the years when the presence of gold miners in the Sierra foothills caused great resentment among the local Indian tribes, who were for some time at war with the newcomers.

Wassama State Historic Park consists of several acres of land on SR 49 at the north edge of the town of Ahwahnee. An Indian roundhouse was built here in 1893; subsequently burned, it was rebuilt by Miwok tribesmen in 1901. After many years of use, the house collapsed in 1978, the year in which the State Department of Parks and Recreation acquired the property. The newly reconstructed roundhouse was dedicated in 1985. The Indian school nearby is a visitors' center. A twenty-hole grinding rock is on display. The area remains an Indian communal and religious center.

The Sierra Mono Museum at North Fork is entirely operated by Mono Indians and is dedicated to the preservation of their heritage and culture; it is located where Roads 225, 228, and 274 converge in the middle of the village.

The Savage Monument

Major James D. Savage arrived in California in 1846 and became active in the southern mines, where he operated at least four trading posts between 1848 and 1852. The first (SRL 527) was on the South Fork of the Merced River in Mariposa County; this was abandoned when war began with the Yosemite Indians in 1850. A second post was established at the mouth of Agua Fria Creek, near the site of Buckeye, while a branch station was started on the Fresno River near Fresno Flats, now Oakhurst. The last post of Major Savage was near Fresno Crossing.

Savage was a colorful figure with a remarkable relationship with the Indians—tradition gives him as many as 33 concubines—and he became a local leader during the troubles known as the Mariposa War in 1851. Commissioned by the state to pacify warlike Indians in the foothills, he pursued them into the Yosemite Valley, thus becoming the second white leader (after Joseph Reddeford Walker and his party) to visit the scenic valley. It was partly because of his efforts that the Mariposa War was ended by a treaty in 1851. Plans to settle recalcitrant Indians on the Fresno Reservation were largely ineffectual, however, and that institution ceased to exist in 1859. Meanwhile, Savage had been instrumental in the establishment of the new government of Tulare County in 1852; later that year, he was killed in a quarrel with a law-enforcement official whom he accused of attacking innocent Indians. A shaft of Vermont granite was placed above his gravesite at Fresno Crossing; the marker and Savage's remains were removed when the site was inundated in 1971 by the creation of Hidden Dam and Hensley Lake. The restored monument now overlooks the eastern shore of the Lake, about eighteen miles northeast of Madera.

A Bit of the Mother Lode

Extending from the northwest to the southeast throughout Madera County, the Mother Lode is marked by the shafts and tunnels of old mines and the sites of one-time mining camps. Before the quartz ledges were opened up in the 1870's and 1880's, however, placer mining began. As early as 1849 settlements sprang up in flats and ravines and along the bars of the San Joaquin and Fresno rivers.

Among the early prosperous placer-mining camps, Coarsegold (at first known as Texas Flat) was the largest in Madera County. There in 1849 five Texans found diggings on the creek where sand yielded particles of gold so coarse that the stream was named Coarsegold Creek. Many fortunes were taken from the surrounding hills, and the settlement grew rapidly.

Other placer-mining centers quickly developed: Grub Gulch, six miles northwest, and Fresno Flats (now Oakhurst), seven miles northeast of Coarsegold; Fine Gold, about six miles southeast near Mountain View Peak; Temperance Flat, on the San Joaquin River four miles east of Fine Gold Gulch; Cassidy's Bar, also on the San Joaquin River in the vicinity of Fort Miller; Soldier Bar; and Rootville—these made up a round of lively little camps that, during the 1850's, composed a small but rich mining district. However, little trace of them is left today.

Throughout this section of the Mother Lode a number of quartz mines likewise earned records as big producers during the 1870's and 1880's. The old mining camp of Coarsegold was located at the confluence of Coarsegold Gulch and Deadwood Gulch, 32 miles northeast of Madera. Radiating from it in all directions were quartz mines, traces of some of which remain today: the Texas Flat Mine, one mile to the northwest, and Topp's Mine (located in 1880), three miles north; the D'Or de Quartz, four and a half miles south; the Five Oaks, one and one-half miles southeast; the Waterloo, a mile and a half further on; and Last Chance, located in 1880, five miles by road from Coarsegold.

At the Grub Gulch camp the Josephine Mine (1880) and the Gambetta (which included the Arkansas Traveler Claim) were located, while two miles to the northeast was the Enterprise Mine.

Other mines located in the Potter Ridge District east of Grub Gulch included the Flying Dutchman, the Crystal Spring, the Rattlesnake, the King's Gulch, and the Victoria. The Potter Ridge Mine was two miles southwest of Fresno Flats.

The Hildreth Mining District was named after Tom Hildreth and his brother, who operated butcher shops in various Sierra mining camps and who ranged their cattle on Madera County foothills. The district, extending ten miles or so northward from the mouth of Fine Gold Creek (which was three miles northeast of old Fort Miller and is now inundated by Millerton Lake), was located in the southern part of the county; Fine Gold Gulch was the western and northern boundary line of the section. Here were the Abbey Mine, a quarter of a mile east of the small camp of Hildreth; the Morrow Mine, located in 1881, in the same section and township as the Abbey Mine; the Hanover, the Golconda, and the Standard. One mile east of Fine Gold, too, was the Mountain View Mine, located in 1880 in the vicinity of Mountain View Peak.

During the 1860's, while the copper excitement was at its height in California, a few copper mines were developed in the foothills of Madera County ten or so miles southwest of Raymond. Two located on the Daulton Ranch, the Ne Plus Ultra and the Jesse Bell, were especially productive, but after World War II, the fall in copper prices brought an end to mining. There was brief revival of activity around 1960.

Oakhurst

Oakhurst is the largest community in the mining area of Madera County today. It keeps alive memories of early days with an annual celebration and an outdoor museum, the Fresno Flats Historical Park. The ex-

Laramore-Lyman House, Fresno Flats Historical Park

hibition contains old buildings from various parts of the county and an interesting display of old wagons; it is located on School Road (Road 427), just off Crane Valley Road (Road 426) near the center of the town. Oakhurst is also the southern terminus of one of California's great highways, fittingly numbered SR 49, which goes north from here through the old towns of the mining days and ends in Plumas County.

Madera

With the construction of the railroad in 1870 an increasing demand came from the East for lumber from the great sugar pine forests of the Sierra Nevada. Some trade developed also in yellow pine, fir, cedar, and other woods. Quick transit from the mountains to the railroad was accomplished by the construction of a V-shaped flume 60 inches wide and 63 miles in length running from the Soquel Basin. This flume, built in 1874 at a cost of half a million dollars and later extended as far as Sugar Pine, carried countless millions of feet of lumber annually from the higher mountains to the railroad. The Sugar Pine Lumber Company and the Madera Sugar Pine Company, with a monthly payroll of $140,000, employed from 900 to 1,000 men. A section of the flume is displayed at the Fresno Flats Historical Park in Oakhurst.

A settlement grew up at the lower end of the flume where it terminated near the Central Pacific Railroad on the south side of the Fresno River. There in 1876 the California Lumber Company laid out the town of Madera. When the county was created in 1893, the

Old Madera County Courthouse, Madera

same name was chosen for it, and the city of Madera became the county seat.

The majestic old Madera County courthouse, constructed in 1900 of granite blocks at 210 West Yosemite Avenue, is now the Museum of the Madera County Historical Society. A distinctive feature of the museum, which has many recreations of rooms and activities from the past, is a photographic collection on the history of Madera County.

Borden, an Early Farm Community

The little town of Borden (originally known as the "Alabama Settlement"), located seventeen miles northwest of Fresno, was the center for a thriving agricultural community before Fresno and Madera even came into existence. It was the earliest farm center in this part of the valley, having been founded in 1868–69 by families from Alabama; Dr. Borden was an early leader. By 1873, Borden had become quite a pretentious place, with two hotels, two stores, and other buildings, as well as aspirations to become the county seat, but a decline set in within the next decade. A souvenir of early days is the old Chinese cemetery, immediately to the west of the settlement (some three miles south of Madera), a reminder of the Chinese laborers who built the Central Pacific Railroad through the San Joaquin Valley.

The Big Trees

There is but one living group of *Sequoia gigantea* within Madera County and that is the Nelder Grove, formerly called Fresno Grove, which stands about five miles south of the Mariposa Grove and immediately east of Sugar Pine. Partly cut over during the years 1888–90, it is now covered with a fine second growth. It derives its present name from John A. Nelder, who had a cabin there in the 1870's. A campground of the Sierra National Forest is nearby.

Devils Postpile National Monument

Devils Postpile is a spectacular mass of basaltic columns like an immense pile of posts—one late nineteenth-century account refers to it as the Devil's Woodpile. These columns vary in size from 10 to 30 inches in diameter and in some cases stand as high as 60 feet. In shape they are irregular polygons with from three to seven sides each but all closely and perfectly fitted together like a vast mosaic.

The group is located near the place where the old Mammoth or French Trail from Fresno Flats (Oakhurst) to Mammoth Lakes crosses the Middle Fork of the San Joaquin River. By automobile, it is accessible only from the eastern side of the Sierra, through Mammoth in Mono County, where SR 203 crosses Minaret Summit and continues west into the canyon of the Middle Fork of the San Joaquin. The Postpile is reached by a four-tenths-of-a-mile footpath from the parking area and ranger station.

Early Californians often regarded geological oddities as being of Satanic origin, and some 150 California place-names (such as Devil's Den in Kern County and the Devil's Cornfield in Death Valley) reflect this feeling. Virtually nothing is known to have been written about Devils Postpile before 1895, although the region was included in the original area of Yosemite National Park in 1890. In 1905, Congress returned some 500 square miles of land, including the Postpile, to the public domain. In 1910, a plan was made to dynamite the Postpile into the nearby San Joaquin River to form a rock-fill dam. Walter Huber of the U.S. Forest Service and members of the Sierra Club were alarmed at this proposal, and their efforts resulted in the creation of Devils Postpile National Monument, proclaimed by President William Howard Taft in 1911, under the authority of the Act for the Preservation of American Antiquities of 1906. It is a unique sight in California and a global rarity of which perhaps only the Giant's Causeway in Ireland is an equal.

Marin County

Marin County was one of the original 27 counties. San Rafael has always been the county seat. "The county is named for an Indian chief who gave California nothing but trouble," relates Jack Mason. "Chief Marin, captured by the Spaniards at Bodega in 1817, was sent to Yerba Buena for safekeeping, but escaped to harass the whites for nine more years. At San Rafael in 1824 he almost met his match in José Antonio Sánchez, 'famous for his skill as an Indian fighter'. Sánchez and Ignacio Martínez chased him onto the little islands at the mouth of San Rafael Estero. But once again Marin got away—only to be caught later and die in captivity in 1834."

Other possible origins of the county name have been suggested. Marin may well be a corruption of "Bahia de Nuestra Señora Rosario de la Marinera" (Bay of our Lady of the Seafarer's Rosary), the name given by Captain Juan Manuel de Ayala in 1775 to that corner of San Francisco Bay now called San Rafael Bay. It is also thought that the name may have been derived from "El Marinero" (the Sailor), the name of a Christian Indian ferryman.

The Indian Past

The Coast Miwok Indians were numerous in Marin County. Many shell mounds have been found by San Francisco and San Rafael bays as well as on the shores of Bolinas and Tomales bays—over 200 throughout the county. Although all of the mounds have been leveled, their contents, such as utensils, beads, and arrow heads, have been placed in several Bay Area museums. When ground was leveled on Hamilton Air Force Base, the razing of two mounds brought to light stone and shell ornaments and conical polished stones pierced at one end and believed to be ceremonial pieces used by a medicine man or possibly the insignia of a chief. An excavation at Fourth and Irwin streets in San Rafael revealed the skeleton of a chief decorated with strings of stone beads and ornaments made of abalone and other shells.

In the Drakes Bay region, mounds going back to the sixteenth century containing European and Oriental material from visiting or wrecked ships have been explored by University of California archaeologists and members of the Drake Navigators Guild.

The Miwok Archaeological Preserve at 2255 Las Gallinas Avenue in Marinwood includes the area where several shell mounds were found along Miller Creek. The Marin Museum of the American Indian at 2200 Novato Boulevard in Novato is at the site of a Coast Miwok settlement and contains displays of local artifacts.

Francis Drake and Nova Albion

Francis Drake set out from England late in 1577 in command of five vessels; his purpose was to probe the defenses of the Spanish New World. The voyage turned into a plundering expedition, and Drake, having aroused the anger of the Spanish, was forced to round Cape Horn and enter the vast Pacific Ocean. His ship, the *Pellican*, which was renamed the *Golden Hind* later in the voyage, was the only one to return to England in 1580.

The ship's log has disappeared. The first published narrative of the voyage, in 1589, was based in part on the diary of Francis Fletcher, chaplain of the expedition—an observant man, but not a sailor. This diary also no longer exists. Heading north along the California coast in the summer of 1579, the ship encountered thick fogs and severe cold, so that the command was given to turn south, where "we fell with a conuenient and fit harborough, and June 17 came to anchor therein, where we continued till the 23 day of July following. During all which time . . . were wee continually visited with like nipping colds as we had felt before; . . . neither could we at any time in whole fourteen dayes together, find the aire so cleare as to be able to take the height of sunne or starre." The dates are those of the Julian Calendar; June 17 would be June 28 by today's reckoning.

At the landing the vessel was reconditioned and contact was made with the local Indians, who were apparently impressed by their white visitors. Word of the strange arrival went through the countryside and each day more and more natives visited the harbor. About a week after their landing, the Englishmen saw a great number of Indians with their leader on the beach.

On this occasion the natives placed a crown of sorts on Drake's head, and "inriched his neck with all their chains, and offering unto him many other things, honoured him by the name of 'Hyoh.' Adding thereunto (as it might seeme) a song and dance of triumph; because they were not onely visited of the gods (for so they judged us to be), but the great and chiefe God was now become their God, their king and patron, and themselves the onely happie and blessed people in the world."

Some days later, Drake with a large company of men journeyed on land and found "a goodly country and fruitfull soyle, stored with many blessings fit for the vse of man." The account continues: "This country our Generall named *Albion*, and that for two causes; the one in respect of the white bancks and cliffes, which lie toward the sea; the other, that it might haue some affinity, euen in name also, with our own country, which was sometimes so called."

Further, "Before we went from thence, our Generall caused to be set vp a monument of our being there, and also of her maiesties and successors right and title to that kingdom; namely, a plate of brasse, fast nailed to a great and firme post; whereon is engrauen her graces name, and the day and yeare of our arriual there, and of the free giving vp of the province and kingdom, both by the king and people, into her maiesties hands: together with her highnesse picture and armes, in a piece of sixpence currant English monie, shewing itselfe by a hole made of purpose through the plate; underneath was likewise engrauen the name of our Generall, etc."

Just where did Drake make his anchorage? Probably no other question in California history has been so extensively debated. The Drake Navigators Guild has made an impressive claim for Drakes Estero, an inlet just inside Point Reyes on Drakes Bay, and in 1916 the Sir Francis Drake Association of California placed a marker at that spot. Yet some other places fit the description made by Fletcher, who noted that the landing was close to the 38th parallel. Bodega Bay and San Francisco Bay have their champions. Partly because Fletcher took the trouble to transcribe some of the Indian words in his journal, modern scholars believe that the Indians in question were of the Coast Miwok, whose territory was almost identical with what is now Marin County.

In 1936 the riddle of Drake's sojourn received new attention when a plate like that described in the narrative was picked up by Beryle Shinn when he stopped his car near Greenbrae. The discovery was made public at a meeting of the California Historical Society in the Sir Francis Drake Hotel in San Francisco on April 6, 1937. Careful study of the plate was made by the eminent historian Herbert Eugene Bolton, of the University of California at Berkeley, and others, and after scientific tests the plate was declared to be authentic. The brass plate, now the property of the University of California, is displayed at the Bancroft Library on the Berkeley campus. It is eight inches wide, five inches high, and about one-eighth of an inch thick; there are square holes at top and bottom to admit the nails that presumably held it to the post. A jagged hole in the lower right corner is about the size of an Elizabethan sixpence. This is the text of the plate:

BEE IT KNOWNE VNTO ALL MEN BY THESE PRESENTS
IVNE 17 1579
BY THE GRACE OF GOD AND IN THE NAME OF HERR
MAIESTY QVEEN ELIZABETH OF ENGLAND AND HERR
SVCCESSORS FOREVER I TAKE POSSESSION OF THIS
KINGDOME WHOSE KING AND PEOPLE FREELY RESIGNE
THEIR RIGHT AND TITLE IN THE WHOLE LAND VNTO HERR
MAIESTIES KEEPING NOW NAMED BY ME AN TO BEE
KNOWN VNTO ALL MEN AS NOVA ALBION.
FRANCIS DRAKE

There was still some skepticism about the authenticity of the plate, and as the quadricentennial of the Drake landing approached in the 1970's, further tests were ordered by the Bancroft Library authorities. Professor Thomas G. Barnes of the Department of History at the University of California at Berkeley had misgivings about the wording and lettering of the plate, as did colleagues from the Folger Shakespeare Library. Metallurgical tests were ordered from the Research Laboratory for Archaeology at Oxford University; the Chemistry Division of the Lawrence Berkeley Laboratory, under Dr. Helen V. Michel and Dr. Frank Asano; and Dr. Cyril Stanley Smith, professor emeritus of the Massachusetts Institute of Technology.

Meanwhile, another scholar, Harvard professor Samuel Eliot Morison, in *The European Discovery of America: The Southern Voyages* (1974), flatly labeled the plate "a hoax perpetrated by some collegiate joker." In July 1977, James D. Hart, director of the Bancroft Library, presented the findings of the investigating groups to the public. The Lawrence Laboratory team declared that for the metal in the plate, "the most probable period is the late nineteenth and early twentieth centuries," a finding more or less corroborated by the other scientists. Hart noted that not everyone would accept these findings as conclusive, and within a year a spirited defense of the authenticity of the plate by Drake scholar Robert H. Power appeared in *California History*. Since the perpetrator of the hoax, if hoax it be, has yet to appear, a second puzzle has been added to the Drake story. (The ubiquitous "Sir" Francis Drake nomenclature in the Bay Area is a historical anomaly, by the way, since Drake was not knighted until after his return to England in September 1580.)

The Prayerbook Cross in San Francisco's Golden Gate Park commemorates the religious services held by Chaplain Fletcher on California soil in 1579. Fletcher's prayer book is a cherished possession of Grace Cathedral (Episcopal) in San Francisco.

Sebastián Cermeño

In January 1594 King Philip II of Spain ordered an exploration of the northwestern coast of North America. The viceroy of New Spain commissioned Sebastián Rodríguez Cermeño, a Portuguese, to take a ship to the Philippines, fill it with Oriental treasure, explore the northern coasts, and then return to Acapulco. On November 4, 1595, the *San Agustín*, a Manila galleon that Cermeño had filled with merchandise, arrived off the California coast at about 41° latitude. Three days later, the ship entered Drakes Bay, where it was wrecked by a storm; Cermeño and his men were forced to proceed in a launch they had constructed there as an auxiliary boat. They did not report any signs of Drake's visit there sixteen years before (if indeed this had been the site of Drake's landing). Before sailing, they explored inland a distance of four leagues and found several rancherias of Indians from whom they obtained acorns for food. Cermeño named the harbor the "Bay of San Francisco," a name that for many years caused great confusion among historians. Hunt and Sanchez say: "The present Drakes Bay was the place first known as 'San Francisco' to the Spaniards, and the name was not transferred to the great inland sea which now bears it until after 1769."

Mission San Rafael Arcángel

At Mission Dolores in San Francisco in the early nineteenth century, the mortality rate of the Indians became alarmingly high. It was suggested that some of the neophytes be sent across the bay to what was perhaps a healthier climate. A trial move proved the wisdom of the proposal, and it was decided to establish there a kind of rancho with chapel, baptistry, and cemetery. The name San Rafael Arcángel was chosen in order that the angel "who in his name expresses the 'healing of God' might care for bodies as well as souls." The mission was founded on December 14, 1817, on a spot called by the Indians "Nanaguani."

An adobe building 79 feet long, 38 feet wide, and 16 feet high was erected and divided by partitions into chapel, padres' house, and other required apartments. San Rafael was at first only an *asistencia* to Mission San Francisco de Asís, but by 1823 it had become self-supporting. Although there is no record that it was raised to the position of an independent mission, all the reports of the fathers refer to it as such, and it is so considered by historians. Father Juan Amorós, known

Mission San Rafael Arcángel, San Rafael

for the zeal with which he undertook every task, served as missionary there from 1819 to his death in 1832. During this period the mission attained maximum strength, although the French mariner Captain August Duhaut-Cilly, passing within sight of it on his way to Sonoma in 1827, did not "deem this poor establishment worth stopping at for purposes of trade." Two years after the death of Father Amorós came secularization, when Ignacio Martínez, a distinguished military officer retired since 1831, was made *comisionado*. For two years he managed the affairs of San Rafael and established the boundaries of the pueblo.

The long, low adobe structure erected at San Rafael was much plainer and simpler than most of the mission structures. Old pictures show that the bells were hung in a wooden frame placed outside the chapel entrance. After secularization the uncared-for walls melted away, and no sign of them now remains. On the site of the chapel (SRL 220) at 1104 Fifth Avenue in San Rafael stands the present St. Raphael's Catholic Church. A replica of the mission was built nearby in 1949, one wing of which is used as the mission museum.

The Mission San Rafael rancho, consisting of sixteen square leagues, was sold by Governor Pico in 1846 to Antonio Suñol, of the San Jose Council, and Antonio María Pico, but they failed to get possession during the period of the American takeover and their title was later declared invalid. In 1859 Bishop J. S. Alemany obtained patent for something over six acres of land for the church.

The Mission Embarcadero and the City of San Rafael

The farthest inland meanderings of the Estero San Rafael de Aguanni are now lost beneath the pavements of San Rafael. On A Street at Third is the probable site of the mission embarcadero. This was the scene of a tragic episode in the Bear Flag Rebellion. Frémont and his men had arrived at the buildings of Mission San Rafael on June 26, 1846, just after the "battle" at Olompali (discussed in the Novato section of this chapter). Searching for the murderers of the Bear Flaggers, Frémont was advised that on the Contra Costa a Californian army under General Castro was planning further resistance to the American conquest. On June 28, a boat landed at the embarcadero, and three men climbed out and headed for the mission. Frémont seems to have assumed that they were Castro supporters carrying messages to Castro's aides in Marin County; he ordered Kit Carson to intercept the travelers and (according to one account) casually mentioned that "we have no time for prisoners." Carson and his men coolly shot the men down. Those killed were Don José de los Reyes Berryessa of Rancho San Vicente near Santa Clara (who was on his way to see his imprisoned son, the alcalde of Sonoma) and his twin sixteen-year-old nephews, Francisco and Ramón, sons of Don Francisco de Haro, former alcalde of San Francisco. For many years a white cross marked the site of this senseless murder.

The oldest part of the city of San Rafael lies west of a line drawn between the site of the mission and that of the mission embarcadero. At the northwest corner of Fourth and C streets stood the adobe residence of Don Timoteo Murphy, started in 1839. Murphy had arrived in California in 1828 to supervise the packing and exporting of beef for Hartnell and Company in Monterey. General Mariano Vallejo befriended him (at one point Murphy was being considered as a possible brother-in-law) and made him administrator of the secularized mission at San Rafael in 1837. The alcaldes transacted their official business in the old mission building until 1850, about the date when freight ceased to be landed at the embarcadero. The seat of justice was transferred to Murphy's house upon his death in 1853 and remained there until the Marin County Courthouse was built in 1872. The principal official functions of the county were transferred to the Marin County Civic Center when the old courthouse burned in 1971. The Civic Center, designed by Frank Lloyd Wright, was the last principal work of the American master; its first unit was completed in 1962, the year after Wright's death.

The striking Civic Center was the scene of a second bloodletting in San Rafael. On August 7, 1970, the courtroom of Judge Harold J. Haley was taken over by gunmen who forced the judge and four hostages from the courtroom in an attempt to liberate a San Quentin convict who was being tried before the judge for the stabbing of a prison guard. The escape van was fired on, and in the melee the judge, defendant James McClain, and two gunmen, Arthur Christmas and Jonathan Jackson, were killed. Two hostages were wounded.

William T. Coleman, chosen leader of the San Francisco Vigilantes in 1856, had extensive interests in Marin County. He was one of the planners of the Mechanics Institute Library in San Rafael. His home, built in 1852, still stands at 1130 Mission Avenue, one of the first frame buildings in the city. The old mission spring is in Boyd Park, donated by the shipping magnate Robert Dollar to the city of San Rafael. Dollar's mansion, built in 1879, at 1408 Mission Avenue is now the Falkirk Cultural Center. At the entrance to Boyd Park at 1125 B Street is the Marin County Historical Society Museum, housed in a building that began as a guest house on the Ira Cook estate in 1879 and was moved here in 1924.

Several houses were erected in San Rafael by convict labor in 1859 and 1860, when prisoners were hired under contract to the firm of Sims and McCauley. Two of these houses were on the public square; one was used as a pharmacy by Dr. Alfred Taliaferro and stands at 1221 Fourth Street. Across the street at 1222 is the other, once called the Central Hotel, a brick structure famous in early days.

Just north of the center of modern San Rafael is the area that was once Rancho San Pedro, Santa Margarita y las Gallinas, granted in 1844 by Governor Micheltorena to Timoteo Murphy. On his deathbed in 1853 Don Timoteo deeded 317 acres of the rancho to Bishop Alemany for the foundation of a school. In 1855 the Sisters of Charity of St. Vincent de Paul established what is now St. Vincent's School for Boys (SRL 630). The beautifully landscaped grounds are approached on a long

Chapel at St. Vincent's School for Boys, North of San Rafael

eucalyptus-lined avenue east of the Redwood Highway about one mile north of the Marin County Civic Center complex.

The grounds on which stand the buildings of Dominican College occupy a large and beautiful tract northeast of the center of San Rafael. The Dominican Sisters, originally from Paris, first located on the West Coast in Monterey in 1851. From Monterey they moved to Benicia in Solano County, where Concepción Argüello became their first native-born novice. From Benicia they moved to San Rafael, where their convent was established in 1889. In 1950 the convent became a women's liberal arts college; it began to admit men in 1971. By gift and by purchase the sisters acquired property that belonged to prominent early-day families. Forest Meadows, the outdoor auditorium, is on land that was owned by William T. Coleman; Meadowlands, the dormitory on Palm Avenue, was the country home of the M. H. de Young family of San Francisco. On the same avenue is the home formerly owned by William Babcock, also of San Franciso. His widow gave this completely furnished home to the convent.

San Quentin

Point San Quentin is named for the Indian companion of Chief Marin. General Mariano Vallejo was impressed by the navigational skills of Quintin, as he was then known, and employed him to command his best lighter operating on Sonoma Creek. Vallejo, according to Jack Mason, "thought newcomers to California added the 'San' to Quintin's name theorizing all local inhabitants were 'zealous Catholics'. The change in spelling to Quentin came at the same time." The Rancho Punta de Quentín took its name from this headland. It extended inland to Larkspur at its southern line and San Anselmo at its northern. The grant was first made in 1840 to Juan Bautista Cooper, who at one time or another owned other ranchos in the state, none of them for very long.

On the eastern part of this rancho at the edge of the bay stands San Quentin Prison, begun in 1853. Before its erection the state's convicted criminals were confined on hulks of ships anchored off Angel Island. It stands on the site of the projected but never-built Marion City. Until the Richmond–San Rafael Bridge was completed in 1956, ferry service was maintained between Point San Quentin and Richmond in Contra Costa County.

San Anselmo and Fairfax

These cities lie on the grounds of Rancho Cañada de Herrera (Vale of the Blacksmith), or La Providencia, granted by acting governor Manuel Jimeno to Domingo Sais in 1839. Dr. A. W. Taliaferro, a skilled surgeon and physician who had come to Marin County in 1849 with a group of young men from Virginia, while wandering one day up San Anselmo Valley "came upon a tract of park-like land, shaded by ancient trees with a sparkling stream of water running through it." He at once began negotiations for its purchase. When Don Domingo learned that he wanted only 40 acres, he said: "It is worth forty acres to us to have a good neighbor. Select your forty acres, we give it to you thankfully." The doctor fenced in his land and built a spacious house on the bank of the "sparkling stream" (Corte Madera Creek), cleared a considerable area of brush, built outbuildings, and settled into the life of a gentleman, as his forebears had done in Virginia. The abundance of wild game and his unstinted hospitality at once made the place popular with his sportsman friends.

Among the visitors in 1856 were Charles S. Fairfax and his wife. Fairfax was descended from English barons of that name, and his wife was famous for her wit and beauty. The couple became fascinated with the place. Some sort of deed of gift was made; they took over the property, and Dr. Taliaferro remained as their permanent guest. Fairfax, in later years always called "Lord Fairfax" because of his ancestry, had come in 1849 as a youth of twenty from the county of Fairfax in Virginia and had spent his first winter in a cabin near Grass Valley. A young man of good education and pleasant bearing, he became a member of the assembly from Yuba County in 1853 and in 1856 was clerk of the state supreme court, which position he held for five years.

The Fairfax home (SRL 679) was located not far from the present business district of Fairfax. Presided over by the gracious Mrs. Fairfax, it became a center of the social life of the period, where notables of the state and nation were entertained. Here also occurred the last politically motivated duel in California history.

A luncheon party had gathered at the house on May 21, 1861, the day following the close of the session of the state legislature, where hot political debate had resulted in a challenge to a duel. The prompt action of an official at that time had prevented the duel from taking place, and the principals, their seconds, and the surgeon had gone to the house of "Lord Fairfax," where their host attempted a reconciliation. The antagonists, Daniel Showalter of Kentucky and Charles W. Piercy of Illinois, had crossed the continent in the same small company some years before but on arriving in California had gone different ways. They had met again as members of the legislature in the opposing Breckinridge and Douglas factions of the Democratic Party. After the luncheon, when all hope of preventing the conflict was abandoned, the hour of three o'clock was set for the duel. Following the first exchange of shots, in which neither man had been injured, Fairfax again attempted to pacify the hot-tempered men, but without success. On resuming their positions and firing, Piercy was instantly killed. Showalter, immediately filled with remorse, pleaded with the surgeon to save his opponent. Leaving California thereafter to join the Confederate Army, he was captured and imprisoned by General Sibley.

In May 1868 the heirs of Domingo Sais deeded this 40-acre tract to the Fairfaxes. In that year Charles Fairfax was made chairman of the California delegation to the Democratic National Convention in New York. He attended the convention and died the following year in Baltimore. After his death the property became the restaurant of Madame Adele Pastori, who, on the decline of her career in Italian opera, came here with her husband, a former master of stagecraft. Her attractive personality and the fine table set by her husband soon drew many artists from San Francisco.

This wooded spot was for many years in the twentieth century the Marin Town and Country Club; it is now privately owned.

The San Francisco Theological Seminary, now located at 2 Kensington Court in San Anselmo, began as the dream of William Anderson Scott, D.D., who arrived in San Francisco in 1854 from Tennessee. He envisioned a training center on the coast for the Presbyterian ministry, and began his school in San Francisco. It moved three times, the last time, in 1877, to a building that still stands at 121 Haight Street. A generous citizen of San Rafael, A. W. Foster, donated the San Anselmo property to the school in 1891. The small hill on which the substantial buildings stand overlooks the town. The Montgomery Memorial Chapel, built at the foot of the hill, was the gift of the chief benefactor of the seminary, Alexander Montgomery, whose remains were interred there.

Ross and Kentfield

The attractive residential town of Ross was named for James Ross, who settled on this part of Rancho Punta de Quentín in 1859, the year of the death of the former owner of the rancho, Benjamin R. Buckelew. Kentfield is on land that passed from the estate of James Ross to Albert Emmet Kent when Kent came to California for his health in 1871. It was called Ross Landing in earlier days, when steamers came up Corte Madera Creek above the present US 101 bridge to load thousands of cords of wood, which they carried to San Francisco. Kent built a spacious house amid old-fashioned formal gardens, with vineyards and orchards at a distance. The Kent Estate is today subdivided into Kent Woodlands.

Rancho Corte de Madera del Presidio
(Corte Madera, Greenbrae, Larkspur, Mill Valley, Belvedere, and Tiburon)

Rancho Corte de Madera del Presidio was granted by Governor José Figueroa to John Reed in 1834. It lay on the peninsula northwest of Racoon Strait and extended inland between the Punta de Quentín and Saucelito Ranchos.

Reed, an Irish sailor, arrived in the area in 1826. As opportunity arose, he ran a boat for hire to Yerba Buena, antedating the regular ferry services by many years. He was naturalized as a Mexican citizen one month before receiving the grant of his rancho. For about five months between the Martínez and Murphy administrations of the secularized San Rafael Mission, he filled that position, beginning on November 30, 1836. His rancho was named for the redwood timbers cut down for the use of the Presidio, and he built the first sawmill in Marin County in the middle of the 1830's. Some of the old timbers still stand (SRL 207) in Old Mill Park on Cascade Drive in Mill Valley, which was named for this early enterprise. A subsequent court case determined that this land was actually owned by Captain William Richardson.

One of the early settlements in this area was Blithedale. This sunny place, through which ran the Arroyo del Corte de Madera del Presidio, was chosen in 1873 by Dr. John Cushing and his wife for the location of a sanatorium. The idealistic agricultural community portrayed by Nathaniel Hawthorne in *The Blithedale Romance*, written twenty years earlier, inspired Dr. Cushing to give the name Blithedale to this place. Dr. Cushing had not been able to establish a sanatorium at the time of his death in 1879, but his widow and son remained on the property and managed it as a summer resort for years afterward. The extensive cement walks that were then made on the place now surround private homes on the site in the 200 block of West Blithedale Avenue near the creek. The original Blithedale Glen, between Eldridge and Cottage avenues, has been subdivided and built up as a part of the town of Mill Valley. The Mill Valley Outdoor Club (SRL 922) at 1 West Blithedale Avenue still has its headquarters in the building created for it in 1902, and still is concerned with the preservation of the local environment.

The town of Larkspur is located in the north corner of Rancho Corte de Madera del Presidio. Here an Indian shell mound formed a knoll, then practically surrounded by marshes, upon which Captain Frémont and some of his soldiers are said to have camped for a time in the summer of 1846. In 1850 a steamboat, plying by way of Corte Madera Creek between what is now Larkspur and San Francisco, made three or four trips a week to carry lumber, hides, beef, and other produce from the country and to return with goods purchased in the city. Today Larkspur is at the end of a regular ferry connecting it with San Francisco. A plaque placed by the Larkspur–Corte Madera Historical Society at the ferry terminal commemorates the maritime life of Larkspur and notes that it was once a busy terminal on the Northwest Pacific Railroad.

The Green Brae brick kiln (SRL 917), last surviving structure of the Remillard Brick Company, is located at 125 East Sir Francis Drake Boulevard in Larkspur. The kiln operated from 1891 to 1915. The Remillard Brick Company was once the largest brick manufacturer on the Pacific Coast, with brickyards at several locations from 1865 until it closed in 1968. Such San Francisco landmarks as Ghirardelli Square and The Cannery are built of Remillard brick.

Present-day Corte Madera began as a station on the Northwestern Pacific line. The site of the station is now a municipal park.

What is now Tiburon was part of the inheritance of Hilarita, daughter of John Reed and his wife Hilaria Sánchez Reed. In 1872 she married Dr. Benjamin F. Lyford, a Civil War surgeon who had arrived in San Francisco in 1866. He was deeply interested in cleanliness and sanitation and was apparently an expert embalmer as well. The Lyfords developed the area as a health resort, which opened in 1888 under the name Hygeia, after the goddess of health. The Lyford home at 376 Greenwood Beach Road has been moved from an earlier site and is open to the public on a limited basis. Old St. Hilary's Church on the hill above the junction of Esperanza and Alemany streets is now a museum of early California history.

Sausalito

William A. Richardson was born in England in 1795 and arrived in San Francisco as first mate on the whaling vessel *L'Orient* in 1822. He procured papers allowing him to remain on land and thereafter became active in the Bay region. He was baptized at Mission Dolores in 1823, and two years later married María Antonia, daughter of Ignacio Martínez, at that time *comandante* of the Presidio. In 1830 he obtained naturalization as a citizen, his name being placed on record as pilot and shipbuilder with a knowledge of Spanish. From 1835 to 1844 he was the first captain of the Port of San Francisco, having been appointed by General Vallejo. In 1838 he was granted Rancho Saucelito by Governor Alvarado, and he made his home thereafter in Marin County. The final patent for 19,572 acres of the rancho was issued to his heirs in 1879, long after his death in 1858.

Richardson's private business was the collection of country produce by means of a launch that visited the various embarcaderos about the Bay. The shore of his own rancho was washed by the waters of Richardson's Bay, thus named at the time of his land ownership there. The site of Richardson's adobe home, built about 1841, is at the northeast corner of Bonita and Pine streets in Sausalito.

Fine hillside springs on Rancho Saucelito gave life to the *sauces* or willows from which the name is derived, and in 1850 Captain Richardson piped water from these springs to a great cistern 30 feet square and 15 feet deep that he had dug for the purpose. From this cistern, located on Richardson Street, Hurricane Gulch, Sausalito, pipes were run on a trestle to the waterfront and thence to a boat, the *Water Nixie*, equipped with tanks and casks for transporting the water to Meiggs' Wharf at San Francisco. From this point Marin County spring water was distributed to dwellers in the growing city by means of mule- and horse-drawn carts for the price of 50 cents a bucket. The mooring place of the old *Water Nixie* is on Richardson Street near Bridgeway, not far from the place of the first settlement of the town of Sausalito, where in 1862 there were a half-dozen houses.

San Carlos Avenue in Sausalito is named for the first known ship to sail through the Golden Gate, on August 5, 1775, under command of Juan Manuel de Ayala. The *San Carlos*, after moving cautiously into the unknown strait, taking frequent soundings, first dropped anchor off Sausalito and later moved to Angel Island.

For many years the Sausalito waterfront was widely known as an anchorage and supply station for whaling vessels and men-of-war. Captain Beechey, in 1826, saw "seven whalers" anchored there. Sir George Simpson, governor-in-chief of the Hudson's Bay Company territories in North America, on entering San Francisco Bay in December 1841, wrote: "We saw on our left in a deep bay known as 'Whaler's Harbor' two vessels, the Government schooner *California* and the Russian brig *Constantine*, now bound to Sitka with the last remnants of [the settlements at Fort] Ross and Bodega on board, . . . about a hundred souls, men, women, and children, all patriotically delighted to exchange the lovely climate of California for the uncongenial skies of Sitka, and that, too, at the expense of making a long voyage in an old, crazy, clumsy tub at the stormiest season of the year."

Captain Richardson in 1855 sold a piece of property near Sausalito to S. R. Throckmorton, who in turn sold it to the Sausalito Land and Ferry Company. This company built wharves, filled in marshy places, and put on a reliable boat for frequent rapid transit across the Bay to San Francisco. Their first boat, the *Princess*, made four round trips daily. It is in the vicinity of this wharf that the newer part of Sausalito has grown up. One of the largest working scale models in the world is the San Francisco Bay Delta Model at 2100 Bridgeway; open to the public since it was built in 1956 by the U.S. Army Corps of Engineers, it is used to study the effects of tides and currents in the Bay complex from the Golden Gate to the Delta cities of Sacramento and Stockton.

On Bulkley Avenue, near Harrison Avenue, on the drive above the waterfront, a crescent-shaped cement seat has been placed honoring the memory of Daniel O'Connell, grandnephew of the Irish patriot of the same name. O'Connell came to California after resigning from the British Navy and was a teacher at Santa Clara College in 1868; later he taught Greek at St. Ignatius College in San Francisco before devoting his time to newspaper and other writing. A poet, he was one of the early members of the Bohemian Club of San Francisco. He lived in Wildwood Glen with his family in "the little house on the hill," which still stands, enlarged and modernized, at 41 Cazneau Avenue.

In 1869, James H. Gardner, former state senator from Downieville and custom house broker, purchased from the Sausalito Land and Ferry Company a parcel of land where he built his house. "The Bower," as he named it, is the oldest house still standing in Sausalito, and is at 47 Girard Avenue. It is privately owned, as is the O'Connell House.

Bolinas

Otter hunting, the first occupation engaged in by settlers in the vicinity of the town of Bolinas, was followed by lumbering in the 1850's, when many sawmills were operating in the tree-filled canyons back from the shore. The only evidence left is the few piles that mark the site of the lighter wharf (SRL 221), about two miles north of Bolinas at the head of Bolinas Lagoon, not far from the junction with SR 1.

From the mills the wood was hauled to the wharf by ox-drawn wagons, which creaked along the uneven roads on wooden wheels made from sawn sections of huge trees. The loads were transferred at the wharf to flat-bottomed boats, or lighters, that carried the cargo to seagoing vessels offshore. These vessels, in turn, transported the lumber and fuel to the growing city of San Francisco. It is estimated that thirteen million feet of lumber were shipped to the city for building purposes from the lighter wharf at Bolinas before the supply was exhausted. After the large trees had been used for lumber, the smaller trees were felled for domestic fuel and sent to the same market.

Ocean gales raked the west shore of Bolinas Bay, and windbreaks in the form of cypress hedges had to be planted before the cottage gardens of the pioneer settlers could grow. In some parts of Bolinas, the roses, fuchsias, and lemon verbenas of early days have now attained tree-like proportions.

Nicasio

Attempts were made to give three grants in the county to Christian Indians. Rancho Olómpali was successfully patented to Camilo Ynitia, but the other two, ranchos Nicasio and Tenicasia, were not confirmed. Twenty square leagues of Nicasio had been granted to Teodosio Quilajuequi and others of his tribe in 1835 by Governor Figueroa, but this was rejected by the Land Commission in 1855. Tenicasia, given by General Mariano Vallejo to the San Rafael Mission Indians in 1841, was rejected by the commission in 1854 because of "failure of prosecution." Vallejo was a valiant friend of the neophytes, but he alone could not carry through the plan of obtaining farms for them where they could use the agricultural knowledge received at the mission. Timoteo Murphy, his friend and co-worker who held the confidence of the Indians and was furthering their interests, had died the year before the matter was settled, and no one else remained to intercede on behalf of the native claimants. "The history of land in Marin," Jack Mason observed, "is one of broken promises, litigation and injustice nurtured on political expediency."

In 1844, another part of Rancho Nicasio, containing ten square leagues, was granted by Governor Micheltorena to Pablo de la Guerra and Juan Cooper, men prominent in political and business affairs, who seem to have parted with the land before 1852. In that year a claim for it was filed by H. W. Halleck and James Black, and a supplementary claim was filed the following year by Benjamin R. Buckelew, Daniel Frink, and William Reynolds. The long and comparatively narrow stretch of this rancho reached from Keyes Creek, flowing into Tomales Bay, to the western boundary of Murphy's Rancho San Pedro, Santa Margarita y Las Gallinas. It was surveyed in the autumn of 1859 and found to contain 56,621 acres, for which patent, signed by President Abraham Lincoln, was issued to all five claimants in 1861.

The extreme northwestern and northeastern ends were claimed by and patented to Henry Wager Halleck, a graduate of West Point, who had come in 1847 with a company of United States artillery to inspect Pacific Coast fortifications. He resigned his commission, was an active and influential member of the constitutional convention in 1849, acted as inspector of lighthouses on the coast, became the leading member of a San Francisco law firm, prepared a report on California land titles, and was the author of several law books. He was also one of the developers of the New Almaden quicksilver mining complex in Santa Clara County. Halleck resumed his military career and during most of the Civil War served as Chief of Staff of the Union Army. The southeastern corner of this large grant was patented to the heirs of Benjamin R. Buckelew, who was also the owner of Punta de Quentín. The two middle tracts, along the eastern shore of Tomales Bay, were patented to the other three claimants, Frink and Reynolds owning the northern piece, and James Black, who also had Rancho Olómpali, the southern.

An interesting old building still standing in the town of Nicasio is the Church of Our Lady of Loretto, established in 1867.

The Pioneer Paper Mill (Samuel P. Taylor State Park)

Samuel Penfield Taylor erected a paper mill in 1856 on what was then called Daniels Creek, afterward Paper Mill Creek, and today Lagunitas Creek. It was the first paper mill on the Pacific Coast and was run by water carried by a flume from a dam in the creek one-half mile above. The warehouse was situated at the end of Tomales Bay, where Point Reyes Station is now.

Rags to supply the mill were gathered by Chinese in San Francisco, made into great bales, and shipped by schooner to the head of Tomales Bay. They were then loaded on a scow and floated on the tide to Taylor's warehouse, from which a team of oxen completed the transportation to the factory. The finished paper was conveyed in reverse manner to San Francisco, where the product found a ready sale and was sent to all parts of the Pacific Coast. The undertaking was prosperous from the beginning and was especially so during the Civil War. By 1884 the demand for paper had become so great that a larger mill was built at a cost of $165,000 and employment there furnished a livelihood for about 100 families. Steam power was added, and the mill did a flourishing business until the depression of 1893.

After lying idle for over twenty years, the red-painted building with windows and doors outlined in white was destroyed by fire. Now only the damaged foundations remain; the columns that acted as supports for the water wheel are still standing, and crumbling bricks mark the site of the boiler. The site of the first paper mill (SRL 552) is marked by a stone monument with bronze plaque in Samuel P. Taylor State Park, off Sir Francis Drake Boulevard between Lagunitas and Olema. The ruins of the later mill are a few yards from the marker.

The Pacific Powder Mill was erected in 1866 about three miles upstream from the paper mill; the exact site is now lost.

Tomales Bay, Inverness, and Olema

"Tomales" is a Coast Miwok word meaning "bay"; thus its present official name is redundant. In 1775, Lieutenant Juan Francisco de la Bodega y Cuadro, commander of the schooner Sonora, discovered Bodega Bay in Sonoma County by chance and "soon afterwards distinguished the mouth of a considerable river, and some way up a large port exactly resembling a dock," according to the Daines Barrington translation of the account of Don Antonio Mourelle. At first, members of the expedition thought that Tomales Bay was the harbor of San Francisco, but later they realized that it was not, because the Farallon Islands were not visible. Indians came in great numbers and rowed their tule rafts between Tomales Point (Punta del Cordon) and Sand Point (Punta de Arenas). They came alongside the ship to present gifts of "rosaries of bone, seeds, and plumes of feathers." Bodega in return gave "bugles, looking glasses, and pieces of cloth."

Bodega named today's Tomales Bay and Bodega Bay for himself—Puerto de la Bodega. The Sonora anchored in the mouth of Tomales Bay on October 3, 1775. After midnight, on the first flow of the tide, the full force of a northeast swell struck the ship and covered it with breaking water. The discovery boat on her side was shattered. By midmorning the Sonora set sail for Monterey. The following day, October 5, the expedition passed two miles from the Golden Gate, unaware that only a month before the San Carlos had departed for Monterey. Bodega was afraid to enter San Francisco Bay because of the loss of the discovery boat.

The town of Tomales, originally located at the head of Keyes Creek, which flows from the northeast into the bay, had its beginning in a store located here in 1852. The North Pacific Coast Railroad ran its first freight train from a warehouse there in 1874; its cargo of 300 sacks of potatoes was the forerunner of many trainloads of produce raised in the vicinity and shipped over this line to Sausalito and thence to San Francisco. The railroad has long since been discontinued.

When on December 28, 1841, the Cowlitz lay becalmed offshore at Drakes Bay after coming from the north, its passengers "began sensibly to feel the influence of a more congenial climate. The sails flapped listlessly against the mast, the vessel heaved reluctantly on the sluggish waters." Sir George Simpson, one of the passengers, continues: "During the whole of the 29th we lay in this state of inactivity about five miles from shore which presented a level sward of about a mile in depth, backed by a high ridge of grassy slopes—the whole pastured by numerous herds of cattle and horses which, without a keeper and without a fold, were growing and fattening, whether their owners waked or slept, in the very middle of winter, and in the coldest nook of the province. Here, on the very threshold of the country, was California in a nutshell, Nature doing everything and man doing nothing. . . . While we lay like a log in the sea, we were glad to be surrounded by large flights of birds—ducks, pelicans, cormorants, gulls, etc."

The land Simpson described is that of Rancho Punta de los Reyes Sobrante, which after the advent of the American settlers became the first great dairy center of the state.

Rancho Punta de los Reyes, on the west side of Tomales Bay, was a 35,000-acre grant made in 1836 to a well-traveled Irish gentleman, James Richard Berry, who had spent much time in Spanish countries. He sold a portion of this land to Joseph Snook, an English-born citizen of Mexico, in 1839, who in turn sold his share to Antonio María Osio in 1843. Osio, a public official, meanwhile had made a successful application for the remaining 48,000 acres of Point Reyes, which was granted to him in 1840 as the Rancho Punta de los Reyes Sobrante ("surplus" or "leftover land"), surrounding the initial grant on three sides. The American takeover in 1846 brought rival claims to the property, complicated by the fact that here, as nearly everywhere in Alta California, no precise surveys had been made and much land was in dispute.

The two ranchos became the property of Dr. Andrew Randall in the early 1850's. Randall, an American resident of Monterey, had been a member of the state legislature and was the first president of the California Academy of Sciences (1853). He overextended himself in land purchases and was murdered in San Francisco by Joseph Hetherington, one of his creditors. (Hetherington was lynched by the Vigilantes within the week.) Oscar L. Shafter, a Vermonter practicing law in California, took on Mrs. Randall's hopelessly debt-ridden inheritance, which finally passed to him and to his brother, James. Both the Shafters became eminent in late-nineteenth-century California, Oscar on the bench of the state supreme court and James as a member of the legislature.

James, who also held judicial office, was a regent of the University of California. At the time of the founding of Leland Stanford Junior University he delivered the dedicatory address and became a trustee of the new institution. His house, "The Oaks," two miles south of Olema, still stands, now in the Golden Gate National Recreational Area.

The Shafter brothers and Charles Webb Howard, president of the Spring Valley Water Company, jointly came to own both Point Reyes ranchos. To their large holding was later added Rancho Tomales y Baulenes,

which had been granted in 1836 by Governor Nicolás Gutiérrez to Rafael García. The combined property stretched south and east from the coast north of Point Reyes to include the top of Mount Tamalpais.

Dairying became the major activity in this part of Marin County. Almost the entire area was leased out by the grantees to dairy farmers, and houses were built for them near clear-flowing springs, of which there were a considerable number. Butter was shipped by schooners to San Francisco. Judge James Shafter was greatly interested in blooded stock, horses as well as cattle, and he frequently entertained friends at his private race track, where his fine horses were trained and shown. After his death many of the customs of the family were continued, for his son Payne Jewett ("Squire") Shafter was also interested in agriculture and the country life. Squire Shafter's daughter Mary had similar interests; her book *American Indian and Other Folk Dances* reveals a historical interest in the people who inhabited the grass-covered hills up to the time white settlers came.

An outcropping of limestone on Olema Creek was worked in the early 1850's by James A. Shorb and William F. Mercer. Four lime kilns were built on the east bank of the creek. The site (SRL 222) is about 100 yards west of SR 1 and about 4.2 miles south of Olema; it cannot be seen from the highway. The structure extended 65 feet against the face of a limestone hill, with openings at the top for loading. The front wall, fifteen feet high, had insets for strength and was three feet thick; the side walls were somewhat narrower. After an estimated four burnings, the kilns were shut down in 1853 and have never been worked again. Here the ravages of time are plainly to be seen; a giant spruce rises from the fire pits; two of the kilns have been destroyed or their stones carried away; two intact chimneys still stand against the sky.

At nearby Olema, a prominent landmark is Nelson's Hotel, built in 1877 and recently renovated and restored. Several other turn-of-the-century frame structures are preserved and privately occupied. Inverness, named after the city in Scotland whence the Shafter family emigrated, was begun by James Shafter in 1889 as a real estate development. In contrast to the lively, six-saloon neighboring town of Olema, Inverness was intended to be a model of sobriety "to the better class of citizens," according to one early announcement.

Rancho Olómpali and Novato

Rancho Olómpali, named for a former Coast Miwok Indian village, Olemaloke, consisted of two square leagues granted by Governor Manuel Micheltorena in 1843 to Camilo Ynitia, who filed claim for it in 1852 and received a United States patent in 1862. The Olómpali rancheria was in a sheltered valley by what is now San Antonio Creek and had an abundance of game and wildfowl. The legend persists that Camilo Ynitia's father, the chief of the Olómpali Indians, lived in the first adobe house built north of San Francisco Bay; this legend is discounted by most historians.

Camilo Ynitia, however, built himself an adobe house, about three miles north of Novato. With 32-inch-thick walls and ceilings eight feet high, it was an impressive structure in the otherwise empty landscape. Nearby were corrals and outbuildings.

On June 24, 1846, there was a surprise skirmish at this spot. The Bear Flag had been raised above nearby Sonoma ten days before, and the Americans were trying to secure their hold on the area. Led by Lieutenant Henry L. Ford, the Bear Flaggers made a raid on the horse corral at Olómpali, unaware that a force of Californians under Joaquín de la Torre and Juan N. Padilla were at breakfast in the ranch house. Padilla was a wanted man in the eyes of the Bear Flaggers, since his force had murdered two Americans a couple of days before. Alerted to the raid, the Californians poured out of the ranch house, took to their mounts, and attacked the Americans, who took cover and sent volleys flying into the midst of the horsemen. Manuel Cantua fell to his death, and three other Californians were wounded; Padilla withdrew his men into the hills and then retreated to San Rafael. Ford's party retreated to Sonoma, and John C. Frémont moved onto the scene, with the tragic consequences recorded earlier in this chapter.

The greater part of this rancho was purchased in 1852 by James Black from Ynitia and his wife, Susana, who retained the southeast corner of the tract for themselves. Black, originally from Scotland, had become the assessor of Marin County and acquired many other tracts of land. He afterward gave this one to his daughter Mary.

In 1863, Mary Black and her husband, Dr. Galen Burdell, came to live at Olómpali. Here the Burdells built their home, using Camilo Ynitia's adobe as its center (SRL 210). This was in turn enlarged by their son James Burdell in 1915, and it became one of the showplaces of Marin County. Lavish gardens were planted and historic artifacts from places such as Mission San Rafael were displayed, all of which have since been returned to their places of origin.

In later years, the home at Rancho Olómpali went through hard times; in 1969 fire gutted the main house. Meanwhile a campaign was begun to persuade the state to acquire this property. Excavations in 1974–75 revealed, among other things, an Elizabethan sixpence, which many believed was the one missing from Drake's Plate of Brass; this has been neither proved nor disproved, however. The property, now Olompali State Historic Park, is being restored to a semblance of its former condition; it is on the western side of US 101 three miles north of Novato.

Rancho Novato was granted in 1939 by Governor Alvarado to Fernando Feliz; it lay along the bay from Black Point to Rancho San José. The town of Novato lies in this district; rail service came through in 1879 and a subdivision made in 1888 marked the beginning of the city. The oldest building in Novato is believed to have been built around 1850, and was the home of postmaster Henry F. Jones for some time. It stood on South Novato Avenue until 1972, when it was donated to the city by its owner, Fabian Bobo. The building was moved to its present location at 901 Sherman Avenue that year and was inaugurated as the Novato History Museum and Archives in 1976. One room of the museum is devoted to the history of nearby Hamilton Air Force Base, now inactive. In 1985 a plaque was placed on the building by the Native Sons of the Golden West.

The Novato City Hall, nearby at Sherman and De Long avenues, was built in 1893. It was once a Presbyterian church and is a good example of Victorian Gothic architecture. Joseph B. Sweetser and Francis De Long were largely responsible for Novato's early prosperity, planting orchards and vineyards and producing high-quality crops that were shipped from the landing on Novato Creek onto the bay and thence to San Francisco. The three-story home they built still stands at 50 Rica Vista Avenue; it is hemmed in by newer houses and almost unrecognizable from contemporary pictures, which show a majestic avenue of fig trees leading to its front veranda.

Rancho San José and Ignacio

Don Ignacio Pacheco, whose father, of the same name, was a Mexican soldier in San Francisco in 1790, was born in San José in 1808. When he was nineteen years old, he became a soldier in the San Francisco Company, and he became a sergeant ten years later. At the expiration of his military service in 1838 he settled on a tract of land bordering San Pablo Bay south of the Feliz grant of Rancho de Novato, and in 1840 the tract was granted to him by Governor Alvarado. Don Ignacio's first wife, Josefa Higuera, named the rancho for her patron saint. The family home still stands in the community of Ignacio and is still in the possession of the family; this is the second-longest occupancy by a single family in California, so far as is known.

The tall palms at 716 Lamone in Ignacio mark the site of the Reichardt villa, a country home of the late

China Camp State Park

nineteenth century. Hamilton Air Force Base nearby was named for Lieutenant Lloyd Hamilton, the first American to fly with the Royal Air Corps in World War I. In operation between 1928 and 1975, it was a major bomber facility during World War II. The future of the base is still uncertain.

China Camp

Farther south along the bay is China Camp, one of the newest state parks (SRL 924). It is situated along Point San Pedro Road just outside the city limits of San Rafael.

In the years after the gold rush, Chinese immigrants in California found many productive occupations. Along the shores of San Francisco and San Pablo bays, shrimp fishing became a major industry after 1870; some 26 camps or fishing villages were recorded. Shrimping was an established trade in China, and the abundance of shrimp in the shallow waters of San Pablo Bay encouraged the start of this activity in California. The shrimp were caught, dried, and sent for export to Asian countries and to the Hawaiian Islands.

The China Camp site is all that remains of this once flourishing industry and community. Relatively isolated, it became a refuge for Chinese who were persecuted in the latter nineteenth century. Chinese families continued to live in the settlement long after its economic heyday had passed. The park itself consists of 1,476 acres of land, of which 36 acres constitute the shoreline village. Fishing is carried on off Point San Pedro as it has been for more than a century.

Islands of Marin County

The eastern boundary of Marin County runs from Petaluma Point in San Pablo Bay south into San Fran-

cisco Bay far enough to include almost all of Angel Island. Within the water area lie several small islands. The Sisters are a little to the northwest of Point San Pedro. The Marin Islands, upon which Chief Marin hid when escaping from his white pursuers, lie midway between San Pedro Point and San Quentin Point. Just south of the mouth of San Rafael Creek is San Rafael Rock. Directly northwest of California Point is Red Rock, an uninhabited area of an acre or so through which pass the boundary lines of Contra Costa, Marin, and San Francisco counties, and about which cling traditions of buried treasure. The largest of all, Angel Island, opposite Tiburon Point, is separated from the mainland by Racoon Strait. The strait took its name from the British 16-gun sloop of war *Racoon*, which was laid up and repaired on the beach at Ayala Cove in the spring of 1814, after suffering damage on a Pacific voyage.

On August 13, 1775, Lieutenant Juan Manuel de Ayala reached an island in San Francisco Bay to which he gave the name of Nuestra Señora de los Angeles, today known as Angel Island. Ayala's mission at that time was to explore in the interest of Spain the estuaries of San Francisco Bay and to determine whether or not a strait connected Drakes Bay and San Francisco Bay. Finding good anchorage and plenty of wood and water, the explorers based at the island for several weeks while making careful surveys of the surrounding topography. The chaplain of the expedition, Father Santa María, and some of the officers landed several times on the mainland, where they visited a hospitable rancheria, undoubtedly that of the Olómpali.

It was the policy of the Mexican government to see that these islands did not fall into foreign hands, particularly the Russians', who were trapping otter here as late as 1835. Angel Island (then called the Island of Los Angeles) was granted by Governor Juan Alvarado in 1838 to Antonio María Osio, who used it for raising horses and cattle. He did not live on it himself, but he subdivided it, built four houses, made a dam for the conservation of water for his stock, and placed part of the land under cultivation.

At the time of the American takeover, the United States government found Angel Island to be too important to national defense to be left in private hands, and despite Osio's protests, it passed into the public domain in 1852. It seems to have been notorious in the 1850's as a den of thieves and as a dueling ground. On August 21, 1858, before a large crowd, state senator William I. Ferguson of Sacramento met San Francisco newspaper editor William Pen Johnson in a duel with pistols: the wounded Ferguson died 24 days later. A more respectable activity was the quarrying of sandstone on the eastern side, which continued into the 1920's. The island was fortified by the military during the Civil War, there being a persistent rumor of imminent attack by Confederate warships on San Francisco Bay. No marauders actually appeared, although a small Russian Imperial fleet visited San Francisco Bay between October 1863 and May 1864 on a peaceable mission; it was even permitted to use the Mare Island Navy Yard to overhaul one of its ships.

Between 1863 and 1946 the island was an Army base. Fort McDowell, the present East Garrison station, was a major induction station. The house once occupied by the commanding officer, General William Rufus Shafter (later of Spanish-American War fame, and a cousin of the Point Reyes Shafter family), still stands, along with other military housing. During World War II some 87,000 soldiers passed through here on their way to the Pacific front. Prisoners of war were interned here as well.

A quarantine station was built in 1888 at Hospital Cove, and Angel Island became a major Immigration and Public Health facility. This "Ellis Island of the West" was in operation until 1946. The island was turned over to Marin County at that time (except for two tiny points of land that are in the City and County of San Francisco), and in turn it became a state property in 1955.

Today, Angel Island State Park (SRL 529) attracts many visitors; the old military and public health facilities can still be seen. Hospital Cove has been named Ayala Cove in honor of the Spanish explorer of two centuries ago. Mount Ida, the 781-foot summit at the center of the island, was renamed Mount Caroline Livermore in honor of the pioneer Marin County conservationist in 1958. A Coast Guard facility is maintained at Point Blunt. Boat service to the island is available from Tiburon, San Francisco, and Berkeley, depending on the time of the year.

Golden Gate National Recreational Area

This magnificent park was created by act of Congress in 1972. It embraces most of the north and west coastal area of San Francisco and sizeable chunks of Marin County. Much of this was once military property and closed to the public. Fort Baker, set aside as a military reservation in 1850, is still occupied by army families, in houses most of which were built between 1901 and 1904. It lies immediately to the east of the Golden Gate Bridge.

The Marin Headlands along the northern side of the Golden Gate are among the most breathtakingly beautiful spots in all of California. They were once part of the defense perimeter of San Francisco Bay. Originally called Lime Point Military Reservation, the region was divided

Golden Gate Bridge

into three posts named for commanding officers: Fort Baker (1897), Fort Barry (1904), and Fort Cronkhite (1937). Visitors can see the huge concrete emplacements for guns that were never used at several places along Conzelman Road leading west from Fort Barry. Battery Spencer, Battery 129, Battery Wallace, Battery Alexander, Battery Mendell, and Battery Smith-Guthrie are to be seen along the drive.

Nearby Point Bonita Light Station, built in 1855, was the last to be automated, in 1980. With it was the first fog signal installed on the coast, an iron cannon transferred from the Benicia Arsenal. Sergeant Maloney, placed in charge at the point with instructions to "fire the gun every half hour during fogs," reported two months later that since there was almost constant fog and no one to relieve him "for even five minutes" he had been unable to get the "two hours' sleep necessary out of the twenty-four." He resigned shortly thereafter. The gun remained in use for two years before its expense and ineffectiveness caused it to be abandoned in favor of another kind of fog signal. The light station is open to visitors on a limited basis, where they can see the huge Fresnel lens that casts a beam that can be seen seventeen miles out to sea under favorable conditions.

Tennessee Cove received its name after the disaster of March 6, 1853, when the steamer *Tennessee* went

Battery Wallace, Marin Headlands, Golden Gate National Recreation Area

aground in a dense fog. There was no light station along the coast at that time. Happily, no lives were lost. The first light station on the coast was erected on Alcatraz Island in the following year.

Muir Woods National Monument has been incorporated into the Golden Gate National Recreational Area. This stand of *Sequoia sempervirens* on the western slope of Mount Tamalpais contains some trees estimated to be as much as 1,700 years old, with a diameter of 12 feet and a height of 240 feet. The forest area was made a national monument by presidential proclamation in 1908, a gift to the nation from William Kent of Kentfield, a member of the 62nd Congress, and his wife, Elizabeth Thatcher Kent. Although President Theodore Roosevelt expressed his desire in accepting the gift to name it for the donors, they wanted it named for John Muir, California's noted naturalist, explorer, and writer, who had long worked in the cause of forest conservation. Muir lived for six years to enjoy the honor conferred on him in the naming of Muir Woods.

Mount Tamalpais State Park

Two Indian words, *tamal* (bay) and *pais* (mountain or country), form the name of the heavily wooded mountain that dominates the landscape on the north side of San Francisco Bay. In the 1860's it was sometimes called Table Mountain. Its three peaks, East, West, and Middle, are all over 2,500 feet high: West Peak is the highest, at 2,604 feet.

Pedestrian trails, some of which were originally made by Indians and others blazed by white pioneers, are still used by hiking parties. These pathways begin at different places around the base of the mountain; a favorite one starts beneath the shadows of the trees behind the old sawmill at Mill Valley. In 1896 the eight-mile Mount Tamalpais and Muir Woods Railroad was laid out, and after its completion a train drawn by a steam engine carried passengers over 283 curves, giving rise to the name "The Crookedest Railroad in the World." About halfway to the top the track described a double bowknot to accomplish a 100-foot rise within a distance of 1,000 feet. The railway has been a thing of the past since 1930, but a highway following another route displays an extensive panorama at every turn.

From the broad trail that circles the summit of East Peak one may see close at hand bays and islands, cities and bridges. If the atmospheric conditions are good, one can see to the north Mount St. Helena and Mount Shasta, to the east Mount Diablo and the distant peaks of the Sierra Nevada, to the south Mount Hamilton and Loma Prieta, and to the west the vast Pacific Ocean.

Mount Tamalpais State Park, a wooded area of about 2,000 acres, includes the East Peak. Below Rock Spring lies the natural amphitheater where performances are given from time to time. The Dipsea Trail has been the site of an annual footrace since 1905. The Steep Ravine area in the park, gift of William Kent shortly before his death in 1928, is an abrupt descent, with redwoods, firs, and thickets of underbrush.

Point Reyes National Seashore

After considerable negotiation between public officials and private landowners, Point Reyes National Seashore was created in 1962 when President John F. Kennedy signed the act of Congress bringing some 71,000 acres under federal control. Plans for such a park had been offered as early as 1935, but a persistent objection was raised by local property owners. The compromise worked out provided for extensive tracts of agricultural land to remain in private hands within the seashore, although such property cannot be sold except to the federal government for inclusion in the park. A distinctive feature of Point Reyes is the lighthouse, built in 1870 and operated until 1975, in the midst of some of the foggiest territory in the United States.

Mariposa County

The name Mariposa (Spanish for "butterfly") was first given in the plural form, Las Mariposas, to a spot in Merced County visited by the expedition of Gabriel Moraga in 1806. The old Mexican grant conferred upon Juan Bautista Alvarado in 1844 and purchased for John C. Frémont in 1847 by his agent, Thomas O. Larkin, likewise took the plural form of the name, while the singular form, Mariposa, was bestowed first upon the creek and later upon the town and the county.

Some have erroneously thought that this place name was derived from "Mariposa Lily," the common name of the many-hued lilies (*Calochortus luteus* and other varieties) that in late spring and early summer give color to the hills of this region. But it is to the butterfly, which at certain seasons of the year is found here in countless numbers, that the source of the delightful place name must be traced.

Mariposa County was one of the original 27 counties. With an area of about 30,000 square miles, it covered one-fifth of the state. Stretching from the Coast Range to the present Nevada state line, and touching Los Angeles County on the south, it contained land now included within ten other counties. The county's present configuration dates from 1880; its area is 1,455 square miles. Agua Fria was very briefly the first county seat, in 1850–51, after which Mariposa became the seat of government.

Walker's Trail over the Sierra

Joseph Reddeford Walker, as early as 1833, came into California over the Sierra Nevada through what are now Mono, Mariposa, and Tuolumne counties. "Reliable knowledge of the Sierra Nevada," says Francis P. Farquhar, "really begins with this expedition."

Passing down the Humboldt River Valley in Nevada and thence south by Carson Lake, Walker and his men struck westward across the Sierra, probably ascending its eastern slope by one of the southern tributaries of the East Walker River. After crossing the summit of the pass, the party was lost for several days "in a maze of lakes and mountains." The description of this region given by Zenas Leonard, chronicler of the expedition, accords well with the character of the country in the vicinity of Virginia Canyon.

From this point, Farquhar says "they would have crossed the Tuolumne, perhaps near Conness Creek.

Passing Tenaya Lake, they probably followed the course of the present Tioga Road" (mostly in Tuolumne County) down the divide between the Tuolumne and Merced rivers. On this stage of the journey the party saw either the Merced Grove or the Tuolumne Grove of *Sequoia gigantea*, thus being the first known white men to see the Big Trees of the Sierra Nevada.

Yosemite Valley

It is fairly certain that the Walker party saw Yosemite Valley in 1833, although they did not camp in the valley itself. Zenas Leonard recorded in his diary what is thought to be the first mention of Yosemite Valley by a white man: "We travelled a few miles every day, still on the top of the mountains, and our course continually obstructed with snow, hills, and rocks. Here we began to encounter in our path, many small streams which would shoot out from under these high snow-banks, and after running a short distance in deep chasms which they have through ages cut in the rocks, precipitate themselves from one lofty precipice to another, until they are exhausted in rain below. Some of these precipices appeared to us to be more than a mile high. Some of the men thought that if we could succeed in descending one of these precipices to the bottom, we might thus work our way into the valley below—but on making several attempts we found it utterly impossible for a man to descend, to say nothing of our horses."

The diary of William Penn Abrams, a Gold Rush pioneer, reveals that he and his companion, U. N. Reamer, saw Yosemite Valley in October 1849. They were following the tracks of a grizzly bear when they came upon the spectacular scene. Bridal Veil Falls was described as dropping "from a cliff below three jagged peaks into the valley." Half Dome looked to the men "as though it had been sliced with a knife as one would slice a loaf of bread." They called it "Rock of Ages." It is possible that historical research may yet uncover other early accounts of Yosemite.

However, it was not until 1851 that the valley can properly be said to have been discovered and made widely known. The first effective discovery was made by Major James D. Savage and Captain John Boling, who, with a strong detachment of mounted volunteers and friendly Indian guides, entered the valley in March of that year to capture the resident Indians in order to put them on the Fresno Indian Reservation. One of this party of discoverers was Dr. L. H. Bunnell, the first man to make the wonders of the Yosemite Valley known to the world.

Major Savage had come to the mines in 1848, enlisted Indian labor in his diggings in Tuolumne County, and soon developed extensive trading relations with the natives. His first post (SRL 527) was set up at or near the mouth of the South Fork of the Merced River in Mariposa County, but this was abandoned when conflict developed between the Yosemite Indians and the whites in 1850. The site of Savage's post is noted by a marker and a modern commercial establishment on SR 140 close to El Portal.

In 1851 and 1852 a number of punitive expeditions against the Indians entered the valley. The last, led by Army Lieutenant Tredwell Moore finally drove the remnants of the tribe over the mountains, where they took refuge with the Monos.

The tourist history of Yosemite Valley began in 1855, when J. M. Hutchings, in company with three friends, formed the first tourist expedition to enter it. Five days of "scenic banqueting" were spent in exploring the region and sketching its wonders. The publicity given to Hutchings' writings and to the accompanying drawings of Thomas Ayers was considerable, and from then on Yosemite Valley attracted ever-increasing numbers of tourists.

The first improved pack trail into Yosemite Valley was made in 1856 by the Mann Brothers, a livery firm in Mariposa. The trail led from Mariposa to the valley by way of the South Fork of the Merced River, crossing at Wawona. Regular tourist travel to the valley began in 1857. The first house was built there in the autumn of 1856, and the first hotel in 1859. The latter was, until its destruction in 1940, a part of the Sentinel Hotel establishment known as Cedar Cottage.

Nearly all the early visitors to Yosemite Valley were Californians, mostly campers. Only a few hundred came yearly until the completion of the Union Pacific and Central Pacific railroads. Today thousands come annually from all parts of the world. The Yosemite Valley Railroad from Merced to El Portal ceased operation in 1945, and the valley is today reached by four main automobile roads. SR 140, called the All-Year Highway when it opened in 1927, enters from the west via Merced, Mariposa, and El Portal, following the Merced River. SR 120, the Big Oak Flat Road, enters from the northwest, originating at Manteca in the San Joaquin Valley. The Tioga Pass Road, open only in the summer months, is an extension of SR 120 to the east, crossing to Lee Vining in Mono County. SR 41 enters from the south, beginning at Fresno, continuing through Oak-

hurst, and entering Yosemite National Park south of Wawona. Besides these, there are two old routes for the traveler with plenty of time and an indifference to steep, rough roads: the road that runs north and east of SR 49 over Chowchilla Mountain to Wawona, and the road that begins in Coulterville and, as the Old Yosemite Road, continues past Bower Cave and the Merced Grove of Big Trees, the first stagecoach road into Yosemite Valley.

Yosemite Valley (SRL 790) was made a state park on June 30, 1864. A national park surrounding the valley was established in 1890, and the present Yosemite National Park was constituted in 1906, when the state of California ceded the Yosemite Valley and the Mariposa Grove of Big Trees to the federal government.

The name "Yosemite," spelled various ways in early accounts, seems to have first been given to the Indians living in the valley by the Mariposa Battalion invading the region in 1851. It is said that in one native dialect a similar word referred to the fierceness of the grizzly bear, and therefore was appropriate for the fierce defenders of their territory.

Yosemite Valley is only a small portion of the 1,189-square-mile National Park, but it has always been the center of visitor interest. In the valley is the Visitors' Center, with a museum established in 1921, comprising departments of history, ethnology, zoology, and botany. The Indian Cultural Museum and the Indian Village are nearby. The Ahwahnee Hotel, named for the Ahwahneechee Indians who lived in the valley for several thousand years, is a world-famous luxury resort built in 1925. Camp Curry, built in 1899, features bungalows and tents. The wooden chapel was first built in 1879, and was moved to its present location in 1901.

Wawona

At Wawona is the site of the log cabin built by Galen Clark in 1857, the same year in which he discovered the Mariposa Grove of Big Trees, only eight miles from his cabin and now within Yosemite National Park. Galen Clark was a member of the first Board of Commissioners for the care of Yosemite Valley and the Mariposa Grove, and was for many years known as the "Guardian of the Valley." For more than 50 years he lived either in Yosemite or at Wawona. At the latter place his cabin was known to all travelers as Clark's Station, where kindly hospitality never failed to be extended.

At the age of 90, in 1904, Galen Clark published his first book, *Indians of Yosemite*; in 1907, he published another, *Big Trees of California*. Clark finished his last book, *The Yosemite Valley*, just two weeks before his death on March 24, 1910, at the age of 96.

Jorgensen Cabin and Studio, History Center, Yosemite National Park

Wawona is now the home of the Pioneer Yosemite History Center, a collection of the park's oldest structures, most of which were moved here from other areas for permanent preservation. Through this outdoor museum the history of Yosemite National Park is meaningfully interpreted for visitors. Among the buildings are a Wells Fargo office, a jail, a wagon shop, and several cabins, including one built by a trailblazer, another by a homesteader, a third by the U.S. Army, and a fourth by the National Park Service. The historical displays center on the old Wawona covered bridge, spanning the south fork of the Merced River, begun about 1858 by Galen Clark, covered in 1875, and restored in 1956. A large collection of horse-drawn wagons is on the same grounds.

Wawona Hotel, Yosemite National Park

Nearby is the charming old Wawona Hotel, still in operation from April through November. The main building was constructed in 1879; one structure of the group, the Clark Cottage, dates from 1876.

Historic Spots Along the All-Year Highway, SR 140

The All-Year Highway (as it was called when completed in 1927), or SR 140 (as it is now known), runs from Merced to the Yosemite Valley. It passes through one of the most interesting and romantic of California's historic regions. Many of the landmarks of mining days have been obliterated, but here and there stark ruined walls of brick or stone marking the site of some ghost city of the hills may be seen, or an occasional hamlet invites the passerby to linger and picture the lively scenes enacted there in the heyday of its past.

Where the modern highway crosses the Merced-Mariposa county line, the route of the old Stockton–Los Angeles Road (locally known as the Millerton Road) is intersected. Following the base of the lower foothills along what is now the boundary line of the two counties, this old road (now almost lost in the grassy hills) avoided the winter freshets and the labyrinthine tulares then covering the floor of the San Joaquin Valley. Along its route, not always precisely the same, the commerce of the rich southern mines flowed in the days of pack trains and stagecoaches. This road was antedated only by the Los Angeles Trail, El Camino Viejo, on the western side of the valley.

About seven miles from the Merced county line the old Yosemite highway branches to the east. A little to the northwest is the site of Indian Gulch, while to the northeast is Guadalupe, both flourishing mining camps at one time. Stone fences built by Chinese labor are in evidence throughout much of this region. After traversing Cathey's Valley, first settled in the early 1850's and still claiming among its inhabitants descendants of original settlers, the road climbs into the lower mountains of Mariposa County. A few miles west of Mariposa, the Agua Fria Road swings to the north to Mount Bullion. The marker (SRL 518) commemorating Agua Fria is on the north side of SR 140 at Carson, now deserted. Both Carson and sites at neighboring Arkansas Flat were operated as mining camps by hardscrabblers in the depression years of the 1930's.

Agua Fria, the exact site of which is just north of SR 140 on the road to Mount Bullion, was the first county seat of Mariposa County. Today scarcely a trace of the place is left except a few foundation stones and abandoned diggings, and it is hard to believe that this place was once the seat of government for one-fifth of California.

Mariposa

Mariposa, founded on John C. Frémont's Rancho Las Mariposas, a grant that occupied a unique position in the mining history of the state (discussed later in this chapter), became the county seat of Mariposa County in September 1851 and was long the center of trade for the mining area covered by the rancho. The town today has preserved some of the features of early mining camps—buildings with substantial walls of brick and stone supplemented by iron doors and shutters, with an occasional overhanging balcony.

Among the several old buildings dating from early mining days the one of greatest interest is the courthouse (SRL 670). Lumber from neighboring forests was used in its construction and the timbers were fitted together with mortise and tenon and held in place by wooden pegs. Built in 1854, it is the oldest courthouse in California still in use. The clock in its tower has been running since 1866. The rear addition dates from 1900. In spite of their years of service the seats and the bar in the courtroom on the second floor remain unchanged. Adding to the historic interest of the building are many documents and newspaper files of priceless value, which are kept in a fireproof vault. Court was conducted in rented quarters in Mariposa from September 1851 until about May 1855, when it moved into the new courthouse. Three of the old houses facing the courthouse are more than a century old.

Mariposa County Courthouse, Mariposa

Other picturesque and historic buildings in Mariposa are St. Joseph's Catholic Church (1862, enlarged 1958), the Trabucco Warehouse, the Schlageter Hotel (1866), the Trabucco Store, and the Odd Fellows Hall (1867), all of which, like the courthouse, are still in use, and the now-abandoned old stone jail. The Jones home on Jones Street (1858) is still a private residence, as is the Counts house (1865 or earlier) across the street. The weekly *Mariposa Gazette* boasts that it has not missed an issue since January 10, 1854; it is now located in a new building, but its old quarters may still be seen at Jones and Ninth streets, a frame structure now housing the Chamber of Commerce.

The Mariposa County Library and History Center at Twelfth and Jessie streets contains furniture belonging to the Frémont family, good displays of turn-of-the-century businesses, much Indian material, and outdoor exhibits connected with mining activities. Dedicated in 1971 and continually expanding, it is one of the most comprehensive collections in the Mother Lode country.

Vanished Towns near Mariposa

Mormon Bar (SRL 323), one and one-half miles southeast of Mariposa on Mariposa Creek, was first settled in 1849 by Mormons, who, however, stayed only a short time. Their places were taken at once by other miners, while at a later period the same ground was worked over by thousands of Chinese. The site of Mormon Bar has been obliterated by the widening of the highway, but the Mariposa County Fairgrounds are today located close to the old townsite. No longer to be seen is the old Chinese graveyard from which the bones of the dead were carried by friends or relatives back to the ancestral burial ground in China.

Buckeye to the west, where James Savage had one of his trading posts, Bootjack to the east, and Ben Hur, about ten miles to the south, all shared with Mormon Bar the prosperity of their neighbor, the town of Mariposa. Virtually nothing remains of these settlements today. The site of the last Ben Hur post office on the Quick Ranch is located about a mile southeast of the older site on the hill. (The first post office, established in 1890, was named for a novel then popular; the post office was discontinued in 1951.) Not far away is the Quick ranch house, into which has been incorporated a portion of the original house built by Morgan W. Quick, who purchased the original 160 acres of his ranch in 1859 from two men having squatters' rights. The garden and orchard about the present house are still watered from the perpetual spring that attracted the first settlers. The 4,000 acres that constitute the present ranch, still owned by the family, are fenced by a stone

Stone Wall on the Road to Ben Hur

wall, built with great labor and remarkable skill by Chinese workmen in 1862. The old wall, which extends for five miles up hill and down, is a truly marvelous piece of workmanship, and appears to be as sound as it was when first laid.

Mount Bullion

Mount Bullion, located on the mountain of that name, on a part of the former Frémont estate, is some five miles northwest of Mariposa on SR 49. The peak was named in honor of Senator Thomas H. Benton, Frémont's father-in-law, whose nickname was "Old Bullion." Only a few buildings remain. On the left side of the road is a wooden-fronted building, long deserted; by the 1980's only a very keen inspection revealed the painted inscription "Princeton Saloon." The building has been getting more run-down with each new edition of *Historic Spots in California* and is perilously close to collapse today. The deserted Princeton Mine nearby produced almost $4.5 million from its ore. Originally one of Frémont's possessions, it has been closed since 1927; there persists a local belief that a fortune remains to be extracted some day.

Mount Ophir

Another vanished town of the Mother Lode is Mount Ophir, which is located one and one-half miles northwest of Mount Bullion off SR 49. A historical marker stands by the road; the site is a few hundred feet to the west in a brush-covered area. Nothing remains of this once busy settlement except fragmentary ruins, long believed to be those of a privately owned mint from the early 1850's. Recent investigations indicate that no such enterprise existed. It has been suggested that the marker was placed as part of an effort to attract tourists in the early 1900's. Just beyond Mount Ophir, on the way to

Bear Valley, further down SR 49, walls of the Trabucco Store stand at the left of the road, "as pretty a ruin as most of the missions can show," as one traveler has described it. This old trading post of the Mother Lode was erected by Louis Trabucco around 1853.

Bear Valley

The present Mariposa County includes what was once Rancho Las Mariposas, sometimes spoken of as the Frémont Grant, a vast estate constituting one of several so-called "floating grants," and located originally in what is now Merced County. A "floating grant," the cause of endless litigation after the American conquest of California, was a grant of land for which the area was precisely given but the actual boundaries were left unspecified, usually because of inadequate surveys of the region in question. After gold was discovered in the Mariposa region in the spring of 1848, Frémont "floated" his rancho up into the hills. The new location proved to be very rich in gold, and for several years large operations were carried on there by Frémont.

The center of his activities was Bear Valley (SRL 331), on SR 49 about eleven miles northwest of Mariposa. At one time it was practically Frémont's own town, built, owned, and lived in by him. The site of his home is on a slight rise just southeast of Bear Valley to the east of the highway. A whitewashed frame structure, local Indians referred to it as "the Little White House," probably without irony, although Frémont had been the unsuccessful presidential candidate of the new Republican Party in 1856, two years before the house was built. It was something of a rural showplace until it burned in 1866 and the site was leveled.

At Bear Valley one can see the iron framework of the Odd Fellows Hall, built in 1862 and now in ruins. The enterprising Trabucco family built yet another store here, the iron doors of which still stand. The Nicholas Pendola Building and the Garbarius Store are other ruins.

Just beyond Bear Valley, continuing northwest on SR 49 toward Coulterville, stand the ruins of Bear Valley's once thriving Chinatown. The climb up the ridge road from this point is so gradual that one is startled, on making a sudden turn, to look down a thousand feet into Hell's Hollow, a winding grade famous for its dangers even with modern roads. To the north, a vista overlooking the hills is of great beauty, particularly when the spring wildflowers are in bloom.

The winding grade down into the hollow passes the Pine Tree and Josephine mines, once big producers for Frémont. The next place of historic interest is Bagby, formerly Benton Mills, the site of one of Frémont's largest mills and river dams. Bagby was a station on the

Ruins of Trabucco Family Store, Bear Valley

Yosemite Valley Railroad. When the New Exchequer Dam was completed in 1966 and the waters of the Merced River began to back up and create Lake McClure, Bagby was one of several locations inundated by the waters of the lake.

Coulterville

The old mining town of Coulterville (SRL 332) is one of the most picturesque and interesting on the Mother Lode. Mexican miners were at work there when George W. Coulter and George Maxwell arrived in 1850 and set up stores. Coulter embellished his goods tent with a small American flag, and "Banderita" (little flag) was the name first given to the settlement. Coulterville, however, became the official name and has persisted.

Like most of the Mother Lode towns, Coulterville suffered a series of disastrous fires, and most of the remaining old buildings are of adobe, stone, or brick, many with iron doors and shutters. Among these are the Jeffrey Hotel (1851), still dispensing hospitality; the picturesque Sun Sun Wo Company store, like the Jeffrey Hotel an adobe structure dating back to 1851, but not in use since 1920; the Gazzola and Jaenecke buildings, the Canova House and Storehouse, and the Magnolia Saloon and Museum. At the northern edge of town the old frame home associated with Coulter, built in 1857, continues to serve as a private residence.

Built around the ruins of the Coulter Hotel is one of the newest and most welcome additions to the Mother Lode: the Northern Mariposa County History Center. Begun in 1983, it has rapidly grown into an interest-ing historical museum. The structure also includes the old Wells Fargo Building (1856) and McCarthy's Store. Nelson Cody, brother of "Buffalo Bill" Cody, was postmaster here in the 1870's. In front of the History Center (and under the town's Hanging Tree) is an eight-ton Porter narrow-gauge locomotive that did its duty on the tortuous line from the Mary Harrison Mine to the Black Creek Potosi stamping mill, one of several rail lines in California claiming to be "The Crookedest Railroad in the World." The locomotive was in service for a number of years, beginning in 1897.

El Portal

This "gateway" on the west to Yosemite Valley was the terminus of the Yosemite Valley Railroad from Merced (1906–45). As the rising waters of Lake McClure filled some of the river valleys below, old equipment from the narrow-gauge railroad was brought to a site a half-mile west of El Portal and is now on display at the Yosemite Valley Railroad Center. El Portal is also a Park Service headquarters and contains housing for employees working in Yosemite National Park, which begins a half-mile east of the settlement. The settlement perches on a ledge above the Merced River and along SR 140.

Unusual Names

In the early mining days millions of dollars in gold was washed from the gravel beds of Mariposa County's many streams. Quartz mining succeeded placer mining, and veins of fabulous wealth were located in the great Mother Lode, which stretches throughout the width of the county. Numerous camps, many of them with odd or unusual names, sprang up all over the county, such as Texas Tent, Cow-and-Calf, Drunken Gulch, Red Cloud, Poison Springs, Hog Canyon, Fly Away, Boneyard, White Rock, Mariposita, Sherlock's Diggings, Whitlock, Pleasant Valley, Hornitos, and Chamisal. Only Hornitos can still be located and visited.

Hornitos

Hornitos ("little ovens"), thirteen miles west of Mount Bullion, derived its name in all likelihood from the presence of many Mexican graves or tombs built of stone in the shape of little bake ovens and set on top of the ground. On the hillside just below the Catholic church and cemetery the ruins of two or three of these interesting relics may be seen. Some authorities believe the name came rather from the outdoor ovens on which the Mexican women cooked. Some early settlers may have come from Los Hornitos in Sonora, Mexico, and bestowed a familiar name on the new location, a common practice throughout much of North America.

Hornitos was settled by Mexican miners and their associates driven from the settlement of Quartzburg, four miles east on the highway, in 1850. The new place had a reputation for rowdiness and violence, with names like Dead Man's Alley and a Chinese colony where gambling dens were run openly. Inevitably, local legends tell that the notorious bandit Joaquín Murieta was a denizen of Hornitos. "Blood was upon nearly every doorstep and the sand was caked with it," says one account.

In time, however, a change came over the place. When the placers at Quartzburg (a short distance up the creek) gave out, many of its citizens came to Hornitos, where the diggings were very rich. In 1870 it became the first and to date only incorporated town in Mariposa County. Ordinances were passed remedying many of the old social abuses, the gambling dens became stores, and children played on the streets. The "city" has never been officially disincorporated, but it has not exercised its municipal functions for many years.

Hornitos (SRL 333) appears today much as it was years ago, with only an occasional electric light bulb visible to indicate the modern age. Some see a distinct Mexican influence in the quaint adobe and stone structures with their massive iron doors, many in ruins and others closed and deserted. Among the interesting buildings from the mining days are the stout stone jail, the Cavagnaro and Gagliardo stores (parts of the interiors of which are on display in the County Historical Center in Mariposa), and two remaining walls of the store run by Domingo Ghirardelli, who left to open his chocolate factory in San Francisco "and has since become a household word," as one contemporary admirer put it. The Masonic Hall, a single-story building erected in 1860 and still in use, was once the only one in California with its meeting hall on the ground floor. A few bullet holes can be seen in the wooden door casings. St. Catherine's Catholic Church, built in 1869, has not held regular services for many years, but it is periodically given a fresh coat of whitewash.

As for virtuous Quartzburg, at one time a populous center of placer mining in Mariposa County, with fraternal societies and all the organizations that made up the social life of the time but no tolerance for the Mexican "rowdies," its last fragments were bulldozed when the highway was widened around 1979. Only the old cemetery on the hill to the north of Road J-16, about four miles east of Hornitos, survives as a reminder that in 1851 this place came close to being chosen the county seat of Mariposa County.

Mendocino County

Mendocino County was one of the original 27 counties, but until 1859 the government was administered by Sonoma County officials. The name was first applied to Cape Mendocino, so named in honor of Antonio de Mendoza, the first viceroy of New Spain, although it is not known when the name was first used. Ukiah has always been the county seat.

Point Arena

Point Arena, or Punta de Arenas ("Sandy Point"), is a prominent headland on the coast in the southwestern part of the county. Captain George Vancouver spent the night of November 10, 1792, offshore at this point in his ship *Discovery*, while on his way from Nootka to San Francisco. Vancouver called the place "Punta Barro de Arena" (sandy clay).

The land stretching back from this point was included in an unnamed and unconfirmed grant made in 1844 to Rafael García, an early soldier of the San Francisco Company and already owner of two grants in what is now Marin County. He stocked the land with cattle; the Garcia River flowing through the land bears his name. This grantee and Antonio Castro were reported to have been the leaders of a party of white men who raided the Indians in the vicinity of Ross in 1845 in search of laborers.

The Manchester Indian Rancheria is located on the Garcia River; the Point Arena Indian Rancheria is located about two miles to the west, off Windy Hollow Road, three miles south of Manchester.

Although a store was in operation on the site in 1859, the town of Point Arena was not incorporated until 1908. It is said that when the lumbering industry was at its

Point Arena Lighthouse

light station is located about three miles north of the town of Point Arena and about a mile and a half west of SR 1.

The Redwoods

The humid coast belt in which this county lies is the natural habitat of the coast redwood (*Sequoia sempervirens*). The rugged shoreline, famous for its vistas of the Pacific Ocean, is cut by wooded canyons formed by numerous mountain streams flowing seaward through fine stands of these and other native trees. The abundant redwood trees, and their superb, durable lumber, induced rapid settlement and exploitation in much the same way that gold brought settlers and adventurers into the Mother Lode and the Sierra Nevada. Fortunately, some of these forests escaped the axe and saw of the pioneer lumbermen. Efforts made by the Save-the-Redwoods League and other conservation groups have resulted in the creation of a series of parks and reserves throughout the Redwood Empire of northern coastal California.

Russian Gulch State Park just north of Mendocino covers 1,103 acres, some of which contain stands of second-growth redwoods. Other coastal preserves are Van Damme State Park to the south; along the coast north of Mendocino, the Jug Handle State Reserve; and, near the Humboldt County line, the large Sinkyone Wilderness State Park, containing a stand of old-growth redwoods, the Sally Bell Grove. North of Laytonville are the Smithe Redwoods State Reserve and the Standish-Hickey State Recreation Area. The Admiral William H. Standley State Recreation Area just south of Branscomb, fourteen miles west of Laytonville, is another redwood preserve, named for a naval officer born in the county. Montgomery Woods State Reserve and Mailliard Redwoods State Reserve are, respectively, northwest of Ukiah and west of SR 128 at Ornbaum Springs. The part of Hendy Woods State Park along the Navarro River contains two large redwood groves; the park is near Philo on SR 128.

Mendocino

A vessel carrying a cargo of silk and tea to San Francisco in 1851 encountered a severe storm and was driven ashore at the mouth of the Noyo River. A party sent from Bodega to salvage the freight saw the timber along this part of the coast, with its readily available lumber supply, and carried the information to Alderman Harry Meiggs of San Francisco. Meiggs, in addition to his political interests, was a mill owner and lumberman, with his main depot at North Beach in San Francisco.

height, Point Arena was the busiest town between San Francisco and Eureka. Asphalt, which exuded from an ocean bluff nearby in quantities insufficient for commercial exploitation—as was proved during the oil excitement of 1865—is used on the streets of the town and makes a satisfactory road surface.

In 1870 a light station was erected well out on the point. The tower, built of brick, was destroyed in the earthquake of 1906; another, of reinforced concrete, was built subsequently a little distance back from the point. The present tower is 115 feet high; it and Pigeon Point Lighthouse in San Mateo County, of the same height, are the two loftiest on the Pacific Coast. Before the establishment of this light, many vessels were lost here. The night of November 20, 1865, is memorable for a disastrous storm in which ten vessels went ashore within a few miles of the point. In 1949, the British cargo ship *Pacific Enterprise* was wrecked near the lighthouse.

The light has been operated automatically since June 1976. The tower is open to the public for tours. A museum is in the adjacent Fog Signal Building. The

With an eye on the opportunity to exploit the territory, Meiggs acquired special equipment to handle immense logs and in July 1852 brought his gear north on the chartered brig *Ontario* to the mouth of Big River. Here William Kasten, one of those who had been driven ashore by the foul weather, claimed the waterfront. Meiggs purchased Kasten's claim and set up the California Lumber Company, the first mill products of which went to build Kasten's new house on what is now Kasten Street in Mendocino.

Along this part of the Mendocino coast, many houses and barns were built of the abundant lumber and painted red with white trim, a style said to be akin to that of the New England coast and described often as "State-of-Maine" architecture. While lumbering remained an important part of the coastal economy, agriculture also developed. In the middle of the twentieth century, a sudden influx of tourists headed for Mendocino, which has become a popular attraction. Many of the old buildings in town have been refurbished and are seeing a second life as inns, shops, or offices. Artists find the place stimulating, and hikers and naturalists enjoy the many nearby attractions.

Landmarks in the small town of Mendocino include the Presbyterian Church (SRL 714), dedicated in 1868, the oldest of its denomination in continuous use in California, and the Masonic Hall, surmounted by a pair of carved wooden figures, the meaning of which is perennially debated. The Ford House Visitor Center at 724 Main was acquired by the State Department of Parks and Recreation as part of the new Mendocino Headlands State Park in 1972 and became a public building in 1983. It has exhibits on the natural and cultural history of the area. The house was built by Jerome Ford for his bride, Martha, in 1854 and was in the family for

many years; Ford was manager of the Mendocino operation of the California Lumber Company, now owned by the Union Lumber Company of Fort Bragg. William H. Kelley, who arrived with Meiggs at the mouth of Big River in 1852, stayed on to build his elegant two-story house at 45007 Albion Street in 1861. Carefully preserved by Mendocino Historical Research, Inc., the Kelley house contains a useful reference library and is set in attractive grounds. The town of Mendocino is a Historic Preservation District listed on the National Register of Historic Places.

Coastal Mill Towns

During the height of the lumbering activity, a number of towns grew up along the coast, each one a shipping point. Twenty mills, including some for making shingles only, were erected in Beaver Township before 1880. In almost every mile, along a creek or gulch or river, could be found a mill with its narrow-gauge railway built up the canyon a few miles for the purpose of bringing lumber or logs from the mountains down to the landing places. Ox teams dragged the logs from where they were felled to the railways. Most of these mills along the coast were operated with no loading facilities other than chutes from the cliffs, down which the lumber was slipped to the vessels lying at anchor below.

From north to south these coast towns and hamlets were Usal, Rockport, Hardy Creek, Westport, Cleone, Fort Bragg, Noyo, Caspar, Mendocino, Little River, Albion, Navarro, Greenwood, Elk River, and, at the very southern edge of the county, Gualala. With the decline of lumbering, many of the old towns lost much of their population, but the increasing tourist business has lured many people back to this picturesque coast, which is enjoying a revival today.

Rockport is an almost abandoned place on a wild and inhospitable coast. Hardy Creek, with its score or two of cottages scattered along a deep canyon opening into a triangle of blue sea, has become a ghost town. Noyo, lying at the mouth of the Noyo River, is a significant fishing center; its deep-water harbor is a coastal landmark. The bridge where SR 1 spans the river is one of the most photographed and painted in the state.

Little River contains two famous hostelries. The Little River Inn is located in the Silas W. Coombs House, built in 1853, and completely modernized. Nearby is Heritage House, the first building of which was put up by the grandfather of the present innkeeper in 1877. The place enjoyed a varied past; among other things, it was a rum-running center for bootleggers during Pro-

Kelley House, Mendocino

hibition. The New England architecture of the coast is prominent in these places, as it is elsewhere. Albion is primarily a fishing town. The second mill in the county was erected there during the winter of 1852–53 under contract with Captain William Richardson of Marin County. In 1845 Captain Richardson applied for a grant of land covering this area, which extended from the Albion River to the Garcia River. This estate, known as the Albion Grant, was never confirmed by the United States.

Navarro, set in a deep valley at the mouth of a broad, winding river, was thus described by J. Smeaton Chase in 1913: "Most of the buildings were out of plumb; the church leaned at an alarming angle; and a loon, swimming leisurely in the middle of the stream, seemed to certify the solitude of the place." Today little remains of this old town, but another community fourteen miles up the river preserves the name. Greenwood is the location of the Elk post office, while Elk River, two miles south, is virtually deserted. Gualala, at the mouth of the picturesque Gualala River, had its lumbering heyday in the 1860's and 1870's.

The Sanel Grant, Sanel, and Hopland

Fernando Felix (Feliz), a former *regidor* at the Pueblo San José and already owner of Rancho Novato, received in 1844 a large tract of land in Sanel Valley lying along the Russian River. He erected an adobe house, 20 by 50 feet, and lived with his family just south of where Hopland now stands. He had lived there for seven years when in 1860 he received the United States patent for the 17,754 acres comprised in his estate.

The settlement that grew up around the Felix home was known by 1859 as Sanel. Then a toll road was built down the east side of the river, which rerouted all the traffic that way, and the town gradually moved over to the road, leaving only one building, a brick store, behind. The new site was called Hopland. Later the building of a railroad drew business back to the original site; and eventually the two places consolidated as Hopland, being called by the residents Old Hopland and New Hopland.

A populous Indian village once existed just south of Old Hopland on the south bank of McDowell Creek. It was called "Sanel," and from this village the grant, the township, and the town preceding Hopland all inherited the name Sanel. Six miles south of Hopland on US 101 is Squaw Rock (SRL 549), also called "Lover's Leap," associated with a Sanel Indian legend. Sotuka, an Indian maiden, is supposed to have jumped from the precipice upon her faithless lover and the girl for whom he

had deserted her, as they lay sleeping below, bringing death to all three.

The first hops grown in this once famous hop-raising center were planted by Stephen Warren Knowles, who settled in Sanel Township in 1858, after arriving in San Francisco on the steamer *Northern Light* a few years earlier. He sold his first crop, dried in the loft of his barn, in Petaluma for 30 cents a pound. The Hermitage post office of early days was on the Knowles's place. Hop growing has now been replaced by the grape industry in this area.

The Yokaya Grant and Ukiah

The Indian word *yokaya* has been translated to mean "south valley" or "deep valley between high hills." The Yokaya Grant of eleven square leagues lay in the fertile valley of the Russian River. It was given by Governor Pío Pico in 1845 to Cayetano Juárez, a native Californian who was a captain of militia and had engaged in many Indian forays. Captain Juárez was also the grantee of Rancho Tulucay in the Napa Valley four years earlier. He had built an adobe there for a permanent home, where he died in 1833 at the age of 75. Patent to this land was received by Juárez from the United States in 1867. Later owners (Hastings, Curry, and Carpenter) surveyed the property and sold it in tracts.

The town of Ukiah, within the boundary of the grant and taking its name phonetically, had its origin in the 1850's. The first settler on the site, Sam Lowry, had established himself there by 1856, but sold out within a year to A. T. Perkins, who became a permanent resident. In 1859, when Sonoma County officials were relieved of the administration of county affairs, the little

Sun House, Ukiah

town was chosen as the county seat. At that time only 100 people were dwelling in the Russian River Valley. The Parducci Winery on the north side of Ukiah, established in 1931, was for many years the northernmost winery in California.

An interesting and unusual building is the Sun House (SRL 926) at 431 South Main Street in Ukiah. This was constructed in 1911 in the California Craftsman style, featuring extensive use of redwood, and has the Hopi Indian sign for the sun deity standing over the front door. This was the home of John Hudson, M.D., and his wife, Grace Carpenter Hudson. He became one of the leading amateur anthropologists of his day, concentrating on the Pomo Indians. Grace Hudson was a well-known artist whose paintings—more than 600—document the life of the Pomo Indians, who were fast dying out in her lifetime. The Sun House Cultural Center, on the extensive grounds of the Sun House, is a showplace for many of Grace Hudson's paintings and for the collections of Dr. Hudson.

Another interesting building in Ukiah is Moore's Flour Mill at 400 South State Street. Still in operation, the water-powered mill employs grindstones more than 100 years old. The Held-Poage Memorial Home and Research Library, built in 1903, at 603 West Perkins Street contains over 3,500 volumes on Mendocino County history and a small display of Indian artifacts.

Fort Bragg

Lieutenant Horatio Gates Gibson was ordered in June 1857 to establish a military post on the Mendocino Indian Reservation. The post was placed one and one-half miles north of the mouth of the Noyo River and was named Fort Bragg in honor of General Braxton Bragg of Mexican War fame. Lieutenant Gibson, who afterward attained the rank of brigadier general, re-

Fort Building, Fort Bragg

mained there for one year. For some years before his death in his nineties he had the distinction of being the oldest living graduate of West Point.

Fort Bragg was located within the city limits of the thriving town that grew up on its site. A historical marker (SRL 615) at 321 Main Street stands upon land that was once part of the fort. The last building from the original fort now stands at 440 Franklin Street and is called the Fort Building. It was moved to its present site around 1890. The location once occupied by the Fort Building is now the Guest House Museum, also known as the Fort Bragg Redwood Museum. This building at 90 West Redwood Avenue was once the C. R. Johnson guest house and is now a logging and lumbering museum.

Next door to the Guest House Museum is the Fort Bragg station of the California Western Railroad. Fort Bragg is the only coastal city in the county to have a railroad connection. The route of the California Western is one of the most scenic in the state, passing along the Noyo River through magnificent redwood forests to Willits on the Redwood Highway. The railroad, over which the Georgia-Pacific Lumber Company ships its product, also offers a passenger service, the "Skunk Train," which has become immensely popular with tourists. The town is also a shipping point for fish and farm and dairy products. From here the coast road runs north through several miles of sand dunes. At Ten Mile River the shore becomes rugged with high cliffs and surf-beaten rocks honeycombed with caves.

Willits

The town of Willits, 40 miles east of Fort Bragg, had its origins in a store opened in 1856 by Kirk Brier from Petaluma. His venture was followed by a blacksmith shop and a saloon. Hiram Willits, who had come to the county in 1857, purchased the store, and the town, incorporated in 1888, was called by his name. The strikingly handsome California Western Railroad station is made of superbly crafted redwood pieces and shingles. The Mendocino County Museum is located at 400 East Commercial Street, an outstanding example of local historic preservation.

Spy Rock

About two miles south of Twin Rocks Creek and 33 miles north of Willits, Spy Rock Road branches east from US 101. About eight miles distant along this road is Spy Rock, an isolated peak in the Eel River Canyon, where Indians in early days built smoke signal fires.

Round Valley

East of Spy Rock and north of the town of Covelo is Round Valley (SRL 674), a circular valley about seven miles in diameter. Here is the Round Valley Indian Reservation, where in 1856, early in the administration of Thomas J. Henley, superintendent of Indian affairs, a farm called the Nome Cult Station (*Nomcult* being a Wintun word meaning "West Tribe") was established by the government, principally as a breeding and fattening station for beef to supply the reservation at Fort Bragg on the coast. Round Valley was declared a reservation in 1858. In 1863 a military post was established there with 70 soldiers under the command of Captain Douglas. Soon afterward a company of cavalry came as reinforcement. This post was maintained until the reservation was turned over to the care of the Methodist Episcopal Church, in accordance with the more peaceable policy of General U. S. Grant toward the Indians.

The Round Valley Indian Reservation is now under the jurisdiction of the Sacramento Indian Agency. Some nine separate tribes still live here. The Round Valley historical monument is located at Inspiration Point on the main road between Dos Rios and Covelo.

Mineral Springs

Ukiah Vichy Springs (SRL 980), known and used by the Indians before the arrival of white settlers, are three miles east of Ukiah. These waters are said to be similar to those of Vichy, France. The place was developed into a summer resort in the 1890's and continued to be popular until the buildings were destroyed by fire. Orr's Hot Sulphur Springs, equipped with a small hotel and a number of cabins, are located on Orr Springs Road at the edge of the redwood belt fourteen miles west of Ukiah.

Black Bart's Rock

A huge boulder on the highway south of Willits, known as Black Bart's Rock, is said to have been the hideout of Black Bart, the bandit, who robbed the mail stage there in pioneer days. Between the years 1875 and 1883 Black Bart became a synonym for elusiveness and mystery. During that time he robbed 27 coaches, traveling on foot for thousands of miles in rough mountain country from the Sierra to the Coast Range. Calaveras, Sierra, Plumas, Yuba, Butte, Shasta, Sonoma, Mendocino, and Trinity counties all knew the terror of this lone highwayman in the linen duster and mask who eluded years of diligent search by detectives. His endurance seemed superhuman, for, although it was said that he always traveled on foot, he was known to have robbed two coaches 60 miles apart in a rough mountain region within 24 hours.

Black Bart was never vicious and seemed averse to taking human life. He was immaculate in dress and extremely polite, a man of refinement and education. Because he was such a quiet, respectable, delicate-looking person, he lived in San Francisco for years under the very eyes of the detectives without once being suspected. He even frequented the favorite restaurant of the police headquarters staff, a bakery on Kearny Street, sometimes eating at the same table with the officers. Black Bart seemed thoroughly to enjoy his own cleverness and notoriety, and a decided sense of humor often expressed itself in facetious rhymes left on empty mail or express boxes for the baffled officers to read.

The mystery of Black Bart's identity was finally unraveled through the combined efforts of Sheriff Thorne of San Andreas, Detective Harry N. Morse, and James B. Hume, special agent of the Wells Fargo Company, whose iron-bound boxes were so frequently rifled in transit. The bandit's propensity for cleanliness finally proved his undoing, for on November 3, 1883, at Funk Hill, on the stage run between Sonora and Milton (Calaveras County), not far from the scene of the first robbery of his career, he dropped a handkerchief while he was busily engaged in opening an express box containing $4,100 in coin. The mark "F.X.o.7." on this piece of linen led Detective Morse, specially hired by Hume, after a most careful search to a laundry on Bush Street in San Francisco to which the fastidious Black Bart had for years carried his little bundle. He had lived in San Francisco all that time under the name of Charles E. Bolton, ostensibly a mining man who made periodic trips to the mines. He was lodged in jail at San Andreas and was shortly sentenced to San Quentin, where he started his term November 21, 1883, and was released January 23, 1888. His whereabouts after that date are unknown.

Anderson Valley

About fifteen miles long and from two to three miles wide, Anderson Valley is crossed by SR 128 halfway between US 101 and the coast. Settled in 1850, it has been a prosperous agricultural region ever since. In recent years wine making has been added to the activities of apple and hop growing.

Boontling is a dialect peculiar to Anderson Valley; it is thought to have begun among the hop growers around the town of Boonville. The more than 1,200 special words of Boontling derive from Pomo Indian speech, Spanish, and the language of the early Scotch-Irish settlers. It is still in use among many of the valley folk. Glossaries of Boontling have been compiled and can be purchased locally.

Boonville, the chief town of the valley, is also the site of the Mendocino County Fairgrounds and the charming Anderson Valley Historical Museum, located in the Little Red School House on the main thoroughfare through the town. The Evergreen Cemetery, still in use, is a well-maintained historic spot on the outskirts of Boonville.

Merced County

Merced County was organized in 1855 from a part of Mariposa County. It was named for the river that Gabriel Moraga, in 1806, had called El Río de Nuestra Señora de la Merced, "The River of Our Lady of Mercy." The county seat first chosen was located on the Turner and Osborn Ranch, but in 1857 it was moved to Snelling's Ranch, and in 1872 to Merced.

Rancheria in Menjoulet Canyon

Menjoulet Canyon, named for a French sheepman of the late 1870's, is today under the waters of Los Banos Creek Reservoir. In 1925 the plateau adjacent to the canyon was excavated, revealing the site of an Indian rancheria three or four hundred years old. Well-defined outlines of six houses were discovered, one of them being 67 feet across and six feet deep. An old barn, fire pits, and the remains of some 40 bodies were also discovered. A second excavation in 1964, just before the inundation began, discovered the first cremations ever found in the region. This seems to have been the earliest known human habitation in Merced County.

First Trails

Little was known of the great interior valleys of the San Joaquin and Sacramento rivers until the beginning of the nineteenth century. During the second administration of Governor José Joaquín de Arrillaga, active exploration of the interior began for the purposes of checking Indian raids on the coastal settlements and establishing missions for Indian conversion. A number of minor expeditions were made into the tulares, or swamps, of the San Joaquin in 1805 and 1806, but scant record is left of these. The first expeditions of which we have much knowledge, as well as the most important from the standpoint of accomplishments, were those made by Gabriel Moraga, called "the greatest pathfinder and Indian fighter of his day."

Moraga, with 25 men and Father Pedro Muñoz as chaplain and diarist, left San Juan Bautista on September 21, 1806, probably entering the valley of the tules by way of San Luis Creek in Merced County. Proceeding across the San Joaquin River, they reached a slough, the haunt of numerous butterflies, which Moraga named "Las Mariposas." Father Muñoz says that here one of the soldiers was sorely afflicted by a butterfly that lodged in his ear. The name, in the singular form, survives in Mariposa Slough, Mariposa Creek, and Mariposa County. The creek has its source in Mariposa County, which lay east of Moraga's march.

Traveling north and northwest, the party toiled for 40 miles through a parched and treeless plain. Coming suddenly upon a clear, sparkling stream, they expressed their gratitude by naming it El Río de Nuestra Señora de la Merced, a name that was applied not only to Merced River but later to the county and to the present city and county seat. The place seemed so beautiful to the tired travelers that Father Muñoz enthusiastically declared it to be an excellent site for a mission.

Moraga explored the lower course of the Merced River in the fall of 1808. He again touched the county in 1810 on his way down the west side of the San Joaquin River from the north. Turning west along San Luis Creek, he returned to San Juan Bautista by way of Pacheco Pass.

The magnitude of Moraga's achievement was never realized by himself or the mission fathers. To them the project was a failure, since it had discovered no sites suitable for the building of an inland mission chain.

The first American to pass through the San Joaquin Valley, although he may not have touched on what is now Merced County, and the first white man to cross the Sierra Nevada, was Jedediah Strong Smith, the great pathfinder and trail breaker of the West. In 1827 he and his party camped on various rivers in the San Joaquin Valley while engaged in trapping beaver. Smith called one of these the Wimmulche (Wimilche) after a tribe of Indians living there. Some historians identify this river with the present Kings River. At any rate, Smith trapped there for a time and then, leaving some of his men encamped on the Wimilche, he crossed the mountains by a route not definitely determined.

Following in Smith's footsteps came other adventurers, and from 1828 until the American occupation, beaver skins may have been gathered along the rivers of Merced County by Hudson's Bay trappers and others, among them Peter Skene Ogden, Michel La Framboise, and Ewing Young.

John C. Frémont, on his way out of California in 1844, proceeded southward from Sutter's Fort, passing through what is now Merced County, and reached the Merced River on April 1. On the following day a raft was constructed, with which the party crossed the river somewhere near its junction with the San Joaquin. Camp was made on the far bank. On April 3 the expedition stopped on the north bank of Bear Creek five miles from its mouth, and the next day they ferried the stream, continuing up the San Joaquin River into today's Madera County.

Westside Trails and Pacheco Pass

Where the foothills of the Mount Diablo Range meet the western rim of the Great Valley, El Camino Viejo, the old westside trail from San Pedro to San Antonio (now part of East Oakland), crossed El Arroyo de Ortigalito ("little nettle"), a link in that long chain of arroyos and *aguajes* (water holes) about which the huts of the Indians had clustered for ages, and along which the Spaniards later laid out their ranchos. From the water holes of Ortigalito, El Camino Viejo proceeded northwest to El Arroyo de los Baños del Padre Arroyo, where fresh water was again found.

Still farther to the north the road crossed El Arroyo de San Luís Gonzaga at Rancho Centinela, where another water hole was found 50 yards to the north. Leaving Centinela, El Camino Viejo skirted the abrupt foothills that led to El Arroyo de Romero, named after a Spaniard from San Juan Bautista who was killed there by Indians. Finally, El Arroyo de Quinto ("fifth creek"), the last watering place in Merced County, was reached. An adobe, probably built before 1840, stood on the plains among the cottonwoods of Quinto Creek as late as 1915.

With the coming of the Americans and the growth of transportation from Stockton to points south, the Stockton-Visalia Road was developed parallel to El Camino Viejo. It followed along the west side of the San Joaquin River, the exact route varying according to the seasonal changes in the river country. The one-story adobe at San Luis Camp on Wolfsen Road, seven and one-half miles north of Los Banos via Highway J-14, was once an important low-water station on this road. Still in good condition, the adobe is rather hard to see because of flanking houses and extensive old trees growing around it; it is on private property. This adobe and other structures built in the early 1840's came under the control of the firm of Miller and Lux; Henry Miller customarily slept in this house whenever he visited this part of his estate.

Joining the Stockton-Visalia Road eight miles northeast of Los Banos, the older Pacheco Pass stage road came in from the west. Long before the Americans came Indians had worn a deep trail over the hills by way of Pacheco Pass, and Spanish explorers in search of mission sites, as well as Spanish officers in pursuit of deserting soldiers or runaway mission Indians, made use of this old mountain path.

A toll road was built over the Pacheco Pass in 1856–57 by A. D. Firebaugh. Two miles west of the summit (in Santa Clara County), and a mile from where the Mountain House later stood, he built a toll station. Portions of the old rock walls of the toll house may still be seen in the narrow defile below the present highway. Along the rocky creek bed, marks of the former stage road lead past the ruins and up the steep hillside, where the route is marked by the remnant of a picturesque split-rail fence of the 1860's.

The early stage road was used by the Butterfield overland stages from 1858 to 1861; on it San Luis Station was an important stopping place. It was eighteen miles from San Luis Ranch east to the Lone Willow Station, and from there the stages passed through a long stretch of desolate alkali wastes to Temple's Ranch and on to Firebaugh's Ferry in Fresno County. During the middle 1860's the loneliness of this part of the road was relieved by the cabin of David Mortimer Wood at Dos Palos, where a lantern was placed in the window at night to guide the drivers of the Gilroy-Visalia stages. Water for the horses was available, too, and in return Wood received supplies and mail brought by the stagecoaches. The part of the old road that lay between Los Banos Creek and Santa Rita ran about one mile and a half north of the present highway, SR 152, which was completed in 1923. Along it were the earliest pioneer American settlements of the Los Banos district. Very little remains to mark any of these places except an occasional black and gnarled tree or faint traces of the former roadbed.

Pacheco Pass is now SRL 829. A plaque has been mounted at the Romero Overlook above the San Luis Reservoir.

A branch of the Pacheco Pass Road crossed El Camino Viejo at Rancho Centinela. From this point it continued northeast to the ford on the San Joaquin River where Hill's Ferry in Stanislaus County was established in the days of the gold rush.

Rancho San Luis Gonzaga

Juan Pérez Pacheco and José María Mejía were granted Rancho San Luís Gonzaga in 1843. Captain Mejía's name had been added to the petition to lend prestige, and by agreement he conveyed his interest to Pacheco. The rancho had previously been granted in 1841 to Francisco Rivera, but he had not met the conditions of the grant, having left the land unoccupied for two years. Grants of land were often made to prominent men, who in return were to help prevent the roving Tulare Indians from raiding the stock at the coast missions. The petitioners, Pacheco and Mejía, indicated that they were prepared to do this, and they received the grant. Juan Pacheco died in 1855, and his property reverted to his father, Francisco Pérez Pacheco, already the holder of much land in present San Benito County.

The Arroyo de San Luís Gonzaga, which had received its name very early in the nineteenth century from Spanish explorers, was chosen by Juan Pérez Pacheco as his homesite. He built his adobe on the ancient *aguaje*, the site of Lis-nay-yuk, a prehistoric Indian village. To it herds of antelope came to drink, and traveling tribes of Indians rested by its springs on their journeys over Pacheco Pass. Later came the Spanish explorers and rancheros, then the stagecoach drivers of the American period, and, finally, the motorists of the twentieth century.

The one-story adobe built by the younger Pacheco soon after he took possession of the rancho stood in good condition at San Luis Station on SR 152 until 1962. Still displaying in its walls the loopholes through which guns could be fired, the adobe served various purposes through the years, including, in the 1920's and 1930's, a roadside refreshment stand. In 1948 it became the home of Miss Paula Fatjo, a fifth-generation direct descendant of Don Francisco Pérez Pacheco and owner of much of the old rancho. With such good care the ancient structure seemed destined to survive many more years. But the rancho was chosen as the site of the San Luis Dam, and the old water hole was to be under several hundred feet of water in the new reservoir. Exca-

vations (which disclosed prehistoric burials estimated to be between 1,000 and 1,500 years old) were begun, with President John F. Kennedy present at the inaugural ceremonies in August 1962. Rather than allow her adobe to disappear, Miss Fatjo decided to move it, at her own expense, to her new ranch headquarters on the western part of the old rancho, just across Pacheco Pass in Santa Clara County, a distance of ten miles. Every precaution was taken to ensure the safety of the building in transit, and, on December 6, 1962, it was inched up the steep grade by truck. Less than a mile short of its destination, unfortunately, the oldest existing adobe in the San Joaquin Valley collapsed into the highway. While portions of the building, including the two ends, were saved, and many of the bricks from the side walls were salvaged, the remains have been placed in storage until the immensely costly work of restoration can be undertaken.

Pacheco also built a two-story adobe at San Luis, but it was destroyed by the earthquake of 1868. It had served as a station on the Butterfield Overland Stage Line from 1858 to 1861.

Until land was sold to the federal government and the State of California, the entire rancho was owned by direct descendants of the Pachecos.

Rancho Centinela was originally a part of San Luís Gonzaga. No traces remain of its old buildings. Centinela, on the road to Gustine at the crossing of San Luis Creek, is one of many places in California where legends of buried treasure long persisted. The name of the current roadside stop at the old site has been corrupted to "Santa Nella."

Rancho Sanjón de Santa Rita

Santa Rita, as well as San Luís Gonzaga, was a place name known to Gabriel Moraga as early as 1806; they were both mentioned in the journal of his expedition of that year. Rancho Sanjón ("deep slough") de Santa Rita was granted to Francisco Soberanes in 1841. With the coming of the Americans the grant changed hands many times. In 1863, a portion of the lands of the rancho came into the possession of Henry Miller, who thus secured his first foothold in the San Joaquin Valley.

By 1866 the remainder of Rancho Sanjón de Santa Rita had been purchased by Henry Miller. From that year the firm of Miller and Lux gradually increased its holdings in this section, until by the 1890's they owned land extending for 68 miles along the west side of the San Joaquin Valley, from Firebaugh's Ferry in Fresno County to Arroyo de Orestimba in Stanislaus County. In addition, they held thousands of acres in the Buena Vista Lake district of Kern County, 200,000 acres on the east side of the valley, as well as thousands of acres in other parts of California (including their original holdings in the Santa Clara Valley) and in Oregon and Nevada. At the time of Miller's death on October 14, 1916, it was estimated that the "Kingdom of Miller and Lux" included a million acres of land and control of a million and half more through leases and grazing arrangements for Miller's herds.

By means of irrigation, Henry Miller turned many desert tracts into flourishing fields. He often seized waters and lands for the purpose, fighting those who tried to prevent him. Once he had acquired water rights by force, he offered part of them to adjacent towns and ranches for a consideration. The immense Miller and Lux holdings are now divided into small farms.

The Miller and Lux headquarters were at the old Rancho Santa Rita. A few of the buildings erected during Henry Miller's lifetime remained for many years, but now all have been demolished except the old company store. The site is north of SR 152 via Indiana Road, four miles west of the San Joaquin River, and thirteen miles east of Los Banos. A little town called Santa Rita Park has grown up nearby.

Rancho Panoche de San Juan y de los Carrisolitos

Throughout the southwestern portion of Merced County old Indian trails may still be traced, and the remains of prehistoric Indian villages have been uncovered at various water holes. In this section, too, early in the nineteenth century, Spanish settlers evidently had sought homes, for it is said that when the survey of Rancho Panoche de San Juan (granted to Julian Ursua in 1844) was completed in 1866, adobes, already of a considerable age, stood on the rancho, which covered five square leagues, over 20,000 acres.

El Arroyo de los Baños

Los Baños (SRL 550) is a Spanish place name meaning "the baths," and was applied to the deep, clear pools on El Arroyo de los Baños near its source. Tradition says that here Father Arroyo de la Cuesta refreshed himself when on missionary trips to the San Joaquin Valley. The name El Arroyo de los Baños del Padre Arroyo (now Los Banos Creek) was derived from this circumstance. Father Arroyo, who served Mission San Juan Bautista for 25 years, from 1808 to 1833, was an accomplished man. He invented a perpetual calendar and became familiar with as many as thirteen Indian dialects, preaching in seven different Indian tongues. He also wrote an Indian grammar and recorded many facts concerning the Indians and their manner of life.

The present town of Los Banos, located about two miles from the creek, has its origins in the Lone Willow Stage Station, built in 1858 on the west bank of what is now called Mud Slough. This place, consisting of a small house for the station keeper and a large barn for the relays of horses, prospered until the Butterfield stages between San Francisco and St. Louis stopped running in 1861; it then became a mere way station on the San Francisco–Los Angeles route and later the shortened Gilroy-Visalia run. By 1865 the countryside was becoming sufficiently settled to require a store, and an enterprising German named Gustave Kreyenhagen opened one in the former residence of the station keeper. He soon realized, however, that he would have better trade if he moved to the junction of the stage road and the Stockton-Visalia freight road; he therefore moved three miles east, taking the store building with him. This junction is eight miles northeast of present-day Los Banos.

Kreyenhagen was not destined to remain there long. Miller and Lux fenced in their property and required that teamsters drive around it. In the summer of 1870, therefore, the storekeeper relocated his trading post twelve miles farther to the west on the Gilroy-Visalia Road, about two miles south of the present Volta. Kreyenhagen had long served as unofficial postmaster, bringing his customers' mail each week from Gilroy, and in 1873 an official post office was established in his store under the name of Los Banos. Other businesses followed, and soon there was a little town. Eventually Miller and Lux took over the settlement and, when the railroad came in 1889, moved post office and businesses five miles east to the tracks. The town is now the center of diversified industry, including fruit and dairy products, and a principal town on the west side of the San Joaquin Valley.

Beginning in 1873, the headquarters of Henry Miller for his Los Banos Division were at Canal Farm (SRL 548), just across the railroad east of the Los Banos business district. None of the original buildings remain at Canal Farm. In 1932 the present inn was constructed on the foundations of the old ranch superintendent's residence, which itself had been built on the ruins of the 1873 ranch house of Henry Miller. Canal Farm derived its name from an irrigation canal, not a Miller and Lux enterprise, built from Mendota Dam to Los Banos Creek in 1871. The orange and olive orchards planted by Miller at Canal Farm still flourish. The Ralph Milliken Museum in Merced County Park in Los Banos is a recently established operation, with materials of local history as well as collections of Indian artifacts and military accoutrements dating back to the nineteenth century.

Rancho Las Mariposas

In 1847 John C. Frémont again figured briefly in Merced history when on February 14 he purchased the Rancho Las Mariposas from Juan B. Alvarado, who had received it from Governor Micheltorena in 1844. This grant, of ten leagues, stipulated that the land be located within the area bounded on the west by the San Joaquin River, on the east by the Sierra Nevada foothills, on the north by the Merced River, and on the south by the Chowchilla River. Alvarado never complied with the usual legal requirements by building a house on the grant and inhabiting it within a year. In fact, he never saw the land, but on account of the hostility of the Indians he did apply to the governor for a military force to enable him to take possession, and in answer to this request General José Castro was sent to the regoin with a company of mounted Californios. Fortifications were begun on the east bank of the San Joaquin River about six miles south of the Merced River, at or near the place where the town of Dover was later located. In December 1844 the Indians stole most of the horses, and the Californios had to make it back to Monterey as best they could. A final effort to take possession of the grant was made by Alvarado in August 1845, but this attempt was frustrated by the revolution against Governor Micheltorena, of which Alvarado was one of the leaders.

According to tradition, Frémont first attempted to locate his grant near the site of the present town of Stevinson, a tradition that seems to be substantiated by the name Fremont's Ford, which still exists at a point on the San Joaquin River near this town, just south of where SR 140 crosses the river. More tangible evidence shows that Frémont endeavored to locate his ranch near the site of the present Le Grand on Mariposa Creek. Early surveyors' maps show a house called Fremont's Ranch south of Mariposa Creek, and it is possible that he lived there in 1848. When gold was discovered in the foothills above this ranch, in 1849, Frémont established himself in the hills of what is now Mariposa County. Through personal influence Frémont was able to secure confirmation of his grant as located by him in the mining regions instead of in the valley. The precedent thus set was to cost the United States government many thousand square miles of territory claimed in other grants of a similar nature.

The First "Cattle King of Merced"

The first bona fide American settlers in Merced County were John M. Montgomery and his partner, Colonel Samuel Scott, two young Kentuckians. In the fall of 1849 they camped under one of the large water oaks on the banks of the Merced River a short distance north of the Cox Ferry Bridge on the left side of SR 59, about four miles west of the present town of Snelling.

John Montgomery became the richest man in Merced County during his time and was known as the "Land and Cattle King of Merced," the predecessor of Henry Miller and others. Before 1852 he had established a permanent home on Bear Creek, on what later became the Wolfsen Ranch, six miles east of Merced.

The Courthouse Tree

The first county seat of Merced was located on the Turner and Osborn Ranch on Mariposa Creek, a place that afterward became known as the Givens Ranch. The Courthouse Tree, under which the first county meetings were held, stood on the bank of the old channel of Mariposa Creek, which was considerably to the south of the present channel. The spot is one and one-half miles to the west of SR 99 and about seven miles southeast of Merced. Floods killed the tree in the winter of 1868–69 and no trace of the site remains.

Snelling's Ranch

Early in the spring of 1851, Montgomery, Scott, and Dr. David Wallace Lewis established a house of entertainment, which was the beginning of the town of Snelling. At first it was only a brush shelter, but Dr. Lewis very soon built what was later known as Snelling's Hotel. In the fall of 1851 the Snelling family arrived and purchased the property.

In 1857 Snelling's Ranch replaced the Turner and Osborn Ranch as the site of the county seat, but in 1872 it was in turn superseded by the new town of Merced, located in the valley fifteen miles to the south. By that time the mines in the mountain regions were giving out, while agriculture was steadily growing in importance. New towns sprang up in the fertile valley regions where railroads were being built, and the old hill towns soon became almost deserted.

Snelling, although not a mining town, was an overflow from the mining regions, and was of considerable importance at one time, being on the well-traveled road to the Mariposa mines. Settled largely by people from the South, it was noted for its spirit of hospitality. Today Snelling is a quiet place, picturesquely situated, where the visitor may find a link with the past in the old courthouse (SRL 409), erected in 1857. The lower story is of stone; the thick walls of that section, which was once used as a jail, are pierced by narrow windows heavily barred. The upper story still serves as a local court of justice. A stone monument dedicated to the

First Merced County Courthouse, Snelling

memory of the pioneers and commemorating the 75th anniversary of the organization of Merced County was placed in front of the courthouse by the Native Sons of the Golden West in 1930.

Old River Towns

As early as 1850 settlers came to the rivers and streams of Merced County and established homes. The vast fertile areas along the streams were used for livestock raising and agriculture, and almost invariably the ranch houses on the through roads became inns. Finally, centers of trade grew up about some of them. After the advent of the railroad, however, trade deserted the old river towns and they became little more than memories.

Located on the Merced River six miles below Snelling was Hopeton, at first known as "Forlorn Hope." It was chiefly notable for the fact that it possessed two churches before Snelling had any.

Merced Falls was one of the principal crossings on the Merced River along the route of the old Stockton–Fort Miller Road. A flour mill and a woolen mill, indicative of two of the county's most important early industries, were located there until they were destroyed by fire in 1893. The lumber mills of the Yosemite Lumber Company were later located there, but now Merced Falls is almost deserted. The falls themselves are now submerged by a power plant of the Pacific Gas and Electric Company.

Dover was a landing place on the San Joaquin River five miles above the mouth of the Merced. Freight was brought by water to this point. The first settlement at the site of Dover was made in the fall of 1844, when General José Castro attempted to build a fort there to facilitate the location of Alvarado's grant, Las Mariposas. Dover was occupied by Americans in 1866. Better boating facilities led to the abandonment of the site in favor of Hill's Ferry (Stanislaus County), six miles down the San Joaquin River.

Plainsburg, first settled in 1853 and once a thriving settlement on Mariposa Creek twelve miles southeast of Merced, began to decline when the railroad came in 1872.

The Old Stage Road

The numerous rivers and streams running from the Sierra Nevada into the San Joaquin Valley made it necessary for the early roads to follow along the base of the foothills and thus avoid the tules or swamps of the lowlands. These foothill roads afforded solid foundation even in rainy seasons. Also, the streams were more easily forded before they spread out over the level valley floor. Population during the 1850's and 1860's was centered on the mines, and supplies had to be freighted into the southern Mother Lode from Stockton along the stage route at the base of the hills. At the time of the formation of Merced County in 1855, the legislature placed the eastern boundary along this old Stockton–Fort Miller Road, which was a part of the Stockton–Los Angeles stage road.

Merced

Merced owes its prominence to the fact that it lay on the line of the Central Pacific Railroad as it pushed south and east through the San Joaquin Valley and that it was the nearest valley town to the southern Mother Lode and Yosemite beyond it. It has always been an important shipping and exchange place, served by two railroads and the nexus of three important highways, SRs 59, 99, and 140, all of which converge and pass through the city. The fertile farmlands nearby have made Merced a major agricultural center as well.

A highlight of the city is the charming Merced County Courthouse Museum, located in the Italianate Renaissance Revival building put up in 1875. Located in its own park at N and 21st streets, the old courthouse was rededicated as the home of the county museum in June 1983. Among the displays are some of the rooms used until 1975 as county offices. The Merced County Historical Society operates the museum, as it does the George Bloss Library in the neighboring town of Atwater.

Old Courthouse, Merced

Rescue Plane, Castle Air Museum, Atwater

Castle Air Museum

Also at Atwater is one of California's most distinctive museums, the Castle Air Museum, next to Castle Air Force Base. On the grounds of the museum are parked some 30 aircraft, mostly fighting planes from World War II and after. Eventually some 90 restored planes will be on display here. An interior museum displays air force uniforms, equipment, and all kinds of historical memorabilia. Inspired by the United States Air Force's Heritage Program, the Castle Air Museum Foundation established and maintains this facility, which is located just off SR 99 at the Buhach off-ramp at Atwater.

Modoc County

Modoc County was formed in 1874 from a part of Siskiyou County. Modoc means "people of the south" and was probably the name given to the inhabitants of this region by the Klamaths, their kin to the north.

Alturas, the first and only county seat, was originally called Dorris's Bridge, after the owner of the ranch on which it was located. The Dorris Ranch was purchased in 1960 by the United States Fish and Wildlife Service, and is now the Modoc National Wildlife Refuge.

The Tule Lake Petroglyphs

At the southeastern corner of Tule Lake, in the Lava Beds National Monument, a high bluff of smooth sandstone projects into the dry lake bed, and a chain of petroglyphs, chiseled deep into the rock, extends for several hundred yards across its face.

Some authorities maintain that these carvings were made by the last of the Rock Indians, who antedated and were exterminated by the Modocs. The Indians living in the region in the early 1850's disclaimed all knowledge of them, regarding them with awe and surrounding them with legends. The elements have obliterated some of the carvings; others, however, remain clear, with accents of black and ochre. The petroglyphs are protected by a fence.

Frémont in Modoc County

John C. Frémont passed through Modoc County when he traveled from Sutter's Fort to Upper Klamath Lake over what was later known as the eastern branch of the California-Oregon Trail. In the vicinity of Newell, the party camped on May 1–4, 1846. Among the group were Kit Carson, Alexis Godey, and Richard Owens. Tule Lake is designated "Rhett Lake" on Frémont's map of the area. The campsite (SRL 6) is about eleven miles southeast of Tulelake, on the Old Alturas Highway about seven-tenths of a mile north of its junction with SR 139.

The Applegate Cutoff and Lassen's Trail

The Applegate Cutoff from Oregon across the northeast corner of California to the Humboldt River in Nevada was opened up by Jesse and Lindsay Applegate with the help of thirteen others in June and July 1846. In the following autumn, more than 90 wagons were piloted by the Applegates from Fort Hall into Oregon over the new road. In 1848 Peter Lassen followed this route, crossing Nevada and entering California by way of Surprise Valley. Passing between Upper Lake and Middle Alkali Lake and up the west side of the valley to Fandango Pass (SRL 546), the trail led down into Goose Lake Valley, where it followed the eastern shore of the lake to a narrow neck at the southern end of the basin, a few miles from Sugar Loaf Hill.

Across this neck at a point on the west shore of Goose Lake, the Applegate Road turned toward Oregon, passing around the north end of both Clear Lake and Tule Lake into the Klamath country. At this same point on Goose Lake, Lassen's Trail began. Running in an almost southerly direction across the Devil's Garden, and striking the Pit River near the mouth of Rattlesnake Creek four miles west of the present city of Alturas, it continued along the north side of the Pit, crossing the river near the mouth of a canyon below the site of Canby. Passing south and west, its course lay through Stone Coal Valley, where it went due west for a few miles and then turned south along the Pit River. Crossing and recrossing the stream several times, or following along the sides of the hills above it, the trail finally led across the river for the last time ten miles above the site of Lookout. From there it proceeded down the east side of the Pit River to Big Valley in Lassen County. Joseph B. Chiles with a company of twelve men, among whom was Pierson B. Reading, had following much the same route into California, by way of Goose Lake and the Pit River, in October 1843.

Tradition has it that the Pit River was so named because of the many holes and pits that had been dug in the region by Indians for trapping game. In his journal, Reading mentions one of these treacherous pitfalls, into which one of his party fell. It should be noted, however, that Commodore Charles Wilkes, in his report and on his map of 1841, designated this stream as ''Pitt's River'' and Goose Lake as ''Pitt's Lake,'' which suggests a different origin for the name. Hudson's Bay trappers had penetrated this region before 1830, a fact recorded by Peter Skene Ogden in his diary of 1829. In this record, also, we find mention of ''Pitt's River'' under the entries of May 21 and 28; the Englishmen of the Hudson's Bay Company might have had in mind William Pitt, who is commemorated in such place names as Pittsburgh, Pennsylvania.

From 1846 on, the Applegate Cutoff was used by emigrants from Oregon, and in August 1848 the first wagon train to enter California from the north came in over the Applegate and Lassen roads. The Oregonians, captained by Peter Burnett (later the first American civil governor of California) and piloted by Thomas McKay, an old Hudson's Bay Company trapper, followed the Applegate Road to Clear Lake, where the party branched off, blazing a new road south to the Pit River. There, Burnett writes, ''to our utter astonishment, we found a new wagon road. Who made this road we could not at first imagine.'' It was later found that this was the trail over which Peter Lassen and his band of emigrants had just passed, on their way to Lassen's Ranch in Tehama County. Southeast of Lassen Peak at the headwaters of the North Fork of the Feather River, the Oregonians came upon Lassen and his party, whom they found stranded and in dire distress, their provisions almost exhausted.

The general course of Burnett's trail was followed by gold-seekers in 1849 and the early 1850's, and the present highway from Klamath Falls in Oregon to Bieber in Lassen County follows closely the trail of the Fortyniners. Trails West, a private volunteer trail-marking organization, has placed markers along these trails in Idaho, Nevada, and California.

A section of the old emigrant trail (SRL 111) may be seen near the Pit River–Happy Camp Road (Bushey Road), 5.5 miles west of SR 299; this road branches from the highway 4.2 miles southwest of Canby.

The Fandango Pass Massacre

Fandango (formerly Lassen's) Pass, over which the Applegate Cutoff and Lassen's Trail crossed the Warner Mountains, was apparently the scene of a tragedy in the early 1850's. The story is that a large emigrant train coming into California over this trail was encamped near a large spring at the edge of the valley beyond the mountains. Rejoicing over the arrival of much-needed supplies, the party was indulging in a fandango (a lively Spanish dance) when the camp was suddenly attacked by Indians and almost the entire company was killed. The name Fandango was given to the valley, the mountain, and the pass.

Another explanation of the origin of the name involves the Wolverine Rangers, a company of California-bound gold-seekers from Michigan, who camped overnight in the valley and disbanded there, burning some of their abandoned wagons. According to one member of the group, the night was so cold that "the men had to dance to keep warm, and named their wild camping place Fandango Valley." Later emigrants, seeing the remains of the burned wagons, assumed that an Indian massacre had taken place. This corner of California has many tales of war between Indians and the incoming white people.

At the head of Fandango Valley in 1866 a battle took place between some settlers and soldiers from Surprise Valley and a band of Paiute Indians, in which the Indians were badly defeated.

Evidences of another early massacre were found on the old Lassen Trail four miles west of Alturas on what was later known as Rattlesnake Ranch. Here in 1870 pioneer settlers came upon a large circle of burned wagons on a flat on the north side of the Pit River close to the present Redding-Alturas highway.

Bloody Point

One of the most terrible of the emigrant massacres in Modoc County took place in 1850 at Bloody Point (SRL 8), seven miles east of Tulelake on the Johnson Ranch and three and one-half miles south of the California-Oregon line. Passing over the old Oregon Trail, a band of more than 90 emigrants were attacked by the Modoc Indians; all of the party were killed except one man, who, badly wounded, escaped to the settlements in southern Oregon with his tragic tale. It is said that old wagon parts were picked up at the spot for many years.

Members of a second emigrant train narrowly escaped death at this point in 1851, and were rescued only by the timely arrival of the Oregon Volunteers. The spot apparently was a natural ambush; several other parties were killed there by the Modocs, who naturally saw the procession of wagon trains as a threat to them and to their existence.

Modoc Wars

The Battle of Infernal Caverns, one of the most famous Indian fights in California, took place on September 26 and 27, 1867, between 110 soldiers led by Lieutenant Colonel George Crook and a band of 75 Paiutes, 30 Pit River Indians, and a few Modocs. For some time the Indians, well equipped with arms and ammunition, had been resisting the influx of settlers throughout southern Idaho, western Nevada, and northeastern California, and Crook and his men had been sent to subdue them. The Indians were finally driven into a rough region on the South Fork of the Pit River. Here,

before a seemingly impregnable fortress of caves and rocks, a pitched battle took place. The Indians were eventually driven from their stronghold, leaving many of their number dead; eight of Crook's command were killed and fourteen were wounded.

The battleground of the Infernal Caverns (SRL 16), where the old fortifications may still be seen, is on the Ferry Ranch, south of Alturas. The graves of six of the soldiers killed in action have been marked by regulation Army headstones at the foot of the slope. Infernal Caverns is reached by going thirteen miles south from Alturas on US 395 and turning right for one mile on a good road leading to ranch homes. At the branch in the road, the right-hand road leads three and one-half miles to the Ferry ranch house. The site of the battle and the graves are on private property, and permission should be obtained before proceeding further. The six graves are about a mile from the house and the caverns are above, in very difficult terrain.

The Modoc War of 1872–73 was a determined resistance mounted by the Modoc tribe against being taken from their homelands and placed on a reservation that they had been forced to share with the Klamaths, a tribe with which they had bad relations. Although they were few in number, the Modocs were exceptionally effective guerrillas and for several months successfully defied the United States Army.

An early engagement of the Modoc War took place on December 21, 1872, on what was then known as Land's Ranch, at a spot (SRL 108) within a stone's throw of the old Frémont campsite on the Oregon Trail. Army supply wagons, escorted by a detachment of cavalrymen, had reached camp in safety, but several of the soldiers who had dropped behind were suddenly attacked by Indians in hiding among the rocks above the road. Two soldiers were killed, and several more were wounded.

Soon after this event, the Modoc tribe retreated into the nearby lava beds in Siskiyou County, in which chapter their story is continued. Early in May 1873, the defeated Modocs broke out of their beseiged stronghold, and in Modoc County, the last engagement of the Modoc War was fought at daybreak on May 10. Kientepoos ("Captain Jack" to the Americans), the leader of the tribe, led a charge on the Army camp at Dry Lake. The soldiers awoke when their horses and mules stampeded and were able to make a fierce and effective counterattack. Kientepoos was captured, the Modocs met their last defeat, and the Modoc War came to an end. The site of this battle is about a half mile west of the Dry Lake guard station on SR 139.

Cressler and Bonner Trading Post, Cedarville

The Cressler and Bonner Trading Post

In Surprise Valley there still stand some of the first log cabins built by white settlers, all provided with loopholes for defense. Among these is the log trading post (SRL 14) that was operated by William T. Cressler and John H. Bonner. This, the oldest structure in Modoc County, was built in 1865 by James Townsend, who was shortly afterward killed by Indians. Townsend's widow sold the building to Cressler and Bonner, and here the partners set up the first mercantile establishment in Modoc County. A thriving trade was carried on, first with the overland emigrants, and later with the early settlers of Surprise Valley. This interesting relic stands in a park in the center of Cedarville, surrounded by a magnificent grove of trees planted by the original owners.

The first road from Cedarville to Alturas followed, in a general way, the course of the present scenic highway SR 299 over the Warner Mountains from Surprise Valley. First constructed in 1869, the road passes over the Bonner Grade (SRL 15), named for John Bonner, a strong advocate of the road. Bonner maintained the road, which became an important stage and freight road to Yreka, until 1871, when Siskiyou County took it over.

Fort Bidwell

Fort Bidwell (SRL 430), at the head of Upper Lake in Surprise Valley, about 30 miles northeast of Alturas and ten miles south of the Oregon boundary line, was named for General John Bidwell. It was established in

1865, and cavalrymen were stationed there to oppose the hostile Indians of northeastern California, southern Oregon, and northwestern Nevada. Fort Bidwell was finally abandoned as a military post in 1893, but until 1930 it was used as a government school for Indians. The boarding school was discontinued that year, and the military barracks, formerly used for dormitories, were torn down. The old military graveyard is about all that remains. Newer homes have taken over this peaceful spot, where life seems to revolve around the general store, erected in 1874 and doing business continously since then. An unusual feature of this building, but not a visible one, is the twelve inches of dirt layered between the main ceiling and the attic, providing both insulation and fireproofing.

Alturas

Originally named Dorris's Bridge for the pioneer ranching family on whose land the town was laid out, Alturas changed its name by community petition to the legislature in 1876. Alturas is Spanish for "heights." Modoc County's largest settlement contains several interesting buildings, including the imposing Modoc County Court House (1914), the charming Sacred Heart Catholic Church (completed in 1910), and the N.C.O. Office Building (1917), which, like the church, is on the National Register of Historic Buildings. N.C.O. stands for the Nevada-California-Oregon Railroad, although local humorists say it also meant "Northern California Outrage" or "Never Come, and Overdue." The station, in Mission Revival style, was later sold to the Southern Pacific Railroad; today it houses the Elks Lodge. The Modoc County Museum at the south end of town has

Sacred Heart Catholic Church, Alturas

an impressive display of artifacts, particularly the enormous collection of Indian arrowheads collected by Mr. and Mrs. Virgil Pratt.

Other Historic Sites

In July 1861, S. D. Evans, Sr., and Joe Bailey were attacked by Indians while they and their men were driving 900 head of beef cattle from Oregon to the mines at Virginia City, Nevada. The site (SRL 125) is on the Centerville Road to Alturas, 4.7 miles southeast of Canby. The Evans and Bailey fight is marked by a white obelisk on a hill near the road.

About seven miles north of Alturas near US 395 is Chimney Rock (SRL 109), the remains of the second building to be erected in the Pit River Valley. Thomas L. Denson, a California pioneer of 1852, built his cabin here in 1860, utilizing the rock as a chimney by cutting the fireplace and flue out of it.

On SR 139 at Newell, seven miles southeast of Tulelake, one building remains from the Tulelake relocation camp (SRL 850.2). The grounds where the camp once stood are now a county public works depot and are usually closed to the public. In front of the surrounding fence a state marker has been placed, and its text is

Tulelake Relocation Camp, Newell

brief but eloquent. The plaque at the site reads: "Tulelake was one of ten concentration camps established during World War II to incarcerate 110,000 persons of Japanese ancestry, of whom the majority were American citizens, behind barbed wire and guard towers, without charge or trial. These camps are reminders of how racism, economic and political exploitation, and expediency undermine constitutional guarantees of United States citizens and aliens alike. May the injustices and humiliation suffered here never recur."

Mono County

Mono County was formed in 1861 of territory taken from Calaveras and Fresno counties. The eastern boundary with the state of Nevada was undetermined for several years, and in 1863, Aurora, the first county seat, was found to be in Nevada. Uncertain too were the northern and southern boundaries of the county; Alpine County to the northwest in 1864 and Inyo County to the south in 1870 were given portions of land originally intended for Mono County. Since Aurora could no longer be the county seat, Bridgeport became the center of government in 1863 and has since retained that position.

"Mono" seems to be a diminutive form of the Shoshonean Indian term "Monache," a name applied to those Shoshones living east of the Sierra and north of Owens Lake. The name was given first to a lake and then to a Sierra pass before being used for the county. The Mono Indians, according to A. L. Kroeber, numbered some 4,000 in 1770 and 1,500 by 1910.

Rock Writings

The small town of Chalfant Valley lies on US 6 near the southern border of Mono County and about seven miles north of Laws in Inyo County. Facing the town on the west is a high volcanic tableland; cut into its eastern escarpment are the petroglyphs known as the Chalfant Valley Group. Near where the present-day gravel Fish Slough Road crosses Chidago Canyon, a towering wall nearly half a mile in length and almost unscalable is covered with petroglyphs, or carvings on stone, and a few pictographs or paintings. The petroglyphs are principally circular in form and are believed to be the largest of this type found in the United States. The most conspicuous of the group is about five and one-half feet in diameter, the other figures being carved in proportion and seemingly connected with the larger one, constituting a series more than twenty feet long.

Chidago Canyon at this point is a labyrinth of carvings and paintings in many intriguing combinations. Many of the minor carvings represent such things as bighorn sheep, bear, deer, a dragonfly, lizards, snakes, human figures, and what may be chicken, bird, or turkey tracks, as well as geometrical designs.

Here and elsewhere in the desert regions of California, Indian rock writings have been wantonly vandalized, and the Bureau of Land Management has discouraged casual visits to these endangered areas. Thus the road west from Chalfant Valley has no signs marking the way to the petroglyphs.

The Sonora Trail

Jedediah Strong Smith, the "Pathfinder of the Sierra," was the first white man to come overland to California and likewise was the first white man to cross the Sierra Nevada, on his way back to the Great Salt Lake in 1827. It is not known for sure precisely which of the mountain passes he used on this trip, but some historians have said that it was the Sonora Pass, which lies high up in the Sierra at the point where Mono, Alpine, and Tuolumne counties meet. The Sonora Trail is the wagon road that later crossed the mountains via this pass.

In October 1841 the Bidwell-Bartleson overland emigrant party, much weakened and disheartened after months of hardship, finally arrived in what is now Mono County and began the ascent of the Sierra on the north side of the Walker River. At last they came to a little stream that flowed west instead of east and realized that they had crossed the dividing ridge of the mountain range. This stream proved to be the headwaters of the Stanislaus River, one of the largest tributaries of the San Joaquin. The river's course through the mountains was rough and precipitous and terribly difficult to follow as the party struggled through what seemed to be endless gorges and canyons. Nearly exhausted and almost out of food, they stumbled through the Sierra foothills and came upon the great San Joaquin Valley.

Difficult as this passage was, the Sonora Trail had been opened, and within a decade or so the first faint trail left by the Bidwell-Bartleson Party (varied somewhat from the original route) had been beaten down and widened into a fairly well-defined road, which led through the very heart of the Mother Lode country and was a close rival in popularity to the Truckee Road.

Dog Town and Monoville

Monoville was the first settlement of any consequence east of the Sierra and south of Lake Tahoe, al-

though some mining had probably been carried on in the region from the time gold had been discovered there in 1852. Continued reports that the Mormons from Nevada were washing out gold in Dog Creek near Mono Lake brought a number of prospectors into the region in 1857, and Dog Town (SRL 792) quickly came into existence as a camp and trading center. "Dog Town" was a popular miner's term for a camp built of huts. The site of Dog Town is along US 395, seven miles south of Bridgeport. After 1859 Dog Town was deserted for its more promising neighbor, Monoville, which soon boasted a population of 700, made up mostly of arrivals from Tuolumne County who came in via the Sonora Pass. Among the early arrivals were brothers Dick and Lee Vining. The nearby town of Lee Vining was named for the latter.

Monoville was different from the majority of mining camps in that it left no notable record of crime. Although the town soon disappeared, it is noteworthy as the starting point from which the discoverers of other mining locations in the region set out. As late as 1864 Monoville was an ambitious contestant for the position of county seat.

Nothing much remains from the brief bonanza days of Monoville except Sinnamon Cut, the result of a hydraulic mining operation that garnered James Sinnamon $90,000 and has scarred the landscape for a hundred and more years since he departed.

Bodie and Its "Bad Men"

Bodie State Historic Park (SRL 341) is unlike any other in California. Its story begins in 1852, with the first discovery of gold ore in the Mono region. The discovery was made by members of Lieutenant Tredwell Moore's detachment of the Second Infantry, U.S.A., who were in pursuit of Yosemite Valley Indians. This discovery led to a good deal of activity; Lee Vining and his party discovered gold in the canyon named for him through which the Tioga Pass Road (SR 120) now runs.

Knowledge of the Mono diggings reached the Tuolumne mines in 1857, resulting in a rush to the new field and the building of the Mono Trail from Big Oak Flat in Tuolumne County through the present Yosemite National Park. In 1859, William S. Bodey made a find, and the district was named for him. (The spelling was changed to Bodie to reflect the correct pronunciation of Bodey's name.)

The sensational Aurora discovery made in 1860 affected Bodie, which was twelve miles southwest, and the Mono Trail became a much-traveled highway for pack trains and miners until the Sonora Pass wagon road was opened in 1864.

Bodie, c. 1877–78

The Standard Mine, discovered in 1861, was the first of Bodie's mines to become famous and is typical of the fluctuating fortunes of mining ventures. During Aurora's boom, the owners of the Standard found it hard to create an interest in their project, then called the Bunker Hill Mine. In 1870, when the Aurora mines became exhausted, Bodie suffered a decline, which ended when a freak cave-in at the mine revealed, not far below the surface, a rich vein of ore. The adjacent Bodie Mine, at first considered a gamble, also rose in value, to the surprise of its owners. Between 1876 and 1880 Bodie was at the height of its success, with a population of more than 10,000 people. It was also known as one of the wildest mining camps in the West. "Good-bye, God! We are moving to Bodie!" a little girl is said to have exclaimed when she learned that her family was joining the bonanza. The "Bad Men from Bodie" acquired a widespread reputation for lawlessness. Legend has it that at least one murder occurred in every 24-hour period; the victims were almost always of the lawless sort, however, and thus the evildoers were somewhat thinned out by their own violent energies.

By 1883 all of the mines except the Bodie and the Standard closed down, and in 1887 these were consolidated. Of all the numerous ventures of the region, this was almost the only one that continued to uphold the fame of Bodie. Operations in later years were sporadic, ceasing altogether in the latter part of the 1950's.

Although Bodie has suffered heavily through the years from fires, the most serious one on June 23, 1932, there are still 168 buildings standing in various degrees of preservation. It is the intention of the Division of Parks and Recreation to maintain Bodie in a state of arrested decay, whereas the buildings in Columbia State Historic Park in Tuolumne County are being restored to their original grandeur. Bodie is a complete ghost town, the only residents being the state park rangers and their families, and there are none of the amenities, such as restaurants, service stations, or overnight facilities, found at other state parks in California.

Bodie lies at the end of a thirteen-mile road (the last three miles of which are dirt) that branches off US 395 to the east some seven miles south of Bridgeport. Among the landmarks to be seen are the Methodist Church, the James Stuart Cain home, the Miners' Union and Odd Fellows halls, and several interesting cemeteries. This fascinating old town has been registered by the Department of the Interior as a National Historic Landmark.

The neighboring camps at Mono Lake, Masonic,

Standard Mill and Town, Bodie

Benton, Tioga, Lundy, and Mammoth City in California, and Aurora in Nevada, are also long deserted. Abandoned miners' cabins, built of massive logs, still linger in Mono's mountain regions, telling tales of primitive life when "great populations" flourished there. At the settlement on the west shore of Mono Lake are two old wooden buildings that were moved from Bodie. Masonic, best reached by a nine-mile dirt road that leaves SR 182 three miles north of Bridgeport, is a photogenic conglomeration of old cabins lying close to the Nevada line. Here is an interesting tram system leading from the mines to the ruined stamp mill. At Benton, four miles west of US 6 on SR 120, are a jail, a schoolhouse, and a thick-walled general store with iron shutters that housed the Wells Fargo office. The population of Benton once reached 6,000.

From Bodie a road, sometimes impassable, leads northeast to Aurora, the first county seat of Mono County before it was determined that it lay in Nevada. At the state line are the ruins of the Sunshine stage station. Until about 1950 Aurora was a very well-preserved ghost town with many buildings standing, but since then most of the old structures have been torn down for their bricks.

Bridgeport

Big Meadows was a grass-covered area that attracted farmers around 1855. A settlement grew up on the East Walker River, which lay across a footbridge from the road up the valley of the river. In time Bridgeport became the name of the settlement, the valley, and a nearby lake. The Mono County Courthouse, erected in 1880, is still in daily use; it stands on US 395, which passes through the center of the small town. This is the second-oldest courthouse in California still in operation. The Mono County Museum nearby is housed in a schoolhouse also built in 1880 and in operation until 1964. A much-needed addition to the structure has recently been built. The collection has much of interest on the history of the many short-lived mining settlements of the county.

Mining Towns of the High Sierra

East of Yosemite Valley high up in the mountains, relics of early silver-mining ventures may still be seen. One of the old camps in the region is Tioga (formerly Bennettville), a mile or two north of Tioga Pass. Here the Tioga Mine was located in 1860 as the Sheepherder

Mine, and in 1874 William Brusky, a prospector, came upon the abandoned diggings and relocated the old claim under its original name.

The Tioga Mining District was organized in 1878 by the Great Sierra Mining Company, made up of men from Sonora. The old Sheepherder Mine was renamed the Tioga Mine, and Bennettville was made the headquarters for the company. Great quantities of supplies and equipment were brought to the camp over very difficult roads from the east side of the mountain, at enormous expenditure of labor and money.

The pressing need for a good road over which to transport heavy machinery from the west side of the Sierra occasioned the expenditure of $64,000 for the construction of the Tioga Road, which was completed in 1883. However, the total expenditure of $300,000 brought about a financial collapse in 1884, and the project was abandoned before any of the ore had been milled.

Bennettville is off SR 120 about ten miles west of Lee Vining; a dirt road a half-mile past Ellery Lake leads to the site. The old livery stable and assayer's building are all that remain.

The Mount Dana Summit Mine (in Tuolumne County), opened in 1878, lay to the south of the Tioga Mine. Here long-deserted rock cabins clustered about a deep mine shaft are the remains of a once-thriving camp. Hikers and fishermen from Yosemite Valley often come upon this interesting mountain ghost town, which is located within Yosemite National Park. The Gaylor Lakes trail, which begins at the Tioga entrance to the park, leads two miles to the remains, which are located on the slope above upper Gaylor Lake.

Lundy, another deserted mining camp a few miles north of Tioga, was established in 1879. Prior to that date, W. J. Lundy had a sawmill there from which he helped supply the enormous demand for lumber at Bodie. Approximately $3 million was taken from the Lundy Mine, and the place remained a substantial town for several years. Lundy Lake was created by the building of a dam that inundated part of the townsite, which is today enjoying a revival as a resort and vacation site. It is located at the western end of Lundy Lake Road, about six miles west of the junction of US 395 and SR 167.

About twenty miles south of Tioga in the Lake District (a region of spectacular scenic grandeur), Mammoth flourished for a brief period. The first discoveries were made there in 1877, but the greatest activity took place in 1879–80. A mill was erected and a trail constructed from Fresno Flats (now Oakhurst, 54 miles west), but the expected ore was not forthcoming. Like many other camps in which enormous capital was expended, little or nothing was produced in return, and in the winter of 1880–81 the place was closed up. Old Mammoth, as the 8,000-foot-high spot is now designated, lies just south of the Mammoth Lakes resort area on Old Mammoth Road.

Mountains and Lakes of Mono County

Mammoth lies in the heart of one of the most superb recreation centers in the Sierra. From it interesting trips may be taken to the hot mineral springs at Whitmore Tubs, the ice-cold or boiling springs of Casa Diablo, the Hot Creek Geyser, Mammoth Rock and the Old Mammoth Mill, the Devils Postpile National Monument (across the line in Madera County), the Earthquake Fault, Minaret Pass, and Shohonk Pass. Pack trips may be taken to Shadow Lake, Thousand Island Lake, and the Upper San Joaquin, while good trails lead to splendid camping and fishing spots about the numerous lakes of the region. This is also a major area for winter sports.

In the vicinity of Convict Lake and Convict Creek in southern Mono County a gun battle took place in 1871 between some desperate fugitives from the prison at Carson City, Nevada, and a posse from Benton. On September 17, 1871, 29 convicts—murderers, robbers, and horse thieves—had broken through the prison guard and escaped. Six of them headed south. On their way they met William A. Poor, a mail carrier, whom they robbed and murdered.

When news of the outrage reached Aurora and Benton, a posse was organized. The men from Benton followed the convicts into southern Mono County, the fugitives having been sighted by Robert Morrison, a Benton merchant, who saw them going up Monte Diablo Creek, henceforth called Convict Creek.

On the following morning the posse followed up the canyon to the lake at its head. There, on September 24, they came upon three of the desperadoes, and in the gunfight that followed, Morrison (for whom Mount Morrison was afterward named) was killed. The convicts escaped toward Round Valley, where they were later captured. Taken to Bishop by irate citizens, the two men who had committed murder were hanged, and the third was returned to the Carson City prison.

Mono Lake lies in the center of the county and is one of the most remarkable features of California's geography. It is estimated that the lake was formed some 700,000 years ago. It has no visible outlet. In recent years, the steady draining of water from the region by Los Angeles County has caused the surface of the lake to drop; two islands named Paoha and Negit are now to be seen rising from its center, along with towers of tufa, formations of calcium carbonate. The chemical buildup in the waters renders them habitable only by tiny brine shrimp and the pupae of the ephydra fly.

Crossing a low divide several miles beyond Mammoth, SR 120 drops down toward Mono Lake, passing the Mono Craters on the right. A beautiful, slightly crescent-shaped range of twenty distinguishable volcanic cones, the Mono Craters have the appearance of sand dunes, the delicate colors of the smooth pumice-stone slopes creating a picture of exceptional symmetry and beauty of form.

Monterey County

Monterey County was one of the original 27 counties. Monterey is Spanish for "hill or wood of the king." It was so named in honor of Gaspar de Zúñiga, count of Monterey and viceroy of Mexico. Monterey was the original county seat, but in 1873 the honor was given to Salinas. The county archives contain many pre-statehood records in Spanish.

The Discovery of Monterey Bay

Juan Rodríguez Cabrillo, in command of the *San Salvador* and the frigate *Victoria*, discovered California in 1542 and sailed up the coast about to the Northwest Cape, at Fort Ross in Sonoma County. On the return voyage, the explorer noted that he had sighted for the second time a place that he had earlier called Cape San Martin, today called Point Pinos. This is the southern headland of Monterey Bay, and the evidence suggests that Cabrillo did not see the bay itself.

The Pacific Grove Lighthouse was established on Point Pinos in 1872, and a marker has been placed there by the Pacific Grove Chapter of the Daughters of the American Revolution in honor of Cabrillo, the first European to see the coast of Alta California.

Probably the first white man to see Monterey Bay itself was Sebastián Rodríguez Cermeño, a Portuguese in command of the Spanish galleon *San Agustín*, in 1595. Cermeño had been sent out to discover a northern port on the California coast where the Manila ships might find protection and supplies and receive warning of enemies. On November 30, the *San Agustín* was wrecked at Drake's Bay, but Cermeño continued his voyage in the *San Buenaventura*, a little launch or open sailboat that he had constructed. In this frail craft he saw Monterey Bay on December 10, 1595, and called it San Pedro Bay.

The Vizcaíno-Serra Landing Place

Sebastián Vizcaíno was a merchant trader who had had much experience on the Spanish galleon route, and who had also been a shipmate of Rodríguez Cermeño on his voyage of discovery in 1595. In the flagship *San Diego*, Vizcaíno entered Monterey Bay on December 15, 1602, the second European to enter its waters and the first to make a landing there.

Vizcaíno was so enchanted with the beauty of this bay that "he wrote almost too enthusiastically to his Majesty concerning it." He spoke of it as a harbor "sheltered from all winds," and a legend grew up concerning this port that would influence all Spanish exploration along the coast for a century and a half to come. Later explorers, having only Vizcaíno's glowing descriptions to go on, failed to realize that Monterey Bay was in fact the San Pedro Bay of Cermeño and Vizcaíno.

The entrance into Monterey Bay and the act of taking possession of it were the principal events of Vizcaíno's voyage. The ceremony was performed under a live oak close to the shore; this was the same oak under which Padre Junipero Serra performed a similar ceremony in 1770, when Mission San Carlos and the Presidio of Monterey were founded. The site of the tree and the landing place (SRL 128), now within the Monterey State Historical Monument, is marked by the Junipero Serra Cross, on the south side of the main gateway to the Monterey Presidio. On Presidio Hill, overlooking the bay, is the Junipero Serra Monument, erected by Mrs. Leland Stanford in 1891. A monument in honor of Gaspar de Portolá, founder of the presidio, has been erected at the landing place, near the Serra Cross, by the state of California.

Portolá's Trail Through Monterey

Leaving San Diego on July 14, 1769, Gaspar de Portolá started north with his men to search for the Bay of Monterey, described in such enthusiastic terms by Vizcaíno in 1602. Traveling up the coast by way of Gaviota Pass, the expedition entered what is now Monterey County and camped, September 21–24, on the banks of the Nacimiento River, near its source. The high ridges of the Coast Range had just been crossed with great difficulty, and the men were in need of rest.

After they had somewhat recuperated, the party pushed on and reached the San Antonio River at a point near Jolon, where they camped on September 24. The next day they camped in the upper Jolon Valley, and on September 26 they descended Quinado Canyon, reaching the Salinas River near King City.

During the days following they camped successively near Metz, Camphora, and Chualar, and on September 30, below what is now Hill Town. From October 1 to October 6 they camped near Blanco and from this point they explored the Monterey Bay region and saw the river and bay at Carmel.

During all this week the party did not recognize Vizcaíno's wonderful harbor "sheltered from all winds" and described in Cabrero Bueno's sailing directions as a bay "round like an O." It was probably shrouded in gray fog, and not until a year later did they know what they had missed.

Leaving a cross planted upon the beach, near Monterey, the party continued the journey northward, camping on October 7 near Del Monte junction and then proceeding across the Pajaro River and camping near the present site of Watsonville, in Santa Cruz County.

Mission San Carlos Borroméo (El Carmelo)

The settlement of Monterey was at the point farthest north in the original plan for the colonization of California, and there the presidio and the mission were to be established. Portolá's party had failed to find the bay in 1769, but a second expedition was organized the following year, Portolá and Father Crespí going by land and Father Serra, who was ill, proceeding by boat.

Portolá reached the Bay of Monterey for the second time on May 24, 1770. He found the cross that he had erected there the year before still standing near the beach, but curiously decorated, "with arrows stuck in the ground and sticks with many feathers, which the gentiles had placed there; suspended from a pole beside the cross was a string of small fish, all fairly fresh, while pieces of meat were deposited at the foot of the cross and a pile of mussels." The Indians later told the padres how, at night, the cross had become wonderfully illuminated, reaching far up into the heavens, and they were afraid and brought peace offerings to it. The day being calm and clear, the entire sweep of the bay was visible, and Crespí and the others realized that this was indeed Vizcaíno's harbor.

Father Serra arrived in the *San Antonio* seven days later, and on June 3, 1770, under the same oak where Vizcaíno had held services 168 years before, the Mission San Carlos Borromeo and the Presidio of Monterey were dedicated.

The first mission building was erected at the presidio on the site where the San Carlos Church stands today. But the presence of the soldiers and the lack of good agricultural land caused Father Serra to look about for a more suitable location. This was found five miles to the south in a fertile valley watered by the Rio Carmelo (so named for the Carmelite Fathers who accompanied Vizcaíno), which empties into the ocean at this point, and the formal transfer of the mission site was made in December 1771. Mission San Carlos Borromeo (SRL 135) became the favorite of Father Serra, where he spent most of his last days and where he died; he lies buried within the sanctuary today. Serra was beatified by the Vatican in 1988.

The present building at Carmel was begun in 1793 and dedicated in 1797. Being beautifully situated and prosperous, it was the headquarters for the Padre Presidente of the California missions until 1803. After 1836, it was not kept in repair and quickly fell into ruins, but in 1882, through the efforts of Father Casanova, the graves of Presidentes Serra and Lasuén and Fathers Crespí and López were discovered within the church. Public interest was then aroused and funds were sought for the restoration, which was accomplished and the church rededicated in 1884. Restoration of the other

Mission San Carlos Borroméo, Carmel

buildings has continued to the present. Carmel Mission, as it is popularly known, is a National Historical Landmark. In 1960 it was raised to the rank of a minor basilica by the Vatican, and was visited by Pope John Paul II in 1987.

The Presidio of Monterey

On the day the mission and presidio were dedicated, Gaspar de Portolá formally took possession of the land in the name of King Carlos III of Spain. A fort of rude palisades and a few huts were erected at once and the second presidio in Alta California was instituted.

Late in the eighteenth century, Spain erected a fort on the hill overlooking Monterey Bay, where the present presidio grounds are located. Count de la Pérouse, who visited Monterey in September 1786, said that the guns of the Castillo greeted him; and in 1793, when George Vancouver sailed into the harbor, he also noted the battery on the hill. Vancouver's party was long and gratefully remembered by residents of the Monterey area (who numbered fewer than 500 by 1800), for they left "grains of the best quality" as well as fruit stones, or pits, which were planted and became productive trees. These added greatly to the variety of foods available in later years.

During the Spanish and Mexican periods, Monterey held first place as the military and social capital of Alta California. It was also the port of entry where American ships and whaling vessels came to trade with the colonists, finally breaking down the barriers placed by the reluctant Spanish government on foreign trade.

The little port, set like a jewel within pine-clad hills beside the blue bay, is described by Richard Henry Dana in *Two Years Before the Mast*. When Dana sailed into the harbor on the brig *Pilgrim* in the year 1834, "the town lay directly before us, making a very pretty appearance, its houses being of whitewashed adobe. . . . The red tiles, too, on the roofs, contrasted well with the white sides and with the extreme greenness of the lawn upon which the houses—about a hundred in number— were dotted about, here and there, irregularly. . . . This, as they are of one story, and of the cottage form, gives them a pretty effect when seen from a little distance. . . . In the centre of it is an open square, surrounded by four lines of one-story buildings, with half a dozen cannon in the centre. . . . This is the Presidio, or fort."

In 1822 the Mexican government built a fort on the present presidio grounds on the hill overlooking Monterey Bay. In 1846, after the American occupation, a blockhouse was erected there and ship guns were mounted. It was named Fort Stockton at first, but later in the same year the name was changed to Fort Mervine in honor of the officer in charge. The old fort is no longer there, but the place where it stood has been marked.

The Sloat Monument, erected in honor of Commodore John Drake Sloat, U.S.N., commemorates the act of taking possession of California for the United States, July 7, 1846, and the raising of the Stars and Stripes over the Custom House at Monterey. The base of the monument was erected by the people of California through popular subscription, and the superstructure was added by the federal government. It was dedicated and unveiled on the hilltop on the present presidio grounds, June 14, 1910.

Fort Halleck was built at the present presidio in 1847 and named in honor of Lieutenant Henry W. Halleck of the Corps of Engineers, which laid out the fort. Halleck later became secretary of state of California during Governor Bennett Riley's military rule, and was chief of staff of the Union army during the Civil War. He was a man of considerable influence during the period of transition from Mexican to American rule. In the early 1850's he was a prominent lawyer in San Francisco. Fort Halleck no longer exists, but the site is marked.

The Presidio Museum, on Corporal Ewing Road, has excellent displays on the history of Monterey.

Mission San Antonio de Padua

Father Junipero Serra, as soon as he had explored the Rio Carmelo and had set his people to work building Mission San Carlos on the new site, set out for the Santa Lucia Mountains to found the third of the missions in Alta California. At length he came to a beautiful valley covered with oaks, which was named Los Robles, and which Portolá, in 1769, had called La Hoya de la Sierra de Santa Lucia.

Close by the little river, which Father Serra named the San Antonio, the bells were hung from the branch of a live oak. Grasping the rope and ringing the bells loud and long, the venerable father cried: "Hear, O Gentiles! Come! Oh come to the holy Church of God! Come, oh come, and receive the Faith of Christ!" And to his companion's plea that it was useless to ring the bells he replied: "Let me give vent to my heart's desires; for I would that these bells were heard all over the world, or at least by all the pagan people who live in this sierra." In fact, after the rustic enramada had been raised and the simple altar placed, a single Indian hesitatingly approached to witness the celebration of the Mass. This was the first instance of a native inhabitant being present at the founding of a mission. By 1805 there were 1,296 neophytes from the neighboring rancherias.

Mission San Antonio de Padua was founded July 14, 1771, at a site one and one-half miles from the present church, which was begun in 1810. The latter is said to have been not only one of the largest but also one of the most picturesque and interesting of all the missions, unsurpassed in its artistic arrangement and the loveliness of its rural setting. The beautiful brick facade withstood the neglect of years and the stress of storm and earthquake, even after the body of the main building and the roofs of the long corridors had crumbled.

Standing in a well-watered valley through which the San Antonio flows southeast to join the Salinas River, the mission became famous for its excellent wheat and its fine horses. A stone mill for grinding the wheat was constructed and operated by water brought for many miles through a stone-walled ditch, or *zanja*. Remains of this feat of engineering still exist in the valley a few hundred yards from the mission, in what was once the garden, or orchard.

After the death of the Reverend Dorotéo Ambris, the last resident priest at San Antonio, the mission structures were deserted and from year to year became a more complete ruin. San Antonio never acquired a neighboring secular village, as did nearly all the missions, and it lay far off the highway that ultimately became US 101. The lands around it became part of the gigantic ranch of William Randolph Hearst. Within sight of the mission, on a nearby hill, Hearst had architect Julia Morgan design a delightful ranch house, still called the Hacienda, which was completed in 1930. Ten years later, the Army acquired 165,000 acres from Hearst and made the area into Fort Hunter Liggett; the Hacienda is the officers' club for the base.

In 1903, the California Historic Landmarks League and the Historic Landmarks Committee of the Native Sons of the Golden West, under the leadership of Joseph R. Knowland, made a plea for restoration of the mission, and in September of that year it was begun. In 1906 much of their effort was destroyed by the earthquake, but the following year renovation of the church proper was completed. The mission stood in loneliness—a vacant but intact church and a long row of brick arches fronting heaps of adobe mud that were once the main wing—until 1949, when the Franciscan Order, aided by the Hearst Foundation, commenced restoration on a large scale.

Mission San Antonio (SRL 232) is twenty miles south of King City and five miles northwest of Jolon, in the Hunter Liggett Military Reservation. The padres' quarters and adjoining reconstructed rooms are now a museum of the life of the mission. Still one of the most tranquil historic spots in California, San Antonio is one of four missions under the care of the founding order of the Franciscans.

Jolon was once a way station on the stage road between Los Angeles and San Francisco. Antonio Ramírez built a one-story adobe inn there, which was later expanded into a two-story hotel by George Dutton. At one point the property was claimed by Faxon Dean Atherton, whose son George (husband of the novelist Gertrude Atherton) chased out a nest of squatters on the land in 1877. Dutton's hotel is now in ruins, on the Jolon Road (county highway G14), just east of the settlement.

Anza's March Through Monterey

Juan Bautista de Anza and his band of settlers crossed the Rio del Nacimiento on March 5, 1776, and proceeded another mile to El Primo Vado ("the first ford") of the Rio de San Antonio, now under the waters of Lake San Antonio. Here they camped for the night, continuing up the river valley the following day to Mission San Antonio, where Anza had made a brief stop on his previous journey in 1774 and where they now remained two days. The fathers welcomed them as royally as had their brothers at San Gabriel and San Luis Obispo.

On the morning of March 8, the expedition once more resumed its march, following up Sulphur Spring Canyon north to Upper Milpitas Road, east to the Jolon Road, northeast over the ridge, and down Kent Canyon to the valley of what was then known as the Rio de Monterey and is now called the Salinas River. Camp was made northwest of the site of King City at Los Ositos ("the little bears"), where Anza had stopped on April 17, 1774. On March 9 they rested at Los Correos (west and across the river from the present town of Gonzales), and the next day, in pouring rain, they reached the Presidio of Monterey.

Father Junípero Serra welcomed the travelers and escorted them to Carmel Mission. Anza was by now very ill. Before recovering fully, he insisted on fulfilling his mission and proceeded north to explore and to map out the site for the new settlement to be established at San Francisco, leaving his people at Monterey until arrangements could be made for their final migration to the new presidio.

On his way north, Anza followed along to the left of what is now the road to Salinas and San Juan Bautista. He made his final camp in Monterey County on March 23, at a place called La Natividad, near Sugar Loaf Mountain. A town and a rancho of that name were later located in the vicinity.

Having finished his work at San Francisco, Anza returned to Monterey on April 8. Governor Rivera was opposed to the settlement of San Francisco and refused to allow Anza to settle his people there. Greatly disappointed, Anza finally set out on his return march to Mexico on April 14, after bidding a sad farewell to his companions on the long and perilous journey from Sonora, who wept bitterly at his departure. On the return trip Anza had several unpleasant encounters with Rivera. The latter maintained his obstructionist policy until a letter from the viceroy forced him to proceed with the founding of a presidio and mission at San Francisco. Others led the settlers to the new outpost, but Anza was the founder in all but name.

Monterey has recognized Anza by a monument, dedicated by the California Centennials Commission, in El Estero Park.

Mission Nuestra Señora Dolorosísima de la Soledad

Soledad Mission (SRL 233) was founded by Father Lasuén on October 9, 1791, 30 miles southeast of Monterey and about a mile west of the Salinas River, with thousands of acres of bare, brown plains stretching away on every side. Although very nearly limitless in acreage, soil and pasturage were only fairly good, and the growth in the number of neophytes was very slow.

Gradually, however, the labors of the fathers surmounted these handicaps, until the Misson of Our Most Sorrowful Lady of Solitude was quite prosperous, and its occupants lived peacefully for about 40 years. Governor Arrillaga died at Soledad in 1814 and was buried under the center of the church. In 1818 the secluded mission became a refuge for the coast missions during the appearance of the pirate Bouchard. In the 1820's the river twice flooded the mission, destroying first the church and then the chapel built to replace the church. After the decree of secularization, Soledad became impoverished, and Father Vicente Francisco de Sarría, who refused to forsake his flock, died there in 1835, destitute and enfeebled by age. The few remaining Indians carried his body 25 miles to Mission San Antonio for burial. The traveler J. Ross Browne has left a mournful description of the site in 1849: "A more desolate place cannot well be imagined. The old church is in ruins, and the adobe huts built for the Indians are roofless, and the walls tumbled about in shapeless piles. Not a tree or shrub is to be seen anywhere in the vicinity."

This description of what was called by many "the forgotten mission" was still accurate a century later. In 1954, the Native Daughters of the Golden West began a project to restore the mission, of which only a few frag-

Ruins at Mission Nuestra Señora Dolorosísima de la Soledad

ments remained. That year a chapel was built and in 1963 a connecting building. More renovation is planned for the future, and visitors can view an interesting archaeological project.

The restored buildings are about four miles west of US 101 on Fort Romie Road. Fort Romie, now vanished, was the site of an experimental Salvation Army farm in 1893.

Royal Presidio Chapel

After the removal of Mission San Carlos Borromeo to Carmel, the old mission building at the Presidio of Monterey became the Presidio Chapel (SRL 105). The present building at 550 Church Street was erected in 1794 and was then called the Royal Chapel because the king's representative worshiped there. When the mission at Carmel was secularized in 1836, the chapel at Monterey became the parish church. The San Carlos Parish Church, as it is now known, was much restored, thanks to the efforts of Governor Romualdo Pacheco, and it is now a National Historic Landmark.

The Custom House

The old Custom House (SRL 1) in Monterey occupies a prominent place in California's history. This picturesque structure of stone and adobe was begun under Spanish rule in 1814. The roof was completed under Mexican rule in 1822, and the towers were added about the time the building came under American rule.

The Monterey Custom House was the most important in the province of Alta California, and all trading vessels were required to enter their cargo on its records. To this quiet harbor came the hunters of seal and sea otter, the pioneers of trade on the Pacific coast, followed closely by whaling vessels, which came to be

Custom House, Monterey

reconditioned after perilous voyages in far northern seas. Most important of all, ships from New England came early, seeking hides and tallow, and with their coming a new era on the coast of Alta California was foreshadowed.

The American flag was raised over the Custom House, temporarily, on October 19, 1842, by Commodore Thomas ap Catesby Jones, commander of the Pacific Squadron of the United States Navy. Relations between the United States and Mexico had been strained since Texas had declared its independence from Mexico in 1836, and there was some fear of British interest in acquiring land on the Pacific. Hearing rumors while at Callao, Peru, that the expected war between his country and Mexico had broken out, Jones brought his four-vessel squadron into the harbor of the capital of Alta California, where he quickly received the surrender of the hapless commander of the presidio. Upon learning from the U.S. consul, Thomas O. Larkin, that he was in error, Jones apologized the next day, hauled down the flag, and sailed away, having demonstrated how easily California could be taken. On July 7, 1846, Commodore John Drake Sloat sent up the colors that announced the passing of California from Mexican rule.

For a while, the Custom House was the property of the U.S. government. In time it was sold to a group of private citizens, who in turn donated it to the state of California. It was restored by the state and marked by the Monterey History and Art Association. A museum of local relics is housed in it, and it is open to the public as a unit of the Monterey State Historical Monument, at the corner of Alvarado and Waterfront streets. Because of its importance in the history of the United States, the Monterey Custom House has been registered by the Department of the Interior as a National Historic Landmark.

Land Grants

In 1773 the Spanish viceroy Bucareli, in preparation for the establishment of future pueblos, authorized Captain Rivera to distribute lands to worthy persons, either native or Spanish, who would devote themselves to farming and stock raising. Among those considered to be worthy persons were Spaniards who had married baptized Indian women. Such a man was Manuel Butron, a soldier, who married Margarita María of the San Carlos Mission and to whom Rivera gave a plot of land 140 varas square near the mission in 1775. This was the first grant of land made by the Spanish in Alta California. The grantee, however, abandoned it later and was living in the Pueblo de San José in 1786.

After the Butron grant, pueblo lots were given to settlers, and by 1784 other tracts of larger dimensions were temporarily granted to individuals by Don Pedro Fages. By 1786 grants of land up to three square leagues were authorized, provided that they did not overlap the boundaries of already established missions, pueblos, or rancherias. By 1793 a few had been granted provisionally to retired soldiers and other settlers on the Salinas River.

Rancho Bolsa de San Cayetano (Lower Pajaro River Valley)

Don Ignacio Vicente Ferrer Vallejo, a Spanish native of Jalisco, Mexico, came to Alta California in 1774 with Lieutenant Ortega and became the progenitor of the Vallejo family in the state. Records show that he was praised for his bravery on many occasions. After the termination of his enlistment he was employed at San Carlos, where he directed agriculture and irrigation. He reenlisted in military service in the Monterey Company and held positions at Soledad, San Jose, and Branciforte. In 1824 he was at San Luis Obispo for the purpose of preventing an Indian revolt, and while there he received the grant of Rancho Bolsa de San Cayetano. The limit of this tract on the north was the Pajaro River; on the west, Monterey Bay; on the east, Rancho Vega del Rio del Pajaro; and on the south, an estuary separating it from the Carneros Rancho. Because it was the first land owned by the Vallejo family within the boundary of California, the original house built on it has been termed the "Casa Materna (Mother House) of the Vallejos."

This adobe was also known as the "Glass House" because of the many glass windows that once enclosed the upper porch. The house was occupied up to 1870; it then served as a barn, and finally fell into ruin. Although efforts were made by the Pajaro Valley Historical Association to renovate the old structure and make it a state park, these were in vain, and in 1962 a later owner removed the remains with a bulldozer. The loss of the "Glass House," the first permanent home of the eminent Vallejo family in California, is one of the most tragic in the annals of the landmarks of the state. The site (SRL 387) is at the junction of Salinas and Hillcrest roads in the town of Pajaro.

In 1790 Don Ignacio married María Antonio, daughter of Francisco Lugo. Their family consisted of eight daughters and five sons. Five of the daughters married men of distinction in the county: Mariano Soberanes, José Amesti, J. B. R. Cooper, J. P. Leese, and José F. Alvarado, all of whom received large grants of government land. Four of the five sons survived their father, who died at Monterey in 1832 at the age of 83. The most distinguished of the sons was Mariano, a leading figure in the annals of California.

José de Jesús, probably the eldest son in the family (since his birthdate is ten years before that of Mariano), lived on his father's rancho and became the owner of it by grant from Governor Figueroa; it was confirmed to him as executor of his father's estate, and he received final patent to it in 1865. He apparently lived on this rancho only a few years after settling the estate, since he became the grantee of Rancho Arroyo de la Alameda in 1842. He spent the last years of his life at Mission San Jose, where he died in 1882 at the age of 84.

An adobe house of two stories, sometimes called the Hipólito adobe and sometimes the Pope adobe, originally constructed four miles from Watsonville on this rancho, was badly wrecked in the 1906 earthquake. Its material afterward was used in the construction of a small one-story cottage at 514 Blackburn Street in Watsonville, which is now a private residence. When in use on the rancho, the structure housed a gristmill in its northwest corner, with millstones on the second floor turned by ox power from the ground floor.

Rancho El Alisal and El Colegio de San José
(East of Salinas)

Rancho El Alisal, consisting of one and one-third square leagues, was granted to Feliciano and Mariano Soberanes in 1834 by Governor Figueroa. Through this tract runs Alisal Creek, on the bank of which W. E. P. Hartnell had established a school of higher learning shortly before.

Hartnell, an Englishman who had married María Teresa de la Guerra in 1825, obtained a grant of land in this vicinity in 1834 for the purpose of building a summer home. Realizing how poor the educational facilities of Alta California were, he decided to establish an institute at his home. El Colegio de San José opened on January 1, 1834, with fifteen pupils. One of these was Pablo de la Guerra, later a member of the constitutional convention and afterward a state senator and chairman of the committee on counties and their boundaries. Two adobe buildings survived until 1960, when their owner, annoyed at the frequent intrusion of sightseers, had them destroyed. Hartnell College in Salinas commemorates the pioneer educator of El Alisal.

The grounds and site of the two adobes are now part of a private stock ranch at 955 Old Stage Road, five miles east of Salinas. The rancho, consisting of 2,971 acres, was patented to "M. T. de la Hartnell" in 1882, passing afterward from the Hartnell heirs to the Spreckels Sugar Company, which later disposed of the property.

The house of the original grantees, the Soberanes adobe, is in the same vicinity but to the west of the road. Hidden by trees, fences, and farm buildings, the place is still used as a family residence on the Silacci Ranch at 960 Old Stage Road.

John C. Frémont camped on the rancho on March 3, 1846. He approached it over the Salinas plain, where "the wild oats were three feet high and well headed." It was here that he received the peremptory order from General José Castro to "return with your people out of the limits of this territory," an order that Frémont ignored. He fortified his party on Gabilan Peak and raised the American flag in defiance.

Rancho Sausal and Salinas

Although a large part of the city of Salinas lies on the Rancho Nacional, the northern part lies on the adjoining Rancho Sausal, which extends north and east of the city. Over this area the Natividad and Gabilan creeks find their way into some of the sloughs that abound in this part of Monterey County.

The American pioneer Jacob P. Leese, who was a landholder in several parts of the state, acquired this property. He filed claim for a confirmation of his right on the basis of two earlier Mexican grants, and received a patent for 10,241 acres in September 1859.

Although the grant had been made to José Tiburcio Castro in 1834, he seems to have resided there much earlier, for his house, only a small part of which is still standing, is said to have been built in 1823. The remnant of the adobe building is in excellent condition, with leather thongs still binding the hand-hewn rafters. Now a private residence, it is located at 803 Sausal Drive, near the corner of Cambrian Drive.

Steinbeck House, Salinas

A more recent and in some ways more celebrated Salinas home is the Steinbeck House, at 132 Central Avenue, where the Nobel Prize–winning novelist John Steinbeck was born on February 27, 1902. The house was built in 1897 and purchased by the Steinbeck family three years later. John lived there until he left to attend Stanford in 1919; he often spent time thereafter at the family cottage in Pacific Grove. The house has been brilliantly restored by the Valley Guild, a volunteer organization that supports Salinas Valley charities and owns and maintains this residence. It is now a restaurant that serves weekday lunches and has an interesting gift shop in the basement, where most of Steinbeck's works can be purchased.

The Salinas Public Library has a special Steinbeck Room devoted to Steinbeck's work and life. It is four blocks from the house at 110 San Luis Street.

World War II had a tragic impact on Salinas. Company C, 194th Battalion of the California National Guard, was called to duty in February 1941. Most of its 107 men came from Salinas. Their appointed place was in the Philippine Islands, and within a year these men and their American and Filipino comrades were battling for their lives as enemy forces closed in. Those who survived the Japanese attacks on Bataan and Corregidor were forced to make the Bataan Death March and were subsequently imprisoned. Only 46 men returned. Salinas has commemorated its soldiers with Bataan Memorial Park, at the junction of Main, Market, and Monterey streets.

Rancho Bolsa Nueva y Moro Cojo (Castroville)

Moro Cojo literally means "lame Moor"; but, since *moro* was used by Spaniards to mean anything black, tradition says that a lame black horse gave the name to this particular tract of land.

This eight-square-league rancho was granted to Simeon Castro in three parts. The first, Moro Cojo, was granted by Governor Luís Argüello in 1825; the second, Bolsa Nueva, by Governor Mariano Chico in 1836; and the third by Governor Juan B. Alvarado in 1837. The last one, according to Bancroft, had been given first to John Milligan, an Irishman who taught weaving at Mission San Juan Bautista. The whole was revalidated to the heirs of Castro by Governor Micheltorena in 1844. Irregular in shape, the rancho reached from the swamp near Monterey Bay to rolling, timbered hills. Its southeastern corner is Lagunita, a lake touched by three other ranchos: Bolsa de las Escarpinas, La Natividad, and Los Vergeles.

The northwestern corner of this grant is near the Elkhorn Slough. The town of Castroville, founded in 1864 by Juan Castro, son of the grantee, is situated within the bounds of this grant.

Rancho La Natividad

Rancho La Natividad consisted of two square leagues of land south of a stretch of Gabilan Creek. The tract was granted to Manuel Butron and Nicolás Alviso by Governor Alvarado in 1837, and their ownership was confirmed by the United States in 1853.

One of the infrequent battles that took place on California soil happened here on November 16, 1846. American rule over California had been proclaimed the previous July, but pockets of Californian resistance persisted. An American recruiting and foraging party of 35 men and 500 horses, led by Captain Charles D. Burrass and Captain Bluford K. Thompson, was on its way to Monterey to join Frémont, who was preparing to go to Los Angeles to reinforce Stockton. Hearing of this, a group of native Californians under Manuel Castro decided to interfere. Making a night march from Monterey toward San Jose, Castro and his men met Burrass and Thompson and their forces. In the skirmish that followed, four Americans were killed and as many wounded; the Californian losses were somewhat greater. The indecisive Battle of Natividad was significant chiefly because it was the only major engagement in the north during the revolt of the Californians against the military occupation by the Americans under Commodore Stockton.

The site of the battle (SRL 651) is marked by a plaque near the junction of Old Stage Road and Crazy Horse Road, seven miles northeast of Salinas. Old Stage Road is the current name for the San Juan Grade; over it stagecoaches traveled between Monterey and San Juan Bautista in the 1850's. Natividad, the small town that grew up here, was a flourishing station on this line. When the line was discontinued and the main traffic was routed through Salinas, the town became deserted. The former schoolhouse has been remodeled and is now a private home, at 661 Old Stage Road.

Rancho El Sur (Point Sur)

In March 1852 Juan Bautista Rogerio Cooper, then harbormaster at Monterey, filed claim to two ranchos in Monterey County: Bolsa del Potrero y Moro Cojo in the vicinity of Salinas, and Rancho El Sur on the seacoast south of the town of Monterey. He received patents for these ranchos in 1859 and 1866, respectively.

Cooper Point on the coast is the southernmost extension of this tract, and the mouth of the Little Sur River is the northern limit. The son, John Baptist Henry Cooper, later relieved his father of a great part of the burden of managing his property and eventually inherited it. The headquarters of this rancho were in a frame house, which is still standing, constructed of timbers brought around the Horn. This area is now Andrew Molera State Park.

Rancho Milpitas (Jolon)

Rancho Milpitas, the grant extending for many miles along the San Antonio River, has its comparatively narrow northwest boundary within Los Padres National Forest. In the fertile level areas by the river and along some of its tributaries were probably located those small plots, cultivated by the natives, that gave rise to the name Milpitas ("little gardens").

Mission Creek was the name given to one of those tributary streams after the establishment of the San Antonio Mission near its bank. From it a supply of water was obtained.

Ygnacio Pastor, a neophyte of the San Antonio Mission, received the grant of Rancho Milpitas from Governor Alvarado in 1838. Patent for 43,281 acres was issued to him in 1875. A small area of 33 acres around Mission San Antonio was patented to Archbishop J. S. Alemany in 1862.

The southeast corner of the rancho is at Jolon (said to be an Indian word for "valley of dead oaks"). The property later passed to Faxon Dean Atherton and then to William Randolph Hearst. It is today part of the Hunter Liggett Military Reservation.

Rancho Los Ojitos (San Antonio River Valley)

Rancho Los Ojitos (in free translation, "ranch of little springs"), adjoining the southern tip of Rancho Milpitas, is a long narrow strip of land lying along the San Antonio River. Most of this land today is in the Lake San Antonio Recreational Area, created when San Antonio Dam was built across the San Antonio River. After the secularization of the mission, the rancho was given to Mariano Soberanes by Governor Alvarado in 1842.

Because the grantee had been active against the American invaders, the place was pillaged by Frémont's men on their way to Los Angeles in 1846. Don Mariano's claim for damages resulted in a very small award by the courts. In 1871 a patent for 8,900 acres was issued to him. Two old houses on the property gradually succumbed to time and the practice maneuvers of soldiers at Hunter Liggett; the ruins are still visible from the Jolon-Pleyto Road about three and one-half miles southeast of Jolon.

Rancho Pleyto (San Antonio River Valley)

Early Spanish travelers through the San Antonio River Valley remarked upon the groups of Indians frequently seen engaged in earnest conversation there. To all appearances, they were endeavoring to settle disagreements that had arisen among themselves, and this valley seemed to be a customary meeting place for that purpose. The Spanish word pleito means "lawsuit," and from it the name of Rancho Pleyto is supposed to have been derived.

The grant of this land was made in 1845 by Governor Pico to Antonio Chavez (Chavis), who two years previously had received Rancho Ciénega del Gabilán. A claim founded on this grant was filed with the Land Commission by W. S. Johnson and Preston K. Woodside. The two were members of the regiment of New York Volunteers brought to California by Colonel Stevenson in 1847. Their claim, first rejected, was settled on appeal in their favor, and 13,299 acres were confirmed to them in 1872.

Through the long narrow valley that comprises this rancho ran the trail between Missions San Antonio and San Miguel; when the days of the stagecoach arrived, it was still the main line of travel between these two points. At the settlement of Pleyto lived J. T. Betts, who was for many years responsible for keeping the horses on the line properly shod. His children grew up in the little town, and his sister kept the hotel there. The town has disappeared; its site is the junction of Pleyto Road and the road to Bradley along the south side of the San Antonio River.

Ranchos Along the Salinas River

Of the 32 private land grants in the Salinas Valley, 26 lie adjacent to the Salinas River. The fertile acres in this region successively attracted Spaniards, Mexicans, and Americans as they traveled over the level country.

Near the mouth of the Salinas River is Rancho Rincón de las Salinas ("corner of the salt marshes"), extending from just east of Twin Bridges (Neponset) to the ocean. This was granted by Governor Figueroa to Cristina Delgado in 1833; Rafael Estrada, having occupied it in 1853, received United States patent for it in 1881.

Across the river from the Rincon de las Salinas was the Bolsa del Potrero y Moro Cojo, or La Sagrada Familia, originally granted to José Joaquín de la Torre, who had arrived in Alta California in 1801. He thereafter had served long and well in the Monterey Company, much of the time as secretary to the governor. In a successful petition to Governor Pablo Vicente de Sola in 1822, Don José Joaquín stated that he owned horses and cattle and that, having been allowed to pasture them on the Bolsa del Potrero y Moro Cojo, he would be pleased to receive a grant of that particular piece of land in order to build houses and fences. Furthermore, it was his belief that the land in question belonged to the government and that no one else had claim upon it.

The tract was almost surrounded by water, lying between the Salinas River and the "Trembladera" (quaking bog), with branching sloughs meandering through it. In 1829 Don José Joaquín sold the entire property, consisting of nearly 7,000 acres, to Juan Bautista Rogerio Cooper, the older half-brother of Thomas O. Larkin. Cooper's house stood about a mile from the Cooper Switch on the railroad.

Southeast of Don José Joaquín de la Torre's Rancho la Sagrada Familia lay the Rinconada del Sanjón (*zanjon*, "deep ditch") of 2,230 acres. Its boundary line on the south and southwest was made up of the curves of the Salinas River and the adjacent sloughs. The grant of this property was given by Governor Alvarado to José Eusebio Boronda in 1840. Confirmed by the United States government in 1854, the grant was surveyed in 1858 and patented two years later.

Don José Eusebio was 30 years old when he received this rancho; four years earlier he had been mayordomo of Rancho Vergeles, which lay along the road from Monterey to San Jose. He married Josefa Buelna. Their home, built on a hill (across the road and railroad from the present Graves School), was so situated that it could be seen for miles over the Salinas plain. Travelers could see, by standing on their saddles, the red tiles of the Boronda adobe over the yellow blossoms of mustard, as Lieutenant William Tecumseh Sherman did in 1849 after crossing the Salinas River on his way from Monterey. That house no longer stands, but a second adobe erected by Don Eusebio in a more protected location may be seen less than three miles northwest of the city of Salinas at 333 Boronda Road. The Boronda adobe (SRL 870) is now owned by the Monterey County Historical Society, which maintains a small museum there.

Antonio Aceves and Antonio Romero had held a four-league grant, called Las Salinas, before 1795. But, as was frequently the case with grants given at that period, when the entire area was unoccupied except by roving bands of Indians, the grantees made very little effort to hold their lands.

One square league out of this area was given by Governor Nicolás Gutiérrez to Gabriel Espinosa in 1839. The western tip of this rancho reached almost to the Bay of Monterey, and the rancho stretched eastward to the Salinas opposite Blanco. Lucinda E. Pogue and the heirs of Don Gabriel filed claim for this property in 1853 and the patent was received fourteen years later, Pogue receiving two-sevenths of the property and each of the five children of Gabriel Espinosa receiving one-seventh.

To the south of Rancho Las Salinas lay part of the City Lands of Monterey, the vast tract extending from the Bay of Monterey to the Salinas, with the title dating back to 1830. Divided from the City Lands of Monterey by the Pilarcitos Canyon was Rancho El Chamisal, granted by Governor Castro to Felipe Vásquez in 1835 and finally patented in 1877 to Nicanor Lugo, Vásquez's widow, and their three children.

Lying parallel with El Chamisal and on the same side of the Salinas River was Rancho El Toro, along which ran Toro Creek. Hill Town is near the northeastern corner of this tract. The rancho was granted to José Ramón Estrada in 1835 by Governor Castro. The grantee had attended school in Monterey and was administrator at Santa Clara for two years after receiving this grant. In 1852 Charles Walters filed claim to the grant and in 1862 received patent for 5,668 acres.

Rancho Nacional lay northeast of the narrow ends of El Chamisal and El Toro across the river. Its corner was at Hill Town, and it extended from the river into Salinas. The cattle, horses, and sheep belonging to Carmel Mission and the Presidio of Monterey were once pastured here. It was one of the *ranchos del rey*, land belonging to the King of Spain, to be used as directed by the government. The grazing was particularly good because of the rich bottom land and the many streams and sloughs. When the Argentine pirate Bouchard was a threat in 1818, people sought refuge here. In April 1839, Governor Alvarado granted two square leagues of

Rancho Nacional to Vicente Cantua; United States patent was obtained by the grantee in 1866 for 6,633 acres.

Hill Town is at the junction of SR 68 and the Spreckels Road, a few miles south of Salinas. In later years Hill Town was the site of one of the first ferries to cross the Salinas River. Operated by Hiram Cory, it was guided across the river by a cable and propelled by the force of the current. Hill Town Ferry (SRL 560) operated until a bridge was built in 1889. A marker on the banks of the stream commemorates the pioneer ferry.

Up the river from Hill Town stretched two ranchos belonging to the Estrada family—Buena Vista and Llano de Buena Vista. Llano de Buena Vista was granted to José Mariano Estrada in 1823. Don José Mariano had come to California in 1797 and was at once made *alférez* of the Monterey Company, a position he held for twelve years. He was rewarded for his service in 1818 against Bouchard by being made brevet lieutenant, and in 1824 he was made full lieutenant for his services in suppressing Indian uprisings. He retired from military service in 1829, and the following year he was made executor of the Luis Argüello estate. His daughter Adelaide married David Spence, to whom this rancho, consisting of 8,446 acres, was patented in 1860. On this grant was the town of Spreckels.

Rancho Buena Vista was granted to José Santiago Estrada and his father, José Mariano Estrada, by Governor Pablo Vicente de Sola in 1822. It consisted of two square leagues. José Santiago and his brothers filed claim for this rancho in 1852, and through the offices of their attorney, Mariano Malarin, they received patent in 1869.

Southeast of Llano de Buena Vista was Rancho Encinal y Buena Esperanza, also bordering on the Salinas River. It was granted to David Spence, the son-in-law of Don José Mariano Estrada, by Governor Figueroa in 1834. The governor at that time stipulated that "within a year at latest he shall build a house thereon and it must be habitable." It was also provided that, when the property was confirmed, the corners should be marked not only by boundary stones but by planting fruit trees, "either wild or tame, of some utility." Any violation of these and other conditions would cause him to forfeit his right to the land. Another square league was granted to Spence by Governor Juan B. Alvarado in 1839. Both of these grants were in due time approved, and a patent for 13,352 acres was issued in 1862.

David Spence was a conservative and widely respected man from Scotland. After living in Peru for a few years, he had come to California, where he lived until his death in 1875. Debarking at Monterey in 1824 from the *Pizarro*, he superintended meat packing for Begg and Company for three years, after which time he went into business for himself and was successful from the first. In 1828 he was baptized at Santa Cruz as David Esteban Spence, and the following year he married Adelaide Estrada. After nearly 40 years of life together, they died within one month of each other. Since their son David had died seven years previously, their large estate was left to their four grandchildren. The station of Spence on the Southern Pacific Railroad is in the northwestern part of this rancho.

South of Don David's property were Ranchos Chualar and Zanjones, both of which finally came into the possession of Don Juan Malarin. On the western bank of the river along this stretch lies the land once contained in Rancho Guadalupe y Llanitos de los Correos, granted to Don Juan between 1831 and 1835. The three grants contained a total of 24,470 acres.

Juan Malarin, the grantee, was a native of Peru. He came to California as master of the *Señoriana* in 1820 and returned in 1824 as master of the *Apolónia*. In 1825 he was chosen by Governor Argüello to take the prizes *Asia* and *Constante* to Acapulco; for this service, which he performed for the government, he was made a lieutenant in the Mexican Navy. He thereafter made Monterey his home between sea voyages and married Josefa Estrada. His fine character and unobtrusive manner made Don Juan an influential citizen and he became president of the Monterey Council. He died at the age of 60, leaving a large family. His eldest son, Mariano, who had been sent to Peru to be educated, was made executor of the estate. The son succeeded in obtaining patents for all three of the ranchos, for Zanjones in 1866, Guadalupe in 1869, and Chualar in 1872.

The town of Chualar stretches along US 101 for a quarter of a mile near the western boundary of Rancho Chualar. The next rancho to the south was Zanjones. The Malarin house stood on the Rancho Guadalupe, the first grant made to Don Juan. In the property settlement, Josefa Estrada, the widow, received one-half of the whole property, the remainder going to the ten children.

Along the river southeast of the Malarin estate was Rancho Rincón de la Puente del Monte, four square leagues granted by Governor Gutiérrez to Teodoro Gonzales on September 20, 1836. A patent for 15,219 acres was given to him in 1866. Don Teodoro, a Mexican otter hunter, became a man of good standing and wealth and at one time served as alcalde in Monterey. His widow and sons later resided in San Francisco. The town of Gonzales, named for this family, lies within the bounds of this irregularly shaped rancho.

Southwest and across the river from the Gonzales property was Rancho Paraje de Sánchez. El Camino Real ran through this grant between Soledad Mission and the missions to the north. The 6,584 acres in this rancho were patented to C. Lugo and others in 1866.

The Salinas River curves in and out of the south-western line of Rancho San Vicente. The town of Sole-dad is in the southern part of this nearly 20,000-acre grant made to Francisco Soto, Francisco Figueroa, and Estévan Munras. Munras was an early Spanish trader at Monterey. His wife was Catalina Manzanelli of Tepic, Mexico, under whose name Ranchos Laguna Seca and San Francisquito were held. Don Estévan, unlike many of his compatriots, was prominent in aiding foreigners and quite ready for a change from Mexican political intrigues.

Across the river from Soledad and Rancho San Vicente lay the lands of Soledad Mission. On behalf of the church, Bishop J. S. Alemany was given patent in 1859 to 34 acres, containing orchards, vineyards, and springs. Feliciano Soberanes purchased 8,900 acres of the mission lands in 1846, reputedly for $800, and his title to them was confirmed. It was reported at the time that the mission was in ruins and that travelers stop-ping there were grossly overcharged.

An adobe occupied by members of the Soberanes family is still standing. Although the largest residence was almost destroyed by fire on January 5, 1935, three of the original eleven rooms were left standing and are in use. This remnant is hidden from view by a modern residence that has been erected on the side of the burned building. These structures stand, with other farm build-ings, at the far left of Fort Romie Road near a bend in the road three-quarters of a mile east of its junction with Foothill Road. Another mile or less down Fort Romie Road is the restored Mission Nuestra Señora de la Soledad.

On Rancho Los Coches ("the pigs"), east of the mis-sion, is an adobe structure that is being preserved by the state of California. It stands directly on the corner of US 101 between Soledad and King City at the junc-tion with the Arroyo Seco Road. This story-and-a-half building, known as the Richardson Adobe (SRL 494), faces the branch road. A porch extends along the entire front. Bancroft says the grant of Los Coches was made in 1841 to María Josefa, daughter of Feliciano Sobera-nes. She was married to William Brunner Richardson, who built the adobe in 1843 and planted the row of black locusts in front in 1846. The building has had various uses, a family residence, a post office, and a stage station among them.

Rancho Arroyo Seco, which adjoined Los Coches on the south, consisted of 16,523 acres. Its northwest cor-ner was near the present junction of Paraiso Springs Road and Clark Road. For this property Joaquín de la Torre filed a claim founded on a grant of four square leagues that Governor Alvarado made to him in 1840.

Richardson Adobe, Soledad

Don Joaquín was a Mexican patriot of energy and cour-age, active against incoming foreigners. Greenfield has grown up on the southeast boundary of this rancho.

Paraiso Springs is at the end of Paraiso Springs Road, in the foothills overlooking the Salinas Valley. The hot springs here have been known since mission times, when the padres dubbed the place Eternidad Paraiso ("eternal paradise"). In the 1890's, a large resort hotel was built here, reached by regular stagecoaches from the Soledad railroad station. The hotel burned for the second and last time in 1954. The privately owned Paraiso Springs resort today is open to the public.

Southeast of Arroyo Seco was Rancho Poza de los Ositos, granted to Carlos Cayetano Espinosa in 1839 by Governor Alvarado. Across the river from this rancho and Arroyo Seco was Rancho San Lorenzo, stretching south along the river as far as San Lorenzo Creek. This grant of 21,884 acres, made by Governor Alvarado to Feliciano Soberanes in 1841, was in addition to Rancho Alisal already held by the grantee, who later purchased some of the land formerly belonging to Soledad Mission.

King City is located on the southern part of this grant. An important stopover on the journey between Los Angeles and San Francisco, the town has long been a traveler's haven. In the San Lorenzo Recreational Cen-ter, just off US 101 west of King City, is the San Lo-renzo Agricultural Museum, displaying antique farm equipment, a working blacksmith shop, the Spreckels farmhouse, and the one-room schoolhouse from La Gloria, a nearby settlement.

Ranchos San Bernabe and San Benito lay further south on the river; no buildings or landmarks remain. The southernmost rancho in the Salinas River region was San Bernardo, granted by Governor Alvarado in 1841 to Mariano and Juan Soberanes. At its northern line it joined Rancho San Lucas. San Ardo, a station on the Southern Pacific Railroad, is about midway on the long narrow tract, which embraces 13,346 acres of rich bottom lands.

Much of the land of Rancho San Lucas is still owned by descendants of Alberto Trescony, who came to California from Italy in 1842 and purchased the estate in 1862. It had first been granted to Rafael Estrada in 1842. The headquarters of the ranch is six miles south and west of the town of San Lucas, one and one-half miles from the Paris Valley Road. The main dwelling house, built in 1865, consists of one story only. It has thick walls and is nearly surrounded by porches. The barn is of two stories, both made of adobe bricks. The blacksmith shop is roofed with handmade tiles removed from a building on Rancho San Benito, also purchased by Alberto Trescony.

The Monterey Peninsula

Rancho Punta de Pinos was a grant of 2,667 acres along the ocean side of the Monterey Peninsula, the northern limit of which was Point Pinos, the southwest headland of Monterey Bay and site of the present light station. South of it was Rancho El Pescadero, extending from near Seal Rocks to Carmel. The shoreline is threaded by the Seventeen-Mile Drive, of which Cypress Point is the westernmost limit and the most famous spot on the route. At this point on the rugged shoreline are found the picturesque Monterey cypress trees, whose branches have been bent and gnarled through long exposure to ocean winds. These trees (*Cupressus macrocarpa Hartweg*) have a restricted habitat and are native only to the coast adjacent to the mouth of the Carmel River. Because of early fishing activities carried on at the water's edge on the southern part of Monterey Peninsula, the name Pescadero ("place where fishing is done") was given to the rocks off the shore in Carmel Bay, to a point to the west of them, and to the rancho itself.

Both of these ranchos passed into the hands of David Jacks, who also owned Rancho Aguajito adjoining El Pescadero on the east. Jacks was more interested in developing these properties than in farming them. He had come to California from Scotland in 1848 and put his business ability to work in the young city of San Francisco. In 1850 he began his lifelong interest in the Monterey region, acquiring the city lands in 1859 by methods that were upheld by the courts but denounced by local citizens. In 1874 he was one of the capitalists who backed the Monterey and Salinas Valley Railroad as a challenge to the dominant and greedy Southern Pacific; the new railroad was to bring the grain of Salinas to the port at Monterey and avoid the high charges of the established railroad. Beset by difficulties of all kinds, the narrow-gauge Monterey and Salinas Valley was forced to sell out to the Southern Pacific in 1879.

In the same year, another Scotsman, Robert Louis Stevenson, wrote a sketch on Monterey that concluded with these words: "Alas for the little town! It is not strong enough to resist the influence of the flaunting caravanserai, and the poor, quaint, penniless native gentlemen of Monterey must perish, like a lower race, before the millionaire vulgarians of the Big Bonanza." Stevenson was referring to the fact that when the Southern Pacific Railroad bought out the Monterey and Salinas Valley line, it built its own broad-gauge track to Monterey and began to plan a luxurious resort at its terminus, Charles Crocker of the Southern Pacific "Big Four" having become interested in the potential of the sleepy town of Monterey. The Del Monte Hotel, "the most elegant seaside establishment in the world," opened in 1880. Transforming Monterey almost overnight into a fashionable and highly successful watering place, the Del Monte Hotel became a California landmark. Twice destroyed by fire and twice rebuilt, it is today the U.S. Naval Postgraduate School.

Jacks also developed a more sober and down-to-earth community to the north of Monterey. The Pacific Grove Retreat began as a summer camp and setting for church meetings, patterned after an earlier undertaking at Ocean Grove, New Jersey. This "haven for the gentle, the refined, the cultured, where carousing and dissipation are unknown" was developed by the Methodist Retreat Association. The community attracted many who sought intellectual and moral uplift. These were uniquely combined in the Chautauqua movement, an Eastern import that first appeared in Pacific Grove in 1879. Lectures, concerts, and seminars in a setting that excluded outside distractions were a feature of the Chautauquas. In 1889, a hall was built at the corner of Sixteenth Street and Central Avenue to house these programs (SRL 839). At one time Pacific Grove was fenced off from its neighbors and imposed strict curfews on its members. Inevitably, the invigorating climate that first brought the Methodist elders into this pine forest attracted others as well, and Pacific Grove had become, by the early twentieth century, a more secular community. One connection with the old days has been preserved: the Asilomar (Spanish *asilo del mar*, "refuge by the sea") conference grounds, begun in 1913 under the sponsorship of Phoebe Apperson Hearst as a campground for the Young Women's Christian Association, are now owned and administered by the state of California, at the western edge of Pacific Grove.

The Carmel Valley

Los Tularcitos, the great triangular tract of 26,581 acres covering the Buckeye Ridge and Burnt Mountain, contains a short stretch of the upper part of the Carmel River. As the river flows through the southwestern corner of the rancho, Los Tularcitos Creek drains into it. This rancho was granted by Governor Figueroa to Rafael Gómez in 1834. In 1852 his widow, Josefa Antonia Gómez de Walters, and his children filed claim for the property and received a patent for it in 1866.

Rancho los Tularcitos passed into the hands of Alberto Trescony, owner of Rancho San Lucas, in the late 1880's; gradually he sold off all but about 2,000 acres, which remain in the family. The main portion, however, which still bears the name Rancho Tularcitos, was acquired by the Marble family in 1924. On a hill south and across the road from the Marble residence is a fragment of adobe wall, all that is left of the original ranch house of Los Tularcitos. The Marble home overlooks a seven-acre tule-bordered lake, from which the ranch received its name of "the little tules." These landmarks are on Tularcitos Road, about two miles east of the junction with Carmel Valley Road.

There were two ranchos Los Laureles along the river; the larger one, through which the river flows, joined Los Tularcitos on the west; the smaller rancho lay to the west of the larger. The larger was patented to José Manuel Boronda and his son, Juan de Mara, in 1866, based on their earlier grant of 1839. The original adobe home, with later additions, is still standing between Carmel Valley Road and the river to the east of Los Laureles Grade Junction. It is on the west side of Boronda Road one-tenth of a mile south of Carmel Valley Road and is occupied as a private residence. The old part of it is of unusual architectural interest. It is 64 feet long and 19 feet wide. The thick-walled rooms are well preserved; roughly squared beams of the simple ceilings are carefully fitted. The ceiling of one room shows an interesting example of veneering done in soft wood.

The smaller Laureles Rancho lay wholly north of the river, as did Rancho Cañada de la Segunda, which reached west to Carmel. On the south bank of the river was Rancho Potrero de San Carlos, which was patented in 1862 to Joaquín Gutiérrez and María Estefana del Real, daughter of the original grantee. This property was purchased in 1858 by Bradley V. Sargent, who also acquired adjoining lands. One of his purchases was Rancho San José y Sur Chiquito, stretching from the lower reaches of the Carmel River southward along the coast. In the northern part of this rancho near the river stood an adobe called "Las Virgenes" because tradition said that local Indians saw there apparitions of the Virgin Mary.

Bradley Sargent also purchased Rancho San Francisquito, lying to the southeast of Rancho Potrero de San Carlos. The San Francisquito ranch house is mentioned in the writings of Robert Louis Stevenson as the place where he was taken by Captain Jonathan Wright to be revived after Wright discovered the writer lying, near death, within a short distance of the house. Stevenson had undertaken a solitary camping trip in the hope of strengthening his precarious health; Wright's kindness, he maintained, saved his life.

Ranchos on the Eastern Boundary of the County

Following the boundary line between Monterey and San Benito counties from north to south, one locates five ranchos, all grants from the Mexican period: Vega del Río del Pájaro, Cañada de la Carpinteria, Los Carneros, Los Vergeles, and Ciénega del Gabilán. No buildings or early landmarks remain on these lands.

Colton Hall

Colton Hall (SRL 126), on Pacific Street between Jefferson and Madison streets in Monterey, was erected in 1847–49 by Reverend Walter Colton, alcalde of the city. Colton came to California as chaplain on the United States frigate *Congress* in 1846 and was named alcalde the same year by Commodore Robert Stockton. A man of great ability, he impaneled the first jury in California and on August 15, 1846, in company with Robert Semple, established the *Californian*, the first newspaper to be published in California. His journal, *Three Years in California*, published in New York in 1850, is one of the most fascinating books on the early American period in California and a mine of information for the historian.

Colton Hall was the first public building in California to be erected for secular purposes; it was "for many years the most useful building in the city, having been used as a constitutional hall, a schoolhouse, a courthouse, a public assembly hall, and a place of religious worship." California's first constitutional convention met here from September 1 to October 13, 1849. The 48 delegates held their sessions on the upper floor, which ran the length of the main building. The large room in which they met has been restored to look as it did in 1849. Robert Semple was chairman of the convention and William G. Marcy was secretary. While Monterey was county seat of Monterey County, from 1850 to 1873, Colton Hall was used as the county courthouse. The jail located at the rear of Colton Hall was constructed in 1854 and served as the city jail until 1956. No one ever escaped from its thick granite walls. Like Colton Hall, the Old Jail is now open to the public.

One of the first schools in California was held in this building, in 1849, by the Rev. Samuel H. Willey. Willey was later prominent in the founding of the College of California, predecessor of the University of California.

Unlike most of Monterey's early buildings, Colton Hall was distinctly of the old New England academy style. Rev. Mr. Willey, who was one of the chaplains of the constitutional convention, says in his reminiscences that when he landed from the steamship *California*, on February 3, 1849, he was struck by the contrast between the architecture of this plain white building and the many Spanish adobe buildings around it. "It might have dropped down from a New England village," was his comment.

The state of California made provisions in 1903 for its preservation, protection, and improvement, and it is now owned by the city of Monterey. The building itself is a two-story structure of stone and remains today in excellent condition; the ground floor houses some of the Monterey city offices. It was marked by a bronze tablet placed by the Native Sons of the Golden West on June 3, 1931.

California's First Convent School

The first convent school in California was established at Monterey in the spring of 1851 by three Dominican Sisters who had arrived in California the previous year. The old adobe building in which the school was held proved to be in very bad condition; furthermore, the population in Monterey was diminishing while that around San Francisco Bay was rapidly increasing. The sisters, therefore, in 1854, decided to move to Benicia, then a more central location.

Concepción Argüello, the story of whose life is closely associated with San Francisco and Benicia, was the first novice to enter the Convent of St. Catherine at Monterey, and when the school was moved to its new location, she was transferred to Benicia.

After the removal of the convent to Benicia, the old building at Monterey was used as a chapel and parish house for a time. Later, it was rented to private parties and rapidly fell into decay; it was torn down soon after 1885. The site where it stood is on the northwest corner of Calle Principal and Franklin Street and is now occupied by the Sheraton Hotel.

The Adobes of Old Monterey

Monterey Old Town Historic District, in which 43 structures from the nineteenth century are located, has been registered as a National Historic Landmark. At the western entrance to Old Monterey stands one of the earliest of its historic buildings, the Casa Munras, one of the first homes to be built outside the original presidio grounds. It was erected by Estévan Munras, who came to California as a merchant. Considerably remodeled, it is now part of the Hotel Munras at 656 Munras Avenue, opposite what was once the southwest corner of the old presidio grounds.

Alvarado Street is the main street of old Monterey (although a parallel street is called Calle Principal); from the waterfront it leads up the hill to a group of dwellings rich in historic interest, centering on the Larkin House.

The Larkin House (SRL 106), located on the corner of Calle Principal and Jefferson Street, is typical of the Spanish-Californian type of architecture that prevailed throughout Alta California: softly tinted adobe walls, cool veranda and picturesque upper balcony, iron-barred windows and walled gardens, with rose and fig trees. It was built in 1834 by Thomas Oliver Larkin, who had come to Monterey as a merchant in 1832 and was appointed United States consul in 1843. Being thoroughly acquainted with conditions in the province, he rendered important service as consul and confidential agent, and his policies helped prepare the way for the American annexation of California. His house is now a unit of the Monterey State Historic Park and has been registered by the Department of the Interior as a National Historic Landmark.

The House of the Four Winds (SRL 353), built about 1830, stands at 540 Calle Principal. It was used as a residence for many years, but in 1846 the first hall of records in the state of California was housed there, and the first recorder in Monterey had his home as well as his office in the building. Now the Monterey Civic Club uses it. The unusual name was derived from the fact that it had a weathervane, the first in Monterey.

Between the Larkin House and the House of the Four Winds is a small one-room adobe built by Larkin in 1834 and known as Sherman's Headquarters. It is an integral part of the architecture of the old Larkin garden, with its redwoods and palms and fig trees, and may be reached through the walled patio of the larger house. In 1847–49 Lieutenant William Tecumseh Sherman of Civil War fame had his civil and military headquarters here.

The Cooper-Molera adobe at 508 Munras Avenue is one of the largest adobes left in northern California. John Rogers Cooper, captain of the trading schooner *Rover*, came to Monterey from New England in 1823. He was born on Alderney, in the Channel Islands, and so was a British subject by birth. It was Cooper who influenced Thomas Larkin, his half-brother by his mother's second marriage, to come to California and to establish himself as a merchant. Recognizing the future of the area, Cooper became a Mexican citizen, took the name of Juan Bautista Rogerio Cooper, and married Encarnación Vallejo, sister of General Mariano Vallejo. The home that he built for his wife in 1826 was divided in 1833, with five rooms being sold off. In 1902, Cooper's daughter Anna purchased these rooms, so that the complex of buildings was one again. Meanwhile, her sister Amelia had married Eusebio Molera, a native of Spain, and in time inherited the complex from her sister. The children of Eusebio and Amelia Molera became great patrons of California history and at various times lived briefly in the adobe. Andrew M. Molera never married and died in 1931; he is commemorated by a state park named for him along the Big Sur coast of Monterey County. His sister Frances also died unmarried, in 1968, and deeded the property to the National Trust for Historic Preservation. The California Department of Parks and Recreation, under a 30-year lease, is undertaking an extensive restoration program of what is now a complex of buildings and courtyards, open to the public.

Adjoining this at 599 Polk Street is a separate adobe that was built about 1832 by Gabriel de la Torre, a Mexican alcalde, and was the first federal court building in California. Across the way at 516 Polk Street is Casa Amesti, a two-story balconied adobe built about 1825 by José Amesti, a Catalonian who had come to California and married Prudenciana Vallejo, another sister of the General, a few years earlier. The building is now a private men's club.

On the northwest corner of Webster and Abrego streets is the one-story Abrego adobe, built by José Abrego in the 1830's. Bayard Taylor, in his *Eldorado*, describes an evening party that he attended in this house in 1849, and also comments that José Abrego, having amassed a substantial fortune within a few years, was the most industrious Californian he had seen in the country. The building is now a private women's club.

The Francisco Pacheco House is a picturesque two-story adobe located on the southwest corner of Abrego and Webster streets opposite the Abrego House. It was built around 1840 by Francisco Pérez Pacheco, a wealthy landowner who had come from Mexico in 1819. He is buried in the San Carlos Church directly in front of the main altar. The building, once used as a hospital, is now a private club.

At 530 Houston Street is the Robert Louis Stevenson House (SRL 352), where the gifted writer lived for a short time in the autumn of 1879. His attachment for Mrs. Fanny Van de Grift Osbourne, whom he had met in France, brought Stevenson to California. This proved to be the most decisive step he had ever taken, for both his character and the entire trend of his life were influenced by this visit to the West. The hills and beaches of the Monterey Peninsula gave Stevenson the landscape he made rich use of in *Treasure Island*. In Monterey some of his greatest friendships were matured; among them were those of Fanny Osbourne, who became his wife; her sister, Nellie Sánchez, his amanuensis and in her own right an important California historian; and

Jules Simoneau, his lifelong friend. Stevenson occupied two airy rooms in the ell of the house, with five sunny windows opening on the balcony to the west. The place is now a unit of the Monterey State Historic Park and contains a collection of Stevenson memorabilia.

Directly behind Colton Hall on Dutra Street is one of Monterey's most picturesque adobes, Casa Vásquez (SRL 351), set in an old-fashioned garden amid a bower of trees. Now a city office building, it was once the home of Dolores Vásquez, sister of Tiburcio Vásquez, California's most ruthless bandit, who terrorized the stage roads up and down the state in the 1870's.

On the northwest corner of Alvarado and Pearl streets is a two-story adobe (SRL 348) now used for stores. This was the home of Juan Bautista Alvarado, governor of California under Mexican rule from 1836 to 1842 and known to his contemporaries as the "silver-tongued" orator because of his brilliant eloquence and great personal magnetism. This Alvarado house is only one of several in various parts of the state in which Don Juan is said to have lived; another in Monterey is at 510 Dutra Street.

On Monterey's waterfront is the so-called Old Whaling Station with its vivid memories of high adventure on many seas. It was built in 1855 by David Wight as a residence. Later it became a boardinghouse for Portuguese sailors. Today it is again a private home, as is its neighbor, the first brick house in California. It was built for Gallant Duncan Dickenson, who arrived in California from Missouri in 1846. The main part of the house was erected in 1847, but the wings were never completed, since the gold rush took the owner away to the mines.

California's first theater (SRL 136), a long rectangular adobe built by Jack Swan in 1843, was originally a sailors' boardinghouse and saloon. It was first used for amateur dramatics by four soldiers and a local group in 1847, and later by members of Colonel J. D. Stevenson's regiment of New York Volunteers. The building, which was restored in 1917, stands at the corner of Pacific and Scott streets and was reopened as a theater in 1937.

The Pacific House (SRL 354), at the junction of Alvarado Street, Scott Street, and Calle Principal, was originally a hotel built by Thomas O. Larkin in 1835 and sold to James McKinley, a Scotsman who had come to California in the 1820's. For many years the Presbyterian Church held services in this building. Now it belongs to the Monterey State Historic Park and is open to the public as a historical and Indian museum. An exceptionally fine patio and garden are at the rear. A short distance away, at Scott and Olivier streets, is the Casa del Oro (SRL 532), also a part of the Monterey State Historic Park. It is said that gold dust was left here for safekeeping, hence the name "house of gold." In the 1850's it was a general store operated by Joseph Boston and Company.

The Gutiérrez Adobe (SRL 713), adjoining buildings at 590 Calle Principal, is a well-preserved example of the domestic architecture of the 1840's. It is now a restaurant. One of the most beautiful adobes in Monterey is also part of the state park; this is the Soberanes adobe (SRL 712), the "House wih the Blue Gate," at 336 Pacific Street. Built about 1830 by José Estrada, its name comes from Feliciano Soberanes, who purchased it from him. In 1941 it became the home of the late Mayo Hayes O'Donnell, noted Monterey historian, and it is now open to the public.

The Casa Bonifacio once stood on Alvarado Street at Bonifacio Place, but has been moved to Mesa Road. There is a legend about the place that is the source of its alternate name, "The House of the Sherman Rose." While Lieutenant William T. Sherman was stationed at Monterey in the late 1840's, he called several times at the home where Señorita María Ygnacia Bonifacio lived. On one of these visits, so the story goes, he unpinned a rose from his uniform (a most unlikely embellishment) and planted it in her garden, saying that if it took root and grew, their love would endure. The flower grew into a marvelous rose tree (or so the story goes) that almost covered the adobe and was the admiration of tourists for many years. Sherman never returned, and Señorita Bonifacio never married.

This house, however, has a more real association with the name of Robert Louis Stevenson, for it was here that his fiancée, Fanny Osbourne, and her sister, Nellie Sánchez, lived with Señorita Bonifacio. Stevenson was of course a frequent visitor, and there he began *The Amateur Emigrant*, gathered notes for "The Old Pacific Capital," and wrote *The Pavilion on the Links*, as well as the unfinished work "A Vendetta of the West."

Many other old buildings are still standing in Monterey. At 177 Van Buren Street is the wood-frame Doud House. The Gordon house, another frame structure, is at 526 Pierce Street. Also on Pierce Street is another Casa de la Torre at 502, and the Casa de Jesús Soto at 460. On Pacific Street one finds the Merritt house at 386, and the Casa Serrano (headquarters of the Monterey History and Art Association) at 412. At the corner of Pacific and Franklin streets is the Capitular Hall, and at the south end of Friendly Plaza facing Pacific Street is the Underwood-Brown adobe. Hartnell Street has the Stokes House at 500 and Frémont's Headquarters at 539. Alvarado Street contains the Casa Sánchez at 412, and the Jacinto Rodríguez adobe at 378. The Estrada adobe, restored in the 1960's, is at 456 Tyler Street. The first French Consulate, an adobe originally standing at Fremont and Abrego streets, was reconstructed in 1932 at the edge of Lake El Estero at the foot of Franklin Street. The Casa Madariaga stands on Abrego Street opposite the Casa Pacheco, and the Casa Buelna is on Mesa Road. Casa Joaquín Soto is at 5 Via Joaquin off El Dorado Street. Casa Boronda (1817), one of Monterey's oldest buildings, is at the end of Boronda Lane south of Fremont Street. Standing two miles southeast of downtown Monterey in the suburbs is the old Castro adobe of Rancho Aguajito, now restored by the Jacks family. It stands at 1224 Castro Road facing the Del Monte Golf Course.

As late as the 1890's, Pacific Street, Alvarado Street, and Calle Principal were lined with old adobe buildings. Most have been demolished to make way for modern structures, and now few can be found on any one of these thoroughfares. Nevertheless, Monterey has done more than most California cities to preserve the tangible evidence of its past. The Monterey History and Art Association has marked virtually all of the city's historic buildings.

Many of these old Monterey buildings function in part as museums, and some have been given over wholly to displays. Situated between the House of the Four Winds and the Casa Gutiérrez at 550 Calle Principal is the Allen Knight Maritime Museum, sponsored by the Monterey History and Art Association. This museum emphasizes the sailing ship era and the local fishing and whaling days in Monterey, drawing on the large private collection accumulated by the late Allen Knight of Carmel. On the grounds of the presidio is the United States Army Museum, with miniatures of early forts, cavalry uniforms, and weapons.

The new Portola Plaza at the foot of Calle Principal is highlighted by a statue of Gaspar de Portolá, a gift of King Juan Carlos of Spain and erected in 1978.

Cannery Row

North of the presidio along the waterfront are some four blocks of buildings that remain from the days when Monterey was the third-largest port in fish tonnage in the world—Cannery Row. The commercial packing of fish in Monterey began modestly when Frank Booth, who had a cannery on the Sacramento River, set up a plant to process Monterey Bay salmon near present-day Fisherman's Wharf. He noticed the large schools of sardines around the wharf and began a small sardine cannery nearby. After this burned, he built another plant at the foot of Alvarado Street and engaged Knute Hovden to develop it. Hovden was a Norwegian living in San Francisco for his health, and he became a major influence in the rising sardine industry. When World War I cut off supplies of European canned fish, the California product was in demand, and by 1918 there were 27 canneries at work along the shores of the bay. Novelist John Steinbeck lived here in the 1920's and early 1930's and immortalized the place in his novel *Cannery Row*. At 800 Cannery Row are the weathered clapboards of Doc Rickett's Western Biological Laboratory and across the street is Wing Chong's, both of which appeared in the book under other names. Experts warned against overfishing, and in 1945 the dangers they had warned of became evident. By 1948, the sardines were gone and the last canning plant had closed.

The area has been revived in recent years as a tourist attraction, highlighted by the stunning Monterey Bay Aquarium, which opened in 1984. The aquarium is housed in part of the old Hovden Cannery on the Monterey–Pacific Grove boundary line.

Del Monte Forest

The Pacific Improvement Company was created in 1878 to control the financial interests of the "Big Four" of railroad fame—Charles Crocker, Mark Hopkins, Collis P. Huntington, and Leland Stanford. This group developed the Del Monte Hotel and held the land of the old Ranchos Punta del Pinos and Pescadero. In 1915, the company was dissolved and began to sell off its properties in the Monterey area. Samuel F. B. Morse, who had been a classmate of Crocker's grandson at Yale, put together a new Del Monte Properties Company with the aid of Herbert Fleishhacker and other San Francisco financiers, and began the systematic development of the nearly uninhabited western side of the Monterey Peninsula.

The result is Del Monte Forest. One of the most carefully controlled areas in California, it was systematically developed for recreation and for privacy. It contains only two commercial establishments, the Pebble Beach Lodge and a small sand-mining company, and seven world-renowned golf courses. The Seventeen-Mile Drive winds through forests of Monterey cypress and pines and great estates; this privately owned road is open to the public upon payment of a toll.

Carmel-by-the-Sea

The community of Carmel-by-the-Sea began as a writers' and artists' colony in the early days of the twentieth century. Mary Austin and George Sterling were among the first to reside here. The picturesque beauty of the area and its quiet isolation appealed to

Robinson Jeffers's Tor House, Carmel

creative artists. Others would follow in time, and today Carmel is a much-visited tourist center and year-round community that yet retains some of the atmosphere of its earlier and simpler days. In addition to the mission, which lies near the mouth of the Carmel River on Rio Road, there are two other historic structures of note in Carmel. The oldest is the two-story stone studio built by Chris Jorgenson on Camino Real, now part of the La Playa Hotel. Nearby is the Tor House, built from native stone and capped by a striking tower of Viking aspect. The poet Robinson Jeffers and his wife, Una, built the Tor House in 1919, shortly after coming to Carmel. Jeffers lived there until his death in 1962. The house, at 26304 Ocean View Avenue, is still occupied by the family and is open to visitors on a limited basis.

At the southern end of Carmel Bay is Point Lobos State Reserve, set aside by action of the legislature in 1933. Here, where a whaling station operated from 1861 to 1884, 1,250 acres of coastal plants, sea lion rookeries, a stand of Monterey cypress, and tide pools and inlets have been preserved.

Moss Landing

One of the most important whaling stations on the coast of California was at Moss Landing, about fifteen miles northeast of Monterey, where Elkhorn Slough flows into Monterey Bay. The whale fishery, one of the chief industries on the coast for nearly 35 years, was finally abandoned in 1888. This landing was named for Charles Moss, who had a farm near the Five-Mile House on the Santa Cruz–Watsonville Road. Before the coming of the railroad, produce was brought down the Salinas River to Monterey Bay and thence to Moss Landing, where a great pier was built for oceangoing vessels. Nothing of this remains today; Moss Landing now shelters a small fleet of fishing vessels and pleasure boats.

Napa County

Napa County was one of the original 27 counties. Napa, accented as Napá in old documents, was the name of a tribe of Indians, said to be the bravest of all the California tribes, who once occupied the valley. Smallpox brought by white settlers was devastating here, and by 1838 the tribe was almost completely annihilated. The city of Napa has always been the county seat.

The Castro Expedition, 1823

The first recorded expedition into what is now Napa County was made in 1823, when a party led by Francisco Castro, and accompanied by José Sánchez and Father José Altamira, made explorations north of San Francisco Bay before founding Mission San Francisco Solano.

The party left San Francisco in a launch on June 25 and went north to Mission San Rafael. Then they explored the valley from Petaluma to Sonoma, Napa, and Suisun. Sites at Petaluma, Sonoma, and Napa were favorably considered, but Sonoma was finally chosen for the mission, while Petaluma and Napa were to be used as mission cattle ranches.

Ranchos Caymus and La Jota (Yountville and Angwin)

George Calvert Yount, a native of North Carolina, came to California from New Mexico with the Wolfskill party in 1831. After he had traveled almost the entire breadth of the continent, his name was linked with many early events in the history of the American occupation of the West. Soon after his arrival in California, he was engaged (1831–33) in hunting sea otter on the Santa Barbara Channel Islands and along the coast of the mainland. While at Santa Barbara, in 1833, he made for Captain A. B. Thompson what were probably the first shingles fashioned in California. During the same year, Yount trapped beaver around San Francisco Bay and along the San Joaquin River. Toward the end of the year he proceeded to the missions at San Rafael and Sonoma, where his resourcefulness and ingenuity appealed to the padres, who engaged him to repair the mission buildings. General Mariano Vallejo had him make shingles for his house in Sonoma.

Mission life pleased Yount, and he stayed for almost three years. In 1835, when he was baptized into the Catholic faith at Mission San Rafael, his name, as was the custom in Alta California on such occasions, was rendered in the Spanish as Jorge Concepción Yount.

It was during this eventful year of Yount's career that he penetrated the Napa Valley with the purpose of making it his home. Here this hardy pioneer lived for many years practically alone except for his Indian neighbors. From the nearest tribe was derived the name "Caymus," which he bestowed upon his estate. Within a territory 50 miles long and 20 miles wide, there were six distinct Indian nations: the Napa, whose villages were situated near the site of the present city of Napa; the Ulucas, on Rancho Tulucay; the Caymus, near Yount's house two miles north of the site of Yountville; the Mayacamas, with their villages located near the mineral hot springs of Calistoga; the Calajomanas, at the Bale ranch; and the Suscols, on Suscol Creek and Rancho Soscol (in Solano County).

Through the influence of Father José L. Guigas of Mission San Francisco Solano at Sonoma and General Vallejo, Yount obtained the princely grant of Rancho Caymus in 1836. It consisted of 11,814 acres, lying in the heart of Napa Valley and including within its southern boundary a bit of what was later to become the northern edge of the town named in his honor, Yountville. Rancho Caymus was the first grant made in Napa County, and Yount's first dwelling was, at the time it was built in 1835 or 1836, the only white habitation inland between Sonoma and the settlements on the Columbia River in Oregon.

A second grant, known as Rancho de la Jota, was made to Yount in 1843. It comprised 4,543 acres of timberland lying on Howell Mountain north of his first estate. In 1882 the Seventh-Day Adventists founded Pacific Union College high on the western slope of the mountain at the village of Angwin. About four miles west of this thriving institution is the St. Helena Sanitarium, also a Seventh-Day Adventist enterprise, located on the lower slopes of the mountain overlooking Napa Valley.

Just below the sanitarium is another important Seventh-Day Adventist building, Elmshaven, the home from 1900 until her death in 1915 of the writer and religious leader Ellen White. Open to visitors, the charming two-story house stands on three acres of grounds at 125 Glass Mountain Lane.

Some of the mission Indians accompanied Yount to Rancho Caymus, where they helped him to build his first dwelling, a Kentucky blockhouse (probably the only one of its kind ever erected in California), as well as subsequent buildings. In 1837 the blockhouse was superseded by a low, narrow building, its massive adobe walls, about 100 feet long, pierced by portholes. This so-called adobe "fort" antedated Sutter's in Sacramento by two years. It is said that the fort was torn down in 1870, but a map of that year shows it standing just below the point where the old road to Chiles Valley crossed the Napa River. Charles L. Camp of the University of California, who made a study of some of California's earliest pioneers, says that after Yount moved into his new adobe house (later the location of the Napa State Farm buildings), his daughter, Mrs. Vines, lived in the old fort.

A man of energy and enterprise, by 1845 Yount had a sawmill on his Rancho de la Jota, another sawmill and a flour mill on Rancho Caymus. The hardy pioneer died in 1865, and his grave (SRL 693) is in the cemetery at the northern edge of Yountville.

The locations of Yount's blockhouse, adobe, and mills (SRL 564) on the Napa River are indicated by a stone monument with bronze plaque on Yount Mill Road about one and one-half miles east of SR 29, at a point about two miles northeast of Yountville.

The Veterans Home of California (SRL 828) at Yountville was founded in 1884 and has been under state ownership since 1897.

Rancho Carne Humana (Upper Napa Valley)

In the 1830's a young English surgeon, Edward Turner Bale, landed at Monterey, where he practiced medicine for five or six years; for part of that time (1840–43) he was surgeon of the California forces by appointment of General Vallejo. Dr. Bale married Carolina Soberanes, a niece of the general, and became a naturalized citizen of Alta California. He received the grant of Rancho Carne Humana in Napa County, to which he went in 1843. By the time of his death in 1849, he was able to leave a rich estate to his widow, two sons, and four daughters.

The name Carne Humana ("human flesh") is as peculiar a title as California history knows. Some authorities believe it to be no more than an attempt to express the name of a local Indian tribe (Calajomanas) phonetically in Spanish. Others explain it as the grotesque joke of Dr. Bale. (No evidence has ever turned up that the Napa Valley Indians were in any way cannibalistic.) Whatever its origin, the name that Bale submitted was accepted by the Mexican authorities and has been rather quickly passed over by later writers of American history.

Although Dr. Bale was a man of good education,

hardy, bold, and adventurous, "his debts and personal quarrels," says Bancroft, got him into many difficulties. Resenting what he considered the too-friendly welcome given by his wife to her uncle Salvador Vallejo, the irate doctor quarreled with Don Salvador and challenged him to a duel. According to Bancroft, Vallejo, a skillful swordsman, "twisted his cumbersome opponent into ridiculous knots. Then sardonically, he beat the Englishman with his sword as though it were a whip. In a rage, Bale drew a revolver and fired. Luckily, the attempted murder was a failure. The intention, however, was counted more important than the deed. The doctor found himself in jail." It was rumored that the Kelseys and other foreigners planned to rescue Bale, and there was much excitement for a time. Narrowly escaping with his life, Bale was finally released.

Rancho Carne Humana comprised the whole of that part of Napa Valley lying north of Rancho Caymus. It consisted of two leagues of fertile land skirted on the west and east by wooded hills and overshadowed on the north by the purple crags of Mount St. Helena. In the 1850's the towns of St. Helena and Calistoga grew up within its bounds.

The Bale adobe was built around 1843 and collapsed in 1931, after which its ruins were cleared away. The site is one mile west of SR 29 on Whitehall Lane beside the small stream known as Bale Creek.

The enterprising doctor had on his lands a sawmill and a gristmill; the former has long since disappeared. It was constructed by Ralph L. Kilburn in 1846 and stood on the banks of the Napa River just north of the present Charles Krug Winery. During the winter of 1847, lumber was shipped from here to Benicia and San Francisco; the mill also supplied the lumber for the first frame structure put up in the city of Napa. John York, who came to the valley in 1845, cut the first logs for Bale's sawmill.

The gristmill (SRL 359) is now the center of Bale Grist Mill State Historic Park, located on the west side of SR 29 three miles north of St. Helena. This was also put up in 1846, the ironwork and blacksmithing being done by F. E. Kellogg, who was paid for his services in land. While the Forty-niners were eagerly searching for gold in the hills and ravines of the Sierra Nevada, the great water wheel of Bale's mill was daily grinding grain from the Upper Napa Valley into flour for the settlers. For 25 years the mill was in operation. Its construction is interesting to the student of pioneer days. The lumber that went into the building (ultimately of three stories with a false storefront) was cut from neighboring forests. The millstones were taken from the hill behind the mill, while the cogs in the great wheel, which made such a clatter when in operation, were all made of wood.

Bale Grist Mill State Historic Park, near St. Helena

The mill's preservation is in part due to the care given it by the family of W. W. Lyman, owner of the mill for many years. In 1923, Mrs. Lyman presented the mill to the Native Sons of the Golden West, who found the task of maintenance against time and vandalism beyond their ability. In 1941, it became a Napa County Park and, in 1974, a State Historic Park. The water-powered grinding wheel resumed operation in 1988.

A number of American pioneers settled on Bale's rancho in the middle 1840's; among them in 1845 were John York, William and David Hudson, William Elliott and sons, William Fowler with sons William and Henry, William Hargrave, and Benjamin Dewell. They found Benjamin and Nancy Kelsey already living on what was soon to become the Kilburn place, owned in later years by Peter Teal and located one mile southeast of Calistoga at 4531 Foothill Boulevard. Here is the nearly buried hearthstone of the Kelsey house (SRL 686), on private property. Nancy Kelsey, the first woman to cross the plains, arrived in California in 1841 with the Bidwell-Bartleson party. Ralph Kilburn came to Napa Valley in

1844. After Kilburn became established on the tract of land that he had received from Dr. Bale, Peter Storm, a Norwegian sailor, lived with him. Storm, in local lore, achieved brief fame in 1846 as the designer of the Bear Flag that flew over Sonoma.

The incoming settlers of 1845 also found Samuel Kelsey living near Bale's Mill with his wife and two or three children, while Elias Barnett already had a log cabin on what later became the George Tucker place. The Tucker house once stood across the highway from the Bothe–Napa Valley State Park. This park is the site of the first church in the valley, the old White Church. Built in 1853, the Methodist Episcopal church was named for its organizer and minister, Rev. Asa White. Behind the marker identifying the site of the church is the oldest cemetery in the valley.

During the winter of 1845–46 John York built a log cabin for himself within the present city limits of Calistoga. The site (SRL 682) is at Foothill Boulevard and Lincoln. York planted the first wheat crop in this section of Napa County. Diagonally across the intersection, where a service station now stands, was David Hudson's cabin (SRL 683), built about the same time as York's. The York cabin site is marked by the familiar bronze state landmark plaque, but nothing marks the Hudson cabin site. Both men moved in later years to larger quarters as their families grew.

It is interesting to note the number of women and children mentioned in the records of the pioneers. The experience of one mother and grandmother, who came early to the valley, is typical of the strenuous life. She was the wife of William B. Elliott, and with her came several grown children and grandchildren. For a time the family lived in a cloth tent, a frail protection against the elements and the wild animals. The entire family had to spend the nights on a platform built in the forks of a mammoth oak tree, often watching helplessly while their uninvited guests plundered the tent for food. During the day the men frequently went on hunting expeditions; and in their absence Mrs. Elliott and the smaller children often had to take refuge in the trees to get away from prowling bears. Mrs. Elliott, however, was herself an excellent shot.

At the head of the valley one and one-half miles northwest of Calistoga on the road to Knight's Valley was the log cabin of Enoch Cyrus, who came to California with his wife and six children in 1846. Then came the Fowlers, who lived with William Hargrave in a log house at the foot of the Mayacamas Range west of Calistoga. Calvin Musgrove and his wife also lived on the Fowler ranch. Wells and Ralph Kilburn lived with their families one mile south of Calistoga.

In 1849 the Owsley family—husband, wife, and eight children—set up a log cabin, an orchard, and finally a frame house two miles south of what is now Calistoga. One-half mile farther south was the home of William Nash, who had come with his wife and fourteen children to California in 1846 in the original overland group from which the ill-fated Donner Party separated. Nash and his party made it to California safely before the early snows began in 1846. Purchasing 330 acres of land from R. L. Kilburn in 1847, Nash settled on his ranch in November 1848, naming it Walnut Grove. There he put up a house of boards cut at Bale's mill, and in January of the following year he planted an orchard from seedlings brought by Elias Barnett from Kentucky. Nash was among the first to inaugurate new and better methods of agriculture in California, practicing, among other things, deep plowing and cultivation. He sold Walnut Grove in 1868 and moved to his prosperous Magnolia Farm five and one-half miles north of the city of Napa.

The chain of pioneer homesteads continued southward to the log house of M. D. Ritchie, who lived with his wife and five children across the road from Reason P. Tucker. Tucker was another member of the historic 1846 overland crossing that the Donner party fatally abandoned, and, like Nash, he arrived safely in California. The Tucker family are still prominent residents of this area. F. E. Kellogg had a frame house one-half mile beyond. Having arrived in the valley in 1846 with a wife and seven children, he had obtained this land for services rendered in building Dr. Bale's gristmill. Kellogg's house still stands, just south of the mill, very much as it was when built in 1849 of lumber cut at Bale's sawmill. It is the oldest house in the Upper Napa Valley and is now owned by the Lyman famly, also important in the history of the old Bale mill.

Across the road from the gristmill Sarah Graves Fosdick opened the second American school in California in July 1847. The first had been established earlier that year by Olive Mann Isbell in the old mission buildings at Santa Clara. Mrs. Fosdick was a survivor of the Donner party who had been brought to the Napa Valley by Reason Tucker, one of the rescuers of that group. The school, a mere shelter of branches, could be used only in good weather. It was replaced in 1849 by a real building erected for Mrs. Fosdick by William Nash. This was used for about five years, until the first public school was opened.

Ranchos Yajome, Napa, and Tulucay (Napa)

Rancho Yajome, an estate of 6,652 acres of fertile land lying on either side of the Napa River north of Rancho Tulucay, was granted to a soldier, Damaso Antonio Rodríguez, in 1841. It appears that he never lived on the land, however, and claim to it was filed by Salvador Vallejo in 1852 and confirmed to him the following year. At what later become Longwood Ranch, north of Napa at 1006 Monticello Road, Vallejo built a handsome two-story adobe ranch house that stood until destroyed by fire in 1970. Now a vineyard, the property is also the site of recent archaeological diggings by the University of California, which have established Indian remains from at least 2000 B.C.

In March 1853, Don Salvador and his wife, María de la Cruz Carrillo, filed a claim for about 3,000 acres of the much larger Rancho Napa granted to them in 1838 by Governor Alvarado. From time to time they had sold parts of their land that lay some distance back from the Napa River. The part retained and for which confirmation was now asked was called "Trancas and Jalapa," which may be translated to mean "Sticks and Morningglories." A Mexican settlement lay in the south end of this area between the road and the river. South of this community was Pueblo de Salvador, a piece of the original grant, where James Clyman purchased a piece of land in 1850 shortly after his marriage to Hannah McComb, a member of the party that he had guided across the plains and mountains in the autumn of 1848.

Rancho Tulucay, comprising two square leagues of land just east of the city of Napa, was granted to Cayetano Juárez in 1841. He had stocked the land as early as 1837 and became a permanent settler there before 1840, having built a small adobe house, no longer standing, and brought his family from Sonoma. About 1847 he built a second and larger adobe, which has been converted into a tavern and stands today at the junction of Soscol Avenue and Silverado Trail. Of all the adobes erected in Napa County before 1848, this is one of only two remaining.

Juárez, a native of California and a military man of some importance, had been a soldier of the San Francisco Company during the years 1828–31, had been promoted to the rank of corporal in 1832, and apparently served as sergeant from 1833. He had engaged in many Indian expeditions, was made mayordomo at Sonoma in 1836, and later served as captain of the militia. In 1845 he was appointed alcalde at Sonoma, the same year in which he received the grant of Rancho Yokoya (Ukiah, in Mendocino County). He distinguished himself somewhat in 1846 by his plans to rescue the prisoners held by the Americans after the Bear Flag Revolt and by a famous swim of nine miles that he made to escape capture. Juárez, who died in Napa in 1883, lies buried in Tulocay Cemetery, for which he had donated the land to the city as early as 1859. The cemetery is in the eastern part of the city and is surrounded by a high wall of exceptionally fine native stone.

Just south of the city of Napa stands the Napa State Hospital, on a site that once lay within the confines of Rancho Tulucay. The institution was initiated by the legislature in 1869–70; in 1872 Napa was chosen by a commission as the site of the hospital, the cornerstone was laid the following year, and the first patient was admitted in 1875.

A few miles farther south, on Suscol Creek, where SR 12 and SR 29 turn briefly to the west and cross the Napa River, is the old Soscol House. Its history is told on an E Clampus Vitus marker placed on the building in 1983: "Soscol House, 1855. Built by Elijah True at the junction of the county road from Napa City and Old Ferry Road, now Soscol, which served the Soscol Ferry crossing at Napa River west of here.

"The thriving transportation center developed here from the stagecoach and wagon traffic was called Suscol; taking that name from the Patwin Indian village site located on the banks of Suscol Creek east of this place, at State Route 29.

"Moved March 1978 to this site, and refurbishing completed by H. & M. Carroll, December 1979." The old way station is now a thriving bar and restaurant. Rancho Soscol, in which it is located, lay mostly within present Solano County.

Other Land Grants

Nicolás Higuera, a soldier in San Francisco from 1819 to 1823 and afterward *alcalde auxiliar* at Sonoma, received two grants from Governor Mariano Chico in 1836. One was Rancho Entre Napa, which lay to the west of the Napa River. The northeast section of this was bought by Nathan Coombs in 1848 and later patented to him; here he laid out plans for the present city of Napa. The other was Rancho Rincón de los Carneros, a tract of 2,558 acres lying to the north and west of the confluence of Carneros Creek and the Napa River. This afterward passed into the possession of Julius Martin, who received United States patent for it in 1858.

Rancho Las Putas, on Putah Creek, covering most of the Berryessa Valley, consisted of eight square leagues. The names of the rancho and the creek come from that of a Patwin Indian tribe. It was granted by Governor Micheltorena in 1843 to two men, probably brothers, who had served as soldiers at San Francisco in the 1830's. The grantees were José de Jesús and Sisto Berryessa, whose wives, probably sisters, were María Anastasia and María Nicolasa Higuera. With the consent of their husbands, the wives filed claim for this tract in 1852 and received confirmation of their rights to 35,516 acres in 1863. Lake Berryessa, created by the construction of Monticello Dam in 1954, has inundated the sites of the old Spanish adobes, as well as the old stage-stop town of Monticello.

Joseph B. Chiles, who came to California first alone in 1841 and for the third time in 1848, bringing family and friends, received a grant of Rancho Catacula in 1844. The grant covered 8,877 acres along the Arroyo de Napa (Chiles Creek), east of Yount's Rancho La Jota. Near the arroyo, Chiles built a house and gristmill. The old mill (SRL 547) stood unused for many years and has now collapsed into the creek. A bronze plaque has been mounted on a boulder on the hillside across the road from the ruins. This location is in Chiles Valley, at the junction of the Chiles and Pope Valley Road with the Lower Chiles Valley Road, three and three-quarters miles north of SR 128, at a point seven miles east of Rutherford. On a ranch just north of the mill ruins on the road to Pope Valley stands, in excellent condition, the old adobe Chiles built in 1846. It has been restored by the Dollar family of San Francisco. Chiles's home at Rutherford is near the Inglenook Winery; his town house in St. Helena still stands at 1343 Spring Street, but it has been remodeled into a church.

In 1841 Manuel Jimeno granted Rancho Locoallomi, consisting of 8,872 acres, to Julian Pope and Rancho Huichica, of two square leagues, to Jacob P. Leese. Leese received an extension of his property three years later, when Governor Micheltorena gave him another three and a half leagues. The Huichica grant lay southeast of Pueblo de Sonoma and the Buena Vista tract of Colonel Haraszthy. Carneros Creek formed its northeastern boundary, with Ranchos Napa and Rincón de los Carneros as neighbors across the stream.

Pope Valley, which is named for pioneer Julian Pope, was thoroughly prospected in the 1860's, along with much of the northern part of Napa County. By 1880 the Aetna cinnabar mine was employing as many as 1,200 Chinese laborers. When this mine closed, many Chinese remained in the area as stonemasons; Napa County's roads are often lined with well-made stone fences dating from this period. Aetna Springs, a later resort north of Pope Valley, was for half a century a favored watering place, but it is not operating now.

The village of Pope Valley is dominated by two structures, closed for some time, but still standing in good order. Henry Haus operated his blacksmith shop here from 1897 until 1950; since his death in 1955 the shop has been unused. An E Clampus Vitus marker was placed here in 1982. Across the street, the Pope Valley Store was first opened in 1888; Thomas Neil added a saloon and a seven-room hotel, which were operated by him and later by his son, Elgy Neil. When the latter died in 1970 the place was closed; it still stands, however, with goods on the shelves and its contents intact.

Napa

The first Napa County courthouse, built in 1856, had to be condemned eight years later when large cracks appeared in the structure. A second building was completed in 1878; this impressive brick building has withstood the ravages of time and earthquakes and is still in use. Public buildings in Napa have often been kept up and refurbished rather than torn down. The Napa Opera House, built in 1880 at 1018–30 Main Street, is undergoing restoration. Old office and business buildings still in use are the Hatt Building at Fifth and Main streets, the Semorile Building at 975 First Street, and the Winship-Smernes Building at 948 Main Street. The Chinese settlers of Napa are remembered in the Sam Kee Laundry building at 1245 Main Street. The Goodman Library building, a gift of George Goodman to the citizens of Napa in 1901, now houses the Napa Historical Society Museum and Library. This beautiful two-story building of native stone is at 1219 First Street. The First Presbyterian Church (SRL 878) has been in continuous use since its construction in 1874; it stands

First Presbyterian Church, Napa

at 1333 Third Street. Although all of these buildings are close to the river, none was seriously damaged by the flood of February 1986, when the Napa River rose to its greatest recorded height during a prolonged rainstorm.

At 1711 Main Street is the Joseph Mathews Winery. Originally the Lisbon Winery, it was built of native stone in 1882 by Joseph Mathews (Mateus), a native of Portugal, who made prize-winning wines here for many years. Recently restored, it is once more in operation; there is a restaurant on the second floor. The building was marked by the Native Sons of the Golden West in 1978.

White Sulphur Springs

The first mineral springs resort in California was White Sulphur Springs, located on Spring Street in the foothills four miles west of St. Helena. Discovered in 1848, the place opened as a resort in 1852, with a wide array of activities for patrons. It is still in business today, with a small museum of artifacts and pictures of its long history.

Calistoga

Samuel Brannan, active in several parts of California, purchased in 1859 a tract of land in the region around the hot springs at the foot of Mt. St. Helena, with the intention of establishing a summer resort. The story is often told that Brannan, at a promotional dinner, boasted that this great resort would be to California as Saratoga Hot Springs was to the state of New York; his toast to the "Saratoga of California" came out as the "Calistoga of Sarafornia." Some historians believe the origin of the name was less spontaneous and more calculated. Near the springs he built a hotel and 25 cottages and laid out elaborate grounds and a race course. The long row of elm trees on Lake Street originally led to the race track. The site of the resort is marked by a series of old palm trees at Indian Springs. One of the cabins (SRL 685) has been moved to 1311 Washington Street, where it is now a part of the Sharpsteen Museum, opened in 1976. Its benefactor, Ben Sharpsteen, a longtime producer for Walt Disney Studios, supervised the making of a remarkable diorama now on display, showing the grounds of the Calistoga resort as they were around 1876. This beautifully kept museum is a repository of Calistoga history.

Another cottage from the resort stands on Cedar Street opposite Pioneer Park and is now a bed-and-breakfast inn. A third cottage, with two sentinel palm trees, is located on Wapoo Street just off Lincoln; this is a private residence. Across the street at the corner of

Sam Brannan Cottage, Sharpsteen Museum, Calistoga

Wapoo and Brannan streets is the store (SRL 684) in which Brannan made $50,000 one year; this is also a private home.

Sam Brannan interested people in the Napa Valley and elsewhere in financing a branch railroad to his resort. Its first trip brought some three thousand people from San Francisco and elsewhere to the grand opening of Calistoga Hot Springs in October 1868. The Napa Valley Railroad Depot (SRL 687), built the same year, later became a Southern Pacific station when that line bought out its predecessor. Railroads no longer run to Calistoga; the station has been made over into shops and offices, and restored Pullman cars on the railroad siding have been transformed likewise.

Calistoga's mineral waters have been famous for over a century; they are bottled by several plants here

Napa Valley Railroad Depot, Calistoga

and in the northern part of the Napa Valley. On Tubbs Lane two miles north of the city an "Old Faithful" geyser is a tourist attraction.

Brannan also turned his attention to the adjacent hillsides. Encouraged by the example of Colonel Agoston Haraszthy in Sonoma County and by a few growers near Napa, he planted the slopes with cuttings of superior wine and table grapes. A century later, the Napa Valley is a world-famous wine-producing region.

Vineyards and Wineries

On the wooded hillsides and in the valleys of Napa County, with its 24,000 acres of vineyards, stand picturesque structures of stone and brick similar to those built long ago in France and Germany. These wineries, however, date back only to the 1860's, when it was realized that the climate and soil were favorable to the culture of the vine.

Both the Spanish and early American settlers had made wine from Napa County vineyards. A notable year, however, was 1859, when Sam Brannan planted his hillside. The previous autumn Charles Krug had made about 1,200 gallons for a Mr. Patchett at Napa. In the year following, Krug went to the Bale Mill place north of St. Helena and made wine for Louis Bruck, and in 1860 he made 5,000 gallons at Yount's place at Yountville. His reputation now established, Krug began in 1868 to build a stone wine cellar (SRL 563) north of St. Helena on the floor of the valley. Additions were made periodically to this winery until it was completed in 1884. Standing amid plantings of shrubbery in a large grove of oaks, and with newer buildings flanking it, it is still a major producer of the Napa Valley, under the ownership of the Mondavi family.

About four miles northwest of the Charles Krug winery on SR 29 is the Hanns Kornell Champagne Cellars, a short distance east of the highway on Larkmead Lane. This operation is located in the buildings at "Larkmead," once the winery of the late Mrs. Howard Coit, better known in San Francisco as Lillie Hitchcock. In 1872, her father, Dr. Charles Hitchcock, bought a thousand acres of Rancho Carne Humana and built a country home, which he named "Lonely." By the time "Lonely" was destroyed by fire in 1929, the property west of the highway was owned by Reinhold Bothe, who made it into a commercial campground. Bothe's property was acquired by the state in 1960, and is now Bothe–Napa Valley State Park, adjacent to the Bale Grist Mill State Historic Park; the entrance is about a mile and a half north of the mill.

The wine industry of the county is centered at St. Helena, where, in its infancy, the custom of a vintage

Charles Krug Winery, St. Helena

festival was established. The Greystone Cellars of the Christian Brothers winery, almost directly across SR 29 from the Charles Krug winery one mile north of St. Helena, is one of the largest stone wineries in the world. Built in 1889, the main structure was temporarily closed in the mid-1980's while renovations were made to comply with state earthquake laws. The winery reopened in 1987.

Closer to St. Helena on the west side of SR 29 is the interesting Beringer winery (SRL 814). Jacob L. Beringer, who had been foreman of the Charles Krug winery, selected this spot in 1875. The winery is built into the western hills, where the limestone formation is peculiarly adapted to the storing and aging of wines. The winery and 800 feet of cellars are cut into the stone—another feat of the Chinese stoneworkers whose activities are evident throughout this part of the Napa Valley. The tunnels running 250 feet directly into the hill are connected by several laterals, honeycombing the entire hill. This underground storage space is filled with oval oak casks, each with a capacity of about 500 gallons. The lower floor of the Rhine House, the former Beringer family home, is now the tasting room for the winery; its beautiful colored glass windows are outstanding.

Chateau Montelena winery, on Tubbs Lane north of Calistoga, is in the huge stone cellar built in 1881 by Alfred L. Tubbs, who desired to copy Château Lafite in the Bordeaux region of France. Only the stone walls are reminders of the past; as in most California wineries, the interior and its workings are very up-to-date.

Three miles south of Calistoga on SRs 29 and 128 and a mile to the west of the highway is the historic Schramsberg Vineyard (SRL 561), begun by Jacob

Schram in 1862. This is one of the many small wineries in the Napa Valley that are open only by appointment.

In 1870 Seneca Ewer came to live at St. Helena. In 1882 he and his partner, Atkinson, built a stone winery near Rutherford. The son, Fred S. Ewer, carried on his father's business and in 1915 sold the wine cellar to Georges de Latour, who enlarged the original stone building by an addition built of concrete. This is now the Beaulieu winery, on SR 29 at Rutherford.

In the foothills just west of Rutherford is the beautifully designed Inglenook winery. The land for this vineyard, formerly the property of a sanatorium, was purchased by Gustav Niebaum in 1880 and planted with cuttings of fine European wine grapes. The three-story winery, built of stone quarried on the estate, was completed in 1887. The taproom contains a rare collection of tankards, pewter and pottery mugs, and valuable old glass.

Stevenson's Silverado

In the spring of 1880, Robert Louis Stevenson and his bride, Fannie Van de Grift Osbourne Stevenson, came to live at the abandoned mine camp of Silverado, on the south slope of Mount St. Helena on the road between Calistoga and Middletown in Lake County. Their honeymoon was in a deserted miner's cabin with its sashless windows "chocked with the green and sweetly smelling foliage of a bay," and its three rooms "so plastered against the hill, that one room was right atop of another." A century later, the modern traveler can see just how the rolling morning fogs can seem to be "a great level ocean." *The Silverado Squatters*, a delightful collection of descriptive and narrative essays, is a rare description of late-nineteenth-century California by a first-rate artist. Completed in France, the book came from the memories of that health-giving summer on the heights of Mount St. Helena.

The Robert Louis Stevenson Memorial State Park (SRL 710) has been established here, but it is undeveloped. The old cabin is gone; its place is marked by the Stevenson Monument, carved from polished granite in the form of an open book, on a base of ore taken from the Silverado Mine. This is not a landmark for the casual tourist; the Stevenson cabin site is up a steep slope.

On the east side of the city of St. Helena is the charming Silverado Museum at 1490 Library Lane, adjoining the St. Helena Library. The Silverado Museum is the creation of the Vailima Foundation, established in 1968 by Mr. and Mrs. Norman Strouse to collect materials associated with the career of Robert Louis Stevenson.

Nevada County

Nevada County was formed in 1851 from territory that had been originally a part of Yuba County. Nevada City was made the county seat. Situated in a region where the entire upper country wears a heavy mantle of snow during the winter months, the name Nevada (Spanish for "snow-covered") was appropriately chosen by its citizens for the town. Later the same name was given to the county. When the Washoe Territory to the east became the Territory of Nevada in 1861 and the state of Nevada was created three years later, the word "City" was added to the name of the county seat, a term that apparently had informally been in use earlier.

The Donner Tragedy

One of the routes into California most frequently used by the emigrants of the 1840's and 1850's was known as the California Trail, or the Truckee Pass Emigrant Road, which followed up the Truckee River valley in Nevada through Donner Pass in the High Sierra.

The first overland party of emigrants to follow the California Trail was the Murphy-Townsend-Stevens party, in the autumn of 1844. In 1845, John C. Frémont, with a small detachment of his company, entered California by the same trail. But the most famous group to negotiate it was the Donner party, whose experiences in the High Sierra during the winter of 1846–47 constitute one of the most heart-rending tragedies in the history of California.

In the spring of 1846 a party of emigrants, led by George and Jacob Donner and James F. Reed, was organized in Sangamon County, Illinois, and started its trek westward. When the party reached Independence, Missouri, the first week in May, it had grown to such proportions that between 200 and 300 wagons were included in the train.

Upon arriving at Fort Bridger, the Reed-Donner party took the fatal step of breaking off from the larger group and following the Hastings Cutoff, a supposed shortcut that passed south of the Great Salt Lake. Instead of taking one week as expected, a whole month of valuable time was consumed in reaching Salt Lake. Struggling on over the great salt deserts west of the lake, where the party suffered many hardships, they finally reached the site of Reno, Nevada, entirely exhausted. Finding forage for their emaciated animals here, the party rested for three or four days. This delay, however, proved to be disastrous, for the storm clouds were already gathering when they reached the mountains. The little band hastened up the eastern side of the Sierra as fast as possible, but on October 28, 1846, before they could reach the summit, heavy snow began to fall—a month earlier than usual.

The emigrants, already weakened and spent, soon found it almost impossible to make progress though the rapidly deepening snow, which quickly obliterated all semblance of a trail. Several attempts to cross the mountain barrier ended in defeat. The party made what pitiful preparations they could for winter camp near the shores of what is now Donner Lake. Shelter was made in three log cabins and a few hastily constructed shacks. The families of George and Jacob Donner, owing to an accident that delayed them, had been forced into camp at Alder Creek, about six miles below the lake. Here their only shelters were crude huts of canvas and boughs banked with snow. With such meager protection from the elements, during what proved to be the most severe winter in 30 years, and with actual famine staring them in the face, the members of the unfortunate party would all have perished had no aid come to them.

On or around December 16, a party of ten men and five women started out in a desperate attempt to obtain help. Struggling on for 32 days over the snow-covered mountains and enduring unbelievable hardships, forced to eat the flesh of their dead companions when nothing else was left, the five women and two of the men finally succeeded in reaching Johnson's Rancho, near the present site of Wheatland, some 35 miles north of Sutter's Fort.

With the aid of John A. Sutter and others, four relief parties were subsequently organized to attempt the rescue of those remaining in the mountains. With great stamina and courage, these parties succeeded in carrying in provisions and brought from their frightful camps of death the emaciated survivors, many of them children.

Of the 89 persons who began the winter at Donner Lake and on Alder Creek, 42 perished. Suffering, despair, and death stalked the camps, and human flesh was eaten here as well. The area at the eastern end of Donner Lake is now Donner Memorial State Park, provided, ironically, with campgrounds that are used in the summer and places where self-contained recreational vehicles may stay overnight in the winter.

The Pioneer Monument (SRL 134), erected by the

Native Sons and Daughters of the Golden West, stands in the park near the entrance and near the site of the Breen cabin, one of the shelters used by the Donner party. The rock pedestal supports a group of four figures in bronze representing a pioneer family; the platform on which they stand, the top of the rock pedestal, is at approximately the level of the snow at this point in the winter of 1846–47, about 22 feet above the ground.

Where the Murphy cabin stood, a huge boulder bears a bronze tablet with the words "Donner Party, 1846–7. The face of this rock formed the north end of the fireplace of the Murphy Cabin. General Stephen W. Kearny, on June 22, 1847, buried under the middle of the cabin the bodies found in the vicinity." The tablet lists the names of the members of the Donner party, those who survived and those who perished. This boulder is 200 yards by trail from the Emigrant Trail Museum, a highlight of the park. The museum has good displays of the natural history of the region as well as its human history.

The area has been recognized also for its significance to the history of the nation and has been registered and marked by the Department of the Interior as a National Historic Landmark.

The Old Emigrant Trail

The old emigrant road, which the Reed-Donner party passed over, was first marked in the 1920's by P. M. Weddell, a San Jose high school teacher, with homemade signs, on some of which the picture of a covered wagon was traced. A few of these still exist. Permanent bronze plaques were later placed by the Native Sons and other groups. The tablet near the summit of Donner Pass on the old Highway 40 bears the inscription "Donner Summit Bridge dedicated to the pioneers who blazed the Overland Trail through these mountains."

One of the first permanent markers along the old emigrant trail was placed near Truckee and stands today in front of the Tahoe-Truckee High School, about a mile east of the Pioneer Monument on the old highway. The tablet contains the following inscription: "The emigrant trail in the pioneer days of California came through the low pass to the north facing this monument. The trail turned west at this point for a distance of approximately twenty-six hundred feet, where a tablet describes the route then followed. Placed by the Historic Landmarks Committee, Native Sons of the Golden West, September 14, 1929."

The second tablet, mentioned in the first and placed on the same day, stands on Coldstream Canyon Road about 150 yards south of its junction with Donner Pass Road (old Highway 40). It reads: "The emigrant trail in the pioneer days of California turned to the south at this point for approximately three miles, then west across the summit of the Sierras about a mile south of the present railroad. It was here that the Donner party missed the trail, owing to the early snows, resulting in tragedy."

The Donner party and most of the other early emigrants who crossed the Sierra Nevada by way of the Truckee River and the Donner Pass traveled down the ridge north of the Bear River, entering the Sacramento Valley by using approximately the same trail as that opened by the Murphy-Townsend-Stevens party in 1844–45.

The point at which the emigrant trail crossed present SR 49 has been marked (SRL 799) at Wolf Creek, halfway between Auburn and Grass Valley. Later a much-traveled emigrant road came down the San Juan Ridge between the Middle and South forks of the Yuba River. This was used mostly by those who had come via the Henness Pass route in Sierra County. This trail followed down the ridge over a soil formation and was preferable to the route over Donner Pass, which was extremely rough and rocky. During the 1860's this route became one of the stage and freight roads for the mines of the famous Comstock Lode in Nevada. In the 1920's a section of this road above Graniteville was rebuilt and utilized during construction of the Bowman Dam.

Toll Roads

During the 1850's and 1860's the rapid development of mines in the recesses of the mountains resulted in an imperative need for the construction of roads—a need that the counties could not meet because of the expense. Consequently, most of the roads and bridges that replaced the pack trails were constructed and owned by individuals or by turnpike companies, and were operated for profit.

The development of a system of state and national highways following roughly the early roads and trails has almost completely eliminated the toll-road system in the state, although all of the San Francisco Bay Area bridges are still toll bridges. Nevada County bought the last of its toll roads and bridges about 1890.

Among the privately owned turnpikes leading from Nevada City were the following: the Nevada–Little York; the Nevada–Grass Valley; and the South Yuba Road, which went from Nevada City to North San Juan, crossing the South Fork of the Yuba River at what was known in 1853 as Robinson's Crossing, later as Black's and then as Purdon's Bridge.

Another important turnpike followed approximately, in part, the route taken by the present SR 49 from Nevada City to Downieville. The first ten-mile stretch of the road, now bypassed on the west by several miles, was known as Purdon's Grade, and is today called Purdon Road. The bridge across the South Fork was at first known as Wall's, then as Webber's, and finally as Purdon's, before its purchase by the county. The bridge at the Middle Fork of the Yuba River is still known as Freeman's Crossing. Thomas Freeman, in 1854, purchased the property from Thomas Hess, who built the first bridge at this point in 1851. The winter floods carried it away, and a second structure, subsequently taken over by Freeman, was erected in 1852. After the flood of 1862, Freeman built a substantial structure that he owned for some 30 years. Two of the old pilings of this bridge may still be seen in the river, less than half a mile west of the present bridge via Moonshine Road. The portion of the tollhouse that served as a stable also stands and has been restored. Between its walls the stagecoaches passed on their way up the mountains.

Just above the massive concrete bridge that carries the modern motorist across the river into Yuba County, Oregon Creek runs into the Middle Yuba. Here is the junction of three roads, one leading up Oregon Creek to Downieville, a second turning right across the creek through an old covered bridge to Alleghany, Forest, and the Henness Pass in Sierra County, and a third proceeding to the left across Moonshine Creek to the Bullards Bar Dam in Yuba County—modern roads of superb scenic grandeur following the routes of historic trails and turnpikes. The covered bridge across Oregon Creek (in Yuba County) was built probably in 1862. A flood in 1883 swept it off its foundations and turned it around, depositing it on the bank 150 feet downstream. By means of ox teams it was inched back to its site on logs and planks, but since no way could be found to reverse it, what had been the south end is now the north. It was at this time, presumably, that the portals at either end of the bridge were curved to meet the road.

Yuba River Bars

Early in 1849 John Rose, who gave his name to Rose's Bar in Yuba County, built a cattle corral at a spot in Pleasant Valley on the lower San Juan Ridge between the sites later occupied by the Anthony House on Deer Creek and Bridgeport on the South Yuba. Apparently Rose's original purpose was to trade with the Indians of the region, but during the early summer prospectors found their way up the South and Middle forks of the Yuba River and Deer Creek, crevassing for gold and finding many rich gravel deposits on the bars along the margins of these streams. The news of these discoveries spread quickly, and by late summer and early fall of 1849 scores of miners were working the Deer Creek

and Yuba River surface diggings. In order to accommodate the increasing trade, Rose established a trading post in a small adobe he had built.

As in practically all the mining regions of the Sierra Nevada, the first prospecting in Nevada County was confined to the gravel bars and the beds of running streams. Scores of river-bar camps sprang up almost overnight. Typical of these mining camps was Bridgeport, on the South Fork of the Yuba, about one and a half miles from its mouth. For two years the town was exceedingly prosperous, but after river mining ceased to be profitable the camp declined. Today the name is preserved only in Bridgeport Township.

The present road to French Corral leaves SR 20 midway between Smartsville and Rough and Ready. The site of the old Anthony House is now buried beneath the waters of Lake Wildwood. After another five miles it crosses the river at Bridgeport or Nye's Crossing by means of an old covered bridge (SRL 390), known to have been erected in 1862 by David I. Wood. It is the oldest housed span in the West, and, at 233 feet, the longest single-span covered bridge in the nation. The road continues to French Corral, less than three miles away, and in another five miles joins SR 49 near North San Juan.

On the Middle Fork of the Yuba additional camps were established in 1850, among them Rice's Crossing (at first known by the rather dubious title of Liar's Flat and then as Lousy Level), Frenchman's Bar, and Condemned Bar (Yuba County). On the South Fork was Jones's Bar, once famous among the river camps.

Panning for gold was, of course, the first and most primitive method of washing the metal from the gravel. The first machine to be employed for the purpose was the rocker, which was introduced in the summer of 1848. This was, in turn, superseded by the long tom. Gradually the miners extended their activities to the gravel of the dry gulches, flats, and hillsides; then ground-sluicing, introduced by William Elwell at Nevada City in February or March of 1850, came into practice. With this innovation an elaborate system of ditches and sluice boxes was developed, out of which, in time, grew the more powerful and extensive hydraulic methods of the 1860's and 1870's. Many old mining ditches of today serve the irrigation needs of orchards and gardens in the hill country of the Sierra Nevada.

Rough and Ready

Coming up from Marysville to Grass Valley on SR 20, the motorist passes near Timbuctoo and Smartsville in Yuba County and climbs the wooded hills through a country that grows richer in historic interest with each curve of the highway. The early farmhouses, tucked among gnarled apple trees, have over the years reminded many travelers of similar views in New England. Among them are the deeply scarred gullies and gravelly hillocks that mark the abandoned diggings of the 1850's and 1860's.

Another turn in the road brings one to a place of green upland meadows where a small town lies sheltered among aging shade and orchard trees. This peaceful spot belies its name—Rough and Ready—but in the feverish days of the 1850's it was a busy mining town, one of the first to be established in Nevada County. A party of men calling themselves the Rough and Ready Company arrived in the vicinity on September 9, 1849, under the leadership of Captain A. A. Townsend, who had served under General Zachary Taylor ("Old Rough and Ready"), hero of the Mexican War, and in 1849 President of the United States. For several months the Rough and Readys were able to keep the richness of this region a secret, preempting all the surrounding land, but by 1850 the incoming tide of miners could not be held back and the place developed into a good-sized town (SRL 294).

One episode in the history of the town makes it unique. During the uncertain days of early 1850, while California's statehood was being debated by Congress, E. F. Brundage conceived the idea of a separate and independent government. Issuing a high-sounding manifesto, he called a mass meeting to organize the State of Rough and Ready. For a short period he had a following of about 100, but the whole affair met with so much ridicule that the State of Rough and Ready soon dissolved into thin air.

On June 28, 1850, Rough and Ready had its first devastating fire. In spite of this discouraging experience, in October it polled 1,000 votes and even aspired to become the county seat of the newly organized Nevada County. A committee to preserve law and order had been elected, a Christian Association was holding services in a little clapboard shanty, and the Masons and the Odd Fellows had joined in forming a benevolent association. The town continued to grow, and during the early 1850's there were more than 300 substantial frame buildings.

Its decline began with the gradual exhaustion of the gold in the creeks and on the flats, and by 1870, after destructive fires in 1856 and 1859, only 24 houses were left in the town, a few of which are still standing. On the hill is the I.O.O.F. building, deeded by the society (now joined with the Grass Valley lodge) to the town of Rough and Ready as a community hall. As one leaves the town, the old Fippin blacksmith shop, deserted and dilapidated, stands on the left of the road. A little farther on to the right is the Toll House, now an antique shop. Scars of old diggings are passed on either side of the road as one leaves Rough and Ready behind and climbs the hills toward Grass Valley, four miles away.

In 1865–66 during the copper-mining excitement, a boom occurred southwest of Rough and Ready, and the towns of Spenceville, Hacketville, Wilsonville, and Queen City were laid out. Only Spenceville endured, being the location of a post office from 1872 to 1932 and the center of a small agricultural community. It is said to have had a population of 150 in the 1920's. During World War II it was used by neighboring Camp Beale as a model German village for war maneuvers. The few remaining old buildings were posted with German signs and became targets for the soldiers' guns. Now the site is practically inaccessible, although a piece of the old road southwest of Rough and Ready is still called Spenceville Road.

About three and a half miles northeast of Rough and Ready, via Beckman Hill Road and Newtown Road, is Newtown, formerly Sailor Flat, while ten miles west and one mile north of SR 20 is Mooney Flat. Both were mining camps in the 1850's but now consist largely of newer homes. The Mooney Flat Road continues past Englebright Reservoir to join the Pleasant Valley Road (to French Corral) above Lake Wildwood Dam.

Grass Valley

The town of Grass Valley, full of memories of the colorful gold-mining days, received its name from the well-watered valley in which it lies. The valley was named by a company of emigrants who in 1849 found their way into the meadows kept green by perpetual springs, after toiling over the Truckee Pass Trail with their half-starved cattle. The gaunt beasts had strayed from camp during the night and in the morning were found enjoying the abundant grass and water of the meadow.

The first white men known to have seen this valley were Claude Chana and a party of French emigrants in 1846. In the summer of 1848, David Stump and two other prospectors came from Oregon to the diggings of El Dorado County, drifting southward into Grass Valley in October. Here they crevassed for gold near the sites of the Eureka and Idaho mines until approaching winter drove them from the mountains.

In August 1849 a party of five men headed by a Dr. Saunders built a cabin on Badger Hill near the eastern edge of what is now the city of Grass Valley. The Saunders party was soon joined by others, making a colony of twenty men who spent the winter in the valley. This became the nucleus of the present town.

Another settlement, which also became a part of the

modern Grass Valley, was established in what came to be known as Boston Ravine, named after the company that arrived there in September 1849 under the leadership of the Rev. H. H. Cummings, its president. Four cabins were erected on the south side of the ravine, where the party spent the winter. For two years Boston Ravine, at the south end of present Mill Street, was the chief settlement in the vicinity, laying the foundation for the flourishing trade of the town that ultimately grew out from it.

Beneath the pines on Gold Hill, at Jenkins Street and Hocking Avenue, stands a monument (SRL 297) bearing the following inscription: "This tablet commemorates the discovery of gold-bearing quartz and the beginning of quartz mining in California. The discovery was made on Gold Hill by George Knight, October 1850. The occurrence of gold-bearing quartz was undoubtedly noted here and elsewhere about the same time or previously, but the above discovery created the great excitement that started the development of quartz mining into a great industry. The Gold Hill Mine, 1850–57, is credited with a total production of $4,000,000. This monument dedicated by Quartz Parlor, N.S.G.W., and Manzanita Parlor, N.D.G.W., October 20, 1929." This discovery aided the development of the city of Grass Valley, although its first prosperity came from the rich placer fields.

Other rich veins about Grass Valley were soon discovered, and crude mills for the reduction of the ore were built. Besides the Gold Hill Mine, where the discovery was first made, there were the Massachusetts Hill; the Eureka, located in 1851 on Wolf Creek; the Allison Ranch, located in 1853 two and a half miles south of the town and for a time one of the richest in the state; and the Idaho, located in 1863 just across Wolf Creek from the Eureka. Of special interest are the North Star, opened in 1851 on Lafayette Hill, and the Empire (SRL 298), located in 1850 on Ophir Hill one mile southeast of town, one of the world's major gold mines.

An incredible amount of tunneling has been done in this area. One vein alone extends for a distance of more than 9,000 feet—nearly two miles. The longest shaft, at the Empire Mine, has been sunk to an inclined depth of approximately 8,000 feet, the bottom of the shaft being 4,000 feet below the earth's surface and 1,500 feet below sea level. It is said that there are over 350 miles of tunnels, shafts, and stopes beneath the Empire Mine alone.

The Empire and the North Star were consolidated under one management in 1929, and continued to operate until the closing of the mines in 1942. In 1945, the Empire reopened, but operations were unprofitable because of the rigid limit set on the price of gold; this mine was permanently closed in 1956. The state ac-

Bourn Cottage, Empire Mine State Historic Park, Grass Valley

quired the property after this time and has gradually been opening sections of it to the public as the Empire Mine State Historic Park, located on East Empire Street, a mile east of town.

Although much of the mining equipment was sold off when the mine finally closed down, there is still much to see here. The park headquarters is in the old Retort Room of the mine. The hoist house at the head of the deep shaft still stands, and visitors can peer down many hundreds of feet into the shaft itself. An old stamping mill, sometimes in operation, can be seen. The grounds adjoining the Empire Mine were the summer home of its owner, William Bourn, Jr., and his family. The Cottage is a well-preserved two-story structure built by Willis Polk for the Bourn family in 1898; adjacent to it is the greenhouse for the extensive gardens of roses and native California trees. The clubhouse (1905) contained facilities for tennis, bowling, dancing, and handball, plus kitchens and bedrooms; it is still used to a limited extent by a private club. The grounds are a delight to stroll through, under tall, stately pines.

The powerhouse (SRL 843) is the one remaining building of the North Star Mine; it too has been converted to public use, as the Nevada County Historical Mining Museum, sometimes known as the Pelton Wheel Museum. Displayed here is the largest Pelton Wheel in the world, 30 feet in diameter, installed here in 1896; at its normal operating speed of 65 revolutions per minute, the rim moved at the rate of 70 miles per hour. Invented by Lester Pelton of Camptonville in neighboring Yuba County, the wheel was rimmed with a series of buckets divided into two chambers by a central barrier. A jet of water delivered from a high-pressure nozzle aimed at the center of the bucket was split by the barrier; the two streams thus formed were turned within the chambers of the bucket into two powerful reverse jets that drove the bucket forward. As a source of power that did not involve petroleum fuel, it was much in demand in mining operations, where asphyxiation was an ever-present danger. The museum also has extensive displays of other kinds of mining equipment; it is located at the south end of Mill Street at Allison Ranch Road, and operated by the city of Grass Valley.

The overwhelming majority of miners came to Grass Valley from Cornwall, England, where hardrock tin mining was a traditional activity. The Cornish pumps they brought were still in use many years later. According to one estimate, the population of Grass Valley in 1890 was 85 percent Cornish, and to this day distinctive Cornish dishes are to be found on Grass Valley restaurant menus. The Holbrook Hotel (SRL 914) at 212 West Main Street was built in 1862 around the Golden Gate Saloon, originally built in 1852, and is the oldest continuously operating saloon in the Mother Lode region.

The churches of Grass Valley reflect a significant historical background. Isaac Owen, the first commissioned Methodist minister in California and later the founder, at Santa Clara, of the University of the Pacific (now located at Stockton), preached his first sermon on California soil under the shade of an oak tree in Grass Valley on the north portion of Clark's Ranch in September 1849, having just come overland by ox team. In January 1852, while Owen was presiding elder of the district, a church was organized in Grass Valley in a building that had been used as a meeting place by the Presbyterians and as a schoolhouse. This building was superseded by a larger one in 1854, and by another in 1872; the present Grass Valley Methodist Church dates from 1937.

Opposite it on Church Street is the Emmanuel Episcopal Church. Bishop William Kip held the first Episcopal services in Grass Valley in April 1854 and the parish was organized the following year. The present building, erected in 1858, has served the community since then. A few blocks up Church Street, old Mount St. Mary's Academy (SRL 853) still stands, but stately old St. Patrick's Catholic Church was replaced by a modern structure in 1949. The adjoining cemetery dates from 1853 and is commemorated by a marker placed in 1981 by the Native Daughters of the Golden West. The Congregationalists erected their first building in 1853 at the corner of Church and Neal streets; it is now a commercial office. The first Women's Christian Temperance Union to be organized in California was formed here in 1874 by the women of the Methodist and Congregational churches.

A tablet placed in the public library in 1933 by the Harvard Club of San Francisco commemorates Josiah Royce, philosopher, historian of California, and noted Harvard professor, who was born in Grass Valley in 1855.

The house (SRL 292) now occupied by the Nevada County Chamber of Commerce, at 248 Mill Street, is a late-1970's replica of the home of Lola Montez. A woman of marked intellectual ability, of almost angelic beauty, and with regal grace, Maria Dolores Eliza Rosanna Gilbert, professionally known as Lola Montez, dancer, was born in Ireland in 1818. She had a sensational European career and was the friend of George Sand, Alexandre Dumas, Victor Hugo, Franz Liszt, and most notoriously King Ludwig I of Bavaria, who made her Countess of Landsfeld and listened to her usually disastrous political advice. Exiled from Bavaria, Lola came to America in 1851, where her Spider Dance took San Francisco by storm. After a tour of the gold country, she settled briefly in Grass Valley and around 1852 built her home, where she kept a pet bear on a leash and was the sensation of the town for a couple of years.

Three doors down from Lola's home stands a two-story building (SRL 293) at 238 Mill Street that in 1853 was a boardinghouse. There a small, precocious child of six shyly admired the glamorous dancer, who became fond of little Lotta Crabtree and taught her the singing and dancing skills that would soon make the child one of the great entertainers of America. Unlike Lola Montez, who died at 42 in New York in humble circumstances, Lotta Crabtree had a solid career that permitted her to retire comparatively young and to live graciously until she died at the age of 77, leaving $4 million to charity in her will. Lotta's Fountain still stands on Market Street in San Francisco as a gift to the city.

There are many ghost towns east and southeast of Grass Valley, with a roster of interesting names: You Bet, Red Dog, Gouge Eye, Little York, Walloupa, and Quaker Hill. Town Talk lay between Grass Valley and Nevada City.

Nevada City

James W. Marshall, the discoverer of gold at Coloma, came to Deer Creek, a tributary of the Yuba River, in the summer of 1848. The first white man to pan for gold at this spot, Marshall did not suspect that the stream contained phenomenal wealth, nor did he dream that just two years later more than 10,000 miners would be at work within a radius of three miles from the spot where he had found the first shining grains.

Early in September 1849 Captain John Pennington and two companions built the first cabin on Gold Run above where that stream empties into Deer Creek, and just above the site of the bridge now known as the

Gault Bridge. In October Dr. A. B. Caldwell erected a log cabin and set up a store on the slope of Aristocracy Hill, about where Trinity Episcopal Church now stands and close to the site of the first public school, which was erected in 1854. For a time the place was known as Caldwell's Upper Store (or Deer Creek Dry Diggings), since Dr. Caldwell previously had had a store seven miles below on Deer Creek at Pleasant Flat, where the town of Deer Creek grew up. Its inhabitants later removed to Newtown, where a number of springs furnished a good water supply.

In the same month the town's first family, the Stampses, settled in a ravine behind the present Coyote Street. In the fall Madam Penn came, an indefatigable worker who customarily took her turn at the rocker. In the spring of 1850 this enterprising woman built a boardinghouse on a site that was continuously occupied by a hotel or lodging house for 109 years and on which the Union Hotel stood from 1863 to 1959.

In March 1850 the miners elected Stamps alcalde of Caldwell's Upper Store, and at the same time they changed the name of the place. In the census of 1850 the name of the town is given as Nevada City, although in an unofficial list of post offices for the year 1851 it appears as Nevada. When a county was established in that section of the Sierra country in 1851, it was also called Nevada, and the town of that name was made the county seat. Ten years later, when the state of Nevada was formed, the citizens of the town of Nevada in California bitterly protested that they had first claim to the name. The matter was appealed to Congress, but that body refused to act. Consequently, its citizens decided that their town should henceforth be known as Nevada City, the name always borne officially by the post office.

The phenomenal growth of this region was due at first almost entirely to surface placers. So eager were the miners to find rich strikes that even the streets of the town were not secure from operations. Finally one irate storekeeper protested. Approaching a miner in the act of digging up the street, the merchant demanded that he stop. The miner refused, pleading that there was no law to prevent him from digging in the streets. "Then I'll make a law," said the indignant merchant, producing a revolver, whereupon the miner beat a hasty retreat. Thereafter the streets of Nevada City were not disturbed.

On the eastern end of Lost Hill gold was discovered early in 1850. The gravel ranges of this section proved extraordinarily rich, and news of the diggings spread rapidly, causing a city to mushroom almost overnight. It was not uncommon for the miners to take out a quart of gold, worth $6,000, in a single day in this region.

Because the peculiar method of mining called "coyoteing," or tunneling, was adopted here, the town was called Coyoteville. During the two years of its existence, a total of $8 million is said to have been taken from the surrounding gravel banks. The site of the old settlement constitutes the northwestern section of present Nevada City.

Nevada City nestles at the foot of a panorama of mountains, and for many years it was perhaps the most idyllic and attractive of all the gold rush cities: always busy, but still retaining much of the charm of the past. In the 1960's, a freeway was built through the very middle of the town despite a chorus of protests, an atrocity that unfortunately happened elsewhere in the state in those days. If one gets away from the bustle of the freeway and has the time to stroll through the streets of the town, something of its old quiet mood may be found still.

The back streets of the county seat follow the old mule trains of the past in a weblike pattern radiating from the center of town, by Broad Street and Deer Creek. Aged, steep-roofed houses, three or four stories high, climb to the precipitous walls of Deer Creek Canyon. One of them, a gabled structure of substantial brick at Clay and Prospect streets, has long been known as The Red Castle. Here and there along the thoroughfares, brick and stone stores with iron bars still stand, doing business as they have for more than a century. At 211 Broad Street, the National Hotel (SRL 899) has been in operation since it opened in August 1856 as the National Exchange Hotel, four adjoining brick buildings. It is today one of the oldest continuously operating hotels west of the Rockies. In a suite on the second floor, businessmen met in 1898 to create the powerful Pacific Gas and Electric Company, which would become a major element in California's twentieth-century history.

Through the doors of J. J. Ott's first assay office, no longer standing, a miner from across the Sierra entered one day in 1859 with puzzling specimens from a new "strike" made near Washoe Lake (now in the state of Nevada). The ore was examined, and the assayer's report proved to be the most sensational bit of news since the announcement of Marshall's discovery of gold at Coloma in 1848, for it heralded the fabulous wealth of the Comstock silver mines, which within a few years produced almost one billion dollars. Some of the contents of the Ott Assay Office have been placed in the Oakland Museum in Alameda County.

Next door to the assayer's office on Coyote Street, the site of the 1853 Wells Fargo Express Office is commemorated by a plaque placed by Wells Fargo and the Native Sons. Another plaque commemorates Ott's assay office. The South Yuba Canal Office (SRL 832) at

134 Main Street is a two-story brick building that until 1880 housed the first incorporated company to supply water for hydraulic mining. Firehouse Number One on Main Street near Commercial, erected in 1861 (the bell tower was added later), is now the Museum of the Nevada County Historical Society, a fascinating mixture of rare documents and the materials of everyday life. Firehouse Number Two, also built in 1861 to house another volunteer fire company, still stands on Broad Street.

Across the street from Firehouse Number Two stands the Nevada Theater (SRL 863), built in 1865, the oldest theater building in the state. It is now in use both as a playhouse and as a community center. Nearby at 325 Spring Street, in the Miner's Foundry building (1856), is the American Victorian Museum, devoted to preserving the art, crafts, and artifacts of the Victorian period. The building itself is the place where the first Pelton Wheel was cast in 1878. The building continued in active use as a foundry until it was acquired by the museum in 1974; regrettably, by then none of the original equipment was still in operation or available.

The first religious services in Nevada City, as in many other mining camps throughout the Sierra, were held under a tree. All the early churches were destroyed by the fires of 1856 and 1863. The Congregationalist structure erected in 1864 during the pastorate of Rev. H. H. Cummings is still standing at Main and Church streets and is now a Baptist church.

The history of this Congregational church is connected with a circumstance of statewide significance, and illustrates the broad influence that radiated from the pioneer ministries of many of these mountain charges. W. W. Ferrier says: "The movement out of which was to come the College of California [forerunner of the University of California] had its inception in May 1853, a few days after the arrival of Professor Henry Durant, in the little mountain town of Nevada City." There, on May 9, a joint session of the Congregational Association of California and the Presbytery of San Francisco (New School) was held, and on the 17th a plan was adopted for establishing an institution of higher learning in California.

Another pioneer church of Nevada City is St. Canice's Catholic Church, built in 1864 and still in use.

The distinctive Nevada City Courthouse on Church Street is the latest in a series of courthouses. The wooden courthouse and log jail that had stood on Broad Street since 1851 were replaced in 1856 by a building on Church Street. That building burned a few weeks after it was put up and was rebuilt at the same location. The new building was likewise destroyed by fire in 1863; the present courthouse was built on the same site in 1864. The courthouse was remodeled and enlarged in 1900 and again in 1936–37, as a result of which it has a somewhat anachronistic appearance in a neighborhood of older buildings.

Across the street from the courthouse at 214 Church Street is the Searls Historical Library. From 1872, this was the law office of Niles Searls, who served as chief justice of the California Supreme Court in 1887–88. His son and grandson followed him as attorneys and used this office until 1970. It is now a documentary repository for Nevada City history, and open to the public during regular visiting hours.

Washington and Its Neighbors

Climbing the Washington Ridge over SR 20, one passes a solitary grave at the right, seven miles northeast of Nevada City. Here in 1858 an emigrant family buried their two-year-old boy, Julius Albert Apperson, and in 1971 the Native Sons of the Golden West placed a plaque above the site "in memory of all lone graves throughout the state of California." The California State Highway Commission ignored the original specifications for the road at this point so as to leave this lone grave undisturbed beneath its sentinel pine.

About seven miles further, the motorist suddenly comes upon a marvelous view of rugged mountain scenery dominated by the majestic Sierra Buttes, which rise above the pine-clad ridges to the north and are visible for 100 miles in every direction. From this point a road branches off to the north and winds down six miles through magnificent pines to the old mining town of Washington, picturesquely situated on the bank of the South Yuba River. Two old store buildings with massive stone walls are still at the center of the village; just beyond it are immense piles of huge granite boulders carried there stone by stone by Chinese miners of long ago presumably for additional structures that were never built.

In the vicinity of Washington during the gold days, numerous mining camps were located at the wealth-producing bars and flats along the river, and some of these camps developed into trading centers of considerable activity. At the mouth of Canyon Creek about three miles up the river from the town was Canal Bar, from which the line of camps extended downstream past several bars to the Brass Wire Bar, across the river from Washington, which in 1880 was worked entirely by Chinese miners. Four miles east of Washington on SR 20, a monument has been erected near a viewpoint overlooking the diggings of Alpha and Omega, now ghost towns. Alpha (SRL 628) was the birthplace of Emma Wixom in 1859. As Emma Nevada, she went on to a brilliant operatic career in Europe and America.

The Alpha mines became exhausted in 1880, but up to that time they had produced no less than $1,500,000 in gold. To the east was its sister camp, Omega (SRL 629), where the deep pit washed out by hydraulic mining reveals the old diggings from which $2,500,000 was taken during the same period. This mine operated on and off until 1949. Across the river from the Washington bridge another road leads about three miles to the Spanish Mine, where Patrick Dillon first panned for gold on Poorman's Creek in 1851.

The San Juan Ridge and the Malakoff Diggins

Hydraulic mining was extensively used on the San Juan Ridge to the north of Nevada City to extract gold from the enormous deposits in the higher mountains. Three companies owned vast mines in the region, which were operated at a tremendous outlay. High up in the Sierra, 6,000 feet above sea level, reservoirs were constructed from which the water supply for hundreds of mines along the ridge was obtained through a system of canals and flumes. Although constructed in 1850–80 merely with pick and shovel and carpenter's level, some are still intact in a few places and exhibit a remarkable workmanship.

The three companies were the Eureka Lake and Yuba Canal Company, with headquarters at North Columbia, which owned four reservoirs and a system of ditches 200 miles long; the North Bloomfield Mining Company, with 43 miles of ditches; and the Milton Mining and Water Company, with offices at French Corral, which owned 80 miles of ditches. The total expenditure of these companies for construction and equipment amounted to $5,568,000.

In order to obtain the most effective management of the ditches and flumes along the ridge, the companies in

Hydraulic Mining Site, Malakoff Diggins State Historic Park

North Bloomfield School, Malakoff Diggins State Historic Park

1878 built, cooperatively, the world's first long-distance telephone line, at a cost of $6,000. This line was 60 miles long and extended up the ridge from French Corral through Birchville, Sweetland, North San Juan, Cherokee, North Columbia, Lake City, North Bloomfield, Moore's Flat, Graniteville, Milton, and Bowman Lake. It was managed by the Ridge Telephone Company and owned jointly by the three mining companies. Edison instruments manufactured in Boston in 1876 were used.

Part of the area over which this line went is now Malakoff Diggins State Historic Park. Here hydraulic mining was carried on so extensively that tons of earth and gravel were washed away, leaving a deeply eroded landscape. The huge hole is second in size only to the LaGrange Mine near Weaverville in Trinity County. Enormous profits in gold were being washed out along San Juan Ridge when Lorenzo Sawyer, a U.S. circuit court judge, handed down the historic decision of January 7, 1884, that virtually outlawed all hydraulic operations in the state. (The Caminetti Act of 1893, a federal statute, permits very limited hydraulic mining and requires the impounding of all debris under the regulations of the California Debris Commission.)

A hundred years have passed, and nature has gradually softened the harsh outlines of the Malakoff; trees now grow in the valleys and the place is a favored campground. The village of North Bloomfield is located within the park, and has an interesting museum and visitors' center, open except for the winter months. A couple of old stores still serve the community. The office of the North Bloomfield Mining and Gravel Company (SRL 852) can still be seen.

St. Columncille's Catholic Church at the western edge of town has had a curious history. It was originally the Bridgeport Union Guard Hall, and was used as a training base for soldiers in the early days of the Civil War. In 1880 it was acquired as a house of worship for the Catholic community of the ridge towns. Later abandoned, it was purchased in 1969 by Mr. Babe Pinaglia and donated to the park, where it now stands. There was once a Catholic church on this site in North Bloomfield.

French Corral

French Corral was the earliest of the mining camps that sprang up along the ancient San Juan River channel. There in 1849 the first settler, a Frenchman, built a corral for his mules; very soon it was discovered that the locality was rich in placer gold, and a town grew up on the site of the Frenchman's corral. Later, as hydraulic mining developed, it became an important town numbering its population in the thousands. Not much remains there today. The office of the Milton Mining and Water Company, in which one terminus of the first long-distance telephone line was located, has been torn down, but the site is marked (SRL 247). The brick walls of the old Wells Fargo Express Office, built in the 1850's and equipped with iron doors and window shutters that once guarded millions of dollars in gold, look as if they will stand for generations to come. A number of old homes are still occupied.

North San Juan

On SR 49 between Nevada City and Downieville lies North San Juan. San Juan Hill to the north was first mined in 1853 by Christian Kientz, who, according to tradition, was the originator of the name. Kientz had been with General Scott's army in Mexico, and saw in the California hill a strong resemblance to the hill on which San Juan de Ulloa in Mexico stands. Later, when the whole hill had been staked out to rich claims, the name was given to the promising camp that grew up close by. By 1857 San Juan was of sufficient importance to be assigned a post office; "North" was prefixed to the name in order to distinguish it from the much older San Juan in San Benito County.

North San Juan today consists of some old brick buildings, some modern houses, a few abandoned old places, and a cemetery. E Clampus Vitus has marked the Wells Fargo Office and the Masonic Hall, built in 1862 and now a general store for the community. Many houses had been built on the hill above town, but when these were found to be standing on "pay gravel" they were bought by mining companies and destroyed. A high cliff forms the southern wall of the chasm washed out by hydraulic operations, along the rim of which today a road winds, while in the distance rise the peaks of the Sierra.

Cherokee and North Columbia

Passing along the scenic Ridge Road, now through groves of pine, now above them, one comes to Cherokee, five miles east of North San Juan. This remnant of the 1850's consists today of a little Catholic church and a handful of weatherworn houses that stand at the edge of the diggings. Just north of Cherokee is the old Badger Hill Mine, once a famous producer.

At North Columbia, originally known as Columbia Hill, three miles beyond Cherokee, a few old homes still stand, notably that of the Coughlan family. The old schoolhouse also remains. At North Columbia begins the Foote's Crossing Road to Alleghany in Sierra County.

North Columbia was originally built on the Pliocene gravel bed of the ancient river channel, but in 1878, when the site was found to contain rich gold deposits, the town was moved to its present location.

Graniteville

Graniteville, a town on the line of the old Ridge Telephone Company, lies in a beautiful forested region near the summit of the mountains 26 miles northeast of Nevada City. Gold was mined in the gulches here as early as 1850, and because the diggings were shallow a number of miners were soon attracted to the spot. The original name of the place was Eureka South, to distinguish it from Eureka in Humboldt County and Eureka North in Sierra County, but when the post office was established there in 1867, the present name was adopted.

Graniteville was threatened with extinction when the surface diggings became exhausted, but during the middle 1860's gold-bearing quartz was found in the vicinity and the town again became a thriving place. A severe fire swept through it in 1878, but because hydraulic-mining companies had reservoirs in the mountains above the town, Graniteville was rebuilt and until 1883 was an active distributing point for these companies. Afterward, however, its existence depended on quartz mining and lumbering. Now its schoolhouse and many of its old residences have been beautifully renovated as summer homes.

Truckee

Off I-80, beyond the summit of Donner Pass, lies the pioneer railroad town of Truckee. The first transcontinental railroad reached Truckee from Sacramento on April 3, 1868, an event marked by a plaque (SRL 780.6) on the Southern Pacific Railroad depot in town; with this, the conquest of the Sierra by iron rails had been made. Thirteen months and seven days later the Central Pacific tracks met those of the Union Pacific at Promontory, Utah.

Truckee has some interesting old buildings, all very much in use today. Gray's Log Waystation, built in 1863, was moved to its present location at 10030 Church Street in 1907 and is marked with an E Clampus Vitus Plaque. The Engelhardt Building at 10020, next door, dates from 1889. The White House was built in 1873 and became the home of banker C. B. White in 1903. It is now a restaurant with a Victorian museum on the second floor, and is listed in the National Register of Historic Places. Another museum is located in the old Truckee Jail, built out of native stone in 1875 and in use until 1964. The building is at 10144 Main Street.

Engelhardt Building, Truckee

Orange County

Orange County was created in 1889 from a portion of Los Angeles County. Santa Ana has always been the county seat.

Although it is generally believed that the county was named for its abundant orange groves, many scholars disagree. The name "Orange" has been given to some 50 places in the United States, including the town founded here in 1873, before the creation of the separate county of Orange. The city of Orange may have been named to advertise a local product, as some think, or it may have been named for another Orange, perhaps in the eastern part of the United States. William Wolfskill first introduced oranges as a commercial crop in 1841, following early attempts at the missions to grow oranges. The first large commercial planting of oranges was made by James Irvine II on his Irvine Ranch in 1886, three years before the creation of the county.

Portolá's Trail

A little company of soldiers and priests led by Gaspar de Portolá entered what is now Orange County on July 22, 1769, on their way north to seek the port of Monterey. Passing through low, open mountain country, they made camp for the night near an Indian village north of San Onofre. Here two little Indian girls, who were very ill, were baptized by the fathers—the first baptism in Alta California. The soldiers named the place Los Cristianitos ("the little Christians"), and it is still called Cristianitos Canyon. The site of the first baptism (SRL 562) is the spring called Aguaje de la Piedra, now within the boundaries of Camp Joseph H. Pendleton and across the boundary line in San Diego County. A marker stands there, off Cristianitos Road, and another marker has been placed at the city hall in San Clemente.

On July 23 the Portolá party "came to a very pleasant green valley, full of willow, alders, live oaks, and other trees not known to us. It has a large arroyo, which at the point where we crossed it carried a good stream of fresh and good water, which, after running a little way, formed in pools in some large patches of tules. We halted there, calling it the valley of Santa Maria Magdalena."

Thus does Father Juan Crespí describe the valley of San Juan Capistrano, in which Portolá and his men stopped. The spot chosen was within a few hundred yards of the present Mission San Juan Capistrano. At the same spot, the explorers camped again on January 20 and April 21, 1770. Juan Bautista de Anza camped there on January 8, 1776, on his way from Mission San Gabriel to San Diego to lend aid to Governor Rivera during the Indian uprising.

From this point, Portolá's trail lay along the foothills east of the Santa Ana Valley and across the Puente Hills into Los Angeles County. On July 24, camp was made on Aliso Creek, near the present site of El Toro, where there was a village of friendly Indians. Here the party rested for two days, moving on a short distance to Tomato Spring on the Irvine Ranch on July 26. Again they pitched camp "near a dry lagoon on a slope, from which [they] examined the spacious plain, the end of which [they] could not see."

On the following day, after crossing the plain, camp was made near a stream that to this day is called Santiago Creek. This campsite was close to the modern city of Orange, at a spot that the Spaniards considered suitable for the building of a city.

Skirting the mountains to the north, Portolá reached the Santa Ana River on July 28. There he pitched camp near the west bank opposite an Indian village. The site of this camp is due east of Anaheim. Here Anza camped on January 7, 1776.

Crossing the swiftly flowing river with great difficulty on July 29, the party traveled northwest until they reached "a very green little valley, which has a small pool of water, on whose bank there is a very large village of very friendly heathen." Camp was made on a hill near the pool and the place was called Santa Marta, now on the south side of La Habra.

Descending the hill on July 30, the little band proceeded north across the valley and over the Puente Hills, coming into the spacious and fertile valley of the San Gabriel. The later main highway, which came from Whittier to La Habra, and then through the hills where Harbor Boulevard runs today, was opened by the Portolá party on their return trips in January and April 1770.

Mission San Juan Capistrano

Owing to the zeal of Padre Presidente Junipero Serra, the founding of Mission San Juan Capistrano was first attempted as early as October 1775. Father Palou writes: "The little troop, composed of Fr. Lasuén, Lieutenant Ortega, a sergeant, and the necessary soldiers, left San Diego toward the end of October. On arriving at the site, an enramada or arbor was hastily erected, near which a large cross was constructed, raised, blessed, and venerated by all. On an altar prepared in the arbor, Fr. Lasuén offered up the first holy Mass. This happened on October 30, 1775, the last day of the octave after the feast of San Juan Capistrano, the

patron of the mission. Formal possession was then taken of the lands and thus the beginning was made amid the rejoicings of the numerous pagans who had flocked thither. They proved their satisfaction by helping to cut and bring down the timber for the chapel and the dwelling." St. John Capistran was an Italian-born Franciscan theologian and preacher of the fifteenth century who participate in the Christian victory over the Turks at Belgrade in 1456.

Hardly had the first founding of San Juan Capistrano taken place than news of the Indian uprising at San Diego forced the fathers to give up the undertaking temporarily. It was not until October of the following year that they returned, this time in company with Father Serra himself. Palou relates that the cross erected by Father Lasuén the year before was found to be still in place and that the two bells that had been left in hiding were disinterred, hung in position, and rung joyously to tell the Indians of the missionaries' return. An arbor was quickly erected, and on November 1, 1776, the formal founding of Mission San Juan Capistrano took place.

The work of building and conversion was left in the care of Fathers Pablo Mugártegui and Gregório Amúrrio, both good and efficient men, who constructed the first chapel and dwelling houses and who increased the prosperity of the mission.

It was long believed by some that the first mission church was erected up the stream four or five miles from the present site at a place known as Misión Vieja, or La Vieja—the Old Mission. The historian Zephyrin Engelhardt, however, believes that the facts point to one location rather than to two, citing statements of Father Palou regarding the finding of the cross and bells and the distance of the first church from the sea as evidence. "From the buildings," writes Palou, "the ocean can be seen and the ships when they cruise there; for the beach is only about half a league [actually a league, says Engelhardt] distant." There is no mention in any of the diaries of a change of location. Engelhardt states that Misión Vieja was only a rancho of the mission.

San Juan Capistrano, which was planned by Father Gregório, was over nine years in the building, the first stone having been laid in 1796 and consecration taking place on September 8, 1806. On December 8, 1812, a great earthquake undid the work of years and took the lives of 40 neophytes. Little attempt was made to rebuild the fallen church until 1860, when some adobe restorations were made, only to be washed away by the first heavy rainstorms. In later years, the Landmarks Club restored the beautiful arched corridors of the patio, the old kitchen with its quaint chimney, and Serra's church, the long building that still stands on the

Mission San Juan Capistrano

east side of the patio. Built in 1777, this is the oldest building now standing in California, and the only remaining church where Father Serra celebrated Mass. Extensive restorations were also carried out by the Catholic Church under the direction of Father St. John O'Sullivan.

San Juan Capistrano (SRL 200) was perhaps the grandest and most beautiful of all the missions. Today the great stone church, which was its crowning glory, lies in magnificent ruins. Its exquisite carvings, done by a master mason over a period of nine years; the great dome, one of the original seven, within which was once the altar; the semi-Moorish architecture, set in a frame of green hills and purple mountains, and softened by the old garden still lingering within its walls, make of San Juan Capistrano an unforgettable Old World picture. The romance of the old mission is enhanced by the legend, celebrated in song, of the return of the swallows each year on St. Joseph's Day, March 19.

The town retains much of its interest and some of its old buildings today. The original registration of San Juan Capistrano as a State Historical Landmark included, for this reason, the town as well as the mission. The restaurant known as "El Adobe de Capistrano," often visited by President Nixon, incorporates two old adobes, the Miguel Yorba on the north (1778) and the *juzgado* (justice court and jail) on the south (1812). The two buildings were originally remodeled as the Van der Leck residence in 1910. To the east across the street is the brick house of Judge Richard Egan, built in the 1880's on the site of an old Aguilar adobe. The Domingo Yorba adobe stands at 31871 Camino Capistrano; like most of these old houses, it is still privately owned. The Manuel García adobe dates from the 1840's and is the only surviving Monterey-style adobe in Orange

County; it is located at 31843 Camino Capistrano. Part of the Juan Ávila adobe, once a huge structure, stands at 31831 Camino Capistrano; the lower floor is a store. The Blas Aguilar adobe is located at 31806 El Camino Real; part of it is said to have been built in 1794 and occupied by the mayordomos of the mission.

At Verdugo and Los Rios streets, across the railroad tracks from the center of town, is the Ríos adobe, built in 1794. It stands on the tiny grant, a fraction more than seven acres, made to Santiago Ríos by Governor Manuel Micheltorena in 1843. The *ranchito* was located on San Juan Creek between the mission and the beach and was entirely surrounded by Rancho Boca de la Playa. The adobe is still the home of the Ríos family and has been marked by E Clampus Vitus as the oldest single-family residence in California continuously occupied by the same family. Rancho Boca de la Playa, 6,607 acres, was granted to Emigdio Vejar by Governor Pío Pico in 1846; it was later owned by Juan Ávila and then by Pablo Pryor. The old adobe ranch house still stands at 33751 Camino Capistrano in Capistrano Beach, under a little point of hill overlooking the ocean at the mouth of San Juan Creek.

On the heights of Costa Mesa, half a mile east of the Santa Ana River at 1900 Adams Avenue, stands the Diego Sepúlveda adobe (SRL 227), built about 1823–25 as an *estancia*, or station, of Mission San Juan Capistrano. An *estancia* was a less important outpost of a mission than an *asistencia*. The adobe was located on Rancho Santiago de Santa Ana, and, when the rancho was later subdivided, it became the home of Diego Sepúlveda, an auxiliary alcalde of Pueblo de Los Angeles. The building is preserved and maintained by the Costa Mesa Historical Society in Estancia Park. The Costa Mesa Historical Society Museum is at Anaheim and Plumer streets; among its collections are memorabilia of the Santa Ana Army Air Base.

The Henry Siever adobe, in Sievers Canyon one-quarter mile east of the San Juan Guard Station on SR 74, is said to have been another *estancia* of San Juan Capistrano. It is located thirteen miles northeast of the mission.

Dana's Cove

On the coast seven and one-half miles southeast of Laguna Beach and west of the outlet of San Juan Creek into the sea lies Dana's Cove. The promontory on the west is Dana Point (SRL 189), and farther west are San Juan Capistrano Point and the San Juan Rocks. In Spanish and Mexican days this cove was the site of the embarcadero, which played an important part in the material life of Mission San Juan Capistrano. Here, in 1818, the pirate Hippolyte de Bouchard landed to raid the mission.

This cove and the high cliff above it are described by Richard Henry Dana in *Two Years Before the Mast*, and they were later named in his honor. The name is also preserved by a modern seaside town, Dana Point. On May 5, 1986, 150 years after Dana's first landing, a marker was placed at the Dana Point Harbor by the Daughters of the American Revolution.

Dana describes how cowhides were thrown from the edge of the cliff to the beach below and loaded onto the *Pilgrim*: "Down this height we pitched the hides, throwing them as far out into the air as we could; and as they were all large, stiff, and doubled, like the cover of a book, the wind took them, and they swayed and eddied about, plunging and rising in the air, like a kite when it has broken its string. As it was now low tide, there was no danger of their falling into the water; and, as fast as they came to ground, the men below picked them up, and, taking them on their heads, walked off with them to the boat. It was really a picturesque sight: the great height, the scaling of the hides, and the continual walking to and fro of the men, who looked like mites, on the beach. This was the romance of hide droghing!"

Rancho Santiago de Santa Ana

Rancho Santiago de Santa Ana extended along the east bank of the Santa Ana River from the mountains to the sea. It was bounded on the east by a line extending from Red Hill to the sea and running parallel to the present Newport Boulevard one mile to the southeast. It is the only rancho lying entirely within Orange County whose history goes back to the Spanish period, some portion of it always having been in the hands of the Yorbas.

José Antonio Yorba first saw this land when he passed over it in 1769 as a corporal in Portolá's company. His father-in-law, Juan Pablo Grijalva, was awarded pasturage rights to the area in 1801, but there is some doubt whether he actually lived on the land. Grijalva had come to California with Anza in 1776. In 1810 the rancho of eleven leagues was formally granted to Yorba and his nephew, Juan Pablo Peralta, by the King of Spain.

The site of the first adobe erected on Rancho Santiago de Santa Ana is on Hoyt Hill, the westernmost point of El Modeno Hills, between El Modeno and Villa Park. Hoyt Hill is on the south side of Santiago Creek directly overlooking the Santiago Boulevard bridge. Another adobe site was west of Orange. A cluster of adobes stood in the vicinity of the present town of Olive.

The community became known as Santa Ana, or Santa Ana Abajo ("lower") to distinguish it from Santa Ana Arriba ("upper") on Bernardo Yorba's Rancho Cañon de Santa Ana, farther up the river. A marker has been placed on the Orange-Olive Road north of Lincoln Avenue in Olive to commemorate the former settlement as Old Santa Ana (SRL 204). An old map designates an adobe just south of Olive as the "Casa de Yorba y tierras."

Red Hill (SRL 203), a prominent landmark three miles northwest of Tustin, near Browning Avenue and La Colina Drive, was known to Indians, padres, rancheros, and early mapmakers. Its name comes from the ores and salts that give its soil a reddish color. It became the dividing line between ranchos. At its base was a swamp, La Ciénega de las Ranas ("the swamp of the frogs"), and some writings erroneously give this name to the hill as well. Between it and the Santiago Hills nearby ran the old trail. Later the stage route also followed this road, crossing the Santa Ana River near Olive and dividing north of the river, one route going through La Habra Valley via Don Pío Pico's Rancho, and the other west of Anaheim via Rancho Los Coyotes, on which Buena Park is situated, and Santa Fe Springs.

In Santa Ana Canyon stands the Ramón Peralta adobe, built in 1871, one of the later and best preserved of the adobes of Orange County. It is situated in a shopping mall on the south side of the Riverside Freeway, one and one-quarter miles east of the Imperial Highway junction. Two other adobes stand on the north side of the freeway within a short distance of the Peralta house, but they are difficult to recognize because of extensive remodeling.

The present city of Santa Ana was founded by William Henry Spurgeon, who settled in the area in 1869. He gave his town the name that had formerly been applied to the settlement near Olive. In 1913, two years before his death, Spurgeon built the present W. H. Spurgeon Block, at the southwest corner of Sycamore and Fourth streets, the first four-story building in Orange County. It replaced a two-story wooden structure on the same site, built by Spurgeon in 1883.

The red Arizona sandstone county courthouse (SRL 837) at 211 West Santa Ana Boulevard is the oldest existing courthouse building in southern California; it was used from 1900 to 1979. Much of Orange County's history is recalled in the collections of the Charles W. Bowers Memorial Museum, a Spanish colonial–style building built in 1933, located at 2002 North Main Street in Santa Ana.

Rancho Santiago de Santa Ana was bounded on the southeast by Rancho Lomas de Santiago, toward the mountains, and Rancho San Joaquín, toward the sea.

Lomas de Santiago, 47,227 acres, was granted to Teodo-cio Yorba by Governor Pío Pico in 1846. San Joaquín was owned by José Sepúlveda, to whom it was granted by Governor Juan B. Alvarado in 1837 and 1842. The United States patent was for 48,803 acres. Sepúlveda's home once stood at the head of Newport Bay. Later he built another in what is now the southwestern part of Santa Ana, near Willits and Bristol streets. He lived in "El Refugio," as he called this home, during the 1850's and 1860's.

Ranchos Lomas de Santiago and San Joaquín, to-gether with a strip along the southeast line of Rancho Santiago de Santa Ana, ultimately came into the hands of James Irvine, and most of this land—close to 120,000 acres—remains today as the Irvine Ranch, one of the last great ranches in California. It covers almost one-fifth of Orange County and stretches from the moun-tains to the sea.

James Irvine, born in Belfast, Ireland, in 1827, came to California during the gold rush, but made his for-tune in merchandising rather than mining. In the 1860's he entered into partnership with Flint, Bixby, and Com-pany, and by 1876 was sole owner of what became known as the Irvine Ranch. Irvine died in 1886, and management of the huge estate eventually passed to his son, James Irvine II, who formed the Irvine Com-pany in 1894. This company holds title to the ranch to-day, but the lands are gradually being subdivided and converted to other uses. The University of California has a 1,500-acre campus on the ranch. The town of Ir-vine (post office, East Irvine) is near the center of the ranch, and five miles north at Irvine Boulevard and My-ford Road are the agricultural offices of the Irvine Com-pany. Across Myford Road from these buildings stands the home built by James Irvine II shortly after the turn of the century. The old residence, with its double row of palm trees, has been converted to offices. The corpo-rate headquarters of the Irvine Ranch are now in New-port Beach.

The Irvine Historical Museum at 5 Rancho San Joa-quin is in the oldest building on the Irvine Ranch, origi-nally the sheep camp headquarters of the ranch under the elder James Irvine.

East Irvine or Old Irvine is the only intact original agricultural shipping center in southern California. Two buildings—the sack storage warehouse, dating from 1895, and the bean and grain warehouse, from 1946—are part of the East Irvine Historical District, as are Irvine's General Store (1909), hotel (1913), and blacksmith's shop (1915). This area, in the middle of a rapidly growing portion of the Irvine Ranch, is sched-uled for a great deal of redevelopment.

Rancho Cañon de Santa Ana (Placentia, Yorba Linda)

The most important ranch house in Orange County during the Mexican period was that of Don Bernardo Yorba, one of California's greatest landowners. It was situated on Rancho Cañon de Santa Ana on the north bank of the Santa Ana River and was a very large estab-lishment. A spacious patio was entirely surrounded by adobe buildings, those on two sides being two stories high. Don Bernardo, a son of José Antonio Yorba of Rancho Santiago de Santa Ana, received his grant of 13,329 acres from Governor José Figueroa in 1834, and construction of the great hacienda began soon after.

The old house stood for years unoccupied and ne-glected. An effort to restore this fine landmark failed, and the owner razed its walls about 1927. Nothing but a historical marker is now left to show where once stood what was one of the greatest of the Mexican ranch houses in California. The site (SRL 226) is at Es-peranza Road and Echo Hill Drive in Yorba Linda; bits of tile and stone from the mansion have been incorpo-rated into the monument. Not far away is the old Yorba Cemetery where Don Bernardo is buried.

Rancho Cañada de los Alisos (El Toro)

Rancho Cañada de los Alisos, an area of 10,668 acres according to the United States patent, was granted to José Serrano by Governor Alvarado in 1842 and by Gov-ernor Pío Pico in 1846. It was acquired in the 1880's by Dwight Whiting. One of Serrano's adobes (SRL 199) still stands at 25151 Serrano Road in El Toro. This par-cel of land has been acquired by Orange County and is now known as Heritage Hill Historical Park. The Se-rrano adobe was built in 1858 and considerably added to by George Whiting, son of Dwight, in 1932. The ex-tensive gardens are graced by three large pepper trees, one well over a century old.

On the same grounds are three historic buildings that have been moved from their original sites. The El Toro Grammar School is a one-room building that once stood on the corner of First Street and Olive Avenue in El Toro. This building was used until 1914, when a new two-room schoolhouse, still visible at that location, was constructed adjacent to it. After service as St. Antho-ny's Catholic Church on El Toro Road from 1914 to 1968, the old schoolhouse suffered a period of neglect before being moved to Heritage Hill. The Bennett Ranch House originally stood at the corner of Second Street and Cherry Avenue in El Toro. It was built in 1908 as a care-taker's home for the Bennett navel orange ranch. St. George's Episcopal Mission was originally located on Whisler Drive in El Toro. It was built in 1891 for a col-

El Toro Grammar School and St. George's Episcopal Mission at Heritage Hill State Historic Park, El Toro

ony of English settlers recruited by Dwight Whiting to become "gentlemen fruit farmers." Most of the interior furnishings are original. All three buildings are open to the public at regular hours.

Anaheim

Anaheim is the pioneer town of the American period in Orange County. It is antedated in the county only by the communities of San Juan Capistrano, Santa Ana Arriba, and Santa Ana Abajo. It is also one of the oldest colony experiments in California, having been started in 1857 by a group of Germans, chiefly from San Francisco. Their plan was to buy a tract of land in common, lay it out in small farms and vineyards, and work it under the supervision of a general manager. Fifty charter members purchased a part of the Rancho San Juan Cajón de Santa Ana from the family of Don Juan Pacífico Ontiveros, the original Mexican grantee.

This fertile tract of 1,165 acres on the north bank of the Santa Ana River and about twelve miles inland from the ocean was divided into 50 twenty-acre lots for the little farms and vineyards, and 50 house lots that were to make up the nucleus of the community. Besides these, there was sufficient public land for schoolhouses and community buildings. A fence made of 40,000 willow poles and five and a half miles long enclosed the entire colony. Most of the willows took root, forming a living wall about the settlement. Gates were erected at the north, south, east, and west ends of the two principal intersecting streets of the colony. The north gate, the site of which is marked (SRL 112) at the corner of Anaheim Boulevard and North Street, was the main entrance to the town, being on the road from Los Angeles. Lucile E. Dickson quotes a writer who says that "the colonists were a curious mixture . . . two or three carpenters, four blacksmiths, three watchmakers, a brewer, an engraver, a shoemaker, a poet, a

miller, a bookbinder, two or three merchants, a hatter, and a musician." Dickson continues, "But in spite of this medley of professions, the colony flourished almost from the beginning, and for many years its name was almost a synonym for prosperity and industry throughout the south."

For many years the town was known as the "Campo Alemán" to its Spanish-speaking neighbors, because of the continued predominance of Germans. Despite the many hardships and financial struggles of the colony's early years, only one of its 50 original settlers abandoned it.

Initially, supplies came to Anaheim through the port of San Pedro. By 1864, however, the colonists had organized the Anaheim Lighter Company and developed a port, with warehouse and dock, closer to the colony. Anaheim Landing (SRL 219), which served the entire Santa Ana Valley until the opening of the Southern Pacific Railroad in 1875, was located on the coast at what is now the town of Seal Beach. The marker is located at the corner of Seal Beach Boulevard and Electric Avenue. Electric Avenue follows the line of the Pacific Electric Railway, which operated between Los Angeles and the coast towns until after the end of World War II. The Pacific Electric Red Car Museum at 707 Electric Avenue in Seal Beach has a display of local transportation history in a converted work car.

The Pioneer House of the Mother Colony (SRL 201) is said to be the first frame house built in the Anaheim Colony. It was built in 1857 by George Hansen, a leader of the group. It has been moved from its original location on North Los Angeles Street and placed at 414 West Street. It contains an interesting collection of relics of pioneer days gathered in the neighborhood. In 1929, the Mother Colony Chapter of the Daughters of the American Revolution opened the museum, now administered by the Anaheim Public Library.

Anaheim has many buildings that reflect the suc-

Pioneer House of the Mother Colony, Anaheim

cessive fashions in domestic architecture in southern California from about 1870 to the early twentieth century. Italianate, Queen Anne, Greek Revival, and Neoclassical Revival houses are to be found in the area bounded by South Olive, East Broadway, South Claudina, and Santa Ana streets. The Ferdinand Backs home at 225 North Claudina is an elegant Colonial Revival building grafted onto an older dwelling; the newer addition was begun in 1902. The remarkably unaltered Kroeger-Melrose Historic District contains more than 70 houses built between 1898 and 1916.

Anaheim is the home of Disneyland, which opened its 185 acres in 1955. The extensive orange groves that once surrounded the park are gone today. Another popular attraction is Knott's Berry Farm at nearby Buena Park, to which Walter Knott moved a number of old buildings from various Western towns. One of these is Maizeland School (SRL 729), the first school in the Rivera district of Los Angeles County. It was originally built on Shugg Lane, now Slauson Avenue. Knott also restored the ghost town of Calico in the Mojave Desert, noted in the San Bernardino County chapter. The Buena Park Historical Society Museum at 7842 Whitaker Street is in the home built in 1887 by Andrew Whitaker.

Rancho San Juan Cajón de Santa Ana, on which Anaheim is situated, was granted in 1837 by Governor Juan B. Alvarado to Juan Pacífico Ontiveros. One of the Ontiveros adobes is still standing at 330 East Crowther Avenue in Placentia and is known as the Ontiveros-Kraemer adobe. The wing built after 1850 was razed in the 1930's; the older part dates from about the time of the granting of the rancho.

Carbon Canyon and Olinda

Carbon Canyon Regional Park, near Brea, contains an area that in the 1870's was used as grazing and cattle land. The arrival of the Santa Fe Railroad in the next decade initiated a land boom in the area that became frantic when Edward L. Doheny discovered oil in the region in 1897. Olinda (SRL 918) burgeoned immediately afterward, becoming a sizable but unincorporated town. At the close of World War II, as productivity dropped in the oil fields, Olinda declined and finally vanished. Today it is remembered only by a plaque in the park.

Richard Nixon

Richard Milhous Nixon was the first native Californian to reach the White House. He was born on January 9, 1913, in Yorba Linda, in a frame house completed the previous year by his father, Frank. The house, privately owned, still stands at 18061 Yorba

Birthplace of Richard Milhous Nixon, Yorba Linda

Linda Boulevard. The grounds in front of the house are marked with various plaques commemorating the political life of Orange County's most famous son: Congressman, United States Senator, Vice President, and finally President of the United States.

Following his resignation from the presidency in 1974, Nixon retired to his home in San Clemente. During his presidency, it was known as the "Western White House." The building, now under other ownership, is near the southern end of the city of San Clemente, on a bluff overlooking the ocean. San Clemente was one of the first planned communities in California, begun in 1925.

Newport Beach

In 1872 Captain S. S. Dunnells of San Diego and D. M. Dorman established a small deck and warehouse at Newport Bay that they called Newport Landing. The following year three brothers, James, Robert, and John McFadden, received a shipment of lumber at the landing for their personal use. Other settlers, however, prevailed upon them to sell their cargo, and the McFaddens decided to go into the lumber business. They purchased Newport Landing in the same year, 1873, and made it their headquarters. It later became known as McFadden's Landing and Port Orange. It was located just below the bluff that divided upper and lower Newport Bay, or near the intersection of Dover Drive with SR 1 (the Pacific Coast Highway) at Newport Beach, where a plaque stands (SRL 198). Eventually it became known as the Old Landing when the McFaddens built a wharf on the ocean side of the peninsula at the present location of the Newport pier. The original wharf (SRL 794) on this site was completed in 1888, and in 1892, the same year the town of Newport was laid out, it became the terminus of the Santa Ana and Newport Railroad.

Until 1907 it was the major commercial port for Orange, San Bernardino, and Riverside counties.

One of the most picturesque landmarks along the southern California coast is the Balboa Pavilion (SRL 959) at 400 Main Street in Balboa on Newport Bay. The Newport Bay Investment Company put up this striking building in 1905 to attract investors to the Balboa Peninsula property; the following year, it became the southern terminus for the Pacific Electric Railway's Red Cars. In the summer months, ferries ply between here and Santa Catalina Island.

On May 10, 1912, Glenn L. Martin flew a hydroplane from the waters of the Pacific Ocean at Balboa to Santa Catalina Island. It was the first known water-to-water flight, and the longest and fastest overwater flight to that date. A monument (SRL 775) at the foot of the Balboa pier commemorates this historic event.

Edward Jackson Martin began the Martin Aviation Company in an abandoned church that stood at Second and Bush streets in Santa Ana. The "father of Orange County aviation" built his first airplane in 1909; later he developed the Orange County Airport.

Orange County During World War II

The open fields of coastal Orange County underwent substantial development because of World War II. The largest lima-bean field in the world, some 17,000 acres, became the El Toro Marine Corps Air Station. At Tustin, one of two Lighter-Than-Air Stations on the West Coast was built to house the huge 14-ZPK-class airships, or blimps. One remaining hangar is among the largest wooden buildings in the United States; it can be visited, as can the nearby Marine Corps station.

Coastal defense consisted in part of huge gun batteries. The gigantic concrete pads for one emplacement may still be seen where Bolsa Chica and Warner avenues meet in Huntington Beach.

Landmarks of the Santa Ana Mountains

In the late 1870's and early 1880's Orange County (then still part of Los Angeles County) experienced a short-lived mining boom. Hank Smith and William Curry discovered silver in 1877 east of Santa Ana in an area that was to become known as Silverado Canyon. The mining camp of Silverado (SRL 202) sprang up the following year and prospered for three or four years. The Blue Light was the principal mine in the district, which is now filled with summer homes.

In 1878 Ramón Mesquida discovered coal nearby, and the town of Carbondale (SRL 228) was built on the flat at the intersection of Santiago and Silverado can-

yons. The Southern Pacific Railroad operated a mine there for a few years. A marker is located at the Silverado Community Church at 8002 Silverado Canyon Road in Silverado Canyon. In 1879 August Witter also discovered coal, this time in the Cañon de los Indios (Canyon of the Indians) to the north. His mine was named the Black Star, and the canyon, a branch of Santiago Canyon, was soon known by the same name as the mine. Black Star Canyon was the scene of a battle between William Wolfskill and other trappers and a band of Indian horse thieves in the early 1830's. The site of the Indian village (SRL 217) is marked by mounds and grinding rocks. It is 6.2 miles up Black Star Canyon Road from the intersection of this road with Silverado Canyon and Santiago Canyon roads.

Rugged Santiago Canyon was chosen by the famous Polish tragedienne Helena Modjeska as the home to which she retired after a long dramatic career that took her all over the world. She had first come to California in 1876 as a member of a small and short-lived Polish colony that attempted to establish itself at Anaheim; another member was Henryk Sienkiewicz, whose novel *Quo Vadis* was a best-seller in the 1890's. After the colony disbanded, Madame Modjeska returned to the stage for a few years. In 1883 she bought the canyon property from Joseph Edward Pleasants and named it "Forest of Arden." About four years later she began construction of a large and beautiful home, under the direction of the famed architect Stanford White. Madame Modjeska sold her property in 1906, three years before her death. The home (SRL 205) is located near highway S-18 and the boundary of the Cleveland National Forest. Privately owned, it is entirely hidden by the forest, and the estate is heavily fenced against intruders. A historical marker is located on the public road nearby.

Across the creek from Modjeska's home is Flores Peak (SRL 225), scene of the capture of a group of bandits in January 1857 by a posse led by General Andrés Pico. Juan Flores, leader of the gang, escaped but was later captured by Pico. Pico's posse was organized after the killing of Sheriff James Barton of Los Angeles by the Flores gang. Flores had escaped from San Quentin Prison earlier in the month. The sheriff's posse encountered the outlaws at what became known as Barton Mound (SRL 218), and there Barton and three others met their deaths. The mound was leveled in the construction of the I-405 freeway, but the marker identifying the site may be found at the end of Sand Canyon Avenue near the junction of the freeway and SR 133 in East Irvine. The East Irvine Historic Area along Sand Canyon Avenue contains several buildings from the early twentieth century that are being preserved.

Placer County

Placer County was organized in 1851 from parts of Sutter and Yuba counties. Auburn was made the county seat. The name Placer is an old Spanish word, the origin of which is obscure, that came to be applied in Spanish countries to surface mining. At the time the name was adopted for the county, placer mining was the principal method employed there, and the placers of the region were among the richest in the state.

Lake Tahoe

Lake Tahoe, located partly in Placer and El Dorado counties and partly in the state of Nevada, lies 6,229 feet above the sea. It is remarkable for its great depth, which, together with its variable bottom, seems to account for the rare and exquisite color of its waters. The exact meaning of the old Indian name Tahoe, sometimes interpreted in poetic phraseology as "Big Water" and considered by modern Indians of the region to mean "deep" and "blue," remains undetermined. The lake has also been known by other names for short periods.

Passing through Alpine County on his way to California in 1844, John C. Frémont climbed the ridge to the vicinity of Carson Pass. From his encampment under the shadow of the Sierra he explored, with Charles Preuss, one of the highest peaks in the area, probably Red Lake Peak. From its lofty summit on February 14, 1844, Frémont and his companion gained the first view of Lake Tahoe ever enjoyed by white men. In his narrative of the expedition Frémont called the newly discovered sheet of water simply the "mountain lake," but on his later map of the expedition he named it Lake Bonpland. Of this circumstance he writes: "I gave to the basin river its name of Humboldt and to the mountain lake the name of his companion traveler, Bonpland [the noted French botanist], and so put it in the map of the expedition."

Frémont's name for the exquisite body of water he had discovered has been practically forgotten. The official mapmaker of the state of California gave to it in 1853 the name of Lake Bigler, after John Bigler, the third governor of California, and people undoubtedly used this official designation for some years. An attempt to change the name to the fanciful Tula Tulia was made in 1861. A successful attempt to find a more appropriate name for this beautiful lake was made in 1862 through the efforts of William Henry Knight.

Knight had come overland to California from Missouri in 1859, and it was on this journey that he had his first view of Lake Tahoe, "from a projecting cliff 1,000 feet above its surface." The scene, wrote Knight, "embraced not only the entire outline of the Lake with its charming bays and rocky headlands but also the magnificent forest of giant pines and firs in which it was embosomed, and the dozen or more lofty mountain peaks thrusting their white summits into the sky at altitudes varying from 8,000 to 11,000 feet above sea level. No imagination can conceive the beauty, sublimity and inspiration of that scene, especially to one who had for weary months been traversing dusty, treeless, and barren plains. The contrast was overwhelming."

In 1861 Knight gathered data for compiling the first general map of the Pacific states, and in 1862 this map was published by the Bancroft Publishing House in San Francisco. On it the name of Lake Bigler had been changed to Lake Tahoe. Knight, who deliberately omitted the name of Bigler, urged John S. Hittell and Dr. Henry De Groot to support him in a change of names. At his request, also, Dr. De Groot had suggested "Tahoe," the Indian name for the lake, as a fit substitute. De Groot had heard the name for the first time in 1859 while on an exploring trip. Knight at once obtained the approval of the Land Office at Washington, D.C., and the new name appeared on all subsequent maps and in printed matter issued from the Department of the Interior. The California state legislature, oblivious to the popular acceptance of the name Tahoe, inexplicably legalized "Bigler" in 1870, and this act was not repealed until 1945.

Very early there were those who sensed the possibilities of the Lake Tahoe region as a pleasure and health resort. With increasing frequency pioneer vacationists from Nevada and elsewhere were lured to the place by the beauty of the lake as well as by its fishing and hunting facilities. The earliest permanent settlements on the lakeshore were those at the mouth of McKinney Creek, at Ward Creek, at Tahoe City (all in Placer County), and at Glenbrook (in Nevada). In the summer of 1862 William Ferguson and Ward Rust built a cabin on the lake at the mouth of Ward Creek. Two other men, John W. McKinney and Thomas Wren, had located a hay ranch on the summit near the county line in 1861, and in 1862 McKinney moved down from his ranch and settled on the shore of Lake Tahoe near the creek that bears his name. There he established a hunting and fishing resort known as Hunter's Retreat. When the place was later acquired by David Chambers its name became Chambers Lodge.

The first survey for Tahoe City was made in 1863, and the Tahoe House was erected by William Pomin the following year. While the nature lover and the tourist contributed to the early prosperity of Tahoe City, the town at first was essentially a lumbering center. After the completion of the Central Pacific Railroad as far as Truckee, a wagon road was constructed from that point to the lake. To accommodate the new influx of visitors, A. J. Bayley built his celebrated Grand Central Hotel at Tahoe City.

While Lake Tahoe receives the flow from over two dozen creeks and streams, its only outlet is the Truckee River. The outlet gates at Tahoe City (SRL 797) were first constructed in 1870; the present ones date from 1913. The gatekeeper's cabin nearby is a replica, built in 1981, of the earlier structure built in 1931 and destroyed by fire in 1978. It is now the museum of the North Lake Tahoe Historical Society and has an extensive collection of historic photographs of the lake. A monument nearby at the Truckee River Bridge on SR 89 commemorates the work of Dr. James E. Church, Jr., who in 1910–11 made possible the accurate prediction and control of seasonal rise in the lake and river levels, thus ending a long dispute between lakeshore owners and downstream Truckee River water users over control of the gates.

· After the decline of the lumber industry, the fame of Lake Tahoe as a summer resort increased. Now it is an all-year playground with an impressive permanent population; many believe, however, that much of its beauty has been spoiled by commercialization and the ever-present noise of speedboats in the summer. Winter sports at nearby Squaw Valley and other resorts draw many visitors during the snowy months. At Squaw

Outlet Gates from Lake Tahoe to the Truckee River, Tahoe City

Valley (SRL 724), the VIII Olympic Winter Games of 1960 commemorated a century of sport skiing in California. The first organized ski clubs and competition in the Western Hemisphere were held in Sierra towns around 1860, mostly in Plumas County to the north. The first ski jump in the area was constructed at Granlibakken, about a mile south of Tahoe City, in 1931. The real boom in skiing, however, came after World War II.

Emigrant Gap and the Old Emigrant Trail

Emigrant Gap, an old lumbering camp and a station on the Central Pacific Railroad, established in the late 1860's, derives its name from a low opening in the mountains at the head of Bear River. A branch of the old California emigrant trail went down into Bear Valley by way of this pass, a region of wild and magnificent scenery.

West of the turnoff to the settlement of Emigrant Gap, a monument at a viewpoint adjacent to the westbound lanes of I-80 commemorates Emigrant Gap (SRL 403), where the covered wagons were lowered over the precipitous cliff to the floor of Bear Valley by means of rope and tackle held by iron spikes driven into the solid rock. It was first used by wagons in the spring of 1845 and continued as a part of the emigrant trail during and after the gold rush.

The early California emigrant trail over Donner Pass skirted the present boundary line between Placer and Nevada counties, following mainly along the Nevada County side. The easier route out of the mountains led north of the Bear River, since the narrow divide between that stream and the North Fork of the American River offered no roadway without improvements, which the emigrants were unable to make.

The Dutch Flat–Donner Lake Road

It was not until the building of the Central Pacific Railroad up the divide between the Bear River and the North Fork of the American River in 1864–66 that a wagon road was constructed along its entire length. In 1849 the head of "wagon navigation" up this ridge was at Illinoistown, and within a few years vehicles had reached as far as Dutch Flat. By 1860, after the discovery of the rich Comstock Lode in Nevada, a great demand had developed for adequate means of transportation over the mountains, and the people of Placer County became anxious to have this very profitable traffic diverted their way. Several attempts made by groups of local citizens to build roads met with failure. Finally, in the fall of 1861, the "Big Four" and others who were building the Central Pacific Railroad over the mountains organized the Dutch Flat and Donner Lake

Wagon Road Company, their purpose being to attract as much of the Nevada traffic as possible. This road was completed in June 1864.

By June 1865 the railroad had been constructed as far as Clipper Gap, and in July the California Stage Company began running coaches from that point to Virginia City, Nevada. As the railroad progressed up the ridge, stations were placed at various points, while the stages and forwarding houses moved on simultaneously, making connections at each terminus. Thus the railroad company forced the stages and freight wagons over its own road. By the time Colfax had become the terminus, in September 1865, the Central Pacific had acquired the greater part of the passenger and freight business between Nevada and California, most of which, up to that time, had gone largely to the Placerville Road in El Dorado County.

Sicard's Ranch

The first settlement in Placer County was Sicard's Ranch, a Mexican grant on the south bank of the Bear River. This grant was given to Theodore Sicard, a French sailor, in 1844, and here in 1845 he built an adobe house about one-half mile above Johnson's Crossing.

Being located on the overland emigrant trail that crossed the valley via Sinclair's Ranch to Sutter's Fort, Sicard's Ranch became of some importance as a stopping place. A fellow countryman of Sicard, Claude Chana (also spelled Chané), arrived at the ranch in October 1846. That same fall, Chana and Sicard planted a few pits of dried peaches brought by an emigrant family and some almonds that Chana himself had; from this beginning came the pioneer commercial orchard of the Sacramento Valley. Chana was also the discoverer of gold in Placer County. After mining at Auburn Ravine, where the discovery was made, and later on the Yuba River, he purchased the Sicard Grant and sold the products of his orchard, vegetable garden, and vineyard to the miners at great profit. The site of Claude Chana's pioneer orchard now lies beneath the debris brought down by the Bear River from the hydraulic diggings in the foothills.

Johnson's Crossing, on the Bear River about three miles east of Wheatland, received a post office in 1853, and for some years it was a lively settlement, being a stopping place for emigrants, as well as for many of the teams engaged in hauling freight from Sacramento to the northern mining camps. The great flood of 1862 nearly destroyed the place, but the real cause of its final desertion was the later avalanche of debris that poured down upon it from the hydraulic mines higher up the river.

Rogers's "Shed," a Crossroads Station

About a half a mile south of present Sheridan stood a very busy crossroads station during the days of the stagecoaches and freighters. It was situated on the Sacramento-Nevada road at a point where four other roads diverged: one running west to Nicolaus in Sutter County (13 miles), one running northwest to Marysville (15 miles) via Kempton's Crossing, a third going northeast toward Grass Valley (28 miles) via McCourtney's Crossing, and a fourth following east to Auburn (20 miles) via Danetown. At this location in 1857 a man named E. C. Rogers built a one-story house with a 150-foot shed in front. The "Shed"—"Union Shed," as it was called—soon became a place of importance. Here the long freight teams that thronged the roads received shelter from the heat in summer and the rain in winter, and here the farmers of the surrounding country brought hay and grain to supply the teams.

The bustling activity about the Shed did not last long, for the building of the California Central Railroad northward from Folsom did away with staging and teaming up and down the valley. In 1861 the railroad had been built as far as Lincoln, named for one of the promoters of the railroad, Charles Lincoln Wilson. From 1861 to 1866 Lincoln was a thriving stage and freight center; but when the terminus of the railroad was changed to Wheatland in 1866, the stage and teaming business was transferred also, and both Lincoln and Rogers's Shed lost their importance as stage centers. In 1868 the Shed, with all its buildings, was consumed by fire.

Manzanita Grove, situated on a wooded knoll in the middle of broad, open fields halfway between Lincoln and Sheridan and east of the highway between them, gained notoriety in early days as a stronghold for thieves. Here, hidden in the center of a thick growth of trees, was a corral where the bandits kept their stolen stock. The robbers were eventually cleared out, and by 1855 the grove had been made the cemetery for the countryside. Today there are only a few of the low-growing manzanitas left among the native oaks, which cast their shadows over the graves of the pioneers buried at this spot. The place has a tranquil beauty that is memorable. Manzanita Grove Cemetery is reached over Wise Road, which turns to the right from SR 65 about four miles north of Lincoln. Wise Road joins the Manzanita Cemetery Road in less than two miles, and from this point it is one mile to the left to the cemetery.

River Bars

Placer County, embracing several branches of the American River besides Bear River, included scores of river-bar camps. Beal's Bar was the first camp above the confluence of the North and South forks of the river. As late as 1853 it polled 96 votes and was an active center of trade for nearby mines. When the old bar immediately upon the river was worked out, the town was moved to a high bench adjoining, and the former site was dug out and its gravel washed for gold.

In this vicinity John Sinclair and some 50 Indian laborers, in the spring and summer of 1848, were among the first to mine on the North Fork of the American River. Governor Richard B. Mason, in his report to Washington in 1848, says: "He [Sinclair] had been engaged about five weeks when I saw him, and up to that time his Indians had used simply closely-woven willow baskets. His net proceeds . . . were about $16,000 worth of gold."

Beal's Bar is now under Folsom Lake, but a marker near Beals Point in Folsom Lake State Park recalls the old express trail (SRL 585) of 1849–54 that led to this and other camps. The Auburn-Folsom Road now parallels this route. Folsom Lake also covers the site of a number of settlements along the North Fork of the American River, chief among them Horseshoe Bar, Smith's Bar, and Rattlesnake Bar. Above the confluence of the North and Middle forks of the river along the North Fork, old sites were washed away or buried by the mass of debris washed down by the hydraulic mines of Gold Run and other places. A number of camps with a marvelous variety of names were located along the Middle Fork: Sailor Claim, Buckner's, Rocky Point Slide, Mammoth, Texas, Quail, Brown's, Kennebec, Buckeye, American, Sardine, Yankee, Dutch, African, Drunkard's, Horseshoe Number Two, and Stony bars among them. Humbug Bar was located in Humbug Canyon, a tributary of the South Branch of the North Fork of the American River. The canyon, first known as Mississippi Canyon, was rechristened Humbug early in 1850 when a group of miners became disgusted with their luck at this place. Later these same prospectors returned with others and struck it rich, proving it to be no "humbug" after all.

Auburn

Early in 1849, Auburn (SRL 404) was known as Woods Dry Diggings. It was one of the earliest mining camps in California, gold having been first discovered there in Auburn Ravine in May 1848 by Claude Chana and a party of Indians en route to Coloma from Sicard's Ranch on the Bear River. A statue in downtown Auburn commemorates Chana's discovery. Chana was soon followed by Nicolaus Allgeier, who had come up from his ranch in Sutter County with his Indian retainers.

Hordes of prospectors and adventurers began to pour in by 1849 and camps sprang up everywhere. According to some authorities, Woods Dry Diggings was called for a time North Fork Dry Diggings. A large group of the miners in the vicinity had come to California in 1846 in Stevenson's Volunteer Regiment from Auburn, New York. It is thought that they changed the name of North Fork Dry Diggings to Auburn in the summer of 1849. Records show that the early diggings here were very rich. During the peak of productiveness it was not unusual for a man to take out $1,000 to $1,500 a day. There is one instance of four cartloads of earth yielding as much as $16,000.

Auburn became the county seat of Sutter County in the spring of 1850. Its favorable location, as well as, in the ironic words of one observer, "its preponderance of population, and the inexhaustible powers of voting possessed by its citizens and partisans, decided the contest in its favor by a majority considerably exceeding the entire population of the county." On April 25, 1851, when Placer County was created from a portion of Sutter County, Auburn was made the seat of justice of the new county. The city was incorporated in 1860, disincorporated about 1866, and reincorporated in 1888. During the 1860's and 1870's, Auburn became quite a cultural and social center, having a private normal school and college and enjoying a reputation as a health resort, the pure air of the lower Sierra being both mild and invigorating.

Devastating fires swept many of the mining camps several times during the early years of their history. After Auburn's first experience, its citizens determined to rebuild the town with more substantial material. In the older section of town, adjacent to I-80, there are a number of solid brick structures dating from the 1850's and 1860's, with the heavy iron doors and iron-shuttered windows common to that period. As one writer has said: "The Auburn of today is a city of contrasts. Entering it from the south, one descries a narrow street, flanked by old brick buildings, and overlooked by the high bell tower of a fire station. A half-mile beyond, upon the summit of a hill, is the modern portion of the community with up-to-date establishments and public buildings. It is plain to see that Auburn, like the chambered nautilus, outgrew the site upon which it was first located. But the shell that it left behind is still a part of its metropolitan area."

A distinctive sight in Old Auburn is the three-story Auburn Hook and Ladder Company Fire House Number Two, built in 1893 for the company that was organized in 1852 and claims to be "the oldest volunteer Fire Department this side of Boston." The bell on the third floor is much older than the structure now housing it, and by custom it tolls the time of day at 8:00 A.M., noon, and 5:00 P.M. Nearby on "Main Street Island" is

Auburn Hook and Ladder Company Fire House Number Two, Auburn

a cluster of buildings that escaped early fires, including Station A of the Auburn Post Office, once occupying a larger corner of the property. Dating from 1852, it is California's oldest operating post office. Three wooden buildings on Sacramento Street also date from 1852 and are collectively called the Chinese Merchants Section, a reminder of the lively commercial life of Auburn's Chinese pioneers. The Empire Livery Stable on Washington Street was built in 1864.

Dominating the skyline and overlooking the old part of town is the imposing Placer County courthouse, built in 1894. It is said that the building is made of bricks and lime from Auburn, marble from Colfax, granite from Rocklin, and slate from Slatington, all Placer County towns.

The Placer County Museum is located at the Gold Country Fairgrounds at 1273 High Street. Within the Historic Museum Complex are to be found the Bernhard Residence, originally constructed as the Travelers' Rest in 1851, and the Bernhard Winery, built in 1874.

Auburn, a Turnpike Center

Auburn has always been the center of extensive staging and freighting operations. In its early days a network of trails radiated from it to the numerous camps springing up in all directions, and over these trails min-

ers' supplies were carried by pack-mule trains. During the 1850's and 1860's most of these rough and narrow trails were gradually superseded by toll roads scarcely less rude and precarious, over which daring "knights of the whip" drove the old stagecoaches at reckless speed or piloted the swaying, creaking freight wagons, aided by the uncanny intelligence of from six to ten horses or mules.

Even after the building of the Central Pacific Railroad up the ridge, the staging and freighting business continued over the many roads reaching out from Auburn. The first passenger train arrived in Auburn on May 13, 1865, an event commemorated by a marker (SRL 780.4) at the Southern Pacific Depot. The advent of the railroad created a demand for additional wagon traffic into Nevada County, and, in 1866, brought about the opening of a new and more direct stage route into El Dorado County, via Lyon's Bridge, where SR 49 now crosses the river. Today, buses and trucks still carry their quota of passengers, mail, and freight over the old mountain roads, most of them improved or reconstructed into modern highways leading to and from Auburn.

There were five main wagon roads centering in Auburn, while many laterals led out from these to all parts of Placer County. The highway from Sacramento up the ridge to Illinoistown went through Auburn, and a branch of this road was one of the main routes to Grass Valley and Nevada City, crossing the Bear River at a place later known as English Bridge and then as Gautier Bridge, ten miles north of Auburn on SR 49. A third road extended northeast to mining camps along the Forest Hill ridge, passing down Auburn Ravine to Ophir and Virginiatown. Still another ran south along the ridge above the American River to Folsom and Sacramento, and connected with roads coming from El Dorado County. On this road six and a half miles south of Auburn stood the Mountaineer House, on the site of which the stone mansion of J. J. Brennan was built, over the foundations of the old stage station. Four miles beyond is the site of the Franklin House, another stage station. Near the Brennan ranch was Auburn Station, the final terminus of California's first passenger railroad, the Sacramento Valley, originally built from Sacramento to Folsom in 1855–56. It was to be extended to Auburn, but the Central Pacific arrived first, and so the Sacramento Valley Railroad was discontinued. Auburn disincorporated to keep from paying the bonds on the railroad that never reached it.

Stupendous difficulties were encountered in transforming devious, threadlike pack trails into roads. The turnpike from Auburn to Forest Hill furnishes an excellent example of the problems met by the builders of these old "High Ways." Leading down into the canyon of the North Fork of the American River where the traveler crossed the stream by means of a crude ferry, the Auburn–Forest Hill trail climbed another steep and meandering path up the opposite canyon wall. Only by a great expenditure of money and labor could the obstacles presented by these mighty canyons be surmounted. Since the county government was unable to raise sufficient funds for the enterprise, the work was taken up by private turnpike companies, the new routes of travel thus becoming toll roads.

The grade of the North Fork Hill Road, as it was called, was improved in 1855 at a cost of $12,000, and in the early 1860's an additional sum of $50,000 was expended upon it. Over a distance of more than 20 miles from Auburn to Yankee Jim's—winding up the deep gorge of the North Fork or clinging to the sides of a mountain far above the stream—this road was carved out of the canyon walls only through herculean effort.

Over this old highland thoroughfare, a continuous stream of life from Auburn poured into the mining camps along the Forest Hill Divide, passing a number of stations and roadhouses along the way, among them the Junction House two and a half miles from Auburn, the Grizzly Bear House, Butcher's Ranch, Sheridan's, Mile Hill Toll House, and Spring Garden.

Auburn Ravine

Extending west from Auburn, down what was once the old Auburn Ravine turnpike, are a number of historic sites reminiscent of early mining activities. Ophir (SRL 463), three miles west of Auburn and north of I-80, was first known as Spanish Corral. Like the biblical Land of Ophir whence came the gold to adorn the temple of Solomon, the region about Spanish Corral was found to be fabulously rich, and the name of the

Adobe, Virginiatown

settlement was changed to Ophir. In 1852 it was, briefly, the most populous community in the county. Today the district about Ophir numbers two or three hundred inhabitants. Orchards and vineyards abound in the surrounding hills, which are scarred with diggings, old pits and dumps, and the foundations of abandoned stamp mills. The Paramount Mine, two miles from Ophir, was once a major producer.

Two miles west of Ophir was Frytown, which had a brief but lively history after it was established in 1849. Gold Hill, four miles west of Ophir, was organized as a town in April 1852; later that year 444 votes were cast in the presidential election. The rich surface diggings of this period were later replaced by fine orchards and vineyards, which continue to flourish today. The little town now consists of newer homes. Only a small cemetery remains from earlier days.

Two miles west of Gold Hill is Virginiatown (SRL 400), a typical ghost town. The protected shell of an adobe building stands where Virginiatown Road and Fowler Road meet. In 1852 Captain John Brislow built California's first railroad here to carry pay dirt one mile, to Auburn Ravine. Virginiatown was the site of Philip Armour and George Aldrich's butcher shop, said to have led to the founding of the famous Armour meat-packing company in Chicago. In decline for many years, the region is today full of attractive modern homes.

Secret Ravine (Newcastle, Penryn, Loomis)

Secret Ravine, extending southwest from Auburn, was the scene of extensive placer mining operations during the 1850's and 1860's and of granite quarrying in the 1870's and 1880's. Commercial orchards were planted up and down the ridges as early as 1870, and these continue to be a chief source of income in the region today. Old mining camps that flourished in the ravine during the gold rush days were soon superseded after the coming of the railroad by other towns built along the ridge.

Newcastle, at the head of Secret Ravine, is the only one of the old 1850 mining camps that thrives today, being a fruit-shipping center on the railroad. The arrival of the first transcontinental railroad at Newcastle on January 10, 1864, is commemorated by a marker (SRL 780.3) at the Southern Pacific Depot. Construction halted on the railroad until April 1865, when it pushed on to Auburn.

Penryn (or Penrhyn, after its patronym in Wales) was established and named in 1864 by Griffith Griffith, a Welshman, whose extensive granite quarries for a number of years supplied the building material for

Griffith Buildng, Penryn

United States. The marker at Rocklin (SRL 780.2) is on Taylor Street, where a small museum of railroad history is displayed in old railroad cars.

Gold Run

The Gold Run region, 25 miles northeast of Auburn, on the ridge south of Dutch Flat between Bear River and the North Fork of the American River, is a good example of early hydraulic mining. A vast bed of auriferous blue gravel two miles long, half a mile wide, and 250 feet deep, with pay dirt all the way down, it yielded immense profit until the early 1880's. O. W. Hollenbeck came to the region in 1854 and mined at a place called Mountain Springs. In 1859 hydraulic mining was begun on the Gold Run claim. In 1862 Hollenbeck laid out a town on Cold Spring Mountain, calling it Mountain Springs. A post office had been established in 1854 under that name, but the name was changed to Gold Run in 1863. The place developed into a mining center long after the other towns of the county and flourished during the 1860's and 1870's. Squire's Canyon, Canyon Creek, Goosling Ravine, Gold Run Canyon, Potato Ravine, and Indiana Canyon all had productive hydraulic mines. After 1884, when the courts outlawed hydraulic mining, the town became almost deserted.

The original town of Gold Run (SRL 405) is near I-80 south of the present Gold Run railway station. The old Union Church built by the miners has been preserved. Deep ravines and high cliffs in the canyon below present striking evidence of the hydraulic forces that once operated there. It is estimated that the total production of the Gold Run mines reached $15 million.

Dutch Flat

Dutch Flat (SRL 397) is unique among the old camps of Placer County. Its main street, lined by huge poplar and locust trees, climbs abruptly from the hollow where the town had its beginning, to a narrow, sloping terrace, on which perches the settlement of later growth, and on up past summer and retirement homes.

Thousands of miners worked the ridges and hills about Dutch Flat, until the entire region was deeply torn by hydraulic operations. Aside from its prominence as a mining center, Dutch Flat was a stage station, making it one of the largest and most important towns of the county around 1865.

The town was first settled by a group of Germans, among them Joseph and Charles Dornbach. The name "Dutch" may have been derived from the nationality of these first settlers (German *Deutsch*), but one looks in

many structures in San Francisco, Stockton, and elsewhere. The quarry (SRL 885) is just off I-80 at the Penryn turnoff. A small museum, stoutly built of granite, is on the edge of Griffith Quarry Park, at the junction of Taylor and Rock Springs roads. A two-story building of hewn granite blocks, erected in Penryn by Griffith in 1878, is still standing in excellent condition. David Griffith succeeded his uncle in 1889 and operated a much smaller granite works until his death in 1918.

About two and a half miles southwest of Penryn is Loomis, the successor of Pino. Pino took its name from the old mining camp of Pine Grove, which was established in Secret Ravine about a mile and a half from the site of Loomis, before the coming of the railroad.

Roseville and Rocklin

The track of the Central Pacific Railroad reached Junction, now Roseville, on April 25, 1864, and Rocklin, four miles east, the following month. At Roseville a marker (SRL 780.1) has been placed at the Southern Pacific depot. Since the railroad moved its roundhouse from Rocklin to Roseville in 1908, the latter has been a major railroad center, one of the largest in the western vain for the "Flat." In 1856 the town was granted a post office under its present designation.

Past the town runs the old road, which from 1864 to 1866 was a much-traveled turnpike; over it the well-braced Concord coaches ran to the rich Washoe silver mines of Nevada, one branch going by way of Bear Valley, Bowman Lake, and Henness Pass, and the other via Donner Lake. The latter route, known as the Dutch Flat–Donner Lake Road, was built by the men who were at that time constructing the Central Pacific Railroad. The names of Governor Leland Stanford, Dr. D. W. Strong, and other promoters of the railway thus became linked with the history of this toll road and with the town. Strong, a resident of Dutch Flat, was the only one of the nine promoters of the railway who lived outside Sacramento. It was he who from the beginning advocated the advantage of the Dutch Flat–Donner Pass route for the railway even when others doubted its feasibility. In the fall of 1866, after the railway had reached Cisco about twenty miles farther up the ridge, Dutch Flat lost much of its importance as a stage center.

During the 1870's hydraulic mining operations at Dutch Flat reached their height. In 1872, the Cedar Creek Company of London purchased as many as 32 claims and worked them on a gigantic scale. Millions in gold were taken from the extensive placers of Dutch Flat, one nugget alone being worth more than $5,000. It is estimated that $30 million more remains in this gravelly ridge.

Every old building in the block that forms the business section of Dutch Flat has a history. The old two-story hotel, built in 1852, now stands vacant. The I.O.O.F. Building, erected in 1858, is still in use, as is the stone store built in 1854. The Masonic Hall dates from 1856, and the Methodist Episcopal Church from 1859–61. Adjoining the American cemetery just above the town is the Chinese burial ground, half-hidden among the pines. Most of the bodies have been removed from the graves and taken back to China. The old site of Chinatown, with a population of 1,000, was on the railroad one mile above Dutch Flat.

Colfax and Illinoistown

Colfax, named after Vice President Schuyler Colfax (1869–73), is a small town about fifteen miles northeast of Auburn in the center of a once prosperous mining region. The Central Pacific Railroad from Sacramento reached as far as Colfax when the first train arrived on September 1, 1865, an event commemorated by a plaque (SRL 780.5) on Main Street. Today the town, located on both the railroad and I-80, is an important shipping point for lumber and fruit.

Across the railroad southeast of Colfax, and now completely absorbed by it, is the site of Illinoistown, first settled early in 1849 under the name of Alder Grove. That year the town became the distributing point for supplies to neighboring camps, and it quickly assumed an importance as a business and trading center second only to that of Auburn.

Goods brought in wagons to Illinoistown were there loaded on pack mules and carried to remote camps over steep and winding mountain trails, later widened into toll roads. One of the most interesting of these old roads is the one that leads from Illinoistown to Iowa Hill and was known as the Mineral Bar Bridge and Road. The cost of constructing the seven miles entering and leaving the canyon of the North Fork of the American River, which, at this point, is 1,500 feet deep, was $75,000. The scenery is magnificent—steep mountainsides threatening to precipitate the traveler into the abyss, where, far below, the sparkling river can be seen with the canyon walls towering over it.

Iowa Hill

The site of the little old town of Iowa Hill (SRL 401) is on the narrow neck of a high ridge between the North Fork of the American River on the north and Indian Canyon on the south. Gold was first discovered there in 1853, and in 1856 the weekly product was estimated at $100,000. The rich lode of the Blue Lead Channel running under the town has been all drifted out, while later hydraulic operations on either side of the town have all but washed the site away. The total gold production up to 1880 has been estimated at $20 million.

Like most of the early mining camps, Iowa Hill had its baptism of fire. In 1857 a conflagration swept away all of the buildings "from Temperance Hall to McCall & Company's Brewery," as an old news item puts it. The last serious fire occurred in 1922, destroying many of the remaining houses in this much-stricken place.

Numerous camps flourished within a radius of five miles of Iowa Hill during the 1850's and 1860's. Independence Hill, Roach Hill, Bird's Flat, Stephen's Hill, Elizabethtown, Wisconsin Hill, Grizzly Flat at the head of Grizzly Canyon, Monona Flat, and Succor Flat—each lived its little day of colorful, polyglot life, only to become again a part of the enveloping wilderness after a few short years. Hundreds of tunnels honeycomb the mountains about these old campsites, constituting tangible evidence of the few extremely profitable claims that were once worked there: the Jamison, the pioneer of the district, producing $500,000; the North Star, $400,000; the Sailor Union, $300,000; and the Iowa Hill, $250,000.

Elizabethtown, on the south side of Indian Canyon from Iowa Hill, was the most important camp north of Shirt-tail Canyon and south of the North Fork in the early 1850's. Wisconsin Hill, separated from Elizabethtown by a deep ravine, was first settled in 1854 and soon had a population of 700, but after 1856 the miners began to scatter. With the completion of a turnpike across Indian Canyon from Iowa Hill and another across Shirt-tail Canyon from Yankee Jim's, the hopes of Wisconsin Hill's businessmen temporarily revived. But instead of bringing more people in, the road furnished the remaining inhabitants with an easy method of transportation to more favored localities.

Forest Hill

Forest Hill (SRL 399), a mining and lumbering camp of some importance in the 1850's and 1860's, was located in a region reported by J. Ross Browne in 1868 as "the most productive cement tunnel-mining district in the state." Situated at an elevation of 3,400 feet, on the summit of the Forest Hill Divide between the Middle Fork of the American River and Shirt-tail Canyon, the town is 2,500 feet above the river. Thousands of acres of virgin pine forests surround it, and the canyon scenery is superb. The auriferous gravel of the Forest Hill Diggings is a part of the Blue Lead Channel, and the early claims, limited to 50 feet each, extended along the side of the hill. The tunnels penetrated the mountain to a distance of from 200 to 5,000 feet.

Early in the spring of 1850 a great rush of miners came to the Forest Hill Divide, lured by the news of rich diggings uncovered there. Coming from the south via Coloma and Greenwood Valley and from the west by way of Auburn, the two groups met about three miles northeast of Todd's store at a place that later became Forest Hill. The brush shanty set up at the latter site as a trading post in 1850 was replaced about 1858 by a substantial house and hotel. The Forest House, as it was known, became the nucleus of an important center of trade and of travel to and from the numerous camps in all directions. The historic hostelry was destroyed by fire on Christmas Day, 1918, with the turkey dinner in the oven. Another hotel replaced it and bears the same name.

The height of activity began early in 1853, after the winter storms had brought down a great mass of loose gravel at the head of Jenny Lind Canyon, exposing many glistening chunks of gold. The Jenny Lind Mine alone later yielded $2,000 or $2,500 daily, the total yield reaching approximately $1,100,000 by 1880. The aggregate production of all the miners in the immediate vicinity of Forest Hill or within rifle shot of the express office was estimated at $10,000,000 up to 1868. Rich mines in the region were the Dardanelles, New Jersey, Independence, Deidesheimer, Fast and Nortwood, Rough and Ready, Gore, and Alabama.

Forest Hill had already assumed a metropolitan air in the late 1850's, boasting a newspaper, fireproof hotels and stores, banks and elegant saloons, and neat homes surrounded by gardens and orchards. It was still one of the larger towns of Placer County in 1880, numbering about 700 inhabitants at that date. The population later dwindled to about 400, but now the place is once again beginning to prosper. Many of the buildings along the broad main street are new, but two old brick stores with iron shutters are still open for business. The old church burned in 1952, but its bell has been preserved. An exceptionally clear, sweet-toned bell brought around the Horn from Boston, it could be heard at times, it is said, twenty miles away through the forest. The Forest Hill Historical Museum on Main Street has displays on local history and artifacts from the Red Point Mine.

Yankee Jim's and Shirt-tail Canyon

A road from Forest Hill leads northwest three miles to Yankee Jim's (SRL 398), high up on the same ridge between the North and Middle forks of the American River. A number of old weathered houses at Yankee Jim's are still standing, reminders of the days when it was one of the largest mining camps in Placer County. Extensive diggings lie on its outskirts.

The origin of the name Yankee Jim's is one of those riddles often encountered in the mining regions. Some hold that the person from whom the camp derived its title was, indeed, a Yankee, but others say he was an Irishman or even an Australian. In any case, Yankee Jim appears to have been somewhat given to banditry, and when not stealing horses did some mining along the river bars of the North Fork. He sought to keep his discoveries a secret, but rumors spread quickly, and by 1850 miners swarmed over the entire ridge country. At the place of Yankee Jim's activities a town sprang up, was named for him, and became famous as a rich mining center.

Nearby is Shirt-tail Canyon, along with its several branches—Brimstone Canyon, Brushy Canyon, Grizzly Canyon, Refuge Canyon, and Devil's Canyon—the scene of extensive gold excitement during the 1850's. The stream bed in each of these canyons was worked and numerous tunnels were dug into the rocky walls above.

The following story is told of how Shirt-tail Canyon got its name. "Early in the summer of 1849 two men, one named Tuttle, formerly from the state of Connecticut, and the other Van Zandt, from Oregon, were prospecting upon Brushy Canyon and in that locality, and at the time supposed there was no one nearer to them than the people who were at work along the river bars. From Brushy they emerged into the valley of the larger stream into which it emptied. It was sultry and hot, and no sound but their own suppressed voices broke the silence of the gorge. A bend in the creek a short distance below them obstructed the view, and they walked down the stream to overcome it. Abruptly turning the point, they were astonished to see before them, but a little way off, a solitary individual—whether white or red they could not at first determine—engaged in primitive mining operations, with crevicing spoon, and sheath-knife and pan. The apparition was perfectly nude, with the exception of a shirt, and that was not overly lengthy. The lone miner was in the edge of the water, and, happening to look up, saw the two men who had intruded upon his domain, at about the same time that they discovered him. Had this not been so . . . they . . . would have stepped back, made some noise, and given the man a chance to don his overalls. As it was, the eyes of both parties met, and an involuntary 'Hello' came from all three mouths. 'What in the devil's name do you call this place?' queried one of the intruders of the *sans culottes*, who proved to be an American. He glanced at his bare legs, and from them to his questioners, took in at a moment the ludicrous appearance he made, and laughingly answered: 'Don't know any name for it yet, but we might as well call it Shirttail as anything else.'"

Michigan Bluff

Looking over into El Dorado County to the south, Michigan Bluff (SRL 402), seven miles east of Forest Hill, clings to the steep slope of the Forest Hill Divide from 1,500 to 2,000 feet above the yawning gorges of the Middle Fork and the North Fork of the Middle Fork of the American River and El Dorado Canyon. Behind it Sugar Loaf towers 250 feet or more above the main street of the settlement, which sits directly at its southern base. The first town, commonly known as Michigan City, was located about half a mile below the present site, on the stretch of comparatively level ground once existing there and later mined out. Scars of hydraulic operations may be seen all up and down the mountainside. Only an old well remains at Michigan City.

The first settlement on this ridge was made one mile to the west at Bird's Valley, where a party of sailors located in the summer of 1848. Later, these men reported at Sutter's Fort the rich diggings that they had worked at Rector's Bar and other places below their camp. A second company, under the leadership of J. D. Hoppe, came up from Sutter's Fort the same fall. Following the trail made by the sailors up the mountainside, they too set up camp in Bird's Valley, crevassing for gold along the rivers in the canyons below. Seeking the precious metal only upon and in the crevices of the bedrock, these first miners used the most primitive tools for their operations—butcher knives, iron spoons, an occasional steel bar, and a pan. As the rainy season approached, the men returned to the valley, believing it to be impossible to winter in that wild country.

In the spring of 1849, hundreds of miners trekked over the rugged mountain trails to the new diggings, and a few stayed through the winter of 1849–50, among them being two men at Bird's Valley. Rich discoveries had been found in El Dorado Canyon and along the bars of the Middle Fork during the summer of 1849, and with the coming of another spring a general stampede began in February 1850. Thousands of men thronged over the trails from Hangtown, Coloma, Georgetown, Pilot Hill, and other places in El Dorado County already overrun with gold-seekers. Finding it impossible to mine along the streams, the rivers still being too high, they camped along the ridges, and Bird's Store became an important rendezvous, with up to 3,000 impatient Argonauts gathered there to wait for the snow to recede and the water to subside.

A few ambitious men camped on the little flat to the east where Michigan City grew up. While grading out the mountainside for enough level ground for their cabins to stand upon, they struck a bed of auriferous gravel. Lack of water delayed the working of the find until 1853, when ditches were dug from the upper reaches of El Dorado and Volcano Canyons, twelve and fifteen miles to the north. Until 1858 the town enjoyed a period of great prosperity, shipping $100,000 worth of gold per month. The North American Mine alone yielded $300,000 up to 1868.

Michigan City had no sooner become established on the narrow shelf at the edge of the diggings than the shelf began to settle and to slip down the mountainside, cracking the walls of the houses and threatening to precipitate the entire settlement into the canyon. This was in 1858, and in 1859 the settlers moved en masse to the present site of Michigan Bluff higher up on the brow of the mountain. Hydraulic mining began in the vicinity in 1858, and during the 1860's and 1870's the town was one of the most prosperous centers on the Forest Hill Divide. By 1880 the numerous smaller claims had been bought up by the owners of the Big Gun Mine.

After 1884, when hydraulic mining was outlawed, Michigan Bluff went quickly into decline until today little of its former prosperity is apparent. Some of the old frame houses are empty and rotting on their foundations, while others have been attractively renovated. Leland Stanford kept a store here from 1853 to 1855, sleeping on the counter at night, for Mrs. Stanford had remained in the East. The business block of Michigan Bluff was destroyed by fire in 1857, in which year Elijah and Lyman Stanford and their families, cousins of Leland, lived in the community.

Deadwood

At the tip of a narrow mountain spur high above the yawning chasms of El Dorado Canyon and the North Fork of the Middle Fork of the American River is the site of Deadwood, a one-time mining camp located seven miles from Michigan Bluff by pack trail. It is 25 miles by the long circuitous road that winds around the head of El Dorado Canyon past the Forks House, continuing across the head of Indian Creek at Westville, and thence down the Deadwood spur.

Gold was first found at Deadwood in 1852 by a group of miners who had previously experienced very indifferent success in the prospecting game. Being greatly elated over this sudden change for the better, the party remarked to all subsequent comers that they "now assuredly had the 'deadwood' upon securing a fortune"—in other words, it was a cinch. Thus Deadwood got its name.

The heartening news of the Deadwood discovery soon spread and a bustling camp sprang up, composed of more than 500 miners who had toiled over fearful canyon trails to this remote spot. It was a wild, austere habitat, to which only the most venturesome came. Deadwood was in a decline by 1855, although mining with moderate returns was carried on in the vicinity for many years. Only a small cemetery and an old well remain at the site.

A high bench or bar in the canyon of the North Fork of the Middle Fork some two or three miles from Deadwood bears the delightful title of Bogus Thunder. A mile or more up the canyon from this place is a waterfall the sound of which reverberates throughout the gorge with such terrific roar that the first comers there thought they were hearing thunder. When they discovered the real cause of the noise, they named the place accordingly.

Last Chance

Almost as difficult of access as Deadwood is Last Chance, above the canyon of the North Fork of the Middle Fork and the great network of narrow gorges and immense canyons that runs into it from the north. Perched at the tip of a promontory on the very brink of this tremendous drop-off, the Last Chance area seems like the jumping-off place.

The search for treasure had led a little group of prospectors into this remote region in 1850. Several rich deposits discovered in the vicinity caused them to linger until all the provisions were gone and starvation threatened. One of the company possessed a good rifle. Saying to his companions, "This is our last chance to make a grubstake," he went into the forest and returned with a large buck. Thus the miners were able to return to their diggings, and a new camp earned its name. This at least is one of several versions of its origin.

Last Chance had become a real town by 1852, and by 1859 the Masons, the Odd Fellows, and the Sons of Temperance had erected halls. Only the cemetery remains today to show that it was once inhabited.

Across Peavine Canyon from Last Chance and about five miles to the southeast, the northernmost group of *Sequoia gigantea* in California stands on a well-watered vale on Duncan Ridge overlooking the Middle Fork of the American River. This grove, known as the Placer County Big Trees, consists of six living trees and two large fallen ones. They are within the Tahoe National Forest.

The motorist to Last Chance and the Placer County Big Trees should take the Mosquito Ridge Road, which branches from the Auburn–Forest Hill Road half a mile west of Forest Hill. The Mosquito Ridge Road, paved for the first nineteen miles and with a wide, graded surface beyond, intersects the road to Last Chance at 24 miles and the road to the Big Trees at 25 miles. The Last Chance road turns north and goes five miles to a junction, thence west a little over three miles to the townsite. The Big Trees road turns south and goes about half a mile to a parking area, from which a trail leads less than a mile to the grove. Other routes to Last Chance are not recommended.

Plumas County

Plumas County was organized in 1854 from a portion of Butte County. The name was derived from El Río de las Plumas, "the river of the feathers," so named by Captain Luís A. Argüello, who led an exploring party up the valley of the Feather River in 1820, and who was impressed by the many feathers of wildfowl that he saw floating on the water. Quincy, originally American Ranch, has been the only county seat.

Beckwourth Pass

Beckwourth Pass (SRL 336) over the High Sierra was discovered in 1851 by James Beckwourth, trapper, scout, and honorary chief of the Crow Indians, while on a prospecting expedition as he and his party crossed the mountains from the American River valley to the Pit River valley. This pass, at 5,212 feet, is the lowest over the summit of the Sierra. It is about two miles east of Chilcoot, on SR 70, which crosses the pass today. Fifteen miles to the west of the pass is the town of Beckwourth, where the old brick Masonic Hall is a landmark in the little community.

Jim Beckwourth subsequently proposed to interested citizens at Bidwell Bar and Marysville that a wagon road be made through this pass, across the Sierra Valley to the Middle Fork of the Feather River, and down the ridge east of the river past Bidwell Bar to Marysville. His plan was eventually adopted, and soon after the completion of the trail, Beckwourth, while at Truckee in the Sierra Nevada, succeeded in persuading a passing emigrant train to try the new road. The party liked it, and others followed in their footsteps until it became a well-beaten trail.

Many emigrants came through this region in 1852. During the spring of that year Beckwourth built a cabin, the first house in Sierra Valley, which served as a trading post and hotel. It stood on a hillside two and a half miles west of the town of Beckwourth. A second cabin was built nearby, but both were burned by Indians. A third log cabin soon replaced the first two, and a part of this historic relic stood for many years on what is now the Harberts Ranch at Walker Mine Road and SR 70. In 1985, the cabin was transported to a new site a quarter of a mile away and is now maintained by Plumas County as a historical landmark.

It was in 1852 that Ina Coolbrith, destined to become California's first poet laureate, then a child of eleven, came through Beckwourth Pass. The party had trekked across the plains and mountains from St. Louis, Missouri, in ox-drawn schooners.

Speaking at a luncheon given in her honor in San Francisco on April 24, 1927, Ina Coolbrith gave this account of the trip: "Ours was the first of the covered-wagon trains to break the trail through Beckwourth Pass into California. We were guided by the famous scout, Jim Beckwourth, who was an historical figure, and to my mind one of the most beautiful creatures that ever lived. He was rather dark and wore his hair in two long braids, twisted with colored cord that gave him a picturesque appearance. He wore a leather coat and moccasins and rode a horse without a saddle.

"When we made that long journey toward the West over the deserts and mountains, our wagon train was driven over ground without a single mark of a wagon wheel until it was broken by ours. And when Jim Beckwourth said he would like to have my mother's little girls ride into California on his horse in front of him, I was the happiest little girl in the world.

"After two or three days of heavy riding we came at last in sight of California and there on the boundary line he stopped, and pointing forward, said: 'Here is California, little girls, here is your kingdom.'"

By action of the United States Geographic Board, through the efforts of officials of the Western Pacific Railroad, a high peak, formerly known as Summit Peak, located six miles due south of Beckwourth Pass, was renamed Mount Ina Coolbrith in her honor. The peak, which rises to an elevation of 8,000 feet in Sierra County, is plainly visible from the pass through which young Ina Coolbrith rode with the famous scout. It lies near the intersection of the county lines of Plumas, Lassen, and Sierra counties, with its slopes reaching out into Plumas and Lassen counties.

Portola

Situated on the Middle Fork of the Feather River, in a region famous for its recreational facilities, the town of Portola is also a noted railroad center. Shortly after 1900, the Western Pacific Railroad came through here on its way from California to Salt Lake City. In 1985, the Feather River Rail Society, with the cooperation of the Union Pacific Railroad (which now owns the Western Pacific), opened the Portola Railroad Museum adjacent to the tracks of the main line. Here are locomotives and rolling stock from Western Pacific and some other lines, in good repair and taken out on the special tracks. The museum is open during the summer.

The Lassen Trail

The 1848 Lassen Emigrant Trail to California passed through Plumas County by way of Big Meadows, now the site of Lake Almanor. In 1849, over 8,000 emigrants to California passed this way, and Big Meadows became an important stopping place for food and water. Trails West, Inc., has placed markers along many parts of this trail; one may be seen at Bunnel Point on the shore of Lake Almanor, another at Prattville just across the lake, others on less accessible sites as the trail heads west into the mountains. The Lassen Trail ended at the Sacramento River at Vina, in what is now Tehama County.

Humboldt-Humbug Roads

The Humboldt and Humbug roads meet SR 89 approximately four miles south of the junction with SR 36. These two roads were the original stage and freight routes into the area from the Sacramento Valley. John Bidwell of Chico obtained the franchise to construct a toll road from Chico to the Honey Lake Valley in Lassen County in the early 1860's. The Chico and Humboldt Wagon Company was incorporated in 1864, and in 1865 stage and freight service was established between Chico and Ruby City, Idaho, the main purpose of the road being to supply the mines of Nevada and Idaho. The Humboldt Road, for the first several miles from the junction with SR 89, follows the route of the original Lassen Emigrant Trail. The Humbug Road, slightly older than the Humboldt, probably grew from early stock trails leading from the Oroville-Marysville area to Big Meadows. Though dirt, the roads are graded and well traveled in summer.

The Gold Lake Excitement

The higher regions of the Sierra Nevada were the last to be prospected during the early days of the gold rush. Several hundred Argonauts in 1849 passed over the Lassen Trail through what is now northwestern Plumas County, but not one stayed to work its streams. One man, however, was instrumental in opening up the country to a later influx of miners. This was J. R. Stoddard, the hero of an adventure whose beginnings are shrouded in mystery. The facts of its later development and the resulting Gold Lake migration are well known, however.

Stoddard, according to his own account, had stumbled upon a lake in the higher mountains somewhere between Downieville and Sierra Valley. The shores of this lake, he declared, were literally covered with chunks of gold. His recital of its exact location and of the circumstances attending its supposed discovery was conflicting and uncertain. The spirit of the times, however, was such as to make the wildest extravaganza seem plausible to credulous gold-seekers, and soon Stoddard found himself the leader not only of the small group originally chosen to go with him to rediscover the fabled lake of gold but of several hundred others, all eager and determined to share in the imagined riches. The number increased, as rumor spread, until 1,000 or more miners left their diggings on the lower reaches of the rivers to join the migration to the new El Dorado.

Gold Lake was never found. Nevertheless, the influx of prospectors into the highlands of the upper Feather River canyons resulted in the opening of the entire region, and many of the tributary streams were found to be very rich. The Gold Lake in Sierra County just across the line from Plumas County, and the much smaller Gold Lake just northwest of Spanish Peak in Plumas County, are reminiscent of this early excitement over the mythical lake with its gold-pebbled shores.

Intersected by the various forks of the Feather River, the land of the fabled "Gold Lake" is one of rugged scenic grandeur. The sculpturing waters have here chiseled the Sierra with canyons 2,000 feet deep, flanked by lofty, forested ridges, magnificent and awe-inspiring. Green and fertile valleys, watered by countless streams, nestle among giant hills and are made still more lovely by the mirrored beauty of numerous lakes. These valleys include Indian, American, Big Meadows, Buck's, Humbug, Mohawk, Genesee, Sierra, Long, Red Clover, Round, Last Chance, and Onion. Near the southern boundary of the county the South Fork of the Feather River rises in the neighborhood of Pilot Peak, while the Middle Fork, a much longer stream with many tributaries, has its headwaters in Sierra Valley. The North Fork rises in the northwestern corner of the county southeast of Lassen Peak. Flowing almost due south through Big Meadows, now largely occupied by Lake Almanor, it waters a considerable section of Plumas County before joining the Middle Fork of the Feather River at Lake Oroville.

Beginning with the gold excitement of the 1850's, mining, lumbering, and agriculture have played important roles in the history of Plumas County. With an increasing horde of gold-seekers pouring into every corner of the region in the early days, mushroom cities of log cabins sprang up almost overnight. Soon there was a great demand for milled lumber with which to erect better buildings. Farmers saw the need for farm and dairy products, and ranches were established in the fertile valleys, where water and pasturelands were abundant. Although many of the old mining camps have since become ghost towns, a few remain, forming a link in the chain reaching back into the historic past. Today, also, many of the pioneer ranches are being farmed by descendants of the original owners.

Plumas County contains scores of mineral springs located in various parts of the county: in Humbug Valley, on the North Fork of the Feather River; at Soda Bar on the East Branch of the North Fork; in Indian Valley near Greenville, where there are warm bathing springs; in Mohawk Valley at the Sulphur Springs Ranch, where both hot and cold water are found; and in many other places. Numerous jets of steam and hot mud accompanied by rumbling noises suggest volcanic activities in Hot Springs Valley near the northwestern corner of the county, and within the limits of Lassen Volcanic National Park. Since early days these places have attracted many visitors.

Rich Bar

Stragglers of the Gold Lake influx, some of whom worked briefly at the now-vanished camps of Onion Valley (a few miles north of Gibsonville on the Quincy Road) and Nelson's Point (where Nelson Creek meets the Middle Fork of the Feather River), made one of the foremost discoveries in Plumas County in July 1850 on the East Branch of the North Fork of the Feather River at a place afterward called Rich Bar. Enormous production records were made at this point, where pans of dirt frequently yielded from $100 to $1,000. It is said that three Germans took out $36,000 in nuggets and gold dust during four days' time. Claims were so rich that they were limited to ten square feet. During the first two years after its discovery, Rich Bar yielded a total of from three to four million dollars in gold, thus earning its name. With the approach of the winter of 1850–51, most of the claims at Rich Bar were deserted, although a few log cabins were erected and occupied until the spring of 1851, when a host of miners again flocked to the region.

A vivid and colorful picture of life in this river camp has been preserved for us in the letters of a woman from New England, Mrs. Louise Amelia Knapp Smith Clappe, who lived at Rich Bar in 1851 and 1852. Written to her sister Molly, in the old home at Amherst, Massachusetts, these letters, playfully signed "Dame Shirley," were penned merely to give her sister "a true picture of mining life," with no thought of subsequent publication. However, two years later they appeared in print, when a friend, the Rev. Ferdinand C. Ewer of San Francisco, made use of them in *The Pioneer*, a monthly magazine of which he was the publisher and in which the "Shirley Letters" appeared during the two years of its existence.

Later writers such as Bancroft, Hittell, and Royce have acknowledged their indebtedness to these letters. Certainly the delightful descriptions, written on the spot, glossing nothing over, form the best firsthand account we have of life in the early gold camps.

With her husband, Dr. Fayette Clappe, "Dame Shirley" came to Rich Bar in the fall of 1851. The journey from Marysville to Bidwell Bar was made in an "excruciatingly springless wagon," with the second stage of the trip negotiated on muleback over winding mountain trails, passing, at long intervals, a rare and welcome farmhouse, where fresh butter, cream, and other luxuries might be had.

Coming at length to the summit of the high ridge overlooking Rich Bar, she was enchanted with the exquisite beauty of the scene that lay before her: "shadowy nooks" and "far down valleys . . . half a dozen blue-bosomed lagoons. . . . It was worth the whole wearisome journey, danger from Indians, grizzly bears, sleeping under the stars, and all."

On the last stretch of her journey, Mrs. Clappe had a narrow escape from death. Although warned that she should walk rather than ride down the precipice, since even the hardiest miners did so, she was determined to ride, for, as she told her sister, "I had much more confidence in my mule's power of picking the way and keeping his footing than in my own." At one point on the trail her saddle slipped and she landed on the tiniest of ledges far above the river bed. "Had the accident happened at any other part of the hill," she writes, "I must have been dashed, a piece of shapeless nothingness, into the dim valleys beneath."

Mrs. Clappe at length found herself safely at "Barra Rica," as the Mexicans called it. The third of the series of letters describes it in vivid tone. "Imagine a tiny valley, about eight hundred yards in length and, perhaps, thirty in width . . . apparently hemmed in by lofty hills, almost perpendicular, draperied to their very summits with beautiful fir trees, the blue-bosomed 'Plumas', or Feather River, I suppose I must call it, undulating along their base. . . . Through the middle of Rich Bar runs the street, thickly planted with about forty tenements, among which figure round tents, square tents, plank hovels, log cabins, etc.—the residences, varying in splendor from 'the Empire' down to a 'local habitation,' formed of pine boughs, and covered with old calico shirts."

Although numerous shanties on the bar claimed the grandiloquent title of "hotel," the Empire was *the* hostelry of the place, and Mrs. Clappe's portrayal of its whimsical splendor equals if not excels her other descriptions: "You first enter a long apartment, level with the street, part of which is fitted up as a bar-room, with that eternal crimson calico which flushes the whole social life of the 'Golden State' with its everlasting red—in the center of a fluted mass of which gleams a really elegant mirror, set off by a background of decanters, cigar vases, and jars of brandied fruit, the whole forming a *tout ensemble* of dazzling splendor. . . . The entire building is lined with purple calico, alternating with a delicate blue, and the effect is really quite pretty. The floors are so uneven that you are always ascending a hill or descending into a valley." Such was "this impertinent apology for a house," a one-time gambler's palace costing its original owners more than $8,000.

On the steep hillside behind the Empire Hotel lay the lonely graveyard where Nancy Ann Bailey, "the second 'Mrs. B.'," one of the two women who preceded Mrs. Clappe at Rich Bar, was buried a week after "Dame Shirley's" arrival. At the head of the bar was the little windowless log cabin in which this pioneer mother died on September 30, 1851, according to the date on the headstone.

Nothing of the mining period remains at Rich Bar (SRL 337) except the decaying headstones in the tiny cemetery on the hill and the heaps of boulders along the river where miners once worked this richest of the northern diggings. Overlooking the river stands the Rich Bar monument dedicated by the Native Sons of the Golden West in 1915 in memory of the pioneers who settled at this spot, some of whom found rest on the hillside nearby, and in special honor of Nancy Ann Bailey. The townsite is just across the river from SR 70, on the old Western Pacific (now Union Pacific) Railroad, about three miles east of Belden.

Indian Bar

In 1852 the Clappes moved to Indian Bar. Mrs. Clappe thus describes the river trail leading to her new home: "The crossings are formed of logs, often moss-grown. . . . At every step gold diggers or their operations greet your vision, sometimes in the form of a dam, sometimes in that of a river turned slightly from its channel, to aid the indefatigable gold hunters in their mining projects. . . . As we approached Indian Bar, the path led several times fearfully near deep holes

from which the laborers were gathering their yellow harvest."

Just across from Indian Bar was Pea Soup Bar (not yet named when Mrs. Clappe wrote her letters), while opposite Rich Bar was a narrow diggings later known as Poverty Bar. It was on this bar that builders of the Feather River Highway (SR 70) established camp while blasting out a roadway from the cliffs of the gorge; the road reached the point opposite Rich Bar in the autumn of 1932. The Western Pacific Railroad was constructed up the canyon in 1909, under the leadership of Arthur Keddie (after whom a small town further up the valley is named). It is interesting to see how the highway and the railroad run up the valley, usually on opposite sides of the river, but occasionally crossing each other.

Spanish Ranch

A quarter of a mile north of the old Oroville-Quincy Road, and about six miles west of Quincy, two Mexicans in July 1850 set up an early camp in that part of Meadow Valley. This circumstance gave rise to the names Spanish Ranch, Spanish Creek, and Spanish Peak. Miners customarily left their horses and pack mules in the care of these Mexicans, who also engaged in cattle raising and slaughtering.

Spanish Ranch soon became a distributing center for surrounding camps. The first hotel, blacksmith shop, and store were erected there in 1852 by Lloyd and Snodgrass. A Wells Fargo Express office was established in 1868. Millions of dollars in gold dust and nuggets passed through its doors. As late as 1881, the year's output in coin and bullion amounted to $114,076. Directly above the townsite towers Spanish Peak (7,047 feet), pierced by the tunnel of the Monte Cristo Mine at an altitude of 6,288 feet, or within 759 feet of the summit.

Two miles southwest of Spanish Ranch is Meadow Valley, an old camp where W. S. Dean settled as early as 1852. A post office called Meadow Valley was established in 1855, but its name was changed to Spanish Ranch in 1861. A change of location may also have been involved. The present Meadow Valley post office was established in 1864. None of the old business buildings remain standing at Spanish Ranch and Meadow Valley (SRL 481). Two and a quarter miles west of Meadow Valley on the old stage road between Quincy and Oroville is the site of Toll Gate, where tolls were collected on one of the first turnpikes in Plumas County. The buildings here, too, have all disappeared.

Seven miles farther southwest the road passed Buck's Ranch, which was first occupied in the fall of 1850 by Horace Bucklin and Francis Walker. It later developed into another important stage station. The site is under the waters of Buck's Lake (SRL 197), which now covers most of Buck's Valley. The dam was constructed in 1925–27. The Buck's Ranch hotel and store served for years as a stage station and express and post office. In the early days it was a haven for pioneers, where miners' pack trains stopped en route to the Feather River mines; later it became an important point in the passenger, express, and mail service to and from Quincy and other towns. In the rich Gravel Range District near Buck's Ranch, miners were known to have found gold, silver, and copper all in one ledge.

Beyond Grizzly Gulch, about three and one-half miles west of Buck's Ranch, is a meadow hemmed in by the forest. Here, visible from the road, stands a granite monument (SRL 212) marking the grave of P. Linthiouh, a nineteen-year-old pioneer who was killed by bandits and buried under a pine tree by his comrade in September 1852. The tree, on which his name and age were carved, no longer stands.

La Porte

La Porte (SRL 213), an old mining camp located on flat benches on both sides of Rabbit Creek, a tributary of Slate Creek in the southwest corner of Plumas County, was known as Rabbit Creek or Rabbit Town from 1850 to 1857. This area was part of Yuba County until 1852 and Sierra County until 1868. During the 1860's and 1870's it developed into a populous center for hydraulic mining. By 1890, some $93 million in bullion had been taken from the area. But after 1884, when hydraulic mining became illegal, La Porte dwindled in population, until today it is a quiet mountain hamlet with only a few dozen inhabitants. The frame hotel,

Ruins, La Porte

now called the Rabbit Creek Lodge, was begun in 1855 and still is in business. Nearby stone walls are all that remain after the 1969 explosion that destroyed the general store. On display is the old stamp mill that was moved from the Oro Fino Mine on Hopkins Creek, where it was powered by a Pelton Wheel on one end and a steam engine on the other. There is a beautiful enclosed cemetery in the town. Nearby, on what is now the La Porte Pines Country Club, is the site of what is claimed to be the world's first recorded ski race, in 1860.

Elizabethtown, or Betsyburg

Miners flocked to the region of Elizabethtown (SRL 231) in 1852 in search of gold. There being only one unmarried lady in the new camp, Elizabeth Stark, the chivalrous miners named the new town in her honor. Elizabethtown, or Betsyburg, as it was sometimes humorously called, was a large camp by 1853, and within two years a post office was established there. However, the surrounding gulches were soon exhausted. After Quincy was made the county seat of Plumas County in 1854 and the post office was moved there in December 1855, Elizabethtown began to decline. Today, only tailings from the old mines indicate its one-time activity. SR 70 passes through the Elizabethtown area two miles north of Quincy, near the campus of Feather River College.

Quincy

The American Ranch was owned by James H. Bradley, one of the three commissioners who organized Plumas County. Owing to his influence, the seat of justice was placed by statute at the hotel on his ranch. With this as a nucleus, he laid out a town, calling it Quincy after his hometown in Illinois, and the people were induced to vote for Quincy as the county seat. The site of Bradley's hotel (SRL 479) is at Main and Fillmore streets.

The part of Quincy bounded by Main, Church, Jackson, and Buchanan streets is full of old buildings, some of which have been marked. The oldest building is the Masonic Hall on Harbison Avenue between Jackson and Main streets, moved from Elizabethtown the year after it was built in 1854. The Methodist Episcopal Church at Jackson and Church streets dates from 1877. Several homes still standing were constructed of lumber brought from abandoned houses in Elizabethtown.

At Court and Main streets is the site of the Plumas House (SRL 480), which was built in 1866, replacing an earlier log structure on the site. The hotel was destroyed by fire in 1923, and the Hotel Quincy built on the site in 1925 met a like fate in 1967. The site is now a city park. The present Plumas County courthouse was built in 1920 in Classic Revival style, replacing the earlier structure from 1859. The courthouse was criticized when it was put up for its large size, but the wisdom of the builders' decision is clear today, county business having increased greatly since 1920. The interior is of Tuolumne County marble.

Quincy was one of the stations of Whiting and Company's Dog Express, which, in the early days, brought the mails over the snowy Sierra. For stretches of twenty miles through snow-covered mountain country, Newfoundlands or St. Bernards, driven tandem, two or four to a team, pulled sledges often carrying loads of over 600 pounds: passengers, express, and mail were all transported. Distinguished service was rendered by these faithful animals and their masters from 1858 until the invention of the horse snowshoe in 1865.

The Plumas County Museum at 500 Jackson Street features displays on the Maidu Indians and several changing exhibits on the commercial activities of the county's past. The mezzanine in this charming old building is an art gallery and has two "period" rooms on display. Two miles east of downtown Quincy and just north of SR 70 the first schoolhouse in Plumas County (SRL 625) has been preserved on the Plumas County Fairgrounds. It was built in 1857 by the residents of the eastern end of American Valley.

Plumas-Eureka State Park

A few miles to the west of Blairsden and Graeagle is Plumas-Eureka State Park, which includes or surrounds several important landmarks of mining days—Jamison

Eureka Mine, Plumas-Eureka State Park

City, Johnsville, Eureka Mills, and the Plumas-Eureka Mine (SRL 196).

Operations started at the Plumas-Eureka Mine, situated on the east slope of Eureka Peak, in the summer of 1851. A company of 36 men was formed, but instead of setting up stamp mills at once, they wisely mined with arrastras, or drag stones, until sufficient money had been made to warrant improvements. Chili wheels, heavy wheels rotated around a pivot, superseded the arrastras, and finally, in 1856, a mill with twelve stamps was erected. In the vicinity of the Plumas-Eureka other quartz mines were opened at various times. To the northeast was the Mammoth Mine, worked by a company of 80 men with the use of arrastras until they, too, erected a twelve-stamp mill. Two other mines in the vicinity, the Washington and the Rough-and-Ready, were not financially successful, because their promoters spent all their profits on equipment. The Washington Mine was owned by a company of 76 men, who laid out an ephemeral town on Jamison Creek, calling it the City of 76.

All of these claims—the Plumas-Eureka, Mammoth, Washington, and Rough-and-Ready—were bought by John Parrott, who sold them to the Sierra Buttes Company of London in 1872. This company operated a consolidated mining venture with considerable success until the early 1890's, when productivity declined and the individual mines were sold off, the last ceasing activity in 1943.

Johnstown, now called Johnsville, was laid out in 1876 on Jamison Creek one-half mile east of the Plumas-Eureka Mine (it is not part of the state park and its buildings are private property). A few old buildings still stand in this village, notably the little firehouse built in 1908 and the rustic Catholic Church. In this region of heavy snows, neglected buildings quickly deteriorate and even those of recent construction soon look very old. The "Johnsville Hotel" is now a private dwelling.

The headquarters of the Plumas-Eureka State Park are a short distance from Johnsville. The charming museum with its excellent displays of natural history, Maidu Indian artifacts, and mining activities is lodged in the former mine bunkhouse and office, and the massive fireplace still gets good use in the winter. A pair of skis (then called snow-shoes) used by John A. ("Snow-Shoe") Thompson is displayed here. Johnsville is the pioneer ski area of America, attested by a monument (SRL 723) across the road from the museum. Winter sports events in the High Sierra were run off annually as early as 1860. La Porte, Onion Valley, Jamison City, and Johnsville, as well as the Sierra County towns of Whiskey Diggings, Poker Flat, Port Wine, and Howland

Flat, organized the earliest ski clubs and held contests that resulted in some notable speed records. The VIII Olympic Winter Games of 1960, held at Squaw Valley near Lake Tahoe, some 60 miles to the south, commemorated a century of sport skiing in California.

Across the parking lot from the museum stands the massive Eureka Mill, a wooden structure 72 feet high, where millions of dollars in gold were produced. The old 48-stamp mill, once leaning precariously and falling into ruin, is being carefully restored. Mining equipment can be seen on exhibit in the grounds; a massive ore crusher is particularly striking.

A short distance from park headquarters along the road to Gibsonville is a monument marking the old trail from Jamison City to Marysville. It consists of a stone taken from one of the early Jamison Creek arrastras and was dedicated in 1932 by the Native Sons and Daughters of the Golden West of Plumas County; a second marker was placed at Split Rock, now on an abandoned piece of road between Johnsville and Mohawk. From this rock early miners obtained the arrastra stones that formed the primitive mills used to grind out the gold. The pioneer trail to Mohawk Valley passed near the site of this marker.

Mohawk and Graeagle

Mohawk, a hamlet near Blairsden and Graeagle, was once a prosperous agricultural center for surrounding mines. It is about three miles east of the site of Jamison. All of the early buildings at Mohawk have been destroyed by fire. This is now a popular resort area.

Graeagle was once a lumber company town, and on the main street of the community one sees still the distinctive red houses, large and small, all trimmed with white. These houses have been maintained for many years and now are all privately owned; some are used as commercial or professional buildings. Most of Graeagle today consists of new homes and resorts.

Indian Valley

Peter Lassen, the first pioneer to settle in Indian Valley, came there with Isadore Meyerwitz in the fall of 1850. Lassen called the spot Cache Valley, but later settlers gave it the name of Indian Valley because of the many Indians living there. Lassen and a Mr. Burton built a log cabin there in 1851, four and a half miles east of the site of Greenville, and developed a thriving trading post. Vegetables were raised and sold to the miners at high prices. The site (SRL 184) is four and one-half miles east of Greenville on the Greenville-Beckwourth Road.

At Greenville, long a center of quartz-mining activity, a bullion ledge was discovered in 1851 and first mined with profit by John W. Ellis in 1856. The Lone Star Mine was first worked there in 1857. At Round Valley, south of Greenville, John Ellis opened up the Ellis Mine in 1862, and quite a camp grew up about the stamp mill. With the abandonment of the mine, the town faded out completely within a few years. Tunnels and rock piles are the only evidence of early-day activity in the locality. Southeast of Greenville at Crescent Mills quartz-mining and milling operations were carried on as late as 1926.

Two famous copper mines in the mountains east of Indian Valley have made fine production records, and continued to employ a large number of men until they were shut down. One was the Engel Mine, closed in 1930, fifteen miles northeast of Crescent Mills; the other was the Walker Mine, northwest of Portola and Beckwourth, which yielded $1,099,000 in copper in 1931, but was closed down in 1932.

Between the broad meadows of Indian Valley and the dense evergreen forests of Mount Hough lies Taylorsville, founded by Jobe T. Taylor, who settled there in 1852. A quaint charm pervades the town, with its great barns, shady streets, white-steepled community church, substantial and dignified old houses, and, close against the hill in a tiny oak wood, the burial ground of the pioneers. A monument here marks the grave of Jobe Taylor. The present school stands on the site of the Taylor Hotel, which was built by the founder in 1859 and burned in 1949. A marker dedicated by the Native Sons of the Golden West stands in front of the school. Millstones from Taylor's gristmill, which was built in 1856 and destroyed by fire in 1918, were incorporated into the marker. At this site in 1852 Taylor built the first permanent residence in Indian Valley, later replaced by his hotel. The original one-room red-brick schoolhouse, built in 1864, still stands at the north edge of Taylorsville. It is now owned and is being preserved by the Native Sons of the Golden West, Plumas Parlor of Taylorsville.

The Indian Valley Museum is located in the Mount Jura Gem and Mineral Society Building next to the cemetery; it contains extensive photographs and artifacts of the region and of the Maidu people, and outside there is an interesting mining display around a mine tunnel entrance built into the adjoining hill.

Big Meadows, Prattville, and Lake Almanor

Big Meadows, consisting of more than 30,000 acres along the North Fork of the Feather River, was an early stock-raising region in the middle of the surrounding mining and lumber country. The salubrious summer air led to the establishment of a resort, Prattville Springs, by Dr. Willard Pratt around 1880. Dr. Pratt, who was born in Pennsylvania and had practiced in Wisconsin, came overland in 1853 and practiced in mining communities. In 1859, he moved to the Sacramento Valley, first to Colusa and then to Chico, where his descendants still live. After retiring from the practice of medicine, he moved to Big Meadows; the town of Prattville developed around the two-story frame hotel he erected there. He died in 1888.

Big Meadows was bought out in 1907 by the Great Western Power Company, which in 1910–14 constructed a dam at the eastern end of the meadows. The lake thus created, Lake Almanor, was for two decades the largest man-made hydroelectric power reservoir in the United States. ("Almanor" was derived from the names of three daughters of Guy Earl, a founder of Great Western.) The cemetery at Prattville was relocated to a hillside where the modern community of Prattville now stands, and Dr. Willard Pratt's grave and monument now lie with others in a grove of tall, shadowing cedars. Now the property of the Pacific Gas and Electric Company, which bought out Great Western in 1930, Lake Almanor is a popular summertime resort,

and the permanent residents of the new Prattville still praise its salubrious air.

Chester

The western end of Big Meadows was a favored summer retreat from the heat of the Sacramento Valley. General and Mrs. John Bidwell had a campsite there and planned a more substantial home for their later years. A year after the General's death in 1900 the house was completed, and it was used by Mrs. Bidwell until her death in 1918. In 1926 it was hauled on skids to its present location on the northeast end of Main Street in Chester. Until the 1960's it was the summer headquarters for the Stover-McKenzie Cattle Company. Known today as the Bidwell-McKenzie House, it is privately owned, but there are plans to make it into a historic site. A downstairs portion is now a business office.

The Chester–Lake Almanor Museum adjoins the Chester Library on First Avenue. Opened in 1985, the museum's displays feature local Maidu Indian culture, nineteenth-century pioneer farming and dairying activities, and early twentieth-century hydroelectric and lumber industrial development.

Riverside County

Riverside County was created in 1893 from territory originally belonging to San Bernardino and San Diego counties. The city of Riverside, founded in 1871 on a channel of the Santa Ana River, has always been the county seat, and gave its name to the county.

Indian Rocks

Riverside County is exceptionally rich in Indian rock writings, those mysterious carvings and drawings depicting stories of hunts, of fires, and of battles. Most of them are painted in a vivid red pigment, the secret of which has been lost. Others are in red and white, and a few in red, black, and white. Nearly always they command a spring or watering place, the camping grounds of the ancient peoples, where these rock pictures may have been left as signboards. Modern Indian tribes do not know their origin or meaning, and only a few of them have been deciphered. Some hold the theory that

the people who made them were of the same race as the Aztecs of Mexico.

There were once seven Indian villages in the San Jacinto Valley: Ivah; Soboba, near Soboba Hot Springs; Jusispah, where the town of San Jacinto now is; Ararah, in Webster's Canyon on the road to Idyllwild; Pahsitnah, the largest in the valley, near Big Springs Ranch; Corova, the most northern, in Castle Canyon; and a small settlement of the Serranos from San Bernardino, near Eden Hot Springs. It is said that the tribes who lived here were among the most powerful of any in the Southwest, and this region about the great peaks of San Jacinto and Tahquitz has an abundance of Indian lore. There may be many carved and painted rocks (petroglyphs and pictographs) in this region that have yet to be discovered.

One of the finest of the Riverside group of pictographs is found in Indian Relic County Park at Fern Valley, on the northeast side of Idyllwild. Painted in

Maze Stone, Maze Stone County Park

vivid red on the face of a huge rock, the color is apparently unfaded in spite of the action of the elements upon it. The design, too, is unusual and constitutes a remarkable piece of workmanship, conforming, so scientists say, to rock paintings and designs found among the early Aztecs of Mexico. According to one theory, it tells the story of a great hunt: the long trail that the hunters follow, their encounter with a bear, the crossing of streams and the climbing of mountains, a skirmish with members of a hostile tribe, the trail again, the final kill, and the great feast.

The Maze Stone (SRL 557) is a remarkable petroglyph in Maze Stone County Park, three miles north of the Perris-Hemet highway (SR 74) and five miles west of Hemet. A huge swastika (a symbol associated with the Indians from ancient times) has been carved into a massive granite boulder. The larger figure is made up of four smaller swastikas, the whole being about four feet in diameter. There is only one other carved rock in the United States known to be like this one, and that is far in the Northwest.

About seven-tenths of a mile east of the Ramona Bowl, on the southern outskirts of Hemet, is the site of the village of Pochea (SRL 104), one of the "seven villages of Pahsitnah." In the vicinity are a number of flat granite rocks the surfaces of which are covered with grinding holes. The Ramona Bowl Museum displays Indian artifacts as well as the history of the Ramona Pageant, held here since 1923.

There are many other Indian rocks, both petroglyphs and pictographs, scattered throughout Riverside County. In Dawson Canyon is an interesting painted rock (SRL 190) that has been marked by the Corona Women's Improvement Club. This rock, found in the right-of-way of the Santa Fe Railroad, was saved from destruction by the club and placed in a cement base by the Santa Fe Railroad Company in 1927.

Chief Lafio of Temecula said the painted rock was the work of the Temecula (Luiseño) Indians, perhaps telling of a three-day fiesta or a religious celebration. Again, it may have been a flood warning, since the San Jacinto River formerly flowed beside the rock and on it are four water signs similar to those found on other rocks listed in the report of the United States Bureau of Ethnography. The painted rock is reached by the Dawson Canyon Fireroad, which turns to the east from the Temescal Canyon Road seven and a half miles south of Corona. A distance of only a quarter of a mile along the Dawson Canyon road brings one to the old Serrano tanning vats, immediately adjacent to the road on the right. From this point the painted rock may be seen across the field on the opposite side of the road. It stands next to the railroad track and is reached by an easy hike. In the vicinity there is also a carved rock (SRL 187), which is reached by the winding road through the clay pits that turns right from the Dawson Canyon Fireroad just one-tenth of a mile past the old tanning vats. A mile or more of twisting and turning along the clay pit road will bring one into clear view of a great natural amphitheater, in the midst of which stands the rock. Its top has been damaged, but many of the carvings are still intact.

In Mockingbird Canyon, between Riverside and Perris, there are two groups of painted rocks near the Mockingbird Springs. Other Indian relics are located on private property throughout southwestern Riverside County.

The Coachella Valley was once a great inland lake, the shoreline of which is still visible in places to the southwest of present-day Coachella. At the western end of Avenue 66, some ten miles south of Coachella, there is a remarkable group of circular depressions among a maze of boulders just below the ancient shoreline. Some authorities believe them to be vestiges of fish traps; others say that they were foundations for primitive houses. Whatever the case, they were made by human hands a long time ago. The ancient shoreline extends down through the Imperial Valley into Mexico.

The ancient village of Ivah once thrived in the region of the present town of San Jacinto, near Massacre Canyon, on the Gilman Hot Springs Road. Many years ago a battle was fought there over a crop of chia, a grain that grew wild on nearly all of the mesa lands. The story goes that a severe drought in southern California caused the total failure of the chia crop in Temecula Valley. The Temeculas, who were a tribe distinctly separate from the seven tribes at San Jacinto, and more warlike, came in search of grain. Proceeding to gather the crop belonging to the village of Ivah, they precipitated a fierce battle. The Ivahs fought valiantly, but being outnumbered they were forced to flee into the narrow ravine now known as Massacre Canyon. There, with their backs against a vertical wall, they fought to their death. Long afterward Massacre Canyon received its name from the white settlers, who had heard the story from elderly Indians.

Perhaps the most inexplicable prehistoric relics in the county, both as to age and as to purpose or meaning, are the giant desert figures (SRL 101) just west of the Colorado River. They represent both humans and animals and are best seen from the air, from which they were discovered. The largest of them is 167 feet long. The mesa is covered with sandstone pebbles that were moved by early people in such a way that bare earth was left to form the figures, the pebbles being placed in windrows about the edge as an outline. Now on the National Register of Historic Places, they have been fenced off by the Bureau of Land Management, which is attempting to protect these artifacts from further vandalism. Their location is about half a mile west of US 95, some seventeen miles north of Blythe.

Palm Springs and Desert Hot Springs

Palm Springs was once the exclusive domain of the Agua Caliente Indians. The world-famous resort is located on and around the Agua Caliente Indian Reservation. At the corner of Indian Avenue and Tahquitz-McCallum Way is the Palm Springs Spa Hotel, on the grounds of which still flow the springs first discovered by the Indians. The first resort hotel was opened in the 1880's.

John Guthrie McCallum was the first permanent white settler in the Palm Springs area; he arrived in 1884 and put up an adobe house. This has been moved from its original location on Palm Canyon Drive, once a rough dirt road, and now stands at 223 South Palm Canyon Drive, where it serves as the Palm Springs Historical Society Museum. The Village Green Heritage Center, where the museum is located, also has Miss Cornelia White's "Little House," built in 1893 by Welwood Murray, the city's first hotel proprietor.

Two miles to the south of Palm Springs in the Palm, Murray, and Andreas canyons are magnificent groves of native date palms, one of the grandest spectacles in all the Southwest. The Washingtonia palms are estimated to be from 1,500 to 2,000 years old. Here, too, in certain spring seasons after heavy rains, may be witnessed the miracle of vast wildflower gardens springing

Cabot's Old Indian Pueblo, Desert Hot Springs

as if by magic from the dry sands of the desert. The Palm Springs Aerial Tramway, two miles west of the city, has been called the "eighth engineering wonder of the world." Completed in 1963, the 13,200-foot line climbs from Valley Station in Chino Canyon (elevation 2,643 feet) to Mountain Station (elevation 8,516 feet) on the slopes of Mount San Jacinto.

Since World War II, Palm Springs and the adjacent region have been favorite vacation spots for such celebrities as presidents Eisenhower, Ford, and Reagan, as well as many entertainers, after whom streets and local landmarks have been named.

Desert Hot Springs, about a dozen miles northeast of Palm Springs, was not discovered until early in the twentieth century. A remarkable structure at 67616 East Desert View Avenue is Cabot's Old Indian Pueblo, a 35-room structure built by Cabot Yerxa, who settled in the area in 1913. A museum and storehouse of Western and Indian artifacts, it contains many curiosities.

Indian Wells, seventeen miles southeast of Palm Springs on SR 111, is the site of an Indian rancheria where a life-giving well was in use until 1910. Mount Eisenhower on the south edge of the community honors a former resident. The Living Desert Reserve in Palm Desert, three miles west, is a 1,200-acre park that preserves much of the desert life and atmosphere.

The Pechanga Burial Ground

About five miles southeast of Temecula is the Pechanga Indian Reservation. A distinctive feature of the place is the old chapel and burial ground, where, it is supposed, Alessandro, hero of Helen Hunt Jackson's novel *Ramona*, buried his father after the massacre at Temecula. Mrs. Jackson's description of the cemetery is still accurate a century later: "The cemetery is quaint. . . . Broken bits of pottery and household utensils are placed on the graves, whether in decoration or with the thought of possible need by those buried there, is debatable. . . . Small metates, bits of colored glass, parts of lamps, children's toys" can still be seen.

San Carlos Pass and Anza's Trail

San Carlos Pass, the first inland gateway to the coast of California, was discovered by Captain Juan Bautista de Anza in 1774 on the first continuous overland journey into the state. The trail and the pass were located by Professor Herbert E. Bolton of the University of California, and in 1924 the Native Sons of the Golden West marked them with a tablet bearing the following inscription: "On March 16, 1774, Juan Bautista de Anza, Indian fighter, explorer and colonizer, led through this Pass (named by him, San Carlos) the first white explorers to cross the mountains into California. The party traveled from Tubac, Arizona, to Monterey, California. On December 27, 1775, on a second expedition into California, Anza led through the Pass the party of Spaniards from Sonora who became the founders of San Francisco."

A marker (SRL 103) stands on the Anza Trail about eight miles southeast of the little town of Anza on the Cary Ranch. About a mile and a half east of Anza the Terwilliger Road turns south from SR 71; at a point just under five miles along Terwilliger Road the Coyote Canyon Road turns east one and one-half miles to the Cary Ranch.

On March 16 the travelers marched through Cahuilla Valley to Laguna Principe, now known as Dry Lake and located on the Contreras Ranch. Another short march on the following day took them as far as San Patricio, at the head of Bautista Canyon. Following this canyon, the expedition descended the mountain to Rio de San Joseph, now the San Jacinto River. This was on March 18, and camp was pitched in a leafy cottonwood grove about three miles above the site of San Jacinto.

On March 19 Anza and his party passed San Jacinto Lake, now dry, camping at its western end. Turning west the next day, they proceeded past the site of Morena through Alessandro Valley, and descended the ridge, probably by way of Sycamore Canyon. Crossing the site of Riverside, the expedition stopped near an Indian village on the banks of the Santa Ana River about three miles southwest of Mount Rubidoux near the Union Pacific railroad bridge (SRL 787). Here, on March 20, a bridge of logs was thrown across the river, and the following day the party crossed the river. On

the 22nd they entered San Bernardino County and on the 24th they arrived at Mission San Gabriel.

Returning from Monterey in April 1774, Anza retraced his steps through Riverside County early in May, stopping again at some of his previous campsites. On May 10 he was once more at Yuma.

In December 1775, Anza again passed over this route as the leader of that remarkable band of pioneers who first settled San Francisco. On Christmas Eve, camp was made near the upper end of Coyote Canyon at Upper Willows, or Fig Tree Spring.

Here, shortly before midnight, a baby boy, Salvador Ignacio Linares, was born, the third and last birth after leaving Tubac. The colonists, forgetting their misery for a time, spent that first Christmas Eve in California singing and dancing and partaking a little too freely, perhaps, of the aguardiente that Anza had given them against the protests of Father Font. On Christmas morning, the train being held in the canyon for another day on account of little Salvador, the priest took the opportunity to rebuke his now-repentant flock by a sermon, at the close of which he wished everybody a happy Christmas.

In 1950 the California Centennials Commission erected a monument in Coyote Canyon near the San Diego county line to commemorate the birth of the first white child in California.

From here, the route was, with one variation, the same as on Anza's previous trip. After leaving Lake San Jacinto, the company went past the site of Lakeview, through Bernasconi Pass, and across Alessandro Valley by way of March Air Force Base to the old campsite on the Santa Ana River.

The route that Anza opened up at this time was used infrequently for a while. By it came the colonists for Los Angeles, and the troops for the presidio of Santa Barbara, but after Fages's expedition in 1782 it was abandoned because of the hostility of the Yuma Indians. A statue of Anza stands at Fourteenth and Market streets in Riverside.

The Old Emigrant Trail and the San Bernardino–Sonora Road

Anza's route across the mountains was superseded by another trail opened in 1782 by Pedro Fages, who, instead of following the older path back to San Gabriel after his expedition against the Yuma Indians, blazed a new one, coming into San Diego County by way of the Carrizo Creek, Vallecito, and over the Cuyamaca Mountains to Mission San Diego.

Santiago Argüello, while in pursuit of Indian horse thieves, rediscovered this trail in 1825. In January 1826 the Mexican government sent Romualdo Pacheco, Lieutenant of Engineers, to investigate it, and with his approval an official mail route was adopted via Carrizo Creek, Vallecito, San Felipe Valley, and Warner's Pass. A small detachment of soldiers was briefly garrisoned on the Colorado River to protect the road but apparently encountered no hostility. From then on the road was occasionally used by mail carriers and traders from Sonora. Probably the first Americans to come this way were David E. Jackson and his party of fur traders, who had come overland from Santa Fe in 1831. Later it came to be known as the Emigrant Trail and formed a part of the Southern Emigrant Trail, a much-traveled route from the East into California during the 1840's and 1850's.

In Riverside and San Bernardino counties there were two branches of the old Emigrant Trail. From the Colorado River to Warner's Ranch and continuing west to Aguanga there was one road. There the San Bernardino–Sonora Road branched north along the western base of the San Jacinto Mountains, while the Colorado Road went directly west and then northwest through the valley north of the Santa Ana Mountains. This section of the road through San Bernardino and Riverside counties to San Gabriel was called the Canyon Road by the mission fathers, who opened it up immediately after Romualdo Pacheco had reestablished the overland route by way of Warner's. It was by the latter route that Jackson traversed Riverside County on his way to San Gabriel, going by way of Temecula, Elsinore, Temescal Canyon, and Corona.

The San Bernardino–Sonora Road passed through Riverside County west of modern Beaumont and turned south, passing through Lamb Canyon to San Jacinto and from there to what is now Hemet. It continued southward along what is now Sage Road to Aguanga, where it merged with another road from San Gabriel that was designated as the Colorado Road. From here the road continued into the desert and to Sonora. The well-traveled road was later used by Americans in their westward marches into California.

The Butterfield Overland Stage Route

The Butterfield route from St. Louis to Los Angeles passed through Riverside County on a route marked by the modern towns of Temecula, Lake Elsinore, and Corona. The long-vanished stage station at 20730 Temescal Canyon Road, four miles southeast of Corona, is marked by SRL 188. A short intact portion of the road lies in the Alberhill section of Elsinore Valley. To the southeast, on the old Machado ranch property, some vestiges of the stage route remain.

One of the old Machado adobes, possibly the one used as a Butterfield stage station, stood until 1964 at 32912 Macy Street near Grand Avenue on the southwest side of Lake Elsinore. It and a small adobe outbuilding have been razed, but the site is marked by three distinctive tall palm trees. Two rooms of another Machado adobe have been incorporated into the home at 15410 Grand Avenue. Agustín Machado acquired the Rancho La Laguna in 1858 from Abel Stearns, who had purchased it from the heirs of the original grantee, Julián Manríquez. The grant of over 13,000 acres was made by Governor Micheltorena in 1844.

Markers of the Bradshaw Road

The Bradshaw Road was a passage between the Colorado River and the Coachella Valley. Only two unconnected, unpaved pieces of the road remain. The easternmost extends twenty miles west from the end of 30th Avenue in the Palo Verde Valley. The other follows the Salt Creek Wash north of the Chocolate Mountains. At Wiley Well, named for the storekeeper and postmaster A. P. Wiley, nine miles west of Blythe at the junction of Bradshaw Trail and Wiley Well Road, E Clampus Vitus has placed a commemorative plaque. Another point marked by the society is at Shaver's Well, on Box Canyon Road. A third site commemorated by the Clampers is at Chiriaco Summit on I-10, a point also known as Romero Pass and as Bradshaw-Grant Pass.

Old Temescal Road

A monument (SRL 638) has been placed at the junction of the Temescal Canyon Road and the road to Glen Ivy Hot Springs, 8.8 miles southeast of the intersection of Ontario Avenue and Main Street south of Corona. It commemorates the old Temescal Road, which has seen the transition from Indian trail to automobile highway, with many an explorer, Argonaut, stagecoach, and military caravan between. I-15 now passes through here, superseding SR 71, but old roads parallel the modern freeway, and along these historical landmarks are still to be found.

The first house in Riverside County was erected by Leandro Serrano in 1824. Don Leandro was the son of a soldier who had come to San Diego with Father Junipero Serra in 1769. He became mayordomo of Pala Chapel, and in 1818, because of his long and faithful service and his influence over the Indians, the priest at Mission San Luis Rey sent him to locate on the mission lands in Temescal Valley where many Indians were then living.

The valley was fair with groves of oak and sycamore, green ciénegas or marshes, and myriad wild-

Tanning Vats, Rancho Serrano, near Glen Ivy Hot Springs

flowers, and at the largest of the ciénegas, Serrano built his first adobe home in 1824. A large Indian rancheria and sweat house or *temescal* were located nearby, and Serrano enlisted the natives in a drive against the bears and mountain cats of the region before bringing in his sheep and cattle.

The site of Serrano's adobe (SRL 185) is marked with a plaque on a boulder at the junction of Lawson Drive and Temescal Canyon Road, just north of Glen Ivy Hot Springs. Nearby, where Temescal Canyon Road meets Dawson Canyon Road, the site of the third adobe Serrano built is marked (SRL 224). Also marked (SRL 186) are the tanning vats, two of which are still visible, used for the preparation of hides on the rancho. Serrano lived in the area until his death in 1852; his family continued to live here until the end of the century.

The city of Corona, largely situated on the Rancho La Sierra of Bernardo Yorba, has honored its founders of 1886 by a monument (SRL 738) in the city park on Sixth Street between Rimpau Avenue and East Grand Boulevard. Corona was formerly called South Riverside.

Rancho Jurupa

Rancho Jurupa, a portion of which later became the Rubidoux Ranch, and on a part of which the city of Riverside now stands, was granted to Juan Bandini in 1838. Don Juan was a well-educated Peruvian gentleman of Italian descent who came to this part of California in 1828. A man of unusual ability, he was a member of the Territorial Assembly and at various times held many important offices in California. One of his daughters married Cave J. Couts and another wed Abel Stearns; thus Don Juan was identified with the emerging American political leadership as well.

Juan Bandini was one of the first white settlers in Riverside County, and in 1839 he built his first home on Rancho Jurupa. The site was on a high bluff along the northwest side of the Santa Ana River, about one thousand feet west of Hamner Boulevard at a point one-half mile north of the Santa Ana River bridge, five and one-half miles north of Corona. This site was three and one-half miles upstream from Bandini's later adobe (the Cota house). Rancho Jurupa consisted of over 32,000 acres of land, which extended for twenty miles along both sides of the Santa Ana River. The plains to the east of the river were considered worthless and were left wild and uncultivated or used for the pasturage of thousands of sheep. Today, the city of Riverside covers the old Jurupa "bench lands." Extensive orange groves replaced the sheep ranges and these in turn have given way in large part to homes. The southeast corner of Rancho Jurupa is the prominent landmark of Pachappa Hill at the eastern end of Jurupa Avenue in Riverside. In 1859, the year of Don Juan's death, most of Rancho Jurupa was sold to his son-in-law Abel Stearns.

Rubidoux Ranch

On May 6, 1843, Juan Bandini sold one and a half leagues of Rancho Jurupa to Benjamin D. Wilson, a native of Tennessee. Wilson, affectionately known as "Don Benito" among the Californians, had been a trader in New Mexico. On coming to California he bought this property and settled down as a ranchero, marrying Ramona Yorba, daughter of Bernardo Yorba, his nearest neighbor. He was held in high regard by the Californians, and among the American pioneers he was a notable friend to the Indians. Robert Glass Cleland said of him: "A man of brave and adventurous spirit, who dealt justly and walked uprightly throughout the entire course of his romantic and richly varied life, B. D. Wilson might well be selected as an example of the most admirable type of manhood bred on the western border in the period immediately preceding the Mexican War. He lived through stirring times in the history of California and contributed abundantly to the making of the state."

Wilson built for himself a fine adobe house, which he later sold to Louis Rubidoux. By 1850, Rubidoux had purchased the remainder of the land that Bandini had sold to Wilson in 1843, obtaining a deed from Wilson on May 3, 1848, for a half-interest in his land, and a deed from Isaac Williams for the other half-interest on December 13, 1849. Louis Rubidoux, a native of St. Louis, was of French descent, his family being prominent in the early history of Missouri. The name was originally Robidoux but was altered in Mexican California. His father was a pioneer merchant in St. Louis and his brother Joseph was the founder of the city of St. Joseph. Louis himself, as well as other members of the family, had been active in the trapping and fur-trading industry in the Southwest before coming to California. Louis Rubidoux exercised considerable influence in building up his community and served as local judge and supervisor. He was a well-educated, genial, kindly man, and his home became a haven for many pioneer families in southern California.

A tablet commemorating Rubidoux placed by the Daughters of the American Revolution is at the community center on Limonite Avenue in the town of Rubidoux, once known as West Riverside. The site of the old Rubidoux adobe (SRL 102) is now in a shopping center on the north side of Mission Boulevard in Rubidoux, about one hundred yards east of Bloomington Boulevard.

Rubidoux built one of the first gristmills in this part of California on the Rancho Jurupa in 1846–47. Being at that time the only mill of its kind in the region, it supplied a great need. It is said that the troops of the Mormon Battalion and Frémont's Battalion in 1847 were the enthusiastic recipients of flour from the Jurupa Mill and beans from the rancho. One of the old millstones has been preserved at the Mission Inn, and another adorns the Rubidoux-Frémont Monument, which stands near the site of the mill (SRL 303) at the intersection of Fort Drive and Molino Way, across Mission Boulevard from the site of the Rubidoux home. The tablet is missing from the marker, which has been vandalized. The monument, erected in 1926, honors two great figures of California history, but John C. Frémont had no direct connection with the Riverside area. Molino Way recalls Rubidoux's industry in the Spanish word for "mill," and Fort Drive commemorates a small military post that never deserved nor officially received the title of fort. A United States Army post was established at this spot on Rancho Jurupa in 1852 by Captain Lovell and Lieutenant Smith, and a small body of troops was kept there until 1854, chiefly as a protection against the Paiute and Mojave Indians. The site of the post is sometimes called "Fort Fremont," although Frémont himself never visited this spot.

Louis Rubidoux died in 1868, and in 1870 a brick house was built on former Rubidoux land—a house that still stands and is one of the Riverside area's oldest. Cornelius Jensen, a native of Denmark who married Mercedes Alvarado, became the storekeeper at Agua Mansa in San Bernardino County in 1854. His adobe house there was one of the few to survive the great flood of 1862. A few years later Jensen came to the Rubidoux ranch, purchased some of it, and built his fine brick home in Danish style. This restored place

Trujillo Adobe, near Riverside–San Bernardino County Line

(SRL 943) is the heart of the Jensen-Alvarado Ranch Historic Park, now being created by the Riverside County Parks Department. The house is at the end of a lane of cottonwoods at 4350 Riverview Drive in Rubidoux. Cornelius Jensen became one of the most respected citizens of Riverside. He is buried in the old cemetery at Agua Mansa, as also, reputedly, is Louis Rubidoux.

There were two settlements on the "Bandini Donation" of Rancho Jurupa—Agua Mansa on the northwest side of the Santa Ana River and San Salvador on the southeast—to which the New Mexican colonists moved from Politana on the Lugo rancho in the mid-1840's. These towns were devastated by flood in 1862, but both were rebuilt on higher ground. Of Agua Mansa only the cemetery remains. At San Salvador, better known as La Placita and called "Spanish Town" by the American pioneers, there remains the Trujillo adobe, preserved by Riverside County, a small, modest structure just a few hundred yards south of the San Bernardino County line, at the junction of North Orange and Center streets. This was the home of Lorenzo Trujillo, leader of the New Mexicans who settled at Politana, Agua Mansa, and San Salvador.

When Trujillo's group left the Lugo rancho for the Bandini Donation, the Lugos replaced them at Politana with Juan Antonio and his band of Cahuilla Indians. This Indian leader also founded the village of Sahatapa (SRL 749) in San Timoteo Canyon, a few miles northwest of Beaumont near El Casco Station on the Southern Pacific Railroad.

Riverside

In 1870, the town of Riverside was founded on the eastern portion of the old Jurupa Grant by Judge J. W. North. North was born in New York in 1815 and educated as a lawyer. He took a prominent part in the material and cultural foundations of three American commonwealths: Minnesota, Nevada, and California. In Minnesota he was active in the territorial legislature, founded the town of Northfield, promoted the Minneapolis and Cedar Valley Railway, and helped to establish the University of Minnesota. He was active in the Republican Convention of 1860, which nominated Abraham Lincoln for the presidency; he was subsequently appointed Surveyor General of the Territory of Nevada, and soon after became a territorial judge. He was president of the Nevada state constitutional convention in 1864.

Judge North went to Knoxville, Tennessee, to open up foundries after the Civil War. While there he became interested in organizing a colony in California. Associating with him men from Massachusetts, Michigan, Iowa, and New York, he went with a committee to California over the Central Pacific Railroad, which had just been opened up. He examined sites in southern California, purchasing a portion of the Rancho Jurupa. In 1870, Riverside was founded on the old rancho. Judge North later moved to Fresno County, where he had acquired land. His busy life ended there in 1880.

The old North residence once stood on the city block now bounded on the west by the Union Pacific depot, on the east by the Santa Fe depot, on the north by Seventh Street, and on the south by Eighth Street. The site was set aside as a city park in 1927, and was named the Judge North Memorial Park in honor of the founder of Riverside.

The city of Riverside was incorporated in 1883, and ten years later it became the seat of a new county. The courthouse, the second built in the county, is a handsome beaux-arts structure at 3050 Main Street, designed by Franklin P. Burnham and built in 1904. Another handsome structure is the Riverside Municipal Museum at Seventh and Orange streets; originally built as the post office in 1912, it has housed the museum since 1945. The museum administers Heritage House at 8193 Magnolia Avenue, a restored Queen Anne mansion from 1891 containing much of its original decor and furnishings. Work is being done to restore some of Riverside's historic Chinatown. An active Chinese community was centered at Brockton and Tequesquite avenues from 1880 to about 1930, the last building of which was removed in 1978.

Three old churches, all of them still active, display different architectural styles. The parish hall of the Magnolia United Presbyterian Church at 7200 Magnolia Avenue is in the Gothic style and was built in 1881. The First Unitarian Church at Seventh and Lemon streets was built in 1891 of red Arizona sandstone and suggests in its design a medieval English parish church.

The First Church of Christ, Scientist, at Sixth and Lemon streets, built in 1900, is the oldest Hispanic Revival structure in the city.

The Tibbets Memorial

The Tibbets Memorial in honor of Mrs. Eliza Tibbets, the woman who raised the first navel orange trees in California, was placed by Aurantia Chapter, DAR, in a small park at the head of Magnolia and Arlington avenues, Riverside, in 1920. Two seedling orange trees were sent to Mrs. Tibbets from Washington, D.C., in 1873 or later by Professor William A. Saunders, the husband of an old friend. Budlings had been sent to Professor Saunders from Bahia, Brazil. Two of these he sent to a friend in Florida, and two he sent to Mrs. Tibbets in Riverside.

The two budlings sent to Florida did not survive, but, owing to Mrs. Tibbets's care and in spite of somewhat adverse circumstances, the two trees entrusted to her lived. From these two budlings grew the great navel orange industry of southern California, adding millions of dollars annually to the state's resources.

The trees were originally planted at the Tibbets home, the site of which is at Central Avenue and Navel Court. At this spot a marker was placed in honor of Eliza's husband, Luther C. Tibbets, in 1935. In 1903 one of the trees (SRL 20) was transplanted a short distance away, at Magnolia and Arlington, and in front of this tree, still producing fruit, is the memorial to Mrs. Tibbets. Offspring trees are on the same plot of land as the Mother Navel Orange, protected by a fence. The other tree was transplanted to the courtyard of the Mission Inn by President Theodore Roosevelt at the time of his visit there, also in 1903, but it died in the 1920's.

The Mission Inn

Captain C. C. Miller came to southern California when it was first emerging from its hacienda days. In 1873 he was made engineer of the new colony of Riverside, which had been established on the old Rancho Jurupa in 1870. As his salary, he received a block of land in the new colony, and there, in 1875, he built an adobe cottage, one of the first solid-walled houses in town, which later became the nucleus of the famous Mission Inn.

The Miller family began to receive guests in the adobe as early as 1876, and the name Glenwood Cottage was given to it. The old-fashioned, homely hospitality of the Millers drew an increasing number of patrons, and a small group of frame buildings grew up around Glenwood Cottage. With this growth, the name

Mission Inn, Riverside

An interesting museum is located at March Air Force Base on the southern edge of Riverside. The March Field Museum is dedicated to the history of the evolution of air power. Over 30 historic aircraft, ranging from the days of World War I to the 1970's, are a feature of the exhibit. The museum is open to the public on a regular basis. March Field is one of the earliest air bases in the United States, established in 1918.

Mount Rubidoux

A local tradition speaks of Indian sunrise services held on Mount Rubidoux. The mountain was named for Louis Rubidoux, who owned part of the Rancho Jurupa on which it is located. In 1906 the Huntington Park Association acquired Mount Rubidoux and developed it as a public park. On April 26, 1907, the Serra Cross was raised on the highest point of the mountain and consecrated to Father Junipero Serra, founder of the California missions. The first annual sunrise pilgrimage to the top of Mount Rubidoux on Easter Sunday was held in 1909, and from that service have come all the subsequent Easter sunrise services of southern California. Every Easter morning thousands of worshippers climb Mount Rubidoux and other mountains for the annual event.

The Land of "Ramona"

Helen Hunt Jackson was a native of Amherst, Massachusetts. Like her childhood friend Emily Dickinson, she spent much time in writing—in her case, from the necessity to support herself after the death of her first husband. A crusader for the rights of Indians, she wrote a scathing account of their mistreatment at the hands of federal officials in *A Century of Dishonor* (1881). This book so impressed the Department of the Interior that she was commissioned to join Abbott Kinney in a survey of the condition of the Mission Indians of southern California.

Journeying through Riverside, Orange, and San Diego counties, Mrs. Jackson developed both a love for a rather romanticized Californian past and a keen dismay at the wretched condition of the Mission Indians. Staying with the Wolf family on the Vail Ranch (about three and one-half miles east of Temecula), Mrs. Jackson investigated the condition of the Temecula Indians. The countryside enchanted her, and the Pechanga Burial Ground, the Pala Chapel, and the Wolf Ranch all became vivid places to her. In 1883 she submitted an extensive report on the condition of the Mission Indians to federal authorities, who apparently paid little attention to it. Mrs. Jackson was determined that her inves-

was changed to Glenwood Tavern, and later to Glenwood Hotel.

Almost from the beginning, Frank A. Miller, son of the pioneer, was proprietor and manager at Glenwood. In 1902 he replaced the old wooden cottages by a new structure of concrete and brick, the building that now surrounds the Court of the Birds. The old adobe cottage stood on its original site in this court until 1948, when it gave way to the swimming pool. Around these two grew the famous Glenwood Mission Inn (now simply Mission Inn, SRL 761), modeled after the old missions of California, and containing rare art treasures from all over the world. Now a National Historic Landmark, the inn has had a special appeal for many celebrities and for some who would later become famous, such as the young Pat and Richard Nixon, who were married there, and Nancy and Ronald Reagan, who honeymooned there. Still on display is the special oversized chair created for President William H. Taft on a 1911 visit. The inn is now being extensively renovated.

Other Riverside Landmarks

In 1907, the University of California established its Citrus Experiment Station on the eastern edge of Riverside, and for many years the development of various citrus crops was carried on there. In 1954, a campus of the university was created at the site, now a major educational facility. The 37-acre botanical gardens of the university and of the experiment station can be visited; they contain many trees that became the basis of important California orchards.

The California Museum of Photography is also located on the campus of the University of California at Riverside.

tigations would produce some amelioration of the living conditions of the Indians. "I'm going to write a novel in which will be set forth some Indian experiences in a way to move people's hearts," she wrote to friends later that year. "People will read a novel when they will not read serious books."

The result was *Ramona* (1884), which used the background of Temecula and Soboba and the San Jacinto Valley to tell the story of the tragedy of Ramona and Alessandro and their people. An instant best-seller, the book was viewed as a picturesque romance rather than a cry for action. Mrs. Jackson may have anticipated this disappointment in another private letter concerning the Soboba Indians: "It breaks my heart," she wrote, "to try to make them understand that all I can do is *tell* about them."

Throughout southern California for many years, tourists were shown aged women who were said to be the "original" Ramona and sites that were the "authentic" locales of the story. The work was really a combination of many stories Mrs. Jackson had gathered and sites she had visited. The Ramona Pageant is held each spring in the Ramona Bowl, a natural amphitheater just south of Hemet. In the San Bernardino National Forest, between Sage and Anza, E Clampus Vitus has placed a plaque at Juan Diego Flats inscribed thus: "In this valley a conflict between the culture of the Indian and the white man resulted in the death of Juan Diego (Alessandro in the play *Ramona*) by the hands of Sam Temple."

San Jacinto

San Jacinto is located on the lands of Rancho San Jacinto Viejo, an area of over 35,000 acres that was granted by Manuel Jimeno, governor pro tem, to José Antonio Estudillo in 1842. Estudillo was a member of the California family that held land also in San Diego and San Leandro in Alameda County. The city of San Jacinto, now located on this old grant, is Riverside County's second-oldest city, having been incorporated in 1888.

At one time the Rancho San Jacinto belonged to Mission San Luis Rey, and a survey of 1827 indicates that an adobe house for the mayordomo of the rancho then existed. Estudillo's petition for a portion of the grant noted the existence of the house, about five miles northwest of San Jacinto, and in time he came to live in the extended home he built around the adobe remains, called Casa Loma. The building still stands by the Ramona Expressway.

Two homes of the Estudillo family stand on the old grant. One is the substantial mansion located on Seventh Street in San Jacinto, with extensive grounds; the other, almost impossible to see from the road, is on the Althouse property on Soboba Road, close to the hot springs resort and formerly a part of it.

San Jacinto received national publicity on July 14, 1937, when a Russian plane that had flown nonstop over the polar route from Moscow missed March Field and landed in Earl Smith's cow pasture.

The museum in this city has an attractive display dedicated to the work of Helen Hunt Jackson. At 181 East Main Street, it also has a wealth of material on the Cahuilla and Soboba Indians and on early ranching in the community.

Banning

Originally a stop on the Southern Pacific Railroad, the town of Banning was named for General Phineas Banning, developer of Los Angeles County's transportation systems. The Malki Museum on the nearby Morongo Indian Reservation is a recently developed source for the history of these people; it is open to the public on a regular basis. The Riverside County Parks Department is developing the Gilman ranch as a historic park. The ranch house was destroyed by fire in 1977, 98 years after it was built, and has been recreated on the original site. Extensive displays of covered wagons and ranch vehicles can be seen. At one time the Gilman Ranch was a stage stop on the Bradshaw line. E Clampus Vitus has placed a plaque at nearby Banning Pass, also known as San Gorgonio Pass.

Idyllwild

A mile above sea level in the San Jacinto Mountains, Idyllwild was developed around the turn of the century as a sanitarium for tuberculosis patients; the clean, dry mountain air was considered very beneficial. A plaque near the center of the community commemorates Camp Emerson, an early resort. The campus of the Idyllwild School of Music and the Arts, originally operated by the University of Southern California, has put on extensive summer programs for many years, making it something of a pioneer in southern California cultural activities.

On the road from Idyllwild to Palm Springs at Garner Valley, a plaque commemorates the Thomas-Garner Ranch, one of the oldest and largest cattle ranches of southern California. It is said that the couple who inspired Mrs. Jackson's Ramona and Alessandro actually lived and worked on the ranch in the later nineteenth century.

Lake Elsinore

The discovery of hot sulfur springs at Lake Elsinore in the 1880's led to the establishment of an early resort. Riverside County has marked its site with a plaque at Graham and Springs streets in Lake Elsinore. At 201 Graham, a two-story wooden building from this period, called the Chimes House, still stands.

The Coachella Valley, Indio, and Date Culture

The dry climate of the Coachella Valley combined with sufficient ground water produces the greatest amount of date culture in the United States. The first dates were imported from Algeria in the 1880's. Date cultivation was encouraged by the U.S. Department of Agriculture in cooperation with private enterprise in the 1920's, and today some 5,000 acres in the Coachella Valley are given over to magnificent groves of many varieties of date palms. Indio, the chief city of the Coachella Valley, began as a railroad center around 1875. Today it hosts the annual Date Festival, which has been a major attraction since the 1930's. The Coachella Valley Museum and Cultural Center at 82616 Miles Avenue in Indio is a repository of artifacts of the region from the days of the Cahuilla Indians to recent times, with special exhibits on the history of railroads and of water resource development in the valley.

Blythe

The town of Blythe was named for financier Thomas H. Blythe of San Francisco, who in the 1870's developed the region known as the Palo Verde Valley, adjacent to the Colorado River. The site of the Blythe Intake (SRL 948) is twelve miles north of the town at the entrance to the Palo Verde Diversion Dam, and marks the first legally filed claim to the Colorado River. The Palo Verde Historical Museum in Blythe is being developed to commemorate the history of the region.

Perris

The Orange Empire Railway Museum, established at Perris in 1958, contains an operating railway, two and one-half miles long, on which are run railway and trolley cars that used to run on Western lines. Of particular interest are the municipal streetcars from the Los Angeles area. The museum is located at 2201 South A Street, just off I-215, south of Perris.

Lake Perris to the north is the southern terminus of the mammoth California State Water Project. Water brought from the northern parts of the state arrives here, 600 miles to the south, where it is impounded behind Perris Dam. Lake Perris has been a recreational center since 1974, but its greater importance is as a reservoir for the thirsty lands of southern California.

Sacramento County

Sacramento County, named for the river so called by Spanish explorers of that region in honor of the Holy Sacrament, was one of the original 27 counties. The only changes made in its boundaries have been those necessitated by the shifting of the stream beds of the Mokelumne and Sacramento rivers. Sacramento has always been the county seat.

An Indian Site

The Nisipowinan village site (SRL 900) near the confluence of the American and Sacramento rivers in Discovery Park, Sacramento, is the most significant extant Indian village and cemetery site in the Sacramento region. Excavation of the mound—locally known as "Joe Mound," after a Portuguese farmer of the area who was called Joe—has shown evidence of habitation as early as 1000 B.C., and has produced artifacts from the encounters of the Indians with Captain John A. Sutter and his contemporaries around 1840.

Old Spanish Trails

Five Spanish expeditions had entered or seen the Sacramento–San Joaquin delta before 1800. In 1772 Pedro Fages, while exploring the "Port of San Francisco" for the purpose of finding a suitable mission site, went up the eastern shore of San Francisco Bay as far as the San Joaquin River and saw the great Sacramento River "from a point of vantage." In 1793 Francisco

Eliza sailed into the Sacramento River and stated that this river had not yet been explored. Sometime before 1808 it was given the name Sacramento.

Long after the mission had been founded at San Francisco, and after 19 of the 21 missions had been established along the coast of Alta California, several expeditions were organized and sent into the river country of the great interior valley to search for suitable sites for new missions. One of the most remarkable of these expeditions was that commanded by Gabriel Moraga in 1808. On October 9 Moraga's party camped on the lower Feather River, which Moraga called the Sacramento, a name he applied also to the great river into which it flows farther down, showing that he believed that the two composed the main stream. He considered the upper Sacramento, which he reached a little later, to be a branch of the main river and called it the Jesús María, a name long retained for that part of its course. It is easy to understand why Moraga reached this conclusion, for at the point where the Sacramento and the Feather come together, it is the Feather that makes a straight line north and south with the lower Sacramento, while the upper Sacramento flows at that point from the west.

An attempt to explore the river country by boat was made by José Antonio Sánchez in 1811, when he proceeded a little way up the Sacramento River. However, an expedition of more importance in the history of Sacramento took place in 1817, led by Father Narciso Durán, accompanied by Luis Argüello and Father Ramón Abella. Various channels that they followed, as well as a number of the places at which they camped, have been identified. At one time a fierce windstorm drove them behind the Montezuma Hills in the vicinity of the present town of Rio Vista (in Solano County), and again, from a vantage point on the site of Clarksburg they had a fine view of the Sierra Nevada. Soon afterward they passed the site of what is now the city of Sacramento, probably being its discoverers.

Opening of the Sacramento Trail

The Sacramento Trail was opened to trade and immigration by an American, Jedediah Strong Smith, who had made the first overland journey into California in 1826. Smith came again, in 1827, to rejoin that part of his company that he had left encamped on one of the rivers of the San Joaquin Valley. Although the Mexican government had demanded his departure from the province, he did not leave the country at once by the way he had come. Instead, he opened a new route that led north up the Sacramento River, called by Smith the Buenaventura.

After several unsuccessful attempts to find a pass through the Sierra Nevada from the river, the Smith party finally left the Sacramento about the middle of April 1828. Going northwest across the Coast Range through the wild regions now included in Trinity and Humboldt counties, Smith and his men came to the seacoast and proceeded along it to Oregon. The route thus opened by this tireless pathfinder of the Far West was soon followed by Hudson's Bay Company hunters and traders from Vancouver by way of Oregon.

A tablet in honor of Jedediah Strong Smith, the man who first opened the doors to California from the north, was placed by the Sacramento Chapter of the Daughters of the American Revolution at the west end of the bridge over the American River on SR 160.

New Helvetia

The first white settlement in the great central valley of California was made by John A. Sutter in 1839. Sutter, who was born in 1803 in Baden, Germany, of Swiss parents, came to the United States when still a young man. Eventually, he drifted to St. Louis and from there to the Pacific Coast by way of the Columbia River.

Slowly, the idea of founding a colony in California took form in the mind of this enterprising young pioneer. Sailing from Fort Vancouver (in what is now the state of Washington) to the Sandwich Islands, he aroused the interest of a handful of Americans and Hawaiian natives (then often called Kanakas) in his project. With this as a nucleus for the future independent state of which he dreamed, Sutter reached Alta California early in July 1839. There he became a citizen of the province and obtained permission of Governor Juan B. Alvarado to establish his settlement.

The great Sacramento Valley was at that time unsettled by white people. A few Spanish expeditions had been made into the interior to search for mission sites or Indians who had run away from life in the missions. Jedediah Strong Smith had explored it in 1828, and Hudson's Bay Company trappers had hunted on its streams. The native peoples who inhabited the river country and the surrounding mountains frequently raided the scattered coastal settlements, and Sutter's proposal to establish a frontier outpost that would act as a buffer against these raids was welcomed by the Mexican government, especially since it meant no expense on their part, other than the granting of a few leagues of wilderness land for the proposed settlement.

With high hopes for the future, Sutter embarked in August 1839 from Yerba Buena up the Sacramento River to choose a location for his estate. About August 15 he landed at what was then the south bank of the

American River, just north of B Street between 28th and 29th streets. A marker has been erected to commemorate the landing place (SRL 591). Soon he moved to a site nearby, where he established a permanent camp and built his fort.

In 1841 Sutter was granted eleven leagues of land in the Sacramento Valley. The construction of a pretentious adobe fort was begun in that year, the outside walls being completed in 1844. In December 1841 Sutter purchased the equipment of the Russian settlement at Fort Ross in Sonoma County, then being disbanded. This purchase included a large number of horses and cattle, a small launch, and several pieces of artillery. The cannon was set up at Sutter's Fort, and armed guards and daily drill became a feature of the place, giving it a decidedly military aspect. Sutter named the little settlement New Helvetia, perhaps hoping one day to make of this semifeudal barony an independent state.

Sutter's Fort

Sutter's Fort, as it soon came to be known, was not merely a fort; it was a trading post and a place of refuge as well. Robert Glass Cleland says that "in addition to Sutter's military activities, he displayed a vast amount of energy in more peaceful endeavors. To care for the ever growing needs of his colony, and especially to meet the pressing demands of his Russian debt, he branched out into a great variety of pursuits and tried all sorts of experiments, most of which impoverished, rather than enriched him. He planted large areas to wheat; built a flour mill; diverted water from the American River for irrigation purposes; grazed large herds of cattle and horses; sent hunters into the mountains and along the rivers for furs and elk skins; set up a distillery; began the weaving of coarse woolen blankets; ran a launch regularly for freight and passengers between his settlement and San Francisco Bay; employed nearly all foreigners who came to him for work, whether he needed them or not; trained the Indians to useful occupations; at times chastised the thieving, war-inclined tribes which the Spanish Californians could not subdue; administered justice as an official of the provincial government; and, in short, made his colony the nucleus of all activity, whether political or economic, in what was then the only settled portion of interior California.

"In addition to these varied activities, with their decided local and personal interest, Sutter contributed in a much larger way to the making of California history through his aid to American immigration. Few people today realize how large a part this hospitable, visionary, improvident land baron of the Sacramento played

in the American advance to California. His fort occupied the most strategic position in all Northern California, so far as the overland trails were concerned, and became the natural objective for parties crossing the Sierras, by the central and northern routes, or coming into the province by way of Oregon.

"At Sutter's, these immigrants, exhausted and half-starved as many of them were, found shelter, food and clothing, and an opportunity to learn something of the new land and people to which they had come. More than one company [the most famous of which was the Donner party], caught in the mountain snows, was saved from destruction by a rescue party sent from Sutter's Fort. The situation of the latter also made it impossible for the California authorities, had they been so inclined, to check or turn aside the stream of overland migration. The passes and trails of the northern Sierras lay open to American frontiersmen so long as Sutter maintained his position on the Sacramento."

Sutter's dream of New Helvetia was ruined by the discovery of gold at his mill at Coloma in 1848. His workers left him to go to the mines. The gold rush was a wave of humanity that swept over his lands. A bustling city grew up on the Sacramento. His splendid isolation was gone. Eventually Sutter moved to Lititz, Pennsylvania, where he spent his last years. He died in 1880 in Washington, D.C., where he had gone to defend his land titles, and was buried at Lititz.

Sutter's Fort fell into the hands of other owners after 1850, and the buildings began to deteriorate. Final destruction was threatened when, in 1889, it was proposed to open 27th Street from K to L streets. This disaster was averted by the efforts of General James G. Martine. The fort was restored by the state in 1891–93, and is now Sutter's Fort State Historic Park (SRL 525). It is located between K and L streets on the north and south and 26th and 28th streets on the west and east, about two and one-quarter miles from the waterfront. It has been registered as a National Historic Landmark by the Department of the Interior.

The original adobe bricks, made by Indians at Sutter's Fort, may be seen in the central building, which is all that remained of the original fort when reconstruction got under way following donation of the property to the state by the Native Sons of the Golden West. This two-story building, with basement, has walls about 30 inches thick, and the original hand-hewn oaken floor joists. Other walls within the fort were reconstructed of kiln-baked bricks, as were the outer walls. The fort was reproduced in its approximate original form and dimensions, with shops, storerooms, living quarters, and the like. About two dozen rooms or sections are devoted to museum purposes, for storage of reserve material, workshops, or displays of historical objects. Several cannon dating from Sutter's time preserve the military aspect of the place. A park, beautifully landscaped, is included in the grounds, which cover two city blocks.

Many interesting objects of pioneer days are housed in Sutter's Fort. These include an outstanding collection of Reed-Donner party items; firearms; stagecoaches and other vehicles; mining tools; costumes; objects made or used by James W. Marshall, who is credited with the discovery of gold at Coloma; equipment used by early fire departments; household furnishings; musical instruments; maps, documents, diaries of Forty-niners, paintings, prints, and rare photographs. The curator's office has files of information relating to California pioneers.

During the reconstruction of the fort, some of the workmen panned dirt near the east gate and recovered a quantity of gold dust that had been dropped years before by miners, or swept from gambling rooms and stores on the premises. Doubtless this was some of the first gold mined after the discovery at Sutter's sawmill in 1848.

The State Indian Museum is located on the property, with the entrance at 2618 K Street. Here is one of the finest and most complete collections of relics representing the workmanship of the prehistoric California Indians. Many artifacts were gathered from the ancient campsites and burial grounds of the San Joaquin and Sacramento valleys. In this remarkable array one sees striking evidence that the California Indian was a skilled craftsman as well as an artist of rare ability. There are pipes, serrated arrow points, and bowls, scores of baskets from all sections, ornaments and implements of stone, bone, and shell—all fashioned with a perfection of line and delicacy of detail found in the finest craftsmanship.

A plaque has been placed at Sutter's Fort to mark the western end of the Coloma Road (SRL 745). The route was first used in 1847 to reach the site of Sutter's sawmill. In January 1848 James Marshall brought to Sutter's Fort over this road the first gold discovered at Coloma. In 1849 James E. Birch established California's first stage line along this route. Other markers on the Coloma Road have been placed near Alder Springs at Nimbus Dam (SRL 746), and at Rescue and Coloma in El Dorado County.

Mexican Land Grants

John A. Sutter was not the first person to receive a land grant in the Sacramento Valley. In 1833 J. B. R. Cooper was granted the land "known by the name of Rio Ojotska," on the present American River three leagues east of the Sacramento. Cooper did not develop the property and renounced the grant in 1835. Four years later Sutter arrived at New Helvetia.

Sutter did not long remain the sole land baron in the Sacramento Valley. The beginning of the American occupation found him already surrounded by neighbors. Many of his former employees had occupied ranchos up and down the length of the great central valley.

John Sinclair, a Scotsman, settled on Rancho del Paso as early as 1841. On this estate of 44,000 acres, granted to Eliab Grimes in December 1844, Sinclair built a house on the right bank of the American River two and one-half miles from Sutter's Fort. This house was, for a time, the first civilized dwelling reached by the overland emigrant trains after crossing the Sierra Nevada. Sinclair was hospitable and kindly in his treatment of those in need, and as alcalde of the Sacramento district he was especially instrumental in sending aid to the Donner party. Part of this rancho was homesteaded in the 1870's by a family named Gibson. This land is today Gibson Ranch County Park on Elverta Road west of Watt Avenue, near the northern edge of the county.

Rancho Río de los Americanos, extending over 35,500 acres on the south side of the American River east of New Helvetia, was granted in 1844 to William A. Leidesdorff, vice-consul of the United States by appointment of Thomas O. Larkin. Leidesdorff died in 1848, leaving the rancho along with other valuable property in San Francisco. Captain Joseph L. Folsom, who had come to California as assistant quartermaster of Stevenson's New York Volunteers, purchased the vast Leidesdorff estate from the heirs for a song, thus becoming one of the wealthiest men in California. The town of Folsom was laid out on his rancho in 1855 and named in his honor. The site of the old Leidesdorff adobe, erected in 1846, is near Routier Road, just south of modern Rancho Cordova.

One summer evening in 1840, William Daylor, an employee of Sutter, climbed a hill southeast of New Helvetia and saw for the first time the rich valley of the Cosumnes River, then thickly populated with Indians. Daylor decided then and there that the lands bordering the north bank of the river were to be his. On returning to the fort he talked the matter over with his friend, Jared Sheldon, also an employee of Sutter. Sheldon, a native of Vermont, had become a naturalized Mexican citizen and held claims against the Mexican government for services in building the Custom House at Monterey. The two men formed a partnership whereby Sheldon was to obtain the grant of land through W. E. P. Hartnell in liquidation of his claim, and also to supply the cattle, while Daylor was to settle upon the land and look after the stock. The first grant, made in 1841, proved to be defective, and a second was drawn up and approved early in 1844 under the designation "Rancho Omochumnes."

Mining Camps of the American River

Mormon Island (SRL 569), in the northeast corner of Sacramento County, was the site of the second important gold discovery in California. Early in the spring of 1848 two Mormons, on their way to Sutter's Mill in Coloma, camped for the night at a bar on the South Fork near its confluence with the North Fork. One of the men remarked: "They are taking gold above us on the river. Let's see if we can find some at this place." Panning out a little dirt in one of their cooking utensils, they revealed a fine prospect. The two Mormons returned to the fort the next day and reported their find to Samuel Brannan, leader of the Mormons in California and associated with C. C. Smith, who kept a store at New Helvetia. Brannan immediately proceeded to the place where the discovery had been made and set up a preemptive claim, demanding a royalty of one-third on all the gold taken out at the bar. This fee continued to be paid to Brannan as long as the Mormons were in the majority. Later, when non-Mormons outnumbered those of the faith, the tithe could no longer be collected. Meanwhile, Brannan had accumulated thousands of dollars, which he invested in merchandising, becoming one of the wealthiest men in California.

By 1853 Mormon Island had become a city of over 2,500 inhabitants, but a fire in 1856 destroyed most of the town and it was never rebuilt. A few rock cellars and the ubiquitous locust tree were all that remained to locate the site of this historic gold town when it was inundated by Folsom Lake in 1955. A marker has been placed on Green Valley Road just over the El Dorado county line, near the cemetery to which graves were moved from the Folsom Dam project area.

Down the American River from Mormon Island were numerous camps, some of which were important towns in the early 1850's. In quick succession came Alabama Bar, on the north bank of the river; Slate Bar, opposite Folsom State Prison, where several stores were located; and Sailor Bar. Bean's Bar was one-half mile below Alabama Bar on the opposite side of the river.

Folsom

Negro Bar was first mined by black people in 1849. By 1851 few blacks remained in a population of 700. The town of Folsom was laid out there in 1855. In the

Wells Fargo Building, Folsom

same year, at Sacramento, Theodore D. Judah began construction of California's first passenger railroad, the Sacramento Valley Railroad, which was completed as far as Folsom—a distance of 22 miles—in 1856. Historical markers have been placed at the Sacramento terminal (SRL 526) at Third and R streets, and at Folsom (SRL 558) on the plaza at Sutter Street near Reading Street. The new town became an important center for stage and freight lines running to the northern mining camps and to Virginia City, Nevada. The greatest prosperity was enjoyed in the early 1860's, when many substantial hotels and business houses were established, as well as an academy and several churches. Some of these sturdy stone and brick buildings still stand. Prominent among them is the Wells Fargo Building, built in 1860, on Sutter Street. This was for one year the western terminus of the Pony Express. The building is now

Folsom Powerhouse, Folsom

the home of the Folsom Historical Society's excellent museum.

The Folsom Powerhouse (SRL 633), a landmark in the history of long-distance high-voltage transportation, operated continuously from 1895 to 1952. It has been presented to the state by the Pacific Gas and Electric Company and can be toured. Below the powerhouse along the river are Maidu Indian grinding rocks. Sacramento Station A (SRL 633.2), built to receive power generated from the Folsom Powerhouse, is located at Sixth and H streets in the capital city. The first transmission of electricity was on July 13, 1895.

Folsom has a ''Nob Hill'' of historic houses; the Cohn House at 305 Scott Street is a National Historic Landmark. The Burnham Mansion at 602 Figueroa Street and the Hyman House at 603 are also late-nineteenth-century houses; all are privately occupied. At the eastern side of the city is Folsom Prison, established in 1880 and still a maximum-security prison. Early convicts did a great deal of stonecutting, which is still in evidence. A museum at the entrance to the facility is open to the public.

Earlier mining methods were replaced by giant dredges that have created some of the most extensive rock tailings to be seen anywhere in California. Although the dredges are no longer in operation, the desolation they created is still very much in evidence between Folsom Boulevard and the American River, on the west side of town. The Natomas Company ceased operations in 1962, by which time millions of dollars of gold had been produced in this area; in the 1920's and early 1930's the average annual production from gold dredging in Sacramento County was $1,300,000.

On or near Alder Creek, two miles south of Folsom, was Prairie City (SRL 464), a mining camp that reached the height of its prosperity in 1853, after the Natoma Water and Mining Company's ditch was completed to that point. A large quartz mill was also erected there in 1857 at a cost of $50,000. For a time, Prairie City was a city in fact as well as in name, being a center of trade for a number of other camps, including Rhoads' Diggings, Alder Creek, and Willow Springs Hill Diggings. The last-named place covered about 2,000 acres and yielded several million dollars' worth of gold.

Cosumnes River Mining Camps

Michigan Bar (SRL 468) was the most prominent of all the early gold camps on the Cosumnes River in Sacramento County. Founded in 1849 by two men from Michigan, it reached a population of 1,500 or more in the early 1850's. The original townsite has since been washed out by hydraulic mining, destroying the last remaining landmarks—the old Heath store and the Wells Fargo Express office. The Addington Pottery Works at Michigan Bar was one of the earliest and largest in the state. The town was located one mile north of the historical marker that stands on SR 16.

Fleeting towns developed in the vicinity of Michigan Bar during those feverish days of 1849 and the 1850's. Cook's Bar, founded in 1849 by Dennis Cook two miles below Michigan Bar, became quite a town in the early 1850's, but by 1860 it had ceased to exist. Five miles southwest of Michigan Bar on the Ione Valley road was Sebastopol, named during the Crimean War, and a lively camp from 1854 to 1859. Katesville, near Cook's Bar, another mining center that arose in 1854, had several stores and saloons, a hotel, and a boardinghouse. By 1862 the place was deserted. Live Oak, northeast of Sebastopol, had rich returns from its diggings from 1854 to 1861. An old brick building stands at this point on the south side of SR 16, about a mile west of the Michigan Bar marker.

Several roads to the southern mines passed through the Cosumnes River region, and ferries, succeeded by toll bridges, as well as a number of hotels, were established by enterprising men at a very early date. William Daylor and Jared Sheldon, as owners of the Omochumnes Mexican grant, were strategically situated and made great profits from mining, ranching, trading, and hotel keeping. In 1850 Sheldon built the Slough House (SRL 575) on Deer Creek (a branch of the Cosumnes River) where the Jackson road crossed that stream. It was destroyed by fire in 1890 and rebuilt the same year on the old site. The second hotel still stands, with gigantic black walnut trees bordering the old highway, and an old cemetery on the knoll above the orchards.

Daylor established himself as a trader and hotel-keeper on the Cosumnes River about a mile east of Slough House. This place, which was at first known as Daylor's Ranch, later became the Cosumnes post office.

In 1846–47 Jared Sheldon built a gristmill on Rancho Omochumnes. Four years later he constructed a dam to provide water to operate the mill. It caused flooding of the claims of miners working along the river below the dam. The miners threatened violence, and Sheldon erected a small fort, placing a cannon there by way of warning. On July 11, 1851, the indignant miners captured the fort, and when Sheldon arrived with reinforcements two hours later, a battle ensued in which he and two of his men were killed. The dam was swept away by high water in the winter of 1851–52. The site of Sheldon's gristmill (SRL 439) is about one mile southeast of Slough House on Meiss Road.

On the west side of SR 99, where it crosses the Cosumnes River between Elk Grove and Galt, was the ranch of Martin Murphy, Jr. (SRL 680). Here the initial action took place in the conquest of California by the

United States. On June 10, 1846, Ezekiel Merritt and a band of settlers overpowered the soldiers of Lieutenant Francisco Arce of the Mexican army and took their horses from the Murphy corral on the north side of the river. Four days later the Bear Flag was raised at Sonoma.

In the Masonic Cemetery at Elk Grove is the grave of Mrs. Benjamin W. Wilder, born Elitha Cumi Donner in 1832 (SRL 719). She came to California in 1846 in the ill-fated party of which her father, George Donner, was one of the leaders. She died in 1923. Elk Grove is the site of the first county free library branch in California (SRL 817), established in 1908. The pioneer effort has been commemorated by a plaque at 9125 Elk Grove Boulevard.

Sutterville

Sutter laid out a townsite in 1844 on his ranch, about two miles below the Sacramento River embarcadero. Here, on high ground overlooking the river, he and his friends built a few dwellings and called the place Suttersville, later Sutterville. The location boasted one of the few elevations above the treacherous waters of the river, and the future of the little settlement seemed promising. It flourished until 1848 as the friendly rival of the fort and the embarcadero. George Zins built a brick building there in 1847, one of the first brick structures erected in California.

The discovery of gold by James W. Marshall in the tailrace of Sutter's Mill at Coloma in 1848 changed the course of events for Sutterville as it did for all California. Sutter's Fort became too small for the business demands that soon crowded in upon it from every side, a new town sprang up by the embarcadero, and Sutterville also became a settlement of some consequence. It was eventually incorporated into the city of Sacramento by an election in 1950. Its original site is now lost, but a marker (SRL 593) stands on Sutterville Road across from the zoo of the William Land Park. The site of the old brick brewery that stood nearby until it was pulled down in 1952 was marked by E Clampus Vitus in 1983.

During the Civil War, Camp Union (SRL 666) of the California Volunteers was located for some months in 1861 and 1862 at Sutterville. A marker has been placed at Sutterville and Del Rio roads.

The Founding of Sacramento

It was around the embarcadero at the foot of the long road leading to Sutter's Fort that the new city of Sacramento first grew up. Sutter had fallen heavily into debt, and finally, in order to evade his creditors, he turned his property over to his son John A. Sutter, Jr., who had arrived at the fort in September 1848. By December the younger Sutter, with Captain William A. Warner, had laid out a town at the embarcadero, naming it Sacramento after the river. By the first part of January 1849 two log cabins had been built, followed soon by the first frame building and a canvas house. In April there were 30 buildings, and by June over 100. On August 1 the first town election was held. Situated at the entrance to the gold fields, Sacramento profited tremendously from the mining trade. By October 1849 it had a resident population of about 2,000 and a floating population of 5,000. Sacramento was incorporated as a city in 1850.

Many home seekers arrived at Sacramento in 1849, expecting to take up homesteads there as they had done in Oregon and the Middle West. Sacramento was being built on the Sutter grant, but these settlers did not see why the laws of a foreign government should have more weight than the rights of free American citizens in the assigning of land. They claimed the right to at least one free city lot each. However, those men who had been buying from Sutter hotly contested this claim, and the Squatters' Riot was the result. The Sacramento River twice flooded the area early in 1850, adding to the uncertainty about what property belonged to whom.

A lot at the southeast corner of Second and N streets was put to the test, when Dr. Charles Robinson, a leader of the squatters, erected a shanty there, only to have it removed by the city authorities. In May 1850 a judgment was rendered in favor of Sutter's title, but on August 14 a body of about 40 squatters contested this decision by attempting to gain possession of the lot from which Robinson had been ousted. When prevented from doing so, they retired up I Street to Third and thence to J near Fourth, where they were met by Mayor Hardin Bigelow with a small band of citizens. The squatters then threw a line across Fourth Street at J and fired upon the citizen group.

In the fight that followed, Mayor Bigelow was seriously wounded, as was Dr. Robinson, while James Maloney and James Morgan, leaders of the squatters, were killed, along with another man and the city assessor. Mayor Bigelow died of his wounds later that year. The insurgents dispersed, but the next day, when Sheriff Joseph McKinney was attempting to arrest some squatters who had fled to Brighton, he too was shot and killed. On August 19, troops having arrived from San Francisco, a proclamation was issued calling for law and order, and the Squatters' Riot was ended. For a number of years, however, property questions were put before the voters in city elections.

In 1982, the New Helvetia Chapter No. 5 of E Clampus Vitus placed a plaque at the entrance of the California Fruit Express Building at 1006 Fourth Street, commemorating the event and listing the casualties.

The Capitol

The state capital, after a brief career in various ambitious young cities, was finally established at Sacramento in 1854. The site of the first courthouse, completed in December 1851, is on the north side of I Street between Sixth and Seventh. It is now occupied by the present Sacramento County Courthouse, dedicated in 1913. The first courthouse was offered for use as the state capitol and the legislative sessions of 1852 and 1854 were held there. The building was destroyed by fire in 1854, but was immediately replaced by a second structure in which the state officials and the legislature were housed until the late fall of 1869 (SRL 869).

The foundations of the state capitol buildings were laid on the present site (SRL 872) in the fall of 1860, only to be washed away by the flood of January 10, 1861. As a protection against recurring floods, two great terraces were constructed, and on this elevation the cornerstone was laid on May 15, 1861, under the auspices of the Masonic Grand Lodge of California. The unfinished structure was occupied by the government late in the fall of 1869, but the building was not finally completed until 1874. In 1951 an annex was completed on the eastern side that houses the offices of the governor and other executives. With the construction of the annex, the terraces were removed and the ground was graded to a gentle slope from the building to the street.

In the 1970's, new state legislation concerning the safety of public buildings in earthquakes caused throughout the state the demolition of old schools, courthouses, libraries, and the like and the erection of safer, but often less attractive, replacements. The state capitol was found to be unsafe according to the new criteria, and, after extensive consideration of other sites and new buildings, it was decided to gut the building, leaving the exterior walls, and replace the interior. Moreover, it was decided that the interior would be rebuilt as it had looked in 1905; the offices of the governor, the treasurer, and the secretary of state, all of which were lodged in the building then, would be restored as display rooms.

In 1975, an army of workers followed by droves of skilled craftspeople began the transformation of the state capitol. In January 1982, the renovated building was returned to use (the legislature had to seek temporary quarters, but the governor's office in the annex had remained unchanged). A total of $67.8 million had been spent, making the project one of the most costly reno-

State Capitol, Sacramento

vations in American history. The verdict of nearly all who have seen the result is that it was worth every penny. Both a museum and a working place, the state capitol is an exceptionally beautiful structure, which guides on regular tours describe in detail. Among the historic rooms is the state library as it was around the turn of the century, with interesting bibliographical displays.

Surrounding the capitol buildings is Capitol Park. The park's 33 acres have been planted with thousands of varieties of trees and shrubs from all parts of the world, all of which seem to thrive in Sacramento's hospitable climate. Virtually all the specimens are labeled. Among the interesting plantings is the Memorial Grove, composed of eastern North American trees transplanted as saplings from the most prominent battlefields of the Civil War by the women's auxiliary of the Grand Army of the Republic and dedicated by them to the state. A space of three acres at the southeast corner of the park is devoted entirely to California flora, where cactus, yucca, and desert willow are close neighbors of fern, azalea, huckleberry, and tiger lily, which thrive in the shade of sequoia and oak and pine, whose native habitat ranges from the Coast Range to the Sierra Nevada.

Since nurseryman James Warren introduced them in 1852, camellias have been closely identified with Sacramento, "the Camellia City." There are over a million camellia bushes in the city and an annual camellia show is held in March.

The California State Fair and Exposition has been held annually in Sacramento since 1859; earlier state fairs were held elsewhere. The extensive fairgrounds along the American River were developed in the late 1970's when the old Stockton Boulevard grounds became inadequate for what was becoming a larger event every year.

The State Library

The California State Library was created on January 24, 1850, by act of the legislature. By July it had acquired 135 volumes, the first donations being made by Colonel J. D. Stevenson, Senator Thomas Jefferson Green, and General John C. Frémont. The collection grew steadily, although little money was made available for the purchase of books. For many years the state library occupied the semicircular central wing of the capitol, additional rooms being assigned to it until it covered about 30 percent of the entire floor space of the building. Today the state library is housed in a building of its own on Capitol Mall (M Street) between Ninth and Tenth streets. Two adjoining rooms in the renovated capitol building commemorate the old library.

Nearby at 1020 O Street are the state archives, where historic documents are preserved and displayed. The oldest document of the collection is a 1798 Spanish-language census taken of the San Francisco Presidio.

Early Churches

The Pioneer Memorial Congregational Church, presently located facing Sutter's Fort, is recorded as having been the first church to be organized in Sacramento, in September 1849, and to hold regular services. The first building was erected in 1850 on a site (SRL 613) on Sixth Street at the southwest corner of the alley between I and J streets. It was destroyed by fire in 1854, and another building was constructed the same year across the street almost opposite the first site. For over 70 years this historic edifice sheltered many significant gatherings. Its open forum, where some of the most distinguished orators of the day held forth, satisfied the intellectual needs of the community.

The founder of the First Congregational Church was the Rev. Joseph A. Benton, who began his long and beneficent career in Sacramento in July 1849. Joseph Benton's parish, however, was boundless and his missionary journeys were often of several weeks' duration. His interests, too, were broad and included education as well as religion. He taught one of the first schools in Sacramento, and in 1849 he and Samuel Willey, with several others, were already planning for public schools and a college in California. Benton was one of the founders of the College of California (forerunner of the Uni-

versity of California), and he later became a professor in the Pacific Theological Seminary in Oakland, now the Pacific School of Religion in Berkeley.

Other religious bodies also organized congregations early in the history of Sacramento. The first Roman Catholic parish was St. Rose of Lima; the church building, which stood at Seventh and K streets, was opened in 1851, although Mass had been said at various locations in 1850. The Cathedral of the Blessed Sacrament, built on Eleventh Street in 1887, was the special project of Bishop Patrick Manogue, who persuaded the authorities in Rome to transfer the seat of the diocese from Grass Valley to Sacramento. The architectural design came from Paris, much of the stained glass came from Austria, and a huge painting was given to the cathedral by Mrs. Leland Stanford in remembrance of the care given by monks in Italy to her son when he was in his last illness.

The Methodist Episcopal Church was housed in a prefabricated building shipped around the Horn from Baltimore in 1849. It was located on the east side of Seventh Street between L and Capitol. In 1852 the Methodists sold the building to the local Jewish congregation and it became the first congregationally owned synagogue on the Pacific Coast (SRL 654).

Old Sacramento

Sacramento has more historic buildings dating from the American pioneer period than any other city in California. Most of them stand in the area bounded by Front, Third, H, and N streets. This was the heart of the city for several decades. As the business center moved closer to the capitol and away from the riverfront, the old district declined and ultimately became a slum. Cheap hotels and stores occupied the solid old brick buildings where much of California's history was made; by the 1930's, they had been modernized beyond recognition by the addition of cement veneers and the removal of ornamentation of an earlier era.

For years, some proponents of slum clearance urged the complete demolition of the blighted area; others, conscious of the priceless heritage at stake, said that the same end could be achieved by restoring the pioneer structures and attracting new businesses to occupy them. But little was done in either way. The issue finally came to a head in the early 1960's when the State Division of Highways announced plans to build a freeway through the old district. The decision was welcomed in some quarters as the answer to two of Sacramento's major problems—transportation and urban renewal—but historians and historically minded persons insisted that the loss of Old Sacramento would be irreparable, and urged an alternate freeway route along the Yolo County side of the Sacramento River. Inventories of the old structures were taken and plans drawn up for the renovation of the area as a historic district. At length a compromise was reached whereby the freeway, although routed through Old Sacramento, would be deflected to spare as many of the important buildings as possible. Their victory at least partly achieved, the historians began to plan in earnest for the careful re-creation of pioneer Sacramento. Construction of the freeway began in the middle 1960's.

Old Sacramento State Historic Park (SRL 812) is now virtually complete. Front and Second streets, and J and K streets between Front and Second, have been restored to the appearance of earlier days, complete with high wooden sidewalks, reminiscent of the days when the river rose and flooded the area almost every year. Deep brick basements are still to be seen here and there, indicating how far above the surface of the soil most of these buildings stand. It is helpful to begin a tour of the area at the Sacramento History Center, which opened in 1985 at 101 I Street, in an exact reconstruction (costing $3,800,000) of the first public building in Sacramento, the City Hall and Waterworks Building of 1854. The exterior blends in with the mid-nineteenth-century look of Old Sacramento, while the interior uses the most modern methods of explaining and showing the history of the city, including extensive video displays.

The following is not a complete guide to Old Sacramento, but is rather an account of some of the buildings that have been designated state historic landmarks within Old Sacramento. One of the most important buildings was the two-story D. O. Mills bank (SRL 609) at 226 J Street, built in 1852. It replaced a small one-story frame building with a stone front that burned in 1852. The first bank's picture was used for many years on the bank's checks. In 1865 the bank was moved to the Heywood building (1857), still standing at the southeast corner of Second and J streets. In 1912 the Mills bank found a new location at the northwest corner of Seventh and J.

Darius Ogden Mills came to Sacramento in 1849 and began his career as a merchant in the new, chaotic city. He was a man who was keen to see a big opportunity and quick to take it, and in October 1849 he opened the first banking house on the Pacific Coast. Mills was not only an astute financier but a man of sound principles and steady, conservative judgment as well. He became a leading figure in the financial life of California, building up the bank at Sacramento on a sound basis and becoming the first president of the Bank of California, established at San Francisco in 1864. He was also inter-

ested in educational and philanthropic movements and gave much of his wealth to these activities. Later, he became a prominent figure in the Bank of New York, and was famous for the three Mills Hotels that he established in New York City for the relief of poor, homeless men.

The B. F. Hastings bank building (SRL 606), built in 1852–53 at the southwest corner of Second and J streets, is better known as the western terminus of the Pony Express. Here began the first overland journey eastward on April 4, 1860.

The Central Overland Pony Express was inaugurated by the firm of Russell, Majors, and Waddell early in 1860, thus preceding the telegraph and the railroad in opening overland communication between the East and the West. Before this, mail had been carried by steamer via Panama, the official mail ship arriving at San Francisco once a month. The Butterfield stages had begun to carry the mail overland via the southern route in 1858, requiring from 20 to 24 days for the trip. In the same year George Chorpenning operated over the central route between Placerville and Salt Lake City. The Pony Express inaugurated a special semiweekly mail service on horseback. Stations were erected about every 25 miles, each rider spanning three stations at the rate of about eight miles an hour. Ten days from St. Joseph, Missouri, to Sacramento was the usual time required.

There were two Pony Express remount stations in Sacramento County. The first was at the Five Mile House (SRL 697), near the present California State University at Sacramento. The Fifteen Mile House (SRL 698), four miles east of Mills on White Rock Road, was next, followed by Mormon Tavern, just over the El Dorado county line. From July 1, 1860, to July 1, 1861, Folsom, rather than Sacramento, was the western terminus of the Pony Express (SRL 702). The mail was carried between the two places by the Sacramento Valley Railroad.

The ponies and their riders, who were picked with care from among the hardiest of young Western men, kept the long trail open between the East and the West until October 26, 1861, when the service was discontinued with the completion of the overland telegraph. The romance of these riders daringly pursuing their path regardless of snow, storm, or hostile Indians has been graphically, and except for a few minor details accurately, portrayed by Mark Twain in *Roughing It*. Although not a financial success for its promoters, the Pony Express was nevertheless a substantial aid to business and undoubtedly helped to hold California, isolated as it was, in the Union.

Another Sacramento building associated with the Pony Express is the stately three-story Adams and

Company building (SRL 607) erected in 1853 at 1014 Second Street. Wells Fargo and Company occupied this structure at the time that it was agent for the western portion of the Pony Express. Across the street at 1015 is the old telegraph building (SRL 366), long thought incorrectly to have been the Pony Express terminus.

Sacramento's first major hotel was the City Hotel, built in 1849 at about 915–17 Front Street. Nearby, at about 923–25, was the Eagle Theater (SRL 595), Sacramento's first, opened the same year. The city's original buildings were not solidly constructed and fell victim to fire and flood. The theater has been reconstructed and is a performing stage. Another early hostelry was the Orleans Hotel (SRL 608), which stood from 1852 to the late 1870's at 1018 Second Street. Typical of the days when thousands of miners thronged the place is the What Cheer House (SRL 597) at the southeast corner of Front and K streets, which has been rebuilt and now caters to the visitors who flock to the sights of Old Sacramento. Ebner's Hotel (SRL 602) at 116 K Street, and the Western Hotel (SRL 601), which is no longer standing, were among other taverns and stopping places in the area.

The Sacramento Theater was opened in March 1853 on Third Street between I and J streets. Ole Bull, Maurice Strakosh, Madame Anna Bishop, and the Robinson Family were among the celebrities who played there. A stock company, including Edwin Booth, took it over in 1855. The old building no longer stands, but nearby, at 917 Third, is the Pioneer Mutual Volunteer Firehouse (SRL 612), erected in 1854 and occupied by Engine Company No. 1. The No. 3 firehouse is at 1112 Second Street. It is now a fine restaurant, having been restored in 1959 in one of the first efforts to rehabilitate Old Sacramento.

Newspapers have played an important role in the life of the state's capital city. The *Sacramento Union* issued its first edition on March 19, 1851, from a site (SRL 605) at 121 J Street; the building there has been restored. The *Union* is still published, as is the *Sacramento Bee*, founded in 1857. One of the early buildings occupied by the *Bee* (SRL 611) is a two-story brick structure at 1016 Third Street.

Sam Brannan's building is located at the southeast corner of Front and J streets. The building now referred to as the Sam Brannan House (SRL 604) at 112 J was built on Brannan's property by Henry E. Robinson in 1853. Across the alley is the slim four-story City Market, a later building (from the 1870's) but one of Old Sacramento's most attractive. Newton Booth, elected governor of California in 1871 and later United States senator, maintained his home, headquarters, and wholesale grocery business (SRL 596) at 1015–17 Front

Street. Part of his block still stands at 1019–21 Front. The beautiful narrow three-story building at 1023 was also owned by Booth. He entered business in Sacramento in 1851. Leland Stanford's wholesale warehouse, built in 1856, still stands at the southeast corner of Front and L. The Lady Adams building (SRL 603) is one of Sacramento's oldest. It was built in 1852 at 113–15 K Street and was named after a ship. The Overton-Read building (SRL 610), at the northwest corner of Third and J, was gone many years before the site was obliterated by the freeway. It housed the Sacramento Post Office from 1852 to 1859.

The structure popularly known as the "Big Four Building" has been moved from its original site on K Street (SRL 600), where the freeway was to be constructed, to the intersection of Front and I streets at the Plaza in Old Sacramento. Built in 1852 and drastically altered through the years, it originally contained the Stanford store and the Huntington-Hopkins hardware store. From their offices here, Leland Stanford, Collis P. Huntington, Mark Hopkins, and Charles Crocker financed and built the Central Pacific Railroad, the western end of the first transcontinental railway, later gaining control of the political and financial affairs of California. The structure is now a bookstore and administrative center for the California State Railroad Museum nearby.

Not an old building at all, but a major attraction in Old Sacramento, is the spectacular California State Railroad Museum, at the northeast entrance to Old Sacramento at Second and I streets. This was opened to the public in 1981, the result of years of planning. In 1937, a group of railroad enthusiasts in the San Francisco Bay Area formed the Pacific Coast Chapter of the Railway and Locomotive Historical Society; members had already begun to acquire historic locomotives and cars in the days when railroads were steadily being cut back, and by 1951 their collection numbered nearly twenty pieces. They hoped to build a museum in San Francisco, but neither funds nor adequate space could be found. In 1964, when the equipment had deteriorated badly because of weather and vandalism, the Bethlehem Shipyard in San Francisco contracted to refurbish and repair many of the more significant pieces.

In 1967, the proposal was made to build a state-sponsored railroad museum in Old Sacramento, birthplace of railroading in California; the State Department of Parks and Recreation soon became custodian of some of the locomotives and cars. In 1976 the Central Pacific Railroad Passenger Station, first phase of the California State Railroad Museum, was opened. In 1984, a steam-train excursion that runs from the station south along the banks of the river for four and a half miles was opened. The steam train operates during the summer months, and plans have been made to extend the line further south.

Among the many attractions within the museum are the Central Pacific Railroad Locomotive No. 1, "Governor Stanford," from 1862; the Virginia and Truckee Railroad Locomotive No. 12, "Genoa," from 1873; the private railroad car "Gold Coast," from about 1895, owned for many years by the authors and historians Lucius Beebe and Charles Clegg; and the Southern Pacific Railroad Locomotive No. 1, "C. P. Huntington," from 1863, which was used as the company's corporate symbol for decades. The museum has become one of the most popular places for Californians and their friends to learn something of the state's history.

The First Transcontinental Railroad

On January 12, 1864, President Abraham Lincoln signed a remarkable document attesting that the western base of the Sierra Nevada began where the Central Pacific Railroad crossed Arcade Creek. Government subsidies for railroad construction through mountainous terrain were considerably higher than those for construction through flatlands. The extra dollars provided by this decree contributed in no small measure to the completion of the transcontinental railroad. A plaque (SRL 780.8) has been placed on the west side of Arcade Creek in the Haggin Oaks Municipal Golf Course, 3645 Fulton Avenue in Sacramento.

On January 8, 1963, Governor Edmund G. Brown dedicated a bronze plaque (SRL 780) at Front and K streets in Sacramento. It was 100 years to the day since Governor Leland Stanford, at the same spot, turned the first spade of earth to begin construction of the Central Pacific Railroad. An earlier plaque had been dedicated by retired railroad employees on the 50th anniversary, January 8, 1913.

Six years and four months after construction began, having conquered seemingly insurmountable obstacles, crews of the Central Pacific met with those of the Union Pacific, which had been building westward, at Promontory, a lonely spot in northern Utah. There, on May 10, 1869, the gold spike was driven to signify completion of the first transcontinental railroad. It also brought to an end the frontier era of California history, although it would be some time before that fact was generally recognized.

It should not be thought that the "Big Four" alone were responsible for this remarkable achievement. The man who planned the Central Pacific and who earlier had built the first passenger railroad in California did not live to see the last spike driven. In his memory a splendid monument of granite boulders stands in front of the Southern Pacific (Amtrak) depot at Fourth and I streets. A bronze tablet on the face of the rock bears this inscription: "That the West may remember Theodore Dehone Judah, pioneer civil engineer and the tireless advocate of a great transcontinental railroad—America's first, this monument was erected by men and women of the Southern Pacific Company, who, in 1930, were carrying on the work he began in 1860. He convinced four Sacramento merchants that his plan was practicable and enlisted their help. Ground was broken for the railroad, January 8, 1863, at the foot of K Street nearby. Judah died November 2, 1863. The road was built past the site of this monument over the lofty Sierra—along the line of Judah's survey—to a junction with the Union Pacific at Promontory, Utah, where on May 10, 1869, the 'last spike' was driven."

The Southern Pacific depot is built on what in gold rush days was China Slough (SRL 594).

Even before the Central Pacific was begun, the corner of Front and K streets was a transportation center. In the early 1850's it was the terminus (SRL 598) for stagecoaches to various places in the Mother Lode country. At the same location, the first successful commercial fruit cannery in the Sacramento Valley, Capitol Packing Company, was established in January 1882.

The California Almond Growers Exchange, founded in 1910, was the first successful grower-owned cooperative for the marketing of California almonds. The principal building (SRL 967), at 1809 C Street, is a shelling plant adjacent to the 1915 brick building that is now a visitors' center, from which tours of the facility are conducted on a regular basis.

Old Sacramento Homes

Under its avenues of fine old trees, Sacramento has many early residences of brick or frame construction. The Stanford-Lathrop home (SRL 614) at 800 N Street was built in the late 1850's. It was purchased by Leland Stanford in 1861 and occupied by him and his wife, Jane Lathrop Stanford, as their residence until 1874. Stanford was governor of California for the single term 1862–63, and the story is told that on his inaugural day early in 1862 the floodwaters of the Sacramento River had once again inundated the downtown district, so that the governor-elect and his lady had to climb through a ground-floor window and depart for the inaugural festivities at the nearby capitol in a rowboat. Leland Stanford, Jr., their only child, who died at the age of sixteen and for whom Stanford University is named, was born in this house in 1868. The house was

Governor's Mansion, Sacramento

extensively remodeled by Stanford and was presented by his widow to the Roman Catholic Diocese of Sacramento in 1900. It is now owned by the State Department of Parks and Recreation, which plans to develop it as a historic site.

The building known as the Governor's Mansion (SRL 823) is a stately white Victorian house at Sixteenth and H streets. It was built in 1877 for Albert Gallatin, president of a pioneer Sacramento hardware firm. In 1887, Gallatin sold the house to Joseph Steffens, dry-goods merchant and father of the author Lincoln Steffens, and in 1903 the state bought it for $32,500 unfurnished. This was the first official residence for California's chief executive; previous governors had had to rent houses, live in hotels, or, as in the case of Governor Stanford, purchase their own houses. Governor George C. Pardee was the first governor to bring his family to live in the mansion, in 1903. The State Fire Marshal declared the building unsuitable for occupancy in 1941, but no alternative official residence being provided, governors Warren, Knight, and Brown lived there throughout their terms of office. Governor Ronald Reagan was the last governor to live there; after a very short residence in 1967, he refused to remain in the house and sought other quarters. California's chief executives have gone back to renting houses, living in hotels, or purchasing their own homes. The Governor's Mansion is open to the public and, whatever its shortcomings as a family residence, is a charming example of a Victorian home. The house has nine fireplaces, each of them fashioned from a different type of marble. The place is still used for some official functions.

The Crocker Art Gallery (SRL 599) stands at 216 O Street. Judge Edwin B. Crocker and his wife collected many fine paintings and drawings during their travels in Europe, especially during the Franco-Prussian War. In the early 1870's a building was erected at the southeast corner of Second and O streets, next to their residence, to house their private collection. In 1884, Crocker's widow donated the building and its contents to the city of Sacramento, with the California Museum Association as co-tenant and administrator. After Mrs. Crocker's death, the old home at the southwest corner of Third and O, built by B. F. Hastings about 1853 and purchased by Crocker about 1868, was also acquired and converted into the gallery annex. Judge Crocker was a brother of Charles Crocker and was legal counsel for the Central Pacific Railroad. His acquisitions are beautifully displayed in the museum, which has many landscapes of California painted in the late nineteenth century, and a very interesting modern art gallery as well.

Sacramento is unusual among American cities in that it has few suburban extensions. A broad span of communities rises eastward through Folsom toward Auburn in Placer County, and there is a small commercial center on the western (Yolo County) side of the river in the new town of West Sacramento, but if one goes either north or south, one is quickly in farming towns and quiet areas with a history of their own.

Sacramento Cemeteries

Sacramento's first cemetery (SRL 592) was established by John A. Sutter in 1849. It was located on Alhambra Boulevard between I and J streets, and is now the campus of Sutter Junior High School. In the same year Sutter and H. A. Schoolcraft gave the land for the Sacramento City Cemetery (SRL 566), at Broadway and Riverside Boulevard. Many pioneers and important persons are buried here, including governors John Bigler, Newton Booth, and William Irwin; Mark Hopkins; E. B. Crocker; and William S. Hamilton.

William Stephens Hamilton, youngest son of Alexander Hamilton, the great Revolutionary War statesman, came to California in 1849. Previous to that time he had served as surveyor of public lands in Illinois, discovered the Hamilton Diggings in southwestern Wisconsin in 1827, engaged in the Black Hawk War, when as colonel he distinguished himself for efficiency and bravery, and was several times a member of the Territorial Legislature of Wisconsin. On coming to California, Hamilton engaged in mining for about a year, after which he went to Sacramento to trade. He died in that city on October 7, 1850.

An unmarked grave in the city cemetery constituted the resting place of William Hamilton until 1879, when friends had the body removed to a more appropriate part of the cemetery and a slab of polished Quincy granite placed over it. In 1889, at the suggestion of John O. Brown, mayor of Sacramento, the remains were again moved, this time to a new plot in the cemetery named Hamilton Square in honor of the deceased. At this time the handsome, oddly shaped monument of massive Quincy granite that still marks the grave was sent out from Massachusetts by a grand-nephew of the pioneer. On one side it bears a bronze medallion of Alexander Hamilton. A small plate below the medallion indicates that the grave is now cared for by the Sacramento Chapter, Daughters of the American Revolution, who thus keep in memory the worthy life of a great man's son.

Chevra Kaddisha, or Home of Peace Cemetery (SRL 654.1), was the first Jewish cemetery in California. The land was acquired in 1850. The site is located at 33rd and K streets in Sacramento.

The Delta Region

The rich delta lands of the Sacramento and San Joaquin rivers cover more than 425,000 acres of immensely

Locke

productive country. It is a section suggestive of the dikes and canals of the Netherlands. First settled in the 1850's by gold-seekers who had failed to make a living in the mines and who had squatted on the river delta in order to raise enough food for their subsistence, the land early demonstrated its extraordinary fertility. After the completion of the Central Pacific Railroad thousands of Chinese workers were employed, for very low wages, in reclaiming the delta country for agriculture. They built the first systems of levees along the various islands, working laboriously with wheelbarrows. Agriculture is still the chief activity of the region, but fishing and pleasure boating are also important.

Towns of the Lower Sacramento Valley

The little town of Franklin lies about four miles east of the Sacramento River, and may be reached from Hood, or directly from Sacramento by Highway J-8, a distance of fifteen miles. In the Franklin Cemetery is the grave of Alexander Hamilton Willard (SRL 657), one of the last surviving members of the Lewis and Clark Expedition of 1804–6. Willard was born in New Hampshire in 1777, came to California in 1852, and died in 1865.

Farther south along the river is the unique town of Locke, which could easily pass for a Mother Lode mining camp or a Western movie set. It is neither. Locke is a community composed almost entirely of Chinese and was built as late as 1916, when fire destroyed the Chinatown of neighboring Walnut Grove. A number of displaced Chinese leased land from George and Clay Locke and began building their homes and shops. The town is centered on a twelve-foot-wide main street overhung by two-story buildings. An interesting feature of the town is the Dai Loy Gambling Hall, now a museum of the town's life. In 1971 the entire community was placed on the National Register of Historic Places.

Walnut Grove nearby has a vigorous Japanese community; its Gakuen Hall, also known as the Walnut Grove Japanese Community Center, is on the National Register of Historic Places. The town, first settled in 1850, is divided by the Sacramento River. The bridge across the river was erected in 1952, replacing an earlier one from 1916, the first cantilevered counterweight bascule bridge west of the Mississippi.

San Benito County

San Benito County derived its name from San Benito Creek, which was named by Father Juan Crespí in 1772; San Benito is Spanish for Saint Benedict. The county was formed in 1874 from a part of Monterey County, and the county seat was placed at Hollister. The area of the county was increased in 1887 by additions from the adjoining counties of Fresno and Merced.

Mission San Juan Bautista

Following the expressed wish of the viceroy, missions were established as fast as possible to fill gaps in the chain from San Diego to San Francisco. Soon after the dedication of Mission San José, Father Fermín Lasuén proceeded to the San Benito Valley, where on the feast day of St. John the Baptist, June 24, 1797, Mission San Juan Bautista was founded. The father had chosen this spot from others suggested to him because this location "promised the most abundant harvest of souls."

Assisting in the ceremonies at the dedication were Father Magín Catalá from Mission Santa Clara and Father Manuel Martiarena, who was to be left in charge of the new establishment. The rites took place before a large assemblage of Indians from the nearby plains. These Indians were at peace with the Spanish, but there were others who inhabited the mountains to the east, including the warlike Asayames tribe, with whom the mission was in conflict for several years.

The first temporary structure was replaced by a new church whose cornerstone was laid on June 13, 1803. Within this stone were placed coins and a sealed bottle containing a narrative of the proceedings at the celebration. Completed in 1812, the main structure was nearly 200 feet long and 30 feet wide, with a high roof about 40 feet above the floor. The church and other buildings were of adobe brick, and made up two sides of a courtyard, the other two of which were completed by a wall. A corridor of twenty arches resting on brick pillars extended across the front of the church.

Father Estévan Tápis, who had succeeded to the office of Padre Presidente on the death of Father Lasuén, officiated at the 1812 dedication. Later that year, at the end of his term of office, Father Tápis went to live at San Juan, remaining there until his death in 1825 at the age of 71. A man of considerable ability, he was familiar with several Indian dialects and enjoyed teaching Indian boys to read and write. Furthermore, he

seems to have gotten on well with the civil authorities who also lived at San Juan.

In 1831, the mission was visited by Captain Alfred Robinson, who wrote: "It is conveniently located in the center of a large valley, with an abundance of rich land and large stocks of cattle. Padre Felipe Arroyo [de la Cuesta] was the missionary, whose infirm state of health kept him confined closely to his chamber. For amusement, when tired of study, he called in the children of the place and set them to dancing and playing their games. In his eccentric taste he had given them the names of all the renowned personages of antiquity, and Ciceros, Platos, and Alexanders were to be found in abundance."

In 1835, when the mission was secularized, José Tiburcio Castro, grantee of nearby Rancho Sausal, was made mayordomo. Sixty-three families of Indians were released from mission discipline at the time, and payments were made to them amounting to over $8,000. The value of the remaining mission property was estimated to be $138,973, with only a debt of $250 standing against it. The mayordomo's final report in 1836 listed 900 head of cattle and 4,000 sheep as the property of the mission and an account of $1,300 against the property.

Mission San Juan Bautista (SRL 195) has been in unbroken service since its founding. The church is the largest of all the mission churches in California, with three aisles. The statues, paintings, and sandstone bap-

Mission San Juan Bautista, at Edge of San Andreas Fault

tismal font are all original, as is the colorful reredos for the statues behind the altar. This was painted by a stranded Boston sailor, Thomas Doak, in 1816, in exchange for room and board. The Convento wing adjoining the church is today used as a museum.

The San Andreas Fault passes immediately to the east of the walled garden of the mission, and seismographic equipment is displayed on the east side of the plaza. The fault creates an abrupt drop of some twelve feet between the mission garden and the flatlands beyond.

San Juan, now San Juan Bautista

In 1835 José Castro became interim governor of California, and in 1836 he and Juan B. Alvarado made San Juan their headquarters in the revolt that resulted in the exile of Governor Gutiérrez and his replacement by Alvarado. Castro petitioned for land in 1839: "Being the owner of a considerable quantity of cattle and horses without possessing any land of my own whereon to place them to increase and prosper I have become acquainted with a suitable place in the neighborhood of this pueblo known by the name of San Justo which does not belong to any owner and is entirely unoccupied." The request was granted. In July 1844, Castro transferred the property to Francisco Pérez Pacheco.

In 1840–41 Castro built a two-story adobe house (SRL 179) on the south side of the plaza diagonally opposite the mission church. With its overhanging balcony, it is considered to be one of the finest examples of California adobe construction remaining from the Mexican era. In 1846, while interim *comandante general*, Castro again organized forces at San Juan; this time he wished to expel John C. Frémont from his temporary stronghold on Gabilan Peak, where the American captain maintained his forces from March 6 to March 9. On July 17, Frémont raised the American flag on the plaza at San Juan and there drilled his ten companies of volunteer troops before starting for Los Angeles to support Commodore Stockton in suppressing the revolt of General Flores.

Castro's house in the pueblo of San Juan was acquired by Patrick Breen and finally deeded to him in 1854. Breen and his family, the first English-speaking settlers in San Juan, were among the members of the Reed-Donner party who survived the tragic winter of 1846–47 in the High Sierra. The room in the Convento Wing of the mission now used as a gift shop was their first home in California. Breen purchased some of the mission property in addition to the Castro house and established an inn, which became famous as a stopping place for travelers between Monterey and the mines in 1849–50. Years later, Helen Hunt Jackson began to write *Ramona* while staying there.

In the 1850's and 1860's San Juan was the site of an exchange station on the route between San Francisco and Los Angeles; at one time eleven stage lines stopped at the Plaza Hotel (SRL 180), on the same side of the plaza as the Castro House. This building consists of two one-story adobes, which were combined, and a second story of wood. The larger of the adobes was built in 1813–14 as armory and barracks for the soldiers of the mission guard. Angelo Zanetta added the second story in 1858 and opened the building as the Plaza Hotel. The old livery stable, built in the 1870's, is still standing and contains an interesting display of old vehicles. Next to it is the Zanetta house, the lower story of which was built by Angelo Zanetta in 1868 with bricks from the old mission nunnery (built in 1815, enlarged in 1832, and torn down in 1868). The upper story above the residence was a wood-frame public hall.

The Castro adobe, Plaza Hotel, stable, and Zanetta house are part of San Juan Bautista State Historic Park; these, with the plaza itself, have also been designated as a National Historic Landmark.

A few other adobes stand along the streets of the old town, as well as several interesting wooden structures from the early American period. Notable among the adobes are the Casa Juan de Anza at Third and Franklin streets and the two-story building on Fourth Street near Washington; the latter was restored by the Native Daughters of the Golden West. Among the American wooden buildings, the Masonic Hall from 1864 is outstanding. US 101 long ago bypassed the little community, and although it has many visitors throughout the year, it has been able to preserve its air of an earlier day.

Plaza Hotel and Livery Stables, San Juan Bautista State Historic Park

The Pacheco Ranchos

Francisco Pérez Pacheco was a Mexican carriage maker who came to California in 1819 with a company of artillery. His bravery and success in quelling Indian revolts won his promotion to junior officer's rank in 1824; afterward, he was commander of the Custom House guard and then of the military post at Monterey.

Since the mission fathers at San Juan Bautista did not need all the land set aside for mission use, they allowed Pacheco to settle upon a part of it some time before 1833. This was the Bolsa de San Felipe, which came by the name Bolsa ("pocket") because it was nearly enclosed by a swamp, a willow grove, and a ravine called Sanjón de Tequisquite. Pacheco allowed the family of the mayordomo of the mission and some of the mission Indians who were living on it to remain. The formalities that attended the legal taking possession of land at that period included pulling up grass, cutting a few tree branches, throwing a few stones, and taking up a handful of earth. After taking possession, Pacheco built a stone house, where he and José Maria Sánchez, owner of the adjoining Rancho Llano del Tequisquite, lived together for a time.

On petition to Governor Figueroa for adjoining property, the Ausaymas tract of two leagues was granted to Pacheco in 1833. In 1836 he petitioned for another two leagues, which he called Guadalaxarita but which the padres called San Felipe, and this tract was probably included in the grant of six leagues made by Governor Gutiérrez that year. Pacheco became an extensive landowner, eventually having in his possession the San Justo Rancho, conveyed to him by José Castro in 1844; the Bolsa de San Felipe near Hollister; the Ausaymas y San Felipe, extending into Santa Clara County; and the San Luis Gonzaga, lying in the counties of Santa Clara and Merced, including the Pacheco Pass and several miles of the Pacheco Pass Road. All of these ranchos were later patented to him by the United States.

In 1844 Don Francisco Pacheco was captain of militia and in 1846 tithe collector. Testimony given in 1852 states that he was then the owner of a house valued at between $15,000 and $20,000, ten cabins for laborers, and thousands of horses, cattle, and hogs, with pens and corrals, and that enough of his land was in cultivation to provide for all living upon it.

Rancho San Justo, through which the San Benito River runs, was sold by Pacheco in 1855, three years before his death, to W. W. Hollister and Flint, Bixby, and Company, men who brought two flocks of sheep from the East and turned the place into a sheep ranch.

Some years later Colonel Hollister sold the eastern portion to the San Justo Homestead Association, a group of businessmen who established the town of Hollister. On the western part, Flint, Bixby, and Company built a three-family ranch house, which still stands as a part of St. Francis Retreat in the hills above San Juan Bautista. The old house and surrounding land were sold to the Franciscan Fathers in 1947.

Rancho Ciénega de los Paicines

Rancho Ciénega de los Paicines was granted by Governor Alvarado to Angel Castro and José Antonio Rodríguez in 1842. Rodríguez died before 1853, when a claim to the property was filed by Angel Castro and Hilaria Castro de Rodríguez, widow of the co-grantee, and her three children. A patent for 8,918 acres was issued to these claimants in 1869. This grant covered the land extending from Tres Pinos Creek on the east to the Cienega Valley at the foot of the Gabilan Mountains on the west. Through it runs a stretch of the San Benito River and its tributary, Pescadero Creek.

Rancho Ciénega de los Paicines has passed through the hands of several owners since the day of Angel Castro; the first of these, Alexander B. Grogan, built the large white ranch house occupied by the present owner. Grogan made extensive improvements to the ranch during his ownership, and his large Red Durham cattle were the prize herd of the county. He sold the ranch to Captain Sudden, a retired English sea captain, who leased it as a cattle and grain ranch. It was then sold to A. Kingsley Macomber, who restored the Grogan ranch house, built a beautiful mansion, and landscaped the grounds extensively. Soon after purchasing the ranch, Macomber sold 1,000 acres east of the old stage road to San Benito and Bitterwater, and south of Tres Pinos Creek, to Colonel George Sykes, who planted part of this acreage with prunes and English walnuts, using the hills for a cattle range. The Sykes Ranch is now owned by Almaden Vineyards, which has planted the hills with wine grapes. The Macomber Ranch proper passed into the hands of Walter P. Murphy, and his estate, in turn, sold it to the present owners, the family of Robert B. Law.

Cienega Road, south of Hollister, follows the main line of the San Andreas Fault for a distance of about fifteen miles. The fault is subject to sudden movement, such as caused the 1906 earthquake, as well as to gradual movement (also known as slow creep). Evidence of fault movement may be seen in the Cienega Winery of Almaden Vineyards, which is slowly being pulled apart and requires constant repair. The present building is the third on the site. The San Andreas Fault at Cienega Winery has been registered by the Department of the Interior as a National Natural Landmark.

Gabilan or Fremont Peak

The highest peak in the Gabilan range of mountains on the border between San Benito and Monterey counties is called Gabilan (Gavilan) Peak, sometimes Hawk's Peak, *gavilán* being Spanish for "sparrow hawk." It is today more commonly called Fremont Peak (SRL 181). To this spot in 1846 Frémont took his little band of followers, after being ordered by Mexican officials to leave the country. Taking possession of the peak, he erected an earthen fort there on March 6. He raised the first American flag to fly over California (a modified version of the flag of the U.S. Army Corps of Engineers) over the fort, which his party held for four days. General José Castro prepared to dislodge the Americans, and Frémont, with his forces outnumbered five to one, slowly retreated north to Sutter's Fort.

On the outcome of the Gabilan episode, Hunt and Sanchez have this to say: "The affair of Hawk's Peak amounts to but little in itself, but the results were unfortunate, both in stirring up antipathy on the part of the Americans toward the Californians and in outraging the feelings of the Californians and giving color to the persistent rumor that the Mexican Government had purposed expelling all foreign residents from the province. In the light of subsequent events, the episode may be regarded as a direct cause of the Bear Flag revolt."

A memorial iron flagstaff was erected in 1908 atop the peak. There are no traces of the fort left. The site is now Fremont Peak State Park.

The Road from the New Idria Mines

The New Idria Quicksilver Mine (SRL 324) lies on the slope below San Carlos Peak. The date of the discovery of this ore deposit is unknown; local Indians were making use of it when the mission fathers arrived. Tradition says that the fathers made assays of the ore and determined it to be cinnabar. Bret Harte, in his *Story of a Mine*, attributes the accidental discovery of the first quicksilver in the region to a group of prospectors who were burning specimens of rock to test it for silver and were surprised to find a pool of "liquid silver" in the ashes of their improvised furnace.

"New Idria" was taken from the name of the Idrija Mine in Austria, and the same square type of furnace used there was initially used here, but it was supplanted long ago by a more effective type. With records

that go back to 1854, it ranks among the most famous quicksilver mines of the world.

In the 1850's and 1860's the town nearest the mine was San Juan, 68 miles away. The stage route between them became a well-traveled road livened by the jangle of bells on the freight teams. The road from the mine followed San Carlos Creek down to Griswold Creek, named for a rancher who lived there. It passed several adobe houses, a few of which stand, vacant or in ruins, beside the road today, and cabins constructed of rough lumber, most of which have disappeared. Next it came to Panoche Creek and ran through Panoche Valley, excellent cattle pasturage, until it reached Tres Pinos Creek, which it crossed and recrossed by means of fords. That part of the road has long been called the "wiggletail." The roadbed of today has been somewhat improved and, for a part of the distance, is now cut out of the canyon side at a higher level. Finally, the settlement that was then called Tres Pinos, now called Paicines, was reached, and the remainder of the journey to San Juan was on a more even grade.

Between 200 and 300 men were employed at the New Idria mines when they were visited by William Brewer of the Whitney Geologic Survey in 1861, who left a description of three mines and their activities. In 1898 the mines were sold to the New Idria Quicksilver Mining Company. During World War I the place was policed by a company of soldiers. The mines were operated by the New Idria Mining and Chemical Company until their closure in April 1972.

Tres Pinos and Paicines

The settlement of Paicines, little more than a post office and general store, stands at the junction of SR 25 and the road to New Idria. This spot used to be called Tres Pinos, named for three stunted pine trees on the bank of Tres Pinos Creek. It was known as Tres Pinos when Tiburcio Vásquez made his last robbery, at Snyder's Store at this junction. The robbery occurred in August 1873. Three men were killed by the bandit: one a deaf man who did not hear the peremptory orders given by Vásquez; one a Portuguese who did not understand the language; and the third the hotelkeeper across the street, who refused to open his door and was felled by a bullet fired through it. The residents of the county became so incensed at the callous crime that Vásquez and his gang sought safety in the south. Trailed by sheriffs and captured, they were brought back to Hollister in May 1874, and after trial in San Jose, Vásquez was executed there on March 19, 1875. The store burned in 1877, but was rebuilt and stands today on the spot where the crime occurred over a century ago.

When the railroad was built out from Hollister to a point west of the original settlement of Tres Pinos, a town grew up at the station and it also was called Tres Pinos. After a time, the older settlement came to be called Paicines, for Rancho Ciénega de los Paicines nearby. The word itself is supposed to be the name of a tribe of Indians that once lived in the region. The main activity of the new Tres Pinos was handling freight for the New Idria mines. The railroad was abandoned in 1944, but the town still prospers on SR 25.

Hollister

In the autumn of 1868 the San Justo Homestead Association was formed by a group of 50 farmers, who each held one share. They purchased from Colonel W. W. Hollister the eastern part of Rancho San Justo, containing 21,000 acres, for the sum of $400,000 and divided the best part of the land into 50 homestead lots, one for each member. One hundred acres in the middle was reserved for a townsite and was laid out in blocks, lots, and streets. This is now the center of Hollister.

A man prominent in the association and the town was T. S. Hawkins, who came to California from Missouri in 1860. He settled first in Santa Clara County but came to what is now San Benito County in 1867, renting 1,000 acres of virgin soil and planting it with grain. In the following year, Hawkins helped to form the San Justo Homestead Association, of which he was made secretary and general manager in 1870. At that time he gave up farming and turned his attention wholly to the advancement of the town.

Because it seemed to be a waste of time to go all the way to the coast to transact legal business at the county seat in Monterey, the suggestion of forming a new county met with approval. San Benito County was organized on February 12, 1874, with the new town of Hollister as its seat.

The Hazel Hawkins Memorial Hospital, completed in Hollister in 1907, was erected by Hawkins as a tribute to his granddaughter, who had died in 1902. A new Hazel Hawkins Hospital was built in 1962, and the original building is now part of a business complex. The San Benito County Historical Museum is at the corner of Ann Alley and West Street in Hollister.

The Pinnacles

On November 19, 1794, George Vancouver, the English navigator, who had been ill for some time in Monterey, had sufficiently recovered to go on an exploring expedition. With a small party on horseback, he set out across the Salinas Valley and reached a point, possibly the southern end of the Gabilan Range, where he "was gratified with the sight of the most extraordinary mountains" that he had ever beheld. One side "presented the appearance of a sumptuous edifice fallen into decay; the columns, which looked as if they had been raised with much labor and industry, were of great magnitude, seemed to be of an excellent form, and seemed to be composed of . . . cream coloured stone." It is thought that Vancouver reached the Pinnacles; if so, his would be the earliest record of a visit to this region.

In *The Days of a Man*, David Starr Jordan wrote: "From 1904 to 1908 it was my pleasure to assist an ardent mountain lover, Mr. C. S. Hain of Tres Pinos, in securing for the people as a Government Forest Reserve, a singular district known as the 'Pinnacles' lying in the Gavilan Range on the line between San Benito and Monterey counties. There the mountain range of yellow Miocene sandstone has been scored into deep gulches by the long action of small streams unaided by frost or ice. The cuts are very narrow and regular, scarcely widened even at the top, and the cliffs assume varied fantastic and picturesque forms. The forests are of little consequence, being of scant oak and digger pines, but many rare flowers are found in the tract, and some of the precipitous walls bear nests of the great California Condor—*Gymnogyps*—a majestic vulture with wing spread of from nine to ten feet."

The area was set aside as a National Monument by proclamation of President Theodore Roosevelt on January 16, 1908. By grants made in 1923 and 1924, the area was increased to 2,980 acres. Further additions were made in subsequent years so that the present size of the monument is 16,222 acres. The spire-like formations of the Pinnacles rise to a height of 1,000 feet, and beneath them are caves and subterranean passages. An amphitheater enclosed by smaller pinnacles has been named in honor of Jordan.

The Pinnacles National Monument is located in San Benito County, except for a very small corner in Monterey County, and is entered about 35 miles south of Hollister.

San Bernardino County

San Bernardino County was organized in 1853 from territory that was at first a part of Los Angeles and San Diego counties. The name comes from the Spanish for St. Bernardine of Siena. The city of San Bernardino has always been the county seat.

The physical extent of San Bernardino County is awesome. Its 20,094 square miles make it by far the largest county in the United States, and nearly twice the size of Inyo County, the next largest within California. Nine of the United States are smaller, so much so that San Bernardino County could contain any two, at least, of the following states: Connecticut, Delaware, Hawaii, Maryland, Massachusetts, New Hampshire, New Jersey, Rhode Island, and Vermont.

In the southwestern corner of the county is the populous San Bernardino Valley, closely linked with neighboring Los Angeles, Orange, and Riverside counties. North and east of the San Gabriel and San Bernardino mountains, beyond Cajon Pass, is the huge Mojave Desert, which rises into the mountains of Nevada. The Mojave region covers some 90 percent of the county's area and contains about one-fifth of its population. In 1988 its residents attempted to secede from San Bernardino County and to form California's 59th county, to be named Mojave County, but the measure was voted down in the June election.

The Pleistocene Land

When the most recent of the Ice Ages joined Alaska with Siberia in the Pleistocene Era, people and animals moved eastward into North America. This era was on the whole wetter and cooler than modern times, so that some of the dry basins of today were once under water, according to geologists. Archaeologists in the twentieth century have been making many discoveries in the Mojave that indicate the presence of human society many thousands of years ago. Near the old silver-mining town of Calico is the Calico Early Man Archaeological Site. Since 1964, this dig has uncovered thousands of stone tools that are claimed to be as much as 50,000 years old, making it the earliest site in the Western Hemisphere where human artifacts have been found. Famed anthropologist Dr. Louis B. Leakey was a consultant on the location of this site, which is on an eroded Pleistocene alluvial fan. Excavations were conducted here by the National Geographic Society and the San Bernardino

County Museum from 1964 to 1981. The Bureau of Land Management currently operates the site, which is open to the public. Some of the finds from the site are on display at the San Bernardino County Museum in Redlands. The presence of so many artifacts in what is now a barren, sparsely populated region suggests a substantial climate change over the ages.

Another discovery, made in 1928–29 in the Turquoise Mountains east of Johannesburg, indicates that Indians were mining the turquoise lodes of the Mojave River sink region centuries ago; many traces of this activity have been obliterated by machinery in modern times. In an excavation of a cave east of Barstow in the Newberry Mountains in the 1950's, organic artifacts were found and were subjected to radio-carbon tests that proclaimed them to be at least 3,000 years old.

Cajon Pass and the Mojave Indian Trail

Professor Herbert Eugene Bolton established that, as early as 1772, Pedro Fages traversed the region of the Cajon Pass, while on his way north into the San Joaquin Valley in pursuit of deserters from the Presidio at San Diego.

The first white man to cross the San Bernardino Mountains into the San Bernardino Valley was Father Francisco Garcés, the famous Spanish priest-explorer, who came in 1776 from the Colorado River. Jedediah Strong Smith, the first American to enter California overland, traveled the same trail from the Colorado in 1826 and again in 1827.

At the eastern entrance to the city of Needles, in a small parkway, a monument (SRL 781) has been placed, calling attention to an old Indian trail, still visible in some places, that ran roughly parallel to the Colorado River on the California side. It was over this route that Garcés and Smith traveled.

Study of the diaries of the Garcés and Smith expeditions has shown that the route taken by these two men did not lead directly through Cajon Pass, as had been supposed. Mojave Indians served as guides from the Colorado on both occasions, and they used the ancient Indian trail, which led across the desert and up the Mojave River to its western headwaters in the San Bernardino Mountains. Crossing the range eight miles east of the present Cajon Pass, it came down into San Bernardino Valley on the ridge between Devil and Cable canyons, crossing Cajon Creek between Devore and Verdemont. From here it skirted the base of the foothills to Cucamonga, and led on to San Gabriel and the sea. The old Mojave Indian Trail is therefore extremely important historically, since it antedates the Cajon as a mountain crossing for the white explorers.

Early in 1827, however, hostilities between the Mojaves and the white explorers broke out, with frequent atrocities committed by both parties. Several alternative routes were developed over the next 30 years, as Indian relations heated and cooled. At the place where the Mojave Trail crossed the summit of the mountains, a marker (SRL 618) has been placed at Monument Peak commemorating both Garcés and Smith and their pioneering journeys across the area.

During the years 1830–31 three pioneer pack trains from New Mexico crossed the San Bernardino Mountains into the valley beyond. The first, forerunner of the Santa Fe caravans, was led by Antonio Armijo, a New Mexican trader, who came in January 1830 by what he called the "San Bernardino Canyon," probably the present Cajon Pass. Ewing Young and his trappers came a little later in the same year, but the trail by which he crossed the mountains is not mentioned. In the fall of 1830 William Wolfskill left Santa Fe with still another band of trappers, and, according to J. J. Warner, went through the Cajon in February 1831. Certainly the last, and possibly all three, of these parties used the Cajon.

At the southbound lanes of I-15 a marker (SRL 576) notes that this was part of the route extending into New Mexico once known as the Santa Fe Trail. North of Cajon Station on the Santa Fe railroad line another marker (SRL 578) notes that from here another road branched east and north to the Great Salt Lake in Utah. On SR 138 at West Cajon Canyon another marker (SRL 577) notes that the Mormons heading westward with their heavy wagons in 1851 passed through here rather than the "Narrows" at the top of the Cajon Pass. A mile and a half south of Devore, close to Glen Helen Regional Park, a monument (SRL 573) commemorates the campsite of the Mormon party in 1851 where they waited to move into the San Bernardino Valley itself.

The Wolfskill passage across the desert set the course for emigrants of the next 30 years. Depending on the destination of a traveler, it might be known as the Santa Fe Road, the Salt Lake Road, or, in more general terms, the Spanish Road or the Mojave Road. Crowder Canyon, which extends into Cajon Canyon from Summit Valley, is reminiscent of the days (1830–60) when stolen animals were pastured in this region, before the long drive across the Mojave Desert. A brisk trade in California mules and horses was car-

ried on with Santa Fe. Most of the mules were destined for Missouri, where there was a great demand for the superior animal then produced in California. While a large proportion of this trade was lawful, there was also much illegitimate and clandestine traffic carried on by Indians and whites alike. Hardly a year passed that the mission fathers and the rancheros did not lose valuable livestock, which was driven off through Cajon Pass by raiding parties of outlaws. Even after the American occupation, these raids continued. One of the reasons settlement was deliberately encouraged in the San Bernardino Valley was the desire to discourage raiders from attacking the more densely settled areas.

Old Trails Across Euclid Avenue

Four historic trails once crossed what is now Euclid Avenue, the long, tree-lined drive that extends north and south through the modern cities of Ontario and Upland.

The first of these trails to be traversed by white men was the Anza Trail, over which Juan Bautista de Anza led the first overland party into California, and again in 1775 the first overland band of settlers, the founders of San Francisco. The Boy Scouts of America and service organizations of Ontario have placed a memorial boulder in honor of Anza in a small park on the corner of Euclid Avenue and Phillips Street. On it a bronze tablet bears the inscription: "To the honor and glory of Juan Bautista D'Anza, Trailmarker, and his band of intrepid followers, who, on March 21, 1774, passed near this spot on their way to San Gabriel and Monterey, the first white men to break a trail overland to California."

The San Gabriel Mission fathers used this trail as far as the Santa Ana River in order to reach their mission station in the San Bernardino Valley until a more direct route was cut shortly after 1822.

The second trail crossing Euclid Avenue, and the oldest of the four, was the Mojave Indian Trail, which was well established when Father Garcés traveled it in 1776. Smith, and probably Ewing Young, followed the same route. On this side of the Cajon Pass, the trail (also known as the Spanish Trail, the Mojave Trail, and the Santa Fe Trail) descended south from the pass and followed the base of the mountains westward approximately where Foothill Boulevard runs today.

At the corner of Euclid and Foothill in Upland stands a striking monument, the "Madonna of the Trail." This is the westernmost of twelve such statues across the United States that mark the trail of the pioneers; the easternmost is at Bethesda, Maryland. The statues were dedicated simultaneously on February 1, 1929. Mrs. Carolyn Emily Cook, then 81 years of age, who had made the trip from Iowa to California as a three-year-old child with her family in an oxcart, unveiled the heroic monument of a pioneer woman and her children. The two speakers at the dedication were Mildred Brooke Hoover and Judge Harry S Truman. Mrs. Hoover was the California State Regent of the Daughters of the American Revolution, who had undertaken the project. Shortly thereafter she began work on the first edition of *Historic Spots in California*, co-authoring one volume and entirely writing another. Her brother-in-law Herbert Clark Hoover was on that date President-elect of the United States. Judge Truman of Missouri had assisted the DAR in the placement of the statues. Later he became a United States senator from Missouri, and in time the 33rd President of the United States. A memory box in the base of the statue, containing coins, books, newspapers, and other printed matter, was opened in 1979 on the 50th anniversary of the dedication.

The third trail crossing Euclid Avenue was the old Emigrant Trail. This trail, which followed Anza's route across the Colorado Desert as far as Carrizo Creek and crossed the mountains via Warner's Ranch, branched in two directions after leaving Aguanga; one branch, known as the San Bernardino–Sonora Road, followed north to San Gorgonio Pass and west through the San Bernardino Valley, while the other, known in mission days as the Canyon Road to the Colorado, and designated by the Los Angeles Court of Sessions on May 19, 1851, as the Colorado Road, took its course along the western mountains via Temecula, Elsinore, Temescal Canyon, Corona, and the Santa Ana River.

The San Bernardino–Sonora Road, the upper branch of the old Emigrant Trail, came from Warner's Ranch via Aguanga and passed down the San Jacinto Valley and across the hills to the site of what is now Beaumont in Riverside County. From there, it continued northwest and west through San Bernardino County via Redlands and Old San Bernardino, or Gauchama, to what is now Colton. From that point the road went southwest past Slover Mountain to Agua Mansa, where it again proceeded westward to what is now Ontario, crossing Euclid Avenue one mile north of the Southern Pacific Railroad. From there it continued west across San Bernardino County to Los Angeles County via Ciénega (Mud Springs) near San Dimas.

The padres, after 1822 and before 1827, were the first to use this road on their way from San Gabriel to their mission outpost at Gauchama. Smith took this route in 1827 on his journey out of California, camping at Jumuba Rancheria a few miles west of Guachama Mission Station. Here he awaited the much-needed supplies that Father Sánchez, of Mission San Gabriel,

had ordered the mayordomo at Guachama to furnish him for his journey.

The last of the four roads crossing Euclid Avenue was the Colorado Road. This was opened from Carrizo Creek to Warner's in 1826 by Romualdo Pacheco, leader of a government expedition seeking an official mail route. Immediately thereafter the missionaries of San Gabriel opened up the road all the way from Warner's to San Gabriel via the canyon route. The first American to use this route was David E. Jackson in 1831, and it was used by other trappers and by those emigrants from Mexico and the East who followed the southern route via Santa Fe and the Gila River, of which the Colorado Road was a continuation. Since this southern trail was the only all-year route into California from the East, it was also used by the Butterfield stages from 1858 to 1861 for carrying passengers and mails.

The route of the Butterfield stages over this section of the Colorado Road may be traced by the adobes that it passed. After crossing the Santa Ana River near the Cota House, in what is now Riverside County, the road followed the base of the hills along Chino Creek, above which the highway from Chino to Santa Ana now runs. About three miles northwest of the Cota House, the stages passed the Raimundo Yorba adobe on Rancho Rincón, now in San Bernardino County. Although it was not one of the official stations along this route, doubtless stages did halt at the old adobe house, which still stands on the brow of the hill, beautifully restored. In 1868 Fenton M. Slaughter purchased this building from Yorba, and lived in it until his death in 1897. His daughter, Julia Slaughter Fuqua, saved it from ruin and brought it back to its former beauty as a memorial to her father. The Yorba-Slaughter Adobe (SRL 191), built in the early 1850's, stands at 17127 Pomona-Rincon

Yorba-Slaughter Adobe, near Chino

Road, about five and one-quarter miles south of Chino; it is one of the outstanding examples of adobe architecture in California.

At Rancho Rincón, the Butterfield route ran along the base of the hill, crossing the extreme southern terminus of Euclid Avenue at that point. From there it continued northwest along Chino Creek for seven miles to Rancho Chino, where a station was maintained on what is now the southern part of the California Institution for Men.

The Mojave Road

Shortly after the admission of California to the Union in 1850, federal officials began to plan an overland railroad to make a closer link between the far-off Pacific state and her 30 sisters. The 1850's saw a massive program of exploration and mapping of all corners of the West. In 1854, a party headed by Army Lieutenant Amiel Weeks Whipple crossed the Mojave Desert and mapped it for a possible railroad line. They discovered a remarkable desert phenomenon, Piute (or Pah-Ute) Springs, a never-failing flow of some 150 gallons of water per minute that gives rise to Piute Creek. The creek flows for nearly a mile before disappearing into the desert, and with the springs creates a remarkable oasis. It seems likely that the Paiute Indians had made some cultivation nearby. The springs, though located in a tangle of mountains and hills that were difficult for teams and wagons to negotiate, became a stopping point on the overland path leading from Fort Mojave on the Arizona side of the Colorado River across the desert to Barstow and from there south over the Cajon Pass into the San Bernardino Valley. In 1867 the United States Army established a small post there, called Fort Piute, which is now in ruins; there are plans to restore the site, but even today it is as remote a spot as can be found anywhere within the state of California. The site is on the Piute Ridge overlooking the Lanfair Valley at the eastern edge of the East Mojave National Scenic Area, and some twelve miles by dirt road from US 95, about 25 miles northwest of Needles.

Until the coming of the railroads, the chief route across this part of California was the Mojave Road. Going west from Fort Piute, the Mojave Road crossed several vital sources of water. Rock Springs and "Government Hole" lay close together; the latter was dug in 1859 by teamsters in the employ of Phineas Banning. West lay Marl Springs, and further on, past an area of volcanic cinder cones, was Soda Springs, where a small army post was put up in 1867.

Soda Springs got a new lease on life in the 1940's when Curtis Howe Springer homesteaded the property and used part of the old rock wall from the fort to build a religious resort with the distinctive name of "Zzyzx." Thirty years later the Bureau of Land Management succeeded in evicting Springer from the place, still shown on some maps as Zzyzx Springs. The Mojave River was first encountered at "The Caves" in Cave (now Afton) Canyon; sixteen miles further west was Camp Cady, where the old commissary and quartermaster store stood until they were destroyed by flood in 1938. The road proceeded along the valley of the Mojave River past modern-day Yermo, Daggett, and Barstow, by which time it had been joined by the Salt Lake Trail, and turned south toward the Cajon Pass. Considerable efforts have been made to have the path of the Mojave Road restored for the enjoyment of modern travelers, but the project is still largely undeveloped. The route of the Mojave Road, from Drum Barracks near Los Angeles Harbor through the Cajon Pass and across the Mojave Desert to the Nevada state line, has been designated as SRL 963.

Rancho and Asistencia de San Bernardino

Mission San Gabriel Arcángel was established in 1771; what is now the San Bernardino Valley was intended to be one of the ranchos that supplied the mission. On May 20, 1810, Father Francisco Dumetz celebrated Mass in an enramada, or temporary chapel, just west of modern Redlands. The day being the feast day of St. Bernardine of Siena, the priest named the chapel "San Bernardino." The name was later to become that of a ranch, a branch mission, a city, a county, a valley, and a mountain range.

In 1819, christianized Indians from the Guachama Rancheria asked the authorities at Mission San Gabriel to teach them to raise cattle and crops. When Father Mariano Payeras visited Guachama ("the place of plenty to eat" in local dialect) in 1821, he found that there were mission cattle grazing in the valley and a number of old houses, probably for the herdsmen of the rancho, at Jumuba, a few miles west of the rancho headquarters. In 1827, Father Sánchez of Mission San Gabriel reported: "Rancho of San Bernardino—The house is of adobe. It consists of one long building. It has an enramada or structure of boughs which serves for a chapel. It has also a building with compartments for keeping grain. The walls of this structure are of adobe."

This was the Guachama Mission Station (SRL 95), or the rancho headquarters, on Rancho San Bernardino, which was owned by Mission San Gabriel. The little mission station was located north of what is now Mission Road and east of where it intersects Mountain

View Avenue, while the site of the Guachama Indian village was on the south side of this road. The marker is on Mission Road in the Bryn Mawr district of Loma Linda.

On what is now known as Barton Hill, one and one-half miles southeast of the old rancho buildings, and about two miles west of the present city of Redlands on Barton Road, an extensive adobe structure was begun about 1830. This was the Asistencia San Bernardino, a chapel under the supervision of Mission San Gabriel. The fathers had planned a chain of interior missions paralleling those near the coast, and San Bernardino, along with San Antonio de Pala and Santa Ysabel, was to have been part of this chain. The program never went beyond these three asistencias, for the decree of secularization in the 1830's ended all mission activity in California.

After secularization, all work on the asistencia ceased and the buildings remained practically deserted until 1842, when a large section of the mission lands was granted to three sons and a nephew of Antonio María Lugo of Los Angeles. The cities of San Bernardino, Redlands, and Colton now stand on the Rancho San Bernardino of the Lugos. One of Don Antonio's sons, José del Carmen Lugo, came to live in the old asistencia buildings, thus saving them from complete disintegration for a time.

After the Rancho San Bernardino was sold to the Mormons by the Lugo brothers in 1851, Bishop Nathan C. Tenney, manager of agricultural operations on the lands formerly cultivated by the missions, occupied the old asistencia buildings. Upon the withdrawal of the Mormons in 1857, Dr. Ben Barton, a prominent pioneer settler, moved with his family into the buildings, occupying them until 1867. From this date the old adobes, untenanted and uncared for, gradually succumbed to the weather, until only a few mud walls remained.

The Asistencia San Bernardino (SRL 42) was meticulously rebuilt in the years 1928–37; wherever possible, materials salvaged from the original structure were incorporated into the replica. It stands at 26930 Barton Road, in the Bryn Mawr district. The striking whitewashed adobe bell tower is a landmark in the neighborhood. The building is used for religious services and also serves as one of the museums of San Bernardino County. This restoration project became a model for similar programs elsewhere in the state.

North of the asistencia, and just beyond the railroad tracks, may be seen the old *zanja*, or water ditch (SRL 43), built in 1819–20 by the Indians under the direction of the Spaniards to bring water for irrigation from Mill Creek Canyon to the Guachama Rancheria. The ditch passes under the business district of Redlands. A little

further north, at 11245 Nevada Street in Redlands, is the much-altered home of Dr. Ben Barton, built for his family in 1866–67, to which they moved from the asistencia. The three-story brick building was one of the largest in the county at the time of its construction.

Mission Ranchos

Mission San Gabriel had three ranchos in the San Bernardino Valley: Rancho San Bernardino, already mentioned as the location of the mission station Guachama and later the asistencia; Rancho Agua Caliente, on which the present city of San Bernardino is located; and Rancho Jumuba, located between the present Loma Linda and Colton. Rancho Jumuba was named for an Indian rancheria that occupied the site beside a bubbling spring of water. It was here that Jedediah Strong Smith camped in 1827 while being outfitted by the mission fathers, just before starting on his return trip to Salt Lake, via the San Joaquin Valley.

San Bernardino

The city of San Bernardino owes its beginnings to a colony of Mormons from Salt Lake City, who arrived in June 1851 and laid the foundation of a thriving community in the six years before their leader, Brigham Young, recalled them. Gradually, the lands purchased from the Lugo brothers were subdivided and sold to the individual members of the Mormon community, who established homes and farms. The town of San Bernardino was founded; in the San Bernardino Mountains, sawmills were erected; roads were constructed, the Mormons opening up the present Foothill Boulevard as far as Cucamonga; extensive agricultural activities were started; and churches and schools were founded.

Adobe and log houses were soon erected on a site originally known as "Agua Caliente," but the name of the neighboring Asistencia San Bernardino was transferred to the new town. Here, because of rumored Indian uprisings, a fort and stockade enclosing eight acres of ground was erected in the form of a parallelogram, 300 feet wide and 720 feet long. The north and south ends were made of cottonwood and willow tree trunks closely fitted together and set three feet in the ground and twelve feet above, while the log houses were moved along the west side, forming a solid wall finished with logs in blockhouse fashion, with loopholes, bastions at the corners, and inset gateways. Within this stockade about a hundred families lived; a few, however, remained outside, camping at a spot now occupied by the Pioneer Memorial Cemetery at Seventh Street and Sierra Way.

The site of the old Mormon stockade (SRL 44) included the present Arrowhead Avenue from Third Street nearly to Fourth Street, and lands to the east, west, and south. Most of this area today is occupied by the striking San Bernardino County Government Center, completed in 1983, and the impressive county courthouse, dating from 1926. On the courthouse site also stood the José Maria Lugo adobe; a plaque was placed at the courthouse by the Native Sons of the Golden West in 1927. A two-story adobe built by the Mormons stood at Third Street and Arrowhead Avenue until 1867, and was used as the first courthouse of San Bernardino County. Jefferson Hunt, an officer in the Mormon Battalion, is sometimes called the "Father of San Bernardino County," for it was he, while a Los Angeles county legislator, who introduced legislation for the creation of a separate San Bernardino County in 1853. The site of his home has been marked by the county on the south side of Fifth Street, between Arrowhead and Mountain View avenues in the city of San Bernardino.

In 1851, the year of their arrival, the Mormons built the first road from the San Bernardino Valley to the summit of the mountains, over which they hauled lumber from their sawmills to be sold in Los Angeles and other expanding communities of southern California. Much of the cost of their colony at San Bernardino was defrayed by the sale of lumber, and, of course, it was needed for construction of their own buildings. Where the Rim of the World Drive crosses the old Mormon lumber road at Crestline in the San Bernardino Mountains, a monument has been erected (SRL 96).

Although they were by and large a peaceable people, a dispute developed between Mormon factions over land titles. The "Independent" group even put up an adobe fortification, Fort Benson (SRL 617), and maintained it for about a year. Its site is indicated by a monument east of Colton, on the west side of Hunt's Lane between I-10 and the Southern Pacific Railroad tracks. This was also the site of the Indian village of Jumuba, where Jedediah Smith camped in 1827. A plaque to the honor of Smith was placed in 1951 in the courthouse plaza by the Native Sons of the Golden West.

In 1857, Mormon activity was halted by the decree of Brigham Young, president of the Mormon church. The decree recalled his coreligionists to Salt Lake City because of the threatened invasion of Utah by United States forces under General Albert Sidney Johnston. The majority of the settlers obeyed the call and left their homes in the San Bernardino Valley, often selling them for very little. Over half the white population of the valley left in a short while, a unique event in the decade in which people were pouring into other parts of California at an unprecedented rate. Their departure seriously hindered the valley's prosperity for some time; the Mormons had been industrious citizens with

great organizing ability, and they had been largely responsible for the development of the agricultural resources of the valley as well as for the sound basis of the city of San Bernardino.

Chino

Rancho Santa Ana del Chino was another of the Mission San Gabriel ranchos. Soon after the secularization of the missions it was granted to Antonio María Lugo. The ranch house (SRL 942) stood about three miles south of the present-day town of Chino; the commemorative marker is at 4440 Eucalyptus Avenue. This adobe was built by Colonel Isaac Williams (known as Don Julián to the Californians), who came to California with Ewing Young in 1832 and became one of the leading citizens of Los Angeles. He married a daughter of the eminent Antonio María Lugo, who in 1841 deeded a half-interest in the Rancho Santa Ana del Chino to his son-in-law, and ten years later deeded the remainder to him.

The Williams adobe was the center of much activity, since it was near the well-traveled southern emigrant trail. Orchards and vineyards were planted; barns, shearing sheds, and adobe huts for a great army of Indian and Mexican laborers were erected; a gristmill, one of the earliest in southern California, was built; the rancho was stocked with fine cattle, horses, and sheep; and an extensive trade in hides and tallow was carried on.

During the Mexican War the adobe was the scene of a battle between the Americans and the Californians. While Colonel Gillespie was shut up in Los Angeles in 1846, a score of Americans, commanded by B. D. Wilson, took refuge on Rancho del Chino, which was 25 miles east of Los Angeles. On September 27 the house was surrounded by a force of 70 mounted Californians; during the short skirmish that followed, one of the Californians, Carlos Ballesteros, was killed, and several Americans were wounded. The Californians, incensed by the death of their friend, who was very popular, set fire to the brea roof of the adobe. At this point, Isaac Williams appeared with a white flag and his two little daughters, whom he insisted on placing in the hands of their uncle Felipe Lugo, one of the attacking party, so they could be taken to their Grandfather Lugo in Los Angeles. The leaders of the Californians, however, persuaded the Americans to surrender, promising them protection as prisoners of war. The success of the Californians in this encounter encouraged them in their attack upon Gillespie.

During the years 1858–61, the Chino adobe assumed additional historical importance as a station on the old Butterfield stage route, which passed its door.

A marker has been placed by San Bernardino County at the corner of Eucalyptus Avenue and SR 71 in Chino.

Very soon after the death of Isaac Williams in 1856, his daughter Francisca married Robert Carlisle, a young southerner, and Mercedes Williams married John Rains, who had been mayordomo at Chino. John Rains and his wife moved to Rancho Cucamonga, while the Carlisles remained at Chino. Robert Carlisle was an energetic, well-educated man and a good business manager, and under his control the prosperity of Rancho del Chino continued until his death in 1865.

Francisca Williams Carlisle married again, and the Chino estate was managed by trustees. In 1881 it was sold to Richard Gird, a miner and engineer, one of the most picturesque characters of the early American period. On Rancho del Chino, Gird lived lavishly in a fine adobe built by Joseph Bridger (the site is on the grounds of the Los Serranos Country Club), and used his influence to persuade entrepreneurs to develop the region. A projected ironworks failed for lack of capital, but sugar beets, first planted on the rancho, had become a major industry of the area by 1900. Gird sold his property in 1894, and soon after it was broken up into small tracts and sold; the Williams adobe has long since disappeared.

Rancho Cucamonga

Rancho Cucamonga derived its name from an Indian village that was on the land when the first white men came there. Tradition tells us that the Cucamonga Indians were unusually intelligent and industrious and that they learned much from the padres, who sometimes came from Mission San Gabriel to visit them. Gradually they acquired cattle and horses and raised good crops of corn and melons in the fertile hills and valleys of "Nuestra Señora del Pilar de Cucamonga," as the padres called the locality.

Tiburcio Tapia, a leading citizen of Los Angeles, petitioned for a grant to the Cucamonga lands in 1839 and received it in that year. Don Tiburcio immediately began the construction of an adobe house on the crest of Cucamonga's highest hill. Its roof was covered with brea from Rancho La Brea near Los Angeles. It was said to be "massive as a fortress, facing south, with east and west wings and a gateway to the north side."

The Indians, who were employed in the building operations, rebelled when they realized that the newcomers were taking their rich grazing lands from them. Retreating to the foothills and canyons, they made occasional raids upon the stock of the white settlers. Desert Indians, too, frequently invaded the rancho lands, and many tales were told by old residents of raids and battles and even attacks upon the Tapia "fortress" on "Red Hill."

In the beginning, Don Tiburcio left his rancho largely in the care of his mayordomo, José María Valdez, who is said to have set out the "mother vineyard." This later developed into one of the large plantings of grapes in California, the first cuttings probably having been obtained at Mission San Gabriel. The history of the old rancho is closely associated with the development of its vineyard.

Among other traditions of those early days at Cucamonga is that of the chest of coins that Don Tiburcio is said to have hidden when rumors of war began to herald the aggression of the United States in Alta California. It is said that this chest contained not only Señor Tapia's own money but that entrusted to him by friends, and also a sum collected for the building of a chapel at Cucamonga.

Tiburcio Tapia died suddenly in 1845. No one knew where the chest had been hidden, except an Indian servant whom Don Tiburcio had sworn to secrecy. Nor would the Indian disclose the whereabouts of the hidden treasure, so great was his fear of the fulfillment of the terrifying oath that Don Tiburcio had placed upon him.

A few years later, Tiburcio Tapia's daughter, María Merced, married Leon V. Prudhomme, and moved with him to the adobe on Red Hill. Doña María, who knew the story of the hidden treasure, slept in her father's room. One night, so the story goes, she saw a mysterious light moving across the chamber wall, and resting upon a particular spot. The apparition was repeated a number of times, greatly disturbing the young wife. In order to prove that the vision was entirely imaginary, her husband plunged a knife into the adobe wall. To his amazement, it went through the wall, disclosing a hollow space behind. In the aperture was a purse containing some silver coins and a scrap of paper with its message faded with age. The paper was studied very carefully and much searching followed, but all in vain. No treasure was ever found, though searchers have not been lacking through the years. The Tapia adobe has long since returned to its native clay.

In 1858, Victor Prudhomme sold Rancho Cucamonga to John Rains and his wife, Mercedes Williams. An unpublished history of the 1890's says: "The coming of John Rains to this place marked not only a new but a progressive epoch in its history. The old Tapia residence on the hill was abandoned and a new one built at the highest point of the east bank of the arroyo, north of the vineyard. Labor and expense was not spared in its construction. . . . The walls were built of heavy brick made of the red clay dug from the hills and roofed with thatches covered with brea mixed with tallow. . . . A little to the east of the Valdez residence was built the store and nearby a blacksmith shop, stables, and several dwellings. . . . The rancho was stocked by Mr. Rains with sheep, horses, and cattle, and 160 acres was set to vines. The small still and winery were proportionately enlarged and improved. The road from Los Angeles to San Bernardino by way of Chino having been abandoned by the stage for the Arroyo San José routes to Bear Valley and the mines, this became a regular station, where the horses were changed and the traveler enabled to obtain refreshments.

"With the vaqueros in charge of the flocks and herds, the laborers in the vineyards and winery, the stable hands in charge of stage relays, mechanics at work on buildings, teamsters, the blacksmiths and a trader and postmaster, the place became not only a hive of industry, but noted as the chief trading post and assembly point for all classes and nationalities east of Los Angeles. The Rains home was a center of social life, and, attracted by the hospitality of its master, the beauty of its mistress, the sparkling wines and festivities, here frequently gathered the representative wealthy and elite of the south."

This rather romantic account tells of what was really but a brief period of years. On November 17, 1862, John Rains was murdered, leaving his 23-year-old widow with four small children and pregnant with a fifth. After a series of accusations, one Manuel Cerradel was arrested and confined to prison. Convicted not of Rains's murder but of an assault on a deputy sheriff, Cerradel was brutally lynched by a group of men while on his way to prison at San Quentin the following year. Ramón Carrillo, a family friend who had been accused by Robert Carlisle, Mercedes Williams Rains's brother-in-law, of the murder of John Rains, was shot to death in Mercedes's presence in 1864; Carlisle was killed in a shooting the following year. The distraught Mercedes married José Clemente Carrillo in 1864 and ultimately the couple became so indebted that they lost their estate. A daughter of John and Mercedes Rains, Francisca, married a young lawyer named Henry T. Gage in 1880. Gage became governor of California in 1899, and Mercedes attended his inaugural in Sacramento.

Meanwhile, the Rains home, also known as Casa de Rancho Cucamonga, had become the property of I. W. Hellman through a mortgage foreclosure in 1871. In the following years the home was for a while a private residence and for a while a hotel. From 1922 to 1948 Mr. and Mrs. Edwin Motsinger lived in the house, which they lovingly restored and to which they welcomed Francisca Rains Gage as a guest in 1946. In 1969 nearby Cucamonga Wash flooded and destroyed much of the

Thomas Winery, Rancho Cucamonga

surrounding area and the house had to be abandoned. After considerable legal difficulties, the property came into the possession of the San Bernardino Museum Association. The restored house is now on the National Register of Historic Landmarks and is open to the public at 7869 Vineyard Avenue, Rancho Cucamonga.

The old adobe winery (SRL 490) built by John Rains stands nearby at 8916 Foothill Boulevard. Established in 1839 by Tiburcio Tapia, this is the oldest commercial winery in California. The winery was restored by H. H. Thomas, the eastern end being replaced after the 1969 flood, and today does business as the Thomas Winery. The Cucamonga District was once among the major wine-producing regions, but urban encroachment has restricted the acreage devoted to vines considerably in recent years.

To the west of the winery, across Cucamonga Creek, is the site of the Tapia adobe (SRL 360) on the southeastern slope of Red Hill, which is now built up with homes and covered by the greens of the Red Hill Country Club.

Yucaipa

The oldest dwelling still standing in San Bernardino County is located at 32183 Kentucky Street, near Dunlap Boulevard and Sixteenth Street, about four miles east of Redlands at the western outskirts of Yucaipa. The two-story Diego Sepúlveda adobe (SRL 528) was built in 1842 in the southeastern corner of the Rancho San Bernardino. Sepúlveda was a nephew of Antonio María Lugo, three of whose sons were co-grantees of the rancho with Sepúlveda. Later owners of the adobe included the Dunlap family, after whom the nearby street is named. In the early 1950's the old house, rapidly falling into ruin, was saved from demolition by a group of public-spirited citizens, who effected its purchase and restoration. Since

1955 it has been operated as one of the San Bernardino County Museums, open to the public on a regular basis as the Sepúlveda-Dunlap adobe.

Although there is no marker at the spot, Yucaipa is the site of an Indian rancheria (SRL 620), from which it received its name. On the hillside just above the house at 33142 Avenue E, excavations by the San Bernardino Historical Society have revealed metates (grinding holes), fireplaces, and implements used by the peaceful Serrano Indians before and during the Spanish period. The place, well watered by springs, a ciénega, and a creek, was a logical site for habitation.

Agua Mansa and San Salvador

These settlements on the "Bandini Donation" on Rancho Jurupa were composed of New Mexican colonists who had moved there in 1845 from the settlement of Politana on Rancho San Bernardino, thought to have been somewhere in the vicinity of the modern city of Colton. Colonists were desirable at that time as protectors against the inroads of unfriendly Indians; and when dissatisfaction with certain conditions at Politana arose, Juan Bandini invited the settlers to leave that place and locate on a parcel of land he donated. It lay on both sides of the Santa Ana River, and later formed part of San Salvador parish. Agua Mansa was on the north and west bank of the river, while the settlement on the south and east side was known as San Salvador. The original parish chapel in San Salvador collapsed before it was completed because it had been built on quicksand.

Agua Mansa ("gentle water") was the site of another chapel erected in 1851 and in use until 1893. The Santa Ana River was anything but gentle in January 1862 when torrential rains caused a disastrous flood that washed away the homes of Agua Mansa and San Salvador on its banks. The chapel and the adjacent cemetery, on higher ground, were spared. The little burial ground is all that remains of Agua Mansa (SRL 121); it is the oldest cemetery in the county, and is located about three miles southwest of Colton on Agua Mansa Road, east of its intersection with Riverside Avenue, and about half a mile north of the Riverside county line. A restoration of the old chapel was made in 1978 and it now serves as part of the San Bernardino County Museum's operations.

Redlands and Loma Linda

Frank E. Brown and Edward G. Judson acquired land from the Southern Pacific Railroad in 1881 and added more to make a parcel of 4,000 acres. This was to

Big Bear Dam, Big Bear Valley

be the planned community of Redlands, named for its reddish earth, and the town was incorporated in 1888. In order to find the water needed to make the community grow, Brown followed the recommendation of Dr. Ben Barton and investigated the nearby mountains. At Big Bear Valley he found a spot where a dam could be built, and in 1884 Big Bear Lake was created. This dam (SRL 725), built by the Bear Valley Irrigation Company, is still visible behind the present, higher dam, built in 1910. Citrus crops thrived in this portion of the valley, and the salubrious climate made Redlands attractive as a winter resort.

The Kimberly Crest Mansion at 1325 Prospect Drive is a reminder of this period of Redlands' history. Built in 1897 for an Eastern industrialist, the French chateau–style building is open to the public with much of its original furnishings and decoration intact.

At 125 West Vine Street is the Redlands A. K. Smiley Library. The Smiley family developed Canyon Crest Park (popularly known as "Smiley Heights") on

Kimberly Crest Mansion, Redlands

the southern edge of the city; beautifully landscaped, it was a highly desirable area of elegant turn-of-the-century homes. The library was given to the city in 1898 and is still in use as a public facility.

The San Bernardino County Museum at 2024 Orange Tree Lane is one of the most spectacular in California. Opened in 1974, it is a large building worthy of a large county, with significant displays of natural history and the history of the people who have lived in the county.

The University of Redlands was the first four-year institution of higher learning in the county. It began as a Baptist institution in 1909; some of its oldest buildings date from that time. The Reverend Jasper Newton Field of the First Baptist Church of Redlands was the first president. It has developed into a distinguished liberal arts institution.

Nearby Loma Linda was the site of several unsuccessful attempts to establish a town, a resort, and a health center. When the only hotel closed for lack of patronage in 1904, "Lonesome Linda" was written off by many as a losing proposition. But the very next year, Seventh-Day Adventists purchased the property and began what turned out to be a highly successful revitalization of the place. The "vegetarian hotel and sanitarium" gradually attracted so many visitors that the facility expanded in 1909, becoming the College of Medical Evangelists. Its medical, nursing, and paramedical programs were consolidated in 1961 with the founding of Loma Linda University. In 1967 the university erected a seven-story medical center, which today has an international reputation for its pioneering work in many surgical techniques. The university and the medical center are the heart of the worldwide Seventh-Day Adventist medical network.

Fontana Rabbit Experimental Station

The only experimental station in the United States devoted to the breeding and raising of rabbits was operated by the Federal government at 8384 Cypress Avenue in Fontana between 1928 and 1965 (SRL 950). The site is now a senior citizens center operated by the city of Fontana.

The San Bernardino Mountains

With the American conquest of California and the imposition of American law, it became urgent to have accurate land surveys made. Three points in the state were selected to serve as the bases for the establishment of meridians and base lines. One was in Humboldt County; another was at the top of Mount Diablo in Contra Costa County; the third was established in 1852 by U.S. Deputy Surveyor Colonel Henry Washington on the west peak of Mount San Bernardino at 116°55'17" west longitude and 34°07'20" north latitude. Base Line Street follows this line for many miles.

High above the San Bernardino Valley the Rim of the World Drive takes motorists to the mountain resorts of Lake Arrowhead and Big Bear Lake, among many others. Several historic spots, appropriately marked, are also to be seen. On the east side of Waterman Canyon in the mountains north of the city of San Bernardino is The Arrowhead (SRL 977), a natural geological formation 1,376 feet in length and 479 feet across at its widest point. The remarkable landmark is the emblem for San Bernardino County and has many Indian legends associated with it.

About three miles north of Big Bear Lake, and roughly parallel to it, lies Holcomb Valley (SRL 619), now a peaceful, sheltered area but in the 1860's the scene of a full-scale gold rush, the largest in southern California. It derives its name from William Francis "Bill" Holcomb, who made the first strikes there in 1860. The area is crisscrossed with good dirt roads, along which Forest Service signs have been placed, indicating the principal landmarks. One of these is at the site of Belleville, the valley's largest town, reputed to have reached a population of 10,000 and to have been a hotbed of Confederate sympathizers during the Civil War. By early 1862 Belleville was challenging the town of San Bernardino to become the county seat. San Bernardino kept its position in a close election, so a mountain story goes, only because a ballot box from Belleville was "accidentally" kicked into a bonfire on election night. The Holcomb Valley gold rush was short-lived, but it was responsible for bringing many new settlers into the county. Another contemporary gold rush occurred in the Lytle Creek–Glenn Ranch area far to the west.

There were a number of lumber roads between the mountains and the valley besides the one built by the Mormons in 1851, and one of the most important was the Daley Toll Road (SRL 579) built in 1870 by Edward Daley and Co. from Del Rosa to the crest near Strawberry Peak. After twenty years as a toll road, it became a county road. A stretch of it can be seen where it crosses the Rim of the World Drive; the Native Sons and Daughters of the Golden West placed a marker there, one-half mile west of Rim of the World High School, in 1935.

Calico

The Calico Mountains, vivid with ever-changing colors, their wild and lofty grandeur wrought by age-old volcanic action, lie in the middle of the Mojave Desert five miles north of Daggett and two miles northwest of Yermo. At their base is the old mining town of Calico (SRL 782). In the 1880's the wealth of the silver mines discovered in this region brought 3,500 people to the place, and Calico became one of the most prosperous as well as one of the wildest camps of the great Southwest. A sensational drop in the price of silver was the cause of its abandonment, and the fury of desert storms caused its final desolation.

In 1952, Walter Knott of Knott's Berry Farm in Buena Park, Orange County, purchased the ruins of the old town and gave it a vigorous restoration. Knott's uncle had been sheriff at Calico in 1882. After several of its buildings had been restored, the town was eventually deeded to San Bernardino County. It is located just off I-15 about four miles northwest of Yermo. To the east, three miles north of the intersection of I-15 and Mineola Road, is the Calico Early Man Archaeological Site, referred to in the beginning of this chapter.

Historic Spots of the Mojave Desert

Chimney Rock (SRL 737), at Rabbit Dry Lake in Lucerne Valley, is the site of the last Indian fight in southern California. In January 1867 Indians from this area raided a lumber camp in the San Bernardino Mountains, looting and burning a number of cabins and a sawmill. A retaliatory posse descended upon the Indians at their Chimney Rock camp and killed and wounded many of them.

The Joshua tree is a giant yucca native to the Southwest. Its twisted, distinctive shape was noted by Mormon pioneers, who, it is said, named the trees after a line from the Book of Joshua: "Thou shalt follow the way pointed to thee by the trees." Joshua Tree National Monument was established in 1936; most of its 870 square miles lie within Riverside County, but the headquarters and visitors' center for the reservation are at Twentynine Palms in San Bernardino County. This oasis was first explored in 1855 by Colonel Henry Washington, who noted that the neighboring Chemehuevi Indians called the area "Mar-rah," or "land of little water." Its present name seems to have come from a slightly later exploration in 1858, when native palms were found at the oasis.

John Searles discovered borax in 1862 on the surface of the lake that now bears his name. In 1873 he and his brother Dennis formed the San Bernardino Borax Mining Company, which they operated until 1897. The now-dry lake today yields many other chemicals besides borax, and the significance of the Searles discovery is indicated by a historical marker (SRL 774) beside the highway at Trona. Borax mining near Calico maintained that old camp in existence for a few years after the end of the silver boom.

Not far from Trona the picturesque remains of the towns of Atolia and Red Mountain mark the Rand Mining District, which straddles the San Bernardino–Kern county line. Across the line, Johannesburg and Randsburg also contain much evidence of a flourishing past.

One of the Argonauts trapped in Death Valley in 1849 led his family to safety by following the dry course of the Amargosa River south to Salt Spring, where they encountered the old Spanish Trail. Harry Wade is commemorated by a monument (SRL 622) 30 miles northwest of Baker at the junction of SR 127 and the graded dirt road into the southern part of Death Valley National Monument.

Another marker of the desert is the Von Schmidt State Boundary Monument (SRL 859) on the east side of River Road about fifteen miles north of Needles. The cast-iron marker was placed by a surveyor, A. W. Von Schmidt, in 1873; subsequent remeasuring put the actual boundary between California and Nevada about three-quarters of a mile to the north.

The Spanish Colonial style was frequently used in the early twentieth century for public buildings in southern California. Two railway stations still stand from this time. At Kelso, the 1906 Union Pacific depot stands in a grove of shade trees. At Barstow, the hotel built by Fred Harvey for the Santa Fe Railroad is commemorated (SRL 892) on the building "Casa del Desierto," erected on the site of the original structure, which burned in 1911. Some 75 Harvey Houses were built along the lines of the Santa Fe Railroad in the late nineteenth century.

Wyatt Earp of Tombstone, Arizona, fame and now an almost legendary character via television, mined gold in the Whipple Mountains near the Colorado River from the early 1900's until his death in 1929. In his honor the little town of Drennan in the southeastern corner of the county renamed itself Earp. The home built by his brother Virgil Earp still stands at 528 West H Street in Colton.

At Daggett the Walter Alf Blacksmith Shop is still standing and contains the old tools and equipment used to repair the vehicles and machinery of miners and pioneers. The family-run private museum is open to the public.

Another private museum, also open to the public, is the Roy Rogers–Dale Evans Museum at 15650 Seneca Road in Victorville. This museum contains extensive memorabilia of the career of this famous pair of entertainers; it is also a fascinating display of the changes in the motion picture industry over the years 1935–60.

San Diego County

San Diego County was named after the harbor that Vizcaíno named in 1602. It was one of the original 27 counties, and the city of San Diego has always been the county seat. San Diego is Spanish for St. Didacus, a native of Spain and a Franciscan saint. Many prestatehood records of deed and wills in Spanish are housed in the courthouse.

The Discovery and Naming of San Diego

The bay of San Diego was first seen on September 28, 1542, by Juan Rodríguez Cabrillo, a Portuguese navigator sent out by Antonio de Mendoza, viceroy of Mexico, to explore the coast of New Spain and to discover, if possible, the elusive strait of Anián. Cabrillo, with his chief pilot, Bartolomé Ferrelo, in the tiny vessels *San Salvador* and *Victoria* anchored in that "port, closed and very good, which they named San Miguel" and that Sebastián Vizcaíno in 1602 renamed San Diego. It is believed by local historians that Ballast Point was the most likely place for Cabrillo to have landed. One-half acre of land within the Fort Rosecrans Military Reservation on Point Loma was set aside by the government in 1913 as Cabrillo National Monument. It is near the end of Point Loma, south and slightly west of Ballast Point. The main feature of the little park is the old Point Loma lighthouse.

It was not until 60 years later that the bay of San Diego was again visited by white men. On May 5, 1602, Sebastián Vizcaíno, with the two ships *San Diego* and *Santo Tomás* and the little frigate *Tres Reyes*, sailed north from Acapulco. He had been sent out by the new viceroy, the Conde de Monterey, to explore the coast of Alta California for safe and convenient harbors in which the Manila galleon might stop for repairs and the recuperation of scurvy-ridden crews, and from which observations on the whereabouts of English pirate ships might be made.

Early in November, Vizcaíno reached the port that Cabrillo had seen before him. In his diary this entry is found: "On the twelfth of the said month, which was the day of the glorious San Diego, the general, admiral, religious, captains, ensigns, and almost all the men went on shore. A hut was built and mass was said in celebration of the feast of San Diego."

Thus was San Diego Bay named, and the first recorded house of Christian worship in Alta California, although a crude and humble one, was erected.

The Settlement of San Diego

In the 1760's, rumors that the Russians were planning to extend their colonies from Alaska down the Pacific Coast to Alta California caused King Carlos III of Spain to order the viceroy of New Spain to investigate the danger. The viceroy transmitted the order to José de Gálvez, visitador general, and Gálvez put into effect what had long been contemplated—the settlement of Alta California. His decision was influenced by personal ambition as well as by fear that the land might become the possession of Russia or England. In 1768, 226 years after the discovery of San Diego by Cabrillo, Gálvez organized the first colonizing project. Gaspar de Portolá was appointed military governor of Alta California and was placed in command of the entire expedition, and Father Junipero Serra was named Padre Presidente of the missions that were to be established in the new province. Officers, priests, soldiers, sailors, laborers, and southern Indian retainers, perhaps 300 men in all, made up the personnel of this, the first band of settlers dispatched to California. The primary aim of the expedition was the protection of the port of Monterey, but a base was also to be established at San Diego. The Franciscan friars were to found missions and convert the Indians, and the soldiers were to guard the country and protect the mission settlements.

The expedition was divided into five companies, three of which went by sea in the ships *San Carlos*, *San Antonio*, and *San José*, and two by land, one under command of Portolá himself and the other under Fernando Rivera y Moncada, his second in command. The second of the sea expeditions to leave La Paz, under command of Juan Pérez in the ship *San Antonio*, was the first to arrive at San Diego, on April 11, 1769, after a voyage of 55 days. On April 19, the *San Carlos*, with Vicente Vila in command and Pedro Fages with his 25 Catalonian volunteers, arrived after a voyage of great suffering, lasting 110 days. Rivera, accompanied by Father Crespí, whose diary is a primary source of California history, arrived on May 14, after a march of 51 days from Velicatá in Baja California. Governor Portolá and a few men of the second land expedition arrived June 29. The rest of this division, with Father Serra, who had made the journey while suffering from an ulcerated leg, arrived last, on July 1. The *San José* and all aboard were lost at sea. Ninety-three Spaniards had died aboard the other ships; many of the Indians had died or deserted. There were left only 126 settlers at San Diego. The site of the landing (SRL 891) is at Spanish Landing Park on Harbor Drive.

Already advanced in years, Father Serra endured experiences of great hardship and privation with a cheerfulness that ignored physical ills and dangers for the cause to which he gave his life. His enthusiasm for the conversion of California's Indians was never dampened by suffering or discouragement.

With him were Father Juan Crespí (a fellow Majorcan who had studied under Serra at the University at Palma and had come with him to Mexico in 1749) and Fathers Gómez, Parrón, and Vizcaíno, besides Portolá and several other government officers. Portolá, with Captain Rivera and a band of soldiers, accompanied by Fathers Crespí and Gómez, and Miguel Costansó, geographer, engineer, and diarist, set out northward to search for the port of Monterey, where the first northern mission was to be established. Father Serra remained at San Diego to undertake the founding of the first of the Franciscan missions to be established in the wilderness of Alta California.

Mission San Diego de Alcalá

Immediately after the departure of Portolá and his men, Father Serra founded Mission San Diego de Alcalá on July 16, 1769, just fifteen days after his arrival. The ceremony was performed in the presence of some 30 men, on what later came to be known as Presidio Hill. Here, overlooking the bay and the river, the first temporary chapel was erected, and the first cross was raised.

The order of ceremony followed at this first founding was much the same as that subsequently used in establishing all of the twenty other missions that finally

Mission San Diego de Alcalá

composed the chain. Helen Hunt Jackson describes the procedure: "A cross was set up; a booth of branches built; the ground and the booth were consecrated by holy water, and christened by the name of a saint; a mass was performed; the neighboring Indians, if there were any, were roused and summoned by the ringing of bells swung on limbs of trees; presents of cloth and trinkets were given them to inspire them with trust, and thus a Mission was founded. Two monks (never, at first, more) were appointed to take charge of the cross and booth, and to win, baptize, convert, and teach all the Indians to be reached in the region. They had for guard and help a few soldiers, and sometimes a few already partly civilized and Christianized Indians; several head of cattle, some tools and seeds, and holy vessels for the church service, completed their store of weapons . . . with which to conquer the wilderness and its savages."

The little settlement at San Diego had, perhaps, greater hardships to endure in the beginning than any of the missions that followed. For a whole year Father Serra labored in vain among the Indians before even one child was baptized. Supplies, too, were insufficient and at the end of six months the whole enterprise was threatened with failure.

Meanwhile, Portolá and his men, under great hardships, were struggling northward on what proved to be an unsuccessful endeavor.

Portolá's Trail to Monterey

Leaving the port of San Diego on July 14, 1769, Portolá, with Father Juan Crespí as chronicler of the expedition, had started north on the long journey to Monterey, where the second mission was to be established.

Passing what is now called Mission Bay, the party came to an Indian village near the northeast point of the cove. Leaving the shore here, they passed into Rose Canyon and camped at some pools. The following day the route lay through Soledad Valley with its Indian villages. Camp made in San Dieguito Canyon, near Del Mar, with another Indian village not far distant.

On July 16 and 17 the trail led by way of the present county road called El Camino Real (the principal highway until the end of the nineteenth century) past San Elijo Lagoon, Batequitos Lagoon, Agua Hedionda Creek, and Buena Vista Creek, near Carlsbad. Many Indian villages were passed along the way, all of them friendly. On July 18, the verdant valley of San Juan Capistrano, the first name given to the valley of San Luis Rey, was reached and camp made. The location was pronounced by Father Crespí to be an excellent site for the placing of a mission, and several years later Mission San Luís Rey was indeed founded near this very spot.

From the valley of San Juan Capistrano northward Portolá passed valleys called by the explorers Santa Margarita and Santa Praxedis de los Rosales (because, it was said, of the numerous "Castilian roses and other flowers" growing there). These sites are commemorated in the name of the old Rancho Santa Margarita y las Flores, north and west of Mission San Luís Rey.

Passing into the region of what is now Orange County on July 22, the party continued north. Six months later, returning from their fruitless search for the port of Monterey, sick and weary, their provisions nearly gone, the little company returned over much the same route, but the homeward marches were long, and several of the old camps were passed without stopping. On January 21, 1770, camp was made apparently on San Onofre Creek, and on January 24 the party rejoined the group anxiously awaiting their return at the newly established Mission of San Diego.

There, Portolá found that the supply ship, which had left for San Blas six months before, had not returned and that provisions were almost exhausted. In his discouragement he considered abandonment of the colony, but he would not yet admit defeat. Father Serra, although greatly concerned about the critical state of affairs, had no intention of giving up the enterprise, and, when the hour seemed darkest, his faith and determination were rewarded by the arrival of the *San Antonio*, and the settlement of Alta California was assured.

The search for the lost port of Monterey was renewed as soon as possible. Father Serra went north by sea, leaving Fathers Luís Jayme and Francisco Dumetz to carry on the work at San Diego. The land expedition under Portolá generally retraced its steps on the northerly route into what is now Orange County.

El Camino Real

El Camino Real, the King's Highway, stretched from San Diego north to San Francisco Bay in Hispanic days. In some places, as between San Diego and Los Angeles, the name was given to two or more parallel courses. Modern US 101 approximately follows this route, which linked the missions and their settlements. In 1906, the El Camino Road Association and the historians Mr. and Mrs. A. S. C. Forbes began the project of marking the old road with several hundred mission-bell guideposts, each surmounted by a bell weighing 100 pounds or more. Through the years these disappeared, but a program to replace the missing bells was begun in the

1960's and the traveler on modern El Camino Real will often find these familiar markers. On November 24, 1963, the 250th anniversary of the birth of Father Serra, bronze plaques were dedicated at the southern and northern ends of El Camino Real (SRL 784) as he knew it and helped to blaze it. One was placed at Mission San Diego and the other at Mission Dolores in San Francisco.

The Second Mission Site

The first site of the mission at San Diego proved to be unsatisfactory because of its proximity to the presidio, and the fathers soon realized that it would be better for the Indian neophytes to be removed some distance from the influence of the soldiers. Furthermore, a location affording more water for agricultural purposes was desirable.

Mission buildings of wood were constructed in 1774 five miles up the valley from the presidio, and considerable progress had been made in the conversion of the Indians by October 1775. At that time, the number of neophytes totaled 76, and 60 additional converts were baptized by the fathers on the day before the feast of St. Francis, October 4.

The resentment of the unconverted Indians, however, finally culminated in a fierce attack upon the unprotected mission on the night of November 4, 1775. Father Jayme, who, "with the shining light of martyrdom in his eyes, and the fierce joy of fearlessness in his heart," sought to quiet the attackers by walking toward them, his hand extended in blessing and with his usual salutation, "Love God, my children!" was ruthlessly slain. Padre Luís Jayme, the first Christian martyr in California, is buried in the mission sanctuary. The other inhabitants of the mission escaped to the garrison on Presidio Hill. The mission buildings were burned to the ground.

The next year, Father Serra returned to the gutted site and began plans for the rebuilding of the mission. Adobe-covered walls and tile roofs made the buildings more resistant to fire. By 1780 most of the reconstruction of the mission and its outbuildings had been completed. The church and other buildings were arranged in a quadrangle around a patio. In 1803, an earthquake damaged the church; the unique buttress-like structure in the front that was added in 1931 has helped the building withstand subsequent shocks.

By 1797, San Diego was the most populous as well as one of the wealthiest of the California missions. Over 1,400 converts had been brought into the Church. The mission owned 20,000 sheep, 10,000 cattle, and

1,250 horses. Within a few years, extensive fields and vineyards were being irrigated by water brought over an aqueduct through Mission Valley. The old mission dam (SRL 52) built across the San Diego River gorge in 1807–16 and constructed of granite and cement twelve feet thick still stands, a remarkable testimony to the quality of California's first irrigation and engineering venture. The dam, recognized by the Department of the Interior as a National Historic Landmark, is in Mission Trails Regional Park on Father Junipero Serra Trail, about five miles north of I-8 off Mission Gorge Road.

At the time of secularization, the mission was given over to Santiago Argüello. The U.S. Cavalry occupied the building from 1846 until 1862, when President Lincoln restored the mission lands to the Church. Decay set in, and by 1931 nothing remained of the buildings except the facade. In that year, restoration was begun by the Native Sons of the Golden West under the scholarly supervision of J. Marshall Miller. The restoration is believed to be exact in every detail. In 1976, Pope Paul VI named the church a minor basilica. It stands at 10818 San Diego Mission Road (SRL 242).

The First Presidio in Alta California

In the shadow of the first cross in Alta California, raised on Presidio Hill on July 16, 1769, both the first mission and the first presidio were established. On the same spot, on July 16, 1915, 146 years later, a group of San Diegans placed the Serra Cross, which stands on Presidio Hill today. From the heap of clay upon which it was raised, old tile from early buildings had been dug up and incorporated into the memorial cross. On it is a bronze tablet bearing this legend:

> Here the First Citizen, Fray Junípero Serra,
> Planted Civilization in California.
> Here he First Raised the Cross,
> Here Began the First Mission,
> Here Founded the First Town
>   —San Diego, July 16, 1769.

Presidio Hill, being situated a little back from the river and the bay, afforded an excellent outlook over the surrounding country and made fortification easy as well. It was near the site of the old Indian village of Cosoy, rancheria of the Diegueños, and here, for over 60 years, San Diego was located within the adobe walls of the Spanish garrison.

The presidio, an essential feature of Spanish colonization, was usually a fortified square, constructed at first of wood and later of brick or stone. Inside the square the commander's residence and the chapel formed the central points around which the garrison

for the soldiers, the officers' quarters, and adobe houses for provisions and military supplies were located.

With the rest of California, San Diego peaceably passed from Spanish to Mexican rule in 1822. A more turbulent period followed, when frequent revolts occurred both between the Californians and the Mexican governors and between the rival factions of the Californians themselves. José María Echeandía, the first governor sent from Mexico, established his headquarters at the Presidio of San Diego, which remained the capital of Alta California during his administration, 1825–31.

It was during this time that the second overland party of Americans to enter California came by way of San Diego County under the leadership of Sylvester Pattie and his son, James Ohio Pattie. The journal of this perilous westward trek of American trappers, written by the younger Pattie, constitutes one of the most stirring narratives of frontier history. This expedition, moreover, opened up a new overland route to the coast and added much to the knowledge of the Southwest.

Coming down the Gila and Colorado rivers as far as the tidewaters of the Gulf of California, the party crossed the desert to the Spanish settlements on the northern coast of Baja California. At Mission Santa Catalina, they were arrested and conducted to San Diego in Alta California under heavy guard, arriving there on March 27, 1828.

Governor Echeandía was fearful and suspicious because of the recent expedition of Jedediah Strong Smith, who on January 1, 1827, had come to San Diego to apply for a passport and was peremptorily refused. Consequently, the governor treated the newcomers cruelly, imprisoning them for several months. Under this harsh treatment, the elder Pattie, already weakened by long privation, died.

Gradually, the younger Pattie was able to soften the governor's attitude by serving as interpreter and by using his knowledge of vaccination to save the population in a smallpox epidemic. Finally, in 1830, he was given passage to Mexico City, whence he made his way back to his native Kentucky.

After Echeandía's administration the presidio was gradually abandoned. Retired soldiers were often given grants of land and went to live on their ranchos or built homes in the town at the foot of the hill. Within a decade the old garrison was deserted and dismantled. On December 25, 1838, earthworks were thrown up on Presidio Hill preparatory to an expected attack from José Castro, leader of a rebel faction from the northern part of the territory, then supposedly threatening the San Diegans. Two cannon from Fort Guijarros were mounted, but the anticipated attack did not materialize.

The earthworks on Presidio Hill were never used by

the Mexicans. On the coming of the Americans in 1846, they were improved by Commodore Robert F. Stockton, and United States troops, including Company B of the famous Mormon Battalion, were stationed there during the brief period of military rule before California's entrance into the Union. The old American fort, of which scarcely a vestige remains, was called Fort Stockton (SRL 54) during that period. The Native Sons of the Golden West have placed a flagstaff and bronze tablet on the site in Presidio Park, off Taylor Street.

The presidio has been almost completely obliterated by storms, earthquakes, and settlers, who used the materials for their homes. The walls of the presidio chapel, the old Spanish garrison, and the first civilian houses long ago crumbled into shapeless mounds of earth, but in 1929 plans were completed for preserving the hill and marking some of its landmarks. Through the consistent and indefatigable efforts of George W. Marston, extending over a period of years, the land was gradually purchased and ultimately presented to the city. Thus, "the cradle of the state's civilization" was finally rescued from oblivion and made a public park.

Here, on July 16, 1929, the 160th anniversary of the founding of San Diego, the Junipero Serra Museum was dedicated. The museum, the Serra Cross, the site of the first mission building, the site of the old Spanish garrison, and the site of Fort Stockton are included within Presidio Park. Beside Taylor Street at the foot of the hill, also within the park, is the marker (SRL 59) noting the site of the presidio, which has been registered as a National Historic Landmark by the Department of the Interior. Nearby another marker (SRL 67) notes the site of the first date palms planted in California by, it is said, Father Serra himself. One stood here until 1957.

Old Town San Diego

The tiny town that began at the foot of Presidio Hill as an overflow from the garrison grew and prospered as the tide of immigration into California increased. Old Town became a state historic park in 1968, when work was begun to restore and stabilize many of the buildings of the area. The plaza (SRL 63) on Washington Square still flies the American flag as it did in July 1846, when the Stars and Stripes were first flown above it. None of the buildings in Old Town are in their original condition, but several have been restored and are open to the public.

The Estudillo adobe (SRL 53) on the plaza is probably the oldest of these. It was built about 1827 by Captain José María de Estudillo, commander of the presidio; when he died in 1830 it passed to his son José

Antonio Estudillo. He and his wife, Doña María Victoria Domínguez, lived here with their twelve children, one of whom continued to live here with her husband until 1887. The house was restored in 1910 with funds provided by the Spreckels family, and is today beautifully furnished, with a lovely patio and well-tended trees and shrubs. For years this was popularly known as "Ramona's Marriage Place," though it is not the spot mentioned in Helen Hunt Jackson's novel *Ramona* (1884).

The Casa de Bandini (SRL 72), at 2660 Calhoun Street, also dates from the late 1820's. It was built by Juan Bandini, who became the son-in-law of José María Estudillo. Although he had held various offices under Mexican rule, Bandini invited Commodore Stockton to make his headquarters at Casa Bandini in 1846. On December 9 of that year, after a harrowing three nights' journey of 35 miles made in bare feet over country luxuriantly covered with prickly pears and guarded by mounted Californians, Lieutenant Edward Beale, with his Indian servant and Kit Carson delivered the message from General Stephen W. Kearny to Commodore Stockton calling for sadly needed reinforcements after the battle of San Pasqual. As a result of the bravery of these men, Kearny and his soldiers, hungry and footsore, many of them wounded, arrived at Old Town on December 12. On the plaza opposite the Estudillo and Bandini houses is a granite boulder with a bronze marker placed by the Daughters of the American Revolution in 1920, marking the end of the Kearny trail.

The Bandini house acquired a second story in the 1860's, when Albert Seely purchased the place and made it into the Cosmopolitan Hotel. It has since served as a store, a pickle factory, and a motel annex, and in its present incarnation is a restaurant serving meals in the patio as well as indoors.

Casa de Pedrorena (SRL 70), at 2616 San Diego Avenue, was the home of Miguel de Pedrorena, Jr. His father was a native of Madrid and a man of high birth and excellent education who came to San Diego in 1838. Being courteous and polite in manner and of a gracious bearing, he won the heart and hand of María Antonia Estudillo. Don Miguel was a member of the constitutional convention at Monterey in 1849, but he died the next year, before he could build on the lot he had acquired next to his in-laws' home. Not until 1869 did his son, Miguel Junior, put up a building, now a bakery.

La Casa de Machado y Silvas (SRL 71), at 2741 San Diego Avenue, is now used for audio-visual programs and park volunteer activities. José Nicasio Silvas, who built this house between 1830 and 1843, lived here for many years with his wife, María Antonia Machado, and children. Their home stayed in the family for over a hundred years; it then became a boarding house, saloon, restaurant, art studio, souvenir shop, museum, and church. It was briefly pressed into service in 1846 as the headquarters of John C. Frémont.

La Casa de Machado y Stewart (SRL 73), at Congress and Mason streets, was built by José Manuel Machado in the 1830's. Jack Stewart, a native of Maine who had visited San Diego in 1835, returned to stay in 1838. He served in the American army and later became a pilot on one of the pilot boats in San Diego Bay. In 1845 he married Machado's youngest daughter, Rosa, and the couple moved into the house to live with the Machados. Stewart had been a shipmate of Richard Henry Dana, Jr., who describes a visit to the house in 1859 in his book *Two Years Before the Mast*. Descendants of the Stewarts lived in the house until 1966; it was acquired by the state in the following year.

Two adobes no longer standing are commemorated as registered state landmarks. The Casa de Cota (SRL 75) stood at Twiggs and Congress streets until it was destroyed during World War II. The Casa de López (SRL 60), at 3890 Twiggs Street, despite its name, was actually built in 1851 by Miguel Alvarez.

Albert Seeley launched the San Diego–Los Angeles Stage Line; his Concord stages could make the 130-mile trip in less than 24 hours if all went well. Soon he had acquired the Bandini house for his Cosmopolitan Hotel. By 1875 he was running daily stages, but gradually competition from the railroad, which reached San Diego in 1887, put the line out of business. The reconstructed Seeley stable and barns at 2648 Calhoun Street now house a collection of Western memorabilia and horse-drawn vehicles as well as Indian artifacts.

The Chapel of the Immaculate Conception (SRL 49), on Conde Street southwest of San Diego Avenue, is a replica of the adobe chapel that was originally built in the 1850's as the home of John Brown. José Antonio Aguirre bought it and presented it to the Catholic congregation, after restoring and altering it to fit the needs of a church. It was dedicated in 1858. The restoration dates from 1937.

The chapel was the special charge of Father Antonio D. Ubach, a native of Catalonia, who was educated at Cape Girardeau, Missouri. He traveled thousands of miles as a missionary among the Indians, and came to San Diego in 1866, where he was placed in charge of the Catholic parish. He brought the first organ to San Diego, and also a football, which he tossed with the boys on the plaza. He had charge of many valuable relics and records of early Spanish days, but the greater part of his work was among the Indians, by whom he was greatly beloved, and with whom he had much influence. It is said that he was the original of the "Father Gaspara" of Helen Hunt Jackson's *Ramona*, and he claimed to have known originals of the characters in the story and their families.

Other Old Town Buildings and Sites

In 1850 a public school was started in San Diego, and in 1865 a structure was built to house it. It still stands (SRL 538) at 3960 Mason Street. The *San Diego Union* Building at 2602 San Diego Avenue was prefabricated in Maine and shipped around the Horn in 1851. The wood-frame structure was the residence of José Antonio Altamirano and later the first home of the *San Diego Union*. It has been restored as nearly as possible to its appearance in 1868, when the first edition of the newspaper came off the press.

The Whaley house (SRL 65), at 2482 San Diego Avenue, in which the San Diego County court met for about twenty years, was the first brick building to be erected in San Diego County. The white cedar woodwork and all of the hardware used in its construction were brought around the Horn, but the bricks were made at Thomas Whaley's own kiln in Old Town in 1856, and the walls were finished with plaster made from ground seashells.

The Derby-Pendleton house at 4017 Harney Street was put up in 1852 by Juan Bandini for his daughter Dolores, the wife of Captain Charles Johnson. Captain George Allan Pendleton, a member of the state constitutional convention of 1849, purchased the place in the 1860's and lived there with his wife, Concepción B. Estudillo. At that time the house was used as the office of the county recorder and the county clerk, both offices being held by Captain Pendleton himself until his death in 1871.

Lieutenant George Horatio Derby of the U.S. Corps of Topographical Engineers lived in the house during the years 1853–55 while engineering the first turning of the San Diego River into False Bay, now Mission Bay. Derby Dike (SRL 244), which can no longer be seen because of the development of the San Diego River Flood Control Channel, was a levee or earth embankment built west from Old Town 1,190 yards across the flats to the opposite high land. Deflection of the river was deemed necessary to avoid silting of the harbor in San Diego Bay. Derby had a secondary profession as a humorous writer, and his columns for the *San Diego Herald*, written under the byline "John Phoenix" and collected by his friend J. Judson Ames under the title *Phoenixiana*, are classics of contemporary California writing.

El Desembarcadero, or the Old Landing (SRL 64), at the mouth of the San Diego River, was the usual landing place for small boats carrying passengers or goods to Old Town. The site, now filled in, is off the ends of Udall and Voltaire streets, just below Rosecrans Street. Congress Hall (SRL 66), the site of which is at 4016 Wallace Street, was a two-story public house that lasted from 1867 to 1939. It was built on the site of the last Pony Express stop, when an adobe structure occupied the location. The old Catholic cemetery, El Campo Santo ("the holy field"), was used from 1850 to 1880 and is the resting place for some distinguished citizens of Old San Diego, including Miguel de Pedrorena, José Antonio Estudillo, and Santiago Argüello. The cemetery (SRL 68) is on the east side of San Diego Avenue at Arista Street. A marker at 2731 San Diego Avenue commemorates the Exchange Hotel (SRL 491), where the San Diego Lodge of the Masons was organized in 1851. In 1855 it became the first three-story building in the city, with two frame stories surmounting the adobe first floor, and was renamed the Franklin House. The hotel was destroyed by fire in 1872.

Historic Point Loma

The ancient Playa trail of the Indians, later used by oxcarts and carretas, horseback riders and pedestrians from the mission, followed the western shore of the bay. It may be roughly identified today as Rosecrans Street, which leads to the United States Government Military Reservation of Fort Rosecrans. A number of the landmarks on Point Loma are located in restricted military areas.

La Punta de Guijarros ("The Point of Cobblestones"), probable landing place of Cabrillo in 1542, was named by Vizcaíno in 1602 and was so designated until early in the nineteenth century, when English-speaking men began to arrive at Old San Diego and La Playa. Captain George Vancouver, who anchored there in 1793, referred to it as "Punta de Guiranos." But it is the memory of long-vanished Boston ships steadied on their stormy homeward voyages around Cape Horn by cargoes of cobblestones within their holds that is preserved for all time by the Yankee translation of the old Spanish name, Ballast Point (SRL 56). The point is within the military area, reached by the lower road that starts where Rosecrans Street ends. The present lighthouse on Ballast Point operated from 1890 until World War II, but no longer displays a beacon.

It was on this small jutting headland that the Spanish castillo, Fort Guijarros (SRL 69), designed by Alberto de Córdoba, was begun about 1797, under the direction of Comandante Manuel Rodríguez. It was completed by the beginning of the nineteenth century and manned by Catalonian soldiers from the San Diego Presidio. Here was fought the so-called "Battle of San Diego" on March 22, 1803, when the American brig *Lelia Byrd*, commanded by Captain William Shaler, was fired on by the Spaniards under command of José Velásquez. The Yankees were attempting to carry on a barter in furs contrary to the Spanish law forbidding foreign trade. "El Júpiter," a cannon cast in Manila in 1783 and used at Fort Guijarros in this early Spanish-American naval engagement, is now mounted on the site of old Fort Stockton on Presidio Hill. Fort Guijarros, built of adobe bricks made by the Indians, stood at the foot of the short hill that runs down to the sea from the later Fort Rosecrans barracks. It was abandoned in 1838.

The first United States government beacon to be placed on this section of the California coast stood on a ridge about half a mile north of the tip of Point Loma. The lighthouse was built in 1854–55 and used for the first time at sunset on November 15, 1855. A few floor tiles from the ruins of Fort Guijarros were incorporated into the building. Because of the heavy fogs that obscured the beacon light at this point, the station was abandoned in 1891 for a lower and more suitable site located at the extreme southwestern tip of Point Loma; this facility is still in operation. The old Point Loma lighthouse (SRL 51) is now the central feature of Cabrillo National Monument.

In the years 1824–46, before the American conquest, the most flourishing hide-droghing (transporting hides in coastal craft) business on the Pacific Coast was probably at La Playa, the eastern side of Point Loma. Here a cosmopolitan town of about 800 men grew up about the ten or twelve great barnlike hide houses established there by the captains of Boston trading ships and named for the vessels they commanded. The most famous of these, the *Brookline*, under Captain James O. Locke, was the first to be erected and the last to disappear. Here the American flag was first raised over California, unofficially, in 1829. The *Brookline* was located near the seawall before the south buildings of the Quarantine Station (SRL 61), the place where ships inbound from foreign ports were examined for contagion. Vessels from almost every maritime nation in the world found anchorage in the little harbor. The crude but colorful life of the day is vividly described by Richard Henry Dana, Jr., in *Two Years Before the Mast*, and by Alfred Robinson in *Life in California*. Old "Hide Park," as the Yankees called it, occupied the sandy tableland that extends from modern La Playa through the Quarantine Station and beyond, and that reaches back to the barren ridge on the west. The site is now within the Naval Electronics Laboratory area off Rosecrans Street.

The site of the old Mexican custom house maintained on Point Loma during this period was probably identified by ruins at the former address, 1036 Bay

Street, in the Roseville district, just north of modern La Playa. Don Juan Bandini was the first custom house keeper.

About halfway out on the inner beach of Ballast Point, headquarters for two New England whaling companies (SRL 50), the Packard Brothers and the Johnson Brothers, were established during the middle of the nineteenth century. The remains of the try-pot fires, the sand still impregnated with oil and soot, could long be seen in this locality, which is also within the Naval Electronics Laboratory.

Military reservation of the outermost three miles of Point Loma was ordered by the United States government in 1852. Possession of the property was not taken, however, until 1870. The post established in 1898 was named Fort Rosecrans (SRL 62) for General William S. Rosecrans, who died the same year; he had come to San Diego with Alonzo E. Horton in 1867. The last remnants of the old Fort Rosecrans are reached by driving to the south end of Rosecrans Street. The Fort Rosecrans National Cemetery (SRL 55), on the crest of Point Loma along the highway to Cabrillo National Monument, was originally designated Cemetery of San Diego Barracks in the late 1870's, although there had been earlier burials in the general area. Here, marked by a granite boulder from the battlefield of San Pasqual, are the graves of those who fell there on December 6, 1846. A granite obelisk memorializes the 60 sailors and marines who lost their lives on July 21, 1905, in a boiler explosion aboard the gunboat USS *Bennington* at anchor in San Diego Bay, and most of whom are buried here.

Landmarks of New San Diego

Long before the establishment of New San Diego, La Punta de los Muertos, or Dead Man's Point (SRL 57), appeared on maps of the area. In 1782, several men from the two ships engaged in the exploration of the coast, *La Princesa* and *La Favorita*, died of scurvy and were buried at this spot. The point is at the corner of Pacific Highway and Market Street and is now surrounded by filled-in lands.

San Diego Barracks (SRL 523), of which no buildings remain, was located on the block bounded by Kettner Boulevard and Market, G, and California streets. It was established in 1851 by Captain Nathaniel Lyon as a supply depot for frontier troops and was first called Post New San Diego. It became subject to Fort Rosecrans around the turn of the century and was abandoned in 1921. A marker is located on Market Street.

The incoming Yankees after 1846 soon saw that the old San Diego was unsuitable for a seaport town, and

New San Diego, located on San Diego Bay, at length superseded it. William Heath Davis built the first wharf there in 1850, but his venture was a financial failure, and nothing more was attempted until 1867, when Alonzo E. Horton arrived and soon afterward laid out the nucleus of the present city. Further growth was made possible by the railroads of the 1880's. A plaque placed by the Daughters of the American Revolution on the Santa Fe Station at Broadway and Kentner Street in 1985 commemorates the linking of San Diego "to the rest of the United States."

The San Diego Maritime Museum at 1306 North Harbor Drive is a floating exhibit of three distinctive vessels. Largest and oldest, its masts silhouetted against the sky, is the sailing ship *Star of India*. Built in England in 1863 and first named the *Euterpe*, it carried passengers and light cargo from Britain to the Antipodes for a number of years, later working the North American coastal trade. It has been berthed at San Diego since 1961. The *Berkeley* was a passenger ferry on San Francisco Bay from 1898 to 1958. The *Medea* was a luxurious steam yacht built in Scotland in 1904 to accommodate Captain MacAllister Hall's grouse and deer-hunting parties.

The Gaslamp Quarter is a section of downtown San Diego built in the late nineteenth century and centered on Fifth Avenue and Broadway. The Horton Plaza honors the name of Alonzo Horton, a civic-minded entrepreneur who did much to develop the area. The blocks are small and without intervening alleys because Horton believed that corner real estate did best and that alleys served primarily to collect trash. John D. Spreckels's office building from the turn of the century occupies a whole block of Broadway between Sixth and Seventh avenues.

Star of India, San Diego Maritime Museum

San Diego State University (SRL 798) on College Avenue was begun in 1897 as a two-year normal school. Four years later it became San Diego State Teachers College, and in 1935 it was fully recognized as a four-year liberal arts college. In 1960 the California State Colleges were authorized to grant doctoral degrees jointly with the University of California, and honorary doctorates independently. On June 7, 1963, San Diego State College conferred upon President John F. Kennedy the first doctorate to be granted by the California State College system. In 1970 the institution, along with several others in the system, became a university.

The Villa Montezuma, at 1925 K Street, is operated as a museum by the San Diego Historical Society. Built by the musician and author Jesse Shepard in 1887, it is an eclectic medley of Victorian architecture, art-glass windows, and ornate woodwork, surmounted by cupolas and domes that add to its fantastic appearance.

Balboa Park, home of the Panama-California International Exposition in 1915–16 and the California-Pacific International Exposition in 1935–36, was set aside as a park in 1868. The first improvements were made in 1889, and three years later the city rented 36 acres in the northwest corner to Kate O. Sessions for a nursery. She paid the rent by landscaping the western portion of the park, and credit is due to her for much of the beauty of San Diego. A beautiful park in Pacific Beach, north of Mission Bay, has been dedicated to the memory of Kate Sessions. Nearby, at Pico Street and Garnet Avenue, a plaque marks the site (SRL 764) of another of her nurseries.

The 1,400-acre Balboa Park is a treasury not only of horticulture but of human activities. The Museum of Man focuses on the history of Native American cultures. The Museum of San Diego History and the House of Pacific Relations have significant displays on the history of the region, while the San Diego Aerospace Museum highlights milestones in aviation history. The Botanical Building and the striking 200-foot-tall California Tower from 1915 are built in the attractive Spanish Colonial style that had so much influence on local architecture. The famous San Diego Zoo was founded in 1916 and has been a much-admired attraction ever since.

La Jolla

Now a northern coastal district of the huge city of San Diego, La Jolla began in the late nineteenth century as a rustic, salubrious town. Its name came from the indentation where La Jolla Bay cuts into the coastline ("La Jolla" is Spanish for "the hollow"; the name is also thought to come from "La Joya" or "jewel"). The La Jolla Caves at the shoreline have been continuously enlarged for over 200,000 years.

Ellen Browning Scripps, who lived here from 1897 to 1932, was, with her brother E. W. Scripps, a major benefactor of the area. The park named in her honor lies to the west of the caves. (Scripps College in Claremont, Los Angeles County, part of the Claremont Colleges, is another of her bequests.) The La Jolla Museum of Contemporary Art on Prospect Street is in the extensively remodeled house where Miss Scripps lived in her last years. The Scripps Institute of Oceanography, north along the coast, was founded in 1903 and in 1912 became a part of the University of California.

Further north, the Salk Institute for Biological Studies was founded in 1961 by Dr. Jonas Salk with support from the March of Dimes National Foundation. It overlooks the ocean at 11010 North Torrey Pines Road. The uplands just east of the Salk Institute were a U.S. Marines training base, Camp Calvin B. Matthews, from 1917 to 1964. The expanding University of California took over the site in 1964, and today it is the San Diego campus of the university. The architecture of the campus has a confidently late-twentieth-century assertiveness which might be seen as descriptive of its age as are the Spanish colonial buildings of Old Town San Diego.

The Torrey Pines

From La Jolla northward for several miles along the precipitous cliffs overlooking the Pacific Ocean, the Torrey Pines grow in a few sheltered spots. These twisted, wind-blown trees are a very rare species, remainders of an ancient forest that was disrupted when glacial and geological movements separated what are now the Channel Islands from the California coast. The Torrey pines were recognized as a distinct species by Dr. Joseph L. LeConte in 1850. Dr. C. C. Parry, then engaged with the Mexican Boundary Survey, was told of the find, and the two men named the trees after their former instructor, Dr. John Torrey of Columbia University, who had reported on the plant collections of Frémont's first two expeditions and had visited California in 1865 and 1872. Torrey Pines State Park, south of Del Mar, encloses most of the trees on the mainland. The only other place where these trees are found is on Santa Rosa Island, one of the Channel Islands.

Mission San Luís Rey de Francia

Four miles inland from Oceanside on SR 76, Mission San Luís Rey de Francia (SRL 239) stands on a

Mission San Luís Rey de Francia, near Oceanside

slight rise overlooking a valley that is today populated and suburban. Local tradition holds that the Indian name for the area was Jacayme, or "pleasant view." It was named for King Louis IX of France, who was sanctified in 1279 for his crusades against the Saracens. On June 13, 1798, Father Fermín Francisco de Lasuén led the solemn ceremonies that celebrated the founding of the mission, on an eminence with great vistas in all directions. The location had already been noted by Father Juan Crespí in 1769 as a likely spot for a mission.

The first substantial church building, which was completed in 1802, was planned by Father Antonio Peyrí and erected under his direction. In 1811 the foundations for the present structure were laid, and on the feast of St. Francis, October 4, 1815, the completed church was dedicated. It was constructed of adobe and faced with burnt brick.

Under the efficient management of Father Peyrí, lasting over a period of 30 years, San Luís Rey prospered. The buildings covered an area of approximately six and one-half acres, and the church building was about 164 feet by 27 feet, with adobe walls 6.5 feet thick and 30 feet high. The "King of the Missions" was not only the largest of the missions but registered more baptisms, marriages, and funerals than any of the others. Its ranches were enormously productive of both cereal crops and livestock.

After secularization, the Indians at San Luís Rey were scattered and the property suffered many years of abuse and neglect—it is said that bullfights were held in the garden courts. On March 15, 1865, President Abraham Lincoln signed the document (a copy of which is on display in the mission museum) returning the mission to Church ownership. It was rededicated as a Franciscan seminary in 1893, and is one of the four missions still in the hands of the founding order. Perhaps

because it is still a vital, active establishment, it remains one of the most attractive historic spots in California.

Asistencia de San Antonio de Pala

Among Father Peyrí's many vigorous activities was the founding in 1816 of the Asistencia de San Antonio de Pala (SRL 243) as a branch of Mission San Luís Rey, located in the Valley of Pala about twenty miles from the mission. A thousand Indian neophytes were soon enrolled from the rancherias of the district.

Pala Chapel is especially noted for its picturesque campanile and for its original Indian frescoes, for many years hidden by a coat of whitewash. The campanile stands apart from the main chapel building, in the old cemetery. It has been restored and is now joined to the main building by a little arched gateway. In its two graceful arches still hang the old bells that for generations have called the Indians to prayer.

Pala Chapel stands on the Pala Indian Reservation, where the Cupeño Indians were moved from Warner Springs in 1903. A resident priest has been there ever since; the Verona Fathers have been in charge of the mission's activities since 1948. This is the only one of the missions of California still serving what is primarily an Indian community. The chapel is about fifteen miles north of Escondido, six miles east of I-15. The highway up the mountain, SR 76, follows somewhat the same route that the old Emigrant Trail took to Warner's Ranch.

Santa Ysabel

The Chapel of Santa Ysabel (SRL 369) was established by Father Fernando Martín in 1818 as an asistencia or outpost of the mission at San Diego. A permanent structure was built there at a later time, but it has since disappeared. The present chapel was built in 1924, just south of the site of the old structure. The historic bells vanished in 1926. Nearby is the picturesque old Indian cemetery. The Chapel of Santa Ysabel is on SR 79 one and one-half miles north of the town of the same name.

The Old Emigrant Trail

Pedro Fages, heading east from San Diego in search of army deserters, made the first entry by a European into Oriflamme Canyon on October 29, 1772. The party eventually reached Mission San Luís Obispo by traveling through Cajon Pass, the Mojave Desert, and the San Joaquin Valley. The Fages Trail (SRL 858) is commemorated by a plaque on county highway S1 about two miles southeast of its intersection with SR 79.

Juan Bautista de Anza, who opened the route across the Colorado Desert into California in 1774, entered the mountains from the desert via San Felipe Creek. On March 12–13, 1774, he camped at San Gregorio (SRL 673) at the entrance to Borrego Valley, where welcome forage refreshed the half-starved animals. A jeep trail to the site proceeds east from the junction of Yaqui Pass Road and Rango Way, six-tenths of a mile north of the intersection of Yaqui Pass and Borrego Springs roads.

Passing through the valley on March 14, Anza's party halted at Santa Catarina (SRL 785) in Coyote Canyon at Reed's Springs, or Lower Willows, just above Beatty's Ranch. The following day the wayfarers entered Riverside County.

Anza's colonizing expedition of 1775–76 camped near San Felipe Creek on December 18, 1775. The next day they marched through the little pass called Los Puercitos (SRL 635), a short distance west of the campsite. A historical marker stands at Los Puercitos on SR 78, 1.7 miles east of Ocotillo Wells. That night they camped at San Gregorio. From December 20 to 22 the party stopped at El Vado ("the ford") at the mouth of Coyote Canyon, and on the 23rd at Santa Catarina. These sites are within Anza-Borrego Desert State Park. El Vado (SRL 634) is about seven miles north of the town of Borrego Springs via Di Giorgio Road and its dirt continuation. Santa Catarina is several miles farther northwest by a jeep trail.

Anza's route was superseded by another trail opened by Pedro Fages on an expedition against the Yuma Indians in 1782. Instead of taking the old path back to San Gabriel, Fages blazed a new one by way of Carrizo Creek and Vallecito and over the Cuyamaca Mountains to San Diego. This route was rediscovered in 1825 by Santiago Argüello in pursuit of Indian horse thieves, and in January 1826 the Mexican government sent Romualdo Pacheco, Lieutenant of Engineers, to investigate it. As a result of his findings, an official mail route was adopted via Carrizo Creek, Vallecito, San Felipe Valley, and Warner's Pass, and from then on it was used occasionally by mail carriers and traders from Sonora. Probably the first Americans to come this way were David E. Jackson and his fur-trading party, who came overland from Santa Fe in 1831. This road, which came to be known as the Emigrant Trail, formed a part of the Southern Overland Trail and was a much traveled path during the 1840's and 1850's. From September 1858 to the beginning of the Civil War it was also the route of the famous Butterfield Stage.

This trail, after crossing the deserts a little south of the international boundary line, entered what is now San Diego County via Carrizo Creek and Warner's Ranch. Passing down the mountain by the old Canyon Road to Sonora, the route proceeded by way of what is now Oak Grove in San Diego County to Temecula and Elsinore in Riverside County, and thence northwest to Mission San Gabriel and Los Angeles.

Another branch of the southern Emigrant Trail passed from Warner's down Palomar Mountain by the old Indian trail behind Pala Chapel to Mission San Luís Rey. Still another route, followed by General Stephen W. Kearny in 1846, led from Warner's to San Diego via Santa Ysabel and San Pasqual.

Rancho Santa Margarita y Las Flores (Camp Pendleton)

For many miles around, Mission San Luís Rey possessed great ranchos on which thousands of head of cattle grazed in mission days. Among these vast domains was Rancho Santa Margarita y las Flores, to the north, long one of the princely estates of California and now, since 1942, Camp Joseph H. Pendleton of the United States Marine Corps. As a military reservation, 125,000 acres of land have been preserved almost intact in the heavily developed coastal area between Santa Barbara and San Diego.

Fragmentary ruins of the stout adobe walls of the outpost of San Pedro, or Las Flores (SRL 616), built by the mission fathers about 1823, and now protected by an overhead roof, may be seen on a knoll not far from I-5 and within sight of the ocean. For many years this building was the hospice where travelers between Missions San Luís Rey and San Juan Capistrano stopped to rest. Nearby, below the hill, is the Las Flores Rancho house erected by Marcos A. Forster, son of Don Juan Forster, who had purchased the large estate from Pío and Andrés Pico in 1864. It is today a Boy Scout headquarters and carefully preserved. These landmarks may be reached via the main gate to the Camp Pendleton grounds; visitors may apply there for admission.

Overlooking the valley of the Santa Margarita River stands the twenty-room adobe Santa Margarita rancho house, now the private residence of the commanding general of Camp Pendleton. There is a museum in the old bunkhouse, built in 1864. The chapel nearby is open to the public for regular services; it is the oldest building on the base, said to have been built by mission Indians in 1810.

Rancho Los Peñasquitos (Rancho Penasquitos)

The first land grant in present San Diego County was made to Francisco María Ruiz by Governor Luis Argüello in 1823. Rancho Los Peñasquitos ("small rocks") lies along the creek of the same name. Ownership was transferred to Francisco María Alvarado in 1837. The Alvarado adobe (possibly built by Ruiz as early as 1827) is mentioned in Major Emory's report of General Kearny's expedition in 1846. The soldiers reached the ranch house on the evening of December 11, after reinforcements from San Diego had enabled them to leave their forced camp on Mule Hill. Emory's report vividly describes the welcome abundance of food that the half-starved soldiers found at Los Peñasquitos. Much of this area is subdivided today; the ruins of the adobe may be seen from the freeway bridge where I-5 crosses Los Peñasquitos Canyon.

Rancho Guajome

Although erected after the Mexican period, one of the most typical of the adobe ranch houses still standing is that on Rancho Guajome ("the big frog"). Guajome was part of the original mission lands of San Luís Rey. In 1845 it was granted to two Indians, Andrés and José Manuel. A few years later they sold it to Abel Stearns, who gave it as a wedding gift to his sister-in-law, Ysidora Bandini, when she married the American Colonel Cave J. Couts in 1851. The house was built in 1852–53.

Added historic interest is attached to the Guajome adobe because it was one of several Spanish-Californian homes in which Helen Hunt Jackson was a guest while gathering material for her novel *Ramona*. The adobe remained in the family for a long time; on July 15, 1943, Cave J. Couts, Jr., son of Cave and Ysidora Couts, died in the same room and in the same bed in which he had been born in 1856. The adobe (SRL 940) and the surrounding land were acquired by San Diego County in 1973 and are today Guajome Regional Park. The park is located two miles southeast of SR 76 at 2210 North Santa Fe Avenue in Vista. On the same property is the Southwestern Antique Gas and Steam Engine Museum, an attractive display of farm machinery.

Other Ranchos and Their Adobes in San Diego County

Old adobes in San Diego County usually stand, remodeled, on private property, or else have fallen into ruin. Rancho Monserate, near the junction of I-15 and SR 76, is today largely a mobile home park. The bunkhouse is the only building still standing from Hispanic times; it has been remodeled and is now the recreational center for the park. In southern San Diego County, Rancho de la Nación gave its name to National City in the northwest corner of the grant. Rancho La Cañada de los Coches (SRL 425) is said to be the smallest Mexican land grant in California; its 28 acres were granted to Apolinaria Lorenzana by Governor Micheltorena in 1843. The marker is at the entrance to Los Coches Trailer Park on Olde Highway, just northeast of El Cajon and about a quarter of a mile from I-8. Rancho Cuyamaca, 35,501 acres in eastern San Diego County, was long the subject of litigation. In 1933, 25,000 acres became Cuyamaca Rancho State Park.

Warner's Ranch

When the Spaniards first visited Agua Caliente (the "hot springs"), they found an Indian rancheria there. All of the land surrounding the springs, about 49,000 acres in all, later came under the joint control of Missions San Diego and San Luís Rey, remaining in their possession until the secularization and confiscation of mission property in 1836. At that time the whole valley, known as the Valle de San José, was granted to Silvestre de la Portilla, but his grant seems to have lapsed later, for when Jonathan Trumbull (Juan José) Warner, a Connecticut Yankee, applied for the land in 1844, the missions still laid claim to it.

Warner, who had come to California with the David E. Jackson party in 1831, was one of the first Americans to become an extensive landholder in California. He dispensed liberal hospitality on his estate, and Warner's Ranch became an objective for all of those early wayfarers who entered California over the old Emigrant Trail, which crossed the Colorado Desert from Yuma. It was the camping place for various divisions of the Army of the West, notably Stephen W. Kearny's regiment and the Mormon Battalion, in 1846 and 1847. In 1853, explorers for a Pacific railroad passed and repassed it in search of a suitable route.

The old headquarters of Warner's Ranch (SRL 311) are located about four miles southwest of Warner Springs and just east of SR 79 on the road to Ranchita and Borrego Springs. The adobe ranch house and barn have been protected somewhat by corrugated-iron roofs, and the ranch has been designated a National Historic Landmark. The house served Warner both as a trading post and as a residence. Warner's Ranch became a stopping place for the Butterfield Overland Stages in 1858.

At Warner Springs (the old Agua Caliente) is an adobe thought to have been built in the 1830's by an Indian named Chungalunga. This is the dwelling in which Warner is supposed to have lived when he first took possession of his ranch in 1844. It is now restored as the Kupa House, a guest house of the resort. Also standing is the picturesque St. Francis Chapel, built about 1830.

The Kearny Trail

The trail that General Stephen W. Kearny and the Army of the West followed through Imperial and San Diego counties, on their way to the fatal Battle of San Pasqual, has been traced by Arthur Woodward, one-time curator of history of the Los Angeles Museum, who went over this section of the old Kearny trail, tracing its route and locating the campsites one by one. He describes the route as follows:

"On November 28, [1846,] they pressed on slowly and came to the large spring near which in later days the Carrizo stage station was erected. . . . From Carrizo, where they camped on the night of the 28th, they pushed on up the dry creek bed to Vallecito, where they camped on the night of the 29th and 30th. . . .

"Beyond Vallecito the road winds across the valley to the base of a small rocky ridge, 4.3 miles distant. On the other side of this low ridge lies Mason Valley. Up this valley marched the troops for a distance of 4.8 miles until they came to the entrance of Box Canyon, a narrow rocky defile through the hills. . . . Here the road emerges and swings west again and after passing over a low ridge of hills drops into San Felipe Valley. The troops marched for about twelve or thirteen miles along this route until they came to the Indian village of San Felipe, which was on the creek. They camped here on the night of December 1 and the next day pressed on up the valley, topped the divide and dropped down to Warner's Ranch. The present road to Vallecito from Warner's probably follows fairly accurately the old trail; indeed, in Box Canyon (the spot where the Mormon Battalion under Cooke had so much trouble, early in 1847) it cannot have changed very much.

"The army camped a trifle south of Warner's Ranch house. . . . The place upon which they camped is probably the rather level grassy flat a few hundred yards south of the house.

"Here they remained recuperating during the days of December 2 and 3. They started for Santa Isabel the morning of December 4th and, after marching for thirteen and a half miles, they camped near the old Mission station of Santa Isabel (probably in the flats southeast of the present site of the chapel on the edge of the creek).

"On the morning of the 5th, the army marched south-southwest to the rancheria of Santa Maria. They were delayed en route by a parley with Captain Gillespie and the naval reinforcements from San Diego, probably at Ballena, about six miles from Santa Isabel. Thence through the hills they travelled southwest, skirting the western edge of what is now the Valley of Santa Maria (in which the town of Ramona is situated)

and probably camping at the head of Clevenger's Canyon. . . . It is about eight or nine miles via the hill trail to the point where they probably emerged in the valley of San Pasqual at a point . . . [about half a mile from] the spot where the Santa Maria River empties into San Pasqual Valley."

The Battle of San Pasqual

The battle of San Pasqual was fought in San Pasqual Valley near an Indian village of that name, east of the present-day city of Escondido. It was the bloodiest of all the battles fought on California soil not involving Indians, and took place on December 6, 1846. Kearny's army, as described above, marched toward San Diego through the narrow San Pasqual Valley. Suddenly they were met by a force of Californians under the command of General Andrés Pico. In rain and fog, the mounted Californians carrying willow lances and sabers inflicted considerable damage on the Americans, eighteen of whom were killed in the first melee. By the time the Americans were able to bring their artillery into play, their gunpowder was damp and nearly useless. The Californians suffered a few wounds but no fatalities; the Americans lost 22 all told, and several more suffered serious wounds, including General Kearny and Captain Gillespie.

Kearny rallied his men on a low, boulder-studded hill, from where Kit Carson and Lieutenant Edward Beale slipped out into the darkness to seek reinforcements from San Diego. The army remained on the hill until December 11, and the men were forced to eat their mules to keep from starvation. Mule Hill (SRL 452) is above Lake Hodges and near Kit Carson Park in Escondido. San Pasqual Battlefield State Historic Park is on SR 78, adjacent to the San Diego Wild Animal Park, an operation of the San Diego Zoo. A monument erec-

San Pasqual Battlefield State Historic Park, near Escondido

ted by the state of California in 1925 commemorates the American dead. A well-appointed visitors' center opened in 1987.

The Butterfield Stage Route

On September 16, 1857, the Butterfield Overland Mail company (closely affiliated with Wells Fargo Express Company) was awarded the contract for the first transcontinental mail and passenger line to California, winning over eight other bidders.

A southern route through Yuma, Arizona, was selected because it was open all year round, and St. Louis was chosen as the central supply depot. Coaches or spring wagons were used, and they carried passengers as well as mail. Stations were erected along the entire route at twenty-mile intervals, horses being changed at every station, and drivers every 200 or 300 miles.

The first stage on the Butterfield line left St. Louis on September 15, 1858, and a second followed the next day. One of the chief remaining landmarks of the old route is at Vallecito ("Little Valley"). This section of the route goes northwest to Warner's Ranch and southeast through Carrizo Canyon, joining the highway from San Diego to Yuma, Arizona, a few miles west of El Centro. In 1847 the men of the Mormon Battalion, under command of Lieutenant Colonel Philip St. George Cooke, passed this way on their journey to San Diego. Their wagons were the first vehicles to use this route.

The Vallecito stage station (SRL 304) was built of blocks of sod rather than adobe bricks. For long it stood deserted, a prey to vandals and earthquakes, its walls rapidly crumbling before the elements. In 1934 it was rebuilt and is now Vallecito Stage Station County Park, within the borders of the Anza-Borrego Desert State Park, on the Overland Stage Route Highway (S2), about nineteen miles southwest of Scissors Crossing.

Vallecito was one of the six stations along the stretch of the Butterfield route through present San Diego County. The first was at Carrizo Creek, just west of the Imperial County line. The next was Palm Spring (SRL 639), about fourteen miles southeast of Vallecito by road and jeep trail. The third was Vallecito.

About ten miles northwest of Vallecito the Butterfield stages passed through Box Canyon (SRL 472), a narrow defile about a mile in length. Here, on January 19, 1847, Cooke's men of the Mormon Battalion had to use axes to hack a wagon road out of solid rock. A trail leads from the historical marker to the edge of Box Canyon. By climbing down into the canyon, one may see the cut made by the soldiers.

The Butterfield route (SRL 647) is still visible at the pass between Blair and Earthquake valleys. The hill six miles south of Scissors Crossing on the road to Vallecito is the divide between the valleys. On the south side, in Blair Valley, a dirt road branches from the main route and circles around to the pass, where a historical marker is located. In this area the Butterfield route passes through Anza-Borrego Desert State Park.

The fourth station was at San Felipe (SRL 793), where Kearny and his men had camped in 1846 on their march to San Diego and the battle of San Pasqual. The site is in San Felipe Valley about a mile northwest of Scissors Crossing. The fifth station was the Warner ranch house.

The last station before Aguagna in Riverside County still stands at Oak Grove on SR 79. It is a long, well-preserved adobe still in use as a store and bar—one of the few Butterfield stations still occupied (SRL 502). It is on the register of National Historic Landmarks. Across the road, from 1861 to 1866, was Camp Wright (SRL 482), established to guard communication between California and Arizona and to cut off traffic to the Confederate states. Troops from this post engaged in the only military action of the Civil War on California soil, the capture of a group of Southern sympathizers en route from El Monte to join the Confederate army. The Oak Grove stage station served as a hospital for Camp Wright.

Julian

Julian (SRL 412) is a town nestled among forests of oak and conifer. Today it is the center of an attractive agricultural community, where apples, pears, and honey supplant the gold of former days. The first discovery of gold in the region was made late in 1869; the first mine was named for George Washington. A small stampede followed, and several other mines with such names as the Cuyamaca, Golden Chariot, and Stonewall Jackson were put into operation. By the time the mines had played out in 1880, some $5 million in gold had been taken.

The Julian Hotel is one of the oldest operating hotels in southern California. It was begun in 1897 by a former slave and his wife, Albert and Margaret Robinson, and was originally named for them. After Mr. Robinson's death, his wife ran the hotel until 1921 when she sold it to Martin Jacobs, who changed the name to the Julian Hotel. It is now on the National Register of Historic Places. The Santa Ysabel School, built at Witch Creek ten miles west of Julian in 1888, was moved to its present site in the town in 1970 and is a museum of local artifacts.

Other Landmarks of San Diego County

An adobe and frame ranch house, built in 1882 by Robert Kelly, then owner of Rancho Agua Hedionda, was restored in the 1930's by the late actor Leo Carrillo, a descendant of prominent early Californians. The Carrillo ranch is located off Palomar Airport Road (S12) two miles east of El Camino Real, and is now owned by the city of Carlsbad, which plans to make it the center of a community park.

Nearby Mount Palomar is the location of the Palomar Observatory, where the largest telescope in the United States, the 200-inch Hale Telescope, was installed in 1950. There is an interesting museum on the grounds.

Olivenhain is the site of a small German colony that was started on Rancho Los Encinitas in 1884. Some old buildings still stand on Rancho Santa Fe Road in Rancho Santa Fe, including the meeting house from 1895.

At Spring Valley, ten miles east of San Diego, is the Bancroft ranch house (SRL 626). The adobe was built in 1863 by A. S. Ensworth and came into the hands of Hubert Howe Bancroft, the great California historian, in 1885. Because of the importance of this occupant, the house has been registered as a National Historic Landmark. It stands on Memory Lane off Bancroft Drive.

At Coronado, across the bay from San Diego, is the Hotel del Coronado (SRL 844), a relic of the Victorian era that is still a showplace and whose 399 rooms are still very much in use. It was designed by the famous architect Stanford White and was formally opened on February 14, 1888. It was the largest building outside

Gaskill Brothers' Store, Campo

New York City to have its own electrical power plant, which supplied the entire city of Coronado until 1922. The Naval Air Station, North Island, Coronado, is the site of the first military flying school in the United States (SRL 818), founded by Glenn Curtiss in 1911.

Eleven miles south of San Diego via National Avenue is Montgomery Memorial State Park (SRL 711), set aside in honor of John Joseph Montgomery, whose glider flight at Otay Mesa in 1883, twenty years before the Wright brothers, was the first successful flight of a heavier-than-air craft. A monument in the shape of a wing has been erected near the site of the historic event. Montgomery died in a glider crash near Evergreen in Santa Clara County in 1911.

In Anza-Borrego Desert State Park, besides the numerous landmarks of Anza and the Butterfield Stage, there is a most unusual monument (SRL 750) in honor of Thomas L. "Peg Leg" Smith, who is supposed to have discovered gold in the vicinity about 1850. Many have sought the "lost" mine in vain. Legend has it that anyone who adds a stone to the monument will have good luck, while the removal of a stone will bring the opposite result. The monument is located about seven miles northeast of Borrego Springs via Palm Canyon Drive and Peg Leg Road.

Campo is a small settlement along SR 94, a mile north of the Mexican border. Here, on December 5, 1875, a gunfight took place to rival the famous incident at the O.K. Corral in Tombstone, Arizona. The battle pitted Silas E. and Lumas H. Gaskill, the Campo storekeepers, against a gang of Mexican bandits from Tecate. Several of the outlaws were killed or mortally wounded. The Gaskill brothers were injured but recovered. Several years later they built a stone store (SRL 411), still standing across the wash from the site of the earlier store where the gunfight began.

In Border Field State Park, a granite shaft marks the

Meeting House, Olivenhain

southernmost point of California and the southwestern corner of the continental United States. The monument was set up in 1851, later taken down, and set back in place in 1894. Border Field State Park is reached from I-5 via Dairy Mart Road and Monument Road. The fence marking the international boundary is so arranged that the monument straddles the border; the fence continues toward the ocean, whence the early voyagers came to explore San Diego county and Alta California.

San Francisco County

San Francisco County derived its name from Mission San Francisco de Asís, established within the present boundary lines of the city in 1776. San Francisco was one of the original 27 counties. Until 1856 the county included what is now San Mateo County, and the city of San Francisco was the county seat. After that date, the government was consolidated, operating as the City and County of San Francisco. Most city records were destroyed in the fire that followed the earthquake of April 18, 1906, but fortunately, many pre-statehood records in Spanish were saved.

Discovery of the Golden Gate

The entrance to San Francisco Bay was discovered on November 1, 1769, by Sergeant José de Ortega, pathfinder of Gaspar de Portolá's expedition and the first white man to see San Francisco Bay.

The expedition was searching for the "lost" bay of Monterey and had proceeded up the coast as far as San Pedro Valley. From this point, Portolá had commissioned Ortega to explore as far north as Point Reyes, which Portolá had seen from the summit of the Montara Mountains just east of Point San Pedro. The channel of the Golden Gate, however, prevented Ortega and his party from reaching their objective. He accordingly proceeded along the south shore of the channel and climbed La Loma Alta (later called Telegraph Hill). From this vantage point, he could see the whole expanse of the bay, its islands, and the hills of the Contra Costa ("opposite coast") beyond.

Having made his observations, Ortega returned to camp to report. Portolá, however, did not realize the tremendous importance of the discovery; he was looking for the bay of Monterey.

Juan Manuel de Ayala, in the historic ship *San Carlos*, and José Cañizares, his subordinate, were the first white men known to have entered San Francisco Bay. In the spring of 1769 the *San Carlos* had carried supplies and colonists for the new pueblo to be founded at San Diego. Again, in 1775, with Ayala in command, it sailed with the fleet sent from Mexico to explore San Francisco Bay. On August 4 the entrance to the Bay was reached. Ayala, suffering from an accidental head injury, sent Cañizares ahead to find an anchorage. The latter did not return all that day, for the currents and tides of the strait were too strong for the little launch in which he made the reconnoitering expedition. Therefore, on the evening of August 5, Ayala, in the *San Carlos*, passed through the strait and into the Bay. Cañizares and Ayala thus are both honored for making the first recorded entrance into San Francisco Bay from the ocean.

For 44 days Ayala and his men remained in the Bay, exploring every arm and inlet and going as far as the mouth of the San Joaquin River, at the same time taking soundings and making a map. Two of the names given at this time are in use today, in slightly different forms. One is that of the island just inside the strait, which was called Isla de Nuestra Señora de los Angeles, "Island of Our Lady of the Angels," and is known today as Angel Island. In a sheltered cove of this island, the *San Carlos* remained during most of its stay in the Bay. Another island was named Isla de los Alcatraces, "Island of the Pelicans," and we have the name today as Alcatraz Island.

It was Ayala's exploration of San Francisco Bay that established the suitability of its shores for settlement, and the location at San Francisco of the mission and the presidio was largely influenced by this expedition. A plaque (SRL 236) commemorating the entrance of the *San Carlos* into San Francisco Bay was placed at Fort Point by the Daughters of the American Revolution in 1955.

The Spaniards had called the gateway to the newly discovered bay "La Boca del Puerto de San Francisco," but an American gave it the name of "Golden Gate." In his *Memoirs* General John C. Frémont says: "To this gate

I gave the name of Chrysopylae, or Golden Gate, for the same reason that the harbor of Byzantium [afterward Constantinople] was called Chrysoceras, or Golden Horn." In a footnote he adds: "The form of the entrance into the bay of San Francisco and its advantages for commerce, Asiatic included, suggested to me the name which I gave to this entrance and which I put upon the map that accompanied a geographical Memoir addressed to the Senate of the United States in June 1848."

The Founding of San Francisco

Juan Bautista de Anza, a major figure in early California history, was a member of the aristocracy of New Spain's frontier provinces. He early distinguished himself, not only as a valiant Indian fighter, but as an officer of unusual abilities and excellent character.

No sooner were the first settlements made in Alta California than practical men such as Father Junipero Serra pointed out the great need for a dependable land route from New Spain. Furthermore, there was the possibility of foreign intervention in Alta California—Russia was becoming active along the northern Pacific coast. Antonio María Bucareli, viceroy of New Spain, decided to send Anza in command of an expedition to find an overland route.

Anza made a successful overland journey to California in 1774, paving the way for further colonization of the province. An important concern here was the project of settling at San Francisco Bay and the region around what the Spaniards called the Río Grande de San Francisco, the delta of the Sacramento and the San Joaquin rivers. These colonies were to be a base for further settlements to the north, as well as buffers against outside enemies.

Accordingly, a second expedition was planned on which Anza was to take settlers and supplies with him to found a presidio and a mission at San Francisco. After fearful hardships encountered in desert and mountains, and needless delays caused by Governor Fernando Rivera, who was opposed to the settlement of San Francisco, this remarkable undertaking was accomplished. Anza himself reached San Francisco on March 27, 1776, but Rivera's lack of cooperation made it necessary for Anza to leave his settlers temporarily at Monterey.

The final lap of the journey had led along the hills, with a "good-sized lake of fresh water," now called Lake Merced, lying to the westward. From this point the company marched toward the Golden Gate, making camp at what the Spaniards called Laguna del Presidio and is now known as Mountain Lake. Arroyo del Puerto

was the name given to the nearby stream known today as Lobos Creek, near the southwestern corner of the presidio military reservation. Anza made a thorough survey of the region, marking out the sites for the presidio and mission. For the presidio fort he chose Cantil Blanco ("white cliff"), above today's Fort Point along the water's edge. The cliff was destroyed early in the American occupancy. He selected a place for the mission near a little rivulet that he named Nuestra Señora de los Dolores. The town was to lie on the plain between the presidio and the mission.

After exploring the Bay and the River of San Francisco up to the junction of the Sacramento and San Joaquin rivers, Anza returned to Monterey. He was greatly disappointed not to be able to settle his colonists in San Francisco, but since he could not do so without the aid of Rivera, he left Monterey "amid the tears and lamentations of the settlers, who had learned to revere and love him in the course of their long march from Sonora." The colonists were settled at San Francisco by José Joaquín Moraga, Anza's capable lieutenant, and by Father Francisco Palou in the summer of 1776. Anza never returned to California, but he is remembered as a major pioneer in its history.

The Presidio of San Francisco

Anza chose the site of the Presidio of San Francisco (SRL 79) on March 28, 1776. On June 27 Lieutenant Moraga and the settlers who had traveled from Sonora to Monterey with Anza made temporary camp at the Laguna de Manantial, about where Eighteenth and Dolores streets intersect today. The next day a shelter of branches was built to serve as a chapel, and on June 29 the first Mass was said. On July 26 most of the expedition moved to the presidio site, where shelters were erected and Mass was offered on July 28. On September 17 the presidio was dedicated, and Moraga took formal possession in the name of King Carlos III.

Neither the Spanish nor the later Mexican government supported the Presidio of San Francisco adequately, and consequently it was never well garrisoned. After 1835 regular troops were no longer stationed there, and by 1840 it was in ruins. Since the American occupation on July 9, 1846, however, it has been one of the principal United States Army establishments on the Pacific Coast.

The presidio reservation, the largest within an American city, consists of about 1,400 acres, originally bare sand hills. In the 1880's large plantings were made of eucalyptus, Monterey cypress, and pines.

The sites of the old Spanish presidio buildings have been marked. At the southwest corner of the original presidio, a bronze tablet has been set in the wall of the Officers' Club and a marker placed by the California Chapter, Daughters of the American Revolution. At the northwest corner, a bronze tablet has been set in a stone near the flagpole on Graham Street. At the northeast corner, a bronze tablet has been set in a stone in the parking lot adjacent to Building T-40 on Mesa Street. The southeast corner is marked by a chromium nail in the aisle of the present Catholic chapel on Moraga Avenue. The only building remaining from the Spanish period is the *comandancia*, now the Officers' Club, on Moraga Avenue. The adobe incorporated into the walls was fashioned in the late eighteenth century. The building has been considerably remodeled and expanded, and has been the Officers' Club since 1848.

Two Spanish cannon, cast in 1673, stand in front of the Officers' Club. The touchhole of one contains fragments of a file thrust there by John C. Frémont when he spiked the guns of the Castillo de San Joaquín during the Bear Flag revolt in 1846. Two other cannon from the Castillo are located elsewhere on the grounds: one, cast in 1628, is at the Presidio Army Museum and the other, cast in 1684, is at Fort Point National Historic Site. Two more Spanish cannon, one cast in 1679 and the other in 1693, flank the post flagpole, 400 feet northwest of the Officers' Club.

Many buildings from the early American period remain. One of the largest of these is the old post hospital, begun in 1857. In 1973, it became the Presidio Army Museum, offering many displays not only of military history but also of such San Francisco events as the earthquake and fire of 1906. The Army gave substantial aid to distressed citizens during that disaster, among other things putting up more than 5,000 one-room

Temporary Shelters Built by the Army after the 1906 Earthquake, Presidio

shacks for temporary shelter. Two of these shelters were saved from oblivion and in 1986 were refurbished and placed in the yard at the rear of the museum, which is located on Funston Avenue near Lincoln Boulevard.

In 1963 the Presidio of San Francisco, then an active post and the headquarters of the Sixth Army, was registered as a National Historic Landmark. The Golden Gate National Recreational Area was established in 1972, and some coastal areas, such as Crissy Field and Fort Point, have been added to its jurisdiction. In 1989 the closure of the post was announced; protestors took some comfort in the fact that the Presidio would become part of the GGNRA and would continue to be enjoyed by the people of San Francisco.

Castillo de San Joaquín and Fort Point

Castillo de San Joaquín (SRL 82) was a Spanish fort located on the Punta de Cantil Blanco at the edge of the Golden Gate, near the old presidio but separate from it. Completed and dedicated on December 8, 1794, Castillo de San Joaquín would never have withstood a siege, for "the structure rested mainly on sand; the brick-faced walls crumbled at the shock whenever a salute was fired; the guns were badly mounted, and, for the most part, worn out." The fort, built principally of adobe in the shape of a horseshoe, gradually became a ruin, and after 1835 no troops were stationed there.

On July 1, 1846, as an aftermath of the Bear Flag Revolt, John C. Frémont and twelve of his men crossed over from Sausalito in the launch *Moscow* and spiked the guns of the Castillo. In his *Memoirs* Frémont says that the guns he spiked were large handsome pieces, but he fails to add that they were dismounted and lying on the ground.

With statehood, new plans were made for the defense of San Francisco Bay. In 1853, digging was begun to level the white cliff where the Castillo stood, and by the following year that natural landmark was no more. At sea level, a new American fort was constructed, which was completed in 1861. The new fort stood about where the old Spanish fort had been and was customarily called Fort Point. In 1882 the Army gave it the name of Fort Winfield Scott, but the name did not catch on in common usage, and by the 1890's the name Fort Point was used again. In 1912 the adjacent area was given the name of Fort Winfield Scott; it continued as a separate, independent post until 1946.

Fort Point was constructed to prevent the entrance of a hostile fleet into San Francisco Bay, though none have attempted it. The three-story fort, with walls between five and twelve feet thick, was designed to mount 126 cannon and to house 600 soldiers. With the advent

Fort Point, Golden Gate National Recreation Area

The Padre Presidente, Junipero Serra, protested this omission, but Gálvez replied, "If Saint Francis wishes a mission, let him show you a good port, and then let it bear his name." Accordingly, when Portolá's party discovered the great bay, the Franciscan chroniclers in the party declared that this must be "the port to which the Visitador referred and to which the Saint has led us."

But it was not until seven years later, in 1776, that Mission San Francisco de Asís was founded. Juan Bautista de Anza had selected the site of the mission in the spring. This was on the bank of the little lake that Anza called Laguna de Manantial, now filled in. The stream that flowed into it he called Arroyo de Nuestra Señora de los Dolores, because it was on the Friday of Our Lady of Sorrows (Viernes de los Dolores) that he found it. The name of the mission itself in later years became popularized to "Mission Dolores."

Father Francisco Palou arrived at the lake on June 27, 1776, and two days later celebrated the first Mass in a temporary chapel. San Francisco celebrates its birthday each year on June 29, the anniversary of the first Mass at the mission site, and thus claims to be five days older than the Declaration of Independence.

The mission was not formally dedicated, however, until early October. The present mission church (SRL 327) was begun, a few hundred yards from the original site, on April 25, 1782, when the first stone was put in place, and dedicated on April 3, 1791. The building has none of the arches, arcades, and towers that adorn most of the other missions, but its massive simplicity makes it none the less impressive.

The shadow of a redwood cross in the enclosed cemetery beside the church falls across old graves. Here lie the remains of Don Luís Antonio Argüello, governor of Alta California from November 1822 to November 1825; he died in 1830. Don Francisco de Haro, first alcalde of San Francisco, is also buried here. Among the other graves are those of James P. Casey and Charles Cora, both hanged by the Vigilantes. Within the church itself are buried Don José Joaquín Moraga, Anza's lieutenant and founder of the presidio, who died in 1795; the Noe family; and William Alexander Leidesdorff, the first black pioneer in San Francisco.

On the south wall of the mission is a plaque erected by the California Historical Society to honor Father Francisco Palou, founder of Mission Dolores and California's first historian. On November 24, 1963, the 250th anniversary of the birth of Father Junipero Serra, a tablet was placed at Mission Dolores to mark the northern terminus of El Camino Real (SRL 784) as Serra knew it and helped to blaze it. A similar plaque was placed at the southern terminus, Mission San Diego de Alcalá.

Today, Mission Dolores is overshadowed by a large

of powerful rifled cannon, brick forts such as this became obsolete, and in 1886 Fort Point was abandoned. The building had a second life in 1933–37 as a base of operations during the construction of the Golden Gate Bridge, which is designed so that the structure passes over the fort but does not touch it. (More than one suicide from the Golden Gate Bridge has landed on the roof at Fort Point.) During World War II, the fort was garrisoned by about 100 soldiers, who manned searchlights and rapid-fire cannon mounted on top of the fort as part of the protection for a submarine net stretched across the entrance to San Francisco Bay. In 1970, the fort was declared the Fort Point National Historic Site and was later incorporated into the Golden Gate National Recreational Area. Today it is a museum of Civil War–era weapons and presents one of the most beautiful coastal views in all California.

Mission San Francisco de Asís (Dolores)

The first plans of the Visitador General of Mexico, José de Gálvez, did not call for a mission dedicated to St. Francis of Assisi, founder of the Franciscan order.

"Mission Dolores," the Mission San Francisco de Asís

parish church built in 1913–18. This church, because of its associations with the old mission, was honored by the Vatican in 1952 with the title of minor basilica. It is in the quiet aisles and peaceful graveyard of the mission, however, that one will find memories of San Francisco's picturesque beginnings.

Yerba Buena Cove

The first Englishman to sail into San Francisco Bay was Captain George Vancouver, who came on the night of November 14, 1792, in the sloop of war *Discovery*, dropping anchor "about a league below the presidio in a place they called Yerba Buena." This is apparently the first reference we have to the little cove that would later mark the beginning of the modern city.

Vancouver was received hospitably by Father Antonio Danti, the priest at the mission, and by the *comandante* of the presidio, Hermenegildo Sal. He has left an interesting description of the country, the Bay, the presidio, and his trip to Mission Santa Clara.

When Vancouver returned the next year, he was not received so warmly, for Don Hermenegildo had been reprimanded for letting an Englishman see the defenseless condition of the settlement.

The Russians in San Francisco

Count Nikolai Rezanov came to San Francisco in 1806. The colonists in Russia's Alaskan settlements were starving and desperately needed a permanent source of food supply. With this in mind, Rezanov sailed south to negotiate with the Spanish officials of San Francisco, well knowing that trade with foreigners was forbidden, as was foreign entry into San Francisco Bay. He

was desperate, however, for his voyage was a race with death, and on April 5, 1806, his ship sailed past the presidio and entered the harbor.

José Darío Argüello, a very influential man and the best friend of Governor José Joaquín de Arrillaga, was *comandante* of San Francisco at this time. His daughter, Concepción, had been baptized at Mission Dolores on February 26, 1791. Concha, as she was affectionately called by her family, was reputed to be the most beautiful woman in Alta California. Count Rezanov was entertained in the Argüello household during his stay in San Francisco, and he and Concha fell in love.

Meanwhile, by gifts and a display of his Russian wares, he had won the favor of the authorities, and was able to make an exchange of his goods for food supplies. On May 21, six weeks after his arrival, Rezanov sailed back to the aid of his starving people in Alaska. From there, he returned to Russia, presumably to obtain royal and ecclesiastical permission for his marriage to Concepción. Somewhere in Siberia Rezanov died, but this was not revealed to his sweetheart for many years.

The aftermath of this romance rightfully belongs to Benicia in Solano County, the place where Concepción spent the closing years of her life and where she was buried. Its political significance concerns the Russian settlements at Bodega and Fort Ross in Sonoma County.

Yerba Buena, the Forerunner of San Francisco

Captain William A. Richardson was the founder of Yerba Buena ("good herb," Spanish for wild mint), which became the nucleus of the modern city of San Francisco. Richardson, an Englishman by birth, came to San Francisco in 1822, when the Mexican flag was flying over the presidio, and Governor Pablo Vicente de Solá, the last Spanish ruler, was just leaving California. From Solá, Richardson gained permission to settle permanently at San Francisco, in return for which he was to teach the young Spaniards the arts of navigation and carpentry, two skills that were much needed. In 1825, Richardson married María Antonia, daughter of Don Ignacio Martínez, *comandante* of the San Francisco Presidio.

Richardson was a master mariner, and besides teaching the trades of carpentry and shipbuilding and the art of navigation to the presidio people, he was also the first to develop trade and communication by water on San Francisco Bay. For three years he managed the shipping that went back and forth between San Francisco and the embarcadero at Mission San José. He piloted vessels in and out of the Bay, and later became Captain of the Port and Bay of San Francisco under the direction of Mariano Guadalupe Vallejo, commanding general in the north.

It was Richardson's plan to found a port town on San Francisco Bay at the best possible anchoring place, and he chose Yerba Buena Cove. José Figueroa, California's most enlightened Mexican governor, acted upon these plans and made Richardson the first harbormaster of San Francisco.

In 1835 Richardson moved to Yerba Buena with his family, living in a tent for three months. It is said that "this tent was the first habitation ever erected in Yerba Buena. At the time, Richardson's only neighbors were bears, coyotes, and wolves. The nearest people lived either at the Presidio or at Mission Dolores." By October 1835 he had put up a board house. He was the "solitary settler" described by Richard Henry Dana, Jr., in *Two Years Before the Mast*. This region is now in the heart of Chinatown, and the site where Richardson's tent stood is at 823–27 Grant Avenue.

In 1836 he built a more elaborate dwelling of adobe. This was the "Casa Grande" of Yerba Buena until 1848, being the largest and most pretentious building there. It withstood several devastating fires, but was taken down in 1852 and replaced by the Adelphi Theater.

From the first, the settlement at Yerba Buena Cove was predominantly English-speaking, a group of foreigners in an area populated by Hispanic and Indian peoples.

The next settler there was Jacob Primer Leese, an American trader, who erected a substantial frame house in 1836. The site of his home is near the intersection of Grant Avenue and Clay Street. The first Fourth of July celebration in San Francisco was held at this house in 1836. Many notable families from around the Bay attended the festivities, among them being the Castro, De Haro, Estudillo, Guerrero, and Martínez families. General Vallejo himself was present, and several ships anchored in the cove took part in the celebration. This redwood house was the center for a large trading business that Leese and his partners, Spear and Hinckley, carried on with the ranchos bordering San Francisco Bay.

Mexican Land Grants

Within the original boundary of San Francisco County lay private ranchos obtained through Mexican governors. When the county was divided in 1856, by far the greater part of the land thus granted was given to San Mateo County. The diminished county of San Francisco occupied the tip of the peninsula, where lands had been reserved for mission and presidio use and where little had been granted to private individuals. The line drawn to separate the two counties passed due west from a point on San Francisco Bay a little east of Visitacion Valley through the southern end of Lake Merced to the Pacific Ocean.

Two of the old ranchos were cut by this line. Rancho Laguna de la Merced, consisting of one-half a square league, was one of these. It was granted in 1835 to José Antonio Galindo, a corporal in the San Francisco militia. After holding it for two years, he sold it to Francisco de Haro for 100 cows and $25 in goods.

Francisco de Haro arrived in California with Governor Argüello in 1819 as a sublieutenant in the San Blas infantry. In 1824 he helped suppress a revolt among Indian neophytes. In that year he married Josefa, daughter of José Antonio Sánchez, and thereafter lived in San Francisco, where they raised their family. In 1838, within a year of purchasing the rancho, he was made alcalde. In that office he was responsible for the guardianship of persons arrested for offenses against law and order. A problem arose when Galindo, former owner of the rancho, was taken into custody for the murder of José Peralta. Lack of a jail compelled Alcalde de Haro to order his fellow townsmen to act as guards. After holding the prisoner under trying circumstances for three months, he finally received Governor Alvarado's permission to send Galindo to the prison at San Jose.

Francisco de Haro held many important positions under the Mexican regime and is frequently mentioned in the annals of San Francisco. He died at a comparatively early age in 1849, his death hastened by grief over the senseless murder of his twin sons by Frémont's men in San Rafael three years before, a tale told in the Marin County chapter.

The second rancho cut by the new county boundary line was the Cañada de Guadalupe, la Visitación y Rodeo Viejo, only a small portion of which was left in San Francisco County. It consisted of two leagues and was granted by Governor Alvarado in 1841 to Jacob Primer Leese. Since the grantee had a house in Yerba Buena, he and his family resided for only a short time on the rancho property, which he afterward sold. The United States patent for the tract was issued in 1865 to Henry R. Payson and William Pierce; the former possessed 5,473 acres and the latter 942 acres.

A tract of 12,643 acres of pueblo land was patented to the city of San Francisco in June 1884.

Other grants of land in the San Francisco area recognized by the United States government were few in number and small in extent. One of these was the Ojo de Agua de Figueroa, 100 varas, granted in 1833 to Apolinario Miranda, a soldier in the San Francisco Company. He constructed an adobe house to replace an earlier temporary structure in 1834. He was once brought before the alcalde for mistreating his wife, Juana Briones; her house in the North Beach section, about where Powell and Filbert streets intersect, was the only dwelling between Yerba Buena and the presidio. She long outlived her husband, who was buried at Mission Dolores, and ended her days in Santa Clara County.

Among the other small grants were Las Camaritas, about nineteen acres, patented to Ferdinand Vassault; two lots in the pueblo land patented to J. P. Leese in 1858; the eight and one-half acres of Mission Dolores, patented to Bishop J. S. Alemany in 1858; and a few others, varying from half an acre to 25 acres, given to various persons.

In 1853 José Y. Limantour made a fantastic claim to the U.S. Land Commission that he had been granted four leagues of land within and adjoining what had become the city of San Francisco. The citizens were aroused and astounded, but the claims were proven to be fraudulent, and Limantour fled the country.

Portsmouth Plaza

Captain John B. Montgomery of the USS *Portsmouth* received orders from Commodore John Drake Sloat, on July 8, 1846, to take possession of Yerba Buena and the northern frontier. On the morning of July 9, Montgomery and his men landed at what is now the corner of Clay and Leidesdorff streets. Nearby, at the southeast corner of Clay and Montgomery streets, is a tablet placed by the Native Sons of the Golden West in 1916. This plaque not only commemorates Montgomery's landing place (SRL 81) but also brings to the attention of all who view it the fact that the waters of San Francisco Bay once came up to the foot of Clay Street almost as far as Montgomery Street. On this site the Bank of Italy, now Bank of America, which had been founded in San Francisco by A. P. Giannini in 1904, built its first main office in 1908. For this reason, the *Portsmouth* is pictured on the bank's official seal.

Montgomery Street was named for Captain Montgomery. The plaza, where the first American flag was raised in San Francisco and where the Custom House stood until 1851, was afterward called Portsmouth Square in honor of his ship; it is now officially Portsmouth Plaza (SRL 119).

In 1849 and the 1850's Portsmouth Square became the place where the principal gambling houses were situated. "Neither tree, shrub, nor grass adorned it, but it contained a rude platform for public speaking, a tall flag staff, and a cow pen enclosed by rough board." Today, Portsmouth Plaza, location of an underground parking garage since 1962, is planted with trees and grass. The pagoda roofs of Chinatown look down upon it, and it is a favorite gathering place for San Franciscans of all races and ages.

On the plaza, near the corner of Clay and Kearny streets, is a monument commemorating the Clay Street Hill Railroad Company (SRL 500), the first cable railway system in the world. Andrew S. Hallidie, English builder of aerial cables for use in Western mines, invented an arrangement whereby heavy cables could be laid underground to draw cars uphill. The first successful car thus equipped ran on Clay Street between Kearny and Leavenworth streets on August 1, 1873, and soon thereafter such lines were in general use. At one time San Francisco had eight lines, but now there are only three. San Francisco's cable cars, among its most famous tourist attractions, have been registered as a National Historic Landmark by the Department of the Interior. At the corner of Mason and Washington streets is the Cable Car Barn and Museum, where visitors may see some retired cable cars and learn about their peculiar operation.

Robert Louis Stevenson, while living in the Bay Area, spent a good many hours at Portsmouth Square, looking at the crowds of people and engaging in long conversations. Scenes in *The Wrecker* are based on his rambles around the square. The first monument erected to him, planned and executed by Bruce Porter and Willis Polk, was put up here in 1897.

Much of the work that Stevenson began in Monterey was completed in San Francisco, notably *Across the Plains* and *The Amateur Emigrant*. The friends he made here were among his most cherished, among them Judge John Boalt and Judge Reardon; Virgil Williams, painter and founder of the California School of Art, and his wife; and the author and professor Charles Warren Stoddard, who influenced Stevenson's move to the South Seas, where he spent his last years.

San Francisco's First Schools

Soon after the American occupation in 1846, it was realized that a school was needed for the children of the rapidly growing town. In April 1847 the first private school was opened by J. D. Marston in a shanty on the west side of Grant Avenue between Pacific Avenue and Broadway. It was attended by some 20 or 30 children, but lasted only a few months.

The site of what has been called San Francisco's first public school (SRL 587) is on the southwest corner of Portsmouth Plaza, and has been marked by the Grand Lodge of Free and Accepted Masons. In the autumn of 1847 a committee met to plan the building, and on April 3, 1848, school was opened by Thomas Douglas, a graduate of Yale. The gold excitement took Douglas off to the mines six weeks later, but the school was resumed in April 1849 by the Reverend Albert Williams, a Presbyterian. This small shanty of a schoolhouse was used for various purposes, "town hall, court house, people's court for trial of culprits by the first vigilance committee, school, church, and finally, jail. Owing to the range and variety of its uses, the building was dignified by the name of Public Institute." The Public Institute School, however (like others of that time), was not a public school in the modern sense, for it was obliged to charge some tuition and was not under complete government control.

In October 1849, John Cotter Pelton, a young New England schoolteacher and a Baptist layman, came to California to establish free public schools. On December 26 of that year he opened a school in the First Baptist church at 878-A Washington Street; soon 50 children were in attendance. Pelton would accept no tuition in his school and worked indefatigably to arouse public interest and action on behalf of the free public school as an established institution.

As a result of Pelton's efforts, his school was adopted by the city in March 1850 and became the first public school in California. On April 8, 1850, the first school ordinance in the state was passed. The site on Washington Street has been marked by a bronze tablet placed by the Northern California Baptist Convention. Another early school was established in Happy Valley in 1850, as noted below.

At the entrance to the Emporium-Capwell store on the south side of Market Street between Fourth and Fifth is a plaque noting that St. Ignatius College was founded on the site in 1855. The Jesuit school was moved to Van Ness Avenue and Hayes Street, near the present Civic Center, in 1880. It is now the University of San Francisco and is located west of the downtown area between Lone Mountain and the Panhandle of Golden Gate Park.

St. Mary's College (SRL 772) was founded in San Francisco in 1863 by Archbishop Joseph Sadoc Alemany, O.P. A marker at College and Crescent avenues near Mission Street indicates the original site. The Christian Brothers took charge of the college in 1868, and in 1889 it was moved to Oakland. In 1928 it was moved to its present campus in Moraga, Contra Costa County.

The First Churches

A party of Mormons, under Sam Brannan, held religious services in Captain Richardson's "Casa Grande" on Dupont Street soon after they arrived in San Francisco in 1846 on the ship *Brooklyn*. In May 1847 a Sunday School was organized by a Methodist missionary, Rev. James H. Wilbur. The Mormon community moved inland by 1847, and the Sunday School was soon disrupted by the gold stampede.

On July 25, 1847, Chaplain Chester Newell, of the United States frigate *Independence*, preached in the C. L. Ross store, on the northwest corner of Montgomery and Washington streets. Although there were probably other services held by ships' chaplains, this is the first recorded Protestant religious service in San Francisco. Protestant worship was carried on in the Public Institute on an irregular basis for the next two years.

At 100 McAllister Street, near the Civic Center, stands a structure originally named in honor of William Taylor, pioneer Methodist preacher of San Francisco. Erected in 1927–30 as the William Taylor Church and Hotel by the united efforts of the Methodist churches of San Francisco and their friends, the building cost over three million dollars. It was vacated by the Methodists in 1937 and now houses federal offices. Taylor and the Rev. Isaac Owen did much to establish religious and educational institutions in California between 1849 and 1856.

St. Francis Church at the northeast corner of Vallejo Street and Columbus Avenue is, after Mission Dolores, the oldest Roman Catholic parish in San Francisco, having been established in 1849. The present building was erected in 1859. Its interior was destroyed by the great fire of 1906, but the walls remained intact and it was fully restored. St. Patrick's Church was founded in 1851. The old wooden building that stood on Market Street about where the Palace Hotel now stands has been moved several times and now stands at the north side of Eddy Street east of Divisadero, where it is in use as the parish hall of Holy Cross Church. It is one of the oldest frame buildings in the city. The present St. Patrick's at 756 Mission Street was rebuilt after the 1906 disaster but incorporates portions of the structure erected about 1870.

Old St. Mary's Church (SRL 810), at California Street and Grant Avenue, San Francisco's first Catholic cathedral, was dedicated in 1854. The bricks came around the Horn, and some of the stone came from China. It was replaced in 1891 by a new cathedral at Van Ness Avenue and O'Farrell Street, and three years later was put in the charge of the Paulist Fathers. Only the walls of Old St. Mary's survived the fire of 1906, but the church was rebuilt within them and rededicated in 1909. St. Mary's Cathedral on Van Ness Avenue was spared in 1906 but was destroyed by fire on September 7, 1962. A new cathedral, of striking design, has replaced it, on the block bounded by Gough, Ellis, Octavia, and Geary streets.

Thomas Starr King, Unitarian preacher and vigorous advocate of the Union cause in the Civil War, came to San Francisco from Boston in 1860. Until his death in 1864, he served as pastor of the First Unitarian Church, the first site of which was on Stockton Street near Sacramento. Since the town was growing southward, a new church was built at 133 Geary Street near Stockton shortly after King's arrival. In this church he preached, and there he was buried. Later, the city's growth necessitated the removal of the church to its present site at Geary and Franklin streets, where the body of King lies in a white marble tomb (SRL 691) before the door of the church.

King used his eloquence to support the Union and the cause of the Sanitary Commission, a Civil War counterpart of the Red Cross. His portrait was hung in the state capitol with the inscription: "The man whose matchless oratory saved California to the Union." A bronze statue was erected in Golden Gate Park as an expression of San Francisco's appreciation of his life and services. A statue of him done by Haig Patigian has been placed, along with one of Father Junipero Serra by Ettore Cadorin, to represent California in Statuary Hall in the Capitol Building in Washington, D.C.

On the west side of Montgomery Street near Columbus Avenue a plaque has been placed to mark the site (SRL 462) of the first Jewish religious services in San Francisco. Here 40 pioneers gathered to celebrate Yom Kippur on September 26, 1849.

At the summit of Nob Hill stands Grace Cathedral, the seat of the Episcopal diocese of California. The cathedral is on the site of the Charles Crocker mansion. The Crocker family donated the land for the cathedral after the mansion was destroyed in the fire of 1906, and the cornerstone was laid by Bishop William F. Nichols in 1910. A distinctive feature of this prominent building is the doors for the east front, which are casts made from the celebrated doors of the Baptistry in Florence, Italy, the work of the fifteenth-century sculptor Lorenzo Ghiberti.

Monuments on Market Street

Perhaps the best known and best loved monument on Market Street is Lotta's Fountain, at the intersection of Geary and Kearny streets. This was presented to the city in 1875 by Lotta Crabtree, famed entertainer who began her career as a child in gold rush days. In 1910 Luisa Tetrazzini sang at midnight on Christmas Eve before thousands massed around the fountain. In commemoration of this event a bas-relief portrait of Madame Tetrazzini by Haig Patigian was added to the fountain.

At Market, Battery, and Bush streets is the Mechanics Monument, dedicated about the turn of the century to the pioneer industrialist Peter Donahue. The sculptor was the deaf-mute Douglas Tilden. The Pioneer Monument, a gift of James Lick, was erected in 1894 at Market, Hyde, and Grove streets.

The Native Sons Monument was given to the city by James D. Phelan to commemorate the admission of California to the Union. It was unveiled on Admission Day, September 9, 1897, and dedicated to the Native Sons of the Golden West. It is in the form of a drinking fountain surmounted by the bronze figure of an angel holding aloft an open book on which is inscribed the date of California's admission to the Union. At the base of the shaft stands a miner with a pick in his right hand, while in his left he holds high an American flag, with California's new star in the field. This monument originally stood at Market, Turk, and Mason streets. It was later moved to Golden Gate Park and subsequently brought back downtown, where it now stands at Market, Montgomery, and Post streets.

Happy Valley

Happy Valley was the name given to a small area between First, Second, Market, and Mission streets. In the winter of 1849–50 about a thousand tents were pitched here, sheltered from the winds by the sand hills along Market Street. In 1850 a successful school was opened here. One of its founders was Rev. Samuel H. Willey, pastor of the Howard Presbyterian Church in Happy Valley, and later one of the founders of the College of California in Oakland. W. D. M. Howard, a prominent merchant, and Thomas J. Nevins greatly aided Willey in building up this Happy Valley Public School. In November 1851 it became the first school operated under the city public school system.

The San Francisco Post Office

When a gold-seeker left home to try his luck in California, he had no mailing address. San Francisco was the one California town well known elsewhere, and families therefore sent their letters care of the Post Office, San Francisco. Mail arrived about once a month in the early gold rush years, and it is reported that long lines stretched from the post office as mail day approached. The San Francisco Post Office had several locations before the present Main Branch at Seventh and Mission streets was erected in 1905, replacing the office on the ground floor of the Customs House, where it had been since 1857.

The Civic Center

San Francisco's handsome Civic Center owes much to the 1906 earthquake and fire, which destroyed nearly 500 blocks of buildings, including the ramshackle City Hall on Larkin Street about where the present City Library stands. The new City Hall, on the block bounded by Van Ness Avenue and Grove, Polk, and McAllister streets, was completed in 1915 and boasts a dome more than eleven feet higher than that of the Capitol in Washington, D.C. The City Hall has been the scene of many gala receptions, such as those connected with the creation of the United Nations in 1945. Tragedy struck here, too, when Mayor George Moscone and Supervisor Harvey Milk were shot to death in their offices by Dan White, a former supervisor, on November 27, 1978.

Across the intersection of Grove and Polk streets from the City Hall is the Civic Auditorium, completed in 1913 and used for numerous exhibitions, performances, and conventions, among them the 1920 Democratic National Convention. The main branch of the City Library, across the Civic Center Plaza from the City Hall, dates back to 1917. The San Francisco Room is a major repository for San Francisco history. Federal and state office buildings in the immediate vicinity add to the impressive quality of the Civic Center.

Across Van Ness Avenue are the complementary buildings of the War Memorial Opera House (SRL 964) and the Veterans Memorial Building. Both were inaugurated in 1932. The Opera House has a special history as the site for two of the most important diplomatic gatherings of the twentieth century. In the spring of 1945, delegates from 46 countries met here to determine ways of maintaining peace once World War II, then raging, had come to an end. On June 26, the United Nations Charter was signed in the Veterans Memorial Building, and a new effort was made toward achieving international amity. The conference ending the war with Japan (the armistice having been signed in September 1945) met here in 1951, and the treaty of peace was signed on September 8. Plaques commemorating these events are to be seen in the foyer of the Opera House. The Veterans Memorial Building houses the San Francisco Museum of Modern Art and the Herbst Theater for the performing arts.

The Shoreline Markers

The location of the shoreline on Market Street as it was in 1848 was marked by two bronze tablets (SRL 83) in 1921 by the Native Sons of the Golden West. One of the tablets was placed at the corner of Market and First streets and reads: "The shoreline of San Francisco reached a point twenty-five feet northeasterly from this spot at the time gold was discovered by James W. Marshall at Coloma, California, January 24, 1848." The other tablet was placed across the street at the base of the Mechanics Monument; on it is reproduced a map of the old shoreline from Howard Street to Pacific Street.

The First Wharves

A little pier for the landing of small boats at high tide was built at the foot of Clay Street in 1846. The principal landing place, however, was at the Punta del Embarcadero, or Clark's Point, now the corner of Battery Street and Broadway. A small wharf was built there in 1847 by William S. Clark, replacing the town's first permanent wharf built there eight years earlier. Clark's Point was first known as the Punta de la Loma Alta. This land was granted in 1839 to Jacob Leese and Salvador Vallejo, who later transferred his interest to Leese. The grant was bounded by what are now Vallejo, Front, and Davis streets and Pacific Avenue. All of San Francisco's present streets east of Montgomery between Broadway and California were originally wharves.

In the spring of 1848 the Central Wharf (also called Long Wharf, SRL 328) was built out from what is now Leidesdorff Street, between Clay and Sacramento streets, some 800 feet into the Bay. The wharf was increased to 2,000 feet in 1850, and Pacific Mail steamers and other large vessels anchored there. The success of Central Wharf (now Commercial Street) caused other wharves to be built, until the whole area was covered with wharves and alleyways. Gradually the entire cove was filled in, mostly with sand from the great dunes extending to the ocean.

In 1853 Meiggs Wharf was built in the area between the foot of Mason Street and the foot of Powell Street. It was constructed by Harry ("Honest Harry") Meiggs, a prominent city official and businessman, who fled San Francisco to South America in 1859 to escape thousands of dollars of bad debts. Meiggs Wharf was enclosed by a seawall in 1881. The present Fisherman's Wharf is close by.

The Buried Ships of San Francisco

The site of the Niantic Hotel (SRL 88) is on the northwest corner of Clay and Sansome streets. Early in the spring of 1849 the ship *Niantic* was anchored on this spot, after it had brought 250 emigrants from Panama at $150 a head. Since it was impossible to obtain a crew for the return voyage because of the lure of the gold fields, the ship was simply left where it was. Storeroom and lodging accommodations were very meager in San Francisco at that time, and any sort of space covered with a roof brought enormous rents. Thus in short order the ship was leased out to various occupants, who used it for stores and offices. The hull was used as a warehouse. The ship was connected to the land by the Clay Street wharf, which before long was lined with structures built on piles.

On May 4, 1851, the *Niantic* was burned to the water's edge in one of the great fires that devastated early San Francisco. On the hulk of the ship the Niantic Hotel was erected. Soon all the area was landlocked, and in 1872 this became the Niantic Block of buildings. In May 1978, workers excavating for the new Pacific Mutual Building at the corner of Clay and Sansome streets struck the old hull of the *Niantic*, and the vessel became newsworthy once again.

Many other ships were abandoned in Yerba Buena Cove in 1849. Although some of them were unseaworthy, even sound ships often had to remain where they had been anchored, owing to the inability of the owners to obtain a crew for the return voyage.

Besides the *Niantic* there were the *General Harrison* (northwest corner of Clay and Battery streets), the *Apollo* (northwest corner of Sacramento and Battery streets), the *Georgian* (between Washington and Jackson streets, west of Battery), and the *Euphemia* (near Battery and Sacramento). Most of them were used as warehouses until they were destroyed in the fire of May 1851. Before 1851 the *Euphemia* had been purchased by the city government and was used as a jail. Balance Street, off Jackson Square, received its name from the ship *Balance* buried there. Lower Market Street covers the remains of the sailing vessels *Bryan*, *Callao*, and *Galen*. At the southwest corner of Sacramento and Front streets is the *Thomas Bennett*. The English brig *Hardie* and the ships *Inez* and *Noble* are in the block bounded by Pacific Avenue and Drumm, Davis, and Jackson streets. The bark *Elizabeth* is under the Embarcadero between Clay and Merchant streets, while the ship *Alida* is beneath Davis Street, between Washington and Jackson streets. These are some of the gold rush ships buried beneath the streets of San Francisco. From time to time, as new construction replaces older buildings, other buried relics of the past turn up.

Pioneer Buildings and Sites

San Francisco is a small city, geographically limited. Throughout its history older buildings have been torn down to give way to newer, and usually larger, structures. Thus there are many plaques and markers throughout the downtown area commemorating long-gone buildings. At Jackson Square, historic preservation has taken place on a large scale. It began with the renovation by wholesale interior decorating firms of several old brick warehouses on what was once the waterfront. Cement veneers and other evidences of modernization were removed, and the buildings stood again as they had in the 1850's and 1860's. Before long, other businesses were attracted, and a once-shabby district was transformed into a handsome, useful center.

On the east side of Montgomery Street between Jackson and Washington streets are several buildings erected in the 1850's, notably those at 722–28 Montgomery. At 722–24 is the building opened as a variety theater on December 15, 1857. A plaque at 728 indicates the site of the first recorded meeting of the Free and Accepted Masons in California (SRL 408) on October 17, 1849.

At the northeast corner of Montgomery and Jackson streets is the building (SRL 453) to which William Tecumseh Sherman moved the branch bank of Lucas, Turner and Company in 1854. He had established the branch in the previous year and headed its operation until 1857. The corner buildings at Jackson Street and Hotaling Place were built about 1860 and served as warehouses for the Hotaling liquor business. The fact that they, like the other solid structures in the present Jackson Square area, escaped the disastrous fire of 1906, inspired a popular jingle by Charles K. Field:

> "If, as they say, God spanked the town
> For being over-frisky,
> Why did He burn the churches down
> And save Hotaling's whisky?"

Remnants of the old Hotaling stables are in evidence in the building at 38 Hotaling Place, and in the basement of No. 42 is the entrance to a brick tunnel, said to have been used by smugglers to bring contraband from the wharf to downtown San Francisco.

The building at 432 Jackson Street has served in the past as the Tremont Hotel and as the French consulate. The Ghirardelli Chocolate Company was once located in the building at 415 Jackson. (This is not to be confused with Ghirardelli Square, another historic center, at 900 North Point Street near Fort Mason.) Close to Jackson Square, and now considered part of this historic district, is the old Barbary Coast on Pacific Avenue, a century ago one of the most infamous sections of any city in the world.

The Montgomery Block (SRL 80) stood on the east side of Montgomery Street with sides on Washington and Merchant streets. It was begun in July 1853 and was opened in December of that year. While the building was new, the owners, the law firm of Halleck, Peachy, and Billings, had their offices on the second floor. Among the tenants were other law firms and financiers. For 30 years a part of the Sutro Library was housed there. The old block, which survived the earthquake and fire of 1906, stood for more than a century before it was demolished in 1959. In its stead is perhaps the most distinctive building on the San Francisco skyline, the Transamerica Pyramid, completed in 1972.

On the southwest corner of Montgomery and Merchant streets stood the western business headquarters of Russell, Majors, and Waddell—a Leavenworth, Kansas, firm that operated the Pony Express (SRL 696). On April 4, 1860, the first westbound rider arrived here carrying mail from St. Joseph, Missouri. The Pony Express ceased operation eighteen months later.

In the days of Spanish and Mexican rule, business in California had been transacted mainly through barter. For a time after the American occupation and the discovery of great quantities of gold, payment was made in gold dust. This led to the coining of the metal. In 1849–50 there were fifteen different operations making coins of various kinds in California. One of these establishments was situated on the south side of Portsmouth Plaza; O. P. Dutton was the director and F. D. Kohler was the assayer. Coins made here were stamped with the name of the Pacific Company and dated 1849.

Although private coins were legal tender until 1856, an act of Congress in 1852 provided for a federal branch mint in San Francisco. This branch was established in 1854 at 608 Commercial Street (SRL 87); the first assayer was Agoston Haraszthy, later famous for his vineyards at Sonoma. Bret Harte was employed at the mint as a bookkeeper for a time. The building, still standing but reduced from three stories to one, was later the United States Subtreasury.

Another mint was constructed in 1870–74 at Fifth and Mission streets. Designed by government architect A. B. Mullett, it is a fine example of the Greek Revival style typical of federal buildings in Washington, D.C. It survived the 1906 fire, only to be supplanted by a new mint in 1937. The structure (SRL 875) is now a National Historic Landmark, registered by the Department of the Interior. The present United States mint is operating at Buchanan Street and Duboce Avenue.

In the early 1840's the Hudson's Bay Company had an office on Montgomery Street between Clay and Sansome streets. In 1846 this San Francisco operation was abandoned and the property was sold to Mellus and Howard. The building was afterward the United States Hotel. The Mellus and Howard Warehouse (SRL 459) once stood at the southwest corner of Montgomery and Clay streets. Here, on August 31, 1850, the Society of California Pioneers, the oldest historical society in the state, was organized. W. D. M. Howard was the first president. The society today maintains an attractive museum at Pioneer Hall at 456 McAllister Street in the Civic Center. This museum has some of the most interesting and unusual displays of California history to be found anywhere in the state.

The office of the *California Star*, the first newspaper published in San Francisco (SRL 85), was on Brenham Place (now Walter Lum Place) at the southwest corner of Washington Street, just west of Portsmouth Plaza. It stood behind the house of its publisher, entrepreneur

Sam Brannan. The first number was issued on January 9, 1847, with Elbert P. Jones as the editor. From 1849 until it expired in 1891 the paper was called the *Alta California*. The site is now identifiable by the building at 743 Washington, the first structure in a purportedly Oriental style to be built in Chinatown. Erected in 1908, it served for many years as the Chinese telephone exchange; today it is a branch office of the Bank of Canton.

At 405 Montgomery Street, at the corner of California, is the site of the Parrott Block (SRL 89), San Francisco's first fireproof building. Constructed in 1852 of granite blocks brought from China, the three-story building came through the holocaust of 1906 relatively unscathed, but in 1926 it was demolished to make way for the Financial Center Building.

On the south side of Clay Street, between Kearny and Montgomery, is the site of the Portsmouth House, operated as California's first hotel in 1846.

The El Dorado and the Parker House (SRL 192), once on the east side of Portsmouth Plaza, were among the most famous of the saloons and gambling resorts clustered about the center of the city's activity in 1849 and the early 1850's. Another hotel, the What Cheer House (SRL 650), opened in 1852 by R. B. Woodward, stood between Montgomery and Leidesdorff streets on the south side of Sacramento Street. The Oriental Hotel (1854) stood on the southwest corner of Battery and Bush streets. The Tehama House (1851), said to be frequented by "the elite of the town," stood at the northwest corner of California and Sansome streets, where the Bank of California is now located.

The International Hotel (1854) stood on the north side of Jackson Street east of Kearny. The Russ Building on Montgomery Street between Bush and Pine today occupies the site of the Russ home and hotel owned by J. C. Christian Russ, who came to California with Company C, New York Volunteers, in 1847.

At 202 Green Street, a marker (SRL 941) notes that on this site, in a simple laboratory, Philo Taylor Farnsworth invented and patented the first all-electronic television system. The first successful transmission of a television image was made by the 21-year-old electronics pioneer on September 7, 1927.

The site of the old California Theater (SRL 86) is at 444 Bush Street. It was built by a syndicate headed by William C. Ralston, William Sharon, C. N. Felton, and H. P. Wakelee. The architect, S. C. Bugbee, was ordered to design a building seating 1,600 and guaranteed to withstand earthquake and fire. It had its grand opening on January 15, 1869. The tablet marking the site was installed by the Commonwealth Club at the suggestion of Emelie Melville, the last surviving member of the cast of the inaugural performance. The California Theater was one of the many casualties of the great fire of 1906.

The site (SRL 937) of the invention of the three-reel Bell slot machine, first manufactured in San Francisco by its inventor, Charles Fey, is commemorated at 406 Market Street. What has been claimed to be the most famous gambling device of all time is no longer legal in San Francisco, nor anywhere else in the state of California.

At the corner of Geary and Stockton streets is the prominent structure still familiarly known as the City of Paris Building (SRL 876), now occupied by Neiman-Marcus. In 1850 the Verdier brothers, immigrants from France, opened a store aboard the ship *Ville de Paris* to serve the Argonauts passing through San Francisco. In 1896 the business moved into the downtown site, considered to be one of the finest examples of the beaux-arts style of commercial building in California.

Union Square (SRL 623), bounded by Post, Stockton, Geary, and Powell streets, was set aside for public use on January 3, 1850, during the administration of the first mayor, John White Geary. Geary was a remarkable man. He had served for a short time as postmaster of San Francisco before becoming mayor; later, he became governor of Kansas and after that governor of Pennsylvania. The square received its name in 1860 when pro-Union meetings were held there. The monument in the center of the square commemorates the victory of the American naval forces commanded by Admiral George Dewey at the Battle of Manila Bay (May 1, 1898) in the Spanish-American War. It was dedicated by President William McKinley in ceremonies held in 1901. An underground parking garage was built beneath the square in 1942.

The main entrance to Woodward's Gardens (SRL 454), a pioneer amusement park, was on the west side of Mission Street between Duboce Avenue and Fourteenth Street. R. B. Woodward built his private home here about 1866 and filled it with works of art. Finding that his collections would be appreciated by the public, he opened his grounds and built an octagonal pavilion with a seating capacity of more than 5,000, to be used for plays, dances, and skating. He added a zoological department across Fourteenth Street, with wild animals and an aquarium. A tunnel beneath the street connected the two parks. Nothing of them remains.

Hubert Howe Bancroft began to accumulate his extraordinary collection in 1859. A successful dealer in books and manuscripts, the Ohio-born businessman decided to collect all the materials he could find for an encyclopedia of the history of the Pacific Coast. Soon he had a remarkable collection of material, which, in 1881, he placed in the first Bancroft Library (SRL 791) at 1538 Valencia Street. This treasury escaped the burning of Bancroft's bookstore on Market Street in 1886.

In 1905, the Bancroft collection was purchased by the University of California for $250,000, after a long debate in the legislature, where many representatives balked at "paying good money for worthless old trash." Bancroft paid $100,000 of the price from his own pocket. The material was taken to Berkeley early in 1906, by the greatest good fortune escaping the San Francisco holocaust in April of that year. The collection is now housed in an annex of the main library on the Berkeley campus, and much material has been added to it over the years, so that it constitutes one of the major repositories of California historical material.

What is believed to be the oldest house now standing in San Francisco is the Phelps House at 1111 Oak Street. It is privately owned today. The house was shipped in sections and brought around the Horn from New Orleans. It was erected in 1850 on Abner Phelps's homestead at the foot of Buena Vista Hill, now by the Panhandle of Golden Gate Park. The first address of the house was 329 Divisadero Street, but over the years the house has been moved (on one occasion being turned around a full 180 degrees), always remaining near the corner of Divisadero and Oak streets. At what is now 321–329 Divisadero is the site of Walter Phelps's haberdashery, built on the original foundation of the Phelps House.

The Haas-Lilienthal House at 2007 Franklin Street was built in 1886 for William Haas, a prosperous wholesale grocer who was born in Bavaria. Haas and his wife, the former Bertha Greenebaum, lived here with their two daughters, Alice and Florine. Both daughters were married in the parlor of the house. When Haas died in 1916, Alice and her husband, Samuel Lilienthal, moved in with her widowed mother. Upon Alice's death in 1972, the family gave the house to the city; today it is open to visitors under the aegis of the Foundation for San Francisco's Architectural Heritage. The unusual and distinctive wooden embellishments along the exterior make the Haas-Lilienthal House a favorite for photographers.

"Fort Gunnybags" and the Vigilance Committees

The site of old "Fort Gunnybags," or Fort Vigilance, the headquarters of the San Francisco Vigilance Committee of 1856, is located at 243 Sacramento Street. The city at that time was given over to a reign of terror. Many San Francisco residents believed that the municipal officials themselves were corrupt and in league with criminal elements.

The occasion for the formation of the Vigilance Committee in 1856 (a previous vigilante group appeared briefly in 1851) was the murder of James King of William by James P. Casey. In his crusading newspaper, the *Bulletin*, King had denounced Casey's political corruption. A cry went up for the immediate punishment of the murderer. Later it was said that the officials of the city could not be depended on, and thus a committee of citizens undertook to see that justice was meted out. William T. Coleman became the chairman of this Vigilance Committee, and thousands of San Franciscans gave him their support. Casey was taken from the jail where he was being held in custody and was hanged along with another accused murderer, Charles Cora, on the evening of May 17, 1856, as King's funeral procession passed nearby. Hubert Howe Bancroft later wrote that the work of the committee was "one of the grandest moral revolutions the world has ever witnessed." It appears that the crime rate of San Francisco decreased after this episode, and that there was a general cleanup of the city, though it cannot be said to have been permanent.

"Fort Gunnybags" (SRL 90) was first marked in 1903 by the California Landmarks League. In the 1906 fire the old building perished, and by the time the tablet was replaced in 1918 by the Native Sons of the Golden West, almost everyone who had taken part in the activities of 1856 had died. At the top of the tablet is a representation of the all-seeing eye that adorned official documents issued by the committee.

The Hills of San Francisco

The hills upon which San Francisco is built separated the three original settlements now lying within one municipality. These settlements were the presidio, the mission, and the commercial area of Yerba Buena. As the latter grew, it spread up and over the hills, so that some modern streets ascend and descend remarkably steep slopes, although the steepest parts have been somewhat lowered. It is said that there are 43 hills in San Francisco.

Telegraph Hill (SRL 91), called by the Spaniards "Loma Alta" (high hill), with an elevation of 275 feet, is first in historic interest. From its top, on October 29, 1850, a fire signal was given to announce the news, brought by the steamer *Oregon*, of the admission of California as the 31st state of the Union. A battery built in 1846 under the direction of Captain John B. Montgomery on the east side of Telegraph Hill gave the name to Battery Street.

Many Chileans had homes near the base of the hill in the 1850's, and in later years Italian families predominated. The Irish lived on the slopes and on the summit. The part between Kearny and Montgomery and Green and Greenwich streets housed what in the 1890's was called the Artist Colony. Since 1930, the hill has been the site of expensive homes and apartment houses.

As early as 1849, Loma Alta was used as a station from which to observe incoming vessels, and was sometimes called "Signal Hill." In September 1849, a 25-by-18-foot two-story house was erected on the top, and this was soon purchased by George Sweeny and Theodore E. Baugh, founders of the Merchants' Exchange. The observers who lived here reported to the people of the city below information on incoming ships—side-wheel steamers, sailing ships, and other craft. Upon the top of this house stood a sort of semaphore by which an elaborate system of signals could be given. The place was known as the Inner Signal Station. The Outer Signal Station was then established near Point Lobos, where incoming craft could first be seen and reported by telegraph to the Inner Station. This was California's first telegraph line, opened in 1853. The same year the North Point Docks were constructed below the hill, and Sansome Street was cut through it. The house that had stood on top of the hill blew down in a storm in 1870 and was not replaced. Some of the oldest houses on the hill, and in the city, stand on Napier Lane, off the Filbert Street stairway.

In 1876 a group of citizens donated to San Francisco a tract 275 feet square between Kearny, Greenwich, and Filbert streets, extending almost to Montgomery Street, as a park; later the city purchased an area of about the same size to extend the park to the summit. In the 1880's a castle-like building stood on the top and a funicular railway ran up Greenwich Street. In the early 1900's the top of the hill was cleared and the area was named Pioneer Park.

Today Telegraph Hill is capped by Coit Tower. The structure, 210 feet tall, was the gift of Mrs. Lillie Hitchcock Coit for the beautification of the city. Lillie was brought to San Francisco by her parents at the age of eight in 1851 and became an enthusiastic supporter of the fire companies, all of which were manned in those days by volunteers. She was made an honorary member of the Knickerbocker No. 5 Company while still a girl, an accolade she never forgot. Although much of her adult life was spent in Paris, she returned to San Francisco before her death in 1929, and bequeathed $100,000 for a memorial to the volunteer firemen of San Francisco. The tower is shaped like a fire-hose nozzle. The interior is decorated with murals which were a W.P.A. project, depicting the kaleidoscopic life of the city in the 1930's. The view from Telegraph Hill on a clear day is magnificent.

Among the writers who have lived on Telegraph Hill are Mark Twain, Joaquin Miller, Frank Norris, Ambrose Bierce, and Bret Harte, who complained that goats browsed on the geraniums in his second-story windowboxes and tramped over the roof at night "like heavy hail-stones"; Harte's story "The Secret of Telegraph Hill" has some good local color. To Charles Warren Stoddard, the wandering goats were "the mascots of the hill." Robert Louis Stevenson called the summit the "Peak of the Wind."

Russian Hill, probably so named because of an early unenclosed Russian sailors' graveyard on its summit at the crest of Vallejo Street, also has superb views over the Bay. At the 360-foot summit an observatory stood about 1861, which was reached by means of a spiral staircase.

Among the writers who have resided on this hill was Helen Hunt Jackson, who died there in 1886. Near her home on the eastern brow a mast was erected for use in the early days of wireless telegraphy. At Vallejo and Taylor streets is the site of Ina Coolbrith's home, now a tiny park named in her honor. She and Bret Harte and Charles Warren Stoddard were known as the "Golden Gate Trinity" in the early days of the *Overland Monthly*, California's first literary journal (1868–1883). Much beloved, Ina Coolbrith was the first poet laureate of the state of California. Between Hyde and Larkin streets Greenwich Street becomes a stairway, and here is another small park, this one dedicated to the poet George Sterling.

On the 1000 block of Green Street are several houses that escaped the fire of 1906. The Feusier Octagon House at 1067 Green, built in 1855, is one of two in San Francisco. The former firehouse at 1088, now an elegant residence, was built two years after the great fire.

Rincon Hill (SRL 84) rose from Rincon ("corner") Point, shown on old maps of San Francisco. On the sheltered southern side of this point was a wooded area favored for picnic outings, and here George Gordon laid out South Park in 1852, patterning it somewhat after the squares then being created in London. Each man who purchased a lot there was required to erect a fireproof house of brick.

Higher upon Rincon Hill grander homes were built, among them those of William C. Ralston, Milton Latham, General Henry W. Halleck, John Parrott, Peter Donahue, General Albert Sidney Johnston, Senator William M. Gwin, Mayor Thomas Selby, Joseph Donohoe, General William Tecumseh Sherman, H. W. Newhall, and the McAllister family. In 1852 the United States Marine Hospital was built on the eastern extremity, and in 1860 St. Mary's Hospital, the first Catholic hospital on the Pacific Coast (now located at the western end of Hayes Street), was built on the hill to the south.

In 1869 Rincon Hill was cut at Second Street, after which the social prestige of the place declined. By that time, the three military men mentioned above had gone East to fight in the Civil War; none returned to San Francisco. A few mansions were maintained by their owners until the fire of 1906, which devastated the area. In *The Wrecker*, Stevenson tells of seeing the hill in its decline in 1879, when he visited Charles Warren Stoddard's residence, then on Vernon (now Dow Place), off Second Street. The economic philosopher Henry George lived at 420 Second Street, just south of Harrison, from 1861 to 1880, and here he wrote *Progress and Poverty*. The "Battle of Rincon Hill" between striking longshoremen and strikebreakers took place on the nearby waterfront on "Bloody Thursday," July 5, 1934. Two maritime workers were killed, several hundred persons were injured, and a general strike followed.

The building of the San Francisco–Oakland Bay Bridge in the 1930's completed the demolition of Rincon Hill; what was left of it was leveled for ramps and the western anchorage of the bridge. Rincon Hill occupied the area that is today bounded by Spear, Second, Folsom, and Brannan streets.

Nob Hill was originally called Fern Hill. Not until the cable car was put into operation was it possible to make this ascent in comfort and safety. Pretentious houses erected on the hill by early nouveaux riches probably gave rise to the name "Nob Hill." The 1906 fire destroyed most of these houses. The pillars of the Grecian doorway of the A. N. Towne residence were left standing among the ruins, and later these "Portals of the Past" were placed in Golden Gate Park, on the banks of Lloyd Lake near the main drive.

Nob Hill was the site of the great houses of the "Big Four," of the Central Pacific Railroad—directors Leland Stanford, Mark Hopkins, Charles Crocker, and Collis P. Huntington. The mansion of Governor (later Senator) Stanford was on the site now occupied by the Stanford Court Apartments at 901 California Street. The Mark Hopkins Hotel stands on the site of the Hopkins mansion; the carriage entrance and the retaining walls along Mason Street are from the original construction. In 1893 Edward Searles donated the mansion to the University of California, in trust for the San Francisco Art Institute, and it became San Francisco's first cultural center, the Mark Hopkins Institute of Art (SRL 754) "for instruction in and illustration of the fine arts, music and literature." (The San Francisco Art Institute is now located at Chestnut and Jones streets on Russian Hill.) Charles Crocker's mansion stood at the present site of Grace Cathedral, now the crowning glory of Nob Hill. Across California Street is the stately Masonic Temple, dedicated in 1958. Collis P. Huntington lived in the mansion built by David D. Colton, now the location of Huntington Park, bequeathed to the city by Huntington's widow in 1915.

Among other notable residents on Nob Hill were the "Silver Kings" of Nevada's Comstock Lode, James G. Fair and James C. Flood. The Fairmont Hotel at 950 Mason Street is on the old Fair estate. The Flood residence is the only one of the great mansions remaining on Nob Hill. This brownstone structure is now the Pacific Union Club, at the northwest corner of California and Mason streets.

Lone Mountain rises to an elevation of 468 feet between Golden Gate Park and the presidio. For years it was surmounted by a cross, first erected in 1862, which was removed to make room for the buildings of the San Francisco College for Women, a Catholic institution established in 1932, now part of the University of San Francisco. At the base of the mountain were four old cemeteries: to the north, Laurel Hill; to the east, Calvary; to the south, the Masonic; and to the west, the Odd Fellows. In 1937, the city voted to remove them.

Laurel Hill Cemetery was laid out in 1854 when earlier burial places in the city had been abandoned. Two earlier ones had been on Telegraph Hill, one on the southern slope near the corner of Sansome and Vallejo streets and one on the North Beach slope in an area bounded by Grant Avenue and Powell, Chestnut, and Francisco streets. Another small one had been near the top of Russian Hill and still another was at Fulton and Hyde streets near the Civic Center. The oldest of these early cemeteries was the Catholic one at Mission Dolores, still intact. Most of San Francisco's cemeteries are now located in Colma in San Mateo County. Laurel Hill Cemetery, the former burial place of many of the most distinguished figures of California's early days, is commemorated by a marker (SRL 760) at 3333 California Street.

Twin Peaks has, as its name implies, two distinct elevations at its top: a north one of 903 feet and a south one of 910 feet. Other names for them were "Los Pechos de la Choca" (the breasts of the Indian maiden) and "the Mission Peaks." The road to the summit was completed in 1916, and on a very clear day one can see the Farallon Islands in the ocean to the west and Mount Diablo in Contra Costa County to the east. A new viewing station on the peaks was completed in 1986.

Mount Davidson, with an elevation of 938 feet, is the highest peak in San Francisco. It was surveyed in 1852 by the United States Geodetic Survey under George Davidson and was named "Blue Mountain." It was included in Rancho San Miguel, later purchased by the public-spirited Adolph Sutro, who began the planting of the trees that now form Sutro Forest. Mount Sutro, with an elevation of 920 feet, is also in this grove. By 1911 the saplings had grown into trees and the highest peak was renamed Mount Davidson in honor of its first surveyor. In 1923 a cross was erected upon its summit

Octagon House, 2648 Gough Street

and the first Easter sunrise service was held there, now an annual event.

Sponsored by the City and County Federation of Women's Clubs, 26 acres of land on the mountain were acquired by the city of San Francisco. This area was dedicated and named Mount Davidson Park on December 20, 1929, the ceremony being part of the celebration of the 83rd birthday of John McLaren, creator of Golden Gate Park and superintendent of the city's parks for 53 years. The first two crosses erected on Mount Davidson were destroyed by fire. A third cross, 103 feet in height and made of concrete, was set up in March 1934.

Some of San Francisco's finest old homes stand on Pacific Heights. One of the city's two remaining octagonal houses is located at 2648 Gough Street. It is owned by the National Society of Colonial Dames and is open to the public on a regular basis. It houses a collection of memorabilia connected with early United States history. Built in 1857, it was moved from its original site at 2645 Gough in 1953. In the same area, old houses are still standing at 1782 Pacific Avenue (built in 1869), 2439 Buchanan Street (1895), and 2209 Jackson Street (1861). The headquarters of the California Historical Society is in the Whittier Mansion at 2090 Jackson Street. This impressive red sandstone building, completed in 1896, is open to the public.

Chinatown

For more than a century, Chinatown in San Francisco was the most picturesque foreign enclave in the United States. The first Chinese immigrants arrived in 1848, and their number had grown to 20,000 within four years, according to Andrew Rolle. Most of these entered through the port of San Francisco, and a substantial number, after their early sojourns in the Mother Lode country, returned to the city. For many reasons, the Chinese population was not integrated with other social groups, and "Chinatowns" developed in many parts of California. By 1885, according to Bancroft, the Chinatown of San Francisco covered about ten blocks "closely packed with some 25,000 souls."

In the late 1870's, the presence of the Chinese in California became a political issue. Denis Kearney, the principal agitator in San Francisco, declared that low-salaried coolie labor was undercutting American workmen. California congressmen took up the matter, and in 1882 the United States banned any further Chinese immigration, the first time such a law had been passed. In 1943 the law was repealed.

Much of the labyrinth of old Chinatown was destroyed in the fire of 1906. The rebuilt area, still heavily populated, is one of San Francisco's principal tourist attractions. The Museum of the Chinese Historical Society of America is at 17 Adler Place, between Columbus and Grant avenues. The bodies of many of San Francisco's early Chinese settlers were returned for burial in their native land, but there is a Chinese cemetery near Colma.

Other Landmarks

Golden Gate Park, one of the glories of San Francisco, is largely the creation of John McLaren, superintendent of parks from 1890 to his death in 1943. The land acquired by the city in 1868 was 1,017 acres of sand dunes. The original plan was for a gigantic park stretching from the ocean to the City Hall. The oldest building in the park is the Conservatory, modeled on the one in London's Kew Gardens. James Lick, the eccentric San Francisco millionaire, had the building imported from England in sections for his San Jose property. At Lick's death in 1876, the building, still in crates, was offered to San Francisco; the 33 tons of glass and steel were purchased by a group of public-spirited citizens and put up in the park in 1879. Fire seriously damaged the building four years later, but it was rebuilt by the generous funding of Charles Crocker. The Children's House in Children's Playground dates from 1885. The gate and tea house in the Japanese Tea Garden are relics of the Midwinter Exposition of 1894. McLaren Lodge, the park's headquarters, was built in 1896. The California Academy of Sciences, founded in 1853, is the oldest scientific institution on the Pacific Coast; the present building was begun in 1924, with additions in 1970. Across the Music Concourse is the Michael H. de Young Memorial Museum, begun in 1916; the works of

art displayed here range from antiquity to the twentieth century. In 1960 a new wing was added to this building to house the Avery Brundage collection of Asian art.

In Lincoln Park is the California Palace of the Legion of Honor, a copy of the Paris building given to San Francisco in 1924 by Mr. and Mrs. Adolph Spreckels. This museum is administered with the de Young Museum, the Asian Art Museum, and the San Francisco Museum of Modern Art by the Fine Arts Museums of San Francisco. Rodin's statue "The Thinker" is featured in the atrium of the palace.

The Southern Pacific Building at 65 Market Street stands on the site of the Preparedness Day bombing of July 22, 1916, in which ten persons were killed and 40 injured. Labor leaders Thomas J. Mooney and Warren K. Billings were falsely convicted of the bombing, and after many years in prison they were finally pardoned.

San Francisco has been host to two world fairs. The Panama-Pacific Exposition of 1915 was held in the Marina district. One of the major buildings, a temporary structure as they all were, was allowed to remain after the fair had ended, and it became a San Francisco landmark. This was the huge Palace of Fine Arts, designed by Bernard Maybeck. It deteriorated over the years, but thanks to a generous gift from Walter Johnson, the building has been renovated and now houses the San Francisco Exploratorium. The Golden Gate International Exposition was held in 1939–40 on man-made Treasure Island, specially created in San Francisco Bay for the event. The island was later taken over by the United States Navy. A few structures from the fair still stand among the buildings erected by the Navy. The airport terminal building from the fair now houses the Treasure Island Museum, devoted to the Sea Services from 1813, and presenting much material on the fair. The museum is open to the public. Treasure Island adjoins Yerba Buena Island (Goat Island), through which the San Francisco–Oakland Bay Bridge traffic passes.

One of California's most interesting museums is the History Room of the Wells Fargo Bank's main office at 420 Montgomery Street. Here are relics of the days when the Wells Fargo Bank and Express Company was one of the mainstays of California.

Golden Gate National Recreational Area

By an act of Congress in 1972, 34,000 acres in San Francisco and Marin counties became the Golden Gate National Recreational Area. Subsequently the area was dedicated to the memory of San Francisco congressman Philip Burton, who was a principal advocate of the project. The San Francisco portion includes most of the coastal frontage of the presidio, highlighted by Fort

Liberty Ship *Jeremiah O'Brien*, Fort Mason

Point. To the east of Fort Point is the National Maritime Museum. The building on the shore displays models and materials from the days of sail to the present. At the Hyde Street pier, several ships from early days are permanently moored and may be visited. One of these, the *Eureka*, was a commuter ferry on the Bay before the San Francisco–Oakland Bay Bridge rendered the ferry fleet obsolete. The *Balclutha*, moved here in 1988 from its previous berth east of Fisherman's Wharf, is a tall British-built square-rigger launched in 1886; it carried California grain around Cape Horn and returned with European cargoes for many years before ending its days in San Francisco. At Pier 45 the USS *Pampanito* can be visited, a World War II submarine with a valiant combat record, docked here since 1982.

Fort Mason, once the Army's port of embarkation, has become the headquarters of the Golden Gate National Recreational Area. Several buildings from the 1850's still stand, among them McDowell Hall, the officers' club off the entrance from Bay Street and Van Ness Avenue, which was once the commanding general's quarters. The Haskell house (Quarters 3), east of the north end of Franklin Street, is where Senator David Broderick died in 1859 following his duel with Judge David Terry. The last Liberty ship from World War II, the *Jeremiah O'Brien*, is moored at one of the Fort Mason piers, and is open to the public. In 1986 the Black Point Battery, a coastal defense briefly operated during the Civil War, was uncovered; it is now being made a permanent part of the Fort Mason historical complex.

Alcatraz Island, in San Francisco Bay, is the location of the first lighthouse to be put to use on the California coast by the federal government, in 1854. Since the 1850's it has also been the site of fortified buildings first put up for defense of San Francisco Bay. It was occasionally used to detain prisoners, such as Confederate sympathizers during the Civil War or Indians en route to reservations, but it was not until 1908 that the Army began to send some prisoners there. Transferred from Army jurisdiction to the Justice Department in 1934, Alcatraz entered its most notorious period as a federal prison. The prison was closed in 1963. Just what will become of Alcatraz Island has been a topic of continual discussion. The island has become one of the most popular tourist attractions in San Francisco, and regular sailings visit it from Fisherman's Wharf.

Ferries and Bridges

As population increased in both San Francisco and the East Bay, the question of convenient transbay travel arose. Ferry lines increased in number, as did the docks along the Embarcadero, the name given to the street at the edge of San Francisco Bay in the commercial district.

On the Embarcadero at the foot of Market Street, where a shed had been erected in 1877, the Ferry Building was constructed of Colusa sandstone in 1896–1903. Through it poured the morning and evening throngs of local commuters as well as overland passengers to and from the Oakland terminal of the transcontinental trains. Ferry service to Oakland ended in 1959, but regular ferries to Marin County were revived in the 1970's and continue to provide service between San Francisco and Sausalito and Tiburon.

Two famous bridges link San Francisco with her neighbors. The San Francisco–Oakland Bay Bridge was opened to traffic in a gala celebration on November 15, 1936. The San Francisco end of the bridge is a short way inland from Pier 26 on the Embarcadero. The eastern and western sections of this bridge are linked by a tunnel through Yerba Buena Island, midway between the two cities and just within the boundary of the city and county of San Francisco.

The Golden Gate Bridge (SRL 975) crosses the channel between old Fort Point in San Francisco and Lime Point on the Marin County shore. Construction began in 1933 and the bridge was opened on May 27, 1937. Converging roadways at either end lead to the single suspension span, which is 4,200 feet long and at its center is 230 feet above the water.

The Farallones

The seven Farallon Islands were probably discovered in 1543 by the Cabrillo-Ferrelo expedition, although no mention was made of them. In 1579 Francis

Drake sent a party ashore to secure a supply of seal meat, birds, and eggs. He named them the Islands of St. James. In 1595 Cermeño called them simply "the islands." The Vizcaíno expedition in 1603 gave them the name of the "Frayles," in honor of the Carmelite fathers on board. In 1743 George Anson, a British naval commander, captured a Manila galleon on which there was a chart indicating the islands as "Los Farallones," but when or by whom they were so named is not known. In 1775 Bodega called them by a combination of two Spanish names, the "Farallones de los Frayles." *Farallón* is a Spanish term for a small, rocky island.

From 1809 to 1812 these islands were developed as a station for the Russian-American Fur Company, and a Russian settlement was made there. The Russians entered the harbor in canoes, hunting the plentiful sea otter under the very guns of the Spanish fort.

The Farallones have always been a natural rookery. In 1849, when fabulous prices were being asked for food in San Francisco, they became a profitable source of supply for egg hunters. This traffic continued for 40 years, until the quarrels of rival egg companies caused United States marshals to interfere. Bird lovers were later aided by Admiral George Dewey in their efforts to have the islands declared a bird sanctuary. It is now one of four in California.

In 1855 a lighthouse was erected on the Farallon Islands. The place has a long record of disastrous shipwrecks; its bays and inlets bear the names of many lost steamers and sailing vessels.

San Joaquin County

San Joaquin County was one of the original 27 counties. San Joaquin, Spanish for St. Joachim, was the name given by Gabriel Moraga to the river in 1813, and was later used to the designate the county. Stockton, which is centrally located, has always been the county seat.

Indian Villages

More than 100 Indian mounds, or kitchen middens, have been located in San Joaquin County, and new discoveries continue to be made from time to time. These mounds, many of which have been leveled, are the sites of aboriginal villages and burial places. They are found on relatively high ground along the banks of the numerous watercourses of the San Joaquin Delta region, such as the San Joaquin, Cosumnes, Mokelumne, and Calaveras rivers, and the Mormon, French Camp, and other sloughs, which furnished almost inexhaustible hunting grounds for the Indians. W. Egbert Schenck wrote that "apparently it would be hard to exaggerate the number of water fowl that were formerly present in the marshy area of the Great Central Valley. Early accounts indicate an abundance and a tameness which it is hard to conceive."

To the inexperienced eye, an Indian mound appears much the same as the land about it. The archaeologist, however, quickly perceives an appreciable difference. "Upon a mound's base," said Schenck, "there is found a mass of earth essentially the same as the base and the surrounding land, but which has been acted upon by man until in color, texture, constituents, or all of these it is readily distinguishable from the base. . . . In color the mounds are characteristically blacker than the surrounding soil. . . . Presumably this darker color is due to the greater amount of organic matter which man has accumulated upon them."

James A. Barr, for many years superintendent of schools in the city of Stockton, became interested in the archaeology of the Stockton region and during the years 1898–1901 made a large collection of specimens. His excellent field notes and carefully cataloged specimens form the main source of information on the archaeology and ethnology of the Stockton region.

The principal aboriginal sites explored by Barr were the Stockton Channel, Walker Slough, Ott, Pool, and Island mounds. There were also three on the Woods Ranch on Robert's Island; one on the Copperopolis road; and others on Martin's Ranch and the O. R. Smith Ranch, at Brandt's Ferry where Bowman Road now crosses the San Joaquin River, on the Lewis Ranch, and on French Camp Slough.

The Stockton Channel mound, located in Stockton between Edison and Harrison streets on the north bank of the Stockton Channel, is probably the site of the Passasimas village described by the 1817 Spanish expedition led by Father Narciso Durán and accompanied by Luis Arguello. It is possible, however, that this village may have been the one covered by the Walker Slough mound. The latter, being only an eighth of a mile from the Island mound, may be regarded as part of the same settlement.

The Ott mound (southeast of Stockton and north of French Camp Slough) and the Pool mound (nine miles southwest of Stockton) were undoubtedly inhabited when the Spanish visited the region in 1805, in 1810, and again in 1811. One of the most interesting localities worked by Barr was that of Union Island near Bethany, where the Spanish expeditions of 1810 and 1811 found the Yokuts village of Pescadero ("fisherman") so named because they saw Indians catching fish there. Rancho Pescadero (35,446 acres), which is located north of Tracy, received its name from this settlement.

The Battle of the Stanislaus

The Stanislaus River, which forms part of the boundary between San Joaquin County and Stanislaus County to the south, was the scene of one of the most notable series of battles fought in Alta California between the Mexicans and the Indians. The encounters took place near the mouth of the river in May and June 1829. The leader of the Indians was Chief Estanislao, who had been educated at Mission San José, (where he was baptized under the Spanish name for St. Stanislaus), but who was now in rebellion against Mexican rule. The Mexican troops, under command of General Mariano G. Vallejo, were victorious. It was one of the few instances in California in which cannons were used in battle. For years afterward farmers in the vicinity plowed up cannon balls and other relics of the Battle of the Stanislaus (the river having been named for the Indian chief). The site (SRL 214) is thought to be in Caswell Memorial State Park on the north side of the Stanislaus within two miles of its junction with the San Joaquin River.

Rancho del Campo de los Franceses (French Camp)

French Camp, four miles south of Stockton, was first occupied about 1832 by French-Canadian hunters employed by the Hudson's Bay Company to trap beaver, mink, bear, and other fur-bearing animals then numerous along the San Joaquin River and adjoining sloughs. Evidences of beaver may still be traced along French Camp Slough. The site of the present town of French Camp (SRL 668) was the terminus of the Oregon Trail, used by these trappers from 1832 to 1845. This trail led from the north across the county along a route later followed by the Sutter's Fort–San Jose Trail, over which Frémont passed in 1844. Michel La Framboise, leader of the fur hunters, came annually to French Camp, and James Alexander Forbes, agent for the company after

1836, likewise made many trips to it. As late as 1845 the place was occupied from spring until fall by the Canadians and their families, who had constructed rude cabins of tules and willow brush, many of which were plastered with mud.

Abandoning their camp hurriedly in the summer of 1845, the trappers left their arms buried in a wood-lined hole or cache on a knoll situated one block and a half northeast of the present road through town. Colonel P. W. Noble, who later kept a store at French Camp, told the story of the buried arms, only to be laughed at. The Reynolds brothers, Eldridge, Edward, and James, then children at the French Camp School, took the story seriously enough to dig for the hidden treasure, and uncovered 40 sabers and muskets. This was in 1856 or 1857. Many years later two of the sabers were presented to the Haggin Museum in Stockton. Mrs. Alice B. Maloney made a study of the weapons and concluded that they were in fact sailors' swords left by a 1846 punitive expedition.

Charles M. Weber, a native of Germany, who was later to become the founder of Stockton, stopped at French Camp in the fall of 1841 while on his way into California with the Bidwell-Bartleson party. Weber was much impressed with the fertile, oak-studded lands that bordered the San Joaquin River. Subsequently, in 1842, he settled in Pueblo de San José and soon after went into partnership with William Gulnac, a blacksmith. Gulnac came to California in 1833, perhaps with the French-Canadian trappers, and later married a Mexican woman, after becoming a naturalized Mexican citizen. For a time the two men engaged in merchandising, manufacturing, and ranching at San Jose. In the spring of 1843 they organized a company of twelve men for the purpose of forming a colony at French Camp. In July Gulnac, being a Mexican citizen, petitioned for a grant of land in the region, and in January 1844 he and others received a large tract, which included both French Camp and the site of the later Stockton. This was named Rancho del Campo de los Franceses. The company organized by Weber and Gulnac was the first colony of white settlers to take up lands in the San Joaquin Valley.

In August 1844, under the leadership of Gulnac, the first settlers arrived at Rancho del Campo de los Franceses. One of the company, Thomas Lindsay, built a tule hut on what is now Lindsay Point behind the city hall at the west end of East Lindsay Street in Stockton, the first dwelling (SRL 178) to be erected by an American within the present city limits. However, in the spring of 1845, Lindsay was killed by Indians, his hut was burned, and his stock and tools were stolen.

To encourage other colonists, Gulnac offered a

square mile of land at French Camp to any prospective settler. One of the first to accept the offer was David Kelsey, who, soon after Gulnac's arrival, reached the settlement with his wife and two children from Oregon en route to Pueblo de San José. Stricken with smallpox within a few months, Kelsey died at the Lindsay cabin and was buried near the present southwest corner of El Dorado and Fremont streets in Stockton. Only one member of the family did not contract the disease. This was America, a child whose care in nursing her family unaided places her among the pioneer heroines of California.

The task of inducing settlers to remain on Rancho del Campo de los Franceses was rather difficult, what with its hostile Indians, plague, poor food, and primitive conditions. Before many months Gulnac became disgusted with the project and in April 1845 he sold the entire estate to Weber for $60, the amount of a grocery bill he owed his partner. In order to persuade settlers to come to the region, Weber virtually gave away the major portion of his estate to those who would settle on it. The testimony and influence of dozens of these colonists ultimately forced the land commissioners to recognize Weber's claim to the grant, the whole of which would otherwise have been lost to him.

Stockton

Captain Weber, in 1847, laid out the town of Tuleburg on the south side of the Laguna, later known as the Stockton Channel. The dense tule swamps that then bordered every watercourse fully justified the name. Even the roofs of the first rude huts were thatched with tules. The head of the channel soon came to be known as the Embarcadero, the location of which was about where Weber Avenue now parallels the water. For a time Weber continued to make his home at San Jose, occasionally going to Tuleburg to carry supplies to his vaqueros, who lived in a tule hut on the north side of Stockton Slough. More houses and corrals were built in the spring of 1848, and wheat was planted.

After the discovery of gold at Coloma, Weber organized the Stockton Mining and Trading Company, which operated for a time on Weber Creek in El Dorado County. José Jesús, an Indian chieftain with whom Weber had made a treaty in 1844 and who remained his lifelong friend, sent many of his own tribesmen to work for Weber in the mines. Believing that it would be more profitable to devote all his time to the building of a city that would serve as a supply and shipping center for the southern mines, Weber dissolved his mining company in September 1848 and took up residence in Tuleburg. In the spring of 1849 the town was resur-

veyed and renamed Stockton, in honor of Commodore Robert F. Stockton, whom Weber had met in Los Angeles in 1846 and admired. By November 15, 1849, the first steamboat from San Francisco, the *John A. Sutter*, had arrived and for a few months made weekly contact between that city and Stockton. By the winter of 1849 Stockton had a population of nearly 1,000, and in 1850 it became the county seat of San Joaquin County, having been incorporated on August 15 of that year.

Thousands of Argonauts bound for the southern mines passed through Stockton in the early 1850's. Some came up the river by boat; others traveled over the Livermore Pass from San Jose and crossed the San Joaquin River at Doak and Bonsell's Ferry, located about where the Mossdale Wye on I-5 and SR 120 is today. From Stockton this restless tide of humanity branched out over the various trails leading to the gold fields— the Mariposa, French Camp, Sonora, Mokelumne Hill, and Lockeford roads, all teeming with life and each one leading to a hoped-for El Dorado. Stockton soon became a flourishing center of trade and commerce. Freighting and staging activities developed to enormous proportions, agriculture and stock raising in the vicinity increased, local commerce grew, and the town became a fixed settlement.

The first house built on Weber Point was of adobe. Adjacent to it Weber erected a second dwelling in 1850 or 1851. This was a two-story frame structure, the lumber for which had been brought around Cape Horn. To this house the Captain brought his bride, Helen Murphy, daughter of Martin Murphy, a large landowner in Santa Clara County. The Weber house, surrounded by gardens, was a notable showplace during the 1850's and 1860's. Some time after Weber's death in 1881 it was destroyed by fire, to be replaced by a second frame house built by the family on the southeast corner of the property facing Stockton Channel. This building was moved in 1984 to the San Joaquin County Museum in Micke Grove south of Lodi. The foundation piers that supported the first mansion, which were made of brick brought around the Horn, could long be seen at the original site on Weber Point (SRL 165); the place is now covered by a modern high-rise hotel, a restaurant, and a parking lot, although the spot is marked with a plaque. The Stockton Channel, which borders the old homesite, has been largely cleared of the many old buildings that lined it for a century and more, and it now provides a clean pathway westward to the port of Stockton, which receives oceangoing vessels.

A few of Stockton's early buildings, dating from the 1850's, remained in the old business section until the 1960's, but most of these were destroyed by the redevelopment project encompassing the nine blocks bordered by Weber Avenue and Hunter, Washington, and Commerce streets. Old St. Mary's Catholic Church at 203 East Washington Street was built in 1861 but includes later additions; the parish was established in 1851. Other old public buildings, all of which are on the National Register of Historic Places, include the Weber Primary School at 55 West Flora Street (built in 1873), the Sperry Union Mill Warehouse at 445 West Weber Avenue (built in the 1870's), the Sperry Building at 146 West Weber Avenue (1888), the Tretheway Building at 229 East Weber Avenue (1892), the Bank of Stockton at 301 East Main Street (1908), the ornate Hotel Stockton at El Dorado Street and Weber (1910), the El Dorado Elementary School at 1525 Pacific Avenue (1915), the one-time Commercial and Savings Bank Building at 343 East Main Street (1915), the California Building at 11 South San Joaquin Street (1917), the modest Nippon Hospital, built by the Japanese for their community at 25 South Commerce Street (1917), and the Federal Building at 401 North San Joaquin Street (1933). Private homes that have been placed on the National Register include the home of Benjamin C. Holt at 548 East Park Street, built in the 1860's and now divided into offices, the Moses Rodgers Home at 921 South San Joaquin Street (1890), and the architecturally interesting Wong Mansion at 345 West Clay Street (1921).

Stockton's old cemeteries are of abiding interest. Stockton Rural Cemetery, at the end of Cemetery Lane, was dedicated in August 1862. Among those buried here is David S. Terry, famed for the 1859 duel in San Mateo County in which he killed U.S. Senator David C. Broderick. Judge Terry's violent life came to an end in 1889 at the railroad station in Lathrop, south of Stockton, where he was shot by the bodyguard of Justice Stephen J. Field. Terry had threatened Field because of the latter's decision against Terry's wife and client, Sarah Althea Hill, in her suit for a part of the fortune of her putative husband, William Sharon. Mrs. Terry went insane a few years later and died in the Stockton State Hospital in 1937.

The monument to Reuel Colt Gridley (SRL 801), erected in 1887, marks the grave of a man who raised $275,000 for the Sanitary Commission, Civil War counterpart of the Red Cross, by selling and reselling a sack of flour. Stockton Rural Cemetery also contains the remains of persons originally buried in the city cemetery located on the block bounded by Weber Avenue and Pilgrim, Main, and Union streets. When this cemetery was abandoned in the 1890's, the body of one John Brown was among those left at the old site, since he had no relatives to pay for the move. Brown, known as "Juan Flaco" ("John the Lean"), was California's Paul Revere. In September 1846 he rode 500 miles in five

days on horseback to bring word of the siege of Los Angeles to Commodore Stockton in San Francisco. A marker has been placed (SRL 513) to honor the last resting place of this forgotten hero of California history who died at Stockton in 1859.

Another early cemetery is the Temple Israel Cemetery (SRL 765), located on the block bounded by Acacia, Pilgrim, Poplar, and Union streets. It was given to the Jewish community of Stockton by Captain Weber in 1851 and is the oldest Jewish cemetery in continuous use in California and west of the Rockies.

Even in pioneer days, although life in Stockton was full of gaiety and excitement, cultural development was not neglected. Churches and schools were established as early as 1850, and during the next two decades a number of prosperous private academies existed. Today it is the home of San Joaquin Delta College and the University of the Pacific, the latter of which was transferred to Stockton from San Jose in 1924. The university has sponsored a good deal of California historical study and writing. The Haggin Museum and Art Gallery in Victory Park contain many interesting relics of San Joaquin County's early days. Of particular interest are the displays related to agricultural machinery, primarily the Holt Tractor Works, which ultimately became the Caterpillar Tractor Company and moved out of Stockton in 1921, and the many aspects of the food canning industry.

The Mariposa Road

Leading from Stockton to the southern mines are various roads that were first used during the days of the gold rush. Along these thoroughfares the first settlements outside the city were established; every house was a wayside inn for the accommodation of travelers. The cost of a meal was usually $1.50, the regular menu comprising pork and beans, with bread and coffee.

Dr. L. R. Chalmers, who settled at the site of Collegeville as early as 1850, persuaded the government teams en route to Fort Miller to pass by his ranch, thereby establishing the Mariposa Road, which became the main route to the southern mines. By 1851 the principal stopping places along this road were Chalmers' Ranch, George Kerr's House, the Fifteen Mile House, the Lone Tree House, and Heath and Emory's Ferry, on the Stanislaus River (since 1860 in Stanislaus County). A settlement grew up at Chalmers' Ranch, and because a college was located there from 1866 to 1874, the name of Collegeville became permanently attached to the place. The college was the work of the Cumberland Presbyterian Church; when the three-story frame structure housing it burned in 1874, it was not replaced. At the corner of Mariposa Road and the Jack Tone Road is a remnant of the Collegeville cemetery, no longer used but still cared for by the local Boy Scouts.

The Lone Tree House, built in the early 1850's from lumber brought around the Horn, stood on the W. P. H. Campbell farm until about 1910. The ranch and hotel were purchased in 1854 by Campbell. The site of the hostelry is on Lone Tree Road near the Lone Tree School, about three miles north of Escalon. In the early days the road at this point branched off to the several ferries on the Stanislaus River—Burney's, Cottle's, and Heath and Emory's.

The French Camp Road

During flood years and always during the winter months the Mariposa Road became impassable, a veritable mire of adobe. The stagecoaches and freighters were then routed over the French Camp Road, which had a sandy loam base. This winter traffic made of French Camp an important staging and freighting center during the early 1850's. Boats landed at the end of French Camp Slough, where goods destined for the mining camps were unloaded. In the summer of 1850 Major Richard P. Hammond laid out a town on the site for Charles Weber, calling it Castoria ("place of beavers"). Colonel P. W. Noble and A. Stevinson, who had come to French Camp in August 1849 and who had become agents for the sale of lots in the new town, built a two-story adobe structure in 1850, using it as a hotel and trading post. As late as 1880 the building was occupied as a home by Noble's widow. This hotel, with its broad fields for the pasturage of livestock, was thronged by travelers during the first years of its existence, but its patronage declined when a second hotel, owned by Le Barron and Company, was erected, this hostelry likewise offering extensive pasturage facilities.

During the 1890's, the partnership of C. A. Bachmann and Charles H. W. Brandt was the largest supplier in the United States of chicory, a coffee additive and substitute. The partners had the finest German equipment to roast and grind the chicory and their own vessel, the *Dora*, to ship their product to market. Formed in 1855, their California Chicory Works (SRL 935) operated until 1911 at 1672 West Bowman Road in French Camp.

The principal stopping place on the French Camp Road between French Camp and Heath and Emory's Ferry, and almost the only one in 1852, was the Zinc House, the material for which had been brought around the Horn from New York early in 1850. The Zinc House consisted of one twelve-by-sixteen room with a seven-foot ceiling. The first school in this part of the county

Dutch Point House, near French Camp

was held in the Zinc House, and for many years the school district retained the name of the unique building in which it had its beginning.

On French Camp Road near Union Road stands the Dutch Point house, commemorated by a plaque placed by the Native Daughters of the Golden West in 1957. A public house was erected here in 1849 and was well situated on a roadway with sandy soil that made travel possible in the winter. The two-story brick structure is privately owned.

At Five Corners, the junction of the French Camp, Jack Tone, and Lone Tree roads, stands the Atlanta Women's Club building, built by the Methodists in 1878 as their church. Nearby, on Lone Tree Road, is the old Protestant cemetery. A Catholic cemetery connected with the defunct St. Patrick's Church to the southeast, near Simms, is still in existence.

Pioneer Farmhouses

San Joaquin County is noteworthy for the number of pioneer farmhouses dating from the 1850's and 1860's still owned by descendants of the original builders. Many of these houses are in excellent condition and are occupied by their owners, while others, which have been abandoned for more modern structures, are being allowed to disintegrate. This is especially true of the frame structures built close to the ground without the protection of stone or brick foundations.

Among the historic homesteads found north of the Calaveras River, one of the most interesting is the Dodge house, situated on the bank of the river and the Waterloo Road to Lockeford (SR 88). A few giant oaks, all that are left of the hundreds that once flourished in the region, surround this fine old mansion. John C. Frémont camped near here on March 26, 1844, and noted that "this place is beautiful, with open groves of oak, and a grassy sward beneath, with many plants in bloom." The present Dodge house was built in 1866. Slight alterations have been made on the interior, while the exterior has assumed a rather modern appearance. It is still quite well preserved.

A two-story brick ranch house stands on the Jack Tone Road and the north bank of the Calaveras River about eleven miles northeast of Stockton. John H. (Jack) Tone and two associates came to California as members of the Webb-Audubon party, under the leadership of Colonel Henry J. Webb and John Woodhouse Audubon, youngest son of the famous ornithologist. Most of the party were bound for the gold fields, but Audubon made the trip to gather specimens of birds and mammals. When Colonel Webb deserted his men in the Rio Grande Valley, Audubon was made leader of the party, which after many hardships reached Stockton in December 1849.

Jack Tone and his partners, in the autumn of 1850, settled on the Calaveras River, where they attempted to raise potatoes. Owing to their lack of skill in irrigating, their initial experiment in California ranching resulted in failure, so the three men tried their luck at mining for a time. In 1851, however, they returned to locate permanently on the Calaveras River, where they built a one-story adobe house on the high part of the riverbank about one-half mile west of the present brick house. The three partners were known thereafter as the "Dobey Boys" by the settlers who had meanwhile taken up land about them. This adobe stood for several years after the brick house was erected in 1873. The homestead is today owned and occupied by descendants of Jack Tone, who treasure the stories of pioneer life on the ranch and are especially proud of that part of the *Audubon Journal* that mentions their ancestor. Tone's wife, Alice Walsh Tone, daughter of Nicholas J. Walsh, another of the original Audubon party, aided Maria R. Audubon in the biographical sketch of her father. The house was marked by a plaque placed in front of it by the Native Daughters of the Golden West in 1937.

The J. H. Cole House, which stands just north of Eight Mile Road and half a mile east of SR 88, was erected in 1863. The former McCall house, on the west side of SR 88 about 1.7 miles north of the Jonathan Dodge House, apparently stands on an ancient Indian mound, since many relics have been dug up in the garden from time to time. The original house, which was built by Samuel Martin about 1858, has been incorporated into the present structure.

Many settlers came to the Mokelumne River in 1851 and took up homesteads along the rich river bottoms. Among these was B. F. Langford, a native of Tennes-

see, who became a California state senator in the 1880's. This enterprising pioneer built the picturesque one-story brick house that stands in the midst of orchards and vineyards on the north side of the river due west of Lockeford, on a segment of Woodbridge Road, just west of Tretheway Road. Beyond its walnut orchard on the opposite side of the river is the site of Staples' Ferry.

South of Lodi and back from the corner of Kettelman and Cherokee lanes stands the ten-room David H. Kettelman house, built in 1858 of brick kilned nearby. Kettelman purchased the place soon after it was built and developed an extensive grain and cattle ranch before the town of Lodi came into existence with the railroad in 1869. He was treasurer and chief promoter of the Mokelumne Ditch and Irrigation Company in 1876.

The John Lyman Beecher house is located east of Stockton on Berne Road near the intersection of Alpine and Copperopolis roads. It was erected in 1860 and stands well preserved today, still in the Beecher family. Beecher crossed the plains from Massachusetts during the gold rush, but soon gave up mining in favor of teaming and freighting out of Stockton, and ultimately purchased the large ranch where he lived the rest of his life. His son John L. became a member of the California legislature.

Seventeen miles east of Stockton was the "Oregon Ranch," first settled by George Theyer and David Wells, who built a tule house there in 1848. When traffic began to flow over the Sonora Road to the southern mines the partners opened the "Oregon Tent," the first stopping place along the road, on a site in what is now Farmington. In 1852 Nathaniel Siggons Harrold, a native of Pennsylvania, who had come by ox team to Woods' Creek, Tuolumne County, in November 1849, purchased the Oregon Ranch, and in 1868 he built a large brick house, still standing at the southern limits of Farmington.

In 1850, about three-fourths of a mile west of the Oregon Tent, James Wasley built the Wisconsin House, which later was moved to Peters, where it was used as a boardinghouse until about 1890. The Marietta House, three miles east, and the Texas Tent, four miles west, were other taverns on the Sonora Road in the 1850's. Harrold served as a cook at the latter establishment before purchasing the Oregon Ranch.

A town was laid out on the Oregon Ranch in 1858 by Dr. W. B. Stamper. It is said that he named the place Farmington because it was the center of an extensive and rich farming country.

After passing Simms, the present French Camp Road becomes part of SR 120 and runs about one-half mile north of the course of the early-day thoroughfare. The original road can be traced, however, by the old-fashioned farmhouses surrounded by tall shade trees that stand south of the present highway. On the north side of the highway, three-fourths of a mile east of Simms, is the J. O'Malley homestead, in a thick grove of orange, olive, and walnut trees.

At Park and Pioneer streets in Escalon is the John Jones house, a square, two-story mansion built in 1867 of bricks fired on the place. Jones, a native of North Carolina, came to California with his family in 1852, and at first kept the Blue Tent Tavern on the French Camp Road one mile east of the site of Escalon. In 1855 he purchased the ranch of 160 acres on which the brick mansion was later built. By 1875 Jones had increased the size of his ranch to 7,000 acres, and in addition he owned several thousand acres in other parts of the valley. In 1894 the town of Escalon was laid out on the home ranch by James W. Jones, son of the original owner.

Near the north bank of the Stanislaus River, about five miles southeast of Escalon, a picturesque two-story brick house stands at the bend of Burwood Road off the River Road. It was built in 1868 by Euphrates Monroe. Nearby, also on Burwood Road, is a two-story white frame house, built in 1862, in which Ishmael Monroe lived and kept the Burwood post office, which operated from 1859 to 1898.

Mokelumne River Ferries

John C. Frémont wrote that on March 25, 1844, his men "halted in a beautiful bottom at the ford of the Rio de los Mukelumnes," which received its name from an "Indian tribe living on the river." "The bottoms on the stream," he continued, "are broad, rich, and extremely fertile, and the uplands are shaded with oak groves." Most of these old woodlands have disappeared, having been supplanted by orchards and vineyards. The Indian rancheria, which existed at the ford when the first white settlers came, has likewise vanished, but the site has been fixed on the Langford ranch some 200 yards east of the present brick house by relics unearthed at the spot.

Among the early wayfarers and emigrants who made use of the ford mentioned by Frémont were Captain Weber, on his journeys between Sutter's Fort and Stockton, and the Murphy-Townsend-Stevens party, who in 1844 were the first to drive wagons along the trail and across the stream at this point. The next few years saw increased travel from Sutter's Fort to Pueblo de San José via this route, which soon came to be known as the Sutter's Fort–San Jose Trail. Later it was also known as the Upper Sacramento Road.

Although the first to settle at the ford was Thomas Pyle in November 1846, records show that in 1849 the place was known as Laird's Ferry. That year David J. Staples, J. F. Staples, and W. H. Nichols took up residence there. Organizing a company known as Staples, Nichols and Company, they acquired possession in February 1850 of the ferry, which was thereafter known as Staples' Ferry. In the fall of 1850 the company built a toll bridge—perhaps the first in the county—across the river west of the ferry. The first to cross on the new bridge, so the story goes, was a grizzly bear, which was given free passage without question. A post office was established at Staples' Ferry in 1851, and until 1854 all stagecoach travel to Sacramento passed that way. After that date the route by way of Woods' Ferry (Woodbridge) was used except in times of flood. Staples' Ferry, however, continued to serve travelers for many years—even as late as 1880, although by that time it was known as Miller's Ferry. The site of the old Staples Hotel, built from lumber brought around the Horn in 1850, is on the south side of the river, about two miles west of Lockeford via Locke Road and Tretheway Road. In the former river bed, just south of the present channel, the steamboat *Pert* lies buried under twelve feet of sand.

After crossing the Calaveras River at the Isbell cabin, the Upper Sacramento Road proceeded via Staples' Ferry to Dry Creek, where in 1849 a Mr. Davis established a crossing that he operated for a few years. Turner Elder, one of the first settlers in the county, had erected a log cabin at this point in the fall of 1846. In 1852 the now extinct Liberty City was established there by C. C. Fugitt. Sixteen years later, when the Central Pacific Railroad was under construction, the town was moved one mile south in the hope that it would be made a station on the new line. This dream, however, was never realized, and before long Liberty became a ghost town. Neither townsite is definitely marked today, although the first location can be approximated from the old pioneer cemetery on Liberty Road just west of Elliott Road, about six miles north of Lockeford.

Benedict's Ferry, about halfway between Woods' and Staples' ferries, was established in 1850 by C. L. Benedict, who had a ranch on the north side of the Mokelumne River at this point. In 1852 the government opened a post office at Benedict's Ferry, and during the same year the Bramlett and Langford sawmill was built there.

Benson's Ferry (SRL 149), started in 1849 by Edward Stokes and A. M. Woods, was purchased by John A. Benson in 1850. After the murder of Benson in 1859 by Green C. Palmer, an employee, and the latter's subsequent suicide, E. P. Gayetty, Benson's son-in-law, took over the operation of the ferry. The two-story Gayetty house, built in the 1870's, still stands near the levee

300 yards west of the present bridge. During the flood of 1862 the earlier Benson house was lashed to a large tree that stood nearby, and was thus saved from being washed down the river.

Mokelumne City (SRL 162) was laid out at the junction of the Cosumnes and Mokelumne rivers in 1854 shortly after the Snap brothers had opened a store there. High hopes were cherished that the place might be made the head of navigation and a center of trade for the mines. For a time the town grew and prospered: boats unloaded at the landing; lots were sold; hotels, stores, shops, warehouses, and dwellings were erected. Then came the flood of 1862. The town was submerged, and as many as nineteen houses were swept away by the rushing, swirling river. Mokelumne City never fully recovered from the disaster, although there was some business activity in the place and people continued to live there until 1878, when the townsite was included in the property purchased by the Barber family for a ranch. The hotel was converted into a barn and stood until replaced by the present structure sometime in the 1890's. The site of the town is on an old stretch of road just east of Benson's Ferry, and three miles north of Thornton via the road to Franklin.

Some of the houses of Mokelumne City were removed to other localities, and a few still stand. One of these is the Jesse Thornton house, situated in a dense grove of oak trees at a beautiful spot on the Mokelumne River directly below the present bridge on the road from Thornton to Galt.

Lodi

The town of Lodi was named in 1874, and has always been the heart of a productive agricultural region. In 1907 the town put up a ceremonial arch (SRL 931) at Pine and Sacramento streets in the popular Mission Re-

Ceremonial Arch, Lodi

vival style (others can be seen at Modesto and at Orland) to celebrate the Tokay Carnival of that year. The word "Lodi" and a California bear were added to the arch in 1908; although probably intended to be a temporary embellishment, the arch is still standing and is now a state landmark.

South of town, in Micke Grove, is the San Joaquin County Historical Museum, which emphasizes in an outdoor location the history of agriculture in the county.

Lockeford

Dr. Dean J. Locke, a native of New Hampshire and a graduate of the Harvard Medical School, came to California in 1849 as physician for the Boston and Newton Joint-Stock Association. For a few months he engaged in mining with his brother George at Mississippi Bar on the American River, but in December 1850 they both came to the Mokelumne River, where another brother, Elmer, had already become an enthusiastic settler. The Lockes purchased 360 acres of land from D. J. Staples for one dollar an acre, and in 1851 they erected a log cabin, since destroyed, on a knoll thickly sprinkled with oaks. Grizzly bears were plentiful in those days, and when night came the hired men "roosted high in the trees like turkeys" for fear of them. The cabin site is now occupied by a pleasant modern farmhouse on La Lomita Rancho about half a mile northwest of Lockeford on Elliott Road. This is the site of the state historical marker for Lockeford (SRL 365).

Lockeford was laid out on the D. J. Locke ranch and named in 1859. Its founders envisioned the town as becoming the head of navigation on the Mokelumne River, an ambition that was strengthened when the little pioneer steamer *Pert* tied up to the Lockeford landing in April 1862. Eventually the Mokelumne Steam Navigation Company was organized, and for three or four years it carried on some business. After 1865, however, the mining population gradually scattered, and the coming of the railroad ultimately put an end to all navigation on the Mokelumne.

Dr. Locke was very influential in the development of the new town, and was especially active in organizing schools, churches, and temperance societies. Even before the town was officially laid out, Locke interested himself in the cultural life of the community. On the second floor of his adobe granary, built in 1858 just west of the site of the present brick house, he fitted up a hall for public gatherings, and here the Sons of Temperance was organized. The Congregationalists held services in this building as early as 1861; in 1869 they erected the building on Elliott Road that is now the Grace Church. The first house on the site of Lockeford

Harmony Grove Church, near Lockeford

was a frame structure erected in 1855, and to it Dr. Locke brought his bride that same year. This first house was outgrown in the succeeding years, and in 1865 the front part of the present two-story brick dwelling on Elliott Road was constructed on the same site. The old brick barn also remains.

Luther Locke, father of the Locke brothers, came to California when Dr. Locke returned with his bride. The following year he built himself a home, a frame structure, in which the first store in Lockeford was opened in 1862. The post office, established in 1861, was located in this building, with Luther Locke as the first postmaster. This landmark, long known as the "White House," stands, very much remodeled, at the northeast corner of Main Street and Elliott Road.

The Harmony Grove Church is a beautiful old brick church a mile and a half southwest of Lockeford on Locke Road. This first and oldest Protestant church in San Joaquin County was built in 1859. Abandoned in 1912, the building was handsomely restored by the Lockeford-Clements Women's Club and rededicated in 1973. Two old cemeteries flank the building. The area is now Harmony Grove County Park.

Four miles northeast of Lockeford is the little town of Clements. One mile north of here near what is now Stillman L. Magee County Park stood the Lone Star Mill (SRL 155) on the Mokelumne River. To this site the Bramlett and Langford sawmill, built near Benedict's Ferry in 1852, was removed in 1854 by the new proprietors, David S. Terry and a man named Hodge. Terry was raised in Texas, and named his mill after the Lone Star state. In 1855 Hodge and Terry added a flour mill. The establishment was destroyed by fire in 1856 and rebuilt on the same site. S. L. Magee bought the Lone Star Mill

in 1860 and continued to operate it until its abandonment about 1885. The present site of Clements was purchased by Thomas Clements from David S. Terry in 1871.

Woodbridge

The first permanent settlers in the vicinity of Woodbridge were George W. Emerson and Ross C. and J. P. Sargent, all from New England. When they arrived in 1850, it is said that they found huts of rived oak left by Hudson's Bay Company trappers. In 1852 Jeremiah H. Woods and Alexander McQueen established a ferry across the Mokelumne River at this point, about where the present bridge and dam span the stream, with the result that before long a new road from Stockton to Sacramento was routed by way of Woods' Ferry. After 1854 the stages that had formerly traveled via Staples' Ferry on the Upper Sacramento Road adopted this more direct route. In 1858 Woods, a very energetic and enterprising man, built a bridge at the site of the ferry (SRL 163), which for years was known as Woods' Bridge. From it the town, which was laid out on the south side of the river in 1859, took the name Woodbridge. For several years the place showed considerable activity, but with the death of Jeremiah Woods in 1864 Woodbridge lost its chief promoter.

Several of the early houses and business buildings

Masonic Hall, Woodbridge

are still to be found at Woodbridge (SRL 358); no markers have been placed for this and the previous landmark sites. On the main street is the I.O.O.F. building, a two-story brick structure, the lower part of which was built in the early 1860's, while the upper story dates from 1874. The older portion was at first the Lavinsky store; later, for a time, it served as a school. The Masonic Hall was built in 1882. A pioneer cemetery contains the grave of William Lewis Manly, hero of the rescue of the Death Valley '49ers.

The Woodbridge Academy, a two-story frame structure erected in the winter of 1878–79 under the leadership of Professor S. L. Morehead, was taken over by the United Brethren in 1881, when it became known as the San Joaquin Valley College (SRL 520). As such it continued to function until the beginning of the twentieth century, when it was superseded by the public grammar school. Today another school building occupies the site on Lilac Street.

The Mokelumne Hill Road

In 1850, seventeen public houses, all located within a distance of 24 miles from Stockton, lined Mokelumne Hill Road, now the Linden Road or SR 26. None of these remains today. The town of Linden, which was laid out in 1862, had its beginnings in the little community that grew up around the Fifteen Mile House. This tavern had been established by Dr. W. D. Treblecock in the fall of 1849. Some years later, C. C. Rynerson erected a flour mill in the vicinity. Soon after, John and James Wasley, cousins of Treblecock, and later brothers-in-law to Rynerson, joined the group and were founders of the town. John Wasley named the new settlement, presumably after his old home at Linden, Ohio. The Rynerson flour mill was destroyed by fire in 1865 and was replaced by a second structure, which met a like fate in 1868. A three-story brick mill, erected in 1871 but no longer used as such, now occupies the site.

San Joaquin and Stanislaus River Crossings

In pioneer days river crossings were important points in the San Joaquin Valley, and it was on the various watercourses that the earliest settlements were planned. Among these first attempts at colonization was New Hope (SRL 436), later known as Stanislaus City, established on the Stanislaus River in November 1846 by a party of Mormons under the leadership of Samuel Brannan. About twenty colonists came up the San Joaquin River in the sailing launch *Comet*, landing on the east branch near the site at which John Doak

and Jacob Bonsell established a ferry two years later. From this point the party proceeded overland to a spot previously selected by Brannan on the north bank of the Stanislaus River one and a half miles from the river's mouth.

By the beginning of 1847 a promising beginning had been made: three log houses had been erected, a crudely improvised sawmill was at work, and 80 acres of grain had been sown. But the stormy winter brought rains and floods, the colonists fell to quarreling among themselves, and by the summer of 1847 only one man remained; he too soon left. The discovery of gold brought an attempt to reestablish a settlement at Stanislaus City; its name is found on a map published in 1851, which also indicated that the road from Stockton to Tuolumne City crossed the Stanislaus River at that point. Nothing, however, came of Sam Brannan's "new hope." A monument commemorating New Hope stands at Ripon, six miles northeast of the site. A similar marker indicating the landing place of the *Comet* (SRL 437) is located on SR 120, west of Manteca near the San Joaquin River.

After attempts to establish Stanislaus City failed, a settlement was started on the west side of the San Joaquin River a little below the mouth of the Stanislaus. Hoping to become a rival of Stockton, San Joaquin City (SRL 777), as it was called, persisted for a number of years. As late as 1880 it had a hotel, a warehouse, and two saloons, as well as stores and homes. Nothing but a historic plaque marks the location today, although the name still appears on modern road maps. North of the site a bridge crosses the river in the vicinity of the old Durham Ferry crossing, established by Titus and Manly in 1850 and later owned by Durham and Fisk. Durham Ferry State Recreational Area commemorates the name.

The first ferry to be operated on the San Joaquin River was that of John Doak and Jacob Bonsell, who in 1848 began to convey passengers in a small yawl across the river at a spot located about where the Southern Pacific Railroad and I-5 cross today. It was here that the old Sutter's Fort–San Jose Trail crossed the river. Traffic to the mines soon grew so heavy that it became necessary to have a larger and more substantial ferryboat, so Doak went to Corte Madera in Marin County, where he built the new craft. With their increased carrying facilities, the partners did an enormous business, reaping equally large returns, for charges on this pioneer ferry were high—one dollar for men on foot, three dollars for men on horseback, and eight dollars for horses and wagons. In 1852, however, Doak sold his share in the business to Hiram Scott, and later in the same year Bonsell died. With the subsequent marriage of Bonsell's widow to James A. Shepherd, the ferry became known as Shepherd's Ferry and was so called until 1856, when it was sold to William T. Moss. The place is still referred to as Mossdale.

The Mossdale area acquired additional historical importance with the construction of the railroad bridge (SRL 780.7) across the San Joaquin River in September 1869, thus completing the transcontinental railroad from the San Francisco Bay Area to Sacramento. Laying of track proceeded from either end until the two parties met at the river, making Mossdale a lesser counterpart of Promontory, Utah, where the Central Pacific and Union Pacific had met on May 10 of the same year.

Corral Hollow

Corral Hollow (SRL 755) may be reached over the Corral Hollow Road, County Road J-2, southwest of Tracy. Many Indian relics, including arrowheads, pestles, and beautifully shaped bowls, have been uncovered along the dry bed of the arroyo, indicating the probable existence of a former Indian encampment in the vicinity. Petrified cedar, as well as fossil leaves and shells, have been found in the arroyo and in the neighboring hills. In early days the hollow was known as El Arroyo de los Buenos Aires, through which an old Spanish trail, El Camino Viejo, ran. According to Bolton, Juan Bautista de Anza passed that way in April 1776. Later, Spanish and Mexican vaqueros made customary use of the trail, along which they drove their herds of cattle. Still later, during the gold days, the old trail was much traveled as a road to the southern mines.

One of the first white settlers in the hollow was Edward B. (Ned) Carrell, who in 1850 took up government land there. For many years it was believed that "Corral Hollow" was a corruption of "Carrell's Hollow," but Carrell's diaries prove this to be untrue. Probably the hollow was named for a corral built there in early days for captured wild horses.

Down on the arroyo among the cottonwoods, directly on the line of the old Spanish trail, Carrell and three associates, Horatio P. Wright, William Breyton, and John A. Stockholm, built, under the leadership of Wright, a tavern called the "Zink House" where the buildings of the present sheep ranch stand. Here for several years meals and liquor were served to wayfarers. A famous visitor at Zink House was James Capen Adams, or, as he was popularly known, "Grizzly" Adams. With his two bears, "Lady Washington" and "Ben Franklin," and his dog, "Rambler," famous actors in Adams's "Mountaineer Museum" in San Francisco, he spent several months in 1855 hunting in the region, his experiences afterward figuring in Theodore Hittell's biographical narrative.

In 1856 John O'Brien, a sheepman who had established his camp in Corral Hollow, discovered an outcropping of a black mineral at the upper end of the canyon about nine miles from the Zink House, which when tested proved to be coal. The Pacific Coal Mining Company was subsequently organized, and this became, in turn, the Commercial Mine and the Eureka Mine.

When Carrell, the only surviving owner of the Eureka Coal Company, died in 1880 at his homestead in the hollow, John and James Treadwell of the Bears' Nest Mine in Alaska purchased the Corral Hollow coal property, naming it the Tesla Mine in honor of Nikola Tesla, the great electrical inventor. During the early 1890's, under the management of the San Francisco and San Joaquin Coal Company, the yield from the Tesla Mine averaged 500 tons of coal daily. From six to ten carloads were shipped each day over the Alameda and San Joaquin, a branch railroad to Stockton, where the coal was transferred to river boats bound for San Francisco.

About this time the Treadwells built a brick and pottery plant two miles down the gulch at Walden Spur on their railroad. Later they built a larger plant four miles down the gulch and organized it as the Carnegie Brick and Pottery Company to manufacture white glazed firebrick. Carnegie (SRL 740) became a town of some 2,000 inhabitants and flourished until 1906, when the earthquake and the failure of the California Safe Deposit Bank in San Francisco ruined the Treadwells financially and caused the abandonment of Carnegie. A great boiler explosion in 1907 and, finally, the floods of 1911, which washed out the railroad, sealed its doom.

The state marker at Carnegie has been vandalized. The area behind it is now Carnegie State Vehicular Recreation Area, which extends westward into a small area of Alameda County.

Southeast of Carnegie, just above the site of the former Camp Thomas of the Hetch Hetchy project, is a manganese mine, first developed by Aurelius Ladd in 1863. During World War I, interest again centered on this mine, when about $80,000 was recovered from the tailings. It was worked again during World War II and the Korean War.

San Luis Obispo County

San Luis Obispo County is named for the Mission of St. Louis, Bishop of Toulouse. It is one of the 27 original counties and was established on February 18, 1850. The city of San Luis Obispo, site of the mission, has always been the county seat.

Unamuno and Cermeño

The coast of San Luis Obispo County was first seen by white men in 1542, but there is no evidence that the Cabrillo expedition landed at any point within the present county. At least two Manila galleon captains, however, paid brief visits. In 1587 Pedro de Unamuno brought his ship into Morro Bay and, according to Henry R. Wagner, penetrated inland about to the present city of San Luis Obispo. Possession was taken in the name of the king of Spain, and a cross was erected. The first Indians encountered by the party were extremely timid, but later the Spaniards were caught off guard by an Indian attack in which two of the explorers were killed and several others wounded. Eight years later Sebastián Rodríguez Cermeño, returning to Mexico in an open launch after the loss of his galleon *San Agustín* at what is today called Drake's Bay, put in at San Luis Obispo Bay. The hungry crew traded with the Indians, who, they recorded, shouted "Cristianos" and "Mexico," evidently memories of their contact with Unamuno. It is probable that Vizcaíno, who named the Santa Lucia Mountains, entered the same bay in 1602.

The Portolá Trail

The present Oso Flaco (Lean Bear) Lake, situated near the coast in southwestern San Luis Obispo County, was so named by the soldiers of Gaspar de Portolá's expedition on September 3, 1769, when a very lean bear was killed near their camp on the shore of the lake. On the 4th, a halt was made in Price Canyon north of Pismo Beach, and on the 5th, one in San Luis Canyon, where the party rested on the 6th. Again the tents were pitched on the 7th, this time at the lower end of Los Osos Creek, where the soldiers spent the day replenishing their food supply with bear meat. This was the occasion for naming the valley La Cañada de los Osos (the Canyon of the Bears), a name it retains today.

Morro Rock (SRL 821), a navigational marker for centuries, stands just off the coast at Morro Bay, and at a location within the present town of Morro Bay and in sight of Morro Rock, camp was made on September 8. Again the expedition was halted on the 9th, at Ellysly Creek just east of Point Estero. Continuing up Ellysly Creek and over Dawson Grade, the band stopped on the 10th somewhat south of present Cambria; and on the 11th, at Little Pico Creek east of San Simeon Point. The following day the party went inland over the hills and stopped above Arroyo de la Cruz. Reaching Ragged Point on San Carpojo Creek on September 13, Portolá found that further progress up the coast was barred by steep mountain precipices. The 14th and 15th were spent in preparing a trail over a most difficult pass by way of San Carpojo Creek to its junction with Dutra Creek, where camp was made on the 16th. On the 17th the march was resumed over very rough country to Wagner Creek, within the present confines of Monterey County.

Three years later Pedro Fages, who had been a leader on the Portolá trek and was now commander of the Presidio of Monterey, had good reason to recall La Cañada de los Osos. The unpredictable supply ships had failed to reach the presidio, and near-famine conditions prevailed there and at Mission San Antonio de Padua. Fages organized California's greatest grizzly bear hunt and, with thirteen soldiers, was able to supply the settlements for months.

The Anza Trail

As far as the site of Mission San Luis Obispo, Juan Bautista de Anza passed over practically the same trail in San Luis Obispo County as Portolá had before him in 1769. The Southern Pacific Railroad follows much the same route today. From the mission, Anza crossed the Santa Lucia Range through Cuesta Pass over the present route of US 101. Continuing along its course to Paso Robles, he turned northwest over the hills along Oak Flat Road (Paso de los Robles) to San Marcos Creek. There the road went almost due north to the Nacimiento River about at Rancho Nacimiento and proceeded to the first crossing of the San Antonio River, about at King Well, now in Monterey County.

On Anza's first trip, in 1774, two stops were made in San Luis Obispo County, one at the mission on April 15, and a second at the Nacimiento River on April 16. On his second trip, in 1776, as leader of the San Francisco colonists, he camped at the following places: the Indian village of El Buchon, in Price Canyon two miles north of Pismo Beach, on March 1; Mission San Luis Obispo on March 2 and 3; and La Asunción, a short distance north of Atascadero, on March 4.

Mission San Luis Obispo de Tolosa

Mission San Luis Obispo de Tolosa was founded by Padre Junipero Serra on September 1, 1772, while on his journey from Monterey to Mexico. Since no other priest was available at the time, Father José Cavaller was left in sole charge of the new post, contrary to the rule that two priests must be stationed at each mission. He continued to serve there until his death in 1789.

The first attempt to manufacture tile in California was made at San Luis Obispo, after the buildings, thatched with tule, had been three times badly damaged by fire. The first of these disasters occurred in November 1776, when hostile Indians shot burning arrows into the roofs. This first experiment in tile making proved successful, and after 1784 all the missions used this method of roofing. At San Luis Obispo an adobe church, completed in 1794, replaced the original chapel.

Mission San Luis Obispo de Tolosa

The mission (SRL 325), at 782 Monterey Street, is now an active parish church in the city of San Luis Obispo. Alterations and makeshift restorations over the years included the boarding over of crumbling walls and the erection of an incongruous steeple, which has since been removed. Since 1934, efforts have been made to restore the mission and some adjoining buildings to their earlier aspect. Plans were made by the city in 1961 to preserve the creek area before the mission and to make an open plaza. This has been achieved,

and the mission today stands in one of the most attractive urban developments in California.

A small historical museum is located in one of the adjoining buildings of the mission.

San Luis Obispo

San Luis Obispo was organized as a town in 1856 and incorporated as a city in 1876. Some beautiful old buildings have been preserved in the downtown area. Outstanding among them is the Pierre Hyppolite Dallidet adobe (SRL 720) on San Luis Obispo Creek at 1185 Pacific Street. This was the home of a French vineyardist who came to the area in 1853. His son Paul presented the old residence and gardens to the San Luis Obispo Historical Society in 1953, in memory of a family that had lived there for a century. The home and gardens are open to the public. Adjoining this is the Ramona Depot, put up in 1889 and moved to its present location in 1980, with its display of old horse-drawn street cars. A marker by the nearby creek notes that this was the first source of water for the mission.

Among the other adobes in San Luis Obispo are the Hays home at 642 Monterey Street, the Simmler adobe in a lovely garden at 466 Dana Street, and the Fisher adobe at 883 Nipomo Street. The Andrews adobe (Casa

Ah Louis Store, San Luis Obispo

de Lobo), built for the mayordomo of the mission, is a wood-sided structure at 1451 Andrew Street. The old Sauer home at 964 Chorro Street and the neighboring art gallery at 970 are old adobes, wood-fronted today. At the end of Lizzie Street, somewhat isolated in a thicket of eucalyptus trees, is the two-story Quintana adobe.

San Luis Obispo's urban history has been rather leisurely, and perhaps as a result, several old downtown business buildings are still in use. These include the Sinsheimer store at 849 Monterey Street and Kluver's cigar factory (1897), now a restaurant, at 726 Higuera Street. The Ah Louis Store (SRL 802) at 800 Palm Street was the first Chinese store in the county. It was established in 1874, and the present iron-shuttered brick store was completed ten years later. In addition to selling herbs and general merchandise, the place also served as a bank and post office for the numerous Chinese laborers employed in digging railroad tunnels through Cuesta Pass in the 1880's and 1890's. Ah Louis died in 1916 in his 99th year.

The San Luis Obispo County Historical Museum is located in the former City Public Library at 696 Monterey Street. The building was erected in 1904 with a Carnegie grant. Among the museum's collections are materials relating to the local Chumash Indians, the history of the coast, and the history of ranching in the county.

Mission San Miguel Arcángel

Mission San Miguel Arcángel (SRL 326) was founded July 25, 1797, by Father Fermín Francisco de Lasuén, assisted by Father Buenaventura Sitjar. It was located on a beautiful spot on the Salinas River where there was plenty of water for irrigation. Some of the canals and dams built by the fathers for irrigating their orchards and crops may still be seen around the mission.

The first temporary wooden buildings were gradually replaced, from 1799 to 1804, by adobe structures. Fire almost destroyed the entire establishment in 1806, and plans were made for reconstruction on a more spacious scale. The church building that was begun in 1816 and completed in 1818 still stands. Secularization took place in 1836, followed by confiscation and neglect. In 1859, the mission was returned to the church, and in 1878 a resident priest took up his office. The principal church building was restored, and services are now held there by the Franciscan Fathers, who maintain the old place as a novitiate. It is one of four California missions still in the hands of the Franciscan order.

San Miguel remains less spoiled by restoration than

Mission San Miguel Arcángel

most of the missions, and contains perhaps the finest examples of the original decorations done by the Indians under the supervision of the fathers, and, in this case, under the particular direction of Estévan Munras of Monterey. Great rafters and corbels hewn from solid trees, carried by Indians 40 miles from the mountains, support the ceiling, and all are colored in light green, pink, blue, and white. The walls are designed to represent fluted pillars tinted in blue, while between these are conventionalized designs of leaves and carved figures. A frieze in reddish brown represents a gallery with railings and pillars. The pulpit, also decorated and colored by the Indians, the confessional built into the adobe wall, the floor of burnt brick laid in alternate rows of squares and oblongs, all remain as they were when first completed with such loving care by the padres and their charges. The monastery with its beautiful low-arched corridor, which extends from the side, is unique in the fact that its arches are of different sizes.

Rios-Caledonia Adobe and Estrella Church

At the south end of the town of San Miguel is the Rios-Caledonia adobe (SRL 936). Petronillo Ríos built this imposing two-story building with Indian labor in 1846. The roof was of handmade tiles and the rafters of pine poles tied in place with strips of rawhide. In time the place passed to George Butchart, who made the building an inn and stage stop and gave it the name "Caledonia," which, he claimed, was a Scots word for "welcome." The coming of the railroad put the stagecoaches out of business, and eventually the Caledonia closed its doors, becoming a private home. Charles Dorries purchased it in 1923 and endeavored to preserve as much of it as he could, but illness and advancing age defeated him, and after his death in 1962 the abandoned structure became the prey of vandals and time. In 1968 a new group called the Friends of the

Rios-Caledonia Adobe, San Miguel

Adobe was organized to save and preserve the building, and after great efforts, the restored adobe was opened to the public in December 1972. It is an excellent example of how the dedication of a small group of people can have good results in historical preservation.

A few miles to the southeast, another old building has come under the care of the Friends of the Adobe. The Estrella Adobe Church (SRL 542) was the first Protestant church in northern San Luis Obispo County. It was built through the cooperation of members of several denominations in 1878. It was restored by the efforts of the Paso Robles Women's Club with the assistance of boys from the California Youth Authority and rededicated in 1952. Located on Airport Road just north of the Paso Robles airport, it is about four miles northeast of Paso Robles.

The Asistencia of Santa Margarita

The Asistencia of Santa Margarita (SRL 364), belonging to Mission San Luis Obispo, was an outpost, or chapel and storehouse, located north of the mission and across steep Cuesta Pass. It was built of stone on a knoll near Santa Margarita Creek, where there lived many Indians whom the padres hoped to enroll as converts. The few ruins of the building may be seen about one-quarter mile west of the town of Santa Margarita, between US 101 and SR 58. A visitor to this place in 1831, while the building was still intact, was Alfred Robinson, who wrote: "We reached 'El Rancho de Santa Rita,' a place used for the cultivation of grain, where, on an eminence that overlooked the grounds, an extensive building was erected. It was divided into store-rooms for different kinds of grain, and apartments for the accommodation of the mayor-domo, servants, and wayfarers. At one end was a chapel, and snug lodging-rooms for the priest who, I was informed, frequently came and passed some weeks at the place during the time of harvest; and the holy friars of the two missions occasionally met there to acknowledge to each other their sins."

Ranchos of Senator Hearst (San Simeon and Cambria)

The ranchos of Piedra Blanca, San Simeon, and Santa Rosa became the property of Senator George W. Hearst. The three stretch along the Pacific from the mouth of San Carpojo Creek southeast to the mouth of Villa Creek and extend far back into the hills.

Rancho Piedra Blanca is the farthest north. It was granted in 1840 to José de Jesús Pico, a former soldier at Monterey. Shortly after receiving this grant he was administrator of San Miguel Mission. Although at one time he was arrested by Frémont and condemned to death, he was pardoned at the intercession of a band of women and children led by Doña Ramona Carrillo de Wilson, wife of Captain John Wilson. Pico afterward became a devoted friend of Frémont and assisted him in bringing about the Treaty of Cahuenga. In 1848 and again in 1849 he made successful trips to the gold mines but later spent his time on his rancho.

Mariano Pacheco purchased a portion of Rancho Piedra Blanca from Pico, and until the 1870's his family lived in the adobe house overlooking the ocean and located about three miles north of the town of San Simeon. Don Mariano was buried in the vicinity. After the departure of the Pacheco family, the extensive two-story adobe was used by tenants until about 1906. Its foundations, marked by a few old cypress trees, are hidden in a tangle of weeds on a hill in what is now a cattle pasture.

The town of San Simeon, which lies on this rancho, was for many years the center of an extensive whaling industry. As early as 1864 Captain Joseph Clark, still active in the 1880's, had a fleet of five boats outfitted for whaling. Many years ago a fire wiped out a large part of the little town, but a few old frame buildings still stand. Sebastian's store (SRL 726), built in the 1860's one-half mile to the west and moved to its present location in 1878, is the oldest store building along the northern coast of San Luis Obispo County. The store and the adjacent post office are still in business. There is also a warehouse built in 1878 by the Hearst interests and bearing the date of its construction. A little farther from the wharf are red-tiled, stucco residences built in more recent times by William Randolph Hearst for his employees.

Up the road behind the town is the large frame ranch house of Senator George Hearst, built soon after he purchased Rancho Piedra Blanca in 1865. It is still the headquarters for the Hearst cattle ranch. This building can be seen from the bus that transports tourists through the private ranch property to Hearst–San Simeon State Historical Monument (SRL 640) on a commanding height overlooking San Simeon Bay.

Here, from 1919 to 1947, William Randolph Hearst, newspaper magnate and son of Senator George and Phoebe Apperson Hearst, created La Cuesta Encantada (The Enchanted Hill) at a cost of millions of dollars. Together with his architect, Julia Morgan, he planned the Spanish Renaissance buildings where he lived and operated his vast empire, entertaining famous guests from far and near, including Calvin Coolidge, Winston Churchill, George Bernard Shaw, and a multitude of motion picture personalities. The main residence, La Casa Grande, has four floors with scores of rooms and twin towers housing carillon bells. The vast structure was never finished. There are also three guest cottages, each a mansion in itself with between ten and eighteen rooms. Casa del Mar faces the Pacific, Casa del Monte the ridges of the Santa Lucia Range, and Casa del Sol the setting sun. The buildings and the grounds are filled with art objects collected by Hearst all over the world. The warehouses at San Simeon contain treasures destined for the castle but still in the packing crates in which they were shipped from European monasteries and palaces. Hearst transplanted exotic trees to his hilltop castle and even established a private zoo. There are both indoor and outdoor swimming pools. Hearst died in 1951 at the age of 88, and in 1958 the Hearst Corporation presented the castle and about 125 acres of surrounding land to the state of California to be opened to the public as a memorial to William Randolph Hearst and his mother, Phoebe Apperson Hearst. The site is also listed as a National Historic Landmark.

Southeast of Rancho Piedra Blanca lies Rancho San Simeon, through which flows San Simeon Creek. This was a grant of one square league made to José Ramón Estrada, son of José Mariano Estrada, and patented to José Miguel Gómez in 1865, shortly before Senator Hearst acquired the property. The San Simeon adobe, gone long ago, was on San Simeon Creek back from the beach about three-quarters of a mile.

The farthest south of the three ranchos is Rancho Santa Rosa, a three-league grant made to Julián Estrada, son of José Ramón Estrada, and patented to him in 1865. The Estrada adobe stood on the road north of Swallow Rock at an elevation of 130 feet; nothing remains to indicate the site. The town of Cambria, first called Rosaville, was located on the property. It originated during the copper excitement of 1863 and was aided in its growth by the quicksilver prospecting of 1871 and by the activities of lumbermen.

Rancho Moro y Cayucos (Cayucos)

Cayuco is a nautical term applied to a small fishing boat that is like a canoe and often made of skins. A point on the coast of San Luis Obispo County that was early used as a port was called by that name because the schooners, pausing offshore from the mouth of a small stream, had commerce with the land by means of these small boats. The creek, the little settlement that grew up near its mouth, and eventually the land nearby were all known by that name.

In 1842, Rancho Moro y Cayucos was granted to Martin Olivera, from Rancho Sausal in Monterey County, and to Vicente Feliz, former mayordomo of another rancho. It was later owned by James McKinley, a Scottish sailor, who married Carmen Amesti, daughter of José Amesti of Rancho Corralitos. McKinley sold it in smaller tracts for dairy farms.

In 1867 this coastal region was served by a weekly stage running from San Luis Obispo to San Simeon. In this year James Cass came to the vicinity of Cayucos Landing and lived first in the hills just behind the settlement, but soon he built a large house that still stands on Ocean Avenue at C Street near Cayucos Creek in the town of Cayucos. He became a leader in the community; in 1870 he built a wharf, and soon afterward a store and warehouse. The broad streets of the town were laid out in 1875, and in the early 1880's a stage bringing passengers from San Miguel and way stations made connections with a weekly boat at Cayucos.

For many years considerable shipping was done from here, but finally a storm destroyed a large part of the pier and motor transportation eliminated the need of steamer calls. Only a small pleasure wharf is now on the site of the wharf built by Captain Cass.

Rancho San Bernardo (Morro Bay)

Vicente Cané (Canet), a Spanish sailor, settled in Alta California before 1828. In 1840 he received a grant of one square league of land lying between San Bernardo and Morro creeks, both of which empty into Morro Bay. The following year Don Vicente was a magistrate at Mission San Luis Obispo. His rancho home was built about that time on a hill above San Bernardo Creek two miles east of Morro Rock. Privately owned, it still stands on the north side of SR 1, to the east of a junction with San Bernardo Creek Road. One and one-quarter miles beyond the Canet adobe, toward San Luis

Obispo, Canet Road leads half a mile to the old family cemetery.

Farther east on SR 1, one mile east of Cuesta College and on the outskirts of the city of San Luis Obispo, is Camp San Luis Obispo, the original home of the California National Guard.

Los Osos Valley

John Wilson, Scottish shipmaster and captain of the *Ayacucho*, who had engaged in trading for years on the coast, settled in California and married Ramona Carrillo de Pacheco. Señora Pacheco owned Rancho Suey and was a widow with two sons, one of whom, Romualdo Pacheco, afterward held many high offices in the state and is the only man of Hispanic origin to serve as governor (1875) since the American conquest. About 1839 Captain Wilson and James Scott, another native of Scotland, entered into a business partnership that continued for several years. Rancho Cañada del Chorro, on the southwest side of the Santa Lucia Range, consisting of 3,167 acres, was granted to them. James Scott died in 1851 and Captain Wilson in 1860, so the patent to it was issued to Wilson's heirs in 1861.

The Cañada de los Osos, so named by Portolá's men in 1769 because of the bears they killed here for food, was a part of the Rancho Cañada de los Osos y Peche y Islay. Once owned by Scott and Wilson (after some earlier and short-lived grants), this too became Wilson's property. Between Rancho El Chorro and Rancho Cañada de los Osos, an Indian named Romualdo cultivated a bit of level land at the base of Cerro Romualdo. This tract of 117 acres was purchased by Captain Wilson and called Huerta (vegetable garden) de Romualdo.

Captain Wilson built an adobe house in the Cañada de los Osos and lived there from 1845 until his death. His widow continued to live there with her son, by then a rising figure in governmental affairs. The property afterward passed to her daughter. What is left of the old house is now a barn on a ranch to the east of Turri Road at a point half a mile north of Los Osos road, about eight miles west of San Luis Obispo via Los Osos Road.

Rancho San Miguelito (Avila Beach)

Rancho San Miguelito lay along the shore of San Luis Obispo Bay with a further shoreline extending northwest along the ocean almost to Pecho Creek. On this rancho an outpost of Mission San Luis Obispo was maintained for a time, and along the valley of the San Luis Obispo River the padres tended fields of corn and beans. The outpost stood near the present town of Avila Beach.

Miguel Ávila, born in Santa Barbara and educated in San Francisco, was a soldier and copyist at Monterey; in 1824 he was a corporal of the guard at Mission San Luis Obispo. One day at the mission, Father Luís Martínez (who appears in Helen Hunt Jackson's *Ramona*) harshly reproved him in the presence of a group of Indians for talking with an Indian at the rancheria. Both padre and corporal apparently became angry; this gave rise to curses and threats of excommunication. The corporal called the soldiers, and the padre rang the bell to call all his assistants and neophytes. "The two forces," so a tale goes, "faced each other in battle array, armed on one side with guns and lances, and on the other with book, holy water, and cross. Martínez began to read and Ávila seized the book, thinking thus to escape damnation; but the padre went on, finished the rite in bad Latin from memory, and retired in triumph to the church." The matter, later sent to the *comandante*, was compromised, and the excommunication of the corporal was annulled.

In 1826, two years after the trouble with the padre, Miguel Ávila married María Inocenta, daughter of Dolores Pico, who was then in charge of Rancho Nacional. He lived in Monterey with his increasing family.

Don Miguel obtained the grant of San Miguelito in three pieces by 1846, and in 1845 he obtained the use of another part of the mission lands, Rancho Laguna, although this was patented in 1859 to Bishop J. S. Alemany. In 1849 Don Miguel was alcalde at San Luis Obispo. In his later years he became interested in the preservation of documents, but the large collection that he kept in his house was lost when that building was destroyed by fire. Avila Beach (formerly Avila) nearby is named in his honor.

Cave Landing

Cave Landing is situated on San Luis Obispo Bay about one-half mile east of Avila Beach, and can be reached from the freeway via Cave Landing Road off Avila Beach Road. The fathers used this landing place for shipping tallow and grain. A pathway leads down to the beach where one can see Arch Rock and the mouth of Robbers' Cave, named in the popular belief that it was a hiding place for contraband. Between Arch Rock and Robbers' Cave is tiny Moonstone Beach, so called from the moonstones among the pebbles and shells washed up by the waves.

From the white sands of Moonstone Beach one may climb over the rocks, ducking through tunnels made by the sea, until, rounding a corner, one comes suddenly upon an immense level rock that juts out 150 feet into deep water and beneath which the tide swirls. This is Cave Landing, an excellent natural pier for deep-sea fishermen. Here Indians fished for hundreds of years and buried their dead in crude graves along the rugged cliffs facing the east. After them came a romantic procession of smugglers and bandits, priests and sea captains.

About 1860, David Mallagh, an Irish sea captain, erected a warehouse on the cliffs above the sea, with a long wooden chute leading down to the water. Huge iron spikes, with immense rings of iron fastened to them, were driven into the solid rock at the top of the cliff. To the rings the great ship cables were fastened. For a decade, Captain Mallagh handled all of the shipping at the cove and hauled passengers and freight to San Luis Obispo. After his death and the advent of the railroad, which reached San Luis Obispo in 1894, Cave Landing was abandoned. The place is still a haven for beach-lovers and hikers.

Ranchos of Francis Ziba Branch
(Pismo Beach, Arroyo Grande)

Francis Ziba Branch, a native of New York, arrived in California with the Wolfskill party in 1831. For a few years he made his home at Santa Barbara, where he kept a store and boardinghouse, leaving occasionally to hunt otter. In 1835 he married Manuela, daughter of Zefarino Carlón, a soldier of the Santa Barbara Company. In 1837 Branch received a grant of over 16,000 acres of land lying to the north of Santa Barbara and named it Rancho Santa Manuela.

When Branch moved to his rancho, which was situated in the Arroyo Grande Valley, Mission San Luis Obispo about thirteen miles to the north was almost the only community in the entire region that was inhabited by white men. The valley that lay in front of his home was an impenetrable swamp—a thicket of willow and cottonwood trees where wildcats, lions, and grizzly bears lived. His stock was often attacked by wild animals and sometimes by the Tulare Indians from the east.

Five years after Branch received his rancho, his father-in-law, Don Zefarino, obtained an adjoining grant of one square league named the Arroyo Grande but frequently called the Ranchita. It lay along the headwaters of the Arroyo Grande and was later patented to his son-in-law.

At the lower end of the Arroyo Grande Valley was Rancho Pismo, two leagues granted to José Ortega in 1840. This was purchased by Isaac Sparks, who resold it, half to Branch and half to John M. Price. To add fur-

ther to his possessions, Branch bought a part of Rancho Bolsa de Chamisal adjoining the Pismo on the south and a tract of land, Rancho Huerhuero, lying several miles to the north of his earlier holdings in the vicinity of the present town of Creston.

The city of Arroyo Grande lies in the Arroyo Grande Valley on the boundary line between Ranchos Santa Manuela and Pismo. Many of its buildings on Branch Street have been preserved from the early years of the twentieth century and restored; the two-story Odd Fellows' Hall on Bridge Street goes back to 1895. Near the town, at the mouth of Corralitos Canyon, long stood the remains of an old adobe believed by some to have been erected by Mission San Luis Obispo as one of the buildings of an asistencia. It is known that farming was carried on by the mission fathers on the rich bottom lands of the Arroyo Grande as early as 1780.

The adobe Branch built on Rancho Santa Manuela was for many years one of the most noted in the county. The unmarked site is located off the Huasna Road about three and one-half miles east of Arroyo Grande, near the Branch School. Nearby, old palms and cypresses indicate the site of the frame house where Branch's son Fred lived; the house has been destroyed by fire.

Another adobe built by the Branch family stands at 2878 Huasna Road, much disguised as a modern stucco residence with Spanish-style arches. Yet another Branch adobe stands on a knoll to the left of the road leading to the county park. It is half a mile beyond the junction of this road and the back road to San Luis Obispo, about five and one-half miles northeast of Arroyo Grande.

John M. Price, who held the half of the Pismo grant not purchased by Francis Ziba Branch, built an adobe home on the land. It still stands but is not occupied. Price also built an adobe schoolhouse nearby, which is now all but ruined. These buildings, together with the frame structure that was Price's last home, stand across the railroad tracks to the right of Price Canyon Road half a mile north of the junction of this road and Bello Street in Pismo Beach. The town of Pismo Beach lies on the coast about in the center of the grant.

Nearby Halcyon began as one of California's utopian colonies. Dr. William H. Dower and Mrs. Francia A. LaDue opened a sanatorium here in 1904. From this grew the theosophical, cooperative, quasi-socialistic colony of the Temple Home Association. On the edge of Halcyon, the old Victorian mansion in which the sanatorium was first located is still to be seen, nearly engulfed in a mobile home park; it is at the corner of 25th Street and SR 1, at the east end of the town of Oceano.

Rancho Nipomo (Nipomo)

One of the most famous old ranchos of California was the vast domain of almost 38,000 acres that constituted Rancho Nipomo (an Indian word said to mean "foot of the mountain"), for many years the first stopping place on El Camino Real south of Mission San Luis Obispo. Many of the early books on California mention Captain Dana, the owner of this rancho, his pleasant home at Nipomo, and his lavish hospitality. In ranchero days, when the great landholders of Alta California were the lords of the country, many travelers stopped here; Colonel John C. Frémont, Edwin Bryant (author of *What I Saw in California*), and General Henry W. Halleck were among those entertained at the Casa de Dana.

William Goodwin Dana, a cousin of Richard Henry Dana, Jr. (who wrote *Two Years Before the Mast*), was born in Boston in 1797 and there received his education. While still a young man, he went to Canton in China and later to India in the service of his uncle, a Boston merchant. Returning home after three years, he soon reembarked, possibly on the *Waverly*, of which he was captain a few years later. In this capacity he engaged for several years in trade between China, the Sandwich (Hawaiian) Islands, California, and Boston.

In 1825 Captain Dana established his business in Santa Barbara, where he soon settled permanently. He became a prominent citizen, holding a number of important office at various times. In 1828 he married María Josefa Carrillo, daughter of Carlos Antonio Carrillo, a resident of Santa Barbara and a short-term provisional governor of California in 1835. About this time Dana applied for Rancho Nipomo. The grant was not confirmed until 1837. In 1839 the captain moved onto his rancho and built the large adobe house of thirteen rooms that still stands; until 1902, Federico Dana, one of his sons, lived there. The adobe, now owned and being restored by the San Luis Obispo County Historical Society, is located at 671 Oakglen Avenue at the south end of the town of Nipomo.

Frémont, on his way from Monterey to Los Angeles in December 1846, camped at Rancho Nipomo with his battalion of 430 hungry and footsore soldiers, soaked to the skin by the rain through which they had tramped on the long march from the north. The campsite was located in an oak grove at a point known as the Summit, not far from Casa de Dana; it is northwest of Nipomo on the west side of US 101.

Rancho El Paso de los Robles (Paso Robles)

Rancho El Paso de los Robles received its name from the many large white oaks that dotted the valley, and the name has survived in the modern town. Well known to the Indians, the hot springs on this rancho were also known to the Franciscan friars who, possibly as early as 1797, placed a rude wall of logs around the edge of the main spring, forming a pool of water. Alfred Robinson, who visited San Miguel in 1830, says that Father Juan Cabot "had erected a small house over the spot for the purpose of shelter and convenience for bathing, and it was resorted to by many persons."

At first an outpost of Mission San Miguel, Rancho El Paso de los Robles was granted to Pedro Narváez in 1844, and later confirmed to Petronillo Ríos. It was purchased in 1857 by Daniel D. and James H. Blackburn and Lazare Godchaux, and improvements were begun at once. James Blackburn built a frame house near the old adobe, said to have been put up by the mission fathers, and used the adobe for servants' quarters. Both stood six and one-half miles south of Paso Robles, near the entrance to the Crescent Dairy.

Drury James, a brother-in-law of James and Daniel Blackburn, purchased the hot springs tract along the west bank of the river where now the town of Paso Robles is situated and built the first substantial house on the site, a duplicate of the James Blackburn house south of town. The site of the original hot springs and the first bathhouse built for it is the northwest corner of Tenth and Spring streets, now a parking lot.

Ranchos Asunción and Atascadero (Atascadero) and Rancho Santa Margarita (Santa Margarita)

Rancho Atascadero, granted to Trifon García in 1842, and Rancho Asunción, granted to Pedro Estrada in 1845, both of which lay between Ranchos Paso de Robles and Santa Margarita, became parts of the large Murphy estate, with headquarters at Santa Margarita. The adobe house in which Pedro Estrada lived on Rancho Asunción is now a fragmentary ruin about two miles out of Atascadero on Traffic Way, a section of old El Camino Real that was left out of the construction of US 101.

After secularization, Rancho Santa Margarita passed from the control of Mission San Luis Obispo and was granted to Joaquín Estrada, the brother of Pedro. In 1860 Martin Murphy, Jr., who lived at Rancho Pastoria de las Borregas in Santa Clara County, came into possession of Rancho Santa Margarita; this, together with Ranchos Atascadero and Asunción and others that he owned, made up a magnificent landed estate totaling 70,000 acres. Martin Murphy's son Patrick took charge of the entire domain, making Santa Margarita his home and his business headquarters. As late as the 1880's, thousands of beef cattle were pastured upon this vast territory.

The Atascadero Administration Building and the Veterans' Memorial Building at 6500 Palma Avenue (SRL 958) are the only remnants of the Atascadero Colony. The beautiful buildings of locally produced brick and reinforced concrete were completed in 1918 and continue to be an important element in the life of the city. The Atascadero Colony, begun in 1914 and ending less than a decade later, was the project of Edward G. Lewis, who envisioned a complex of food-processing operations and business ventures, none of which came to realization.

James Dean Memorial

California is full of monuments, and one of the more unusual is at the little crossroads town of Cholame, where SR 41 meets SR 46. In the late afternoon of September 30, 1955, James Dean was killed in an automobile accident at this spot. Only 24 years old, Dean was a rising Hollywood actor who is best remembered for the film *Rebel Without a Cause* and was already attracting a good deal of attention as a symbol of a younger, restless generation. His death was much lamented, and he became a hero for many young Americans.

James Dean Memorial, Cholame

A Japanese man, Seita Ohnishi, decided to erect a monument to Dean on the site of his death, and on the 22nd anniversary of the accident, September 30, 1977, the monument was placed directly in front of the tiny Cholame Post Office. It consists of a cast aluminum and stainless steel structure enclosing a tall ailanthus tree, the "tree of heaven," which is neither irrigated nor fertilized, receiving "only what heaven sends it." Mr. Ohnishi's inscription says that the monument "stands for James Dean and other American Rebels who taught us the importance of having a cause." The anniversary of Dean's death brings carloads of fans annually to the memorial.

San Mateo County

San Mateo County was organized in 1856 from the southern portion of San Francisco County. San Mateo is Spanish for St. Matthew. The county seat, located through fraudulent election at Belmont in May 1856, was changed within a year to Redwood City, where it has remained, although the question of its removal came up in 1861 and at other times.

In 1868, by an act of the state legislature, the southern boundary, which had been a line running due west from the source of the south branch of San Francisquito Creek and reaching the coast at San Gregorio, became an irregular line running southwest to the coast below Point Año Nuevo. This change transferred a large tract, including Pescadero, from Santa Cruz County to San Mateo County.

History and geography have tended to separate the county into coastal and bayside regions. As Alan Hynding notes: "Beauty and isolation typified the San Mateo coast in the last century. Rugged, forested mountains and a rocky shoreline broken by occasional stretches of white beach made access by both land and sea difficult. As a result, significantly fewer people settled there than on the bayside. As time passed, the coast became a backwater. . . . The first part of the county to be colonized by Europeans, the coast was the last to feel the impact of the twentieth century."

Indian Mounds

Indian villages were widely scattered along the shores of both ocean and bay. Near Point Año Nuevo, the southernmost corner of the county, are acres of dunes, where the shifting sands have revealed from time to time such evidences of Indian occupation as are usually found in kitchen middens: broken shells, arrow points, bones of wild animals that were used for food, and occasional human skeletons that were buried near tribal dwellings. Farther north on the coast at Half Moon Bay are several mounds.

Perhaps the largest mounds in the county were in the vicinity of South San Francisco and Brisbane on the shore of the bay, but here, as elsewhere, most of the material was taken away years ago for road surfacing, fertilizer, and other purposes.

On and near the banks of San Mateo Creek, once a favorite haunt of native tribes, have been found many indications of early human habitation. During excavations for house foundations on Baywood Avenue west of SR 82, as many as six skeletons were taken out of one small area. The ground in this vicinity is largely impregnated with broken shell. Across the highway where the creek, for a little distance, is held within bounds by concrete walls, larger shell mounds were found. About two feet of surface shell, in which a few relics such as mortars were found, were removed before the erection of school buildings on the Civic Center site. It was probably from this village that the helpful visitors, mentioned by Anza, came to his camp on San Mateo Creek in March 1776.

In Redwood City the part of Main Street that runs between El Camino Real and the railroad track traverses the site of another Indian village. A small triangular park now marks the site.

La Punta de Año Nuevo

Sebastián Vizcaíno set sail from Mexico on May 5, 1602, to survey the California coast for a good harbor to be used by the Spanish galleons on their trips to and from the Philippines. He found a harbor that pleased him at Monterey and remained there at anchor for a few days. When he resumed the voyage on January 3, 1603, the first conspicuous point he sighted was a low headland to which the name La Punta de Año Nuevo (New Year's Point) was given—the name that the extreme southwestern point of San Mateo County still bears. It was the point that mariners following Vizcaíno described as the northwestern extremity of Monterey Bay.

The Mexican grant of land made in this vicinity in 1842 perpetuated the name. The extreme tip of land is now an island frequented by sea lions. The point and beach are now part of Año Nuevo State Reserve, a protected breeding ground for northern elephant seals.

The Portolá Trail

On Monday, October 23, 1769, Gaspar de Portolá and the members of his party, including Father Crespí and Ensign Miguel Costansó, diarists of the expedition, having rested over Sunday in the Cañada de la Salud, which is now Waddell Creek in Santa Cruz County, resumed their march in search of the elusive bay of Monterey. Traveling two leagues that day, they entered the region now included in San Mateo County, passed La Punta de Año Nuevo without being sure of its identity, and camped for the night at an Indian village they called "La Casa Grande," for an unusually large house in its center. This site was identified by Bolton as Gazos Creek (SRL 23), but later evidence seems to point to Whitehouse Creek as the location. Here they seem to have heard rumors of a port and a ship to the north, and were confirmed in their decision to continue.

During the following days they pursued their journey north, following the present Cloverdale Road inland to the site of Pescadero on Pescadero Creek, then over the hills near the shore to camp on San Gregorio Creek at the present townsite of San Gregorio. They remained there for two days for the benefit of sick and tired soldiers. Father Crespí was impressed by the surroundings of the two Indian settlements, and proposed the place for a mission site. A historical marker on the coast highway (SRL 26), close to where the Indians' permanent village was situated, memorializes the explorers' stop.

On October 27 they halted on the south bank of Purisima Creek (SRL 22) and the next night they pitched camp (SRL 21) near the town of Half Moon Bay. Pillar Point, probably first seen by the navigator Francisco de Gali in 1585, could be discerned from this place, lying to the north-northwest. Here a halt was made over Sunday, October 29, because Portolá himself was ill. On October 30 they stopped on the bank of Martini's Creek (SRL 25), just north of Montara Beach, having had to bridge some of the creeks on the way. Here the route was blocked by Pedro Mountain, and Sergeant Ortega was sent to break a trail over the barrier.

Next morning the party ascended the mountain and looked down upon the Gulf of the Farallones. Some of the leaders identified this as the Bay of San Francisco of the ancient navigators, for Point Reyes was visible 40 miles to the north-northwest. A base camp (SRL 24) was established on October 31 on the south side of

Pedro Valley near a lagoon at its mouth. From this point Sergeant Ortega made an extended exploring trip, discovering not the long-sought bay of Monterey, but the inner or present-day Bay of San Francisco instead. A hunting party, which left camp on November 2 and returned at nightfall with news of an inland sea, was the first to report the discovery of the bay, since Ortega did not return until the night of November 3. He had been drawn inland by a report from the Indians of "a port and a ship therein" only two days distant from their camp. The site of the discovery (SRL 394) is on Sweeney Ridge, just east of Pacifica, and is reached by a trail. It is now in the southernmost part of the Golden Gate National Recreational Area and is also a National Historic Landmark.

On November 4, Portolá and his men crossed Sweeney Ridge just south of the present radar station behind San Bruno, paused beyond the summit to view the great arm of the sea drawing down far to the southeast on their right and disappearing on their left behind San Bruno Mountain. They then went down to camp by a pond now covered by the waters of San Andreas Lake, where a historical marker (SRL 27) now stands on Skyline Boulevard. The trail they followed on November 5 is today mostly covered by the Crystal Springs Lakes; camp was made near a lake later called the Laguna de Raymundo or Laguna Grande (SRL 94), now included in the upper reservoir, west of Ralston Avenue. Here the mountains on the right were covered with oak, redwood, and madrone trees. The party saw many herds of deer on the valley floor. This section is today the San Francisco State Fish and Game Refuge, where numerous deer may often be seen grazing.

On November 6 the party turned east over the low hills along the Redwood City–Woodside city limits and again established a base camp one league from the bay on San Francisquito Creek in Menlo Park (SRL 2), on the opposite bank from the huge old redwood tree known as the "Palo Alto." From this point Ortega explored to the south and then up the east side of the bay, possibly as far as San Lorenzo. On November 10, he returned with the discouraging news that hostile Indians and another great arm of the sea barred further progress. After conferring with the other members of the party, Portolá decided to discontinue the search for Cermeño's harbor of Monterey.

Retracing their steps, the little company returned to the unrecognized Monterey Bay over the route by which they had come, camping on November 11 north of Woodside (SRL 92), on the 12th again at San Andreas Lake, and on the 13th at Pedro Valley. From there they proceeded down the coast, stopping to relieve their hunger with shellfish at Martini's Creek and with fowl

at the "Plain of Wild Geese" at Half Moon Bay. Camping at Tunitas Creek (SRL 375), Butano Creek, and New Year's Creek, they entered Santa Cruz County once more on November 20. On November 27 they were back at Monterey Bay, and again they did not realize that this was the harbor for which they were searching.

Rivera's Trail in 1774

The Spanish Viceroy in Mexico, Antonio María Bucareli, wanting to establish a mission at the port of San Francisco, ordered Fernando de Rivera y Moncada to go there to look for a suitable site. Rivera had been a member of the expedition led by Gaspar de Portolá, which had discovered that port.

Setting out from Monterey by Pedro Fages's inland route on November 23, 1774, the party of twenty reached San Francisquito Creek at the southern boundary line of San Mateo County on November 28. Accompanying Captain Rivera on this journey was Father Francisco Palou, who, like the captain, kept a journal. Their camping place at the creek seemed to them suitable for a mission, since it met the requirements of wood, water, and native people to be Christianized. Therefore a cross made of two beams was erected to mark the spot for future consideration.

On the next day's march northward, they turned into the hills between present Redwood City and San Carlos, where they found friendly Indians; Father Palou, in his religious zeal, "embraced them" and made them gifts of beads, hoping to hold their friendship until the time for gathering them into the fold of the mission. As the day wore on, more and more natives joined the travelers, pressing them to enter their villages, of which there were many along the route both in the hills and near the shore of the Bay.

On November 30, the day of the feast of St. Andrew, Rivera and his party came to a pleasant valley (where Portolá had camped) that since that day has borne the name they gave—San Andreas. On that day, too, friendly Indians seemed to enjoy the company and the food of the strangers, and again Father Palou intimated that he would return and would bring seeds for planting so that they could grow similar food for themselves.

For the next few days they explored in the territory now included in northern San Mateo County and San Francisco, being the first white men to see the views from San Bruno Mountain and Mount Davidson. Then, deciding not to retrace their steps but to follow down the coast as the Portolá expedition had done, they reached Pedro Valley, crossed Pedro Mountain, and on December 6 camped at Purisima Creek south of Half

Moon Bay. Spending a day at an Indian village there, they continued south to Butano Creek on December 8. They crossed the present border of Santa Cruz County on December 10 and returned to Monterey on the 12th. Rivera and Palou recommended the establishment of Mission San Francisco on what later became known as San Francisquito Creek, but Father Serra decided instead in favor of the northern end of the peninsula, though the explorers had thought the place unsatisfactory.

Anza's Trail in 1776

Juan Bautista de Anza, on his way from Monterey to the port of San Francisco with a party of thirteen, including Lieutenant José Joaquín Moraga and Father Pedro Font, entered what is now San Mateo County by crossing San Francisquito Creek on March 26, 1776. An Indian village of about twenty huts was near the creek, and on the north bank stood the cross erected by Father Palou when he had passed the place with Captain Rivera two years before. Font's diary gives the information that along this arroyo were various trees: laurel, ash, and "a beautiful cypress called redwood."

After making gifts of beads to the women in this village, they proceeded through a plain of oak and soon were met by a group of shouting natives whose long-haired chief was recognized by Corporal Robles as being one of a group whom his companions of a former journey had called the "Shouters." Approaching the place where Redwood City now stands, they came to another village, where they saw a large heap of mussel shells. During the day's march, they passed four Indian villages. The last one was located on San Mateo Creek shortly before they made their camp for the night (SRL 48)—in the present city of Burlingame, perhaps at Barroilhet Avenue—on one of the arroyos bordered with scented trees that they called laurel.

With an early start on March 27, the party's line of travel led past Millbrae, San Bruno, and Daly City, toward the port of San Francisco. Two days later half of the party with the camp equipment returned to await their commander at San Mateo Creek. Anza, accompanied by his chaplain and five soldiers, spent the day exploring the hills for timber for the new settlements. In the course of the afternoon, Corporal Robles shot an immense bear that appeared out of the woods near the Crystal Springs Lakes. The skin of this animal was preserved as a gift for the viceroy.

On reaching camp at the site of the city of San Mateo, they found most of the men from the Indian village congregated there. After a heavy rain during the night, they set out in the morning in a southeasterly direction. When San Francisquito Creek was reached, Father Font set the graphometer 36 varas from the foot of the tallest redwood tree there and found that its height was a little more than 50 varas, a vara being a measure of approximately 33 inches. The native Indians watched this proceeding quietly. The tree measured has long been assumed to have been the famous "Palo Alto" beside the Southern Pacific Railroad tracks. It may, however, have been another redwood farther downstream.

From this point the party passed on into Santa Clara County. Soon the route thus established was again traveled, this time by Anza's company of settlers that, bound for San Francisco from Mexico, had rested for a time at Monterey while their leader went ahead. The colonists camped at San Mateo on June 24, 25, and 26, 1776; a historical marker (SRL 47) on Arroyo Court, north of Third Avenue and west of El Camino Real, commemorates the campsite.

El Camino Real, the San Jose Road

Although the Bayshore Freeway (US 101) has replaced it as the route of high-speed transportation, El Camino Real, the old road leading south from San Francisco, has an interesting story of its own, distinct from the histories of the ranches, estates, and large cities that have sprung up beside it.

When Mission San Francisco was founded in 1776, the trail from the south had already been established by Anza's exploration earlier that year. San Jose Avenue follows part of this route. Mission Street is part of the road built across the sand hills between downtown San Francisco and the mission in 1850 and extended southward by San Francisco County in 1851. The original San Jose road also remained open in the same period because it was a boundary between land grants. Its common Spanish designation as "camino real" was retained on title papers and property maps.

At the top of the hill in the Mission Street Gap, now the center of Daly City, Mission Street and San Jose Avenue come together, and the original trail to the presidio branched off to the northwest. South from this point the Spanish trail and the partly planked stage road of the early 1850's ran considerably uphill and east of today's El Camino Real, which was relocated for two miles within the city limits of South San Francisco in 1914–15. Mission Street across the railroad tracks represents the old route, once famous for its taverns and roadhouses. One that remains is Molloy's Springs, or the Old Brooksville Hotel, at 1655 Mission in Colma. Built in 1883, it is commemorated by a plaque placed by E Clampus Vitus. Through San Bruno and Millbrae the old Spanish trail and modern El Camino Real run parallel, skirting the edge of the bay marsh.

Just south of present Broadway in Burlingame, the

road in Spanish times crossed a narrow neck of land between a natural salt-pan and a lake (on present California Drive), and thence went over a grassy knoll to present El Camino Real in a northward extension of its line south of Peninsula Avenue. From this point to San Mateo Creek, where a toll bridge was built at the present crossing in 1851, El Camino Real still follows its original route, with a shallow bend around the site of the adobe San Mateo outpost of Mission San Francisco.

At San Mateo the traveler left the summer fogs and entered a country of oak groves and natural clearings, spread between the hills and the sloughs. Somewhere south of here, Captain George Vancouver with his officers and an escort of seven Spanish soldiers stopped for a picnic on November 20, 1792, on their way to Santa Clara. The great British navigator, the first foreign visitor to San Francisco, was impressed with the scene, particularly "a very pleasant and enchanting lawn, situated among a grove of trees at the foot of a small hill, by which flowed a very fine stream of excellent water. This delightful pasture was nearly inclosed on every side."

Leaving the steep south bank of San Mateo Creek, the road as traveled before the late spring of 1853 bore rapidly to the right of the present route, running nearly as far west as the present Alameda de las Pulgas in order to avoid the adobe soil north of Laurel Creek. South of present Hillsdale was a narrow pass and gap between hills and marsh at Belmont, then called the Portezuelo de las Pulgas, very near the Old County Road. This road was bypassed when present El Camino was built west of the tracks in 1917–18, through Belmont and San Carlos.

At San Carlos the wide oak plain begins. To Vancouver in 1792 it was "a country I little expected to find in these regions. For about twenty miles it could only be compared to a park, which had originally been closely planted with the true old English oak; [with] the stately lords of the forest in complete possession of the soil, which was covered with luxuriant herbage, and beautifully diversified with pleasing eminences and valleys; which, with the range of lofty rugged mountains that bounded the prospect, required only to be adorned with the neat habitations of an industrious people, to produce a scene not inferior to the most studied effect of taste in the disposal of grounds." In the White Oaks district the well-defined Spanish trail turned to the west, keeping in the edge of the trees, and crossed Cordilleras or Finger Creek (Arroyo de los Cadillos) into Redwood City just east of Stanford Lane.

Turning sharply to the right to avoid the low-lying adobe lands, the original route—called the stage road in a deed of 1851—went by the foot of Eagle Hill at Jefferson Avenue, thence to the Indian village near Union Cemetery, and diagonally across El Camino and the tracks south of Five Points to Semicircular Road and Fifth Avenue in North Fair Oaks, the site of Steinberger's Woodlawn roadhouse, which was built early in 1852 and stood for many years.

From this point south the original Spanish highway is now called Middlefield Road. For the first half-mile the slight curve of the old trail is followed exactly by the modern street, but from Marsh Road through Menlo Park to the county line at San Francisquito Creek, the route was straightened by Steinberger's Middle Field Fence, the original trail having wandered slightly to the west in many places. The first bridge was built here in 1851, but it collapsed a few years later and was not replaced until the turn of the century.

Although Middlefield Road was considered the main highway in Spanish times, this crossing could be used only by horsemen and pedestrians. In 1784, we learn from a letter of Father Palou, high water still stopped communication between San Francisco and San Jose, but by the time of Vancouver's visit in 1792 horsemen could get through by an alternate route. By 1803 there was cart traffic, which followed a well-marked detour crossing San Francisquito Creek farther downstream. This route left Middlefield Road in North Fair Oaks and ran down toward the bay to the Indian mound at Ninth and Fair Oaks avenues and thence to Marsh Road. From that point the *camino carretero* is still in use as present Bay Road, winding gently with the invisible contour of the land through two and a half miles of oaks and laurels. Just short of University Avenue in East Palo Alto the Spanish road bent away to the right, crossed an old channel of the San Francisquito, zigzagged through and around the mosquito-ridden willow swamps on both sides of the *paso de carretas* just below the Bayshore Freeway crossing, and rejoined the main bridle trail at the Mesa rancho in Palo Alto.

Old Land Grants

The northern boundary line of the county runs through the Mexican grant of Rancho Laguna de la Merced, only a small portion of which extends from San Francisco County into San Mateo County. South of this, on the ocean side of the peninsula, are the lands of eight ranchos, each having one boundary line at the low-tide mark on the beach. The southernmost rancho reaches to the border of Santa Cruz County.

Rancho San Pedro (Pacifica)

One of Father Palou's last plans for Mission San Francisco, before his retirement from California in 1784, was the removal of farming operations to a fertile valley on the ocean shore fifteen miles to the southwest, called by him the Cañada de las Almejas, in memory of the shellfish feast held by the Portolá expedition in 1769. The chief of Prúrstak, the largest Indian village, had been baptized in 1783, and a great harvest of souls was to be expected from the coast farther to the south. Accordingly, in 1786, Fathers Cambon and Noriega dedicated a chapel in the valley to Saints Peter and Paul, and work was pushed forward on a quadrangle of buildings with an entrance looking east up the valley. Half or more of the mission's 800-odd neophytes were moved to the new establishment, and for some years most of the new converts from the peninsula and down the coast were baptized—and buried—at the chapel, which in time became known simply as San Pedro. A devastating pestilence struck the settlement in the early 1790's. The white man's diseases wreaked havoc on the Indians of California, nowhere more murderously than in San Mateo County. It is estimated that there were at least 1,500 natives in the county in 1770; by 1860 there were fewer than 50, most of whom had been brought in from elsewhere to supplement the dwindling labor force.

In 1834, shortly after secularization, Don Francisco de Haro, military *comandante* of San Francisco, petitioned the Mexican government for a grant of San Francisco Mission lands. The following year he specifically requested San Pedro, including a sketch map that showed the old building "in ruins." One of de Haro's company presented a similar petition the same year, but none of these petitions was granted. In 1836 de Haro's successor in command, Francisco Sánchez, copied his predecessor's map and petition, and in 1839 he was finally given a formal grant of the two leagues of land.

Don Francisco, son of José Antonio Sánchez, who owned Rancho Buriburi, was a native of San Francisco and a highly respected citizen. As a member of the San Francisco Company, he attained the rank of captain and finally that of acting commander. In 1846, on the occupation of San Francisco by American forces, he moved down to his ranch. In December 1846, annoyed by the depredations of Americans, Sánchez headed the short-lived revolt in which Alcalde Bartlett of San Francisco was captured and held hostage. The revolt ended in surrender after the battle of Santa Clara. Sánchez lived largely at Mission Dolores until his death in 1862, by which time his country home had fallen into decay. The large two-story Sanchez adobe (SRL 391) now stands refurbished as a county historical monument in Pedro Valley, a suburb of Pacifica, one mile east of the coast highway via Linda Mar Boulevard. A thicket of cypress and pine trees borders the property.

Sanchez Adobe, Pacifica

Rancho San Pedro, patented in 1858 with 8,926 acres, occupied very nearly the same bounds as the present city of Pacifica, incorporated in 1957; it includes the districts of Edgemar, Pacific Manor, Sharp Park, Vallemar, Rockaway Beach, Pedro Point, and Linda Mar. The Pedro Valley district, though now filled with modern homes, still has a few small houses from the 1850's and 1860's in the side canyons, witnesses to a century of large-scale irrigated truck gardening, an economic mainstay of coastal San Mateo County.

Rancho El Corral de Tierra
(Montara, Moss Beach, Princeton)

This rancho, extending from the south face of Pedro Mountain to Pilarcitos Creek, was first known as El Pilar or Los Pilares, from the rocks off Pillar Point, and was occupied by the horse and ox ranches of Mission San Francisco as early as the 1790's. It very nearly became the location of the town of Branciforte, established instead at Santa Cruz in 1797.

Rancho Corral de Tierra contained one and three-quarters leagues, granted in two parts. The northern and larger part was given in 1839 to Francisco Guerrero Palomares, whose widow, Josefa Haro de Guerrero Denniston, filed her claim in 1852 and received the patent for the land fourteen years later. The ranch home stood on a hillside near a creek about one mile northeast of Princeton until the earthquake of 1906.

Princeton-by-the-Sea is about two miles south of Point Montara Lighthouse, now a youth hostel. Like other coastal towns, it had a notorious career connected with rum-running in the Prohibition era. The respectable history of Princeton began with an early pier from which produce was sent by schooner to San Francisco.

Nearby Miramar began with the building of a wharf

Point Montara Lighthouse

at Amesport Landing near the mouth of Arroyo de en Medio, a small stream dividing the property of the two owners of Rancho Corral de Tierra. Warehouses for the shipping of grain from this fertile region were built just south of the mouth of the creek. J. P. Ames, who headed this venture, came west with Stevenson's Regiment at the time of the Mexican War. Honorably discharged at Monterey in 1848, he came north to San Mateo County and became its treasurer in 1862. He represented the county in the state legislature in 1876–77. Amesport Landing was afterward acquired by the Pacific Mail Steamship Company, which disposed in 1917 of the site of the old warehouses to the owner of a small hotel there.

The southern end of Rancho Corral de Tierra, granted to Tiburcio Vásquez in 1839, extended south from Arroyo de en Medio to Arroyo de los Pilarcitos, the latter name also used for the rancho. His claim was filed with the Land Commission in 1853, but the patent was not issued until 1873. The Vásquez adobe home was built on the north bank of Pilarcitos Creek a little west of the Main Street bridge, now at the northern edge of the city of Half Moon Bay. Don Tiburcio's youngest son, Pablo Vásquez, built a one-story wooden house in 1869. Known today as Pilarcitos House and still standing at 270 Main Street in Half Moon Bay, it is one of the oldest wooden structures in San Mateo County.

The Main Street bridge, built in 1900, was the first in the county, and indeed one of the first anywhere, to be made of structurally reinforced concrete. A plaque on the bridge gives some of its history.

Above the gateway of a well-enclosed cemetery on the San Mateo highway a few hundred yards north of this bridge may be read "Pilarcitos Cemetery 1820–1923," though the cemetery was actually established in 1857. Many of the graves within this Catholic cemetery

are of settlers of old Spanishtown. The International Order of Odd Fellows Cemetery, immediately to the east, was established by the Odd Fellows and the Masons in 1856.

Rancho Miramontes (Half Moon Bay)

This rancho, known also as San Benito, was granted to Candelario Miramontes by Governor Alvarado in 1841. When the first members of the Miramontes family, the sons Vicente and Rodolfo, took up residence there, grizzly bears and other predators native to the country were still present and proved destructive to the roaming herds of cattle. Miramontes built an adobe near the intersection of Johnston and Mill streets in Half Moon Bay; it became his daughter's home, where all of her children were born, and survived until the twentieth century.

The Vásquez and Miramontes families were company—and protection—for each other. Around their houses the settlement called Spanishtown grew up. About 1860 the Yankees began to arrive, one of the first being Henry Bidwell, nephew of California pioneer John Bidwell, who ran a blacksmith shop and was the first postmaster. The town was platted in 1863 in the southwest angle formed by the confluence of Arroyo Leon and Pilarcitos Creek. The post office was named Half Moon Bay for the section of the adjacent ocean, and in time the name replaced Spanishtown as the name of the settlement.

Half Moon Bay today is proud of its well-preserved downtown district. The Estanislao Zaballa house at 326 Main Street dates from 1863. Zaballa, a native of Spain, married Dolores, daughter of Candelario Miramontes, in 1853, and began the San Benito General Store and Saloon. He platted Spanishtown in 1863. The oldest continuously operating place of business in town is Boitano's General Merchandise Store and Saloon at 527 Main Street, which has been in business since 1873. One of the oldest Protestant churches in the county is the handsome Methodist Episcopal Church (1872) at the northeast corner of Johnston and Miramontes streets.

James Johnston was an American pioneer who in 1853 purchased a half-league of land from the southern part of the Miramontes grant, and with his brothers went into cattle raising and farming. His house, begun around 1855, is a striking saltbox built using mortise and tenon construction and wooden pegs. In its heyday the elegantly furnished house boasted a chapel on the second floor and an enclosed patio. Long abandoned, the house is now being restored by a local foundation and has been placed on the National Register of

Historic Places. It stands on Higgins Purisima Road east of SR 1 about one-half mile south of Half Moon Bay. Across the road from James's house is the William Johnston house, built by his brother and still in use, although much modified since the second story was added in 1878. The property includes two original barns.

Rancho Cañada Verde y Arroyo de la Purísima (Purisima and Tunitas)

This grant was made provisionally by Governor Alvarado in 1838 to José María Alviso, a military officer in San Jose. The following year Alviso transferred his claim to his brother José Antonio Alviso, who received the final grant from Prefect José Castro. In 1864 José Antonio Alviso received a United States patent for 8,906 acres lying between Purisima and Tunitas creeks.

The town of Purisima was once flourishing, with a hotel, repair shops for wagons and farm machinery, a school, and a post office. Nothing remains of the town today except the old cemetery, marked by an E Clampus Vitus plaque in 1963. The plaque is on Verde Road, one-quarter mile east of its northern intersection with the coast highway.

Just before crossing Tunitas Creek by the long bridge at the southern edge of this rancho, one encounters the road from Kings Mountain, which leads on as a private road toward the beach and the site of Tunitas Glen, the terminal of the defunct Ocean Shore Railroad from San Francisco. Plans had been made by a group of San Franciscans to connect their city and Santa Cruz by trains running through this scenic coastal region, but the line never got beyond this point. A stage service completed the journey, and the railroad, which struggled against constant landslides along the coast, was discontinued in 1920.

Rancho San Gregorio

Rancho San Gregorio, consisting of four square leagues, was granted by Governor Alvarado in 1839 to Antonino Buelna. The rancho included the whole of the lower San Gregorio Creek watershed and extended along the coast from Tunitas Creek to Pomponio Creek. At the time of receiving his grant, Don Antonino was in command of an expedition against Indians and foreigners in the San Joaquin Valley.

The settlement of San Gregorio is an old one. Early houses, not much more than shacks, quickly disappeared. When the La Honda road was completed, stores sprang up where the road intersected with the Stage Road paralleling the coast, about three-quarters of a mile east of SR 1 on SR 84 today. The "San Gregorio House," built in 1866, has been a summer resort, a stage stop, a hotel, a saloon, and a gas station. Today it is a private residence. A nearby general store built at the turn of the century still supplies tourists.

Pomponio Creek is named for Chief Pomponio, who ran away from a mission and was captured by Mexican authorities in Monterey in 1824. His mountain hideout had been at the headwaters of Pomponio Creek, a short stretch of which formed the southern line of Buelna's Rancho San Gregorio.

Rancho El Pescadero, or San Antonio (Pescadero)

Rancho El Pescadero ("the fishery"), or San Antonio, was granted in 1833 by Governor José Figueroa to Juan José Gonzales, mayordomo of Santa Cruz Mission, and was patented to his descendants by the United States government in June 1866. It consisted of 3,282 acres in the vicinity of the town of Pescadero on Pescadero Creek.

By 1842 Gonzales was living in a small adobe on the north bank of the creek one block east of the bridge over that stream at the north end of town. The Bartlett V. Weeks family, natives of Maine who came to California in 1859 via Nicaragua, purchased in 1860 the 157-acre tract upon which this adobe stood. No vestige of it now remains; its site is at the south end of Goulson Street, formerly Pescadero Street, which was the original Spanish trail to the crossing of the creek.

The first American to take up permanent residence in this area was Alexander Moore, who after traveling across the plains by covered wagon reached California in 1847 with his father and other members of the family. Alexander went to the mines on the Tuolumne River for a while. In 1853, attracted to the Pescadero region by the fertile soil, he put up a large L-shaped house north of Pescadero Creek, using lumber hauled by ox team from Santa Cruz. Two miles north of town Thomas W. Moore founded the Willowside Farm, and the drive to the house, between gigantic eucalyptus trees, is now part of the public road.

Pescadero is an unusual San Mateo County coastal town in that its historical buildings are all American; indeed, it has been compared to a New England village. One manifestation of this is the white, steepled First Congregational Church (SRL 949) on San Gregorio Street. Now designated the Pescadero Community Church, the building dates from 1867 and is claimed to be "the oldest church building on its original site within the San Mateo–Santa Clara county region." The steeple was added in 1890, and the social hall dates from 1940. Services are still held regularly.

Across the street is the McCormick House, built in the late 1860's by James McCormick in the popular Classical Revival style, and now privately owned. St. Anthony's Catholic Church on North Street is also in the New England style.

Rancho Bútano (South of Pescadero)

Rancho Bútano consisted of one square league lying along the ocean between Butano Creek and Arroyo de los Frijoles ("Bean Hollow"), south of Pescadero. It was given originally to Ramona Sánchez in 1838, confirmed by Governor Micheltorena six years later, and patented to Manuel Rodríguez by the United States government in 1866. The property was held for many years by Loren Coburn, who vainly tried to establish a resort along the coast. His hotel stood until it was demolished in the 1930's. Coburn faced frequent battles with other landowners and with his own family, and was a leading promoter of the Ocean Shore Railroad from San Francisco to Santa Cruz that never was completed. On the coast south of Butano Creek is Pebble Beach, a deposit of varicolored, water-worn pebbles. They lie several feet deep over an area of approximately two acres; agate, chalcedony, jasper, moonstones, and sardonyx are found among them. Removal of pebbles is illegal today.

East of Rancho Bútano is Butano State Park, containing within its 2,100 acres the last small stand of virgin timber in this part of the mountains. Extensive logging was a principal economic activity here until the mid-twentieth century.

Rancho Punta de Año Nuevo

Rancho Punta de Año Nuevo was a vast tract of 17,753 acres granted in 1842 by Governor Alvarado to Simeón Castro, already the owner of two ranchos in Monterey County. The grant extended from Butano Creek, where an earlier grant was in dispute, to south of Point Año Nuevo. In 1866 the part of the ranch that lay between Butano Creek and Arroyo de los Frijoles was patented to Manuel Rodríguez as Rancho Bútano.

In 1851 Rancho Punta de Año Nuevo was sold to Isaac Graham of Santa Cruz, who leased parts of it. Van Houten, a tenant, built a prefabricated home (shipped around the Horn from the East) on what is now called Whitehouse Creek: Van Houten's white two-story residence was said to be so conspicuous a landmark that mariners sailing north reckoned the distance to San Francisco by sighting it. Eventually hidden from view by a eucalyptus grove, it burned in 1976.

In 1862 Loren Coburn came into possession of the greater part of Simeón Castro's original rancho. In that year he leased it to a group of dairymen; in this group were Horace Gushee, Charles H. Willson, and three members of the Steele family: Rensselaer, Isaac, and Edgar. The Steeles were natives of Delaware County, New York, who arrived in California in the mid-1850's. They located first north of San Francisco Bay, where they made butter and cheese of the highest quality and shipped it to San Francisco. After moving to Rancho Punta de Año Nuevo, they continued the same line of work. A brother of Isaac and Edgar and cousin of Rensselaer was General Frederick Steele of the Union Army in the Civil War. As a donation to the Sanitary Fund (the forerunner of today's American Red Cross), the Steeles made a 3,850-pound cheese for display at the Mechanics' Fair in San Francisco. After the fair ended, slices of the cheese were sent to President Lincoln, General Grant, and General Steele, and the remainder sold for one dollar a pound. The project realized some $2,820 for the Sanitary Fund by January 1864.

In 1869, the Steeles purchased over 7,000 acres of the rancho lying south of Gazos Creek and established a chain of highly successful dairies. Important structures remaining from the dairies include the Cascade Rancho House and Dairy Building, the Ramsey-Steele House, the Año Nuevo Rancho House, and the Dickerman Barn. The enterprise is marked (SRL 906) on SR 1, "the Cabrillo Highway," about thirteen miles south of Pescadero and about two miles north of the Santa Cruz county line.

Just north of Gazos Creek is Pigeon Point Lighthouse, built in 1872. Its height of 115 feet is equaled on the Pacific coast only by Point Arena Lighthouse in Mendocino County. The name comes from the clipper ship *Carrier Pigeon*, wrecked there on May 6, 1853; happily, the captain and crew survived the ordeal. The worst disaster on the San Mateo County coast occurred here in dense fog in August 1929; at least 77 lives were lost when the steamship *San Juan* collided with another vessel. Pigeon Point Lighthouse (SRL 930), still in operation, now shares its grounds with a youth hostel, and is one of the most photographed and painted spots on the California coast.

Rancho Feliz and Crystal Springs

Three of the old land grants later recognized by the United States government lay entirely in the interior of the county, with no border on the coast. They are Ranchos Feliz, Cañada de Raimundo, and Cañada del Corte de Madera.

The northernmost rancho of this group, Rancho

Feliz, was granted in 1844 by Governor Manuel Michel-torena to Domingo Feliz, to whom 4,448 acres were confirmed by United States patent in 1873. Don Domingo built a house situated, according to a grant-map of 1856, on the southern edge of his property west of a slough. Near it passed the road leading from San Mateo to the coast, converging near the location of his house with the road leading from Belmont to the coast. Skyline Boulevard coincides with the old San Mateo road where it crosses between Upper and Lower Crystal Springs Lakes on an earthen causeway.

The upper lakes of the San Andreas Valley (which gave its name to the great fault along which the 1906 earthquake occurred) lie on Rancho Feliz. The lakes were made by damming sloughs and lagoons to form reservoirs for the San Francisco water system. They hold the water brought from Hetch Hetchy Reservoir in Yosemite, 200 miles away. The enormous project of providing water for San Francisco and the Peninsula began at the turn of the century, but not until 1934 was Hetch Hetchy water actually brought to the lakes. At the south end of Upper Crystal Springs Lake is the Pulgas Water Temple, a Roman Renaissance–style structure, located at the outfall of the Hetch Hetchy tunnel. The inscription around the entablature reads: "I will give water in the wilderness and rivers in the desert to give drink to my people" (Isaiah 43:20). The present monument, built in 1938, replaced an earlier, temporary structure built for the ceremonies held in October 1934 when the first flow of Hetch Hetchy water poured into the San Francisco reservoirs. The Pulgas Water Temple is on the west side of Cañada Road, two miles south of its junction with SR 92.

Lower Crystal Springs Lake now covers the site of the settlement of Crystal Springs, near where Colonel Agoston Haraszthy made an experimental planting of

Pulgas Water Temple, Woodside

European wine grapes in the early 1850's. Haraszthy, a Hungarian nobleman, was a naturalized American citizen before he came to the West Coast and was a member of the state assembly in the early days of California's statehood. After a test of his 25-acre vineyard had proved that the fruit would not ripen properly in this location, he sold his property and removed the vines to Sonoma County, where soil and climate were more fitted to viticulture. There he established the Buena Vista Vineyard.

Rancho Cañada de Raymundo (Woodside)

Rancho Cañada de Raymundo was granted by Governor Alvarado in 1840 to John Copinger, "a man of ability and learning," once a British naval officer and later, in California, a lieutenant in charge of the artillery company that had brought about the success of Alvarado's revolution and put the governor in power. The rancho was bounded on the north by Rancho Feliz, on the south (at Arroyo Alambique) by Rancho Corte de Madera, and on the northeast by a line long in dispute with Rancho de las Pulgas.

John Copinger died in 1847, and in 1859 this property of 12,545 acres was patented to his widow, María Luisa (daughter of Rafael Soto), who in 1851 had married Captain John Greer, and to his daughter, Manuela Copinger, who afterward married José Antonio Miramontes and lived in a large house that long stood near present Woodside and Miramontes roads.

The Mountain Home Ranch, on Portola Road just southeast of the junction with La Honda Road (SR 84), is a part of Rancho Cañada de Raymundo sold by John Copinger to Charles Brown, a Baltimorean who left his whaling vessel in San Francisco in 1833. Brown lived at Sonoma and around San Jose before coming to this region. He built an adobe house here, probably about 1838, and a sawmill in 1849 near Alambique Creek, southwest of the house. A historical marker (SRL 478) at the junction of Woodside and Portola roads indicates the location of the first sawmill in San Mateo County.

At the time of the American occupation in 1846, there had been a settlement at Woodside for some ten years. As early as 1832, William Smith, an Englishman, came here to saw lumber for barter and sale. Other sawyers followed, and by 1849–50 sawmills were erected in the redwoods. Lumber was supplied to the incoming settlers of Santa Clara Valley and also shipped to San Francisco.

The old Woodside Store (SRL 93), the first store opened between San Francisco and Santa Clara, is the one surviving landmark of pioneer days in Woodside.

Woodside Store, Woodside

Now owned by the county of San Mateo, it is open to the public as a museum of the pioneer lumbering days, at 471 Kings Mountain Road.

"Searsville" is commemorated by a marker (SRL 474) at the junction of Portola and Sand Hill roads. John H. Sears emigrated to San Mateo County from New York via Cape Horn and in 1854 built a house later used as a hotel, known as the Sears House. A town grew up near this house, the location being a convenient stopping place for drivers of mule and ox teams hauling lumber from the mills east of La Honda ridge for loading on schooners at the Embarcadero at Redwood City. The little settlement was the scene of considerable activity on Sundays, when ox-pulling, horse racing, and cockfighting were popular amusements. Searsville Lake covers a part of the old town; it now supplies water for the Stanford University campus and is included in the university's Jasper Ridge Biological Preserve.

The La Questa Vineyard and House are located off Woodside Road at 240 La Questa Road. A vineyard was established here in the 1880's by Emmett H. Rixford with vines imported from France. The two-story winery was constructed by a Swiss mason of stones dug from the fields when the vineyard was laid out. The winery has been converted into a private residence.

Filoli (SRL 907), now owned by the National Trust for Historic Preservation, is on the western side of Cañada Road. The great Georgian Revival mansion was designed by Willis Polk for William Bowers Bourn II and occupied by his family in 1917. The Bourn family motto ("Fight, love, live") inspired the name. It later passed into the hands of the William B. Roth family, Mrs. Roth being Lurline Matson of the famed navigation company. Surrounded by beautifully landscaped gardens, Filoli represents the high point of the era in which country estates were owned by wealthy San Franciscans.

Rancho Cañada del Corte de Madera (Portola Valley)

This rancho, which lay above the confluence of Los Trancos and San Francisquito creeks, covered a large tract between the streams. Portola Road runs across it, and Searsville, Coon, and Felt Lakes, which are named for men who held property near them, are within the boundaries of the old rancho.

Governor Figueroa gave one square league of land there to Domingo Peralta and Máximo Martínez in 1833. Peralta, who had also part of Rancho San Ramón and a share of his father's great San Antonio Rancho across the bay, kept his part of the Corte de Madera grant for only a short time and divided it between his co-grantee, Martínez, and Cipriano Thurn in 1834. In 1879 some 3,566 acres of the rancho were patented to Thurn and Horace W. Carpentier.

More land appears to have been granted to Martínez at later dates, and the United States patent for 22,980 acres, of which a part extended across Los Trancos Creek, was given to him in 1858. His family resided in various houses on the property until 1901.

The name Corte de Madera means "timber choppings," and in fact the redwoods in this area had been exploited from a very early date by the Pueblo of San José and Mission Santa Clara. In the 1830's a new draying road (arrastradero) was opened to get lumber to the southern markets. Following a trail made by wild cattle through the hills to the southeast, it crossed Los Trancos Creek at the present Arastradero Road bridge. Felix Buelna built a gambling retreat and meeting place for his friends here in the 1850's. In 1868, when a section of the never-completed Menlo Park and Santa Cruz Turnpike was opened, the building at the junction was taken over by an American; it still stands today (SRL 825) as a wayside tavern. This place at the corner of Alpine and Arastradero roads has for several generations been a favorite haunt of Stanford University students.

The name Portola Valley is a local shortening of the name "Portola-Crespi Valley," which a landowner and newspaper editor bestowed on the area from Crystal Springs to Searsville in 1886. The settlement of Portola grew up on land purchased in 1883 by Andrew S. Hallidie, inventor of San Francisco's cable cars. Here he later experimented with another approach by building an aerial tramway suspended from an overhead cable from bottom to top of the mountainside on his property.

Early Catholic residents of Portola Valley found that their first church, a reconditioned dance hall, was inadequate and set out to construct a new one. Many residents participated in the construction in some fashion. The Church of Our Lady of the Wayside (SRL 909) at

930 Portola Road, designed by Timothy L. Pflueger and dedicated in 1912, is a charming fusion of the Georgian and Mission Revival styles of architecture.

Rancho Cañada de Guadalupe, la Visitación y Rodeo Viejo (Brisbane)

Of all the old land grants in the county, those bordering on San Francisco Bay have become the most widely known and most thickly settled. There ran El Camino Real of Hispanic days, and there today run the great highways that lead south from San Francisco.

The northernmost of these ranchos was Rancho Cañada de Guadalupe, la Visitación y Rodeo Viejo, consisting of two square leagues given in 1841 by Governor Alvarado to Jacob P. Leese. The grantee appears frequently in the early history of California because he engaged in commercial ventures in Monterey and in San Francisco and because he married Rosalía, sister of General Mariano Vallejo. Leese's ranch house was in the sheltered and oak-covered corner of the hill now occupied by the city of Brisbane, near Alvarado Street just west of Visitacion Avenue.

When in 1856 San Mateo County was formed by the division of San Francisco County, the dividing line ran through this rancho, placing most of its area in the new county.

Rancho Buriburi (South San Francisco, San Bruno, Millbrae)

Rancho Buriburi was granted to José Antonio Sánchez by the provincial government in 1835, confirming an earlier, tentative grant of 1827. The patent for the land was given to Sánchez's heirs in 1872 for 14,639 acres extending from the salt marshes on the Bay to the Spring Valley lakes and from the Colma cemeteries to the middle of what is now Burlingame.

This land had hitherto been a government cattle ranch; in 1797 Governor Borica had sent 265 head of cattle to it to provide meat for the Presidio of San Francisco. Immediately upon the formal grant of the Buriburi tract in 1835, the Sánchez family constructed two identical adobe houses in the area now occupied by the city of Millbrae; the houses stood until 1871.

On Rancho Buriburi are located the cities of South San Francisco, San Bruno, Millbrae, and the northern part of Burlingame. South San Francisco's first landholder was Charles Lux, a cattle baron, who purchased 1,500 acres of land from the Sánchez family in 1856 and erected a stately home between what are now Oak and Chestnut avenues. The land was used to hold cattle for grazing before they went to market. In time the meat-packing industry developed in this region, and other industries followed, until South San Francisco, incorporated as a city in 1908, became known as "The Industrial City." A prominent feature is its city hall, a copy of Independence Hall in Philadelphia, constructed in the early 1920's.

Millbrae received its name from Darius Ogden Mills, a native of New York and a man of influence in both the East and the West, who in 1860 became owner of the 1,100-acre headquarters tract of this rancho. In 1866 he erected a three-story, towered wooden mansion that he named Millbrae. In 1872, by employing a large group of Chinese laborers to drain marshland, Mills reclaimed many acres that he used as pasturage for his fine dairy herd. After his death, his daughter, then the widow of Whitelaw Reid, former United States ambassador to the Court of St. James, erected the Mills Memorial Hospital in San Mateo as a tribute to her father.

During World War II the old Mills mansion was used as a merchant marine convalescent home. In the 1950's the entire estate was razed for apartments and a shopping center; some doors, windows, and furnishings from the mansion were saved and incorporated into a building housing a restaurant on the south edge of St. Helena in Napa County. The mansion and grounds were located about where the block of apartments west of Ogden Drive now stands, and the entrance way is represented by Murchison Drive. The Millbrae station for the Southern Pacific Railroad, in Colonial Revival style, is listed on the National Register of Historic Places.

Rancho San Mateo (Burlingame, Hillsborough)

Rancho San Mateo was given in 1846 by Governor Pío Pico to his secretary, Cayetano Arenas, as a reward for military service. The two leagues (confirmed for 6,438 acres) were taken from an old rancho of Mission Dolores and were the last parcel of land in San Mateo County to be granted by the Mexican government. The rancho lay along San Francisco Bay between Rancho Buriburi on the north and San Mateo Creek on the south and was bounded on the west by Rancho Feliz along the course of the San Andreas Creek, which is now covered by Crystal Springs Lakes.

In November 1827, when some of the officers of the British ship *Blossom* passed through this region on their way to Monterey, they were impressed by its strong resemblance to "a nobleman's park; herds of cattle and horses were grazing upon the rich pasture, and numerous fallow deer, startled at the approach of strangers, bounded off to seek protection among the hills. The resemblance, however, could not be traced farther. Instead of a noble mansion in character with so fine a country, the party arrived at a miserable hut dwelling before the door of which a number of half naked Indians were basking in the sun." The litter scattered about the building "sadly disgraced the park-like scenery. This spot is named San Matheo, and belongs to the mission."

What the British sailors saw was the San Mateo outpost of Mission San Francisco de Asis (SRL 393). There were two long adobe structures, located end to end on the north bank of San Mateo Creek, with one end in what is now the intersection of Baywood Avenue and El Camino Real. The ruined state of the outpost is mentioned in *Eldorado* by Bayard Taylor, who saw it in 1849. The earthquake of 1868 completely wrecked the walls, and in 1870 all that remained of them was leveled. Some of the tiles from the roof were preserved and, with tile from Mission San Antonio in Monterey County, were used to build the roof of the railroad station at Burlingame (SRL 846). This station, at California Drive and Burlingame Avenue, is an early example of Mission Revival architecture, and has served the community since it opened in 1894.

In 1848 this rancho passed into the hands of William Davis Merry Howard, a Bostonian who had first come to California as cabin boy of a hide-drogher (a ship that transported hides along the coast). Later, with Henry Mellus, he purchased the abandoned office buildings of the Hudson's Bay Company in San Francisco, where they carried on mercantile persuits. Wishing to have property in whatever city might prove to be the metropolis of the new state, Howard bought large tracts of land in the towns of San Francisco, Sacramento, and Vallejo. Because of his philanthropic and commercial activities, Howard Street in San Francisco was named in his honor, and a memorial to him stands in St. Matthew's Episcopal Church in San Mateo, at the southern edge of his vast holdings. The church was organized in 1865 after preliminary services had been held in various locations, and was constructed of stone taken from a quarry on the Howard property on Crystal Springs Road. Situated at Baldwin Avenue and El Camino Real, the English Gothic church of today stands on the site of the 1865 structure, a victim of the 1906 earthquake. San Francisco architect Willis Polk designed the 1909 replacement, incorporating a small portion of the original building.

The city of San Mateo began with Nicholas de Peyster's roadhouse, situated in the old mission adobe in 1849 but moved the following year across the creek to a tall wooden structure called the San Mateo House. It stood until 1964, serving as a nurses' residence for the adjacent Mills Memorial Hospital.

In 1863, after the railroad had been built down the peninsula from San Francisco, a town was platted by C. B. Polhemus, and the San Mateo station became the northern terminus of the San Mateo, Pescadero, and Santa Cruz Stage Company lines owned by Taft and Garretson. Outlying places thus afforded communication with the railroad were Crystal Springs, San Felix, Byrnes's Store, Eureka Gardens, Spanishtown, Purisima, Lobitos, San Gregorio, Pescadero, Pigeon Point, Seaside, Davenport, and Santa Cruz, the last three lying within Santa Cruz County.

The town was eventually hedged around on three sides by large properties; that of W. D. M. Howard, who had purchased Rancho San Mateo on the north; that of Frederick Macondray, one of the first great merchants of San Francisco, who chose land just south of San Mateo Creek for a country home in 1854; and that of Alvinza Hayward, retired mine operator and financier, on the southeast.

The Macondray home in time became the property of John Parrott, identified with shipping and financial interests along the Pacific Coast. He developed the home and gave it the name Baywood; after its destruction in 1927 the site became the residential subdivision called Baywood. Hayward's home, afterward a hotel, stood near the tall palms on what is now Hayward Avenue.

Burlingame is named for Anson Burlingame, one-time United States minister to China and a purchaser of part of the Howard property. The nearby community of Hillsborough, noted for its beautiful estates, has two mansions of particular historical interest. Willis Polk designed an Italian-style mansion in 1917 for Templeton Crocker that was one of the last great buildings of the Peninsula. It is now the Crystal Springs School at 400 Uplands Drive. At 565 Remillard Road is Carolands (SRL 886), a huge French Renaissance mansion inspired by the Chateau of Vaux-le-Vicomte and designed by the French firm of E. Saint-Saens. The name comes from its builder, Francis Carolan, whose wife, Harriet Pullman, heiress to the Pullman fortune, was determined to have a house that outshone all other California residences. It fell into disuse upon the death of its last owner, Countess Lillian Remillard Dandini, and it may be torn down.

Rancho de las Pulgas (San Mateo, Belmont, San Carlos, Redwood City, Atherton, Menlo Park)

The Argüellos took a leading role in the Spanish days of Alta California, and the history of Rancho de las Pulgas is traced through the children and grandchildren of this pioneer family.

Don José Darío Argüello, one of the finest characters of those days, arrived at San Gabriel with his bride in 1781. They had traveled overland from Mexico in the company that Rivera had formed for the Santa Barbara presidio, which was soon to be established. In June 1787 Argüello was promoted to lieutenant in the San Francisco Company, where he served as *comandante* until March 1791 and again for a ten-year period beginning in 1796. He was holding a similar position in Santa Barbara in 1814 when, at the death of Governor Arrillaga, he was made acting governor of Alta California. He continued to live at Santa Barbara during the year that he held the two offices simultaneously. Receiving a commission as governor of Baja California in October 1815, he traveled overland with his wife and some of his children; although he would have liked to return to Alta California, he never did. His wife, Ignacia, niece of Lieutenant José Joaquín Moraga, first *comandante* of San Francisco, made both arduous overland journeys with him in those days when riding a horse or traveling in a creaking carreta were the only alternatives to walking.

The nine children of Don José Darío and Doña Ignacia Argüello were all born in California, and all received a careful home education. The eldest son, José Ignacio Máximo, was sent to Mexico to be trained for the priesthood and in later years came back to California to officiate on special occasions. Gervasio, of some military importance, married Encarnación Bernal during the year that his father was acting governor in Santa Barbara and spent his last years in Mexico. Concepción, whose story is told in the chapter on San Francisco County, accompanied her parents to Baja California during the time she was awaiting word from her long-absent lover, Count Nikolai Rezanov. She stayed for a time before returning to Alta California to spend the rest of her life.

Santiago, one year younger than his sister Concepción and a cadet at the San Francisco Presidio when Rezanov made the acquaintance of the family, married Pilar, daughter of Francisco Ortega of Santa Barbara, when he was very young and became the father of 22 children. He became grantee of several tracts of land, held many important military positions, and left an honorable record in all parts of the state when he died in 1862 at his Tijuana Rancho (San Diego County) at the age of 71. The most prominent among the children of Don José Darío was Luís Antonio Argüello, born in San Francisco in 1784. Having been elected acting governor of California in 1822, a position he held until 1825, he had the distinction of being the first native-born governor of the territory. He was frequently involved in controversies and, although he was concerned with the welfare of his country, he did not win universal approval as his father had.

Two tracts of land appear to have been granted to Don José Darío Argüello before the year 1800. One,

called "El Pilar," was given "in consideration of his large family." Of this, little is known: according to Hittell, it was an indefinite tract on the coast between Point San Pedro and Point Año Nuevo, and the grant was never confirmed. The other, known at that time as "Cachanígtac" but afterward called "Las Pulgas" (the fleas), contained about twelve square leagues and was situated on San Francisco Bay between San Mateo Creek on the north and San Francisquito Creek on the south. The western boundary line of this tract was the cause of much litigation.

The precise location of the Pulgas ranch house is unknown. The best interpretation of available evidence is that it was a crude building of palisade construction, rather than adobe, with a thatched roof, and that it stood on a little bend of Pulgas Creek on the south edge of present San Carlos Avenue in San Carlos.

This rancho consisted of very rich and accessible land, and the vague description of its western boundary, "back to the sierra or range of mountains," caused misunderstandings and disputes. The matter was finally settled in 1856 when a patent for 32,240 acres was issued to Doña María Argüello (widow of Don Luís Darío), her two sons, and an attorney, Simón Monserrate Mezes, who had been given a part of the land in return for his services in defending the title against squatters. About this time Mezes built a frame house at present Cedar Street and Magnolia Avenue in San Carlos, a location formerly thought to have been that of the original ranch headquarters.

Since the 1850's the vast grant has been cut into uncounted portions of varying sizes, and the land that comprised this old rancho is now densely populated. El Camino Real, on whose borders the cities of San Mateo, Belmont, San Carlos, Redwood City, Atherton, and Menlo Park have clustered runs through the grant from San Mateo Creek on the north to San Francisquito Creek on the south, and beyond into Santa Clara County. The close proximity of the cities makes the road for the entire distance like a city street. To carry the congested traffic, the parallel Bayshore Freeway (US 101) was constructed, and now the cities have stretched some of their streets over to the freeway and beyond. To the west, the Junipero Serra Freeway (I-280), extending from Daly City to San Jose, is now another important artery.

A bridge crossing the lower part of the Bay extends from San Mateo to Hayward in Alameda County. The San Mateo Bridge—twelve miles long, seven over water—was the longest highway bridge in the world when it opened in 1929. A new bridge replaced the old one in 1970. At the lower end of the rancho, a railroad bridge and the Dumbarton Toll Bridge cross the Bay from East Palo Alto to Newark. The Dumbarton Bridge, the first to span the Bay, opened in 1927; it too has been replaced by a new structure.

South of these bridges, at the very southeastern corner of the grant, the now almost forgotten town of Ravenswood was platted. The John Beal Steinberger property at this point was purchased in 1852 by I. C. Woods, Rufus Rowe, D. H. Haskell, John K. Hackett, and C. D. Judah, who laid out the town. Promoters hoped that the Central Pacific Railroad would choose this spot for the end of a bridge across the Bay. When that plan did not materialize, the town was abandoned, and the temporary structures that had been erected soon disappeared. The site of the old Ravenswood wharf is known as Cooley's Landing. The Ravenswood area is now East Palo Alto, but the old name survives in the local elementary school district.

Belmont and San Carlos

The first permanent settler at present Belmont was Charles Aubrey Angelo, an Englishman, who in 1850 opened a stage station called the Angelo House on a spot now 1,200 feet south of Ralston Avenue between the railroad tracks and Old County Road. The town that grew up, which became the first county seat of San Mateo County in 1856, centered about the Ralston Avenue–Old County Road intersection in its early years. The Belmont Hotel at the northeast corner, begun by John T. Ellet in 1853, stood there for many years. A store begun by Matthew J. O'Neill and Walter A. Emmett in 1880 still stands on the northwest corner of the intersection. Here as elsewhere throughout the Peninsula, older buildings by the score have been pulled down to make room for newer and more commodious structures.

West of the town lies the Cañada del Diablo, chosen by S. M. Mezes, one of the patentees of the Pulgas rancho, for his home. There, too, lived Leonetto Cipriani, Mezes's one-time law partner, in a small villa set on the hillside. Cipriani returned to his native Italy in the excitement of the Risorgimento in the early 1860's, and William C. Ralston bought the villa and acreage. With discriminating taste, Ralston made his estate a place of unusual charm, where he entertained people of worldwide distinction during the 1860's and 1870's.

William Chapman Ralston, a native of Ohio, who had already gained valuable experience in the shipping world before his arrival in San Francisco in 1854, became a powerful Western financier. He maintained both a city and a country home, and upon the latter he spent lavishly. From the modest villa of Count Cipriani he evolved a residence of great magnificence. With his wife, Elizabeth, he became "the perfect host," giving delightful weekend parties, banquets, and balls. From his stone-built, mahogany-stalled stables, he was able to provide mounts for a score of guests.

For the illumination of his country seat he erected costly gas works that also benefited the town of Belmont; for his own use he built a wharf on the bayshore but generously shared it with the public.

After his death by drowning in August 1875, the marvelously developed estate was taken over by his former business associate, William Sharon, of Comstock Lode fame. Sharon built a great dam and reservoir in the hills to provide irrigation for the plantings that have now grown to parklike proportions.

Following its occupancy by Senator Sharon, the house at Belmont was used for a private school kept by the widow of Alpheus Bull, a business associate of both Ralston and Sharon. Later, the house was turned into a hospital by Dr. Gardiner.

In 1923 the place was taken over by the Sisters of Notre Dame, who removed to it their convent and college established in San Jose in 1851. The Ralston mansion is now Ralston Hall (SRL 856), restored to the character of the Ralston era. The Cipriani villa is identifiable as one wing of the house, which is on the register of National Historic Landmarks.

Although San Carlos was the site of the original Pulgas Ranch, the town dates only from 1887 and its name from the beginning of the following year; it is said to be called after the first ship to enter San Francisco Bay, the *San Carlos* (1775), which in turn had been named as a patriotic compliment to King Carlos III of Spain. In 1886 S. M. Mezes and others laid out the road called Alameda de las Pulgas, thereby preserving the original name of the area. The principal landmark of San Carlos is the Southern Pacific railroad station, built in 1888 in an ornamental style of sandstone blocks and somewhat resembling the Stanford University architecture of the same period and material. Indeed, Italian stonemasons imported to build the Stanford quadrangle also worked on this building. The Museum of San Carlos History is at 533 Laurel Street.

The San Mateo County Historical Museum is located on the grounds of the College of San Mateo at 1700 West Hillsdale Boulevard in San Mateo. It contains materials on the history of the county going back to prehistoric times as well as an impressive collection of horse-drawn carriages.

Embarcadero de las Pulgas, Redwood City

A little creek, running through Rancho de las Pulgas where Redwood City, the county seat, now stands and emptying into a slough or arm of the bay, formed a natural shipping point or embarcadero.

Lumbering became an important industry wherever the redwoods grew, and there were many of these trees in the mountains within a few miles of this place. In 1850 the shipment of lumber from the Woodside and Searsville mills began, and the Embarcadero became a busy wharf. Several schooners were launched there that year. Wagon making and blacksmithing were important adjuncts to the business of hauling the product of the mills to the Embarcadero and were early established there. This was the nucleus around which the present Redwood City developed. Redwood Creek flows under the city today, and Redwood Slough is filled in.

William Carey Jones, who had come to the West Coast in 1849 as a special government agent to investigate the condition of land titles in California, acquired over 2,000 acres near Redwood City from the Pulgas Ranch. It extended from Five Points to Whipple Avenue and from El Camino Real to the brow of the hill. This property was put up for sheriff's sale early in 1858, when it was purchased by Horace Hawes. Hawes was a native of New York who had been named by President Polk to be American consul for the Society Islands and other South Sea islands in 1847. By an unanticipated routing of the vessel on which he took passage, he arrived in San Francisco, where he remained and became prefect. He resided in San Francisco and at Redwood Farm, his country home, until his death in 1870. He was a staunch supporter of the Union side during the Civil War. The western part of Redwood City stands on this property. If the original plans of the owner had been carried through, a seat of learning called "Mount Eagle University" would have been located in the area. On Woodside Road in this part of Redwood City is the Union Cemetery (SRL 816), which was actually created and named in 1859, reflecting two years before the Civil War broke out the patriotic sentiments of the community.

The first Protestant church in the county was organized in Redwood City in 1862. Land was purchased at the present corner of Middlefield Road and Jefferson Avenue for a building for the First Congregational Church, which had been meeting in the courthouse for some months.

Downtown Redwood City contains several interesting old buildings fairly close to one another. The oldest building in town, the Offerman House at 1018 Main Street, was built in 1857 and is now an antique store. The Lathrop House at 627 Hamilton Street is a handsome, restored two-story structure, whose establishment in 1863 is commemorated by a plaque placed by the Native Daughters of the Golden West. An interesting commercial structure is the old Bank of San Mateo County building from 1900, at the corner of Broadway and Main Street.

Dominating the Redwood City skyline is the impressive San Mateo County courthouse. This is the fourth courthouse in the county's history, and an unusual example of Roman-Renaissance architectural style. Designed in 1903, the building had been accepted by the board of supervisors but not yet occupied when the 1906 earthquake struck. The building was severely damaged, but the 116-foot-high dome and its massive panels of stained glass came through the earthquake unharmed. In 1910 the board of supervisors held its first meeting in the new courthouse. The courthouse, at Broadway and Hamilton, has a large annex, added in 1939.

Menlo Park and Atherton

The adjoining areas of Menlo Park and Atherton lie near the southern part of the county along El Camino Real. Their common boundaries are so irregular that it is difficult to distinguish the territory of the earlier-named Menlo Park from its newer neighbor.

Dennis J. Oliver and his brother-in-law, D. C. McGlynn, became owners of a 1,700-acre tract on the Pulgas rancho and in the 1850's erected a gate with a wooden arch across its top. This was at the corner of the present Middle Avenue and El Camino Real. The arch bore the inscription "Menlo Park" in memory of "the most beautiful spot in the world"—their former home in Menlough, County Galway, Ireland. This gate became weatherworn, but it was preserved while Camp Fremont, used for the concentration of troops during World War I, was in the area. The arch was destroyed in an automobile accident in 1922. The Camp Fremont buildings were gradually pulled down after the war, with the exception of one building designed by the noted California architect Julia Morgan. The building was the Y.W.C.A. Hostess House at the camp during the war and was later moved south across the county line to Palo Alto to a site near the intersection of University Avenue and El Camino Real (SRL 895) for use as a community center and veterans' building. After significant restoration in the late 1970's, it now houses a restaurant.

Upon the building of the San Francisco–San Jose Railroad down the Peninsula in 1863, a station called Menlo Park was placed a short distance from this old gate. The Victorian "gingerbread" station (SRL 955), built in 1867, still stands, now converted to other uses. Men of wealth, many of them San Francisco businessmen, chose this locality for the luxurious country homes that they built on ample estates at convenient driving distances from the railroad station. A town of small houses, hotels, and stores grew up near the station, and in 1873 the first church in the town was organized by a group of Presbyterian residents. In the following year a house of worship was erected upon land donated for that purpose, and in it Protestant families of the town and the surrounding countryside attended services. This frame structure was located on Santa Cruz Avenue a little west of El Camino Real. The Roman Catholic Church of the Nativity, built in the same period, still stands on Oak Grove Avenue east of El Camino. On March 23, 1874, the town was incorporated, but the incorporation was allowed to lapse and was not renewed until November 15, 1927.

Not far from the station a fine residence was built by Milton S. Latham, an Ohioan who had arrived in California in 1850 and had purchased land from John T. Doyle in 1871. He eventually bought several other small tracts adjoining his original purchase. He was elected governor of California in 1859, only to renounce that honor later in the same year to fill the unexpired term of United States Senator David C. Broderick, who had been slain in a duel that took place within the county. Latham entertained extensively in this country home. The house, with its stately pillars, costly interior, and elaborate fountains placed in well-landscaped grounds among large native oaks, became the property of Mary Hopkins, the widow of Mark Hopkins, one of the pioneers of the state who had arrived from New York in 1849 and one of the "Big Four" who put through the building of the Central Pacific Railroad. After her remarriage in 1888, the great house passed to their adopted son, Timothy, who followed in the footsteps of Mark Hopkins by becoming treasurer of the Central Pacific Railroad Company. The mansion was badly damaged in the earthquake of 1906, and eventually it was pulled down, having stood for decades at the end of a once well-kept drive far back in the grounds entered at

Latham Gate House, Menlo Park

the keeper's gate on Ravenswood Avenue. The Latham Gate House still stands at 555 Ravenswood, and is now occupied by the offices of community organizations as part of the Menlo Park Civic Center.

Besides the wealthy residents who came to the region of Menlo Park for rest and recreation on their large estates there were permanent residents who worked there. One such family was established by John and Margaret Murray, who came around the Horn from New York in 1854. They purchased various lands within the confines of the present county. From Menlo Park they shipped milk to San Francisco by stage, and there twin sons were born to them. In later years Margaret divided 28 acres of land that she held on San Francisquito Creek among her four children. One son, John Jarvis, was given the part nearest the creek and on it erected a house and barn about the year 1880. In 1930 the land was acquired from James, son of John Jarvis, by the Allied Arts Guild of California. On these three acres are ateliers, shops, and a restaurant; the proceeds of the latter help support the Childrens Hospital at Stanford. The old Murray barn is incorporated into this attractive and philanthropic complex at Arbor Road and Creek Drive.

Atherton, incorporated in 1923, extends in its longest direction from Bay Road between Ringwood Avenue and Marsh Road, across Middlefield Road, the railroad, and El Camino Real, and to a little distance west of the Alameda de la Pulgas. Within this area are many large modern homes and the sites of older ones no longer standing.

Faxon Dean Atherton, originally from Massachusetts, first visited California in 1836 while a resident of Chile and a member of a firm engaged in the hide-and-tallow trade. In 1860 he acquired a tract of over 400 acres, formerly occupied by James King of William, and built a country mansion among the native oaks growing there. He named his estate "Valparaiso Park," from the city in Chile where his wife had been born and where he had spent his early manhood. Life in this house is depicted by his daughter-in-law, Gertrude Atherton, in her *Adventures of a Novelist*, written of the period when the country was sparsely settled and quiet afternoons on a comfortable veranda had few interruptions.

After the Atherton family was gone, the place was used as a school for boys by Ira G. Hoyt, a former state superintendent of public instruction, and during the occupancy of this school the mansion was destroyed by fire. The location, near the intersection of Elena and Isabella avenues (names of two of the Atherton daughters), is now owned by the Menlo Circus Club, which was organized primarily for the purpose of raising funds for the Stanford Home for Convalescent Chil-

Watkins-Cartan House, Atherton

dren. Valparaiso Avenue, not far off, carries the name of the old house, and the name of the former Fair Oaks station where a post office was established in 1867 has been superseded by the name Atherton.

The Watkins-Cartan House at 25 Isabella Avenue in Atherton is said to be the oldest house in the Menlo Park–Atherton area. The Victorian Gothic house was prefabricated in Connecticut and originally erected on the site of the Atherton railroad station. It was the summer residence of Captain James W. Watkins, of the Pacific Mail Steamship Company, and dates from 1860; it is still a charming, well-preserved private residence.

John T. Doyle, a "scholar of rare culture and refinement" and one of the foremost lawyers of his day, in 1856 purchased land in the vicinity from Horace P. Jones and gradually added to the acreage until he owned a large tract. One of his accomplishments for the welfare of the new state was the final disentangling of the affairs of the missions at the request of Archbishop Alemany. In the course of his duties he often traveled the ill-kept roads between the missions, always receiving a welcome from the resident fathers.

General William Tecumseh Sherman was one of the frequent honored visitors at the Doyle home, a palatial frame house. The ample veranda was shaded by a wisteria vine of huge proportions. Although the old house no longer stands, the tall palms of the drive leading to its site still border Toyon Road off Ringwood Avenue. Not far from the Doyle house was the Joseph

A. Donohoe residence on Middlefield Road, now the location of Menlo-Atherton High School.

Another man who had one of the early houses in the Menlo Park–Atherton vicinity was Charles N. Felton, who entertained there extensively. Originally from New York, he became subtreasurer at San Francisco and also served from March 1891 to March 1893 as United States Senator, completing the term of George Hearst. He built his house in 1870 and lived in it until his death in 1913. The mansion is no longer standing, but the property, near Encinal Avenue and the Southern Pacific Railroad, is now a residential subdivision called "Felton Gables."

James Clair Flood, who arrived in San Francisco in 1849 and became one of the "Bonanza Kings" of the Comstock Lode, bought a tract of land along Middlefield Road in 1876 and two years later began the erection of a great white mansion upon it. The house was called Linden Towers and was placed well back from the road and surrounded by lawn and fine trees. Eventually it passed to his son James L. Flood, who purchased neighboring land as well and enclosed the estate by placing a brick wall along the entire frontage on Middlefield Road. James L. Flood died in 1928, and the house was torn down in 1934; the brick wall still stands, now bordering a residential subdivision.

Until 1956 the oldest building in the Menlo Park–Atherton area was a unique structure that stood near the corner of Ringwood and Colby avenues, probably the only surviving example in California of an early Spanish type of construction, the *encajonada* or "boxed-house." The walls were made of rammed earth columns tamped down inside a movable frame, in this case a lattice of redwood laths, rather than the usual wattle covering. It was probably built in the Mexican period to house herdsmen of the Rancho de las Pulgas. There is evidence that it was constructed before 1846; its redwood laths, therefore, must have been hand-sawed in the sawpits of Woodside.

After standing for over a century, the strange adobe found itself face to face with bulldozers clearing the land for a subdivision. The owner, John Wickett, a man with more than a passing interest in California history, could not bring himself to destroy it, and local authorities would not permit him to move the "substandard structure" to another site in the same area. He therefore had it raised on jacks and transported many miles over a winding mountain road to property he owned near Skyline Boulevard—no mean accomplishment, when it is remembered that what was moved were unframed, unsupported, foundationless walls held together only by their own compaction. The adobe stands on private grounds off Skyline Boulevard across from the Skeggs Point observation area.

La Honda

John H. Sears moved from Searsville in the winter of 1861–62 and settled seventeen miles from Redwood City in the mountains. The place eventually acquired the name La Honda, from the creek, Arroyo Hondo ("deep"), so named for its deep and redwood-filled canyon. About 1877 Sears began the construction of a store, and in 1878 he became low bidder to build the present winding Old La Honda Road, the first road through the isolated region. The Sears store (SRL 343) was often called the "Bandit-built Store," because the owner employed in its construction two newcomers to the vicinity who, after their departure, were believed to have been the Younger brothers, Jim and Bob, outlaws from the Midwest, where the pair were jailed soon after they left California. The old store stood at the northwest corner of La Honda and Sears Ranch roads until it was torn down early in 1960.

The Broderick-Terry Duel

An aftermath of the bitter political campaign of 1859 in California was a duel that reverberated throughout the nation because of the prominence of the participants and the death of one. Both men were pioneers of 1849 and members of the same political party, although they espoused opposite factions.

David C. Broderick, born in Ireland in 1820, had lived in New York as a boy and had come from there to California, where he became a power in the Democratic party. He was acting lieutenant governor in 1851 and became United States senator in 1857.

David C. Terry, born in Kentucky in 1823, had seen military service in Texas and Mexico before coming to the West Coast in 1849. He became chief justice of the California Supreme Court and was active in politics, first as a Whig, then as a leader in the American or Know-Nothing party. In the campaign of 1859 he allied himself with the "Chivalry" (pro-Southern) faction of the Democratic party. Incensed by certain statements made by Senator Broderick of the "Tammany" (opposing) faction in his campaign speeches, Terry challenged him to a duel at a site outside the jurisdiction of San Francisco County.

A plaque in the parking lot at 1100 Lake Merced Boulevard in Daly City (SRL 19) is about one-quarter of a mile from the actual field of combat, which was located and marked in 1917 by the Landmarks Committee of the Native Sons of the Golden West. The site is in a small ravine just off a park that can be reached from the aforementioned parking lot or from El Portal Way between Cliffside and Lakeview drives. Two granite shafts were later erected where the principals stood, marked with their names. On the eminence nearby, where spectators witnessed the duel, there is a bronze tablet on a foundation of granite, stating the historic facts of the event. The text is as follows: "U.S. Senator, David C. Broderick, and Chief Justice of the Supreme Court, David S. Terry, met here in the early morning of September 13, 1859, Senator Broderick receiving a mortal wound. This was the last of the great duels fought in California. With the exception of the Burr-Hamilton affair, no duel has taken place in the United States where the principals were as well known or occupied as high official positions."

Broderick was carried back to San Francisco, where he died three days later. The story went about that his pistol had misfired and that Terry had coolly shot him. Public opinion in California, disgusted by the rift in the dominant Democratic party, began to move to the newly formed Republican party. Abraham Lincoln, a Republican, was elected to the presidency in 1860 with the help of California's four electoral votes, and Leland Stanford, also a Republican, was elected governor of California the following year.

Terry, a combative man, soon joined the Confederate Army, where he became a brigadier general. After the war he spent some time in Mexico. He later returned to California, settling in Stockton, where his fiery temper embroiled him in many an altercation. In 1889 he was shot to death in the railway station at Lathrop (San Joaquin County) by United States Marshal David Neagle, bodyguard of United States Supreme Court Justice Stephen J. Field, whom he had attacked.

Santa Barbara County

Santa Barbara County took its name from Santa Barbara Channel, so called by Vizcaíno when his ship entered it on December 4, 1602, the feast day of Saint Barbara. This was one of the original 27 counties of the state, and the city of Santa Barbara has been the county seat from the beginning.

Chumash Painted Cave State Historic Park

In a canyon near the summit of San Marcos Pass, some 2,600 feet high and about twelve miles northwest of the city of Santa Barbara, is a remarkable cave filled with Indian pictographs. This site is on Painted Cave Road, about two miles north of its junction with SR 154, the San Marcos Pass Road. Conventionalized pictures of human figures, trees, snakelike creatures, and the sun, including what may be a depiction of a solar eclipse, and circular designs and crosses, done in red, white, yellow, and black, cover the interior of the cavern. Modern research has come up with some tentative conclusions about these unusual paintings: they were made by some of the numerous Chumash family of Indians; they were probably shamanistic and used for rituals of some kind; and they were shown only to the initiates of a cult, for no more than two people can fit into the cave at the same time. The cave has been protected from defacement and injury by a locked gate.

In the early 1970's the land around the Painted Cave was purchased by a citizens' committee and the private, nonprofit California State Parks Foundation, which presented it to the state of California. Today Chumash Painted Cave State Historic Park is operated as a satellite unit of El Capitan State Beach, and permission to visit the cave must be obtained from the office of the latter.

Burton Mound and the Puerto de Santa Barbara

Burton Mound (SRL 306), located within circular Burton Drive between Natoma Avenue and Mason Street in Santa Barbara, is today merely a gentle rise surrounded by city streets and dwellings, about a block and a half from Santa Barbara Harbor. It is thought that this mound is the site of the Indian village of Syujtun, recorded by Cabrillo in 1542 on his voyage of discovery. In 1769 Portolá and Father Crespí also noted the existence of this Indian village. Excavations conducted here by the Museum of the American Indian, Heye Foundation, of New York City in 1923 confirmed the antiquity of the site.

The old Puerto de Santa Bárbara, an early landing place for the mission and presidio, was located at the foot of the present Chapala Street west of the mouth of Mission Creek and due east of and comprising Burton Mound. During mission days this land was owned by Mission Santa Barbara and was called El Rancho de la Playa ("The Ranch of the Beach"). After secularization it became the property of the Mexican government, which granted it to James (Santiago) Burke, who, in turn, sold it to Joseph Chapman, the young New Englander who had escaped from Bouchard's pirate ship in 1818. Chapman, it is said, erected a small adobe house on the mound, later conveying the land to Benjamin Foxen.

According to tradition, the massive adobe that stood on the mound for over 70 years, long the most conspicuous landmark on the Santa Barbara waterfront, was erected by Thomas Robins. For about ten years, during the 1840's, it was the home of Captain George C. Nidever, who, it is said, planted trees and gardens and added two outbuildings to the adobe house. In 1851, Nidever sold the place to Augustus F. Hinchman, Santa Barbara attorney and prominent citizen, who in 1860 sold it to Lewis T. Burton. Burton had come to California with the Wolfskill party in 1831. He became a wealthy merchant and ranchero and in 1839 married María Antonia Carrillo, daughter of Carlos Carrillo. Burton lived in the home until his death in 1879, by which time Santa Barbara had become famous as a resort; the Seaside Hotel Association acquired Burton's property with the intention of building a hotel on the site. Not until 1901–2, however, was the Potter (later the Ambassador) Hotel built, and beautifully landscaped gardens soon covered the historic Indian mound. The hotel burned in 1921, and the site was released for archaeological investigations.

Carpinteria

One-quarter of a mile southwest of the historical monument on US 101 at Carpinteria, on the east bank of Carpinteria Creek, is the site of an Indian shell mound, now subdivided and built up with homes. This was the location of the Chumash village of Mishopshnow (SRL 535), discovered by the Cabrillo expedition in 1542. One-half mile east of the mouth of the creek were asphalt pits, now excavated. The tar exuding from the banks along the shore was used by the Chumash people for caulking boats, baskets, and vessels for carrying liquid. The story of the Spanish naming of the village is told by Father Crespí, diarist of the Portolá expedition of 1769: "Not very far from the town we saw some springs of asphaltum. These Indians have many canoes, and at that time were constructing one, for which reasons the soldiers named the town Carpintería [carpenter shop] but I baptized it with the name of San Roque."

Excavations have revealed the presence not only of human inhabitants over long periods of time, but also of prehistoric animals similar to those taken from the famous La Brea Pits in Los Angeles. An old tar pit may be seen at the end of Calle Ocho in Carpinteria Beach State Park. In the early days of Santa Barbara County, wharves were built at this asphalt deposit and the material was taken out for shipment to San Francisco and elsewhere in California.

The Carpinteria Valley Museum at 956 Maple Avenue has displays of artifacts from both Chumash and more recent times.

The Santa Barbara Channel Islands

Four islands lie in the Santa Barbara Channel off the coast of Santa Barbara County. San Miguel Island has long been thought to be the burial place of Juan Rodríguez Cabrillo, discoverer of Alta California. In 1542, Cabrillo's ships, the *San Salvador* and the *Victoria*, lay anchored for eight days in a bay at San Miguel awaiting the abatement of the autumn storms that delayed their passage north. During this time Cabrillo suffered a fall, breaking his arm near the shoulder.

In spite of his injury and in the face of many misfortunes, he continued his voyage, going as far as the Northwest Cape near Fort Ross. Forced back by storms at this point, Cabrillo turned south. Although tradition holds that he died and was buried on San Miguel on January 3, 1543, the historian Harry Kelsey has argued that his final resting place was on Santa Catalina Island, in the southern Channel Islands group. A bronze tablet mounted on a granite boulder was placed in honor of Cabrillo by the Santa Barbara Chapter, Daughters of the American Revolution, in 1919, in the palm garden along the waterfront on East Cabrillo Boulevard between Santa Barbara and Punta Gorda streets.

Most of the Channel Islands are now part of Channel Islands National Park. Three of the islands within the jurisdiction of Santa Barbara County—San Miguel, Santa Barbara, and Santa Cruz—are also archaeological districts noted on the National Register of Historic Places.

Point Conception

Point Conception, which marks a change in the direction of the California coastline, was discovered by Cabrillo on October 18, 1542, and sighted by many other early explorers. Bolton says that, sailing up the coast from San Diego, the ships had anchored on October 14 off Carpinteria, on the 15th five miles west of Point Goleta, on the 16th off Cañada del Refugio, and on the 17th off Gaviota Pass. Cabrillo had difficulty rounding Point Conception because of storms, and for eight days he was forced to anchor his ships at San Miguel Island before again attempting the passage. After several days of buffeting by the winds, he was driven back to anchorage off Gaviota Pass, where he remained for three days, taking on wood and water. On November 6 he was finally able to round Point Conception, the "Cape Horn of the Pacific."

The Point Conception Light Station, one of the remotest anywhere along the Pacific coast, was built in 1855. The station was too high on the bluff for its light to pierce the coastal fog, and it was abandoned for a lower site in 1882, which is still in operation.

Point Arguello

Point Arguello, a rocky headland twenty miles southwest of Lompoc, forms, with Point Conception, the corner where the California coastline turns from a generally north-south direction to a line running east and west. Its historic interest is largely associated with the many ships that have been wrecked there.

The first of these was probably the USS *Edith*, wrecked in 1849. The story is told that the sailors aboard the *Edith*, being anxious to join the gold rush, deliberately ran the ship up on the beach, where it was broken up by the waves. Some of the crew and passengers stayed for a short time at Rancho Nipomo (San Luis Obispo County), where the hospitable ranchero, Captain William G. Dana, gave them horses and money so they could continue to the mines. Afterward the ship was salvaged by Dana, and the materials were used on the rancho. The smokestack on the forge in the blacksmith shop was part of the wreckage put to good use by this thrifty Bostonian. The sidewheel steamer *Yankee Blade* was wrecked in 1854, allegedly carrying $153,000 in gold bullion, none of which seems to have been recovered.

The greatest disaster along the California coast in

recorded history occurred here on September 8, 1923, when seven United States Navy destroyers southward bound in a thick night fog piled on the rocks three miles north, one after the other. Twenty-two men were lost, and every ship was damaged beyond repair.

Since then, the toll taken by the rocky point from the procession of ships that constantly pass that way has included the passenger steamer *Harvard*, which went aground about one and one-half miles north of Point Arguello on May 30, 1931; the freighter *Iowan* in 1941; and the Greek freighter *Ionnes Kulkundous* in 1949. Remains of some of these vessels may be seen just offshore. The first lighthouse at Point Arguello was fairly late in appearing, compared to others along the Pacific coast; not until 1901 was a light station erected here. It was replaced in 1934 by another, and that in turn has been replaced by a fully automatic beacon and an electronic sensing device called Loran.

Along the coast some distance east of points Arguello and Conception and a few miles west of Goleta is the Ellwood Oil Field. On the night of February 23, 1942, the Japanese submarine *I-17*, under Commander Kozo Nishino, came to the surface a little more than a mile offshore and shelled the oil field for twenty minutes without any significant American reprisal. There were no casualties, and the damage was minor; one oil well was hit and a pier was partially destroyed. Two large gasoline storage tanks, the primary target of the Japanese, were untouched. The Tokyo press, however, reported that Santa Barbara had been devastated. Lumber from the damaged pier was subsequently sold as salvage and was later incorporated into a building on the north side of US 101 that has since been used as a restaurant.

The Trail of Gaspar de Portolá

On the southwest corner of the grounds of Santa Barbara's courthouse is a boulder placed by the Santa Barbara Chapter, DAR, and set with a bronze tablet bearing the inscription: "In honor of Governor de Portolá, his officers and soldiers, and Fray Juan Crespí (diarist), the first white men to march through the wilderness of California. Arrived at Santa Barbara, August 18, 1769, and camped in this vicinity two days."

The land expedition from Mission San Diego to Monterey Bay, under direct command of Gaspar de Portolá, left San Diego on July 14, 1769. Traveling up the coast, the party blazed a trail that was later the route followed approximately by El Camino Real ("the king's highway"), along which the California mission chain was established.

On August 16 Portolá and his men made camp at an Indian village near what is now known as Rincon Point, on Rincon Creek. The following day they reached another village where they found the inhabitants building a canoe and accordingly called the place La Carpintería. On August 18, Portolá reached a very large Indian town, where downtown Santa Barbara now stands, and pitched camp there.

Proceeding up the coast along the Santa Barbara Channel, the party passed many Indian villages. The people of this region were fishermen with large, well-made canoes, in which they plied between the mainland and the Channel Islands.

In the days following, the party passed up the coast, camping successively on the west side of what is now Santa Barbara, at Goleta, Dos Pueblos Canyon, Tajiguas Creek, Gaviota, Wild Horse Canyon under Point Arguello, Cañada Honda, and, on August 30, the mouth of the Santa Ynez River at Surf. The next day camp was made near San Antonio Creek on the present Vandenberg Air Force Base, and on September 1 the party traveled northward to Guadalupe Lake, beyond which lay present-day San Luis Obispo County.

The Anza Trail

Juan Bautista de Anza in 1774 followed a welltrodden path from San Gabriel to Monterey, broken first by Gaspar de Portolá and followed later a halfdozen times by Pedro Fages and also by Father Junipero Serra on his way to Mexico in 1772. On his hurried trip in the spring of 1774, Anza made only three camps in Santa Barbara County: west of Goleta, April 12; east of Rocky Point, April 13; and on the south bank of the Santa Ynez River near its mouth, April 14. On April 15 Anza rode all the way from the Santa Ynez River to Mission San Luis Obispo, a distance of over 50 miles. On his return from Monterey, he camped on the north bank of the Santa Ynez River, April 26. On the 27th he met Father Serra on his way back from Mexico City. At the friar's urging, Anza recounted the story of his overland journey, and camped with him that night somewhere east of Point Conception and west of Goleta. On the 28th Anza continued, camping that night at Dos Pueblos Canyon.

The San Francisco colonists led by Anza in 1776 made camp at the following sites: Rincon Creek, west of Rincon Point, on February 24; near Carpinteria Landing at an Indian village, February 25; west of Goleta, February 26; El Cojo Canyon, east of Point Conception, February 27; near Surf, at the mouth of the Santa Ynez River, February 28; and near the mouth of San Antonio

Creek, February 29. A tablet in honor of Anza has been placed in the courthouse grounds at Santa Barbara.

The Santa Barbara Presidio

Founded April 21, 1782, the Santa Barbara Royal Presidio was the last in a chain of four military fortresses built by the Spanish along the coast of Alta California. The others had been founded at San Diego, San Francisco, and Monterey. The dedication was made by Father Junipero Serra in the presence of Governor Felipe de Neve and Lieutenant José Francisco Ortega and his 55 soldiers.

El Presidio de Santa Barbara State Historic Park (SRL 636) encompasses the original presidio site. It is located in downtown Santa Barbara at the intersection of Santa Barbara and Canon Perdido streets. Two bronze markers in the sidewalk, placed by the Native Sons of the Golden West, indicate where the lines of the old presidio quadrangle crossed the streets. (Canon Perdido, "lost cannon," derived its name from an incident that occurred during the American military occupation of Santa Barbara. In the spring of 1848, a six-pounder brass gun from a wrecked American brig disappeared and was presumed to have been stolen. The military governor imposed a $500 fine upon the townspeople, to their outrage. Ten years later, a storm uncovered the cannon on a beach.)

Lieutenant Ortega, the first *comandante* of the presidio, directed construction of the temporary fortifications and living quarters for the first settlers, the 55 soldiers and their families. Construction of the permanent adobe presidio structure was directed by his successor, Lieutenant Felipe de Goycoechea, who served from 1784 to 1804. The buildings of the presidio formed a quadrangle enclosing a central parade ground, surrounded by an outer defense wall.

Two adobes of the original presidio quadrangle have survived, and work has begun on the reconstruction of the entire presidio. One of the two surviving adobes is known as El Cuartel ("the soldiers' quarters"), located at 122 East Canon Perdido Street. El Cuartel is the oldest building in Santa Barbara, and the second oldest in California, (the Serra Chapel at San Juan Capistrano is the oldest). El Cuartel houses a museum and gift shop. The other surviving structure, the Canedo adobe, stands across the street at 123 East Canon Perdido. The reconstructed padre's quarters adjoin the Canedo adobe, both of which have museum exhibits. The largest building of the quadrangle, the reconstructed presidio chapel, is adjacent to the padre's quarters.

El Presidio de Santa Barbara State Historic Park is operated and is being developed by the Santa Barbara Trust for Historic Preservation under an agreement with the state Department of Parks and Recreation.

Mission Santa Barbara

Mission Santa Barbara (SRL 309) was not founded until four years after the establishment of the presidio. Father Serra had selected the site, and after his death in 1784, the work of building the mission was carried on by his successor, Father Fermín Francisco de Lasuén. Father Lasuén performed the ceremonies of consecration on December 4, 1786, the feast day of St. Barbara, and held a second ceremony upon the arrival of Governor Fages twelve days later.

The building of the first temporary chapel and adjoining dwellings and storehouses was begun the following year. Gradually the establishment grew in size and prosperity until, in 1807, there were over 1,700 neophytes living in the Indian village of 250 adobe huts that surrounded the mission.

In 1789 a new church of adobe roofed with tile replaced the temporary structure. In 1793 this church was replaced by a larger one, which was finished in 1794. This, in turn, was superseded by a more magnificent structure, the earthquake of 1812 having damaged the former building. The new structure, built on the same site, was dedicated in 1820. This building, with the marks of storm and earthquake upon it, has been maintained in keeping with its ancient aspect. The massive walls, six feet thick, the stone steps and tile floors, two of the six chapels built in the solid walls, which are of double thickness at these points, all make it the most solidly built of any of the missions. The temblor of 1925, however, necessitated almost rebuilding the church. Fa-

Mission Santa Barbara

ther Augustine Hobrecht, superior of the mission, was tireless in seeing that the minutest detail was restored as before, only reinforcing the structure by modern methods so that the building might withstand future shocks. Problems arising from the restoration of 1925–27 necessitated yet another rebuilding of the towers and facade in 1950–53.

In the beautiful old tree-shaded cemetery are the graves of 4,000 Indians and 500 white people. One grave is said to be that of Juana María, an Indian woman reputed to have lived alone for eighteen years on San Nicolas Island in the Santa Barbara Channel. Juana María was found and brought to Santa Barbara by Captain George Nidever in 1853. She died in 1854, and it is thought that she was buried in the mission garden, although no record of the burial has been found in the mission archives, nor is there any document bearing testimony of her baptism and the bestowal of her Christian name, Juana María, after her rescue. However, Captain Nidever's veracity and the high regard in which he was held in Santa Barbara, where he lived for over 50 years, lends sufficient weight to the story, to which he was the chief witness, to give it credence. A bronze tablet was placed at the grave by the Santa Barbara Chapter, DAR, in 1928.

Before the church stands a stone fountain of simple, harmonious design, and near it is a long stone trough, once used by the Indian women for washing clothes. These were constructed in 1808. About 500 feet north of the mission church, in what is now Mission Historical Park of the city of Santa Barbara, is a square stone reservoir, constructed in 1806, part of the irrigation system to collect water for the mission orchards and gardens. This reservoir, still in excellent condition, forms part of the water system of the city of Santa Barbara. Across Pedregoso Creek, about a mile and a half north of the mission in what is now called Mission Canyon, a dam was constructed in 1807. Now much silted up, it may be seen in the Santa Barbara Botanic Garden. Portions of the aqueduct may also be found there and at various points in the canyon. A bronze tablet has been placed just above the dam by La Cumbre Chapter, DAR.

Below the reservoir are ruins of the pottery kiln built in 1808, where utensils, adobe bricks, and tiles were made by the neophytes under the fathers' supervision. Northeast of the reservoir is the filter, or settling tank, where the water was purified for domestic use. Fairly well preserved, this interesting relic is decidedly picturesque, resembling an ornamental vault or tomb. East of the reservoir and above it are the ruins of a gristmill (1827) with its own irregularly hexagonal reservoir.

Mission Santa Barbara has never suffered from the neglect and decay of the other missions after secularization. In 1842 the bishop's residence was changed from San Diego to Santa Barbara, and in 1853 a petition to Rome resulted in making the mission a hospice, the beginning of an apostolic college for the education of Franciscan students for the priesthood. St. Anthony's Seminary was completed in 1901 and adjoins the mission. This was the influence that saved Santa Barbara from neglect. Since its founding, it has been used continuously for religious observances. It is the only one of all the missions that has remained in the hands of the Franciscan Fathers since its founding, and it is one of four now under their administration. For its historical and architectural importance to the United States, Mission Santa Barbara has been registered as a National Historic Landmark by the Department of the Interior.

The newest addition to the mission is the archive-library, added to the west wing, which houses original documents of mission days and old and rare books of the Hispanic period of California. This facility, completed in 1969, is open to qualified scholars and writers.

Mission La Purísima Concepción

The first site of Mission La Purísima Concepción is on the 500 block of South F street in Lompoc (SRL 928). Father Fermín Francisco de Lasuén founded the mission on December 8, 1787, the Feast of the Immaculate Conception of Mary. A temporary building was begun in 1788, but this was soon replaced by an adobe structure roofed with tile, which was finished in 1802. This building was totally destroyed by the earthquake of 1812, but fragmentary ruins can be seen to this day—the only instance among California's missions of physical evidence at a site other than the present one. The great gash made by the earthquake may still be seen on the hillside above the ruins.

A new church, about four miles northeast of the first site, was promptly erected by Father Mariano Payéras, who did effective work in both the old and the new locations. His death in 1823 was a great loss to the mission. The Indian uprising that spread from Mission Santa Inés in 1824 struck heavily at La Purísima, which was captured and held for several weeks. Soldiers from Monterey finally dispersed the Indians.

At one time La Purísima was very prosperous, but the neglect that followed secularization and confiscation and the inroads of the elements caused its steady disintegration. Finally it became a crumbling ruin, its roof gone, its walls fallen and half choked with wild mustard and elder bushes. Only the stately row of white pillars, in Grecian beauty, testified to its past. Such was its state when, in the mid-1930's, it was restored and rebuilt by the Civilian Conservation Corps and the National Park Service. Subsequently it became La Purísima Mission State Historic Park (SRL 340), one mile north of SR 246 and two miles northeast of Lompoc. It is one of two missions owned by the state, the other being San Francisco Solano at Sonoma. La Purísima, in its lovely rural setting, is the only one of California's twenty-one missions to be restored as a complete mission establishment. The state property consists of almost 1,000 acres, an area large enough to take in the water system in Purisima Valley. A self-guiding round-trip hike of one mile enables the visitor to gain a complete picture of mission life at its height. Besides the main buildings—church, shops and quarters, and padres' residence—restoration has included numerous outbuildings, gardens, soap factory, tannery, and reservoirs. This is also a National Historic Landmark. A visit to Mission La Purísima Concepción is an educational experience unparalleled in California.

The Lompoc Museum is at 200 South H Street, in the Carnegie Library Building (1910). Among its features are extensive Chumash Indian artifacts and a collection of modern aerospace exhibits. The Lompoc Valley Historical Museum at 207 North L Street is in the Fabing-McKay-Spanne House from 1875, the first two-story house built in the Lompoc Valley.

Mission Santa Inés

Mission Santa Inés (SRL 305) was founded in order to reach the Indians living inland. Father Estévan Tápis made a survey of the country in 1798, and from his report a site for the proposed mission was chosen in the beautiful valley of Calahuasa, 45 miles northwest of Santa Barbara via Gaviota Pass. Thirteen Indian rancherias in the vicinity, with an estimated population of over 1,100, gave promise of many converts.

Mission Santa Inés, Solvang

After the death of Father Lasuén in 1803, Father Tápis succeeded him as Padre Presidente, and in 1804 he founded the new church at Santa Inés. A simple chapel was erected at first; this was replaced, after the earthquake of 1812, by a building of brick and adobe, roofed and floored with tile. This structure, completed in 1817, still stands in the open fields with its background of rugged, purple mountains. There is an especially lovely garden with a fountain. Near the mission are the stone ruins of an old gristmill, built by Joseph Chapman in 1820.

The Indian uprising of 1824 started at Mission Santa Inés, as a result of their harsh treatment by the soldiers. The Indians revolted, burned a large number of the mission buildings, but left the church unharmed, and escaped to La Purísima, where they were finally overcome by soldiers from Monterey.

After the secularization of the missions in the 1830's, Pope Gregory XVI took steps to establish California as a diocese with its own bishop. In 1840 one of the Franciscan friars, Francisco García Diego y Moreno, was appointed and consecrated Bishop of Both Californias, his territory including Baja California in Mexico as well as the present state of California. Bishop Diego established the first seminary for the training of priests in California at Mission Santa Inés in 1844. The seminaries of the several Roman Catholic dioceses of California can all trace their beginnings to Santa Inés.

Santa Inés suffered materially from the effects of secularization, as did nearly all of the missions. It was in a sad state of ruin until early in the twentieth century, when restoration was begun. The mission retains much of its old charm: Indian frescoes and hand-carved doors, harmonious arcades and flower-filled patio, and a beautiful campanile, its plain wall pierced, as at Mission San Gabriel, by niches for the bells that ring for prayer.

Mission Santa Inés is located just south of SR 246 at the east end of the Danish community of Solvang. It is now administered by the Capuchin Fathers, a branch of the Franciscan order.

Santa Barbara's Adobe Heritage

Santa Barbara, like Monterey, is a city of beautiful old adobe homes. Through the efforts of the Santa Barbara Trust for Historic Preservation and the Santa Barbara Historical Society, steps have been taken by the city to ensure the permanent preservation of its architectural heritage. After a state law was passed in 1959 enabling cities to take such steps, Santa Barbara enacted "El Pueblo Viejo" ordinance in 1960, setting aside the sixteen blocks bounded by State, Figueroa, Laguna, and Ortega streets as a historic area. Within these boundaries no building of historical or architectural value is to be destroyed or altered, and no new construction is to be undertaken that does not conform to the style of architecture of the old adobes.

Casa de la Guerra (SRL 307) is, after the mission, perhaps the most interesting remaining landmark of old Spanish days in Santa Barbara. It was built with Indian labor by José Antonio Julián de la Guerra y Noriega during the years 1819–27. One of the adobe bricks in the front corridor of the old house still bears the date 1826 plainly marked on it.

Don José Antonio, a native of Spain, came from Mexico to California as a lieutenant in 1806. There he married María Antonia Juliana Carrillo, and in 1815 he was made *comandante* of the Presidio of Santa Barbara, an office he held until 1842. De la Guerra was a man of strong character and ability. His home was the center of social life in Santa Barbara and a stopping place for many distinguished visitors. Among others, Richard Henry Dana, author of *Two Years Before the Mast*, visited the adobe mansion in 1834 and again in 1859.

El Paseo, initially called "The Street in Spain," was designed by James Osborne Craig and built in 1923. This walkway passes by the De La Guerra adobe and the two adjacent Gaspar Oreña adobes (1849 and 1858). Taking its style and decorative motifs from Spanish architecture, El Paseo greatly influenced the rebuilding of this part of Santa Barbara after the earthquake of June 29, 1925.

Across from the adobes is De la Guerra Plaza, one of the city's original parks, dedicated in 1855. Santa Barbara's first city hall was built in the center of the plaza in 1874 and demolished in 1924; the two tall palm trees that still stand there were located at the rear of the building. The current city hall, designed in Spanish Colonial Revival style, was built in 1923. Complementing it is the News-Press Building, from 1922.

The Hill-Carrillo adobe (SRL 721) at 11 East Carrillo Street was built about 1825 by Daniel Hill, a native of Massachusetts who came to California in 1823 and married Rafaela Ortega. In this house, in 1833, was born the first child of American parents in California, Isobel, daughter of Thomas Oliver Larkin, first American consul in California, and Rachel Holmes Larkin. It became the home of Captain John Wilson and Doña Ramona Carrillo de Wilson and, later, of Guillermo Carrillo. The building was purchased in 1928 by philanthropist Max C. Fleischmann, and was given to the Santa Barbara Foundation to be preserved as one of the historic buildings of Santa Barbara.

The Covarrubias adobe (SRL 308), located at 715 Santa Barbara Street, was built in 1817 by Domingo Carrillo, whose daughter María married José María Covarrubias in 1838. This house is a fine example of California architecture. Owing to the fact that sunshine was permitted to enter the rooms through skylights, the building is in a remarkable state of preservation. Adjacent to this adobe is the so-called "Historic" (or Malo) adobe. It is supposed to have been built about 1836 near the present corner of State and Carrillo streets for Concepción Pico de Carrillo, sister of Governor Pío Pico. In 1903 it was taken down brick by brick and reconstructed at Carrillo and Anacapa streets. In 1922 it was again moved and rebuilt in the same fashion at its present location by John R. Southworth. In 1938 the Covarrubias and "Historic" adobes were acquired by Los Rancheros Visitadores, an equestrian organization. They are now the property of the Santa Barbara Historical Society, which built its museum—of adobe, in authentic style—on the adjoining land at 136 De la Guerra Street in 1964.

The Gonzales-Ramirez adobe at 835 Laguna Street was built in 1825 and occupied by members of the Gonzales family for many years afterward. This building is a National Historic Landmark. The Rochin adobe at 820 Santa Barbara Street, built in 1856, is sheathed in shiplap siding and is still occupied by a descendant of the original owner. The Santiago de la Guerra adobe at 110 East De la Guerra Street (reputedly built about 1812 but now much altered) housed the lieutenant of a Spanish-speaking cavalry unit that was formed to join the Union forces in the Civil War. The Lugo adobe, built about 1830, was remodeled in 1922 into the Meridian Studios at 114 East De la Guerra Street. The little Pico adobe, built about 1820, was built for the family of a retired soldier, Santiago Pico, founder of the Pico family; still occupied, it stands at 920 Anacapa Street behind the Cota-Knox home at 914–916 Anacapa. The latter is a brick structure built in 1871. The Miranda adobe, built about 1840, and the old guardhouse have been incorporated into a restaurant and office complex at De la Guerra Street and Presidio Avenue. The two Cordero adobes stand at 304 East Carrillo Street and, at 906 Garden Street, behind a store. The two-story Botiller-Grand adobe is at 1023 Bath Street; the family retained ownership of the house for well over a century after it was built, about 1844. The Arellanes-Kirk adobe, built about 1860, is the most recent; it stands at 421 East Figueroa Street and has always been in residential use.

Other Buildings of Santa Barbara

Santa Barbara has many historic buildings that come from what might be called the "post-adobe" period. At the corner of State and De la Guerra streets a bronze tablet was placed by the Native Sons of the Golden West in 1929, commemorating the first raising of the

American flag in Santa Barbara. The Lobero Theater, at 33 East Canon Perdido Street, stands on the site (SRL 361) of the old adobe theater and opera house operated by José Lobero, who in 1873 enlarged a wood and adobe school to make Santa Barbara's first theater. This was torn down in 1923 when renovation proved to be infeasible. The present structure opened in August 1924, and Santa Barbara's annual Old Spanish Days Fiesta dates from the celebration of this opening. The Fox-Arlington Theater at 1317 State Street is on the site of the Arlington Hotel (1875) and a later hotel (1910) that was wrecked in the 1925 earthquake. When Fox West Coast Theaters planned to build a motion-picture theater on this site, the architect Joseph Plunkett conceived the building in the Spanish Colonial Revival style, and it was so created in 1930–31. In 1976 it became the Arlington Center for the Performing Arts.

The culmination of Santa Barbara's architectural renaissance is the county courthouse on the 1100 block of Anacapa Street, designed by William Mooser and dedicated on August 14, 1929. County oil revenues covered the $1,500,000 cost of the building. It is one of the most beautiful adaptations of Spanish-California architecture in the entire state and one of the notable public buildings of the United States. It is listed on the National Register of Historic Places.

The Upham Hotel at 1404 De La Vina Street was built in 1871 in the Italianate style. The two-story redwood structure is surmounted by a cupola. The name comes from Cyrus Upham, who owned and operated the hotel from 1898 through 1911. The Upham is the oldest Santa Barbara hotel in continuous operation. Down the street at 925 is another Italiante structure, the former St. Vincent's School, later the Knights of Columbus Hall. Built in 1874, the building was completely renovated as an office building in 1983.

A small architectural-historical area centers on the Trussell-Winchester adobe (SRL 559) at 412 West Montecito Street. Captain Horatio Gates Trussell, a native of Maine, built it in 1854, shortly after his arrival in California. Into it he incorporated timbers from the SS *Winfield Scott*, wrecked in 1853 on Anacapa Island. The adobe was later acquired by the Winchester and Hastings families. It is an important example of the transition from adobe to frame construction in the early American period. The Judge Charles Fernald house, one of the best examples of the Victorian period in Santa Barbara, was moved to its present location at 414 West Montecito in 1959. Built in 1862, the house was lived in by the Fernald family until 1958, and like the Trussell-Winchester adobe, it is open to the public.

The Hunt-Stambach house is an Italiante structure that has been moved to three different locations since its erection in 1873 at State and Anacapa streets. Its

Trussell-Winchester Adobe, Santa Barbara

present location is at 821 Coronel Street. Peter J. Barber, who built many houses in Santa Barbara in the late nineteenth century, was the architect. "Crocker Row" is a series of five Mission Revival houses built for William H. Crocker of San Francisco in 1894–95 as exclusive rentals for winter visitors. Located at 2010–2050 Garden Street, each house is set back slightly from the next in order to provide ocean views.

A second historic district has been created by the city of Santa Barbara—the Brinkerhoff Avenue Landmark District. This block-long street and its environs were developed in the late nineteenth and early twentieth centuries. It was named for a local physician, Dr. Samuel Brinkerhoff, who owned the block but did not subdivide it. The district's earliest existing houses were built in 1887–88. Over the past two decades protective and enterprising property owners have established antique shops, galleries, and other businesses in the old homes. Of particular distinction are the buildings at 519, 523, 528, and 533 Brinkerhoff Avenue, at 501 Chapala Street, and at 124 and 136 West Cota Street.

Stearns Wharf, extending from the foot of State Street, was built by John Stearn in 1872. It served the town as a port for cargo, passenger, and fishing ships. It was damaged by wind and waves and a waterspout, but was always rebuilt, until it was destroyed by fire in 1973. In 1981 a new Stearns Wharf was opened to the public.

Nearby, just off US 101 at Chapala and Montecito streets, is the gigantic Moreton Bay Fig Tree, one of the sights of the city. The tree arrived as a seedling from its native Australia and, in the belief that it was a rubber plant, was planted by a local family on this spot in 1877. It has become so enormous that it is said that 10,000 people can stand in its shade at noon.

Montecito

Montecito, Santa Barbara's neighbor to the east, is a community of beautiful homes. Here, too, are relics of adobe days. The Pedro Masini house, the oldest two-story adobe in the Santa Barbara area, was reputedly built in 1820. Still occupied, it stands at the junction of Sheffield Drive, Ortega Hill Road, and North Jameson Lane, just north of US 101. The Hosmer adobe, at 461 Ysidro Road, is still occupied by members of the Hosmer family. The same road leads to the San Ysidro Guest Rancho at 900 San Ysidro Lane, where one room of the old Casa San Ysidro (1829) still stands, incorporated into a building of this handsome resort hotel.

Goleta

West of Santa Barbara is Goleta, location of the University of California at Santa Barbara. Here stands an adobe built in the 1840's by Daniel Hill, who also built the Carrillo adobe in the city. Enlarged and modernized by James G. Williams early in the twentieth century, it is covered with wooden siding and not easily recognizable as an adobe. It continues to serve as a private residence and is located at 35 La Patera Lane, north of Hollister Avenue.

The La Patera ranch consisted of 1,043 acres in the eastern portion of the Dos Pueblos grant. In 1872 William Whitney Stow of San Francisco purchased this land; his 21-year-old son Sherman moved to La Patera immediately afterward and started planning his house. The house, begun the following year, was the home of Sherman and his heirs for the next 95 years. W. W. Stow became interested in the cultivation of lemons, and in 1874 3,000 lemon trees were planted on the ranch, probably the first commercial lemon planting in California. These early plantings were at the site of the present Crestview Oaks subdivision. In 1967, after many years of family use, the Stow House was given to the county of Santa Barbara. Since then the house has

Stow House, Goleta

been looked after and opened to the public by the Goleta Valley Historical Society, by arrangement with the county. Stow House is located at 304 Los Carneros Road in Goleta.

On the grounds, in an old barn-warehouse, is the Horace A. Sexton Memorial Museum, named in memory of a native of the area who was a major contributor to the growth of the Goleta Valley Historical Society. The museum, which has many outdoor displays, focuses on farm equipment and early relics of the automobile in Santa Barbara County.

El Refugio and Gaviota

About twenty miles west of the city of Santa Barbara, the Cañada del Refugio once marked the eastern boundary of the great Rancho Nuestra Señora del Refugio, which ran westward along the sea for 25 miles to the Cañada del Cojo. Here in the Cañada del Refugio the Ortega family lived for many years. José Francisco de Ortega, who had accompanied Portolá on his expedition to Monterey in 1769 and had assisted in the founding of the Presidio of Santa Barbara in 1782, was rewarded for his services with permission to occupy this land in 1794. After his death, it was granted to his son, José María Ortega.

The coast of El Refugio is closely linked with romance, for here on the beach Don José had his embarcadero, where he engaged in genteel smuggling, and here the pirate Hippolyte Bouchard landed in 1818 and sacked and burned the adobe casa that stood at the canyon's entrance facing the sea and El Camino Real. Here, too, the Yankee Joseph Chapman deserted from the pirate ship. He later married into the Ortega family and proved to be a very useful citizen.

Don José built his second adobe about three miles back in the Cañada del Refugio. It and the old vineyard, once famous in California, have disappeared. The road that winds through the canyon and up the mountain, almost inaccessible toward the summit, leads down into the valley of Santa Ynez by way of Refugio Pass. Former President Ronald Reagan's Rancho del Cielo lies to the west of this road in a secluded portion of the Santa Ynez Mountains.

West of El Refugio two Ortega adobes still stand, one of them completely rebuilt, the other much as it was originally and until recently still owned by the Ortega family. Two and a half miles west of Cañada del Refugio and Refugio Beach State Park a private road turns north from US 101 and leads two miles up Tajiguas Creek to one of California's most beautiful adobe homes. It was built perhaps as early as 1800 and enlarged and improved in 1879. It later fell into ruin, and in 1924 was taken down and rebuilt by Kirk B. Johnson, according to the designs of the architect George Washington Smith. It has since passed out of Johnson's hands and has undergone further renovation.

The other Ortega adobe was built by Pedro and José Ortega about 1850. It is situated deep in the ravine of Arroyo Hondo, less than four and one-half miles east of Gaviota. Clarence Cullimore in *Santa Barbara Adobes* notes that when this adobe is seen from above, it is "a rare gem, in a perfect setting."

North of Gaviota, US 101 crosses Gaviota Pass (SRL 248). Soldiers from Santa Barbara waited in ambush here on Christmas Day, 1846, to prevent John C. Frémont and his battalion from reaching the city. Frémont, however, was warned of the plot and accomplished his objective by using San Marcos Pass instead.

The San Marcos Pass

San Marcos Pass, about fifteen miles northwest of Santa Barbara, was one of the passes over which the early explorers and mission fathers crossed from the coast to the inland valleys. Gaviota Pass, the northernmost of these passes, is 28 miles farther up the coast from Santa Barbara.

In 1846, on his way from Monterey to reinforce Commodore Stockton in Los Angeles during the period of American occupation, John C. Frémont eluded the Californian soldiers who were waiting for him in ambush in Gaviota Pass by taking the route over the San Marcos grade instead. The latter route was known to few and presented many difficulties. Guided by Benjamin Foxen, the Americans succeeded in reaching the top after swinging the artillery across the intervening chasms on ropes, an all-day struggle. From the summit, Foxen's eldest son, William, led the men down the mountain and into Santa Barbara.

Foxen Canyon

Located in Foxen Canyon about fifteen miles northwest of Los Olivos and 25 miles southeast of Santa Maria is the site of the old Foxen home. Rancho Tinaquaic, on which it was located, comprised two leagues of land and was granted in 1837 and 1842 to William Benjamin Foxen, an Englishman who had settled in California in 1828. He was baptized a Catholic as William Domingo Foxen, married Eduarda Osuna, and became a citizen of Alta California. The Californians often referred to him as Don Julián.

Here in December 1846, Frémont arrived with his army of 700 men on their way to Santa Barbara and Los Angeles. Frémont had been told by William G. Dana at Rancho Nipomo (San Luis Obispo County), where he had camped on December 18, that the Californians were waiting for him in ambush at Gaviota Pass, the main passage through the mountains, a narrow defile between towering walls of granite from which huge boulders could be rolled down upon a passing enemy. In an account published in 1931, William Dana's son Juan Francisco declared that Frémont was advised to seek the services of Foxen, a man familiar with the country to the southwest where an alternate and more difficult pass might be crossed. (According to other accounts, it was Foxen himself who warned Frémont of the ambush.)

Proceeding to Rancho Tinaquaic, Frémont camped on December 20 in the woods near the Foxen home. There, according to Dana's account, he solicited the aid of Foxen, who, though "torn between loyalty to the Californians and the tie of English blood which bound him to the invaders," granted the request and led the little army on its difficult passage over San Marcos Pass and into Santa Barbara unharmed. As a consequence of this deed, Foxen for some time afterward suffered at the hands of his neighbors, who on more than one occasion set fire to his rancho buildings.

Foxen is commemorated by a memorial chapel built in 1875 by his daughter and son-in-law, Ramona and Frederick Wickenden (SRL 877), at the head of Foxen Canyon, four miles southeast of Sisquoc at the junction of Foxen Canyon Road and Tepusquet Road. Foxen lies buried under a marble column in the family cemetery nearby.

From the chapel and cemetery it is less than two miles southeast on Foxen Canyon Road to the Frederick Wickenden adobe. Wickenden married Ramona Foxen in 1860 and two years later built the central portion of the structure of adobe, making frame additions through the years. The house, now designated as headquarters for Rancho Tinaquaic, served also as store, post office, and stage station. Wickenden died in 1918 at the age of 93. Another mile and a half along the road brings one to the approximate site of Frémont's camp on the old Foxen ranch, which has been marked by the Pioneers Section of the Minerva Literary Club of Santa Maria. Less than two miles southeast of this marker, on the right side of the road, is an adobe mound, all that remains of Benjamin Foxen's home. It has also been marked.

Santa Ynez Valley

On the south side of the Santa Ynez River at Buellton, just west of US 101, is the adobe built in 1853 by Dr. Ramón de la Cuesta. It has thirteen rooms and remains much in its original condition. De la Cuesta came to California in 1849 and two years later purchased Rancho de la Vega, some 8,000 acres. The old adobe is a private residence.

Three miles east of Buellton is the Danish town of Solvang, home of Mission Santa Inés. The old mission stood practically alone until the founding of the settlement in 1911. Solvang ("sunny field" in Danish) was founded by the Danish-American Corporation, which included Danish professors from Illinois, who established the now-defunct Atterdag College in 1914. The town has become a major tourist center.

Two miles east of Solvang is the town of Santa Ynez. The Santa Ynez Valley Historical Society Museum, begun in 1961, has an excellent display of the varying stages of life in the valley. There is a small research library in a room of this museum. Next door, the Parks-Janeway Carriage House, also operated by the Santa Ynez Valley Historical Society, has a stunning display of more than 30 carriages and stagecoaches, restored to immaculate condition. The exhibits come from all over the state. Saddles from various periods in California history are also displayed. These two facilities are excellent examples of how California history can be preserved and displayed even in areas of comparatively low population.

North of Solvang is Ballard, a former stagecoach stop. Santa Barbara County has granted landmark status to its old Presbyterian church and its one-room schoolhouse, built in 1883 and still used by students up to the third grade, at 2425 School Street. Two miles north of Ballard is the town of Los Olivos, in the middle of a small, choice area of vineyards. From early times a stage station had been maintained at Los Olivos, and the narrow-gauge Pacific Coast Railway, coming through in 1887, increased the community's economic base. Mattei's Tavern was built here on Railway Avenue in 1886. The rail line shut down in 1934, but Mattei's Tavern still serves the public at its accustomed spot.

West of Buellton was Rancho Santa Rosa, a grant of some 17,000 acres made to Francisco Cota in 1839. The old ranch house, built of adobe on a knoll overlooking the property, is still standing, although greatly remodeled. Plans to make it a county park in 1938, when it had been long abandoned, did not materialize, but fortunately it has since been renovated and again serves as a private residence. It is located on Mail Road near Santos Road, less than a mile south of SR 246 six miles west of Buellton.

The Lompoc Oil Field lies in the Purisima Hills north of the old mission and the city of Lompoc. Here is a historic well, Hill 4 (SRL 582). It was the first oil well in which a water shutoff was attained by pumping cement through the tubing and behind the casing. The development of the modern cementing technique, of which this well was the forerunner, has increased the productive life of thousands of oil wells and made available millions of barrels of oil that might otherwise have remained underground. Hill 4, spudded in 1905 and completed the following year, was drilled to a final depth of 2,507 feet by the Union Oil Company of California. It produced for over 45 years.

Rancho Jesús María, over 40,000 acres, was granted to Lucas Antonio and José A. Olivera in 1837. The old adobe ranch house is somewhat altered and is now used as a guest house by the military at Vandenberg Air Force Base, a missile-testing center that was once Camp Cooke, an army base. About four miles northwest of the Vandenberg main gate on the Lompoc-Casmalia road, and not far from the San Antonio Creek Road junction, a turnoff to the left is marked "Marshallia Ranch." From this point it is about one mile to the adobe. Vandenberg Air Force Base also includes Point Sal, an important shipping point for Santa Maria Valley grain in the 1890's. Only a little cemetery and a few old trees remain here from earlier days.

Santa Maria Valley

The first settlement in Santa Maria Valley was known as La Graciosa and was located a short distance southwest of Orcutt. It is on Bradley Road, off Clark Avenue, about two and one-half miles southeast of town. Six miles northwest of Orcutt, the old Elizalde adobe still serves as a private home on the Righetti Ranch, to the north side of SR 1.

The town of Guadalupe in the northwestern corner of Santa Barbara County was named for the old Mexican rancho on which it was located. Rancho Guadalupe, of 43,681 acres, was granted to Diego Olivera in 1840. A large one-story adobe built by the Arrellanes family about 1849 still stands on Tenth Street near Guadalupe Avenue (SR 1).

Santa Maria Valley, about 35 miles long and from three to ten miles wide, is known as the "Valley of the Gardens" because of its extensive agricultural development. The city of Santa Maria, first called Grangeville and then Central City, was founded in 1874.

Los Alamos, fifteen miles southeast of Santa Maria, became a stage stop in 1877; before that time it was part of Rancho Los Alamos, a 48,803-acre grant made in 1839 by Governor Alvarado to José Antonio de la Guerra y Carrillo, son of José Antonio de la Guerra y Noriega of Santa Barbara. Subsequently the rancho was acquired by Gaspar Orena, brother-in-law of the younger

De la Guerra. The De la Guerra–Orena adobe, beautifully preserved, is now a National Historic Landmark. It is located three and one-half miles west of Los Alamos just off the road leading to Vandenberg Air Force Base. Part of Rancho Los Alamos eventually came into the hands of the oil magnate Edward L. Doheny.

Much of Santa Barbara County is rugged mountainous area included in Los Padres National Forest and penetrated by few roads. As early as 1925 Robert E.

Easton led the efforts to establish a sanctuary in the upper Sisquoc region for the vanishing California condor. It was an appropriate gesture in a county where the preservation of California's fast-disappearing past is so strongly pursued. The last known California condor in the wild was captured in April 1987, and unless breeding in captivity is successful, the species will be extinct.

Santa Clara County

Santa Clara County was named after Mission Santa Clara, which was established in that region in 1777. It was one of the original 27 counties. San Jose has been the county seat from the beginning, and was California's first state capital. Many pre-statehood records written in Spanish are filed in the county courthouse.

Indian Mounds

Indians in considerable numbers dwelt in the region of Santa Clara County when the first white explorers came this way. Portolá's party reported in 1769 "many large villages" of natives at the lower end of San Francisco Bay. Anza, in 1776, saw three large rancherias with many residents on the Guadalupe River and another about two miles to the north, possibly near the lower end of Moffett Field, where Chief Íñigo later had his ranch.

Even after homes had been established by the Spanish, some of the old Indian villages were occupied at times, for the wife of Don Secundino Robles said that three groups of natives were within a short distance of their house, which had been built about where Alma Street meets San Antonio Avenue in Palo Alto. Nearby was the place known as the Castro Indian mound, until its destruction the largest mound in the lower Bay region. Spreading out to a width of 290 feet, it had a length of 450 feet and a height of ten feet or more. Excavations were made by archaeologists from Stanford University and the University of California at Berkeley, both of which have museum specimens from the place. The mound was reduced by scrapers and eventually leveled; much of the soil was hauled away for fertilizer, and a subdivision now covers the site.

The principal artifacts discovered were mortars, pestles, bone scraping blades, awls, needles, chains of small beads, and an occasional bowl of a soapstone pipe evidently obtained through barter. The few obsidian implements found must also have been brought in. This kitchen midden, unlike those further north along the bayshore, showed a scarcity of certain ordinary species of shell and a preponderance of a small species less desirable for food but common throughout the Bay Area. The almost exclusive appearance of this small species of shell throughout the depth of the mound suggests that the salt marsh along the Bay has been an effective barrier to more desirable species of edible shellfish from the time of the earliest habitation of the mound.

On the northeast side of Middlefield Road south of Marion Avenue in Palo Alto is the site of an Indian village, commemorated by a plaque placed at Marion and Webster Street by the city of Palo Alto and the Palo Alto Historical Association.

Five miles west of Gilroy on the former Adams School grounds stationary mortars in large flat boulders may be seen. Arrowheads and stone implements have been plowed up in several neighboring fields.

Old Trails of Santa Clara

In 1769, Gaspar de Portolá was sent by José de Gálvez, visitador general of New Spain, to take possession of and to fortify the ports of San Diego and Monterey in Alta California. Portolá failed to find Monterey on this expedition but discovered instead the Bay of San Francisco.

Leaving their camp on San Pedro Creek on November 4, Portolá's party journeyed down into the Santa Clara Valley, by way of what are now the Crystal Springs Lakes and Woodside, to the northwest bank of San Francisquito Creek at Menlo Park. Father Juan Crespí, chronicler of the expedition, wrote: "We pitched camp in a plain some six leagues long, grown with good oaks and live oaks, and with much other timber in the neighborhood. This plain has two good arroyos with a good flow of water, and at the southern end of the estuary there is a good river, with plenty of water, which passes through the plain mentioned, well wooded on its banks [Guadalupe River]. . . . This entire port is surrounded by many and large villages of barbarous heathen who are very affable, mild, and docile, and very generous."

The site of the camp under a tall redwood is generally thought to be across the creek from the lone redwood tree that still stands beside the Southern Pacific railroad tracks at Palo Alto. Beneath this tree is a boulder on which is a bronze tablet carrying the following inscription: "Under this giant redwood, The Palo Alto, November 6–11, 1769, camped Portolá and his men on the expedition that discovered San Francisco Bay. This was the assembling point for their reconnoitering parties. Here in 1774, Padre Palou erected a cross to mark the site of a proposed mission. The celebrated Pedro Font topographical map, of 1776, contained the drawing of the original double-trunked tree, making The Palo Alto the first official living California landmark. Placed by the Historic Landmarks Committee, N.S.G.W., November 7, 1926."

This tree was long a landmark for the Indians and later for the Spanish explorers and the missionaries and soldiers traveling up and down the peninsula between San Francisco and the missions of Santa Clara and San José. The Spaniards called it the *palo alto* (tall tree), and the name passed on to the modern city that grew up beside it. The tree is now in somewhat weakened condition, despite both private and public efforts to maintain it.

From this central camp at the tall redwood, José Francisco de Ortega went up the eastern shore of the Bay, and it is thought that he explored as far as Alameda Creek, near Niles, or farther. On the return journey to Monterey, Portolá's party retraced its former trail through San Mateo, Santa Cruz, and Monterey counties.

Pedro Fages was the first white man to go inland from Monterey Bay to San Francisco Bay. His first expedition was made in 1770. In 1772 he made a second trip, which was also recorded by Father Crespí. Fages left Monterey on March 20, 1772, and, passing over the Salinas River and through the valley that bears its name, he climbed the Gabilan Mountains, dropping down into the valley on the other side where Mission San Juan Bautista was to be established by Father Lasuén in 1797. From there, continuing north, he entered the Santa Clara Valley north of Hudner (a Southern Pacific station in San Benito County), passed Tesquisquita Slough and San Felipe Lake, traveled the broad valley that he named San Bernardino de Siena, and on March 22 pitched camp on Llagas Creek a little north of Gilroy.

The next day the party followed along the west side of the Santa Clara Valley and climbed the low hills that extend eastward into the valley near San Martin. Camp that night was made near Coyote Creek, on the shores of a lake named San Benvenuto by Crespí. On March 25 the party passed along the edge of the eastern foothills and camped at San Lorenzo Creek in Alameda County.

After discovering the Sacramento Valley, Fages reentered the Santa Clara Valley by way of Mission Pass, continuing around the head of San Francisco Bay to a point near Milpitas. Retracing their old course, on April 3, the party made camp at the spur of hills near San Martín. On April 4 camp was pitched near the site of San Juan Bautista.

Juan Bautista de Anza, in 1775–76, made his second expedition from Sonora, Mexico, to San Francisco. After stopping a few days at Monterey, he proceeded northward on March 23, 1776, by way of the Salinas River and the Gabilan Mountains to the "San Bernardino Valley," the southern end of what is now the Santa Clara Valley. There he camped at Llagas Creek. On March 24 he entered the valley through the low hills above the Coyote River and named the plain before him the Llano de los Robles del Puerto de San Francisco ("Plain of the Oaks of the Port of San Francisco"). The party kept to the western side of the valley along the foothills, camping on the Arroyo de San José Cupertino on March 25, from where they had a broad view of San Francisco Bay.

On March 26 the little band reached the tall redwood tree on the banks of San Francisquito Creek and found the cross that Palou had placed there on November 28, 1774, five years after Portolá had passed that way. A plaque at the corner of Middlefield Road and Coleridge Avenue in Palo Alto was placed two hundred years later, during the celebration of the United States bicentennial, commemorating the passage of the Anza party through the region. From this point Anza proceeded northward up the peninsula, where he explored and located the sites for the Presidio and Mission of San Francisco.

Over this old trail up the Santa Clara Valley, marked out by Pedro Fages, the mission fathers came later. It became a part of El Camino Real, "the Royal Road," linking the missions of the south with the settlements in the San Francisco Bay Area.

Mission Santa Clara de Asís

The founding of Mission Santa Clara de Asís took place on January 12, 1777, with Father Tomás de la Peña from Mission San Francisco de Asís officiating, and José Joaquín Moraga and his soldiers from the Presidio of San Francisco present at the ceremonies. The site chosen for the new mission was on the banks of Río Guadalupe, the chief camping and fishing grounds of the local Costanoan Indians and called by them So-co-is-ta-ka, meaning "at (the) laurel." Another name for the place seems to have been Thamien. Here the mission cross was planted on the bank of a stream on a spot later forming a part of the Laurelwood Farm. The site of the original mission has been determined to be the west bank of now-dry Mission Creek, about one-quarter mile south of the confluence of this creek and the Guadalupe River. A bronze plaque (SRL 250) has been placed at Kifer Road and De la Cruz Boulevard in Santa Clara commemorating the site.

Twice within the next two years the Guadalupe River, swollen by the winter rains, flooded the church, and in 1779 the fathers moved a short distance south. This second location is now marked by a cross in a small city park at the northeast corner of Martin Avenue and De la Cruz Boulevard. The mission remained here until 1784, when a site on higher ground was selected as a better location. The third site was at the southwest corner of Franklin Street and Campbell Avenue, near the Santa Clara station of the Southern Pacific Railroad. The building erected here is said to have been one of the most elaborate and beautiful of all the mission struc-tures in California. It was begun by Father José Antonio Murguía on November 19, 1781, and was dedicated by Father Junipero Serra in one of his last public appearances on May 15, 1784. The Indian name for this site was Juquensen, or "The Valley of the Oaks." The cornerstone of the third Mission Santa Clara was unearthed during construction in 1911, and a cross was placed at the street corner to mark the spot.

The earthquakes of 1812 and 1818 caused serious damage to the buildings at the third site, and the fathers were obliged to move again. This they did in 1819, to a point on the east side of the present campus drive (Alviso Street) of the University of Santa Clara, opposite the south half of the Jesuit residence. The mission remained here until the completion of the church at the fifth and last site (SRL 338), a stone's throw away, where the university chapel now stands. The fifth church was begun in 1822 and dedicated on August 11, 1825.

After the secularization of the California missions in 1836, the lands of Mission Santa Clara were confiscated and the buildings became sadly neglected. In 1850 the Rt. Rev. Joseph S. Alemany, O.P., bishop of the new Diocese of Monterey, invited the Society of Jesus to Santa Clara to restore the church and to build up a college. Accordingly, on March 19, 1851, Santa Clara College was established in the old mission buildings by Rev. John Nobili, S.J., who adapted what was left of the old adobe buildings to the requirements of a school. Changes necessitated by the growth of the school finally altered the mission buildings until little of the original remained. By 1855 frame structures had replaced many of the former adobes. The 1825 adobe church, used as students' chapel and parish church, was encased in wood and given two towers quite out of keeping with mission architecture.

In 1855 the state granted a university charter to the college, but it was 57 years before it became the University of Santa Clara, on April 29, 1912. Since then, many fine buildings have been placed by the Jesuits around the site of the old mission. Fire destroyed the 1825 church on October 25, 1926, and in its place a concrete replica of the Franciscan adobe church was built in 1928–29 on the same site. Part of the altar end of the adobe church was saved after the fire and was incorporated into the replica; the bricks may be seen through glass in the sacristy. Many relics dating from the beginning of the mission's history were rescued and preserved. Part of the 1777 cross from the first site is encased in the large cross standing in front of the present church. To the right of the church is a gate leading into the old "Campo Santo" or cemetery. In the garden at the rear of the church one adobe building and an adobe wall from the original cloisters of 1822 still stand. In the

Adobe Wall, Mission Santa Clara de Asís

arch south of this wall are grinding stones used in the mission period for making flour and olive oil.

El Pueblo San José de Guadalupe

Because the Spanish government had difficulty in supplying provisions for the religious and military establishments in Alta California, Governor Felipe de Neve, during his journey in 1777, under orders of Viceroy Antonio María Bucareli, selected certain locations for the placing of agricultural settlements. One of these was near the newly established Mission Santa Clara. The governor appointed Lieutenant José Joaquín Moraga to found a settlement on the Guadalupe River two and one-quarter miles from the mission. Moraga was to take with him nine soldiers "of known skill in agriculture," two settlers, and three laborers.

On November 29, 1777, the new town was founded on the bank of the small river from which it derived its name. El Pueblo de San José de Guadalupe (SRL 433) began at what is now the corner of Hobson and Vendome streets in San Jose, although the state marker has been relocated at the city hall on Mission Street.

The floods of March 1778 inundated the marshy land on which this first settlement had been started during the previous dry season and washed away the nearly completed dam built for irrigation purposes. In July a new dam was constructed farther upstream, and the small group of settlers moved to high ground. This move caused some confusion in land titles, and Moraga was instructed by Governor Pedro Fages in 1782 to clear up the tangled property claims, to make the allotments uniform and regular, and to designate what were vacant lands and what were common lands. The hastily constructed first houses were gradually replaced by adobes.

San José de Guadalupe was visited by Captain George Vancouver in 1792, who praised the beauty of its broad, oak-studded fields and the fertility of the valley in which it was located. The yearly winter floods worked against this settlement, however, and a new town was established on higher ground in 1797, near what is now the corner of Market and San Fernando streets; some buildings may have been erected there at an earlier date.

In 1803 the mission fathers built a small adobe church on the new plaza. It was improved in 1835 and later encased in brick, but was ultimately destroyed by fire. In 1877, the present stone structure, St. Joseph's Church, was completed at the corner of Market and San Fernando streets (SRL 910), on the site of the old adobe chapel. The park enclosed by South Market Street is a part of what was the plaza.

San Jose, as the city is known today, is California's oldest civil settlement. For over a century and a half the seat of municipal government was maintained at the second site of the pueblo, on or around the plaza. A new civic center was built in the 1960's on Mission at First street near the Guadalupe River, practically within sight of the original pueblo location of 1777.

El Embarcadero de Santa Clara (Alviso)

Mission Santa Clara had its embarcadero, or landing place, at the head of the navigable slough that extends south from San Francisco Bay and is known today as Alviso Slough. In early mission days it was called the Embarcadero de Santa Clara de Asís, and played a very important part in the life of the settlers at Mission Santa Clara and the pueblo of San José.

Yankee ship captains, from 1835 to 1850, opened up an extensive trade with the dons who owned the vast ranchos bordering on San Francisco Bay; every rancho had its embarcadero. The Embarcadero de Santa Clara was one of the principal landings, as noted by Richard Henry Dana, Jr., in *Two Years Before the Mast:* "The Mission of Dolores, near the anchorage, has no trade at all, but those of San José, Santa Clara, and others situated on the large creeks or rivers which run into the bay . . . do a greater business in hides than any in California. Large boats, or launches, manned by Indians . . . are attached to the missions, and sent down to the vessels with hides, to bring away goods in return."

Ygnacio Alviso settled at the Embarcadero de Santa Clara in 1840, and shortly thereafter the name of the landing was changed to Alviso. He had been granted Rancho Rincón de los Esteros in 1838. Alviso was mayordomo at the mission and was engaged in construction work there at about the time the fifth and last church was built. Alviso prospered as a port with the development of the mercury mines at New Almaden, opened in 1845, and the discovery of gold in the Sierra three years later increased the flow of trade substantially. A steamer was run between Alviso and San Francisco, and the first warehouse was built there in 1849–50. It was during this time that the first state capital was located at nearby San Jose.

After 1865 the railroads began to divert trade from the embarcaderos on the Bay, and although a branch of the railroad was built through the town in 1876, Alviso went into a steep decline in the latter years of the nineteenth century. The old brick Wade warehouse is one of the few landmarks remaining from these days.

Thomas Foon Chew opened his successful Bayside Canning Company in Alviso in 1906, and by 1921 it was the third-largest cannery in the United States. The en-

terprise did not long survive Chew's death in 1931. Today Alviso is a historic district on the National Register
of Historic Places, and the Department of the Interior
has included parts of it in its 23,000-acre San Francisco
Bay National Wildlife Refuge. The town was annexed
to San Jose in 1968. The South Bay Yacht Club, organized in 1896, continues to function, and its 1906 clubhouse is in regular use.

The Alameda

The tree-lined avenue known as The Alameda was
first planted by the padres for the benefit of wayfarers
between Mission Santa Clara and the Pueblo de San
José. The planting of the trees was begun in 1799 by Father Magín Catalá, who employed 200 Indians to trans-
plant common black willows from the riverbank and to
water and protect the young grove until the trees should
be large enough to withstand the presence of roving
herds of cattle that pastured in this unfenced territory.
Bordering one side of this grove was a three-mile *acequia*,
or ditch, taking water from the Guadalupe to irrigate the
mission garden and other land. Three rows of willows
grew there in the early days, and they served as shade
from the hot summer sun and as protection from the
wild cattle that resented the intrusion of pedestrians.

Captain Alfred Robinson, who visited here several
times before 1841, says of this road that "it is frequented
generally on the Sabbath or feast days when all the town
repair to the church at Santa Clara. On a Sunday may
be seen hundreds of persons of both sexes, gaily attired
in silks and satins, mounted on their finest horses, and
proceeding leisurely up the road. No carriages are used,
and, of course, the scene is divested of all the pomp
and splendor which accompanies church-going in the
larger places of the republic, yet in one respect it excells
them all, that is, in the display of female beauty. No
part of Mexico can show so large a share of bright eyes,
fine teeth, fair proportions, and beautiful complexions."

For almost a century the grove remained unde-
spoiled, but as the region was opened up and traffic
grew heavier over this highway, it became evident that
a more solid roadbed would be necessary. Although it
was the most important road in the region, winter rains
made travel difficult. In the winter of 1852 it became impassable, and all traffic was compelled to use a route to
the west, making the journey from the mission to the
town much longer. In 1856 Crandall Brothers established an omnibus line to carry passengers along The
Alameda, but the roadbed was still far from satisfactory.
In order to secure maintenance, a franchise to collect
tolls was granted to the Alameda Turnpike Company in
1862 in return for making and maintaining a good road.

Upon the expiration of this franchise in 1868, a railroad
with horse-drawn cars began operations, two years later
changing to steam locomotion and extending the line
some miles at the southern end.

When electrification of the line came in 1887, public
opinion finally consented to the destruction of the center line of trees. One of the county papers on November 24, 1887, announced: "The last of the beautiful grove
of trees which has stood for a century in the Alameda,
San Jose's lovely drive, has been cut down to make room
for the electric road to Santa Clara." Tradition has it
that three willows on the east side of the Alameda that
survived until 1961 were of the original 1799 planting.

The Alameda is now a paved modern highway, much
of it SR 82, and in 1984 it was designated by the San
Jose City Council as a City Historic Landmark, taking
in all the lots fronting The Alameda between SR 17 and
Race Street.

Adobes in San Jose

Many buildings in the old pueblo were constructed
of adobe, but travelers writing of them as late as 1850
had little to say in their favor. One by one they were replaced by better structures. In later years, when the
adobes of California had begun to be regarded as historical landmarks, only two remained.

The first of these adobes stands at 184 West St. John
Street. This adobe is believed to have been built in 1799
by Manuel González, an Apache Indian, who died in
the adobe in 1804. It was later owned by Luís María
Peralta, *comisionado* of the pueblo from 1807 to 1822 and
grantee of the huge Rancho San Antonio in Alameda
County. Jacob Bowman believes this "Peralta Adobe"
(SRL 866) to be the second-oldest adobe in the nine Bay
Area counties, Mission Dolores in San Francisco being
the first. In the days of the pueblo the adobe was at the
extreme northern edge of the plaza.

Don Luís preferred to live here rather than at his
land grant, which he gave to his four sons, and here he
died in 1851 at the age of 92. The adobe and fourteen
acres of land were left to his unmarried daughters Josefa
and Guadalupe. Today only two of the original rooms
remain. In 1949 a concrete structure was built so close
to it that the adobe lost part of a wall to accommodate
the newer building. The adobe was acquired by the San
Jose City Council in 1966, and through the efforts of the
Peralta Restorations Fund Committee, it was restored
to its original state. A park enclosed by adobe walls
now surrounds the building. In August 1976 the park
was dedicated as a part of the U.S. bicentennial festivities; the adobe is also listed on the National Register
of Historic Places.

The second remaining adobe in San Jose stands at 770 Lincoln Avenue. Here on the grounds of Rancho Los Coches a low one-room adobe had been built by an Indian known as Roberto around 1836, eight years before he received the grant of the rancho. When Antonio María Suñol purchased the rancho from Roberto in 1847, he added three large brick rooms to the structure. A Dalmatian sea captain, Stefano Splivalo, purchased the building and 55 acres in 1853, and he made major architectural changes, further enlarging the house and adding a complete second story and balcony. The deterioration that inevitably ensued was halted over a century later when John Bruzzone purchased the building and set out to restore it. Today, identified as the Suñol adobe (SRL 898), it has been converted into law offices and is open to the public. The nearby freeway, I-280, was rerouted to pass to the north of the building, sparing it and the garden with its 150-year-old fig tree, the branches of which form a canopy over a redwood arbor in the garden.

Adobes in Santa Clara

At 3260 The Alameda (SR 82 between Franklin and Benton streets) is a one-story adobe building (SRL 249) that was part of José Peña's house, and may have been constructed as early as the 1790's as an Indian dwelling of the third Mission Santa Clara. It is being preserved by the Santa Clara Women's Club and is used by the group as their clubhouse. It stands back from the street in an old garden of pear and apricot trees, succulents, and flowering shrubs. Nearby on the grounds of the University of Santa Clara an adobe remnant of the old mission has been converted into an administration building.

At 373 Jefferson Street stands a modest family residence of one and one-half stories now called the Berryessa adobe. A narrow porch runs along the north side; at the rear is a wooden stairway leading to the one-room upstairs attic. A large olive tree shades the front corner of the home, privately owned.

The Courthouse

The first tribunal of the region, the *juzgado,* was built within the original Pueblo de San José in 1783. After the removal of the pueblo to higher ground, a second *juzgado* was erected about 1798 in what is now the center of Market Street at the intersection of Post Street. The second adobe structure, before it was torn down in 1850 and the brick removed for use elsewhere, saw the growth of the Spanish and Mexican pueblo into an

Santa Clara County Courthouse, San Jose

American town. It was a low building with a sloping, tiled roof, and in front of it Thomas J. Fallon hoisted the United States flag on July 13, 1846. (Fallon later became mayor of San Jose, and his home, built about 1859, still stands at 173 West St. John Street.)

The first county court convened in March 1850 in an adobe building on the west side of South First Street opposite the passageway then known as Archer Alley, later Fountain Alley. Over the next few years the court met in several other buildings, including the former state capitol, none of which stand today. In 1866 work began on an imposing two-story domed building on North First Street opposite St. James Square, and this county courthouse was occupied by the authorities on January 1, 1868. It was still the seat of county government when fire destroyed the interior on May 18, 1931. The outer walls remained intact, and the restoration of the interior was complete by September 1932. In the process of restoration, a third story replaced the dome. Further restoration costing more than $700,000 was done to update the building, which was rededicated in 1973.

The Monterey Road

El Camino Real stretches southward from Santa Clara and San Jose toward Monterey. In Spanish times the road to the capital ran from the south end of the plaza between the double row of mud houses that was San Jose. To avoid the pueblo's reservoir (a pond 800 feet in length, lying just south of Duane Street and east of Almaden Avenue), the road skirted the Canoas marshes on the right and continued south through the low bare hills called Las Lagrimas, approximately in the line of present South First Street. Continuing down the valley parallel to US 101 and the Southern Pacific

Railroad line, the road passed through the settlements of Coyote and Morgan Hill. A marker (SRL 259) at the northwest corner of Old US Highway 101 and Tennant Avenue in Morgan Hill commemorates the site of the Twenty-One Mile House, one of a chain of taverns catering to travelers in the mid-1850's, and the now-gone Vasquez Tree, inexplicably connected with the name of the bandit Tiburcio Vásquez. The southernmost settlements on the road in Santa Clara County were Gilroy and San Martin, after which the road headed through the low hills toward the Pajaro River, often turbulent and difficult to cross in those days, and from there into San Benito County. The first permanent span across the Pajaro was made in 1866.

The San Francisco Road

The first road north from San Jose led to Santa Clara Mission, and beyond that point it followed the trail opened by Juan Bautista de Anza on March 30, 1776. Beginning in the plaza between the church and the royal granary, the road ran close among the adobes, emerging on the west side of a pond at the intersection of present Santa Clara and Market streets. The pueblo's main *acequia* ran parallel at some distance to the left, and a branch of it was crossed at present St. James Street. Between Market and First streets, at Julian Street, the highway to Mission San José (in Alameda County) and the Contra Costa forked off to the right, over a plain strewn with the bleached bones of slaughtered cattle, until it reached an immense sycamore grove near Coyote Creek and became one with the present Old Oakland Road. At the road fork began the *suertes* or farming lots of the residents of the pueblo. The first lot on the right was inhabited by the family of Plácido Californio, one of the first Lower Californian Indians brought north by the Franciscans, who retired from Mission Santa Clara and settled in the pueblo in 1796.

The road to San Francisco continued through the *suertes*, which were bordered by willow hedges and little alleys stretching to the riverbank, and went on past the area called the Pueblo Viejo, where the town had first been founded. As it reached the open country, the road bore more and more west of present North First Street, finally reaching the Guadalupe River near the place where Anza's men had opened a ford. At this point, near the original site of Mission Santa Clara, the river was crossed, at first by the bridge built by the missionaries. In 1797, when the crossing began to be used by travelers between Mission San José and the third Mission Santa Clara as well as between the Pueblo de San José and San Francisco, the civil-military authorities erected a more satisfactory bridge. In its later state, this consisted of two tree trunks supporting a roadbed of five-foot squared timbers topped with planks, the whole suspended above bank level by a heavy chain anchored from four tall sycamores. The "Old Spanish Bridge" remained a landmark until the 1880's, and a piece of the chain, said to have come from a Portuguese ship, is preserved in the museum at the University of Santa Clara.

From the Guadalupe River northwest, the original trail became a boundary between ranchos, and for this reason the present Bayshore Freeway (US 101) still follows the same general line. Where Moffett Field now is, the trail swung first to the right of the freeway, then inland to the left. In records of 1836–53 this route is called the old or summer road, the lowlands near the Bay being nearly impassable during the winter. Nevertheless, the first American squatters found the northern end of the trail useful; they fenced and improved it, and it is now the longer portion of Charleston Road in Palo Alto.

After Mission Santa Clara was moved to near its present site, a better if slightly longer road was opened. This road began at the plaza and ran slightly north and east of the present El Camino Real. Near the western side of the present city of Santa Clara the road passed to the north of the main rancheria inhabited after secularization by the mission Indians.

Where present El Camino Real runs due west along a section line to the Lawrence Expressway and Fremont Avenue, the main highway in use before the 1850's swung slowly to the right across what was known as the Baijo, an open area grown with mustard and intersected with sloughs, where the battle of Santa Clara was fought in 1847. Where the present Lawrence Expressway passes over the railroad (site of the Lawrence post office from 1887 to 1935) was the easternmost point of the Roblar, a great forest of white oaks and live oaks extending down the west side of the valley between the low adobe lands and the chaparral nearer the hills. In the 1830's and 1840's travelers coming from the north caught sight here of the mission church, glistening white with its bell tower beside it.

Northward the main trail lay for several miles in the edge of the woods, east of the present railroad. The oaks in this section succumbed first to charcoal burners, then to the insatiable wood-burning locomotives and the needs of mechanized large-scale wheat farming, and finally to fruit orchards. In present Mountain View the oak woods and the road formed a semicircle extending three-fourths of a mile east of the railroad, around the alluvial fan of Stevens Creek, which was fringed with willow swamps. After swinging west again to the mission's Corral de Pastoria near present Central Expressway just south of Rengstorff Avenue, the Spanish road bore off to the right across Adobe Creek and the nearby black-adobe flats and continued north past what is now the Palo Alto Cultural Center to the Middlefield Road crossing of San Francisquito Creek. A plaque at the corner of Middlefield Road and Palo Alto Avenue, placed by the city of Palo Alto and the Palo Alto Historical Association in 1969 adjacent to the present-day bridge over the creek, commemorates this crossing.

Spanish and Mexican Land Grants in Santa Clara County

Some fifty grants of land in what is now Santa Clara County were made by the Spanish and Mexican authorities before the official annexation of California to the United States in 1848. Virtually all of this territory was accessible, habitable, and productive land and thus became the site of most of the twentieth-century cities and towns in the county. Two land grants originate from the Spanish period: Rancho San Ysidro, in southern Santa Clara County, and Rancho Los Tularcitos.

Rancho San Ysidro (Old Gilroy)

According to Bancroft, Rancho San Ysidro, one of the finest in the district, was granted in 1810 to Ygnacio Ortega, son of Captain José F. Ortega, who probably came with his father from Mexico between 1769 and 1773. Don Ygnacio, whose wife was Gertrudis Arce, was a *soldado distinguido* of the San Diego Company in 1792.

After Don Ygnacio's death in 1833, Governor Figueroa granted the lands of this rancho to his heirs, divided approximately equally between Ysabel Ortega (the wife of Julian Cantua), Quentin, and María Clara de la Asunción (the wife of John Gilroy). Ysabel received the portion called Rancho La Polka, in the hills east of San Martin and northeast of Gilroy. Rancho San Ysidro was divided between Quentin Ortega and John and Clara Gilroy. Their houses lay close to each other, the dividing line between the property roughly following present-day SR 152, the Pacheco Pass Road. The buildings on these properties have long ago vanished.

John Gilroy, the first non-Hispanic foreign settler in California, deserted the *Isaac Todd* in Monterey in 1814. He was of Scots descent, born John Cameron, and when he became ill with scurvy and left his ship, he adopted his mother's maiden name as his own, a suc-

cessful ruse to avoid being retaken. By September of that year he had been baptized at Mission San Carlos as Juan Bautista María Gilroy. In 1821, he was married at Mission San Juan Bautista to Clara, daughter of Ygnacio Ortega.

Gilroy, a man of fine physique and pleasant manners, though possessed of little education, had much natural ability and became influential in his locality. When he became a naturalized Mexican citizen in 1833, he produced certificates to show that he was a soapmaker and a millwright of good character, with a wife and four children, and had also some livestock on Rancho San Ysidro. As the years passed, he lost all his property, and toward the end of his life became dependent upon charity. He died in 1869, aged 75 years. The little settlement of San Ysidro, over which he was alcalde for a time, stretched along the Pacheco Pass Road, and is now known as Old Gilroy.

While John Gilroy was still living, the first American to locate permanently in the vicinity came upon the scene. This was Julius Martin, born in North Carolina in 1804, who had come overland from his former home in Missouri with his wife and daughters and arrived at San Ysidro in 1843. For a part of the overland journey this family had been with a larger group, most of whom proceeded to Oregon. Near Fort Laramie they met Joseph Reddeford Walker, who, returning to California as leader of the smaller group, brought them across Walker Pass. During the ensuing years Walker was a frequent and welcome visitor at the Martin home.

Julius Martin settled in San Ysidro, where he constructed a small horsepower flour mill with a capacity of twenty bushels a day, as well as three houses, none of which are still standing. He became a captain of the American Scouts under Frémont and saw the Bear Flag raised in Sonoma. When Charles Bennett, Sutter's messenger, paused in San Ysidro on his way to report the discovery of gold to government headquarters in Monterey, his story so interested the settlers that most of them left for the diggings. Julius Martin was among the number who went, and he did well enough that after he returned in 1850 he was able to pay cash for 1,220 acres of Rancho San Ysidro, which had 4,460 acres all told. Martin held this property until his death in 1891. Although blind for the last 30 years of his life, he was able to come out victorious in litigation that threatened to deprive him of his land. He was a man of good education and had an excellent memory. To his reminiscences, told to interviewers during his last years, are due many of the details of the early history not only of the immediate vicinity but also of other parts of the state.

Rancho Los Tularcitos (Milpitas)

Rancho Los Tularcitos lay in the north part of Santa Clara County near the lower end of San Francisco Bay. It extended south from the confluence of Calera and Penitencia creeks along the latter stream to present-day Calaveras Road in Milpitas, and east to include the mountains at the heads of Calera Creek and the Arroyo de los Coches. The southeastern point was marked by a live oak tree, which also denoted the northeastern point of the outlying lands of the Pueblo de San José.

This rancho was granted by Pablo Vicente de Solá, the last of the Spanish governors of Alta California, to José Higuera in 1821. The grant was renewed by the Mexican governor Juan B. Alvarado in 1839; patent for 4,394 acres was issued by the United States government to Higuera's heirs in 1870. This land was afterward purchased by Henry Curtner, a native of Vermont.

The old adobe built by Higuera on the rancho still stands in a well-landscaped Milpitas city park, at the end of Rancho Higuera Drive, and is open to the public.

Rancho Milpitas (Milpitas)

Rancho Milpitas (from *milpa*, Spanish for "maize field") lay immediately to the south of Rancho Los Tularcitos. The right to the lands of the rancho was claimed by two men, Nicolás Berryessa and José María de Jesús Alviso. Both men were sons of Spanish pioneers in Alta California and soldiers of the military company in San Francisco, where they served together from 1819 to 1827. Both were leading men in the Pueblo de San José, Alviso being alcalde in 1836, at which time Berryessa was *regidor*, and both were residing in San Jose in 1841.

Berryessa was an unlucky man: his cattle were plundered by Frémont's battalion; his brother, José de los Reyes, was killed by Frémont's men; squatters settled on his land; and, as the last straw, his claim to Rancho Milpitas, based on a decree from Alcalde Pedro Chaboya, was rejected by the Land Commission in 1855. He died insane in 1863.

José María de Jesús Alviso, who received Rancho Milpitas, was the son of Francisco Javier Alviso, a member of the Anza expedition. (The name Alviso is of Basque origin, and was originally spelled "Albizu"; José María de Jesús Alviso signed his name "Albizu.") His claim to the rancho was based on a grant from Governor José Castro in 1835. His home on the rancho was about two miles from the town of Milpitas, near the intersection of present-day Calaveras and Piedmont roads. One adobe of the hacienda remains, probably built in the 1830's. The second story of this adobe above the upper veranda is covered by weatherboarding to protect the original material. The house is occupied, and the remnant of the old rancho on which it stands is still farmed.

The town of Milpitas lies on the western boundary of the rancho. The Spanish originally named the town Penitencia, after the nearby creek. According to tradition, the creek was named for a "house of penitence" on its banks, a small adobe where priests from the missions came at stated intervals to hear confessions.

José María de Jesús Alviso's cousin Ygnacio owned the Rancho Rincón de los Esteros to the west; no buildings remain on this property from the Hispanic past.

Rancho Ulistac (Agnew)

Lying between the Guadalupe River and Saratoga Creek, Rancho Ulistac was first granted by Governor Pío Pico in 1845 to Indian claimants; in 1857 the heirs of Jacob D. Hoppe were confirmed in his claim to the property. Hoppe, a native of Maryland, reached California in 1846 at the age of 33. A year after his arrival on the West Coast, he became interested in the establishment of a weekly newspaper. The printing materials that he had were afterward turned over to the proprietors of the *Alta California*. He lived in San Jose, where he was the first American postmaster and a delegate to the constitutional convention, finally becoming one of the unfortunate victims of the explosion of the steamer *Jenny Lind* in San Francisco Bay on April 11, 1853.

On a portion of this property James Lick built his mansion. A native of Pennsylvania and a piano maker by trade, Lick arrived in California in 1848 and bought up land there and elsewhere at low prices. Later this property greatly increased in value until it was worth millions. Lick's mansion and gardens and the round brick warehouse from his water-powered flour mill still stand on the west bank of the Guadalupe River just north of the present Montague Road, which was named after a neighbor of Lick. The property today is privately owned and not open to the public. Across the river is the town of Agnew and the Agnews State Hospital.

Lick began giving away his vast wealth in 1873; at his death in 1876 a board of trustees was still coping with the distribution of his fortune. The amount of $700,000 was allocated to the establishment of Lick Observatory. The site, on the summit of Mount Hamilton, about twenty miles east of San Jose, was granted by act of Congress in 1876, and, with additional grants, the reservation now totals 3,133 acres. The observatory was opened to the public by the University of California in 1888. Lick lies buried under the supporting pier of the 36-inch refracting telescope.

Mount Hamilton, 4,209 feet above sea level, was named in honor of the Rev. Laurentine Hamilton, a pioneer missionary preacher in San Jose and also superintendent of schools. With William H. Brewer and Josiah D. Whitney, Hamilton was one of the first white men to climb the mountain, on August 26, 1861.

Rancho Posolmi and Moffett Field

The land at the lower end of San Francisco Bay was inhabited for countless years by an Indian tribe whose chieftain, Lope Íñigo, was granted formal possession by Governor Micheltorena in 1844. This Rancho Posolmi, some 1,697 level acres of salt marsh, proved to be ideally suited for the West Coast's first lighter-than-air base. In 1931 President Herbert Hoover established the Sunnyvale Naval Air Station to house the navy's newest airship, the dirigible USS *Macon*. Eight days before the formal dedication of the base on April 12, 1933, tragedy struck when the *Macon*'s sister ship, the USS *Akron*, crashed off the coast of New Jersey with the loss of 73 lives, including that of Rear Admiral William A. Moffett. The Sunnyvale Naval Air Station was subsequently renamed Moffett Field. Shortly after the *Macon* itself crashed on the California coast near Point Sur in 1935, the Navy abandoned its dirigible program. Moffett Field remains a major aeronautical facility, highlighted by the Ames Research Center, operated by the National Aeronautic and Space Administration.

Rancho Pastoría de las Borregas (Mountain View and Sunnyvale)

Adjacent to Rancho Posolmi and lying mostly to the south of what is now the Bayshore Freeway is Rancho Pastoría de las Borregas, also called Rancho Refugio. It was originally granted in 1842 to Francisco Estrada. A series of decrees by the Land Commission in the years between 1856 and 1881 divided the property into two tracts, with Permanente Creek as the dividing line. A city park at the corner of Rengstorff and Crisante avenues in Mountain View is the site of the home of the Castro family, who owned the northern half of the old rancho. Mariano Castro was the father-in-law of Francisco Estrada and inherited his claim upon the early deaths of his daughter and her husband.

The southern half of the rancho was purchased by Martin Murphy, Jr., who arrived with his father in California in 1844. The Murphys came from Ireland and first settled in Canada. The family was prominent in the life of the community, particularly in the activities of the Catholic church; Murphy had an important part in the establishment of Santa Clara College and the

Convent of Notre Dame. The picturesque house they lived in was framed on the East Coast and brought around the Horn about 1851; it was occupied continuously for over a century by members of the same family. It was demolished in 1961, but the site is marked (SRL 644) in the Murphy Historic Park at 252 North Sunnyvale Avenue in Sunnyvale.

Rancho Rincón de San Francisquito (Palo Alto)

In 1824 José Peña built a wood house on what is now the Stanford University campus, then outlying land of Mission Santa Clara. His son, Narciso Antonio Peña, later justice of the peace in the area, built a small adobe some time later near the mission horse corral. In 1841, while teaching at Santa Clara, José Peña received a formal grant of the land from Governor Alvarado. The Rancho Rincón de San Francisquito, about two square leagues in area, lay between the creek of that name and San Antonio (Adobe) Creek, on the former mission cattle range.

Secundino Robles, born in Santa Cruz either in 1811 or 1813, was mayordomo at the mission in 1841. In 1846 he was commander of some of Francisco Sánchez's troops, when he was taken prisoner and distinguished himself by breaking his sword in two before surrendering to his American captors. Some years before his marriage in 1835 he had discovered the location of an outcrop of cinnabar on Alamitos Creek—the secret source of the red paint so long prized by the Indians for the decoration of their bodies. Afterward, when the cinnabar deposit proved to be rich in mercury, he and his brother Teodoro received a payment of $13,000 in cash, besides a certain interest in the company that was formed for the development of the mine at New Almaden.

The brothers traded their interest in the mine to José Peña for his rancho and the buildings upon it, "orchard, corrals, and all property he may have on said land." The deed was drawn up in September 1847; Secundino took immediate possession with his wife and four children and set about enlarging the small Peña adobe.

In its heyday the Robles home was famous for its hospitality; for a while it was even a stage stop between San Francisco and San Jose. Twenty-five more children were born to Secundino and María Antonia Robles after they took possession of the estate, making 29 in all. By the end of the century, the house was unoccupied, and it collapsed in the April 18, 1906, earthquake. The site of the adobe has been marked by a plaque at the corner of Alma and Ferne avenues placed by the city of Palo Alto and the Palo Alto Historical Association.

The rancho dwindled over the years. Jeremiah

Clarke of San Francisco purchased a portion of it from María Rosalía Robles, former wife of Teodoro Robles, in 1859. Clarke held a good deal of land in the area; his holdings extended to Mayfield Slough by the Bay. At the Clarke-Wilson landing, goods were shipped to San Francisco. The bayshore property belonging to Clarke was in time sold and developed; a wooden building that was a hammer factory in the late nineteenth century still stands at 2995 Middlefield Road at Matadero Creek.

Rancho Rinconada del Arroyo de San Francisquito (Palo Alto)

Don Rafael Soto, born in the Pueblo de San José, was the son of Ignacio Soto, a member of the Anza expedition. He had received a small piece of land in a bend (*rinconada*) of San Francisquito Creek on loan from Mission Santa Clara after its secularization, a place that had been the headquarters of the mission's sheep ranch. Soto petitioned for title to the Rancho Rinconada del Arroyo de San Francisquito in 1835, which was denied him on a technicality.

Don Rafael had discovered the navigability of San Francisquito Creek up to the point at which he established an embarcadero for the loading and unloading of boats. The way between the embarcadero and El Camino Real, some three miles away, was not a properly defined road until 1874, when the present Embarcadero Road was opened by the county.

After the death of Don Rafael, his widow, Doña María Antonia, married into the Mesa family and received the grant for Rancho Rinconada del Arroyo de San Francisquito in 1841 from Governor Juan B. Alvarado. The 2,230 acres of the property bordered San Francisquito Creek from the Bay to the Palo Alto, the landmark tree that stands beside the railroad bridge in the city of that name. The house in which the Mesas and the large Soto family lived stood for many years at the corner of Middlefield Road and North California Avenue; the site is marked by a plaque placed by the city of Palo Alto and the Palo Alto Historical Association.

Rancho San Francisquito (Stanford University)

Rancho San Francisquito lay along the eastern side of San Francisquito Creek to the south of Rancho Rinconada del Arroyo de San Francisquito. It was formally granted by Governor Alvarado to Antonino Buelna, who had been active in the revolt that put Alvarado into power, in 1839, two years after Don Antonino had begun the building of his adobe house near the northern edge of the Stanford University golf course. In time

this became known as "El Paso del Arroyo" ("the crossing of the creek") for the nearby and much-used ford at the creek. Ox teams, hauling logs and lumber from mills on the mountainside, could at this point take on a double load for the easy grade in the valley.

After American rule began, the rancho had a large number of squatters, whose claims caused a good deal of confusion in the 1850's. Most of the squatters were bought off by George Gordon, a wealthy San Francisco businessman, who in 1863 secured title to most of the original land. Before his death in 1869 he had built for himself a country home on the property and laid out Eucalyptus Avenue and other drives.

Leland Stanford purchased the property from the executors of the estate and used the Gordon house as a nucleus for his larger and finer residence. He greatly enlarged his holdings by the purchase of adjoining lands, so that he eventually possessed 9,200 acres, which in time became the site of Stanford University.

Rancho San Antonio (Los Altos)

This rancho was an oblong strip of land stretching from San Antonio (Adobe) Creek to Cupertino (Stevens) Creek along the foothills. It was granted to Juan Prado Mesa in 1839 by Governor Alvarado. Don Prado was a soldier stationed at the presidio in San Francisco who had become *alferez* (officer in command) in 1837. He erected a large square adobe, which survived long into the twentieth century as a crumbling ruin locally thought of as a fortification. The site today is on a hill on the southeast side of El Monte Avenue near Summerhill Avenue in the community of Los Altos, most of which is situated on the territory of the rancho.

Rancho La Purísima Concepción (Los Altos Hills)

Rancho La Purísima Concepción was granted in 1840 to José Gorgonio, an Indian who had been at Mission Santa Clara, by Governor Alvarado. He and another Indian, José Ramón, occupied the land for some years before the formal grant; their home was on a hill on the west side of Adobe Creek near present Fremont Avenue. The grant was sold to Juana Briones de Miranda in 1844. Juana was the daughter of a pioneer family that arrived in California in the 1790's. Her marriage to Apolinario Miranda, a soldier at the San Francisco Presidio, seems to have been unhappy: in 1843 he was sent before the subprefect for not living harmoniously with his wife.

In the North Beach district of San Francisco, where she had an adobe house, Juana frequently acted as doctor, nurse, or midwife. She continued this activity after

moving with her seven children to the Rancho La Purísima Concepción, a hilly tract of land in which rise several small streams that unite to form Adobe Creek. A
glimpse of rancho life can be gained from a description
of a shopping trip to San Francisco, which required a
full week, three days going, and three days returning,
and one day for the necessary errands in the city. The
carreta, drawn by a team of oxen and piled with hides
to be sold, got an early start and, jolting over the uneven road, reached the first night's destination at the
Argüello rancho, Rancho de las Pulgas. The next day, a
fresh team of oxen was supplied for the second lap of
the journey, which ended at the Sánchez rancho, Rancho Buriburi (both ranchos are in what is now San
Mateo County). There another exchange of oxen took
place and Mission Dolores was reached the third night.
On the fourth day, the travelers greeted old friends and
took the hides to Davis or to Leidesdorff, the two most
successful merchant-shipowners of the time, exchanging them for supplies. The return journey saw all the
oxen returned to their home corrals, and the travelers
reached home with their own animals the night of the
seventh day.

The Juana Briones de Miranda adobe (SRL 524) is located at 950 Old Trace Road on the border between Palo
Alto and Los Altos Hills, just west of the intersection of
Arastradero Road and the Foothill Expressway. Dr.
Charles Palmer Nott, a botanist at Stanford University,
purchased the place in 1900 and made many improvements to both the house and the grounds. The long
and narrow adobe, found falling into decay, was protected by being covered with boards. Dr. Nott added
rooms, including a second story, for his growing family.
The property was acquired in 1925 by Dr. George Lee
Easton of San Francisco and remains in the family. The
adobe is open to the public on a limited basis through
the Palo Alto–based Women's Heritage Museum. Old
Trace Road was originally a trail over which redwood
logs were hauled from the hills to the Bay for shipping.

Rancho Quito (Saratoga)

Rancho Quito lay in the fertile country between the
town of Saratoga and SR 82, watered by Saratoga and
Calabasas creeks, with the Arroyo San Tomás Aquino
as its eastern boundary. The rancho was granted in
1841 by Governor Alvarado to José Noriega and José
Zenon Fernández. Both men arrived in California as
part of a colonizing expedition organized by José María
Padrés and José María Híjar. They settled in San Jose,
where Fernández taught for a time in nearby Santa
Clara. At the time of the grant he was secretary to the
council of the pueblo of San José. Both owners transferred the property to Manuel Alviso in 1844. Noriega
continued to live in the vicinity. The American patent
of 1866 was granted jointly to Alviso and to the heirs of
Fernández. Meanwhile, in 1859, Alviso had sold part of
his interest in the property to Don José Ramón Argüello, son of Don Luís Argüello and grandson of Don José
Darío Argüello. Argüello's Quito Farm was at the junction of modern-day Saratoga Avenue and Quito Road.
There Argüello planted olive trees, a fruit orchard, and
a small vineyard, which passed in 1882 into the possession of Edward E. Goodrich, who further developed
the property by building a winery, an oil mill, and
houses for his employees.

The city of Saratoga lies at the southwest corner of
Rancho Quito on Saratoga Creek. The old settlement of
Gubserville (SRL 447) was on the road from Santa Clara
that extends through this rancho. The settlement was
the first place on the stage route out of Santa Clara at
which the driver paused to leave mail. The post office
existed here from 1882 to 1899, and Frank Gubser was
postmaster as well as saloonkeeper. Gubser's "Half-
Way House" stood on the northwest side of Saratoga
Avenue about opposite Los Felice Drive, where the
state marker is located. Nearby, at Payne and Saratoga
avenues, is the site of the Moreland School (SRL 489),
which, when it was marked by the state of California in
1953, was the center of the oldest known rural school
district in the state.

Before the boundary lines of Rancho Quito were
definitely known, several families made homes in the
region east of Cupertino on land they supposed to be
public land. When court proceedings were decided
against these families, they either moved elsewhere or
were given the option to buy their lots within five years'
time. Robert Glendenning was one of those who remained; a Scotsman who arrived in California via Australia in 1850, he and his family settled in the area and
eventually built a home in 1871. Their home still stands
on a private road leading south from 19160 Homestead
Road in Saratoga.

Rancho Rinconada de los Gatos (Los Gatos)

Rancho Rinconada de los Gatos, consisting of one
and one-half square leagues, was granted by Governor
Alvarado in 1840 to Sebastián Peralta and José Hernández. The Arroyo San Tomás Aquino formed its western
boundary and separated it from Rancho Quito. The
rancho extended south of present-day Los Gatos into
the broad lower end of the canyon, which is described
by John C. Frémont in his *Memoirs* as a valley "openly
wooded with groves of oak, free from underbrush, and
after the spring rains covered with grass. On the west it

is protected from the chilling influence of the northwest winds by the Cuesta de los Gatos [Wildcat Ridge], which separates it from the coast."

It is said that a fight took place there in 1831 between the Indians of the region and soldiers from Mission Santa Clara. Several legends, too, are connected with the naming of the place, all having to do with the number of large native cats. These seem to have been both plentiful and fierce, since the legends tell of several encounters with them. The ridge was known by the name of Los Gatos as early as 1831, and the rancho and the modern city of Los Gatos adopted the name from the ridge.

Sebastián Peralta sold 2,500 acres of the rancho to Claud Simond in 1852, and on this land Simond built an adobe home of one and one-half stories that is still standing at 14610 Quito Road. A private residence, the adobe has been remodeled over the years, but it still retains its Mexican charm, with its deep-set windows and doors. A commemorative bronze tablet was affixed to the outer wall of the old part in 1927 by the Colonial Dames of America.

Rancho Santa Teresa (San Jose)

Rancho Santa Teresa originally consisted of 9,647 acres granted to Joaquín Bernal, a native of Mexico. The land he chose lies today within the southeastern part of the city of San Jose, bounded on the east by Coyote Creek. Much of the territory is now Santa Teresa County Park. On this rancho was signed the Treaty of Santa Teresa on November 29, 1844. Governor Manuel Micheltorena, who was opposed by Juan Bautista Alvarado and José Castro, agreed by its terms to send his army of cholos, an unpopular band of ex-convicts, out of California within three months. In fact he did not do so, and the "battle" of Cahuenga Pass, near Los Angeles, took place the following February; it resulted in Micheltorena's finally being unseated as governor.

Rancho El Potrero de Santa Clara (San Jose)

One of the earliest boundary markers in California was placed between Mission Santa Clara and the Pueblo de San José to fix the extent of the mission pastures. The Potrero (pasture lands) de Santa Clara was enclosed by a willow hedge and running ditch at its northwest end; the Alameda was built around its southern end. This ditch and the other early irrigation ditches were fed from the Posa de Santa Clara, a natural pond excavated into a shallow well, which had a perennial flow. This source is recognizably described in the early mission reports; its location has been identified as the middle of the block bounded by Mission Street, Park Avenue, and The Alameda.

After the secularization of the missions, this land reverted to the Mexican government, and in 1844 Governor Micheltorena granted Rancho El Potrero de Santa Clara, purportedly consisting of one square league, to James Alexander Forbes, who was then the British vice-consul for California. A native of Scotland, Forbes had arrived in California around 1830, had become a naturalized Mexican citizen, and in 1834 had married Ana María, daughter of Juan Crisóstomo Galindo, claimant of mission lands near Milpitas. According to some authorities, El Potrero de Santa Clara was given as a marriage dower to the bride. A number of former mission Indians also claimed this property.

In 1847 Forbes sold the property to Commodore Robert Field Stockton, U.S.N. Born in 1795, Stockton had seen long service with the Navy, beginning with the War of 1812; he commanded the squadron that accepted the surrender of the Mexican garrisons at Santa Barbara and Los Angeles, and was military governor of California from the summer of 1846 until early the following year. He did not spend much time in California (he represented his native New Jersey in the United States Senate in 1851–53, after his resignation from the Navy), but he is credited with three new business ventures that proved important for the region: a nursery for the propagation of fruit trees, a residential subdivision called Alameda Gardens, and the importation of houses from the East brought around the Horn. Agents established a nursery with stock imported from Massachusetts; it is said that the first strawberry plants in the Santa Clara Valley were brought in at this time, the beginnings of what was to become an important crop in the area. Stockton also imported bees from Italy; a marker at the San Jose Airport (SRL 945), however, incorrectly ascribes the introduction of the honeybee in California to Christopher A. Shelton in 1853.

For the Alameda Gardens subdivision, Stockton ordered houses to be made in New England ready to be erected in California after being shipped around the Horn. Ten houses were put up; a house now standing at another location on 968 Emory Street is thought to be one of these, the others all having disappeared.

Rancho Los Coches (San Jose)

The first case decided for property in Santa Clara County by the Federal Land Commission, following the terms of the Treaty of Guadalupe-Hidalgo, was that of Rancho Los Coches (called "The Pigs" because it had been the mission's swine pasturage), consisting of one-half square league lying southwest of the Alameda.

The boundary began on the Alameda at the Ciénega de Santa Clara and extended westward to the Roblar del Torotal, thence southeast along this forest to the Arroyo de los Gatos, thence to the Guadalupe River. This rancho had been granted in 1842 by Governor Micheltorena to Roberto, a Christianized Indian of Mission Santa Clara who had been living on the land with his wife and children before that date. The question in this case was concerned with the legality of a grant to an Indian and further with his right to dispose of the property. The question being decided in the affirmative by the commission, a claim, based on Roberto's ownership, was filed in 1852 by Antonio Suñol, his daughter Paula Suñol de Sansevain, and Henry M. Naglee, and the claimants received the patent to the rancho in 1857.

Antonio María Suñol, a Spaniard once in the French naval service, left the *Bordelais* in Monterey harbor in 1818. He settled in San Jose, where he kept a shop, and about 1824 married María Dolores Bernal. He was postmaster from 1826 to 1829, *síndico* (receiver) from 1839 to 1840, and subprefect from 1841 to 1844. During his ranch activities, he sold cattle to Captain John Sutter on credit and had difficulty in obtaining payment. The Suñol adobe, still standing, has been described earlier in this chapter.

Henry Morris Naglee, a distinguished officer in the Civil War and one of the three joint patentees of Rancho Los Coches, long held a portion of it in his name. Naglee Park, which extended from Eleventh Street to Coyote Creek in the city of San Jose, was once his property (although not on Los Coches), and here on a 140-acre tract stood his residence, reached by a driveway one and one-half miles long. Now remodeled as an apartment house, the building stands at the northwest corner of San Fernando and Fourteenth streets. The redwood trees and the stately palms remaining from his planting, which line some of the streets in this vicinity, give some idea of the extent and beauty of the grounds laid out around his home in 1865.

Rancho Las Animas (Southern Santa Clara County)

The first census of San Jose, taken in 1778, lists thirteen-year-old José Mariano Castro, eldest son of Joaquín Castro and his wife, María Botiller, both of whom came to California in 1776 with the Anza colonists. This boy, grown to manhood and married to Josefa Romero, journeyed back to Mexico in 1801 and obtained the grant of Rancho La Brea. The document, directly from the Spanish Viceroy Marquinas, was dated August 17, 1802. Together with an addition to it granted in 1810 by Viceroy Lizano y Beaumont, it was the only rancho in

California granted directly by a viceroy, according to Theodore Hittell. In later years some difficulty regarding the title was encountered, but in 1835 the matter was adjusted by the regranting of it under the name of Rancho Las Animas by the Mexican governor, José Figueroa, to the widow of Don José Mariano, Doña Josefa.

In time this rancho passed into the possession of José María Sánchez. The 26,519 acres patented to his heirs in 1873 extend from the border with San Benito County across US 101 south of Gilroy to Mount Madonna County Park in the Santa Cruz Mountains. On this rancho, the Carnadero Creek flows for miles through a series of rolling hills, after it leaves the higher region in the vicinity of Mount Madonna. Excellent pasture lands are on these hills, and here around Miller's Station was the celebrated Bloomfield Ranch of Henry Miller, the German boy who climbed to success through his ability to raise and market cattle and sheep.

Heinrich Alfred Kreiser was the name of this young German in his native land, but in his journey from New York via the Isthmus of Panama he had used a ticket purchased from a chance acquaintance named Henry Miller. On March 30, 1858, eight years after he had reached California, he changed his name by legal procedure to Henry Miller. In that year he entered into partnership with Charles Lux, a partnership that lasted until the death of Lux 25 years later. As time passed, the firm of Miller and Lux became familiar throughout the West. Henry Miller seemed to succeed in all that he undertook; his ability to foresee the outcome of his plans was remarkable. The lands and herds of this firm stretched over the state; in several counties large feeding grounds and fields for cultivation were acquired. More than a dozen of the old ranchos were owned in whole or in part by Miller and Lux, and the number of their employees was legion. When the animals were driven to market in San Francisco, no matter how long the journey, feeding and resting places on their own property were always convenient.

The Bloomfield Ranch is easily recognized by three large concrete silos, built relatively recently, along US 101 three and one-half miles south of Gilroy. It is said that one of the dwellings on the ranch, visible from the highway, is part of the old ranch house.

On Mount Madonna (elevation 1,897 feet), in the mountains on the northwest part of this rancho, Henry Miller built an elaborate country home overlooking the broad valley below. There he entertained his friends. After his death in 1916, the house, which had been purchased for rebuilding elsewhere, was removed piece by piece, and the fountains, terraces, and choice trees and shrubs that graced the grounds were left untended. The ruins of the estate may be seen in Mount Madonna County Park.

Rancho Ojo de Agua de la Coche (Morgan Hill)

An epic of the Western movement might be written using as a theme the Martin Murphy family. Martin Murphy, Sr., nearing the age of 60 years, arrived in California in 1844 with his sons and daughters and several grandchildren. Murphy was born in 1785 in Ireland, where he married and where his elder children were born. Disliking his prospects in his native land, he took his family (with the exception of his eldest son and daughter, who joined him later) and moved in 1820 to Frampton, Canada, where he settled and remained twenty years.

At the end of this period another move was made, this time to a pioneer part of the United States west of the Mississippi River near St. Joseph. The new location proved unsatisfactory because of the lack of religious and educational opportunities and because of the presence of malaria, to which his wife, Mary Foley, and three of his grandchildren succumbed. Again he took up his family and moved on; this time his destination was chosen because of the influence of a priest who had visited California and who described it enthusiastically. Selling all his land, he put the proceeds into provisions, wagons, oxen, and equipment for the long trek to the Far West in 1844. At a point on the Missouri River, the Murphy and Stevens parties joined forces for mutual protection and aid; in the long westward journey Captain Elisha Stevens was co-leader with Martin Murphy.

With the young men of the party on horseback accompanying the wagons drawn by oxen and containing the family and all their household goods, the long journey was finally ended in safety around Sacramento. Here most of the men in the group enlisted at once under Sutter's leadership to go to the aid of Governor Micheltorena in putting down the Alvarado-Castro insurrection of 1845. When this episode was ended, the immigrants were free to settle where they chose, and the party disbanded. Martin Murphy, Jr., bought land nearby on the Cosumnes River, where he lived until the gold rush of 1849 enabled him to sell his land and livestock at a considerable profit, when he again followed his father.

Martin Murphy, Sr., had settled in Santa Clara County near the present town of Morgan Hill. Purchasing Rancho Ojo de Agua de la Coche, which had been granted by Governor Figueroa to Juan María Hernández in 1835, he built an adobe residence between the town of Morgan Hill and the hill that rises to the west of the town, known as, among other things, Murphy's Peak or Twenty-One Mile Peak. Martin J. C. Murphy, a grandson, received the United States patent to the rancho in 1860. US 101 and the Southern Pacific Railroad pass through the town, which was named for Hiram Morgan Hill, who married Martin Murphy's granddaughter Diana. Hill's home, built in the 1880's or 1890's, still stands at 350 North Monterey Street.

Rancho Cañada de Pala (Eastern Santa Clara County)

Beginning just south of Alum Rock Canyon and extending to the present highway to Lick Observatory, the mountainous Rancho Cañada de Pala takes in 15,714 acres. It was granted in 1839 to José de Jesús Bernal by Governor Alvarado. About seven miles along Mount Hamilton Road from its junction with Alum Rock Avenue, a small adobe, the history of which is uncertain, stands on the Tiernan Ranch to the left of the road, not far from the junction with Quinby Road. The old adobe, partially wood-covered, is just north of the former Hall's Valley schoolhouse, now in use as a residence.

New Almaden

Since ancient times the Indians of the Santa Clara Valley visited the hill of red earth (cinnabar) above the poplar-lined stream that the Spaniards later called the Arroyo de los Alamitos ("the River of the Little Poplar Trees"). The red earth made excellent pigment, which the Indians used for adornment.

As early as 1824 the Spanish settlers of the valley knew about the red hill and its pigments. In that year an attempt was made by the Robles brothers, Secundino and Teodoro, and by Don Antonio Suñol, a member of the San Jose Council, to find silver or gold in the deposit; in time their excavation was called "La Mina Santa Clara."

In the year 1842 Governor Alvarado made grants of land in this vicinity to two men: Rancho Cañada de los Capitancillos was granted to Justo Larios, and Rancho San Vicente to José de los Reyes Berryessa. On November 22, 1845, Andrés Castillero, a deputy of the Mexican government, filed with Alcalde Pedro Chabolla in San Jose a document in which he claimed discovery of "silver with a ley of gold" on the rancho of José Berryessa. In conformity with the mining ordinances he asked that notices of his discovery and of his intention to develop it be affixed in public places. After making certain crude tests he filed a second document in the following month reporting the discovery of "liquid quicksilver" in the deposit, and shortly thereafter went back to Mexico.

Soon there began long-drawn-out litigation over the ownership of the mine. In 1846, Barron, Forbes and Company of Tepic, Mexico, owned the controlling interest in the project, and after the discovery of gold at Coloma in 1848, there was a tremendous increase in the demand for mercury, used in the reduction of gold ore. New Almaden (SRL 339), named for the great Almaden mine in Spain, became the most famous and one of the most productive mercury mines in the world. Mining operations ended in 1975.

The Department of the Interior designated New Almaden a National Historic Landmark District in 1958. The district encompasses the *hacienda*, or mining community, that evolved along the banks of the Alamitos Creek, and the Cinnabar Hills where the actual mining operation took place. Santa Clara County purchased 3,500 acres of Cinnabar Hills open space for the creation of Quicksilver Park in 1975. Still standing is the pretentious "Casa Grande," home of the mine superintendent, with two-foot-thick walls and magnificent hand-carved fireplaces. The building dates back to 1854; the original formal landscaping was done by John McLaren. The picturesque settlement continues up to the furnaces and reduction works. Small wooden houses, many marked with historic plaques, line the main street. The Hacienda Cemetery has been restored and maintained by the California Pioneers of Santa Clara County and is located on Bertram Avenue in back of the hacienda.

The Almaden Vineyards (SRL 505), planted by Charles LeFranc in 1852, are located at 1530 Blossom Hill Road in San Jose; the present winery goes back to 1876.

Casa Grande, New Almaden, San Jose

The Battle of Santa Clara

The American conquest of California was not unchallenged, but the so-called battles that took place were, on the whole, mere skirmishes with few casualties. On January 2, 1847, one such skirmish, known as the Battle of Santa Clara, was fought about two and one-half miles west of Mission Santa Clara at a spot marked at 2780 El Camino Real by a plaque placed by E Clampus Vitus. The American leaders were captains Joseph Aram, Charles M. Weber, and John W. Murphy; Francisco Sánchez was the Mexican captain. Four Californios were killed and four wounded; two Americans suffered wounds. The site of the Armistice Oak (SRL 260), under which the battle is said to have ended, is in Civic Center Park, on El Camino Real at Lincoln Street. A five-day armistice followed the battle, during which time Sánchez and his forces retreated to the Santa Cruz Mountains and then surrendered to the American authorities.

California's First State Capital

San Jose became the first state capital of California after the adoption of the first state constitution on November 13, 1849. The first legislature convened there on December 17, delayed by heavy rains, which kept many legislators from reaching the town for the announced December 15 opening. Nine months later Congress passed the act that formally admitted California to the Union. Although serious work was accomplished at San Jose, this session is known as "the Legislature of a Thousand Drinks" because of the freely imbibing Senator Thomas Jefferson Green and his advocacy of adjournment to the local saloon.

The capital was removed from San Jose to Vallejo by act of the second legislature on February 14, 1851, and the removal took effect on May 1 of that year. The building that served as the first state capitol was a little two-story structure, adobe below and frame above, which stood on a site (SRL 461) directly across South Market Street from the spot now marked by a granite boulder and bronze plate on the east side of the old plaza. The tablet, placed by the Native Sons of the Golden West, bears an image of the old adobe capitol, which was destroyed by fire in 1853.

The First American School in California

The first American school in California was held in the crumbling buildings of Mission Santa Clara in the spring of 1847 by Mrs. Olive Mann Isbell. She and her husband, Dr. James C. Isbell, had just arrived from Ohio with other members of an overland emigrant party. While the men were called to do military duty, the women and children were left at the mission. Partly to relieve mothers of the constant care of their families, Mrs. Isbell began to give rudimentary instruction to the children with the slender means at her disposal, lacking books, paper, pencils, and no chalk. One of the pupils later recounted that letters of the alphabet were drawn on the back of the hand with a stick of charcoal and thus made visible to the beginners. When the men returned from their short period of military service and the reunited families went their separate ways, this unique school ended; Mrs. Isbell taught for many years in other parts of the state.

The College of Notre Dame

Two sisters from the Order of Notre Dame de Namur established the College of Notre Dame in San Jose in 1851; the college was officially chartered as an institution of higher learning four years later. The flourishing establishment occupied a tract of land extending from West Santa Clara Street to West St. John Street and from Notre Dame Street to Santa Teresa Street. In 1923 the college was moved to the less urban atmosphere of Belmont in San Mateo County, some 25 miles to the north.

The University of the Pacific

The University of the Pacific, founded under Methodist auspices in San Jose, is the oldest incorporated educational institution in California, having received its charter on July 10, 1851, under the name California Wesleyan University. In 1870 the college, by then called the University of the Pacific, was moved to College Park, about halfway between Santa Clara and San Jose, and now within the San Jose city limits. In 1921 the name was changed to the College of the Pacific, and in 1924 the entire establishment was moved to Stockton, where in 1961 it once more took the name of the University of the Pacific. The site on the old College Park campus is now occupied by Bellarmine College Preparatory School, operated by the Jesuits and originally the high school department of the University of Santa Clara.

San Jose State University

The first normal school (an institution specifically designed for the training of teachers) in California began in San Francisco in 1857 as a private enterprise,

Minns's Evening Normal School, taking its name from the first principal, George W. Minns. By act of the legislature in 1862 it was made a public normal school. In 1870, after a spirited contest over the location, the school was moved to San Jose. In 1921 all the normal schools in California were changed to teachers' colleges. The institution became San Jose State College in 1935 and was raised to university status in 1972, along with many other state colleges. SRL 417, commemorating the original normal school, is located at Tower Hall, a structure dating from 1910.

Other Historic Spots in San Jose

The French prune, for which the Santa Clara Valley became famous, was introduced into California at San Jose in the winter of 1856–57 by Louis Pellier, aided by his brothers Pierre and Jean. A native of France, Pellier came to California in 1849, and the following year opened a nursery called City Gardens (SRL 434). On November 29, 1977, the two hundredth anniversary of the founding of the pueblo, Pellier Park was dedicated on the site at St. James and Terraine streets by the city of San Jose.

At 432 South Eighth Street is the Edwin Markham Cottage (SRL 416), the house where the poet lived from 1869 to 1889 and wrote the first draft of his most celebrated work, "The Man With the Hoe." After a boyhood spent in Solano County, Markham attended the normal school at San Jose and upon graduation began teaching school at Evergreen.

The Hayes Mansion (SRL 888) at 200 Edenvale Avenue is a 1904 example of what is called Mission Revival–Italian Renaissance architecture, designed by George W. Page. The Hayes family was prominent in religious and political activities in San Jose for many years.

A larger building is the Winchester House (SRL 868) at 525 South Winchester Boulevard at I-280 and SR 17. Sarah Winchester was heiress to the Winchester Repeating Arms Company fortune. Following the deaths of her husband and baby daughter, she came to California in 1880 and set out to enlarge a country house. A spiritualist, she became convinced that her life depended on constantly adding to her house; some 160 rooms had been completed at the time of her death in 1922. The Winchester Mystery House is a public attraction today, where visitors can see staircases ending in the ceiling, doors that open onto blank walls, and five fully equipped kitchens.

Another striking building in San Jose is the Rosicrucian Egyptian Museum at Park and Naglee avenues, containing remarkable displays of ancient artifacts collected by the Rosicrucian fellowship.

The San Jose Museum of Art at 110 South Market Street is located in the old post office (SRL 854), the first federal building in San Jose, constructed in 1892. Nearby are two churches that, like the post office building, are on the National Register of Historic Places. St. Joseph's Catholic Church (SRL 910) at Market and San Fernando streets was completed in 1877 and is currently undergoing a thorough renovation. The First Unitarian Church (SRL 902) at 160 North Third Street has been in continuous use since its completion in 1892. A third church, Trinity Episcopal, at Second and St. John streets, is a redwood structure, built in 1863, and is the oldest church building still standing in San Jose.

A plaque at the northwest corner of First and San Fernando streets (SRL 952) commemorates the site of the first broadcasting station in the world, established by Dr. Charles Herrold in 1909. It later became known as KQW and is now KCBS, located in San Francisco. Another plaque, at 79 North Market Street, marks the birthplace of Amadeo Peter Giannini, born in what was then the Swiss Hotel in 1870. In 1904 Giannini founded the Bank of Italy, now Bank of America, in San Francisco, and in 1910 he opened the bank's first out-of-town branch, in San Jose at the corner of Santa Clara

Restored Firehouse, San Jose Historical Museum

and Lightston streets. The bank structure has been moved to the San Jose Historical Museum.

The San Jose Historical Museum, situated in Kelley Park at 635 Phelan Avenue, contains a number of historic buildings from the city and from the Santa Clara Valley, including the old Coyote Post Office, dating from 1862. Dominating the site is a replica of the San Jose Electric Tower; this was the inspiration of J. J. Owen, owner of the *San Jose Mercury*, who in 1881 printed an editorial suggesting that if the city provided one high and immense source of arc light, the night would become as day for the downtown area. The idea met with public approval, and the 237-foot tower was installed by the end of the year. Straddling the intersection of Santa Clara and Market streets, the tower's light of 24,000 candlepower failed to illuminate the area as expected; it was damaged in a windstorm in 1915 and collapsed later that year. The 115-foot replica is scaled to fit the streets of the museum.

Campbell

William Campbell, a native of Kentucky and a veteran of the War of 1812, arrived in Santa Clara County with his family in 1846, having traveled on the first part of the overland journey with the Donner party. The following year he assisted in the surveys of the towns of San Jose and Santa Clara, and in 1847–48 he built a sawmill, about three miles above present Saratoga near Long Bridge, on the creek long called by his name. His elder son, David, went to another county to live, but Benjamin, a boy of nineteen when the family arrived in California, purchased land some miles northeast of his father's mill, on which he raised wheat until 1887. In that year he subdivided the tract and sold lots for the town of Campbell.

The town was at one time the center of fruit-raising activities in the Santa Clara Valley. The Campbell Fruit Growers Union cooperative was taken over by the George W. Hyde Company, which operated one of the world's largest drying grounds. The largest prune dehydrating plant in the world was in the Sunsweet Plant No. 1 in Campbell. On a visit to the area in 1903 (in the course of which Mrs. Winchester refused to receive him in her home), President Theodore Roosevelt planted a redwood tree on the Campbell High School grounds, an offshoot of which still stands at the intersection of Winchester Boulevard and Campbell Avenue. The Campbell Historical Museum at First Street and Civic Center Drive contains relics and displays of the area's agricultural history. By 1965, houses and apartments had entirely taken over the orchards and food-processing activities of the past.

Los Gatos

Situated on the Arroyo de los Gatos after it flows from the canyon into the broader open space at the foot of the Santa Cruz Mountains is the city of Los Gatos. It had its beginning in the Santa Rosa Flour Mill (SRL 458) built on the east side of Los Gatos Creek by James Alexander Forbes in 1854.

The mill had three stories of stone taken from the nearby canyon and a fourth story of redwood. A dam was built half a mile upstream and water was carried from it through a wooden flume to power the two water wheels that ran the totally automatic machinery. Forbes overextended himself in constructing the mill and by 1856 had declared bankruptcy. Other entrepreneurs followed, until the mill was closed in 1887. The earthquake of 1906 badly damaged the building, and in 1916 the Pacific Gas and Electric Company, the current owner, pulled down the four-story mill, leaving intact a two-story stone addition from 1880 to serve as an electrical substation. The building today serves as the Forbes Mill Regional Museum, established by Eureka Federal Savings Company. It is accessible from East Main and Church streets in Los Gatos, on the east side of SR 17.

El Camino Real, from Mission Santa Clara to Mission Santa Cruz, passed just to the east of Forbes's Mill. A flood in 1862 demolished the road. Beginning in 1847, sawmills were operated in the canyons above the present town, and at that period the trail through the canyon was used for hauling the lumber down to a lumberyard at the present corner of College and Main streets, so that teamsters from San Jose would not have to travel the dangerous one-lane road to the mills.

A good wagon road into the redwoods and over the mountains to Santa Cruz was needed. In 1857, the first meeting of the Santa Cruz Gap Turnpike Joint Stock Company was held in the tollhouse, which still stands at 142 South Santa Cruz Avenue, at the corner of Wood Road. In October 1858 the toll road was completed from Los Gatos, up the west side of Los Gatos Canyon to Lexington, and on to the summit. There it connected with the Santa Cruz Turnpike near the cabin of Charles Henry "Mountain Charley" McKiernan, the first permanent white settler in the Santa Cruz Mountains.

Royce Street in Los Gatos is named for Josiah Royce, historian, philosopher, and psychologist, who spent a part of his early years on that street in the house of his mother, Sarah Eleanor Royce.

At 17535 Santa Cruz Highway one can see the statues of two cats, eight feet high, flanking the entrance to the estate once owned by Colonel and Mrs. Erskin Scott Wood. The concrete felines are the work of sculptor Charles Paine and were put up when the estate was built in 1922. They are now regarded as the official symbol for the town, which is named for the wildcats in the area.

Kotani-En (SRL 903) at 15891 Ravine Road is a classical Japanese residence surrounded by gardens covering an acre and a half of land. It was commissioned in 1918 by San Francisco financier Max H. Cohn.

The Los Gatos Museum at 4 Tait Avenue is housed in the city's old firehouse, where changing displays on local history can be seen.

Historic Spots of the Santa Cruz Mountains in Santa Clara County

Rising toward the ridge marking the Santa Cruz County boundary, the Santa Cruz Mountains south of Los Gatos contain a few remaining historical landmarks and some names of historical interest. When the Lexington Dam was completed in 1953, impounding the waters of Los Gatos Creek, the historic area of Lexington and Alma was inundated. Here the first sawmill in Santa Clara County was erected in 1848. As roads into the area were constructed, John Pennell Henning of Lexington, Missouri, laid out a "city of Lexington" in 1858. A number of commercial enterprises were in operation at its height in 1867, including the Lexington House Hotel, which catered to sportsmen who fished for trout in Los Gatos Creek or hunted bear and deer in the nearby mountains.

Alma originated in 1862 as the Forest House, a roadside hotel. The Lexington post office was moved there in 1873 and given the name Alma (Spanish for "soul"), for Alma was the soul of the redwood district. A mile up the canyon from Lexington, Alma prospered when James Fair's South Pacific Coast Railroad began its run from Alameda in 1878; the passengers left the narrow-gauge line at Alma and took stagecoaches over the mountains to Santa Cruz. The railroad to Santa Cruz was completed in 1880 and seven years later was taken over by the Southern Pacific Railroad, which converted the line to standard gauge in 1909. The last trains ran between Los Gatos and Santa Cruz on March 4, 1940.

The oldest building believed still to be standing in the Santa Cruz Mountains is at 22849 Summit Road, built in 1852 by the German cabinetmaker John Martin Schultheis for his family. Closer to the main road, at 22951 Summit, is the frame house built in 1880 by Volney Averell, who married Alice Schultheis. The Summit Opera House, run by Averell and Charles Aitken, was at nearby Patchin (SRL 448), commemorated by a plaque at Mountain Charley Road and Old Santa Cruz Highway Road, east of today's SR 17.

"Bohemia" is a picturesque building at 241 Loma Prieta Road. This was built in the mid-1870's by Z. A. Catton to serve as both a private residence and an inn. In the latter capacity, it was a haven for writers such as Ambrose Bierce, Jack London, and George Sterling, whose patronage gave it a Bohemian tone.

Austrian Dam stands at the junction of Austrian Gulch and Los Gatos Creek. Austro-German immigrants in the 1870's settled on these mountain slopes and with their industry and thrift soon made a prosperous settlement of orchards and vineyards. A terrific cloudburst in 1889 swept away their possessions; the foundations of their immense winery were so loosened that it collapsed and thousands of gallons of red wine poured down Los Gatos Creek. Although a few undaunted souls remained, most of the colony returned to Europe or sought employment elsewhere in California. A forest fire in 1923 destroyed the few wooden buildings left in Austrian Gulch.

Holy City is still marked on road maps, but no longer exists in fact. It was founded in 1918 by William E. "Father" Riker, the leader of a white-supremacist religious cult and perennial candidate for governor of the state. The colony became a tourist attraction on the highway between Santa Cruz and the San Francisco Bay Area; its wooden buildings plastered with garish signs housed a print shop, a mineral water concern, a radio station, and tourist facilities for "the world's perfect government." After SR 17 was rerouted in the 1950's, Holy City began its terminal decline.

Saratoga

William Campbell and his sons, David and Benjamin, began construction of a sawmill on Arroyo Quito late in 1847. Before the mill was finished, word reached them of the discovery of gold in the Sierra Nevada. They rushed to the mines, but soon returned to complete their mill, only to find that one was already in operation on Arroyo de los Gatos, even though it had been begun a month later than their own. The Campbell mill was thus the second operating sawmill in Santa Clara County. It was located at or near Long Bridge, about three miles west of Saratoga at the junction of SR 9 and Sanborn Road. In the early 1950's, Campbell Creek was officially renamed Saratoga Creek.

In 1850–51 Martin McCarty, another lumberman, built a toll road up the canyon to what had become known as Campbell's Redwoods. At the lower end of the road, a little settlement began to grow, known at first simply as Toll Gate. In 1855 a post office was established under the name of McCartysville. McCarty's tollgate crossed the present Big Basin Way (formerly Lumber Street) near the corner of Third Street, about where 14477 Big Basin Way is today.

Meanwhile, in 1854, William Haun and John Whisman had established a gristmill called Redwood Mills. It was later purchased by Charles Maclay, who added a tannery and changed the name to Bank Mills. The McCartysville post office was also renamed Bank Mills, but in 1865 it became Saratoga (SRL 435), because, like New York state's Saratoga, it was close to valuable and popular medicinal springs.

Pacific Congress Springs, a short distance west of Saratoga on SR 9, was one of the earliest and most fashionable recreational resorts in California. The mineral springs were discovered in the early 1850's by Jerd Caldwell. Wealthy men, including D. O. Mills and Alvinza Hayward, became interested in the place and formed a corporation, and in June 1866, Congress Hall opened to the public. The building stood about five minutes' walk from the springs. The management owned about 720 acres of wooded hillside, and eventually other buildings were added. The mineral water was proclaimed to be "a refreshing beverage and invigorating tonic." The resort was closed in 1942, and all the buildings are now gone.

Although efforts were made to establish manufacturing in Saratoga, it continued to be chiefly a hub of the lumbering industry and also pioneered in fruit raising, drying, and packing. Today Saratoga is a city of beautiful homes, some of them of considerable age. The James Springer house at 20770 Wildwood Way (1851) is the oldest in town, a prefabricated house brought around the Horn. Martin McCarty's widow, Hannah, lived in a house still standing at 20600 Lomita Avenue, thought to have been built in 1877. Remodeled now as an office building, the John Henry home at 14630 Big Basin Way (1869) is also of interest. The earlier McWilliams house (1865) has been moved to 20460 Saratoga–Los Gatos Road, in the Saratoga Historical Park. Next door at 20450 Saratoga–Los Gatos Road stands the Saratoga Historical Museum, in what was a commercial building built in 1904. The Saratoga Foothill Clubhouse at 20399 Park Place was designed by Julia Morgan, and has been in continuous use since 1915. Welchhurst at 15808 Sanborn Road was built as a family retreat by Judge James R. Welch in 1914. It is interesting for its use of indigenous materials and now serves as a youth hostel. Both Welchhurst and the Saratoga Foothill Clubhouse are on the National Register of Historic Places.

In Madronia Cemetery, at Oak and Sixth streets, are buried A. T. Dowd, discoverer of the Calaveras Big Trees; Riley Moutry, one of the heroic rescuers of the Donner party; and Mrs. Mary Ann Brown, the widow of John Brown, famous abolitionist of Harper's Ferry. Mrs. Brown came to California in 1864, five years after her husband's execution. She and her family settled at Red Bluff, where the home built for her by the townspeople is still standing. In 1870 the Browns moved to Humboldt County, and eleven years later to Saratoga. Mrs. Brown's home from 1881 to 1883 was on the side of the mountain three miles above town, overlooking a wide sweep of the Santa Clara Valley. The building no longer stands, but the site is on the property of the Stuart Camp of the Boy Scouts. It is reached by Bohlman Road, a continuation of Oak Street, a steep and winding mountain road bordered on either side by a tangle of wildflowers and native shrubs. In 1883, before moving to San Francisco, Mrs. Brown sold the mountain farm and lived a short time in a rented house, no longer standing, on the site of the present Sacred Heart Church at 13915 Saratoga Avenue. Mary Ann Brown died in San Francisco in 1884, but her remains were returned to Saratoga for funeral services and burial.

Senator James Duval Phelan, philanthropist, statesman, and patron of the arts, named his Saratoga country place Villa Montalvo in honor of the early Spanish author Ordoñez de Montalvo, in whose *Las Sergas de Esplandian* ("The Exploits of Esplandian"), published in 1510, the name California appears for the first time. The house, built in 1912 on an estate of 175 acres, is situated in the foothills of the Santa Cruz Mountains in a region of great natural beauty with an extensive view over valley and mountains. In the nineteen-room mansion, which surrounds three sides of a colorful court, the owners placed priceless works of art gathered from many lands during a long period of years. Here this native son of San Francisco entertained his many friends in the social, political, commercial, and artistic circles in which he moved.

At the death of Senator Phelan in 1930, the place with all its precious furnishings was left to the San Francisco Art Association. It is now administered as an art gallery and cultural center by the Villa Montalvo Association, and is on the National Register of Historic Places. The gates at the beginning of a long driveway to the mansion are located at 15400 Montalvo Road, Saratoga, just southeast of the business section of the town.

The Hakone Japanese Garden at 21000 Congress Springs Boulevard has been a City of Saratoga Park since 1966. The fifteen-acre property was originally owned by Mr. and Mrs. Oliver C. Stine of San Francisco, who in 1917 constructed here a Japanese house in the old-country style, using neither adhesives nor nails. The extensive and exquisite gardens were completed by N. Aihara, a relative of the court gardeners to the emperor of Japan, the following year. Mrs. Stine called the estate Hakone because, lying in the Congress Springs area, it reminded her of Fuju Hakone National Park, with its mineral springs, in Japan.

The Paul Masson Winery (SRL 733) is at 13150 Saratoga Avenue. One of the first wineries in California, the sandstone walls dating from 1852 have twice been swept by fire and twice rebuilt.

Stevens Creek and Cupertino

Stevens Creek was originally known as Arroyo de San José Cupertino. SRL 800, in the west parking lot of Monte Vista High School at 21840 McClellan Road in Cupertino, marks the approximate spot where on March 25, 1776, on the second Anza expedition, Father Font wrote in his diary the name that had been bestowed on the stream. The stream now bears the name of Captain Elisha Stevens, an early settler in the area, a South Carolinian who led the first successful passage of wagons over the Sierra Nevada in 1844. He settled on the banks of the Arroyo de San Joseph Cupertino in 1859, but by 1864 headed south to the Kern River area, claiming there were too many people in the region for his liking. The oldest house still standing in the Stevens Creek area is that built by W. T. McClellan at 22221 McClellan Road, in the Cupertino city facility now called the McClellan Ranch Park.

The first millionaire in the region, Charles Baldwin, started a large estate in 1887, which he named "Beaulieu," with 70 acres of vineyards. Cupertino was then noted for its wine production. The estate is now the campus of De Anza College. The well-known San Francisco architect Willis Polk designed for Baldwin a large home, which has been moved to its present location at 21250 Stevens Creek Boulevard on the college campus; it is now the home of the California History Center. Other reminders of the early estate are the stone winery and underground cellars, now used as the college bookstore and cafeteria.

"Woodhills" at 22800 Prospect Road, built in 1913, was the country home of Fremont Older, a distinguished San Francisco newspaper editor, and his wife, Cora, who was active in California historical work. An adjacent adobe tile structure was built in 1923 from materials Mrs. Older salvaged from an 1847 adobe in San Jose that was being dismantled.

"The Frenchman," Peter Coutts

An almost legendary character is the "Frenchman" of Frenchman's Tower and Frenchman's Road on the property now owned by Stanford University. Known as "Peter Coutts" during his residence in California, Jean-

Baptiste Paulin Caperon was his real name. In France he was a wealthy banker and the publisher of the anti-Royalist newspaper *La Liberté*. Leaving his homeland as a political exile, he lived for a while in Switzerland under the name of a cousin, Peter Coutts. Using a passport in this name, he came with his family to America, settling on the Matadero Ranch in the vicinity of Mayfield around 1874. "Ayrshire Farm," as he called it, soon became a showplace, with prizewinning Ayrshire cattle and extensive orchards and plantings of trees. Coutts spent much time and money in tunneling into the hillside in search of an adequate water supply. A round red brick tower still standing on Old Page Mill Road was to house the tank for some portion of a hoped-for water supply. He laid out a race track between his house and El Camino Real, and his horses were among the noteworthy features of his estate. His house still stands at 859 Escondido Road on the Stanford campus. In 1891 this cottage was occupied by the young president of the newly founded Leland Stanford Junior University, Dr. David Starr Jordan, who gave it the name "Escondite," or "hiding place."

It was generally believed that this was only a temporary residence for Coutts until a more appropriate, grand structure was built. His many activities gave rise to wild rumors as to who he was, why had he settled in California, and what he was up to. Suddenly, one morning in 1880, the Coutts family disappeared almost as mysteriously as it had arrived. In time his true identity was revealed. The political situation in France had become favorable for his return, and his last years before his death in 1890 were spent in wealth and comfort.

Two other buildings remain from Coutts's ranch. At 860 Escondido is the two-story brick building that was Coutts's library, and at 830 Escondido is a much-remodeled Spanish-style adobe residence known as "the Hacienda."

Stanford University

Leland Stanford, a native of New York, came to California in 1852 at the height of the gold fever. Stanford, however, did not seek gold but with his three brothers at once went into extensive mercantile operations in Sacramento. He amassed a fortune in the following eight years. The first Republican governor of California, elected in 1862, he materially aided the Union cause during the Civil War. His considerable energies thereafter were devoted toward the building of the first transcontinental railroad. He was one of the "Big Four" Sacramento businessmen who built and owned the Central Pacific Railroad (the others were Charles Crocker, Mark Hopkins, and Collis P. Hunt-

ington). This railroad was subsequently merged with the Southern Pacific Railroad, a major force in the life of California in the last decades of the nineteenth century and the first decade of the twentieth. Stanford resumed his political career in 1885 as United States senator from California and was in that office when he died in 1893.

In 1870, Stanford purchased the land that had been the Rancho San Francisquito. The Stanfords remodeled and enlarged the house built by the previous owner, George Gordon. In time this became the Stanford Convalescent Home, which stood at 520 Willow Road until 1965, when it was torn down to make room for expansions to the Stanford Medical Center.

Stanford University lies in large part on the Palo Alto Farm, which Stanford had used for the breeding and training of pedigreed race horses. The Red Barn, still standing from this period on Junipero Serra Road, is on the National Register of Historic Places. Over the years, Stanford's horses held nineteen world records. Nearby is the grave of Palo Alto, the most famous of Stanford's horses, and a statue of Electioneer, the horse that sired nine world record holders. Of particular interest is the plaque (SRL 834) noting that motion pictures were born here.

Did all four hooves of a running horse leave the ground at the same moment? The question had long interested Stanford and other horse fanciers. He made arrangements with San Francisco photographer Eadweard Muybridge to bring his cameras to the farm in 1878–79. According to the plaque on the site, "men and animals in motion" were photographed in "consecutive instantaneous exposures . . . provided by a battery of 24 cameras fitted with electro-shutters." The pictures reveal that a horse, while running rapidly, can have all four hooves off the ground at the same time.

Tragedy struck the Stanford family when Leland, Jr., their only son, died in Florence, Italy, in 1884 at the age of sixteen. On November 11, 1886, the Stanfords founded the university that was to be not only a memorial to their adored child but a gift of love to all the children of California. To provide an adequate campus, the senator purchased adjoining tracts: the Ayrshire Farm or Matadero Rancho of Peter Coutts lying to the southeast, Coon Farm lying between San Francisquito and Los Trancos creeks, and Felt Farm or Rancho de los Trancos lying along Los Trancos Creek. The university's cornerstone was laid on May 14, 1887, and in October 1891 its doors were opened to students.

Time has brought many changes to what was once the tranquil, secluded campus situated at the end of the impressive Palm Drive leading to nearby Palo Alto. The heart of the university is the Quadrangle, built of native sandstone with archways and tile roofs reminiscent of California mission-style architecture. At the center of the inner quadrangle is the Stanford Memorial Church, dedicated by Mrs. Stanford to the memory of her husband. It was completed in 1901, four years before Mrs. Stanford's death. The campus was badly hit by the 1906 earthquake, and the church steeple was toppled into the midst of the ruins. The restored church was built without the architecturally incongruous steeple. The Italian-made mosaics, both inside and out, were fortunately little damaged. The style of the Quadrangle is reflected in the Thomas Welton Stanford Art Gallery, funded by a younger brother of the senator and opened in 1917.

Several other buildings on the campus are of historical interest. The oldest university building, constructed at the same time as the Quadrangle, is Encina Hall on Serra Street, modeled after a Swiss hotel that the Stanfords once visited. Long a men's dormitory, it now houses university offices. "The Knoll" on Lomita Drive was built to be the home of the president of the university and was first occupied by Ray Lyman Wilbur and his family in 1916. The Hanna-Honeycomb House at 737 Frenchman's Road was designed by Frank Lloyd Wright in 1935 for Professor and Mrs. Paul Hanna, and is considered to be one of his most important buildings; it now belongs to the university.

The Stanfords, father, mother, and son, lie in a mausoleum on campus not far from the Leland Stanford Junior Museum, which displays, among many collections, the original gold spike driven at Promontory Point in Utah by Stanford on May 10, 1869, completing the first transcontinental railroad. The two-story museum is adjoined by the striking Rodin Sculpture Garden (1985), a gift of Bernard G. Cantor.

Stanford Family Mausoleum, Stanford University

The first graduating class of 1895 included Herbert Hoover, president of the United States from 1929 to 1933. He received the news of his election at his home on the campus, at 623 Mirada Avenue. The 21-room house (SRL 913) was largely designed by his wife, and is officially called the Lou Henry Hoover House. After her death in 1944, it became the home of the president of the university. A university landmark since 1941 has been the 280-foot tower of the Hoover Institution on War, Revolution, and Peace. The nucleus of this library and research organization is a body of materials that Hoover began assembling in 1919 at the conclusion of World War I.

Mayfield, College Terrace, and Palo Alto

Mayfield and College Terrace are the oldest parts of the city of Palo Alto. A plaque placed by the city and the Palo Alto Historical Association at the corner of Sherman Avenue and Birch Street marks the site of the "Herring Box School" (so called for its small size), the first school in Mayfield, from 1855. Another plaque notes the site of "Uncle Jim's Cabin" at the corner of California Avenue and El Camino Real, a public house and post office built in 1853 by James Otterson.

Mayfield became a town in 1867; its name came from Mayfield Farm, the home of Sarah Wallis (SRL 969). The site of her home, which no longer stands, is on the south side of La Selva Drive midway between Military Way and Magnolia Drive in Palo Alto. The house was destroyed by fire in 1936, but some unusual trees in the vicinity mark its site. Sarah Wallis was the first president of the California Suffrage Association in 1870; in 1873 she was the first president of the California State Woman Suffrage Education Association.

College Terrace is a somewhat later development lying between Mayfield and the Stanford campus. The Kee House at 2310 Yale Street, built in 1889, is probably the oldest house in the neighborhood.

Where Palo Alto now stands, only grain fields existed when the cornerstone of the university was laid in 1887. The Stanfords were unhappy that nearby Mayfield permitted the sale of alcohol. At their urging, Timothy Hopkins, a financial associate of Stanford, acquired some 740 acres along El Camino Real south of Menlo Park, and a new town named University Park came into being. A distinctive feature of the Hopkins tract was the restriction prohibiting the sale of alcoholic beverages within its boundaries, a restriction not lifted until after World War II.

Palo Alto, the name of Stanford's stock farm, soon became the preferred name of the new town, officially incorporated in 1894. Adjoining tracts were added to the city, largely to the south, Mayfield being annexed in 1925. In addition to the landmarks already mentioned, Palo Alto has a number of historic sites. Professorville Historic District comprises the blocks bounded by Lincoln, Waverley, Kingsley, and Emerson streets. The neighborhood was the earliest off-campus residential area for professors at the university and their families. The university's policy of granting a long-term lease, rather than outright ownership, of campus property was an incentive for professors to build in town. One of the many historic homes in the area, at 345 Lincoln Avenue, is of interest as the home of Professor C. B. Wing, who with his neighbor, Professor C. D. Marx, helped develop Palo Alto's unique system of municipally owned utilities.

The Ramona Street Historic District is a block between University and Hamilton avenues designed in the 1920's by Pedro de Lemos, director of the Stanford University Art Museum, and Birge Clark, a prominent Palo Alto architect. A unifying theme of Mediterranean and California Colonial Revival styles characterizes the design of the buildings in the area.

The Squire House at 900 University Avenue (SRL 857) was designed in Classic Revival style by T. Paterson Ross of San Francisco for John A. Squire. The Hostess House at 27 University Avenue (SRL 895) was originally part of Camp Fremont, in nearby Menlo Park, San Mateo County. Designed by Julia Morgan in 1918, it was moved to its present location the following year and became the first municipally sponsored community center in the nation. In the 1970's, after many years of service as a community center, it was transferred by the city to private ownership under terms insuring appropriate use and restoration; it currently houses a restaurant.

The site of the laboratory of Dr. Lee De Forest (SRL 836) is at 913 Emerson Street. The two-story frame house was demolished in 1978; the landmark plaque reads: "Electronics Research Laboratory. Original site of the laboratory and factory of Federal Telegraph Company, founded in 1909 by Cyril F. Elwell. Here, with two assistants, Dr. Lee De Forest, inventor of the three-element radio vacuum tube, devised in 1911–1913 the first vacuum tube amplifier and oscillator. World-wide developments based on this research led to modern radio communication, television, and the electronics age." Elwell's house at 1451 Cowper Street still stands; here in 1908 he transmitted radio signals to Mountain View and Los Altos, the first radio-telephone station on the West Coast. At 1044 Bryant Street is the childhood home of Russell and Sigurd Varian, who, with William Hansen, invented the Klystron tube, a key component

of radar, and established the pioneer electronics firm of Varian Associates in Stanford Industrial Park after World War II.

At the rear of the driveway at 367 Addison Avenue (SRL 976) is the one-car garage that William Hewlett and David Packard used as a laboratory in 1938. Newlyweds David and Lucile Packard occupied the two-story house, Hewlett the small shingle cottage behind it. In the garage they invented electric machines for the nearby Palo Alto Medical Clinic as well as other devices for other clients, notably an audio oscillator for which they began receiving orders in 1939 from, among others, the Walt Disney Studios. By the mid-1950's, the Hewlett-Packard Company they founded had become a world leader in electronics and computer design and manufacturing. This was the beginning of "Silicon Valley," the area around Palo Alto where these industries have flourished since.

Montgomery Hill

John Joseph Montgomery, born in Yuba City in 1858, is remembered for flying a glider at Otay Mesa, south of San Diego, in 1883, thus becoming the first man to go aloft in a heavier-than-air craft. Montgomery Hill (SRL 813), on Yerba Buena Road in Evergreen, commemorates this aviation pioneer whose 55 successful flights demonstrated aerodynamic developments of great importance to aviation. Montgomery, a professor at Santa Clara College, was killed in a glider crash at the site in 1911.

Gilroy

The chief town of southern Santa Clara County is named for pioneer settler John Gilroy, as described in the section on Rancho San Ysidro. Several buildings of historic interest still stand. The Christian Church at 160 Fifth Street originally stood on Third Street, but was moved to this location in 1887. The frame structure was built in 1857, making it the oldest church building in continuous use in Santa Clara County. Another old church, in the next block at 214 Fifth Street, is the Presbyterian Church, much expanded since it was built in 1869.

Fifth Street is a gallery of fine old buildings. The Baxter House at 323 was built in 1875 for hardware merchant J. A. Baxter; it was later the home of Millie Lewis Sargeant, a great-granddaughter of Julius Martin, also mentioned in the Rancho San Ysidro section of this chapter. The Ball House at 314 was saved from condemnation in 1973, its hundredth year, and completely

Holloway House, Gilroy

grown nearby. An annual Garlic Festival in July has attracted many visitors to Gilroy since the first celebration in 1979.

Near Redwood Retreat, ten miles west of Gilroy in the Mount Madonna region, is a log cabin built by the novelist Frank Norris a short time before his death in 1902. He and his wife established themselves there near the forest cabin of their friend Fanny Stevenson, the widow of Robert Louis Stevenson. Here Norris planned to write *The Wolf,* which was to complete the trilogy begun by *The Octopus* and *The Pit,* but his sudden death following an appendectomy at the age of 32 intervened before the manuscript was finished. A semicircular seat, built of stones brought from the nearby stream, is a memorial erected near the cabin by friends of the novelist. The cabin is on a private road reached from Gilroy by a route including the Hecker Pass highway, Watsonville Road, Redwood Retreat Road, and Sanders Road. The cabin is about three-quarters of a mile from the site of the old Redwood Retreat Hotel.

Gilroy Hot Springs, about fifteen miles northeast of Gilroy, was a resort built around springs discovered by Francisco Cantua, a sheepherder, in 1865. By 1874 a post office had been established at the springs and small cottages had been built to accommodate guests. The Gilroy Hot Springs Hotel was built in 1879, its three stories made entirely of redwood. Soon it was a popular retreat patronized by those who liked to fish and to hunt as well as to "take the waters." The waters flowing from the spring at 105 degrees contained soda, magnesium, iron, sulfur, and iodine, among other trace minerals; they were claimed to cure almost everything except consumption. The resort declined in the twentieth century to the point that, in 1963, all the buildings were condemned for public use. The property was up for sale in 1980 when fire destroyed the hotel, the clubhouse, and five of the nearby buildings. The place is presently closed to the public, but it is reported that 105-degree water still flows unceasingly from the springs.

restored. The Hoxett House at 338, begun in 1869, was the home of Gilroy benefactress Caroline Amelia Hoxett; it became the site of the Women's Civic Club after her death in 1927. She provided the clocks in the old city hall building at Sixth and Monterey streets (built in 1905 and now housing a restaurant) and gave land for the I.O.O.F. Children's Home as well as for the Carnegie Library building. The latter building, begun in 1910 at 195 Fifth, is now the location of the excellent Gilroy Historical Museum, which has a rich repository of materials on southern Santa Clara County. The Holloway House at 7539 Eigleberry Street is a Queen Anne home designed in 1903 for the Edgar Holloway family by William Weeks and is now on the National Register of Historic Places.

Gilroy has always been a farming center. Large acreages of garlic were planted near the town in the 1920's by Kiyoshi Hirasaki and by Joseph Gubser, Sr. By 1955 Gilroy proclaimed itself to be the "Garlic Capital of America," with 90 percent of the U.S. garlic crop being

Santa Cruz County

Santa Cruz County was named after Mission Santa Cruz ("holy cross") and was one of the original 27 counties. It was created on February 18, 1850, and called Branciforte County, but the name was changed to Santa Cruz in March 1850. The northwestern part of its original area, including the town of Pescadero, was annexed to San Mateo County in 1868. The county seat is at Santa Cruz. Pre-statehood documents are housed in the Special Collections of the McHenry Library on the campus of the University of California at Santa Cruz.

The Portolá Trail

Leaving the region of Monterey County and proceeding northward, Gaspar de Portolá and his men crossed the Pajaro River on October 8, 1769, unaware that they were leaving behind them the bay they sought. The Rio de Pajaro ("Bird River") was named by the soldiers for a gigantic stuffed bird that looked like an eagle set upon the riverbank, presumably an Indian totem. In this valley the Spaniards were amazed by gigantic trees, taller than any they had ever seen, which they called *palos colorados* because of the color of the wood. This is the first mention of a redwood tree in California's written history. The trees they saw were a stand of coast redwoods, *Sequoia sempervirens*, to be distinguished from their giant cousins of the High Sierra, the *Sequoia gigantea*.

During the following week the party traveled up Corralitos Creek, camping east of Corralitos Lagoon and again just east of modern Aptos. They then crossed Soquel Creek about three miles from the coast, their route having been close to the present SR 1 from Watsonville to Soquel.

On October 17 the party camped on the west bank of a large river, which they called the San Lorenzo, the name it still bears. Here they again saw many redwoods and "roses of Castile" but, much to the disappointment of Father Crespí, no Indians. The city of Santa Cruz is now located at this place.

From October 17 to the end of the month, the expedition traversed the route now covered by SR 1, along the coast of Santa Cruz and San Mateo counties. This route, for a few miles northwest of Santa Cruz, lies across the ancient sea beaches now raised to form fertile benches on which vegetable crops are grown. The region is well known to geologists because of the plainly pictured story of changes shown by the series of sea terraces between the hills and the present tide line.

The going was sometimes arduous in this region; at one arroyo a bridge of poles and earth had to be made before men and animals could get across. Seven gulches of varying difficulty were crossed in one day alone. On October 20 they arrived "at the mouth of a very deep stream that flowed out between very high hills of the mountain chain," and camped there for three nights.

On Sunday, October 22, Father Crespí wrote: "The day dawned, overcast and gloomy; the men were wet and wearied for want of sleep, as they had no tents, and it was necessary to let them rest. . . . What excited our wonder on this occasion was that all the sick, for whom we feared the wetting might prove exceedingly harmful, suddenly found their pains very much relieved. This was the reason for giving the canyon the name of La Salud." La Salud ("health") is now known as Waddell Creek, and still becomes, after heavy rains, the "very deep stream" that the travelers found. From here the expedition proceeded northward and its subsequent story belongs to the history of San Mateo County.

Mission Santa Cruz

The Viceroy Condé de Revilla Gigedo and Father Matías de Noriega decided in 1789 to establish a mission on the spot called Santa Cruz between those missions already established at San Carlos (Carmel) and Santa Clara. Two years after this decision was made, Father Fermín Francisco de Lasuén consecrated a site at the lower end of the San Lorenzo Valley. Here, on St. Augustine's Day, August 28, 1791, he said Mass in the presence of many Indians and raised a cross.

The following month Fathers Alonzo Salazar and Baldomero López, accompanied by Hermenegildo Sal, *comandante* of the San Francisco Presidio, and his military escort, arrived at the prospective site. Christian Indians brought along from Santa Clara were set to work at once cutting wood for the construction of a brush shelter, or *enramada*, for the fathers.

On Sunday morning, September 25, 1791, the formal ceremony for the founding of Mission la Exaltación de la Santa Cruz was celebrated. The fathers had brought with them as a nucleus for the mission a painting of Our Lady of Sorrows and an image of Saint Francis. From the neighboring missions at Carmel, Santa Clara, and San Francisco came donations of horses, cows, oxen, mules, sheep, and two bushels of barley for seed. At the end of three months 87 Indians had been baptized. It is thought that the first church was constructed about where North Pacific Avenue and River Street now intersect, with the southern end of the spacious plaza at the present juncture of Pacific Avenue and Mission and Water streets. Soon the establishment was found to be too near the river, and in the move to higher ground only the garden was left on the lower level.

The first stone of the new Mission Santa Cruz was laid on February 27, 1793, and the completed structure was dedicated in the spring of 1794, with Commander Sal and Father Tomás de la Peña of Mission Santa Clara present. The church, built on the mesa above the river, was a substantial building 112.5 feet long, 29 feet wide, and 25.5 feet high, with walls five feet thick. The lower part of the walls was made of native rock and the upper part of adobe. The vaulted roof, at first covered with thatch, was later recovered with tile.

Other buildings, erected as needed, formed an open square about where the present park is situated, bounded by High, Emmet, Mission, and Sylvar streets. The mission church and the priests' quarters were on what is now High Street. On the present Sylvar Street were storehouses and rooms for looms. Back from Emmet Street, along what is now known as School Street, were the women's quarters; and on the other side of School Street was the adobe building, still standing, that is believed to have been the guardhouse. This, the only building remaining from the mission of 1793–94, has been designated Santa Cruz Mission State Historical Monument. The building was divided into two residences around the time of secularization and is known as the Neary-Rodriguez adobe, after the early owners. The building is at 136 School Street and is marked by a plaque placed by the Daughters of the American Revolution.

All went well with the mission for more than twenty years; trouble then arose with the secular Branciforte Pueblo nearby. To add to the troubles of the mission, the pirate Hippolyte de Bouchard, flying the insurgent flag of Buenos Aires, threatened an attack in 1818. Because of a storm at sea the attack, fortunately, never took place, but in the frantic effort to save mission properties in this emergency, much damage was done to the church and its furnishings by misdirected zeal.

The mission was secularized by Governor Figueroa in 1834. In 1840 an earthquake weakened the walls; and on January 9, 1857, another tremor caused the final destruction, for a month later at three o'clock in the morning the southwestern corner fell with a loud crash.

On the site of the ruined mission (SRL 342), at 126

Restoration Work, Neary-Rodriguez Adobe, Santa Cruz Mission State Historical Monument

High Street, a wooden frame church, now called Holy Cross Church, was dedicated in 1858. This served the parish until the present English Gothic Holy Cross Church, designed by Thomas J. Welsh of San Francisco, was completed in 1889. In 1891, on the centennial of the founding of the original mission, a memorial arch of granite was erected in front of this brick church. The bell that rings out from the church was recast from the old bells salvaged from the earthquake-ruined mission.

In 1931 a concrete replica of the original mission was built on Emmet Street facing the upper plaza. It is identical in proportions to the first structure, but about half its size, and is approximately 75 yards from the original site. In this replica are housed many objects that were in the original mission, notably a chandelier now altered for electricity and hanging near the entrance. A statue of Our Lady of Sorrows occupies a niche in the front part of the little church, while in a room off the outer corridor are preserved richly ornamented vestments.

Holy Cross School was founded by the Sisters of Charity in 1862 in an adobe that stood next to the Neary-Rodriguez adobe. The school adobe is no more, but the kindergarten and grammar school occupy the site and the high school is diagonally across the plaza.

Villa de Branciforte

Three pueblos were established in California by the Spanish: San Jose, Los Angeles, and Branciforte. The last, named in honor of the Marquis de Branciforte, viceroy of Mexico, was established in 1797 under the direction of Governor Diego de Borica and was located across the San Lorenzo River from Mission Santa Cruz. Governor Borica showed his practical mind when he chose this place: good building material was close at hand, there was a plentiful supply of fish in the waters of the bay, and the facilities for shipping could easily be developed to handle the future produce of the pueblo. His recommendations were likewise sensible: "An adobe house to be built for each settler so that the prevalent state of things at San José and Los Angeles, where the settlers still live in tule huts, being unable to build better buildings without neglecting their fields, may be avoided; the houses not to cost over $200." Each colonist was to receive from the government a musket, a plow, a few necessary animals, and a subsidy of 116 pesos on a plan of easy repayment. The observance of religious duties was to be enforced. He called for farmers, mechanics, artisans, and sailors as settlers. Gabriel Moraga was taken from his position as *comisionado* of San José and placed in charge of the new pueblo.

On May 12, 1797, the schooner *Concepción* arrived

in Monterey Bay with colonists from Guadalajara, but no houses were ready for them. Don Alberto Córdoba, lieutenant of engineers in the Spanish Army who had visited there the previous year, arrived in August with instructions to follow a plan that had been drawn up in Mexico. He began a canal for irrigation, erected a few temporary houses, and sent estimates for further work to the governor and the viceroy, before the work was suspended in October.

Among the passengers on the *Concepción* were three men who became alcaldes. José Vicente Mojica, who brought a wife and five children, was alcalde in 1802; José Antonio Robles, who married first Rosalía Merlopes and at her death her sister, Gertrudis, and reared several children, held a number of offices before becoming alcalde in 1842; and Agustín Narvaez, nineteen when he arrived, stayed at Branciforte only a few years before becoming alcalde in San José in 1821. Among the disabled soldiers sent there in 1798 were José Joaquín Castro and José Antonio Rodríguez, both of whom played an important part in the affairs of their time and whose descendants are now widely scattered throughout the state.

In 1799 Gabriel Moraga was succeeded by Ignacio Vallejo as *comisionado*, and the pueblo continued under the military jurisdiction of Monterey (except for two years under the civil jurisdiction of San José) until the time of its dissolution. The fathers at Mission Santa Cruz seem to have regarded the pueblo and its easygoing ways as detrimental to their work of the salvation of the Indians, who declined in number greatly as the nineteenth century wore on.

After the American occupation and the coming of American pioneers, Branciforte became a township of attractive homes. By a special election in 1907, it became part of the city of Santa Cruz. The mile-long race track, laid out in 1797 by Córdoba, is now Branciforte Avenue, and the intersection of this avenue with Water Street is the center of the old Villa de Branciforte (SRL 469), which occupied a rectangle one-half mile wide from east to west and one mile long from north to south. A bull-and-bear-fight arena was located on the flats near the Soquel Avenue Bridge, between the San Lorenzo River and Branciforte Creek. As late as July 13, 1867, four bulls "from the Gabilan and Taurian mountains" fought here, with lances, firecrackers, and red flags adding to the excitement. "Admission and seats— $1.00. Standing room on the sunny side—50 cents."

Santa Cruz

A period of disintegration followed the Mexican order to secularize the missions, but before the gold rush several industries had developed in the town of Santa Cruz, which had grown up around the plaza of the mission.

Thomas Fallon, who had arrived in Branciforte in 1845 and who had raised the flag of the United States in San Jose in 1846, put up a building on the plaza. This had an outside staircase and did double duty as a residence and saddlery shop. The county later purchased this property for use as the county courthouse, paying Fallon $3,500.

William Blackburn, a Virginia cabinetmaker who had come overland to California with the Swasey-Todd company in 1845, worked as a lumberman in the Santa Cruz Mountains before joining the California Battalion Artillery, Company A, as a second lieutenant. He was alcalde of Santa Cruz from 1847 to 1849 and became county judge in 1850, at which time the decisions of his court became famous for their originality. His orchards were one of the chief attractions of Santa Cruz during his lifetime. His home grounds, extending from Chestnut Avenue to Walnut Avenue and to the Neary Lagoon, covered the present site of the Southern Pacific Railroad yards. The old Blackburn house still stands at 152 Cedar Street.

Richard C. Kirby, born in England in 1817, left a whaling boat in Oregon in 1845 and came by land to California, where he became associated with Paul Sweet in a tannery business on the San Agustín rancho shortly after his arrival. In the fall of 1850 he put up a small establishment for tanning leather in Squabble Hollow, now Glen Canyon. Kirby leather soon became famous; he tanned not only hides from local sources but also those shipped from South America. In 1852 he married Georgiana Bruce, who had been a member of the Brook Farm Colony near Boston in the 1840's and had come to California to establish a school. She too was Englishborn and had come to America as a governess; while teaching in the South, she had become an ardent abolitionist. Mrs. Kirby has left a vivid picture of life in Santa Cruz in the 1850's in her journal. She was much interested in the beautification of her home and surroundings and imported rare shrubs and trees. The Kirby home, a frame house, stood at 321 Mission Street, and has now been moved to 117 Jordan Street.

The oldest wood-frame house in Santa Cruz is the Alzina house, at 109 Sylvar Street. Francisco Alzina was the first sheriff of Santa Cruz County, serving from 1850 to 1868. He and his wife, the former María Gonzáles, built their little house at the corner of Mission and Sylvar streets; it was later moved to its present location and the Willey house was erected in its place. The Willey house at 105 Sylvar Street is a late-Eastlake-style mansion with stained glass windows and handsome porch

Alzina House, Santa Cruz

railings. Henry Willey had the redwood house built in 1893 for his bride. Like the Alzina house, this is a private residence today. Other old houses from this era are to be found on Green and Mission streets.

The Branciforte adobe is the name given to the one remaining structure from the Villa de Branciforte. Located at Goss and North Branciforte avenues, it was commemorated by a plaque placed by E Clampus Vitus in 1980. Not much is actually known about the early history of the house, although the plaque suggests that it may have been the residence of the *comisionado* in the early 1800's.

The Cowell House at 1001 High Street goes back to about 1850, when it was the ranch house for the Cowell Ranch, north and west of the city of Santa Cruz. The property originally belonged to Albion P. Jordan, pioneer lime industrialist, who later established a partnership with Isaac E. Davis. In 1865 he sold his share and his home to Henry Cowell. Cowell and his brother John, originally from Massachusetts, developed limestone deposits and operated limekilns on the ranch. The family lived in this house from 1865 to 1897, when they moved to San Francisco. Father Henry feared fortune-hunters and forbade his children to marry. One son, Ernest, married without parental blessing and was ostracized. He was later reinstated, however, when he broke with his wife. Ernest left $250,000 to the University of California for the establishment of Cowell Hospital.

The University of California also benefited from the Cowell family when, in 1961, the Regents of the university announced that a new campus would be built on the 2,000-acre Cowell Ranch. One building that survives from the ranch days is the Cook House, put up about 1880, which stands on the first quarry on the property. It took on a new existence as the chancellor's office when the campus went into operation in 1965 and to-

day houses the campus security services; it is located at the south end of the campus just north of High Street.

The Santa Cruz County Historical Museum is located in the octagonal County Hall of Records at Cooper and Front streets, built in 1882. The unusual shape is said to have been inspired by a $50 gold piece minted in San Francisco in 1851–52. With the aid of a grant from the U.S. Department of Housing and Urban Development, the building was refurbished after its records were moved to the new County Governmental Center in 1968. Since 1972 it has presented changing displays of local historical interest as well as a fine photographic collection of county history. The Santa Cruz County Society for Historical Preservation, Inc., which operates the museum, also owns and maintains the 1914 Davenport Jail.

The Mark Abbott Memorial Lighthouse has a museum open to visitors on a limited basis at Lighthouse Point at the western side of Santa Cruz Harbor. This lighthouse is one of the newest structures on the Pacific Coast. It was erected in 1967 to replace an earlier structure that was being undermined by three large sea caverns.

The Santa Cruz City Museum, while emphasizing the natural history of the city and the coastal area, also has many displays connected with local history. The attractive building is along the shore at 1305 East Cliff Drive.

Rancho San Andrés (Monterey Bay Coast West of Watsonville)

Three grants, given to members of the Castro family in 1833, stretched along the shore of Monterey Bay from the mouth of Soquel Creek to the mouth of the Pajaro River and extended far inland. The southernmost of these ranchos had been occupied for possibly ten years by a pensioned soldier, José Joaquín Castro. As a boy he had come to California in Juan Bautista de Anza's party. He held several minor positions in the pueblo of Branciforte and was alcalde in 1831. His Rancho San Andrés, consisting of two square leagues, was confirmed to his eldest son, Guadalupe, in 1854.

The first house of Don José Joaquín on the rancho was located not far from the beach, but when he erected his large adobe house he chose a site on a hill above Larkin Valley, overlooking in the distance a great sweep of the Pajaro Valley. The house stands today, a large two-story adobe with an upper and a lower veranda stretching the whole length of the front. A ballroom on the upper floor has windows giving a broad view of the family domains that spread out on all sides.

This house, at 184 Old Adobe Road, is one of the few large ones remaining from the times of the earliest settlers. Neglected for many years and often mistaken for an old barn, it deteriorated so much that it appeared unsalvageable. Happily, it was purchased in the 1950's and beautifully restored. The narrow road over which this dignified adobe is reached climbs a hill from the crossroads of Larkin Valley Road and Buena Vista Drive, a few miles northwest of Watsonville.

Rancho Aptos

Rancho Aptos, of one square league, was granted by Governor José Figueroa in 1833 to Rafael Castro, an industrious and prosperous ranchero who had held a few minor official positions. The southeast line of this grant adjoined the larger Rancho San Andrés belonging to his father, José Joaquín Castro, and extended north along the bay to present-day Borregas Creek. In the early 1870's he donated property for a Catholic chapel, the Church of Our Lady of Mount Carmel, at the present corner of Seacliff Beach State Park Drive and the old Santa Cruz–Watsonville highway (Soquel Drive). Excessive deterioration caused it to be abandoned in 1925. A bell from this church is preserved at Mission Santa Cruz, and a statue of Our Lady of Mount Carmel, originally from Spain, is now in St. Joseph's Catholic Church in Capitola. A new church was constructed on the Aptos property in the 1960's.

In a niche in the tall marble monument that marks his grave in the cemetery near the church is a miniature bust of Don Rafael, who died in 1878. In the family plot his wife, Soledad Cota, and other members of his family are buried. In the outlying part of this churchyard but still within the confines of the old cypress hedge lie the bones of many Indians removed from an early In-

dian burying ground not far away when the property was taken over by Claus Spreckels.

On the coast of modern Aptos is Seacliff State Beach. At the end of a wooden pier about halfway along the beach is the 435-foot concrete supply ship *Palo Alto*. This was one of several concrete-hulled ships built during World War I, in a project that came to naught. The *Palo Alto* was purchased by promoters and brought to Seacliff, where it has been ever since. For some time the moored ship was an amusement pier with a dance floor on deck; the inevitable ravages of time and surf have made it unsafe to venture upon the ship, and in time it will probably crumble into Monterey Bay. Meanwhile, the fishing pier leading to it is a busy place most of the year.

Ranchos Soquel and Soquel Augmentación

Martina, a daughter of José Joaquín Castro, obtained the grant of Rancho Soquel, 1,668 acres, from Governor Figueroa in 1833. To her was given also the larger grant, Rancho Soquel Augmentación, of 32,702 acres, on which lies the greater part of the watershed of Soquel Creek, containing vast forests of redwood, live oak, and madrone. A good part of this is today the State Forest of Nisene Marks, which has been intentionally left undeveloped. The grant stretched over the mountaintops of the county boundary to Loma Prieta. Both of these grants were confirmed and patented to her in 1860.

Martina's second marriage was to Michael Lodge, a sailor from Dublin, and when her grant was confirmed, they built an adobe house on a point of high ground near a ravine and springs of pure water. The empty field where the Lodge adobe once stood is at the end of Hill Street beyond Capitola Avenue. On the property there was an ox-powered flour mill, no longer standing, and the millstones are now mounted in Pringle Grove, the property of the Soquel Pioneer Club, off north Main Street.

The Bay View Hotel in Aptos is the oldest such establishment operating in Santa Cruz County and is commemorated by a plaque placed by E Clampus Vitus in 1974. It was built about 1870 by José Arano, said to be a French immigrant, who married María de la Augustia, youngest daughter of Don Rafael Castro. It is said that while the hotel was under construction, Arano personally inspected every bit of lumber that went into it, and every stick of furniture, much of which is still there today. The Bay View was a luxurious watering place for many years; its patrons included King Kalakaua of the Hawaiian Islands and the entertainer Lillian Russell, as well as local entrepreneur Claus Spreckels,

Concrete Ship *Palo Alto*, Seacliff State Beach, Aptos

who had purchased a large part of Rancho Aptos. Falling into decline after World War I, the hotel was purchased in 1944 and subsequently moved about 100 feet back from the railroad tracks; it is on Soquel Drive near Trout Gulch Road.

The First Congregational Church on Soquel Drive in the middle of Soquel was erected in 1870. It was the creation of S. A. Hall, a ship's carpenter from Maine, who dreamed of creating a New England–style church for the Congregationalists of the area. Land was donated by Joshua Parrish, and the building was truly a congregation-wide effort. In the years since 1870 a social hall and a new steeple have been added; the latter burned in 1964 but has now been completely restored.

Rancho de los Corralitos

In the eastern part of the county lies Rancho Corralitos, which was granted in 1823, 1841, and 1844 to José Amesti, a native of Spain who came to California on the *Panther* in 1822 and became a prominent citizen and merchant in the land of his adoption. He married Prudenciana, daughter of Ignacio Vallejo, in 1824. The 15,000 acres of this property were patented to his heirs in 1861 by the federal government. The Amesti adobe is located at 162 Amesti Road, on a hill northwest of the Amesti schoolhouse.

The town of Corralitos in the northern part of the rancho was a place of bustling activity in the pioneer days of the 1860's. It was surrounded by forests in which sawmills were moved from place to place as each location became "sawed out." As early as 1865 several families living there had the luxury of water in their homes, running through pipes made by boring a hole lengthwise through redwood logs.

The first sawmill in this region was in Brown's Valley near Garcia's bridge three and a half miles above Corralitos and was owned and operated by Brown and Williamson from 1865 to 1867. The same company later built Gamecock Mill farther up the canyon. The narrow, rough logging roads, when abandoned by their original users, were improved for general travel by the settlers "working out" their taxes by filling chuckholes, hauling gravel, and widening the track.

In 1855 Benjamin Hames bought a site just above the present town, where the city of Watsonville's filter plant is now located, and built a flour mill to which settlers as far away as Salinas hauled grain to be ground. The water from a dam in Eureka Canyon was brought through redwood flumes to operate the mill. In 1877 the site and buildings were bought by Peter and James Brown for a paper mill, where sun-dried strawboard was made from straw grown on Pajaro Valley ranches.

For a few years the binding boards used in making textbooks for the schools throughout the state were manufactured here.

The first school serving the settlement was built among oak trees one and a half miles south of the town on the road leading to Watsonville and was called Oak Grove. The oaks are now gone, but a redwood grove on the opposite side of the road identifies the spot. The school was next moved one mile nearer the town, and the third schoolhouse was built in the town itself. The present school is about a mile south of Corralitos.

Rancho Salsipuedes (Eastern Pajaro Valley and Northward)

The Salsipuedes grant of 31,201 acres was made to Francisco de Haro in 1834 and regranted to Manuel Jimeno in 1840, the final grant being for a total of eight leagues. These lands extended on the south from the Pajaro River north to the mountains at the county line, and a small part near Bodfish Canyon lay in Santa Clara County.

Don Manuel, who came to California from Mexico in 1830, was a man of great influence and was much respected in civil affairs. His wife, said to have been as vivacious as he was witty, was Agustías, daughter of José de la Guerra y Noriega. He was secretary of state for several years under governors Alvarado and Micheltorena. Two of his sons, Antonio and Porfirio, went east with William T. Sherman for their education. After many years of poor health he died in Mexico in 1853. The site of his now almost forgotten adobe is on the Chittenden Pass Road, which runs for many miles through this rancho.

William F. White, who had come from Pennsylvania with his young wife in 1849, acquired land from Don Manuel five miles east of Watsonville, and in 1853 he built the first substantial American-owned house in the Pajaro Valley. The exterior lumber for this house, shipped from Maine, was of outstanding quality. White installed a pump, which was a great curiosity. The family residence was used as a place of worship one Sunday a month, the officiating priest coming from Mission San Juan Bautista. The house still stands, at 508 Riverside Road, and has been the property of the Silliman family for more than a century.

Associated with White in the purchase of this rancho were three other influential men: William Tecumseh Sherman, of Civil War fame; Montgomery Blair, postmaster general in Abraham Lincoln's cabinet; and Edward D. Baker, an early United States senator from Oregon. A United States patent for this land was issued to "James Blair et al." on March 2, 1861, two days before Lincoln became president. White was a bank commissioner, appointed by Governor Irwin, and was a member of the constitutional convention of 1878 before becoming a candidate for governor on the Workingman's ticket in 1879.

Rancho Bolsa del Pájaro and Watsonville

Rancho Bolsa del Pájaro consisted of two separate grants that stretch along both sides of the Pajaro River northeast of its mouth. It was granted by Governor Alvarado in 1837 to Sebastián Rodríguez, who also claimed the Rincón de la Ballena in present San Mateo County, a claim that was rejected by United States authorities.

Don Sebastián, a sergeant of the Monterey Company and *comisionado* of Santa Cruz in 1831, died in 1855, leaving a large family and an estate on which many troublesome squatters had arrived. The litigation concerning Rancho Bolsa del Pájaro after American occupation was finally ended when a patent was issued to the heirs in 1860 for one of the grants.

D. S. Gregory and Judge John H. Watson, the latter a native of Georgia, obtained the other grant before the death of Don Sebastián and laid out the town of Watsonville in 1852. W. L. Thrift, one of its first settlers, put up a tent that served as a hotel; when a post office was established the following year, he became the first postmaster of the town.

These riverine lands were once proclaimed to be "acre for acre the richest land on earth." Potatoes were the first principal crop, followed by apples; Watsonville is now famous for its apple orchards.

Watsonville's City Plaza was donated to the city in 1860 by Sebastián Rodríguez, son of Don Sebastián. Located on the plaza are two cannons, one a large field piece, made in 1899, and the other from the mail steamer *Oregon*. When the *Oregon* entered San Francisco harbor on October 18, 1850, this cannon fired the shots announcing that California had been admitted to the Union as the 31st state. The Mansion House building, put up in 1871 at the corner of East Beach and Main streets, was a hotel for many years and was moved to its present location at 420 Main Street in 1914. Today it houses offices and a restaurant and is listed, along with the City Plaza, the Judge Lee house (1894) at 128 East Beach Street, and the Resetar house (1925) at Madison and East Lake streets, on the National Register of Historic Places. The history of the Pajaro Valley is the theme of the William Volck Memorial Museum at 261 East Beach Street, named for the entomologist who made important contributions in combating the codling moth that had threatened the valley's apple industry.

An interesting adobe house stands at 514 Blackburn Street. It was constructed by Jesús Vallejo on his Rancho Bolsa de San Cayetano on the San Juan Road in Monterey County. Damaged by the 1906 earthquake, it was about to be pulled down when Dr. Saxton T. Pope purchased it and had the material reerected on his own property. Now a one-story, three-room dwelling, it retains its original oak doors.

Rancho Arroyo del Rodeo (Capitola and Soquel)

This rancho consisted of one-quarter of a square league lying on the shore of Monterey Bay between Soquel and Rodeo creeks. Most of today's cities of Capitola and Soquel lie on its land. It was granted by Governor Figueroa in 1834 to Francisco Rodríguez, the early California poet. On Soquel Creek a dam and a flour mill were constructed in 1858; over the years the flour mill became a sawmill and later a paper mill, the name of which survives in Paper Mill Road today. Frémont and his party camped at the spot on March 1, 1846.

The name of the rancho was derived from the cattle roundups or rodeos of the herds of the Castro and Rodríguez families, which took place in a natural amphitheater a half-mile south of the present Soquel Avenue bridge across Rodeo Creek. The amphitheater is now covered by a huge freeway fill.

Rancho San Agustín and Scotts Valley

An archaeological dig in 1983 at the site of the present Scotts Valley City Hall on Kings Drive unearthed an Indian cutting tool believed to be from 8,000 to 10,000 years old, perhaps the oldest artifact ever unearthed in northern California. More recent history begins with the granting of Rancho San Agustín in 1841 to Juan José Crisóstomo Majors, the name that Joseph L. Majors of Tennessee had assumed when he became a Mexican citizen three years earlier. He received a United States patent for his land, in his original name, in 1866. In 1841 he also received a grant of the Zayante rancho, discussed below.

Hiram Daniel Scott came into Monterey Bay in 1846 as second mate on the *C. Whiting*, and in 1852 he purchased Rancho San Agustín. The father, also named Hiram, followed his son west and took the ranch over. This area is now known as Scotts Valley; it was incorporated as a city in 1964. The Scott home, built in 1853 and since moved a few hundred yards from its original site, is being restored and preserved. It serves as a meeting place for the Scotts Valley Historical Society, at 4603 Scotts Valley Drive.

Rancho Carbonera (San Lorenzo River)

Rancho Carbonera, bordering the San Lorenzo River north of Santa Cruz, was granted by Governor Alvarado to José Guillermo Bocle in 1838. It was patented to him in 1873.

Bocle was a man of many aliases—Boc, Buckle, Thompson, and Mead being a few. He and his brother Samuel (who had come to California in 1823, according to his own statement, and who was naturalized in 1841) both took the name of Thompson after the American occupation. William Thompson or Guillermo Bocle was an English sailor who came to California in 1823, married María Antonia Castro, and became the father of a large family. At his death, unable to sign his own name, he left "to those now living with me" 15,000 acres of land along with horses, cattle, and money. Thompson's Flat, a section of his old holdings, includes the campsite of John C. Frémont, then lieutenant in the topographical engineering corps of the United States Army, and his 60 men on February 25–28, 1846. All this is now located on the Pasatiempo Golf Course.

Paradise Masonic Park, established and incorporated in August 1924, is also within the boundaries of this rancho. A sawmill was erected here in 1855. James Waters, a carpenter from Maryland who was in charge of this mill, later erected many buildings in the counties of Santa Cruz and Monterey and rose to a position of importance in the Pajaro Valley. Here in 1860 a paper mill was established with a reputed peak daily output of a ton of coarse brown paper, the first pulp mill on the West Coast. It survived only two years, until high water carried away the flume.

In 1865 the California Powder Works were constructed with an entrance about where the gates to Paradise Park now stand. A 1,300-foot tunnel through the mountain brought water from the San Lorenzo River to operate the grinding mills, the output of which was used for blasting in the construction of the Central Pacific Railroad. It was here that smokeless powder was first produced. Work continued at the plant until 1916.

Santa Cruz County is the only county in the state to have as many as three covered bridges still intact. Only the one in Paradise Park, however, still carries vehicular traffic. Constructed in 1872 from local wood, it is used daily by residents of the community. Built by the San Francisco Bridge Company to serve the California Powder Works, it is the only covered span in the West to be equipped with fire hoses at both ends. Other distinctive features are the diamond windows in its siding and the center doorway leading to an observation platform overlooking the San Lorenzo River. The 180-foot-long

Covered Bridge, Paradise Masonic Park

structure is in Paradise Park, about three miles northwest of Santa Cruz, on the east side of SR 9.

Rancho Zayante and Felton

Rancho Zayante was granted in 1834 to Joaquín Buelna, who had previously held the post of alcalde at Branciforte. It was regranted in 1841 to Joseph L. Majors (who also held Rancho San Agustín), who immediately sold it to Isaac Graham, to whom it was patented in 1870, although Graham had died in 1867. One stake on the west line was placed between Felton and Ben Lomond in the big curve of the San Lorenzo River near Brackney Road.

Graham, a hardy frontiersman, had come from Hardin County, Kentucky, in 1833. Three years after his arrival he assisted Juan B. Alvarado in expelling Governor Gutiérrez, with the understanding that the country thereafter should be free from Mexican domination. However, shortly after Alvarado came into power, Graham and his associates were arrested as dangerous foreigners and placed in confinement on a boat in Monterey harbor. A few of the group were released before Don José Castro sailed with the prisoners for Mexico, and all were released by the Mexican authorities after their arrival. It was reported that Isaac Graham received $36,000 as compensation and that a part of this sum was used in the purchase of the rancho. Within a year after he came into possession of the land, he built on the west bank of the Zayante Creek opposite Bean Creek the first power sawmill in California. This was in 1842, about two months before the one at Bodega Bay was established.

Both Mount Hermon and Felton in the southern part

of this rancho are near the junction of Zayante Creek and the San Lorenzo River. Between these two settlements is another covered bridge (SRL 583), built across the San Lorenzo River. Settlers had attempted to get a bridge in place of the ford at this location and succeeded in having one erected in 1879; it was replaced in 1892 by the covered bridge now standing. The Felton covered bridge is the tallest covered span in the nation. It was built of local redwood and is 186 feet long. It was replaced in 1938 by a concrete span nearby and is the first example in the West of a bypassed covered bridge that has been preserved.

The county's third remaining covered bridge once crossed Branciforte Creek on the Glen Canyon road after it leaves Santa Cruz via Market Street. Only 83 feet long, it was built in 1892 and used until 1939, when it was moved half a block into De Laveaga Park for preservation. Though not in use, it still graces the same creek and looks so much a part of the surroundings that one would think it had been there from the beginning. It is said to be the most photographed of all the covered bridges, having been featured in several motion pictures and television productions. Its location is about two miles northeast of Santa Cruz.

Felton is named for Senator Charles N. Felton, attorney for one of the owners of Rancho Zayante. About 1878 Mr. and Mrs. George Day ran the first hotel in Felton, the Big Tree House. Supplies for the hotel had to be brought across the river, and when the river was in flood, a horse had to swim across, carrying both rider and food. In addition to his hotel, Day conducted a livery stable and ran a stage line. George U. Collins, brother of Mrs. Day, a lumberman from Maine who was then operating a shingle mill on Bean Creek, built a road from Felton to the Big Trees, placing a tollhouse at the point where the Toll House Resort now is.

Rancho Refugio (West of Santa Cruz)

This rancho was situated on the shore of Monterey Bay southwest of Rancho de la Cañada del Rincón. Its northwestern boundary was Laguna Creek. Smaller creeks—Coja, Baldwin, and Meder—flow from the hills through this tract into the bay. The old coast road, successively used by the Portolá expedition, vaqueros, lumber wagons, and stagecoaches, extended across this rancho, as does SR 1 over the same route today.

In 1839 this land was apparently granted to María de los Angeles Castro and her three sisters, one of whom was the wife of José Antonio Bolcoff, to whom it was definitely granted by Governor Alvarado in 1841. It was later claimed by his sons, Francisco and Juan, as executors of the estate.

José Antonio Bolcoff was one of the earliest foreign settlers in Spanish California. A native of Kamchatka, he deserted a Russian sailing vessel when it visited Monterey Bay in 1815, settled in Santa Cruz, and in 1822 married Candida, one of the daughters of José Joaquín Castro. They raised a family of eleven children. After being naturalized as a Mexican citizen, he became alcalde at three different times and held that office when the American flag was raised over California.

Following the order of secularization, he was put in charge of the buildings and properties of Mission Santa Cruz, and assumed these duties in July 1839. To govern the little group of people over which he had control, he immediately promulgated 22 statutes. These laws, intended for a few Spanish families and about 70 Indians, dealt with precautions to be taken against fires spreading to grass and timber, the responsibility of each resident for keeping the street in front of his house clean, prohibition of the sale of liquor after eight o'clock, and an eight o'clock curfew, the hour later being changed to ten.

On receiving the grant of Rancho Refugio, he built an adobe house, part of which is still standing at the Wilder Rancho on Meder Creek, about four miles west of Santa Cruz on the coast road. The original tiles remain on one end of the long, low building now used as a storeroom, the other end of which fell years ago. Excavation for the foundation of the Wilder family home, a frame house now standing between the old adobe and the road, uncovered the base of the old fireplace, and in the earth about it were found old knives, spoons, and crockery.

This land passed from the Bolcoff heirs to Moses Meder, one of the Mormons brought by Sam Brannan to San Francisco on the ship *Brooklyn* in 1846. The place had been in the possession of the Delos Wilder family for nearly six generations when it was bought for a state park. Plans call for maintenance of the buildings, including an interpretive museum that will recall the use of this property as the Baldwin and Wilder Dairy, established in 1871. One of the frame ranch houses standing within a few yards of the adobe and the later Wilder residence was built during the early pioneer days and shows on its roof the original hand-split and hand-planed shingles.

Rancho Arroyo de la Laguna

Adjoining Rancho Refugio on the northwest at Arroyo de la Laguna, now Laguna Creek, was Rancho Arroyo de la Laguna, which extended along the coast as far as San Vicente Creek, just south of the present-day settlement of Davenport. This grant was made in

1840 by Governor Alvarado to Gil Sánchez, a tithe collector at Branciforte.

James Williams, a lumberman and blacksmith, who with his brother Isaac came overland to California with the Chiles-Walker party, settled near Santa Cruz. Another brother, Squire, a former member of Frémont's Battalion, died in the Yuba mines in 1848. In 1852 James and the heirs of Squire filed claim for the lands of this grant, and it was patented to them in 1881. On the edge of this rancho, at the mouth of San Vicente Creek, is the site of Williams Landing, where in the 1850's lumber from the hills was loaded on schooners.

Rancho Agua Puerca y las Trancas (Davenport and Swanton)

This square league of land, given by Governor Micheltorena in 1843 to Ramón Rodríguez and Francisco Alviso, extends along the coast from the mouth of the Arroyo Agua Puerca at the old Davenport landing on the east to the Cañada de las Trancas on the west. Scott Creek, flowing almost the entire length of the rancho, enters it from the hills at its northeast corner and near the southwest corner joins the Pacific Ocean.

Near the confluence of Big Creek, Little Creek, and Scott Creek is a country settlement, formerly the stage station Laurel Grove, now called Swanton after one of the men who built a powerhouse further up Big Creek; the powerhouse is now gone.

James Archibald purchased this rancho. He employed Ambrogio Gianone, who came from Switzerland via the dairies of Marin County in 1869, and the Gianone name since that time has been closely identified with this locality. The ranch headquarters at that date were on Archibald Creek, where now an old barn and other farm buildings stand beside the Swanton Road, one

Gianone Storehouse, near Swanton

and a quarter miles north of its junction with SR 1. Across the road is a small, substantial "rock" house, which young Gianone built soon after his arrival. Set into the hillside, it was erected for the making of Swiss cheese. No longer a cheese factory, it is now known as the Gianone storehouse.

Other Mexican Grants

Stretching back from the coast between San Vicente and Molino creeks is Rancho San Vicente, granted in 1846 to Blas A. Escamilla and patented to him in 1870 (although Bancroft states that it was previously granted to Antonio Rodríguez in 1839). On this tract was the Agua Puerca School, which, although it changed location several times for the convenience of families with children of school age, always retained the name Agua Puerca because its earliest site was near the creek of that name.

In the northwestern part of the city of Santa Cruz a grant of less than 200 acres was given in 1844 to Nicolas Dodero, an Italian sailor who left the María Ester at San Francisco in 1827 and spent most of his life in San Jose and Branciforte. He received his patent in 1866 to this Rancho Tres Ojos de Agua ("three eyes of water"), referring to the springs near High Street south of the University of California campus, whence a stream flows down through the town. Nothing remains of several other small grants in the Santa Cruz region.

Schooner Landings

Santa Cruz County lies along the northeastern shore of Monterey Bay. With few wagon roads and no railroads in the pioneer days, and with the products of its kilns, tanneries, and mills too great for local needs, the active residents of this region depended upon water transportation for a wider market. Inlets at the mouths of streams were used as landing places for schooners, and loading was sometimes done through the surf before wharves were built.

The southernmost landing was that of Pajaro at the mouth of the Pajaro River. A mile north of Pajaro a wharf was built in 1903 at a spot named Port Rogers, later Port Watsonville. A storm in 1912 destroyed the pier, whose pilings may occasionally be seen at low tide. The landing at the mouth of Soquel Creek was in use as early as 1849. Near Soquel Landing is the present town of Capitola, developed in 1869 by Frederick A. Hihn as California's first seaside resort. The superintendent's office from this project still stands at 201 Monterey Avenue (SRL 860).

A wharf was built in 1849 near the mouth of the San

Lorenzo River at Santa Cruz by Elihu Anthony. It was purchased two years later by Isaac E. Davis and Albion P. Jordan, who maintained a fleet of small schooners to haul lime to San Francisco and who, in 1855, had the $150,000 schooner *Santa Cruz* built in the East and brought around the Horn. Davis and Jordan had the largest industry in the town of Santa Cruz in the 1850's. Both Forty-niners from New England, they had been engineers on a Sacramento River steamboat before coming to this region. Their original kiln was at the upper end of Bay Street; later they moved farther north to the Rincón rancho. The names of these two American pioneers were given to two streets, Davis (now part of Escalona Drive) and Jordan, which intersect north of Mission Street.

In the shale on the beach, about one-half mile northwest of Meder Creek, are a number of mooring irons used by schooners that once called there for the produce of the Cowell Lime Company. The brick-built kilns, now unused, are located about three miles up Meder Canyon behind the Wilder Ranch, and from the kilns ox teams hauled the burned lime to this natural wharf.

Williams Landing was at the mouth of San Vicente Creek. Lime from the kilns in the vicinity was shipped from there, and in 1851 W. W. Waddell shipped lumber from the mill he had established there, the first of four mills that he eventually operated within the county.

At the mouth of the Arroyo del Agua Perca farther northwest, Davenport Landing was the site of extensive whaling operations. The French explorer La Pérouse, in 1786, wrote while in Monterey Bay, "It is impossible to conceive the number of whales by which we are surrounded." Captain John P. Davenport, an old whaling master, who 55 years later was residing on the shore of the bay, also observed the great number of whales. According to Hittell's 1885 *History of California*, he devised a scheme whereby he could go out from shore in a whaling boat, capture a whale, and tow it to land, where the blubber could be removed and prepared in great pots, instead of completing the whole operation at sea. While directing this work, which began in the 1850's, Captain Davenport lived in a frame house on the west side of the arroyo overlooking the 450-foot wharf that he had built. His men lived in cabins or in the hotel that stood a little way up the arroyo and served as headquarters for the lumber and lime men of the region.

Despite the action of wind and wave, the captain's wharf outlasted a newer one built by the Reese Lime Works near their storehouse on the opposite side of the arroyo.

The hotel that housed the workers in these early industries and the few small houses of the time have all disappeared, along with the old wharves, giving way to a one-room country school, no longer in use, and a few scattered homes just west of SR 1. Old Davenport shows no trace of its former shipping or other activities, but a new Davenport, about one mile south on the hillside above San Vicente Creek, has grown up around a busy cement plant.

The landing farthest north and west in the county was between Punta de Año Nuevo and the mouth of Waddell Creek. Through the change of county line made in 1868, this spot is now in San Mateo County. But at the time of its operation it was a part of Santa Cruz County, and pickets, posts, and sawn lumber from the forests in the canyons for miles around were shipped from there. This wharf was erected by W. W. Waddell for the purpose of transporting the lumber to the mill on the creek that still bears his name.

Waddell Creek, Cañada de la Salud

Waddell Creek, the perennial coast stream that rises in Big Basin Redwoods State Park, is fed by water trickling down from springs on the mountain slopes bordering its banks and continues downward to its lagoon on the Pacific. The valley through which this stream flows has a history paralleling, in miniature, that of the state.

Little is known of the earliest human inhabitants of this canyon. But the discovery, as late as 1920, of broken arrowheads and chips of flint on a knoll on the west side of the creek bank about a quarter of a mile back from the lagoon, and the unearthing, in 1916, of a large and perfectly made obsidian spearhead in the clearing out of a spring on the mountainside about 500 feet west of this knoll, prove that at least a few Indians used this place as a camping ground.

The name "Cañada de la Salud," or "Canyon of Health," was bestowed on the valley by the Portolá expedition in 1769. The place is easily identified because the engineer of the party, Don Miguel Costansó, appended a note to his diary stating that Punta de Año Nuevo, which had been discovered and named by the Vizcaíno sea expedition of 1602–3, was in approximately the same latitude as their camping place.

After the establishment of the mission at Santa Cruz, the mission herds roamed the coast up to a point where they mingled with the cattle from the mission at San Francisco, according to Duhaut-Cilly, who voyaged along the coast in 1827. The land of this valley, however, was never included in any Spanish or Mexican grant but lay between Rancho Agua Puerca y las Trancas and Rancho Punta de Año Nuevo.

After the American annexation, the wooded sides of the canyon resounded with the blows of the woodsman's axe and the buzz of his saw. At this time the place became known and recorded on maps as "Big Gulch." There William W. Waddell, who had been born in 1818 in Kentucky and had arrived in California in 1851, established his fourth and last sawmill in 1862 (others were at Williams Landing, at Rincón, and at Branciforte). To transport lumber to the wharf built between the mouth of the creek and Punta de Año Nuevo, he constructed a five-mile horse tramway in as straight a line as possible, following the course of the stream, and built twelve bridges across the meandering channel. The mill was located on high ground between, and at the confluence of, the east and west forks of the creek known from that time to the present as Waddell Creek.

After Waddell died in 1875 of an injury inflicted by a grizzly bear, lumbering and woodcutting in the valley gradually ceased. The wharf was finally destroyed in a storm. At the mill the huge boilers were left in place and are still there, although they are now hedged round by second-growth redwoods. In the vicinity were found fire-scarred tires of the oxcarts used in the logging; a heavy, square timber, once part of a manger for oxen; and heaps of stones on the flats that were once fireplaces in the simple cabins. Along the downward course of the stream, fern-covered piles in alder groves are all that remain of the bridges over the stream bed, now long abandoned as the creek has changed course.

The lower part of the valley was owned at one time by the Ocean Shore Land and Investment Company. When it abandoned the prospect of building the Ocean Shore Railway from San Francisco to Santa Cruz, it sold the property in 1914 to Theodore J. Hoover, who had previously purchased the upper part of the valley. Hoover was the brother of President Herbert Hoover and dean of the Stanford School of Engineering, and was much interested in the conservation of natural resources.

An interesting note on this family comes from the Santa Cruz historian Margaret Koch: "Theodore Hoover spent his last years in the valley he loved and the large home he and his wife had planned. He died in 1955 and lies buried on Grateful Mountain, high in the Rancho range. Beside him is his wife, Mildred Brooke Hoover, who died in 1940. Mrs. Hoover became a well-known California historian with the publication of her book entitled *Historic Spots in California*, in 1933 and 1937. It was published in three volumes originally, and Mrs. Hoover collaborated on it with her brother-in-law and sister, Hero Eugene Rensch and Ethel Grace Rensch." Much of the Waddell Creek Valley is now part of Big Basin Redwoods State Park. Theodore J. Hoover Natural Preserve, which includes Waddell Marsh, is located at the mouth of Waddell Creek at the ocean.

Mountain Charley

Charles Henry McKiernan, formerly an Irish quartermaster in the British army, arrived in San Francisco during the gold rush and went directly to the mines. In 1850, coming with his wages as a miner into the Santa Cruz Mountains, he followed a rough trail through the Los Gatos region to a place near the Laguna del Sargento, where earlier the Indians and Spanish had camped from time to time. Using whipsawed lumber from the redwood trees, which grew thickly around him, he built a house near a spring and with redwood pickets enclosed corrals for the livestock. Grizzly bears, mountain lions, coyotes, and eagles took a heavy toll of the calves and lambs. However, he became so adept with his muzzle-loading blunderbuss that he won fame as a bear hunter. An attack by a wounded mother bear nearly cost him his life, and he ever after wore in his skull a plate made by a Santa Cruz physician from two Mexican silver dollars.

McKiernan was for two years the only resident of this region, and he was known to later arrivals as "Mountain Charley." He made many trails and roads through his property; one of them was a cutoff down the old Indian trail near his home through the Moody Gulch territory to Los Gatos Creek. When the Santa Clara Turnpike was organized, he became a stockholder, and one of his roads became part of the route from Los Gatos to Santa Cruz. Leaving Los Gatos, this stage road curved to the west above the later site of Alma and climbed to the summit. A relic of it, designated by a sign reading "Mt. Charley Road," may be followed from Summit Road south to a junction on the Glenwood Highway at a point two and one-half miles southwest of Glenwood. Narrow and winding, the road is little changed since stagecoach days and provides an interesting glimpse into the past.

Mountain Charley, after settling down as stockman and stage owner, did not forget his experience as a miner but carried on investigations of the mineral possibilities of his property. Other parts of his story belong to Santa Clara County and are told in that chapter. He moved to San Jose in 1884 so that his children might be closer to schools, and died there in 1892. As a memorial to this pioneer, a redwood tree, one of the largest of its kind, has been named the "Mountain Charley Big Tree." It stands 300 feet back from the road and is one-half mile north of Glenwood.

Stage Lines out of Santa Cruz

After the close of Mexican rule in California, the former methods of travel—on foot, on horseback, and in bumping, creaking carts—became inadequate, and various kinds of omnibuses and stages were put to use as soon as roads connected the pivotal points.

A stage line was established between Santa Cruz and San Jose, via San Juan Bautista, in 1854. Passengers for San Francisco stopped overnight in San Jose and in the winter season proceeded by boat from Alviso the next morning; in summer it was possible to continue the journey on another stage line.

A driver on this line between Santa Cruz and San Jose was "Cock-eyed Charley," written on the Great Register in 1867 as Charley Darkey Parkhurst, aged 55, a farmer and a native of New Hampshire. A typical stage driver, Charley took a nip at roadhouses, carried the U.S. mail, swore at the horses, and voted as a good citizen. After giving up public driving, Cock-eyed Charley retired to a ranch near the Twelve Mile House out of Santa Cruz and began stock raising on a small scale. Not until death came in 1879 was it learned that Charley was a woman. Her grave is in the Watsonville Cemetery on the west side of Freedom Boulevard.

Another old stage road to San Jose left Santa Cruz by fording the San Lorenzo River, where the Water Street bridge is now. From there it turned up the Graham Grade, used by Isaac Graham in hauling lumber to the wharf on the Santa Cruz beach, and turned again to pass over what is now the Pasatiempo Golf Course and on to the first stop, the ranch of Abraham Hendricks in Scotts Valley, where two horses were added for the long pull ahead. From this station the road led up to Mountain Charley's station on Mountain Charley Road at the summit and thence over the county line and down to San Jose. Mountain Charley was owner and operator of this line until he sold it in 1874 to George Colgrove, the capable and spectacular driver of the yellow-bodied Concord coach that for a number of years swayed on its leather springs over the narrow mountain roads. This route had been put through in 1857, and Charles C. Martin gave the right of way across his land in the forest north of Rancho San Agustín, now Scotts Valley. He established a stage stop on Mountain Charley Road at the present Station Ranch, which is still in the Martin family.

By 1858 a road over the mountains from Soquel, now called the "Old San Jose Road," had been completed through the efforts of Frederick A. Hihn, a native of Germany and a public-spirited resident of Santa Cruz since 1851. A stage immediately put on between Santa Cruz and San Jose used this route, which today joins the old Los Gatos–Santa Cruz highway beyond Burrell at the site of Schultheis Lagoon in Santa Clara County.

Above the old Soquel–San Jose road in this same area is the small community of Skyland, with a picturesque old Presbyterian church, built in 1887, standing with its detached bell tower under spreading oaks. This place had its own post office from 1884 to 1886 and from 1893 to 1910, and even boasted a small newspaper at one time. The economy was based on the vineyards and fruit orchards in the vicinity, and also on the lumbering activities in the surrounding forests, most of which were owned by Frederick Hihn, who at one time paid one-tenth of all Santa Cruz County's taxes. A few old ranch homes still stand in the area.

In an old directory of 1875 appears an advertisement of a stage line of which Charles G. Sykes was proprietor: "A new stage line Santa Clara to Santa Cruz, via Saratoga, Congress Springs, Ocean View, San Francisco Saw-Mills, San Lorenzo Flume and Transportation Company Mills, Boulder Creek, and Felton. This delightful route . . . for fourteen miles follows the San Lorenzo V-Flume and passes one paper mill, ten saw mills, one fuse factory, three lime kilns, and the California Powder Company's works. It also passes Boulder, Bear, Newell, Love, Fall, and Sayante [sic] creeks whose waters are well stocked with mountain trout, the forests abounding with game of all kinds." The stage left the Cameron House in Santa Clara on Mondays, Wednesdays, and Fridays at seven in the morning and, returning, left Santa Cruz on the alternate mornings at seven, making connections with the Alviso boat. The one-way fare was $2.50.

In 1872 a horse-drawn stage was driven by "Billy" Bias up the coast from Santa Cruz to San Gregorio. Turning inland here, the stage followed a road winding over the mountains to Redwood City via La Honda, similar to the present SR 84. This route was a hazardous one, not only because of narrow and poorly built mountain roads but also because of the precipitous cliffs at Waddell Beach, which had to be passed by driving over the sand at low tide. A road has since been cut in the face of the cliff at this point; but even today, in wet weather, slides of crumbling rock sometimes block the road.

Nathan P. Ingalls, a native of New Hampshire, who had driven a four-yoke cow team across the Plains in 1853, succeeded Bias as owner and driver on this line. Commencing July 1, 1874, he took the mail contract, in addition to others, from Santa Cruz to San Mateo and drove the route to Pescadero once a day for over twelve years, a distance of 37 miles. A veteran stage driver, he had previously put on the first stage from Napa to Clear Lake and had driven a stage for Wooly and Taft from San Mateo to Pescadero for three years before taking the Santa Cruz route. It was his boast that he had never been held up in his life. After being county supervisor in 1890, he again became interested in stage lines, this time in Monterey County.

Glenwood

Charles Christopher Martin, born in Nova Scotia, came around Cape Horn from Maine in the late 1840's. Arriving in California, he worked for a time as a teamster in the lumbering area of Lexington in Santa Clara County, and in 1851 he began homesteading land adjoining that of Mountain Charley McKiernan. He operated a tollgate and stage station on Mountain Charley Road at a point now called the "Station Ranch" and still owned by his descendants.

In the 1860's, while engaged in lumbering, Martin built a home in a quiet, sheltered valley below the stage route. There he and his wife, Hannah Carver Martin, raised their family. By 1873 he had built and opened a store. The place was at first called Martinville but soon became known as Glenwood (SRL 449, marker at 4175 Glenwood Drive). The post office was established in 1880, and Martin became first postmaster.

That same year, 1880, saw the passage of the first train over the completed narrow-gauge South Pacific Coast Railroad of the James G. Fair interests. By 1877 it had been built from Alameda, along the eastern side of San Francisco Bay, to San Jose and Los Gatos. Then came the task of tunneling through the Santa Cruz Mountains to join the previously built Felton–Santa Cruz line. Two of the tunnels were over a mile long, and one of these emerged at Glenwood. Southern Pacific took over the line in 1887, and it was converted to broad gauge early in the twentieth century.

Many resorts were developing in the mountains, and they became even more popular now that there was rail service from the Bay Area. The railroad that passed through Glenwood became known as the "Picnic Line." Charles Martin himself built a hotel in the 1890's that became a social center for San Francisco millionaires. Perhaps the biggest boost to the local economy came when the main automobile road to Santa Cruz was constructed through the settlement in 1916, a project Martin had been encouraging for some time. Not long after, the old pioneer died at the age of 90.

But Glenwood's prosperity as a tourist stop on a main highway was to be short-lived. In 1934 the highway was realigned, and Glenwood was left off the beaten track. The store, which had been remodeled and to which had been added a gasoline station, was closed the same year, and it was razed in 1949. Another blow was dealt when the Southern Pacific discontinued its Los Gatos–Santa Cruz service and pulled up the tracks. The line had been failing for several years, and final abandonment was caused by storm damage during the severe winter of 1939–40. The last train passed through Glenwood on March 4, 1940.

In the spring of 1948 many of the location scenes of what was to be Jeanette MacDonald's last motion picture, *The Sun Comes Up*, were filmed in Glenwood. The town's last post office, finally discontinued in 1954, was built of lumber from one of the movie sets; the last postmaster was Margaret Koch, great-granddaughter of Charles C. Martin, who has written extensively on Santa Cruz County history.

Few historic buildings still stand at Glenwood. Part of Martin's old winery on Bean Creek remains. The last home of Mr. and Mrs. Charles C. Martin remains, and across Glenwood Drive is the foreman's house, from the days of the narrow-gauge railway; both are in good use as private residences. The Glenwood Hotel was torn down in 1976, long after most of its adjacent property was sold to the Catholic Order of St. Mary of the Palms, which still maintains a few outlying cabins as a summer retreat.

Boulder Creek

One of the early post offices in the county was Boulder Creek, situated at the point where Boulder Creek from the northwest and Bear Creek from the east flow into the San Lorenzo River, a lumber center for many years. An older settlement, called Lorenzo in the 1870's, is now within its limits.

The timber from the site of the town had been cut out by James F. Cunningham, a man who had come West after considerable military service in the East and had taken up government land on the San Lorenzo River and who, after the early 1870's, was identified with the lumber interests in the county. J. W. Peery was another mill proprietor. He had the Silver Lumber Mills and in connection with them operated a tannery. Peery's Toll Road ran up the San Lorenzo River across to Saratoga. The Bear Creek Toll Road also ran across the mountains to Lexington. Completed in 1875, it never even paid the wages of a tollkeeper, and was finally sold to the county in 1891.

The lumber produced in the vicinity of Boulder Creek was sent over the V-flume built by the San Lorenzo Flume and Transportation Company. This V-flume originally extended from a point about five miles north of Boulder Creek to a point in the lower end of Felton. The "Flume House" stood at its upper end; and, although the structure has been removed, the spot is marked by the very large eucalyptus trees that were planted about it as saplings. From Felton the lumber was shipped to the wharf at Santa Cruz over a narrow-gauge railroad. The "dump" at the end of the flume was at about the point where the Felton Bowl now stands in the lower end of the town and extended some 300 or 400 feet.

Around Boulder Creek during timber cutting, over

50 saw and shingle mills operated within a radius of seven miles. Because of the size of this operation, the Southern Pacific changed the railroad line to standard gauge in 1907. But in 1934, when the timber was exhausted and the mills were closed, the last train was run, and the rails between Felton and Boulder Creek were removed.

Boulder Creek has an interesting museum at 12788 State Highway 9, with much information on the floods that have caused such havoc in the region. Four country newspapers have been published at Boulder Creek, and their names suggest the tenor of their reportage. The first one was *The Boulder Creek Hatchet*, the second was *The Boulder Creek Blast*, the third was *The Mountain Echo*, and the fourth, which printed its last page in 1924, was *The Valley Echo*.

Ben Lomond

Ben Lomond Mountain was named by Thomas Burns, a native of Scotland. The town that grew up in the 1880's on the river at the base of the mountain took on the name. James J. Pierce, of Santa Clara, owned much timberland there and operated a mill at a site between Mill Street and the river. He laid out the town, and two bridges, still located on the highway passing through the town, are built on the site of two early ones that he gave to the county in exchange for bringing the main road through his new townsite.

At the confluence of Love Creek and the San Lorenzo River stood a waterpower sawmill first operated by Vardamon Bennett, a native of Georgia, who brought his large family to California in 1834. This mill was later owned by Harry Love, a former captain of spies appointed by General Zachary Taylor during the Mexican War. In 1853, when the California state legislature raised a special force to run down the bandit Joaquín Murieta, Harry Love was made its captain. Love and his rangers overtook and killed a man who they claimed was the outlaw at a place now in Fresno County, in which chapter the story is told. In 1854, Love was rewarded for his services by an additional state appropriation of $5,000. With this money he began logging in the mountains, and, by marrying the widow of Vardamon Bennett, he came into possession of the mill. To get the logs to the mill, he built a road since known as the "Harry Love Grade," and the creek where the mill stood is Love Creek, over which one of the bridges on the main street of Ben Lomond extends.

Redwoods

The many coast redwoods, *Sequoia sempervirens*, throughout the Santa Cruz foothills and mountains have made the region famous. Because it was in this county that these trees were first glimpsed and named for posterity—by the Portolá expedition in October 1769 in Pajaro Valley—it is fitting that here the first state park was set aside for their preservation. A few virgin groves and many acres of second-growth trees became the inspiration for the California State Park system.

Big Basin Redwoods State Park (formerly called the California State Redwood Park), situated in the northwestern part of the county in the heart of the "Big Basin" in the Waddell Creek drainage area 23 miles from Santa Cruz, contains over 15,000 acres of redwoods and other native foliage in an extensive preserve that extends from the crest of the mountains to the Pacific shore. Apparently the first person to mention the desirability and necessity of acquiring redwood forests for posterity was Ralph Smith, whose editorials in the *Redwood City Times and Gazette* awakened general interest before his untimely death in 1887. The cause was then taken up by Captain Ferdinand Lee Clark and Andrew P. Hill. Hill, then living in San Jose, made many trips to photograph the trees in the Big Basin and was tireless in his efforts to bring the matter of their preservation before the public and to produce legislative action.

A group of interested persons was called together on May 1, 1900, in the library of Stanford University and a committee was appointed to visit and report upon this remote region. On the last evening of their inspection visit, May 18, 1900, sitting on the west bank of Sempervirens Creek, they organized the Sempervirens Club, the main object of which was the acquisition and preservation of the surrounding forest.

The idea of state parks was new. Parks hitherto had been the creation of communities or the bequest of local families. That the state should own and administer a huge area called a "park" was a disturbing idea to those who thought that the less the state or any government had to do with anything, the better it was for the private citizen.

Editors of newspapers in the two counties most interested united in giving publicity to the project of a state redwood park. Among these papers were the *Boulder Creek Mountain Echo*, the *Santa Cruz Surf*, the *Santa Cruz Sentinel*, and the *San Jose Mercury*.

In 1901 the California legislature passed an enabling act whereby 3,800 acres were purchased by the state in the next year for a quarter of a million dollars. Subsequently, Governor Gage appointed the following men to the first state board of commissioners: Father Robert E. Kenna, S.J., president of Santa Clara University; Professor William Russell Dudley, botanist of Stanford University; A. W. Foster, regent of the State University and president of the Northwestern Railway; and William H.

Mills, land agent of the Southern Pacific Railway Company. The governor of the state was ex officio chairman.

Big Basin Redwoods State Park (SRL 827) was established in 1902, the first of the many state parks that have been created since then. Another group of redwoods twenty miles south of the Big Basin park is the Henry Cowell Redwoods State Park, formerly Santa Cruz Big Trees County Park. It became a state park in 1954. The largest tree in this group is the "Giant," 306 feet high.

World War II's Strangest Naval Battle

On the afternoon of December 20, 1941, off the California coast in view of the Santa Cruz Mountains, an incident took place that has been called "World War II's strangest naval battle." The opponents were the Japanese submarine I-23, under Commander Genichi Shibata, and the Richfield Oil Company tanker Agwiworld, commanded by Captain Frederico B. Goncalves, bound for San Francisco from Los Angeles Harbor with a full cargo of oil. When the submarine surfaced and began to shell the unarmed tanker, Captain Goncalves, in a moment of audacity, headed his ship toward the Japanese vessel with the intention of ramming it. The submarine withdrew, but by this time the Agwiworld's master realized the futility of counterattack and headed full speed for Santa Cruz. The I-23 pursued and continued firing, but the tanker, by following a zigzag course and heading directly into a heavy wind and a rough sea, escaped being hit. Meanwhile, the sailors of the Agwiworld replied to the shots by hurling potatoes at the I-23. The submarine, her low deck awash in the turbulent seas, finally abandoned the attack, and the oil tanker reached Santa Cruz in safety.

The I-23, strangely, made no attempt to torpedo the defenseless Agwiworld. On the same day, several hundred miles to the north, another Japanese submarine successfully torpedoed the tanker Emidio with a loss of five lives; this story is told in the Del Norte County chapter.

Shasta County

Shasta County was one of the original 27 counties and at first included within its boundaries all of the territory that later became Modoc and Lassen counties, as well as parts of the present Siskiyou, Plumas, and Tehama counties. "Shasta" is apparently a corruption of the name of a tribe of Indians living in the vicinity of Mount Shasta. The county seat was placed first at Reading's Ranch, but was transferred to Shasta in 1851, and finally was moved to Redding in 1888.

Newcomers to California history and geography can be pardonably confused by the fact that Lassen Peak and more than half of the area of Lassen Volcanic National Park lie within Shasta County, not neighboring Lassen County, while Mount Shasta, the great landmark of northern California, lies in neighboring Siskiyou County.

Lassen Volcanic National Park

Lassen Peak (10,453 feet) was called Monte San José by the padres who accompanied Luís Argüello on an exploring expedition in 1821 to seek for mission sites. Early maps of California, however, give it as Mount St. Joseph. It was later named Lassen Buttes after Peter Lassen, the Danish-born pioneer of northeastern California, and finally Lassen Peak. The Maidu Indians called it "La Lapham Yerman y'aidum," meaning "the long, high mountain that was broken." On May 30, 1914, after having been quiescent for more than 200 years, Lassen Peak began a series of about 300 eruptions. Since 1915 the old volcano has been relatively quiet, although quantities of smoke, at decreasing intervals, have issued from its crater.

Lassen Peak and Cinder Cone were set aside as National Monuments in May 1907. On August 9, 1916, the region was designated the Lassen Volcanic National Park, and in January 1929 it was enlarged to its present area of 163 square miles.

The park contains other interesting volcanic cones, such as Prospect Peak and Harkness Peak, as well as numerous fumaroles, hot springs, mud pots, and boiling lakes, since the entire region is of volcanic origin. The park lies at the southern end of the Cascade Range, which includes the volcanically active Mount St. Helens in Washington, and at the northern end of the Sierra Nevada; it presents a magnificent skyline. Within the area are outstanding scenic features—multicolored lava crags of varied and fantastic forms rising to a height of over 8,500 feet above sea level, impressive canyons, and primeval forests.

Among the most beautiful of the individual wonders included in the park is Lake Tartarus, or Boiling Springs Lake, which lies jade-green and ominous (as one writer described it) amid the encircling forest. Lake Tartarus is part of a group of volcanic phenomena to the south of Lassen Peak that includes the Devil's Kitchen, Willow Creek Geyser, Bumpass Hell, and many other mud pots and hot springs.

Old Trails

A number of old trails crossed the Upper Sacramento Valley in the vicinity of Redding. The earliest to be blazed, known as the Trinity Trail, was made by Jedediah Strong Smith in the spring of 1828. Smith's route led across what are now Trinity and Humboldt counties and on up the coast through the Del Norte region into southern Oregon. Learning of the new pathway from Smith, a party of Hudson's Bay Company trappers, led by Alexander Roderick McLeod, almost immediately set out for California, with John Turner, a former member of Smith's expedition, acting as guide. McLeod probably reached the Upper Sacramento Valley by this trail, and for a number of years trappers no doubt continued to follow it into California.

The Trinity River was discovered and named in 1845 by Pierson B. Reading, who was trapping in the Trinity country at that time. In 1848 he found the first gold in the region. Somewhere between Kennett (an old copper-mining town now inundated by Shasta Lake) and Castle Crags, Reading's earliest trail into the Trinity country crossed over the stretch of steep mountains separating the Sacramento and Shasta valleys known as the "Devil's Backbone." On his way back he crossed the same mountains at a point between Castella and Delta. In 1848 he took a new route, this time over the mountains that lie at the head of the Middle Fork of Cottonwood Creek, and on his return he blazed the trail later known as the Shasta-Weaverville Road, followed by thousands of miners in 1849 and the 1850's. Supplies for the mines of the Trinity, Scott, and Salmon rivers, brought in by way of the town of Shasta, were taken over this trail by muleback. In 1861 the main section of the trail—that going west from Shasta to Weaverville—was widened into a wagon road by Charles Camden. The Redding-Eureka highway (SR 299) today follows roughly this early thoroughfare.

In 1859 a through stage road to Oregon was opened up, which ran from Shasta to Yreka by way of French Gulch, Carrville (Trinity County), and Callahan and Fort Jones (Siskiyou County). Part of this is today SR 3. During the 1860's it was the principal wagon road to the north. At the junction of this road and the Shasta-Weaverville Road formerly stood the Tower House, a landmark famous in the early days.

When Levi H. Tower and Charles Camden arrived at this spot in November 1850, they found a log cabin, occupied by a man named Schneider. Here Tower built the Tower House Hotel with lumber hewn from the surrounding forests and split by hand. For many years after it was abandoned, remains of the old hostelry still stood near the highway. The residence of Charles Camden, erected some time later near the old hotel, now belongs to the National Park Service and is being restored. In its beautiful mountain setting, Tower House with its lands was the showplace of the county in early days, and it is still a magnificent estate.

The second oldest trail through the Upper Sacramento Valley may have been the east branch of the California-Oregon Trail, although no absolute proof of this has yet been found. It seems likely that McLeod took this route on his way out of the valley in 1829. It is known that he lost most of his supplies in the snowdrifts and was forced to cache his furs at the approach of winter and that on his return the following spring he found them spoiled, a circumstance that led to his discharge from the Hudson's Bay Company. At the headwaters of the North Fork of the McCloud River on Bartle's Ranch in Siskiyou County, a wooden trough and some guns were uncovered in 1874. At the time it was believed that these were the remains of McLeod's cache. In any event this early trail was followed by explorers and trappers before 1829, for in Ogden's diary of that year "Pitt's River" is mentioned. In 1841 Pitt's Lake (now Goose Lake) and Pitt's River (since known as the Pit River) were accurately mapped by Charles Wilkes, whose source of information had been the Hudson's Bay Company, which indicates that its trappers had explored the region through which the trail passed.

The east branch of the California-Oregon Trail, after leaving the Sacramento Valley, crossed a ruggedly mountainous country before passing out of the state between Tule and Clear lakes in the north. In crossing this difficult region, early travelers developed variations of the road. One such route was taken by Frémont and his men in the spring of 1846. In the latter part of April they had passed up the east bank of the Sacramento River as far as its confluence with Cottonwood Creek, opposite which they turned east and then northeast across what is now Shasta County. In Lassen County, some distance east of Fall River, Frémont's party forded the Pit River. Crossing the mountains to Big Valley (called by Frémont "Round Valley"), they spent the night of April 30 at its upper end. From there the party journeyed north over the route followed later by emigrants from Oregon.

In the fall of 1848 the first wagon train into California from Oregon followed the Applegate Road as far as Clear Lake in Modoc County. The lure of gold brought many Oregonians into California in 1849 and the early 1850's. From Big Valley, most of the Argonauts bound for Shasta and the Trinity mines climbed the mountains to the west and crossed the Pit River west of Fall River Mills. Leaving the Pit at this point, they went south for some distance and then turned west through Burney Valley and thence southwest to Shasta, the trading center of the Trinity region. In 1856 a road to Yreka was built by way of the Pit River crossing, and shortly thereafter the California Stage Company inaugurated a daily schedule from Sacramento to Yreka, the first through stage service to that point. Because of Indian massacres in Fall River Valley and attacks on the stage, this line was discontinued in January 1857 for a short time.

It is not known who first blazed the west branch of the California-Oregon Trail, which followed up the Sacramento River canyon and around the west side of Mount Shasta, but it is certain that Hudson's Bay Company trappers used it annually from 1832 to 1845. Ewing Young, the trapper, making his way into Oregon to settle in 1834, followed this route, being the first to travel the entire length of the Oregon Trail from San Bernardino in southern California to the Methodist mission in northern Oregon. In 1837 the demand for cattle in the Willamette Valley led to Young's second expedition over the Oregon Trail, when he accomplished the arduous task of driving 700 head of cattle and 40 horses over the Devil's Backbone. Young's party included P. L. Edwards, the diarist of the company, and twenty others, among whom were settlers bound for Oregon.

In 1841 a contingent of the Wilkes Exploring Expedition, consisting of about eighteen persons under the command of Lieutenant George F. Emmons, came down the Oregon Trail across the Siskiyou Mountains and through what are now Siskiyou and Shasta counties to New Helvetia and Yerba Buena. A number of Oregonians had joined the party, making a total of 39 persons and about 76 animals. On his map Wilkes designated that part of the Sacramento River above its confluence with the Pit River as "Destruction River," a name that may have been given originally by Hudson's Bay Company trappers to the McLeod (now spelled "McCloud") River, on the banks of which McLeod met disaster in the winter of 1829. That part of the Pit River in Shasta County was called the Sacramento.

The largest early expedition to use the west branch of the California-Oregon Trail was led by Joseph Gale, who in May 1843, in company with 42 settlers bound for Oregon, drove 250 head of cattle, 650 horses, and 3,000 sheep northward over this difficult path. On May 30 of the same year Lansford W. Hastings started for California with a party of discontented Oregonians. At the Rogue River they met Joseph Gale, who persuaded about two-thirds of the party to return to the Willamette Valley. With the remaining emigrants Hastings continued to California over the route just traveled by Gale. In 1845 James Clyman, with 35 men, one woman, and three children, also passed over this trail on the way south.

All of these parties had to cross the Devil's Backbone, and over these lofty, barren mountains they struggled slowly and painfully. The Wilkes party, while traversing these precipitous slopes, which Clyman described as "almost too steep for brush to grow . . . and in many places too narrow for a rabbit to walk over," lost their way but were guided to safety by the Indian wife of one of the company.

Late in 1848 gold-seekers from the north began using the Oregon Trail; and after the Siskiyou region was opened up in 1850, miners poured over it from the south. Because of the mountainous character of the route, it remained a pack trail until 1860, when a wagon road was constructed from Upper Soda Springs to Yreka. Today I-5 and the Shasta Route of the Southern Pacific Railroad follow the old California-Oregon Trail closely—many of the railroad stations are on the exact line of the trail—making this the oldest continuously used road in northern California.

Where the California-Oregon stage road crossed the present highway two miles north of Anderson, a marker (SRL 58) has been placed by the Native Sons of the Golden West. On the banks of the Sacramento River opposite this point was an early steamboat landing. This place, designated on a map of 1862 as "Reading," was the northernmost point on the Sacramento to be reached by river boats.

At the Bridge Bay off-ramp on I-5 a marker (SRL 148) notes that nearby Bass Hill on the old stage road was a notorious spot for holdups and memorializes Williamson Lyncoya Smith, division stage agent of the California and Oregon Stage Company, and the pioneer stage drivers along this road.

The McCloud River north of its junction with the Pit (now within Shasta Lake) was the site of a Wintun Indian settlement, and the home of Consalulu, the last Wintun chief. About two miles above the mouth of the McCloud River, fossil remains of at least 25 distinct species, including the mastodon, elephant, giant sloth, large extinct lion, and cave bear, were taken from the Potter Creek Cave. In the same area was a place known as Joaquin Miller's Pass, where the poet is said to have forded the McCloud River on muleback.

On the park highway in the Lassen Volcanic National Park, a few hundred yards northwest of the checking station at Manzanita Lake, is a monument

(SRL 11) marking the Nobles Pass Road followed by the pioneers of 1852. A large lava rock about five feet high, bearing a bronze plaque, stands at the junction of the two park highways, one going down to Lost Creek and Hat Creek to Burney, and the other turning west to Viola, Shingletown, and Redding. The latter was the route used by early emigrants who came over Nobles Pass. It was at this point that they caught their first glimpse of the Sacramento Valley. The summit of Nobles Pass is about three miles to the northeast.

SR 44 closely parallels Nobles Trail from Viola to Redding. Trails West, Inc., a private organization, has placed markers along this road at Deer Flats, Battle Creek, Shingletown, Charley's Place, Dersch Ranch, and Emigrant Ferry, in addition to others that are not easily accessible to the average motorist.

Rancho Buena Ventura (Anderson and Redding)

The Reading adobe once stood just south of Ball's Ferry on the west bank of the Sacramento River near its confluence with Cottonwood Creek. The original rancho consisted of a strip of land three miles wide extending for nineteen miles along the west bank of the Sacramento River from the mouth of Cottonwood Creek at the head of Bloody Island in the south to Salt Creek in the north. Later the towns of Anderson and Redding were established on the rancho. (The town of Redding was named for B. B. Redding, land agent for the Central Pacific Railroad, and not, as may be thought, for Major Reading.)

Pierson Barton Reading, a native of New Jersey, came West with the Chiles-Walker party in 1843. He and twelve other men, among whom was Joseph B. Chiles, separated from the main party at Fort Hall, coming into California by an uncharted trail, now known as the Yellowstone Cutoff. Passing through what is now Shasta County, Reading and his companions arrived at Sutter's Fort on November 10, 1843.

A comparison of Reading's descriptions of the trail followed by the Chiles party in 1843 with the geographical features in northern California indicates clearly the route traveled. Leaving Big Valley (in Lassen County) on October 25, the band of thirteen men followed the course of the Pit River through the mountains, camping on the stream eighteen miles to the southwest. The next day they continued over mountainous country above the Pit River Canyon. "In some places," Reading writes, "the descent from the top of the bank to the water must have been 1,200 feet, the stream pitching over rocks and ledges, forming beautiful cascades, one of which had an abrupt fall of about 150 feet." This was, without doubt, Burney Falls, in McArthur–

Burney Falls Memorial State Park, whose actual drop is 128 feet.

Successive halts were made by Reading and his companions at Goose Valley on October 28, at the head of Hatchet Creek on the 29th, and on Cow Creek on the 31st. On the first day of November they traveled sixteen miles down Cow Creek, again pitching their tents on its banks. The next day, camp was made on Battle Creek, a part of the present boundary line between Shasta and Tehama counties, and the day after, upon traveling eight miles, they passed through Iron Canyon, where they found the course of the stream "very crooked." Camp was made at the end of the day in the valley east of Red Bluff, whence the journey was continued to Sutter's Fort.

Here Reading worked for a time in Captain Sutter's employ. In December 1844, through Sutter's friendship and influence, Reading obtained a grant of 26,000 acres from Governor Micheltorena, the most northerly grant in California, which he took over in August 1845. A house was built for Reading's overseer on Rancho Buena Ventura, as Reading called his new estate, and the land was stocked with cattle. This first house was burned by the Indians the following spring.

Reading participated in the Bear Flag Revolt at Sonoma in June 1846, and on July 5 or 6 he enlisted in Frémont's Battalion, serving first as lieutenant of artillery and then as paymaster with the rank of major, which office he held until May 31, 1847. In June he returned to his rancho and erected a permanent adobe house (SRL 10), which stood for many years, seven miles east of Cottonwood via Balls Ferry Road and Adobe Lane.

Ranch life, however, did not claim all of Reading's attention this early. In February 1848 he was among the first to visit the scene of Marshall's momentous discovery of gold at Coloma. An examination of the soil satisfied him that gold must be present on his own rancho, and he returned at once to investigate. In March he and his Indian laborers washed out the first gold to be found in Shasta County, at the mouth of Clear Creek Canyon on a spot later known as Reading's Bar. In July of the same year he found gold on the Trinity River. On his return journey he camped on the site of the present town of Shasta, known for a time as Reading's Springs.

When Shasta County was established in 1850, Reading's Ranch, as Rancho Buena Ventura had come to be known, was designated as the county seat. But with the organization of the Court of Sessions at the Major's adobe on February 10, 1851, the county seat was ordered removed to Shasta. "In the lonely still of the night," the tale is told, the court packed up the county records and carried them on horseback 25 miles to the new location, perhaps "the most quiet county-seat removal on record in California." No one rejoiced more heartily over the change than Major Reading.

In 1852 Reading was appointed United States Special Indian Agent, and for several years, without remuneration, he carried on work among the Indians. His kindliness was one of Reading's outstanding characteristics.

Going to Washington in 1855 to settle his land grant title, Reading met Miss Fannie Wallace Washington, whom he brought with him to California as his bride. With her coming the adobe on Rancho Buena Ventura was enlarged, and became noted for its unfailing hospitality. About the great fireplace many celebrities gathered—Bidwell, Frémont, Sutter, Lassen, and Joaquin Miller, among others. Here at his home on May 29, 1868, Pierson B. Reading died. A simple granite slab bearing a bronze memorial plate marks his grave, on Adobe Lane a quarter of a mile from the historic adobe, on a slight eminence overlooking the Sacramento River and the valley beyond. The old house, built with thick walls and high windows for protection from Indian arrows, has now eroded away to a shapeless mound. The site has been given by the Shasta Historical Society to the county of Shasta in the hope of an ultimate restoration.

Samuel Burney

The grave of Samuel Burney, a Scotsman, who was the first settler in Burney Valley, is close beside the Redding-Alturas Highway (SR 299) one-half mile east of Burney. Numerous place names in the vicinity perpetuate the memory of this pioneer—the mountain, the valley, the falls, and the town all bear his name. Burney Falls, one of the most beautiful natural phenomena in California, is the chief attraction in McArthur–Burney Falls Memorial State Park, a tract of 160 acres deeded to the state in 1920 by Frank McArthur as a memorial to his father and mother. Burney Creek wells up from the ground within the southern boundary of the park and falls 128 feet in two streams that water the ferns and mosses on the rocks. Although the creek goes dry in the summer between the park and the town of Burney, some ten miles to the south, the falls flow all year around with an unvarying temperature of 48 degrees.

Burney came to the valley early in 1857 and built a log cabin, barn, and corral a mile north of the present town of Burney. Although friendly with the Indians and speaking their language, he met death at their hands in March 1859.

Building Facade, Shasta State Historic Park

Shasta State Historic Park

Shasta (SRL 77), five miles west of Redding on SR 299, was a bustling place in the 1850's. It was called Reading's Bar by the first settlers who arrived in May 1849, but by the following year the present name was adopted. Shasta was the main center of wagon transportation for the Trinity mines and the roads north. As many as 100 freight teams have been known to stop in Shasta on a single night. Its favored location soon made it the commercial shipping center of northern California, and its merchants did a thriving business.

The decline of the mining industry and the coming of the railroad along the banks of the Sacramento River both contributed to the decline of Shasta. By 1888 the county seat had been moved to Redding. Guidebooks written as late as 1948 described the place as a virtually abandoned town. Soon afterward, McCloud Parlor No. 149 of Redding, Native Sons of the Golden West, acquired much of the property and presented it to the state of California, which in turn began the work

Courthouse Museum, Shasta State Historic Park

of restoring the old site. Today it is Shasta State Historic Park.

The restored county courthouse has been renovated and is now a museum of the boom years. The Masonic Lodge nearby has an interesting history. It was the first to be established in the state, its charter having been brought to California by Peter Lassen in 1848. The lodge was first organized at Benton City on Lassen's Ranch (Tehama County), but in May 1851 it was moved to Shasta. The present hall, which has been in use since 1853, is owned and carefully preserved by Western Star Lodge, No. 2.

At the eastern edge of town a marker indicates directions to the foundation of a Catholic church that was never built (SRL 483). Father Raphael Rinaldi, an Italian priest who arrived in the Shasta diggings in 1855, was dissatisfied with the small church in which the Catholics of the camp worshiped, and determined to build a magnificent basilica-like edifice of cut stone, modeled on the architecture of his homeland. The cornerstone was laid in 1857 by Archbishop Joseph Sadoc Alemany, O.P., of San Francisco, but the church never rose above its foundation, which remains today in a cluster of brush and high grass; unless one is looking very hard for it, this historical landmark can easily be missed. The nearest point of reference is the corner of High and Main streets.

A little less than a mile west of town off SR 299 is the grave of a baby boy (SRL 377), all that remains of a pioneer Jewish cemetery. The headstone was discovered in 1923 by engineers planning the highway. When it was found that the grave, with a little iron fence surrounding it, was directly in the line of the proposed highway, the officials altered the route. This road has since been abandoned in favor of a higher routing. The

headstone is now gone. It is reported that the stone's Hebrew inscription was: "Here lies buried Elchanan, son of Eliakim Broinshstein from the city of Red Bluff, born the 29th day of the month of Adar in the year 5624. Died the 15th day of Kislav of the year 5625 from the Creation of the Worlds (according to the Hebrew calendar)." There was also an English inscription: "Charles, son of George and Helena Brownstein. Born May 4, 1864, died December 14, 1864."

Shasta Mining Camps

Reading's Bar, where Major Reading in 1848 discovered the first gold in Shasta County, and where he washed out as much as 52 ounces daily with the aid of his Indian workmen, is now only a memory. On a flat adjoining the bar a camp grew up that was known at first as Clear Creek Diggings and later as Horse Town. By October 1849, 300 to 400 miners had congregated at Clear Creek Diggings, and considerable gold was taken out, although most of the miners did little more than prospect.

One of these prospectors, who had arrived in camp with one pack horse, settled there permanently and later built a hotel. As a result, so the story goes, the name of the place was changed to "One-Horse Town" in 1851. It did not remain a one-horse town, however, for before many years it boasted 1,000 inhabitants and had two hotels, stores, shops, a Catholic church, a newspaper (*The Northern Argus*, established in 1857), and fourteen saloons.

The marked site (SRL 32) of Reading's Bar and Horse Town is at the Clear Creek bridge seven miles west of SR 273 on Clear Creek Road, which intersects the highway at a point four miles south of Redding and less than a mile north of Clear Creek itself. Horse Town was destroyed by fire in 1868, and the site has been thoroughly dredged out.

Reading's discovery of gold at this place is also commemorated by a native boulder bearing a bronze tablet placed by the California Highway Commission on a now-bypassed stretch of SR 273 at the end of the Clear Creek Bridge (SRL 78).

In the vicinity of Horse Town were other early mining camps: Centerville to the north, Muletown to the northwest, and Piety Hill, Igo, and Ono to the west. The latter two still exist as small settlements, sharing the Igo-Ono School. There seems to be no single recognized source for their names, although it is said that the pioneer preacher Rev. William Kidder chose one from the Biblical "plains of Ono."

Whiskeytown (SRL 131), on SR 299 between Shasta and Weaverville, was settled in 1849. It was a lively place, as its name might imply, where money was plentiful and freely spent. The U.S. Post Office Department refused to allow the name Whiskeytown as a postal designation until 1952. Prior to that, the post office had been called Blair, later Stella, and finally Schilling. The old town now lies beneath Whiskeytown Lake, created by the Whiskeytown Dam; a new Whiskeytown lies on higher ground on what is now the lakeshore. Whiskeytown Dam was dedicated by President John F. Kennedy on September 28, 1963, on his last trip to California and less than two months before his assassination.

At French Gulch (SRL 166), originally called Morrowville, the diggings were very rich. In their avid search for gold, some of the miners even tore down their cabins to follow the leads extending under them. This once wild camp is today a peaceful community, on Trinity Hill Road three miles north of SR 299; the turn-off is five miles west of Whiskeytown.

Southern's Station

Simeon Fisher Southern arrived in Shasta in 1855, where at first he operated the Eagle Hotel, and later the St. Charles. In the next few years he ran hotels in French Gulch and Dog Creek on the Oregon Trail. In 1859 he built a cabin of shakes and hand-hewn logs at a spot 45 miles north of Redding that would later be known as Southern's. This developed into a busy trading post for miners from Hazel Creek and the Upper Sacramento River. When stagecoaches replaced pack-mule trains on the Oregon Trail in 1871, Southern's became an important station on the old road. Gradually the place took on the aspect of a summer resort, as the fame of the surrounding region spread. In 1882 a two-story extension was added to the original cabin. Eventually the old cabin was torn down and the two-story addition was considerably enlarged to care for the increasing number of summer visitors.

After the death of Southern in 1892, changes crept in. With the sale of the property to lumber interests in 1902, the surrounding forests were cut and the old hotel disappeared, to be replaced by modern facilities. The spot on which the old hotel stood (SRL 33) is marked by a few old apple trees, planted in the 1860's, and by a native boulder bearing a bronze tablet on which is an engraving of the original Southern cabin and its two-story addition. The site is about eight miles south of Castella, on the west side of I-5. The names of many famous people appear on the old hotel register, which is still treasured by the family; among them are President Rutherford B. Hayes, Generals William T. Sherman and Philip H. Sheridan, Robert Ingersoll, Mrs. Jay Gould, George Jay Gould, and the "Big Four": Charles

Crocker, Mark Hopkins, C. P. Huntington, and Leland Stanford.

The American Ranch (Anderson)

Elias Anderson, one of Shasta County's first settlers, purchased the American Ranch in 1856, and on his land grew up the nucleus of what is now the town of Anderson. The ranch also was an early stopping place for teamsters and travelers on the California-Oregon Trail, and from it a trail branched off to the Trinity mines. The first buildings of the old stage station, the site of which is near the highway across the creek from central Anderson, were of adobe.

Bell's Bridge

Five miles south of Redding off SR 273, a few hundred yards above the Clear Creek Bridge, is the old Bell hostelry, built by J. J. Bell, who settled on the road to Oregon in May 1851. During the gold rush the place teemed with activity, and thousands of men and animals found refreshment there on their way to the Shasta, Trinity, and Siskiyou gold fields. Fabulous prices were paid for food and lodging, and with the proceeds Bell was able to make extensive improvements on his ranch. He also operated a toll bridge (SRL 519) across Clear Creek at this point. The tavern now serves as a hay barn. The marker commemorating Bell's Bridge has been placed just off Clear Creek Road on the frontage road of SR 273, at a point 2,200 feet north of the actual site of the bridge.

Fort Reading

Fort Reading (SRL 379), named in honor of Major Pierson B. Reading, was established in May 1852 on Cow Creek on the Nobles Pass Road at a site six miles northeast of the present town of Anderson on Dersch Road. It was abandoned in 1867 as part of the demobilization of the army at the end of the Civil War. Nothing remains of the old fort itself, but the site, now in a cultivated field, has been marked. The location is 3.4 miles east of the junction of Dersch and Airport roads.

The Dersch Homestead

Northeast of Anderson stood the Dersch homestead (SRL 120). In 1850 a Mr. Baker had set up a tent hotel there, making the place an emigrant station on the Nobles Pass Road. George Dersch followed him, using Indian labor from rancherias flourishing at Jelly's Ferry

Dersch Homestead, near Anderson

(Tehama County), Cottonwood, Reading's adobe, and Millville. Roving Indians raided the ranch in 1863, driving off the cattle, stealing the household provisions, and leaving the family destitute. In 1866 a second raid was made, in which Mrs. Dersch was killed. The soldiers at Fort Reading were appealed to but with no results. This led to an uprising of the settlers, resulting in the extermination of most of the Indians in the surrounding rancherias.

The old house stood until it burned in 1934 on the northeast side of Dersch Road at the Bear Creek Bridge. A replica of the original house has been built; it is located on Dersch Road 7.8 miles east of its junction with Airport Road. A small Trails West marker identifies the site, but there is no state plaque.

Millville

Fourteen miles east of Redding on SR 44 is Millville, a thriving place with a distinctive atmosphere of pioneer days. It was settled in 1853 by S. E. and N. T. Stroud, who built the first house there on the banks of Clover Creek. The first gristmill in Shasta County was built in Millville in 1856 by D. D. Harrell and Russell Furman, who named the place Bunscombe Mills, in honor of Harrell's birthplace in North Carolina. Eventually the name was changed to Millville.

Shingletown

Shingletown was established before 1860 as a lumber center. One of the pioneer families there, the Ogburns, established themselves in the region as early as 1848.

The Ogburn Ranch, just off SR 44 near Charley's Place, has been in operation since that time; an E Clampus Vitus plaque commemorates the place. Nearby is the Ogburn-Inwood Cemetery, whose earliest gravestones bear the date of 1860; it too is still in use.

Fall River Valley and Fort Crook

On July 1, 1857, a fort was established by Lieutenant George Crook on Fall River at the upper end of Fall River Valley to serve as a buffer against Indian attacks on the early settlers. The post consisted of twenty small log buildings placed in the form of an oblong. With the abandonment of Fort Crook in 1869 and the transfer of the soldiers to Fort Bidwell, the buildings were used for a time as a school, but were later sold and moved to Burgettville, now Glenburn. The site of the fort (SRL 355) is now in a cultivated field on private property about ten miles northwest of Fall River Mills on the road through Glenburn.

The first settlers in Fall River Valley were two men named Bowles and Rogers, who came there from Yreka in 1855. They brought heavy mill machinery with them by ox team and at once set to work cutting trees—some of which still lie where they fell. In the autumn other settlers joined them, among whom were the Lockhart brothers, who located on the site of Fall River Mills. Bowles, Rogers, and William Lockhart spent the winter at this place but were killed by Indians early the following spring. When Sam Lockhart returned to the valley, he was saved from a similar fate only by the timely arrival of a company of men from Yreka. The remains of "Lockhart's Fort," in which he made a gallant five-day fight for life, may be seen today on the hill near Fall River Mills. Shortly after his arrival, Sam Lockhart established a ferry (SRL 555) where the California-Oregon stage road crossed the Pit River just below the mouth of the Fall River. There, also, he built a bridge across the Pit River in 1859, only to have it washed away in the flood of 1862.

The first school in Fall River Valley (SRL 759) was built in 1868 at a spot that is now three and one-half miles east of McArthur on the south side of SR 299. It was a simple log building, 20 by 30 feet, without floor or windows. About two years later the first sawmill in the valley was set up at Dana, and lumber from this mill was used to floor the school and to construct desks.

The Fort Crook Historical Society operates and maintains the handsome museum at Fall River Mills, on SR 299 at the edge of the town. Both Indian and settler are represented in this interesting collection. The building, dedicated in 1963, is twelve-sided, patterned after a twelve-sided "Round Barn" built in the valley in 1910 and now being renovated. Buildings from other places have been moved to the museum grounds; these include a one-room schoolhouse built in 1884, a very old log cabin built in 1860, and a building housing a farm equipment display, showing specimens of this equipment from the beginning of white settlement in the valley.

Castle Crags State Park

Sharply outlined against the sky, the lofty gray turrets of Castle Crags offer a striking contrast to the dark green of the pine-covered mountains that surround them. This superb group rises more than 6,600 feet above sea level and includes among its towers the Cathedral Spires, Castle Dome, and Battle Rock. Hidden high up in the recesses of Castle Crags lies Castle Lake, discovered by Crook and his men while in pursuit of Indians.

Below these crags, at first known as Castle Rocks, lay historic Lower Soda Springs (called Castle Crag with the advent of the railroad in 1886) in a green meadow east of the Sacramento River at its confluence with Soda Creek. It was long the favorite camping ground of the Shastas and other mountain Indian tribes. It is known that Lansford Hastings and sixteen companions, who had started from Rogue River, Oregon, in May 1843, camped at the springs. It is said that Hastings was so pleased with the magnificent location of Lower Soda Springs that he applied for a grant of land that should include both Castle Rocks and its snow-covered neighbor to the north, then known as Shasta Butte and now as Mount Shasta. The grant never materialized, since Hastings would not become a Mexican citizen.

The first permanent settler in the region of Lower Soda Springs was Joe Doblondy, "Mountain Joe," frontiersman and guide for Frémont. It is not known just when Mountain Joe came to this spot. On the Lower Soda Springs Ranch he tilled the soil, built houses, kept a sort of hotel, guided travelers up the Oregon Trail past Mount Shasta, and fought the Indians. He was also the friend of Joaquin Miller, who in 1854 ran away from school in Oregon and came to live with Mountain Joe under the shadow of the crags. "He was my ideal, my hero," wrote the poet in later years, and it was from Mountain Joe's seemingly inexhaustible store of tales (first heard in Oregon), as well as from the majesty of the surroundings in which he lived, that Miller gained the inspiration for much of his poetry.

The first mining on Soda Creek was carried on in the early 1850's by Bill Fox, who had escaped from the Yreka jail and hid in this isolated spot. He took out a large amount of gold, but was discovered and had to leave the country. Mountain Joe's tales of the fabulous Lost Cabin Mine and other supposedly rich diggings lured a large number of miners to Soda Creek and the Upper Sacramento River in the spring of 1855. According to one account, "the little valley was soon a white sea of tents. Every bar on the Sacramento was the scene of excitement. . . . The rivers ran dark and sullen with sand and slime. The fish turned on their sides and died, or hid under the muddy clouds that obscured the deepest pools."

But the tales of wealth told by Mountain Joe proved unfounded, and the army of angry, disgusted miners soon left the region. The results of their short sojourn, however, were not so easily removed. The fish and game on which the Indians depended had been killed or driven out, and the desire for vengeance stirred the warriors to action. One morning in June 1855, while Mountain Joe was absent, a band of Indians, descending from Castle Rocks, plundered and burned the settlement at Lower Soda Springs. On his return, Mountain Joe and Joaquin Miller traced the flight of the Indians up the rocks by the flour they had spilled. With recruits from the neighboring settlements of Portuguese Flat and Dog Creek, Mountain Joe soon gathered together a company to take revenge on the Indians. Judge R. P. Gibson, who had married the daughter of the chief of the Shastas, persuaded this tribe to join with the white settlers against the Pits and the other hostile tribes.

The Battle of the Crags, graphically described by Joaquin Miller, youthful participant in the fight, took place on Battle Rock (SRL 116), the most prominent of all the spires and domes of the group. Directly under the highest crag in the northwest corner of the great mass, the settlers, led by Gibson and his Shasta allies, fought face to face with the Modocs. Many on both sides were killed or wounded; among the wounded was young Miller, who afterward told how he was carried down the mountainside in a large buckskin bag tied to the back of a wrinkled old Indian woman. Camp was made on the riverbanks below the site of the later Soda Springs Hotel, and there Joaquin was cared for by Mountain Joe until he recovered from his wounds. The Battle of the Crags was one of a long series of conflicts between the Indians and the white settlers of northeastern California that culminated in the Modoc War nearly twenty years later.

After passing through several hands, Lower Soda Springs came into the possession of G. W. Bailey in 1858, who operated a ranch, a wayside inn, and a summer resort at this spot. In 1887 he sold the place to Leland Stanford for a summer home, but apparently it was not used.

In 1892 the new owners, the Pacific Improvement

Company, built the Castle Crag Tavern, the largest summer hotel in Shasta County. It became famous and people from all parts of the world visited it, but it was destroyed by fire early in 1900 and was never rebuilt. A number of log cabins were erected in its stead and the place was operated as a summer camp until 1930, when it passed into private hands and was closed to the public. It is now known as the Berry Estate.

Redding

Redding, named in honor of B. B. Redding, for many years land agent for the Central Pacific Railroad, was founded in the summer of 1872. It was the temporary railhead of the line until construction began up the Sacramento River gorge in 1883; the line was connected to Portland, Oregon, in 1887. The town was incorporated the same year, the first municipality in Shasta County. It became the county seat in 1888. Because of its central location on roads leading east and west as well as north and south, it has always been an active center of trade and transportation. The city maintains a museum with departments of ethnology, the fine arts, and history at 1911 Rio Drive, on the riverside, in Caldwell Park.

Shasta College was opened in Redding in 1950 and in 1967 was moved to its present site. Its museum and research center at 1065 North Old Oregon Trail, housed in a modern-day replica of Major Reading's adobe, is open to the public on a limited basis; it contains extensive material on upper Sacramento Valley history in the early twentieth century as well as displays on natural and Indian history.

The Copper Boom

Around the turn of the century Shasta County enjoyed a copper-mining boom. In 1906 five copper smelters were in operation: Keswick (in operation from 1896 to 1907), Coram (1906–11), Kennett (1905–19), Bully Hill (1901–10), and Ingot (1905–9). The copper-refining process produced sulfur fumes that killed surrounding vegetation, and some smelters were closed for this reason.

Shasta Dam and Shasta Lake

On the Sacramento River, ten miles northwest of Redding, the U.S. Bureau of Reclamation constructed Shasta Dam between 1938 and 1944. This is the principal unit of the great Central Valley Water Project. The 602-foot-high dam, the second-highest in California, is open to the public for tours; there is also a visitors' center and museum. The impounded waters of the Sacramento and its tributaries, including the Pit and Mc-Cloud rivers, now form Shasta Lake, 29,500 acres of water with 365 miles of shoreline. The lake is now a major recreational area, as well as a site of vital importance for water storage, flood control, and hydroelectric power.

The construction of the dam led to the founding of several small towns in the area: Pine Grove, Project City, Central Valley, Toyon, and Summit City. After the dam was finished, these towns, unlike earlier ones, did not become ghost towns, and they are well populated today.

Lake Shasta Caverns, now a commercial enterprise, was discovered on November 3, 1878, by James A. Richardson, a federal fisheries employee, whose inscription, written in carbide from his miner's lamp, can still be seen within the caves. It is located on the northern side of Shasta Lake, off the O'Brien Recreation Area turnoff from I-5.

The Whiskeytown-Shasta-Trinity National Recreation Area now embraces Whiskeytown Lake and its environs, Shasta Lake and its environs, and Clair Engle Lake and Lewiston Lake and their environs in Trinity County. These are all man-made lakes with abundant camping and recreational facilities.

On June 17, 1950, during the Shasta Centennial celebration, the California Centennials Commission dedicated an official state plaque on Shasta Dam. The tablet is inscribed: "If you seek their monument, look about you. To pioneer mothers and fathers of California—whose urge to envision what lay beyond the far horizon and whose courage to overcome hardship opened the unknown West, converting wilderness into empire."

Sierra County

Sierra County was organized from a part of Yuba County in 1852, and Downieville was made the county seat. The name Sierra Nevada ("snow-covered, saw-toothed mountains") is applied to the mountain range that extends from Tehachapi Pass on the south to Lassen Peak on the north.

Goodyear's Bar

Superb mountain peaks look down upon the old river camps at Goodyear's Bar—Saddle Back, Monte Cristo, Fir Cap, Grizzly Peak, and others—where the jade-green North Fork of the Yuba River is joined by the tumbling waters of Goodyear Creek. The small tri-angular flat on which a horde of miners once lived and worked has today not more than a few dozen inhabit-ants, with only a scattering of houses that stand almost upon the abandoned diggings. The old two-story-and-attic frame hotel is the town's principal landmark. The old school, built in 1862, is now the community center.

Goodyear's Bar, settled in the summer of 1849 by Andrew and Miles Goodyear and two companions, was one of the first mining camps on the North Fork of the Yuba. By 1852 the place had become the center for a number of lively camps up and down the river as well as on the neighboring ridges. Nearby were the Ranse Doddler and Hoodoo bars, with St. Joe's Bar two miles below and Woodville, at first known as Cutthroat Bar, farther up the river.

The diggings in the vicinity yielded rich returns. At Kennedy Ranch, located at the upper end of Good-year's Bar, Peter Yore's men cleaned up $2,000 in gold dust from a single wheelbarrow load of earth, a find that was kept secret from the other miners until a con-siderable harvest had been gathered.

Goodyear's Bar prospered through the 1850's, but it declined in the early 1860's, with the gradual exhaus-tion of ore deposits along the river. Decline was further hastened by the devastating fire that swept through the town in 1864.

Downieville

Downieville, in one of the highest and most rugged regions in the state, is set in a magnificent wooded am-phitheater surrounded by lofty, pine-clad mountains. At its door the Downie River (also called the North Fork of the North Fork of the Yuba River) flows into the larger stream of the Yuba, a part of that network of forks and tributaries that reach through deep canyons upward into the higher altitudes of the Sierra.

William Downie (usually called "Major" Downie), a Scotsman, for whom the town was later named, arrived at "The Forks" in November 1849. With him were ten black sailors, an Indian, an Irish boy, and Jim Crow, a Kanaka, who later became a notorious character in the North Yuba River country and for whom Jim Crow Can-yon was named. Erecting a few log cabins, the Major and his men wintered at the flat just above the present townsite. Some of the men spent their time digging into the rocky crevices under the snow, taking out $100 to $200 in gold each day.

There was a rush of miners into the area the follow-ing spring, accompanied by rich strikes on all the neigh-boring bars and flats. "The Forks" soon became the center of the wide circle of camps reaching up and down both rivers and their tributaries, and before long the name of the place was changed to Downieville. By 1851 the population of the town had increased to more than 5,000.

Stories told of the miners and their life on the Yuba indicate the phenomenal richness of the placers. On Durgan Flat, where the courthouse now stands, Frank Anderson and three companions in eleven days took out ore valued at $12,900 from a claim only 60 feet square. One day's yield was valued at $4,300, while the total yield during the first six months that the loca-tion was worked brought over $80,000. Jersey Flat, just above the present town, at the spot where Downie and his party first made temporary camp, was a close sec-ond to Durgan Flat in production. According to the Major, Jim Crow killed a salmon weighing fourteen pounds here, and after the fish had been cooked for supper gold was found at the bottom of the kettle. At Zumwalt Flat each man averaged five ounces a day for three and one-half hours' labor, while at Tin Cup Dig-gings, opposite Zumwalt Flat, three men who worked there in 1850 were said to have made it a rule to fill a tin cup with gold before quitting work at night, which they had no trouble doing.

But the miners were not satisfied, and in order to get out the gold that still lay in the bedrock of the river, they flumed the entire Yuba between Downieville and Goodyear's Bar out of its channel. When the winter floods came, however, their flume was swept away like so much straw.

Other diggings in the canyon country brought vast wealth. At Gold Bluff, two miles above Downieville, in the fall of 1850 a nugget of pure gold was taken out that weighed 25 pounds, the largest ever found on the North Yuba. The black slate of this area continued to produce thousands of dollars up to the time of World War I, when mining activities were discontinued. Below Slug Canyon, so called because of the coarse lump or slug gold found there, the Steamboat Company on Steamboat Bar took out an average of $5,000 a day for several weeks during 1851. At the head of this canyon and about three miles south of Downieville is the City of Six Quartz Mine, a famous producer in the early days. Another famous mine, Monte Cristo, is located on the south slope of Monte Cristo, 1,000 feet above Goodyear Creek and three miles northwest of Downieville. It was opened in 1854, and at one time the adjoining camp had a population as large as that of Downieville.

Downieville remains much as it was in the gold days. Along the crooked main street (SR 49, following the bank of the river), which is still lined in part by boardwalks, stand the same buildings. Along the riverbanks and up the mountainsides the old-fashioned houses, set amid aged locust and fruit trees, line the shady streets and alleyways, making the residential part of Downieville one of the town's most charming features.

One of the first buildings in Downieville, thought to have been erected in 1852, a stone structure with heavy iron doors and shuttered windows, was restored and presented to the town for use as a museum by the heirs of J. M. B. Meroux, a pioneer. The walls of this building are made entirely of flat rocks laid horizontally, a very

Gallows, Downieville

early type of construction. The nucleus of the museum is a collection of valuable relics gathered by former sheriff George C. Bynon.

The Hirschfelder house, now a grocery store, is another stone structure that dates from 1852, as does the Craycroft Building across the main street. The frame Masonic Hall was built in 1864 to replace an earlier structure. The Catholic and Methodist Episcopal churches, both built in the 1850's, have been marked by official state plaques, although neither has been assigned a registration number.

Across the river from the business section stands the courthouse, a modern structure that was built after fire destroyed the old courthouse in 1947. Here there are two old cannon, an arrastra wheel that was used by the pioners to grind the gold-impregnated quartz, and at the rear of the building the old gallows (SRL 971), first used in 1858. A more noteworthy hanging, which made Downieville notorious for a while, took place in 1851 where the highway bridge crosses the river today. Jack Cannon, a popular Australian miner, was stabbed to death by Juanita (Josefa in some accounts), a Mexican woman who claimed she had been mortally insulted by Cannon. Anti-Mexican feelings were high—Cannon's group had broken the door to Juanita's shanty the night before the murder—and in short order Juanita was lynched, an event that aroused much criticism both in the United States and abroad.

Main Street, Downieville

Near the courthouse are the diggings—huge piles of granite boulders marking the rich river claims where miners in 1850 and 1851 averaged $100 to $200 daily. Here the Chinese came after others had ceased to consider the location worthwhile. Lifting the heavy stones one by one, they cleared out the bed of the North Yuba, leaving mammoth heaps as evidence of their great labors.

·Heritage Park stands by the river on the town side, displaying old monitors, mining equipment, and a stamping mill.

Sierra City

Following the line of the old stage road from Downieville, SR 49 sweeps up the scenic canyon of the North Fork of the Yuba River. Above green alpine meadows and old apple orchards, where an occasional old farmhouse may still be seen, the road leads past the little old settlement of Loganville, eleven miles from Downieville, to Sierra City, two miles further. Towering almost a mile above the town are the majestic Sierra Buttes, jagged granite peaks that can be seen from miles away. In the gold rush days they witnessed feverish activity along the creeks leading into the North Fork, and even the almost perpendicular sides of the granite pile were climbed in the search for gold.

In the spring of 1850 P. A. Haven and Joseph Zumwalt located on the site of Sierra City, in a region thickly populated with Indians. In the same year a Mr. Murphy discovered the Sierra Buttes quartz ledge. By 1852 tunnels penetrated the craggy buttes in all directions, and the miners were using as many as twenty arrastras, run by mules, to pulverize the rock. During that winter a heavy blanket of snow and avalanches from the steep mountain above crushed every house in the mining camp. In the face of this disaster it was not until 1858 that a permanent settlement was established on the townsite.

Another rich quartz deposit of the Sierra Buttes was opened up at the Monumental Quartz Mine, where in August 1860 an immense gold nugget, weighing 1,596 troy ounces and valued at $25,500, was taken out, the second largest to be found in California.

One mile east of Sierra City on SR 49 is the Kentucky Mine Museum, operated by Sierra County, containing a six-level stamping mill that is still in operation and is demonstrated by docents. The grounds also contain a miner's cabin and a museum of Sierra City history.

Among the interesting historic structures still standing in Sierra City are the Busch Building on Main Street, erected in 1871, the Catholic Church, and the Masonic Hall. The Busch Building at one time housed the Wells

Kentucky Mine Museum, near Sierra City

Fargo Express Office, and is currently being refurbished. Its lower two stories of brick survived a fire about 1948 that destroyed the third story of wood. The building was begun during the Fourth of July celebration and the ceremonies were conducted by E Clampus Vitus, which had been organized in Sierra City in 1857. The letters "ECV" still mark the doorway in the building through which the "Clampers" passed.

E Clampus Vitus (the name is nonsensical) was in part a fraternal organization charitable toward widows and orphans and in part a prankish group that mocked the solemn lodges of its day. It died out but was reorganized as E Clampus Vitus Redivivus in 1931 by a few members of various California historical organizations who were interested in preserving the lore and fun of gold rush days. The group's plaques are to be seen throughout the state today.

Sierra City is unusual among the gold towns in never having suffered a serious fire, owing in part to abundant supplies of water from its many mountain streams. These watercourses have been harnessed to furnish power not only for the mills at the mines, as in the old days, but to generate electricity and to supply the needs of the town.

Forest

Forest, fourteen miles south of Downieville via Goodyear's Bar, was one of the liveliest camps in Sierra County during the middle 1850's. It was once called Brownsville, after an early settler; then Yomana, an Indian name said to designate the high bluff above the town, and finally Forest City; the latter part of the name was dropped in the 1890's.

Having worked out the streams, bars, and banks

about Forest, the miners began to tunnel into the mountains to the south. The name of one of these tunnels, the Alleghany, was given to a flourishing camp on the opposite side of the mountain, where pay dirt was struck in 1855. The town of Alleghany increased in importance so rapidly the following year that the entire population of Forest flocked to the new camp, leaving the older place an empty shell. When a rich strike was made in the Bald Mountain district in 1870, Forest awoke from its sleep, only to relapse after a few years into the quiet hamlet of today. A few empty stores stand along the main street, and a little Catholic church crowns the hill above; steep-roofed houses cling to the mountains on either side of the canyon, reaching only over narrow, precipitous roads.

Alleghany

Alleghany may be reached by a variety of routes, all of them winding mountain roads with sections that are narrow, steep, and rough. From Downieville on the north, one may proceed by way of Goodyear's Bar and Forest, a trip of nineteen miles in all. From Camptonville on the west, the road along Gold Ridge joins the route from Downieville at the site of Mountain House, between Goodyear's Bar and Forest. From Freeman's Crossing at the Nevada-Yuba county line, the main road to Alleghany, fully paved in contrast to the others, is about nineteen miles in length. From North Columbia, eighteen miles to the southwest, a road leads to Alleghany by way of Foote's Crossing on the Middle Fork of the Yuba River. Alleghany may also be reached from the east over the Henness Pass route.

Of all these roads, the most interesting, and most recently built, is the Foote's Crossing approach; a portion of the route, on the Nevada County side above the Middle Fork, has been described as "America's most spectacular mile of mountain road." This dizzying thoroughfare was built by A. D. Foote as a toll road in the first decade of the twentieth century, just as the automobile was coming into general use. The road is a marvel of engineering skill. Cut into the face of a stupendous precipice high above the deep gorge of the Middle Fork, it takes a narrow, threadlike course along the almost perpendicular cliffs; in places huge iron bars had to be anchored far into the solid rock underneath the roadbed. At the bottom of the canyon is Foote's Crossing Bridge, where a roadhouse once stood. Beyond, the great gorge of the Middle Fork converges with that of Kanaka Creek to make one immense canyon.

Kanaka Creek was discovered in May 1850 by one of several parties of Hawaiian prospectors sent out by a certain Captain Ross, the reputed son of King Kamehameha. (The term Kanaka was at that time used for a native of the Hawaiian Islands and was not considered a derogatory term.) A general rush of miners followed. Kanaka Creek proved to be extraordinarily rich in gold and some very large nuggets were taken out.

Up the north side of Kanaka Creek Canyon to Alleghany, new vistas of scenic grandeur successively unfold. Evidences of one-time mining activities are visible on every hand: masses of green serpentine rock, polished and of great beauty; old "glory holes" and deserted mines visible far up the wooded ravine. Nearer Alleghany the country becomes increasingly rocky, and one can glimpse a few mines of this famous district: the Madden, Rainbow, Oriental, Spoohn Gold, and others, the smaller ones having produced $1,500 to $2,000 each year and the larger ones millions. According to record, one chunk of ore found in this region weighed 163 pounds and brought $27,000 from the mint, and from one pocket as much as $80,000 was taken. Some of these rich deposits have been lost through faulty surveys or the sudden caving in of a tunnel and have never been relocated. This happened in the case of the old Red Star Mine, from which as much as $80,000 was taken from one chute in 1912. Hope of recovering such leads is continually reviving, and the fascination of the quest lures the modern treasure hunter as it did the Argonauts of old. Virtually every year brings newspaper reports of some new gold strike in the Alleghany area.

Alleghany is still essentially a "gold camp"—one of the few left in California—where most of the hundred or so citizens have some connection with the gold-mining industry. Clinging "like a cluster of cliff swallows' nests to the side of the mountain," the houses of the town are built on a series of terraces connected by streets. Fires, one as recently as 1987, have steadily reduced the town; in the words of a citizen, "When we lose something now, nothing gets replaced." A general store and one tavern remain.

Just below Alleghany the famous Original Sixteen-to-One Mine, so called to distinguish it from the Sixteen-to-One above Washington in Nevada County, was located in 1896 by Thomas J. Bradbury. Year after year Bradbury lived at Alleghany and worked his claim on a small scale. Then in 1907 the rich Tightner Mine was discovered nearby. In 1916 it was found that this location and the Original Sixteen-to-One were tapping the same vein, its apex in the backyard of the Bradbury home. This discovery led to the consolidation of the Tightner and the Twenty-One, another adjacent property, with the Sixteen-to-One as the Original Sixteen-to-One Company, which continued to work the claim until December 1965. Most of the mining done around Alleghany since then has been on a smaller scale.

Following the line of the ancient Blue Lead river channel across Kanaka Creek Canyon, one finds auriferous gravel deposits on the opposite slopes at Chips Flat, and again at what was once the mining camp of Minnesota Flat on the other side of the ridge. An outcropping of blue gravel at the latter location was discovered in July 1852 by an old English sailor, known to his fellows as "Chips" because he had previously been employed as a ship's carpenter. Later Chips located even richer diggings on the northern slope of the same ridge, at Chips Flat.

The old scenic road from Camptonville in Yuba County to Downieville along the backbone of Gold Ridge overlooked the heavily timbered canyons of Oregon Creek to the south and the North Yuba River to the north. A fairly good dirt road, over which Alleghany may be reached, follows the same course today, passing the sites of several historic stopping places along the way. A little over three miles east of Camptonville, across the Sierra County line, long stood the old Sleighville House, a two-story hotel. The original structure, built in 1849 by Peter Yore, was added to from time to time as the needs of the family increased. Not far from the site of the old hostelry lies the burial ground of the Yore family. Dense evergreen forests enclose the place on all sides, and in winter the landscape is heavily mantled in snow. At this point, in early days, it was necessary to transfer goods from wagons to sleighs during the winter months, and from this circumstance the house took its name.

The next historic point on the Gold Ridge route, about five miles beyond Sleighville House, is the site of Nigger Tent. On this spot in 1849 a black man put up a tent with a cabin, on the site of which a subsequent owner erected a substantial frame hotel. In spite of changes, the original name of Nigger Tent stuck to the locality. Several miles beyond, where the road forks, is the site of the Mountain House, burned long ago, where a magnificent panorama of wooded mountains and deeply chiseled canyons may be seen. From here one road goes south to Forest, while the other leads north to Goodyear's Bar and Downieville.

The main road to Alleghany begins at SR 49, in the area of Freeman's Crossing on the Nevada-Yuba county line between North San Juan and Camptonville. The road crosses Oregon Creek over the famous old covered bridge built about 1862 and, a few miles beyond, enters Sierra County. At a point about six miles beyond the bridge a road leads north to what remains of Pike City, a few old cabins and foundations. About four miles beyond the Pike turnoff a handsome monument stands beside the main road at the site of the Plum Valley House (SRL 695), built in 1854 by John Bope. Deriving its name from the wild plums that grow in this area, it was a toll station on the Henness Pass Road (SRL 421) between Marysville and Virginia City, Nevada. This route had been in use as an emigrant trail as early as 1849. A dirt Forest Service road still follows its course across Henness Pass (6,806 feet) to join SR 89 nine miles southeast of Sierraville.

Gold Beyond the Mountains

Towering thousands of feet above the towns of the North Yuba River canyon, a huge mass of mountains crowned with castellated peaks and knife-like crests, of which the Sierra Buttes are a part, forms an effective barrier to direct travel into the old mining district of northwestern Sierra County. In order to drive to this area one must turn north above Sierra City and follow a circuitous route by way of Gold Lake, Mohawk, and Johnsville to Gibsonville, or else retrace to Bullard's Bar in Yuba County and from there proceed northward via Challenge and Strawberry Valley, through La Porte in Plumas County, and thence to Gibsonville on the road to Quincy.

This remote section of Sierra County was first prospected in the spring of 1850, when gold was found along the ridge between the North Fork of the Yuba River and the South Fork of the Feather River by an old sea captain named Sears, whose name was later given to the ridge.

Returning to the Yuba, Sears prepared to lead a company of prospectors to the scene of his discovery. But the news that Sears had struck it rich spread, and before proceeding very far his party found that they were being followed by a group under the leadership of a man named Gibson. When ordered to turn back, Gibson's men refused, saying that the mountains of California were as free to them as to any man, and that if there was gold beyond those mountains they were going to get their share. A compromise was at length reached and the two parties proceeded to Sears' Ridge, where operations were begun at a place afterward known as Sears' Diggings.

Before long a number of other locations were staked out in the vicinity, some of which proved to be richer than the original strike. Gibson, who was an especially enterprising prospector, discovered very rich deposits on an adjoining ridge overlooking Little Slate Creek, a site later developed into the large and thriving camp of Gibsonville, which as late as 1870 was a busy place. With the passing years Gibsonville, in windswept isolation, has grown more deserted. The few remaining wooden houses straggle up and down the crooked street, bleached bone-white by the action of the elements.

The enterprising Gibson struck another rich deposit at a place that became known as Secret Ravine because he had kept the location a secret from his comrades, who charged him with playing them false. The resultant dissension among Gibson's followers and growing dissatisfaction among Sears' men caused a scattering of the two groups, resulting in new discoveries in all directions. Many new camps were established, among them Howland Flat (or Table Rock), Pine Grove, Potosi, St. Louis, Queen City, Poker Flat, Craig's Flat, Deadwood, Chandlerville, Port Wine, Scales, Poverty Hill, Brandy City, Hepsidam, Whiskey Diggings (or Newark), McMahon's, Morristown, and Eureka City at the source of Goodyear Creek.

At La Porte a good dirt road turns southeast across the Sierra County line and runs four miles to Queen City, marked by a few old cabins. At this point a road running northeast and southwest is intersected. The branch to the northeast goes to Howland Flat via St. Louis. St. Louis, staked out on the site of Sears' Diggings in the fall of 1852 by a party of Missourians, enjoyed a brief period of prosperity until it was swept by fire in 1857. Later, during the 1860's, a short-lived hydraulic boom revived the place. Howland Flat, where the post office (1857–1922) was always called Table Rock, is situated on the north side of Table Rock at an elevation of 6,000 feet. A fair number of old houses remain from its more populous days. From here a trail leads three miles to Poker Flat on Canyon Creek. The road continues from Howland Flat to join the Johnsville road east of Gibsonville.

The road southwest from Queen City goes to Port Wine, Poverty Hill, and Scales. Less than a mile from Queen City is a magnificent old stone building, a strange sight in this wilderness. This former store, with its iron doors, plus an old cemetery and piles of long-forgotten diggings are all that remain of Port Wine, named by prospectors who found a cask of port wine hidden in a nearby canyon. The road continues past the turnoff to Poverty Hill to the little community of Scales with its neat white homes. From here the motorist can follow the road west into Yuba County, joining the main road to La Porte about two and a half miles northeast of Strawberry Valley.

Sierra Valley

In Sierra Valley, across Yuba Pass and 23 miles east of Sierra City on SR 49, is the old town of Sierraville, a supply center rather than a mining camp. The old Globe Hotel, now outfitted as a motel, and the Monte Carlo Saloon remain from earlier days. Cut off from the rest of the county by the snows of winter, Sierraville recently made an unsuccessful bid to replace Downieville as county seat. Nearby Sattley and Calpine are towns connected with the lumber industry, the latter having been a company town for the Davis-Johnson Lumber Company at the beginning of this century.

Loyalton, near the northern terminus of SR 49, is the site of the Sierra Valley Museum, opened in 1984, which has displays on the ranching and logging industries of Sierra Valley. An old school building, later used as a Catholic place of worship, has been moved onto the grounds, which are at the Loyalton City Park.

Siskiyou County

Siskiyou County was created in 1852 from the northern part of Shasta County and a part of Klamath County. Yreka has always been the county seat. After Klamath County was dissolved in 1874, Siskiyou County received still more of its territory.

The name Siskiyou, according to Erwin G. Gudde, meant "bobtailed horse" in the Cree Indian language and was borrowed by the Chinook jargon, the trade language of the Oregon Territory. A mountain pass was given this name after Alexander McLeod of the Hudson's Bay Company lost a horse while going through it in 1828. The boundary between Oregon and Alta California, along the 42nd parallel, follows the natural border formed by the Siskiyou Mountains, although the two men who made the boundary by treaty in 1819 (U.S. secretary of state John Quincy Adams and the Spanish minister in Washington Don Luís Onís) had no reliable geographic knowledge of the area. The Siskiyou Pass is in southern Oregon, about four miles north of the California boundary, and is crossed today by I-5.

Mount Shasta

"Lonely as God, and white as a winter moon, Mount Shasta starts up sudden and solitary from the heart of the great black forests of Northern California."

Thus did the picture of this majestic peak imprint itself upon the mind and heart of Joaquin Miller, who spent several years of his youth within the radius of its influence. The beautiful legend of how the Great Spirit "made this mountain first of all" was told to him by the native people among whom he lived. That story included the long-held Shasta Indian tradition that "before the white man came they could see the fire ascending from the mountain by night and the smoke by day, every time they chose to look in that direction."

"Shasta," wrote John Muir, "is a fire-mountain, an old volcano gradually accumulated and built up into the blue deep of the sky by successive eruptions of ashes and molten lava." Periods of quiescence intervened between eruptions. Then the glacial winter came on, "a down-crawling mantle of ice upon a foundation of smouldering fire, crushing and grinding its brown, flinty lavas, and thus degrading and remodeling the entire mountain." The summit was a mass of ruins, considerably lowered, and the sides deeply grooved and fluted. Beneath the snowy surface the fires still glowed, but the glaciers still flowed on, "sculpturing the mountain with stern, resistless energy."

Five of these glaciers—Bolam, Hotlum, Whitney, Wintun, and Konwakiton—still scour the sides of the great mountain, principally on the north and east slopes above the 10,000-foot level. Hundreds of streams are fed by these ice rivers; Big Spring, one source of the Sacramento River, gushes from the mountainside in a cold flood just one mile north of Mount Shasta City. John Muir describes the fountainhead of the McCloud River thus: "Think of a spring giving rise to a river, a spring fifty yards wide at the mouth, issuing from the base of a lava bluff with wild songs—not gloomily from a dark cavey mouth, but from a world of ferns and mosses gold and green."

The Mud Creek area, four miles northeast of McCloud, was devastated in August 1924 by a vast flow of mud washed down by the melting snows of the Konwakiton Glacier. Water and sediment spread out from the creek bed over the country, killing a vast extent of timber and leaving a desolate waste.

Shasta's snowy summit, at 14,162 feet, dominates the landscape for a hundred miles and is visible for almost twice that distance. The first recorded mention of it, as "Shatasla," was in 1814, in the journal of Alexander Henry, an early mountain man. It is possible that Spanish explorers in 1817 observed it from a distance when Father Narciso Durán, accompanied by Luís Argüello, led an expedition from San Francisco by boat up the Sacramento River, reaching as far north as the mouth of the Feather River. Durán made this entry in his journal on May 20: "At about ten leagues to the northwest of this place we saw the very high hill called

by soldiers that went near its slope 'Jesus Maria.' It is entirely covered with snow." There is no way of knowing, however, whether this mountain was in fact Mount Shasta.

Peter Skene Ogden, a Hudson's Bay Company trapper, wintered on the streams east and north of the mountain in 1826–27, and on February 14, 1827, he wrote in his journal: "There is a mountain equal in height to Mount Hood or Vancouver I have named Mt. Sastise." In reference to the stream he wrote: "I have named this river Sastise River."

Shasta is undoubtedly a word of Indian origin, although both derivation and meaning are uncertain. Odgen says that he derived "these names from the tribes of Indians" living there, and according to Stephen Powers, Shas-ti-ka was the tribal name of the people in this region. (Alleged Russian or French origins for the name—*tchastal*, "white," and *chaste*, "pure"—are now generally discredited.)

English and American explorers during the early part of the nineteenth century viewed the great mountain and placed it on their maps under variant spellings. Lieutenant Emmons, of the Wilkes Exploring Expedition, who saw it on October 3, 1841, mentioned it in his report and on accompanying maps as "Mount Shaste"; Frémont, who five years later saw it while on his third expedition, referred to it in his subsequent report as "Shastl" and on his map of 1848 as "Tsashtl"; Lieutenant Robert S. Williamson, of the United States Topographical Engineers, in his report of the expedition that surveyed for a railroad route from Oregon to the Sacramento Valley in 1851 and 1855, designated the mountain "Shasta Butte," *butte* being a name freely used by American trappers in the West.

The first recorded ascent of Mount Shasta appears to have been made by Captain E. D. Pearce in August or September 1854. Shortly after, Pearce led a party of thirteen adventurous citizens from Yreka, Humbug, and Scott valleys to the summit. Other ascents followed. Israel S. Diehl, of Yreka, climbed to the top alone on October 11, 1855. He was followed by a German, Anton Roman, in April 1856. Joaquin Miller, who ascended the mountain several times, climbed it for the last time in 1858 at the age of seventeen. It was his book, *Life Amongst the Modocs,* written in London in 1873, that made Mount Shasta known to the world.

The first scientific ascent of the mountain was made in September 1862 by Josiah Dwight Whitney, head of the state Geological Survey, his chief assistant, William H. Brewer, and Chester Averill. Clarence King discovered the glaciers on Mount Shasta in 1870. Captain A. F. Rodgers, of the United States Coast and Geodetic Survey, began a series of observations from the summit in 1875. In October of that year he erected a steel monument, some fourteen feet high and capped by a nickel reflector, on the highest point. This monument stood for many years. In the summer of 1877 John Muir visited Mount Shasta's forests and wild gardens with Sir Joseph Hooker, the great English botanist, and Professor Asa Gray, America's foremost botanist at that time. B. A. Colonna, of the Coast and Geodetic Survey, spent nine successive days and nights on the summit of Mount Shasta in July and August 1878. At the end of that period he succeeded in exchanging heliograph flashes with observers posted on Mount St. Helena, 192 miles to the south.

Mount Shasta is in the middle of the 29,260 acres of the Mount Shasta Wilderness, which lies entirely within Shasta National Forest. The Sierra Club erected the stone Shasta Alpine Lodge in 1922 at Horse Camp (7,992 feet), nine miles from Mount Shasta City.

The Modoc Lava Beds

For the archaeologist and the student of early Western history, as well as for the lover of unique natural formations, the Modoc Lava Beds in the Lava Beds National Monument hold a great fascination. This region was once the domain of the Modoc Indians. The Modoc name for the region is said to have meant "the land of burned-out fires," and its labyrinthine caves, seemingly bottomless fumaroles, and extinct craters testify to the fitness of that designation. This vast mesa-like formation is broken here and there by buttes or cinder cones several hundred feet high; the harsh outlines of these volcanic masses are relieved by the contrast of blossoming plants and shrubs, clumps of pine and juniper, and beautiful varicolored rock.

Lava Beds National Monument, established in 1925, lies at the eastern edge of Siskiyou County, a portion extending further east into Modoc County. A good road traverses the region, leaving SR 139 at Newell in Modoc County in the north and returning to that road near Tionesta, also in Modoc County, in the south.

From the visitors' center near the southeast entrance to the monument, a short drive takes one past a series of remarkable natural phenomena. Indian Well, for instance, has two pools of crystal-clear ice water that never seem to diminish, even during the driest seasons. Near Indian Well are Labyrinth Cave, Skull Cave, Symbol Cave, and Symbol Bridge. Labyrinth Cave is a series of subterranean cells connected by a maze of tunnels running in all directions, the main gallery being almost two miles in length, with a part of the distance navigable only in a crouching position. Skull Cave, the largest cavern in the region yet explored, has three stories at its lower end. A river of ice covers the floor of the lower chamber and in it are imbedded numerous skulls of Rocky Mountain sheep and pronghorn antelope, bones of now-extinct animals, and even scattered human bones. On the rocks and about one of the entrances to Symbol Cave are clear and unfaded Indian pictographs. In a separate portion of the monument are striking Indian petroglyphs, described in the Modoc County chapter.

Beyond Symbol Bridge and Antelope Well, with its abundant, clear, sweet water, is Bearpaw Cave, a series of rock and ice chambers connected by underground corridors. One of the chambers contains a river of ice that lasts throughout the year, while at the opposite end of the abyss another immense cavity holds an unfailing water supply. Sentinel Cave, Crystal Cave, Chocolate Bridge, Painted Cave, Jove's Thunderbolt, and "The Chimneys" (large vents projecting twenty feet or more above the ground and extending straight down into the earth to a depth so great that a rock dropped from the top cannot be heard to strike bottom) are among the natural phenomena most accessible to the tourist. The Catacombs Cavern, the most beautiful of the entire group, resembles a medieval cathedral, its roof buttressed by massive columns and the walls and ceilings frescoed by a delicate coral-like formation traced in fanciful designs. About 150 caves in this interesting group have been discovered and explored.

North of the lava beds is the Tule Lake National Wildlife Refuge. To the northwest and extending into Oregon is the Lower Klamath National Wildlife Refuge, which has been declared a National Historic Landmark. Established in 1908, this was one of the first major waterfowl reserves in the United States.

Sheep Rock

At the foot of Shasta Pass twenty miles north of Sisson's Station (now Mount Shasta City), the first wagon road from the Sacramento Valley to Yreka led over a low divide from the eastern slopes of the mountain into Shasta Valley. There the bold and craggy summit of Sheep Rock rises 2,000 feet above the gray sagebrush and sand of the valley and 5,714 feet above sea level. The rock's several square miles of comparatively level surface, dotted with bunch grass, were one of the chief winter pastures of the wild mountain sheep that came down from the high ridges of Mount Shasta to the warm lava crags and plateaus of Sheep Rock, where the snow never lies deep. Stockmen still follow the ruts of the old stage road at Sheep Rock.

A marker has been placed on US 97 about fifteen miles northeast of Weed at a point 600 feet south of the crossing of the old emigrant trail (SRL 517). The marker stands at the intersection of the old Military Pass Road from Fort Crook in Shasta County.

John Muir, who loved and explored Mount Shasta from summit to base, wrote with characteristic enthusiasm: "Far better than climbing the mountain is going around its warm fertile base, enjoying its bounties like a bee circling around a bank of flowers. The distance is about a hundred miles, [and] a good level road may be found all the way round, by Shasta Valley, Sheep Rock, Elk Flat, Huckleberry Valley, Squaw Valley, following for a considerable portion of the way the old Emigrant Road, which lies along the east disk of the mountain, and is deeply worn by the wagons of the early gold-seekers." Portions of this old road are still used by the Forest Service and it is possible during the summer months to drive around Mount Shasta, a distance of 65 miles from Weed or Mount Shasta City. The road takes one through aspen thickets and forests of Shasta fir, across glacial washes, and to points where superb views may be had, all within a few miles of the snow belt.

Marble Mountain

The Marble Mountain Wilderness Area in the Klamath National Forest is a region of magnificent mountains and forests covering 237,527 acres. In it lies Marble Mountain, from which the area derives its name.

Lying between the Klamath River and its tributary, Scott River, the Marble Mountain Range culminates in a castellated peak, 7,396 feet in elevation. Composed of limestone, a large proportion of which is marble of high commercial value, the rugged grandeur and the "monumental purity" of this massive upheaval inspired the traditions and beliefs of the Indians, who knew the peak as the "White Mountain."

Owing to its striking appearance, Marble Mountain served as a landmark for early pioneers, and the Kelsey Trail, lying almost directly at its base, was one of the first paths ever blazed across these mountains into Scott Valley. Travelers over this rugged trail almost invariably halted to gaze upward with wonder and amazement at the beetling cliffs and towering domes of Marble Mountain rising above them. This route, at best a rough and dangerous one for man and beast, was long ago abandoned for more accessible passes through the mountains.

The California-Oregon Trail

Lying halfway between San Francisco Bay and the Columbia River, the Siskiyou region, first crossed by trappers and settlers, was soon marked by a well-defined route of travel. This trail was the principal thoroughfare during the gold period. Today's trade and commerce continue to flow over it. In general, it has been called the California-Oregon Trail, but it should be noted that this term has been applied to several other routes to and from Oregon through northern California. The earliest was the coast route, through what is now Del Norte County, blazed by Jedediah Strong Smith in 1828 and followed for a time by Hudson's Bay Company trappers. Alexander R. McLeod, for whom the McCloud River is named, was the first of these, in 1829.

In 1830 Peter Skene Ogden, another Hudson's Bay agent, opened up a route by way of Klamath Lake, and in his footsteps came Michel La Framboise, the leader of trapping expeditions from the north during the years from 1830 to 1845. The central route leading up the Sacramento River Canyon was first crossed in its entire length by Ewing Young in 1834. During the 1850's, when gold mining was the chief industry of the Siskiyou region, two variations of the latter route developed, one of which led around the eastern base of Mount Shasta while the other crossed over Trinity and Scott mountains into Scott Valley and thence to Yreka.

Ewing Young, on his way to settle in Oregon in 1834, was the first to follow the California-Oregon Trail around the western base of Mount Shasta. A scarcity of cattle in the Willamette Valley led Young to return to the San Francisco Bay region in 1837. Driving 700 Spanish longhorns, he and about twenty other men started for Oregon, and succeeded in bringing 680 of the animals over the rugged mountains of the Sacramento River Canyon into Shasta Valley. In 1843 the enterprising Joseph Gale, with a much larger herd of livestock, made the same difficult climb.

The old trail and the difficulties experienced by the many early travelers who passed over it are described in the journals of Philip L. Edwards, diarist of the Young party of 1837; in the George Emmons report of the Wilkes Expedition in 1841; in the account by Lansford W. Hastings of his trip in 1843; and in the diary of James Clyman, depicting vividly a journey in 1845. By 1840 California began to attract settlers, and every year of that decade saw an increasing number of emigrants passing over the California-Oregon Trail from the Willamette Valley to the Sacramento Valley, the climax being reached during the years of the gold rush, 1848–53.

Lieutenant Emmons and his men camped on September 28, 1841, at the foot of the Boundary Range (the Siskiyou Mountains) within sight of Pilot Rock, "a singular, isolated rock, which stands like a tower on the top of the ridge, rising above the surrounding forest with a bare and apparently unbroken surface. . . .

From its top an extensive country is overlooked, and as soon as the party came in sight of it a dense column of smoke arose, which was thought to be a signal made by the Klamet Indians, to the Shaste tribe, of the approach of our party." Charles Wilkes, commander of the entire expedition, named this Emmons' Peak, in honor of the officer in charge of the California contingent of the expedition, but the name Pilot Rock has since been applied to it. Located in southern Oregon, it is visible for many miles on both sides of the mountains.

When the Wilkes Expedition passed through the Siskiyous they feared attacks by hostile Indians, who were determined to keep the white invaders out. The party avoided all contact with the natives and thereby frustrated one of the main objectives of the trip, that of making detailed observations of the Indians in their natural habitat. Ascending the Siskiyou Mountains on September 29, the party was in constant fear of these so-called "Rogues." To the travelers the whole mountainside seemed "admirably adapted for an ambuscade." However, little difficulty was encountered and at the summit the men had their first glorious view of the "Klamet Valley," and of "Mount Shaste, a high, snowy peak, of a sugar-loaf form, which rose through the distant haze."

Descending the southern slope of the Siskiyous, the expedition pitched their tents on "Otter Creek [now Camp Creek] within a mile of the Klamet River," and on October 1 they camped on the Shasta River, somewhere near the site of the present town of Montague. There they found Indians spearing abundant quantities of salmon. Near the present Gazelle, not far from Sheep Rock, large herds of antelope, as well as long-horned mountain sheep, were seen the next day. At midday the party left the Shasta Valley and camped on a stream near the site of the present town of Edgewood, formerly Butteville. This place was the camping ground of a tribe of Indians, which Emmons observed closely and which he pronounced "a fine-looking race," extremely skillful in the manufacture and use of the bow and arrow. Continuing their journey on October 3, the travelers "entered the forest on the slopes of the Shaste Range. . . . After passing this ridge, they soon met the head waters of the Sacramento, flowing to the southward, and their camp was pitched on the banks of another stream, that came from the Shaste Peak." This was in Strawberry Valley.

Little escaped the observation of James Clyman when he climbed the Siskiyous and made his way down the Sacramento River Canyon in 1845. His diary is full of vivid descriptions revealing the rugged character of the old trail. Like other early travelers he was constantly on guard against Indian attacks. Climbing the

"Siskiew mountain" on June 23, the party neared the summit, where there was "a bad thicket to pass whare nearly all the parties passing this Trail have been attacted." The Clyman company, however, met with no misadventure and soon came in sight of the vast wilderness lying to the south, "wild and awfully sublime." On June 24, the "Clamet" (Klamath) River was crossed, a few hundred feet east of the present bridge near the site of the now extinct lumbering camp of Klamathon (1890–1900) near the mouth of Willow Creek. Following up Willow Creek on June 25, the emigrants passed over Little Shasta River, where they made camp and where Clyman noted the striking volcanic character of Shasta Valley. A modern traveler, looking on its strange beauty for the first time, may share Clyman's wonder at this unique landscape.

Clyman's party traversed the valley the next day; after crossing the Shasta River, they set up camp on a site near the present town of Edgewood. From this point Clyman describes Pilot Rock, plainly visible across the Oregon border to the north. They resumed the line of march on June 28, and passed through what would later be known as Wagon Valley. To the east of the pass rose the snowy peaks of Mount Shasta, while on the west stood Mount Eddy, the whole region magnificently timbered.

The first wagon party to cross the Siskiyou Mountains into California was led by Lindsey Applegate in June 1849. After climbing the mountains with their six wagons, the little party crossed Shasta Valley to what became known as Wagon Valley. The feelings of remoteness and the anxiety about the Indians caused the emigrants to abandon their project and return to Oregon, leaving four of the cumbersome wagons to rot in the wilderness. Governor Joseph Lane of Oregon Territory, en route to the California gold fields in 1850, also abandoned a wagon in this locality. The iron from these vehicles was salvaged and sold during World War I.

The first wagon team (1854) and the first transportation by stage and freight team (the California Stage Company, 1856) from the Sacramento Valley crossed the Pit River at Fall River Mills in Shasta County. Continuing northwest, the road passed around the eastern base of Mount Shasta, down through Sheep Rock Pass into Shasta Valley, and then again northwest to Yreka. From there it continued northeast, crossing the Shasta River about five miles northwest of Montague. The Klamath River was ferried just north of its junction with Willow Creek, where the road became identical with the older trail followed by trappers on their way over the Siskiyou Mountains. The part of the road that passed east of Mount Shasta was used for about a year, until Indian troubles caused traffic to be transferred to the Yreka-Callahan-Shasta route. This route became known as the California-Oregon Stage Road and was operated until the advent of the railroad in 1887–88.

Henry Slicer had already opened a stage line to Callahan's in 1854. After abandoning the route around the eastern base of Mount Shasta, the California Stage Company bought out Greathouse and Slicer and began, at great expense, to complete the road to the town of Shasta (in early days sometimes called Shasta City). This road was pushed over Trinity Mountain in 1857, and in 1859 Scott Mountain was also crossed. Meanwhile the Oregon Stage Company had completed its turnpike over the Siskiyous. It connected with the California Stage Line at Yreka in 1860, and a through route was thus staged for the first time from Portland, Oregon, to Sacramento, California. It was over this route that the first telegraph line from California to Oregon was constructed.

After 1870 the route from Yreka to the Klamath River went by way of the Anderson Grade, crossing the Shasta River about four miles north of Yreka. On this road the Ten Mile House, a stage station of the 1870's, still stands. Ascending the mountain over a high-line grade, the road descended to the Klamath River about six miles south of Cottonwood (now Henley), where the river was ferried. The trail of the trappers over the Siskiyous continued to be used from this point on. Pioneer Bridge on SR 263 was erected over the Shasta River three miles north of Yreka in 1931 and dedicated to the memory of the early-day stage drivers who traveled this road.

Stopping Places on the California-Oregon Trail

Along the old California-Oregon Trail many historic spots, stopping places for a long succession of travelers, invite the interest of the present-day visitor. They were, at first, mere campsites (in some cases, on or near the old Indian rancherias) where the trailblazers and their immediate successors, the trappers and explorers of the 1830's and 1840's, stopped on their way through the wilderness. The sites have been identified by means of diaries and journals kept by a few of these earliest travelers. Before long, the faint trails of the pathfinders were being widened by the feet of settlers seeking new homes, and they, too, have left records of favored campsites.

With the discovery of gold in California, the procession down the Oregon Trail became a flood of humanity bound for the numerous El Dorados that California had opened. Hotels or inns were built on the early campgrounds and proved popular stopping places for gold-seekers and settlers. With the coming of the first wagons a road was constructed, and soon the picturesque mule trains were superseded by freighters and stagecoaches. Then the wayside inns became stage stations, with towns growing up about them. When the Southern Pacific Railroad was constructed from Redding into Oregon in 1886–87, its route was practically identical with that of the California-Oregon Trail and portions of the early stage road. Many of the railroad stations are on the exact line of the first trail, or very close to it.

Upper Soda Springs, the southernmost Siskiyou County station on the Oregon Trail, is today in the northern part of Dunsmuir. The stage station is long gone. An important railroad center, Dunsmuir was first called "Pusher" because extra engines were added to northbound trains at this point to push them over the summit. When Alexander Dunsmuir passed through in 1886, he was so charmed by the place that he offered to give a fountain to the town if it were renamed after him, and the bargain was made. The central part of Dunsmuir, flanked by the large old brick railroad hotel, is on the National Register of Historic Places. The Dunsmuir Museum at 4101 Pine Street has an excellent collection on the history of the railroad and the community. Near Upper Soda Springs, in Railroad Park, Southern Pacific engine 1727, which was in service on the line over the summit, is on permanent display.

The next camp on the old trail, which here ran about half a mile west of the present I-5, was located in Strawberry Valley, where a settlement grew up in the early 1850's. A post office was established in 1870 under the name of Berryvale. For twelve years J. H. Sisson was postmaster and hotelkeeper. When the railroad came through in 1887, the station, one mile east of Berryvale, was named Sisson's, and the town that soon grew up on the new site was called Sisson, a name it bore until 1924, when it was changed to Mount Shasta.

Southern Pacific Locomotive, Railroad Park, Dunsmuir

Sisson's Hotel at Berryvale was a favorite summer resort and outfitting point for early-day mountain climbers. From there, trails radiated in all directions: Mount Shasta, with its glaciers and panoramas of northern California, southern Oregon, and western Nevada; Black Butte, an odd cinder cone that sits like a dwarf in the shadow of Mount Shasta; Mount Eddy, with its lovely Shasta lilies and Castle Lake; and the flowery fringes and wooded streams of Strawberry Valley.

The Old Stage Road still exists in Mount Shasta and runs by the State Fish Hatchery on the west side of town. The hatchery was established in 1888 and can be visited by the public. At the time it was built it was the largest in the world. The building closest to the road, old Hatchery A, built in 1909, is now the Sisson Hatchery Museum, opened in 1983. The history of both the town and the mountain named Mount Shasta is chronicled here. The museum houses many changing as well as permanent exhibits and much interesting material on the history of railroading in the area.

Sisson's Hotel stood from 1865 to 1916 almost at the top of the low hill just before the hatchery gate. Across the road is the site of the Strawberry Valley stage station (SRL 396). On the same side of the road as this site is a small white house with a red roof; this was the old post office and store kept by Mrs. S. J. Fellows, who followed J. H. Sisson as postmaster.

About fifteen miles north of Berryvale the old trail passed the site of Butteville (now Edgewood), a camping ground mentioned in most of the early journals. From Butteville the trail proceeded to Edson's (now Gazelle) and thence across the Shasta Valley. The Shasta River was forded near the site of Montague, where there was an important campsite, and continued to Willow Creek. After 1850 the trail, which had developed into a stage road, made a detour to Yreka and rejoined the old trail before it reached Willow Creek.

Near where Willow Creek runs into the Klamath River from the south, the next stopping place on the old emigrant trail was not far from the site of the later settlement of Klamathon. Proceeding downstream three miles to Cottonwood Creek, which runs into the Klamath from the north, the trail followed up Cottonwood Creek Canyon and crossed the summit of the Siskiyous about where the present railroad passes over. The last camp before reaching Oregon was made in the canyon of Cottonwood Creek just before the trail began climbing over the mountain.

In 1870 the stage road into Oregon was rerouted over the so-called Anderson Grade. Cottonwood (later Henley) was the place where stagecoaches and freighters en route from Yreka to Oregon changed horses

from 1860 to 1887, when the completion of the railroad ended stage operations.

Trails of the Northern El Dorado

The first Argonauts from Oregon passed through Siskiyou County without stopping to prospect its streams, and no mining was done there until the summer of 1850. In June of that year gold-seekers penetrated the wild and rugged Salmon Mountains. Crossing the ridge from the North Fork of the Trinity River, they came upon the South Fork of the Salmon River, down which they followed to the mouth of the North Fork, where rich diggings were found. The camp established at this point came to be known as the Forks of the Salmon, and during the summer several hundred men gathered there. From this central point they spread up the North Fork of the Salmon River and over the divide into the Scott River Valley.

Meanwhile, a party of miners had traveled the length of the Klamath River from its mouth to the Shasta River, panning for gold at every bar. "It was this group of miners," says David Rhys Jones, "that established the course of the Klamath River below the junction of the Shasta. From that time on, the river that had been variously known as the Clamitte, the Klamet, Indian Scalp River, and Smith River, has borne the name by which it was known near its source." Again, Jones says that "prior to 1850 all maps delineating the Klamath River represented its source and upper course correctly—as it had been observed by trappers. The course of the river below Shasta River was unexplored, but the mouth of a large stream in southern Oregon had been crossed by Jedediah S. Smith in 1828. This was the mouth of the Rogue. So the Hudson's Bay Company map presented to Wilkes, and published as part of his travel records, shows the Klamath River turning back into Oregon through the Siskiyous, below the Shasta, and emptying into the ocean at the mouth of the Rogue."

When winter approached, the miners on the Klamath left for the settlements of the Sacramento Valley, following a southerly course and passing the future sites of Yreka and Greenhorn, where gold was discovered on the creek. A few miles to the east they came upon the Oregon Trail, where they found a fresh wagon track. Camping that night near the site of Edson's, they reached Wagon Valley the following day. There they found the abandoned wagon that Governor Joseph Lane had recently transported across the Siskiyou Mountains. Later they overtook Lane himself, bound for the gold fields.

In San Francisco two years before, while on his way to organize the Oregon territory, Lane had resisted the gold fever, but in the summer of 1850 it hit him. With the gold fields on the Sierra Nevada as an objective, he crossed the border into California. Lane's party did a little incidental prospecting on the Klamath River and on the Shasta River at Joe Lane's Bar near the mouth of Yreka Creek. The following year Lane came to Siskiyou County at the head of a large company of men bound for Scott Bar, where they did considerable mining.

Scott Valley was first explored in 1850 by a group of miners led by John Scott, who had crossed the Salmon Mountains from the North Fork of the Salmon River. These men panned for gold at a point on Scott River named Scott Bar for their leader. Indians soon drove them from this location. Returning to the Salmon River and crossing the mountains to the Trinity River, they spread the news of their discovery of gold at Scott Bar. Many parties started at once for the new location and the place was soon overcrowded with miners. As a result, prospecting parties spread over the entire region, and many new diggings, the scene of thriving camps in 1851, were uncovered.

One such find was the chance discovery of gold on the site later occupied by Yreka. This location attracted little attention at the time, for a rich bonanza was found at Ingall's Gulch on Greenhorn Creek soon afterward. Its discoverers came to Scott Bar for provisions, where they organized as secretly as possible and returned to Ingall's Gulch. They were followed, however, and while they lay asleep their claims were occupied by others. This was the beginning of mining on Greenhorn Creek, in January 1851.

Salmon River Camps

The first mining camp up the Salmon River from its mouth is Somes Bar. Today a country store there serves a small scattered population. Continuing up the river, one finds it difficult to imagine that in the early 1850's every bar, creek, and gulch along the river's course teemed with miners.

Forks of Salmon had a population of several hundred in the summer of 1850, although fewer than 50 spent the winter of 1850–51 there. Before winter had passed, the report of rich diggings attracted miners from all directions, many rushing to the spot without supplies. As a result, when late snows blocked the trails in March, thousands all up and down the Salmon River and its branches were on the verge of starvation. Apparently supplies were somehow gotten through. Forks of Salmon still exists as a small settlement.

Sawyer's Bar, on the North Fork of the Salmon River, has been hard hit by fires, and the only historic building remaining there is St. Joseph's Catholic Church, built in the 1850's of whipsawed lumber. Father Florian Schwenninger, a Benedictine monk from the Austrian Tyrol, was the pastor here until 1866, a tireless school-teacher, musician, and artist as well as missionary to the mining towns of Siskiyou County. The oil painting of the Crucifixion that Father Florian brought from Austria still hangs over the altar in St. Joseph's Church, which has been restored and is used for services on a limited basis. Paradise Flat, the little piece of ground on which it stands, has never been mined and is thought to contain a small fortune in gold. South of Sawyer's Bar are a number of quartz mines, chief among them being the Black Bear Mine seven or eight miles to the southwest. Material for the mill of this mine was carried over the mountains on muleback or dragged in on sleds by oxen.

Scott Valley

Scott Valley, named for John Scott, the discoverer of gold at Scott Bar, is still the beautiful, "rich bottom, with fertile ranches, surrounded with high and very steep mountains, rough and rugged, and furrowed into very deep canyons," described by William H. Brewer, who visited the region in the autumn of 1863. Formerly famed for its rich gold production, the valley is now devoted to agriculture.

The Scott Bar of 1850 was located a few hundred yards above and on the opposite bank of Scott River from the Scott Bar of 1851 and succeeding years. The old trail of the 1850's zigzagged for three miles through the precipitous canyon that lay between Scott Bar and the mouth of the Scott River, the canyon proper being, in many places, at least 3,000 feet deep. In the early 1850's this great gorge was teeming with life. Among the bustling camps of the region were French Bar, Johnson's Bar, Poorman's Bar, Lytle's Bar, Slapjack Bar, Michigan Bar, and Junction Bar. Governor Lane worked Lane's Gulch on Whitney Hill near Scott Bar in 1851.

Some of the old buildings in the vicinity of Scott Bar are still intact. The Quartz Hill Mine has yielded millions, and continued to operate into the twentieth century.

Etna Mills (now Etna), originally known as Rough and Ready Mills, grew up around the flour mill established there in 1856 in competition with a neighboring concern known as the Etna Mills, erected in 1854. There was considerable rivalry between the two communities, but the newer place finally won out as a town in 1863, when the post office was shifted from Etna Mills to the more successful Rough and Ready. Since there was already a Rough and Ready in Nevada County, the name of its rival, Etna Mills, was given to the new post office.

Etna, now a town of about 600 inhabitants, lies in the midst of a rich agricultural district shut in by the heavily forested Salmon Mountains to the west and the Scott Mountains on the south and east. Its main street has several charming old buildings and willow-shaded sidewalks.

Callahan

Callahan's Ranch, or Callahan, near the junction of the East and South forks of the Scott River, was the first stopping place after crossing Scott Mountain from the south. Here in the autumn of 1851 M. B. Callahan opened a public house and store. Soon after Callahan sold out in 1855, the place became the terminus of Greathouse and Slicer's stage line from Yreka, which used the two Concord coaches that Henry Slicer had brought over the Siskiyou Mountains from Oregon in 1854, the first in Siskiyou County. At Callahan's, passengers were transferred to mules for the difficult journey over Scott Mountain to the Trinity River and over the Trinity Mountains to French Gulch and the town of Shasta.

The Callahan Ranch Hotel, built in 1854, was originally a stage stop and later a hotel; it is now closed. Across the street is a general store, The Emporium, that has been in business at the same spot since the early days of this century.

Fort Jones

Fort Jones was established in 1852 as an army station protecting settlers and miners against hostile Indians. It was named for Colonel Roger Jones, Adjutant General of the Army from 1825 to 1852. The fort was abandoned in 1858, and the frame houses that had replaced the first log cabins were purchased and moved into town. The site of the fort (SRL 317) is one mile south of the town of Fort Jones on SR 3 and Scott Valley Road. Three of the men serving at Fort Jones, upon their discharge from the Army, became pioneer settlers of the valley. The town of Fort Jones was originally named Wheelock and was a stage station on the road from Yreka to Shasta. The Fort Jones House on East Main Street has been marked by E Clampus Vitus as the principal building of the community since the 1850's. Callahan, Etna, and Fort Jones are today linked by SR 3.

Yreka

In March 1851 a gold strike was made at Yreka Flats, an event that brought 2,000 men to the spot in less than six weeks. This discovery was made by Abraham Thompson in a ravine later known as Black Gulch. The camp that grew up was called Thompson's Dry Diggings and was located on a knoll near a spring at the intersection of the present Yama and Discovery streets in Yreka.

Meanwhile, miners' cabins were built for three miles along Yreka Creek from Greenhorn to Hawkinsville, and business soon moved away from the flats and nearer to the creek. A town, at first called Shasta Butte City, was laid on in May 1851. To avoid confusion with the older Shasta City (in Shasta County), the name was changed to Yreka, which phoneticized the Indian name for Mount Shasta, I-e-ka. (Gudde says that the intended spelling was "Wyreka" and that the present version is due to a clerical error.) When Siskiyou County was formally organized by the state legislature in 1852, Yreka was designated the county seat, and so it remains.

Among the episodes that enlivened the early history of Yreka, the Greenhorn War of 1855 was perhaps the most exciting. This was a contest over water rights waged by two mining factions, the Yreka Flats Ditch Association and the miners on Lower Greenhorn Creek. The latter precipitated the war when they cut the Yreka Flats Ditch because it was diverting water from their claims on the creek. The matter was taken before the local court, which supported the Yreka faction and enjoined against further cutting of the ditch. The injunction was disobeyed and the guilty party arrested. This was the signal for the Greenhorn miners to act. In a body they marched to the Yreka jail and got the prisoner released after an encounter with the law. Nevertheless, the decision of the court stood, and the Yreka Flats Ditch Association continued to use the water brought from Greenhorn Creek.

Law and order gradually emerged in Yreka, but only after the first excitement of gold fever died away and more sober industries such as lumbering became the basis of the town's economy. On July 4, 1871, one-third of the town of Yreka burned within one terrifying hour. The brick structures downtown survived and today are part of the Historic District (SRL 901) of Yreka, centered on Third Street from Lennox Street to Center Street and branching out along Miner Street from Main Street to Oregon Street. A walking-tour guide to the houses and buildings, most of which are marked with the date of their building, can be ob-

Van Choate-Rosborough House, Yreka

tained in town. A walk through this district is a delightful experience, and the plaques on the old houses are clear and readable. The historic district was first identified and marked in 1972.

On Miner Street, then as now a commercial thoroughfare, one can see the City Meat Market at 319, built in 1854 and now a restaurant; the Livingston and Bro. building at 311–313, from either 1854 or 1855; and a dozen others, all well marked. The I.O.O.F. building at 107–111 Miner Street, built in 1859, is perhaps the most imposing of these structures.

Third Street is principally residential, and its many charming old buildings are all marked and all still lived in. At 301 Third Street is the Van Choate–Rosborough house (1858), a one-and-one-half-story house with red siding and white trim; at 216 is the Ivy house (1899), with an elegant veranda on the two stories facing the street; at 122 is the Cummins-Forest home (1855), a frame house with apple trees in the side yard. Walking through the old, preserved neighborhoods of California towns is one of the great pleasures for the historian and traveler.

At the south end of Yreka is the Siskiyou County Museum, housed in a replica of the Callahan Ranch Hotel at 910 South Main Street. On the museum's grounds are log cabins from mining and lumbering days and a remarkable and extensive collection of mining gear. Within the Siskiyou County courthouse on Fourth Street is a special adjunct of the county museum, a display focusing on the mining activities of the county, with information on the differences between the gold nuggets found in different regions.

Hawkinsville and Greenhorn

Many mining camps formerly existed near Yreka. Two miles to the north was Frogtown, founded in 1851.

The following year, when the Oregon Trail went through, Frogtown was moved to higher ground and renamed Hawkinsville. An E Clampus Vitus plaque commemorates Frogtown two miles north of Yreka on SR 263. The brick Catholic church at Hawkinsville was remodeled from a structure originally built in 1858. This church is no longer in use, although it stands in the center of the village. To the south of Yreka was Greenhorn, a settlement of miners' cabins.

The name Greenhorn is typical of the unique nomenclature that grew out of the rough life of the Argonauts. A company of miners had dug a ditch some distance back from the creek, but finding their claims unprofitable they had abandoned the location. A new arrival, at once dubbed a "greenhorn" by his more experienced companions, asked where he could find a good place to work. Thinking to enjoy a joke at his expense, the miners directed the young fellow to the hill they had just vacated. The "greenhorn," setting to work on the abandoned ditch, was rewarded by a rich strike, which he kept a secret. When the jokers finally learned that the "greenhorn" had been quietly working the richest ground along the creek, there was a rush for claims on the new lead. To perpetuate the joke, so the story goes, the creek was called "Greenhorn," a name it still bears. Similar stories have been told in other sections of the mining regions in California to explain the origin of the name.

Vast piles of rock and gravel that fill the canyons and gullies with debris in the hills to the south of Yreka give evidence of early mining operations. These relics will long disfigure the landscape with their gaunt, gray sterility, covering spots once made beautiful with the delicate hues of wildflowers, the pale blue of juniper berries, and the autumn flame of the Oregon grape.

The story of Indian Peggy forms a romantic episode in Yreka's history. In the 1850's Peggy's people, the Klamaths, were preparing to attack the encroaching white settlers. Trying to avoid bloodshed, Peggy traveled twenty miles over rough mountains to warn the settlers. When the Klamath warriors approached the town along the devious trails of the brush-covered hills, they found it strongly guarded by sentries and were forced to retreat.

For years after this event, Peggy, fearing to associate with her kinfolk, lived among the people of Yreka, who never forgot the service she had rendered. When the remnants of her tribe were finally placed on the reservation four miles to the south of town, Indian Peggy was pensioned and cared for until her death at the advanced age of 105 years. Her grave, on private property, memorializes her deed.

Humbug City

Ten miles northwest of Yreka, Humbug City once flourished on Humbug Creek, where gold was discovered in May 1851. The story goes that a company of men on their way to mine on the creek were met by a returning group who said it was all a humbug. Undaunted, the first group continued to the stream, where they set to work with pan and rocker. Their diligence was rewarded, and with a wry twist they called it Humbug Creek. News of the find spread quickly, and before long the stream was thronged with miners and dotted with camps.

Joaquin Miller, who as a youth lived among the Indians of the Siskiyous, often joined the miners in their search for gold along the various streams. He draws a rather gloomy picture of the Humbug mining region: "It lay west of the city [Yreka], a day's ride down in a deep, densely timbered cañon, out of sight of Mount Shasta, out of sight of everything—even the sun; save here and there where a landslide had ploughed up the forest, or the miners had mown down the great evergreens about their cabins, or town sites in the camp."

It was a rough place, and as wild as the mountains that hemmed it in. "A sort of Hades, a savage Eden, with many Adams walking up and down, and plucking of every tree, nothing forbidden here; for here, so far as it would seem, are neither laws of God or man." The Forks, where "three little streams joined hands, and went down from there to the Klamat together," was the center of the region. Miller's cabin stood on the steep bank of the main stream, not far from the river. He was particularly impressed by the "Howlin' Wilderness," the principal saloon in the town. It was an immense log cabin with a huge fireplace, "where crackled and roared, day and night, a pine-log fire," the memory of which spelled enchantment to the poet for years after. The "Howlin' Wilderness" was the scene, too, of many a fight "in this fierce little mining camp of the Forks," and the saying, "We will have a man for breakfast tomorrow," was a common one.

The Modoc War

The coming of American miners and settlers into the Klamath Basin threatened the existence of the Modoc Indians, who began retaliation against the invaders. Federal officials set aside a reservation in southern Oregon for both the Modocs and the Klamaths, but the arrangement did not work out, and the Modocs returned to their traditional land on the Lost River. Attempts to force the tribe to return to the reservation

Cross Commemorating the Modoc War, Lava Beds National Monument

met with armed resistance on November 29, 1872, and thus began the six-month Modoc War. The Modocs, under Kientepoos, or Captain Jack, retreated into the lava beds, where the terrain gave them many advantages. An attempt in January 1873 to storm their stronghold ended in 37 Army casualties and no Modoc losses.

To avoid further bloodshed, peace talks were arranged between the Army and the Modocs. Wi-ne-ma ("Toby") Riddle, Kientepoos' cousin and the wife of a white man, acted as interpreter. Meanwhile, the Army was bringing in reinforcements. Virtually compelled to assert his leadership by agreeing to an act of violence, Kientepoos had General Edward Canby and the Rev. Eleazar Thomas shot from ambush as they came unarmed for a peace parley on April 12, 1873. Wi-ne-ma, who had warned the whites of treachery, helped their two companions to safety. With this act, any chance of a negotiated settlement was lost. Within three days, the Army had moved mortars and howitzers onto the field, and within three more days, the Modocs began a retreat that ultimately forced them to surrender. Kientepoos and three other leaders were hanged in October for the murders of Canby and Thomas, and the remainder of the tribe was exiled to far-off Oklahoma.

The battleground lies within Lava Beds National Monument. "Captain Jack's stronghold" (SRL 9), at the southern end of Tule Lake, remains almost unchanged. Rude rock forts, used by soldiers and Indians alike, are now overgrown with sage and bitterbrush. An interesting half-mile trail, marked with signposts, has been made through the area. It helps one to comprehend how fewer than 60 warriors held off an army of over 600 men for nearly five months in this half-acre of lava outcroppings. Canby's Cross (SRL 110), three miles to the west, marks the site of his murder; the Native Daughters of the Golden West have placed a monument nearby. Nine-tenths of a mile west of Canby's Cross is Guillem's Graveyard (SRL 13), where almost 100 Army casualties were buried in one spot. The bodies were removed to the National Cemetery in Washington, D.C., in the 1890's, but the rock wall surrounding the old cemetery may still be seen. Hospital Rock, an Army refuge, and Captain Jack's Cave, the Modocs' headquarters, are also in the vicinity and well marked.

This is a haunted landscape; once visited, it is not forgotten.

Solano County

Solano County, named in honor of an Indian chief, was one of the original 27 counties. The first county seat was at Benicia, but in 1858 it was removed to Fairfield.

Solano, Chief of the Suisuns

The last of the missions established in California by the Franciscan friars was at Sonoma in 1823 and was called San Francisco Solano after an illustrious Franciscan missionary to the New World who died in Peru in 1610. Father Altamira, founder of the mission, bestowed this name in baptism upon Sem Yeto, who was an exceptionally able chief over most of the rancherias between Petaluma Creek and the Sacramento River. The chief accepted the title and the new faith.

At Soscol Creek (Napa County) in 1835, a skirmish took place between Chief Solano's people and a force led by Mariano Vallejo, commandant at Sonoma. The Indians were defeated, but the two leaders became friends thereafter. One of the tribes over which Solano was chief was the Suisun ("west winds"), which occupied the valley east of the Soscol Hills, with a rancheria at present-day Rockville. When a county was formed in this area, General Vallejo suggested that it be named Solano County in honor of his friend.

Dr. Platon Vallejo, the general's son, described the relationship between the two men: "The *comandante* always held Solano . . . as a personal friend and equal. He consulted him on all things. The chief was a most welcome guest at the hacienda when the *comandante* settled at Sonoma. He might be savage still in some things. When enemies opposed him he killed them if he could, but he also had the primitive virtues of truth, honor, and everlasting good faith, and the trust placed in him was never betrayed. My father has often told me that he never came in contact with a finer mind. He was a keen, clear-headed thinker, readily grasped new ideas, learned to speak Spanish with ease and precision, and was so ready to debate that few cared to engage him in a contest of wit."

A heroic bronze statue of the chief stands on the county library grounds at the southwest corner of Texas Street and Union Avenue in Fairfield, the work of sculptor William Gordon Huff. A plaque on the grounds of Solano Community College near Rockville, placed by the Native Sons of the Golden West in 1971, marks the vicinity of the grave of the chief, the exact site of which is unknown.

Ranchos Suisun and Tolenas (Fairfield)

Rancho Suisun was the first of five Mexican grants in this county that were confirmed with patents issued by the United States government after 1848. Francisco Solano made a petition in 1837 describing himself as the "principal chief of the unconverted Indians and born captain of the Suisun" and asked for four square leagues. The land, he said, belonged to him "by hereditary right from his ancestor," and he wished to "revalidate his right." The grant was temporarily made to him and confirmed by Governor Pío Pico in 1845. The land was afterward purchased by General Vallejo, who sold it to Archibald A. Ritchie, who received patent to its 17,754 acres in 1857. On the border of this grant is Fairfield, the county seat, which was established by Ritchie's partner, Captain R. H. Waterman.

Rancho Tolenas was granted to José Francisco Armijo, "by birth a Mexican, having four sons of the same country without any lands to cultivate," in 1840, the year after he petitioned for three square leagues of land. Governor Alvarado made the grant with the proviso that Armijo should not in any manner molest the Indians already located there. The title to the 13,315 acres of the rancho was acquired by Antonio Armijo upon his father's death in 1850 and was confirmed by U.S. patent in 1868. The adobe home built on this rancho, five miles northwest of Fairfield, is long gone, but the name of Armijo lives on in a Fairfield high school.

Rancho Río de los Putos, the Wolfskill Grant

John Reed Wolfskill, the first American settler in Solano County, arrived in California in 1838 and lived in the southern part of the province with his brother William, a trapper, who had reached California a few years earlier. In 1842 John drove 96 head of cattle north to a point near the bank of Putah Creek (named for a Patwin Indian tribe), where he erected a wattle hut. The Río de los Putos grant was made in 1842 to William Wolfskill, who had acquired Mexican citizenship; the patent of 1858 awarded him 17,754 acres, partly in Solano County and partly in Yolo County, on either side of the creek. William's home, however, was in Los Angeles.

Three other brothers, Sarchel, Milton, and Mathus, eventually acquired this vast tract of land, along with John, and all four made homes along the fertile banks of Putah Creek, or Río de los Putos. John erected a house one and a half miles southeast of Sarchel's and farther from the creek, using smooth, white volcanic tufa, the native stone. A true horticulturist, he planted many acres of black walnuts, pecans, pomegranates, apricots, oranges, figs, and olives which became the basis of Solano County's orchards. The stone house fell in the earthquake of 1892 and was replaced the following year by a seventeen-room frame house. This stood, as did the former one, at the end of a long driveway lined with olive trees. Emblazoned on this later house was the number 96, the Wolfskill cattle brand, a reference to the cattle John had driven north in 1842. This house, in which John Wolfskill lived until his death in his nineties in 1897, burned in 1948.

Over a hundred acres of this property, owned by John Wolfskill and after him by his daughter and then by his grandchildren, was willed to the University of California at Davis for an agricultural experimental station, with the provision that the old olive plantings be retained. The spot (SRL 804) is two miles southwest of Winters, off Putah Creek Road. It is easily identifiable by the magnificent avenue of gnarled olive trees leading to two university buildings erected on the site of John Wolfskill's house.

Rancho Los Putos and the Vaca Valley

Among the names of immigrants arriving in Pueblo Los Angeles in November 1841 with the Rowland-Workman party appears "J. Manuel Vaca and families." Juan Manuel Vaca and Juan Felipe Peña then went north to Sonoma, where General Vallejo housed the women and children, and the men journeyed on to look for desirable land and to build homes. By June 1842, they petitioned for a grant of land, which was made the following year by Governor Micheltorena. The language of the grant was so vague that it appeared to include lands that were part of the prior Wolfskill grant, and a heated controversy developed that was finally resolved by Micheltorena in Wolfskill's favor.

The settlers' adobe homes were built about two miles southwest of the present city of Vacaville in the lower end of Vaca Valley and its lateral Lagoon Valley. Vaca's house was razed before the end of the century. The Peña adobe (SRL 534), still standing beside I-80, was occupied by descendants of the Peña family until 1918. Its restoration was begun in 1963 through the initial efforts of the Solano County Historical Society. The adobe structure, 50 by 18 feet, was found to be in good condition, since it had been sheathed in frame about 1875. Replacement bricks have been made with adobe from the nearby lagoon. The Peña adobe and its grounds are now owned by the city of Vacaville; the Mowers-Goheen Museum, housed in an adjacent building, contains Indian artifacts and natural history exhibits. The Willis Linn Jepsen Memorial Garden has an interesting collection of native plants.

Ulatis Creek, which flows through this rancho, was named for the Indian tribe sometimes designated the "Ooloolatis," who occupied the area and left many artifacts. The Ulatis were wiped out by the smallpox epidemic of 1837–39. The life of Chief Solano of the neighboring Suisuns was saved by vaccination.

Rancho Los Ulpinos and John Bidwell

John Bidwell, a naturalized Mexican citizen, petitioned in 1844 for the grant of Rancho Los Ulpinos, 17,726 acres in the eastern part of the county along the bank of the Sacramento River. Governor Micheltorena made the grant in the same year. After the American conquest of California, Bidwell sold parts of the grant to several persons, until the boundary lines were in a state of chaos. In 1855 these properties were all defined amicably when the entire rancho was divided into twenty equal tracts made by measurements along the riverfront extending back one league. The tracts were sold in Benicia, and the proceeds were allocated to the various claimants. The land was finally patented to Bidwell in 1866, thus making all titles valid.

Unpatented Land Grants

The Soscol grant, eleven square leagues extending northward from Carquinez Strait, was claimed by General Vallejo, who said it had been given to him by Governor Micheltorena in 1843 in consideration of his services as an officer and of the large sums of money that he had furnished the Mexican government. Although the American courts ultimately declared his title to be invalid, purchases made under it were allowed when further small payments were made. Within the borders of the Soscol grant lies much of modern-day Benicia, Cordelia, and Vallejo.

The Sobrante grant came into the public domain when the courts rejected the claim of brothers José and Juan Luco. Within its 50 square leagues are present-day Birds Landing, Collinsville, Denverton, and most of the Montezuma Hills.

Collinsville

Lansford W. Hastings, a lawyer from Ohio, reached California by way of Oregon in 1843 in command of the emigrant party that bore his name. He was active in the early American settlement of the region, traveling extensively in his effort to attract new residents. Returning to the eastern part of the United States, he published there in 1844 *The Emigrant's Guide.* Coming back to California, he became agent for the Mormons and selected a site for the location of one of their colonies on the north side of the Sacramento River near its junction with the San Joaquin. There in 1846 he laid out a town and built an adobe for himself. This building was called "Montezuma House," and Bayard Taylor, in *Eldorado* (1849), mentions it thus: " 'City of Montezuma,' a solitary house on a sort of headland, projecting into Suisun Bay, and fronting the rival three-house city, New-York-of-the-Pacific" (now Pittsburg, in Contra Costa County). Hastings had hoped to obtain a large grant of land from the Mexican government, but after the American flag was officially raised over California on July 7, 1846, the Mormons lost interest in the site. During his stay, Hastings established a ferry across to the Contra Costa side. After leaving Montezuma, he became attorney for the northern district of California and was a member of the constitutional convention, where his geographical knowledge was useful in fixing boundaries.

The adobe built by Hastings stands at the end of Stratton Lane a little more than a mile east of Collinsville overlooking the place where California's two great

House on Stilts, Collinsville

rivers meet. The building is gradually decaying and is fenced to keep visitors away; the adobe was sheathed in redwood many years ago. Numerous machines for fabricating and stamping coins were found in the house after the builder left it; it is thought that they were intended for the use of the Mormons.

Collinsville was named for C. J. Collins, who settled in the area in 1856. In the next decade, a planned city attracted much interest but few residents, since many of the lots were under water at high tide. F. E. Booth and Company erected a salmon cannery here in 1873 and employed many Italian fishermen, who lived in homes built on stilts to allow free circulation of flood tides beneath them. But the salmon decreased, and there were fires, and there was only one road to the outside world; today only a few occupied houses remain in this town on stilts, once called "Little Venice" and one of the strangest historic spots in California.

Benicia

Benicia lies on the north side of Carquinez Strait, between San Pablo and Suisun bays. In 1850 it rivaled San Francisco as the metropolis of northern California. The town was a pioneer military, religious, and educational center. Benicia was laid out in 1847 by Dr. Robert Semple, who had taken part in the Bear Flag revolt in 1846 at Sonoma, in which General Vallejo was captured. Dr. Semple, impressed with Carquinez Strait as the possible site for a city, made a bargain with his prisoner (whose estate covered much of the present Solano, Napa, and Sonoma counties) for a part of his Soscol grant, the land now occupied by the city of Benicia. The site was deeded to Dr. Semple and his friend Thomas O. Larkin after General Vallejo had been released from imprisonment at Sutter's Fort. The city covered 2,100 acres, according to the survey of 1847.

The name first selected for the town was Francisca, in honor of the wife of General Vallejo. For a while, Francisca's enthusiasts expected it to become the chief city of the greater San Francisco Bay area. When it was learned that the older city of Yerba Buena had changed its name to San Francisco in the same year, Francisca's name was changed to Benicia, one of Sra. Vallejo's other names.

Dr. Semple established the first ferry across Carquinez Strait in 1847. It proved to be a very lucrative operation in the ensuing years of the gold rush. There was continuous ferry service between Benicia and Martinez (laid out in 1849) for 115 years, until the present highway bridge was completed in 1962.

Many noted men and women connected with the early history of California are associated with Benicia. General Vallejo was the donor of the land; Dr. Robert Semple founded the city and was president of the state constitutional convention at Monterey in 1849; Thomas O. Larkin was the first and only United States consul in California; General Persifer F. Smith was the commanding officer of the Pacific Division of the United States Army after California became a state; General Bennett Riley located the Benicia Arsenal; and Concepción Argüello, whose romantic tragedy was unfortunately quite real, ended her days here.

On the west side of First Street between C and D streets was the adobe built in 1847 and rented to Captain E. H. von Pfister. The captain was keeping a store in the building in May 1848, when Charles Bennett stopped by on his way to Monterey to have tests made on some gold nuggets picked up by James Marshall on the American River on January 24, 1848. Bennett told the story of Marshall's discovery, showed the nuggets, and thus helped to precipitate the rush to the gold fields. The site where the adobe once stood has been marked.

One of the first hotels in northern California was built in 1847 for Major Stephen Cooper. Here Cooper's daughter Frances married Dr. Semple soon after the opening of the hotel in the town's first wedding ceremony, performed by the former governor of Missouri, L. W. Boggs, then alcalde of Sonoma. Cooper's California House was sold in 1854 to John Rueger, who turned it into a brewery. The remodeled building stood at the south side of West H Street near First until it was consumed by fire in 1945; the site is now occupied by a tavern called "The Brewery," which contains interesting murals of Benicia's pioneer days.

Benicia's oldest hotel building still standing is the Washington House at 333 First Street. The frame structure was first erected in the 1850's as a hotel and was remodeled in 1897. It was a speakeasy in Prohibition days, and later a Chinese lottery operated there until 1946. Today it is divided into several shops.

Dr. W. F. Peabody established a hospital in Benicia in 1849 and is said to have prospered from the patronage of miners returning from the Sierra. He served on the Benicia Seminary Board until 1852 while mayor of the city, where he resided until 1864. The hospital at 245 West H Street has been completely rebuilt into a private residence; here as elsewhere in downtown Benicia, a marker on the sidewalk designates the site.

The first Masonic Hall built in California (SRL 174) was formally dedicated at Benicia at the end of 1850. The two-story frame building is located at 106 West J Street. The lower floor was used as the county courthouse until 1852. About 1880 the Masons sold the hall, reacquiring it in 1950. Many of California's prominent pioneers received their degrees in this building, including George C. Yount, early settler of the Napa Valley. Still in use, the hall is one of three places in California where any Masonic lodge may hold meetings to confer degrees.

The first Pony Express relay rider from St. Joseph, Missouri, William Hamilton, reached Benicia on April 23, 1860, and was ferried across the strait. A bronze marker commemorating the event is set at the southeast corner of First and A streets. The old railway station is nearby. From here the transcontinental railroad crossed to Contra Costa County by the steamboats *Port Costa* and *Solano*. The latter transported 48 cars and a locomotive in one trip and served until the completion of the Southern Pacific Railroad bridge in 1929.

Near the Pony Express marker is a plaque commemorating Jack London. The young writer frequented the Benicia waterfront while gathering firsthand impressions for his *Tales of the Fish Patrol* and *John Barleycorn.*

First Protestant Church in California

On the site of what is now the Benicia City Park, the first Protestant church in California (SRL 175) was established on April 15, 1849, by Rev. Sylvester Woodbridge, a missionary sent to California by the Presbyterian Church of New York. Until 1854, it was the only Protestant church in Benicia. Reverend Woodbridge exerted considerable influence in the community, for he was the keeper of the town records in addition to being a successful farmer and a teacher. In the latter capacity, he established Benicia's first school, which was one of the first in California. The site is marked on the north side of West K Street. The church membership became divided over the question of secession and loyalty during the Civil War; the church declined and was closed in 1871, and Woodbridge moved to San Francisco.

The Benicia Arsenal and Barracks

The Benicia Barracks (SRL 177), one of the first United States military posts in California, was established in 1849 by Lieutenant General Silas Casey, commanding two companies of the Second U.S. Infantry. The first buildings were erected that year, since Benicia promised to become the central military post of the region. It was strategically located on Carquinez Strait, into which both the Sacramento and the San Joaquin rivers empty, and thus stood at the gateway to the interior of California and the mining regions. However, San Francisco, instead of Benicia, became the metropolis of San Francisco Bay and the port of entry to central California; consequently, the Benicia military post was superseded in importance by the presidio at the Golden Gate. In 1908 the barracks was placed under the control of the Benicia Arsenal. A marker at the east end of Hillcrest Avenue indicates the site of the barracks.

In August 1851, the Army began setting up the first ordnance supply depot in California. A small wooden powder magazine was erected, soon to be followed by others of brick, frame, and stone. Benicia Arsenal (SRL 176) was officially designated as such in April 1852. The oldest stone magazine, built in 1857 at a cost of $35,000, has walls four and a half feet thick, with a vaulted ceiling and modified Corinthian pillars, constructed by French artisans recruited by the federal government. The beautiful interior makes it hard for one to realize that the building was intended for so prosaic a purpose as the storage of gunpowder. The building is now owned by the Benicia Historical Museum and Cultural Foundation, and preparations are under way to restore the building and to open it for displays. This and other structures of hand-hewn sandstone blocks from the surrounding hills are among the finest examples of the stonecutter's art in California. Some of the other structures, still standing in excellent condition, are the first hospital, built in 1856, which served as the post chapel during World War II (thus accounting for the small belfry on the roof); the famous clock-tower building of 1859; and two fine stone warehouses built in 1853–54 and today known as the Camel Barns. The sandstone clock-tower building, with fortress-like walls pierced by gun ports, overlooks the strait. It was originally a three-story building with two towers, but it was damaged by an explosion and fire in 1912 and reduced to two stories and the single massive tower housing the clock, which still keeps time.

The Camel Barns derive their name from a brief moment in their history. In 1856 a herd of camels was imported from the Near East by the Army as an experiment in the transportation of military supplies across the deserts of the Southwest. The experiment was unsuccess-

Camel Barns Museum, Benicia Arsenal

ful, and in 1863 the camels were driven to Benicia and housed in the two stone warehouses on the arsenal grounds. In February 1864, the camels were sold at auction; it is believed that the last of these camels died in Los Angeles's Griffith Park in 1934. One of these buildings is now a museum of Benicia history, while the other remains closed. Between the two buildings is a small machine shop that is part of a proposed museum complex. The Camel Barn museum is open to the public.

In its first decade, the arsenal housed many soldiers, including the young Army lieutenants William T. Sherman and Ulysses S. Grant. Its facilities were continuously used for ammunition storage and ordnance repair, even after the last of the troops moved out. Through the years more buildings were erected, reflecting the architectural modes of different eras, until the arsenal grounds contained structures from virtually every period of the state's history. World War II brought an increase of the arsenal's size from 345 acres to 2,192 acres. For the storage of high explosives, 109 concrete bunkers were built into the neighboring hills. Most of this ammunition was later removed inland to Utah, where it was thought to be safer from enemy attacks. The arsenal was never attacked, however, and it was a major shipping center of war materiel for the Pacific theater of operations.

For more than a century the arsenal and its magnificent buildings were closed to the general public. In 1961 the Army began deactivation of the post, which was completed in March 1964. Much of the property has been converted to commercial and industrial use, but most of the principal historic structures have been preserved.

Other landmarks at the arsenal include the cemetery, with burials as early as 1849 and as recently as World War II, when eight German prisoners of war were interred; the headquarters building from 1870; the guardhouse and the permanent barracks, both from 1872; three shop buildings erected in 1876, 1884, and 1887; and the commanding officer's residence, a two-story building with an imposing east entrance overlooking the strait, built in 1860. The commanding officer in 1906–11 was Colonel James W. Benét, father of the poets Stephen Vincent Benét and William Rose Benét. In 1985, when the building housed a restaurant, a fire in the kitchen temporarily ended its latest public function.

The main entrance to the arsenal grounds is at the end of Military Road East.

The Old State Capitol Building

The most prominent structure of early Benicia is the third state capitol building (SRL 153), located at the northwest corner of First and G streets. The imposing two-story brick building, built in 1852 at a cost of $24,800, was ostensibly intended for the city hall but was promptly offered for the use of the state. The offer was accepted, and Benicia became the third capital of the state of California, following San Jose and Vallejo. It held the honor from February 4, 1853, to February 25, 1854, three days after which the "capital on wheels" made its final journey to Sacramento.

The stately building was designed to resemble a Greek temple. Two fluted columns are set flush with the entranceway. Brick walls, plastered on the interior, support the iron-covered roof. Two angular staircases connect the senate chamber on the lower floor with the assembly room on the second story. The building has been restored and furnished as it was in 1853 when it was the center of California government.

Next to the capitol is the Fischer-Hanlon house (SRL 880) at 137 West G Street. This was once part of a hotel on First Street, begun in the gold rush era. Following a fire in 1856, the unburned half of the building was purchased by Joseph Fischer, a Benicia merchant of Swiss birth, who had the building moved to its present loca-

Old State Capitol Building, Benicia

tion and added a kitchen, porches, and servants' quarters. It was donated to the state in 1969 by his descendants, having been used as a family home since 1856. Completely renovated, it is now open to the public.

The Benicia Seminary

Benicia was home to a number of early educational institutions, most of them short-lived. The Benicia Seminary, established in 1852, was one of the first Protestant girls' schools in California. Miss Mary Atkins, who became its principal in 1854 and its owner the following year, gave the school fame and success. A strict disciplinarian, she insisted that "no student [was] to tarry before a mirror for more than three seconds" and admonished parents against "over indulgence in spending money." Ill health forced her to sell the seminary in 1865 to Reverend Cyrus T. Mills and his wife, who conducted the school until 1871, when they moved to Oakland and there established Mills College. After a time, Miss Atkins, now Mrs. Lynch, repurchased her old school and led it from 1878 until her death in 1882. The "Mother of Seminaries" closed its doors in 1886. Many members of its faculty went out to teach elsewhere in the state, and several founded other seminaries. Some of Miss Atkins's pupils also became prominent teachers in public and private California schools.

The seminary site (SRL 795) is on the north side of I Street west of First. It is indicated by a small marker, but, for reasons of space, the state bronze plaque and monuments were placed in the Benicia City Park facing Military Road West.

St. Augustine College and St. Paul's Episcopal Church

When Dr. Robert Semple founded Benicia in 1847, he set aside some land for a college. A nondenominational boys' school was established in 1852, which in 1867 became the Episcopalian College of St. Augustine, under the management of Rev. J. L. Breck, leader of a missionary company from the East. Reverend Breck was unable to carry out his plans for developing the college, and, still under Episcopalian auspices, it later became a military school. The campus covered 52 acres and was adjacent to the entire block occupied from 1870 by its sister school, St. Mary's College of the Pacific. Gertrude Horn (later Atherton) was a pupil at St. Mary's, which closed in 1885; St. Augustine continued until 1889.

Bishop J. H. D. Wingfield of the Sacramento diocese supervised both schools for a time and had his residence on the campus from 1876 to 1898. The bishop's house, today a private residence at 36 Wingfield Way, is the only building remaining from either campus. The bishop now has his headquarters in Sacramento, and the campus has been subdivided.

St. Paul's Episcopal Church (SRL 862), in downtown Benicia, is a picturesque and significant landmark of early days. Its ceiling, like an inverted ship's hull, was designed by Captain Julian McAllister, commander of the Benicia Arsenal. The church was consecrated in January 1860, with Captain McAllister as lay reader until the arrival of Reverend James Cameron in October of that year. The church stands in excellent condition today at First and East J streets. The rectory at 120 East J Street was originally a New England saltbox home, built in 1790 in Torrington, Connecticut. Captain McAllister purchased the house in 1864 and had it dismantled, shipped around the Horn, and reassembled at the present site in Benicia. The original fireplace and staircase remain, with a master bedroom and kitchen added in 1865.

St. Dominic's Church and Priory

Catholic families in Benicia at first drove by oxcart to Sonoma Mission for Mass. The first Catholic church in Benicia was built at the corner of Fourth and East I streets in 1852. The present stone and concrete Church of Saint Dominic, on the north side of East I Street between Fourth and Fifth streets East, was solemnly blessed in March 1890, shortly before the demolition of the earlier building.

Saint Dominic's parish was formally established on March 16, 1854, when the Very Reverend Francis Sadoc Villarasa, O.P., arrived from Monterey with his whole religious community and accepted the care of the parish in the name of the Order of the Preachers. Father Villarasa and the Most Reverend Joseph Sadoc Alemany, O.P., had arrived in San Francisco late in 1850. The latter, who became the first archbishop of San Francisco in 1853, gave to the former for the use of the order the church already built in Benicia. Near the church the first residence for the community was built in 1854. This was used until 1887, when a new priory was erected on Fifth Street East near East I Street.

The work most dear to Father Villarasa on his arrival in California was the establishment of a convent and a novitiate for the education of Dominican priests. These he had established in Monterey, but he had them moved to Benicia when he came there in 1854. The Dominican priory existed until 1935, when it became a vicariate. By this change valuable old books brought from Spain in early years and protected within these walls were made available to interested historians.

St. Catherine's Convent and Sister Mary Dominica Argüello

The Dominican Sisters arrived in California in 1850. They settled first at Monterey, where in the spring of 1851 they established the first convent school in California. However, the old adobe building in which they were located was in bad condition, and since the population in Monterey was diminishing and that around San Francisco Bay was rapidly increasing, the Sisters decided to move to Benicia, which seemed to be a more central point. Here they established St. Catherine's Convent in 1854. It was operated as a convent and a school until 1959. Luisa and María Vallejo were among the young women who received their education here, and many orphan children were given shelter and schooling. In 1889 the Sisters moved to what is now the Dominican College of San Rafael, but they continued to operate St. Catherine's in Benicia until it was razed in 1966. The site, where First and L streets meet, is now a commercial center.

One of the saddest romances of early California history is the story of Concepción Argüello and the Russian Count Nikolai Rezanov. Bret Harte, Richard White, and Gertrude Atherton are among the writers who have given their versions of the story to the world. At the Presidio of San Francisco the two pledged their engagement in 1806. Rezanov returned to Alaska and thence to Russia to get imperial permission for his marriage. For years, Concepción waited for her lover, refusing all suitors. After several years, a rumor reached California

Grave of Sister Mary Dominica Argüello (Concepción Argüello), St. Catherine's Convent, Benicia

of the count's death while crossing Siberia; it was confirmed only in 1847, 36 years after his departure.

Concepción at length joined the Third Order of St. Francis, giving her life to teaching the poor and caring for the sick. When the Dominican Sisters founded their convent school in Monterey in 1851, she became their first native-born novice, and when the convent was moved in 1854, she came to Benicia with the Sisters. Sister Mary Dominica Argüello died at the Convent of St. Catherine on December 23, 1857, at the age of 66. She is buried in St. Dominic's Cemetery on Hillcrest Avenue at the northeastern corner of the town. Her simple tombstone is in the second row in the section reserved for Sisters' graves; a modern memorial to her stands nearby.

Other Benicia Landmarks

Benicia was of great importance as a port of entry for many years. It had the advantage of deep water at the shore, where seagoing vessels could discharge their cargoes directly on the land. Captain John Walsh, having led a seafaring life, settled there in 1849 and became collector of the port. His house still stands, in fair condition, at 235 East L Street. The house is one of three almost identical houses prefabricated in Boston and brought around the Horn to California in 1849. The second house, now gone, ended up in San Francisco, and the third became Lachryma Montis, General Vallejo's home in Sonoma.

The site of the Pacific Mail and Steamship Company docks is at the end of East H Street. The company began operations here in 1850 with a fleet of six sidewheelers. California's first large industrial enterprise flourished here, as docks, foundries, machine shops, and repair drydocks were established; here the great seagoing ships of that era were repaired and coaled.

At the foot of West Eleventh, Twelfth, and Thirteenth streets, along the waterfront, is the site (SRL 973) of the Turner-Robertson Shipyard, which operated here from 1883 to 1918.

The *California*, first steamer of the line to make the journey around the Horn from New York, arrived in San Francisco on February 28, 1849, crowded with passengers. Coal for refueling for the return journey had to be brought to California by sea, and since the first shipload had not arrived, the steamer was forced to wait. Refueled, the *California*, with Captain Forbes in command, made an excursion to Benicia with a party of invited guests in April before setting off in May to return to New York. After the establishment of the docks, all the great ships of this company, the *California*, the *Oregon*, and the *Panama*, berthed in Benicia between

regular trips until the company removed its headquarters to San Francisco in the early 1860's.

The competition of the overland railway, completed in 1869, was felt keenly by the Pacific Mail and Steamship Company, and by 1881 it had left Benicia altogether. Some of its waterfront property was taken over by the Benicia Agricultural Works. The area today is a thriving commercial center.

Cordelia and Green Valley

The town of Cordelia, next to Benicia the oldest in the county, was named in honor of the wife of Captain R. H. Waterman, founder of Fairfield. Situated at the lower end of Green Valley on the route from Benicia to Sacramento, it was a stopping place for stages, and a hotel for the accommodation of travelers was operated there in 1855 by John Charles Pitman, an Englishman. Stone quarried near Cordelia was taken by barges through the Cordelia Slough and across the bay to San Francisco, where it was used in building and in paving the streets. The shipping point was then called Bridgeport; and when in 1868 the California Pacific Railroad was routed through, the community of Cordelia was moved a short distance south to the newer site. The Pitman House was succeeded by the Cordelia Hotel, which years later became a family residence and survived until it burned in 1937. The Thompson Bar in Cordelia is said to be one of the oldest in the county. Cordelia is just south of the junction of the highways I-80 and I-680.

North of Cordelia on the other side of I-80 stretches Cherry Valley, an area now more residential than agricultural. About three and one-half miles north along Green Valley Road, set back some distance to the west of the road, is the imposing stone residence started in 1860 by Granville P. Swift, Bear Flagger and builder of Temelec Hall near Sonoma. After 80 years in the related Swift and Jones families, the building is now the clubhouse for the Green Valley Country Club.

Rockville and the Rockville Stone Chapel

Rockville was a settlement on the old stage road between Benicia and Sacramento and today is a settled crossroads on Suisun Valley Road about two miles north of I-80. Through this area runs the northern boundary of the unconfirmed Soscol grant.

By 1852 summer camp meetings were being held regularly on Suisun Valley Creek, where baptism by total immersion was possible. The settlers gathered from afar with their tents and cookstoves and even the family milk cow, prepared to spend a week. Circuit riders preached at the meetings and services lasted into the night, with the aid of lanterns hung in the oak trees. At two such camp meetings, in 1854 and 1855, $5,000 was raised to build a permanent structure, the Rockville Stone Chapel. Landy and Sarah Alford, pioneers in the area, gave five acres for the site of the church and a cemetery. The cornerstone was laid on October 3, 1856, the stone coming from the adjacent hills; the church was built by volunteer labor.

Many pioneers were highly sensitive to the split in the Methodist Episcopal Church caused by the slavery question. One Sunday in 1863 the predominant Northerners sang the "Battle Cry of Freedom." Indignant Southerners in the congregation promptly installed a stone plaque, still visible, reading "M. E. Church South 1856," and the Northerners began to worship elsewhere.

Regular services were held in the chapel (SRL 779), just north of the Rockville crossroads, until 1895, and occasional services were held until 1919. The building gradually deteriorated except for the stone walls, which had withstood the 1906 earthquake. In 1929 the reunited Methodist Episcopal Church deeded it to the Rockville Public Cemetery District on condition that it be restored as a pioneer monument, and this was done in 1940.

Suisun City

In October 1850, Dr. John Baker and Curtis Wilson sailed up the Suisun Slough to Suisun Island, a bit of hard upland rising from the marsh, and landed at the present site of Suisun City, where they discovered a herd of elk among the tules. In the same year Captain Josiah Wing began to run various watercraft to the island. In 1852 he erected a warehouse on this "embarcadero" (the name by which the place was then known), and his schooner, the *Ann Sophia*, transported the produce of the valley, beginning an industry that assumed vast proportions as the country became more populous. In 1854 the Captain and John Owen, who later became a merchant in the place, laid out the town of Suisun west of the wharf and just below the southern boundary line of the Suisun grant. In 1857 the first church was built under Presbyterian auspices, the land and building being donated by the people of the vicinity. In 1858 Captain Wing built a residence for himself in the town. Suisun was incorporated as a city in 1868, when the railroad arrived.

The old plaza is formed by the broadening of Main Street between Solano and Morgan streets. The Lawler house is the oldest surviving dwelling in the city; it was built in 1856 and moved to its present location, at 712 East Main Street, in 1982, where it is used as an office building.

The Mothball Fleet

At the end of World War II, some 300 seaworthy cargo vessels were moored in Suisun Bay just east of Benicia. As they were needed, they were taken from reserve and put into service, as in the Korean and Viet Nam wars. Between 70 and 80 vessels were still anchored there in 1987. They can be seen from I-680 just east of the Benicia-Martinez Bridge.

Vallejo, California's Second Capital

California's first state capital was at San Jose; at the urging of General Mariano Vallejo, it was moved in 1852. Vallejo promised to grant land on which to build a capital city and also promised to erect a capitol building, lodgings, and such social institutions as schools and churches. As a compliment to their benefactor, the legislature named the new city "Vallejo," although he himself had suggested "Eureka."

On January 5, 1852, the legislature met for the first time in the new frame capitol building. But it was dissatisfied with the poor housing facilities, and, since Vallejo found himself unable to fulfill his promises of accessory buildings, the legislature moved hastily to Sacramento on January 12. A devastating flood in Sacramento caused them to adjourn on May 4, 1852, to meet again in Vallejo on January 3, 1853. On February 4 this "Peripatetic Government," or "Capital on Wheels," as it has been variously designated, was carried to the neighboring town of Benicia, where it remained until February 25, 1854, when Sacramento finally won the fight for the state capital.

The site of the capitol building (SRL 574) is marked at 219 York Street near Sacramento Street, in downtown Vallejo. Nearby, in the old city hall at 734 Main Street, is the Vallejo Naval and Historical Museum, exhibiting materials connected with the history of the city and of neighboring Mare Island Naval Shipyard.

A Methodist Episcopal church was organized in Vallejo in 1855, the outcome of a Sunday school that Mrs. David G. Farragut, wife of the first commandant of the Mare Island Navy Yard, and others had been conducting for some months. In 1856 General John B. Frisbie donated a site for the edifice, giving a deed to five men, one of them being Commander Farragut, "in trust for the Methodist Episcopal Church in the town of Vallejo." Upon this lot and largely through the exertion of Farragut, a small rough structure was built, which served for a time the double purpose of chapel and schoolhouse—the first record of a publicly supported school in Vallejo. The site is at 420 Virginia Street.

Vallejo was the site of one of California's earliest orphanages, built by the Good Templars of California and Nevada in 1869 and operated until the early 1920's. The site of the large home and school is on the hilltop near the present intersection of La Crescenda and Rincon Way.

Mare Island

The United States Naval Shipyard (SRL 751) is located on Mare Island, just across the Napa River from Vallejo. The island was first named "Isla Plana" in 1775 by Juan Manuel de Ayala of the *San Carlos*. The legend of its present name is connected with General Vallejo. One day a barge transporting horses and cattle across Carquinez Strait was caught in a sudden squall. The frightened animals stampeded, capsizing the frail craft. Some of them were lost, but one white mare, much prized by the General's wife, swam to a neighboring island, where she was rescued a few days later. General Vallejo in gratitude named the island "La Isla de la Yegua" (Mare Island).

In 1851 Congress authorized a floating drydock for the West Coast; in 1852 a naval commission headed by Commodore John D. Sloat was sent to the San Francisco Bay Area to investigate and recommend a site for a navy yard and depot. Mare Island was selected and purchased by the federal government for $83,401. The first commandant arrived on September 16, 1854, and immediately began construction of a shipyard. This young officer was David G. Farragut, who was later to become the hero of the battles of Vicksburg and Mobile Bay in the Civil War and to be named the Navy's first full admiral.

The naval shipyard has built over 500 craft for the Navy, including the battleship *California*. It built the first warship on the coast (*Saginaw*, 1859), converted the Navy's coal burner to oil (*Cheyenne*, 1908), built the first flight deck on any ship in the world (cruiser *Pennsylvania*, 1911), and built the hull of the world's first aircraft carrier (*Langley*, 1921–22). The nuclear-powered attack submarine *Drum* (1970) was the last vessel completed here. Today the ships are built elsewhere, but the shipyard is still important for overhaul and repair of naval vessels.

Mare Island had the first radio station in the Pacific. The Navy's oldest chapel, St. Peter's, dedicated in 1901, stands here. Mare Island's cemetery was established in 1856 and contains 900 graves, including those of sailors of eight nationalities and the daughter of Francis Scott Key, author of our national anthem.

Mare Island's gun park includes the two guns from the Union ship *Kearsarge*, which sank the Confederate blockade raider *Alabama* off the French coast in 1864; the two forward guns of Farragut's flagship *Hartford*,

which helped to silence the forts at the entrance to Mobile Bay; and the figurehead of the frigate *Independence*, built in 1812 and station ship at Mare Island from 1855 to 1913. Mare Island is joined to the mainland by an earthen causeway. Visitors may apply to the Public Information Officer for permission to enter the grounds.

Vacaville

In 1850 Don Manuel Vaca deeded nine square miles of Rancho Los Putos to William McDaniel, who paid the sum of $3,000 in cash and agreed to lay out a townsite on one of the square miles, to name it Vacaville, and to give to the former owner certain town lots. The streets were given Spanish names, which were not retained by the American settlers. The earliest occupation of the settlers here was cutting the rank growth of wild oats and transporting the hay to landings on the Sacramento River. The Vacaville Museum at 213 Buck Avenue has displays on the history of Solano County and Vacaville.

A private school called Ulatis Academy was started in Vacaville in 1855 by a Professor Anderson from San Francisco. The academy was succeeded about 1861 by the Pacific Methodist College under the auspices of the Methodist Episcopal Church, South; the poet Edwin Markham was one of the students. The college was moved to Santa Rosa in 1871. The one surviving college building, at 712 East Main Street, is thought to have been a girls' dormitory.

The "Nut Tree" wayside place, now within Vacaville's city limits, was started with a black walnut planted in 1860 by Josiah Allison, a pioneer of 1854. His small niece, Sally Fox, had picked up the nut in Arizona on the westward journey. A huge tree grew beside the Western Wagon Road, now I-80, and became shelter for a fruit stand. The tree is gone, but from this humble beginning Allison's descendants have developed the famous "Nut Tree" restaurant.

Silveyville and Dixon

Silveyville, on the old route between Napa and Sacramento, was established by Elijah S. Silvey, who made two trips from Missouri to California, accompanied by his wife and two children, before settling permanently here.

On his second arrival, in 1852, he built a house for his family and a corral for the herd of 100 milk cows he had brought. His house became a country hotel, and the corral accommodated horses of the stagecoaches and freight wagons. It became his custom to place a red lantern aloft at night to guide travelers. A trading center called Silveyville developed there, only to be moved bodily five miles east to the new California Pacific Railroad in 1868. Thomas Dickson donated ten acres on the line of the railroad for a station, and at that spot a town grew up, taking the name of its benefactor but misspelling it Dixon. Silveyville gradually disappeared. Some of the frame buildings were moved intact, while the bricks of the merchandise store were hauled to the new town and employed in constructing the Capitol Hotel, which stood until 1920. The old Methodist Episcopal Church was moved in the spring of 1870 to Dixon, where services are still held at its present location on the corner of North Jefferson and B streets.

Fairfield

The location of the county seat at Benicia provoked complaint because it was on the very edge of the county, a serious defect in those days of slow travel, when residents of outlying sections had business to transact. The agitation for a change became acute in 1857. As a result, R. H. Waterman, an old sea captain born in New York and once warden of the Port of San Francisco, who in 1848 had purchased with Archibald A. Ritchie four leagues of the Suisun grant, made a gift of a block of land and money to place the county buildings upon it. On September 2, 1858, a vote of the people chose Fairfield to replace Benicia, and Captain Waterman's offer was accepted. The name Fairfield, after Captain Waterman's boyhood home in Connecticut, was given to the place. An effort in 1873 to move the county seat to Vallejo was unsuccessful.

The home in which Captain Waterman lived is one mile north of Fairfield off Mankas Corner Road. The well-built two-story frame house, standing at the end of a long drive between eucalyptus trees planted by him, is in excellent condition, as are the marble fireplaces, high ceilings, and curved staircase. Old fig trees planted by the Captain grow near the house, which was begun in 1852. It is now a private residence.

Travis Air Force Base, a huge installation primarily involved with transpacific military air traffic, is located four miles northeast of Fairfield. It is named in honor of Brigadier General Robert T. Travis, who was killed there in an airplane accident on August 5, 1950. An Air Force Museum on the base is open to visitors by appointment.

Rio Vista

In the fall of 1857 a town called "Brazos del Rio" (Arms of the River) was laid out by Colonel N. H. Davis on his land at the upper end of the Ulpinos grant near the junction of Cache Slough and the Sacramento River. The wharf constructed by Colonel Davis in 1858 was sold the following year to the Steam Navigation Company, which doubled the size of the wharf to accommodate large steamers.

The name of the settlement was changed to Rio Vista, but on January 9, 1862, heavy rains swept the town away. The inhabitants began to look for a better location, and negotiations were entered into with Joseph Bruning for a location in the upper edge of the Montezuma Hills, in the northeast corner of his ranch. The new town plat was surveyed and recorded; part of the site was on the Bruning property and part on the adjoining ranch of T. J. McWorthy. The main street of the new Rio Vista now runs between the sites of these old farms.

Saint Gertude's and Saint Joseph's were academies begun in the 1870's; these two schools did not survive the 1920's, and no trace of them remains. The Catholic church built in 1862 at the northwest corner of California and Fourth streets is still in use. The oldest residence, also built in 1862, is still occupied and is located at 198 Logan Street.

The Rio Vista Museum at 16 North Front Street has interesting displays on various events of the community's history including the discovery of the largest gas field in northern California in 1936.

California Railway Museum

Halfway between Rio Vista and Fairfield is the California Railway Museum, the creation of the Bay Area Electric Railroad Association, Inc. The purpose of the association is to preserve cars from the days of interurban electric rail transport. The present site, acquired in 1960, is at 5848 State Highway 12 (Suisun City being the postal location). The museum is open to the public, and rides on a mile-and-a-quarter track are offered on weekends.

Landings

Solano County, bordered on the south and east by the Sacramento River, Suisun and San Pablo bays, and Carquinez Strait, began at an early date to make use of water transportation for freight and passengers. Embarcaderos were placed in many inland sloughs and landings along the river. Maine Prairie, at the head of navigation on the Maine Prairie Slough, shipped much of the wild oat hay and wheat from northern Solano County; 50,000 tons were said to be transported in one season. The flood of 1862 swept the community away, and although some rebuilding occurred, the advent of the railroads decreased the prosperity of this community and others; beyond place names, virtually nothing remains of them.

Birds Landing, south of the California Railway Museum and on Montezuma Slough northwest of Collinsville, was originally a shipping point for John Bird, a New Yorker who arrived in California in 1859. He purchased 1,000 acres of land and started a storage and commission business; the building of the wharf around 1869 afforded an easy means of shipment of hay and wheat. Only a few piles remain today. The general store, still standing, was established in 1875, at the crossroads about half a mile northeast of the embarcadero and was given the same name. The post office at Bird's Landing, which operated out of the general store until 1968, was officially cited in June 1988 as one of the three smallest post offices in the United States (the others being Ochopee in Florida and Salvo in North Carolina).

On the slough northwest of the Collinsville were Mein's and Dutton's landings. At Mein's Landing, one mile due west of the Birds Landing crossroads, the house built about 1880 by Captain Mein is still standing. It is now used as headquarters for a private duck club. Dutton's Landing, about two miles northwest of Collinsville, was once the site of a ferry; it can now be reached only by the Grizzly Island Road, across that island.

On Miner Sough is berthed the old barge *Golden Gate*, which was built in the 1890's and last saw service in the building of the Golden Gate Bridge. It was acquired by John Stringer in 1970 and is now a tavern and restaurant under the name "The Golden Gate Island Resort."

Sonoma County

Sonoma County was one of the original 27 counties. "Sonoma" is the name of an Indian tribe whose village site was taken over by Father Altamira in 1823 for Mission San Francisco Solano. The county seat was located at the town of Sonoma from 1850 to 1854; since 1854 it has been at Santa Rosa.

Discovery and Naming of Bodega Bay

The Vizcaíno expedition of 1602–3 made a lengthy and perilous voyage along the coast of Alta California. Searching for harbors and suitable anchorages, the fleet of the three vessels put in at several places as far north as Cape Mendocino, and it was on the northern leg of the voyage that Bodega Bay was discovered. It remained for a later explorer to map the bay and give it the name by which it is now known.

On October 3, 1775, the Spanish explorer Juan Francisco de la Bodega y Cuadra entered the bay that now bears his name in the little schooner *Sonora*. Bodega's voyage was a part of Spain's plan to approach California from the sea. His careful observations and acts of possession were of great importance to succeeding explorers and colonizers.

On October 20, 1793, Archibald Menzies, a naturalist of the expedition led by Captain George Vancouver, landed on the northwestern shore of Bodega Bay near an island (probably Bodega Rock) that the party named Gibson Island. His party was in search of botanical specimens. Partly because the ground had been burned over recently by the Indians and partly because of the season of the year he found few plants, and, to his disappointment, these few were similar to those he had already found at Monterey and San Francisco. The party, which also encountered a small group of peaceful Indians, did find something of interest—described as "a cross formed of a piece of stave of a cask fastened to a pole by rope yarn." Its origins are unknown. The various landings made at Bodega Bay are commemorated by a marker (SRL 833) in Doran Park.

Coming of the Russians

In 1741, Admiral Vitus Bering discovered the sea and the strait that bear his name. On this voyage he also discovered Alaska, whose waters were alive with fur seals. Another expedition followed in 1765.

These activities on the part of the Russians undoubtedly had some influence in rousing Spain to the danger of losing California and led to a speedier occupation of San Diego and Monterey. Subsequently, they led also to the founding of missions, military posts, and pueblos north of San Francisco Bay.

By the close of the eighteenth century, the Russian-American Fur Company had established itself on the Aleutian Islands and on the coast of Alaska. These colonies were rich in furs but lacked trade connections by which they could obtain food and necessary supplies. Russia began to look southward to California, with its warm climate and fertile soil, from which she might feed her needy colonists.

In 1806, the czar's chamberlain, Count Nikolai Rezanov, went to Sitka on official business. He found the colonists starving and stricken with fever and scurvy. Temporary relief was obtained from an American ship, but something more permanent was needed. Accordingly, Rezanov sailed south to open negotiations with the Spanish officials of San Francisco, well knowing that trade with foreigners was forbidden.

The advent of the Russians into California is closely associated with the names of two women, the lovely Concepción Argüello and the Russian princess Helena de Gagarin. The story of Concepción and her love for County Rezanov is told in connection with the San Francisco Presidio, where the romance began, and with Benicia (Solano County), where Concepción spent the closing years of her life in the Convent of St. Catherine. The story of Princess Helena is told later in this chapter.

Undoubtedly, Nikolai Rezanov had political ambitions for Russia when he visited California in 1806. Doubtless, too, his courtship of Concepción Argüello was sincere, though mixed with diplomacy. Certainly, its result was propitious for his enterprise. The account of Doctor Georg von Langsdorff, his friend and companion, shows quite clearly that his ultimate purpose was to establish a Russian colony in northern California. Rezanov's untimely death on the steppes of Siberia prevented him from carrying out this plan himself. A few years later, however, his purpose was fulfilled by Ivan A. Kuskov, an agent of the Russian-American Fur Company.

Founding of Bodega Bay, Kuskov, and Fort Ross

Rezanov had taken careful observation all along the coast on his return voyage to Alaska in 1806, and his report was most favorable. In 1809, Kuskov came down from Sitka prepared to make temporary settlements. One was made at Bodega Bay and another in the Salmon Creek Valley six miles inland. Wheat was sown and harvested, and in August, with the precious store of food and 2,000 otter skins, Kuskov returned to Alaska.

In 1811 Kuskov came again, as governor of the Russian settlements to be established in California. Although he went through no ceremony of taking possession of the land for Russia, he made permanent settlements at Kuskov (in Salmon Creek Valley) and, in 1812, at Fort Ross, twelve miles north of the mouth of the Russian River on a high bluff overlooking the sea. These settlements were fortified and the Russian flag raised over them. Title to the territory for a considerable distance had been secured from the Indians who inhabited the region.

Today nothing remains to mark the site of the Salmon Creek Valley village. This location, where Stephen Smith later settled, is about a mile northwest of Bodega.

Fort Ross

The Russian settlements flourished; the one at Fort Ross became the center of activities. Not only did the settlers gather rich fur harvests on land and sea, but they became a prosperous agricultural community, supplying food to the Alaskan colonies as well as to their own people. During the years 1810–22, they also carried on a considerable trade with their Spanish neighbors, who were eager to secure the finely made manufactured articles that the Russians exchanged for food supplies. This trade was carried on in spite of the fact that it was still officially forbidden; the Californians made opportunities for it, and almost no friction arose between the two peoples.

Nonetheless, it seems clear that fear of the Russian advance in northern California led the Spanish authorities to explore and settle the regions north of San Francisco Bay in what are now Sonoma, Solano, and Marin counties.

In December 1823 President James Monroe asserted that the United States had a special interest in the Western Hemisphere, and warned the Powers of Europe not to meddle in the internal affairs of an independent New World state nor to seek to extend their territorial claims in the Western Hemisphere. In this statement, subsequently called the Monroe Doctrine, Monroe was referring not only to the newly liberated colonies in South America but also to the growing menace of the Russian Empire in North America. His warning was heeded by the Russians. In 1824, Russia agreed to limit all future settlements to Alaska, but for nearly twenty years longer the colony at Fort Ross remained independent of Mexican control. By 1840, however, the sea otter had been almost exterminated, and the Russian-American Fur Company could no longer maintain American colonies. The political aspect was no longer significant, moreover, and by 1839 Russian officials had sent orders for the withdrawal of all colonists from California. In 1841 the entire property was sold to Captain John Sutter of New Helvetia (Sacramento), and the colonists returned to Alaska.

The original inhabitants of Fort Ross consisted of about 100 Russians and 80 Aleuts, the maximum population never exceeding 400. The settlement stood on a bluff above a little cove in the sea. The land sloped gently upward to the base of a range of hills covered with pine, fir, cedar, and laurel.

The fort itself was enclosed by a palisade built of heavy redwood timbers and mounted with cannon. Two blockhouses, one octagonal and the other heptagonal, surmounted the corners of the palisade, facing the sea on the southwest and the land on the northwest corners. Within the enclosure were nine build-

Fort Ross State Historic Park

Mission San Francisco Solano, Sonoma

ings, among them the commander's quarters and the chapel. Outside were 50 buildings, besides blacksmith, carpenter, and cooper shops and a large stable for 200 milk cows. At the landing place on the beach below was the boathouse, where seagoing vessels were built.

Fort Ross State Historic Park (SRL 5) has been owned by the state since 1906 and is partially restored. The distinctive Russian Orthodox chapel with its hexagonal tower and round cupola, all built of redwood, was destroyed by fire in 1970 and has been completely reconstructed. The commandant's house and the bastions, as well as the bastions surrounding the fort, have also been restored. SR 1, which formerly ran through the grounds, has been diverted to the east of the quadrangle. The visitors' center contains many interesting displays on Russian colonial life. Fort Ross is a registered National Historic Landmark, as is the separately designated commandant's house.

Founding of Mission San Francisco Solano

In 1823, Governor Argüello became anxious to check the Russian advance into the interior north of San Francisco Bay, a region that Gabriel Moraga had already explored during the years 1812–14 and earlier. The governor advised Father José Altamira, a young priest newly stationed at San Francisco, to transfer the Missions of San Francisco de Asís and San Rafael Arcángel to Sonoma without delay. The Sonoma site was chosen for its proximity to the Russians and because its climate was more favorable for the Indian neophytes than that of the established missions. Without waiting for the final approval by the proper church authorities, the zealous Father Altamira set out at once to choose the site for the new mission, the foundations of which were laid perhaps as early as 1823.

So radical and unauthorized a step occasioned much dissatisfaction among the Church leadership. A com-

promise was ultimately arranged whereby Missions San Francisco de Asís and San Rafael Arcángel were to continue as before and approval was given for the establishment of a new mission. It was called Mission San Francisco Solano (SRL 3), in honor of St. Francis Solano, an illustrious Franciscan missionary to the New World who died in Peru in 1610, and was thus distinguished from Mission San Francisco de Asís at San Francisco, named in honor of St. Francis of Assisi.

This, the last and northernmost of the 21 California missions, was a plain, low building with an overhanging roof covering the corridors of the wing. After secularization in 1834, the mission chapel was rebuilt by Mariano G. Vallejo, who was appointed *comisionado*, and then became the parish church. It was sold in 1881 to Solomon Schocken by Archbishop Alemany and subsequently was used for secular purposes. In 1903 a public fund was raised and the old mission was deeded to the state of California. Part of Sonoma State Historic Park today, it is located diagonally across from the northeast corner of Sonoma Plaza. The padres' house, built about 1825, is the oldest structure in Sonoma. The adobe church dates from about 1840, the earlier church having stood east of the padres' quarters.

Founding of the Pueblo of Sonoma

In 1833 Governor José Figueroa directed the occupation and settlement of what are now Sonoma and Marin counties. His primary object was to force the Russians out of California. The man who was entrusted with this task was Mariano Guadalupe Vallejo, then military commander and director of colonization on Mexico's northern frontier. In the summer of 1833 Vallejo made an official tour of the Russian settlements, where he made his mission clearly known to the Russian governor.

Mexican settlements were attempted at what are now the towns of Petaluma, Santa Rosa, and Fulton, but the hostility of the Indians caused their abandonment. Sonoma Valley was then chosen as the place of settlement, and there in 1835 General Vallejo founded the Pueblo de Sonoma next to Mission San Francisco Solano.

The Sonoma Plaza

General Vallejo himself laid out the new pueblo around a square or plaza, which was used as a drilling ground for the soldiers who defended the town between 1835 and 1846. On the northeast corner of the plaza stood the mission church and next to it the padres' house. Adjoining the padres' house on the right was a larger adobe, in which Vallejo is said to have lived temporarily; this has long since disappeared. To the west of the church stood the barracks, a two-story building with a balcony. This house (SRL 316), which is still standing, was begun around 1837 by Vallejo for his soldiers and was occupied by American troops from 1846 to 1848. It became part of Sonoma State Historic Park in 1958 and is now used as a museum of local history.

Next to the barracks, a large two-story adobe mansion, known as the Casa Grande, was erected soon after the founding of Sonoma. Here General Vallejo lived during the years preceding California's annexation to the United States. The Vallejo adobe had a balcony extending across the front, and on the southwest corner there was a tall square tower, giving a view on all the surrounding country. Eleven of Vallejo's children were born here. Only the long, low adobe in the rear, used as a kitchen and as a servants' quarters, survived a fire in 1867; it can be seen today as one of the park buildings.

Other adobes were gradually built around the open plaza. A few of these remain today, some of them encased in wood but still retaining the picturesque Spanish balconies. One of these is the Leese-Fitch adobe at 487 First Street West. Here Jacob Leese introduced commercial activity to Sonoma County in 1841. During the American occupation it was the residence of General Persifer F. Smith. Sold to Mrs. Fitch in 1850, the building next housed the St. Mary's Academy for young ladies, and since then has been a private residence under a succession of owners.

Don Salvador Vallejo, brother of the general, first lived in Sonoma directly west of the Casa Grande. His house was finished in September 1840, in time for him to bring to it his bride, María de la Luz Carrillo, sister of the general's wife. This home was torn down and re-placed by the Sebastiani Apartments in 1938. In 1850 Don Salvador built a wing adjacent to his original adobe, and this still stands as the Swiss Hotel (SRL 496), at 18 West Spain Street.

Another picturesque remnant is the Blue Wing Inn (SRL 17), at 133 East Spain Street, opposite the mission. The building is being restored by the California Department of Parks and Recreation. At 415–417 First Street West, opposite the northwest corner of the plaza, stands the Salvador Vallejo adobe (SRL 501), with a balcony extending across the front, now housing a hotel and other businesses. Don Salvador built this as a one-story adobe in the early 1840's. A second story of wood was added in the 1850's, in a brief period when the building was a well-regarded hotel; from 1858 the place was the home of the Sonoma Academy, later Cumberland College, a Presbyterian coeducational boarding school from 1858 to 1864. In the 1880's it was the home and winery of Camille Aguillon.

The site of the Union Hotel and Union Hall (SRL 627) is marked by a plaque across from the southwest corner of the plaza. The plaza has seen many changes since the raising of the Bear Flag here in 1846. In the 1870's the plaza was a treeless open area crossed by paths, and its perimeter was flanked by buildings of one or two stories. In 1880, the Sonoma Valley Railroad laid tracks down Spain Street to the plaza, where the company built a depot and a roundhouse. By 1890, the railroad property had been removed north to what is now Depot Park, and the Ladies Improvement Club (later the Sonoma Valley Women's Club) began a successful campaign to make the plaza into a parklike area. The Sonoma City Hall was built in the center of the plaza in 1906–8; architect A. C. Lutgens of San Francisco designed the unusual Mission Revival building so that all four facades were identical. The Sonoma Plaza has been designated a National Historic Landmark.

Other old adobe buildings stand at some distance from Sonoma's plaza. The John G. Ray house, at 205 East Spain Street, was built about 1847, and the so-called Nash adobe (SRL 667), at 579 First Street East, was built around 1847 by H. A. Green. John H. Nash was the first American to be alcalde of Sonoma during the Mexican regime. He was living here in July 1847 when Lieutenant William Tecumseh Sherman of the United States Army arrested him because he refused to turn over his office to the American-appointed alcalde, Lilburn W. Boggs. Nancy Bones Patton, a survivor of the Donner Party, and her husband purchased the house in 1848, and it was carefully restored in 1931 by Nancy's great-granddaughter Zolita Bates. Today this privately owned dwelling looks much as it originally did, as does another old adobe, "La Casita" at 143 West Spain Street.

The Vasquez house in the El Paseo Complex off First Street East is one of the first wooden frame houses in Sonoma. Built for General Joseph Hooker, it first stood across the plaza on First Street West and was moved to its present location to serve as the headquarters for the Sonoma League for Historic Preservation.

North on First Street West is the old Sonoma Valley Railway Depot in Depot Park. Relocated here from the plaza in 1890, it eventually became the Sonoma Valley Historical Society Museum, devoted to preserving the artifacts of the region.

In Sonoma's Mountain Cemetery is the grave of the only known veteran of the American Revolutionary War to be buried in California. Captain William Smith, who joined the Virginia Navy as a boy of eleven in 1779, died in Sonoma in 1846. His grave was marked by the California State Society, Daughters of the American Revolution, in 1965.

The Bear Flag Revolt

In the spring of 1846 many American settlers in the Sacramento Valley and neighboring valleys believed they were in danger of being driven from the country by General José Castro, commander of the Mexican army. Encouraged by Captain John C. Frémont of the United States forces, a group of 33 men surprised General Vallejo at Sonoma and took possession of the town on June 14, 1846. Although Vallejo had always been favorable to the United States, he, his brother, Salvador, and Victor Prudon (or Prudhomme) were taken prisoner and carried to Sutter's Fort, where the were kept for two months.

William B. Ide was left in command of the rebel forces at Sonoma. Since the action of the insurgents did not represent the United States government, the Stars and Stripes could not be raised in place of the Mexican flag. A new flag was therefore created, called the Bear Flag of the California Republic. The banner had a white field and a lower red border; a bear and a star were its emblems. On July 9, 1846, the Bear Flag was lowered, and the American flag was raised over the plaza by Lieutenant Joseph Warren Revere, grandson of Paul Revere, the American Revolutionary War patriot.

A slightly modified version of this flag was adopted as the California state flag by the legislature in 1911. The original Bear Flag was displayed in San Francisco and was destroyed in the fire of 1906.

The Bear Flag Monument (SRL 7), in the form of a bronze statue representing a young pioneer clutching the staff of the Bear Flag, which floats above him, was placed on the old Sonoma plaza by the state of California and dedicated June 14, 1915. A bas-relief on the face of the pedestal shows the raising of the Bear Flag in 1846; nearby, on a plain wooden staff, the modern Bear Flag is flown daily.

Temelec

One of the Bear Flaggers later settled about four miles southwest of Sonoma. In 1858 Captain Granville Perry Swift constructed Temelec Hall (SRL 237), a magnificent stone mansion, using forced Indian labor. Its cost was estimated at $250,000, the most expensive home in the county at the time. It was for many years a private home, with about twenty large rooms and nine fireplaces, all with marble mantels. Today it is a clubhouse of a retirement subdivision off Arnold Drive.

Mariano Vallejo and His Lands

Mariano Guadalupe Vallejo, born on July 4, 1807, was the son of Ignacio Vallejo and his wife, María Antonia Lugo, who lived in Monterey County. His schoolmates at Monterey included Juan B. Alvarado and José Castro. A military career being his choice, he entered the Monterey Company in 1823 as a cadet and was promoted to *alférez*, or ensign, in San Francisco in 1827. In 1830 he was elected to the *diputación*, and in 1832 he married Francisca Benicia, daughter of Joaquín Carrillo.

José Figueroa, governor of Alta California from 1833 to 1835, chose him *comisionado* to secularize Mission San Francisco Solano and to establish the town of Sonoma. In compensation for his services, the governor gave him large tracts of land north of San Francisco Bay and in 1835 a plot of ground in Pueblo de Sonoma. Here Vallejo built his Casa Grande, only the servants' quarters of which are still standing.

Vallejo was the outstanding native Californian of his day; his position came to him because of his ability and experience. Advanced to the rank of colonel in 1836, he assumed the position of commander general, took the oath of allegiance to the new governor, and issued a patriotic proclamation on that occasion. From this time his efforts and money were expended to an even greater extent than before to serve his country. He induced the Mexican government to unite the military and civil commands in one officer and turned over his command to Governor Micheltorena in 1842. Rancho Soscol, a large area in Solano County, was granted to him. His ranch home, however, was at Rancho Petaluma in Sonoma County, the ten leagues of which were granted to him by Governor Micheltorena in 1843; in the following year he received five additional leagues. The large holding was confirmed by a United States patent issued by President Ulysses S. Grant in 1874.

On Rancho Petaluma, which he may have occupied for several years before the formal granting, the farseeing General Vallejo carried out a plan of agriculture that benefited not only himself but also the Indians who labored for him. In the foothills of the Sonoma Mountains, he built between 1834 and 1844 a large adobe house, which still stands above the open fields of Petaluma Valley. It was built on a grander scale than any other adobe in northern California. Its three facades, the main one 200 feet long, are shaded by broad balconies, while the spacious patio, open on the fourth side, overlooks the valley below. The adobe brick walls are three feet thick, and the framework is constructed of beams hewn from solid trees and bound together with strong rawhide thongs; nails are not to be seen. Stout iron grilles and solid shutters provided protection in the event of attack.

The Petaluma Adobe State Historic Park (SRL 18), four miles east of Petaluma, was deeded by the Native Sons of the Golden West in 1951, who in turn had acquired the property from the heirs of William D. Bliss, the second owner of the property after Vallejo sold it in 1857. The State Division of Parks and Recreation has carried out an extensive program of restoration, with superb results. Many authorities consider this building

Vallejo House, Sonoma

to be the finest example of an adobe constructed during the Mexican period in California.

General Vallejo purchased a part of Rancho Agua Caliente, which had been given to Lázaro Piña in 1840 by Governor Alvarado. It stretched along Sonoma Creek beyond the outer line of the lands of the Pueblo de Sonoma to the east. Thaddeus M. Leavenworth, who had come to California as chaplain with Stevenson's regiment of New York Volunteers, became the owner of that part of the grant lying closest to Sonoma.

Adjoining the property of Leavenworth, the General put up a frame house (SRL 4) in 1850. It was prefabricated in the eastern United States and, with two others, was shipped around the Horn. He called it Lachryma Montis or "Tears of the Mountain" because of the large hot and cold springs in the nearby hillside. He lived there many years before his death in 1890, and his burial place is on a hill north of Sonoma quite near Lachryma Montis. In the immediate vicinity of the residence is a building called the Swiss Chalet. Its exterior is of brick and wood, the lumber having been brought around the Horn in 1849–50. Lachryma Montis and the Swiss Chalet, together with the surrounding seventeen acres of land, were purchased in 1933 by the State Park Commission. The Vallejo Home State Historical Monument is at the northern end of Third Street West in Sonoma; a museum is maintained in the Swiss Chalet.

One old adobe still stands on Rancho Agua Caliente, the Justi home, about three miles southwest of Kenwood on Dunbar Road. Built around 1850, it was at one time the Glen Ellen post office. It is wood-covered today. In the same area, at 13255 Sonoma Highway, is Glen Oaks, a beautiful stone mansion built in 1860.

Santa Rosa

Several tracts of land in Sonoma County were granted to relatives of General Vallejo's wife, Francisca Benicia Carrillo. These tracts included Rancho Cabeza de Santa Rosa, given to her widowed mother in 1837; Rancho Sotoyome, to Henry Fitch, a brother-in-law; Rancho Los Guilicos, to John Wilson, another brother-in-law; and Rancho Llano de Santa Rosa, to Joaquín Carrillo, a brother.

Both Fitch and his mother-in-law were residents of San Diego. Fitch continued to live in the south. Señora María Ignacia López de Carrillo moved to her Rancho Cabeza de Santa Rosa with her unmarried children and continued to reside there for the remainder of her life. The city of Santa Rosa is situated on part of her grant.

Her residence was located on the south side of Santa Rosa Creek. One ruined building remains near the corner of Hartley Drive and Franquette Avenue, just north of Montgomery Drive, in eastern Santa Rosa. There is a local tradition that the Carrillo adobes were originally built as an outpost of the mission at Sonoma, but records of the Franciscan order do not substantiate this claim. In his later years Salvador Vallejo confessed that he had mentioned the "Mission of Santa Rosa" in jest to Duflot de Mofras, a visitor to California in the early 1840's. Evidently the Frenchman took him seriously, for he included the "Mission" in the voluminous account of his travels published in Paris in 1844. Frank Marryatt's *Mountains and Molehills* (1855), however, specifically mentioned the ranch house as being adjacent to an adobe mission building. It is known that a chapel was maintained at the Carrillo home, but this was common practice in rancho days. In any event, whatever its ecclesiastical connections, the Carrillo adobe may safely be said to be the first dwelling erected in the vicinity of Santa Rosa.

The name of Santa Rosa Creek was supposedly bestowed by Father Juan Amoros of San Rafael when he baptized an Indian girl there in honor of Saint Rose of Lima in the late 1820's. A monument along the highway on the north side of Santa Rosa Creek, roughly opposite the Carrillo adobe, commemorates this event, but the baptism is recorded neither at San Rafael nor at Sonoma.

In 1853, the son Julio Carrillo filed claim for a part of his mother's property, two square leagues lying between Rancho San Miguel and Santa Rosa Creek. He built his house near the stream on a site that is now Second Street in Santa Rosa. In the early days of the settlement, he gave land for a plaza where the courthouse now stands.

The eldest son of the Carrillo family, who was named Joaquín after his father, received the grant of Llano de Santa Rosa from Governor Micheltorena in 1844. This tract of three square leagues adjoined his mother's property and lies due west of Santa Rosa. The tract previously had been granted to Marcus (Mark) West, who had allowed his right to lapse; upon petition, it was regranted to Joaquín Carrillo, who at once built a small house and later built a larger one, long ago torn down. This adobe faced the east on what is now Petaluma Avenue in Sebastopol. This street was once part of the old Spanish Trail and later was used by the stage lines.

A Santa Rosa landmark is the Church Built From One Tree. In 1873, a giant redwood growing near Guerneville was cut down, and the 78,000 board feet of lumber it produced went entirely into the construction of the First Baptist Church in Santa Rosa. The church was located for many years on B Street, but when the congre-gation moved to a new facility in 1957, the old building was moved to its present location on Sonoma Avenue near Santa Rosa Avenue and backed by Juilliard Park. Shortly thereafter, the church entered a new existence as a museum devoted to the spectacular career of Robert L. Ripley, Santa Rosa's native son, whose "Believe It Or Not" was a newspaper feature for many years and who died in 1949. In addition to displays about Ripley and the Church Built From One Tree, the museum features displays on Santa Rosa and the neighborhood.

The Sonoma County Museum is in the old post office building, now located at 425 Seventh Street in Santa Rosa. It displays changing exhibitions on various aspects of Sonoma County history.

Rancho Sotoyome and Alexander Valley

Henry Delano Fitch, a dashing young sea captain from Massachusetts, met Señorita Josefa Carrillo upon his arrival in San Diego in 1826. Three years later, plans were made for their marriage, but certain legal technicalities arose that forced them to postpone the wedding. The fact that the young captain was a foreigner was the main obstacle, but since the bride's parents gave consent, the date for the ceremony was set for April 15, 1829. At the last moment the friar who had planned to officiate weakened and decided he could not do so. Sympathetic relatives and friends made it possible for the young people to elope on the captain's boat the next day, and one story has it that the marriage took place in Valparaiso on July 3. (According to a document in the Bancroft Library at Berkeley, the wedding in Valparaiso occurred on January 18, 1831.)

Difficulties beset the pair on their return to California. Finally, as penance, Captain Fitch was asked to give "a bell of at least fifty pounds in weight for the church at Los Angeles," which he did. Thereafter he lived in San Diego, where he kept a store.

In 1841 Captain Fitch received a grant of three square leagues of land lying in Sonoma County, where his wife's sister and her husband, Mariano Vallejo, lived. Eight more leagues were added to this Rancho Sotoyome in 1844. Instead of residing on the property, Captain Fitch traveled north, inspected it, made arrangements for its upkeep, and returned to his business in the south. He sent an acquaintance, Cyrus Alexander, to live there and offered to give him, as remuneration, two leagues of land. Alexander, a trapper and trader, who had reached San Diego in 1833, agreed. Alexander Valley, northeast of Healdsburg, is named for him. His old adobe was restored as a private dwelling about 1970 and stands on the ranch at 8644 Highway 128, across the road from the old Alexander School, now also a private home.

On the southwestern boundary of Rancho Sotoyome, six miles south and west of Healdsburg, stands the hop kiln (SRL 893) of the former Walters ranch, a tripartite stone structure dating from 1902–4. Located at 6050 Westside Road, it remains as a monument to what was once a major hop-growing center of the United States. This area of the Russian River Valley is now an important vineyard region, known as the Sweetwater Historic District, and the building has been transformed into the Hop Kiln Winery.

Ranchos of the Russian River

In 1836 a tract of land along the Russian River was granted to Juan Bautista Rogers Cooper, who, after a seafaring life, settled in Monterey, where he met and married Encarnación Vallejo.

When Mariano Vallejo, Cooper's brother-in-law, returned to Monterey from an official visit to Bodega and Fort Ross, he told Cooper of the productive region he had seen. The area lying between the Estero Americano on the coast and the Russian River was then inhabited by only a few Russians and Indians. Vallejo encouraged Cooper to make a tour of inspection. This Cooper did and obtained a grant of four leagues along the Russian River in exchange for two tracts previously held by him on the American River.

On his new grant he built a sawmill in 1834, and called the tract Rancho El Molino. The sawmill, believed to be the first power-operated commercial sawmill in California, was actually put up in 1834, two years before the grant became official. The site (SRL 835) of Cooper's mill is about two miles north of Forestville on Mark West Creek, near the eastern end of the Mirabel Resort Trailer Park, off the River Road about 1,000 feet above the junction of the creek and the Russian River.

No buildings or sites remain from three other ranchos established in the region between Estero Americano and the Russian River. Ranchos Estero Americano, Cañada de Pogólimi, and Cañada de Jonive were granted to Americans recommended by Cooper. In 1858, the latter was patented to Jasper O'Farrell, who is remembered for having laid out the streets of San Francisco.

Rancho Bodega

Rancho Bodega, consisting of eight square leagues on the coast between Estero Americano and the Russian River, was granted to Stephen Smith by Governor Micheltorena in 1844. When the land was confirmed in 1859 and patented to the heirs of the grantee, the more than 35,000 acres claimed were accepted by the court as being "the same land described in the grant to Stephen Smith (now deceased)."

Smith, a native of Maryland who visited California in 1841, came from Peru, where he had spent a little time. On this visit, he made plans to return to California after a trip East and to set up a sawmill. The mill machinery was brought from Baltimore and set up in the redwood region east of Bodega Head. Although confident that the country would eventually belong to the United States, Smith obtained Mexican citizenship in order to become a landowner. Within two years after receiving the grant of Rancho Bodega, he had the pleasure of raising the American flag over his property. The eastern boundary line of his rancho lay a little way to the east of his mill, which was placed to the north of Salmon Creek. His house stood near the creek and north of the Estero Americano, the boundary between Ranchos Bodega and Blucher, the latter of which lay partly in neighboring Marin County. To both of these tracts he laid claim, and both were awarded to his descendants.

A year after the death of Stephen Smith in 1855, his widow married another Southerner, Tyler Curtis. Squatters caused trouble, resulting in what is called the "Bodega War"; and Curtis was forced to sell land, including an area that had been the site of the Russian settlement in 1811. The Curtis family moved to San Francisco, and in time Smith's adobe mansion succumbed to fire and erosion.

In the town of Bodega itself is the charming St. Teresa of Avila Catholic Church (SRL 820), built in 1859, a much-photographed white-painted frame building high on a hill.

Rancho Los Guilicos and Kenwood

John Wilson, who reached California in 1837 and married Ramona Carrillo, was the grantee of Rancho Los Guilicos, containing 18,833 acres and given by Governor Alvarado. It was patented in the name of William Hood in 1866. Afterward it was owned jointly by Mrs. Wilson and Hood, who had purchased a part of it. Hood's old home (SRL 692), built of fired brick in 1858, still stands, now within the grounds of the Los Guilicos Juvenile Facility, some nine miles east of Santa Rosa off SR 12. This rancho lies between Santa Rosa and Sonoma, the town of Glen Ellen being on its southern tip. The former Southern Pacific stations of Kenwood and Melita are on this old grant. In the old Pagani winery nearby, built in 1906, the Kenwood Vineyards Winery has been established.

Rancho Mallacomes and Knight's Valley

This rancho, lying in the upper part of Knight's Valley, consisted of 17,742 acres granted in 1843 by Governor Micheltorena to José de los Santos Berryessa. The grantee was a soldier at Sonoma from 1840 to 1842 and alcalde there in 1846.

Knight's Valley, in which this grant lay, was named for Thomas P. Knight, a native of Maine who came to California in 1845. After he reached the Sierra on his overland journey, an explosion of a keg of powder under his wagon destroyed all of his possessions, including a stock of goods that he had planned to sell. He took part in the Bear Flag Revolt and then went to the mines before settling down to be a farmer in Napa and Sonoma counties.

Knight lived in the two-story adobe built by Berryessa and made additions to it. A small part of the house still stands beside a newer dwelling in Knight's Valley, about seven and one-half miles northeast of Calistoga on SR 128, on the east side of the highway three-tenths of a mile south of the intersection of Franz Valley Road.

Rancho Cotati

Rancho Cotati, granted to Juan Castañeda in 1844, was patented to Thomas Page in 1858. Its 17,238 acres lay to the south of Santa Rosa. The Northwestern Pacific Railway passed through it early in the twentieth century, and the station of Cotati is in the southwestern quarter of the rancho. Cotati's hexagonal town plan was designed during the 1890's by Newton Smyth as an alternative to the traditional grid. (Only one other American city—Detroit, Michigan—is known to have a hexagonal street pattern.) Each of the streets surrounding the six-sided town plaza (SRL 879), where Dr. Page's barn once stood, is named after one of his sons. "Cotati" recalls the name of a local Indian chieftain.

Healdsburg

The valley of the Russian River was home to thousands of the Pomo family of Indians when the white settlers arrived. As elsewhere in California, diseases spread by the newcomers soon all but destroyed the indigenous population, beginning with the smallpox epidemic of 1837. It has been estimated that upwards of 10,000 Pomo villagers lived in the area in the 1830's; only twelve were recorded in 1916.

Much of this region became part of Rancho Sotoyome. As the quarrel between squatters and the widow Fitch erupted following Captain Fitch's death in 1849, disputes over rightful ownership of land became frequent. Thanks to the support of the pioneer lawyer Colonel L. A. Norton, Mrs. Fitch was ultimately confirmed in the title to most of her property, and the squatters, many of whom had already settled and begun farming, bought and paid for their land.

One such settler was Ohio-born Harmon Heald, who had come to the area with his brothers in 1850 after a failed attempt at gold mining. Heald noted the advantageous location of that part of Rancho Sotoyome bordering the trail between San Francisco and the northern mines. In 1851 he built a cabin along this route at what is today the 300 block of Healdsburg Avenue. He added a store the following year and opened a post office in 1854. Buying up what land he could, he obtained title to it when the Fitch claim was cleared, and in 1857 he officially subdivided and laid out a town he named Healdsburg. He donated lots for a central park, a school, a cemetery, and churches; the remaining lots were sold for $15 apiece.

The town was incorporated in 1867, eight years after Heald's death. With the arrival of the Northwestern Pacific Railroad in 1871, Healdsburg began to flourish as an agricultural exporting center, which in large part it remains today. Wine making is now its principal activity.

Healdsburg's plaza remains a center of activity. It is bordered by many well-preserved buildings, such as the old Schwab Brothers Show Store at 113 Plaza Street, built in 1883, and two structures from 1885, the Gobbi Building at 312 Center Street and the Cook Hardware Building next door at 318 Center Street. Healdsburg is also a city of well-preserved homes, of which the John Hassett house (1853) at 239 Center is the oldest known. Two interesting Greek Revival homes, both built in 1871, are the Polly Reynolds house at 105 Fitch Street and the Samuel Meyer house at 308 Tucker Street. An earlier Greek Revival house (1854) is associated with the name of Lindsay Carson, brother of Kit Carson, who settled here in the 1850's and 1860's. The building is now a law office at 641 Healdsburg Avenue. The Healdsburg Museum is located at 133 Matheson Street, just east of the plaza.

Petaluma

The Petaluma River, actually a slough, runs northward from San Pablo Bay to the present-day city of Petaluma. It is thought that it was first ascended by a Spanish expedition under Ferdinand Quiros in 1776. In 1819, Father Mariano Payéras visited the Llano de los Petalumas ("the plain of the Petaluma Indians"). Mariano Vallejo began the construction of his impressive adobe nearby in 1834.

It was the river that determined the placement of

the city of Petaluma. Hunters' camps and trading posts to supply the gold miners appeared on its banks in 1849. The valley became an important source of grain, exported to San Francisco. Waterborne commerce between San Francisco and Petaluma throve until August 1950, when the last steamer, the *Petaluma*, moored for the last time at Gold Landing in McNear Canal. In addition to cereal and vegetable crops, Petaluma became known for its poultry. In 1879 L. C. Byce won a gold medal at the California State Fair for his new incubator and soon thereafter began to make in Petaluma the brooders and incubators that made the mass production of poultry both possible and profitable. In 1918, Bert Kerrigan, secretary of the Petaluma chamber of commerce, dubbed the town "The Egg Basket of the World."

Petaluma today is a more diversified place than it was fifty years ago, when "Chicken Is King" was its motto. It retains some striking older buildings, mostly along Kentucky and Fourth streets and Petaluma Boulevard North. The "Iron Front" buildings from the 1880's and 1890's, early examples of prefabrication, are outstanding; their factory-made fronts, usually of cast or sheet iron, were fashioned in San Francisco and then shipped to Petaluma. The 1906 earthquake, so destructive to Santa Rosa and San Francisco, spared Petaluma, and consequently many of these buildings are unaltered from their original design. On the south side of Western Avenue, between Kentucky Street and Petaluma Boulevard North, is a matchless row of iron fronts, including the Masonic Hall, the former Arcade Saloon, the New Model Saloon, and the Mutual Relief Building. The smaller, graceful iron front of the McNear building (1886) can be seen where Petaluma Boulevard North bends at Center Park. Extending west for some blocks on D Street west of Fourth is an attractive row of houses from many different periods. The Petaluma Museum is housed in the old Carnegie Library at the corner of Fourth and B streets.

A few miles northwest of Petaluma, on Stony Point Road at Roblar Road, stands the Washoe house, once an important stage stop and today one of the diminishing number of typical roadhouses to be found along the old routes of California. It was built about 1859. Farther to the west are Two Rock, a community that has all but disappeared, although the two large boulders that gave it the name are still prominent landmarks on the hillside, and Bloomfield, a collection of photogenic old homes and business buildings.

The Vineyard of Colonel Haraszthy

Wine grapes from Europe were first grown successfully in Sonoma County, which has remained an area of exceptionally productive vineyards and wineries. Colonel Agoston Haraszthy, a Hungarian nobleman who has often been called "the father of wine making in California," attempted first to ripen grapes from his imported stock at Crystal Springs in San Mateo County in 1852, but met with slight success there. Looking for a proper soil and climate for his purpose, he moved to the protected Sonoma Valley, where General Vallejo had already made one variety of wine from the ordinary mission grape.

In 1856 Colonel Haraszthy purchased a piece of land east of the town of Sonoma that became known as the Buena Vista Vineyard and placed his son Attila in charge. In 1857 he employed Chinese labor to dig a tunnel into the hillside, where he stored five thousand gallons of wine as an initial vintage. This tunnel was followed by another in 1858 and a third in 1862. In that year the first stone cellar was built of rock excavated from the tunnels. Another and larger cellar, also with three tunnels, was begun in 1864. In 1862 Haraszthy's winery was the first in the world to use California redwood for wine tanks. Redwood tanks are now standard storage for wines in many areas. The old cellars (SRL 392) may still be seen at the Buena Vista Winery at the end of Old Winery Road, two miles northeast of Sonoma.

In 1861, Governor Downey appointed a committee to report on the ways and means of improving viticulture in California. One member of the committee was Colonel Haraszthy, who went to Europe and brought home cuttings of every obtainable variety. One of these, the Zinfandel of much-disputed origin, later became a major California product. In 1868, the colonel went to

Buena Vista Winery, near Sonoma

Nicaragua, where his mysterious disappearance was reported the following year; it is supposed that he met his death while crossing a river.

Arpad Haraszthy, his son, went to Europe in 1857 to be educated. After having spent two years in the study of wine making, particularly the making of champagne, and in visiting vineyards and wineries, he returned to California. Years of experimental work were necessary before he was satisfied with the champagne made under Western conditions. Arpad Haraszthy was the first president of the California Viticultural Commission.

The Sebastiani Winery (SRL 739) at Fourth Street East near Spain Street is another interesting Sonoma winery. Around the turn of the century, Samuele Sebastiani purchased the original vineyard of Mission San Francisco Solano, first planted in 1825. It was here that General Vallejo, after the secularization of the mission, produced many prizewinning wines. The Grundlach-Bundschu Winery at the end of Thornsberry Road goes back to 1858.

The Asti Colony

The Italian Swiss Agricultural Colony (SRL 621) was organized in 1881 under the leadership of Andrea Sbarboro. Its membership consisted of 100 immigrants living in San Francisco who had been thrown out of work by hard times. The members paid one dollar per month for each share of stock they owned. The committee appointed to select a location for the colony chose the Truett Ranch, a tract of 1,500 acres bordering the Russian River. This was a succession of rolling hills with red soil on which oak trees grew. Higher hills beyond, thickly covered with forests of fir, oak, madrone, and pine, made this a sheltered basin. Similar in appearance to the famed wine district of Mount Ferrat in northern Italy, it was put to a like use in the planting of vineyards.

In 1887 a substantial concrete winery 150 by 52 feet was built. Adjoining it was a cooper shop where trained men from Germany put together large casks and puncheons, while the outside work of the vineyards was done entirely by Italians. As the colony prospered, the acreage was increased, and larger equipment was needed. To celebrate the completion of a wine vat with a capacity of 500,000 gallons built for blending purposes, a dance was given at which 50 couples and a ten-piece band were accommodated on the floor of the vat.

The quaint little church of Our Lady of Mount Carmel, built in the shape of half a wine barrel, remains as a landmark, although it has been replaced by a newer church. The current name for the winery is Colony; it is located at the Asti turnoff of US 101, four miles south of Cloverdale.

Fountain Grove

At the northeastern edge of Santa Rosa, where Business Highway 101 joins the US 101 freeway, Fountain Grove stands as a memorial to one of the several utopian colonies that flourished in northern California in the late nineteenth century. Thomas Lake Harris, spiritualist leader of the Brotherhood of the New Life, moved some of his followers here from the East in 1875. Robert V. Hine writes that the Brotherhood of the New Life was "the product of ecclesiastical revolt, a deep feeling for social reform, Christianity, spiritualism, and Swedenborgianism mixed in the mind of Harris with later additions of Oriental mysticism and late nineteenth-century anti-monopoly socialism." Much of the 1,500 acres that Harris acquired was planted with vineyards. About 30 colonists, most of whom lived in a community house, thus supported themselves until 1891, at which time difficulties, including rumors of scandalous activities, caused the downfall of the colony. After the dispersal of the colonists, Kanaye Nagasawa, Harris's disciple, remained at Fountain Grove, of which he became the sole owner in the 1920's. Nagasawa managed the Fountain Grove Winery until his death in 1934. The community house burned long ago, but other buildings remain, including the disused winery, Harris's home, and some interesting round barns. The area is currently being developed as a light industry and recreational park as well as a large residential tract.

The Burbank Experimental Farm

Luther Burbank, whose name first was brought prominently before the public with the Burbank potato, was born in Massachusetts in 1849. A student of nature from his earliest years, he desired a mild climate in which to work, and in 1878 he purchased four acres of land at the edge of Santa Rosa. On this tract he grew specimens from many parts of the world and carried on extensive research in plant life. He developed a marked improvement in certain vegetables, fruits, and flowers and, by hybridization, produced striking changes in size, form, and color. As time went on, more space was needed, and in 1885 he purchased eighteen acres near Sebastopol, where he established the Burbank Experimental Farm and where by planting large fields he was able to carry on more extensive experiments than before. He became known as "the Plant Wizard," and the results of his labors can be seen in orchards and gardens throughout the world. At his death in his late seventies, he left behind him an extraordinary record of accomplishment. He lies buried beneath a tree in his Santa Rosa garden.

After her husband's death in 1926, Mrs. Burbank moved into the charming two-story cottage that, with its adjoining gardens, is now administered by the city of Santa Rosa (SRL 234). The Luther Burbank Home and Gardens have also been registered as a National Historic Landmark. There is a small museum of Burbank memorabilia in the old carriage house, and since Mrs. Burbank's death in 1977, the home has been open to the public for a limited tour.

Jack London's Cottage, Jack London State Historic Park, Glen Ellen

Cloverdale

Cloverdale, in the Russian River Valley at the northern edge of the county, was famous early in the twentieth century for its citrus crops; it is the most northerly point in the state where citrus fruit is grown. Each February the town has a well-attended Citrus Festival. An interesting museum of local history is maintained by the Cloverdale Historical Society at 215 North Cloverdale Boulevard.

Three miles south of Cloverdale, on Bluxome Creek, the short-lived Icaria-Speranza Community (SRL 981) was established in 1881. This was the only French utopian ("Icarian") colony founded in California. Like other Icarian communities started in Iowa and in the Mississippi Valley in the 1870's, this one believed in liberty, brotherhood, and freedom, as well as the importance of marriage, family life, and education.

Jack London State Historic Park

On a wooded hillside overlooking the orchards and vineyards of the Valley of the Moon is the ranch that was once the home of Jack London, author of *The Call of the Wild*, *The Sea-Wolf*, and other tales of adventure as well as of social criticism. Although he was often elsewhere for months at a time, London lived here from 1905 until his death in 1916 at the age of 40. His widow, Charmian, continued to live on the property, and in 1919 she built the "House of Happy Walls" of native fieldstone as a memorial to her husband. Although the Sonoma Valley is known to have been called the Valle de la Luna as early as 1841, Jack London's writings made the name "Valley of the Moon" world-famous.

In 1959 Irving Shephard, nephew of Jack London and heir of Charmian London, gave 40 acres of the ranch to the state of California. This includes Chairmian's home, now a museum of Jack London artifacts, and the au-

thor's grave, marked by a red lava boulder and close to the graves of two pioneer children that were on the land when London bought it. By far the most unusual landmark, however, is the ruined "Wolf House," which was to have been the Londons' permanent home and was nearly completed when it burned on September 22, 1913. Although London hoped to rebuild, nothing was done except to clear away debris. The remaining four-story exterior, with its archways, chimneys, and staircases built of native volcanic stone, is one of California's most-photographed historic spots.

Jack London State Historic Park (SRL 743) has recently acquired the author's "Beauty Ranch" adjoining the 40 acres of the original grant. At this ranch, London built experimental (and expensive) quarters for his livestock; the stallion barn and the circular "pig palace" can still be seen. "The Cottage," where London died on November 22, 1916, is not open to the public, but there are plans to restore it. A short distance northwest of Glen Ellen, the park has also been registered by the Department of the Interior as a National Historic Landmark.

Mount St. Helena

Mount St. Helena is at the point where Sonoma, Lake, and Napa counties meet. On one of the northwest spurs of the mountain, seven miles in a straight line northeast of Geyserville, are the Geysers, while near its southern slope, partly in Napa County and partly in Sonoma, lies the Petrified Forest—indications of the mountain's volcanic origin.

The mountain was named in honor of the patron saint of Russia by Princess Helena de Gagarin. The princess, wife of Count Alexander Rotcheff, governor-general of Siberia and of the Russian colonies on the shores of the North Pacific, had read the fascinating descriptions of California made by the great navigator Otto Kotzebue. Arriving at Fort Ross in 1841, she organized an expedition to the interior of California that included the first recorded ascent of the peak, which she and her companions made on June 20 of that year.

In May 1853 the tablet placed on Mount St. Helena by the Russians twelve years before was found by Dr. T. A. Hylton of Petaluma. It was later placed in the museum of the Society of California Pioneers in San Francisco, only to be destroyed in the fire of 1906. Dr. Hylton had made a paper facsimile of the tablet, from which a replica was made in 1912. The replica was placed on the summit of Mount St. Helena in commemoration of the centenary of the founding of Fort Ross.

The Geysers

The Indians believed that the Great Spirit dwelling within the mountain worked miracles, and their sick went to the healing springs and hot-water jets that welled up in the vicinity of the Geysers. In April 1847, the pioneer hunter and trapper William B. Elliott came suddenly upon the region while tracking a wounded bear. Back in Sonoma, he told his friends that he had found the gates to the Inferno.

The Geysers became a tourist attraction, and in 1854 an inn was built nearby, which registered twenty visitors its first year. A larger hotel, built from lumber sawed on the spot, was erected in 1857–58. Its register displayed the signatures of presidents Ulysses S. Grant, William McKinley, and Theodore Roosevelt, as well as those of Giuseppe Garibaldi, Horace Greeley, Mark Twain, J. Pierpont Morgan, and William Jennings Bryan. The hotel was destroyed by fire in 1937.

The Geysers are now closed to the public and there is little to be seen at the end of the long roads twisting up the mountain. The region is being developed as a source of thermal power by the Pacific Gas and Electric Company and some other firms.

The Petrified Forest

Surrounded by groves of living oak, fir, and redwood, the Petrified Forest lies across a small valley from the southwestern base of Mount St. Helena at an eleva-

tion of 1,000 feet. The petrified trees that form the group are mainly redwood, silicified and opalized. They lie in two tiers in a parallelogram a mile in extent from east to west and about a quarter of a mile from north to south. The trees, measuring from three and one-half to twelve feet in diameter and as much as 126 feet in length, were buried millions of years ago by lava from the now-extinct volcano five miles to the north. The fact that the trees are all lying with their tops pointing away from Mount St. Helena seems to indicate that lava streams from the cone caused their downfall and their ultimate preservation in forms of stone.

The forest was discovered in the 1850's, but excavation was not begun until 1870, when the prospector Charles Evans, "Petrified Charlie," homesteaded the land. Much of the brush, volcanic ashes, and deposits of silica that had pressed upon the trees for ages was removed by Evans, who enclosed the ground and charged a small fee to visitors, one of whom was Robert Louis Stevenson. In *The Silverado Squatters* (1880) Stevenson gives a more detailed description of the proprietor than of the property, which is still a privately owned attraction.

In all the specimens found in this ancient stone forest, the transmutation from wood to stone has been so perfect that texture and fiber are completely preserved, making it easy for scientists to determine species. Many of the trees are of great size and, though broken, retain the relative positions of the pieces. The largest tree in the group was uncovered in 1919 at a depth of 90 feet. It lies intact and is one of the most perfect specimens known. In 1930 Professor Erlingdorf of Princeton University found twelve varieties of prehistoric fossilized leaves on the property.

The Petrified Forest (SRL 915) can be reached by leaving US 101 at Santa Rosa on Mark West Springs Road and continuing twelve miles northeast on this road and its continuations, Porter Creek Road and Petrified Forest Road. The forest lies five miles west of Calistoga in Napa County on Petrified Forest Road. En route from Santa Rosa is Mark West Lodge, now a restaurant. Mineral hot springs were discovered here by William Travis in 1857, and the place was operated as a resort for many years.

Stanislaus County

Stanislaus County was named for the river that forms part of its border with San Joaquin County to the north. The river was named for an Indian chief who was baptized by the padres under the Spanish name Estanislao, for one of the two Polish saints, Stanislaus Kostka or Stanislaus of Krakow. The county was organized in 1854 from a part of Tuolumne County, and the first county seat was placed at Adamsville. Within a few months the seat of justice was moved to Empire City; in December 1855 it was transferred to La Grange; in 1862 to Knight's Ferry; and in 1871 it was finally located at Modesto.

The Stanislaus River

The Stanislaus is one of the major rivers flowing from the Sierra Nevada into the San Joaquin Valley. It is one of the few "wild" rivers in California, which means that for most of its length it is not barred by dams or reclamation projects. The first white man to arrive at the Stanislaus was Gabriel Moraga, who discovered it in 1806 while on one of his several exploring expeditions through the river country of the north in search of mission sites. He explored it again on that remarkable expedition of 1808 when he crossed for the second time all the Sierra rivers as far north as the Upper Sacramento and discovered the territory of at least ten additional counties. In 1810 he again ranged the country watered by the Stanislaus, in an unsuccessful attempt to capture runaway Indians.

Estanislao was such an Indian. Baptized at Mission San José, he was educated by Padre Narciso Durán, and one story says that he was especially proficient in music. In 1827 or 1828 he ran away from the mission and took refuge in the San Joaquin Valley, where he became a leader of the Indian people. The Mexican authorities believed that he and his followers were preparing a general uprising, and three separate military expeditions were sent against them. The third, led by Mariano Vallejo in 1829, brought defeat to Estanislao and his people. The site of the battle (SRL 214) is in San Joaquin County, near Ripon, on the north bank of the Stanislaus River, which seems to have been named at this time for the redoubtable chieftain.

John C. Frémont, who ferried the river on March 30, 1844, and camped on the Stanislaus County side, described its scenery thus: "Issuing from the woods, we rode about sixteen miles over open prairie partly covered with bunch grass, the timber reappearing on the rolling hills of the River Stanislaus, in the usual belt of evergreen oaks. The level valley was about forty feet below the upland, and the stream seventy yards broad, with the usual fertile bottom land which was covered with green grass among large oaks. We encamped on one of these bottoms, in a grove of the large white oaks previously mentioned."

The Old West Side

Recently occupied Indian campsites existed on the arroyos along the west side of the San Joaquin Valley when the first white men came to the region. Remains of some of these ancient villages were long in evidence, the most noteworthy being located on Arroyo de las Garzas, about six miles from the edge of the valley, and on arroyos de Orestimba, del Puerto, and del Hospital.

El Camino Viejo, the old road of the Spanish and Mexican periods, followed along the west side of the San Joaquin Valley and crossed many creeks that are known today by their Spanish names. Among those in Stanislaus County are Arroyo de las Garzas ("the herons"), Arroyo de Orestimba ("the meeting place," so called because the padres, when first gathering Indian neophytes in the region, made an agreement with the remaining natives to meet them there again the following year), Arroyo Salado Grande ("big salty creek," where the pioneer known as "Salty" Smith settled in 1855), Arroyo del Puerto ("the gate," so named because of the natural cut in the hills west of Patterson through which the creek flows during the rainy season), and Arroyo del Hospital (named for the experience of a party of Spaniards who, overcome by sickness, rested beside this stream and were healed).

Spanish settlement on the west side seems to have had an early beginning, for at least one Spaniard, a deserter from the cavalry, settled on Arroyo de las Garzas as early as 1820. A battle took place in the vicinity that year, when a detachment of Spanish troops came to get both the fugitive soldier and some Indians who had run away from missions. American pioneers in 1852 found the mestizo son of this former cavalryman living in an adobe on Arroyo de las Garzas just across the line in Merced County several miles west of the present town of Gustine.

Above the sycamore grove on Arroyo de Orestimba stood the ranch house of Rancho Orestimba y las Garzas, granted in 1844 to Sebastián Núñez, a son-in-law of Francisco Pacheco.

Jesse Hill, one of the owners of Hill's Ferry on the San Joaquin River, settled on the Arroyo de las Garzas in 1854, where he built a house from lumber brought around the Horn and hauled to Las Garzas by ox team. The site was later occupied by one of the Simon Newman Company sheep camps.

Hill's Ferry

A ferry across the San Joaquin River at the site later known as Hill's Ferry was first operated in the autumn of 1849, when a man named Thompson carried emigrants from Mexico who were traveling to the mines via Pacheco Pass across the river at this point. Jesse Hill and John de Hart later purchased the ferry from Thompson. After De Hart's death, Hill became the sole owner, until in 1865 the ferry passed into the hands of C. G. Hubner.

By this date the town of Hill's Ferry had achieved some importance as a shipping point for grain. During the high-water season, from April to July, boats customarily came up the river this far to exchange their cargoes for grain and other farm produce. But during the rest of the year the isolation of the town was complete. There was no telegraph service, and the mails had to be brought in by stage from Banta, a day's journey away. Nevertheless, during its heyday, Hill's Ferry was a lively place. Its very isolation infused it with a decidedly "Wild West" spirit. Horse thieves and outlaws found it a convenient crossing place en route to mountain hideouts. The place became noted for its tough characters, and there was much drinking, gambling, and shooting.

In 1886–87, at the time the west side railroad was being constructed, Simon Newman, who was the chief merchant at Hill's Ferry, donated some land to the railroad. When the town of Newman was laid out on this land in 1887, the people of Hill's Ferry and those living at Dutch Corners, two miles away, were induced to move to the new town. With this change Hill's Ferry literally ceased to exist, since most of the houses were soon carted away to other locations. The site of Hill's Ferry is on the west bank of the San Joaquin River about five miles northeast of Newman.

Knight's Ferry

Knight's Ferry (SRL 347), an old mining town and trading post on the Stanislaus River 40 miles southeast

of Stockton, was founded in the spring of 1849 by William Knight, an Indianan who was educated as a physician but in the West was a hunter and trapper. He first came to California with the Workman-Rowland party in 1841. The following year he brought his family from New Mexico, and in 1843 they settled on the banks of the Sacramento in Yolo County at a place still called Knight's Landing.

The first ferry to be established on the Stanislaus River was the one at Knight's Ferry, on the old Sonora Road from Stockton to the southern mines. As early as 1850 thousands of miners passed this way, when ferry receipts could scarcely have been less than $500 a day. The importance and prosperity of Knight's Ferry were further enhanced by the fact that the river bars and banks, hills and gulches, were rich in gold for miles in all directions. Above the ferry was Two Mile Bar, and below it was Keeler's Flat, where Keeler's Ferry, in the shadow of what is now called Lover's Leap, was started later in 1849.

After the death of William Knight in a shoot-out on November 9, 1849, John and Lewis Dent came into possession of the ferry. In 1854 it was superseded by a bridge built on the site of the present structure. During the same year the Dents and David Locke erected a gristmill and a sawmill on the riverbank some 300 yards above the ferry. In 1856 a town was laid out on the north bank of the river. This was referred to by some as Dentville, since by now three Dent brothers and their families lived there, but the name was always officially Knight's Ferry. The place continued to grow and prosper, and from 1862 to 1871 it was the county seat of Stanislaus County.

Knight's Ferry is still one of the most picturesque of the old river towns. Perhaps its most striking feature is a wooden covered bridge, built in 1864 to replace the bridge from 1854, which was destroyed in the flood of 1862. At 330 feet it is the longest covered bridge in the

Covered Bridge, Knight's Ferry

western United States. It is now open only for pedestrian traffic. The house built in 1851 by Lewis Dent, the oldest building in town, still stands on Ellen Street. The Dents' brother-in-law, U.S. Army Captain Ulysses S. Grant, who was stationed on the Pacific Coast while his wife, Julia Dent Grant, remained at home in Indiana, visited the house on three occasions between 1852 and 1854.

The general store on Main Street has been doing business steadily since it was constructed in 1852, making it the oldest continuously operating general store in California. Excepting regular holidays, it has been closed only once, for three days in the flood of 1955. The Isaac Dakin home (1853) and a modern replica of Dakin's Smithy are other sights of the town. The Village Church was built in 1900 on the foundation of the original building of 1860 and was first known as the Knight's Ferry Methodist Episcopal Church. Another old building that has seen much service is the Masonic Hall, built in 1870 and still in use. Knight's Ferry is an outstanding example of an old town that is very much alive today, still flourishing around its well-preserved buildings. About two miles southeast on Willms Road is the headquarters of the Willms Ranch (SRL 415). John R. Willms, a German-born Forty-niner, and his partner, John H. Kappelmann, began to acquire land here in 1852 and eventually had 3,600 acres. Kappelmann died in 1881, and Willms carried on alone until, at his death in 1910, the ranch totaled 8,600 acres. The present ranch house, built in 1892, replaced an earlier one destroyed by fire. The ranch remains private property; members of the Willms family still own and live on it.

La Grange

La Grange was first known as French Bar, French miners having come to that region to prospect as early as 1852. Later the settlement was moved higher up on the bank of the Tuolumne River away from the original bar. By 1855 La Grange had become a thriving center of trade, since the bulk of the population in the county had moved up into the mining regions. The county seat was transferred from Empire City to La Grange in December 1855, and there it remained until 1862, when another contest took it to Knight's Ferry by a majority of only 29 votes.

At the height of its prosperity, La Grange had from 4,000 to 5,000 inhabitants and was served daily by three or more stage lines. During the 1870's extensive hydraulic operations were carried on in the vicinity, when ditches were built at a cost of $5 million to convey water to the diggings. The La Grange Dam near the Tuolumne County line was built in 1891–93, and today it is part of

the system of Stanislaus County reservoirs that supplies the Modesto and Turlock irrigation districts. The Tuolumne River is the life force of the region.

For several miles along the banks of the Tuolumne, thousands of rock mounds and pyramids stand as monuments to the Herculean efforts of early miners to harvest gold from the river's bed. The tiny town of La Grange has a very attractive setting on the Tuolumne River. The National Register of Historic Places includes the entire town in its listing, and the Stanislaus County Historical Society has marked historic spots. Most of these are congregated at the east end of Main Street, by the modern Fire Department.

Several deserted old stone buildings, with heavy iron doors, can be seen in town. Among them is the oldest remaining structure in La Grange, identified as the trading post built in 1850–51 by John Inman and William Sanders. The old jail was marked with a plaque by E Clampus Vitus in 1976. Part of the old adobe post office has been incorporated into a barn. St. Louis's Catholic Church and the deserted Odd Fellows Hall are other landmarks. The most recent plaque commemorating La Grange (SRL 414) was placed by the Native Daughters of the Golden West in 1984 at SR 132 and San Pedro Dam Road.

A ferry was operated at La Grange, first by Nathan McFarland and later by Anthony B. McMillan, from the early 1850's until about 1880, when a bridge was built across the Tuolumne at this point. Two miles below the town, where the present highway bridge spans the river, is the site of Branch's Ferry, which George C. Branch operated from 1851 to 1862; this is now a boat-launching spot in La Grange Regional Park.

Adamsville and Empire City

When Adamsville, which was founded in 1849, was made the first county seat of Stanislaus County in 1854, there were so few buildings in the place that the initial session of court was held out of doors, under a large tree. Before many months the county government was moved to nearby Empire City, and Adamsville, on the south bank of the Tuolumne River, ceased to exist. No marker indicates its precise site.

Empire City (SRL 418) was originally situated on the Tuolumne River twenty miles from its mouth. It was laid out on the south side of the river by John G. Marvin, a lawyer from Boston, who later became the first California state superintendent of schools.

Because it was at the head of navigation on the river, Empire City was made the Army supply station in 1851 for outlying forts, including Fort Miller and Fort Tejón. Floods nearly destroyed the place in 1852, but it was rebuilt and became the county seat in 1854 after a hard political fight, only to have the seat of justice moved to La Grange little more than a year later. Today the cemetery is all that remains of the first Empire City, which had lost its importance some time before the later Empire City was laid out as a trade center for a growing farm community. The pioneer burial ground has been incorporated into Lakewood Memorial Park, about one mile south of the present town of Empire on Highway J-7; a plaque placed by the Native Daughters of the Golden West is to be seen at the entrance to the park. A monument has been placed by E Clampus Vitus to the memory of the citizens of old Empire City, at the turn-off from the highway to the park.

Tuolumne River Ferries

There were a number of ferries up and down the Tuolumne that served as crossings to the Mariposa mines in the 1850's. Dickenson's Ferry, located below the present Roberts' Ferry Road Bridge about eight miles east of Waterford, was established in the early 1850's by Gallant Duncan Dickenson and developed into one of the most important stopping places on the old Fort Miller Road. Dickenson, who came overland with his family from Missouri in 1846, was an active, energetic man who engaged in many pioneer enterprises. Shortly after his arrival in California he became a member of Aram's garrison at Santa Clara, and in 1847 he built at Monterey what is said to be California's first brick house. The following year he mined for gold at Dickenson's Gulch in Tuolumne County, and from there he went to Stockton, where he built and operated a hotel and served as Prefect of the San Joaquin District in 1849–50.

In 1862 John W. Roberts, who had come from Boston in 1849, purchased the properties at Dickenson's Ferry, which now became known as Roberts' Ferry. When the original Dickenson Hotel was destroyed by fire in 1865, Roberts immediately replaced it with a two-story brick structure, the lower story of which still stands near the river.

At Horr's Ranch, near Roberts' Ferry, an unsuccessful attempt was made in the 1860's by Dr. B. D. Horr to found the town of Horrsville, a name that may have been doomed from the outset. A little pioneer cemetery located near the present highway a half-mile north of the river and a half-mile west of Roberts' Ferry Road Bridge marks the approximate site of the town.

Among other early ferries on the Tuolumne was Salter and Morley's Ferry. Calvin Salter and his partner, I. D. Morley, took up ranch land two miles east of Dickenson's Ferry and four miles below Branch's Ferry. There they established a ferry, stage station, and post office. Salter's farm was on the river near the ford, while Morley's land occupied the site on which the Turlock Reservoir now stands.

Tuolumne City

Many development schemes throughout California in the early American days, 1846–56, came to naught. Newcomers with no knowledge of California learned to their grief that water and weather and soil conditions in the region paid no heed to the plans of the new entrepreneurs.

Among the several towns founded with great expectations along the Tuolumne River was Tuolumne City, located about three miles from the mouth of the river where it joins the San Joaquin. Paxson McDowell, its promoter, dreamed of great wealth when he established the town in the spring of 1850. Lots were staked out on a plot of 160 acres and were sold at high prices. Unfortunately, when summer came it was found that the river was too low for navigation, and the place soon became deserted.

In the middle 1860's Tuolumne City was revived as the center for a small farming community, and navigation on the river during high water was resumed. When nearby Modesto became the county seat in 1871, however, it seems that virtually all the inhabitants of Tuolumne City moved there, along with the newspaper that became the *Modesto Bee*.

A rival of this town existed for a time in Paradise, laid out in 1867 by John Mitchell on his ranch in Paradise Valley five miles east of Tuolumne City. A flour mill, a warehouse, and a number of stores were built. During the several years of prosperity that Paradise experienced, regular weekly and tri-weekly boat service from Stockton was maintained. But with the founding of Modesto, Paradise also came to an end. At least two houses still standing in Modesto were first erected in Paradise and brought into the new city: they are the Church home at 302 Burney Street and the house at 1016 Franklin Street, which has been in Modesto since 1870.

A. J. Grayson, in 1850, established a ferry on the San Joaquin River eight miles above the mouth of the Tuolumne, and a settlement known as Grayson grew up there. After 1852 the place was practically deserted for several years, although the ferry was still operated. In 1868, after the development of grain farming in the region, the place was surveyed and a town was laid out by J. W. Van Benschotten, who had purchased the ferry. A brisk upriver trade caused the place to flourish until the building of the west side railroad in the middle 1880's. Grayson today is a small town two miles north-east of Westley.

Langworth and Burneyville, Oakdale and Riverbank

The present towns of Oakdale and Riverbank, which date from the 1870's, are the successors of Langworth and Burneyville, respectively, which had been established before the coming of the railroad. Langworth, plotted as a town in 1860 by Henry Langworthy, was located on the Mariposa Road on the hill above the ferry owned by James Burney. Burney was a former sheriff of Mariposa County and a member of the Mariposa Battalion under Major James D. Savage in 1851. He moved down the river to begin Burneyville in 1867. When the railroad was run east of this site in 1871, the post office moved to the new town of Oakdale, and Langworth was finished. A plaque commemorating the town was placed by E Clampus Vitus at the junction of Langworth Road and SR 108, about three miles west of Oakdale. Oakdale has been an agricultural processing and shipping center for many years, as well as a stopover for travelers on the way to Yosemite from the San Francisco Bay Area.

At the corner of First and High streets in Riverbank, an E Clampus Vitus plaque notes that Burneyville was founded on the riverbank below the bluff by Major James Burney in 1867. Burney operated a second ferry at this point for a few years. He then served with distinction, in the words of the plaque, as "public servant, school superintendent and justice of the peace; Burney lived a full life [and] died 1901 at the age of 87 years." The small community of Burneyville has been absorbed by the expanding town of Riverbank.

Modesto

Modesto is the offspring of the railroad. The Central Pacific reached the site in 1870, and it was two years before the next thrust down the San Joaquin Valley carried the line farther south and east. Although early accounts seem to agree that the railroad terminus was not an attractive spot, it was clear to many people that the future of Stanislaus County lay along this central route. Within a year the new community was chosen to be the county seat, even though accommodations were so few that the county offices were scattered among boarding houses, the back rooms of commercial buildings, and similar improvised quarters.

The explanation most often given for the distinctive name of the town—Modesto is Spanish for "modesty"—goes as follows. The directors of the Central Pacific named railroad stops for officials of the company or members of their families. The name of William C. Ralston was proposed for the new town, but the San Francisco banker declined the honor. The chosen name reflects his unusual modesty in so doing.

Modesto's early history is full of stories of Wild West hell-raising in saloons and dens of iniquity. Vigilantes frequently purged the undesirable elements, who returned after a short while. At the same time, the undeniable progress in agriculture and the prosperity brought by the railroad ensured that a more serious, permanent quality would eventually take over in the community. In 1912, the energetic Modesto Business Men's Association received permission to erect an ornamental iron arch at the intersection of Ninth and I streets in what was then the commercial heart of town. (Other Central Valley towns, such as Lodi and Orland, made the same kind of construction.) Although the slogan to be written on the arch was originally NOBODY'S GOT MODESTO'S GOAT, sanity mercifully prevailed and the runner-up in the competition for the slogan—MODESTO: WATER WEALTH CONTENTMENT HEALTH—was chosen. It can be seen to this day, smartly embellished with electric lights at night, as the planners intended.

The McHenry Museum at 1402 I Street is housed in what was once the city library building, given to the city in 1912 by the McHenry family. Among its treasures are reconstructed offices, a large collection of guns and cattle brands from Stanislaus County, and a research and archive center for Modesto and Stanislaus County history. The McHenry Mansion, in which this prominent family lived, is nearby at Fifteenth and I

McHenry Mansion, Modesto

streets. It has been restored to its Victorian grandeur, including the distinctive cupola on top, visible, it was said, for miles around when it was constructed in 1883. The mansion is open to the public on a regular basis.

Patterson

An interesting example of a planned community, Patterson was founded in 1909. Thomas W. Patterson, one of the heirs to his uncle's Rancho del Puerto, was impressed by the colonization projects in other parts of the Central Valley, which had brought many settlers into the region. His town was laid out in the shape of a wagon wheel, the streets converging on a plaza where the Hotel del Puerto stands. The hotel, built in 1910, was the first building in town, along with the office of the Patterson Ranch Company, which stands in the center of the plaza and is now the home of the Patterson City Museum. The handsome palm-lined thoroughfare of Las Palmas Avenue, leading into the town from the west, was planted by Patterson, it is thought in emulation of Kearney Avenue in Fresno.

Hotel del Puerto, Patterson

A complex irrigation project, bringing water from the San Joaquin River to the town, insured its success, and within a few months of its establishment, Patterson was on the way to becoming a principal town on the west side of the San Joaquin Valley.

Sutter County

Sutter County, named in honor of John Augustus Sutter, was one of the original 27 counties. During the first two years of its existence the county seat was claimed by four towns in succession: Oro, Nicolaus, Auburn, and Vernon. Auburn was later included in Placer County when that county was created. The county seat was finally located at Yuba City, where it has remained.

Spanish Expeditions

Gabriel Moraga explored the great inland valley of California several times. On his second expedition, in 1808, he ventured farther north than he had gone on the expedition of 1806. His habit of naming every geographical feature he encountered caused much confusion later on in California's history, when names were mixed up owing to the sketchiness of his records and those of other travelers. Moraga declared that the Feather River was the principal stream of the great northern valley, and that the Sacramento was its principal tributary. It is true that at the point where the Sacramento and Feather come together it is the latter that makes a straight course

north and south with the lower Sacramento, whereas the upper Sacramento flows in at that point from the west. The Moraga expedition also saw "a mountain range, in the middle of the valley"—surely the Sutter Buttes.

Interest in the great river country lagged for several years, but in 1817 the founding of missions in the interior was again urged by Padre Presidente Mariano Payéras. As a result, in May of that year, a voyage was made by boat up the Sacramento, probably as far north as the mouth of the Feather River, or within sight of the Sutter Buttes. This expedition was led by Father Narciso Durán, accompanied by Luís Argüello and Father Ramón Abella.

The Sutter Buttes

The Sutter Buttes are a short range of volcanic hills that rise abruptly from the level floor of the valley in northern Sutter County. They bear within their rugged declivities the same marks and fossils found in the Coast Range to the west. In the spring their slopes blossom with many wildflowers and shrubs. First discovered by the Spaniards, the Buttes were seen by Jedediah Strong Smith in 1828, and by a Hudson's Bay Company trapper, Michel La Framboise, as well as others who followed after him. In the various documents relating to Sutter's Grant, these peaks were designated simply as "los tres picos," and John C. Frémont, who camped there from May 30 to June 8, 1846, spoke of them as "the three Buttes." A monument in Frémont's honor was placed three miles northwest of Sutter City in the South Pass of the Buttes on the old stage road to Colusa in 1923 by the Bi-county Federation of Women's Clubs of Sutter and Yuba counties.

Sutter's Hock Farm

One of General John A. Sutter's several ranchos was Hock Farm (SRL 346), a corruption of the German word *hoch* or "upper." An Indian village nearby was called after the farm. On this rancho, which was located on the west side of the Feather River about eight miles below Yuba City, Sutter kept agents to look after his cattle from 1841 until 1850. An adobe house was put up on the estate in the winter of 1841–42, followed by other structures from time to time. Hock Farm, also referred to as Upper Farm, became Sutter's principal stock ranch, the animals ranging freely over the entire countryside between the Feather and Sacramento rivers and south of the Buttes.

By 1850 gold-seekers had despoiled Sutter of the greater part of his lands at New Helvetia. It was at this time that he retired to a plot of ground at Hock Farm that he had reserved for his home. There he built a mansion one and a half miles above the site of the adobe house. The grounds were laid out with beautiful gar-

Wall of Old Iron Fort, Sutter's Hock Farm, south of Yuba City

dens, an orchard, and a vineyard, and there Sutter kept open house to the many travelers and friends who called to pay their respects. Following the flood of 1862, debris from the mines gradually buried the best part of the gardens and orchard at Hock Farm. In 1868 Sutter left the land he so loved and found a home among the Moravians at Lititz, Pennsylvania, where he is buried. He died in Washington, D.C., on June 18, 1880.

The old adobe and the later mansion have disappeared. For many years the remnant of the garden and orchard was used as a picnic grounds. Today the site is marked by one wall of the old iron fort, which stands on the Garden Highway eight miles south of Yuba City. The memorial tablet on it was placed by the Bi-county Federation of Women's Clubs of Sutter and Yuba counties in 1927.

Nicolaus

Nicolaus, the ranch and trading post of Nicolaus Allgeier, was established on the road between New Helvetia and Hock Farm because of the need for ferry transportation at this point on the Feather River. Allgeier, a native of Germany and for a time a Hudson's Bay Company trapper, was employed by Sutter to help build the adobe at Hock Farm. In compensation for this work, as well as for anticipated services as ferryman, Allgeier was given a plot of land one mile square at the crossing. Here he put up a hut of mud-covered tules, and in 1843 he constructed a primitive ferry, which he maintained with Indian labor.

The ferry at Nicolaus was one of many places in California to come into the hands of land speculators. The arrival of a United States government barque in 1849, with supplies for Camp Far West, was the signal for a broadside issued by its promoters, in August 1850, to the effect that Nicolaus was "the head of navigation," and that it was "the only port of entry that has ever been established north of Sacramento—the only town north of that city that has ever had a full-rigged seagoing vessel lying at her landing." Its advantages were already "too manifest to be any longer denied and doubted. Furthermore, the close proximity of the town to the rich placers on the Feather and Yuba rivers, Deer, Dry, and Bear creeks, and the forks of the American ensures its continuance as a depot for the supplies for all the northern mines."

Allgeier, who had put up an adobe house at his landing place in 1847, built a two-story adobe hotel there in 1849. During the following year, as a result of advertising, over 300 lots were sold, and three hotels, a dozen stores, and over 100 dwellings were erected. For a time the little river town showed such business ac-

Old Two-Story House, Nicolaus

tivity that it presented a more flourishing appearance than Marysville, twenty miles to the north.

Realization that Nicolaus was not at the head of navigation fell heavily upon that hopeful town in the winter of 1849–50. Boats could usually reach Marysville, but when the river was low they were compelled to unload at Vernon, nine miles below Nicolaus. By 1853 many of the houses had been torn down and carted away, and the town was almost deserted. Until the building of the railroad, however, the place served as a shipping point and center of trade for surrounding ranches.

Nicolaus was the second county seat of Sutter County, from 1850 to 1851; it lost that honor, first to Auburn and then, after Auburn had become the county seat of the newly created Placer County, to Vernon. The seat of justice was reestablished at Nicolaus in 1852, but in 1854 it was transferred to Yuba City for a few months. Returned again to Nicolaus for a period of two years, the county seat was permanently established at Yuba City after 1856. Nicolaus still exists as a small farming community in the southeastern part of the county. It lies under the levee protecting it from the Feather River. There are a few of the old residences left as landmarks, including a substantial two-story house with lower story of brick and upper story of wood.

Oro

Thomas Jefferson Green purchased a tract of land at the junction of the Bear River with the Feather River, just north of Nicolaus, from John Sutter, and immediately announced a new city, named Oro, to be built on the spot. An influential state senator, he caused his "paper city" to be designated county seat when Sutter County was created by the legislature in 1850.

In order to win over his rivals at Auburn, Nicolaus, Vernon, and Yuba City, each better fitted for the position than Oro, Green exercised to its full extent the power of a shrewd, energetic, and imposing presence, a persuasive tongue, and a bluff, good-natured personality. The outcome was that the senator won the day.

Since there was not a house in town for any purpose, much less for the holding of court, a zinc structure 20 by 20 feet was put up, we are told, "without glass or shutters at the windows, or doors for the entrances. Not a tree, or bush, or shrub grew near enough to give its shade to the building." Under a brilliant May sun the first court met in the zinc house, but "law and equity, lawyers and litigants, jurors and witnesses, with a spontaneity of action that would astonish nothing but a salamander, rushed out of and fled that building, never to return." Oro remained a paper city.

Vernon (Verona)

In April 1849 Sutter sold a strip of land along the Sacramento and Feather rivers three miles in length and one mile back. The group of men who purchased this tract laid out at the junction of the rivers a town one mile square. This was Vernon, another of the short-lived river towns of 1849–50.

The winter of 1848–49 was such a dry one that the Feather River was not navigable. Vessels were compelled to unload at Vernon, and hopes were aroused that the place would become the head of navigation. The prospects for a glorious future seemed bright indeed, and lots were sold rapidly at a high figure. One hotel was built entirely of mahogany from a shipment bought in Chile; originally intended for New York, this expensive cargo had been brought to California because the ship's captain desired to reach the gold fields.

The heavy rains of 1849–50 caused the rivers to rise so that it was possible for ships to go as far as Marysville. This was a deadly blow to Vernon, as well as to most of the infant cities along the river. Erstwhile enthusiastic speculators transferred their affections to other towns farther up the river. But Vernon did not expire without a struggle. E. O. Crosby, a property owner who was a member of the state senate, succeeded in having the county seat transferred from Auburn to Vernon in 1851. The position was lost the next year, however, and in 1853 the hotel ceased to be a public house and the post office was closed. No vestige of Vernon remains today. Only its name is preserved in Vernon Township and Vernon Road. A settlement called Verona was later established on the site and still exists.

Yuba City

Samuel Brannan, Pierson B. Reading, and Henry Cheever laid out Yuba City in July 1849 on the site of the Indian village found at this spot by the first white men in the region. Where the round earthen huts of the Indians once clustered on the riverbank at the foot of what is now Second Street, a levee and terraced lots now stand, and no vestige of the old mound is visible.

Yuba City and Marysville, its "twin city" across the Feather River where it is joined by the Yuba River, are situated in a natural flood plain. In 1955 a large portion of the town was inundated. Dams on the mountain streams and higher levees have since then kept flood damage to a minimum, but 1986 witnessed considerable flooding in the lower part of Sutter County. Rich farmland has made Sutter County, small in size and population, a major agricultural region. To this area immigrants have come ever since 1850. Among the most recent arrivals are Sikhs from India, the largest settlement of this group in the United States. Since 1970 they have erected two huge temples in the Yuba City area, Gurdwara on Tierra Buena Road, and Guru Nanak on Bogue Road. Their white walls, blue trim, and onion-shaped domes make these temples picturesque additions to the lower Feather River landscape. They are open to the public.

The Community Memorial Museum of Sutter County at 1333 Butte House Road is housed in a handsome building dedicated in 1975. Its displays range from Maidu Indian artifacts to souvenirs of the home front in World War II and the Korean War—a good introduction to the history of Sutter County.

Camp Bethel

Though no trace of its existence is to be seen now, Camp Bethel was once one of the largest of the old religious camp meetings in northern California. It was founded by Reverend George Baker in 1862 on land donated by Gilbert Smith of East Butte, two miles north of what is now the town of Sutter. Methodist camp meetings were held in a board pavilion 100 feet square for three weeks in the summer. Families from all over the state lived in little wooden cabins, doing their own cooking or boarding with Mrs. Smith. When attendance dwindled in the 1880's, the land reverted by agreement to the Smith family, and later the site became the Lang Ranch. A mile south of Camp Bethel stood a house belonging to the Bland Ranch. Henry Meade Bland, California's second poet laureate, spent his boyhood here, at "Saint's Rest," as his father, a pastor, called it.

The Thompson Seedless Grape

William Thompson, an Englishman, settled west of the town of Sutter in 1863 and began farming. In 1872 he sent to New York for three cuttings of "Lady de Coverly" grape vines. One cutting survived to produce the Thompson Seedless grape, first displayed in Marysville in 1875 and an instant success. Thousands of acres of this grape have been planted in California to produce raisins, wine, and table grapes. A marker (SRL 929) has been placed on SR 20 near Thompson's farm site at 9001 Colusa Highway near West Butte Road.

Tehama County

Tehama County was organized in 1856 from parts of Colusa, Butte, and Shasta counties, and the county seat was located at the town of Tehama. In 1857 the seat of government was changed to Red Bluff, where it has remained to the present.

Tehama, a word of undetermined meaning, may have been an Indian term. Nellie Van de Grift Sanchez says that "two definitions have been offered: 'high water,' in reference to the overflowing of the Sacramento River, and 'low land,'" but also notes that these may be an attempt to make the name fit the circumstances.

First Trails

The first recorded expedition into Tehama County was that of the Spanish explorer Luis Argüello, who in 1821 probably pushed as far north as Cottonwood Creek. Then came the American Jedediah Strong Smith in 1828, and in his footsteps came a stream of hunters and traders from the south. Hudson's Bay Company trappers from the north followed much the same general course during the years 1830–45. This old Sacramento Valley route, known at first as the California-

Oregon Trail and later as the California-Oregon Road, was soon beaten into a well-defined path by trappers and explorers, among them Ewing Young, Lieutenant Emmons of the Wilkes expedition, and Joseph Gale. Sometimes proceeding all the way down the western side of the river, and at other times crossing over to the east side somewhere between Red Bluff and Tehama (a variation used most frequently by the gold-seekers of 1849 and the 1850's), this historic road has been used through the years by pack-mule trains, herds of cattle and sheep, stagecoaches and freighters, and finally cars, trucks, and buses.

In 1843 John Bidwell, accompanied by Peter Lassen and John Burheim, chased a band of horse thieves over this trail, pursuing them as far north as Red Bluff, where the thieves were overtaken and the property was recovered. It was on this trip that Lassen selected the land that was later granted to him by the Mexican government.

Returning to this region the following year, Bidwell brought with him five other men who were destined to become the first settlers in the upper Sacramento Valley. Of them, Pierson B. Reading settled in what is now Shasta County, while Job Francis Dye, William George Chard, Robert Hasty Thomes, and Albert G. Toomes followed Lassen as the earliest white settlers in Tehama County. Each of them located on Mexican grants chosen on this trip with Bidwell in 1844. On this trip also Bidwell mapped the valley, giving those names to its streams that they still bear.

Bloody Island

Samuel J. Hensley, who had accompanied Reading to California in 1843, while rafting logs on the Sacramento River in the northern part of Tehama County early in 1844, had an encounter with some Indians on an island that lies in the river just below the mouth of Cottonwood Creek. It is said that Hensley named the place "Bloody Island" because of this experience. During his stay in the region, Hensley noted the fine land north of Cottonwood Creek (in what is now Shasta County), and later recommended it to Reading as suitable for a ranch. This was the southernmost part of the grant made to Reading in 1844.

Lassen's Ranch

Through the influence of John A. Sutter, Rancho Bosquejo ("the wooded place"), comprising 26,000 acres of excellent farming land, was granted in 1843 to Peter Lassen, a pioneer blacksmith who was a native of Denmark and who had come overland to Oregon in

1839. He set sail for California in an English ship and landed at Fort Ross. From there he went to Pueblo de San José, where he spent the winter of 1839–40. After ranching at Santa Cruz in 1841, he was at Sutter's Fort in 1842–43. In December 1843, according to some accounts, Lassen started for Rancho Bosquejo, but he did not reach his destination until the following February, because high water forced him to camp at the Sutter Buttes. Other authorities place these events one year later, in 1844–45. Surrounded by hundreds of Indians, Lassen established a trading post near the mouth of Deer Creek on the east side of the Sacramento River. There is no trace left of the buildings today, but the site is near Vina, eighteen miles south of the present city of Red Bluff on SR 99.

In 1847 Lassen laid out a town on his ranch, calling it Benton City in honor of Senator Thomas H. Benton of Missouri. That same year he returned to Missouri to induce settlers to come to his ranch in California, and to obtain a charter for a Masonic lodge that he wished to establish in the new town. This charter, granted on May 10, 1848, antedates by six months any other charter granted to a Masonic lodge in California.

The Lassen Trail

Lassen's Ranch was at the end of the Lassen Trail across the Sierra Nevada, the first northern emigrant route into California from the East. The earliest emigrant party to come over this trail started from Missouri in the spring of 1848 under the leadership of Peter Lassen, reaching his ranch in California in the fall of the same year after much hardship. A considerable number of emigrants undertook to shorten their journey overland in 1849–50 by using the same route. While it never became popular, since it proved to be a long cutoff, steep and precipitous, and passing through the territory of hostile Indians, it did serve to introduce many emigrants to northern California, thus quickening an early interest in that part of the state.

Lassen's Trail came into California from northwestern Nevada through Surprise Valley and over the Fandango Pass. It continued southeast, following the Pit River part of the way and on to Big Meadows, now covered by the waters of Lake Almanor. The historic trail entered Tehama County over Deer Creek Pass to Deer Creek Meadows before following the ridge between Mill Creek and Deer Creek over the once precipitous "Narrows," now less risky since it has been widened for logging trucks. Other historic spots along the way include Bruff's Camp high in the forest belt, and Steep Hollow and Emigrant Springs in the rocky foothill slopes, before the trail emerged into the Sacramento Valley near Toomes Creek, at a point near the railroad two miles below Los Molinos and some four miles above Vina.

The End of Lassen's Ranch

Lassen's party arrived in California in the fall of 1848 to learn of the discovery of gold, and at once the entire plan of settlement on Lassen's Ranch was abandoned as the members of the party headed for the mountains. In May 1851 the Masonic chapter was moved from Benton City to Shasta in Shasta County. Benton City no longer exists, but the Masons of Shasta and Tehama counties have erected a monument on the site. It stands on the east side of SR 99 just north of Deer Creek.

In 1848 Lassen gave to Daniel Sill, a trapper, one league of land on which the latter built an adobe and on which the town of Danville was later projected but never settled. In 1852, Lassen conveyed his remaining lands to Henry Gerke, a German, who settled there in 1869. In 1881 the former governor Leland Stanford (later a U.S. senator and founder of Stanford University) purchased from Gerke 9,000 acres of the original Lassen grant. Subsequently Stanford purchased additional lands, all of which were included in the famous Vina Ranch of 55,000 acres, which the senator conveyed to Stanford University by the Founding Grant, November 11, 1885. The name Vina was derived from the fact that here Senator Stanford planted a vast vineyard, one of the largest in the world. After the ranch became the property of the university, plans for developing the vineyard were abandoned. In 1955, 580 acres of the Lassen Grant, including the headquarters buildings of the original Stanford-Vina Ranch, were purchased by Our Lady of the New Clairvaux Trappist Monastery, which now occupies the spot.

Trails West, Inc., a private organization, has placed a marker near the stone cross at the entrance to the monastery, commemorating the end of the Lassen Trail.

Frémont at Lassen's Ranch

John C. Frémont, coming up from New Helvetia in March 1846 on his way to Oregon, spent a month at Lassen's Ranch, from which he made a local exploring trip through what is now Tehama County. Arriving at the ranch on March 30, he noted that Lassen had a vineyard, that he was experimenting with cotton, and that his wheat crop was large.

On April 5 Frémont and his men set out up the valley, camping that night "on a little creek on the Sacra-

mento, where an emigrant 'from the states' was establishing himself and was already building a house." This was probably Albert Toomes on his Rancho de los Molinos. On April 6 the expedition crossed the river in canoes to another farm on the right bank, no doubt that of Toomes's friend and partner, Robert Thomes. There Frémont made camp on "a creek wooded principally with large oaks."

During the next few days the party crossed Red Bank Creek and Cottonwood Creek (later the boundary line between Tehama and Shasta counties), and on April 9 they crossed to the east side of the Sacramento River, camping on Cow Creek in what is now Shasta County. Two days later they were back at Lassen's Ranch, where they remained until April 24, when the march to Oregon was resumed. A month later, on May 24, when returning from Oregon to participate in the stirring events of the American occupation, Frémont again stopped at Lassen's Ranch.

First Settlers

Robert Hasty Thomes, a native of Maine, came to California with the Bidwell-Bartleson party in 1841. For a time he was engaged as a carpenter and builder in San Francisco and Monterey in partnership with Alfred Toomes, as is evidenced by the frequent appearance of the firm name of Thomes and Toomes in Thomas O. Larkin's books and other records.

In the winter of 1844, Thomes received the Mexican land grant of Rancho de los Saúcos ("elder trees"), located south of Elder Creek in what is now Tehama County. Although he stocked the place in 1845, he did not settle there permanently until 1846 or 1847, when he built an adobe house on his property. This house was burned in 1858. In the late 1860's or early 1870's Thomes erected the brick house that stood until 1945, when it was destroyed by fire, on what was long known as the Finnell Ranch, later as the El Camino Colony, and now as the Elder Creek Ranch. A hotel, known as the Tehama House, was built on the site of the old adobe at the corner of Fourth and C streets in the town of Tehama.

Robert Thomes was a man of character and influence in his community. He died in 1878 and lies buried under the largest and most ornamental monument in the Tehama Cemetery, a monument composed of granite from the quarries of Penryn, Placer County.

William George Chard, a native of New York, came to California from New Mexico in 1832. He was at Los Angeles until 1836 and at Santa Cruz from 1837 to 1841. During the years 1843–45 he was in partnership with

Josiah Belden in a store and boardinghouse at Monterey. In 1844 Chard obtained a grant of land on the north side of Elder Creek (in Tehama County), naming it Rancho de las Flores ("the flowers"). In the same year Josiah Belden obtained Rancho de la Barranca Colorada north of Chard's grant. Chard took his cattle to Rancho de las Flores in 1845 and in 1846 erected a log cabin on the Sacramento River at a site four miles north of the present Tehama, but he did not go to his rancho to live until the following year because he was employed at the New Almaden Mine (in Santa Clara County) from 1845 to 1847. The log house at Rancho de las Flores came to be known as the Sacramento House, and it was a popular stopping place on the road to the northern mines.

Across the river from Chard's rancho, Job Francis Dye built an adobe in 1847 on Rancho de los Berrendos ("the antelopes"). Dye, a Kentucky trapper who came from New Mexico with Ewing Young in 1831–32, for a time engaged in hunting sea otter along the coast. Later he ran a store and distillery at Santa Cruz, where he also had a ranch. Until the 1880's, Dye's adobe stood on the west bank of Antelope Creek on what later became known as the Cone Ranch. It was located on a spot not far from where the Cone Methodist Church now stands. This old adobe was long distinguished by the hospitality of its owner, who kept open house and entertained "in true Southern manner" the many guests who gathered there.

Albert G. Toomes, a native of Missouri who came to California with the Workman-Rowland party in 1841, was given the grant of Rancho Río de los Molinos ("river of the mills") in 1844. Toomes visited his rancho in 1845 and again in 1847, to stock it with cattle, and in 1846 he erected an adobe near where the settlement of Los Molinos grew up. That Toomes did not go to live permanently on the estate until 1849 is evident from the fact that the firm of Thomes and Toomes is mentioned in records at Monterey until the end of 1848.

William C. Moon, who also came to California with the Workman-Rowland party in 1841, settled on the west side of the Sacramento River opposite the mouth of Deer Creek as early as 1845, and ran a ferry at this point during the gold rush. The ferry was located about where the present Squaw Hill Bridge crosses the Sacramento River on the road from Vina to Corning. Moon lived on his ranch until his death in 1878. The original post-office desk where mail was sorted at the Moon House may be seen at the Tehama County Museum in Tehama.

The William Ide Adobe

William B. Ide, a native of Rutland, Massachusetts, came with his family from New Hampshire to what is now Tehama County in 1845. He built a log cabin on the R. H. Thomes ranch and spent the winter there. In the spring of 1846 he moved to the Belden ranch, where he put up another log house in Ide's Bottom south of what was later Red Bluff. In 1847 Ide purchased from Belden the Rancho de la Barranca Colorada ("Ranch of the Red Bluff"), so called because of an adjacent cliff on the river, 50 feet high, composed of sand and gravel of a reddish hue.

Ide was the commandant of the Bear Flag Revolt in 1846. After 1850 he resided much of the time at Monroeville, Colusa County, where he eventually held virtually all the county offices and where he died in 1852. The spot is now in Glenn County.

One and one-half miles northeast of Red Bluff on the west bank of the Sacramento River stands an adobe house built in the late 1840's or early 1850's. For years it has been known as the Ide adobe (SRL 12), presumably built by William B. Ide. Careful research, however, fails to prove conclusively that Ide built the house or owned the land on which it stands, or that he established the ferry that crossed the river at that point. The Adobe Ferry, as it was known, operated for more than three decades, being abandoned in the autumn of 1876 when the Centennial Bridge across the Sacramento River at Red Bluff was completed. The restored adobe is the main feature of the four-acre William B. Ide Adobe State Historic Park, dedicated in 1960. Though it is almost certain that Ide did not build the adobe, it seems proper that this historical site be set aside in memory of a man who helped to shape decisively, though briefly, the destiny of the state.

Tehama

Robert Thomes's adobe was built on a spot later covered by Tehama, the first town in the county. It has been authentically established, however, that before Thomes settled on the site he had given to his friend Albert Toomes a small tract of land where Tehama now stands, thus making Toomes the founder of the town. In 1849 Tehama (then known as Hall's Ranch), located on the west side of the Sacramento River twelve miles south of Red Bluff, was an important center of trade and freighting on the Oregon Road as well as the principal ferry crossing between Marysville and Shasta. Other ferries were soon established at Moon's Ranch, Ide's adobe, and Red Bluff. When the steamer *Orient* landed at Red Bluff in 1850, Tehama at once lost its prestige as a river town. As a stage center, however, it held its own for a number of years.

The first stage line from Colusa to Shasta was opened up by Baxter and Monroe in 1851. An opposition line

Old Tehama County Jail, Tehama

from Marysville, via Hamilton, Neal's Ranch, and Bidwell's Ranch, in Butte County, was started by Hall and Crandall in 1852. The two lines converged in Tehama, creating a prosperous activity that continued until the coming of the railroad.

Tehama, with its old buildings and tree-lined streets, is today a quiet settlement. The old Masonic Lodge building, erected in 1859, was used as a school for the first twenty years of the town's existence, and used by the Masons for over 100 years; it stands at Third and C streets. A museum is operated there by the Tehama County Museum Foundation, with interesting materials on the history of the county. A replica of the old Tehama County Jail, built in 1884, stands on the western side of the museum building. The first courtroom in Tehama, in a structure no longer standing, is commemorated by a plaque (SRL 183) at Second and D streets.

The Nomi Lackee Indian Reservation

The Nomi Lackee Indian Reservation was established in 1854 by the United States government to provide a home for Indians who were displaced as white settlers moved onto the land. Grain was the major crop raised on the more than 25,000 acres of land that formed the reservation. From 300 to 2,500 Indians lived there until 1866, when they were moved to Round Valley in Mendocino County, near the town of Covelo.

Colonel B. F. Washington, great-grandson of Law-rence Washington, brother of George Washington, came overland to California from Virginia in 1849, finally settling in Tehama County. He acquired title to a considerable tract of land near the Nomi Lackee Indian Reservation. His home, located by a spring, was known for many years as Washington's Gardens, but it has long since disappeared.

William Nixon Henley also acquired land nearby; hence, the name Henleyville was given to the small community to the east. A monument with a descriptive plaque (SRL 357) marks the location of the Nomi Lackee Indian Reservation four miles north of Flournoy on Osborn Road.

Red Bluff

First mapped in 1851 as a settlement in southern Shasta County, Red Bluff began to prosper when the steamboat service reached it in the early 1850's. The railroads reached Red Bluff in 1871, and the city continued to grow as a transportation center. The first courthouse of 1860 has given way to the graceful pillars of the 1922 courthouse, with its modern brick addition from 1979. The Odd Fellows Building at 382 Oak Street was built in 1883 and is still in use; the cast-iron details around the ground-floor veranda are very distinctive. The Kelly-Griggs Museum at 311 Washington Street is located in the Griggs house, built in 1885, and contains a beautiful collection of Victorian furniture and glassware as well as Indian artifacts. A number of houses in the vicinity are listed on the locally available map of a walking tour.

In 1864, near the close of the Civil War, Mary Ann Brown, the widow of John Brown, the famous abolitionist of Harper's Ferry, came to Red Bluff with her

Kelly-Griggs Museum, Red Bluff

House of Mrs. John Brown, Red Bluff

A. Veatch, who purchased the property in 1854. Two years later, in Lake County, he discovered the first borax ever found in California, but the quantities were insufficient for commercial development.

Tuscan Springs was developed as a health resort by several successive owners, one of whom was Ed Walbridge. In the years 1892–1912 he built a two-story hotel to accommodate 125 guests, ran a daily stagecoach from Red Bluff, and established a post office. Walbridge's first hotel was destroyed by fire in 1899 and was replaced with a three-story hotel. From the spring waters, he developed and sold bottled mineral salts for medicinal purposes. A second fire in 1916 ended the days of this popular health resort. The rise and fall of Tuscan Springs was closely paralleled in many places throughout California in just these years.

The Sierra Lumber Company

When lumbering operations were developed in the pine belt of the northern Sierra Nevada, a major problem in the early days was transporting the lumber to shipping points in the valley. C. F. Ellsworth designed and constructed the first V-flume in the state. His original Empire Flume was built in the early 1870's and was over 40 miles in length, extending from Lyman Springs in the mountains east of Red Bluff to Sesma, a site near present-day Los Molinos. The high-trestle flume followed Belle Mill Road, entering the valley near Antelope Flouring Mills. In 1881 the route was changed so that it ended along the east bank of the Sacramento opposite Red Bluff.

By 1878, several small lumber mills had combined to form a large corporation known as the Sierra Lumber Company, which operated mills at Lyonsville. Lumber was shipped to the large mill at the end of the flume in Antelope, where it was finished and shipped by steamboat, barge, or rail. In 1907, the Diamond Match Company purchased from Sierra Lumber its large timber holdings and the mills at Chico and Red Bluff, as well as the mill at Lyonsville, since torn down. Following severe flooding and fires, the mill at Antelope was closed, and Diamond moved west across the Sacramento. Its integrated forest products plant south of Red Bluff was completed in 1958. Diamond International celebrated its 100th year in business in 1981.

Corning and Gerber

Corning, named for John Corning, a railroad superintendent for the Central Pacific Railroad, was founded in 1882. Like the Lindsay region in Tulare County, Corning is a center for the cultivation of olives. Before 1920, the University of California planted test plots here, and

children. So great was the town's admiration for John Brown that a sum of money was raised to provide the family with a home. The house (SRL 117) was built at what is now 135 Main Street, and there Mrs. Brown lived until 1870, when she and her three daughters moved to Humboldt County. The house, somewhat remodeled, has been occupied as a private dwelling. In 1988, the owner of the building announced that it was no longer economically feasible to make the necessary repairs, and let it be known that he was about to tear it down. Local historical groups protested. Designation as a State Registered Landmark, however, does not guarantee the preservation of a building; a number of landmarks in California commemorate structures no longer standing. As this is written, the fate of Mary Ann Brown's house is uncertain.

Andrew Jelly built a brick house northeast of Red Bluff in 1856. Jelly came to California in 1848 and gained title to his land by buying scrip that soldiers of the Mexican War had received instead of pay for military service. The scrip entitled the holder to 160 acres of frontier land. Jelly was a brickmason by trade. He built the house large enough to take care of his family and to accommodate travelers, using brick made and baked from the clay soil on the ranch. At one time a post office was established and maintained there. In the 1890's the Haakonson family purchased the Jelly Ranch; members of that family still live on the ranch in the remodeled ranch home. The location is on Jelly's Ferry Road, about six miles northeast of Red Bluff.

Tuscan Springs

Tuscan Springs is located near the head of Little Salt Creek, approximately nine miles east of Red Bluff. The springs were named after the similar sulfur-type springs of Tuscany, Italy, by their first owner, Dr. John their success started the olive industry. Five miles northwest of Corning on Davis Road is a two-story adobe house with a facing of cobblestones, built in 1859 by Henry Clay Wilson, later state senator. Since 1900 this home has been owned by the Clark family.

Gerber, named for a Sacramento family, became a center for the Southern Pacific Railroad, which moved its roundhouse from Red Bluff to Gerber in 1916. The Humann Ranch, a tourist attraction, displays a scale model of the Southern Pacific operations that were the economic foundation of the town. The last train was dispatched from Gerber in 1972.

Mineral

About 42 miles east of Red Bluff on SR 36 is the small community of Mineral. Here are the headquarters of Lassen Volcanic National Park, very little of which actually lies within Tehama County. Mineral was first known as Hampton's and was an overnight stop on the Red Bluff–Susanville wagon road when the first post office was established there in 1902. Just inside the southwest entrance to the park, north of Mineral on SR 89, is the Lassen Park Ski Area, first opened in the winter of 1938–39, and still in operation.

Trinity County

Trinity County was one of the original 27 counties, and Weaverville has always been the county seat. The Trinity River, which flows across the county, was named in the erroneous belief that it flowed into the ocean at Trinidad Bay in Humboldt County.

Early Explorations

Jedediah Strong Smith and his party were among the first white men to explore Trinity County. In early April 1828 Smith came up the eastern side of the "Buenaventura" (the present Sacramento River) to the vicinity of Red Bluff. There he found "the rocky hills coming in so close to the river as to make it impossible to travel." After scouting parties had been sent north and northwest, it was decided that the most practicable route was to the northwest. He crossed the Sacramento River on April 11, 1828, and, traveling in very rough country, passed over the divide made by the Trinity Mountains into the present Trinity County on April 17. So far Smith's route seems to have followed approximately that of the present Red Bluff–Eureka highway, SR 36.

The next day Smith's party followed down one of the tributaries of the South Fork of the Trinity River, probably Hayfork Creek. On April 21 they reached "a small valley on the river which turned in its course nearly North and . . . received a branch from the South." Smith states in his diary that he named the river he had been following Smith's River. Many of the early maps label as Smith's River the rivers now known as the Trinity and the Klamath, into which the Trinity flows. Later the name was transferred to the present Smith River in Del Norte County.

On April 24 he had to cross to the west bank because the mountain came so close to the east bank of the river that it was impossible to proceed. There he found the traveling rough; the ground was so rocky that the horses' feet were being mangled. Climbing the high ridge to the west of the river, the party crossed over into Humboldt County. Jedediah Smith had opened up the coast route to Oregon on the first journey ever made by a white man from California into Oregon. This route was followed in later years, at least in part, by trappers of the Hudson's Bay Company from Oregon. Ewing Young, noted trapper, made his first passage to the north this way in 1832.

The Old Trinity Trail

SR 299, which crosses the mountains of Shasta and Trinity counties between Redding and Weaverville, follows, approximately, the old Trinity Trail opened up by early trappers and gold-seekers. Trappers of the Hudson's Bay Company may have used this route to some extent in the 1830's and 1840's. The first trails were made by Indians, and the first white men to travel this country used these paths. The first definite knowledge (apart from Smith's recorded journey) comes from Major P. B. Reading, who says that in 1848 he had crossed the mountains "where the travel passed . . . from Shasta to Weaver." Reading had previously visited the area for the purpose of trapping as early as 1845, and it was he who gave the Trinity River its present name, not realizing that the river flows into the Klamath, not into Trinidad Bay on the coast.

The Forty-niners also used the Trinity Trail on their

way to the Trinity gold fields, and the need for safe transportation of gold in the early 1850's led to the establishment of express offices and what were known as Pony Express lines. Over these trails mail and bullion were carried on horseback. The mail route for Trinity County led from Red Bluff in Tehama County to Shasta and thence over the mountains to Weaverville, 50 miles northwest. These trails were for pack trains of horses and mules only. Such slow and laborious means of transportation delayed the development of the county and the coming of families.

The Buckhorn or Grass Valley Creek Toll Road

The route of the old Trinity Trail was followed until the first wagon road in the county was built. The Buckhorn–Grass Valley Creek Toll Road, connecting Weaverville, Shasta, and Redding, was begun in 1857 and completed in 1858. The credit for the construction of this road is given to William Spencer Lowden of Lowden's Ranch, located on Grass Valley Creek. Lowden, a deputy United States surveyor, was a relay Pony Express rider in the celebrated ride made in January 1854, when two express companies, Adams and Wells Fargo, raced the text of President Franklin Pierce's annual message to Congress from San Francisco to Portland, Oregon. Lowden was then a young man of 24, and it is said that he rode his relay of 60 miles from Tehama to Shasta in 2 hours and 37 minutes. While another rider took the bags and dashed on to Yreka, Lowden continued west 40 miles farther to Weaverville. In his ride from Tehama to Shasta it is reported that he changed horses nineteen times, touching the ground only once.

During the early 1860's, the Lewiston Turnpike Road, a variation of the Shasta–Weaverville Road, was constructed from near the Tower House in Shasta County to Lewiston in Trinity County. This, like the Grass Valley Creek Road, was originally a private toll road.

The Hyampom Trail

An important pioneer line of travel called the Hyampom Trail passed through the settlement of Hyampom. A wagon road came from Humboldt Bay as far as Hydesville in Humboldt County, in the center of an agricultural region. From Hydesville the road became a trail that ran east through Carlotta and Yager. Beyond Yager the trail passed by the Redwood House and Fort Baker and over Coyote Flat. Crossing Mad River and climbing Hohn Ridge, it reached Pilot Creek, where it turned northeast over South Fork Mountain to Hyampom. Here the trail branched, one branch going to Big Bar and the other up Hayfork Creek to the Sacramento Valley.

The Hyampom Trail was always a pack trail. The country was rough, and the way often steep and dangerous. Parts of it are still used by ranchers to bring in winter supplies. In 1922 a road was completed between Hyampom Valley and Hayfork.

The Oregon Road

Although a road had been built over Trinity Mountain, Scott Mountain still had to be crossed by mule pack. In 1859, however, this obstacle to travel to Oregon was overcome, when Scott Mountain Road was built at an expense of $25,000. The road went from Shasta and French Gulch in Shasta County over Trinity Mountain into Trinity County. From there it went through Trinity Center and Carrville, after which it climbed over Scott Mountain into Siskiyou County to Yreka. This road became the main artery for interstate commerce between California and Oregon until the railroad up the Sacramento Canyon was built in the 1880's. In spite of heavy snowfall, this road was kept open all winter. Oxen housed at the summit were driven back and forth over the road after a snowstorm in order to tramp down the loose snow. Because of difficulties, the stage to Jacksonville had been run only in the summertime up to the fall of 1859. That year the Oregon Company spent $10,000 in improving the road over the Siskiyous, and in 1860 a daily line of stages was established between Sacramento and Portland. When the railroad was built, this road did not pay as a toll road and was taken over by the county. Today SR 3, a state scenic highway, follows this old route over Scott Mountain.

The First Discovery of Gold

In 1858 Major Pierson B. Reading described his discovery of gold at Reading's Bar ten years earlier: "In the month of July 1848, I crossed the mountains of the Coast Range at the head of Middle Cottonwood Creek, struck the Trinity at what is now called Reading's Bar; prospected for two days, and found the bars rich in gold; returned to my home on Cottonwood, and in ten days fitted out an expedition for mining purposes; and crossed the mountains where the travel passed about two years ago from Shasta to Weaver.

"My party consisted of three white men, one Delaware, one Chinook, and about sixty Indians from the Sacramento Valley. With this force I worked the bar bearing my name. I had with me one hundred and twenty head of cattle with an abundant supply of other provisions. After about six weeks' work, parties came in from Oregon, who at once protested against my Indian labor. I then left the stream and returned to my home where I have since remained in the enjoyment of the tranquil life of a farmer."

The identity of the parties from Oregon who caused Reading to abandon his mining operations is not known. But Reading's Bar, on which the major and his Indians worked, is located on Trinity River at the mouth of Reading's Creek immediately below the Douglas City bridge.

River and Creek Mining

It has been said that the first settler in Trinity County may have been a Frenchman named Gross who came here from Oregon in 1849. After discovering gold at a place he named Rich Gulch, he settled at Evans' Bar on the Trinity River and built what may have been the first cabin in this part of the county.

"During 1850 a large number of gold-seekers came into the county, some crossing the mountains to the east of the Trinity River from Shasta County, others coming up the Klamath and Trinity rivers, after coming up the coast from San Francisco by vessel and making a difficult and dangerous landing at Trinidad Bay. By the end of 1851 all the gold-bearing sections of the county had been explored and prospected, and in the spring of 1852 there were occupants of every bar along the Trinity River from Salyer to Carrville, and every tributary stream leading into the Trinity River within the county had been traversed and prospected. The mountains lying to the west of Trinity River had been crossed, and the agricultural lands in Hayfork and Hyampom valleys were at that period being located and improved."

The early mining was done on the river bars and along the creeks. On the Trinity River below Lowden's Ranch at the mouth of Grass Valley Creek were numerous river-bar camps; Ingrams, Union, Ferry, Douglas, Trinity, and Texas bars were all active before 1856. The placers at the mouth of Weaver Creek, which flows into Trinity River at Douglas City a few miles below Lowden's Ranch, were among the richest in the country. Down the river, near Douglas City, was the Kanaka Bar. Farther down were Reading's Bar and Cape Horn Bar, where German and Danish miners erected neat houses. Opposite Cape Horn Bar was Turner's Bar, from which six Germans and Danes took $32,000 in one year. One-half mile below Turner's was Buckeye Bar, with a water dip-wheel 42 feet in diameter. Steiner's Flat, four miles below Douglas City, is one of the few places worked intermittently from 1850 to the present day.

Eight miles downriver from Steiner's Flat is the site of the Arkansas Dam across Trinity River, about four miles above Junction City. Some sixty miners made the first attempt to construct this dam during the summer and fall of 1850. The dam had been completed, turning the water from the bed of the river into a canal, and some work in the bed of the river was proving the gravels of high value when the first rain of the season came, swelling the waters of the river so much that the dam was washed away. The dam was again constructed in the following year, to be once more destroyed by the rise in the river at the first rainfall, and it was not until some three years later that a log dam placed across the river withstood the waters passing through it in the late fall and winter months.

Near Junction City were Hocker's Ranch, Ferry Bar, and Red Hill. In 1851 Joseph McGillivray, a Scotsman of wonderful resource, persistence, and ability, came to Cooper's Bar, five miles down the river from Junction City, and began to develop it into a home, ranch, orchard, and garden spot. He employed William Berber, a trained horticulturist from New York. All the leading varieties of fruit trees, flowering shrubs, and other plants were introduced, and before long he was supplying the whole county. McGillivray's Ranch became famous as a beautiful spot. Now it is a waste of heaped-up dredge tailings.

At Junction City was located the sawmill of Seeley and Dowles. In later years a grave was discovered on Slattery Creek near Junction City. The fallen headboard had the following inscription: "Col. H. Seeley, September 2, 1852, aged 54 years." The grave was fenced and at one time had been well cared for.

Canon City, located above Junction City on Canon Creek, was one of the first mining camps, originally known as Jackass Bar. It became one of the largest gold-producing settlements in the county. The last trading post there closed its door in 1885.

At the mouth of the North Fork of the Trinity River was an important town called North Fork, later renamed Helena. Here Herbert Hoover worked for a time as a young mining engineer. Until 1926 this was the end of the road; from here the traveler west had to follow a trail. In that year the state highway was opened all the way down Trinity River. Helena is listed on the National Register of Historic Places.

Big Bar, eight miles below Helena, was an important mining center in the 1850's. Weaver and Company, who mined there in 1850, spent $10,000 diverting water from Little Weaver Creek and took out $100,000 in gold.

The canyon of the Trinity River between North Fork and Big Bar was once the scene of much mining activity in the bed of the river. Chinese miners were the last to work there. Manzanita Flat, worked for many years, had a twentieth-century revival with the use of the water of Manzanita Creek.

Cox's Bar was quite famous in the early days, but no evidence remains of the extensive mining done there except moss-covered tailing piles and scarred banks. Mosses have been taken from the rock there and burned, the ashes yielding fine "flour" gold. At Big Flat, near Cox's Bar, was a large settlement—450 people in 1856.

The largest gold nugget ever found in Trinity County, valued at $1,800, was discovered on Digger Creek by George Van Matre. Minersville, near the mouth of Stewart's Fork, was a center of rich pocket mines. In 1880 the noted Brown Bear Quartz Mines were discovered on Deadwood Creek; they have produced more than a million dollars' worth of ore. Crow's Bar, of 80 acres, was mined by water brought from Rush Creek through a ditch eight miles long, built at a cost of $20,000.

Since the 1850's much gold has been taken from the banks and bed of the Trinity River and its tributaries, but none of them has been worked completely. During the depression of the 1930's, a large number of men worked along the bars with equipment such as was used by the early miners: the pan, the rocker, the sluice. Many earned enough to live on. Today, one can see small dredging operations along the length of the river after the winter storms have abated.

La Grange Mine

Mining in Trinity County goes back to 1851. In 1873 several mining claims were consolidated into the Weaverville Ditch and Hydraulic Mining Company. In 1879 the Trinity Gold Mining Company was formed and purchased the property in Oregon Gulch, four miles northwest of Weaverville. Five years later a Frenchman, Baron La Grange, formed the La Grange Hydraulic Mining Company and purchased the mine for $250,000. The La Grange Mine (SRL 778) was for years one of the most important hydraulic mines in California.

Water for washing the gravel in this tremendous deposit was first obtained through ditches from Weaver Creek. As this supply proved inadequate, a water right on the East Fork of Stewart's Fork 30 miles away was acquired. The tailings of this mine were run into a narrow valley owned by the company and from this valley drained directly into the Trinity River. Since this stream is not navigable and the surrounding country is not farmland, this was considered an ideal dumping ground for mine waste.

For many years the La Grange Mine was known as the largest operating hydraulic mine in the world, but it has been closed since World War I. A vast quantity of low-grade gravel is left, but the cost of reopening the works would be considerable because of the necessity of driving tunnels and cuts.

The Bridge Gulch Massacre

When the first settlers came to Trinity County, they were constantly annoyed by the depredations of the Indians, who resented the invasion of the settlers and the brutal destruction of the forests and mountains. A number of expeditions were organized to drive the Indians out. In 1852 the killing of a man named Anderson aroused high feeling among the white settlers. Anderson had gone alone to the range to bring in some of his cattle when he was attacked and killed by several Indians, who drove off the cattle. When Anderson failed to return to Weaverville and his riderless mule appeared at the corral, a search party was formed, which found his arrow-pierced body. A portion of the party set out after the Indians, while the remainder went back to Weaverville to spread the alarm. Soon afterward 70 men were ready to start. Joining the advance party, whose position was relayed by messengers sent back to Weaverville, they again picked up the Indians' trail. After tracking them to their camp at Bridge Gulch in Hayfork Valley, the whites surrounded the camp and, in an attack from four sides, massacred 153 Indians. Only two little Indian girls, who were overlooked, survived. These children were brought back to town and reared by white families. One of them, Ellen Clifford, was long a resident of Weaverville. At a later date "Indian Bob" of Douglas City claimed that he was a boy of nine at the time of the massacre and had hidden behind a log until the whites had left the scene. There is no one to verify or discredit his story.

The natural bridge where the massacre took place is located on Hayfork Creek, about nine miles above the town of Hayfork and a mile from the Leach Ranch–Wildwood Road. Carved from limestone by the action of the water, it has a span of 150 feet and is 30 feet high. The highway to Hayfork makes this point easily accessible.

Weaverville

The mining town of Weaverville, named in 1850 for John Weaver, a gold prospector who arrived in the vicinity in 1849, is located in what was one of the wildest and most inaccessible regions of California. Now it is easily reached by SR 299 from Redding and Eureka. It was the center of great mining activity in the days of '49, and in 1850 it became the county seat of Trinity County. Many old buildings, some with iron shutters and winding outside stairways, give charm to the narrow streets of Weaverville. It is probably one of the best preserved of all the old towns, and for many years was far from the beaten path, though always an important center in the Trinity region.

Main Street and Spiral Staircase, Weaverville

Like many other towns of the county, it has suffered heavily from fires. The first fire, in March 1853, destroyed 35 of the 41 buildings in the town, but immediately the inhabitants started reconstruction, this time replacing the wooden and canvas buildings wherever possible with brick ones. During the summer of 1853, the first courthouse and jail were built; and the Masonic Lodge, chartered in the summer of 1852, was for a time housed on the second floor of the first courthouse building.

Early in the winter of 1855 fire once more swept the town, but again the citizens began rebuilding immediately. More brick buildings were constructed in 1855, some of red-burnt brick and some of adobe, and by 1858 there were 25 brick buildings on Main Street. Some of these were two-story structures, and nearly all were equipped with the iron doors and shutters that many now believe were necessary for the protection of the gold stored within but that were in reality for protection against fire.

In 1986 nineteen brick buildings erected between 1855 and 1859 were still in use in Weaverville. One of these built in 1856 as a saloon, store, and office building, was purchased by Trinity County in 1865 and has been used continuously as a courthouse ever since. Three buildings, including the halls of the Native Sons of the Golden West and the International Order of Odd

Fellows, have outside spiral staircases from the sidewalks to the overhanging balconies of the second floors. These iron staircases were handmade by the town blacksmiths. When the buildings were erected, they had the distinction of having two owners, one for the lower floor and one for the upper. Since space was at a premium and all the buildings were wall to wall, the only solution was an outside front stairway. The Historic District is centered on four blocks along Main Street; Weaverville is on the National Register of Historic Places.

The Chinese population of Weaverville in the early days numbered at one time about 2,000, and Chinatown was a busy two blocks on both sides of the street. After the toll taken by repeated fires, the last of which was in 1905, and the changes wrought by time, there are now remaining only one adobe house and the Joss House. The Weaverville Joss House State Historical Monument (SRL 709) is situated back from Main Street on a knoll across the bridge over Weaver Creek. The present building was built in 1874 to replace one that had burned. It is still a place of worship and is open to the public. The furnishings, for the most part, are those saved from the fires and are the very ones brought from China in 1854. In a small room there is a sort of frieze near the ceiling, on which are the names of hundreds of Chinese who once constituted a part of Weaverville's Chinatown.

The Chinese Tong War of 1854 occupies a place of note in the town's history. About 600 Chinese took part in the battle on a flat near Five Cent Gulch, about a mile east of town on SR 3, which leads toward Trinity Alps. The site of the battle has since been mined, so that little of the 1854 contours remains. However, in the collections of the J. J. Jackson Memorial Museum at 508 Main Street, there are sword, pike, and spear relics of this war between the tongs.

The Jackson Museum is housed in a structure dedicated in 1968. On its two floors are excellent displays of materials tracing the history of Trinity County, includ-

Joss House State Historical Monument, Weaverville

ing an outstanding photographic collection. The adjacent property is the Trinity County Historical Park, like the museum administered by the Trinity County Historical Society. In the park are several interesting displays. The 1849 hand-pump fire engine saw service in San Francisco before being purchased by Weaverville in 1906. A restored steam-powered two-stamp mill from the Paymaster Gold Mine near Lewiston is fully operable and is demonstrated from time to time. An old miner's cabin from the La Grange Mine region can also be seen here.

Historic Townsites and Stopping Places

In the 1850's and 1860's, settlements equipped with homes, store, sawmill, blacksmith shop, and meat market flourished at Carrville, Trinity Center, Minersville, Lewiston, Douglas City, Indian Creek, Hayfork, Evans' Bar, Junction City, Canon City, North Fork, Logan Gulch, Big Bar, Cox Bar, Burnt Ranch, and Campbell Ranch. Much of the travel in those days was over trails on foot, requiring frequent stopping places, and making them remunerative places of business. The Trinity House, long since vanished, was a famous inn on the north bank of Trinity River below the old Lowden Bridge. The present bridge is one mile above the site.

Carrville, formerly the ranch of Curry and Noyes, became one of the best-known resorts in northern California. James E. Carr was the founder of the family that owned the place. It is one mile south of Coffee Creek. The Bonanza King Quartz Mine, lying on the mountain east of Trinity River, is one of the valuable mines of the county. There has been much gold dredging along the river here and below.

Trinity Center was a lively and populous place in the early 1850's and for over a century was the center of one of the principal mining sections of Trinity County. The water ditches built in 1853 leading from Swift Creek were still in use a hundred years later. The district was settled in 1851, and by 1853 it had become a famous mining center. Trinity Center and the old camp of Minersville have been inundated by the Trinity Dam project, which was completed in 1962. A new town of Trinity Center has been built on the lakeshore. Nine buildings from old Trinity Center were moved to the new townsite and stand today as reminders of the town's origin. The lake created by Trinity Dam has been named Clair Engle Lake in honor of a U.S. senator who sponsored the project. It is known locally as Trinity Lake. This is now part of the Whiskeytown-Shasta-Trinity National Recreation Area, as is Lewiston Lake, created by the Lewiston Dam, part of the same project.

Lewiston is one of the oldest settlements and the site of the first ferry for pack horses between Shasta and Weaverville. The route was from the Tower House to the summit of Trinity Mountain, thence down Hoadley Gulch to Lewiston, and along the Trinity River until it turned north over Brown's Mountain to Weaverville. Lewiston was always a trade center. A toll bridge located at this place was owned by Olney Phillips for many years.

Rush Creek was formerly mined actively. At the mouth of the creek was Dutch John's Trading Post, later Jacob Paulsen's, a well-known spot. Logan Gulch, midway down the canyon from Helena to Big Flat, was a leading trade center in the 1850's. Rich returns were obtained from the bed of the river.

Burnt Ranch, or McWhorter's, was one of the oldest settlements of Trinity County, first occupied in 1853. Destroyed by Indians, the charred remains of the house caused the place to be named Burnt Ranch. In this section of the county—a choice fruit-growing region—are Salyer, Fountain's, Hawkins' Bar, Daily's, Lake City, and New River. Lake City was an important settlement, but it was destroyed by Indians in 1865 and never rebuilt. During early gold rush days, an average of 400 to 500 miners worked the mountainous New River area, and in the 1880's New River itself was the scene of a large quartz-mining boom. Heavy milling machinery was packed in by mules, and gold worth millions of dollars was taken out.

Hayfork is an important agricultural and mining area, the site of the Trinity County Fair. There, in the pioneer period, Bayles's sawmill and flour mill supplied nearly all the flour used in Trinity County. Hyampom is another agricultural section, where ranching began in the 1850's.

The National Forests and the Salmon–Trinity Alps Primitive Area

Although gold mining brought the pioneer population to Trinity County, the chief importance of this county is now as a recreational and lumbering center. The major part of the land area of the county lies within Trinity National Forest. This forest, covering approximately 77 percent of the county, comprises 1,780,960 acres of timberland, in which Douglas fir predominates, with sugar pine and yellow pine second. Within the Trinity National Forest lies the Salmon–Trinity Alps Primitive Area, 500,000 acres, which is being preserved as nearly as possible in its original state.

Other parts of Trinity County lie within portions of Shasta National Forest on the east and Six Rivers National Forest on the west. The Forest Service has constructed good trails through many of these forests, and jeep roads lure the motorist off the beaten track.

Tulare County

Tulare County was created in 1852 from the southern part of Mariposa County and the northern part of Los Angeles County. Tulare is Spanish for "a place of tules, or rushes." The first county seat was at Wood's Cabin, afterward known as Woodsville, but later in 1852 it was removed to Visalia, where it has remained.

Hog Wallows

Parts of the San Joaquin Valley were once covered by curious mounds called hog wallows. Fairly regular in shape, they were as much as 50 feet long, 20 feet wide, and 6 feet high; at their bases, water collected in the winter and encouraged the growth of tules. All kinds of theories have been advanced to explain them. The Yokuts Indians believed they were leftover earth dumped from work baskets after the building of the great Sierra Nevada. Since hardpan underlies most of them, early theories held that pressure from gas and water escaping through cracks below caused the mounds. A modern theory, not accepted by all, is that the common pocket gopher is largely responsible.

Leveling the hog wallows was necessary to make the land suitable for agriculture, and over the years most of this area has been filled in and cultivated. In order to preserve a fragment of this land in its unplowed, natural state, the Buckman family of Exeter presented a plot of ten acres in 1979 to the Tulare County Historical Society. A marker has been placed by the society at the road on the northern edge of the preserve, which is located on Avenue 314 just west of Road 220, near Lindcove.

Indian Mounds

As in other areas of California, most sites of early Indian habitation in Tulare County have been all but obliterated.

The largest of a group of remarkable mounds, once surrounded at flood time by the waters of Tulare Lake, was situated fifteen miles due west of Tulare on what is known as the old Jacobs Ranch. This mound, about 150 yards long and six feet above the surrounding country, was composed of a solid mass of the common soft-shell clams of Tulare Lake, which were found in layers "as clean and closely packed as if they had been washed and stacked by hand." Wagon loads of these thin, white shells were gradually hauled away for chicken feed.

Locally known as the Paige Mound, one of the largest rancherias ever reported in that section of the San Joaquin Valley was located along an old channel of Cameron Creek about two miles east of the settlement of Paige, southwest of Tulare. Many years ago an irrigation ditch was cut along the top of this mound, disclosing old burials and Indian artifacts. Gradually over a period of years the mound was leveled.

Several miles from the eastern shore of Tulare Lake there was a long island or series of islands that remained unknown to American settlers for many years on account of the dense screen of tule swamps that stretched for miles along the lakeshore in both directions. These islands always escaped the winter floods. Said to have been discovered in 1853 by a cattleman, the land was acquired soon afterward by Judge J. J. Atwell, of Visalia, who used it as a pasture for hogs. Atwell's Island, as it came to be known, formed at least two islands during the highest water. The one to the west was called Skull Island, because the remains of Indian houses and skeletons uncovered by wave action were found there by the first white settlers to visit it. Another was called Pelican Island. The present town of Alpaugh is located on what was once Atwell's Island, and a little to the south and west of town many artifacts and remains of Indian villages have been found along old stream beds.

The Derby Expedition, which entered the San Joaquin Valley in April 1850, a few weeks after the Wood Massacre on the Kaweah River, reported that there were two large rancherias at Outside, Cameron, and Deep creeks; and that the 200 inhabitants of these villages had treated them with great hospitality. The Broder family, which settled on Cameron Creek in the early 1850's, also found several hundred Indians living on what came to be known as Broder's Mound and along the ridge to the southwest. Various epidemics, however, soon reduced this number to not more than twenty. The Broders built their first house in this region about 200 yards from the old mound, but later a more pretentious house was erected on the mound itself. This house became a refuge for neighboring white settlers during the flood of 1862, when the mound was the only dry land for miles around. The Broder mound property finally came into the hands of a Visalia bank in 1927, when, owing to a series of delays in leveling and building operations, local archaeologists working under the supervision of F. F. Latta succeeded in making one of the most extensive studies of ancient Indian cultures in the

San Joaquin Valley. Perhaps the most remarkable example of Yokuts burial customs ever unearthed was found at this site, yielding more than 800 specimens within an area of not over 45 by 60 feet. Three distinct cultures were uncovered, including that of what was probably the first migration into the valley, as well as that of the later Indians found at the site by the first white settlers.

The Sweet mound, found on the west bank of Elk Bayou, four and a half miles south of Waukena, was the site of one of the most extensive permanent rancherias on the east shore of Tulare Lake. This mound was found by two boys on the property of Adolph Sweet on Thanksgiving Day, 1928, and was subsequently excavated by local archaeologists. Early American settlers had noted that this site was occupied by Indians as late as 1860. The burials and house sites unearthed at the Sweet mound appeared to be extremely ancient, showing no signs of contact with later Indian cultures or with whites.

Many rock writings made by the Indians of prehistoric times may be seen along the western slope of the eastern foothills throughout Tulare County. The most remarkable of these are located north and slightly east of Visalia at Woodlake, Dillon's Point, and Kaweah Caves.

The Old Spanish Trail Through Visalia

Gabriel Moraga, in 1806, went into the river country on the western side of the Great Valley to search for mission sites. On his return trip he ascended the Kings River a short distance, crossing what is now Tulare County seven miles east of Visalia at Venice Hills, known as Kaweah Hills to local Indians and early pioneers.

Another party (possibly under the leadership of Juan Ortega), accompanied by Father Juan Cabot, chronicler of the expedition, went into the tulares in 1814, also in search of mission sites. In 1815, Juan Ortega and Father Cabot led an expedition from Mission San Miguel to hunt for Indians who had run away from the mission. Proceeding up the Kings River, the party crossed over to the Kaweah River in Tulare County and from there went on to the area of Venice Hills.

These expeditions reported favorably on the region near the present city of Visalia. They considered it especially suitable for mission sites, and in the biennial report for the years 1815–16 Padre Presidente Mariano Payéras renewed his recommendation to found a mission and presidio in the valley. The site selected was approximately the area of Mooney Grove Park, which had the three requisites of water, timber, and receptive Indians. When Lieutenant José María Estudillo went into the valley in 1819 in an attempt to subdue uprisings among the Indians, he was emphatic in his report that a presidio would be necessary in connection with any mission established in that country. To be sure, there were numerous Indians in the area, but, in his judgment, they were very unfriendly. At any rate, nothing was done in either the Spanish or the Mexican period to make permanent white settlements in Tulare County.

American Pathfinders

The first American to travel the Tulare Trail was Jedediah Strong Smith, in 1826 and 1827. Skirting the Sierra foothills along the eastern side of the valley, he probably followed much the same route as that taken later by the Stockton–Los Angeles Stage Road, and now followed approximately by modern highways SR 65 and SR 245 through Porterville, Lindsay, Exeter, and Woodlake. Smith was followed in 1834 by Joseph Walker, who led the Bonneville hunters out of California over the Sierra by way of the pass that now bears his name, which forms an outlet from the South Fork of the Kern River to the eastern side of the divide.

John C. Frémont, in 1844, followed the old trail out of California. In the winter of 1845–46, a second expedition under Frémont reached Walker's Lake in Nevada. There the company divided, Frémont himself crossing the mountains with a few men to Sutter's Fort, while the main body, under the leadership of Joseph Walker, went through Walker Pass and down the Kern River, where they camped for three weeks early in 1846. Frémont, who had hurried south to meet his men, and who had understood the Kings River to be the appointed meeting place, waited for several weeks before returning to Sutter's Fort. During this time he ascended the Kings River along the right bank to its junction with the North Fork, up which he climbed to an altitude of 10,000 feet. Walker with the main body, after waiting in vain at the Kern River camp for Frémont's arrival, pushed on northward through Tulare County, finally rejoining Frémont near Mission San José.

Woodsville

Under the leadership of John Wood, a party that was said to have come from the Mariposa mines settled on the southern bank of the Kaweah River either late in 1849 or early in 1850. A substantial log cabin was built a short distance south of the Kaweah River delta, seven miles east of the site of the present city of Visalia.

Wood and his party had been established only a few months when a group of Kaweah Indians arrived and, because of earlier mistreatment at the hands of the Wood party, demanded that they leave the region within ten days. The white men were slow in making preparations to leave and delayed beyond the alloted time; all but three were massacred.

Another settlement had been made at the same time, about half a mile distant, by Loomis St. Johns, for whom the St. Johns River was named. Although it was near the Wood cabin, the St. Johns settlement was left unmolested by the Indians. Also about the same time two brothers, A. A. and C. R. Wingfield, claimed squatter's rights on land along the Kaweah River from the Wood cabin south.

When Tulare County was created in April 1852, the legislature provided that the seat of justice be placed at the cabin on the south side of Kaweah Creek, near the bridge built by Dr. Thomas Payne, and that it be called Woodsville.

The first election board, a party under the command of Major James D. Savage, opened its polls on July 10, 1852; instead of voting in the cabin, the election was held out of doors under the shade of a great oak tree on the south side of Kaweah Creek. Many years later, markers were placed designating as the Election Tree or the Charter Oak (SRL 410) a tree on the north side of the St. Johns River, which was created in the flood of 1862 and is, in fact, slightly north of Kaweah Creek. In 1905 some surviving participants in that election claimed that the tree thus marked was the actual Election Tree. Modern travelers can understand the confusion when they try to find the Election Tree amid the magnificent stands of oak in the countryside east of Visalia. The tree marked is on Charter Oak Drive east of Road 168 and about eight and a half miles from the city.

Visalia

In 1852 a group of settlers from Iowa and Texas located a few miles to the southwest of the Wood cabin. In November they erected a log fort on the north bank of Mill Creek for protection against the Indians. To this they gave the name of Fort Visalia, probably suggested by one of their number, Nathaniel Vise, whose family home was in Visalia, Kentucky. Visalia thus claims to be the oldest town in California between Stockton and Los Angeles. Fort Visalia stood in the area now bounded by Oak, Center, Garden, and Bridge streets, and is commemorated by a marker placed there in 1981 by the Boy Scouts and the Tulare County Historical Society.

An election in September 1853 resulted in the removal of the seat of justice from Woodsville to Visalia. The county board of supervisors subsequently decreed that the name of the county seat should be Buena Vista, but petitions and protests caused them to rescind this action, and since March 1854 Visalia has been the official name of the Tulare County seat. It was not incorporated until 1874, long after it was well established as the most important town in the San Joaquin Valley south of Stockton.

California was admitted as a free state in 1850, and officially remained loyal to the Union in the Civil War. Nonetheless, pockets of Confederate or "secesh" (from "secessionist") sympathies persisted, one of which was in Visalia. Officials felt it necessary to establish a military camp at the town, and in October 1862 a company of the Second California Cavalry arrived to establish Camp Babbitt, named for the quartermaster general of the Pacific. Within a month, violence broke out between the townspeople and the soldiers after one of the latter was shot and killed in a saloon brawl. The alarmed camp commander sent off to Army headquarters in San Francisco the message that "this command does not number more than 100 men and the rebels can bring against it 250 men in 24 hours and 400 men in 2 days all of them well armed." Two additional companies were dispatched to join the garrison in Visalia. A pro-Confederate newspaper was shut down, prominent citizens (including the future founder of Bakersfield, State Senator Thomas Baker) were arrested and released only after taking a loyalty oath, and another soldier was shot and killed. As the Confederate fortunes waned, so too did "secesh" sympathies, and at the war's end, Camp Babbitt was disbanded. The camp had been established in the 400 block of East Race Street and moved later to Ben Maddox Way and East Houston Avenue. It is said that resentment against the government continued in a quiet way for many years; not until twenty years after Appomattox did the Republican Party elect any officeholders in Visalia.

Few of Visalia's early buildings are still standing. A huge eucalyptus tree in what is now the courtyard of the Visalia Visitors Center is commemorated as having been planted by an early settler, David R. Douglass, in 1860. The "City of Beautiful Trees" is one of the most wooded in the state, and the ubiquitous valley oak is the official city symbol.

Mooney Grove and Tulare County's Pioneer Park

About five miles south of the center of Visalia on Mooney Boulevard (SR 63) is Mooney Grove County Park, 100 acres of virgin oak purchased from the heirs of Michael Mooney in 1909 and preserved as a remnant of the forest of valley oaks that formerly covered much of the Kaweah River delta. In the park is the Tulare County Museum, which was founded by a grant from Hugh Mooney. The museum is a repository of Tulare County's past, ranging from Yokuts Indian basketry and projec-

Facade of Masonic and Odd Fellows Hall, Tulare County Museum, Mooney Grove County Park

tile points to life in the county during World War II. The museum's Pioneer Village is a collection of old and historically important buildings that have been moved from various parts of the county and reconstructed. In this way preservation has been assured for these links with the past that would otherwise inevitably have been destroyed in the name of progress. Among them are a log cabin (1854), the Cramer residence and post office (built perhaps as early as 1863) from a settlement in the North Tule River Valley, and the Surprise School (1908). One of the most interesting relics is the ornate Gothic facade from the Masonic and Odd Fellows Hall in Visalia, erected in 1873 and torn down in 1963.

Stone Corral

Possibly the oldest surviving structure in Tulare County built by white men is the 50-foot-square stone corral on the southeast corner of Stokes Mountain, east of Cutler and northeast of Seville. It was constructed of large rocks in 1853 by James Smith as a hog pen. Near here, on the night of June 11, 1893, occurred the fight between a sheriff's posse and the notorious outlaws John Sontag and Chris Evans. Sontag was killed, and his companion was wounded and captured the next day. Cedar rails split by Evans are on display in Pioneer Village.

Tule River Indian Reservation

In 1857, after hostilities between the Tule River Indians and the white settlers had ended, a reservation was established near the present city of Porterville. To it were brought Indians from several tribal groups of a widespread area. The reservation was placed near the rancherias of the Koyeti and Yaudanchi tribes, both of which were branches of the Yokuts, who occupied the San Joaquin Valley. The first Tule River Indian Reservation was located on both sides of the Old Springville Highway, where, for about a quarter of a mile, it runs south to join the later highway at the Alta Vista School. A marker (SRL 388) is on Reservation Road, two miles east of Porterville. The location did not prove satisfactory, and in 1873 the reservation was moved ten miles southeast, into the mountains, to its present location.

The Stockton–Los Angeles Road

The old Stockton–Los Angeles Stage Road crossed the Kaweah River delta at a place long known as Four Creeks, that portion of the delta lying south of the Venice Hills. Stages and freight teams used this road, which went from Los Angeles north to Fort Miller and the mines.

The route was divided into the Upper and Lower Detours, as they were called. These detours paralleled each other as they passed along the base of the hills a few miles apart, and the southern junction of the two was near the base of the Venice Hills and a little to the southwest, where the Southern Pacific Railroad now crosses the St. Johns River. The Lower Detour came in from the west, while the Upper Detour passed to the east of Twin Buttes and skirted the western side of the Venice Hills. Uniting at the junction on the St. Johns, the road then passed the Election Tree at Woodsville and followed the base of the Venice Hills about a quarter of a mile before crossing the St. Johns River. For a half-mile it continued south and then turned to the southwest for a quarter of a mile, crossing the Kaweah River a half-mile south of the Election Tree.

Butterfield Stage Stations

During dry weather the northbound Butterfield Overland Stages, in the years 1858–61, turned off from the old Stockton–Los Angeles route east of Visalia (where one of the main stage stations was located at what is now the southeast corner of Main and Court streets) and crossed the country to the Kings River Station (Whitmore's Ferry). When the river was too high to be crossed at Whitmore's, a route along the base of the hills was followed to Smith's Ferry near present Reedley in Fresno County.

Proceeding southeast from Visalia, one passed the following stations: the "Pike" Lawless Ranch, one mile south of the present Outside Creek Bridge; the Tule River Station, later Porterville; and Fountain Springs. At the Tule River Station, Peter Goodhue erected the first building, a shake house with a fireplace at each end and a porch on the south side. The site of this old overland station (SRL 473) is at the foot of Scenic Hill, Main and Henderson streets, at the north city limits of Porterville.

Porterville

In 1859 a young man named Porter Putnam arrived at the Lawless Ranch, where he obtained a job caring for the stage horses. Soon afterward he went to the Tule River Station. Putnam was an enterprising young man, with an affable, hospitable nature. He bought out Goodhue and developed the station into a popular stopping place and hotel, and the place came to be known as Porter's Station. The town that grew up around it was called Portersville, later Porterville. A marker commemorating the site of the Putnam House and Store was placed at the corner of Main and Oak streets by the Historical Committee of the City of Porterville in 1955. Another historical marker, on East Putnam Avenue between Plano Street and Leggett Drive, commemorates the site of the Porterville Flour Mill, which operated there from 1868 until it closed in 1912. The buildings were deeded to the city along with several acres of land to form Murray Park in 1929, but they were torn down in 1938.

A charming relic of the past is the Zalud house at the corner of Hockett and Morton streets. Built in 1891 for Bohemian-born John Zalud and his family, the two-story home with its distinctive mansard roof sits in a lovely garden, especially noted for its summer display of roses. Pearle Zalud, the last survivor of the six children of the family, bequeathed the house and its garden to the city of Porterville upon her death in 1970. The house is open to the public on a regular basis and contains articles brought back from family travels and furniture from the late nineteenth century.

Nearby, at 257 North D Street, in the building constructed in 1913 as the passenger depot for the Southern Pacific Railroad, is the Porterville Historical Museum. Begun in 1963, the museum emphasizes the highly successful citrus industry that from the beginning of the century has contributed to Porterville's prosperity. As urbanization has taken over more and more land along the southern coast, the high-quality oranges from this region have become a major California product.

Other Points on the Butterfield Route

A monument (SRL 648) stands at the small crossroads community of Fountain Springs to commemorate the early stage station that stood one and one-half miles to the northwest at the junction of the Stockton–Los Angeles Road and the road to the Kern River gold mines. The actual site of the station is on private rangeland half a mile from the road.

Ducor, originally Dutch Corners, lies west of Fountain Springs, and is commemorated by a marker placed by E Clampus Vitus in 1980. The little settlement was a way station on a Southern Pacific route put through in 1888, a line parallel to the Butterfield route.

Another marker (SRL 473) has been placed just west of Lindsay on a portion of the old Butterfield stage route where SR 65 meets SR 137. A nearby marker from 1928 commemorates John C. Frémont's passage through the area.

Tailholt, a Ghost of the White River

The present hamlet of White River, also known as Tailholt (SRL 413), a little over seven miles southeast of Fountain Springs, was at one time a mining camp almost as well known as Angel's, Columbia, or Sonora. Not more than a handful of people make it their home today.

It was first established about 1856, during the Kern River gold rush. Placer gold was discovered on a small tributary stream in Coarse Gold Gulch about two miles east of the present town, and the original settlement called Dogtown grew up. When the first road into Linns Valley was built, old Dogtown was left one and one-half miles to the east. A new settlement, for a short time also known as Dogtown, was established at the present site. An interesting happening gave it the curious name of Tailholt. The story, as told by F. F. Latta, is as follows: "'Yank' Booth, the old stage driver, while en route to Visalia, stopped at [Dogtown] to change horses. He had with him a society lady who was returning from the Kern River Mines after having visited her husband, a mine operator at that place. This lady seriously offended the dignity of Yank by effectively 'high-hatting' him. She further aroused the ire of Yank by carrying with her in the stage a pet poodle.

"As the horses were being changed at Dogtown, a large cat crossed the street ahead of them, leaving the restaurant of Mother Cummings and proceeding to the hotel of Levi Mitchell. The dog spied the cat and attempted to jump from a small window at the side of the stagecoach. The lady made one wild grab for the dog and succeeded in catching it by the tail as it was leaving the stage. Yelping at the top of its voice, the dog hung suspended from the window, and the lady screamed for help. Yank took in the situation at a glance and went ahead changing horses. Mother Cummings came to the rescue. While lifting the dog through the window she remarked, 'Well, ma'am, a tail-holt is better than no holt at all.' When Yank reached Visalia he told the postmaster and keeper of the stage station that the name of the new place on White River was Tailholt."

Two old cemeteries at Tailholt are especially interesting. One, situated on the crest of a hill to the north of the river, was reserved for respectable people, while to the other, located on "Boot Hill," south of the river, were relegated the renegades—desperate characters who died with their boots on. Of the seven burials at Boot Hill, five were the result of gunfights.

Tulare

Throughout the West in the late nineteenth century, it was a common practice for agents representing a railroad-building project to approach the city fathers of a community and demand favors for the railroad. Without them, it was warned, the railroad would be built via a rival settlement, to the great economic disadvantage of the unfriendly city. When Visalia authorities refused to cooperate with the Southern Pacific, the railroad's officials deliberately routed the San Joaquin Valley line westward, founding the town of Tulare to be the local station in 1872. Visalia was by then well established enough to survive this deprivation and in time it did become a way station on the Southern Pacific line.

Tulare never became a sizable city, as did other railroad-favored spots such as Bakersfield and Fresno, but it remains one of the principal towns of the county whose name it bears—a unique example of a town taking its name from the county and not the other way around.

The old Tulare Woman's Club House at West Tulare and I streets, built in 1882, was constructed for its employees by the Southern Pacific Railroad. Its original name was Library Hall, since the railroad provided books for employees and townspeople (most of whom worked for the railroad). It was also a social and recreational center for the town. After many of the railroad's operations were moved to Bakersfield in 1890—causing a considerable loss of revenue to Tulare—the building served as a public library. When the Carnegie Library was built in 1905, the building was abandoned; some time later, it was turned over to the Tulare Woman's Club rent-free in return for maintenance. In time the

burden of maintenance became too great, and the city of Tulare took over the building in 1969. It continues to be a social center for the town.

Zumwalt Park at the corner of Tulare and M streets was named in 1971 for an illustrious Tulare family. Dr. Elmo Zumwalt, son of Tulare pioneers, was for many years a practicing physician and public official of the city, twice its mayor, and administrator of the Tulare County Hospital. His son Admiral Elmo Zumwalt, Jr., a graduate of Annapolis, has had a very distinguished career; in 1971 he was named Chief of Naval Operations, the youngest man to hold that honor.

Traver

The traveler through the mining districts of California often comes upon ghost towns, tiny settlements that thrived for a few months or years before meeting an early death. A rare example of such a place in an agricultural region is Traver, some sixteen miles north of Tulare on SR 99.

For intensive agriculture, it was realized, the San Joaquin Valley had to depend on irrigation. In 1882 Peter Y. Baker, a civil engineer, conceived the idea of a large irrigation project that would furnish water to some 130,000 acres of land on the south side of the Kings River in both Tulare and Fresno counties. Enough investors participated in the project to allow the newly formed corporation to acquire 30,000 acres. The corporation was called the 76 Land and Water Company, after the cattle brand of Senator Thomas Fowler, owner of part of the new holding and a principal stockholder. The main settlement of the project was named after Charles Traver, company director. The 76 or Alta Canal was built to bring water into this hitherto unplanted area, and the townsite was platted while railroads offered excursion rates to bring prospective settlers into the area.

After some initial setbacks, Traver was soon in full swing. Annie Mitchell continues the story: "When the first contingent of buyers arrived on April 4, 1884, water was flowing through the canal. On that auspicious day the depot was the only completely finished building, but by the end of the day buyers had invested $65,000. Two months later Traver had two general stores, a drug store, a hardware store, two lumber yards, two hotels, two barber shops, two livery stables, three saloons, a postoffice, a school, an express office, a large Chinatown and a lively red light district.

"Fruit, grapes, vegetables and alfalfa did well, but basically Traver was a storage and shipping point for grain. Each of three warehouses held 30,000 tons of sacked grain. Most of the time they were filled and sacks of grain were piled outside and along the railroad right of way. Teamsters waited hours and even days to unload their wagons. By 1886 Traver was one of the largest grain shipping towns in the nation." Since the Bonanza gold rush days, very few California towns had boasted such rapid growth and apparent prosperity.

By a terrible irony, Traver was already beginning to die in the middle of this boom; in Annie Mitchell's words, "Traver was ruined by the same thing that created it—water." The soil was highly alkaline, and as intensive irrigation brought the alkali to the surface, virtually all of the plants were destroyed. Like a blight, the alkali spread until the fertile fields were a desert plain. At the same time, the railroad opened a new line on the eastern side of the valley, developing the new towns of Dinuba and Reedley. And in 1887 Traver experienced the first of five fires that discouraged settlers from remaining.

Traver still stands, marked by the plaque E Clampus Vitus placed there in 1974. Better farming methods have restored some of the land, though it remains a rather bare patch in the luxuriant fields of Tulare County. On or about April 8 of every year, descendants of former Traver residents join the inhabitants of today in a homecoming festival.

Allensworth

The unsuspected alkali that wiped out Traver's hopes worked with equal destructiveness in the southwestern corner of the county, in another kind of Promised Land, the town of Allensworth.

Allen Allensworth was born into slavery in Kentucky in 1842. During the Civil War he escaped and entered service with the Union forces. After the war, he and his brother operated restaurants in St. Louis while he pursued a formal education, becoming a minister in 1871. In 1886, by then married, he returned to the military as chaplain of the all-black 24th Infantry, where his service took him as far away as the Philippine Islands. When he retired in 1906, Colonel Allensworth was the highest-ranking chaplain and the highest-ranking black U.S. Army officer of his time.

The Colonel's dream was to find some place in the United States where black Americans might live and create "sentiment favorable to the intellectual and industrial liberty" of their people, a dream shared by Professor William Payne. In 1908 Allensworth and Payne and three other black men incorporated the California and Home Promotion Association and in the same year acquired several thousand acres by the Santa Fe Railroad tracks, a few miles east of Alpaugh. Proximity to

the railroad was important for a community that hoped to send its produce to market easily and to provide a refreshment and rest stop.

The settlement grew rapidly, many of the arrivals coming from parts of the United States where segregation was enforced by both custom and law. Allensworth became a remarkably self-sufficient community. The church and the school soon developed, as, in time, did the blacksmith shop and the livery stable, the barber shop, and the drug store. But the economic life of the community depended on agriculture, and the irrigation needed for Allensworth's crops brought to the surface the same alkaline poisons that destroyed Traver. The accounts of Allensworth's brief years of prosperity (1910–15) are bright with the promise of crops that seldom saw a third yield.

Like Traver, a series of mishaps doomed Allensworth. The Colonel was killed in an automobile accident in southern California in 1914, just when the first evidence of alkali was being found in the wells of his town. Allensworth believed that the railroad's prosperity would also benefit the town, but this was not to be, for after World War I the new highways and the growing trucking industry bypassed the town. Bereft of their leader, painfully conscious of being aliens in a strange land, and confronted with the implacable alkalinity that killed most vegetation, the people of Allensworth gradually moved elsewhere.

Established in 1976, Allensworth State Historic Park is something of a ghost town today, although unlike Bodie State Historic Park in Mono County, it has restored buildings, and a few inhabitants. It is easily accessible from SR 43 some eight miles west of Earlimart on SR 99. The home of Colonel and Mrs. Allensworth is among those still preserved, as is the schoolhouse, where a commemorative jubilee is held annually in the middle of May. Projects for further development can be seen in the park's visitors' center.

School, Allensworth

Sequoia National Forest and Park

Sequoia National Forest and Sequoia National Park (in which is the General Sherman Tree, the largest *Sequoia gigantea* of all) comprise the most extensive as well as the most remarkable group of trees in the entire Sierra Big Tree belt, numbering 53 individual groves in all. Within this vast assemblage some of the most magnificent of the Sierra groves are to be found, a few of the most notable being Little Boulder Grove; the General Grant Grove section of Kings Canyon National Park, containing the General Grant or the Nation's Christmas Tree, one of the three largest of the Big Trees; the Muir Grove; Giant Forest, generally considered to be the largest and finest of all the Sierra Big Tree forests, where scores of separate groves merge, one into another; Redwood Canyon, another magnificent stand of over 3,000 trees; Redwood Meadow; Atwell; Garfield; Dillon Wood; and Mountain Home or Balch Park.

Giant Forest, in what is now Sequoia National Park, was discovered by Hale Tharp, a stockman, who in the summer of 1856 had located in the Three Rivers district at what became known as the Tharp Ranch, now inundated by Lake Kaweah, about two and one-half miles below the present town of Three Rivers. Friendly Indians told Tharp of the existence of a neighboring forest of "big trees," and in the summer of 1858, wanting to see for himself and needing summer pasture for his cattle, he made his first trip into the Giant Forest, accompanied by two Indians.

A huge hollow sequoia log still lying at Tharp's old camp in Log Meadow testifies to this first visit of a white man to the great forest. On this log Tharp carved his name and the year, 1858, on the day he arrived. The inscription has now been obliterated by vandals. In this log Tharp built a unique home, where he spent many summers. It was fitted with a door, a window, and a stone fireplace, and contained one large room 56.5 feet long. The tree itself is 24 feet in diameter at the base and is estimated to have been 311 feet high when it fell. It is now carefully preserved by the National Park Service and is reached by a paved road extending six-tenths of a mile from the Crescent Meadow parking area.

Tharp was the first white man not only to enter the Sequoia National Park region but also to live there, and his discovery led to further search and discovery of other important groves—Kings River, Tule River, and Deer Creek. By the summer of 1862 all of the groves in the state had been made known.

A movement for the protection of the groves of giant sequoias in the mountains of Tulare County for purposes of permanent drainage, lumber supply, recreation, and scenic beauty was begun in 1878. A long, hard fight followed with the private interests that were seeking to buy up the Big Trees for commercial purposes. The leader in this fight was Colonel George W. Stewart, who, as publisher and editor of the *Visalia Delta* in 1890, was also the chief promoter of the campaign for the creation of the Sequoia and General Grant National Parks. The latter is now part of Kings Canyon National Park.

Because of his unselfish and persistent work in pushing the cause of the giant trees, George Stewart has been justly acclaimed the "Father of the Sequoia National Park." A mountain in the Great Western Divide, rising almost 13,000 feet above sea level and about 5,000 feet above the Big Trees of the park, has been named Mount George Stewart in his honor.

The John Muir Trail

For years a ridge trail from Yosemite to the headwaters of the Kern River had been the dream of many lovers of the High Sierra. In 1914, on the annual trip of the Sierra Club, Meyer Lissner suggested that the state legislature be requested to appropriate money to build such a trail. While plans were being made, John Muir, for many years leader and president of the club, died. "In seeking a fitting memorial to the man who had done so much to explore and make known to the world the wonders and beauty of the High Sierra, it seemed but fitting that a trail to be constructed near the crest of his 'range of light' should bear his name."

The first appropriation of $10,000 was approved by Governor Hiram Johnson in 1915, and another $10,000 was made available in 1917. No further appropriations were secured until 1925, and work on the trail was then resumed.

Walter L. Huber described the trail thus: "In its course the trail passes Thousand Island Lake and the Devil's Post Pile National Monument, rounds the flanks of the loftiest and most famous mountain peaks, from Mt. Ritter and Banner Peak on the north to the Evolution Group, Mt. Goddard, the Palisades and Mt. Tyndall on the south, zigzags up a succession of the highest and most impregnable divides, and affords approach to the Tehipite Valley, Kings River Canyon, and the Canyon of the Kern. It is the gateway to the best fishing, the most ambitious mountaineering, the sublimest and most diversified scenery that the High Sierra has to offer.

"The southern terminus of the trail is Mount Whitney, the highest point in the United States, exclusive of Alaska. Along the route are 148 peaks rising to elevations of more than thirteen thousand feet, including twelve of the fourteen summits in California which attain elevations of more than fourteen thousand feet. The crest of the Sierra is more than thirteen thousand feet in elevation for eight and a half miles continuously adjacent to Mt. Whitney. Even these cold statistics give an inkling of the grandeur of the region which this trail has made accessible, but not *too* accessible; for here is, I am glad to say, one of the most extensive areas in any of our Western states yet remaining practically free from automobile invasion."

Huber added that with the John Muir Trail should be mentioned the High Sierra Trail, constructed by the National Park Service in Sequoia National Park from the Giant Forest to Mount Whitney. This trail opened some of the finest mountain scenery on the American continent and, with the John Muir Trail, made a complete loop through one of the most scenic areas of the High Sierra.

The Kaweah Cooperative Commonwealth

Tulare County was the home, from 1886 to 1892, of a socialist utopian colony, the Kaweah Cooperative Commonwealth. Under the leadership of Burnette G. Haskell and James J. Martin, several dozen people established themselves on the banks of the Kaweah River "for the purpose of demonstrating the advantages of cooperation in social and industrial life." The population of the colony at its peak reached about 300, but for long periods it averaged only 50 to 75. One of the objectives of the colonists was to support themselves by cutting timber in what is now Sequoia National Park, and they did succeed in building a sawmill and an eighteen-mile lumber road. It is debatable whether they would ever have cut the magnificent sequoias in the Giant Forest, for they recognized their value to scientists and

Post Office, Kaweah

tourists. What is now known as the General Sherman Tree was called by the colonists the Karl Marx Tree.

The dissolution of the colony was due to internal troubles as well as to external pressure—from the large timber interests, the press, and the federal government, which established Sequoia National Park on September 25, 1890, and a few days later declared the adjacent lands a national forest. The colonists were never able to secure title to their land and soon disbanded, but many of them remained residents of Tulare County. The road from Kaweah to Old Colony Mill, painstakingly built by hand in 1886–90, was completed to the Giant Forest by the government in 1903. It was the only road into the forest until the Generals Highway was completed in 1927. Today, the old road is maintained as a fire road. Another tangible reminder of the hopes of the colonists is the tiny wood-frame Kaweah post office (SRL 389), about three miles north of Three Rivers.

Tuolumne County

Tuolumne County was one of the original 27 counties, and Sonora has always been the county seat.

Prehistoric Landmarks

Table Mountain, frequently mentioned by Bret Harte in his tales, is a conspicuous feature of the Tuolumne County landscape. For many miles its rocky entablature and splintered capitals dominate river gorge or spreading valley. A particularly fine view of its long, level top is obtained while crossing Rawhide Flat on the road from Tuttletown to Jamestown. The topography in the Miocene period consisted of an andesite lava flow that filled the hollows. Table Mountain is a part of this huge mass of lava, a quarter of a mile wide on the average and 40 miles long, that filled one of the ancient stream beds. Ages of erosion have cut away the banks that hemmed in this ancient river, leaving the hard andesite mountain standing out in bold relief. Deep beneath this once molten mass have been found bones of extinct animals, traces of early flora, and implements of stone. Water-worn pebbles, gravel, and smoothly polished gold nuggets have been taken from the ancient river channel by miners, who tunneled great distances into the heart of the mountain until it was honeycombed with subterranean passageways. Even today, Table Mountain, once the maker of vast fortunes, holds millions of dollars in gold within it.

Southeast of Dardanelle, a resort on SR 108, is the largest and oldest known specimen of the western juniper, called the Bennett Juniper for Clarence Bennett, who discovered it in 1932. Several thousand years old, it is over 40 feet in circumference and about 85 feet tall. The ancient tree is reached by a seven-mile trail from Dardanelle or a twelve-mile dirt road via Niagara Creek and Eagle Meadow.

There are two groups of *Sequoia gigantea* in Tuolumne County, the South Grove of the Calaveras Big Trees and the Tuolumne Grove. The South Grove, seven miles southeast of the North Grove of the Calaveras Big Trees in Calaveras County (both of which are in the Calaveras Big Trees State Park) is reached only by trail. It is a magnificent stand of 974 giant trees, all over twelve feet in diameter. Among them is the Louis Agassiz, one of the largest of all the Big Trees. The Tuolumne Grove, on the western boundary of Yosemite National Park on the Big Oak Flat Road, contains only a small number of trees.

In Pate Valley, a wooded flat in the Grand Canyon of the Tuolumne River below Muir Gorge, there are a number of Indian picture writings, the first of them discovered by Harnden and McKibbie while exploring the river in 1907. These pictographs, colored with red ochre, are painted on the face of a high cliff on Piute Creek a little way from its junction with the Tuolumne River. Near the middle of the precipice there is a small cave, partly natural and partly hollowed out by human hands, in which other pictographs may be seen.

The Gabriel Moraga Expedition

Gabriel Moraga named the Tuolumne River in 1806. Charles E. Chapman says that "the Indian village of Tualamne, visited by them, is perhaps the origin of the modern name in Tuolumne River and County, although it was located on the Stanislaus." A diary kept by Father Pedro Muñoz contains these lines, which indicate the origin of the name: "On the morning of this day the expedition went toward the east, along the banks of the river, and having traveled about six leagues, we came upon a village called Tautamne. This village is situated on some steep precipices, inaccessible on account of their rough rocks. The Indians live in the *sótanos* (cellars or caves)."

Tuolumne, according to Bancroft, is a corruption of the Indian word *talmalamne,* meaning "a group of stone huts or caves." Although Kroeber thinks this interpretation is unlikely, since the California Indians did not build stone houses and lived in caves only in mountain regions, the extract from the diary of Father Muñoz is worthy of consideration. Kroeber also says that "the word Tawalimni, which perhaps was really Tawalamni or Tawalumni, would easily give rise, in either English or Spanish, to Tuolumne," and that it was the name of a tribe of Indians, "possibly Miwok, but more probably Yokuts," living in the vicinity of the lower Tuolumne and Stanislaus rivers as far up as Knight's Ferry. The river, meadows, canyon, and county now bear the name.

Sonora Pass

In the early days of California's development, the Sierra Nevada stood as an almost insurmountable barrier between the western American plains and the Pacific slope. The jagged crest on the eastern edge of Tuolumne County, which is also the eastern boundary line of parts of both Stanislaus National Forest and Yosemite National Park, was one of the most impassable stretches in the entire range. The great difficulty was neither in the ascent of the eastern side, nor in passing the summit, but rather in the western descent, which, though spoken of figuratively as a slope, is in reality a series of granite domes, lakes, and canyons with almost perpendicular walls.

Sonora Pass, in the northeastern corner of Tuolumne County near its conjunction with Alpine and Mono counties, rises to an elevation of 9,624 feet. Wagons hauling supplies to the mines east of the Sierra have used this pass since 1864. It was also the route of the early passenger stage on its weekly journey from Sonora to Bodie. The Sonora-Mono Highway (SR 108) of today, as it winds through scenic Stanislaus Forest, over the crest, and on down to Bridgeport, 110 miles from Sonora, follows the old road approximately. Portions of the former roadbed can be seen clearly from the highway at several points. Historical signs have been placed near the summit and along the route to call attention to points of interest. Fourteen miles northeast of Sonora a monument has been erected commemorating the Sonora-Mono Road (SRL 422).

In 1841 the Bidwell-Bartleson party, the first overland group of American settlers to enter California by crossing the Sierra Nevada, used a pass located ten miles south of the present Sonora Pass. By the time the party had begun the western descent, the last ox had been consumed and the travelers had begun to eat crow and wildcat. In the attempt to add to their provisions, young John Bidwell left the party to hunt, planning to cut across country and rejoin them later. When night overtook him he found himself in a grove of large trees. In the darkness he had particular difficulty in getting around a fallen tree, the butt of which seemed to extend some twenty or more feet into the air. In after years he visited the North Grove of the Calaveras Big Trees and found what he believed was the same spot. However, since the route of the party followed down the south side of the Stanislaus, rather than the north side, it is likely that Bidwell discovered the South Grove rather than the North Grove.

The emigrant trails to the west of Sonora Pass were not easy to follow, and various parties became entangled in the vast labyrinth of canyons, mountains, and rivers through which it was necessary to travel. In the early 1850's a party of gold-seekers was caught in a heavy snowstorm on the eastern slope of the mountains. As a result, they were forced to abandon their wagons, but finally succeeded in crossing the pass and finding a comparatively sheltered spot on the western side. From this place a few members of the party proceeded as far as the Jarboe ranch, about where the town of Tuolumne now is, and from there assistance was sent back to the men in camp. It is from this episode that Relief Valley got its name.

Among the first wagon trains to cross Sonora Pass were the Duckwall party and the Washington Trahern party, named after a Cherokee Indian who was the leader of the outfit. The former, consisting of W. J. Duckwall, his wife, six children, and three other men, found themselves marooned on one of the granite domes southwest of Sonora Pass, but managed to extricate themselves by hitching one pair of oxen to the front of a wagon and three pair to the rear and letting the vehicles down the precipitous granite wall. The Duckwalls arrived at Upper Relief Valley on September 27, 1853. The Washington Trahern party, who had lost most of their wagons in crossing the summit, reached the valley a day later. No road has ever been built over this stretch of the old emigrant trail, and the country has remained primitive and isolated.

From Strawberry and Pinecrest to Burst Rock (also known as Birth Rock because in the natural chamber formed by the great boulder a baby girl was born to an emigrant mother) a trail follows the old emigrant road marked by trees on which blazes made by the pioneers are still visible. Near Emigrant Lake there is a blazed tree upon which has been carved the epitaph of a traveler who perished at that spot in October 1853. For many years parts of ox wagons abandoned by the snowbound emigrants were to be found at Upper Relief Valley.

Virginia Pass and Conness Pass

Long before white settlers came, the passes of the High Sierra were used by Indians to reach the deer and acorns that abounded on the western side and the pine nuts on the eastern slopes or to get the choice larvae that are found at Mono Lake at certain seasons.

Two of the lesser-known passes that cross the eastern border of Tuolumne County and are reached only by trail are the Virginia and the Conness, both of which lead from Yosemite National Park into the Hoover Primitive Area on the western side of Mono National Forest. The Hoover Primitive Area contains 30 square miles at the headwaters of Green and Lee Vining creeks, and within it are Tioga, Conness, Excelsior, and Dunderberg peaks, as well as several glacial lakes. Two of these lakes, lying close together not far from the summit, are the Hoover Lakes, so named in honor of Theodore J. Hoover, mining engineer, who explored and mapped this region in the summers of 1904 and 1905 while in charge of the Standard Consolidated Mines at Bodie. Conness Peak was named in 1863 for John Conness, later United States senator, in appreciation for his efforts in promoting the bill that organized the California Geological Survey. Dominating the landscape, it lifts its majestic summit 12,565 feet above the sea.

Tioga Pass

Of the several Sierra passes on the eastern border of Tuolumne County, the Tioga Pass is one of the most used at present time. Over this pass the Tioga Road crosses the summit at an elevation of 9,941 feet. The pass is dominated on the southeast by Mount Dana, 13,050 feet elevation, named in 1863 by the Whitney Survey in honor of James Dwight Dana, professor of geology at Yale University from 1850 to 1894.

Mining carried on in the Tioga district by the Great Sierra Consolidated Silver Mining Company, incorporated in 1881, necessitated a road from Sonora to the summit. The Tioga Road, or the "Great Sierra Wagon

Road," which was completed in 1883 at a cost of $61,000, was built in part over the Mono Trail, but from the point where the latter turned south toward Mono Pass, the Tioga Road was continued eastward to Tioga Pass. When the mines in this rugged eastern part of Yosemite National Park were closed in July 1884, the road also was abandoned. A few of the buildings at the mines can still be found in a fair state of preservation.

The Tioga Road was donated to the United States Department of the Interior in 1915 and is now one of the most scenic in California. Passing south of the Hetch Hetchy Valley through the Yosemite National Park via Lake Tenaya and Tuolumne Meadows, it bisects the park from east to west. At the first ranger station west of the pass is a bronze plaque, which bears the following legend: "This tablet commemorates the successful labors of Stephen T. Mather, Director of the National Park Service, in securing for the people the Tioga Pass Road. Dedicated to the enduring memory of a faithful public servant by the members of the Brooklyn Daily Eagle National Park Development Tour, July 20, 1924." The last stretch of the original Tioga Road in use, extending 21 miles west of Lake Tenaya, was reconstructed in 1956–60.

The Grand Canyon of the Tuolumne

One of the most spectacular scenic canyons in the United States is the Grand Canyon of the Tuolumne, lying wholly within Tuolumne County fifteen miles due north of Yosemite Valley. Within a distance of twenty miles the Tuolumne River descends this majestic gorge from the level of Tuolumne Meadows to Hetch Hetchy Valley, a drop of almost 5,000 feet, the greater part of which occurs within the two miles immediately west of the California Falls. John Muir describes the marvelous beauty of the canyon's superb, cascading river: "It is the cascades of sloping falls of the main river that are the crowning glory of the Canyon. . . . For miles the river is one wild, exulting, onrushing mass of snowy purple bloom, spreading over glacial waves of granite without any definite channel, gliding in magnificent silver plumes, dashing and foaming through huge bowlder-dams, leaping high in the air in wheel-like whirls . . . doubling, glinting, singing in exuberance of mountain energy."

Tuolumne Meadows, one of the most beautiful of the numerous alpine meadows found in the Sierra, lies at the junction of the Dana and Lyell forks of the Tuolumne River about fifteen miles northeast of Yosemite Valley. It is surrounded on all sides by the highest peaks of the Sierra Nevada, and many trails wind up from it into the very heart of the range. Conness, Dana, Mam-

moth, and Lyell peaks stand guard at the north and east. On Mount Lyell there is a small glacier, the southernmost in California, which scientists believe is a remnant of larger and older glaciers that, among other things, carved Yosemite Valley. Cathedral Range, with its unique and picturesque Cathedral Peak, protects the southern boundary of the meadow. Out of the floor of the valley itself rises Lembert Dome, while at the lower end, at the entrance to the Tuolumne Grand Canyon, towers beautiful Fairview Dome. The Tuolumne Meadows Visitors Center, where the highway crosses Unicorn Creek in the middle of the meadows, is a striking building from 1934 originally used as the mess hall for the local Civilian Conservation Corps. It is built in the distinctive style found in many public buildings throughout the Sierra: cemented boulders forming a foundation and lower walls, and upright peeled logs framing a front porch or veranda.

Hetch Hetchy (originally spelled Hatchatchie), a deep valley at the lower end of Tuolumne Canyon, was discovered by Joseph Screech in 1850 while hunting game. The valley was then occupied by Indians. John Muir is the authority for the statement that the name is a Miwok Indian word for a certain grass with edible seed that grew in the vicinity. The valley was visited in 1863 by Professor J. D. Whitney and in 1871 by John Muir, who called it the "Tuolumne Yosemite." Muir explored the valley later, in 1875, with Galen Clark. Over the protests of Muir and other conservationists, the city of San Francisco, in the early 1900's, asked the federal government for the right to dam the Tuolumne, flood the Hetch Hetchy, and provide San Francisco with its water system. In 1913 President Woodrow Wilson and Secretary of the Interior Franklin Lane (a Canadian-born Californian) reversed previous federal denials of the request and allowed the Hetch Hetchy project to proceed. The O'Shaughnessy Dam, named for San Francisco's city engineer, was completed and the reservoir filled in 1923. The height of the dam was increased in 1938. The dam, giving a view onto the Hetch Hetchy Reservoir, is reached by road from SR 120 just west of the Big Oak Flat entrance station to Yosemite National Park. In 1988, Secretary of the Interior Donald Hodel caused a furor when he proposed that the dam be taken down and the valley drained and restored. Protests from the city of San Francisco so far seem to have defeated this scheme.

River Camps

Activity on the bars of the Tuolumne and Stanislaus rivers began early in 1849. Hawkins' Bar, below Jacksonville, was the site of the first river diggings on the

Tuolumne. Its population increased from fifteen in April 1849 to 700 by the following September. Extensive plans for damming and diverting the river were made but had to be abandoned because of an unexpected rise in the flow of the water. By 1852 Hawkins' Bar was practically deserted.

The history of Swett's Bar, where mining was begun in November 1849, is typical. A company of 70 men cut a race to divert the stream, but here, too, the sudden rise of water caused the project to be abandoned temporarily. In August 1850 the work was resumed, and after 59 days of hard labor the dam was completed— only to be washed away that very evening. The process was repeated a third time, with the same result. The season being then too far advanced to resume the project, the work was laid aside for the year. In August 1851 the camp, although reduced to 27 men, completed a dam in a few weeks, and for some time thereafter an ounce of gold per man was taken out each day.

During 1850 the river camps along the Tuolumne were among the largest in the county, thousands of miners being engaged in attempts to divert the river in order to mine its bed. Few of the camps, however, enjoyed any great prosperity, and all of them, Hawkins', Swett's, Stevens', Payne's, Hart's, Morgan's, Roger's, Signorita, York, and Texas bars, have completely disappeared. Not a vestige of former days remains to show where the cabins of the miners once stood. Not even the bars themselves remain as they were, for the river has changed its course several times since the 1850's.

Along that part of the old channel now covered by Lake Don Pedro lay the bars of Don Pedro, Indian, and Red Mountain. From one claim at Don Pedro's Bar, gold valued at $100,000 was taken out before 1889, the cost of operation being only $5,000. At the time of Lincoln's election to the presidency in 1860, as many as 1,500 votes were cast at Don Pedro's Bar. Indian Bar, the scene of active mining in the 1850's, continued to exist until the building of Don Pedro Dam.

Moccasin, once a thriving camp at the mouth of Moccasin Creek, is now the site of the Moccasin Creek Power House, a unit in the Hetch Hetchy water system.

Woods' Crossing

The first discovery of gold in Tuolumne County was made in August 1848 at Woods' Crossing on Woods' Creek by a party of men led by James Woods. James Savage, J. H. Rider, and Charles Bassett were members of the party. The richness of the field proved remarkable, and for a time gold in the amount of two or three hundred dollars a day per man was taken out with pick and knife alone. It is said that more gold was taken from this creek than from any other stream of its size in California. Almost as famous were two of its branches, Sullivan's Creek and Curtis Creek.

At Woods' Crossing, on SR 49 one mile southwest of Jamestown, a small monument of gold-bearing quartz has been erected by the Tuolumne County Chamber of Commerce commemorating the finding of gold there. The spot at which the discovery was made is located 500 feet southeast of this marker where the old road crosses Woods' Creek.

Sonora

Very soon after the discovery of gold at Woods' Crossing, settlements were made at Jamestown and at Sonora, farther up on Woods' Creek. Located in a famous gold region, Sonora is one of the most picturesque and beautiful of all the old mining towns on the Mother Lode. Changing conditions have brought innovations that have somewhat altered its charm and individuality, but much of interest still remains. Along Washington Street, some of the heavy iron shutters of earlier days have been replaced by plate-glass windows, which display relics of the mining era and recently found gold nuggets as well as current merchandise. On Saturday evenings in summer the street is like a plaza on fiesta day. A walk along the same route in the daytime reveals narrow side streets, along which may be seen old stone buildings with iron shutters, old trees, houses, gardens, and stone walls covered with ivy that must have been planted in the very earliest years.

Sonorian Camp, as it was first known, was located by a party of Mexicans who pushed up Woods' Creek beyond Woods' Crossing and were the sole occupants of this region for several months. In the spring of 1849 the first Yankee settlers arrived, including R. S. Ham, who apparently assumed the office of alcalde, and George Washington Keeler. Others soon followed. In July 1849 fully 1,500 foreigners, largely Mexicans and Chileans, poured into the camps of Tuolumne County, and by autumn there were 5,000 people in Sonora. The narrow streets were constantly thronged and on Sundays were almost impassable. A tax on foreigners, which incited a bloodless war in June 1850, brought an exodus that cut the population almost in half.

In spite of frequent fires from which Sonora has suffered, some buildings reminiscent of the gold rush days still remain in and about the town. At 286 South Washington Street stands the Gunn house, oldest residence in Sonora. Dr. Lewis C. Gunn, who had arrived in Jamestown in 1849, built the house and in 1851 brought his wife and family of young children from the East to

Street-Morgan Mansion, Sonora

live there. At that time the house, a two-story adobe, had a balcony across the entire front of the second story. The parlor at the left was used as a printing office. Here the first issue of the *Sonora Herald* came out on July 4, 1850. Across the hall was the county recorder's office, Dr. Gunn having been elected recorder in 1850. After the Gunn family moved to San Francisco in 1861, the house was converted into a hospital, and in 1899 was remodeled as a private residence. Only the middle part of the present structure comprises the original Gunn adobe. The house is now a motel and is an outstanding example of a building in keeping with its historic theme.

St. James Episcopal Church (SRL 139), built in 1859, is one of the most attractive small churches in the Mother Lode or anywhere in California, as well as one of the oldest Episcopal churches in the state. It is easily seen at the north end of Washington Street, commanding a view over the business district. To the west, the Street-Morgan mansion stands across the way from the church; this outstanding Victorian home, built in 1896, has been converted to offices and is beautifully preserved. St. Patrick's Catholic Church (1862) is another beautiful old building still serving the community. The Tuolumne County courthouse, built in 1898 and set back from Washington Street by a small park, is an impressive structure suggesting the vitality that resurged in the town in the year that the railroad arrived.

The Tuolumne County Museum at 158 West Bradford Street is housed in the old jail, which operated from 1865 until 1961; it has many fascinating exhibits related to gold mining. The Tuolumne County Historical Society, which operates the museum (open to the public on a regular basis), has printed guides for walking tours of this small, charming city. The City Hotel (1852) was originally an adobe structure and has been extensively remodeled, now presenting its 1890's appearance. A modern building, but an outstanding example of period architecture, is the Security Pacific Bank. Other noteworthy public buildings are the Odd Fellows Hall on Washington Street and the Wells Fargo Building at Washington and Linoberg streets. Old residences still standing (all of which are privately owned and not open to the public) are the Burden, Burgson, Rosasco, Cady, and Sugg homes, the latter two being on the National Register of Historic Places.

On a hill at the edge of town beyond the 1909 grammar school building is the Masonic cemetery, in which the graves of many early residents lie shadowed by oak and cypress trees. Here stands the monument of gold-bearing quartz put up by Tuolumne Lodge No. 8, F.&A.M., of Sonora, the Sonora Welfare Club, and the Tuolumne County Chamber of Commerce in honor of Jacob Richard Stoker, 1820–96. The inscription reads in part: "His heart was finer metal than any gold his shovel ever brought to light." Dick Stoker was a Mexican War veteran who came to California in 1849. He was intimately associated with Mark Twain and the Gillis brothers on Jackass Hill in the 1860's, and was a member of Tuolumne Lodge No. 8. With a reputation for being just and fair, Dick settled many miners' disputes and served his community faithfully.

The Big Bonanza Mine in the heart of Sonora is the greatest pocket mine ever discovered. (A pocket mine is one which yields a large and usually compact amount of pay dirt in a very small area.) It is located on Piety Hill less than 100 yards north of the St. James Episcopal Church and within a short distance of four other churches. It was first worked in 1851 by Chileans, who took out a large amount of surface gold. In the 1870's it was purchased by three partners, who worked it for years and then one day broke into a body of almost solid gold. The next day they shipped gold valued at $160,000 to the San Francisco Mint. Within a week $500,000 was taken out and another half-million was mined before the property was again sold.

Among other mines in this vicinity were the San Giuseppe, located about a quarter of a mile northwest of the center of Sonora, and the Golden Gate, renowned for the pureness of its gold. It has been estimated that $41 million worth of gold has been mined within a radius of two miles of Sonora.

Jamestown and its Neighbors

Jamestown (SRL 431), also called Jimtown, lies in the shadow of Table Mountain about four miles southwest of Sonora on SR 108. Colonel George F. James, a lawyer from San Francisco, located at this point on Woods' Creek in 1848. James fell into disfavor, and after his departure the inhabitants changed the name of the settlement to American Camp. The old name, however, had more appeal to the miners and was revived. In the years 1890–1915 $30 million in gold was removed from the Jamestown area alone—evidence that the gold rush was not confined to 1849 and the 1850's.

The coming of the railroad in 1898 made Jamestown an important transportation center, although there was not much railroad activity beyond here. The Sierra Railroad maintained its lines long after the end of World War II, and until 1985 an excursion along a length of track from the railroad station was run by a historic railroad organization. Limited service resumed in 1987.

Jamestown is a busy, modern place today; on its main street one can see old brick stores and hotels, many with balconies. The building formerly occupied by the St. James Masonic Lodge has been partly remodeled and the original stone has been covered with stucco, but the thickness of the walls is evident at the entrance. It is located on the west side of Main Street two doors north of the picturesque Emporium. The Methodist Episcopal church was built in 1852 and is still in use.

At Montezuma (SRL 122), three miles south of Jamestown on SR 49, mining operations were begun in the summer and fall of 1852. Deep and extensive mines in this neighborhood produced exceptionally pure gold. Two stage lines passed through this settlement: the line from Stockton to Sonora, and Dr. Clarke's line from Sonora and Columbia to Don Pedro's, La Grange, and other points. The old Fox Building at Montezuma has been rebuilt and is now used as a private dwelling. Remains of a cemetery are near the corral.

Yorktown, Curtisville, Sullivan's Creek, Green Springs, Campo Seco (or Dry Diggins), and Hardtack were other camps in the vicinity of Jamestown.

At Quartz Mountain, south of Jamestown and east of SR 49, is the famous App Mine, which produced $6,500,000 in gold up to the year 1909. The mine was closed down a few years after this date, and in 1927 the town of Quartz was destroyed by fire. John App and others became interested in property on this mountain as early as 1856, when they located the quartz claim on the west side. App married Leanna Donner, one of the six Donner girls orphaned by the famous Donner Pass tragedy of 1847. Mrs. App, who reached the age of 95, lived for 78 years in Tuolumne County.

South of Quartz is Stent, formerly known as Poverty Hill, where an old cemetery is about all that remains of pioneer days. To the southeast stood Algerine, once a notoriously wild mining camp, which boasted two streets lined with business houses. Today only a few cellars show the sites of the old stores.

Climbing Table Mountain west of Jamestown one comes to Rawhide, or Rawhide Flat, the location of the famous Rawhide Quartz Mine, which had a production record of over $6 million up to 1909. At one time this mine, owned by Captain William Nevills, was considered one of the greatest gold mines in the world. There has been much pocket mining in the vicinity of Rawhide.

Jeffersonville, a thriving town in the 1850's and a stage stop between Rawhide and Tuttletown, was the scene of extensive tunnel mining under Table Mountain. Nothing remains to mark the site of the town but a small tree-shaded graveyard on top of a hill. West of Jeffersonville is the site of French Flat, now overgrown with chaparral. The Humbug Mine, on the east slope of the mountain a little way from the road leading from Jamestown to Rawhide, was the richest of all the tunnel mines, with a total yield of more than $4 million; nuggets the size of hen's eggs were found there.

Columbia

Columbia (SRL 123) was a city of several thousand people, one of the largest mining camps in California. From an area of 640 acres on the outskirts of the town, more gold was recovered from gravel than in any equal area in the Western Hemisphere. Most of the topsoil here, averaging from 20 to 60 feet in depth, was removed by hand cart, leaving an expanse of rocks, fantastic and unreal in appearance.

The rush for gold at Columbia had few parallels. On March 27, 1850, Dr. Thaddeus Hildreth, his brother George, and some other miners made camp for the night under an oak tree in the vicinity of what is now Columbia. Rain during the night obliged the men to remain the next morning in order to dry their blankets, and while there, John Walker found "color" in a nearby gulch. The party remained and located at this promising point, which is where the bridge at the foot of Main Street crosses Columbia Gulch.

For a time the place was called Hildreth's Diggings, but was soon named Columbia. Almost from the first the camp was troubled by a lack of water. The winter of 1850–51 provided little rain to remedy the situation. In

June 1851 the Tuolumne County Water Company was organized at Columbia. Its attempt to build a ditch to Five Mile Creek was at first frustrated, however, by the fact that there was insufficient waterpower to operate its sawmill. Heavy steam equipment had to be hauled to it, and by late November the mill was in operation. The ditch was completed by the following spring. In the meantime merchants were coming in to supply the needs of the 200 men working on the ditch. About the first of September 1851 a citizens' committee was appointed to lay out the streets and lots, and subsequently the town was platted on its present site. It was incorporated in May 1854, only to be almost destroyed by fire in July of the same year. The reconstructed buildings were substantial and more nearly fireproof. In the summer of that year another ditch company, the Columbia and Stanislaus Water Company, was formed, but eventually it was absorbed by the older company. Ultimately, after years of supplying the county with water for mining and irrigation, the Tuolumne County Water Company and its successors were absorbed by the Pacific Gas and Electric Company, which continues to furnish power and electricity for the entire county.

Families had begun to settle in Columbia as early as the fall of 1851, and soon gardens were planted and ranches cultivated in the vicinity. From January 1858 to January 1860 Columbia was illuminated by gas made from pitch, the lamps being set on cedar posts. Churches and public buildings were illuminated free. The gasworks were located on the east side of Gold Street, midway between Washington and State streets, about opposite the end of Fulton Street. After two years this system was found to be unsatisfactory and was discontinued.

Marble from the Columbia Quarry is of even grain and is remarkable for its elasticity. In color it ranges from white to gray and is either banded or rose-mottled. The sidewalks laid around the Palace Hotel in San Francisco in 1878 were made of this marble.

The town was often spoken of as "Columbia, the Gem of the Southern Mines," because of the great extent and rich character of its placer deposits. With the decline of mining, its population diminished to a few hundred, but it never became a ghost town. Columbia's post office has operated continuously since November 16, 1852. Through the years its sturdy old brick buildings weathered the vicissitudes of age and neglect. As the centennial of the gold rush approached, the Mother Lode country began to attract the attention of historians, and Columbia was adjudged the best preserved of the old camps and the most worthy of restoration as a memorial to the pioneers and a piece of "living his-

tory" for the enjoyment and education of future generations. Thus the picturesque old town was purchased by the state of California and in 1945 became Columbia State Historic Park. It has since been registered as a National Historic Landmark.

Columbia remains a town fully lived in, with all kinds of everyday functions going on, on a site that is deliberately maintained to present the appearance, as far as possible, of a town of the late 1850's. Two terribly destructive fires, in 1854 and 1857, were convincing reasons for rebuilding most of the public structures in brick or stone and embellishing them with iron shutters and doors.

The little engine house contains one of the oldest pieces of fire-extinguishing apparatus in the state, the hand-pumper "Papeete," polished and painted to look as it did when it arrived in Columbia in December 1859. (It is said that the engine was constructed for use in Papeete, Tahiti, but the Columbia committee visiting San Francisco to purchase a municipal wagon prevailed upon the builder to sell it to Columbia instead.) The adjoining two-story building contained the office where four short-lived newspapers were printed. The post office is located in an old grocery store building on Jackson Street and displays the earliest set of boxes to be used in Columbia, built locally in 1861. Among the oldest buildings in town are the Franklin & Wolf and Brainard buildings, adjacent and having a common wall. The Stage Drivers' Retreat and the Pioneer Saloon (Alberding's) are just two of the numerous establishments where miners gathered to slake their thirst and pass the time. The City Hotel, from 1856, is a charming establishment operated by Columbia College; the view of Columbia from its second-story balcony is a favorite of photographers. The Fallon Hotel and Theater have been restored and are likewise open for business; Owen Fallon built the oldest part of it in the fall of 1859. Nearby stands a replica of Eagle Cottage, the original of which was put up as a boardinghouse in the middle 1850's. A stone monument on the west side of Broadway opposite the restored Masonic Hall bears a bronze tablet recounting major events in Columbia's history.

Todd & Company's Express maintained an office at Columbia at least as early as 1852, the year in which William Daegener took charge, at a location unknown to historians. By September 1853 Todd had sold out to Wells Fargo & Co., and within the next few months the office was moved to the American Hotel. This was at the site of the present brick Wells Fargo Building, which Daegener built in 1858. Now thoroughly renovated and restored, it is another favorite subject for photographers. Wells Fargo operated there until 1914.

Wells Fargo Building, Columbia

At Columbia there are several residences that were built between 1854 and 1860. Some have been remodeled beyond recognition, but a few maintain the beauty of their original construction. One of these, located directly across the street from the restored post office, was built as a combination store and residence by Louis Braquihai in the spring of 1856.

The brick Columbia school on the hill was opened for its first term by John Graham on March 18, 1861, using furnishings from the old school. By September new desks and seats were all in place. Restoration of the schoolhouse was effected through the efforts of the California Teachers' Association. On a hill beyond the school is the cemetery of Columbia Lodge No. 28, F.&A.M., which has been restored by the Grand Lodge, which also rebuilt the Masonic Hall in the town itself.

St. Ann's Church, a favorite subject for photographers and painters, crowns Kennebec Hill, overlooking the world's richest placer grounds, with the ghostlike rocks of the diggings encroaching to the very edge of the little cemetery. The church was erected in 1856 with funds donated for its construction by the miners. The walls of this historic church were built of brick fired in a kiln that was located on the Sonora-Springfield Road, while the timbers used in its construction were obtained from Saw Mill Flat about three miles southeast of Columbia. The belfry was added in 1857. The interior decorations and altar paintings are the work of

pioneer hotelkeeper James Fallon, son of Owen Fallon. After having stood for half a century, the walls of the old church were considered to be unsafe, and its doors were closed, but through the united efforts of the Native Sons of the Golden West and the Knights of Columbus, the structure was repaired and was rededicated in 1906. It is now in regular use.

Between Columbia and Vallecito was Parrott's Ferry (SRL 438) on the Stanislaus River. Thomas H. Parrott established it in 1860, and it operated until 1903, when the first bridge was built. An incised boulder at Parrott's Ferry Outlook reads: "Inspiration Point: The Inspiration to revive the Ancient and Honorable Order of E Clampus Vitus, a benevolent society prominent in gold rush days, occurred fifty years ago to Carl I. Wheat as he travelled from Columbia down to Parrott's Ferry on the Stanislaus River. ECV Redivivus, now a fraternal historical society dedicated to preserving Western history and lore, has thirty-five active chapters throughout California and Nevada. Plaque dedicated May 26, 1980 [Memorial Day]. Co-sponsored by Matuca Chapter 1848, Quivira Chapter, Yerba Buena Capitulus Redivivus, New Helvetia Chapter, Paltrix Chapter, Lord Sholto Douglas Chapter. Credo Quia Absurdum."

Gold Springs

In the sands of a large spring, which is still visible about a mile and a half northwest of Columbia, a Mr. Hatch and others discovered gold in the latter part of April 1850. This spring and another were the source of a stream that was used for mining operations employing some 300 miners. A camp boasting a two-story brick building, at least three food stores, several boardinghouses, a soda works, and a number of mechanics' shops and hardware stores, with an area population of 500, had grown up at the springs by 1856. Its citizens were quiet, orderly, and enterprising. Several gardens and small ranches in the immediate vicinity supplied fresh fruits and vegetables to the miners at Columbia and Yankee Hill to the southeast, and to Red Dog, Dow's Flat, Heavy Tree Hill, Wayne's Bar, Simpson's Bar, Italian Bar, and Texas Bar to the north.

Saw Mill Flat

Saw Mill Flat (SRL 424), so named because of the two sawmills erected there to supply mining timbers in the early 1850's, was situated on a fork of Woods' Creek, three miles southwest of Columbia and one and a half miles south of Yankee Hill. At first it was a great resort for Mexicans and Peruvians, and it is said that

Joaquín Murieta, at that time a monte dealer, operated in the town, where injustices done to him by some Americans set him on his career of banditry.

Shaw's Flat

Shaw's Flat (SRL 395), on the eastern edge of Table Mountain, was named by Mandeville Shaw, who planted an orchard there in 1849. A number of substantial cottages surrounded by gardens planted with fruit and ornamental trees give the place an attractive appearance today. The Mississippi House, built in 1850 and serving as a store, bar, and post office, is still to be seen, but is near collapse. Also preserved at Shaw's Flat is the old miners' bell, used to announce the convening of court and to summon the men to work; it may be seen at the school.

In 1855 miners sinking a shaft at Caldwell's Gardens discovered river gravel under the lava. At this point, the ancient stream was wide and flat and the lava coat consequently thin. Caldwell's claim is said to have yielded $250,000 in gold. Following this discovery, tunnels, some of great length, were made under Table Mountain and immense fortunes were taken out.

Brown's Flat and Squabbletown

Brown's Flat, located on Woods' Creek one mile north of Sonora, had its beginning in 1851. Extensive hill and surface diggings independent of the creek bed were worked in the vicinity. Among these mines were the Page, the Ford, and the Sugarman, the last-named producing crystallized gold of great beauty. After 1852 steam and horse power were used in draining the many claims.

Squabbletown, a small camp farther north on Woods' Creek, has practically disappeared. Only a few old cabins show where the settlement once stood.

Tuttletown

Tuttletown (SRL 124), about six miles west of Sonora on SR 49, was named after Judge A. A. H. Tuttle, who built a log cabin there in 1848. The earliest dwellings consisted of tents and Mexican *ramadas*, or brush houses. It was a stopping place for packers carrying miners' supplies over the old Slum-gullion Road from Angels Camp to Sonora, and by 1849–50 it was a flourishing camp. Since that time its population has dwindled to a dozen or so families. Here are the ruins of a little country store built of stone, known as Swerer's, where Mark Twain once traded. On the outskirts of Tuttle-

Mark Twain's Cabin, Jackass Hill, near Tuttletown

town, opposite the Patterson Mine, are three old Spanish cork trees.

Jackass Hill

Jackass Hill, just west of Tuttletown, achieved much notoriety in 1851 and 1852. The diggings were rich in coarse gold and excitement was intense. Hundreds of men rushed to the scene, and many a lucky miner made his "pile" in a few hours. Some claims of 100 square feet yielded as much as $10,000, and one quartz pocket produced from $100 to $300 a day for three years. Numerous small pocket mines made rich yields of ore.

The hill received its name from the braying of the jackasses in the pack trains that paused overnight on their way to and from the mines. As many as 200 of the animals are said to have been picketed on the hill at one time.

Mark Twain spent five months on Jackass Hill in 1864–65 as the guest of William R. Gillis. A replica of the cabin (SRL 138) stands on the hilltop about one mile from Tuttletown. It is built around the old fireplace, which survived the destruction of the original cabin by fire in 1906. It is surrounded by modern homes and is set apart by a fence. A tablet telling the story of Jackass Hill was placed near the cabin in 1929 by the Tuolumne County Chamber of Commerce.

Springfield

Springfield (SRL 432), a camp southwest of Columbia near the head of Mormon Creek, received its name from the fine springs there, which afforded sufficient water for the placer-mining operations of several hundred men who worked the rich gold claims in the vicinity. The miners often uncovered Indian mortars and pestles, showing that Indians had camped at the springs.

The town, with its stores, shops, and hotels, was well laid out about a plaza. The erection of a Methodist church before that of a gambling house makes Spring-field unique in the annals of mining towns. It was noted for the quiet orderliness and sobriety of its citizens, many of whom worked in the mines under Table Mountain nearby. Today the site of the town is indicated by an abandoned brick schoolhouse, which formerly served as a church, and was an arsenal in the Civil War.

Chinese Camp

Some ten miles southwest of Sonora is Chinese Camp (SRL 423), which in 1856 had a population of 1,000 and boasted a church, several stores and hotels, a bank, an express office, and two fraternal orders, the Masonic Lodge and the Sons of Temperance. Mining there consisted principally of surface diggings on the hilltop and in the valley. Water was brought to the mines in the vicinity from Woods' Creek by means of a flume and ditch.

One of several stories told of the origin of this old place name is that the town was founded by a ship's captain who deserted his vessel (the brig *Eagle*) in San Francisco Bay and brought his entire Chinese crew there to mine. A less dramatic version is that Chinese miners were employed there by English prospectors. A third story says that after gold became exhausted up over the hill at Campo Salvado, the miners working there ultimately joined the Chinese on the other side and named the new location after them. It is estimated that at one time 5,000 Chinese worked there, but there seems to be no Chinese population in the town today. One may still see at Chinese Camp a few old stone and brick buildings with heavy iron doors typical of the early gold days. The Wells Fargo Building (SRL 140) has entirely vanished, although its iron doors are in the Wells Fargo Museum in San Francisco. On a hill at the edge of Chinese Camp is picturesque little St. Francis Xavier Catholic Church, built in 1854 and restored in 1949 and again in 1976.

Chinese Camp was the rallying place of the second big tong war in California. Two Mile Bar on the Stanislaus River was the scene of the incident that led to this war. Twelve members of the Sam-Yap Tong were working near six members of the Yan-Wo Tong when a huge stone rolled from one property to the other. Words and blows ensued. Calls went out for assistance. American blacksmiths in neighboring camps were engaged to make crude weapons—pikes, daggers, and tridents—and a few firearms were supplied from San Francisco. On September 26, 1856, 900 members of the Yan-Wo Tong went forth from Chinese Camp to meet 1,200 members of the opposing tong near Crimea House. The battle took place amid the beating of gongs and the reverberations of random shots from inexperienced marksmen. The casualties were four killed and four wounded. American officers of the law finally arrested 250 of the combatants. The State Historical Museum at Sutter's Fort, Sacramento, has specimens of these locally manufactured weapons.

Jacksonville

Jacksonville (SRL 419) on the Tuolumne River was established by Colonel Alden Jackson in June 1849 and by the summer of 1851 it ranked second only to Sonora. At Jacksonville was planted the first orchard in that part of the state, known as Smart's Garden, and for many years a sparse scattering of old apple trees remained. Mining through the orchard brought about its final destruction. In the early 1850's Jacksonville was the scene of extensive river operations, including the building of great dams and wing dams at high cost in labor and materials. A modern dam finished off the town, which now lies at the bottom of Lake Don Pedro.

Priest's Hotel and Big Oak Flat

Priest's Hotel (named after its original owner) was on the main road to Yosemite Valley in the 1860's. A wagon road over this route was not completed to the floor of the valley until 1874. The steep and winding road up Old Priest's Grade (now bypassed by SR 120) is one of the most picturesque in the Sierra, and one of the most challenging for the driver. The original Priest's Hotel and its successor have long disappeared from the site, simply known as Priest today. From a hill at about the middle of the settlement a panorama touching seven counties may be observed on a clear day.

About a mile from the hotel stood a famous landmark during mining days, the big oak (*Quercus lobata*) from which Big Oak Flat (SRL 406) derived its name. This huge tree, eleven feet in diameter, was eventually killed by miners digging about its roots for gold.

James Savage, with a retinue of Indian laborers in 1850, was the first man to mine Big Oak Flat, originally called Savage Diggings. In the vicinity, the Lumsden, Big Oak Flat, Longfellow, Cosmopolite, and Mississippi mines were notable producers. A large stone building, the Odd Fellows Hall, still stands at Big Oak Flat.

First and Second Garrote

Groveland (SRL 446), formerly known as Garrote or First Garrote, on the Big Oak Flat Road (SR 120), is still a thriving community. On its main street stands a memento of the past, the old stone Tannehill store, and at the opposite end of the block is the Masonic Hall, an old two-story adobe. About two miles above Groveland, near the edge of the Stanislaus National Forest, is Second Garrote (SRL 460), a small mountain town. When the stage line opened on the Yosemite road in 1876, it is said that the operators of the line wished to provide something of interest for travelers at the otherwise featureless stage stop; they selected a large oak and christened it Hangman's Tree. Across the road from the marker and enclosed by a fence is a two-story frame house, formerly the home of Chaffee and Chamberlain, alleged to have been the originals of Bret Harte's stories. Mines in the vicinity of Second Garrote were the Kanaka, the Big Betsy, and the Mexican.

Tuolumne

Tuolumne, just west of the border of the Stanislaus National Forest, was a lumber center and terminus of the Sierra Railway. It is less than a mile from the old mining camp of Carter's, first known as Summersville (SRL 407), named in honor of Mrs. Elizabeth Summers, wife of an early settler. Just north of the town is the Tuolumne Indian Rancheria, the home of about 150 Miwok Indians, whose ancestral home this area was.

The Buchanan Mine ten miles east of Tuolumne has yielded more than $2 million over the years.

The East Belt Mines

Mining activity in the East Belt began early in the 1850's. The Soulsby Quartz Mine at Soulsbyville was discovered by Benjamin Soulsby in 1856. It seems to have been worked exclusively by Cornish miners. By 1909 it had produced $7 million. Other mines in the vicinity were the Black Oak, the Live Oak, the Golden Treasure, and the Platt and Gilson. Soulsbyville (SRL 420) has always been a place of well-kept homes, pretty gardens, and law-abiding people, so the chroniclers say.

Over the lava ridge just east of Soulsbyville was Cherokee (SRL 445), near neighbor to Arastraville. The Confidence Mine at Confidence, thirteen miles northeast of Sonora on SR 108, was discovered in 1853 and was one of several good producers in this vicinity. This group of claims included the Independence, the Little Jessie, the Mary Ellen, and the Plowboy. The Excelsior Mine at Sugar Pine produced $420,000 worth of gold before the quartz vein was lost; many attempts to relocate the vein have failed.

Ventura County

Ventura County was organized in 1873 and the city of Ventura was made the county seat. Ventura is a shortened form of San Buenaventura, so called after Mission San Buenaventura. The name was derived from the saint whose title, Bonaventure (good fortune), is said to have been bestowed after he was healed by Saint Francis. The city is still officially known as San Buenaventura, although the post office has been designated Ventura since 1889. The Roman Doric courthouse with its white marble facade (SRL 847), erected in 1913 at 501 Poli Street, became Ventura's city hall in 1973. In the plaza in front of the city hall stands a statue of Father Junipero Serra, founder of the mission, carved by John Palo-Kangas in 1936.

Cabrillo's Landing Place

Once there were many Chumash Indian villages along the shore of what is now Ventura County. When Cabrillo, the discoverer of California, sailed up the coast in 1542, it is thought by some historians that he came ashore on October 10 at a place where there was a large village, called Shislolop in the local dialect. Cabrillo called the place El Pueblo de las Canoas ("the Town of the Canoes"), because he was so impressed by the large, finely built boats that these Chumash Indians used. The boats carried from fifteen to twenty persons, were built of boards hewn by hand, and were caulked with asphalt from the neighboring hills. Their boats, homes, implements, and utensils, as well as their mode of life, exhibited a skill in workmanship and a high level of culture that placed a distinguishing mark upon the Chumash Indians of Ventura and Santa Barbara counties and of the Channel Islands. Being also friendly and numerous, they provided many converts for the zealous Franciscans who followed Cabrillo some 200 years later.

Relics of the Chumash civilization have been found throughout the region and are preserved in the Ventura County Historical Museum located at 100 East Main Street in Ventura. Water baskets lined with native asphalt, skillfully wrought bowls and mortars, and finely shaped arrowheads are among the many interesting treasures displayed.

The old village at which Cabrillo landed may have been the one located on the seashore at the foot of what are now Figueroa and Palm streets in Ventura. In the 1870's a kitchen midden was still visible very near the sea, on Figueroa Street, on land now occupied by oil storage tanks. There is, however, some difference of opinion among historians as to the location of Pueblo de las Canoas, Mugu Lagoon southeast of Oxnard and Rincon Point also having been noted as possible sites. Modern opinion favors the Ventura location.

Cabrillo remained at the Pueblo de las Canoas until October 13, when he sailed "six or seven leagues, passing along the shores of two large islands," anchoring off Rincon Point.

The Trail of Portolá

Leaving the campsite near Castaic in Los Angeles County on August 10, 1769, Captain Gaspar de Portolá and his men continued down the rich valley that was later called the Santa Clara, after a village that Father Juan Crespí had named, halting for the night on the banks of an arroyo in the vicinity of Rancho Camulos very near the county line. On the three succeeding days the tents were pitched near Indian villages in the neighborhood of Fillmore, Santa Paula, and Saticoy, where the friendly inhabitants gave the strangers gifts of seeds, acorns, and baskets of pine nuts in exchange for beads. Monuments have been erected at Warring Park in Piru (SRL 624) and the eastern edge of Santa Paula (SRL 727) in commemoration of Portolá's visit. On August 14 the party stopped near the site of Mission San Buenaventura, where a large rancheria was located. Father Crespí, who named the village La Asunción de Nuestra Señora, expressed the hope "that such a fine site, where nothing is lacking, will become a good mission." The next night found the travelers at another town where the father wrote that the villagers

"kept us awake playing all night on some doleful pipes or whistles." The name bestowed upon this place by the soldiers has persisted in Pitas ("whistles") Point, location of Faria County Park. On August 16, Rincon Point was rounded and camp was made at a fishing village on Rincon Creek.

When Portolá's men twice again traversed this county in the first half of 1770, their route was the shorter one followed by the present US 101 via Conejo Grade and Calabasas.

The Anza Trail

Juan Bautista de Anza, on April 10, 1774, traveling north on his overland journey from Sonora to San Francisco, camped near Triunfo (a former post office at the junction of El Camino Real and the road to Lake Sherwood) in Russell Valley west of Calabasas. "Passing among many docile heathens," the party continued their march the next day, halting for the night near San Buenaventura on the river of the same name. Returning from the north a little later, Anza camped on April 29 east of Camarillo at the foot of Conejo Grade, this being his only stop in Ventura County on that trip. In 1776 Anza passed this way again as leader of the first overland emigrant trains to California. Retracing his former route, he made only one halt in Ventura County, near El Rio, on February 23, 1776.

Mission San Buenaventura

In the midst of these populous villages with their friendly people, halfway between San Diego on the south and Monterey on the north, Father Junípero Serra at length planted the ninth of the missions and named it San Buenaventura. It was the last to be dedicated by the zealous founder of the California mission chain, for his death occurred just two years later, on August 28, 1784.

From the very beginning of his work in California the Padre Presidente had contemplated the founding of this halfway station in the fruitful valley of San Buenaventura. However the Indian uprisings at San Diego and, more especially, the difficulties between the mission fathers and the civil authorities had long delayed the fulfillment of his wish. It was thirteen years after the founding of San Diego de Alcalá, the first of the missions, before Mission San Buenaventura was finally established on March 31, 1782. In the vicinity of the Indian village locally known as Mitz-Khan-a-Khan, Father Serra put up the first crude enramada for the celebration of the first Mass.

It was the custom, when a mission was dedicated, to erect a cross, not only as an emblem of faith but as a beacon to guide travelers to the mission. Along the coast a site was usually chosen that was visible both by land and by sea. At Ventura, the place selected was a lofty hill called La Loma de la Cruz ("the Hill of the Cross"), which rises immediately behind the mission church in the present city of Ventura.

For nearly 50 years Serra's cross (SRL 113) stood upon the hilltop above the mission. At last, however, rain and wind so weakened it that it fell. The old central timber was replaced by a new one, but the original scroll and crosspiece were retained. Thus it stood for another half-century, when in 1875 it was again blown down. After that, for 38 years, the hillside was without a cross. The scroll of the original cross, however, was saved and is now preserved in the Ventura County Museum of History and Art. In 1913 a new cross was raised on the original hilltop site, now located within Grant Park.

Very soon after the erection of the first enramada, the first mission church was built. According to Captain George Vancouver, this was destroyed by fire. Church records indicate that if such was the case, the disaster occurred between December 9, 1791 and June 21, 1792. The site of this first church may have been at what is now the corner of Palm and Thompson streets. There in 1792 a small chapel dedicated to San Miguel Arcángel was built to be used as the mission church while the principal church was being built at its present location at 211 East Main Street. This chapel was in use when the 1812 earthquake severely damaged the building, and in 1816 it was pulled down. Another chapel built nearby suffered from flood damage and its last ruins were removed in the 1870's.

Another chapel, dedicated to Santa Gertrudis, was built for the Indian community at the entrance to Casitas Pass, about seven miles north of the mission. This chapel was used intermittently for many years until about 1868. Many Indians of the community settled about the Chapel of Santa Gertrudis, and the great numbers of their little willow-thatched houses gave the name Casitas ("Little Houses") to the entire region. The site of the chapel now lies under the Ojai Freeway, by the turnoff to Foster Park.

The present mission church was begun early in 1793 but not completed for some years. Even before the dedication of the present mission structure on September 10, 1809, the mission garden had become famous. In the autumn of 1793, Vancouver, on his second visit to California, wrote in his journal about the gardens of San Buenaventura, describing them as "far exceeding anything" he had seen elsewhere in California. At a

Mission San Buenaventura, Ventura

later date, Richard Henry Dana declared them to be "the finest in the whole country."

The old walled garden, now entirely vanished, was bounded approximately by Main Street on the north, Ventura Avenue on the west, Meta Street on the south, and Colombo Street on the east. The beautiful Ventura County Museum of History and Art (1977) at 100 East Main Street now occupies the northeast portion of the old mission garden.

The present mission structure on the north side of East Main Street (SRL 310) was at one time the center of what was considered to be one of the richest of all the missions, being especially famous for its horticulture. After the secularization of the missions, it suffered with the rest. It was roofless for many years after the earthquake of 1857 and, while in this condition, was abandoned, for how long is not known, but we do know that the Chapel of Santa Gertrudis was being used in its stead in 1868. In 1895 the present mission structure was described by J. Torrey as a "well-preserved building, its walls still bearing traces of the rude frescoing affected by the builders of that time."

In 1957 the interior of the church was restored, as nearly as possible, to its original condition, undoing the work of an earlier regrettable "restoration," which had obliterated much of its ancient charm. Ceiling and flooring were torn out in 1957 to reveal the original beams and floor tiles. The crudely beautiful Indian frescoes, which had been covered up by ornate scroll work, unfortunately could not be saved, but a small section of them, which had escaped modernization, may be seen in the Father Serra Chapel. Many relics are on display in the mission museum, including part of the old wooden pulpit, carved and painted by the Indians, which had been torn out of the church in the earlier restoration, and the original confessionals, also showing Indian handiwork. Old records in Father Serra's handwriting and a pair of unusual wooden bells, probably used during the last three days of Holy Week and the only ones extant in the California mission chain, are also to be seen there.

A fascinating display at 113 East Main Street immediately to the west of the mission is the Mission Plaza Archaeological Interpretive Facility, opened in 1980. Several years before, a team of archaeologists sifted through 3,500 years of historical remains to piece together the life story of one city block. The Albinger Archaeological Museum has displays from the Oak Grove people of prehistoric times through the later settlers of Ventura, the Chumash, Spanish, Mexicans, Americans, and Chinese. Outside, the excavated remains of four old mission buildings can be seen superimposed on the foundation of one of the first church structures, as well as middens and wells. Up Valdez Alley on the hill behind the facility are the remains of the excellent system of pipes and aqueducts built by the padres and their laborers to bring water from the Ventura River and San Antonio Creek to the fountains and fields of the mission. At the end of the system they built a settling tank and receiving reservoir (SRL 114), called "Cabeza del Caballo" from the horse's head that once adorned its water spout. The area is now known as Eastman Park.

The great water ditch or stone aqueduct, which was also a part of the padres' seven-mile-long water system, was demolished by the floods and landslides of 1866–67. The massive ruins may still be seen near the mouth of the Cañada Larga, eloquent testimonials to the workmanship of the mission fathers and their Indian laborers. The remnants are about one-fourth mile east of the Ojai Road on Cañada Larga Road.

The Mission Town

Standing on a slight elevation at the foot of La Loma de la Cruz, the mission church dominated the tiny town that grew out from it westward to the San Buenaventura River. Two irregular bridle paths formed the streets of the little settlement and along these the adobe homes were built, sometimes flat-roofed and covered with brea, sometimes more picturesquely tiled, and, occasionally, shingled. Only the Ortega adobe remains today.

Seventy years before the Ortega house was built on the east bank of the San Buenaventura River, an adobe

Ortega Adobe, Ventura

home had been erected on the Rancho Sespe near the site of Fillmore, 28 miles east of Ventura. The unknown builders of this homestead were murdered by a band of Mojave Indians, leaving the house deserted and forgotten until 1857, when it was remembered by Miguel Emigdio Ortega, who needed its sturdy timbers for his new home. Four arduous days were taken for the journey, a bodyguard of mounted horsemen accompanying the expedition as a protection against the Indians. The house was dismantled and the coveted timbers were hauled back to Ventura, where they were incorporated in the new house. In 1897, E. C. Ortega, son of the original builder, had occasion to repair the old home. The center beam, brought from the Sespe house 40 years before, was found to be in perfect condition and so solid that a 20-penny spike could not penetrate it more than a quarter of an inch.

In the flood of 1861–62, the swollen waters of the San Buenaventura swept away half of the Ortega adobe and a portion of the orchard of pear, peach, and fig trees. The remaining portion of the house is still in good condition and has been added to slightly at the eastern front end. It is owned by the city of Ventura and is open to the public at 215 West Main Street.

In the beginning all the lands about San Buenaventura belonged to the mission. After secularization of the missions, grants were made, and the people to whom the land was given began establishing homes and building their adobe *casas* throughout the county. These tracts were very large, those over 4,000 acres being considered to be among the smaller units. Consequently, the country homes scattered over the entire area were few, and only a handful remain.

On what was formerly the Lower Ojai Rancho stands the López adobe, called the "Barracks" because it once defended the lower Ojai Valley against the threat of marauding Indians. Extensively renovated but preserving a flavor of earlier days, it is beautifully situated on the McCaleb Ranch just to the left of the highway about two and one-half miles northwest of Ojai. About nine miles north of Ventura, and just east of the Ojai highway on Old Creek Road, stands the Santa Ana Rancho adobe house of Don José de Arnaz.

Frémont's Camp

Don José de Arnaz was mayordomo of San Buenaventura at the time of General Frémont's arrival at the mission in 1846. Frémont, on his way south to the reconquest of Los Angeles, wished to gain possession of Mission San Buenaventura for the United States. In order to obtain the knowledge that would enable him to carry out his plan, he arrested Arnaz and tried to get the desired information out of him. Arnaz, however, claimed that he was unable to give this information and was finally released.

Until the publication in 1928 of the memoirs of Don José de Arnaz, the site of General Frémont's camp while at Ventura was unknown or forgotten. Arnaz wrote that he "established his camp on the west side of the mission orchard." This places the site of the camp south of Main Street near Garden Street. Arnaz's town house was on what is now West Main Street, midway between South Ventura Avenue and the river. In the late 1850's he moved to his Santa Ana Rancho, and his old home in town became the American Hotel.

Rancho San Miguel and the Olivas Adobe

Perhaps the best preserved of the historic adobes around Ventura is the Olivas adobe (SRL 115), which stands near the Santa Clara River about one and one-half miles south of East Main Street on Olivas Park Drive. Don Raimundo Olivas, the original owner, was born in Los Angeles in 1801 and came to Santa Barbara as a soldier twenty years later. In 1841 he and another retired soldier, Felipe Lorenzana, received the grant of 4,693 acres that constituted Rancho San Miguel; Lorenzana sold his half, the western portion, to Dixie Thompson at a later date. This is roughly where the eastern portion of the city of Ventura stands today.

The Olivas adobe is a long two-story building with balcony and veranda overlooking a walled garden below, and fields, park, and marshlands beyond. The Olivas family, with its 21 children, was famous for its fine entertainment and generous hospitality, and many stories are locally told of the place, such as the time that Olivas was surprised and robbed by bandits. Beautifully restored and open to the public, the adobe stands in a park maintained by the City of Ventura Parks and Recreation Department, a gift from the Max C. Fleischmann Foundation in 1963.

Rancho Camulos

About 30 miles east of Ventura, on the road to Los Angeles by way of Santa Paula and Newhall (SR 126), is one of the most famous adobes in California. Located on Rancho Camulos, it was the home of the Del Valle family until the mid-1920's and was the setting for part of the novel *Ramona*, written by Helen Hunt Jackson. Rancho Camulos was originally a part of Rancho San Francisco, granted to Antonio del Valle in 1833 and 1839. Gradually, Don Antonio purchased 2,000 acres of the Rancho Temescal, and on this he built his home in the early 1860's. Travelers between missions San Buenaventura and San Fernando often stopped at Rancho Camulos, where the hospitality of the Del Valles was famous.

The Camulos adobe is probably the best preserved and most typical of all of California's old rancho houses. From Rancho Camulos, Mrs. Jackson drew largely for her remarkable pictures of Spanish life in early California. Her visit there in 1881 inspired the opening scenes of the tale.

The charming Del Valle family chapel is a separate wooden building on the property where for many years Mass was regularly offered to the family, employees, neighboring Indians, and guests. Long a literary and historic shrine, Rancho Camulos has remained much the same externally for many years. Its gates are now closed to visitors, but a monument (SRL 553) stands on the highway. Rancho San Francisco is commemorated by a marker (SRL 556) just across the Los Angeles County line one-quarter mile south of the junction of SR 126 and I-5, at Valencia.

Piru, closest town to Camulos, was founded by David Cook in 1887, during the triple boom in railroad, health resorts, and real estate. Cook's beautiful mansion at 829 North Park Avenue burned in 1981 but has been faithfully restored by the owners, who maintain it as a private residence.

Rancho Simi

SR 118 parallels SR 126 as a highway from Ventura to Los Angeles; for much of its length it passes through the Simi Valley, location of the old Spanish Rancho Simi, first grant in Ventura County. The huge ranch, whose 113,009 acres made it one of California's largest, includes the valley and surrounding hills and a bit of Los Angeles County. The original grant was made in 1795, a second following in 1825, to Patricio, Miguel, and Francisco Javier Pico, whose interests were sold soon thereafter to José de la Guerra y Noriega of Santa Barbara, who also acquired part of adjoining El Conejo Rancho. The name "Simi" comes from the Chumash Simih or Chimii (place or village).

In 1889 the Chicago Mutual Benefit Company advertised "Simiopolis" in Chicago and Cincinnati, and shipped out twelve prefabricated "colony" houses for buyers. One of these stands today in Strathearn Memorial Park (SRL 979) at 137 Strathearn Place in the town of Simi Valley. An adobe built by De la Guerra, probably in the 1820's, is also on the site; additions to it were made by the Strathearn family in 1892. The first Simi Library, opened in 1930, also stands in the park, and houses exhibits about local pioneer families.

Rincon Point

The jagged cliffs of Rincon Point rise above the sea some twelve miles west of Ventura, a place reputed to be a battleground of the ancestors of the Chumash tribe. It is chiefly associated with the Battle of San Buenaventura, fought between rival factions of Californians on March 27–28, 1838, and for the dramatic poem "The Fight of the Paso del Mar," written by Bayard Taylor.

The rival factions concerned in the Battle of San Buenaventura were led by Juan Bautista Alvarado in the north and by Andrés and Pío Pico in the south. Alvarado's forces, commanded by General José Castro, seized Rincon Point, believed to be of great strategic importance, before their enemies, under Carlos Antonio Carrillo, had arrived at the scene. From Rincon Point, Castro marched down to San Buenaventura and took it by surprise with only a few shots fired, although Alvarado lost one man.

When the Eastern journalist Bayard Taylor wrote "The Fight of the Paso Del Mar" in 1840, he had never seen the place of which he wrote. In 1849 he visited California for the first time, and early in the following year saw Rincon Point. In his book *Eldorado*, written after this visit, he said: "We touched at Santa Barbara on the third morning out. . . . We ran astray in the channel between the Island of Santa Rosa and the mainland, making the coast at about twenty-five miles south of the town. I did not regret this as it gave me an oppor-

tunity of seeing the point where the Coast Mountains come down to the sea, forming a narrow pass. . . . It is generally known as the Rincon, or Corner. . . . I had made it the scene of an imaginary incident, giving the name of Paso Del Mar—the Pass of the Sea—to the spot. I was delighted to find so near a correspondence between its crags of black rock, its breakers and reaches of spray-wet sand, and the previous picture in my imagination."

Taylor evidently was geographically confused in the writing of his poem, for it seems that the story it immortalizes was a folktale from Point Loma connected with the days of hide droughing or transport at La Playa, when old San Diego was the shipping point for the great ranchos of the Southwest. The story, as related in full by A. M. Loop in *The Silver Gate* (January 1900), an early San Diego magazine, seems to have been substantiated by old residents of San Diego. But although the tragic climax of this tale was in reality set at Point Loma, Taylor himself, by his reminiscence in *Eldorado*, made it also a legend of Ventura's Rincon.

Other Historic Spots in Ventura County

The town of Camarillo, usually associated with the nearby State Hospital and St. John's Seminary (location of the Edward L. Doheny Memorial Library), was named for Juan Camarillo, who purchased Rancho Calleguas from the heirs of the grantee, José Pedro Ruíz. The Camarillo home at 3771 Mission Oak Boulevard, built in 1892, remains as the family's private residence.

About eight miles east of Camarillo, at 51 South Ventu Park Road in Newbury Park, is the reconstructed Stagecoach Inn (SRL 659). The original white frame two-story inn was built in 1876 by James Hammell as a stage stop under the name of the Grand Union Hotel. Moved to its present location in 1966 when the Ventura Freeway widened US 101, it burned down in 1970, but was completely rebuilt and reopened in 1976. It is today the museum of the Conejo Valley Historical Society.

Nearby Moorpark was apparently named for the Moorpark apricot, which flourished in this area around 1900. Most of this part of Ventura County has had the rapid changes of increased population dramatically thrust upon it. In 1955, Moorpark replaced its last hand-cranked telephone with a dial model. Four years later, it became the first town in the United States to receive all its electricity from a nuclear power plant!

Where Sycamore Road joins SR 126, four miles east of Santa Paula, there stands a giant sycamore that was fully mature when John C. Frémont passed that way with his men on their march south to Los Angeles in

Sycamore Tree, near Santa Paula

Bard's name is remembered in the little settlement of Bardsdale, just across the Santa Clara River from Fillmore. He was also associated with the development of the Simi Valley and with Port Hueneme. The port was once, according to W. W. Robinson, "the biggest California shipping point south of San Francisco" and, during World War II, the harbor through which was shipped "the major portion of all the supplies for our Armed Forces in the Pacific." It is the location of the Naval Construction Battalion Center, "Home of the Seabees"; the Seabee Museum on the Port Hueneme Naval Base, open to the public, commemorates this historic unit. The Port Hueneme Museum and Historical Society, in the former Bank of Hueneme building at 220 North Market Street in Port Hueneme, has special displays on pioneer families of the region.

The nearby city of Oxnard now exceeds Ventura in population. It owes its early success to the incredible richness of its soil; lima beans and sugar beets were among the crops that flourished in abundance in the vicinity. The Oxnard Historical Society Museum at 424 South C Street is housed in the basement of the 1906 Carnegie Library. In the vicinity are El Rio, once called New Jerusalem, and Montalvo, named for the early Spanish author who first used the word "California." The Fillmore Historical Museum at 447 Main Street is in the old Southern Pacific Railroad Depot.

Northern Ventura County is a ruggedly beautiful area included in Los Padres National Forest and penetrated by few roads. The Sespe Wildlife Area north of Fillmore and Piru was dedicated to the preservation of the California condor, a venture that unfortunately failed. The last wild California condor was captured in 1987.

Ventura County also includes two of the Channel Islands—Anacapa and San Nicolas. The lighthouse on Anacapa Island, built in 1932, was one of the last to be constructed in the United States. The headquarters of the Channel Islands National Monument is in the city of Ventura; the visitors' center is at 1901 Spinnaker Drive in the Ventura Harbor area.

1846 (SRL 756). A kind of long-standing "community center," it has seen service as a meeting place, post office, and outdoor chapel.

Oil is today one of Ventura County's principal industries, and the California Oil Museum is located here, in a building at Tenth and Main streets in Santa Paula. Interesting exhibits of early-day oil machinery may be seen in this well-kept structure, in which the Union Oil Company was organized in 1890. Lyman Stewart and Wallace L. Hardison, oil men from Pennsylvania, consolidated their California interests with those of Thomas R. Bard, who became the first president of the corporation and later served in the United States Senate. Although Bard had drilled the first well in the county as early as 1865, Ventura County did not achieve real prominence in the oil industry until the 1920's, when spectacular discoveries were made near the city of Ventura.

Yolo County

Yolo County was one of the original 27 counties. Yolo, or Yo-doy, was the name of a tribe of Patwin Indians, and is said to mean "a place abounding in rushes." Fre-

mont was the first county seat, from 1850 to 1851, when the honor was bestowed upon Washington, now Broderick. In 1857 the county seat was moved to Cacheville, now Yolo, but after four years, in 1861, Washington again became the county seat. In 1862, Woodland was finally chosen as the permanent seat of justice.

The Trail of the Fur Hunter

In the marshlands west of the Sacramento River lived the Yo-doy, a tribal branch of the Patwin or Southern Wintuan Indians. To the south lay fertile, unbroken plains where game abounded. These plains were bounded on the north and south by Cache and Putah creeks, while on the east flowed the great river, and on the west lay a range of hills. The area supported a fairly large indigenous population; some 147 archaeological sites have been recorded in Yolo County. The diseases of the white settlers devastated the native people, some remnants of whom still live in the Capay Valley.

For hundreds of years, Indian hunters roamed this region undisturbed. In 1808, Gabriel Moraga led an expedition that sailed up the Sacramento to what is now Sutter County, noting Indian villages along the river. A second upriver expedition was led in 1817 by Father Narciso Durán, Luís Argüello, and Father Ramón Abella to look for mission sites in the great Central Valley. They landed near the present town of Clarksburg and put up a cross on the opposite shore near Freeport in Sacramento County. In 1821, the Spanish government's last expedition into the Central Valley of California was the first to pass overland through what is now Yolo County. Led by Luís Argüello, the party crossed what are now Solano and Yolo counties before reaching the Sacramento River at a point in Colusa County in the vicinity of Grimes. Father Blas Ordaz, chaplain and chronicler of the expedition, noted the existence of an Indian rancheria by Putah Creek, near present-day Winters, and estimated its population at 400 souls.

In 1828 the American explorer Jedediah Strong Smith is thought to have hunted and trapped on the streams of Yolo County, followed by the great army of Hudson's Bay Company trappers, who found this a rich field. They cached their furs along the river and smaller streams, one of which became known as Cache Creek. One of their camps, known to early settlers as French Camp, was situated in a grove of oaks on the north bank of Cache Creek one mile east of the present town of Yolo, formerly Cacheville.

In the spring and summer of 1830 another band of hunters, led by Ewing Young, trapped along the San Joaquin and Sacramento rivers and remained for a time on Cache Creek. Two years later, on his way to Oregon, Young again passed through Yolo County territory, camping on Cache and Putah creeks before proceeding to the coast and northward to Oregon by way of Putah Canyon.

Joseph Gale, who had come to California with Ewing Young in 1831, had a cattle rendezvous on Cache Creek in 1843. The need for more livestock in the Willamette Valley in Oregon was the incentive for a daring project begun by Gale in 1841. Undaunted by the difficulties of getting the cattle to Oregon, he set to work to construct an oceangoing vessel that he proposed to take to California and there exchange for livestock. Through the intervention of Charles Wilkes, the Hudson's Bay Company equipped the vessel, and Gale, after passing a seaman's examination, was granted a seaman's license. The schooner, *Star of Oregon*, was launched in May 1841, and toward the end of August 1842 Gale and his crew started down the Columbia River toward California. At San Francisco, José Y. Limantour, a Frenchman, purchased the vessel in exchange for 350 cows.

Needing more men for the vast stock-driving venture over the mountains as well as for the Oregon settlement project, Gale waited until the spring of 1843 before starting north. Circulars had been sent out describing the advantages of the Willamette Valley for settlement, and by the middle of May, 42 men, among them Jacob P. Leese, had gathered at Cache Creek. From a tall cottonwood tree trimmed into the form of a flagstaff the Stars and Stripes floated for several weeks that spring. The expedition finally started northward on May 14, driving 1,250 head of cattle, 600 horses and mules, and 3,000 sheep, most of which were safely guided over the northern mountain barrier after a journey of 75 days.

Mexican Land Grants

Within what is now Yolo County, eleven grants of land for permanent settlement were made by the Mexican government between 1842 and the American conquest in 1846. Only five of these titles, however, were later confirmed by the United States government.

The first, Rancho Río de los Putos, was situated on both banks of Putah Creek in the vicinity of Winters. ("Los Putos" and "Putah" seem to be Spanish approximations of the name of a local Indian tribe.) The grant of four leagues was made to William Wolfskill, an American residing in Los Angeles; it was occupied in July 1842 by his brother John, who began the plantings that would make him the father of the horticultural industry in northern California. While his initial plantings of vines and trees were on both sides of the creek, his permanent residence was on the south bank, in what became Solano County.

William Gordon, a native of Ohio who brought his family to California with the Workman-Rowland party in 1841, settled on Rancho Quesesoni in July 1842. This pioneering venture was located on a grant of two square leagues bisected by Cache Creek west of what is now Woodland. (The boundaries can be followed on county roads 94B, 19, and 89 and SR 16.) "Uncle Billy" Gordon had been a trapper and hunter in New Mexico, "rough, honest, and hospitable." His place on Cache Creek became a "general rendezvous for settlers and hunters" from 1843 to 1846. James Clyman, in his diary for July 12, 1845, noted that at the time of his visit Gordon was the only permanent settler on Cache Creek. On this rancho the first wheat in Yolo County was grown, and in 1847, in a primitive building one mile from Gordon's home, the county's first school was started with an enrollment of eight pupils. Gordon sold land and water rights to James Moore, resulting in construction in 1856 of the first irrigation dam and ditch system to utilize the natural water supply of Cache Creek, which flows out of Clear Lake in the mountains of Lake County.

Rancho Quesesoni, more commonly known as Gordon's Ranch, was sold in 1866, when William Gordon moved to Cobb Valley in Lake County, where he lived until his death in 1876. All that remains today is a family cemetery situated north of Cache Creek, near the former homesite on County Road 19, and marked with a plaque in 1948 by the Native Daughters of the Golden West.

The third grant made in Yolo County territory was given to Thomas M. Hardy, a Canadian, in 1843, and consisted of 26,637 acres along Cache Creek east of Gordon's Ranch, reaching as far as the Sacramento River. It was called Rancho Río de Jesús María, an early name given to the Upper Sacramento River. Hardy built a tule shack on the west bank of the Sacramento near the mouth of the Feather River, but he spent very little time there, having enlisted in military service under the Mexican government.

After Hardy's death by drowning in Suisun Bay in 1848 or 1849, his property was sold by the public administrator. Among those who purchased portions of the original rancho was James H. Harbin, who had come to this part of California in 1847. On Harbin's land the town of Fremont was afterward laid out. In 1857 Harbin moved to Lake County, where he settled at the springs that bear his name.

Rancho Cañada de Capay was located on Cache Creek and was granted to Francisco Berryessa and his brothers, Santiago and Demisio, in 1843. (Kroeber says that Capay is from the Indian *kapai*, meaning "stream.") Their great holdings were later taken over by incoming Americans, one of whom was George Dickson Stephens. In 1850 Stephens camped on Cache Creek on what he supposed was government land, but he afterward learned that it was part of the Berryessa grant. With his brother John he acquired the property that

Stephens Adobe, between Madison and Esparto

same year and erected an adobe dwelling. This house, around which a larger frame structure was built as the needs of the family grew, is the only adobe standing in Yolo County today. The building is well preserved and is still occupied by Stephens's descendants. It stands half a mile south of SR 16 midway between Madison and Esparto; the wooden balcony and veranda overhang the adobe walls.

Almost simultaneously with the building of Moore's canal on Gordon's Ranch, another dam and ditch were begun by David Quincy Adams in 1857. The Adams Canal, which was completed in 1870, was laid out by Adams on Rancho Cañada de Capay, 4,693 acres of which he had purchased with money made in the mines of the Mother Lode during the years from 1849 to 1852. Adams built his canal for the purpose of irrigating 150 acres of alfalfa and 40 acres of gardens cared for by Chinese. This alfalfa, probably the first to be grown in California, was raised from seed obtained by Adams from Chile, and nearly all of the alfalfa grown in northern California today is known as Chilean alfalfa. The Adams Dam, which was located on Cache Creek about two miles west and a little north of Capay, no longer exists, but a newer Capay Dam diverts water southward to the Winters Canal.

Washington (Broderick) and West Sacramento

In December 1844 Rancho Nueva Flandria, the fifth Mexican grant in Yolo County, consisting of three square leagues of land bordering on the west bank of the Sacramento River, was granted to John Schwartz, also called Juan de Swat, an eccentric Dutch immigrant who had come to California with the Bidwell-Bartleson party in 1841.

In the spring of 1846 Schwartz sold 600 acres of his

rancho to James McDowell, who had come overland with his wife and daughter in 1845. McDowell built a cabin on the northwest corner of his ranch opposite the site of the present city of Sacramento, where he took his family to live. He died in 1849, and in 1850 his widow had a townsite laid out on the land. This was the beginning of the little town of Washington, later known as Broderick.

When the town of Fremont began to decline in 1851, Washington became the center of commerce as well as of judicial and political activity in Yolo County. From 1851 to 1857 it was the county seat, and again from 1861 to 1862.

Washington was the site of the first Pacific Coast salmon cannery, established in the spring of 1864 on the west side of the Sacramento River opposite the foot of Sacramento's K Street. William and George Hume and Andrew Hapgood, fishermen from Maine, began with crude equipment in a converted cabin and scow, performing every operation by hand. During the first year, at least half the cans burst at the seams in cooking, but the partners managed to produce 2,000 cases of a dozen cans each, selling them at five dollars a case. As the business became more successful, other salmon canneries sprang up. By 1882, the peak year, there were twenty canneries along the Sacramento River and San Francisco Bay producing 200,000 cases of salmon a year. Decline set in when the number of salmon entering the Sacramento River was sharply reduced, a consequence of the silting of the river by hydraulic mining in the Sierra. In recognition of the fact that the multi-million-dollar salmon canning industry of the Pacific Coast is a direct outgrowth of this pioneering effort, the Department of the Interior has registered the site of Hapgood, Hume, and Company as a National Historic Landmark, and in April 1964 a plaque was placed in Broderick just up the river from Tower Bridge.

For several years most of the traffic from the northern and western sections of Yolo County passed through Washington. So great was its early promise that the citizens for a time had hopes of its becoming a great city. Later, with the transfer of growth and activity from Washington to Sacramento across the river, and with the coming of the railroad, which decreased its importance as a center of navigation, Washington's boom days were ended.

On January 3, 1987, Broderick became part of California's newest municipality, the town of West Sacramento.

Fremont

On the west shore of the Sacramento River one-half mile below the mouth of the Feather River, within the boundaries of the Harbin Ranch, Jonas Spect, a native of Pennsylvania, who had come overland to Oregon in 1847 and from there to San Francisco on the *Henry* early in 1848, established the town of Fremont in March 1849. Spect erected a temporary store of tules, willow poles, and canvas, and with the help of the Indians established a ferry across the Sacramento River. A sand bar at this point made an excellent ford across the Feather River; this seemed to be the head of navigation for both streams.

With miners, teamsters, and packers constantly passing through on their way to the mining regions, Fremont grew by leaps and bounds, and at the height of its prosperity claimed a population of 3,000. But its promise was short-lived. In the winter of 1849 heavy storms washed away the sand bars and the Feather River became navigable as far as Marysville. Commerce on both rivers passed Fremont by, and it was soon superseded in importance by Washington.

The loyal citizens of Fremont did not give up their town at once, and by means of desperate lobbying succeeded in making it the first county seat in 1850. In July 1851, however, popular vote took the seat of government to Washington, and Fremont, its last hope gone, gradually disappeared. Some of its buildings were moved to Knights Landing, some to Marysville, and others to newly established ranches in the vicinity. Soon empty lots were all that remained of the little river town. Today the site is privately owned farmland.

Cacheville (Yolo)

In September 1849 Thomas Cochran camped on the north bank of Cache Creek about ten miles west of Fremont, on the site of the present town of Yolo, and put up a hotel for the accommodation of travelers along the west side of the Sacramento River. The place grew and became known as Cochran's Crossing. In 1853 James A. Hutton arrived and built a large, commodious structure that he opened to the public. The hospitality of Hutton and his family became so well known that the name of the place was changed to Hutton's Ranch, or Travelers' Home. The old Hutton house is still standing at 325 Main Street. In 1857 the place became the county seat of Yolo County and was renamed Cacheville. The post office had been established under the name of Yolo in 1853.

Located in a rich farming region, Cacheville grew rapidly for a few years, but was outstripped by the more promising Yolo City, later known as Woodland, a few miles to the south. The Pacific Methodist (South) College was established at Cacheville in 1859 but was moved to Vacaville in 1861 and to Santa Rosa in 1871. The Methodist church, built in 1867, is still standing.

Knights Landing

William Knight, a native of Baltimore, Maryland, who was said to have been educated as a physician, came to California with the Workman-Rowland party in 1841. In 1843 he settled at a natural landing place on the Sacramento River later known as Knights Landing. In 1846 he received a grant to this land, but the title was never confirmed.

Knight's first home on the river rancho was made of tules and willow poles fastened with rawhide and plastered with mud. It was built in 1843 on an ancient Indian mound. Since this site was at the junction of the lower Sycamore Slough with the Sacramento River, it proved suitable for a ferry, which was established by Knight soon after his arrival, and the place became an important landing and shipping point on the Sacramento. Knight later moved to Stanislaus County, where he founded Knight's Ferry; when he died there on November 9, 1849, his lack of business foresight resulted in his estate being lost to his intended heirs.

An attempt to start a town at Knights was made in 1849 under the name of Baltimore, but it never materialized because of disagreements over the sale of lots. In 1853, however, Charles F. Reed laid out another townsite and the place was officially named Knights Landing. The same year, J. R. Snowball, Knight's son-in-law, and J. J. Perkins opened a general store on the Indian mound. Snowball was later elected judge and became a prosperous businessman and landowner. In 1877 he built an imposing two-story house that still stands near the river, a prominent local landmark.

Snowball House, Knights Landing

Knights Landing, which is located about twelve miles north of Woodland, retained the early river-town atmosphere in the older portion of the settlement so perfectly that in the 1920's it was chosen by film directors as the locale for the making of Mississippi River scenes in *Showboat* and *Steamboat Round the Bend*. Most of the picturesque buildings along Front Street were destroyed in a fire that swept the town in 1938; since then, the town has turned away from the river, although it is still a center for fishing and boating activities.

Woodland

The fine groves of oak trees just south of Cache Creek, where the city of Woodland now stands, were centrally located in the midst of an extensive and fertile region, which later became one of the principal agricultural belts of the county. "Uncle Johnny" Morris, a Kentuckian, was the first white man to settle in what is now Woodland. He arrived with his family in November 1849 from Missouri and lived for two years in a log cabin on the south side of Cache Creek. During this time he planted two acres of the Mission variety of grapes, the first in the county. In 1851 he settled at what is now the corner of First and Clover streets. He was joined two years later by Henry Wyckoff, who set up the first store in what he called "Yolo City." By 1857 Frank S. Freeman had purchased 160 acres and laid out a town that he envisioned as a trading center for one of the richest grain-growing counties in the nation. The following year he opened the town's first post office, which his wife, Gertrude, named Woodland.

Freeman donated a city block to the county when Woodland was chosen as county seat in 1862, and an imposing courthouse was erected there the following year; this was replaced by the present Neoclassical Revival structure in 1917. On the northwest corner of First and Main streets is the brick commercial building Freeman built in the 1860's; across the street is the old Capitol Hotel building from 1868. The Woodland Opera House (SRL 851) at Second Street and Dead Cat Alley, first opened in 1896, is currently enjoying a revival as a performing theater.

Among the many fine old houses on College and First streets built in the last quarter of the nineteenth century, the Gable House (SRL 864) at 659 First Street is an excellent example of what is often called Victorian architecture; it is on the National Register of Historic Places. The small wooden Gothic-style church on First Street, from 1874, is one of the oldest public buildings in the county; originally a Congregationalist house of worship, it is today the First Church of Christ, Scientist.

Clarksburg

Clarksburg lies on the west bank of the Sacramento River in an area first settled by an adventurous German named Frederick Babel in 1849. Other farmers moved into the area, where the fertile soil produced rich crops. Floods, however, were an annual threat, and not until the second decade of the twentieth century were high levees and canals created that transformed this land into what was called "The Eden of California." The present town dates from the 1920's. On the River Road north of Clarksburg one can see some of the two-story houses built by Portuguese settlers before 1900; typically, the family living quarters were placed on the second floor in anticipation of floods. Near the Freeport Bridge, St. Joseph's Catholic Church, built in 1923 to replace a structure from 1886, is still an important element in the life of the Portuguese community.

Davis

Where the little town of Davisville grew up in the late 1860's and where the University of California at Davis now draws thousands of students annually, Jerome C. Davis settled in the early 1850's. An energetic entrepreneur, by 1864 his ranch totaled approximately 13,000 acres, more than 8,000 of which were fenced; he raised cattle, horses, and sheep, had extensive wheatfields, and raised profitable crops of peaches and grapes.

William Dresbach leased the Davis home in 1867 and made it into a hotel, which he called the Yolo House. As a settlement began to grow up, Dresbach named it Davisville. With the advent of the railroad the place became a thriving grain-shipping point. In 1868, however, when a branch of the Central Pacific Railroad was extended north to Marysville, Davisville began to decline as a trade center, a decline hastened when the Vaca Valley Railroad was constructed to Madison in 1875.

The rich farming lands that surrounded Davisville continued to be developed, however, and in 1905 the University Farm was established by an act of the state legislature. The first buildings were erected there in 1907 (three are still standing), the same year that the name of the Davisville post office was shortened to the present Davis. The first courses for adult farmers were given in the autumn of 1908, and the following January the farm school for young men and boys was opened. In 1922 it was officially organized as a branch of the College of Agriculture of the University of California at Berkeley. Even at this early date, a gradual shift had begun in the educational mission of the school. More and more courses not directly related to agriculture were

offered, and finally, in 1951, these were combined into the College of Letters and Science. In 1959 Davis was authorized as a general campus of the University of California, and a graduate division was established in 1961.

Winters

The city of Winters is located on a tract of Rancho Río de los Putos, just above the old Wolfskill Ford, where a town was laid out by developers of the Vaca Valley Railroad in 1875. This independent line, initially built from Vaca Station, now Elmira, to Vacaville in 1869, was extended to the north bank of Putah Creek, with plans for connecting lines to Berryessa Valley and the north coastal lumber district through Cache Creek Canyon. A 40-acre townsite was named for the former landowner, Theodore Winters, a well-known breeder of horses who had purchased a large tract of the Wolfskills' rancho in 1865.

Three brick business houses constructed in 1875–76 still stand in a one-block historic district. The Bank of Winters, organized locally in 1885 to finance the rapidly growing fruit industry, built a large facility in 1904, which stands on the corner of Main Street and Railroad Avenue.

Seven miles west of Winters on SR 128 is scenic Putah Canyon, where the Putah Creek Turnpike, an early toll road to Berryessa Valley, was operated by the Adam See family from 1858 to 1875, when a county road was opened. Stone quarries in the upper canyon furnished grinding stones for some of the first gristmills in northern California as early as 1846. Later, stone for many public and private buildings was extracted from the Bertholet Quarry. Devil's Gate, a jagged rock outcropping at the head of Putah Canyon where Yolo, Napa, and Solano counties meet, became the site of Monticello Dam, a federal reclamation project completed in 1957. The 304-foot-high concrete arched dam impounds the waters of Putah Creek, creating Lake Berryessa.

Eastern Yolo County

The eastern part of Yolo County is crisscrossed by a maze of roads, highways, railroad tracks, and bridges. The first bridge across the Sacramento River was a wooden wagon bridge constructed in 1857 between Washington and Sacramento's I Street. When the transcontinental railroad was completed in 1869, the bridge was rebuilt to accommodate railroad tracks. Today the I Street Bridge is on the National Register of Historic Places, as is the Tower Bridge, a striking twin-towered automobile bridge several blocks downstream, which leads directly to the state capitol.

Downriver from the two bridges is the Port of Sacramento, which was opened to deep-sea traffic in 1963. The Port is the terminus of a 42.8-mile ship channel, 30 feet deep, that was constructed between Collinsville in Solano County and West Sacramento. California's sole inland navigation lock may be seen on the barge canal here.

Travelers on I-80 cross the Yolo Bypass on the three-mile-long Yolo Causeway. The bypass is part of an elaborate system to control flooding of 101,000 acres of the Sacramento Valley. The system, which was begun in 1911, extends from Shasta Dam to Rio Vista and includes 980 miles of levees, 438 miles of flood-control channels and canals, 31 bridges, six weirs, and seven bypasses. The Yolo Causeway is now a six-lane divided elevated highway, widened and reinforced in 1985–86. When it was constructed in 1916, it was the first all-year, all-weather road across what was then a vast wilderness of tules.

Yuba County

Yuba County was one of the original 27 counties established in 1850. Nevada and Sierra counties were later created from its territory. Marysville has been the only county seat.

There are two explanations for the origin of the name Yuba. According to one, the Gabriel Moraga expedition of 1808, while naming the rivers flowing from the Sierra into the valley, gave one the name of Río de las Uvas ("River of the Grapes") for the wild grapes that grew on its banks; "Yuba" is thus a corruption of "Uvas." A second account holds that Yu-ba was the ancestral village of a Maidu Indian tribe, located where the Feather River was joined by a great river flowing from the mountains, and that this name was used for both the river and the county.

Yuba Trails

Before the arrival of white men in the territory of what is now Yuba County, its dim trails were trodden only by the Maidu people. John C. Frémont, in his *Memoirs*, describes their villages as he saw them in 1846: "We traveled across the valley plain, and in about sixteen miles reached Feather River, at twenty miles from its junction with the Sacramento, near the mouth of the Yuba, so called from a village of Indians who live on it. The Indians aided us across the river with canoes and small rafts. Extending across the bank in front of the village was a range of wicker cribs, about twelve feet high, partly filled with what is there the Indians' staff of life, acorns. A collection of huts, shaped like bee-hives, with naked Indians sunning themselves on the tops, and these acorn cribs, are the prominent objects in an Indian village."

Hudson's Bay Company trappers occasionally crossed the region during the years 1830–41. In the 1840's a branch of the old California Emigrant Trail crossed the High Sierra through Donner Pass and followed down the mountains to Johnson's Rancho, an outpost of civilization at that time, located on the Bear River about three miles east of where Wheatland now stands.

Marysville

A large portion of what is now Yuba County became a part of the princely domain of John A. Sutter after 1841, but, since the lands included on his map covered a much larger area than the Mexican laws allowed, he resorted to the practice of subletting parts of his estate to other settlers. Some of these farms were in what are now Sutter and Placer counties, while others lay within the present boundaries of Yuba County.

The land on which the town of Marysville was later founded was located on a part of Sutter's Ranch that was leased in the fall of 1842 to Theodore Cordua, a Prussian, for a period of nineteen years. Cordua made it a stock ranch and in 1842–43 built an adobe dwelling, with a trading room and outbuildings, at what is now the foot of D Street in Marysville.

Cordua, described as "a fat, jolly, whist-loving man, popular with everybody," called his settlement "New Mecklenburg" after his native land, but his neighbors called it Cordua's Ranch. It stood on the California-Oregon Trail through the Sacramento Valley, and by 1846 travel over this route from Oregon had become so extensive that Cordua's adobe became an important way station and trading post for emigrants, hunters, and, later, miners. The adobe with its thick walls, seemingly built to withstand a siege, was destroyed by fire in 1851. In 1844, Cordua obtained a grant of seven leagues of land from the Mexican government north of the Yuba River in what is now Yuba County, but not included in his former lease from Sutter.

Charles Covillaud, a native of France and a former employee of Cordua, purchased a half-share in the ranch at New Mecklenburg in 1848. In January 1849, the other half was sold to two brothers-in-law of Covillaud's wife; they were Michael C. Nye, who married Mrs. Harriet Murphy Pike, a survivor of the Donner party tragedy, and William Foster, also a member of the Donner party and husband of Sarah Murphy. Nye and Foster sold out to Covillaud in September 1849, and in October Covillaud in turn sold all but one-fourth to José Manuel Ramírez, John Sampson, and Theodore Sicard. Discovery of gold at Coloma in 1848 had brought a period of great development to the region, and a town was laid out in January 1850. Covillaud's wife, Mary Murphy Covillaud, another member of the Donner party, received the honor of having the new town named for her, Marysville.

Marysville became the actual head of navigation on the Feather River and a center of trade for the northern mines. Its location gave it a decided superiority over all other candidates for such a position on the river, above and below. The distance to the mines, north and east, was not great, and cargoes from the river boats could be transported readily by pack-mule trains to the outlying gold fields. These proved to be rich producers, and as a result Marysville experienced a phenomenal growth.

Freight and passenger boats landed at a point adjoining the old plaza, on Front between D and E streets. Today the river, held in leash by stone levees, actually flows above the city streets. In the early days the plaza looked down upon the stream and its rich bottom lands, which were originally covered with groves of cottonwood, willow, and sycamore, but which soon became dotted with the homes and orchards and vineyards of the early settlers. Hydraulic mining, however, changed the face of the entire countryside, burying homes and settlements beneath acres of debris, raising the bed of the river 70 feet or more, and necessitating the construction of miles of levees. Most of the tailings from mining days are now buried under suburban homes.

A Chinese temple (SRL 889), one of the oldest in the state and the only one in the nation erected to the water god Bok Kai, still stands on Front Street near E, but no longer does it watch the passing of ships upon the river as it did in the stirring days of the 1850's. The roof of this sturdy brick shrine is now about on a level

Entrance to Bok Kai Temple, Marysville

with the levee, which keeps the river from washing the whole structure down to the sea. It is still used by worshipers.

Among Marysville's many interesting old houses is the José M. Ramírez residence at 220 Fifth Street between B and C. Of elaborate construction, with marble basement and Gothic windows, it is known locally as "The Castle." It later became the home of W. T. Ellis, the father of the Marysville levee system, for whom Ellis Lake in downtown Marysville is named.

The brick house at 630 D Street, said to have been built by Stephen J. Field, still serves as a private dwelling. Field, a young New York lawyer who came to Marysville in 1849, worked with Sutter, Covillaud, Ramírez, Cordua, Sicard, Sampson, and others in laying out the town of Marysville and organizing the county. He purchased 200 lots within the prospective city and named the first streets after his associates, Covillaud, Ramírez, Sampson, and Sicard. Later he became the first alcalde of the town, a state legislator, and, in 1857, Chief Justice of the California Supreme Court. Appointed to the United States Supreme Court in 1863 by President Abraham Lincoln, Field served until 1897, making his the second-longest tenure on that bench.

The old Aaron home at 704 D Street was willed to the city of Marysville and opened as the Mary Aaron Memorial Museum in 1960. The two-story building, built in 1856, contains displays relating to mining activities, agriculture, and early county government.

Marysville is one of the cities in California where modern priorities and interests have prevailed over the past, and most of the old buildings in the downtown area have been pulled down since 1960. One that has survived is St. Joseph's Catholic Church, built in 1855 at Seventh and C streets, a handsome neo-Gothic structure.

Mary Aaron Memorial Museum, Marysville

Among the graves of pioneers in the Marysville Cemetery are those of Mary Murphy Covillaud and Father Florian Schwenninger, a Tyrolean-born Benedictine monk, who labored heroically in the churches of the mining camps during the gold rush. Particularly known for his work at Sawyer's Bar in Siskiyou County, he spent his last years, 1866–68, at St. Joseph's Church in Marysville.

Nearby Beale Air Force Base was established as Camp Beale in 1942. It was named for Edward Fitzgerald Beale, prominent in the history of Kern County, where he developed Rancho El Tejón; he also was the Federal Superintendent of Indian Affairs for the state of California.

Johnson's Rancho (Wheatland)

Pablo Gutiérrez, an employee of Captain Sutter, received a grant of five leagues of land on the north side of Bear River in 1844. Here he built an adobe house at a point later called Johnson's Crossing, about three miles east of present Wheatland.

Gutiérrez was killed late in 1844, and his grant and cattle were sold at auction by Captain Sutter, magistrate of the region. The land was purchased for $150 by William Johnson and Sebastian Kayser, Johnson taking the eastern half and Kayser the western half. Just below the crossing they built an adobe house.

This place came to be known as Johnson's Ranch (SRL 493), on which Wheatland was later located, and was the first settlement reached by the Argonauts who crossed the Sierra over that branch of the California Trail that went through Donner Pass and down the ridge north of Bear River into Yuba County. Here many footsore emigrants rested and obtained supplies. Among them were the seven members of the Donner

party who succeeded in getting over the mountains in the winter of 1846–47, finally reaching Johnson's Rancho, where they sought aid for those imprisoned at snowbound Donner Lake.

Johnson was the first husband of Mary Murphy of the Donner Party, who later married Charles Covillaud.

Camp Far West

Camp Far West was established upriver from Johnson's Rancho by the United States government in 1849 for the protection of American settlers in the Yuba region. Two companies of soldiers were stationed there under command of Captain Hannibal Day. The post was abandoned in 1852, and the grounds now lie under the waters of the Camp Far West Reservoir. The site, about four miles east of Wheatland, has been marked by the Native Sons of the Golden West.

Gold Bars on the Yuba

The first prospectors in the Sierra worked along the rivers and especially on the sand bars, which were rich in gold. Like other gold-bearing streams, the Yuba River above Marysville was dotted thickly with river-bar settlements by 1850, a camp to every one or two miles. According to some authorities, Jonas Spect was the first to find gold in the county, on June 2, 1848, at a place later known as Rose's Bar. Almost simultaneously Michael Nye and William Foster found pay gravel on Dry Creek near its junction with the Yuba.

In the fall of 1848 John Rose and William J. Reynolds opened a store at Rose's Bar, where they supplied the miners with goods from Sacramento as well as fresh beef and farm products brought from their ranch south of Marysville. In the spring of 1849 Rose's Bar was so overcrowded with miners that at a meeting called for the purpose it was decided to limit claims to 100 square feet per man. By 1850, 2,000 men were at work on this bar alone.

The floods of 1850 drove the miners away from the sand bars to higher ground, where more gold was uncovered. Gatesville, or Sucker Flat (virtually an extension of Rose's Bar away from the river), grew up at this time and had developed into a town of some importance by the time the bars along the river became depleted of their gold. Squaw Creek, another rich locality, enjoyed its brief heyday in common with such neighboring camps as Cordua, Sawmill, Lander's, and Kennebec bars. Opposite Lander's Bar near the mouth of Deer Creek was Malay Camp, worked by miners from the Malay Peninsula.

The richest of all the Yuba River bars was Parks'

Bar, located two or three miles west of Rose's Bar. To this location came David Parks with his wife and children in September 1848. Since a man with a family was very unusual in the earliest camps, the place was named in his honor. Parks' Bar, which had become a populous camp by 1849, reached the height of its prosperity in 1852, when it rivaled Marysville for a time. When gold along the river bars became worked out, in 1855, decline set in, and Parks', as well as its neighbors, Barton's and Union bars, was soon depopulated.

Near Parks' Bar was Sicard's Bar, where Theodore Sicard was the first to find gold. The name Sicard Flat was given to the town that grew up about a mile back from the river and is still perpetuated in the Sicard Flat School District with its handful of scattered ranch houses.

The first mining camp of importance above Marysville was Swiss Bar, opposite Sand Flat, nine miles up the river. Little mining was done there before 1850, and the place was never the equal of Long Bar, a little farther up the river. Long Bar, in addition to being the longest bar on the Yuba, also boasted the longest period of success. It was occupied as early as October 1848, and the first organized body of miners to come to California from the outside stopped there in November. By 1851 there was a ferry in operation between Long Bar and Kennebec Bar across the river. Above Long Bar was Chimney Hill, and at the mouth of Dry Creek was Owsley's Bar, named for a Dr. Owsley, who mined there in the early days.

After 1857 hydraulic mining slowly destroyed the old river bars and their camps along the Yuba. They became buried cities, lying at least 70 feet beneath the debris washed down from the titanic diggings in the Sierra. Today the names of a few remain as school districts or townships, such as Foster's Bar Township, Rose Bar Township, Parks' Bar Township, and Long Bar Township.

Gold still lies in the bed of the Yuba River, and in later years extensive dredging took out vast sums from the old tailings. In 1905 the Yuba Consolidated Goldfields began operations nine miles east of Marysville, with a capital of $12,500,000. The towns of Marigold and Hammonton, the latter named after Wendell P. Hammon, moving spirit of the company, grew up, direct descendants of the mining camps of the 1850's. During the depression of the 1930's the field was taken over by men, otherwise unemployed, who were learning to wield pan and rocker in approved pioneer style. On Parks' Bar alone, from 50 to 100 people were mining by these primitive methods in the summer of 1932.

Today, small portable dredges are often seen in operation along the Yuba and other streams coming from the Sierra highlands, and nearly every year reports are made of the finding of a choice nugget or other discovery.

"Speculative Cities"

Population increased so rapidly in the fall of 1849 and in 1850 that land speculators saw possibilities of accumulating wealth by laying out cities on paper. Alonzo Delano said in 1854 of these pioneer real estate booms: "There seemed to be a speculative mania spreading over the land, and scores of new towns were heard of which were never known, only the puffs of newspapers, the stakes which marked the size of lots, and the nicely drawn plot of the surveyor." Delano spoke from experience, for he took part in some of the speculation, buying lots in Marysville and losing half of his earnings in the operation. In an effort to recoup his losses he and a friend laid out a town on the Feather River twenty miles north of Marysville, but they were unable to attract population to their town.

Marysville, as it turned out, survived and became a thriving city. Linda, on the south bank of the Yuba River above Marysville, had a short boom, and a store there remained in business about two years. The arrival of the little stern-wheel steamer *Linda* at the site was the occasion for the establishment of the town in 1850, but its hope to become the head of navigation and to rival Marysville was never realized. The site is now buried more than 30 feet beneath the tailings washed down from the hydraulic mines in the hills, and the only reminder of this would-be city is the modern Marysville suburb called Linda.

Early in 1851, the *Linda* was converted to a dredge, probably the first in the history of California mining. The *Linda* made it up the river as far as Owsley's Bar, and came to an unprofitable end.

Smartsville

The first building at Smartsville (SRL 321) was a hotel built in the spring of 1856 by a Mr. Smart. The Catholic church, which had first been organized at Rose's Bar by Father Peter Magagnotto, C.P., had its building erected here in 1861; it burned in 1870, but another took its place the following year, and still stands at Main and O'Brien streets. As the present-day traveler approaches the town, the most conspicuous feature of the landscape is still its church, which stands like a faithful guardian among the handful of old homes half-hidden among trees. The old frame Masonic Temple on O'Brien Street, moved to Smartsville from Rose's Bar, is still in use. The post office designation, strangely, has always been Smartville. Remains of the rich mines developed at Smartsville in the late 1850's, as well as scars of the hydraulic operations of the 1860's and 1870's, may still be seen in the surrounding hills. By 1878 the Excelsior Company at Smartsville had washed eight million cubic yards of detritus into the Yuba River, while ten times that amount remained in the company's claims when hydraulic activities ceased in 1884.

To the north of Smartsville is a great gash in the hillside, the site of the once populous mining camp of Sucker Flat.

The Empire Ranch Station

In the early 1850's, the heyday of stagecoaches before the advent of railroads, the California Stage Company carried passengers from one end of the state to the other. One of the many stations used by this company was maintained on the Empire Ranch near the town of Smartsville, where meals were served and horses changed. The old Empire Ranch Station stood there for over a century, one of the last remaining California Stage Company stops. Now only a pile of debris marks the site, on the road to Beale Air Force Base just south of Smartsville and a stone's throw from SR 20. The barn, built in 1852 with rough hand-hewn timbers held together by wooden pegs, still stands across the road from the site of the station. Halfway up the hill, hidden among the oaks on the right side of the road, is a neglected graveyard. Beyond this graveyard on the opposite side is another cemetery that has seen more recent use.

In 1849 a Mr. Berry and his wife built a log cabin on the site of the later Empire Ranch Station, and by 1851 this location had become the rallying point for miners for miles around. Thomas Mooney and Michael Riley bought the place that year and established a trading post and hotel there. Sunday was a gala day at the Empire Ranch, when hundreds of miners gathered in a convivial mood for sports and other pleasures.

Timbuctoo

Timbuctoo (SRL 320), also a neighbor of Smartsville, has only one of its original buildings left, the old Wells Fargo Express Office from 1855. Although the building, which was also known as the Stewart Brothers Store, was restored in 1928 by the Native Sons of the Golden West, the structure has partly collapsed, and it is fenced to prevent injuries from falling bricks. The town bears a forlorn and neglected look today. It is on Timbuctoo Road half a mile north of the junction with SR 20, about half a mile west of Smartsville. The first mining in this region was done as early as 1850 in the ravines nearby, one of which was named Timbuctoo after a black African man who was one of the first miners in the locality.

The town of Timbuctoo was started in 1855. During the period when hydraulic mining flourished, it was the largest town in the eastern part of Yuba County, with a population of 1,200 at the height of its prosperity. Looking about the site today, it is difficult to imagine it as it was in those days, with a church, a theater, and the usual cluster of saloons, stores, and hotels.

Brown's Valley

On the old road to Downieville, thirteen miles northeast of Marysville and one mile north of SR 20, is Brown's Valley. An early settler named Brown, who came to this spot in 1850, discovered gold near a huge boulder adjoining the temporary camp he had set up. After taking out over $12,000 in quartz, Brown "was satisfied to retire." Not long after his discovery four Frenchmen developed the famous Jefferson Mine in the vicinity; other rich discoveries followed rapidly, among them the Flag, the Donnebroge, the Pennsylvania, and the Sweet Vengeance mines. One of the first stamp mills to be erected in California was put up at the Sweet Vengeance Mine by a French company, which purchased the mine from Spaniards who had been milling the ore by means of an arrastra on Little Creek.

Ruins of some of the old mills still rise above the shafts of once prosperous mines, and within the town a stone store is another vivid reminder of the past. The present hamlet once possessed five hotels, 24 saloons, and numerous stores, hard though this may be to visualize today.

Along the old Marysville-Downieville road the sites of many taverns and stage stations are passed. All of them have totally vanished, although a few survive in place names; for example, the Peoria Cemetery and Peoria Road are named after the long-vanished Peoria House, about fifteen miles northeast of Marysville.

The Oregon House

Where the branch turnpike to La Porte turned north from the Downieville Trail, 24 miles northeast of Marysville, the Oregon House was built in 1852. It became one of the most popular of the several hostelries along that trail, and many a traveler in search of gold found rest and entertainment awaiting him within its hospitable doors. The original Oregon House was destroyed by fire many years ago, but the name is preserved in a country post office, where County Road E-20 and Frenchtown Road meet.

Indiana Ranch and Greenville

The Downieville Trail and, later, the first wagon road from the Oregon House to Camptonville went by way of Foster's Bar, passing through Indiana Ranch and the town of Greenville. Beyond the Oregon House several stopping places broke the loneliness of the old trail, among them the California House and the Keystone House, the latter a large hotel with a racetrack attached. Indiana Ranch was at one time a thriving town. It was first settled in 1851 by the Page brothers from Indiana, Peter Labadie, and John Tolles; the latter two kept the first hotels in the place. After 1860 mining declined in the vicinity, and although rich pockets have been found from time to time, not one of them has proved lasting.

Greenville, now a tiny settlement on Oregon Hill Road northwest of Bullard's Bar Dam, was originally known as Oregon Hill. Gold was first found there in 1850, but the place did not become prosperous until a ditch was constructed to bring water to the diggings. The company responsible for the building of this ditch was composed of nine members, and in order to let everyone know that it was no "one-horse" affair that they were putting in, they named it the Nine-Horse Ditch.

Brownsville and Northeastern Yuba County

Brownsville, located on what was known in early days as the Central Turnpike to La Porte, was named after I. E. Brown, who erected a sawmill in the vicinity in 1851. For a decade or more a number of sawmills and lumbering camps, as well as mining camps, existed in the surrounding country. Among these were the Sharon Valley Mills, two miles northeast, completed in 1853 by L. T. Crane; the Challenge Mills, a mile farther to the northeast, built in 1856; and the short-lived Washington and Page mills, located on Dry Creek, south of Challenge.

Brownsville was a "temperance town" and in 1878 became something of an educational center with the establishment there of the Knoxdale Institute by Martin Knox and his wife, with Professor E. K. Hill acting as principal. Knox, in partnership with P. E. Weeks, had purchased Brown's mill in 1852 and conducted the business until 1857; they also ran a hotel there.

North and northeast from Challenge Mills to La Porte a number of stage stations were passed, all important stopping places on the way to the gold mines of northwestern Sierra County and Plumas County. Woodville, now Woodleaf, just south of the present Butte County line, was formerly known as Barker's Ranch,

first settled in 1850 by Charles Barker. James Wood bought the place in 1858 and built a beautiful two-story brick hotel, the Woodville House, still standing.

Leaving Woodleaf behind, the traveler passes through a corner of Butte County at Clipper Mills and again enters Yuba County at Strawberry Valley, known to the Indians as "Pomingo." Once in the midst of a large mining area, the Strawberry Valley district included the rich diggings on Deadwood Creek, Kentucky Gulch, Rich Gulch, and Whiskey Gulch. The town of Strawberry Valley became a lively center of trade for the surrounding mines, and in the late 1850's its main street was lined with stores, shops, saloons, and dwellings, the leading hostelry being the Columbus Hotel, still standing with its old well. The buildings on one side of this street were originally in Butte County, while those on the opposite side were located in Yuba County, but in 1860 the legislature moved the county line a short distance north. All that is left of the town today is in Yuba County.

Dobbins' Ranch

Located in the lovely foothill valley of Dobbins' Creek, Dobbins' Ranch was first settled in 1849 by William M. and Mark D. Dobbins. By 1850 it had become the terminus for the stage-carried express business of Langton's Pioneer Express. From that point the express had to be transported over the mountains to Downieville on muleback. Turnpikes ultimately took the place of the narrow pack trails, and in 1860 Atchison and Rice, with others, constructed a road to Downieville by way of Dobbins' Ranch, Bullard's Bar, and Camptonville, a course followed today by Yuba County Road E-20. The pioneer store that still stands in Dobbins, as it is called today, was opened in 1867 by William Slingsby and Dan Gattens, who formed a partnership, maintaining a pack train on the Downieville Trail continuously for a number of years, and furnishing the surrounding country with supplies.

Gold Bars of the North Yuba River

The early miners of northeastern Yuba County had a wild and rugged country to contend with. Carl I. Wheat, in a note to the De Long Journals, describes this section as follows: "The map of Northeastern Yuba County gives no hint of the wildly broken nature of the terrain. The general contour of the ridges suggests an old plateau, slightly tilted to the west, greatly cut away by erosion during recent geologic times. The Yuba River and its many branches have cut deeply into this old plateau, its gorges being from five hundred to over a thousand feet in depth. Oregon Creek canyon just south of Camptonville falls away on a grand scale. The 'bars' were located along the rivers, with mountains towering up on both sides. The other towns and 'diggins' were generally located on or near the tops of the highest ridges, where the miners discovered the rich, gold-bearing gravels left by the rivers of earlier geologic ages. To one familiar with this broken terrain, De Long's active journeyings to and fro, on foot and on muleback, take on a new significance. It is a heavily wooded country, and to become lost was, and is, very easy, if one were to leave the beaten paths. . . . The very names of many of the populous mining camps of these wild ridges have been lost, and in other localities only a lone cabin or an ancient apple tree remains to recall the teeming life of the early 'fifties,' for the pines have grown up even over the burying places of the dead, and Nature has hastened to take back her own."

The Bullard's Bar Reservoir now covers most of the old mining sites in this area. Impounded by Bullard's Bar Dam, 12,000 acre-feet of water are stored to operate generators in the powerhouse at the base of the structure. Bullard's Bar was named for a Dr. Bullard who had been shipwrecked off the California coast on his way from Brooklyn, New York, to the Sandwich Islands. He made his way here and turned to mining. Foster's Bar, the other historically important town of the region, was named for William M. Foster, a survivor of the Donner party tragedy, who established a store along the river in 1849. Both these places are now under the waters of the reservoir.

Camptonville

Camptonville's present buildings date from after the gold rush, the town having been completely destroyed by fire several times. SR 49 passes it a quarter of a mile to the west. In a fenced enclosure at the entrance to the town from the highway is a monument placed in 1929 by the Masons, with a plaque testifying that "On this spot in 1878 Lester Allen Pelton invented the Pelton Water Wheel." A miniature wheel surmounts the monument. Also within the enclosure is a memorial stone to Robert Campton (1820–84), a blacksmith for whom the town was named. William Bull Meek, "stage driver– Wells Fargo Agent–mule skinner–teamster–merchant," is memorialized with a plaque placed by the E Clampus Vitus chapter that bears his name. A small building marked "Town Jail" completes this remarkable assemblage.

A hotel was built on the site of Camptonville as early as 1850, when it was on the main road from Marys-

Pelton Wheel Monument, Camptonville

ville and Nevada City to Downieville, and pack-mule trains stopped there daily on their way to the higher mountains. The toll road via Foster's Bar was completed to Camptonville in 1854, and the California Stage Company began running stages that far in the following year. The first great boom, however, came to the town in 1852, when gold was discovered on Gold Ridge to the east. Among the new arrivals at that time was Campton. By 1866 Camptonville numbered 1,500 residents and was the center for hydraulic operations that produced $500,000 annually. A plank road a mile long formed the main street of the town. This was lined by more than 30 stores, numerous hotels and boarding-houses, as well as the ubiquitous saloons. Most of this ground was soon washed out by the activities of giant hydraulic monitors. The place today is a charming village of perhaps 600 residents.

Rich strikes other than that of Gold Ridge soon caused a number of settlements to spring up throughout the region. Two miles north of Camptonville a group of men from Galena, Illinois, found gold in 1852, and the camp that grew up there was known as Galena Hill, a sizable place by 1856, and abandoned soon thereafter. The site is on Weeds Point Road west of SR 49.

Young's Hill, three miles northwest, also had its beginnings in 1852 when William Young and his brother settled there. The camp is mentioned frequently in the diary of the writer Charles E. De Long, who lived there for some time. By 1856 it was a thriving center of trade, with hotels, stores, saloons, blacksmith shops, and even a theater flanking its main street.

Ramm's Ranch to the southwest was located early by John Ramm, who saw the value of the perpetual spring that existed on the spot and that he used to advantage later in his grape culture. Early settlers in the region had found there a large Yuba Indian rancheria.

The Wheatland Riot

East of Wheatland was the Durst Ranch, scene of one of California's most famous riots. The ranch had first been planted with hops in 1874; by 1913 it was a major producer. Ralph Durst was the state's largest employer of migratory labor, and, in response to advertising, as many as 2,800 men, women, and children showed up on August 1, 1913. They found that there were fewer jobs than people, pay was very low, and the company store gouged the workers for food and supplies. As was not unusual in California's labor camps at that time, sanitation and housing were woefully insufficient. There were, for example, only eight or nine crude toilets for these thousands of people.

On August 2, a protest meeting was called by the Industrial Workers of the World (I.W.W.), and a strike was organized. This led to a personal confrontation between Durst and the I.W.W. leader Richard "Blackie" Ford; on August 3, the sheriff and his deputies were called out. A deputy fired a warning shot into the air, starting a full-scale riot by the outraged hop pickers that ended in the deaths of the sheriff, the district attorney, and two workers; about a dozen more people were injured. Ford and another I.W.W. leader, Herman Suhr, were arrested, convicted of murder, and sentenced to life imprisonment.

The shock of this episode reverberated outside Yuba County. Governor Hiram Johnson sent in the National Guard to keep order and created a Commission on Immigration and Housing to investigate the condition of migratory farm laborers. Although some legislative action resulted from the report of the commission, written by Carleton Parker, it did virtually nothing to improve the condition of migratory workers in California, whose lives remained dismal and who continued to be exploited for decades. The influence of the I.W.W., which had already been labeled a radical organization, was all but wiped out in the Sacramento Valley.

Later in 1913, "General" Charles T. Kelley led unemployed migratory farm workers and unskilled workers in a march on Sacramento to demand legislative aid. Twenty years before, Kelley had led a California detachment (which included Jack London) in Coxey's Army's march on Washington, D.C. Like Coxey's Army, Kelley's Army was broken up by police deputies on reaching its destination. The condition of itinerant labor remains a perennial issue in California.

Bibliography

As with previous editions of *Historic Spots in California,* this bibliography lists sources by county. There are, however, many writings in California history with a scope wider than that of a single county. To avoid unnecessary repetition, this edition begins the bibliography with a series of listings by area—California in General, Coastal California, the Gold Country, the San Francisco Bay Area, and Southern California—followed by the counties in alphabetical order.

California in General

Atlas of California. Culver City: Pacific Book Center, Inc., 1979.

Bancroft, Hubert Howe. *California.* Vols. 18–24 of *The History of the Pacific States of North America.* San Francisco: The History Company, 1884–90. [Most of the California material was written by Henry L. Oak].

Barth, Gunther. *Bitter Strength: A History of the Chinese in the United States, 1850–1870.* Cambridge: Harvard University Press, 1964.

Batman, Richard. *James Pattie's West: The Dream and the Reality.* Norman: University of Oklahoma Press, 1986.

Bean, Walton, and James J. Rawls. *California, an Interpretive History.* 5th ed. New York: McGraw-Hill, 1988.

Beasley, Delilah L. *The Negro Trail Blazers of California.* 1919. Reprint, San Francisco: R & E Associates, 1968.

Beck, Warren A., and Ynez D. Haase. *Historical Atlas of California.* Norman: University of Oklahoma Press, 1975.

Beilharz, Edwin. *Felipe de Neve, First Governor of California.* San Francisco: California Historical Society, 1972.

Biggs, Donald C. *Conquer and Colonize: Stevenson's Regiment in California.* San Rafael: Presidio Press, 1977.

Bland, Henry Meade. [Robert Louis] *Stevenson's California.* San Jose: The Pacific Short Story Club, 1924.

Bolton, Herbert Eugene. *Anza's California Expeditions.* 5 vols. Berkeley: University of California Press, 1930.

———, ed. *Historical Memoirs of New California, by Fray Francisco Palou, O.F.M.* 5 vols. Berkeley: University of California Press, 1926.

Boutelle, Sara Holmes. *Julia Morgan, Architect.* New York: Abbeville Press, 1988.

Boyd, William Harlan. *Stagecoach Heyday in the San Joaquin Valley, 1853–1876.* Bakersfield: Kern County Historical Society, 1983.

Brooks, George R., ed. *The Southwest Expeditions of Jedediah S. Smith: His Personal Account of the Journey to California, 1826–1827.* Glendale, Calif.: Arthur H. Clark Co., 1977.

Bunje, Emile T. H., and James C. Kean. *Pre-Marshall Gold in California: Discoveries and Near-Discoveries, 1840–1848.* 1938. Reprint, Old Sacramento: Hammon's Archives and Artifacts, 1983.

Chapman, Charles E. *A History of California. The Spanish Period.* New York: Macmillan, 1921.

Chartkoff, Joseph, and Kerry Kona Chartkoff. *The Archaeology of California.* Stanford: Stanford University Press, 1984.

Clark, George T. *Leland Stanford, War Governor of California, Railroad Builder, and Founder of Stanford University.* Stanford: Stanford University Press, 1931.

Cleland, Robert Glass. *From Wilderness to Empire, a History of California.* Edited by Glenn S. Dumke. New York: Knopf, 1959.

Cook, Sherburne F. *Colonial Expeditions to the Interior of California's Central Valley, 1800–1820.* Berkeley: University of California Press, 1960.

———. *The Conflict Between the California Indians and White Civilization.* Berkeley: University of California Press, 1943.

———. *Expeditions to the Interior of California's Central Valley, 1820–1840.* Berkeley: University of California Press, 1962.

———. *The Population of the California Indians, 1769–1970.* Berkeley: University of California Press, 1976.

de Roos, Robert. *The Thirsty Land: The Story of the Central Valley Project.* Stanford: Stanford University Press, 1948.

Eargle, Dolan H., Jr. *The Earth Is Our Mother: A Guide to the Indians of California, Their Locales, and Historic Sites.* San Francisco: Trees Company Press, 1986.

Eldredge, Zoeth Skinner. *History of California.* 5 vols. New York, 1915.

Farquhar, Francis P., ed. *Up and Down California in 1860–1864: The Journal of William H. Brewer.* 1930. Reprint, Berkeley and Los Angeles: University of California Press, 1966.

Fowler, Harlan D. *Camels to California, a Chapter in Western Transportation.* Stanford: Stanford University Press, 1950.

Fox, Stephen. *John Muir and His Legacy: The American Conservationist Movement.* Boston: Little, Brown, 1981.

Frémont, John C. *The Expeditions of John Charles Frémont.* Vol. 1, *Travels from 1838 to 1844,* edited by Donald Jackson and Mary Lee Spence. Vol. 2, *The Bear Flag Revolt and the Court-Martial,* edited by Mary Lee Spence and Donald Jackson. Vol. 3, *Travels from 1848 to 1854,* edited by Mary Lee Spence. Urbana: University of Illinois Press, 1970, 1973, 1984.

———. *The Exploring Expeditions to the Rocky Mountains, Oregon, and California.* Buffalo, N.Y.: George H. Derby & Co., 1849.

———. *Memoirs of My Life, Including in the Narrative Five Journeys of Western Exploration.* Chicago: Belford, Clarke & Co., 1887.

Garr, Daniel. "Power and Priorities: Church-State Boundary Disputes in Spanish California." *California History* 57 (1979): 364–75.

Geiger, Maynard J. *Franciscan Missionaries in Hispanic California, 1769–1848: A Biographical Dictionary.* San Marino: Huntington Library, 1969.

———. *The Life and Times of Fray Junipero Serra.* 2 vols. Washington, D.C., 1959.

Gelber, Steven M. "Working to Prosperity: California's New Deal Murals." *California History* 58 (1979): 98–127.

Goode, Kenneth. *California's Black Pioneers.* Santa Barbara: McNally & Loftin, 1973.

Gudde, Erwin G. *California Place Names.* Berkeley: University of California Press, 1960.

———. *1000 California Place Names.* Berkeley: University of California Press, 1979. [A shortened edition of the preceding title].

Guest, Francis F. *Fermin Francisco de Lasuen, 1736–1803, a Biography.* Washington, D.C., 1973.

———. "Junipero Serra and His Approach to the Indians." *Southern California Quarterly* 67 (1985): 223–61.

———. "Municipal Government in Spanish California." *California Historical Society Quarterly* 46 (1967): 307–36.

Hague, Harlan. "'Here Is the Road': Indian as Guide." *The Californians,* Mar.–Apr. 1985, pp. 28–33.

Hart, James D. *A Companion to California.* 2d ed. Berkeley: University of California Press, 1987.

Hastings, Lansford Warren. *The Emigrants' Guide to California.* Facsimile of the 1845 edition with introduction and notes by Charles H. Carey. Princeton: Princeton University Press, 1932.

Heizer, Robert F. *Languages, Territories, and Names of California Indian Tribes.* Berkeley: University of California Press, 1966.

———, ed. *California.* Vol. 8 of *Handbook of North American Indians.* Washington, D.C.: Smithsonian Institution, 1978.

———, ed. *The Destruction of the California Indians, 1847–1865.* Salt Lake City and Santa Barbara: Peregrine Smith, 1974.

Heizer, Robert F., and Albert B. Elsasser. *The Natural World of the California Indians.* Berkeley: University of California Press, 1980.

Helfrich, Devere, Helen Helfrich, and Thomas Hunt. *Emigrant Trails West; A Guide to Trail Markers Placed by Trails West, Inc., Along the California, Applegate, Lassen, and Nobles' Emigrant Trails in Idaho, Nevada, and California.* Reno: Trails West, Inc., 1984.

Herr, Pamela. *Jessie Benton Frémont: American Woman of the 19th Century.* New York: Franklin Watts, 1987.

Hine, Robert V. *California's Utopian Colonies.* 1953. Reprint, Berkeley: University of California Press, 1983.

Hittell, Theodore. *History of California.* 4 vols. San Francisco, 1885–97.

Hornbeck, David. "Land Tenure and Rancho Expansion in Alta California, 1784–1846." *Journal of Historical Geography* 4 (Oct. 1978).

Hornbeck, David, and Phillip Kane. *California Patterns: A Geographical and Historical Atlas.* Palo Alto: Mayfield Publishing Co., 1983.

Hunt, Rockwell, and Nellie Van de Grift Sanchez. *A Short History of California.* New York, 1929.

Hutchinson, W. H. "Southern Pacific: Myth and Reality." *California Historical Society Quarterly* 48 (1969): 325–34.

Jackson, W. Turrentine, and Alan M. Peterson. *The Sacramento–San Joaquin Delta: The Evolution and Implementation of Water Policy, an Historical Perspective.* Davis: California Water Resources Center, University of California at Davis, 1977.

Jaeger, Edmund C. *The California Deserts.* Stanford: Stanford University Press, 1965.

Jelenik, Lawrence J. *Harvest Empire: A History of California Agriculture.* San Francisco: Boyd & Fraser, 1979.

Kroeber, A. L. "California Place Names of Indian Origin." *University of California Publications in American Archaeology and Ethnology* 12, no. 2 (1916–17).

Lapp, Rudolph. *Afro-Americans in California.* Rev. ed. San Francisco: Boyd & Fraser, 1987.

Liebman, Ellen. *California Farmland: A History of Large Agricultural Landholdings.* Totowa, N.J.: Rowman & Allenhold, 1983.

McGloin, John B. *California's First Archbishop: The Life of Joseph Sadoc Alemany, O.P., 1814–1888.* New York: Herder & Herder, 1966.

McGowan, Joseph A. *History of the Sacramento Valley.* 3 vols. New York: Lewis Historical Publishing Co., 1961.

MacMullen, Jerry. *Paddle-Wheel Days in California.* Stanford: Stanford University Press, 1944.

McWilliams, Carey. *California: The Great Exception.* New York: A. A. Wyn, 1950.

———. *Factories in the Field: The Story of Migratory Farm Labor in California.* 1939. Reprint, Santa Barbara and Salt Lake City: Peregrine Publishers, 1971.

Marinacci, Barbara and Rudy. *California's Spanish Place-Names: What They Mean and How They Got There.* San Rafael: Presidio Press, 1980.

Moratto, M. J. *California Archaeology.* New York: Academic Press, 1984.

Nadeau, Remi. *Ghost Towns and Mining Camps of California.* Los Angeles: Ward Ritchie Press, 1965.

Nevins, Allen. *Frémont, Pathmarker of the West.* New York: Longmans, Green, 1955.

Nunis, Doyce B. *The Hudson's Bay Company's First Fur Brigade to the Sacramento Valley: Alexander McLeod's 1829 Hunt.* Fair Oaks: Sacramento Book Collector's Club, 1968.

Powers, Stephen. *Tribes of California.* Berkeley: University of California Press, 1977.

Rawls, James J. *Indians of California: The Changing Image.* Norman: University of Oklahoma Press, 1984.

Rice, Richard B., William A. Bullough, and Richard J. Orsi. *The Elusive Eden: A New History of California.* New York: Knopf, 1988.

Robinson, W. W. *Land in California.* 1948. Reprint, Berkeley: University of California Press, 1980.

Rolle, Andrew. *California, a History.* 4th ed. Arlington Heights, Ill.: Harlan Davidson, 1987.

Royce, Josiah. *California.* Boston: Houghton Mifflin, 1886.

Salley, H. E. *History of California Post Offices, 1849–1976.* La Mesa: Postal History Associates, 1977.

Sanchez, Nellie Van de Grift. *Spanish and Indian Place Names of California.* San Francisco, 1914.

Schoneberger, William A., with Paul Sonnenburg. *California Wings: A History of Aviation in the Golden State.* Woodland Hills: Windsor Publishing Co., 1984.

Starr, Kevin. *Americans and the California Dream, 1850–1915.* New York: Oxford University Press, 1973.

———. *Inventing the Dream: California Through the Progressive Era*. New York: Oxford University Press, 1985.

Sullivan, Maurice S. *The Travels of Jedediah Strong Smith*. Santa Ana: Fine Arts Press, 1934.

Thompson, John, and Edward A. Dutra. *The Tule Breakers: The Story of the California Dredge*. Stockton: Stockton Corral of Westerners International, 1983.

Uzes, Francois D. *Chaining the Land: A History of Surveying in California*. Sacramento: Landmark Enterprises, 1977.

Watkins, T. H. *California, an Illustrated History*. Palo Alto: American West Publishing Co., 1973.

Weber, David J. *The Mexican Frontier, 1821–1846: The American Southwest Under Mexico*. Albuquerque: University of New Mexico Press, 1982.

Weber, Francis J. *Documents of California's Catholic History*. Los Angeles: Dawson's Book Shop, 1965.

Weitze, Karen. *California's Mission Revival*. Los Angeles: Hennessey & Ingalls, 1984.

Wood, Raymund F. "Anglo Influence on Spanish Place Names in California." *Southern California Quarterly* 58 (1981): 392–413.

Ziebarth, Marilyn. "California's First Environmental Battle." *California History* 63 (1984): 274–79.

Coastal California

Bolton, Herbert Eugene. *Fray Juan Crespí, Missionary Explorer on the Pacific Coast, 1769–1774*. Berkeley: University of California Press, 1927.

———, ed. *Font's Complete Diary, a Chronicle of the Founding of San Francisco*. Berkeley: University of California Press, 1933.

Brandes, Ray, trans. and ed. *The Costanso Narrative of the Portolá Expedition*. Newhall: Hogarth Press, 1970.

Brown, Joseph E. *Monarchs of the Mist: The Story of Redwood National Park and the Coast Redwoods*. Point Reyes: Coastal Parks Association, 1982.

Burgess, Sherwood D. "Lumbering in Hispanic California." *California Historical Society Quarterly* 41 (1962): 237–48.

California Coastal Access Guide. Berkeley and Los Angeles: University of California Press, 1983.

The California Missions, a Pictorial History. Menlo Park: Lane Publishing Co., 1964, rev. ed. 1979.

Chase, Joseph Smeaton. *California Coast Trails: A Horseback Ride from Mexico to Oregon*. Boston: Houghton Mifflin, 1915.

Costo, Rupert, and Jeanette Henry Costo, eds. *The Missions of California: A Legacy of Genocide*. San Francisco: The Indian Historian Press, 1987.

Coughlin, Magdalen. "Boston Smugglers on the Coast, 1797–1821; an Insight into the American Acquisition of California." *California Historical Society Quarterly* 46 (1967): 99–120.

Dana, Richard Henry, Jr. *Two Years Before the Mast*. 1840. Reprint, ed. by Thomas Philbrick and with appendix, "Twenty-Four Years Later." New York: Penguin Books, 1985.

Doran, Adelaide LeMert. *Pieces of Eight: Channel Islands, a Bibliographical Guide and Source Book*. Glendale: Arthur H. Clark Co., 1981.

Ehlers, Chad, and Jim Gibbs. *Sentinels of Solitude: West Coast Lighthouses*. Portland, Oreg.: Graphic Arts Center Publishing Co., 1981.

Engelhardt, Zephyrin. *The Missions and Missionaries of California*. Santa Barbara: Santa Barbara Mission, 1930.

Hutchinson, W. H. *California Heritage: A History of Northern California Lumbering*. Rev. ed. Santa Cruz: Forest Historical Society, Inc., 1974.

Jacobs, Julius L. "California's Pioneer Wine Families." *California Historical Quarterly* 54 (1975): 139–75.

Kelsey, Harry. *Juan Rodríguez Cabrillo*. San Marino: Huntington Library, 1986.

———. "Mapping the California Coast: The Voyages of Discovery, 1533–1543." *Arizona and the West* 26 (1984): 307–24.

Martin, Wallace. *Sail and Steam on the North California Coast, 1850–1900*. San Francisco: National Maritime Museum Association, 1983.

Mathes, W. Michael. *Vizcaíno and Spanish Expansion in the Pacific Ocean, 1580–1630*. San Francisco: California Historical Society, 1968.

Nickerson, Roy. *Robert Louis Stevenson in California: A Remarkable Courtship*. San Francisco: Chronicle Books, 1982.

Older, Mrs. Fremont. *California Missions and Their Romances*. New York: Coward-McCann, 1938.

Schrepfer, Susan R. *The Fight to Save the Redwoods: A History of Environmental Reform, 1917–1978*. Madison: University of Wisconsin Press, 1983.

Shanks, Ralph C., and Janetta Thompson Shanks. *Lighthouses and Lifeboats on the Redwood Coast*. San Anselmo: Costanso Books, 1983.

Smith, Wallace E. "The Reverend Stephen Bowers, 'Curiosity Hunter' of the Santa Barbara Channel Islands." *California History* 62 (1983): 26–37.

Stanger, Frank M., and Alan K. Brown. *Who Discovered the Golden Gate: The Explorers' Own Accounts*. San Mateo: San Mateo County History Association, 1969.

Taylor, Bayard. *Eldorado, Or Adventures in the Path of Empire; Comprising a Voyage to California, Via Panama; Life in San Francisco and Monterey*. New York: G. P. Putnam, 1850; reissued 1864.

Treutlein, Theodore E. "Fages As Explorer." *California Historical Quarterly* 51 (1972): 338–56.

———. "The Portolá Expedition of 1769–1770." *California Historical Society Quarterly* 47 (1969): 291–334.

———. *San Francisco Bay: Discovery and Exploration*. San Francisco: California Historical Society, 1968.

Underhill, Reuben L. *From Cowhides to Golden Fleece—A Narrative of California, 1832–1858—Based upon Unpublished Correspondence of Thomas Oliver Larkin, Trader, Developer, Promoter, and Only American Consul*. Stanford: Stanford University Press, 1939.

Wagner, Henry R. *Spanish Voyages to the Northwest Coast of America in the Sixteenth Century*. San Francisco: California Historical Society, 1929.

Weber, Francis J. "California's Caminito Real." *California Historical Quarterly* 5.1 (1975): 63–76.

Wheeler, Eugene, and Robert Kallman. *Shipwrecks, Smugglers, and Maritime Mysteries of the Santa Barbara Channel.* Santa Barbara: McNally & Loftin, 1985.

Wilbur, Marguerite Eyer. *Vancouver in California, 1792–1794.* Los Angeles, 1953.

The Gold Country

Burnett, Peter H. *Recollections and Opinions of an Old Pioneer.* New York: D. Appleton & Co., 1880.

Caughey, John W. *The California Gold Rush.* 1948. Reprint, Berkeley and Los Angeles: University of California Press, 1975.

Clark, William B., ed. *Gold Districts of California.* San Francisco: California Division of Mines and Geology, 1970.

Delano, A. *Life on the Plains and Among the Diggings.* Buffalo, N.Y.: Miller, Orton, & Mulligan, 1854.

Engbeck, Joseph H., Jr. *The Enduring Giants.* Berkeley: University Extension, University of California, 1973.

Farquhar, Francis P. *History of the Sierra Nevada.* Berkeley and Los Angeles: University of California Press, 1965.

Gay, Theressa. *James W. Marshall, the Discoverer of California Gold.* Georgetown, Calif.: Talisman Press, 1967.

Geologic Guidebook Along Highway 49: Sierra Gold Belt, the Mother Lode Country. San Francisco: State Division of Mines, 1948.

Giffen, Helen S., ed. *The Diaries of Peter Decker: Overland to California in 1849 and Life in the Mines, 1850–1851.* Georgetown, Calif.: Talisman Press, 1966.

Glasscock, C. B. *A Golden Highway: Scenes of History's Greatest Gold Rush Yesterday and Today.* Indianapolis: Bobbs-Merrill, 1934.

Gudde, Erwin G. *Bigler's Chronicle of the West: The Conquest of California, Discovery of Gold, and Mormon Settlement as Reflected in William Henry Bigler's Diaries.* Berkeley: University of California Press, 1962.

Holliday, J. S. *The World Rushed In: The California Gold Rush Experience.* New York: Simon and Schuster, 1981.

Jackson, Joseph Henry. *Anybody's Gold: The Story of California's Mining Towns.* 1941. Reprint, San Francisco: Chronicle Books, 1982.

Jackson, W. Turrentine. "Wells Fargo Staging over the Sierra." *California Historical Society Quarterly* 49 (1970): 99–134.

Littlefield, Douglas R. "Water Rights During the California Gold Rush: Conflicts over Economic Points of View." *Western Historical Quarterly* 14 (1983): 415–34.

Masri, Allen. *The Golden Hills of California.* Vol. 1 (with Peter Abenheim), *A Descriptive Guide to the Mother Lode Counties of the Southern Mines.* Vol. 2, *A Descriptive Guide to the Mother Lode Counties of the Northern Mines.* Santa Cruz: Western Tanager Press, 1979, 1983.

Reading, Pierson Barton. "Journal of Pierson Barton Reading," *Quarterly of the Society of California Pioneers* 7, no. 3, (1930).

Robins, Winifred. *Gold Country Renaissance: A Guide to the Artists and Artisans of California's Historic Mother Lode.* San Francisco: Chronicle Books, 1983.

Sargent, Shirley, ed. *Seeking the Elephant, 1849: James M. Hutching's Journal.* Glendale: Arthur H. Clark Co., 1980.

Todd, Arthur Cecil. *The Cornish Miner in America: The Contribution to the Mining Industry by Emigrant Cornish Miners, the*

Men Called Cousin Jacks. Glendale: Arthur H. Clark Co., 1967.

Wagner, Jack R. *Gold Mines of California: An Illustrated History of the Most Productive Mines with Descriptions of the Interesting People Who Owned and Operated Them.* Berkeley: Howell-North Books, 1970.

Weston, Otheto. *Mother Lode Album.* Stanford: Stanford University Press, 1948.

San Francisco Bay Area

Bowman, J. N. "Adobe Houses in the San Francisco Bay Region," in *Geologic Guidebook of the San Francisco Bay Counties.* San Francisco: Department of Natural Resources, Division of Mines, 1951.

———. "The Peraltas and Their Houses." *California Historical Society Quarterly* 30 (1951): 217–31.

France, Edward E. *Some Aspects of the Migration of the Negro in the San Francisco Bay Area Since 1940.* San Francisco: R & E Research Associates, 1974.

Gifford, E. W. "Composition of California Shellmounds." *University of California Publications in American Archaeology and Ethnology* 12, no. 1 (1916): 1–29.

Gudde, Erwin G. "Place Names in the San Francisco Bay Counties," in *Geologic Guidebook of the San Francisco Bay Counties.* San Francisco: Department of Natural Resources, Division of Mines, 1951.

Kemble, John Haskell. *San Francisco Bay: A Pictorial Maritime History.* 1957. Reprint, New York: Bonanza Books, 1979.

Kennard, Charles. *San Francisco Bay Area Landmarks: Recollections of Four Centuries.* Palo Alto: Tioga Publishing Company, 1987.

Kinnaird, Lawrence. *History of the Greater San Francisco Bay Region.* 3 vols. New York and West Palm Beach: Lewis Historical Publishing Co., 1966.

Liberatore, Karen. *The Complete Guide to the Golden Gate National Recreational Area.* San Francisco: Chronicle Books, 1982.

Nelson, Nils Christian. "Shellmounds of the San Francisco Bay Region." *University of California Publications in American Archaeology and Ethnology,* 8, no. 4 (1909).

Schwendinger, Robert J. *International Port of Call: An Illustrated Maritime History of the Golden Gate.* Woodland Hills: Windsor Publications, 1984.

Scott, Mel. *The San Francisco Bay Area: A Metropolis in Perspective.* 2d ed. Berkeley: University of California Press, 1985.

Whitnah, Dorothy L. *Guide to the Golden Gate National Recreational Area.* Berkeley: Wilderness Press, 1978.

Wilson, Mark A. *East Bay Heritage: A Pot-Pourri of Living History.* San Francisco: California Living Books, 1979.

Wollenberg, Charles. *Golden Gate Metropolis: Perspectives on a Bay Area History.* Berkeley: University of California Press, 1985.

Southern California

Bean, Lowell John. *Mukat's People, the Cahuilla Indians of Southern California.* Berkeley: University of California Press, 1972.

Bolton, Herbert Eugene. *Spanish Exploration in the Southwest.* Vol. 17 of *Original Narratives of American History.* New York: Scribner, 1916.

Faulk, Odie B. *Too Far North—Too Far South.* Los Angeles: Westernlore Press, 1967.

Hague, Harland H. "The Search for a Southern Overland Route to California." *California Historical Quarterly* 55 (1976): 150–61.

Hine, Leland D. *Baptists in Southern California.* Valley Forge, Pa.: Judson Press, 1966.

James, George Wharton. *Through Ramona's Country.* Boston: Little, Brown, 1909.

Johnson, Hank. *The Railroad That Lighted Southern California.* Long Beach: Anglo Books, 1965.

Lyman, Edward L. "Outmaneuvering the Octopus: Atchison, Topeka, and Santa Fe." *California History* 67 (1988): 94–107, 145–46.

McWilliams, Carey. *Southern California Country: An Island on the Land.* New York: Duell, Sloan, and Pearce, 1946.

Moses, Vincent. "'Oranges for Health—California for Wealth': The Billion-Dollar Navel and the California Dream." *The Californians,* July–Aug. 1985, pp. 27–37.

Nunis, Doyce B., Jr., and Abraham Hoffman, eds. *A Southern California Historical Anthology.* Los Angeles: Historical Society of Southern California, 1975.

Orsi, Richard. "*The Octopus* Reconsidered: The Southern Pacific and Agricultural Modernization in California, 1865–1915." *California Historical Quarterly* 54 (1975): 197–220.

Pitt, Leonard. *The Decline of the Californios: A Social History of Spanish-Speaking Californios, 1846–1890.* Berkeley and Los Angeles: University of California Press, 1966.

Stowe, Noel J., ed. "Pioneering Land Development in the Californias: An Interview with David Otto Brant." *California Historical Society Quarterly* 47 (1968): 15–40, 141–56, 237–50.

Thompson, Gerald. *Edward F. Beale and the American West.* Albuquerque: University of New Mexico Press, 1983.

Alameda County

Abeloe, William N. *St. Leander's, 1864–1964.* San Leandro: St. Leander's Church, 1964.

Bagwell, Beth. *Oakland, Story of a City.* Novato: Presidio Press, 1982.

Berhardi, Robert. *The Buildings of Berkeley.* Oakland: Holmes Book Company, 1973.

———. *The Buildings of Oakland.* Oakland: Forest Hill Press, 1979.

Berkeley Gazette. Special Centennial Edition. Oct. 26, 1977.

Burgess, Sherwood D. "Oakland's Water War." *California History* 64 (1985): 34–41.

Davis, William Heath. *Seventy-Five Years in California.* 1889. Reprint, edited by Harold A. Small, San Francisco: John Howell Books, 1967.

McArdle, Phil, ed. *Exactly Opposite the Golden Gate: Essays on Berkeley's History.* Berkeley: Berkeley Historical Society, 1983.

McCarthy, Francis F. *The History of Mission San Jose, California, 1797–1835.* 1958. Reprint, San Jose: Commission for the Restoration of the Mission San Jose, 1977.

Martin, Imelda. *Alameda: A Geographical History.* Alameda: Friends of the Alameda Free Library, 1977.

Mosier, Page, and Dan Mosier. *Alameda County Place-Names.* Fremont: Mines Road Books, 1986.

Newton, Janet. *Las Positas: The Story of Robert and Josefa Livermore.* Livermore: Ralph and Janet Newton, 1969.

———. *Stories of the Vineyards and Wineries of the Livermore Valley.* 2d ed. Livermore: Janet Newton, 1987.

Noble, John Wesley. *Its Name Was M.U.D.* Oakland: East Bay Municipal Utility District, 1970.

Pattiani, Evelyn Craig. *Queen of the Hills: The Story of Piedmont, a California City.* 1954. Reprint, Oakland: DiMaggio Publications, 1982.

Pettit, George A. *Berkeley: The Town and Gown of It.* Berkeley: Howell-North Books, 1973.

———. *History of Berkeley.* Oakland: Alameda County Historical Society, 1976.

Sandoval, John. *History of Washington Township.* Fremont: Washington Township Historical Society, 1986.

Schenck, William E. "The Emeryville Shellmound." *University of California Publications in American Archaeology and Ethnology* 23, no. 3 (1926).

Studer, Jack J. "The First Map of Oakland, California: An Historical Speculation as Solution to an Enigma." *California Historical Society Quarterly* 48 (1969): 59–72.

———. "Julius Kellersberger, a Swiss as Surveyor and City Planner in California, 1851–1857." *California Historical Society Quarterly* 47 (1968): 3–14.

Thompson & West. *Official Historical Atlas of Alameda County.* 1878. Reprint, Fresno: Valley Publishers, 1976.

Verbarg, Leonard. *Celebrities at Your Doorstep.* Oakland: Alameda County Historical Society, 1972.

Webb, Catherine, ed. *Stories of Albany.* Albany: Albany Historical Society, 1983.

Weber, David. *Oakland: Hub of the West.* Tulsa, Okla.: Continental Heritage Press, 1981.

Weber, Francis J., comp. and ed. *The Patriarchal Mission: A Documentary History of San Jose.* Los Angeles: Libra Press, 1986.

Willard, Ruth Hendricks. *Alameda County: California Crossroads.* Northridge: Windsor Publications, 1988.

Alpine County

Alpine Heritage. Alpine County Centennial Book Committee, 1964.

Gianella, Vincent P. "Where Frémont Crossed the Sierra Nevada in 1844." *Sierra Club Bulletin* 44, no. 7 (Oct. 1959).

Quille, Dan de [William Wright]. "Snow-Shoe Thompson." *Overland Monthly* 8, no. 46 (Oct. 1886): 419–35.

White, Chester Lee. "Surmounting the Sierras, the Campaign for a Wagon Road." *California Historical Society Quarterly* 7 (1928): 3–19.

Amador County

Andrews, John R. *Ghost Towns of Amador.* Rev. ed. Fresno: Book Publishers, 1979.

Garbarini, Evelyn. *The Kennedy Wheels.* Jackson: Amador Press-News, 1975.

Glover, Choice M. *History of Amador County, California.* Sutter Creek: C. M. Glover, 1987.

Mason, J. D. *History of Amador County, California.* Oakland: Thompson & West, 1881.

Noble, John Wesley. *Its Name Was M.U.D.* Oakland: East Bay Municipal Utility District, 1970.

Butte County

Bidwell, Annie E. K. *Rancho Chico Indians (1891–1913).* Edited by Dorothy J. Hill. Chico: Bidwell Mansion Cooperating Association, 1980.

Bidwell, John. *Echoes of the Past.* 1889. Reprint, California Department of Parks and Recreation, 1987.

Bleyhl, Norris A. *Three Military Posts in Northeastern California, 1849–1863.* Chico: Association for Northern California Records and Research, 1984.

Book, Susan W. *The Chinese in Butte County, California, 1860–1920.* San Francisco: R & E Research Associates, 1976.

Butte County Branch, National League of American Pen Women. *Butte Remembers.* Chico, 1973.

Dunn, Forest, comp. *Butte County Place Names: A Geographical and Historical Dictionary.* Chico: Association for Northern California Records and Research, 1977.

Joslyn, Evelyn. *Memoirs of the Lott-Sank Family.* Oroville, 1973.

Kroeber, Theodora. *Ishi in Two Worlds.* Berkeley: University of California Press, 1961.

Mansfield, George C. *History of Butte County, California, with Biographical Sketches.* Los Angeles: Historic Record Co., 1918.

Talbitzer, Bill. *Butte County: An Illustrated History.* Northridge: Windsor Publications, 1987.

———. *The Days of Old, the Days of Gold.* Oroville: Las Plumas Publications, 1973.

———. *Lost Beneath the Feather.* Oroville, 1963.

Wells's and Chambers's History of Butte County, California, 1882, and Biographical Sketches of Its Prominent Men and Pioneers. Reprint, Berkeley: Howell-North Books, 1973.

Calaveras County

An Album of Pioneer Schools of Calaveras County. San Andreas: Calaveras County Historical Society, 1986.

Castro, Kenneth M., and Doris Castro. *Murphys, California: Short History and Guide.* Murphys: Kenneth M. Castro, 1972.

Elliott, W. W. *Calaveras County Illustrated and Described.* 1885. Reprint, Fresno: Valley Publishers, 1976.

Fry, Walter, and John R. White. *Big Trees.* Stanford: Stanford University Press, 1930.

Merriam, John C. "The True Story of the Calaveras Skull." *Sunset* 24, no. 2 (1910): 153–58.

Noble, John Wesley. *Its Name Was M.U.D.* Oakland: East Bay Municipal Utility District, 1970.

Stewart, George R., Jr. *Bret Harte, Argonaut and Exile.* Boston: Houghton Mifflin, 1931.

Colusa County

Benet, George. *A Place in Colusa.* San Pedro: Singlejack Books, 1977.

Carter, Jane Foster. *If the Walls Could Talk.* Colusa: History Preservation Committee, 1988.

Green, Will S. *Colusa County, California.* 1880. Reprint, Willows: Elizabeth Eubank, 1950.

McCornish, Charles Davis, and Rebecca T. Lambert. *History of Colusa and Glenn Counties, California.* Los Angeles: Historic Record Co., 1918.

Young, Helen D. *Arbuckle and College City.* Fresno: Pioneer Publishing Company, 1978.

Contra Costa County

Andrews, Edna May, et al. *History of Concord, Its Progress and Promise.* Concord: Concord Historical Society, 1986.

Bogue, Lucille. "O'Neill at Tao House: California's Best-Kept Secret." *The Californians,* July–Aug. 1986, pp. 34–39.

Bohakel, Charles A. *Historic Tales of East Contra Costa County.* Antioch: Charles Bohakel, 1984.

———. *The Indians of Contra Costa County.* Amarillo, Tex.: P & H Publishers, 1977.

———. *Mount Diablo, The "Devil" Mountain of California.* Rev. ed. Antioch: Charles Bohakel, 1975.

———. "Tragic Tales of the Mount Diablo Coalfields." *The Californians,* July–Aug. 1984, pp. 39–41.

Cole, Susan D. *Richmond: Windows to the Past.* Richmond: Wildcat Canyon Books, 1980.

Conley, Frances. *First Settlers: The Castros of Rancho San Pablo.* San Pablo: San Pablo Historical and Museum Society, 1980.

Contra Costa Sun. "How It All Began." Issues of July 15–17, 1977, July 5–7, 1978, and July 28, 1982.

Emanuels, George. *California's Contra Costa County.* Fresno: Panorama West Books, 1986.

———. *Walnut Creek, Arroyo de las Nueces.* Walnut Creek: Diablo Books, 1984.

Fink, Leonora Galindo. "The San Ramon Valley." *Contra Costa Chronicles* 1, no. 3 (1966): 17–27.

Hurwitz, Karen E. *The History of John Marsh and Rancho de los Meganos.* Martinez: Contra Costa Development Association, 1973.

Illustrations of Contra Costa County, California, with Historical Sketches by Smith and Elliott. 1879. Reprint, Fresno: Valley Publishers, 1979.

Kimball, Sandy. *Moraga's Pride: Rancho Laguna de los Palos Colorados.* Moraga: Moraga Historical Society, 1987.

Loud, Lewellyn L. "The Stege Mounds at Richmond, California." *University of California Publications in American Archaeology and Ethnology* 17, no. 6 (1924).

Mollenkopf, Jacquelyn. "The Byron Rail Disaster." *California History* 61 (1983): 292–301.

Munro-Fraser, J. P. *History of Contra Costa County, California.* 1882. Reprint, Oakland: Brooks-Sterling Co., 1974.

Murdock, Dick. *Port Costa, 1879–1941: A Saga of Sails, Sacks, and Rails.* Port Costa: Murdock-Endom Publishers, 1977.

Nelson, N. C. "The Ellis Landing Shellmound." *University of*

California Publications in American Archaeology and Ethnology 7, no. 6 (1910).

Noble, John Wesley. *Its Name Was M.U.D.* Oakland: East Bay Municipal Utility District, 1970.

Russi, Alice McNeil. "Elam Brown." *Contra Costa Chronicles* 1, no. 3 (1966): 4–16.

Sorrick, Muir. *The History of Orinda, Gateway to Contra Costa County.* 1970. Reprint, Orinda: Friends of the Orinda Library, 1987.

Whitfield, Vallie Jo. *History of Pleasant Hill, California.* Pleasant Hill: Whitfield Books, 1988.

Winkley, John. *Dr. John Marsh, Wilderness Scout.* Nashville, Tenn.: Parthenon Press, 1962.

Del Norte County

Bledsoe, A. J. *Indian Wars of the Northwest.* San Francisco, 1885.

Carranco, Lynwood. "Two Tragic Shipwrecks of the 1860's." *The Californians,* May–June 1987, pp. 9–21.

McBeth, Frances Turner. *Lower Klamath Country.* Berkeley: Anchor Press, 1950.

———. *Pioneers of Elk Valley.* Angwin: Pacific Union College Press, 1960.

Smith, Esther Ruth. *History of Del Norte County.* Oakland: Holmes Book Company, 1953.

El Dorado County

Bradley, Glen D. *The Story of the Pony Express.* Chicago: A. C. McClurg & Co., 1913.

Davis, Leonard M. *Georgetown, Pride of the Mountains.* Roseville: Georgetown Divide Rotary Club, 1976.

Dillon, Richard. *Fool's Gold: The Decline and Fall of Captain John Sutter of California.* 1967. Reprint, Santa Cruz: Western Tanager Press, 1981.

Greuner, Lorene, comp. *Lake Valley's Past.* South Lake Tahoe: Lake Tahoe Historical Society, 1976.

Paul, Rodman W. *The California Gold Discovery: Sources, Documents, Accounts and Memoirs Relating to the Discovery of Gold at Sutter's Mill.* Georgetown: Talisman Press, 1966.

Sanborn, Margaret. *The American, River of El Dorado.* New York: Holt, Rinehart, and Winston, 1974.

Yohalem, Betty, ed. *I Remember: Stories and Pictures of El Dorado County Pioneer Families.* Placerville: El Dorado County Chamber of Commerce, 1977.

Zauner, Phyllis. *Lake Tahoe.* Tahoe Paradise: Zanel Publications, 1982.

Fresno County

Clough, Charles W., et al. *Fresno County in the Twentieth Century.* Fresno: Panorama West Books, 1986.

Clough, Charles W., and William B. Secrest, Jr. *Fresno County: The Pioneer Years from the Beginnings to 1900.* Fresno: Panorama West Books, 1984.

Donelan, John. "Coalinga, 4:42 P.M." *California History* 64 (1986): 42–47.

Eaton, Edwin M. *Vintage Fresno: Pictorial Recollections of a Western Town.* Fresno: Huntington Press, 1965.

Fresno Bee. "Fresno Centennial Issue." Sept. 22, 1985.

Fresno Past and Present, 1885–1985. Fresno: Fresno City and County Historical Society, 1985.

Genini, Ronald. "Industrial Workers of the World and Their Fresno Free Speech Fight, 1910–1911." *California Historical Quarterly* 53 (1974): 100–114.

Imperial Fresno. Fresno, California. 1897. Reprint, Fresno: Fresno City and County Historical Society, 1979.

Johnston, Hank. *They Felled the Redwoods.* Glendale: Interurban Press, 1983.

M. Theo Kearney's Fresno County, California, and the Fruit Vale Estate. 1903. Reprint, Fresno: Fresno City and County Historical Society, 1980.

McFarland, J. Randall. *Centennial Selma: Biography of a California Community's First 100 Years.* Selma: Selma Enterprise, 1980.

McGee, Lizzie. *Mills of the Sequoias.* Visalia: Tulare County Historical Society, 1952.

Secrest, William B. [Sr.] "The Horrifying History of a Highwayman's Head." *The Californians,* Nov.–Dec. 1986, pp. 28–34.

———. *Joaquin, Bloody Bandit of the Mother Lode.* Fresno: Saga-West Publishing Company, 1967.

Teilman, I., and W. H. Shafer. *The Historical Story of Irrigation in Fresno and Kings Counties in Central California.* Fresno: Williams and Son, 1943.

Tweed, William C. *Sequoia–Kings Canyon: The Story Behind the Scenery.* Las Vegas: KC Publications, 1980.

Winchell, Lilbourne Alsip. *History of Fresno County and the San Joaquin Valley, Narrative and Bibliographical.* Fresno: Arthur H. Cawston, 1933.

Glenn County

McCornish, Charles Davis, and Rebecca T. Lambert. *History of Colusa and Glenn Counties, California.* Los Angeles: Historic Record Co., 1918.

Russell, Gene H. *Orland's Colorful Past.* Orland: Orland Community Scholarship Association, 1977.

Humboldt County

Adams, Kramer A. *Covered Bridges of the West.* Berkeley: Howell-North Books, 1963.

Anderson, Mary. *Backwoods Chronicle: A History of Southern Humboldt [County], 1849–1920.* Redway: Southern Humboldt Press, 1985.

Beal, Laurence. *The Carson Mansion: America's First Victorian Home and the Man Who Built It.* Eureka: Times Publishing Company, 1973.

Bledsoe, A. J. *Indian Wars of the Northwest.* San Francisco, 1855.

Carranco, Lynwood. "Maritime Fiasco on the Northern California Coast." *California History* 60 (1981): 210–27.

———. "Two Tragic Shipwrecks of the 1860's." *The Californians,* May–June 1987, pp. 9–21.

Coy, Owen C. *The Humboldt Bay Region, 1850–1875: A Study in the Americanization of California.* Los Angeles: California State Historical Association, 1929.

Hoopes, Chad L. "Redick McKee and the Humboldt Bay Region, 1851–1852." *California Historical Society Quarterly* 49 (1970): 195–220.

Nelson, Byron, Jr. *Our Home Forever: A Hupa Tribal History.* Hupa: Hupa Tribe, 1978.

Sachs, Benjamin. *Carson Mansion and Ingomar Theater.* Fresno: Valley Publishers, 1979.

Zahl, Paul A. "Finding the Mt. Everest of All Living Things." *National Geographic* 126 (July 1964): 10–51.

Imperial County

Davis, Arthur P. "The New Inland Sea." *National Geographic* 18 (Jan. 1907): 36–49.

deStanley, Mildred. *The Salton Sea, Yesterday and Today.* Los Angeles: Triumph Press, 1966.

Farr, F. C. *History of Imperial County.* Berkeley: Elms and Franks, 1918.

Farris, William H. *The 1847 Crossing of Imperial County, California, and Baja California, Mexico, by the U.S. Mormon Battalion.* El Centro: Imperial Valley College Museum Society, 1977.

Gillett, Paul, and Peter Gillett. *Imperial Valley's Lost Gold.* Yuma, Ariz.: Southwest Printers, 1974.

Hanna, Phil Townsend. "The Wells of Santa Rosa of the Flat Rocks." *Touring Topics* 20 (Jan. 1928): 18–20, 31.

Harris, Elizabeth. *Townsite of Silsbee and Indian Well.* Holtville: Imperial Valley Pioneer Society, 1979.

James, George Wharton. *Wonders of the Colorado Desert.* Boston: Little, Brown, 1906.

Love, Frank. *Mining Camps and Ghost Towns Along the Lower Colorado in Arizona and California.* Los Angeles: Westernlore Press, 1974.

Inyo County

Austin, Mary. *The Land of Little Rain.* 1903. Reprint, New York: Penguin, 1988.

Chalfant, W. A. *Death Valley.* Stanford: Stanford University Press, 1930.

Cronkhite, Daniel. *Death Valley's Victims: A Descriptive Chronology, 1849–1980.* 3d ed. Morongo Valley: Sagebrush Press, 1981.

DeDecker, Mary. *Mines of the Eastern Sierra.* Glendale: La Siesta Press, 1966.

Kahrl, William. "The Politics of California Water: Owens Valley and the Los Angeles Aqueduct, 1900–1927." *California Historical Quarterly* 55 (1976): 2–25, 98–120.

———. *Water and Power: The Conflict Over Los Angeles' Water Supply in the Owens Valley.* Berkeley: University of California Press, 1982.

Lingenfelter, Richard E. *Death Valley and the Amargosa: A Land of Illusion.* Berkeley: University of California Press, 1986.

McAdams, Cliff. *Death Valley, Past and Present. Guide and Reference Book.* Boulder, Colo.: Pruett Publishing Company, 1981.

Nadeau, Remi. *The Water Seekers.* New York: Doubleday, 1950.

Paher, Stanley. *Death Valley Ghost Towns.* Las Vegas: Nevada Publications, 1973.

Richards, Frederick L. "The Commander's House." *Westways,* Feb. 1965, pp. 16–17.

Rose, Dan. "The Legend of Winnedumah." *Touring Topics* 19 (Aug. 1927): 35, 39.

Walton, John. "Picnic at Alabama Gates: The Owens Valley Rebellion, 1904–1927." *California History* 65 (1986): 192–207.

Williams, George, III. *The Guide to Bodie and Eastern Sierra Historic Sites.* Riverside: Tree by the River Publishers, 1981.

Kern County

Bailey, Richard C. *Explorations in Kern.* Bakersfield: Kern County Historical Society, 1962.

———. *Heart of the Golden Empire: An Illustrated History of Bakersfield.* Woodland Hills: Windsor Publications, 1984.

———. *Heritage of Kern.* Bakersfield: Kern County Historical Society, 1957.

Bolton, Herbert Eugene. "In the South San Joaquin Ahead of Garcés." *California Historical Society Quarterly* 10 (1931): 211–19.

Boyd, William Harland. *A California Middle Border: The Kern River Country, 1772–1880.* Richardson, Tex.: Havilah Press, 1972.

———. *Kern County Wayfarers, 1844–1881.* Bakersfield: Kern County Historical Society, 1977.

———. *Land of Havilah.* Bakersfield: Kern County Historical Society, 1952.

Burmeister, Eugene. *The Golden Empire: Kern County, California.* Beverly Hills: Autograph Press, 1977.

Crowe, Earle. *Men of El Tejon.* Los Angeles: Ward Ritchie Press, 1957.

Darling, Curtis. *Kern County Place Names.* Bakersfield: Kern County Historical Society, 1988.

Gifford, E. W., and W. Egbert Schenck. "Archaeology of the Southern San Joaquin Valley, California." *University of California Publications in American Archaeology and Ethnology* 23, no. 1 (1926): 1–122.

Inside Historic Kern. Bakersfield: Kern County Historical Society, 1982.

Kreiser, Ralph F., and Thomas Hunt. *Kern County Panorama.* Bakersfield: Kern County Historical Society, 1961.

Ludeke, John. "The No-Fence Law of 1874: Victory for San Joaquin Valley Farmers." *California History* 59 (1980): 98–115.

Peirson, Emma. *Kern's Desert.* Bakersfield: Kern County Historical Society, 1956.

Robinson, W. W. *The Story of Kern County.* Bakersfield: Title Insurance & Trust Co., 1961.

Saunders, Charles Francis. *The Southern Sierras of California.* Boston: Houghton Mifflin, 1923.

Street, Richard Steven. "A Kern County Diary: The Forgotten Photographs of Carleton E. Watkins, 1881–1888." *California History* 61 (1983): 242–63.

Where the Railroad Ended: Delano Centennial Yearbook. Delano: Delano Historical Society, 1974.

Kings County

Bolton, Herbert Eugene. "In the South San Joaquin Ahead of Garcés." *California Historical Society Quarterly* 10 (1931): 211–19.

Brown, James L. *Mussel Slough Tragedy.* 2d ed. Hanford: Old-town News, 1980.

———. *The Story of Kings County, California.* Berkeley: Lederer, Street, and Zeus, 1941.

Brown, Robert R. *History of Kings County.* Hanford: A. H. Cawston, 1940.

Buckner, Leona Kreyenhagen. *The Lemoore Story.* Lemoore: Lemoore Chamber of Commerce, 1962.

Mitchell, Annie. *Sites to See.* Fresno: Panorama West Books, 1983.

Preston, William L. *Vanishing Landscape: Land and Life in the Tulare Lake Basin.* Berkeley: University of California Press, 1980.

Lake County

Anderson, Winslow. *Mineral Springs and Health Resorts of California.* San Francisco: Bancroft Company, 1892.

Benson, William Ralganal. "Narrative of the Stone and Kelsey Massacre." *California Historical Society Quarterly* 11 (1932): 266–73.

Carpenter, Aurelius, and Percy H. Millberry. *History of Mendocino and Lake Counties.* Los Angeles: Historic Record Co., 1914.

Case, Suzanne D. *Join Me in Paradise: The History of Guenoc Valley.* Middletown: Guenoc Winery, 1982.

Harris, Henry. *California's Medical Story.* San Francisco: J. W. Stacey, 1932.

History of Napa and Lake Counties, California. San Francisco: Slocum, Bowen & Co., 1882.

Lewis, Ruth, et al. *Stories and Legends of Lake County.* 1949 rev. ed.; orig. pub. 1935. Reprint, Kelseyville: Lake County Historical Society, 1983.

Mauldin, Henry K. *Your Lakes, Valleys and Mountains: History of Lake County.* San Francisco: East Wind Printers, 1960.

Lassen County

Dozier, Dave F. *Main Street, Susanville 1910.* Susanville: Lassen County Historical Society, 1979.

Fairfield, Asa Merrill. *Fairfield's History of Lassen County, California.* San Francisco: H. S. Crocker, 1916.

Fariss & Smith. *History of Plumas, Lassen, and Sierra Counties, California.* 1882. Reprint, Berkeley: Howell-North Books, 1971.

Purdy, Tim I. *Sagebrush Reflections: The History of Amedee and Honey Lake.* Stamford, Conn.: Distribution Publications, 1983.

Strong, Douglas H. *"These Happy Grounds," a History of the Lassen Region.* Red Bluff: Walker Lithograph, 1982.

Swartzlow, Ruby Johnson. *Lassen, His Life and Legacy.* 1964. Reprint, Mineral: Loomis Museum Association, 1972.

Los Angeles County

Acuna, Rodolfo. *A Community Under Siege: A History of Chicanos East of the Los Angeles River.* Los Angeles: Chicano Studies Research Center, University of California at Los Angeles, 1984.

Basten, Fred E. *Santa Monica Bay: The First Hundred Years.* Los Angeles: Douglas-West Publishers, 1975.

Belderrain, Francisca Lopez. "First to Find Gold in California." *Touring Topics* 22 (Nov. 1930): 32–34.

Bottles, Scott L. *Los Angeles and the Automobile: The Making of the Modern City.* Berkeley: University of California Press, 1987.

Carpenter, Virginia L. *The Ranchos of Don Pacifico Ontiveros.* Fullerton: Friis-Pioneer Press, 1982.

Caughey, John, and LaRee Caughey, eds. *Los Angeles: Biography of a City.* Berkeley: University of California Press, 1976.

Chapin, Lon F. *Thirty Years in Pasadena, with an Historical Sketch of Previous Eras.* 2 vols. Los Angeles: Southwest Publishing Co., 1924.

Clark, David L. *Los Angeles: A City Apart.* Woodland Hills: Windsor Publications, 1981.

Conner, E. Palmer. *The Romance of the Ranchos.* Los Angeles: Title Insurance & Trust Co., 1930.

Dakin, Susanna B. *A Scotch Paisano in Old Los Angeles: Hugo Reid's Life in California, 1832–1852.* 1939. Reprint, Berkeley: University of California Press, 1978.

"A Double Look at Utopia: Llano del Rio." 1. Aldous Huxley, "Ozymandias, the Utopia That Failed." 2. Paul Kagan, "Portrait of a California Utopia." *California Historical Society Quarterly* 51 (1972): 117–54.

Driver, Les. "Carrillo's Flying Artillery: The Battle of San Pedro." *California Historical Society Quarterly* 48 (1969): 335–49.

Fink, Augusta. *Time and the Terraced Land* [Rancho Los Palos Verdes]. Berkeley: Howell-North Books, 1966.

Fogelson, Robert M. *The Fragmented Metropolis: Los Angeles, 1850–1930.* Cambridge: Harvard University Press, 1967.

Gebhard, David, and Robert Winter. *Architecture in Los Angeles: A Complete Guide.* Layton, Utah: Gibbs M. Smith, 1984.

Goodwin, H. Marshall, Jr. "The Arroyo Seco: From Dry Gulch to Freeway." *Southern California Quarterly* 47 (1965): 90–94.

Grenier, Judson A., et al., eds. *A Guide to Historic Places in Los Angeles County.* Dubuque, Iowa: Kendall-Hunt Publishing Co., 1978.

Grenier, Judson A., with Robert C. Gillingham. *California Legacy: The James Alexander Watson–Maria Dolores Dominguez de Watson Family, 1820–1980.* Carson, Calif.: Watson Land Company, 1982.

Hager, Anna Marie. "A Salute to the Port of Los Angeles, from Mud Flats to Modern-Day Miracle." *California Historical Society Quarterly* 49 (1970): 329–36.

Harrington, Marie. *Mission San Fernando: A Guide.* Mission Hills: San Fernando Valley Historical Society, 1971.

Johnson, Faye. "William S. Hart, Cowboy's Cowboy." *The Californians* May–June 1986, pp. 39–43.

Kelsey, Harry. "A New Look at the Founding of Old Los Angeles." *California Historical Quarterly* 55 (1976): 326–39.

King, William E. *Mission San Gabriel: Two Hundred Years, 1771–1971*. San Gabriel: The Claretian Fathers, 1971.

Leadabrand, Russ. *A Guidebook to the San Gabriel Mountains of California*. Los Angeles: Ward Ritchie Press, 1963.

Los Angeles: An Instructional Resource Guide. Los Angeles County Office of the Superintendent of Schools, 1980.

"Los Angeles, 1781–1981; A Special Bicentennial Issue." *California History* 60, no. 1 (1981).

Marquez, Ernest. *Port Los Angeles: A Phenomenon of the Railroad Era*. San Marino: Golden West Books, 1976.

Matson, Charles A. *Building a World Gateway*. Los Angeles: Pacific Era Publishers, 1945.

Meyer, Larry J., and Patricia L. Kalayjian. *Long Beach, Fortune's Harbor*. Long Beach: Historical Society of Long Beach, 1983.

Outland, Charles F. *Man-Made Disaster: The Story of St. Francis Dam*. Glendale: Arthur H. Clark Co., 1977.

Owen, J. Thomas. "The Church by the Plaza, a History of the Pueblo Church of Los Angeles." *Historical Society of Southern California Quarterly* 42 (1960): 5–28, 186–204.

Parks, Marion. "In Pursuit of Vanished Days, Visits to the Extant Historic Adobe Houses of Los Angeles County." *Annual Publications of the Historical Society of Southern California* 14, parts I and II (1928–29): 7–63, 135–207.

Perry, Edward Casewell. *Burbank: An Illustrated History*. Northridge: Windsor Publications, 1981.

Pflueger, Donald H. *Covina: Sunflowers, Citrus, Subdivisions*. Covina: Donald H. Pflueger, 1964.

———. *Glendora: The Annals of a Southern California Community*. Claremont: Saunders Press, 1951.

Pomona Centennial History. Pomona: Pomona Centennial-Bicentennial Committee, 1976.

Prudhomme, Charles J. "Gold Discovery in California: Who Was the First Real Discoverer of Gold in the State?" *Annual Publications of the Historical Society of Southern California* 12, part II (1922): 18–25.

Queenan, Charles F. *Long Beach and Los Angeles, a Tale of Two Ports*. Northridge: Windsor Publications, 1986.

Quinn, Charles Russell. *History of Downey*. Downey: Elena Quinn, 1973.

Rand, Christopher. *Los Angeles, the Ultimate City*. New York: Oxford University Press, 1967.

Rios-Bustamente, Antonio, and Pedro Castillo. *An Illustrated History of Mexican Los Angeles, 1781–1985*. Los Angeles: University of California Press, 1986.

Robinson, W. W. *Los Angeles: A Profile*. Norman: University of Oklahoma Press, 1968.

———. *Ranchos Become Cities*. Pasadena: San Pasqual Press, 1939.

Rogers, Warren S. *Mesa to Metropolis; the Crenshaw Area, Los Angeles*. Los Angeles: Lorrin L. Morrison, 1959.

Rolle, Andrew. *Los Angeles: From Pueblo to City of the Future*. San Francisco: Boyd & Fraser, 1981.

Rowland, Leonore. *The Romance of La Puente Rancho*. Covina: Neilson Press, 1958.

San Pedro, a Pictorial History. San Pedro: San Pedro Bay Historical Society, 1983.

Scheid, Ann. *Pasadena: Crown of the Valley*. Northridge: Windsor Publications, 1986.

Schiesl, Martin J. "City Planning and the Federal Government in World War II: The Los Angeles Experiment." *California History* 59 (1980): 126–43.

Tanner, John Douglas, Jr. "Campaign for Los Angeles—December 29, 1846, to January 10, 1847." *California Historical Society Quarterly* 48 (1969): 219–42.

U.S. Works Progress Administration, Writer's Program. *Los Angeles: A Guide to the City and Its Environs*. 1939. Rev. ed., New York: Hastings House, 1951.

Weber, Francis J., comp. and ed. *The Mission in the Valley: San Fernando Rey de España*. Los Angeles, 1975.

———, comp. and ed. *The Pride of the Missions: A Documentary History of San Gabriel Mission*. Los Angeles, 1979.

Wright, Judy. *Claremont, a Pictorial History*. Claremont: Claremont Historic Resources Center, 1980.

Madera County

Clough, Charles W. *Madera*. Fresno: Valley Publishers, 1968.

Crampton, C. Gregory, ed. *The Mariposa Indian War, 1850–51; Diaries of Robert Eccleston*. Salt Lake City: University of Utah Press, 1975.

Farquhar, Francis P. *Place Names of the High Sierra*. San Francisco: Sierra Club, 1926.

Foster, Doris, and Clyde Foster. "One Hundred Years of History—Foster's Hogue Ranch." *The Madera Historical Society Quarterly* 1 (1961): 1–7.

Fry, Walter, and John R. White. *Big Trees*. Stanford: Stanford University Press, 1930.

LeConte, J. N. "The Devil's Postpile." *Sierra Club Bulletin* 8 (Jan. 1912): 170–73.

Matthis, Francois E. "Devil's Postpile and Its Strange Setting." *Sierra Club Bulletin* 15 (Feb. 1930): 1–8.

Marin County

Andrews, Kenneth R. *Drake's Voyages*. New York: Scribners, 1967.

Armentrout-Ma, L. Eve. "Chinese in California's Fishing Industry, 1850–1914." *California History* 60 (1981): 142–57.

Bancroft Library Publications. *The Plate of Brass Reexamined* (1977). *Supplementary Report* (1979). Berkeley: Bancroft Library, University of California at Berkeley.

Carlson, Pamela McGuire, and E. Breck Parkman. "An Exceptional Adaptation: Camillo Ynitia." *California History* 65 (1986): 238–47.

Colley, Charles C. "The Missionization of the Coast Miwok Indians of California." *California Historical Society Quarterly* 49 (1970): 143–62.

Dwyer, John T. *One Hundred Years an Orphan; St. Vincent's Home for Boys at San Rafael, 1855–1955*. Fresno: Academy Library Guild, 1955.

Evans, Elliott A. P., and David W. Heron. "Isla de los Angeles: Unique State Park in San Francisco Bay." *California History* 66 (1987): 24–39.

Fairley, Lincoln. "Literary Associations with Mount Tamalpais." *California History* 61 (1982): 82–99.

"The Francis Drake Controversy: His California Anchorage,

June 17–July 23, 1579." Marilyn Ziebarth, ed. *California Historical Quarterly* 53, no. 2 (1974).

Futcher, Jane, and Robert Conover. *Marin: The Place, The People*. New York: Holt, Rinehart, and Winston, 1981.

Glimpses of Belvedere and Tiburon; the Early Decades. Belvedere-Tiburon: The Landmarks Society, 1964.

Hanna, Warren L. *Lost Harbor: The Controversy over Drake's California Anchorage*. Berkeley: University of California Press, 1979.

Heizer, Robert F. *Elizabethan California*. Ramona, Calif.: Ballena Press, 1974.

Killion, Tom. *Fortress Marin*. San Rafael: Presidio Press, 1979.

McKenna, Clare V., Jr. "The Origins of San Quentin, 1851–1880." *California History* 66 (1987): 49–54.

Martin, N. B. "'Portus Novae Albionis': Site of Drake's California Sojourn." *Pacific Historical Review* 48 (1979): 319–31.

Mason, Jack. *Point Reyes: The Solemn Land*. Inverness, Calif.: North Shore Books, 1970.

Mason, Jack, and Helen Van Cleave Park. *Early Marin*. Rev. ed. Inverness, Calif.: North Shore Books, 1976.

Morison, Samuel Eliot. *The European Discovery of America*. Vol. 2, *The Southern Voyages, 1492–1616*. New York: Oxford University Press, 1974.

Pictorial History of Tiburon, a California Railroad Town. Belvedere-Tiburon, 1984.

Teather, Louise. *Discovering Marin: Historical Tour by Cities and Towns*. Fairfax: The Tamal Land Press, 1974.

Thrower, Norman J. W., ed. *Sir Francis Drake and the Famous Voyage, 1577–1580: Essays Commemorating the Quadricentennial of Drake's Circumnavigation of the Earth*. Berkeley: University of California Press, 1984.

Treganza, Adan E. "Old Lime Kilns Near Olema." *Geologic Guidebook of the San Francisco Bay Counties*. San Francisco: State of California, Division of Mines, 1951, pp. 65–72.

Mariposa County

Burchfield, Chris. "Demolishing Two Mariposa Legends." *The Californians*, Nov.–Dec. 1986, pp. 42–43.

Clark, Galen. *The Yosemite Valley*. Yosemite Valley, 1911.

Crampton, C. Gregory, ed. *The Mariposa Indian War, 1850–51: Diaries of Robert Eccleston*. Salt Lake City: University of Utah Press, 1975.

"The Early Days in Yosemite," reprinted from the *Mariposa Democrat* of August 5, 1856, with introduction by Ansel F. Hall. *California Historical Society Quarterly* 4 (1925): 2–58.

Mendershausen, Ralph. *Treasures of the South Fork: A History and Guide for the South Fork of the Merced River in Mariposa County*. Mariposa: Ralph R. Mendershausen, 1983.

Muir, John. *The Yosemite*. New York: Century Company, 1912.

Phillips, Catherine Coffin. *Coulterville Chronicle: The Annals of a Mother Lode Mining Town*. 1942. Reprint, Fresno: Valley Publishers, 1978.

Robertson, David. *West of Eden: A History of Art and Literature of Yosemite*. Yosemite: Yosemite Natural History Association, 1984.

Sargent, Shirley. *Mariposa County Guidebook*. Yosemite: Flying Spur Press, 1984.

———. *Yosemite's Historic Wawona*. Yosemite: Flying Spur Press, 1984.

Trexler, Keith A. *The Tioga Road, a History; 1883–1961*. Rev. ed. Yosemite: Yosemite Natural History Association, 1975.

Wood, Raymund F. *California's Agua Fria*. Fresno: Academy Library Guild, 1954.

Mendocino County

Boynton, Searles R. *The Painter Lady: Grace Carpenter Hudson*. Eureka: Interface Corporation, 1978.

Carpenter, Aurelius O. *A History of Mendocino County*. 1914. Reprint, Mendocino: Pacific Rim Research, 1977.

Kortum, Karl, and Roger Olmsted. "A Dangerous-Looking Place—Sailing Days on the Redwood Coast." *California Historical Quarterly* 50 (1971): 43–58.

Landsman, David, ed. *Mendocino County Historic Annals*. 2 vols. Mendocino: Pacific Rim Research, 1977.

Stebbins, Beth. *The Noyo: Being an Account of the History at the Mouth of the Noyo River, on the Mendocino County Coast of California, from 1852 into 1920 and a Little Beyond*. Mendocino: Bear and Stebbins, 1986.

Merced County

Cabezut-Ortin, Delores J. *Merced County: The Golden Harvest*. Northridge: Windsor Publications, 1987.

DePertuis, Jeff. *Homes of Old Merced*. Merced: Merced Historical Society, 1987.

Outcalt, John. *History of Merced County*. Los Angeles: Historic Record Co., 1925.

Pimentel, Wayne. *Dogtown and Ditches: Life on the Westside*. Los Banos: Loose Change Publications, 1987.

Shumate, Albert. *Francisco Pacheco of Pacheco Pass*. Stockton: University of the Pacific, 1977.

Treadwell, Edward F. *The Cattle King*. New York: Macmillan, 1931.

Veronico, Nicholas. *Castle Air Museum*. Castro Valley: Pacific Aero Press, 1985.

Modoc County

Dillon, Richard. *Burnt-Out Fires: California's Modoc Indian War*. Englewood Cliffs, N.J.: Prentice-Hall, 1973.

French, R. A., comp., and Gertrude P. French, ed. *A Historical, Biographical, and Pictorial Magazine Devoted to Modoc County*. Alturas, Calif.: 1912.

Sagebrush Corner—Opening of California's Northeast. New York: Garland Publishing, 1973.

Thompson, Erwin N. *Modoc War: Its Military History and Topography*. Sacramento: Argus Books, 1971.

Mono County

Bean, Betty. *Horseshoe Canyon: A Brief History of the June Lake Loop*. Bishop: Chalfant Press, 1977.

Briggs, Carl. "Goodbye, God; We're Going to Bodie." *The Californians*, July–Aug. 1986, pp. 30–32.

Cain, Ella M. *The Story of Bodie*. San Francisco: Fearon Publishers, 1956.

———. *The Story of Early Mono County*. San Francisco: Fearon Publishers, 1961.

Calhoun, Margaret. *Pioneers of Mono Basin*. Lee Vining: Artemisia Press, 1984.

Chalfant, W. A. *Gold, Guns, and Ghost Towns*. 1947. Reprint, Bishop: Chalfant Press, 1975.

DeDecker, Mary. *Mines of the Eastern Sierra*. Glendale: La Siesta Press, 1966.

Johnson, Russ, and Anne Johnson. *The Ghost Town of Bodie, as Reported in the Newspapers of the Day*. Bishop: Chalfant Press, 1967.

Reed, Adele. *Old Mammoth*. Genny Smith, ed. Palo Alto: Genny Smith Books, 1982.

Russell, Carl P. "Early Mining Excitements East of Yosemite." *Sierra Club Bulletin* 13 (Feb. 1928): 40–53.

Von Blon, John L. "Rock Writings of the Owens Valley." *Touring Topics* 21 (May 1929): 14–17, 51.

Williams, George, III. *The Guide to Bodie and Eastern Sierra Historic Sites*. Riverside: Tree by the River Publishers, 1981.

———. *The Murderers of Convict Lake*. Riverside: Tree by the River Publishers, 1984.

Monterey County

Colton, Walter. *Three Years in California*. New York: A. S. Barnes & Co., 1850.

Dakin, Susanna B. *The Lives of William Hartnell*. Stanford: Stanford University Press, 1949.

Davenport, William. *The Monterey Peninsula*. Menlo Park: Lane Books, 1964.

Fink, Augusta. *Monterey: The Presence of the Past*. San Francisco: Chronicle Books, 1972.

———. *Monterey County: The Dramatic Story of Its Past*. Fresno: Valley Publishers, 1978.

Fisher, Anne B. *The Salinas, Upside-Down River*. New York: Rinehart, 1945.

Guinn, James Miller. *History and Biographical Record of Monterey and San Benito Counties*. Los Angeles: Historic Record Co., 1910.

Horne, Kibbey M. *A History of the Presidio of Monterey, 1770 to 1970*. Monterey: Defense Language Institute, 1970.

Howard, Donald M. *Prehistoric Sites Handbooks: Monterey and San Luis Obispo Counties*. Carmel: Monterey County Archaeological Society, 1979.

King City, California: The First Hundred Years. King City: San Antonio Valley Historical Association, 1986.

Kirker, Harold. "The Larkin House Revisited." *California History* 65 (1986): 26–33.

Lewis, Betty. *Monterey Bay Yesterday*. Fresno: Valley Publishers, 1977.

O'Donnell, Mayo Hayes. *Monterey's Adobe Heritage*. Monterey: Monterey Savings and Loan, 1965.

Orth, Michael. "The Founding of Carmel." *California Historical Society Quarterly* 48 (1969): 195–210.

Perry, Frank. *Lighthouse Point: Reflections on Monterey Bay History*. Soquel: GBH Publishing, 1982.

Planer, Edward T. "The Short but Valuable Life of the M & SV RR." *Monterey Peninsula-Herald*, Oct. 19, 1975, pp. 4–11.

Reinstedt, Randall A. *The Monterey Peninsula, an Enchanted Land*. Northridge: Windsor Publications, 1987.

———. *Shipwrecks and Sea Monsters of California's Central Coast*. Carmel: Ghost Town Publications, 1987.

Smith, Frances Rand. *The Mission of San Antonio de Padua*. Stanford: Stanford University Press, 1932.

Smith, Gene A. "The War That Wasn't: Thomas ap Catesby Jones's Seizure of Monterey." *California History* 66 (1987): 104–14.

Spencer-Hancock, Diane, and William E. Pritchard. "El Castillo de Monterey, Frontline of Defense." *California History* 63 (1984): 230–41.

Stevenson, Robert Louis. *From Scotland to Silverado*. Edited by James D. Hart. Cambridge: Belknap Press of Harvard University, 1966.

Van Nostrand, Jeanne. *Monterey: Adobe Capital of California, 1770–1847*. San Francisco: California Historical Society, 1969.

Weber, Francis J., comp. and ed. *California's Sorrowful Mission: A Documentary History of Nuestra Señora de la Soledad*. Los Angeles: Archdiocese of Los Angeles Archives, 1986.

———. *Father of the Missions: A Documentary History of San Carlos Borromeo*. Hong Kong: Libra Press, 1984.

Napa County

Archuleta, Kay. *The Brannan Story*. St. Helena: Illuminations Press, 1982.

Camp, Charles L., ed. *George C. Yount and His Chronicles of the West, Comprising Extracts from his "Memoirs."* Denver: Old West Publishing Co., 1966.

Dutton, Joan Perry. *They Left Their Mark: Famous Passages Through the Wine Country*. St. Helena: Illuminations Press, 1983.

Gregory, Tom. *History of Solano and Napa Counties, California*. Los Angeles: Historic Record Co., 1912.

History of Napa and Lake Counties, California. San Francisco: Slocum, Bowen & Co., 1882.

Stevenson, Robert Louis. *From Scotland to Silverado*. Edited by James D. Hart. Cambridge: Belknap Press of Harvard University, 1966.

Verardo, Denzil. *In the Valley of Bottled Poetry: Napa Valley Architectural Survivors*. Pacific Grove: Boxwood Press, 1983.

Verardo, Denzil, and Jennie Verardo. *Napa Valley: From Golden Fields to Purple Harvest*. Northridge: Windsor Publications, 1986.

Nevada County

Best, Gerald M. *Nevada County Narrow Gauge*. Berkeley: Howell-North Books, 1965.

Browne, Juanita Kennedy. *Nuggets of Nevada County History*. Nevada City: Nevada County Historical Society, 1983.

California Mining Journal [featuring Nevada and Sierra county mines] 1, no. 1 (Aug. 1931).

Comstock, David A. *Gold Diggers and Camp Followers: The Ne-vada County Chronicles, 1845–1851.* Grass Valley: Comstock-Bonanza Press, 1982.

Comstock, David A., and Ardis Comstock. *Index to History of Nevada County by Thompson and West.* Grass Valley: Comstock-Bonanza Press, 1979.

Houghton, Mrs. Eliza Cook (Donner). *The Expedition of the Donner Party and Its Tragic Fate.* Chicago: A. G. McClurg & Co., 1911.

Lardner, W. B., and M. J. Brock. *History of Placer and Nevada Counties, California.* Los Angeles: Historic Record Co., 1924.

McGlashan, C. F. *History of the Donner Party, a Tragedy of the Sierra.* 1881. Reprint, Stanford: Stanford University Press, 1940, 1977.

Mann, Ralph. *After the Gold Rush: Society in Grass Valley and Ne-vada City, California, 1849–1870.* Stanford: Stanford University Press, 1982.

Meschery, Joanne. *Truckee, an Illustrated History of the Town and Its Surroundings.* Truckee: Rocking Stone Press, 1978.

Rourke, Constance. *Troopers of the Gold Coast, or the Rise of Lotta Crabtree.* New York: Harcourt, Brace, 1928.

Slyter, Robert I., and Grace I. Slyter. *Historical Notes of the Early Washington, Nevada County, California, Mining District.* Washington, Calif.: Robert I. Slyter, 1972.

Smith, Paul B. "Highway Planning in California's Mother Lode: The Changing Townscape of Auburn and Nevada City." *California History* 59 (1980): 204–21.

Stewart, George. *Ordeal by Hunger.* 1936. Reprint, New York: Washington Square Press, 1960.

Wells, Harry L. *History of Nevada County, California.* Oakland: Thompson & West, 1880. Reprint, Berkeley: Howell-North Books, 1970.

Wyckoff, Robert M. *The Compleat Pedestrian's Partially Illustrated Guide to Greater Nevada City.* 2d ed. Nevada City: Nevada City Publishing Co., 1979.

———. *Walking Tours and Twice-Told Tales of Grass Valley.* Nevada City: Nevada City Publishing Co., 1979.

———, ed. *Never Come, Never Go! The Story of Nevada County's Narrow-Gauge Railroad.* Nevada City: Nevada City Publishing Co., 1986.

Orange County

Cleland, Robert G. *The Irvine Ranch.* 1952. Revised with an Epi-logue by Robert V. Hine, San Marino: Huntington Library, 1984.

Dickson, Lucile E. "The Founding and Early History of Ana-heim, California." *Annual Publications, Historical Society of Southern California* 2, part I (1918).

Friis, Leo J. *Campo Aleman: The First Ten Years of Anaheim.* Santa Ana: Friis-Pioneer Press, 1983.

———. *Historic Buildings of Pioneer Anaheim.* Santa Ana: Friis-Pioneer Press, 1983.

———. *Orange County Through Four Centuries.* Santa Ana: Friis-Pioneer Press, 1982.

Gibson, Wayne Dell. *Tomas Yorba's Santa Ana Viejo, 1769–1847.* Santa Ana: Santa Ana College Foundation Press, 1970.

Hallan-Gibson, Pamela. *The Golden Promise: An Illustrated His-tory of Orange County.* Northridge: Windsor Publications, 1986.

Lee, Ellen K. *Newport Bay: A Pioneer History.* Newport Beach: Newport Beach Historical Society, 1973.

Marsh, Diann. *Anaheim's Architectural Treasury.* Anaheim: Ana-heim Historical Society, 1973.

Meadows, Don. *Historic Place Names in Orange County.* Balboa Island: Paisano Press, 1966.

Miller, Edrick J. *The S.A.A.A.B. [Santa Ana Army Air Base] Story.* Costa Mesa: Edrick J. Miller, 1981.

Olin, Spencer, Jr. "Bible Communism and the Origins of Orange County." *California History* 58 (1979): 220–33.

O'Neill, Ynez Viola. "Father Serra Plans the Founding of Mis-sion San Juan Capistrano." *California Historical Quarterly* 56 (1977): 46–51.

Osterman, Joseph D. "Venture, Gain, Loss and Change in Old El Toro's Orange County." *The Californians,* July–Aug. 1983, pp. 6–12.

Roley, Margaret, et al. *100 Years of Laguna Beach, 1876–1976.* Laguna Beach: Laguna Beach Historical Society, 1974.

Schultz, Elizabeth, ed. *Visiting Orange County's Past.* Santa Ana: Orange County Historical Commission, 1984.

Sleeper, Jim. *Santa Ana Mountains.* Trabuco Canyon: California Classics, 1976.

Smith, Gail Vinje, and William A. Allen. *The Picture History of Balboa Island, 1906–1981. A Celebration of the Diamond Jubi-lee.* Newport Beach: Gailliard Press, 1981.

Weber, Francis J., ed. *The Jewel of the Missions: A Documentary History of San Juan Capistrano.* San Juan Capistrano: San Juan Capistrano Mission, 1976.

Placer County

Davis, Leonard M. *Profiles Out of the Past: A Biographical History of Roseville.* Roseville: Roseville Community Projects, 1982.

Gilberg, M. E. *Auburn: A California Mining Camp Comes of Age.* Newcastle: Gilmer Press, 1986.

History of Placer County, California, with Illustrations and Bio-graphical Sketches of Its Prominent Men and Pioneers. 1882. Re-print, Auburn: Placer County Historical Society, 1986.

Lardner, W. B., and M. J. Brock. *History of Placer and Nevada Counties, California.* Los Angeles: Historic Record Co., 1924.

Robie, Wendell. *Auburn: A Century of Memories.* Auburn: Placer County Historical Society, 1988.

Smith, Paul B. "Highway Planning in California's Mother Lode: The Changing Townscape of Auburn and Nevada City." *California History* 59 (1980): 204–21.

Zauner, Phyllis. *Lake Tahoe.* Tahoe Paradise: Zanel Publica-tions, 1982.

Plumas County

Beckwourth, James P. *The Life and Adventures of James P. Beck-wourth.* Edited by T. D. Bonner. 1856. Reprint, New York: Knopf, 1931.

Clappe, Louise Amelie Knapp Smith ("Dame Shirley"). *The Shirley Letters, Being Letters Written in 1851–1852 from the*

California Mines. 1854. Reprint, Salt Lake City: Peregrine Smith, 1983.

Dunn, Mary E. Phelps. *A Review of the History of Plumas County and Explanation of Many Place Names*. 1960. Reprint, Quincy: Plumas County Historical Society, 1982.

Fariss & Smith. *History of Plumas, Lassen, and Sierra Counties, California*. 1882. Reprint, Berkeley: Howell-North Books, 1971.

Hall, Jacqueline, and JoEllen Hall. *Italian-Swiss Settlement in Plumas County, 1860–1920*. Chico: Association for Northern California Records and Research, 1973.

Little, Jane Braxton. *Plumas Sketches*. Canyondam, Calif.: Wolf Creek Press, 1983.

Paul, Rodman W. "In Search of Dame Shirley." *Pacific Historical Review* 33 (1964): 127–46.

Riverside County

Ainsworth, Katherine. *The McCallum Saga: The Story of the Founding of Palm Springs*. Palm Springs: Palm Springs Desert Museum, 1973.

Beattie, George William. "Development of Travel Between Southern Arizona and Los Angeles, as Related to the San Bernardino Valley." *Annual Publications, Historical Society of Southern California* 13 (1925): 228–57.

Brumgardt, John R., and Larry L. Bowles. *People of the Magic Waters: The Cahuilla Indians of Palm Springs*. Palm Springs: ETC Publications, 1981.

DeStanley, Mildred. *The Salton Sea, Yesterday and Today*. Los Angeles: Triumph Press, 1966.

Eldridge, Fred, and Stanley Reynolds. *Our History: Corona, California Commentaries*. Corona: Heritage Committee, Corona Public Library, 1986.

Gunther, Jane Davies. *Riverside County, California, Place Names: Their Origins and Their Stories*. Riverside: J. D. Gunther, 1984.

Jackson, Helen Hunt. *Ramona*. 1884. Reprint, New York: Avon, 1970.

James, George Wharton. *Through Ramona's Country*. 1909. Reprint, Boston: Little, Brown, 1970.

Kennedy, Don H. "Ramona's People." *The Californians*, Sept.–Oct. 1986, pp. 46–49.

Klotz, Esther, and Joan H. Hall. *Adobes, Bungalows, and Mansions of Riverside, California*. Riverside: Riverside Museum Press, 1985.

Lopez, Barry. "California Desert, a Worldly Wilderness." *National Geographic* 171 (Jan. 1987): 42–78.

Moses, Vincent. "Machines in the Garden: A Citrus Monopoly in Riverside, 1900–1936." *California History* 61 (1982): 26–35.

Patterson, Tom. *Landmarks of Riverside*. Riverside: Press-Enterprise Co., 1964.

Robinson, W. W. *The Story of Riverside County*. Riverside: Title Insurance & Trust Co., 1957.

Stonehouse, Merlin. *John Wesley North and the Reform Frontier*. Minneapolis: University of Minnesota Press, 1965.

Vickery, Joyce Carter. *Defending Eden: New Mexican Pioneers in Southern California, 1830–1890*. Riverside: Riverside Museum Press, 1977.

Sacramento County

Blenkie, Joe. *Folsom-Auburn and the Mother Lode: Gold, Blood, Water*. Sacramento: Western Wonder Publications, 1976.

Bradley, Glen D. *The Story of the Pony Express*. Chicago: A. G. McClurg & Co., 1913.

Briens, Marvin. "Sacramento Defies the Rivers, 1850–1878." *California History* 58 (1979): 2–19.

Chu, George. "Chinatowns in the Delta: The Chinese in the Sacramento–San Joaquin Delta, 1870–1960." *California Historical Society Quarterly* 49 (1970): 21–38.

Dillon, Richard. *Fool's Gold: The Decline and Fall of Captain John Sutter of California*. New York: Coward-McCann, 1967.

Gillenkirk, Jeff, and James Motlow. "This Was Our Place: Memories of Locke." *California History* 66 (1987): 170–87.

Graham, Kathleen Mary, et al., eds. *Historic Houses of the Sacramento River Delta*. Walnut Grove: Sacramento Delta Historical Society, 1984.

Hall, Carroll D., Hero Eugene Rensch, Jack R. Ryson, and Norman L. Wilson. *Old Sacramento, a Report on Its Significance to the City, State and Nation, with Recommendations for the Preservation and Use of Its Principal Historic Structures and Sites*. 3 vols. Sacramento: State Division of Beaches and Parks, 1958, 1960.

Hume, Charles V. "First of the Gold Rush Theatres." *California Historical Society Quarterly* 46 (1967): 337–44.

Hussey, John A., ed. *Early Sacramento: Glimpses of John Augustus Sutter, the Hock Farm and Neighboring Indian Tribes, from the Journals of Prince Paul, H.R.H. Duke Paul Wilhelm of Wurttemburg*. Translated by Louis C. Butscher. Sacramento: Sacramento Book Collectors Club, 1973.

Lokke, Janet. "'Like a Bright Tree of Life': Farmland Settlement of the Sacramento River Delta." *California History* 59 (1980): 222–39.

McGowan, Joseph A., and Terry R. Willis. *Sacramento, Heart of the Golden State*. Woodland Hills: Windsor Publications, 1983.

Neasham, V. Audrey. *Old Sacramento, a Reference Point in Time*. Sacramento Historic Landmarks Commission, in cooperation with the Redevelopment Agency of the City of Sacramento, 1965.

Neasham, V. Audrey, and James E. Hensley. *The City of the Plain: Sacramento in the Nineteenth Century*. Sacramento: Sacramento Pioneer Foundation, 1969.

Severson, Thor. *Sacramento: An Illustrated History, 1839–1874*. San Francisco: California Historical Society, 1973.

Smith, Jesse M., ed. *Sketches of Old Sacramento*. Sacramento: Sacramento County Historical Society, 1976.

Thompson, John. "From Waterways to Roadways in the Sacramento Delta." *California History* 59 (1980): 144–59.

Wheat, Carl I. "A Sketch of the Life of Theodore D. Judah." *California Historical Society Quarterly* 4 (1925): 219–71.

Zauner, Phyllis. *Sacramento: A Mini-History*. Tahoe Paradise: Zanel Publications, 1979.

San Benito County

Flint, Dorothy. *Escarpment on the San Andreas: The Probing of a California Heritage*. Hollister: Marjorie Flint, 1978.

Hoyle, M. F. *Crimes and Career of Tiburcio Vasquez, the Bandit of San Benito County and Notorious Early California Outlaw*. Hollister: Evening Free Lance, 1927.

Iacopi, Robert. *Earthquake Country*. Menlo Park: Lane Books, 1964.

Jordan, David Starr. *The Days of a Man*. 2 vols. Yonkers, N.Y.: World Book Co., 1922.

Milliken, Ralph LeRoy. *San Juan Bautista, California, the City of History*. Los Banos: Los Banos Enterprise, 1961.

San Bernardino County

Beattie, George W. "Development of Travel Between Southern Arizona and Los Angeles, as Related to the San Bernardino Valley." *Annual Publications, Historical Society of Southern California* 13 (1925): 228–57.

———. "San Bernardino Valley in the Spanish Period." *Annual Publications, Historical Society of Southern California* 12, part III (1923) 10–28.

Beattie, George W., and Helen P. Beattie. *Heritage of the Valley*. Oakland: Biobooks, 1951.

Bishop, M. Guy. "The San Bernardino Mormon Colony: 'To Establish a Standard of Righteousness.'" *The Californians*, Sept.–Oct. 1987, pp. 12–17.

Black, Esther Boulton. *Rancho Cucamonga and Dona Merced*. Redlands: San Bernardino County Museum Association, 1975.

———. *Stories of Old Upland*. Upland: Chaffey Communities Cultural Center, 1979.

Casebier, Dennis. *Fort Pah-Ute, California*. Norco: Tales of the Mojave Road Publishing Company, 1974.

———. *The Mojave Road*. Norco: Tales of the Mojave Road Publishing Company, 1975.

Conley, Bernice Bedford. *Dreamers and Dwellers: Ontario and Neighbors*. Ontario: Stump Printing Services, 1982.

Historical Landmarks of San Bernardino County. Redlands: San Bernardino County Museum, 1980.

Houston, Flora Belle. "When the Mormons Settled San Bernardino." *Touring Topics* 22 (Apr. 1930): 32–34, 52.

Keeling, Patricia J., ed. *Once Upon a Desert: A Bicentennial Project*. Barstow: Mojave River Valley Museum Association, 1976.

Kroeber, A. L., and C. B. Kroeber. *A Mojave War Reminiscence, 1854–1880*. Berkeley: University of California Press, 1973.

Lawrence, Eleanor. "Mexican Trade Between Santa Fe and Los Angeles, 1830–1848." *California Historical Society Quarterly* 10 (1931): 27–39.

Leadabrand, Russ. *A Guidebook to the Mojave Desert of California*. Los Angeles: Ward Ritchie Press, 1966.

———. *A Guidebook to the San Bernardino Mountains of California*. Los Angeles: Ritchie & Simon, 1973.

Moore, William G. *Redlands Yesterdays: A Photo Album, 1870–1920*. Redlands: Moore Historical Foundation, 1983.

Peirson, Emma. *The Mojave River and Its Valley*. Glendale: Arthur H. Clark Co., 1970.

Robinson, John W. *Mines of the San Bernardinos*. Glendale: La Siesta Press, 1977.

Robinson, W. W. *The Story of San Bernardino County*. San Bernardino: Title Insurance & Trust Co., 1962.

Schuiling, Walter C. *San Bernardino County: Land of Contrasts*. Woodland Hills: Windsor Publications, 1984.

———, ed. *Pleistocene Man at Calico*. Redlands: San Bernardino County Museum Association, 1979.

San Diego County

Berger, Dan, Peter Jensen, and Margaret C. Berg. *San Diego: Where Tomorrow Begins*. Northridge: Windsor Publications, 1987.

Booth, Larry, Roger Olmsted, and Richard F. Pourade. "Portrait of a Boom Town: San Diego in the 1880's." *California Historical Quarterly* 50 (1971): 363–94.

Brackett, R. W. *The History of San Diego County Ranchos*. San Diego: Union Title Insurance Co., 1960.

Brown, Joseph E. *Cabrillo National Monument*. San Diego: Cabrillo Historical Association, 1981.

Engstrand, Iris H. W. *San Diego: California's Cornerstone*. Tulsa, Okla.: Continental Heritage Press, 1980.

———. "Serra and the Founding of San Diego." *The Californians*, Sept.–Oct. 1984, pp. 24–26.

Hill, J. J. *History of Warner's Ranch and Its Environs*. Los Angeles, 1927.

Holland, F. Ross. *The Old Point Loma Lighthouse, San Diego*. San Diego: Cabrillo Historical Association, 1978.

Jackson, Helen Hunt. *Glimpses of California and the Missions*. Boston: Little, Brown, 1923.

Kuhn, Gerald C., and Francis P. Shephard. *Sea Cliffs, Beaches and Coastal Valleys of San Diego County*. Berkeley: University of California Press, 1984.

Lemenager, Charles R. *Off the Main Road, San Vicente and Barona; A History of the Rancho Cañada de San Vicente y Mesa del Padre Barona*. Ramona: Eagle Peak Publishing Co., 1983.

Lindsay, Diana. *Our Historic Desert: The Story of the Anza-Borrego Desert*. San Diego: Copley Books, 1973.

McKeever, Michael. *A Short History of San Diego*. San Francisco: Lexikos, 1985.

MacMullen, Jerry. *They Came by Sea: A Pictorial History of San Diego Bay*. San Diego: Ward Ritchie Press, 1969.

MacPhail, Elizabeth C. *The Story of New San Diego and of Its Founder Alonzo E. Horton*. San Diego: San Diego Historical Society, 1979.

Mills, James. *Historical Landmarks of San Diego County*. San Diego: San Diego Historical Society, 1960.

O'Neal, Lulu R. *The History of Ramona, California, and Environs*. Ramona: Ballena Press, 1976.

Ryan, Frances B., and Lewis C. Ryan. *Escondido As It Was, 1900–1950*. Escondido: Frances B. and Lewis C. Ryan, 1980.

Stein, Lou. *San Diego County Place Names*. San Diego: Tofus Press, 1975.

Weber, Francis J., ed. *King of the Missions, a Documentary History of San Luis Rey de Francia*. Los Angeles, 1980.

————, ed. *The Pronto Mission, a Documentary History of San Diego de Alcala.* Los Angeles, 1980.

San Francisco County

Averbach, Alvin. "San Francisco's South of Market District, 1858–1958: The Emergence of a Skid Row." *California Historical Quarterly* 52 (1973): 196–223.

Baird, Joseph Armstrong, Jr. "The Mansion of the California Historical Society, 2090 Jackson Street, San Francisco." *California Historical Society Quarterly* 48 (1969): 309–24.

Brant, Michelle. *Timeless Walks in San Francisco.* Berkeley: Bookpeople, 1979.

Bullen, Isabel. "A Glimpse into the *Niantic's* Hold." *California History* 58 (1980): 326–33.

The California Star: Yerba Buena and San Francisco—Volume 1, 1847–48; a Reproduction in Facsimile. Introduction by Fred Blackburn Rogers. Berkeley: Howell-North Books, 1965.

Cather, Helen V. *The History of San Francisco's Chinatown.* San Francisco: R & E Research Associates, 1974.

Daniels, Douglas Henry. *Pioneer Urbanites: A Social and Cultural History of Black San Francisco.* Philadelphia: Temple University Press, 1980.

Delgado, James. "A Dream of Seven Decades: San Francisco's Aquatic Park." *California History* 64 (1985): 272–82.

————. "'No Longer a Buoyant Ship'—Unearthing the Gold Rush Steamship *Niantic.*" *California History* 58 (1980): 316–25.

DeLuca, Richard. "'We Hold the Rock': The Indian Attempt to Reclaim Alcatraz Island." *California History* 62 (1983): 2–23.

Dicker, Laverne M. "The San Francisco Earthquake and Fire: Photographs and Manuscripts from the California Historical Society Library." *California History* 59 (1980): 34–65.

Doughty, Robin W. "The Farallones and the Boston Men." *California Historical Quarterly* 53 (1974): 309–16.

Fey, Marshall. "Charles Fey and San Francisco's Liberty Bell Slot Machine." *California Historical Quarterly* 54 (1975): 57–62.

Fritzsche, Bruno. "San Francisco in 1843: A Key to Dr. Sandels' Drawing." *California Historical Quarterly* 50 (1971): 3–14.

Geiger, Maynard. "New Data on the Buildings of Mission San Francisco." *California Historical Society Quarterly* 46 (1967): 195–205.

Jewett, Masha Zakheim. *Coit Tower, San Francisco.* San Francisco: Volcano Press, 1986.

Lewis, Oscar. *San Francisco: Mission to Metropolis.* 2d ed. San Diego: Howell-North Books, 1980.

Lockwood, Charles. "Rincon Hill Was San Francisco's Most Genteel Neighborhood." *California History* 58 (1979): 48–61.

Loewenstein, Louis K. *Streets of San Francisco: The Origins of San Francisco's Street and Place Names.* San Francisco: Lexikos, 1984.

Lotchin, Roger. *San Francisco, 1846–1856: From Hamlet to City.* Lincoln: University of Nebraska Press, 1979.

McGloin, John B. *San Francisco: The Story of a City.* San Rafael: Presidio Press, 1979.

Mawn, Geoffrey. "Framework for Destiny: San Francisco, 1847." *California Historical Quarterly* 51 (1972): 165–78.

Mullen, Kevin J. "San Francisco: City on the Wrong Side of the Bay." *The Californians,* Mar.–Apr. 1984, pp. 34–42.

Page, Charles Hall, et al. *Splendid Survivors: San Francisco's Architectural Heritage.* San Francisco: California Living Books, 1979.

Parker, Elizabeth L., and James Abajian. *A Walking Tour of the Black Presence in San Francisco During the Nineteenth Century.* San Francisco: San Francisco African-American Historical and Cultural Society, 1974.

Watkins, T. H., and R. R. Olmsted. *Mirror of the Dream: An Illustrated History of San Francisco.* San Francisco: Scrimshaw Press, 1976.

Weber, Francis J., comp. and ed. *Mission Dolores: A Documentary History of San Francisco Mission.* Los Angeles: Archdiocese of Los Angeles Archives, 1979.

San Joaquin County

Audubon, John W. *Audubon's Western Journal, 1849–1850.* Cleveland, Ohio: Arthur H. Clark Co., 1906.

Baltich, Frances. *Search for Safety: The Founding of Stockton's Black Community.* Stockton: Frances Baltich, 1982.

Brotherton, I. N. ("Jack"). *The Annals of Stanislaus: River Towns and Ferries.* Santa Cruz: Western Tanager Press, 1982.

Curtis, Mrs. Dwight. *Old Cemeteries of San Joaquin County.* 2 vols. Stockton: San Joaquin Genealogical Society, 1960.

Davis, Olive. *Stockton: Sunrise Port on the San Joaquin.* Woodland Hills: Windsor Publications, 1984.

Hardeman, Nicholas P. *Harbor of the Heartlands: A History of the Inland Seaport of Stockton, California, from the Gold Rush to 1985.* Stockton: Holt-Atherton Center for Western Studies, 1986.

Hillman, Raymond, and Leonard Covello. *Cities and Towns of San Joaquin County Since 1847.* Fresno: Panorama West Books, 1985.

Hittell, Theodore H. *The Adventures of James Capen Adams, Mountaineer Grizzly Bear Hunter of California.* 1860. Rev. ed. New York: Scribner, 1911.

Mazet, Horace S. "The Man Who Loved Grizzlies." *The Californians,* Sept.–Oct. 1985, pp. 27–35.

Minnick, Sylvia Sun. *Samfow: The San Joaquin Chinese Legacy.* Lodi: San Joaquin County Historical Society, 1988.

Schenck, W. Egbert. "Historic Aboriginal Groups of the California Delta Region." *University of California Publications in American Archaeology and Ethnology* 25, no. 4 (1929): 289–413.

Spencer, Horace A. *A Guide to Historical Locations in San Joaquin County.* 3d ed. Stockton: San Joaquin County Superintendent of Schools Office, 1978.

Tinkham, George H. *History of San Joaquin County, California.* Los Angeles: Historic Record Co., 1923.

Wood, R. Coke, and Leonard Covello. *Stockton Memories.* Stockton: Valley Publishers, 1977.

San Luis Obispo County

Angel, Myron. *History of San Luis Obispo County.* 1883. Reprint, San Miguel: Friends of the Adobes, 1983.

Darling, Velva G. "Cave Landing, a San Luis Obispo County Scenic Spot." *Touring Topics* 18, Mar. 1926.

Howard, Donald M. *Prehistoric Sites Handbook: Monterey and San Luis Obispo Counties.* Carmel: Monterey County Archaeological Society, 1979.

Kocher, Paul H. *Mission San Luis Obispo de Tolosa, 1772–1972, a Historical Sketch.* San Luis Obispo: Blake Printing and Publishing, 1972.

Robinson, W. W. *The Story of San Luis Obispo County.* Los Angeles: Title Insurance & Trust Co., 1957.

Romney, Joseph B. *A Research Guide to the History of San Luis Obispo County, California.* Rexburg, Idaho: Milhollow Publications, 1985.

Swanberg, W. A. *Citizen Hearst.* New York: Scribner, 1961.

Weber, Francis J., comp. and ed. *Mission in the Valley of the Bears: A Documentary History of San Luis Obispo de Tolosa.* Los Angeles: Archdiocese of Los Angeles Archives, 1985.

Winslow, Carleton M., and Nickola L. Frye. *The Enchanted Hill: The Story of Hearst Castle at San Simeon.* Los Angeles: Rosebud Books, 1980.

San Mateo County

Atherton, F. D. *The California Diary of Faxon Dean Atherton, 1836–9.* Edited by Doyce R. Nunis, Jr. Special Publication 29. San Francisco: California Historical Society, 1964.

Atherton, Gertrude. *Adventures of a Novelist.* New York: Liveright, 1932.

Blum, Joseph A. "South San Francisco—the Making of an Industrial City." *California History* 63 (1984): 114–34.

Brown, Alan K. "Rivera at San Francisco, a Journal of Exploration, 1774." *California Historical Society Quarterly* 41 (1962): 325–41.

———. *Saw Pits in the Spanish Redwoods.* San Mateo: San Mateo County Historical Association, 1966.

Carter, Charles Franklin. "Duhaut-Cilly's Account of California in the Years 1827–28." *California Historical Society Quarterly* 8 (1929): 131–66, 306–36.

Chandler, Samuel C. *Gateway to the Peninsula: A History of the City of Daly City.* Daly City: Daly City Public Library, 1973.

Coastside Cultural Resources of San Mateo County, California. Redwood City: San Mateo County Department of Environmental Management, Planning Division, 1980.

Historic Resources Element of the San Mateo County General Plan. Redwood City: San Mateo County Department of Environmental Management, 1982.

Hynding, Alan. *From Frontier to Suburb: The Story of the San Mateo Peninsula.* Palo Alto: Star Publishing Company, 1983.

The Illustrated History of San Mateo County. 1878. Reduced facsimile, Woodside: Gilbert Richards, 1974.

Kauffman, Linda. *South San Francisco: A History.* South San Francisco, 1976.

Richards, Gilbert. *Crossroads: People and Events of the Redwoods of San Mateo County.* Woodside: Gilbert Richards, 1973.

Shumate, Albert. "Correspondence Concerning 'Murder, by God!'" *The Californians*, May–June 1986, pp. 6, 7, 51.

Stanger, Frank M. "'The Hospice' or 'Mission San Mateo.'" *California Historical Society Quarterly* 23 (1944): 247–58.

———. *Sawmills in the Redwoods: Logging on the San Francisco Peninsula.* San Mateo: San Mateo County Historical Association, 1967.

———. *South from San Francisco: San Mateo County, California, Its History and Heritage.* San Mateo: San Mateo County Historical Association, 1963.

Wyatt, Roscoe D. *Historic Names and Places in San Mateo County.* Redwood City: San Mateo County Title Insurance Company, 1947.

Santa Barbara County

Bookspan, Rochelle, ed. *Santa Barbara by the Sea.* Santa Barbara: McNally & Loftin, 1983.

Caldwell, Joyce Craven. *Carpinteria as It Was.* Carpinteria: Papillon Press, 1979.

Cullimore, Clarence. *Santa Barbara Adobes.* Santa Barbara: Santa Barbara Book Publishing Co., 1948.

Geiger, Maynard. *Mission Santa Barbara, 1782–1965.* Santa Barbara: Franciscan Fathers of California, 1965.

Hageman, Fred C., and Russell C. Ewing. *An Archaeological and Restoration Study of Mission La Purísima Concepción.* Edited by Richard Whitehead. Santa Barbara: Santa Barbara Trust for Historic Preservation, 1980.

Harrington, John P. "Exploration of the Burton Mound at Santa Barbara, California." *Forty-Fourth Annual Report of the Bureau of American Ethnology.* Washington, D.C.: U.S. Government Printing Office, 1928, pp. 30–168.

Hawley, Walter A. *The Early Days of Santa Barbara, California: From the First Discoveries by Europeans to December, 1846.* 1920. 3d ed., enlarged, edited by John C. Woodward. Santa Barbara: Santa Barbara Heritage, 1987.

Hudson, Travis. *Guide to Painted Cave.* Santa Barbara: McNally & Loftin, 1982.

Rife, Joanne. *Where the Light Turns Gold: The Story of the Santa Inez Valley.* Fresno: Valley Publishers, 1977.

Rogers, David Banks. *Prehistoric Man of the Santa Barbara Coast.* Santa Barbara: Santa Barbara Museum of Natural History, 1929.

Sandos, James A. "'Levantamiento!' The 1824 Chumash Uprising Reconsidered." *Southern California Quarterly* 57 (1985): 109–33.

Tompkins, Walker. *Old Spanish Santa Barbara.* Santa Barbara: McNally & Loftin, 1984.

———. *Santa Barbara History Makers.* Santa Barbara: McNally & Loftin, 1983.

———. *Stagecoach Days in Santa Barbara County.* Santa Barbara: McNally & Loftin, 1984.

Weber, Francis J., comp. and ed. *Our Lady's Mission: A Documentary History of La Purísima Concepción.* Los Angeles: Libra Press, 1986.

———, ed. *Queen of the Missions: A Documentary History of Santa Barbara.* Hong Kong: Libra Press, 1979.

Santa Clara County

Allen, Peter C. *Stanford, from the Foothills to the Bay.* Stanford: Stanford Historical Society, 1980.

Arbuckle, Clyde, and Ralph Rambo. *Santa Clara County Ranchos.* San Jose: Rosicrucian Press, 1973.

Butler, Phyllis F. "New Almaden's Casa Grande." *California Historical Quarterly* 54 (1975): 315–22.

———. *The Valley of Santa Clara: Historic Buildings, 1792–1920.* Novato: Presidio Press, 1981.

Cupertino Chronicle. Cupertino: California History Center, De Anza College, 1975.

Curtis, James R. "New Chicago of the Far West: Land Speculation in Alviso, California, 1890–1891." *California History* 61 (1982): 36–45.

Fox, Theron, ed. *After Harper's Ferry: John Brown's Widow—Her Family and the Saratoga Years.* Saratoga: Saratoga Historical Foundation, 1964.

Jacobson, Yvonne. *Passing Farms, Enduring Values: California's Santa Clara Valley.* Los Altos: Kaufmann, 1984.

Khorsand, Seonaid, and Alice Marshall. *Lingering Legacy: A Historical Tour Guide in and Around the Santa Clara Valley.* Cupertino: California History Center, De Anza College, 1973.

McKay, Leonard. *Luis Maria Peralta and His Adobe.* San Jose: Smith-McKay Printing Company, 1976.

McKevitt, Gerald. *The University of Santa Clara: A History, 1851–1977.* Stanford: Stanford University Press, 1979.

Palo Alto Times-Tribune. Stanford Centennial Issue. Nov. 10, 1985.

Payne, Stephen M. *Santa Clara County: Harvest of Change.* Northridge: Windsor Publications, 1987.

Santa Clara County Heritage Resource Inventory. San Jose: Santa Clara County Historical Heritage Commission, 1979.

Spearman, Arthur Dunning. *The Five Franciscan Churches of Mission Santa Clara, 1777–1825.* Palo Alto: National Press, 1963.

Sullivan, Charles L. *Like Modern Edens: Winegrowing in Santa Clara Valley and Santa Cruz Mountains, 1798–1981.* Cupertino: California History Center, De Anza College, 1982.

Thompson & West. *Historical Atlas of Santa Clara County.* 1876. Reprint, San Jose: Smith and McKay Publishing Company, 1973.

Weber, Francis J. *The Laurelwood Mission: A Documentary History of Santa Clara de Asis.* Los Angeles: Dawson's Book Shop, n.d.

Weymouth, Alice Jenkins. *The Palo Alto Tree.* Stanford: Stanford University Press, 1930.

Santa Cruz County

Adams, Kramer A. *Covered Bridges of the West.* Berkeley: Howell-North Books, 1963.

Chase, John. *The Sidewalk Companion to Santa Cruz Architecture.* Rev. ed. Santa Cruz: Paper Vision Press, 1979.

Clark, Donald Thomas. *Santa Cruz County Place Names.* Santa Cruz: Santa Cruz Historical Society, 1986.

Gant, Michael S., ed. *Santa Cruz, the Early Years; the Collected Historical Writings of Leon Rowland.* Santa Cruz: Paper Vision Press, 1980.

Koch, Margaret. *Santa Cruz County, Parade of the Past.* Fresno: Valley Publishers, 1979.

———. *The Walk Around Santa Cruz Book.* Fresno: Valley Publishers, 1980.

Lewis, Betty. *Watsonville: Memories That Linger.* Fresno: Valley Publishers, 1977.

MacMullen, Jerry. "World War II's Strangest Naval Battle." *Westways* 48, no. 6 (June 1955): 10–11.

Sullivan, Charles L. *Like Modern Edens: Winegrowing in Santa Clara Valley and Santa Cruz Mountains, 1798–1981.* Cupertino: California History Center, De Anza College, 1982.

Weber, Francis J., ed. *Holy Cross Mission: A Documentary History of Santa Cruz.* Hong Kong: Libra Press, 1984.

Young, John V. *Ghost Towns of the Santa Cruz Mountains.* Santa Cruz: Paper Vision Press, 1979.

Shasta County

Bleyhl, Norris A. *Three Military Posts in Northern California, 1849–1863.* Chico: Association for Northern California Records and Research, 1984.

Frisbie, Mabel Moores, and Jean Moores Beauchamp. *Shasta: The Queen City.* San Francisco: California Historical Society, 1973.

Giffen, Helen. *Man of Destiny: Pierson Barton Reading, Pioneer of Shasta County, California.* Redding: Shasta Historical Society, 1985.

Johnson, Paul C., and Mabel Moores Frisbie. "Shasta Revisited." *California Historical Quarterly* 51 (1972): 331–37.

Jones, William A. "Prosperity v. Pollution: The Shasta Copper Mining Controversy." *The Californians,* Mar.–Apr. 1985, pp. 34–37.

Lawson, John D. *Redding and Shasta County: Gateway to the Cascades.* Northridge: Windsor Publications, 1986.

Miller, Joaquin (Cincinnatus Heine). "The Battle of Castle Crags." *Leslie's Monthly,* Mar. 1893.

———. *Life Amongst the Modocs.* London: Richard Bentley & Son, 1875.

Neasham, Ernest R. *Fall River Valley . . . from the Earliest Times Until 1890.* Sacramento: Citadel Press, 1985.

Reminiscence of the Fort Crook Historical Society. Fall River Mills: Fort Crook Historical Society, 1965 (subsequently reprinted).

Strong, Douglas H. *"These Happy Grounds": A History of the Lassen Region.* Red Bluff: Walker Lithography, 1982.

Sierra County

California Mining Journal [featuring Nevada and Sierra County mines] 1, no. 1 (Aug. 1931).

Downie, Major William. *Hunting for Gold.* San Francisco: The California Publishing Company, 1893.

Fariss & Smith. *History of Plumas, Lassen and Sierra Counties, California.* 1882. Reprint, Berkeley: Howell-North Books, 1971.

Sinnott, James J. *Alleghany and Forest City.* Downieville: James J. Sinnott, 1974.

———. *Sierra City and Goodyears Bar.* Downieville: James J. Sinnott, 1974.

Siskiyou County

Camp, Charles L., ed. *James Clyman: American Frontiersman.* San Francisco: California Historical Society, 1928.

Dillon, Richard. *Burnt-Out Fires: California's Modoc Indian War.* Englewood Cliffs, N.J.: Prentice-Hall, 1973.

Hall, Ansel F. "Mount Shasta." *Sierra Club Bulletin* 12 (1926): 252–67.

Jones, David Rhys. "Pre-Pioneer Pathfinders, California-Oregon Trail, 1826–1846." *Motor Land*, 29 (1931).

Jones, William A. "Yreka's Chinese and the Great Flood of '90." *The Californians*, Sept.–Oct. 1986, pp. 31–35.

Miller, Joaquin (Cincinnatus Heine). *Life Amongst the Modocs.* London: Richard Bentley & Son, 1875.

Palmberg, Walter H. *Copper Paladin: A Modoc Tragedy. A Story of the Two Principal Role-Players of the Modoc Indian War of 1872–73.* Bryn Mawr, Pa.: Dorrance & Company, 1982.

Palmquist, Peter E. "Silver Plates Among the Goldfields. The Photographers of Siskiyou County 1850–1906." *California History* 65 (1986): 114–25.

Riddle, Jeff C. *The Indian History of the Modoc War.* 1914. Reprint, Eugene, Oreg.: Urion Press, 1974.

Thompson, Erwin N. *Modoc War: Its Military History and Topography.* Sacramento: Argus Books, 1971.

Wells, Harry L. *History of Siskiyou County, California.* Oakland: Stewart & Co., 1881.

Solano County

Dillon, Richard. *Great Expectations: The Story of Benicia, California.* Benicia: Benicia Heritage Books, 1981.

Emparan, Madie Brown. *The Vallejos of California.* San Francisco: The Gleeson Library Associates, 1968.

Gregory, Tom. *History of Solano and Napa Counties, California.* Los Angeles: Historic Record Co., 1912.

Lemmon, Sue, and E. D. Wichels. *From Sidewheelers to Nuclear Power: A Pictorial Essay Covering 123 Years at the Mare Island Naval Shipyard.* Vallejo: Mare Island Historical Record, 1984.

Limbaugh, Ronald H., and Walter A. Payne. *Vacaville: The Heritage of a California Community.* Vacaville: Vacaville City Council, 1978.

"Yee Ah Chong Remembers Vacaville's Chinatown." *California History* 63 (1984): 247–51.

Young, Wood. *Vaca–Peña Los Putos Rancho and the Pena Adobe.* Vallejo: Wheeler Printing & Publishing, 1965.

Sonoma County

Alexander, James B. *Sonoma Valley Legacy: Histories and Sites of 70 Historic Adobes In and Around Sonoma Valley.* Sonoma: Sonoma Valley Historical Society, 1986.

Clar, C. Raymond. *Out of the River Mist: History of the Russian River Area and the Lumber Town of Guerneville.* Sacramento: Argus Books, 1973.

Claybourn, Hannah, et al. *Historic Homes of Healdsburg.* Healdsburg: Healdsburg Historical Society, n.d.

Donohoe, Joan Marie. "Agostin Haraszthy: A Study in Cre-

ativity." *California Historical Society Quarterly* 48 (1969): 153–64.

Emparan, Madie Brown. *The Vallejos of California.* San Francisco: The Gleeson Library Associates, 1968.

Heig, Adair. *History of Petaluma, a California River Town.* Petaluma and San Francisco: Scottwall Associates, 1982.

Munroe-Fraser, J. P. *History of Sonoma County.* 1880. Reprint, Petaluma: C. B. Verona, 1973.

Parmelee, Robert D. *Pioneer Sonoma.* Sonoma: Sonoma Index-Tribune, 1972.

Smilie, Robert S. *The Sonoma Mission.* Fresno: Valley Publishers, 1974.

Spencer-Hancock, Diane, and William E. Pritchard. "The Chapel at Fort Ross: Its History and Reconstruction." *California History* 61 (1982): 2–17.

Tuomey, Honoria, and Luisa Vallejo Emparan. "Historic Mount St. Helena." *California Historical Society Quarterly* 3 (1924): 171–77.

Weber, Francis J., comp. and ed. *Last of the Missions: A Documentary History of San Francisco de Solano.* Los Angeles: Archdiocese of Los Angeles Archives, 1986.

Stanislaus County

Bare, Colleen S. *The McHenry Mansion: Modesto's Heritage.* Modesto: McHenry Mansion Foundation Press, 1985.

Beard, Franklin. *The Way We Were Fifty Years Ago: East of Modesto to Empire and Beyond.* Modesto: The McHenry Museum, 1985.

Branch, L. C. *History of Stanislaus County.* 1881. Reprint, Stanislaus County Historical Society, 1974.

Brotherton, I. N. ("Jack"). *The Annals of Stanislaus: River Towns and Ferries.* Santa Cruz: Western Tanager Press, 1982.

Criswell, John F. *Knight's Ferry's Century-Old Structures.* Knight's Ferry: John F. Criswell, 1981.

———. *Knight's Ferry's Golden Past.* Knight's Ferry: John F. Criswell, 1982.

Elias, Solomon P. *Stories of Stanislaus.* 1924. Reprint, Modesto: McHenry Museum Guild, 1979.

Gray, Thomas B. *Quest for Deep Gold: The Story of La Grange, California.* Modesto: Southern Mines Press, 1973.

Lucas, Mildred D. *From Amber Grain to Fruited Plain: A History of Ceres and Its Surroundings.* Ceres: Ceres Unified School District, 1976.

Maino, Jeanette Gould. *One Hundred Years.* Modesto: Belt Printing & Lithography Company, 1970.

Patterson Irrigator. Diamond Jubilee of Patterson, 1909–1984. May 31, 1984 issue.

Tinkham, George H. *History of Stanislaus County, with Biographical Sketches.* 1921. Reprint, Modesto: McHenry Museum Guild, 1979.

Sutter County

Bayless, Dorothy Martin. *Index to Thompson and West's 1879 History of Sutter County, California.* Sacramento: Dorothy M. Bayless, n.d.

Delay, Peter J. *History of Yuba and Sutter Counties, California.* Los Angeles: Historic Record Co., 1924.

Hendrix, Louise Butts. *Sutter Buttes, Land of the Histun Yani.* Yuba City: Louise B. Hendrix, 1980.

Hussey, John A., ed. *Early Sacramento: Glimpses of John Augustus Sutter, the Hock Farm and Neighboring Tribes, from the Journal of Prince Paul, H.R.H. Duke Paul Wilhelm of Wurttemburg.* Translated by Louis C. Butscher. Sacramento: Sacramento Book Collectors Club, 1973.

Sullivan, Janet R., and Mary-Jane Zall. *The Survivors: Existing Homes and Buildings of Yuba and Sutter Counties' Past.* Marysville, 1974.

Thompson & West. *History of Sutter County.* 1879. Reprint, Berkeley: Howell-North Books, 1974.

Tehama County

Bruff, J. Goldsborough. *Gold Rush: The Journals, Drawings and Other Papers of J. Goldsborough Bruff, April 2, 1849–July 20, 1851.* Edited by Georgia Willis Read and Ruth Gaines. New York, 1944.

Grimes, Mary Lee. *The First Fifty Years: A Pictorial Essay of Tehama County, 1856–1906.* Red Bluff: Tehama County Heritage, 1984.

Hisken, Clara Hough. *Tehama: Little City of the Big Trees.* New York: Exposition Press, 1948.

Hislop, Donald L. *The Nomee Lackee Indian Reservation, 1854–1870.* Chico: Association for Northern California Records and Research, 1978.

Hitchcock, Ruth Hughes. *Leaves of the Past, 1828–1880. A Pioneer Register, Including an Overview of the History and Events of Early Tehama County.* Chico: Association for Northern California Records and Research, 1982.

Lewis, E. J. *Tehama County, California, with Historical Reminiscences.* San Francisco: Elliott & Moore, 1880.

Sherman, Edwin A. *Fifty Years of Masonry in California.* 2 vols. San Francisco: George Spaulding & Co., 1898.

Zelinsky, Edward Galland, and Nancy Olmsted. "Upriver Boats—When Red Bluff Was the Head of Navigation." *California History* 64 (1985): 86–117.

Trinity County

Bell, Horace. *Tales of the Trinity.* 1879–80. Reprint, edited by Dewey and Nola Mosier. Weaverville: Trinity County Historical Society, 1983.

Cox, Isaac. *The Annals of Trinity County.* San Francisco: Commercial Book and Job Steam Printing Establishment, 1858.

Dale, Harrison Clifford. *The Ashley-Smith Explorations and the Discovery of a Central Route to the Pacific, 1822–1829, with Original Journals.* Cleveland, Ohio: Arthur H. Clark Co., 1918.

McDonald, Douglas, and Gina McDonald. *The History of Weaverville Joss House and the Chinese of Trinity County, California.* Medford, Oreg.: McDonald Publishing, 1988.

Miller, William P. "Trinity County." Report by State Mineralogist. Sacramento: State Office, 1890.

Mosier, Dewey, and Nola Mosier. "The Giants and the Mountain—Mining Machines Make a Highway." *California History* 61 (1982): 188–95.

Trinity County Historic Sites. Weaverville: Trinity County Historical Society, 1981.

Tulare County

Bunch, Lonnie G., III. "Allensworth: The Life, Death, and Rebirth of an All-Black Community." *The Californians,* Nov.–Dec. 1987, pp. 26–33.

Fry, Walter, and John R. White. *Big Trees.* Stanford: Stanford University Press, 1930.

Gifford, E. W., and W. Egbert Schenck. "Archaeology of the Southern San Joaquin Valley, California." *University of California Publications in American Archaeology and Ethnology* 13 no. 1 (1926): 1–122.

McCraw, Donald J. "The Tree That Crossed a Continent." *California History* 61 (1982): 120–39.

McCubbin, J. C. *Papers on the History of the San Joaquin Valley, California.* Collected and edited by Raymund F. Wood. Fresno: California State University at Fresno Library, 1960.

McGee, Lizzie. *Mills of the Sequoias.* Visalia: Tulare County Historical Society, 1952.

Mitchell, Annie. *Jim Savage and the Tulareno Indians.* Los Angeles: Westernlore Press, 1957.

———. *A Modern History of Tulare County.* Visalia: Limited Editions of Visalia, 1974.

———. *Sites to See: Historic Landmarks in Tulare County.* Fresno: Panorama West Books, 1983.

———. *The Way It Was: The Colorful History of Tulare County.* Fresno: Valley Publishers, 1976.

Porterville Recorder. "The Porterville Museum, 20th Anniversary Issue." Nov. 9, 1985.

Robinson, W. W. *The Story of Tulare County and Visalia.* Los Angeles: Title Insurance & Trust Co., 1955.

Small, Kathleen. *History of Tulare County.* Chicago: S. J. Clarke Publishing Co., 1926.

Stewart, George W. *Big Trees of the Giant Forest.* San Francisco: A. M. Robertson, 1930.

Tweed, William C. *Sequoia–Kings Canyon: The Story Behind the Scenery.* Las Vegas: KC Publications, 1980.

Tuolumne County

Holmes, Roberta Evelyn. *The Southern Mines of California; Early Development of the Sonora Mining Region.* San Francisco: Grabhorn Press, 1931.

Lang, H. O. *A History of Tuolumne County, California.* 1882. Reprint, Columbia: Tuolumne County Historical Society, 1973.

Mark Twain's Sojourn in Tuolumne County, California: Genesis of a Literary Giant. Sonora: Tuolumne County Historical Society, 1988.

O'Neill, Elizabeth Stone. *Meadow in the Sky: A History of Yosemite's Tuolumne Meadows Region.* Fresno: Panorama West Books, 1983.

Paden, Irene D., and Margaret B. Schlichtmann. *The Big Oak Flat Road*. San Francisco: Lawton Kennedy, 1955.

Robertson, David. *East of Eden: A History of Art and Literature of Yosemite*. Yosemite: Yosemite Natural History Association, 1984.

Stewart, George R. *Bret Harte, Argonaut and Exile*. Boston: Houghton Mifflin, 1931.

Trexler, Keith A. *The Tioga Road: A History, 1883–1961*. 1961. Rev. ed. Yosemite: Yosemite Natural Historical Association, 1975.

Ventura County

Bandurraga, Peter L., David W. Hill, and G. Belden Holland. *Ventura County's Yesterdays Today: Looking Back at Ventura County*. Ventura: Anacapa Publishing, 1980.

Belknap, Michael R. "The Era of the Lemon: A History of Santa Paula, California." *California Historical Society Quarterly* 48 (1968): 113–40.

Bicentennial San Buenaventura, 1782–1982. Ventura: San Buenaventura Mission, 1982.

Del Castillo, Richard Griswold. "The Del Valle Family and the Fantasy Heritage." *California History* 59 (1980): 2–15.

Engelhardt, Zephyrin. *San Buenaventura, the Mission by the Sea*. Santa Barbara: Mission Santa Barbara, 1930.

Fry, Patricia. *The Ojai Valley: An Illustrated History*. Ojai: P. L. Fry, n.d.

Outland, Charles F. *Man-Made Disaster: The Story of St. Francis Dam*. Glendale: Arthur H. Clark Co., 1977.

Ricard, Herbert F. *Place Names of Ventura County*. Ventura: Ventura County Historical Society, 1972.

Robinson, W. W. *The Story of Ventura County*. Los Angeles: Title Insurance & Trust Co., 1956.

Smith, Wallace E. *This Land Was Ours: The Del Valles and Camulos*. Ventura: Ventura County Historical Society, 1977.

Triem, Judith. *Ventura County: Land of Good Fortune*. Northridge: Windsor Publications, 1985.

Weber, Francis J. *A History of San Buenaventura Mission*. Los Angeles: Roman Catholic Archdiocese of Los Angeles, 1977.

Yolo County

Clyman, James. "James Clyman, His Diaries and Reminiscences." Edited by Charles L. Camp. *California Historical Society Quarterly* 5 (1926): 109–28.

Gregory, Tom. *History of Yolo County, California, with Biographical Sketches*. Los Angeles: Historic Record Co., 1913.

Hill, Joseph J. "Ewing Young in the Fur Trade of the Far Southwest, 1822–1834." *Oregon Historical Society Quarterly* 24 (1923): 1–23.

History of Yolo County, California, Its Resources and Its People. Edited by William O. Russell. Woodland: Nelle S. Coil, 1940.

Larkey, Joann, ed. *Davisville '68: The History and Heritage of the City of Davis, Yolo County, California*. Davis: Davis Historical Landmarks Commission, 1969.

Larkey, Joann, and Shipley Walters. *Yolo County: Land of Changing Patterns*. Woodland: Yolo County Historical Society, 1987.

McDermott, Douglas, and Robert K. Sarlos. "The Woodland 'Hershey' Opera House: The End of an Era in California Theatre." *California Historical Society Quarterly* 48 (1969): 291–308.

Walking Tours of Historic Woodland. Woodland: City of Woodland, 1976.

Winters' Architectural Heritage. Winters: Winters Historic Landmarks Advisory Commission, 1985.

Yuba County

Bal, Peggy. *Pebbles in the Stream: A History of Beale Air Force Base and Neighboring Areas*. Chico: Easter Publishing Co., 1979.

Bleyhl, Norris A. *Three Military Posts in Northeastern California, 1849–1863*. Chico: Association for Northern California Records and Research, 1984.

Delay, Peter J. *History of Yuba and Sutter Counties*. Los Angeles: Historic Record Co., 1924.

The History of Yuba County. Marysville: Yuba County Historical Commission, 1976.

Smith, Louise A. *Reclamation: A History of the Linda-Olivehurst Area of California, 1850–1975*. Marysville: Louise A. Smith, 1975.

Sullivan, Janet R., and Mary-Jane Zall. *The Survivors: Existing Homes and Buildings of Yuba and Sutter Counties' Past*. Marysville, 1974.

Wells, Henry L., and William H. Chamberlain. *History of Yuba County, California*. Oakland: Thompson & West, 1879.

Wheat, Carl I. "'California's Bantam Cock'—The Journals of Charles E. DeLong, 1854–1863." Edited with an introduction by Carl I. Wheat. *California Historical Society Quarterly* 8, 9, 10 (1929–31): *passim*.

Index

Library of Congress Cataloging-in-Publication Data

Historic spots in California. — 4th ed. / by Mildred Brooke Hoover
. . . [et al.]; revised by Douglas E. Kyle.
p. cm.
Bibliography: p.
Includes index.
ISBN 0-8047-1734-6 (alk. paper) — ISBN 0-8047-1735-4
(pbk.: alk. paper)
1. Historic sites—California.   2. California—History, Local.
I. Hoover, Mildred Brooke.   II. Kyle, Douglas E., 1935–
F862.H57   1990
979.4—dc20
89-31682
CIP

∞